The Worthies of England

EDITED BY JOHN FREEMAN

THE ENGLISHMAN AT WAR

An Anthology

THOMAS FULLER
from the painting by Isaac Fuller at Berkeley Castle

THOMAS FULLER
from the painting by Isaac Fuller at Berkeley Castle

The Worthies of England

THOMAS FULLER

EDITED
WITH AN INTRODUCTION AND NOTES
BY
JOHN FREEMAN

George Allen & Unwin Ltd
RUSKIN HOUSE MUSEUM STREET LONDON

THIS EDITION FIRST PUBLISHED IN 1952

PRINTED IN GREAT BRITAIN
in 10 on 11 point Georgian type
BY THE BLACKFRIARS PRESS LIMITED
LEICESTER

PREFACE

THIS, being the first abridged edition of Fuller's *Worthies*, and the first reprint for over a century, requires a few words explaining the principle on which the work has been carried out. My aim has been to knit together the vast materials supplied by Fuller, and to provide an edition reduced in compass but faithful in spirit to the original. The bulk of the work has been retained, but the lists of gentry, of mayors and sheriffs are omitted altogether, except for a figure here and there sufficiently fully treated to be retained. The largest omission is from Fuller's lengthy introduction ("The Design of the Ensuing Work") most of which, in view of the abridgement and rearrangement, lost much of its point. Fuller's classification of worthies under their respective professions has been discarded; in abridging the work I have found it more satisfactory to follow chronological order, with slight deviations here and there to achieve better grouping, such as the grouping of certain worthies together because of their original treatment together. Except for the heading for the worthies, the cross-headings are Fuller's own.

I have adhered to Fuller's alphabetical order of counties, except that I begin with Bedfordshire instead of Berkshire (originally spelled Barkshire); and the arrangement of the material in each county, except for the worthies, is more or less as in the original edition. With Wales, however, I have not included the separate counties (except Monmouthshire, which is placed in England) as they are treated very sketchily. I have, therefore, grouped all the selected Welsh worthies under the general heading of Wales, which in the original edition receives general treatment before the counties are dealt with separately; and I have taken a larger liberty with the text than elsewhere by substituting the name of the county, without the use of square brackets, where Fuller says "born in this county."

The text is modernized, but not with slavish consistency, and such words as *unpartial*, *intituled*, *anticronism*, among others, are left as preserving something of the essential flavour of the work. The punctuation, sometimes chaotic, according to our ideas, has been revised in accordance with modern practice; but here again I have found the retention of the original practice necessary at times to elucidate Fuller's meaning on the few occasions when he is not at his clearest.

Annotation proved a particular difficulty. My hope is to present the *Worthies* with sufficient annotation to help the reader to enjoy the work more fully. Any attempt at complete annotation would probably have been misguided, and would have resulted in an even more voluminous work. I have, therefore, confined annotation in the main to the worthies themselves, and then chiefly to the less well-known figures, especially when Fuller overlooks important facts such as a worthy's chief title to fame, or when he makes definite mistakes. The more interesting of

Fuller's own notes are retained, and where it may not be clear that the note is by him, I have appended the initial "F". Editorial interpolations of dates, names and translations are clearly marked off within square brackets. Where Fuller gives Latin and Greek passages of any length followed by his own translations, the originals are generally omitted and the fact noted. Inaccuracies of date and name are silently corrected. I have preferred to pass uncorrected certain other inaccuracies, such as ascriptions of nativities to wrong localities, rather than burden the work with further annotation.

I have taken the liberty of incorporating material from the *Church History* and from *The Holy State* on the rare occasions that Fuller excuses himself from writing a life because he had done so already in one of those works. Such interpolations are always noted.

This edition has been the labour of several years, in the course of which I have received much willing and generous help, which it is a pleasure to acknowledge. My very grateful thanks are due to Mrs. B. Carolyn Wells for help with the preparation of the text and the problem of selection; to Mr. D. J. Benger for wise guidance especially over annotation; to Miss J. Hobbs for the typing of all this material; to my cousin Mr. T. B. F. Ruoff for the elucidation of historico-legal and other points; and to Mr. and Mrs. Richard Grindle for help with Fuller's Latin. None of these worthies, however, is in any way answerable for the errors, omissions and other defects of this edition, for which I alone am responsible; and at this stage I will plead in Fuller's own words: "Thus imperfections may occasion perfection; which makes me to hope that hereafter the defects of this my book (without prejudice to my profit or credit) will be judiciously discovered, and industriously amended by others."

J. F.

CONTENTS

INTRODUCTION

I

THOMAS FULLER was born in June, 1608, at the village of Aldwinkle St. Peter's, Northamptonshire, twin parish to Aldwinkle All Saints, where Dryden was born twenty-three years later. His father, also named Thomas, had been educated at Trinity and St. John's Cambridge, and was presented to the living of Aldwinkle St. Peter's under the patronage of Thomas Cecil Lord Burghley. He knew Robert Browne, founder of the sect named after him, and rector of Achurch nearby, possessed slight puritan leanings himself, and had thereby come in for punishment under the court of high commission.[1] He married Judith Davenant, widow of a Stephen Payne, and sister of John Davenant, later bishop of Salisbury. Davenant's other sister married, as her second husband, Robert Townson, who as dean of Westminster attended Ralegh to the scaffold,[2] and in 1621 was appointed bishop of Salisbury.

Fuller, the eldest of seven children, was educated for four years at the village school by the Rev. Arthur Smith, who claimed kinship with John Smith the colonist, but learned little until his father took his education in hand.[3] "A boy of a pregnant wit," says Aubrey, he was entered at the age of thirteen at Queens' College, Cambridge, just after his uncle Davenant, who was president of the college and Lady Margaret professor of divinity, had been elected bishop of Salisbury in succession to Dr. Townson, who died in the year of appointment. Fuller's tutors were Edward Davenant, nephew of the bishop, and the "ever honoured" John Thorpe. He proceeded B.A. in 1625, and M.A. in 1628.

Davenant tried to obtain a fellowship for Fuller at Queens', but for some reason he was passed over, and in 1629 entered Sidney Sussex College as a fellow-commoner, but never obtained a fellowship. Next year he was appointed, by Corpus Christi College, to the perpetual curacy of St. Benet's, Cambridge, taking orders at the same time. In January 1631 he preached the funeral sermon of Hobson the Cambridge carrier, celebrated in Milton's sonnet, and eponymously famous as 'Hobson's choice.' Later in the same year appeared his first published work, *David's Heinous Sin, Hearty Repentance, Heavy Punishment,* a poetical effusion of no merit. He was appointed by Davenant to the prebend of Netherbury in Ecclesia, Dorset, which he considered "one of the best prebends in England."

His father died intestate in 1631 or 1632, and Fuller was granted administration of his estate. A year or so later he resigned the curacy of St. Benet's and in 1634 Davenant appointed him to the living of Broadwindsor in Dorset. He took his B.D. degree the following year; four

(1) See note 1, p. 447 on this incident. (2) Townson's life is given under Cambridgeshire, p. 57. (3) John Smith's life is given under Cheshire, p. 75.

parishioners accompanied him for the occasion, and the hospitality dispensed cost him £140.

The date of Fuller's marriage has remained largely a matter of conjecture. We know only for certain the date of baptism of Judeth, apparently his first child, on April 29, 1639. His wife was Ellen Grove, daughter of Hugh Grove, of Chisenbury, Wiltshire, and M.P. for Shaftesbury. Her brother Hugh, a royalist captain, was later involved in Penruddock's rising, and beheaded for treason. Her sister Katherine married Fuller's cousin and tutor, Edward Davenant.[1]

Fuller's first characteristic work, *The History of the Holy War,* a racy history of the crusades, appeared in 1639, went quickly into a second edition, and continued in popularity until the Restoration. He was elected to the convocation of 1640 as one of the proctors for the diocese of Bristol. Fuller, who belonged to the moderates, probably objected to some of the measures passed, but eventually conformed. The House of Commons passed a bill fining those who agreed to the measures, and he was down for £200, but the bill did not pass in the Lords.[2]

The year 1641 was an eventful one for Fuller. His uncle Bishop Davenant died in April; his son John[3] was born in June; he abandoned both livings, though he claims that he was never formally sequestered; he settled in London, preached at the Inns of Court, and became curate at the Chapel Royal, Savoy. He also completed *The Holy and Profane State,* though the printer took a full year to produce it. It was his most popular work during his life-time, and probably since, and has been aptly described as "an effective medley of four distinct types of literature . . . character-writing, essay, biography, and courtesy-book in little."[4]

When the civil war broke out, Fuller, a man of moderation, was for peace, and he was one of the six chosen to carry a petition for peace from the city of Westminster to the king at Oxford. At Uxbridge the party were held up and searched, and found in possession of "two scandalous books arraigning the proceedings of the House," as well as letters with ciphers to royalist peers. It was found that the House of Lords had given the party the pass. Eventually the party were remanded by a joint order of both houses, and imprisoned for a short time. The Westminster petition eventually reached the king through other channels.

When, some three months later, it was expected that the negotiations at Oxford would prove successful, Fuller preached in Westminster Abbey a sermon on the return of "our English Zion." The occasion, March 27, 1643, was the anniversary of Charles I's accession, and he

(1) The identity of Fuller's first wife was not known until 1879, when it was published by his biographer, J. E. Bailey. The fact appears to have escaped notice until 1918, when J. F. Fuller, F.S.A., relying on information supplied by John J. Hammond, published the fact as a new discovery. See *Notes and Queries,* 12S.IV, May and July, 1918. The present writer is indebted to Sir Henry L. L. Denny, president of the Genealogical Society, and who claims Fuller as his ancestral uncle by marriage, for confirmation of the above. (2) The convocation, which passed an oath for conformity to the church of England and canons for the restraint of sectaries, etc., as well as subsidies for the king, was a momentous one, for among the charges finally brought against Archbishop Laud was that he had sanctioned its illegalities. (3) Educated at Sidney Sussex College. He became rector of Great Wakering, Essex, where he died in 1687. (4) M. G. Walten, *Thomas Fuller's "The Holy and Profane State," vol. I,* 7.

gave offence in the City, which was strongly parliamentarian. His wife died about this time, and in April the Lords gave him a pass to and from Salisbury for her obsequies.

As a result of the discovery of Waller's plot in June 1643 (the object of which was to seize the city of London for the king) parliament imposed a covenant which Fuller took with reservations. In July he preached an important sermon "Of Reformation." The storm aroused, and the order to take the covenant without reservations, resulted in his secret flight to Oxford. His property, mainly books, was confiscated. He took up residence at Lincoln College, but he was not really happy at Oxford; he was outspoken in desiring peace, and extreme royalists therefore regarded him as lukewarm, whereas puritans and his Calvinistic opponent John Saltmarsh[1] regarded him as popish. It was therefore probably with relief that after a few months' residence in Oxford he accepted the chaplaincy to the forces under Sir Ralph (later Lord) Hopton, a moderate royalist much respected by his opponents. While following Hopton on campaign he conceived the idea of "a more exact collection of the worthies general of England," and he began to collect the materials both from persons and from local records.[2] At the siege of Basing House he was encouraging the garrison, then preaching again at Oxford, and by the autumn he was at Exeter, where the king appointed him chaplain to the infant Princess Henrietta, and he resigned the chaplaincy to Hopton.

Good Thoughts in Bad Times, a book of devotional and moral applications (a companion volume, *Good Thoughts in Worse Times,* followed in 1647) was composed and published during his stay of eighteen months in Exeter. He was appointed, March 1646, to a lectureship founded by Laurence Bodley, canon of Exeter and elder brother of Sir Josias Bodley the military engineer, but in a few weeks Exeter was to surrender to Fairfax. Fuller went to London, claiming protection under the articles of surrender, but was unable to obtain terms that would enable him to practise his profession. He therefore engaged himself in writing, and was resident at the Crown, the address of his publisher, living possibly on the accumulated profits of the sales of *The Holy War* and *The Holy and Profane State.* He enlarged for separate publication one of the lives that had appeared in the latter volume, entitled *Andronicus, or the Unfortunate Politician,* which was probably directed, in its mild way, against the party in power.

Fuller possessed influential friends on both sides, and fared better than most of the ejected clergy, but was always willing to give a helping hand to the less fortunate. No doubt it was influence that enabled him to resume preaching, though at some time during 1647 he was again inhibited. His contemporary at Sidney Sussex College, Edward, second Baron Montagu of Boughton, a parliamentarian since 1644, received him at Boughton House in the winter of 1646/7, and gave him financial assistance, thus enabling him to carry on with his research. Another influential friend was Sir John Danvers the regicide, whom he acknowledged as having, by a liberal annual payment, raised up his fortunes

(1) His life is given under Yorkshire, p. 665. (2) *Life,* 1661.

when they were cast to the ground. The friendship survived until Danvers' death in 1655.

The execution of Charles I affected him so deeply that he put aside the *Worthies* for the time being. Later in the same year he received the perpetual curacy of Waltham Abbey in Essex from the second earl of Carlisle, who had joined the parliamentarians in 1644, and he also became the earl's chaplain. He was able to complete his large *Pisgah-Sight of Palestine,* a topographical and historical description of the holy land, written with typical gusto and infectious enjoyment, but owing to difficulties with the plates, publication was delayed until 1650. This was followed in 1651 by seven lives contributed to a collection, entitled *Abel Redevivus,* containing the biographies of modern divines. His visits to London were frequent, and restraint upon his preaching appears again to be removed, for we find him preaching at Chelsea and elsewhere. The Chelsea sermon, a mixture of boldness, tactful evasion and astuteness, is an interesting commentary on his character. The king's execution was still fresh in men's minds, and he chose the text "There is a just man that perisheth in his righteousness; and there is a wicked man that prolongeth his life in his wickedness." The innuendo could not have been missed, yet the whole sermon is masterly in its evasion of direct reference, and somewhat reminiscent of Latimer's reply to his inquisitors. On publication it received the title of *The Just Man's Funeral.*

Some time after 1651 Fuller received from Lionel Cranfield, third earl of Middlesex, what remained of the library of the latter's father;[1] and also about this time most of his own books were returned to him. He was hard at work on the *Church History,* lectured every Wednesday at St. Clement's, Eastcheap, and was allowed the use of a chamber at Sion College,[2] where he was familiar with John Spencer the "learned library keeper," who kept jottings, which have survived, of Fuller's sermons.

Either late in 1651 or early in 1652 Fuller married again, his bride being Mary Roper, the younger sister of Thomas, Viscount Baltinglas, and a descendant of James Pilkington, the first protestant bishop of Durham.[3] A son, James, was born in December 1652, but died in July 1654; a daughter, Anne, born in November 1653, died in April 1655; and another son, Thomas, was born in May 1655. Nothing certain is known of the last, though it is conjectured that he eventually went to live in Ireland.

The great *Church History* appeared early in 1656. The immense folio contained also an excellent *History of the University of Cambridge,* and a *History of Waltham Abbey.* Some critics consider the *Church History* Fuller's greatest work.[4] It was, for a time, the favourite of Pepys, and Lamb revelled in it as much as he did in the *Worthies.* The period

(1) He succeeded his brother James in 1651. The life of the father, the first earl, is given under London, p. 369. All three were Fuller's patrons. (2) Founded in 1623 for the use of London clergy. It possessed an excellent library, constantly augmented by benefactions. The building and most of the contents perished in the Great Fire. (3) His life is given under Lancashire, p. 297. (4) See especially E. E. Kellett's penetrating essay, "A Church Historian," in *Reconsiderations.*

covered is from the birth of Christ to the execution of Charles I, and there is a moving account of the king's last hours and of his burial. The book was later sharply attacked, chiefly on points of detail, by Dr. Peter Heylyn, a strong Laudian, and who therefore disliked the views of a moderate like Fuller. Heylyn was annoyed also by "trencher-jests" and by the large number of dedications to patrons (an early form of publication by subscription) and castigated them as being "like prayers of some old mendicants at the doors of their good masters and dames." In allusion to the same practice another opponent, Robert South, later famous as a divine, spoke of Fuller as running around London with his big book under one arm and his little wife under the other, and recommending himself as a dinner guest by his facetious talk. In the *Appeal of Injured Innocence,* a small folio (1659) Fuller replied with firmness, though with his usual good humour, and scored not a few points off Heylyn. He later visited his opponent, and they became truly reconciled.

During 1655 occurred the royalist rising in the west under John Penruddock. Hugh Grove, the brother of Fuller's first wife, took part and was beheaded. The famous Cromwellian board of "triers," set up in the previous year to supervise appointments to the ministry, now increased its vigilance, and possibly due partly to his brother-in-law's treason, Fuller was requested to appear before the board. He consulted John Howe, then domestic chaplain to Cromwell. "Sir," he said, "you may observe that I am a pretty corpulent man, and I am to go through a passage that is very strait; I beg you would be so good as to give me a shove, and help me through." Fortified by Howe's advice, and exercising his usual superb adroitness in such matters, he managed to satisfy the board, and continued with his functions.

After the publication of the *Church History* he pressed on with the *Worthies,* but the differences with Heylyn, to whom he had replied at great length, retarded progress. In 1658 he was presented by George, Baron (later first earl of) Berkeley, with the living of Cranford in Middlesex. It appears that he had some time previously been appointed Berkeley's chaplain. His pamphlet entitled *An Alarum to the Counties of England and Wales,* appealing for a free parliament, appeared in February 1660. It fitted well with the mood of the time, and quickly ran into three editions. This was soon followed by *Mixt Contemplations in Better Times,* similar to the volumes of *Good Thoughts.* He accompanied Berkeley to meet Charles II at The Hague, and celebrated the Restoration with a set of verses ("Loyal Panegyrick") that does more credit to his loyalty than to his literary powers.

After the publication of the *Church History* he enjoyed greatly enhanced fame, and was possibly the most popular author of the day. He was created D.D. by royal letter, and resumed his lectureship at the Savoy. Pepys, who referred to him in his diary as "the great Tom Fuller," was disappointed with a sermon at the Savoy on May 12, though formerly he had conceived a high opinion of Fuller as a pulpit orator. The living of Broadwindsor was restored to him, but after hearing the incumbent preach he decided not to displace him. He took up the prebend of Netherbury again, and was appointed chaplain in extraordinary to the king. During the summer of 1661, on returning from a visit to Salisbury in connexion with the prebend, he suddenly became very ill of a fever, probably typhus, but insisted on carrying out a promise to preach a marriage sermon for a kinsman. He died a few days later, on the 16th of August, and was buried at Cranford Church the following day, followed to the grave by two hundred clergymen from London. He had only recently been supervising the *Worthies* for the press, "crying out for pen and ink to the last," but the work was not published until February 1662; it was dedicated to the king by the "author's orphan" John Fuller.

II

Fuller "was of stature somewhat tall, exceeding the mean, with a proportionable bigness to become it, but no way inclining to corpulency."[1] A very popular man, he had a large acquaintance in all walks of life. He was entirely without rancour. Among the earliest writers to make something near a living by his books, he supervised them with particular care, and took trouble, when necessary, to correct each new edition. It was his boast that "no stationer hath ever lost by me." He had a very remarkable memory, the cultivation of which was no doubt sharpened by the exigencies of authorship under the conditions of civil war. Some ascribed to him an "art of memory"; he disclaimed any trick or art, but gave the advice, "Marshal thy notions into a handsome method."

Much has been written, for and against, of Fuller's attitude in the civil war. He has been accused of "trimming" and time-serving. He has made his own position perfectly clear in several places, and most fully in an essay "Of Time-Serving" in the *Holy State,* where he distinguishes four kinds of time-serving, descending in degree from the first kind, "out of Christian devotion." He believed in no sacrifice of principle, but asserted that it was a matter of necessary policy to be pliant over inessentials. Like most men, he had no doubt a constitutional aversion to martyrdom: he told Heylyn, when excusing himself for not writing more strongly in favour of Laud when feeling against the latter was very strong, that "it had been madness for me to run my neck into the halter." He constantly preached moderation, which he defended as being very different to mere lukewarmness, and in the early stages of the civil war was all for peace by "accommodations," or as we should say, by compromise. His royalism, however, grew stronger as the struggle intensified,[1] though it did not cool his natural warmth of heart for every man of goodwill, royalist or parliamentarian, Laudian or puritan. He counted among his friends the regicide Sir John Danvers, and this particular friendship must have lent most colour to the charge of time-serving, but it was quite in accordance with the higher courtesies of the age.[3] Nevertheless, Fuller must have made certain mental reserva-

(1) *Life,* 1661. (2) This is Gardiner's view. See *History of the Great Civil War* (ed. 1893) vol. I, ch. 14. (3) For instance, Waller to his opponent Hopton before battle: "Let us do it in a way of honour without personal animosities." As for Danvers, he was a very determined opponent of the king, and only twice failed to attend the commission that sentenced him. Fuller's opinion of another regicide, the famous Bradshaw, will be found in an oblique reference on p. 70.

tions, for neither Danvers nor other figures among parliamentarians, except divines, find a place in the *Worthies*.

A word should be said of the part played by Fuller in the development of religious liberty in this country. His moderation, "the silken chain running through all virtues," and his belief in compromise, found constant expression in books and sermons, and helped to create a more tolerant attitude toward dissent.[1] What he said of Richard Vines the puritan is equally true of himself: "He was most charitably moderate to such as dissented from him."

He emerges as a great man even in a period of intellectual giants. It was an age of variegated intellectual and spiritual strains, and is too easily regarded as merely puritan. Puritan literature was certainly poured out in a flood of pamphlet, book and sermon, but side by side with it there was intellectual ferment of a very different kind, the ferment of powerful thought from minds rapidly discarding mediaevalism and ushering in modernism. Sir Thomas Browne could combine his peculiar scepticism with devotionalism and the crudities of witchcraft; Hobbes' infernal logic produced a frightful Erastianism; Milton was bellicose with republicanism; Selden's grave and varied learning disturbed conservative spirits; Sir Thomas Urquhart flouted all with a glorious translation of the humanism and unabashed sensualism of Rabelais; and a curious blend of rationalism and puritanism found its outlet in the formation of the Royal Society. Amid these cross-currents we find the figure of Fuller, the "least prejudiced great man in an age of great men," infusing every subject he undertook with a charitable humour quite uncharacteristic of the period. It is not surprising, in an age of fierce controversy, when "the fury of the merciless pen" wounded far too often, that he should become one of its most popular authors, appealing widely because his pen was taken up, not to wound, but to instruct and to delight.

III

Fuller's reputation, high at his death, had sunk more or less to that of a literary buffoon by the eighteenth century. When Charles Lamb made his *Selections* in 1811 he stated that Fuller was scarcely read except by antiquaries, but in that year (a century and a half after publication) appeared the first reprint of the *Worthies,* and several other works were reprinted in the course of the nineteenth century, when Fuller enjoyed a considerable vogue. In the last half century or so he has again been very largely neglected.

The neglect has been due probably to three factors: reaction following the excessive praise of Coleridge, the reputation of being merely a quaint and witty eccentric, and the voluminous nature of his work. Nearly every writer on Fuller has stressed his wit and quaintness, and thus helped to obscure his real achievement.[2] Wit and humour are certainly prominent features in nearly all his work, but these are subsidiary to a wonderful narrative power and the ability to write a perfect short life

(1) See W. K. Jordan, *Development of Religious Toleration,* 1603-1640, ch. 2, §4.
(2) Coleridge's famous "wit was the stuff and substance of Fuller's intellect," a somewhat loose pronouncement, has been repeated *ad nauseam.*

or character.[1] In fact, Fuller is the master of the miniature life. Swiftly flowing narrative is a particular feature of the *Church History,* and is also prominent in his history of the Crusades, *The Holy War,* as well as in much else of his work, but the *Church History* contains also many a life on the miniature pattern used in extenso in the *Worthies.* Nothing could be better in its kind than the lives of Richard Mulcaster the schoolmaster, Thomas Taylor the puritan, John Barkham the antiquary, Thomas Coryate of the *Crudities*—the instances could be readily multiplied. He cannot resist a story, "purposely interlaced, not as meat, but as condiment," though sometimes it is irritatingly trivial or at other times he fails to observe any artistic proportion. Nevertheless, the *Worthies* is a wonderful collection of lives, being in addition a magnificent storehouse of topography, proverbs and antiquarian and other lore. By dealing with the manufactures, the natural commodities, the buildings and other matters within each county, he presents a lively picture of the English scene and of some aspects of the life and work of the people in seventeenth-century England.

Except for his assiduity in collecting material, much would have been lost to us. Besides the "learnedst and gravest persons," he would never "refuse to light his candle in investigating Truth from the meanest person's discovery. He would endure contentedly an hour's or more impertinence from any aged church-officer or other superannuated person for the gleaning of two lines to his purpose." A great deal of the material thus quarried has found its way into our standard compilations and histories.[2] He provides the *locus classicus* for the stories, among others, of Ralegh's cloak in a "plashy place," and Shakespeare and Ben Jonson's wit combats. He has preserved for us the lives of minor but interesting worthies that would otherwise have had no memorial; and not a little of the interest of Fuller derives from his acquaintance with many of whom he wrote.

His character emerges clearly from his writings. His moderation and charity are seen time and again in his lives of "painful and pious" pastors, many of them puritans; story, joke and witticism fairly jostle each other as they did his conversation; benefactions to charity, church or university receive especial warmth of praise; he delights in oddities of character and circumstance; and the low-church protestant shews through the references to "Romish superstitions," but these are so often forgotten in his charity that he is carried away by the sterling qualities of the "papist."[3] Throughout it all, as Leslie Stephen says, he suffers from a sort of rude intellectual health: there is always immense gusto and no trace of dullness, and he enjoys immediate and intimate contact with the reader.

(1) The two of course are not synonymous: Fuller wrote several "characters" on the Theophrastean model popular in his day, and especially in *The Holy and Profane State,* but in the main he keeps to the short life. As a character writer he does not generally stand comparison with Clarendon, who in a paragraph could contain the essence of a personality. (2) In this connexion it is worth noting that Anthony à Wood, in his *Athenae Oxonienses,* used Fuller freely without acknowledgement, often reproducing the exact phrases. This has led several contributors to the *Dictionary of National Biography* to ascribe to Wood what was actually written by Fuller. (3) Fuller was rather more strongly anti-Roman than most Anglicans of his day.

Fuller was not a philosophic historian in the usual sense, but he was among the earlier "documentary" historians, and careful in the use of authorities. He owed much to Camden, Leland, Godwin, "bilious" Bale, Pits, Speed, and others, all constantly acknowledged in his notes. As a divine he did not possess the depth of learning of some of his contemporaries, and as a pulpit orator, though very popular in his day, he cannot compare with his friend Jeremy Taylor; but then, of course, he would not have been the Fuller of *The Holy State,* the *Church History* and *The Worthies of England.* His learning, though wide, was rather that of the annalist and antiquary.

His style is somewhat uncharacteristic of his time, and in its comparative simplicity looks forward to the Augustan age. He does not produce the magnificent Latinesque sonorities that we expect from Sir Thomas Browne or Milton, but he could command a moving eloquence, as when he tells of the dispersal of Wycliffe's ashes and doctrine,[1] or delineates the character of Sir Francis Drake, or when his "pen is sensible of no higher preferment than when it may be permitted to draw the curtains about those who have died in the bed of honour." "The pyramids themselves, doting with age, have forgotten the names of their founders," is worthy of Sir Thomas Browne. He is fond of alliteration, and abounds in aphorisms, and they are so like proverbs that the reader will frequently take them for such, e.g., *The fox thrives best when he is most cursed, Better ride alone than have a thief's company, It is a needless work for a blackamoor to besoot his own face.* Very few works in English literature contain so much sustained aphoristic fancy as *The Holy State,* and the book was to Fuller but the "leakage of his soul" whilst amassing material for the *Church History.*

The more the matter is studied, the more surprising it appears that there has been such long neglect of the most lively of antiquaries, who wrote the most readable of all works of collective biography and the brightest of all ecclesiastical histories.

(1) *Church History,* Bk. IV, Cent. 15.

THE DESIGN OF THE ENSUING WORK

ENGLAND may not unfitly be compared to an house, not very great, but convenient; and the several shires may properly be resembled to the *rooms* thereof. Now, as learned Master Camden and painful Master Speed, with others, have described the rooms themselves, so it is our intention, God willing, to describe the *furniture* of these rooms; such eminent commodities which every country doth produce, with the persons of quality bred therein, and some other observables coincident with the same subject.

Cato, that great and grave philosopher, did commonly demand, when any new project was propounded unto him, *Cui bono?* What good would ensue, in case the same was effected? A question more fit to be asked than facile to be answered in all undertakings, especially in the setting forth of new books, insomuch that they themselves who complain that they are too many already, help daily to make them more.

Know then, I propound five ends to myself in this book: first, to gain some glory to God; secondly, to preserve the memories of the dead; thirdly, to present examples to the living; fourthly, to entertain the reader with delight; and lastly (which I am not ashamed publicly to profess) to procure some honest profit to myself. If not so happy to obtain all, I will be joyful to attain some; yea, contented and thankful too, if gaining any (especially the first) of these ends, the motives of my endeavours.

First, glory to God, which ought to be the aim of all our actions, though too often our bow starts, our hand shakes, and so our arrow misseth the mark. Yet I hope that our describing so good a land, with the various fruits and fruitful varieties therein, will engage both writer and reader in gratitude to that God who hath been so bountiful to our nation. In order whereunto, I have not always taken, but often sought to exhort to thankfulness, hoping the same will be interpreted no straggling from my subject, but a closing with my calling.

Secondly, to preserve the memories of the dead. A good name is an ointment poured out, smelt where it is not seen. It hath been the lawful desire of men in all ages to perpetuate their memories, thereby in some sort revenging themselves of mortality, though few have found out effectual means to perform it. For monuments made of wood are subject to be burnt; of glass, to be broken; of soft stone, to moulder; of marble and metal (if escaping the teeth of time) to be demolished by the hand of covetousness; so that, in my apprehension, the safest way to secure a memory from oblivion is (next his own virtues) by committing the same in writing to posterity.

Thirdly, to present examples to the living, having here precedents of all sorts and sizes; of men famous for valour, wealth, wisdom, learning, religion and bounty to the public, on which last we most largely insist. The scholar, being taxed by his writing master for idleness in his absence, made a fair defence when pleading that his master had neither left him paper whereon or copy whereby to write. But rich men will be without excuse, if not expressing their bounty in some proportion, God having provided them paper enough ("the poor you have always with you") and set them signal examples, as in our ensuing work will plainly appear.

Fourthly, to entertain the reader with delight. I confess, the subject is but dull in itself, to tell the time and place of men's birth, and deaths, their names, with the names and number of their books; and therefore this bare skeleton of time, place and person must be fleshed with some pleasant passages. To this intent I have purposely interlaced (not as meat, but as condiment) many delightful stories, that so the reader, if he do not arise, which I hope and desire, *religiosior* or *doctior,* with more piety or learning, at least he may depart *jocundior,* with more pleasure and lawful delight.

Lastly, to procure moderate profit to myself in compensation of my pains. It was a proper question which plain-dealing Jacob pertinently propounded to Laban his father-in-law: "And now when shall I provide for mine house also?" Hitherto no stationer hath lost by me; hereafter it will be high time for me (all things considered) to save for myself.

The matter following may be divided into real and personal, though not according to the legal acception of the words. By *real,* I understand the commodities and observables of every county; by *personal,* the characters of those worthy men who were natives thereof.

THE REAL TOPICS INSISTED ON IN THE RESPECTIVE COUNTIES

THE NATIVE COMMODITIES

No county hath cause to complain with the Grecian widows, "that they are neglected in the daily ministration." God hath not given *all* commodities to one, to elate it with pride, and *none* to others to deject them with pensiveness; but there is some kind of equality betwixt the profits of counties, to continue commerce and balance trading in some proportion.

We have therefore in this work taken especial notice of the several commodities which every shire doth produce. And indeed God himself enjoineth us to observe the variety of the earth's productions in this kind. For speaking of the land of Havilah, where, saith he, "there is gold, and the gold of that land is good; there is bdellium, and the onyx-stone." See here how the Holy Spirit points at those places where God hath scattered such treasure, and the best thereof in all kinds, that man, if so disposed, may know where to gather them up.

I confess England cannot boast of gold and precious stones with the land of Havilah; yet affordeth it other things, both above and beneath ground, more needful for man's being. Indeed some shires, Joseph-like, have a better coloured coat than others; and some, with Benjamin, have a more bountiful mess of meat belonging unto them. Yet every county hath a child's portion, as if God in some sort observed gavelkind in the distribution of his favours. "Oh that men would therefore praise the

Lord for His goodness, and declare the wondrous works which He doth for the children of men."

Know, reader, when a commodity is general to all England, then, to avoid repetition, it is entered in that county where there was the first, or else the most and best of that kind. And we have so contrived it that, generally, *three commodities* are treated of in every county.

THE MANUFACTURES

Some heathen have causelessly complained of Nature as a step-mother to mankind, because other creatures come into the world clothed with feathers, furs, or fleeces &c., or armed with paws, claws, beaks, tusks, horns, hoofs, whilst man is exposed naked into the world: I say a causeless charge, because Providence having given men hands, and reason to use them (two blessings denied to other creatures) all clothing and fencing is eminently and transcendently bestowed upon him.

It is very remarkable to see the manufacturers in England, not knowing whether more to admire the rarity or variety thereof. Undoubtedly the wealth of a nation consisteth in driving a native commodity through the most hands to the highest artificial perfection, whereof we have taken especial cognizance in the respective counties, yet so as, though briefly naming, not largely handling that manufacture whereon we have formerly insisted.

It must not be forgotten that there be some things which cannot properly be termed natural commodities, because of their quality altered and disguised by men's industry, and yet they attain not the reputation of manufactures. As salt, being water boiled; malt, barley dried; cider, apples pressed. Seeing therefore they have a mixed nature, they are promiscuously placed as suiteth best with my own conveniency.

MEDICINAL WATERS

The God of Nature hath not discovered himself so variously wonderful in anything as in the waters of fountains, rivers, &c. England hath as large a share herein as any country, and her springs wonderful on several accounts. 1. Colour: black, red, yellow &c. 2. Taste: sweet, bitter, salt, acid, corroding, astringing &c. 3. Odour: stinking of sulphur, like the scouring of a gun very foul. 4. Sound: beating sometimes like a march, sometimes like a retreat on several occasions. 5. Heat: lukewarm, and gradually hot even to scalding. 6. Weight: considerably heavier or lighter in proportion to other waters. 7. Motion: though many miles from the sea, sympathizing therewith, ebbing and flowing accordingly. 8. Effects: some being surgeons to heal sores, others physicians to cure diseases.

The last is proper for our pen, being the largess of Heaven to poor people, who cannot go to the price of a costly cure. Of these more have been discovered by casualty than industry, to evidence that therein we are not so much beholden to man's pains as God's providence. Many springs formerly sovereign have since lost their virtue, yet so that other springs have found it, so that their sanative qualities may seem not taken away, but removed. And as there are many mean men of great ability yet depressed in obscurity, so no doubt there are in our land *aquae incognitae* of concealed worth and virtue, in effect no whit inferior to those which in fame are far above them. However, the gift which Nature holdeth forth may be doubled in the goodness thereof, if the hand of Art do but help to receive it, and the patients be prepared with physic, in the using of such water; otherwise *fons vitae* may be *fons mortis,* if diet, due time and quantity be not observed.

Some will say that our English waters must needs be raw, because so far from the fire: whilst those are better boiled which, lying more south, are nearer the sun. But experience avows the contrary, that England affordeth most sanative waters for English bodies, if men were as judicious in taking as Nature is bountiful in tendering them.

As for the proprietaries of such (or rather of the ground surrounding such) medicinal waters, as I would not have them detrimented in the least degree by the conflux of people unto them, so it is injurious in my judgment for them to set them to sale, and make gain of God's free gift therein.

THE BUILDINGS

Next we take notice of the signal structures which each county doth afford. Indeed the Italians do account all English to be Gothish buildings, only vast (and greatness must have something of coarseness therein). However, abating for their advantage above us in materials, marble, porphyry, &c., their palaces may admire the art in some English fabrics, and in our churches especially.

THE WONDERS

Of these England affordeth many, which by several authors are variously reckoned up. One reckoneth four as most remarkable; another accounted six; a third bringeth them up to thirteen, which since some have increased. Indeed if so many men had all agreed in one number, that had been a wonder indeed.

But under this title we comprehend all rarities which are out of the ordinary road of Nature, the illustration whereof may minister unto us matter of profitable discourse. Of these wonders, some were transient, lasting only for a time (like extraordinary ambassadors employed on some great affair); others liegers and permanent, the most proper for our pen to observe. And to prevent vacuity in some counties (that this topic of wonders might be invested with some matter) some artificial rarities are, but very sparingly, inserted, such as transcend the standard of ordinary performance; but these are cast in as overweight, the former being only our proper subject.

Our great design herein is, that men may pay the tribute of their admiration, where the same is due, to God himself, who, as David observeth, "only doth great wonders." A secondary end I have herein, to show that England falls not short of foreign countries in wonderful sights, the same in kind, though not in degree. Italy hath her Grotta della Sibilla, we in Somersetshire our Wookey Hole; Spain her Anas, we our Mole, &c. But wonders, like prophets, are not without honour save in their own country, where constancy, or at least commonness of converse with them abateth their respect and reputation.

LOCAL PROVERBS

A proverb is much matter decocted into few words. Some will have a proverb so called from *verbum*, a *word*, and *pro*, as in *proavus*, signifying *before;* being a speech which time out of mind hath had peaceable possession in the mouths of many people. Others deduce it from *verbum*, a *word*, and *pro* for *vice*, as in *propraeses*, *in stead of*, because it is not to be taken in the literal sense; one thing being put for another.

Six essentials are required to the completing of a perfect proverb, namely, that it be

1. Short 2. Plain 3. Common 4. Figurative 5. Ancient 6. True	Otherwise it is no proverb, but a(n)	1. Oration 2. Riddle 3. Secret 4. Sentence 5. Upstart 6. Libel

I have only insisted on such local proverbs in their respective counties wherein some proper place or person is mentioned; such as suggest unto us some historical hint, and the interpretation thereof afford some considerable information, and conduce to the illustration of those counties wherein they are used.

Herein I have neglected such narrow and restrictive proverbs as never travelled beyond the smoke of the chimneys of that town wherein they were made, and though perchance significant in themselves, are unknown to the neighbouring counties, so far they are from acquiring a national reception. Besides, I have declined all such which are frivolous, scurrilous, scandalous, confining ourselves only to such whose expounding may contribute to the understanding of those shires wherein they are in fashion.

We have not confined ourselves to proverbs in the strict acception thereof, but sometimes insist on such which have only a proverbial tendency, or lie, as one may say, in the marches betwixt proverb and prophecy, where they afford us a fit occasion to sally forth into such discourse as may conduce to the history of our nation.

THE MEDICINAL HERBS

Some maintain this position, "that every county cures the diseases which it causes, and bringeth remedies for all the maladies bred therein." An opinion which, grant not true, yet may have much truth therein, seeing every country, and England especially, affordeth excellent plants, were it not partly for men's laziness, that they will not seek them; partly for their ignorance, that they know not when they have found them; and partly for their pride and peevishness, because, when found, they disdain to use and apply them. Indeed, *quod charum, charum;* what is fetched far, and bought dear, that only is esteemed; otherwise, were many English plants as rare as they are useful, we would hug in our hands what we now trample under our feet.

Now the reason why I have been so sparing in this topic, and so seldom insist thereon, is because these herbs grow equally for goodness and plenty in all counties, so that no one shire can, without manifest usurpation, entitle itself thereunto. Besides, they are so common and numerous, they would jostle out matter of more concernment. However, we have noted it where the herb is rare and very useful; and in our following book (though here the method be transposed) have placed medicinal herbs next medicinal waters, conceiving that order most natural.

MUSICIANS

Music is nothing else but wild sounds civilized into time and tune. Such the extensiveness thereof, that it stoopeth as low as brute beasts, yet mounteth as high as angels; for horses will do more for a whistle than for a whip, and, by hearing their bells, jingle away their weariness.

Such as cavil at music because Jubal, a descendant from wicked Cain, was the first founder thereof, may as well be content to lie out of doors, and refuse all cover to shelter them, because Jabal, of the same extraction, being his own brother, first invented to dwell in tents.

I confess there is a company of pretenders to music, who are commonly called *crowders*, and that justly too, because they *crowd* into the company of gentlemen, both unsent for and unwelcome; but these are no more a disgrace to the true professors of that faculty than monkeys are a disparagement to mankind.

Now right ancient is the use of music in England, especially if it be true what I read in a worthy Father;[1] and I know not what more to admire, either that so memorable a passage should escape Master Camden's, or that it should fall under my observation:

> They say, even those which compose histories, that in the island of Britain, there is a certain cave, lying under a mountain, in the top thereof gaping. The wind therefore falling into the cave, and dashing into the bosom of a hollow place, there is heard a tinkling of cymbals, beating in tune and time.

Where this musical place should be in Britain, I could never find; yet have been informed[2] that Dr. Miles Smith, bishop of Hereford, found something tending that way (by the help of an active fancy) in Herefordshire. But waiving this *natural*, the antiquity of *artificial* music in this island is proved by the practice of the bards, thereby communicating religion, learning and civility to the Britons.

Right glad I am, that when music was lately shut out of our churches, on what default of hers I dare not to inquire, it hath since been harboured and welcomed in the halls, parlours and chambers of the primest persons of this nation. Sure I am, it could not enter into my head to surmise that music would have been so much discouraged by such who turned our kingdom into a Commonwealth, seeing they prided themselves in the arms thereof, an impaled harp being moiety of the same. When it was asked what made a good musician, one answered a good voice, another that it was skill. But he said the truth who said it was encouragement. It was therefore my constant wish that, seeing most of our musicians were men of maturity, and arrived at their full age and skill before these distracted times began, and seeing what the historian wrote in another

(1) Clemens Alexandrinus, *Stromata*, lib. vi. (2) By Master Stephens, a learned servant to the bishop.

sense is true here in our acception and application thereof, *Res est unius seculi populus virorum;* I say, I did constantly wish that there might have been some seminary of youth set up, to be bred in the faculty of music, to supply succession, when this set of masters in that science had served their generation.

Yet although I missed of what I did then desire, yet, thanks be to God, I have lived to see music come into request (since our nation came into right tune) and began to flourish in our churches and elsewhere; so that now no fear but we shall have a new generation skilful in that science, to succeed such whose age shall call upon them to pay their debt to nature.

In recounting up of musicians, I have only insisted on such who made it their profession, and either have written books of that faculty, and have attained to such an eminence therein as is generally acknowledged. Otherwise the work would be endless, to recount all up who took it as a quality of accomplishment; amongst whom King Henry the Eighth must be accounted, who (as Erasmus testifies to his knowledge) did not only sing his part sure, but also compose services for his chapel, of four, five and six parts; though as good a professor as he was, he was a great destroyer of music in this land; surely not intentionally, but accidentally, when he suppressed so many choirs at the dissolution.

BUILDERS OF CHURCHES

Such centurions who have erected us synagogues, places for God's public worship, seem to me to have given good testimony of their love to our nation. Bitter was the brave[1] which railing Rabsheca sent to holy Hezekiah, proffering him 2,000 horses, on condition that the other were but able to find riders for them. But it grieves me to see the superstitution of the former insult over the religion of this present age, bragging that she left us ten thousand churches and chapels, more or less ready built, if we can find but repairers to keep them up.

It is in my opinion both dishonourable to God, and scandalous to all good men, to see such houses daily decay; but there is a generation of people who, to prevent the verifying of the old proverb, "*Pater noster* built churches, and *Our Father* plucks them down," endeavour to pluck down both churches and our Father together, neglecting, yea, despising the use both of the one and the other. Be it here remembered, that it is not only equal but just, that such as have been founders of churches, or grand benefactors unto them, should have due respect in preserving their monuments from violation or encroachment of others. I urge this the rather, because abuses have been frequent in this kind, even to those that have deserved best. I cannot with patience remember the story of Henry Keble, lord mayor of London 1511, who, besides other benefactions in his lifetime, rebuilded Aldermary Church run to very ruins, and bequeathed at his death a thousand pounds for the finishing thereof. Yet within sixty years after, his bones were unkindly, yea inhumanly, cast out of the vault wherein they were buried, his monument plucked down for some wealthy person of the present times to be buried therein.

(1) *Brave,* strictly a verb, but used here as a substantive in the sense of 'challenge'.

I could wish this was the last barbarism in this kind, and am sorry that, upon small inquiry, I could insist on later instances.

FREE SCHOOLS AND COLLEGES

I place schools before colleges, because they are introductory thereunto, intended for the breeding of children and youth, as the other for youth and men. And seeing much of truth is contained in our English proverb, "It is as good to be unborn as unbred," such may in some sort seem their second parents, who have provided for their education.

These schools are of two kinds. First, those wherein only a salary is given to the schoolmaster to teach children *gratis;* and these, I confess, are good. Secondly, such wherein a select number of scholars have competent maintenance allowed towards their living in the university; and these, all will acknowledge, are better. Some do suspect a surfeit in our land of the multitude of schools, because the nursery is bigger than the orchard, the one breeding more plants than the other can maintain trees, and the land not affording sufficient preferment for them, learning is forced to stoop to mean courses to make a livelihood. But I conceive that "store in this kind is no sore;" and if we must not "do evil that good may come thereof," we must not forbear doing that which is good, for fear of accidental evils which may arise from the same.

BRIDGES

Builders of bridges (which are highways over water) and makers of caused-ways or causeways, which are bridges over dirt, though last in order, are not least in benefit to the commonwealth. Such conveniences save the lives of many, ease the labour of more painful travellers, and may be said in some sort to lengthen the day, and shorten the way to men in their journeys; yea, bridges make and keep this island a continent to itself. How great the care of the ancient Romans to repair them, for the safety of passengers, appears by the origination of *pontifex,* having the inspection over bridges by his primitive institution.

Indeed the word bridge appears not in all Scripture, whereof this the reason. The rivers of Palestine were either so shallow, that they were passable by fords, as of Jabbok, Arnon, and Jordan before it grew navigable; or else so deep, that they were ferried over, as Jordan when near his fall into the Dead Sea; but most of ours in England are of a middle size; so deep, that they cannot be forded; so narrow, that they need not to be ferried over. Hence come our so eminent bridges, insomuch that such structures are accounted amongst our English excellences.[1]

However, Palestine was subject with England to the same inconveniences of bad highways; and therefore, in the list of charitable actors reckoned by the prophet, he is accounted as a principal, "the restorer of paths to dwell in;" for indeed some ways may be said not-habitable, being so deep and dirty that they cut off all intercourse, the end general of all men's dwelling together.

I will conclude this topic of bridges with this memorable accident.

(1) *Anglia, mons, pons,* &c.

Maud, queen to King Henry the First, being to pass the River Lea about Stratford, near the falling of the said river into the Thames, was almost drowned in riding over it. But this proved the bad cause of a good effect; for hereupon she built the beautiful bridge there, for the benefit of travellers; and the village, probably from a fair arch or bow therein, received (as some conceive) the addition of Stratford Bow. Far be it from me to wish the least ill to any who willingly would not have their fingers to ache, or an hair of their heads lessened. Yet this I could desire, that some covetous churls, who otherwise will not be melted into works of charity, may, in their passing over waters, be put into peril without peril—understand me, might be endangered to fright, but not hurt—that others might fare the better for their fears; such misers being minded thereby to make or repair bridges for public safety and convenience.

OF MODERN BATTLES

Immediately before our Farewell to the respective counties, we have inserted a breviate of modern battles since our civil distempers.[1] I need here premise nothing of the difference betwixt a skirmish, being only the engagement of parties, and a battle, being an encounter betwixt generals with their armies. Nor yet of the difference betwixt *praelium* a fight or battle, and *bellum* a war; the former a fight in field, the latter the continuance of hostility (which may be for many years) whilst the difference dependeth undecided. *Peracto praelio, manet bellum* [the battle done, the war continues]. And though a truce may give a comma or colon to the war, nothing under a peace can put a perfect period thereunto.

In describing these battles I am, for distinction sake, necessitated to use the word Parliament improperly, according to the abusive acception thereof for these latter years. Let us think and judge with the wise; but if we do not speak with the vulgar, we shall be dumb to the vulgar. Otherwise I know a parliament properly is a complete syllogism, the lords and commons being two propositions, the king the conclusion thereof; and our English tongue wanteth one word to express the dissenting part of a parliament; and I trust in God, as our language doth not afford the name, so our land shall not hereafter behold the nature thereof.

These battles are here inserted, not with any extent (God knows my heart) to perpetuate the odious remembrance of our mutual animosities, that heartburnings may remain when houseburnings are removed, but chiefly to raise our gratitude to God, that so many battles should be fought in the bosom of so little a land, and so few scars and signs thereof extant in their visible impressions. Such who consider how many men we have lost, would wonder we have any left, and such who see how many we have left, that we had any lost. In a word, as it is said of the best oil, that it hath no taste, that is, no *tang*, but the pure natural gust of oil therein, so I have endeavoured to present these battles according to plain historical truth, without any partial reflections.

(1) In this edition the accounts of battles have been placed immediately before the Worthies.

WHY THE WORTHIES IN THIS WORK ARE DIGESTED COUNTY-WAYS

First, this method of marshalling them is new, and therefore, I hope, nevertheless acceptable. Secondly, it is as informative to our judgments, to order them by counties according to their place, as by centuries (so oft done before) according to the time; seeing *where* is as essential as *when* to a man's being. Yea, both in some sort may be said to be *jure divino* (understand it ordered by God's immediate providence) and therefore are coupled together by the Apostle: "And hath determined the times before appointed, and the bounds of their habitation." If of their habitation in general, then more especially of the most important place of their nativity.

The Spirit of God in Scripture taketh signal notice hereof: "The Lord shall count when he writes up the people, *that this man was born there.*" "Philip was of Bethsaida, the city of Andrew and Peter." And all know how St. Paul got his best liberty where he saw the first light "in Tarsus, a city of Cilicia."

When Augustus Cæsar issued out a decree to tax the whole world, it was ordered therein that "every one should go into his own city," as the most compendious way to prevent confusion and effectually to advance the business. I find the same to expedite this work, by methodizing the Worthies therein according to the respective places of their nativities. If some conceive it a pleasant sight, in the city of London, to behold the natives of the several shires, after the hearing of a sermon, pass in a decent equipage to some hall, there to dine together, for the continuance and increase of love and amity amongst them; surely this spectacle will not seem unpleasant to ingenuous eyes, to see the heroes of every particular county modelled in a body together, and marching under the banners of their several eminencies.

Here you may behold how each county is innated with a particular genius, inclining the natives thereof to be dexterous, some in one profession, some in another; one carrying away the credit for soldiers, another for seamen, another for lawyers, another for divines, &c., as I could easily instance, but that I will not forestall the reader's observation, seeing some love not a rose of another's gathering, but delight to pluck it themselves.

Here also one may see how the same county was not always equally fruitful in the production of worthy persons; but as trees are observed to have their bearing and barren years, so shires have their rise and fall in affording famous persons, one age being more fertile than another, as by annexing the dates to their several worthies will appear.

In a word, my serious desire is to set a noble emulation between the several counties, which should acquit themselves most eminent in their memorable offspring. Nor let a smaller shire be disheartened herein, to contest with another larger in extent, and more populous in persons, seeing *viri* do not always hold out in proportion to *homines*. Thus we find the tribe of Simeon more numerous than any in Israel (Judah and Dan only excepted) as which, at their coming out of Egypt, afforded no fewer than "fifty-nine thousand and three hundred." Yet that tribe did not yield prince, priest, prophet or any remarkable persons, Apocrypha, Judith only excepted; *multi gregarii, pauci egregii,* and multitude with amplitude is never the true standard of eminency, as the judicious reader, by perusing and comparing our county catalogues, will quickly perceive.

OF THE AUTHORS FROM WHOM OUR INTELLIGENCE IN THE FOLLOWING WORK HATH BEEN DERIVED

The plain English saying hath very much of downright truth therein: "I tell you my tale, and my tale-master," which is essential to the begetting of credit to any relation. Indeed when one writeth with St. John (waiving his infallible inspiration) "that which we have heard, which we have seen with our eyes, which we have looked upon, and our hands have handled," such clogging a book with authors were superfluous, which now is necessary in him that writeth what was done at distance, *far from,* in time *long before* him.

First, to assert and vindicate the writer. When Adam complained that he was naked, God demanded of him, "Who told thee that thou wast naked?" Intimating thus much, that if he could not produce the person who first so informed him, he might justly be suspected (as indeed he was) the author as well as utterer of that sad truth. Our Saviour said to Pilate, "Sayest thou this thing of thyself, or did others tell thee?" And all things reported are reducible to this dichotomy: 1. *The Fountain of Invention;* 2. *The Channel of Relation.* If one ignorantly buyeth stolen cattle, and hath them fairly vouched unto him, and publicly in an open fair payeth toll for them, he cannot be damnified thereby: the case I conceive of him who writeth a falsehood, and chargeth his margin with the author thereof.

Secondly, to edify and inform the reader: *frustra creditur, quod sine agnitione originis creditur* (it is vainly believed, which is believed without the knowledge of the original thereof). Yea, properly it is no rational belief, but an easy, lazy, supine credulity.

Such as designingly conceal their authors, do it either out of guiltiness or envy. Guiltiness, when conscious to themselves that, if inspection be made of such quotations, they will be found defectively, redundantly or injuriously cited, distorted from their genuine intention.

Or else they do it out of envy. Tyrants commonly cut off the stairs by which they climb up unto their thrones (witness King Richard the Third beheading the duke of Buckingham) for fear that, if still they be left standing, others will get up the same way. Such the jealousy of some writers, that their readers would be as, if not more, knowing than themselves, might they be but directed to the original, which they purposely intercept.

Some, to avoid this rock of envy, run on as bad of ostentation; and in the end of their books, muster up an army of authors, though perchance they themselves have not seriously perused one regiment thereof, so that the goodness of their library, not greatness of their learning, may thence be concluded, that they *have* (if with the prophet's axe some were not borrowed) for I will not say *have read,* many books in their possession.

I have endeavoured to steer my course betwixt both these rocks, and come now to give in the particulars whence I have derived my information, knowing full well *quantas auctor, tanta fides.* These may be referred to three heads: first, *Printed Books;* secondly, *Records in Public Offices;* thirdly, *Manuscripts* in the possession of private gentlemen. To which we may add a fourth, viz., *Instructions* received from the *nearest relations* to those persons whose lives we have presented.

We pass by printed books, cited in the margin, and obvious to all who are pleased to consult them, and first pitch on the Records of the Tower. Master William Ryley[1] was then master of those jewels, for so they deserve to be accounted, seeing a scholar would prefer that place before the keeping of all the prisoners in the Tower. I know not whether more to commend his care in securing, dexterity in finding, diligence in perusing them, or courtesy in communicating such copies of them as my occasions required, thanks being all the fees expected from me.

I place next the records in the exchequer; for, although I had a catalogue of the sheriffs of England lent me by Master Highmore of the Pipe Office, which I compared with another of that learned knight Sir Winkefield Bodenham, yet, being frequently at a loss, I was forced to repair to the originals in the exchequer. Here let not my gratitude be buried in the graves of Master John Witt, and Master Francis Boyton, both since deceased, but, whilst living, advantageous to my studies.

To these authentic records let me add the Church Registers in several parishes, denied indeed by our common lawyers, but stickled for by some canonists to be records-fellows at least, and having, though not the *formality* in law, the force thereof in history, very useful to help us in many nativities.

And here I cannot but bemoan the μέγα χάσμα, that great gulf, or broad blank, left in our registers during our civil wars, after the laying aside of bishops, and before the restitution of his most sacred majesty. Yea, hereafter this sad vacuum is like to prove so thick, like the Egyptian darkness, that it will be sensible in our English histories.

I dare maintain that the wars betwixt York and Lancaster, lasting by intermission some sixty years, were not so destructive to church records, as our modern wars in six years; for, during the former, their differences agreed in the same religion, impressing them with reverence of all sacred muniments; whilst our civil wars, founded in faction, and variety of pretended religions, exposed all naked church records a prey to their armed violence.

Let me add, that it conduced much to the exactness of Jewish genealogies, that their children were solemnly circumcised and named on the eighth day. On the contrary, the omitting the baptizing of infants till they be adult (which causeth, that though the weekly births exceed the burials, the burials exceed the christenings in London) will perplex those who in the next age shall write the nativities of such persons. Say not it matters not though their nativities be utterly forgotten; for though their fathers were factious fanatics, the sons, by God's grace, may prove sober Christians, and eminent in their generations.

(1) See p. 297 for a note on William Ryley.

The last port to which I trafficked for intelligence, towards our issuing work, was by making my addresses, by letters and otherwise, to the nearest relations of those whose lives I have written. Such applications have sometimes proved chargeable; but, if my weak pains shall find preferment, that is, acceptance from the judicious reader, my care and cost is forgotten, and shall never come under computation.

Here I cannot but condemn the carelessness, not to say ingratitude, of those (I am safe whilst containing myself in general terms) who can give no better account of the place where their fathers or grandfathers were born, than the child unborn; so that sometimes we have been more beholden to strangers for our instructions herein than to their nearest kindred. And although some will say sons are more comfortably concerned to know the time of their fathers' death than place of their birth, yet I could almost wish that a moderate fine were imposed on such heirs, whose fathers were born before them, and yet they know not where they were born. However, this I must gratefully confess, I have met with many who *could not,* never with any who *would not,* furnish me with information herein.

It is observable that men born a hundred years since, and upwards, have their nativities fixed with more assurance, than those born some eighty years since. Men's eyes see worst in the twilight, in that interval after the sun is set, and natural light ended, and before candles are set up, and artificial light begun. In such a *crepusculum* of time those writers lived, who fall short of the history of Bale and Leland, yet go before the memory of any alive, which unhappy insterstice hath often perplexed us, and may easier be complained of than amended.

To conclude, should I present all with books, who courteously have conduced to my instruction, the whole impression would not suffice. But I remember the no less civil than politic invitation of Judah to the tribe of Simeon, "Come up with me into my lot (to conquer the Canaanites) and I likewise will go with thee into thy lot." If such who have lent me theirs, shall have occasion to borrow mine assistance, my pains, brains and books, are no more mine than theirs to command, which, besides my prayers for them, and thanks to them, is all my ability in requital can perform.

BEDFORDSHIRE

BEDFORDSHIRE hath Northamptonshire on the north, Huntingdon and Cambridge-shires on the east, Hertfordshire on the south, Buckinghamshire on the west thereof. It lieth from north to south in an oval form, and may be allowed two and twenty miles in length, though the general breadth thereof extendeth not to full fifteen.

The soil consisteth of a deep clay, yet so that this county may be said to wear a belt or girdle of sand about, or rather athwart, the body thereof, from Woburn to Potton, affording fair and pleasant, as the other part doth fruitful and profitable places for habitation, which partakes plentifully in the partage of all English conveniences.

Here let this caveat be entered, to preserve its due, but invaded right to much grain growing in this county; for corn-chandlers (the most avouchable authors in this point) will inform you that when Hertfordshire wheat and barley carries the credit in London, thereby much is meant (though miscalled) which is immediately bought in and brought out of Hertfordshire, but originally growing in Bedfordshire, about Dunstable and elsewhere. But let not the dry nurse, which only carried the child in her arms and dandled it in her lap, lay claim to that babe which the true mother did breed and bear in her body.

NATURAL COMMODITIES

Barley

White, large, plump and full of flour. The countryman will tell you that of all our grains this is most nice, and must be most observed in the several seasons thereof. It doth not only allay hunger, but also in a manner quencheth thirst, when ordered into malt. It is, though not so toothsome, as wholesome as wheat itself, and was all the staff of bread which Christ's body leaned on in this life; eating, to attest his humanity, barley loaves, to evidence his humility.

Malt

This is barley with the property thereof much altered, having passed both water and fire, steeped and dried on a kiln. What great estates maltsters got formerly in this county may be collected from the wealth of the ale-brewers therein, there being so near a relation betwixt the two callings. For I read in the reign of King Henry the Fifth of William Murfley, an ale-brewer of Dunstable (accounted, I confess, a lollard, and follower of the Lord Cobham) who, when taken, had two horses trapped with gilt armour led after him, and had a pair of gilt spurs in his bosom, expecting (say they) knighthood from the Lord Cobham. And although I believe not the report in full habitude, it is enough to intimate unto us that in that age it was a wealthy employment.

FULLER'S EARTH

Great store of this is digged up not far from Woburn in this county, whence it is commonly called Woburn earth. Such the use thereof in drapery that good cloth can hardly be made without it, foreign parts affording neither so much, nor so good of this kind.[1] No wonder then if our statutes strictly forbid the transportation thereof, to preserve the perfection of clothing amongst ourselves. But were this fuller's earth like *terra lemnia,* or *sigillata,* and all the parcels thereof locked up under a seal, yet the Dutch (so long as they are so cunning, and we so careless) will stock themselves hence with plentiful proportions thereof.

LARKS

The most and best of these are caught and well dressed about Dunstable in this shire. A harmless bird whilst living, not trespassing on grain, and wholesome when dead, then filling the stomach with meat, as formerly the ear with music. In winter they fly in flocks, probably the reason why *alauda* signifieth in Latin both a lark and a legion of soldiers; except any will say a legion is so called because helmeted on their heads and crested like a lark, therefore also called in Latin *galerita.* If men would imitate the early rising of this bird, it would conduce much unto their healthfulness.

THE MANUFACTURES

Fat folk (whose collops stick to their sides) are generally lazy, whilst leaner people are of more activity. Thus fruitful countries (as this is for the generality thereof) take to themselves a writ of ease; the principal cause why Bedfordshire affords not any trades peculiar to itself.

THE BUILDINGS

This county affordeth no cathedral, and the parochial churches entitle not themselves to any eminency. Only I hear such high commendations of a chapel and monument erected at Maldon by Thomas earl of Elgin to the memory of his deceased lady Diana Cecil, that I am impatient till I have beheld it, to satisfy myself whether it answereth that character of curiosity which credible persons have given thereof.

Toddington, Ampthill, and Woburn carry away credit amongst the houses of the nobility in this county.

THE WONDERS

At Harleswood, commonly called Harrold, in this county, the river of Ouse, anno 1399, parted asunder, the water from the fountain standing still, and those towards the sea giving way, so that it was passable over on foot for three miles together, not without the astonishment of the beholders. It was an ominous presage of the sad civil wars betwixt the two houses of York and Lancaster.

There is a rivulet in this county (though confining on Buckinghamshire) near a village called Aspley, and take the strange operation thereof from his pen who, though a poet, is a credible author:

(1) See more hereof in Surrey, title NATURAL COMMODITIES.

The brook which on her bank dost boast that earth alone,
Which, noted of this isle, converteth wood to stone.
That little Aspley's earth we anciently instyle,
'Mongst sundry other things, A Wonder of the Isle.[1]

But, by his leave, there is another of the same nature in Northamptonshire; which because less known I will there enlarge myself on that subject.

PROVERBS

As crooked as Crawley brook. This a nameless brook arising about Woburn, running by Crawley, and falling immediately into the Ouse. But this proverb may better be verified of Ouse itself in this shire, more *meandrous* than *Maeander,* which runneth above eighty miles in eighteen by land. Blame it not if, sensible of its sad condition, and presaging its fall into the foggy fens in the next county, it be loath to leave this pleasant place; as who would not prolong their own happiness?

The Bailiff of Bedford is coming. This proverb hath its *original* in this, but *use* in the next county of Cambridge. The River Ouse running by is called the Bailiff of Bedford who, swelling with rain, snow-water and tributary brooks in the winter, and coming down on a sudden, arresteth the Isle of Ely with an inundation. But I am informed that the drainers of the fens have of late with incredible care, cost, art and industry, wrested the mace out of this bailiff's hand, and have secured the country against his power for the future.

THE WORTHIES

HENRY DE ESSEX. He is too well known in our English chronicles, being baron of Rayleigh in Essex and hereditary standard-bearer of England. It happened in the reign of this king [Henry II] there was a fierce battle fought in Flintshire, at Coleshill, betwixt the English and Welsh, wherein this Henry de Essex, *animum et signum simul abjecit* (betwixt traitor and coward cast away both his courage and banner together) occasioning a great overthrow of English.

But he that hath the baseness to do, had the boldness to deny the doing of so foul a fact, until he was challenged in combat by Robert de Momford, a knight, eyewitness thereof, and by him overcome in a duel; whereupon his large inheritance was confiscated to the king, and he himself partly thrust, partly going into a convent, hid his head in a cowl, under which, betwixt shame and sanctity, he blushed out the remainder of his life. [*fl.* 1157]

SILVESTER DE EVERDON, for so he is written in the records of Carlisle (though Eversden and Everseen in other books) which are most to be credited, as passing under the pens of the best, and to his particular the most knowing clerks, no doubt took his name from Everton, a village in this (but the confines of Cambridge) shire. He was a man memorable for his preferment, and very able to discharge the lay part thereof, receiving the great seal anno the 29th of King Henry the Third, 1244, and is commended for one most cunning in customs of chancery. The

(1) Drayton's *Polyolbion.*

same year he was chosen bishop of Carlisle, though demurring on the acceptance thereof (conscious to himself, perchance, as unqualified) his consecration was deferred to the next year.

He, with the rest of the English bishops, addressed themselves to King Henry the Third, and boldly enough *requested-required* of him, that all foreigners and insufficient persons might be put out of their bishoprics. Now as to the point of insufficiency the king, singling out this Silvester, thus bespake him:[1] "And thou, Silvester of Carlisle who, so long licking the chancery, was the little clerk of my clergyman, it is sufficiently known to all how I advanced thee to be a bishop before many reverend persons and able divines."

His expression "licking the chancery" hath left posterity to interpret it, whether taxing him for ambition, liquorishly longing for that place; or for adulation, by the soft smoothing of flattery making his way thereunto; or for avarice, licking it so that he gained great, if good, profit thereby. As for his expression "little clerk," it is plain it referred not to his stature, but drawfness in learning. However, all this would not persuade him into a resignation of his bishopric, though it was not long before he lost both it and his life, by a fall from a skittish horse, Anno Domini 1254.

MARGARET BEAUFORT, countess of Richmond and Derby [*b.* 1443]. No person of judgment or ingenuity will find fault with her posture under this title, who was great-great-grandchild to King Edward the Third, and mother to King Henry the Seventh, besides her (almost incredible) alliance to so many foreign princes.[2]

Thus reader, I am confident I have pleased thee as well as myself in disposing her in this place. And yet I am well assured that were she alive she would (half-offended hereat) be more contented to be ranked under another and lower topic of benefactors to the public; yea, if left to her own liberty, would choose that reposing-place for her memory. This is not only most consonant to her humility and charity (desiring rather to be good than great) but also more conformable to her remarkable expression, according to the devotion of those darker days, "that if the Christian princes would agree to march with an army for the recovery of Palestine, she would be their laundress."

This is she who, besides a professor of divinity placed in both universities, founded the two fair colleges of Christ's and Saint John's in Cambridge. By the way, be it observed that Cambridge hath been much beholden to the strength of bounty in the weaker sex. Of the four halls therein two, viz., Clare and Pembroke were (as I may say) feminine foundations; and of the twelve colleges one third, Queens', Christ's, Saint John's and Sidney owe their original to worthy women; whereas no female ever founded college in Oxford, though bountiful benefactors to many; seeing Queen's College therein, though commended to the queens of England for its successive patronesses, had Robert Eglesfield[3] for the effectual founder thereof.

And Cambridge is so far from being ashamed of, she is joyful at and

(1) Matthew Paris [Latin original omitted]. (2) See their number in her funeral sermon preached by Bishop Fisher. (3) See Cumberland, p. 101.

thankful for such charity, having read of our Saviour himself that "Mary Magdalene, and Joanna, and Susanna, and many other women, ministered unto him of their substance." But this worthy Lady Margaret, being too high for a mean man to commend, is long since gone to the great God to reward, dying [1509] in the beginning of the reign of her grand-child King Henry the Eighth.[1]

THOMAS CHASE, an ancient and faithful labourer in God's vineyard, led his life most in Buckinghamshire, but found his death in this county; long kept in durance, and hanged at last, in the bishop's prison at Woburn. His executioners, to palliate their murder, and asperse his memory, gave it out that he had destroyed himself; a loud lie, seeing he was so loaden with chains that he could not lift up his own body. But the clearing hereof must be remitted to that day wherein all things done in secret shall be made manifest. His martyrdom happened in the reign of King Henry the Seventh, Anno Domini 1506.

GEORGE JOYE was born in this county, though the exact place be not expressed. He was a great friend to Master Tyndale, and therefore perfectly hated by Wolsey, Fisher and Sir Thomas More. The particulars of his sufferings, if known, would justly advance him into the reputation of a confessor. He translated some parts of the Bible into English, and wrote many books reckoned up by Bale; notwithstanding many machinations against his life, he found his coffin where he fetched his cradle, *in sua patria sepultus,* being peaceably buried in his native county 1553, the last year of King Edward the Sixth.

JOHN MORDAUNT [FIRST BARON MORDAUNT OF TURVEY]. He was extracted of a very ancient parent in this county, and married one of the daughters and heirs of Henry Vere of Addington in Northamptonshire, whereby he received a great inheritance, being by aged persons in those parts remembered by the name of John of the Woods (reader, I was born under the shadow, and felt the warmth of them); so great a master he was of oaks and timber in that county, besides large possessions he had in Essex and elsewhere. King Henry the Eighth, owning him deservedly for a very wise man, created him Baron Mordaunt of Turvey.[2] [1490?-1562]

WILLIAM SCLATER was born [1575] at Leighton Buzzard in this county,[3] son to Anthony Sclater, the minister thereof for fifty years together, who died well night an hundred years of age. This William his son was bred in Eton, then in King's College in Cambridge, where he commenced bachelor, and (after many years' discontinuance) doctor of divinity. Hence he was invited to be preacher at Walsall in Staffordshire, where he began his sermons (afterwards printed) on the first three chapters of the Romans. Afterwards John Coles, esquire, of Somersetshire, over-entreated him into the western parts, where he presented him vicar of Pitminster. Here he met with manifold and expensive vexations, even to the jeopardy of his

(1) Margaret Beaufort is memorable also for being an early patron of Caxton and Wynkyn de Worde. (2) He was general surveyor of the king's woods, 1526; a supporter of the Reformation, and took part in the trial of Anne Boleyn. (3) So was I informed by his son, Dr. Sclater, late minister of St. Peter-le-Poer, London.

life; but, by the goodness of God, his own innocency and courage, with the favour of his diocesan, he came off with no less honour to himself than confusion to his adversaries.

He was at first not well-affected to the ceremonies of the church; but afterwards, on his profound studying of the point, he was reconciled to them, as for order and decency; and by his example others were persuaded to conform.

Constancy of studying contracted the stone upon him, which he used to call *flagellum studiosorum.* Nor was his health improved by being removed to a wealthier living, when John Lord Poulett of Hinton (at the instance of Elizabeth his lady, in whose inheritance it was, a worthy favourer of piety and pious men) preferred him to the rich parsonage of Limpsham in Somersetshire, where indeed there was scarce any element good, save the earth therein. Whereupon, for his own preservation, he was re-persuaded to return to Pitminster, there continuing till the day of his death, which happened in the year of our Lord 1626, in the fifty-first year of his age, leaving many learned works behind him.

FRANCIS DILLINGHAM was born at Dean in this county, and bred fellow in Christ's College in Cambridge. He was an excellent linguist and subtle disputant. My father was present in the bachelors' schools when a Greek Act[1] was kept, between him and William Alabaster, of Trinity College, to their mutual commendation; a disputation so famous that it served for an era, or epoch, for the scholars in that age thence to date their seniority.

He was afterwards chosen, anno 1607, to be one of the translators of the Bible; and, being richly beneficed at Wilden in this county, died a single man, leaving a fair estate to his brother Master Thomas Dillingham, who was chosen one of the late assembly (though, for age, indisposition and other reasons, not appearing therein) and for many years was the humble, painful and faithful pastor of Dean, the place of his nativity. [*fl.* 1611]

HENRY GREY, son to Henry Grey, was born at Wrest in this county. Something must be premised of his extraction. Richard Grey, third earl of Kent of that family, was so profuse a person, that he wilfully wasted his estate, giving away what he could not spend to the king and others; so little he reflected on Sir Henry Grey his brother (but by a second venter) of Wrest in this county. Hereupon the said Sir Henry, though heir to his brother Richard after his death, yet perceiving himself over-titled, or rather under-stated for so high an honour (the undoubted right whereof rested in him) declined the assuming thereof. Thus the earldom of Kent lay, though not dead, asleep in the family of the Greys almost 50 years, viz., from the 15th of King Henry the Eighth till the 13th of Queen Elizabeth, when she advanced Reginald Grey, grandchild to Sir Henry Grey aforesaid (who had recruited himself with competence of revenues) to be earl of Kent, anno 1571.

This Reginald dying issueless within the year, Henry his brother (the subject of our present description) succeeded to his honour; a person truly

(1) *Act*=a thesis publicly maintained by a candidate for a degree. Francis Dillingham was one of the translators of the Authorized Version.

noble, expending the income of his own estate and of his lady's fair jointure (Mary the relict of Edward earl of Derby) in hospitality.

He was a most cordial protestant, on the same token that, being present at the execution of the Queen of Scots, when she requested the nobility there to stand by and see her death, he (fearing something of superstition) hardly assented thereunto. Yet was he as far from the faction as superstition, deserving the character given unto him, *Omnibus verae nobilitatis ornamentis vir longe honoratissimus.*[1] He left no issue, except some will behold him in some sort parent of Sidney College in Cambridge, as one of the executors to the foundress thereof, who did both *prove* and *improve* her will, besides his personal benefaction thereunto; and, being the surviving executor, he did perpetuate the fellowships (formerly temporary) according to the implicit trust deposited in him, to the advantages of that foundation. He died Anno Domini 1613.

FRANCIS CLEARK, knight, was born at Eaton Socon in this shire, near to Saint Neot's, in the lordship there commonly called the Parsonage. He was a noble benefactor to Sidney College, augmenting all the scholarships of the foundation, and erecting a fair and firm range of building. Such his skill in arithmetic and architecture that, staying at home, he did provide to a brick what was necessary for the finishing thereof. He founded four new fellowships; and, had he been pleased to consult with the college, the settlement with the same expense might have proved more advantageous; for though in gifts to private persons it be improper that the receiver should be the director thereof, a corporation may give the best advice to improve the favours conferred upon it. But it is a general practice that men desire rather to be *broad* than *thick* benefactors.

However, seeing every one may do with his own as he pleaseth, blessed be the memory of this worthy knight, whose gift in effect was felt by the college before the giver thereof was seen, being himself a mere stranger unto it. Some say that because this was the youngest foundation in the university (generally the last child hath the least left it) his charity pitched upon it. But I have been informed that Sir Francis coming privately to Cambridge, to see *unseen,* took notice of Doctor Ward his daily presence in the hall, with the scholars' conformity in caps and diligent performance of exercises, which endeared this place unto him. Thus observing of old statutes is the best loadstone to attract new benefactors. His death happened Anno Domini 163—.

THE FAREWELL

Being to take my farewell of this county, I am minded of the mistake (what writer is free from them?) in Mr. Stow, telling us of tide-boats, tillboats and barges which come from Bedfordshire down the Thames to London, which surely must row over many miles of dry land in their passage thereunto. But if there be a possibility of such a conveyance by art and industry to be effected, may his words prove true by way of prediction, seeing certainly such a conveniency must needs be advantageous to this county.

(1) Camden's *Britannia* ['A person plentifully endowed with all the distinctions of true nobility'].

BERKSHIRE

BERKSHIRE hath Wiltshire on the west, Hampshire on the south, Surrey on the east, Oxford and Buckinghamshire (parted first with the Isis, then with the flexuous river of Thames) on the north thereof. It may be fancied in a form like a lute lying along, whose belly is towards the west, whilst the narrow neck or long handle is extended toward the east. From Coleshill to Windsor it may be allowed in length forty miles. But it amounteth to little more than half as much in the broadest part thereof. It partaketh as plentiful as any county in England of the common commodities, grass, grain, fish, fowl, wool and wood, &c., and we will particularly instance on one or two of them.

NATURAL COMMODITIES

Oaks

It was given in instruction to the spies sent to search the land of Canaan that, amongst other enquiries, they should take particular notice "whether there be wood therein or not?" An important question, the rather because at that time the Israelites were in Arabia the Desert, where they saw not a tree in many months' travel (insomuch that it is recorded for a wonder that in Elim were "seventy palm trees") and now knew the worth of wood by wanting it.

But Berkshire affordeth abundance of trees of all kinds, though her oaks in Windsor Forest for the present come only under our commendation. First, for their firmness, whereof our ships are made. The oak in other kingdoms may be called cowardly, as riving and splitting round about the passage of the bullet, fearing as it were the force thereof; whilst our English, as heart of oak indeed, though entered with bullet, remaineth firm round about it.

Secondly, for the convenience of portage. The wealth of a covetous man (wanting an heart to make use thereof) may not unfitly be compared to the oaks and fir-trees, good and plentiful indeed, in the highlands in Scotland, but growing on such unaccesible mountains, no strength or art can render them useful, Nature in this kind having given them full coffers, but no key to unlock them. Whereas, so indulgent is Divine Providence to England, that our four principal forests lie either on the sea or navigable rivers, viz., New Forest on the sea, Shire Wood on the Trent, Dean on the Severn, and this Windsor Forest on the Thames; and I could wish more care were taken for preserving the timber therein.

Bark

The very name of this shire justly entitles us here to handle this commodity, though common to other counties, because *Barkshire* (as some will have it) was so called from a stripped or *bark-bared oak,* to which signal place the people repaired in time of trouble to make their general defence. It is essential for making good leather, though lately one hath propounded a way to tann it solid and saleable without the help thereof, on condition (and good reason too) he may be allowed reasonable profit for so rare an invention. But many think that he that waits for dead men's shoes, and he that stays for leather shoes made without bark, may both of them go a long time barefoot.

TROUTS

This is a pleasant and wholesome fish, as whose feeding is pure and cleanly in the swiftest streams and on the hardest gravel. Good and great of this kind are found in the river of Kennet nigh Hungerford, though not so big as that which Gesner affirms taken in the Leman lake, being three cubits in length. They are in their perfection in the month of May, and yearly decline with the buck. Being come to his full growth, he decays in goodness, not greatness, and thrives in his head till his death. Note by the way that an hog-back and little head is a sign that any fish is in season.

Other commodities of this, return in other counties, where they may be mentioned with more convenience.

THE MANUFACTURES

CLOTHING

It is plied therein, and because we meet with the best of our manufactures in the first of our shires,[1] a word of the antiquity thereof.

1. *Cloth* sure is of the same date with civility in this land. Indeed the ancient Britons are reported to go naked, clothed only with colours painted, custom making them insensible of cold, with the beggar who, being demanded how he could go naked, returned, "All my body is face." But no sooner had the Romans reduced this island, but cloth, though coarse, such as would hide and heat, was here generally made and used.

2. *Fine Cloth* (though narrow) for persons of worth at home to wear, and for foreign exportation, began in England about the beginning of the reign of King Edward the Third; before which time our statutes take no cognizance of clothing, as inconsiderable (wool being transported in specie) and needing no rules to regulate it, save what prudence dictated to private husbands with their own families.

3. *Broadcloth* (wherein the wealth of our nation is folded up) made with broad looms, two men attending each of them, began here in the reign of King Henry the Eighth. And I have been informed that Jack of Newbury[2] was the first that introduced it into this county. Well may the poets feign Minerva the goddess of wit and the foundress of weaving, so great is the ingenuity thereof.

THE BUILDINGS

Windsor Castle was a royal seat ever since the Conquest, but brought to the modern beauty chiefly at the cost of King Edward the Third. It is a castle for strength, a palace for state, and hath in it a college for learning, a chapel for devotion, and an almshouse (of decayed gentlemen) for

(1) In the original edition Berkshire (then spelt Barkshire) was placed first in alphabetical order. (2) See p. 28 below.

charity. In this palace most remarkable the hall for greatness, Winchester tower for height, and the terrace on the north side for pleasure, where a dull eye may travel twenty miles in a moment. Nor boasteth so much that it consisteth of two great courts, as that it contained two great kings, John of France and David of Scotland, prisoners therein together; as also that it was the seat of the honourable order of the Garter.

Many neat houses and pleasant seats there be in this county, both on the Kennet and Thames, which seem dutifully to attend at distance on Windsor Castle, as Aldermaston, Englefield, &c., most sweet in their situation.

PROVERBS

The Vicar of Bray will be Vicar of Bray still. Bray, a village well known in this county, so called from the Bibroces, a kind of ancient Britons inhabiting thereabouts. The vivacious vicar hereof living under King Henry the Eighth, King Edward the Sixth, Queen Mary, and Queen Elizabeth, was first a papist, then a protestant, then a papist, then a protestant again. He had seen some martyrs burnt (two miles off) at Windsor, and found this fire too hot for his tender temper. This vicar being taxed by one for being a turncoat and an unconstant changeling, "Not so," said he, "for I always kept my principle, which is this, to live and die the vicar of Bray." Such many nowadays, who though they cannot turn the wind, will turn their mills, and set them so, that wheresoever it bloweth their grist shall certainly be grinded.[1]

THE BATTLES

NEWBURY (the first) September 20, 1643. The earl of Essex having raised the siege of Gloucester, and returning towards London, was rather followed than overtaken by the king's army. Both sides might be traced by a tract of bloody footsteps, especially at Aldbourne in Wilts, where they had a smart encounter. At Newbury the earl made a stand. Here happened a fierce fight on the east side of the town, wherein the Londoners did shew that they could as well use a sword in the field as a mete-wand in a shop. The parliament was conceived to lose the most, the king the most considerable persons; amongst whom the earls of Carnarvon and Sunderland, the Viscount Falkland, Colonel Morgan, &c. Both armies may be said to beat and be beaten, neither winning the day, and both the twilight. Hence it was that both sides were so sadly filled with their supper overnight, neither next morning had any stomach to breakfast; but, keeping their stations, were rather contented to face, than willing to fight, one another.

NEWBURY (the second) October 27, 1644. One would wonder where the earl of Essex, so lately stripped out of all his infantry in Cornwall, so soon reinvested himself with more foot, save that London is the shop-general of all commodities. Recruited with fresh (but not fresh-water) soldiers, he gave the king battle. This fight was as long and fierce as the

(1) See Fuller's account, in Norfolk (p. 412) of Andrew Perne, a 'Vicar of Bray' in grain.

former, but the conquest more clear on the parliament's side. The Cornish, though behaving themselves valiantly, were conceived not to do so well, because expected to have done better.

The royalists were at night fain to hang lighted matches on the hedges (so to simulate their abode thereabouts) whilst they drew off, securing their cannon in Donnington Castle, the governor whereof, Sir J. Boys, did the king knight's service; and so, in a pace slower than a flight and faster than a retreat, returned in as good order as their condition was capable of. Many here lost their lives, as if Newbury were so named by a sad prolepsis, fore-signifying that that town should afford a *new burying* place to many slain in two bloody battles.

THE WORTHIES

ALFRED, the fourth son to King Ethelwulf, was born [849] at Wantage, a market-town in this county; an excellent scholar, though he was past twelve years of age before he knew one letter in the book. And did not he run fast, who starting so late came soon to the mark? He was a curious poet, excellent musician, a valiant and successful soldier, who fought seven battles against the Danes in one year, and at last made them his subjects by conquest, and God's servants by Christianity. He gave the first institution, or (as others will have it) the best instauration, to the university of Oxford. A prince who cannot be painted to the life without his loss, no words reaching his worth.

He divided, 1. Every natural day (as to himself) into three parts: eight hours for his devotion, eight hours for his employment, eight hours for his sleep and refection. 2. His revenues into three parts: one for his expenses in war, a second for the maintenance of his court, and a third to be spent on pious uses. 3. His land into thirty-two shires, which number since is altered and increased.[1] 4. His subjects into hundreds and tithings, consisting of ten persons, mutually pledged for their good behaviour; such being accounted suspicious for their life and loyalty that could not give such security.

He left learning where he found ignorance; justice where he found oppression; peace where he found distraction. And, having reigned about four and thirty years, he died, and was buried at Winchester, anno 899. He loved religion more than superstition, favoured learned men more than lazy monks; which, perchance, was the cause that his memory is not loaden with miracles, and he not solemnly sainted with other Saxon kings who far less deserved it.

THOMAS COLE, commonly called the Rich Clothier of Reading. Tradition and an authorless pamphlet make him a man of vast wealth, maintaining an hundred and forty menial servants in his house, besides three hundred poor people whom he set on work; insomuch that his wains with cloth filled the highway betwixt Reading and London, to the stopping of King Henry the First in his progress; who notwithstanding,

(1) Wessex was apparently divided into shires before Alfred's day, but the division of the whole of England into shires was not accomplished until probably late in the tenth century.

for the encouraging of his subjects' industry, gratified the said Cole, and all of his profession, with the set measure of a yard, the said king making his own arm the standard thereof, whereby drapery was reduced in the meteing thereof to a greater certainity.

The truth is this: monks began to lard the lives of their saints with lies, whence they proceeded in like manner to flourish out the facts of famous knights (King Arthur, Guy of Warwick, &c.) in imitation whereof some meaner wits in the same sort made description of mechanics, powdering their lives with improbable passages, to the great prejudice of truth; seeing the making of broadcloth in England could not be so ancient, and it was the arm, not of King Henry, but King Edward the First, which is notoriously known to have been the adequation of a yard.

However, because *omnis fabula fundatur in historia* [all fables are founded on fact] let this Cole be accounted eminent in this kind; though I vehemently suspect very little truth would remain in the midst of this story, if the gross falsehoods were pared from both sides thereof.

ST. EDMUND RICH, son to Edward Rich and Mabel his wife, was born [1170?] at Abingdon in Berkshire, and bred in Oxford. Some will have St. Edmund Hall in that university built by his means, but others, more probably, named in his memory. He became canon of Salisbury, and from thence, by the joint consent of pope, king and monks (three cords seldom twisted in the same cable) advanced archbishop of Canterbury, where he sat almost ten years, till he willingly deserted it, partly because offended at the power of the pope's legate, making him no more than a mere cipher, signifying only in conjunction, when concurring with his pleasure; partly because, vexed at his polling and peeling of the English people: so grievous, he could not endure, so general, he could not avoid to behold it. For these reasons he left the land, went (or shall I say fled) into France, where he sighed out the remainder of his life, most at Pontigny, but some at Soisy, where he died anno 1240.

Pope Innocent the Fourth canonized him six years after his death, whereat many much wondered, that he should so much honour one a professed foe to papal extortions. Some conceived he did it *se defendendo,* and for a *ne noceat,* that he might not be tormented with his ghost. But what hurt were it, if all the enemies of his holiness were sainted, on condition they took death in their way thereunto? Sure it is that Louis king of France a year after translated his corpse and, three years after that, bestowed a most sumptuous shrine of gold and silver and crystal upon it; and the 16th of November is the festival appointed for his memorial.

ROBERT RICH, son to Edward and Mabel his wife, brother of St. Edmund, archbishop of Canterbury, was born at Abingdon in this county. He followed his brother at very great distance both in parts and learning (though accompanying him in his travels beyond the seas) and wrote a book of the life, death and miracles of his brother, being much to blame if he did not do all right to so near a relation. [*fl.* 1185-1240]

ELEANOR, eldest daughter to King Edward the First and Queen Eleanor, was born at Windsor, Anno Dom. 1266. She was afterwards married by a proxy, a naked sword being in bed interposed betwixt him and her body, to Alfonso king of Aragon, with all ceremonies of state. And indeed they proved but ceremonies, the substance soon miscarrying, the said King Alfonso dying Anno Dom. 1292, before the consummation of the marriage. But soon after this lady found that a living earl was better than a dead king, when married to Henry the third earl of Berri in France, from whom the dukes of Anjou and kings of Sicily are descended. This lady deceased in the seven and twentieth of her father's reign, Anno Dom. 1298.

MARY, sixth daughter of King Edward the First and Queen Eleanor, was born at Windsor, April the 12th, 1279. Being but ten years of age, she was made a nun at Amesbury in Wiltshire without her own and, at the first, against her parents' consent, merely to gratify Queen Eleanor her grandmother. Let us pity her, who probably did not pity herself, as not knowing a veil from a kerchief, not understanding the requisites to, nor her own fitness for that profession, having afterwards time too much to bemoan, but none to amend, her condition.

RICHARD OF WALLINGFORD was born [1292?] in that market-town, pleasantly seated on the River Thames, wherein his father was a blacksmith. He went afterwards to Oxford, and was bred in Merton College, then a monk, and at last abbot of St. Alban's, where he became a most expert mathematician, especially for the mechanical part thereof, and (retaining somewhat of his father's trade) was dexterous at making pretty engines and instruments.

His master-piece was a most artificial clock, made, saith my author,[1] *magno labore, majore sumptu, arte vero maxima* (with much *pain*, more *cost*, and most *art*). It remained in that monastery in the time of John Bale, whom by his words I collect an eyewitness thereof; affirming that Europe had not the like, so that it seemed as good as the famous clock at Strasburg in Germany, and in this respect better, because ancienter. It was a calendar as well as a clock, shewing the fixed stars and planets, the ebbing and flowing of the sea, minutes of the hours, and what not?

I have heard that when monopolies began to grow common in the court of France, the king's jester moved to have this monopoly for himself, viz., a *gardesque* of every one who carried a watch about him, and cared not how he employed his time. Surely the monks of Saint Alban's were concerned to be careful how they spent their hours, seeing no convent in England had the like curiosity, this their clock gathering up the least crumb of time, presenting the minutary fractions thereof; on which account, I conceive Richard the maker thereof well prepared for the time of his dissolution, when he died of the leprosy, Anno Dom. 1336.

(1) Bale.

EDWARD THE THIRD, son to Edward the Second and Queen Isabella, was born at Windsor, November 13, 1312, and proved afterwards a pious and fortunate prince. I behold him as merely passive in the deposing of his father, practised on in his minority by his mother and Mortimer. His French victories speak both of his wisdom and valour; and though the conquests of King Henry the Fifth were *thicker* (achieved in a shorter time) his were *broader* (in France and Scotland by sea and land) though both of *length* alike, as lost by their immediate successors.

He was the first English king which coined gold, which with me amounts to a wonder, that before his time all yellow payments in the land should be made in foreign coin. He first stamped the rose-nobles, having on the one side,

IESUS AVTEM TRANSIENS PER MEDIVM ILLORUM IBAT

and on the reverse, his own image with sword and shield, sitting in a ship waving on the sea. Hereupon an English rhymer, in the reign of King Henry the Sixth,

For four things our Noble sheweth to me,
King, Ship, and Sword, and Power of the Sea.

He had a numerous and happy issue by Phillippa his queen, after whose death, he cast his affection on Alice Perrers his paramour, much to his disgrace; it being true what Epictetus returned to Hadrian the emperor asking of him what love was: *In puero, pudor; in virgine, rubor; in femina, furor, in juvene, ardor; in sene, risus* (in a boy, bashfulness; in a maid, blushing; in a woman, fury; in a young man, fire; in an old man, folly). However, take this king altogether, at home, abroad, at church, in state, and he had few equals, none superiors. He died Anno Dom. 1377.

HENRY THE SIXTH, son to Henry the Fifth, was born [1421] in Windsor Castle against the will of his father, by the wilfulness of his mother. He was fitter for a cowl than a crown; of so easy a nature, that he might well have exchanged a pound of patience for an ounce of valour; being so innocent to others, that he was hurtful to himself. He was both over-subjected and over-wived, having married Margaret the daughter of René king of Jerusalem, Sicily and Aragon, a prince only puissant in titles, otherwise little able to assist his son-in-law. Through home-bred dissensions, he not only lost the foreign acquisitions of his father in France, but also his own inheritance in England to the house of York. His death, or murder rather, happened in 1471.

This Henry was twice crowned, twice deposed, and twice buried (first at Chertsey, then at Windsor) and once half sainted. Our Henry the Seventh cheapened the price of his canonization (one may see *for his love,* and buy *for his money,* in the court of Rome) but would not come up to the sum demanded. However, this Henry was a saint (though not with the pope) with the people, repairing to his monument from the farthest part of the land, and fancying that they received much benefit thereby. He was the last prince whom I find expressly born at Windsor. It seems that afterwards our English queens grew out of conceit with that place, as unfortunate for royal nativities.

JOHN WINCHCOMBE [*alias* SMALWOODE] called commonly JACK OF NEWBURY, was the most considerable clothier (without fancy and fiction) England ever beheld. His looms were his hands, whereof he kept one hundred in his house, each managed by a man and a boy. In the expedition to Flodden Field, against James king of Scotland, he marched with an hundred of his own men (as well armed, and better clothed, than any) to shew that the painful to use their hands in peace could be valiant, and employ their arms in war. He feasted King Henry the Eighth and his first queen Catherine at his own house, extant at Newbury at this day, but divided into many tenements. Well may his house now make sixteen clothiers' houses, whose wealth would amount to six hundred of their estates. He built the church of Newbury from the pulpit westward to the tower inclusively; and died about the year 1520; some of his name and kindred of great wealth still remaining in this county.

HENRY BULLOCK was most probably born in this county, where his ancient name appears in a worshipful estate. He was bred fellow and doctor of divinity in Queens' College in Cambridge; a good linguist and general scholar, familiar with Erasmus (an evidence of his learning, it being as hard to halt before a cripple as to deceive his judgment) calling him Bovillus in his epistles unto him.

By the way, our English writers, when rendering a surname in Latin, which hath an appellative signification, content them to retain the body of the name, and only disguise the termination; as Cross, Peacock, *Crossus, Peacocus,* &c. But the Germans, in such a case, do use to mould the meaning of the name, either into Latin, as J. Fierce they translate *I. Ferus,* Bullock, *Bovillus;* or into Greek, as Swarts they render *Melancthon,* Reecklin, *Capnio.*

'Tis confessed our Bullock, compelled by Cardinal Wolsey, wrote against Luther, but otherwise his affections were biased to the protestant party. [*d.* 1526]

SIR JOHN MASON, knight, was born [1503] at Abingdon, where he is remembered among the benefactors to the beautiful almshouses therein; bred in All Souls in Oxford. King Henry the Eighth, coming thither, was so highly pleased with an oration Mr. Mason made unto him, that he instantly gave order for his education beyond the seas, as confident he would prove an able minister of state. This was the politic discipline of those days, to select the pregnancies of either universities, and breed them in foreign parts for public employments. He was privy councillor to King Henry the Eighth and King Edward the Sixth. One maketh him his secretary of state, which some suspect too high; another, but master of the requests, which I believe as much beneath him. He continued councillor to Queen Mary and Queen Elizabeth, to whom he was treasurer of the household, and chancellor of the university of Oxford.

Mr. Camden gives him this true character, *Vir fuit gravis, atque erunditus*; which I like much better than that which followeth so far as I can understand it: *Ecclesiasticorum beneficiorum incubator maximus.*[1]

(1) These words are absurdly rendered by Abraham Darcy, who understood not Latin, and translated Camden out of the French translation: "He was diligent and

Surely he could be no canonical incumbent in any benefice, not being in orders, which leaveth him under the suspicion of being a great engrosser of long leases in church livings, which then used to be let for many years, a pitiful pension being reserved for the poor curate; though possibly in his younger time he might have *tonsuram primam*, or be a deacon, which, improved by his great power, might qualify, at least countenance him for the holding of his spiritual promotions. He died 1566, and lieth buried in the quire of St. Paul's (over against William Herbert, first earl of Pembroke) and I remember this distich of his long epitaph:

> *Tempore quinque suo regnantes ordine vidit,*
> *Horum a consiliis quatuor ille fuit.*
> He saw five princes which the sceptre bore;
> Of them was privy councillor to four.

It appears by his epitaph that he left no child of his own body, but adopted his nephew to be his son and heir.

THOMAS GODWIN was born [1517] at Oakingham in this county, and first bred in the free school therein. Hence he was sent to Magdalen College in Oxford, maintained there for a time by the bounty of Doctor Layton, dean of York, till at last he was chosen fellow of the college. This he exchanged on some terms for the schoolmaster's place of Berkeley in Gloucestershire, where he also studied physic, which afterwards proved beneficial unto him, when forbidden to teach school in the reign of Queen Mary. Yea, Bonner threatened him with fire and faggot, which caused him often to obscure himself and remove his habitation. He was an eloquent preacher, tall and comely in person; qualities which much endeared him to Queen Elizabeth, who loved good parts well, but better when in a goodly person. For 18 years together he never failed to be one of the select chaplains which preached in the Lent before her majesty. He was first dean of Christ Church in Oxford, then dean of Canterbury, and at last bishop of Bath and Wells.

Being infirm with age, and diseased with the gout, he was necessitated, for a nurse, to marry a second wife, a matron of years proportionable to himself. But this was by his court enemies (which no bishop wanted in that age) represented to the queen, to his great disgrace. Yea, they traduced him to have married a girl of twenty years of age, until the good earl of Bedford, casually present at such discourse: "Madam," said he to her majesty, "I know not how much the woman is above twenty; but I know a son of hers is but little under forty."[1]

Being afflicted with a quartan fever, he was advised by his physicians to retire into this county, to Oakingham, the place of his birth, seeing in such cases native air may prove cordial to patients, as mothers' milk to

careful to the preservation of benefits." [Mason was not in holy orders, but was appointed dean of Winchester 1549. He was an astute politician, pliant in principle, profiting by every turn of the wheel, and held high office under four sovereigns. He actually signed the letter to Mary informing her that Lady Jane Grey was proclaimed queen, but, seeing how the tide was running, arranged with the lord mayor for the proclamation of Mary]. (1) Ralegh, who had been trying to secure a manor on a 100 years' lease in Godwin's see, was the author of this story. Godwin was the father of Francis Godwin (see Northamptonshire, p. 437) Fuller's chief authority for the accounts of bishops in this work.

(and old men are twice) children. Here he died, breathing his first and last in the same place, November 19, 1590, and lieth buried under a monument in the south side of the chancel.

JOHN MARBECK was an organist in the choir of Windsor, and very skilful therein; a man of admirable industry and ingenuity, who not perfectly understanding the Latin tongue, did, out of the Latin, with the help of the English Bible, make an English *Concordance,* which Bishop Gardiner himself could not but commend as a piece of singular industry, professing that there were no fewer than twelve learned men to make the first Latin *Concordance.* And King Henry the Eighth, hearing thereof, said that "he was better employed than those priests which accused him." Let, therefore, our modern concordances of Cotton, Newman, Bernard, &c., as children and grandchildren, do their duty to Marbeck's *Concordance,* as their parent at first endeavoured in our language.

This Marbeck was a very zealous protestant, and of so sweet and amiable nature, that all good men did love, and few bad men did hate him. Yet was he condemned, Anno 1544, on the statute of the Six Articles, to be burnt at Windsor, had not his pardon been procured, divers assigning divers causes thereof: 1, That Bishop Gardiner bare him a special affection for his skill in the mystery of music. 2, That such who condemned him procured his pardon out of remorse of conscience, because so slender the evidence against him, it being questionable whether his *Concordance* was made after the statute of the Six Articles or before it, and if before, he was freed by the king's general pardon. 3, That it was done out of design to reserve him for a discovery of the rest of the party. If so, their plot failed them; for, being as true as steel (whereof his fetters were made which he wore in prison for a good time) he could not be frighted or flattered to make any detection.

Here a mistake was committed by Mr. Foxe in his first edition whereon the papists much insult, making this Marbeck burnt at Windsor for his religion, with Anthony Peirson, Robert Testwood, and Henry Filmer.[1] No doubt Mr. Foxe rejoiced at his own mistake, thus far forth, both for Marbeck's sake who escaped with his life, and his enemies, who thereby drew the less guilt of blood on their own consciences. But hear what he pleads for his mistake:

1, Marbeck was dead in law, as condemned; whereon his error was probably grounded. 2, He confessing that one of the four condemned was pardoned his life, misnaming him Filmer instead of Marbeck. 3, Let papists first purge their lying legend from manifest and intentional untruths, before they censure others for casual slips and unmeant mistakes. 4, Recognizing his book in the next edition, he with blushing amended his error. And is not this penance enough, according to the principles of his accusers, confession, contrition, and satisfaction?

All this will not content some morose cavillers, whom I have heard jeeringly say "that many who were burnt in Foxe in the reign of Queen

(1) Marbeck was pardoned through the instrumentality of Bishop Gardiner. The statute of Six Articles (its preamble read "an act abolishing diversity in opinions") was designed to curb heterodoxy. The act was inspired by Henry VIII though he, more than others, had surreptitiously encouraged such heterodoxy.

Mary, drank sack in the days of Queen Elizabeth." But enough is said to any ingenuous person. And it is impossible for any author of a voluminous book, consisting of several persons and circumstances (reader, in pleading for Master Foxe, I plead for myself) to have such ubiquitary intelligence, as to apply the same infallibly to every particular. [*d.* 1585?]

SIR THOMAS SMITH, knight, was born [1556?] at Abingdon, bred in the university of Oxford. God and himself raised him to the eminency he attained unto, unbefriended with any extraction. He may seem to have had an ingenuous emulation of Sir Thomas Smith[1] senior, secretary of state, whom he imitated in many good qualities, and had no doubt equalled him in preferment, if not prevented by death. He attained only to be master of the requests and secretary to King James for his Latin letters; higher places expecting him, when a period was put to his life November 28, 1609. He lieth buried in the church of Fulham in Middlesex under a monument erected by his lady, Frances, daughter to William Lord Chandos, and afterwards countess of Exeter.

HENRY [UNTON or] UMPTON, knight, was born [1557?] as by all indications in the Heralds' Office doth appear, at Wadley in this county. He was son to Sir Edward Umpton, by Anne, the relict of John Dudley, earl of Warwick, and the eldest daughter of Edward Seymour, duke of Somerset. He was employed by Queen Elizabeth ambassador into France, where he so behaved himself right stoutly in her behalf, as may appear by this particular.

In the month of March, anno 1592, being sensible of some injury offered by the duke of Guise to the honour of the Queen of England, he sent him this ensuing challenge:

Forasmuch as lately, in the lodging of my Lord Du Mayne, and in public elsewhere, impudently, indiscreetly and over-boldly, you spoke badly of my sovereign, whose sacred person here in this country I represent, to maintain both by word and weapon her honour, which never was called in question among people of honesty and virtue; I say you have wickedly lied, in speaking so basely of my sovereign; and you shall do nothing else but lie, whensoever you shall dare to tax her honour. Moreover that her sacred person (being one of the most complete and virtuous princes that lives in this world) ought not to be evil-spoken of by the tongue of such a perfidious traitor to her law and country as you are. And hereupon I do defy you, and challenge your person to mine, with such manner of arms as you shall like or choose, be it either on horseback or on foot. Nor would I have you think any inequality of person between us, I being issued of as great a race and noble house (every way) as yourself. So, assigning me an indifferent place, I will there maintain my words, and the lie which I gave you, and which you should not endure if you have any courage at all in you. If you consent not to meet me hereupon, I will hold you, and cause you to be generally held, for the arrantest coward and most slanderous slave that lives in all France. I expect your answer.

I find not what answer was returned.[2] This Sir Henry, dying in the French king's camp before La Fère, had his corpse brought over to London, and carried in a coach to Wadley, thence to Faringdon, where he was buried in the church on Tuesday the 8th of July, 1596. He had allowed him a baron's hearse, because dying ambassador lieger.

(1) See Essex, p. 175. (2) Nothing came of the challenge, though repeated thrice.

WILLIAM LAUD was born [1573] at Reading in this county, of honest parentage, bred in St. John's College in Oxford, whereof he became president; successively bishop of St. David's, Bath and Wells, London, and at last archbishop of Canterbury. One of low stature, but high parts; piercing eyes, cheerful countenance, wherein gravity and pleasantness were well compounded; admirable in his naturals, unblameable in his morals, being very strict in his conversation. Of him I have written in my *Church History*, though I confess it was somewhat too soon for one with safety and truth to treat of such a subject. Indeed I could instance in some kind of coarse venison, not fit for food when first killed, and therefore cunning cooks bury it for some hours in the earth, till the rankness thereof being mortified thereby, it makes most palatable meat. So the memory of some persons newly deceased are neither fit for a writer's or reader's repast, until some competent time after their interment. However, I am confident that unpartial posterity, on a serious review of all passages, will allow his name to be reposed amongst the heroes of our nation, seeing such as behold his expense on St. Paul's as but a cipher, will assign his other benefactions a very valuable signification, viz., his erecting and endowing an almshouse in Reading, his increasing of Oxford library with books, and St. John's College with beautiful buildings. He was beheaded January 10, 1645.

JOHN KENDRICK was born at Reading in this county, and bred a draper in the city of London. His state may be compared to the mustard-seed, very little at the beginning, but growing so great, that the birds made nests therein; or rather he therein made nests for many birds, which otherwise, being either infledged or maimed, must have been exposed to wind and weather.

The worthiest of David's Worthies were digested into *ternions* and they again subdivided into two *ranks*. If this double dichotomy were used to methodize our protestant benefactors since the Reformation, sure I am that Mr. Kendrick will be, if not the last of the first, the first of the second three. His charity began at his kindred; proceeded to his friends and servants, to whom he left large legacies; concluded with the poor, on whom he bestowed above twenty thousand pounds, Reading and Newbury sharing the deepest therein. And if any envious distrustful miser (measuring other men's hearts by the narrowness of his own) suspecteth the truth thereof, and if he dare hazard the smarting of his bleared eyes to behold so bright a sun of bounty, let him consult his will, publicly in print. He departed this life on the 30th day of September, 1624, and lies buried in St. Christopher's, London, to the curate of which parish he gave twenty pounds per annum for ever.

WILLIAM TWISSE was born [1578?] at Speen in this county, which was an ancient Roman city, mentioned by Antonine in his Itinerary by the name of Spina. This mindeth me of a passage in Clemens Alexandrinus, speaking of sanctified afflictions: *Nos quidem e spinis uvas colligimus.* And here, in another sense, God's church gathered grapes, this good man out of this thorny place. Hence he was sent by Winchester School to

New College in Oxford, and there became a general scholar. His plain preaching was good, solid disputing better, pious living best of all. He afterwards became preacher in the place of his nativity (Spinham lands is part of Newbury); and though generally our Saviour's observation is verified, "a prophet is not without honour save in his own country"—chiefly because *minutiae omnes pueritiae ejus ibi sunt cognitae* [all the particulars of his youth are known there]—yet here he met with deserved respect. Here he laid a good foundation, and the more the pity if, since, some of his fanciful auditors have built hay and stubble thereupon. And no wonder if this good doctor toward his death was slighted by sectaries, it being usual for new-lights to neglect those who have borne the heat of the day. His Latin works give great evidence of his abilities in controversial matters. He was chosen prolocutor in the late assembly of divines,[1] wherein his moderation was very much commended; and, dying in Holborn, he was buried at Westminster, Anno Domini 1646.

WILLIAM LYFORD was born [1598] at Peasemore in this county, and bred in Magdalen College in Oxford, where he proceeded bachelor of divinity 1631. He was also fellow of that foundation, on the same token that his conscience *post factum* was much troubled about his resigning his place for money to his successor, but, as his friends have informed me, he before his death took order for the restitution thereof.

The modesty of his mind was legible in the comeliness of his countenance, and the meekness of his spirit visible in his courteous carriage. He was afterwards fixed at Sherborne in Dorsetshire, where his large vineyard required such an able and painful vinedresser. Here he laid a good foundation, before the beginning of our civil wars, with his learned preaching and catechizing; and indeed, though sermons give most sail to men's souls, catechizing layeth the best ballast in them, keeping them steady from "being carried away with every wind of doctrine." Yet he drank a deep draught of the bitter cup with the rest of his brethren, and had his share of obloquy from such factious persons as could not abide the wholesome words of sound doctrine. But their candle (without their repentance) shall be put out in darkness, whilst his memory shall shine in his learned works he hath left behind him. [*d.* 1653]

THE FAREWELL

Being to take my leave of this shire, I seriously considered what want there was therein, so that I might wish the supply thereof. But I can discover no natural defect, and I therefore wish the inhabitants a thankful heart to that God who hath given them a country so perfect in profit and pleasure. Withal it is observed that the lands in Berkshire are very skittish, and often cast their owners, which yet I impute not so much to the unruliness of the *beasts* as to the unskilfulness of the *riders*. I desire heartily that hereafter the Berkshire gentry may be better settled in their saddles, so that the sweet places in this county may not be subject to so many mutations.

(1) *The late assembly of divines,* referred to several times in this work, was the Westminster Assembly of 1643, established by parliament and directed to confer on the liturgy, discipline and government of the Church of England.

BUCKINGHAMSHIRE

IT is a long narrow county, the miles therein proportioned accordingly, stretching forty-four miles from north to south, whilst the breadth is content with fourteen at the most. A fruitful county, especially in the Vale of Aylesbury, where one (lately) entire pasture, called Beryfield, now part of the inheritance of Sir Robert Lee, baronet, in the manor of Quarrendon, is let yearly for eight hundred pounds, the tenant not complaining of his bargain.

This county takes its name from Buckingham, the chief town therein, as that from beeches (called in the Saxon tongue *buccen*) growing plentifully thereabouts, as in other places in this county, and therefore placed first amongst its

NATURAL COMMODITIES

Beech

This was esteemed sacred amongst the Romans. *Manius Curius juravit se ex praeda nihil attigisse, praeter guttum faginum quo sacrificaret* (protested that he touched nothing of the prey besides a beech-cup, wherewith he should sacrifice).[1] It is also medicinal, though we would wish none sore lips or eyes to try the truth of Pliny's report, whether beech-leaves cure the one, or the ashes of beech-mast heal the other. Our ordinary use thereof, besides making of many utensils, if for building of houses. One asked, when beech would make the best timber, meaning what season of the year was best to cut it down for that purpose. It was answered that "beech would make the best timber when no oak was to be had"; a time, I assure you, which daily approacheth in our land.

Hence it was that such care was taken in the reign of King Henry the Eighth, when woods were in a far better condition than nowadays, for the preserving of the standels of beech.[2] As also it was provided in the first of Queen Elizabeth, that no timber trees of oak, beech and ash (where beech deservedly is made second) being one foot square at the stub, and growing within fourteen miles of the sea, or any navigable river, should be converted to coal or fuel, as the debasing of that which, if Nature did not first intend, necessity must employ for better service.

Sheep

The best and biggest-bodied in England are in the Vale of Aylesbury in this county, where it is nothing to give ten pounds or more for a breed-ram. So that, should a foreigner hear of the price thereof, he would guess that ram rather to be some Roman engine of battery, than the creature commonly so called.

(1) Pliny. (2) Stat. 35 Hen. VIII, cap. 17 [an act passed in 1543 for the preservation of timber. The monasteries had owned a large number of woods and after the Dissolution the property passed to the crown and private hands, and most woods were cleared of timber. *Standel* is a young tree left standing for timber].

I know not whether his observation, with the reason thereof, be worth inserting, who first took notice that our cattle for food are English when feeding in the fields, but French when fed on in a family.

English	1. Sheep	2. Ox	3. Calf	4. Hog	5. Pig
French	1. Mutton	2. Beef	3. Veal	4. Bacon	5. Pork

Whereof he assigned this reason, that after the Norman Conquest, the French so tyrannized over the English tenants that they forced them to keep and feed their cattle; but the Monsieurs ate all their good meat after it was slaughtered.

Foreigners much admire at our English sheep, because they do not (as those beyond the seas) follow their shepherds like to a pack of dogs, but wander wide abroad; and the popish priests tell their simple flocks that this disobedience of our sheep happeneth unto us because (*risum teneatis, amici?* [can you help laughing, friends?]) we have left the great shepherd the pope; whereas they did so long before our separation from Rome, because, freed from the fear of wolves (infesting them in foreign parts) they feed safely in the fields, needing neither guide to direct, nor guard to defend them.

TAME PHEASANTS

They first took their name from Phasis, a river in Asia, and long their flight thence into England: a fowl fair in the feathers, a cock especially (males by *nature,* though female by *art,* the finest of both sexes) and dainty in the flesh. Abundance of these are kept about Wycombe; the care being more than the cost, seeing their general repast is on pismires. Whether these tame be as good as wild pheasants, I leave to palate-men to decide.

THE MANUFACTURES

It is true of this county that it liveth more by its lands than by its hands. Such the fruitfulness, venting the native commodities thereof at great rates (thank the vicinity of London, the best chapman) that no handicrafts of note, save what common to other counties, are used therein, except any will instance in bone-lace, much thereof being made about Olney in this county; though more, I believe, in Devonshire, where we shall meet more properly therewith.

PROVERBS

Here if you beat a bush, it's odds you'll start a thief. No doubt there was just occasion for this proverb at the original thereof, which then contained satirical truth, proportioned to the place before it was reformed; whereof thus our great antiquary:[1] "It was altogether unpassable in times by reason of trees, until that Leofstane, abbot of Saint Alban's did cut them down, because they yielded a place of refuge for thieves."

But this proverb is now antiquated as to the truth thereof, Buckinghamshire affording as many maiden assizes as any county of equal populousness. Yea, hear how she pleadeth for herself that such highwaymen were never her natives, but fled thither for their shelter out of neighbouring counties.

(1) Camden's *Britannia.*

THE WORTHIES

SIR WILLIAM DE WINDSOR, knight [BARON WINDSOR]. I am confident herein is no mislocation, beholding him an ancestor to the right honourable Thomas Windsor Hickman, Lord Windsor, and fixed at Bradenham. He was deputed by King Edward the Third, in the forty-seventh year of his reign, lord lieutenant of Ireland, which country was then in a sad condition, for the king was so intent on the conquest of France, as a land nearer, fairer, and due to him by descent, that he neglected the effectual reduction of Ireland.

This encouraged the Irish grandees (their *O's* and *Mac's*) to rant and tyrant it in their respective seigniories, whilst such English who were planted there had nothing native (save their surnames) left, degenerating by degrees to be Irish in their habits, manners and language. Yea, as the wild Irish are observed to love their nurses or fosters above their natural mothers, so these barbarizing English were more endeared to the interest of Ireland which fed them, than of England which bare and bred them.

To prevent more mischief this worthy knight was sent over, of whose valour and fidelity the king had great experience. He contracted with the king to defray the whole charge of that kingdom (as appeareth by the instrument in the Tower) for eleven thousand two hundred and thirteen pounds, six shillings and eightpence per annum.

Now Sir William undertook not the conquest, but custody of the land in a defensive war. He promised not with a daring mountebank to cure, but with a discreet physician to ease this Irish gout.

Indeed I meet with a passage in Froissart, relating how Sir William should report of himself "that he was so far from subduing the Irish, he could never have access to understand and know their countries, albeit he had spent more time in the service of Ireland than any Englishman then living"; which to me seems no wonder, the Irish vermin shrouding themselves under the scabs of their bogs, and hair of their woods. However, he may truly be said to have left that land much improved, because no whit more impaired during those dangerous distractions, and safely resigned his office (as I take it) in the first of King Richard the Second.[1]

[*d.* 1384]

JOHN BUCKINGHAM (for so his name is truly written) alias Bokingham and Bukingham, took his name and nativity, no doubt, from Buckingham, in this county, *à-la-mode* of that age. He was bred at the university of Oxford; and, although since by some causelessly slandered for want of learning, was a great disputant and well-studied scholar, as his works do declare. He was afterwards preferred bishop of Lincoln, where several contests happened betwixt him and Pope Boniface the Ninth, who, in revenge, *ex plenitude potestatis,* removed him from Lincoln to Lichfield; that is, from the hall into the kitchen, a bishopric of less credit and profit. Buckingham grew sullen hereat, and would rather shut himself out than play at a less game; and so, quitting episcopacy 1397, lived and died [1398]

(1) He was actually recalled because Edward would not support his policy, though later he became viceroy of Ireland. He took a prominent part in quelling the peasants' revolt of 1381-2. He married Alice Perrers, the mistress of Edward III.

a private monk at Canterbury, where he lies buried the lowermost in the body of Christ Church, under a very fair gravestone, as my industrious friend hath well retrieved his memory,[1] though the brass of his monument be worn or rather torn away. He indented with the prior and convent at Canterbury to build him a chantry chapel near his sepulchre, which I find not performed.

JOHN MATHEW, Mercer, son to Thomas Mathew, was born at Sherrington in this county; lord mayor of London, Anno Domini 1490. He is eminent on this account, that he was the first bachelor that ever was chosen into that office. Yea, it was above a hundred and twenty years before he was seconded by a single person succeeding him in that place, viz., Sir John Leman, lord mayor 1616. It seemeth that a lady mayoress is something more than ornamental to a lord mayor; their wives' great portions, or good providence, much advantaging their estates, to be capable of so high a dignity.

JOHN SCRIVENER was martyred at Amersham, Anno Domini 1521, on whom an extraordinary piece of cruelty was used, his own children being forced to set the first fire upon him: for which the law (Deut. xiii. 6) was most erroneously pretended, as will appear by the perusing thereof: "If thy brother, the son of thy mother, or thy son, or thy daughter, or the wife of thy bosom, or thy friend which is as thy own soul, entice thee secretly, saying, Let us go and serve other gods: thou shalt not consent unto him, nor harken unto him; but thou shalt surely kill him; thine hand shall be first upon him to put him to death."

See we here how in the case of idolatry one is to spare none related unto them, either as equals or inferiors. But this law enjoins not children to accuse or execute their own parents, as Scrivener's children were compelled to do. A barbarous cruelty, especially seeing the civil law among the heathen Romans did provide that *filius non torquetur in caput parentis* (a son shall not be examined on the rack to accuse his father, in such cases wherein his life is concerned). Others, besides Scrivener, were martyred, and more confessors molested in this small county, anno 1521, than in all England elsewhere for twenty years together.

ROBERT ALDRICH [or ALDRIDGE], although he lived but in the twilight of religion, he is justly to be placed not on the dark but light side of Reformation; for, though his actions were but weak, his affections were sincere therein. Born he was at Burnham in this county, bred in King's College in Cambridge, proctor of that university, anno 1525; about which time many letters passed betwixt him and his familiar friend Erasmus, who styleth him *blandae eloquentiae juvenum*. He was afterwards schoolmaster, then fellow and provoster of Eton, and at last made bishop of Carlisle, anno 1537, by King Henry the Eighth. He was never a thorough-paced papist (much less a persecutor of protestants) though a complier with some superstitions. He died at Horncastle in Lincolnshire (a house belonging to his see) in the reign of Queen Mary, 1556.

(1) William Somner, in his *Antiquities of Canterbury*.

JOHN HOLYMAN was born [1495] at Coddington in this county, bred in New College in Oxford, and afterwards became a Benedictine in Reading, until that monastery was dissolved. Queen Mary, in the first of her reign, preferred him bishop of Bristol whilst his predecessor, Paul Bush (deprived for being married) was yet alive. He lived peaceably, not imbruing his hands in protestants' blood, and died, seasonably for himself, a little before the death of Queen Mary, 1558.

JOHN HARLEY was born in the parish of Newport Pagnell in this county, as a learned antiquary,[1] a native of the same place, hath informed me, where some of his kindred were lately, if not still, in being. He was bred first, fellow, then schoolmaster in Magdalen College in Oxford. In the dangerous days of King Henry the Eighth he was an hearty but concealed protestant.

In the first week of the reign of King Edward the Sixth, whilst most men's minds stood at a gaze (it being dead water with them which way the tide would turn) Master Harley, in the parish church of Saint Peter's in Oxford, in a solemn Lent sermon, publicly preached anti-papal doctrine, and powerfully pressed justification by faith alone; whereupon the over-officious vice-chancellor hurried him up to London for an heretic, there to answer for his contempt.

But the case was soon altered: Harley was acquitted, commended, preferred to be tutor to the sons of John earl of Warwick, afterwards duke of Northumberland. He was thence made bishop of Hereford.

It is said of Abraham, "He was buried in a good old age." It cannot be said of our Harley, he died in an *old* age, finding him not above fifty, though expiring in a *good* age, in two respects: in relation to the piety of his life past, and in reference to the future troubles which immediately followed. Surely, had he survived a little longer, he had lost his life, as he did his bishopric, for being married, in the first of Queen Mary. He died Anno Domini 1558, shifting from place to place, the cause why there is no certain intelligence where he was interred.

RICHARD COX was born [1500] at Whaddon in this county, and bred for some years in King's College in Cambridge, even when Cardinal Wolsey was erecting Christ Church in Oxford. This great prelate, desiring that his college should be as fair within as without, and having learning answerable to the building thereof, employed his emissaries to remove thither the most hopeful plants of Cambridge, and this Richard Cox amongst the rest. He became afterwards schoolmaster of Eton, which was happy with many flourishing wits under his endeavours, and Haddon[2] amongst the rest, whom he loved with filial affection. Hence he was sent for to be instructor to Prince Edward, which, with good conscience, to his great credit he discharged. Here, reader, forgive me in hazarding thy censure, in making and translating a distich upon them.

Praeceptor doctus, docilis magis an puer ille?
Ille puer docilis, praeceptor tu quoque doctus.
Master more able, child of more docility?
Docile the child, master of great ability.

(1) Mr. Martin, beneficed near Northampton. (2) Walter Haddon—see below, p. 39.

At last he was preferred bishop of Ely, 1559, commendably continuing therein, whatever causeless malice hath reported to the contrary, twenty-one years, and dying Anno Domini 1581.[1]

WILLIAM ALLEY was born [1510?] at Wycombe in this county, bred first at Eton, then in King's College, where he was admitted Anno Domini 1528. Hence he went away being bachelor of arts, and afterwards became lecturer in Saint Paul's; I say lecturer, which name, though since it hath sounded ill in some jealous ears as infected with faction,[2] was an ancient office founded in some cathedrals, to read divinity there; and this Master Alley's learned lectures (according to that age) are extant in print. He was consecrated bishop of Exeter July 14, 1560; and dying 1570, lieth buried under a fair marble in his own cathedral.

WALTER HADDON was born [1516] of a knightly family in this county; bred at Eton, afterwards fellow in King's College, where he proceeded doctor of law, and was the king's professor in that faculty, chosen vice-chancellor of Cambridge 1549; soon after he was made president of Magdalen College in Oxford, which place he waived in the reign of Queen Mary, and sheltered himself in obscurity. Queen Elizabeth made him one of the masters of her requests, and employed him in several embassies beyond the seas. Her majesty, being demanded whether she preferred him or Buchanan for learning, wittily and warily returned, "*Buchananum omnibus antepono, Haddonum nemini postpono*" [Buchanan I place before all; Haddon I put second to none]. Indeed he was a most eloquent man, and a pure Ciceronian in his style, as appeareth by his writings, and especially in his book against Osorius. [*d.* 1572]

THOMAS BICKLEY was born [1518] at Stowe in this county, bred first chorister, then scholar, then fellow in Magdalen College in Oxford. In the first of Edward the Sixth, his detestation of superstition may rather be commended, than his discretion in expressing it, when, before the public abolishing of popery, at evening prayer he brake the consecrated Host with his hands, and stamped it under his feet, in the college chapel. Afterwards he fled over into France, living an exile in Paris and Orleans all the reign of Queen Mary. Returning into England, he became chaplain to Archbishop Parker, who preferred him warden of Merton College, wherein he continued twenty years. When passed the age of a man (eighty years old) he began the life of a bishop, and was rather contented than willing to accept the bishopric of Chichester, freely offered unto him; yet lived he eleven years therein, and died ninety years of age, April 30, 1596,[3] and had a most sumptuous funeral; all the gentry of the vicinage doing their homage to "the crown of his old age, which was found in the

(1) Cox, a favourite of Cranmer, was on the commission to draw up the English liturgy, 1548-50. When vice-chancellor of Oxford he was somewhat ruthless in destroying MSS, books, etc., and was referred to as 'cancellor' of the university. He was in exile in Mary's reign. As bishop of Ely he alienated much church property to court favourites. (2) Fuller refers to the 'lecturers', often of puritan sympathies, employed simply for preaching by individuals or corporations. They were odious to the bishops, and Laud, when bishop of London, was especially hostile. (3) Actually he was 67 when he became bishop, and 78 when he died.

way of truth." He led a single life, left an hundred pound to Merton College, and other moneys to pious uses.

LAURENCE HUMPHREY was born [1527?] in this county, bred in Magdalen College in Oxford; a great and general scholar, able linguist, deep divine, pious to God, humble in himself, charitable to others. In the reign of Queen Mary he fled into Germany, and there was fellow-commoner with Mr. Jewel (whose life he wrote at large in Latin) in all his sufferings. Here he translated Origen *De Recta Fide* and Philo *De Nobilitate* out of Greek.

Returning into England in the reign of Queen Elizabeth, he was made president of Magdalen College in Oxford, and dean of Winchester. Higher preferment he never attained, because he never desired it; though a learned author seems to put it on another account, *fortasse eo quod de adiaphoris non juxta cum Ecclesia Anglicana senserit.*[1] I deny not but he might scruple some ceremonies, but sure I am he was much molested in his college with a party of fierce, not to say furious, nonconformists from whom he much dissented in judgment. He died Anno Domini 1590.

ARTHUR GREY [FOURTEENTH BARON GREY DE WILTON, *b.* 1536] is justly reckoned amongst the natives of this shire, whose father had his habitation (not at Wilton, a decayed castle in Herefordshire, whence he took his title) but at Whaddon, a fair house of his family, not far from Buckingham.

He succeeded to a small estate, much diminished on this sad occasion. His father William Lord Grey being taken prisoner in France, after long ineffectual soliciting to be (because captivated in the public service) redeemed on the public charge, at last was forced to ransom himself with the sale of the best part of his patrimony.

Our Arthur endeavoured to advance his estate by his valour, being entered in feats of war under his marital father, at the siege of Leith 1560, where he was shot in the shoulder, which inspirited him with a constant antipathy against the Scotch. He was afterwards sent over lord deputy[2] into Ireland, anno 1580, where, before he had received the sword, or any emblems of command, *ut acrioribus initiis terrorem incuteret* (to fright his foes with his fierce beginning) he unfortunately fought the rebels at Glendalough, to the great loss of English blood. This made many commend his courage above his conduct, till he recovered his credit, and finally suppressed the rebellion of Desmond.

Returning into England, the queen chiefly relied on his counsel for ordering our land forces against the Spaniards in '88, and fortifying places of advantage. The mention of that year (critical in church differences about discipline at home, as well as with foreign foes abroad) mindeth me that this lord was but a back-friend to bishops, and in all divisions of votes in parliament, or council-table, sided with the anti-prelatical party.

(1) Camden's *Elizabeth* ['Perhaps because on indifferent matters his opinions did not fall in line with the Anglican church.' Humphreys objected to the priest's cap and popish surplice, which his opponents considered indifferent matters. Elizabeth told him that he was 'strait-laced'.] (2) Edmund Spenser was appointed his secretary.

When Secretary Davison, that state-pageant (raised up on purpose to be put down) was censured in the star-chamber about the business of the Queen of Scots, this Lord Grey only defended him, as doing nothing therein but what became an able and honest minister of state. An ear-witness saith, *Haec fuse, oratorie, et animose, Greium disserentem audivimus* [We have heard Grey discoursing on these matters at length, oratorically and with courage]. So that besides bluntness (the common and becoming eloquence of soldiers) he had a real rhetoric, and could very emphatically express himself. Indeed this warlike lord would not wear two heads under one helmet, and may be said always to have borne his beaver open, not dissembling in the least degree, but owning his own judgment at all times what he was. He deceased Anno Domini 1593.

ROGER GOAD was born [1538] at Horton in this county, and was admitted scholar in King's College in Cambridge 1555. Leaving the college, he became schoolmaster at Guildford in Surrey. But pity it is that a great candle should be burning in the kitchen, whilst light is lacking in the hall, and his public parts pent in so private a profession. He was made not to guide boys but govern men. Hence, by an unexpected election, he was surprised into the provostship of King's College, wherein he remained forty years. He was thrice vice-chancellor of Cambridge; a grave, sage and learned man. He had many contests with the young fry in this college, chiefly because he loved their good better than they themselves. Very little there is of his in print, save what he did in conjunction with other doctors of the university. By his testament he gave the rectory of Milton to the college; and dying on St. Mark's day 1610, lieth buried in a vestry on the north side of the chapel.

JOHN KING was born [1559?] at Warnhall, nigh Thame, in this county; Robert King, the last abbot of Oseney, and first bishop of Oxford, being his great uncle. He was first dean of Christ Church, then bishop of London, being full fraught with all episcopal qualities; so that he who endeavoureth to give a perfect account thereof will rather discover his own defects than describe this prelate's perfections. He died Anno Domini 1621, being buried in the quire of Saint Paul's, with the plain epitaph of *Resurgam*.[2]

SIR GEORGE CROKE, knight, son of Sir John Croke and Elizabeth Unton his wife, was born [1560] at Chilton in this county, in the second year of the reign of Queen Elizabeth, bred first in Oxford, then a double reader in the Inner Temple, serjeant at law, and the king's serjeant, justice first of the common bench, 22 Jacobi, and then of the upper bench, 4 Caroli.

His ability in his profession is sufficiently attested by his own printed

(1) Camden's *Elizabeth* [William Davison (1541?—1608) referred to in the previous sentence, was on the commission (of which Lord Grey was also a member) for the trial of Mary Queen of Scots. He was unjustly charged by Elizabeth for undue haste in securing her signature on Mary's death-warrant, and was imprisoned in the Tower, 1587-8]. (2) He was the father of Henry King, poet and bishop of Chichester, whose life follows below, p. 44.

Reports; eight eminent judges of the law, out of their knowledge of his great wisdom, learning and integrity, approving and allowing them to be published for the common benefit.[1]

He was against the illegality of ship-money, both publicly in Westminster Hall, and privately in his judgment demanded by the king, though concluded to subscribe (according to the course of the court) by plurality of voices. The countryman's wit (levelled to his brain) will not for many years be forgotten: "That ship-money may be gotten by *Hook,* but not by *Crook*"; though since they have paid taxes (loins to the little finger, and scorpions to the rod of ship-money) but whether by *Hook* or *Crook,* let others inquire.

His piety, in his equal and even walkings in the way of God through the several turnings and occasions of his life, is evidenced by his charity to man, founding a chapel at Bletchley in Buckinghamshire, two miles at least distanced from the mother church, and an hospital in the same parish, with a liberal revenue.

Considering his declining and decaying age, and desiring to examine his life, and prepare an account to the Supreme Judge, he petitioned King Charles for a writ of ease, which, though in some sort denied (what wise master would willingly part with a good servant?) was in effect granted unto him. He died at Waterstock in Oxfordshire, in the eighty-second year of his age, Anno Domini 1642.

DAME HESTER TEMPLE, daughter to Miles Sands, esquire, was born at Latimer in this county, and was married to Sir Thomas Temple of Stowe, baronet. She had four sons and nine daughters, which lived to be married, and so exceedingly multiplied, that this lady saw seven hundred extracted from her body. Reader, I speak within compass, and have left myself a reserve, having bought the truth hereof by a wager I lost. Besides, there was a new generation of marriageable females just at her death; so that this aged vine may be said to wither, even when it had many young boughs ready to knit.

Had I been one of her relations, and as well enabled as most of them be, I would have erected a monument for her, thus designed. A fair tree should have been erected, the said lady and her husband lying at the bottom of the root thereof; the heir of the family should have ascended both the middle and top bough thereof. On the right hand hereof her younger sons, on the left her daughters should, as so many boughs, be spread forth. Her grandchildren should have their names inscribed on the branches of those boughs; the great-grandchildren on the twigs of those branches; the great-great-grandchildren on the leaves of those twigs. Such as survived her death should be done in a lively green, the rest (as blasted) in a pale and yellow fading colour.

I confess very many of her descendants died before her death; in which respect she was far surpassed by a Roman matron, on whom the poet thus epitapheth it, in her own person.[2]

(1) The *Reports,* written in Norman-French, extend over sixty years. (2) Ausonous [Latin original omitted].

Twenty-nine births Callicrate I told,
And of both sexes saw none sent to grave,
I was an hundred and five winters old,
Yet stay from staff my hand did never crave.

Thus in all ages God bestoweth personal felicities on some far above the proportion of others. The Lady Temple died Anno Domini 1656.

WILLIAM OUGHTRED was, though branched from a right ancient family in the north, born [1575] in the town, bred in the school of Eton, became fellow of King's College, and at last was beneficed by Thomas earl of Arundel at Albury in Surrey. All his contemporaries unanimously acknowledged him the prince of mathematicians in our age and nation. This aged Simeon had, though no revelation, a strong persuasion that before his death he should behold Christ's anointed restored to his throne;[1] which he did accordingly, to his incredible joy, and then had his *Dimittis* out of this mortal life, June 30, 1660.

SAMUEL COLLINS, son to Baldwin Collins (born in Coventry, a pious and painful preacher, prodigiously bountiful to the poor, whom Queen Elizabeth constantly called Father Collins) was born [1576] and bred at Eton, so that he breathed learned air from the place of his nativity. Hence coming to King's College in Cambridge he was chosen successively fellow, provost and regius professor. One of an admirable wit and memory, the most fluent Latinist of our age; so that as Caligula is said to have sent his soldiers vainly to fight against the tide, with the same success have any encountered the torrent of his tongue in disputation. He constantly read his lectures twice a week for above forty years, giving notice of the time to his auditors in a ticket on the school doors, wherein never any two alike, without some considerable difference in the critical language thereof. When some displeased courtier did him the injurious courtesy to prefer him downwards (in point of profit) to the bishopric of Bristol, he improved[2] all his friends to decline his election. In these troublesome times (affording more preachers than professors) he lost his church, but kept his chair; wherein he died [1651].

RICHARD MONTAGU [or MOUNTAGUE] was born [1577] at Dorney, where his father was vicar of the parish, within three miles of Eton, and so, though not within reach, within sight of that staple place for grammar-learning, wherein he was bred.[3] Thence was he chosen successively fellow of King's College in Cambridge, fellow of Eton, parson of Stanford Rivers in Essex, canon of Windsor, parson of Petworth, elected bishop of Chichester, and at last of Norwich. He spent very much in repairing his parsonage-house at Petworth, as also on his episcopal house at Aldingbourne near Chichester.

He was most exact in the Latin and Greek; and, in the vindication of

(1) Fuller refers to the Restoration. Oughtred invented trigonometrical abbreviations and introduced the multiplication and proportion signs. (2) *Improved*=exerted pressure on, pressed. (3) So am I informed by his son-in-law, Doctor David Stokes.

tithes, wrestled with the grand antiquary of England,[1] and gave him a fair flat fall in the point of a Greek criticism, taxing him justly for mistaking a *god* (amongst the Egyptians) more than there was, by making a *man* amongst the grammarians fewer than they should be.

He hath many learned works extant against the papists, some in English, some in Latin; and one, called his *Appello Caesarem,* which (without his intent and against his will) gave occasion of much trouble in the land. He began an ecclesiastical history, and set forth his apparatus, and alas! it was but an apparatus, though through no default of his, but defect of his health; sickness, troublesome times, and then death surprising him. Had it been finished, we had had church-annals to put into the balance with those of Baronius; and which would have swayed with them for learning, and weighed them down for truth. He died Anno Domini 1641.

HENRY KING, D.D., son to John King (lately mentioned) bishop of London, and his wife (of the ancient family of the Conquests) was born [1592] in this county, in the same town, house, and chamber, with his father, a local coincidence, which in all considerable particulars cannot be paralleled.

We know the scripture proverb, used in exprobation, "As is the mother, so is the daughter"; both wicked, both woeful. But here it may be said, by way of thankfulness to God and honour to the persons, "As was the father, so is the son"; both pious, both prosperous, till the calamity of the times involved the latter.

Episcopacy, anno 1641, was beheld by many in a deep consumption, which many hoped would prove mortal. To cure this, it was conceived the most probable cordial to prefer persons into that order, not only unblameable for their life and eminent for their learning, but also generally beloved by all disengaged people; and amongst these King Charles advanced this our doctor bishop of Chichester.

But all would not do: their innocency was so far from stopping the mouth of malice, that malice almost had swallowed them down her throat. Since, God hath rewarded his patience, giving him to live to see the restitution of his order.

David said that "the good tree (man) shall bring forth his fruit in due season"; so our doctor varied his fruits, according to the diversity of his age. Being brought up in Christ Church in Oxford, he delighted in the studies of music and poetry; more elder, he applied himself to oratory and philosophy; and in his reduced age fixed on divinity, which his printed sermons on the Lord's Prayer, and others which he preached, remaining fresh in the minds of his auditors, will report him to all posterity.[2] [*d.* 1669]

(1) John Selden (see Sussex, p. 574) whose *History of Tithes* Montague criticized in his book *Diatraebae upon the first part of the late History of Tithes.* In a passage in Wiltshire, omitted from this edition, Fuller refers to "Mr. Selden, from whom it is a sin to dissent in a criticism of antiquity." (2) Henry King was deprived in 1643, recovering his see at the Restoration. He wrote, among other poems, the beautiful 'Exequy to his Dead Wife.' He was a friend of Izaak Walton, Ben Jonson and Donne (who was ordained by his father).

JOHN GREGORY was born November 10, 1607, at Amersham in this county, of honest though mean parents, yet rich enough to derive unto him the hereditary infirmity of the gout, which afflicted him the last twenty years of his life. He was bred in Christ Church in Oxford, where he so applied his book that he studied sixteen hours of the four-and-twenty for many years together. He attained to be an exquisite linguist and general scholar, his modesty setting the greater lustre on his learning. His notes on Dr. Ridley's book of civil law gave the first testimony of his pregnancy to the world, and never did text and comment better meet together.

He was first, chaplain of Christ Church, and thence preferred by Bishop Duppa prebendary of Chichester and Sarum, and indeed no church preferment compatible with his age was above his deserts. He died at Kidlington in Oxfordshire, 1646, and was buried at Christ Church in Oxford.

His *Opera Posthuma* are faithfully set forth by his good friend John Gurgany, and deservedly dedicated to Edward Bysshe, esquire; one so able that he could, charitable that he would, and valiant that he durst, relieve Master Gregory in his great distress.[1]

THE FAREWELL

On serious consideration, I was at a loss to wish to this county what it wanted; God and the kings of England have so favoured it with natural perfections and civil privileges. In avowance of the latter, it showeth more borough towns (sending burgesses no fewer than twelve to the parliament) than any shire, though thrice as big, lying in the kingdom of Mercia. Now seeing, at the instant writing hereof, the general news of the nation is of a parliament to be called after his majesty's coronation, my prayers shall be that the freeholders of this county shall (amongst many therein so qualified) choose good servants to God, subjects to the king, patriots to the county, effectually to advance a happiness to the church and commonwealth.

(1) Gregory was a noted orientalist in his day.

CAMBRIDGESHIRE

CAMBRIDGESHIRE hath Lincolnshire on the north, Norfolk and Suffolk on the east, Essex and Hertfordshire on the south, Huntingdon- and Bedford-shires on the west, being in length thirty-five, in breadth not fully twenty miles. The tables therein as well furnished as any; the south part affording bread and beer, and the north (the Isle of Ely) meat thereunto. So good the grain growing here, that it out-selleth others some pence in the bushel.

The north part of this county is lately much improved by draining, though the poorest sort of people will not be sensible thereof. Tell them of the great benefit to the public, because where a pike or duck fed formerly, now a bullock or sheep is fatted; they will be ready to return, that if they be taken in taking that bullock or sheep, the rich owner inditeth them for felons; whereas that pike or duck were their own goods only for their pains of catching them. So impossible it is that the best project, though perfectly performed, should please all interests and affections.

It happened in the year 1657, upon the dissolution of the great snow, their banks were assaulted above their strength of resistance, to the great loss of much cattle, corn, and some Christians. But, soon after, the seasonable industry of the undertakers did recover all by degrees, and confute their jealousies who suspected the relapsing of these lands into their former condition.

This northern part is called the Isle of Ely, which one will have so named from the Greek word, Ἕλειος, fenny or marshy ground. But our Saxon ancestors were not so good Grecians, and it is plain that plenty of eels gave it its denomination. Here, I hope, I shall not trespass on gravity in mentioning a passage observed by the reverend professor of Oxford, Doctor Prideaux, referring the reader to him for the author's attesting the same.[1] When the priests in this part of the county would still retain their wives, in despite of whatever the pope and monks could do to the contrary, their wives and children were miraculously turned all into eels (surely the greater into congers, the less into grigs) whence it had the name of *Eely*: I understand him a *Lie of Eels.* No doubt the first founder of so damnable an untruth hath long since received his reward. However, for this cause, we take first notice, amongst the county's

NATURAL COMMODITIES

Of Eels

Which, though they be found in all shires in England, yet are most properly treated of here, as most, first and best; the courts of the kings of England being thence therewith anciently supplied. I will not engage in the controversy whether they be bred by generation as other fish; or

(1) John Prideaux—see Devonshire p. 137.

equivocally, out of putrefaction; or both ways, which is most probable; seeing some have adventured to know the distinguishing marks betwixt the one and other. I know the silver eels are generally preferred, and I could wish they loved men but as well as men love them, that I myself might be comprised within the compass of that desire. They are observed to be never out of season (whilst other fishes have their set times) and the biggest eels are ever esteemed the best. I know not whether the Italian proverb be here worth remembering: "Give eels without wine to your enemies."

HARES

Though these are found in all counties, yet because lately there was in this shire an hare-park nigh Newmarket, preserved for the king's game, let them here be particularly mentioned. Some prefer their sport in hunting before their flesh for eating, as accounting it melancholic meat, and hard to be digested, though others think all the hardness is how to come by it. All the might of this silly creature is in the flight thereof.

Whether or no they change their sex every year (as some have reported) let huntsmen decide. These late years of our civil wars hath been very destructive unto them; and no wonder if no law hath been given to hares, when so little hath been observed toward men.

SAFFRON

Though plenty hereof in this county, yet, because I conceive it first planted in Essex, we thither refer our description thereof.

WILLOWS

A sad tree, whereof such who have lost their love make their mourning garlands; and we know what exiles hung up their harps upon such doleful supporters. The twigs hereof are physic, to drive out the folly of children. This tree delighteth in moist places, and is triumphant in the Isle of Ely, where the roots strengthen their banks, and lop affords fuel for their fire. It groweth incredibly fast, it being a byword in this county "that the profit by willows will buy the owner a horse, before that by other trees will pay for his saddle." Let me add that if green ash may burn before a queen, withered willows may be allowed to burn before a lady.

THE MANUFACTURES

PAPER

Expect not I should, by way of preface, enumerate the several inventions whereby the ancients did communicate and continue their notions to posterity. First, by writing in leaves of trees, still remembered when we call such a scantling of paper a folio or leaf. Hence from leaves men proceeded to the bark of trees, as more solid, still countenanced in the notation of the word *liber*. Next they wrote in labels or sheets of lead, wherein the letters were deeply engraven, being a kind of printing before printing; and to this I refer the words of Job, an author allowed contemporary with, if not senior to Moses himself: "Oh that my words were now written, oh that they were printed in a book."

To omit many other devices in after-ages to signify their conceptions, paper was first made of a broad flag (not unlike our great dock) growing in and nigh Canopus in Egypt, which it seems was a staple commodity of that country, and substantial enough to bear the solemn curse of the prophet: "The paper-reeds by the brooks shall wither, be driven away, and be no more."

Our modern paper is made of grinded rags, and yet this new artificial doth still thankfully retain the name of the old natural paper. It may pass for the emblem of men of mean extraction, who by art and industry, with God's blessing thereon, come to high preferment. "He raiseth the poor out of the dust, and lifteth the needy out of the dunghill, that he may set him with his princes, even with the princes of his people." One may find, if searching into the pedigree of paper, it cometh into the world at the *doungate,* raked thence in rags, which, refined by art (especially after precious secrets are written therein) is found fit to be choicely kept in the cabinets of the greatest potentates. Pity it is that the first author of so useful an invention cannot with any assurance be assigned.

There are almost as many several kinds of paper as conditions of persons betwixt the emperor and beggar: imperial, royal, cardinal, and so downwards to that coarse paper called *emporetica,* useful only for chapmen to wrap their wares therein. Paper participates in some sort of the characters of the countrymen which make it: the Venetian being neat, subtile and courtlike; the French, light, slight and slender; the Dutch, thick, corpulent and gross, not to say sometimes also *charta bibula,* sucking up the ink with the sponginess thereof.

Paper is entered as a manufacture of this county, because there are mills nigh Stourbridge Fair, where paper was made in the memory of our fathers. And it seemeth to me a proper conjunction, that seeing Cambridge yieldeth so many good writers, Cambridgeshire should afford paper unto them. Pity the making thereof is disused, considering the vast sums yearly expended in our land for paper out of Italy, France and Germany, which might be lessened were it made in our nation. To such who object that we can never equal the perfection of Venice paper, I return, neither can we match the purity of Venice glasses; and yet many green ones are blown in Sussex, profitable to the makers, and convenient for the users thereof, as no doubt such coarser (homespun) paper would be found very beneficial for the commonwealth.

BASKETS

These are made of the osiers plentifully growing in the moist parts of this county, an acre whereof turns to more profit than one of wheat; a necessary utensil in the house, whereby many things are kept, which otherwise would be lost. Yea, in some sort it saved the life of St. Paul, when "let down by the wall of Damascus in a basket"; whence some (not improbably) conjecture him *hominem tricubitalem* (a man of low stature). Martial confesseth baskets to have been a British invention, though Rome afterwards laid claim thereunto:

Barbara de pictis veni bascauda Britannis,
Sed me jam mavult dicere Roma suam.

I, foreign basket, first in Britain known,
And now by Rome accounted for her own.

Their making is daily improved with much descant of art, splitting their wickers as small as threads, and dyeing them into several colours, which daily grow a greater commodity.

THE BUILDINGS

Cambridge is the chief credit of the county, as the university is of Cambridge. It is confessed that Oxford far exceeds it for sweetness of situation, and yet it may be maintained that though there be better air in Oxford, yet there is more in the colleges of Cambridge; for Oxford is an university in a town, Cambridge a town in an university, where the colleges are not surrounded with the offensive embraces of streets, but generally situated on the outside, affording the better conveniency of private walks and gardens about them. But, having formerly written of the fabrics of Cambridge,[1] I forbear any further enlargement.

ELY MINSTER

This presenteth itself afar off to the eye of the traveller, and on all sides, at great distance, not only maketh a promise, but giveth earnest of the beauty thereof. The lanthorn therein, built by Bishop Hotham (wherein the labour of twenty years, and five thousand ninety-four pounds eighteen shillings tenpence halfpenny farthing was expended) is a masterpiece of architecture. When the bells ring, the woodwork thereof shaketh and gapeth (no defect, but perfection of structure) and exactly chocketh into the joints again, so that it may pass for the lively emblem of the sincere Christian who, though he hath *motum trepidationis* (of fear and trembling) stands firmly fixed on the basis of a true faith. Rare also is the art in the chapel of Saint Mary's, the pattern or parent of that in King's College in Cambridge, though here (as often elsewhere) it hath happened, the child hath outgrown the father. Nor must the chapel of Bishop West be forgotten, seeing the master-masons of King James, on serious inspection, found finer stone-work herein, than in King Henry the Seventh his chapel at Westminster.

It grieved me lately to see so many new lights in this church (supernumerary windows more than were in the first fabric) and the whole structure in a falling condition, except some good men's charity seasonably support it. Yet was I glad to hear a great antiquary employed to transcribe and preserve the monuments in that church, as all others in the late-drowned land. And it is hard to say which was the better office, whether of those who newly have dried them from the inundation of water, or of those who shall drain them from the deluge of oblivion, by perpetuating their antiquaries to posterity.

(1) In my *History* of that university.

WONDERS

Let me here insert an artificial wonder, of what is commonly called Devils Ditch, countryfolk conceiting that it was made by the devil, when the devil he made it, being the work of some king or kings of the East Angles. See the laziness of posterity, so far from imitating the industry of their ancestors, that they belibel the pure effects of their pains as hellish achievements. But, if the aforesaid kings merely made this ditch to get themselves a name, divine justice hath met with them, their names being quite forgotten. More probably it was made to divide and defend their dominions from the kingdom of Mercia, or possibly to keep the people in employment, for diversion of mutinous thoughts, laziness being the mother of disloyalty, industry of obedience.

PROVERBS

Cambridgeshire Camels. I cannot reconcile this common saying to any considerable sense. I know a camel passeth in the Latin proverb either for *gibbous* and distorted, or for one that undertaketh a thing *awkly or ungeenly* (*camelus saltat*) or else for one of extraordinary bulk or bigness; all unappliable in any peculiar manner to the people of this county, as straight and dexterous as any other, nor of any exorbitant proportions.

All that I can recover of probability is this: the fen-men dwelling in the northern part of this county, when stalking on their stilts, are little giants indeed, as Master Camden hath well observed. However, that mathematician who measured the height of Hercules by the bigness of his foot, would here be much mistaken in his dimensions, if proportionably collecting the bulk of their bodies from the length of their legs.

A boisten horse and a Cambridge master of art are a couple of creatures that will give way to nobody. This proverb we find in the letter of William Zoone written to George Bruin, in his *Theatre of Cities;* and it is objected against us by an Oxford antiquary,[1] as if our masters wanted manners to give place to their betters, though, all things considered, it soundeth more to their honour than disgrace.

For mark what immediately went before in the same author:[2] "Walking in the streets, they require, not only of the townsmen, but also of every stranger, except they excel in dignity, that they go out of the way unto them." Herein two things are observable in the scholars: 1. Their *manners,* or *civility.* If the party, whatever he be, appear dignified above them, they willingly allow him superiority. What is this but to give what is due to another? 2. Their *manhood* or *courage.* If he seem beneath them, then they do *uti jure suo,* and take what is their own to themselves.

An Henry-Sophister. So are they called who, after four years' standing in the university, stay themselves from commencing bachelors of art, to render them (in some colleges) more capable of preferment. Several reasons are assigned of their name.

That tradition is senseless (and inconsistent with his princely magnificence) of such who fancy that King Henry the Eighth, coming to

(1) Brian Twine, Ant. Acad. Oxon. (2) Gulielmus Zoone [Latin original omitted].

Cambridge, stayed all the sophisters a year, who expected a year of grace should have been given unto them. More probable it is, because that king is commonly conceived of great strength and stature, that these *Sophistae Henriciani* were elder and bigger than others. The truth is this: in the reign of King Henry the Eighth, after the destruction of monasteries, learning was at a loss, and the university (thanks be unto God! more scared than hurt) stood at a gaze what would become of her. Hereupon many students stayed themselves two, three, some four years, as who would see, how their degrees (before they took them) should be rewarded and maintained.[1]

THE WORTHIES

MATTHEW PARIS is acknowledged an Englishman by all (save such who mistake *Parisius* for *Parisiensis*) and may probably be presumed born in this (as bred in the next) county, where the name and family of Paris is right ancient, even long before they were settled therein at Hildersham, which accrued unto them by their marriage with the daughter and heir of the Buslers. Sure I am, were he now alive, the Parises would account themselves credited with his, and he would not be ashamed of their affinity.

He was bred a monk of Saint Albans, skilled not only in poetry, oratory and divinity, but also in such manual as lie in the suburbs of liberal sciences, painting, graving, &c. But his genius chiefly disposed him for the writing of histories, wherein he wrote a large *Chronicle*, from the Conquest unto the year of our Lord 1250, where he concludes with this distich:

> *Siste tui metas studii, Matthæe, quietas:*
> *Nec ventura petas, quae postera proferat aetas,*
> Matthew, here cease thy pen in peace, and study on no more;
> Nor do thou roam at things to come, what next age hath in store.

However he, afterwards resuming that work, continued it until the year 1259. This I observe, not to condemn him, but excuse myself from inconstancy; it being, it seems, a catching disease with authors, to obey the importunity of others, contrary to their own resolution.

His history is unpartially and judiciously written (save where he indulgeth too much to monkish miracles and visions) and no writer so plainly discovereth the pride, avarice and rapine of the court of Rome, so that he seldom "kisseth the pope's toe without biting it." Nor have the papists any way to waive his true jeers, but by suggesting *haec non ab ipso scripta, sed ab aliis falso illi ascripta,* insinuating a suspicion of forgery in his last edition: understand them in what some eighty years since was set forth by Matthew Parker; whereas it was done with all integrity, according to the best and most ancient manuscripts; wherein all those anti-papal passages plainly appear as since in a later and exacter edition, by the care and industry of Doctor William Watts. This Matthew left off living and writing at the same time, viz., anno 1259. I will only add, that though he had sharp nails, he had clean hands; strict in his own as well

(1) The sophister ('Henry-sophisters' apart) was, at Cambridge, a student in his second or third year.

as striking at the loose conversations of others; and, for his eminent austerity, was employed by Pope Innocent the Fourth, not only to visit the monks in the diocese of Norwich, but also was sent by him into Norway, to reform the discipline in Holm, a fair convent therein, but much corrupted.

NICHOLAS OF ELY was so called (say some) from being archdeacon thereof; which dignity so dyed his denomination in grain, that it kept colour till his death, not fading, for his future higher preferments; though others conjecture his birth also at Ely. When the bold barons obtruded a chancellor (a king's tongue and hands by whom he publicly speaks and acts) anno 1260, they forced this Nicholas on King Henry the Third for that office, till the king some months after displaced him; yet (knowing him a man of much merit) voluntarily chose him lord treasurer, when ousted of his chancellor's place; so that (it seems) he would trust him with his coffers, but not with his conscience; yea, he afterwards preferred him bishop of Worcester, then of Winchester. Here he sat twelve years, and that cathedral may (by a synecdoche of a novel part for the whole) challenge his interment, having his heart enclosed in a wall, though his body be buried at Waverley in Surrey, 1280.

HUGH DE BALSHAM (for so is he truly written) was born in this county, as may easily be spelled out of the four following probabilities put together. First, it was fashionable for clergymen in that age to assume their surnames from the place of their nativity; secondly, Balsham is an eminent village in this county, whereof an ancient author taketh notice, naming thence the neighbouring ground *amoenissima Montana de Balsham;*[1] thirdly, there is no other village of that name throughout the dominions of England; fourthly, it is certain this Hugh was bred in this county, where he attained to be sub-prior, and afterwards bishop of Ely.

This Hugh was he who founded Peterhouse in the university of Cambridge, the first *built* (though not first *endowed*) college in England. This foundation he finished anno 1284, bestowing some lands upon it, since much augmented by bountiful benefactors. He sat 28 years in his see, and died June the 15th, 1286.

WILLIAM OF [BOTTISHAM or] BOTTLESHAM, made by the pope first bishop of Bethlehem in Syria; afterward, anno 1386, bishop of Llandaff, and thence removed to Rochester. A famous preacher, confessor to King Richard the Second, and learned writer; but by Walsingham and Bale called John by mistake. He died in February, anno 1400. Nor must we forget that he was once fellow of Pembroke Hall.

WILLIAM CAXTON, born [1422?] in that town (a noted stage betwixt Royston and Huntingdon). Bale beginneth very coldly in his commendation, by whom he is charactered *vir non omnino stupidus, aut ignavia torpens;*[2] but we understand the language of his *liptote,* the rather because

(1) Henry of Huntingdon. (2) "A man not altogether dull or listless with idleness." Caxton was born at Tenterden, Kent. He came of the Caustons of Kent, and his name was often thus spelt.

he proceedeth to praise his diligence and learning. He had most of his education beyond the seas, living thirty years in the court of Margaret duchess of Burgundy, sister to King Edward the Fourth, whence I conclude him an anti-Lancastrian in his affection. He continued *Polychronicon* (beginning where Trevisa ended) unto the end of King Edward the Fourth, with good judgment and fidelity. And yet, when he writeth that King Richard the Second left in his treasury money and jewels to the value of seven hundred thousand pounds, I cannot credit him, it is so contrary to the received character of that king's riotous prodigality. Caxton carefully collected and printed all Chaucer's works; and on many accounts deserved well of posterity when he died [1491].

JOHN TIPTOFT, son and heir of John Lord Tiptoft and Joyce his wife (daughter and co-heir of Edward Charlton Lord Powis by his wife Eleanor, sister and co-heir of Edmund Holland, earl of Kent) was born [1427?, at Everton in Bedfordshire]. . . He was bred in Balliol College in Oxford, where he attained to great learning; and by King Henry the Sixth was afterwards created first, viscount, then earl of Worcester, and lord high constable of England, and by King Edward the Fourth knight of the Garter.

The skies began now to lour and threaten civil wars, and the house of York fell sick of a relapse. Meantime this earl could not be discourteous to Henry the Sixth, who had so much advanced him, nor disloyal to Edward the Fourth, in whom the right of the crown lay. Consulting his own safety, he resolved on this expedient for a time to quit his own and visit the Holy Land. In his passage thither, or thence, he came to Rome, where he made a Latin speech before the pope, Pius the Second, and converted the Italians into a better opinion than they had formerly of the Englishmen's learning; insomuch that his holiness wept at the elegancy of the oration.

He returned from Christ's sepulchre to his own grave in England, coming home in a most unhappy juncture of time. If sooner, or later, he had found King Edward on that throne, to which now Henry the Sixth was restored, and whose restitution was only remarkable for the death of this worthy lord. Thus those who, when the house of the state is on fire, politicly hope to save their own chamber, are sometimes burned therein.

Treason was charged upon him for secret siding with King Edward, who before and afterward *de facto*, and always *de jure*, was the lawful king of England. On this account he lost his life. Then did the axe at one blow cut off more learning in England than was left in the heads of all surviving nobility. His death happened on Saint Luke's Day 1470.[1]

SIR WILLIAM HORN, salter, son to Thomas Horn, was born at Snailwell in this county. He was knighted by King Henry the Seventh; and, anno 1487, was lord mayor of London. He gave bountifully to the preachers at Saint Paul's Cross, and bestowed five hundred marks to the mending

(1) Excessively cruel even in an age of cruelty, Tiptoft earned for himself the name of the 'Butcher of England'. He was an accomplished scholar and munificent patron of learning.

of the highways betwixt Cambridge, the county town where he had his first life, and London, the city where he got his livelihood.

Know, in that age, Horn's five hundred marks[1] had in them the intrinsic value of our five hundred pounds, which in those days would go very far in the wages of labourers.

SIR THOMAS (son of John) KNEESWORTH, was born at Kneesworth in this county, bred a fishmonger in London, whereof he was lord mayor anno 1505. He appointed the water-conduit at Bishopsgate to be built, to the great convenience of the city, formerly much wanting that useful element. Be it here observed, for the encouragement of the industry of Cambridgeshire apprentices, that by the premises it doth appear that this small county, in the compass of eighteen years, afforded three lord mayors and benefactors, which no other shire of equal or greater quantity ever produced.

SIR THOMAS ELYOT. He was son to Sir Richard Elyot and born [1490?] some say, in Suffolk, but his house and chief estate lay in this county. After his long sailing into foreign parts, he at last cast anchor at home, and being well skilled in Greek and Latin, was the author of many excellent works. Of these, one in Latin was styled *Defensorium Bonarum Mulierum,* or the *Defence of Good Women,* though some will say that such are hardly found, and easily defended.

He wrote also an excellent *Dictionary* of Latin and English, if not the first, the best of that kind in that age; and England then abounding with so many learned clergymen, I know not which more to wonder at, that they missed, or he hit on so necessary a subject. Let me add, Bishop Cooper grafted his *Dictionary* on the stock of Sir Thomas Elyot, which worthy knight deceased anno 1546, and was buried at Carlton in this county.[2]

SIR EDWARD NORTH [FIRST BARON NORTH]. He was a prudent person, and in managing matters of importance of great despatch; not unskilled in law, and eminently employed in the court of augmentation; a court short-lived (erected in the end of Henry the Eighth, dissolved in the beginning of King Edward the Sixth's reign) yet very beneficial to the officers therein.[3] This Sir Edward was made, by Queen Mary, baron of Kirtling in this county; and was a considerable benefactor to Peterhouse in Cambridge, where he is remembered in their parlour, with this distich under his picture:

> *Nobilis hic vere fuerat si nobilis ullus,*
> *Qui sibi principium nobilitatis erat.*
> [He was truly noble, if any man were noble,
> who was himself the founder of his nobility.]

(1) A mark was originally worth 13s. 4d. (2) Sir Thomas Elyot is now remembered mainly for his *Boke named the Governour,* a politico-educational treatise, strongly tinged with classical influence, one of the earliest products of the Renaissance in England. It contains the earliest reference to the apocryphal story of Henry V being arrainged, when Prince of Wales, before Sir William Gascoigne, which story Fuller quotes in this judge's life in Yorkshire, p. 648. The Bishop Cooper referred to is Thomas Cooper (1517?—1594) son of an Oxford tailor, who rose to be bishop of Winchester. (3) The court of augmentation, constituted in 1536 when the smaller monasteries were suppressed, dealt with the spoil and augmented the king's revenues.

He was father to Roger Lord North, and great-grandfather to Dudley Lord North, now surviving. [1496?-1564]

THOMAS THIRLBY, doctor of laws, was, as I am assured by an excellent antiquary,[1] born [1506?] in the town, and bred in the university of Cambridge, most probably in Trinity Hall. He was very able in his own faculty, and more than once employed in embassies by King Henry the Eighth, who preferred him bishop of Westminster. Here, had Thirlby lived long, and continued the course he began, he had prevented Queen Mary from dissolving that bishopric, as which would have dissolved itself for lack of land, sold and wasted by him. And though probably he did this to raise and enrich his own family, yet such the success of his sacrilege, his name and alliance is extinct.

From Westminster he was removed to Norwich, thence to Ely. He cannot be fellowed (as some other of his order) by the light of the faggots kindled by him to burn poor martyrs, seeing he was given rather to prodigality than cruelty, it being signally observed that he wept at Archbishop Cranmer's degradation.[2] After the death of Queen Mary, he was as violent in his opinions, but not so virulent in his expressions; always devoted to Queen Mary, but never invective against Queen Elizabeth. He lived in free custody; died, and is buried at Lambeth, 1570.

RICHARD HULOET was born at Wisbech in this county, and brought up in good learning. He wrote a book called *The English and Latin A B C,* and dedicated the same to Thomas Goodrich,[3] bishop of Ely and chancellor of England. Some will condemn him of indiscretion in presenting so low a subject to so high a person, as if he would teach the greatest statesman in the land to spell aright. Others will excuse him, his book being, though of low, of general use for the common people, who then began to betake themselves to reading (long neglected in the land) so that many who had one foot in their grave, had their hand on their primer. But I believe that his book (whereof I could never recover a sight) though intituled an *A B C,* related not to literal reading, but rather to some elemental grounds of religion. He flourished Anno Domini 1552.

SIR THOMAS RIDLEY, knight, doctor of the laws, was born [1550?] at Ely in this county, bred first a scholar in Eton, then fellow of King's College in Cambridge. He was a general scholar in all kind of learning, especially in that which we call *melior literatura.* He afterwards was chancellor of Winchester, and the vicar-general to the archbishop of Canterbury. His memory will never die whilst his book called *A View of the Civil and Ecclesiastical Law* is living; a book of so much merit, that the common lawyers (notwithstanding the difference betwixt the professions) will ingeniously allow a due commendation to his learned performance in that subject. He died Anno Domini 1629, on the three and twentieth day of January.

(1) Mr. Martin beneficed near Northampton. (2) He assisted at his old friend Cranmer's degradation, though, as Fuller says, he wept. He was deprived in 1559 and imprisoned soon after for continuing to preach against the Reformation. He was the first and only bishop of Westminster. (3) See Lincolnshire, p. 334.

ANDREW WILLET, D.D., was born [1562] at Ely in this county, bred fellow of Christ's College in Cambridge. He afterwards succeeded his father in the parsonage of Barley in Hertfordshire, and became prebendary of Ely. He confuted their cavil who make children the cause of covetousness in clergymen, being bountiful above his ability, notwithstanding his numerous issue. No less admirable his industry, appearing in his *Synopsis, Comments,* and *Commentaries;* insomuch that one, considering his polygraphy, said merrily that he must write whilst he slept, it being impossible that he should do so much when waking. Sure I am, he wrote not sleepily nor *oscitanter,* but what was solid in itself, and profitable for others.

A casual fall from his horse, in the highway near Hoddesdon, breaking his leg, accelerated his death. It seems that God's promise to his children, "to keep them in all their ways, that they dash not their foot against the stone," is (as other temporal promises) to be taken with a tacit cause of revocation, viz., if God's wisdom doth not discover the contrary more for his glory and his children's good. This doctor died Anno Domini 1621.

R[ICHARD] PARKER, for so is his Christian name defectively written in my book, was born in Ely [1572] (therefore place-naming himself *Eliensis*) was son, as I am confident, to Master Parker, archdeacon of Ely, to whom that bishopric in the long vacancy (after the death of Bishop Cox) was proferred, and by him refused, *tantum opum usuram iniquis conditionibus sibi oblatum respuens* [rejecting so much wealth offered to him as being interest on unjust terms]. Our Parker was bred in, and became fellow of Caius College; an excellent herald, historian and antiquary, author of a short, plain, true and brief manuscript called *Sceletos Cantabrigiensis;* and yet the bare bones thereof are fleshed with much matter, and hath furnished me with the nativities of several bishops who were masters of colleges.

I am not of the mind of the Italian (from whose envy God deliver us) Polydore Vergil who, having first served his own turn with them, burnt all the rare English manuscripts of history he could procure, so to raise the valuation of his own works. But from my heart I wish some ingenious person would print Mr. Parker's book for the use of posterity.[1] He was a melancholy man, neglecting all preferment to enjoy himself; and died in the place of his nativity [1629].

THOMAS (son to William) WESTFIELD, D.D., was born Anno Domini 1573 in the parish of Saint Mary's in Ely, and there bred at the free-school under Master Spight till he was sent to Jesus College in Cambridge, being first scholar, then fellow thereof. He was curate, or assistant rather, to Bishop Felton, whilst minister of Saint Mary-le-Bow in Cheapside; afterward rector of Hornsey nigh, and Great Saint Bartholomew's in, London, where in his preaching he went through the four evangelists. He was afterwards made archdeacon of Saint Albans, and at last bishop of Bristol, a place proffered to and refused by him twenty-five years before: for then the bishopric was offered to him to maintain him, which this contented meek man, having a self-subsistence, did then decline; though accepting

(1) First published in 1715.

of it afterwards, when proffered to him to maintain the bishopric, and support the episcopal dignity by his signal devotion. What good opinion the parliament (though not over-fond of bishops) conceived of him, appears by their order ensuing:[1]

The thirteenth of May, 1643. From the Committee of Lords and Commons for Sequestration of Delinquents' estates.

Upon information in the behalf of the bishop of Bristol, that his tenants refuse to pay him his rents; it is ordered by this committee, that all profits of his bishopric be restored to him, and a safe conduct be granted him to pass with his family to Bristol, being himself of great age, and a person of great learning and merit.

JO. WYLDE.

About the midst of his life he had a terrible sickness, so that he thought (to use his own expression in his diary) that "God would put out the candle of his life, though he was pleased only to snuff it." By his will (the true copy whereof I have) he desired to be buried in his cathedral church, near the tomb of Paul Bush, the first bishop thereof. "And as for my worldly goods,"—reader, they are his own words in his will—"which (as the times now are) I know not well where they be, nor what they are, I give and bequeath them all to my dear wife Elizabeth, &c." He protested himself on his death-bed "a true protestant of the Church of England"; and dying Junii 28, 1644, lieth buried according to his own desire above mentioned.

Thus leaving such as survived him to see more sorrow, and feel more misery, he was seasonably taken away from the evil to come; and according to the anagram made on him by his daughter, "Thomas Westfield, 'I dwel the most safe'," enjoying all happiness, and possessing the reward of his pains, who converted many, and confirmed more by his constancy in his calling.

ROBERT TOWNSON, D.D., was born [1575] in Saint Botolph's parish in Cambridge, and bred a fellow in Queens' College, being admitted very young therein, but 12 years of age. He was blessed with an happy memory, insomuch that when D.D. he could say by heart the second book of the *Aeneid,* which he learnt at school, without missing a verse. He was an excellent preacher, and becoming a pulpit with his gravity. He attended King James his chaplain into Scotland, and after his return, was preferred dean of Westminster, then bishop of Salisbury.

Doctor Townson had a hospitable heart, a generous disposition, free from covetousness, and was always confident in God's providence that, if he should die, his children (and those were many) would be provided for, wherein he was not mistaken. He lived in his bishopric but a year; and being appointed at very short warning to preach before the parliament, by unseasonable sitting up to study, contracted a fever, whereof he died, and was buried in Westminster Abbey, Anno Domini 1621.

THOMAS GOAD, D.D. was son of Dr. Roger Goad[2] (for more than forty years provost of King's College) but whether born [1576] in the provost's

(1) The particulars of this were procured for me by my worthy friend Mathew Gilly, esquire, from Elizabeth, the bishop's sole surviving daughter. (2) See Buckinghamshire, p. 41.

lodgings in Cambridge, or at Milton in this county, I am not fully informed. He was bred a fellow under his father; afterwards chaplain to Archbishop Abbot, rector of Hadleigh in Suffolk, prebendary of Canterbury, &c.; a great and general scholar, exact critic, historian, poet (delighting in making of verses till the day of his death) schoolman, divine. He was substituted by King James in the place of Doctor Hall (indisposed in health) and sent over to the synod of Dort. He had a commanding presence, an uncontrollable spirit, impatient to be opposed, and loving to steer the discourse (being a good pilot to that purpose) of all the company he came in. [*d.* 1638]

JOHN RICHARDSON was born of honest parentage at Linton in this county; bred first, fellow of Emmanuel, then master of Peterhouse, and at last of Trinity College in Cambridge, and was regius professor in that university. Such who represent him a dull and heavy man in his parts, may be confuted with this instance. An extraordinary act in divinity was kept at Cambridge before King James, wherein Doctor John Davenant was answerer, and Doctor Richardson amongst others the opposers. The question was maintained in the negative, concerning the "excommunicating of kings." Doctor Richardson vigorously pressed the practice of Saint Ambrose excommunicating of the emperor Theodosius; insomuch that the king, in some passion, returned, *"Profecto fuit hoc ab Ambrosio insolentissime factum."* To whom Doctor Richardson rejoined, *"Responsum vere regium, et Alexandro dignum. Hoc non est argumenta dissolvere, sed desecare."* And so, sitting down he desisted from any further dispute.[1]

He was employed one of the translators of the Bible, and was a most excellent linguist, whose death happened Anno Domini 1625.

ANDREW MARVELL was born [1586?] at Meldreth in this county,[2] and bred a master of arts in Trinity College in Cambridge.

He afterwards became minister in Hull, where for his lifetime he was well beloved; most facetious in his discourse, yet grave in his carriage; a most excellent preacher who like a good husband never broached what he had new brewed, but preached what he had pre-studied some competent time before; insomuch that he was wont to say that he would cross the common proverb which called "Saturday the working day, and Monday the holiday of preachers." It happened that, Anno Domini 1641, Jan. 23, crossing Humber in a barrow-boat, the same was sandwarped, and he drowned therein, by the carelessness, not to say drunkenness, of the boatmen, to the great grief of all good men.[3] His excellent comment upon Saint Peter is daily desired and expected, if the envy and covetousness of private persons, for their own use, deprive not the public of the benefit thereof.

(1) The altercation runs thus: "Assuredly this was insolently done by Ambrose." . . . "A truly royal answer, and worthy of Alexander. This is not refuting, but slaughtering the argument." (2) So his son-in-law informed me. [This Marvell was father of the poet]. (3) With Mrs. Skinner (daughter to Sir Edward Coke) a very religious gentlewoman.

WILLIAM COLLET was born at Over in this county, bred a clerk in London, till at last he attained to be keeper of the records in the Tower, none equalling him in his dexterity in that office. He went the same path with his predecessor in that place, Master Augustine Vincent, but out-went him as survivor. And because method is the mother of memory, he orderly digested all records, that they were to be found in an instant. He abominated their course who by a water would refresh a record, to make it useful for the present, and useless ever after. He detested, under the pretence of mending it, to practise with a pen on any old writing, preserving it in the pure nature thereof. Indeed Master Selden and others, in their works, have presented posterity with a plentiful feast of English rarities; but let me say that Collet may be called their caterer, who furnished them with provision on reasonable rates. He died, to the great grief of all antiquaries, Anno Domini 1644.

MICHAEL DALTON, esquire. He was bred in the study of our municipal law in Lincoln's Inn, and attained great skill in his own profession. His gravity graced the bench of justices in this county, where his judgment deservedly passed for an oracle in the law, having enriched the world with two excellent treatises, the one of the office of the sheriffs, the other of the justices of peace. Out of the dedicatory epistle of the latter I learnt this (which I knew not before) that King James was so highly affected with our English government by justices of peace, that he was the first who settled the same in his native country of Scotland. [*d.* 1648?]

EDWARD NORGATE, son to Robert Norgate, D.D., master of Benet College, was born in Cambridge; bred by his father-in-law[1] (who married his mother) Nicholas Felton bishop of Ely who, finding him inclined to limning and heraldry, permitted him to follow his fancy therein; for parents who cross the current of their children's genius (if running in no vicious channels) tempt them to take worse courses to themselves.

He was very judicious in pictures, to which purpose he was employed into Italy to purchase them for the earl of Arundel. Returning by Marseilles, he missed the money he expected; and being there unknowing of and unknown to any, he was observed by a French gentleman (so deservedly styled) to walk in the Exchange, as I may call it, of that city many hours every morning and evening, with swift feet and sad face, forwards and backwards. To him the civil monsieur addressed himself, desiring to know the cause of his discontent; and if it came within the compass of his power, he promised to help him with his best advice. Norgate communicated his condition; to whom the other returned, "Take, I pray, my counsel; I have taken notice of your walking more than twenty miles a day in one furlong, upwards and downwards; and what is spent in needless going and returning, if laid out in progressive motion, would bring you into your own country. I will suit you (if so pleased) with a light habit, and furnish you with competent money for a footman." Norgate very cheerfully consented, and footed it (being accommodated accordingly) through the body of France (being more than five hundred

(1) *Father-in-law* = step-father.

English miles); and so leisurely, with ease, safety and health, returned into England.[1]

He became the best illuminer or limner of our age, employed generally to make the initial letters in the patents of peers and commissions of ambassadors, having left few heirs to the kind, none to the degree, of his art therein. He was an excellent herald, by the title of [Windsor Herald] and, which was the crown of all, a right honest man. Exemplary his patience in his sickness (whereof I was an eye-witness) though a complication of diseases, stone, ulcer in the bladder, &c., seized on him. He died at the Heralds' office, Anno Domini 1650.

JOHN CRANE was born [1572] in Wisbech in this county, bred an apothecary in Cambridge, so diligent a youth that some judicious persons prognosticated that he would be a rich man. Dr. Butler[2] took so great a fancy unto him, that he lived and died in his family; yea, and left the main body of his estate unto him.

This Mr. Crane had a large heart to entertain his friends, and annually very nobly treated all the Oxford men at the commencement. He gave at his death no less than three thousand pounds to charitable uses, bestowing the house he lived in (and that a very fair one) after his wife's death, on the public professor of physic; and, in settlement of his other benefactions, discreetly reflected on Wisbech, where he was born (to which he gave £100 to build a town hall); Cambridge, where he lived; Lynn, where he was well acquainted; Ipswich, where Dr. Butler (the first founder of his estate) was born; and Kingston, where his lands lay. He in some sort gives preventing physic to the scholars, now he is dead, by giving £100 to be lent gratis to an honest man, the better to enable him to buy good fish and fowl for the university, having observed much sickness occasioned by unwholesome food in that kind. He bequeathed to Dr. Wren bishop of Ely, and Dr. Brownrig bishop of Exeter, one hundred pounds apiece by his will, and as much by a codicil annexed thereunto. Besides his concealed charities, his hand was always open to all the distressed royalists. [*d.* 1652]

THE FAREWELL

It is hard for a physician to prescribe proper physic to such a patient, who hath a hot liver and a cold stomach, because what is good for the one is bad for the other. As hard it is, for weather to please the concernments of this county, whose northern part, being moist and fenny, desireth fair weather; south and south-eastern, dry and healthy, delighteth so much rain that it can well digest (save in harvest time) one shower every day, and two every Sunday. But the God of heaven, "who can make it rain on one place, and not on another," can fit the necessity of both; and I remit them both to his providence.

(1) This story is of his own relation. (2) William Butler the physician—see Suffolk, p. 534.

CHESHIRE

CHESHIRE lieth in form of an axe, Wirral being the handle thereof, having Lancashire (parted with the River Mersey) on the north; a corner of Yorkshire on the north-east; Derby- and Stafford-shires (severed with mountains) on the east; Shropshire on the south; Denbigh, Flintshire and the Irish Ocean on the west thereof. The longest part (advantaged with excursions) is four and forty, the broadest twenty-five miles.

This county was reputed a palatinate before the Conquest, and since continued in the same dignity. It is much senior to Lancashire in that honour, which relateth to Cheshire as the copy to the original, being palatinated but by King Edward the Third, referring the duke of Lancaster to have his regal jurisdiction, *adeo integre et libere sicut comes Cestriae,* &c. And whereas records are written in the common law, *contra coronam et dignitatem Regis,* in this county they run thus, *contra dignitatem gladii Cestriae.*

It aboundeth with all things necessary to man's life; and it is observable that all the rivers and rivulets therein rise in, or run through, some *meer* or *pool,* as Combermere, Bagmere, Pickmere, Ridley Pool, Petty Pool, &c.; so that Cheshire hath more lakes in this kind than all the neighbouring counties, affording plenty of carps, tenches, trouts, eels, &c. therein.

The gentry of this county are remarkable upon a four-fold account: 1. For their *numerousness,* not to be paralleled in England in the like extent of ground. 2. Their *antiquity,* many of their ancestors being fixed here before the Norman Conquest. 3. Their *loyalty,* especially against a northern enemy, heartily hating a Scot; understand it before the union of the two kingdoms. 4. *Hospitality,* no county keeping better houses, which, because all grows on their own, may be the better afforded.

One said pleasantly that it appeared to all people that the Cheshire gentry were good housekeepers, because they gave so many wheat-sheaves (bread being the staff of hospitality, wheaten the best of bread) in their coats of arms. Indeed, I have told no fewer than six and twenty, called *garbs* in heraldry, which are borne in the several coat-armours of the gentry of this county; the original whereof is sufficiently known to be out of conformity to Hugh Cyveiliog, the fifth earl-palatine of Chester, who gave *Azure, six Garbs or.* And many of the gentry of the county, being his dependants, had assigned them, or did assume in their shields, something in allusion thereunto.

NATURAL COMMODITIES

Salt

This is most essential to man's livelihood, without which neither sacrifice was acceptable to God, nor meat savory to man. It is placed on the board with bread, to shew that they are equally necessary to man's sustenance.

A general in our late wars soundly chid a captain for his so soon surrendering of a castle, seeing he had store of powder therein. "I had," returned the captain, "plenty of black, but no white powder at all."

And here it is remarkable to observe the defects which sundry places have herein: 1. Some countries have salt without flesh within many miles, as in the south part of Africa. 2. Some have plenty of flesh, but no salt to make use thereof, as in many parts of Tartary. 3. Some have flesh and salt, but the flesh utterly uncapable of seasoning, as about Nombre de Dios and other places near the meridian in America. 4. Some have flesh, salt, and flesh capable thereof, but so unconscionably dear, that common people have little comfort therein, as in France, no country having salt more plentiful, and (for reason of state) most excessive in the rate thereof.

These things considered we, who have flesh, salt, salt at reasonable prices, and flesh capable thereof, have cause to profess,

O fortunati nimium bona si sua norint
Angligenae.

The manner of making salt in this county is so largely and exactly described by Mr. Camden, that nothing can be added thereunto.

Cheese

Poor men do eat it for hunger, rich for digestion. It seems that the ancient British had no skill in the making thereof till taught by the Romans, and now the Romans may even learn of us more exactness therein. This county doth afford the best for quantity and quality, and yet their cows are not (as in other shires) housed in the winter, so that it may seem strange that the hardiest kine should yield the tenderest cheese. Some essayed in vain to make the like in other places, though hence they fetched both their kine and dairymaids. It seems they should have fetched their ground too (wherein surely some occult excellency in this kind) or else so good cheese will not be made. I hear not the like commendation of the butter in this county; and perchance these two commodities are like stars of a different horizon, so that the elevation of the one to eminency is the depression of the other.

Millstones

Stones, they are natural; as fitted for that purpose, artificial. Very great and good are digged up at Mow Cop Hill in this county, though one moiety thereof be in Staffordshire, out of which the River Trent doth arise. How necessary these are for man's sustenance, is proved by the painful experience of such aged persons who, wanting their molar teeth, must make use of their gums for grinders; and such bad shifts should men be put to, if wanting mills where stones turn corn into bread.

Manufactures considerable I meet with none in this county, and therefore proceed.

THE BUILDINGS

Beeston Castle, situated on a steep hill, carried away the credit of this county for building; it was erected by Randulph the third earl of Chester, when he returned victorious from the Holy Land. I am much taken with the neatness of the structure, though, I confess, my eye never did, and now never shall behold it.

When some justly quarrel at Virgil's fiction, making Dido fall in love with Aeneas, who indeed was dead many years before her cradle was made, others have sought ingeniously to salve the anticronism in history, by the plea that she fell in love with his picture, which she saw in tapestry; yet I may truly allege for myself, that I was affected with the delight of this castle, though by me never seen, and now levelled to the ground (since the late wars), beholding the delineation thereof cut by the charge of John Savage, esquire.

Veraque cum desunt moenia picta juvant.
When real walls are vanish'd quite,
Painted ones do us delight.

I confess learned Leland is very confident that this castle shall see better times, deriving his intelligence from ancient predictions:

Tempus erit quando rursus caput exerat altum,
Vatibus antiquis si vas mihi credere vati.
Beeston in time its head aloft shall heave,
If I, a prophet, prophets may believe.

But I give credit to Leland's *history,* when he tells what is past, more than to his *prophecy,* when he foretells what is to come.

THE WONDERS

It is reported by credible and believed by discreet persons, that there is a pool adjoining to Brereton, the seat of the honourable family of the Breretons, wherein bodies of trees are seen to swim for certain days together before the death of any heir of that house. If so, let not all men look for so solemn summons to pay their debts to Nature. God grant us that grey hairs, dimness of sight, dulness of other senses, decay in general of strength, death of our dearest relations, especially when far younger than ourselves, before our eyes, &c. may serve us (instead of swimming logs) and be sanctified unto us, for sufficient and effectual monitors of our mortality.

We must not forget the many fir-trees found here buried under ground, whereof largely hereafter in a more proper place. The people of this county cut such pieces of wood very small, and use them instead of candles, which give a good light. My author adds that "such wooden candles have long snuffs; and yet," saith he, which to me amounts to a wonder, "in falling do no harm, though they light into tow, flax, or the like."[1] Strange that the least fire should be so dead as not to be revived with such cordials. Let not this encourage careless servants to tempt Providence with such combustible conjunctions; no county being more sadly sensible of casualties by fire: Nantwich, a fair market therein, being twice burnt down to the ground within the compass of one hundred and fifty years.[2]

PROVERBS

Cheshire chief of men. Say not this proverb carries a challenge in it, and our men of Kent will undertake these chief of men for engrossing

(1) W. Smith, in his Vale Royal of England.—F. (2) Once anno 1438, and again 1583.—F.

manhood to themselves. And some will oppose to this narrow county-proverb an English one of greater latitude, viz., *No man so good, but another may be as good as he.* For, rather than any difference shall arise, by wise and peaceable men, many chiefs will be allowed.

Indeed, the Cestrians have always demeaned themselves right valiantly in their undertakings. This was well known to King Richard the Second, who in dangerous times sent for two thousand Cheshire men, all archers, to attend him; which number, in time of a suspicious parliament, was doubled by him, all having *bouche of court* (bread and beer) and sixpence a day, large wages in that age.

Pity it was that the valour of these Cheshire men was once wasted against themselves, in a terrible battle betwixt King Henry the Fourth and Henry Percy surnamed Hotspur, not ill described by our author:

> There Dutton, Dutton kills; a Done doth kill a Done,
> A Booth, a Booth; and Legh by Legh is overthrown;
> A Venables against a Venables doth stand;
> And Troutbeck fighteth with a Troutbeck hand to hand;
> There Molyneux doth make a Molyneux to die;
> And Egerton the strength of Egerton doth try;
> O Cheshire, wert thou mad, of thine own native gore;
> So much until this day thou never shedst before![1]

Nor doth this abate our former commendation of their loyalty, the cause they maintained being so intricate and perplexed; one side fighting for Mortimer, who should be king by right; the other for Henry the Fourth, who actually was so; and politic men, who know the one were loyal, will be loth to say that the others were traitors.

Let no ill-natured wit urge, in opposition to the manhood of Cheshire men, their late miscarriage under a worthy knight, whom I forebear to name; partly because he nameth himself (though I say nothing of him); partly because, before my pains pass the press, he will probably he honourably additioned.[2] For, had other counties seasonably contributed their promised assistance, what now proved an abortive birth would have been a vital infant. Besides, better things were provided for our gracious sovereign, that he the copy, as God the original, might not come in the tempestuous wind of war, fire or fury, or earthquake of open enmity, but in the still voice of a peaceable composition. And, to shew that this not be man's work, God suffered both the men of Kent, and Cheshire chief of men, to fail in their loyal endeavours, that it might only be God's work, and justly marvellous in our eyes.

Better wed over the Mixon than over the Moor. "Over the Mixon"; that is, hard by or at home, Mixon being that heap of compost which lieth in the yards of good husbands.

"Than over the Moor"; that is, far off or from London; the road from Chester leading to London over some part of the moorlands in Staffordshire. The meaning is, the gentry in Cheshire find it more profitable to match within their county than to bring a bride out of other shires:

(1) Drayton's *Polyolbion.* (2) Fuller probably alludes to Sir William Brereton (1604—1661) who led the parliamentary cause in Cheshire, and had the distinction of defeating Rupert at Tarvin in 1644.

1. Because better acquainted with her birth and breeding. 2. Because (though her portion perchance may be less) the expense will be less to maintain her.

Such intermarriages in this county have been observed both a prolonger of worshipful families, and the preserver of amity betwixt them; seeing what Mr. Camden reported of the citizens of Cork[1] is verified of the Cheshire gentry: they are all of an alliance.

THE BATTLES

ROWTON HEATH, 1645, Sept. 24. His majesty, being informed that Colonel Jones had seized the suburbs and strong church of Saint John's in Chester, advanced northward for the relief thereof. Poyntz, one of the parliament's generals, pursued his majesty. At Rowton Heath, within three miles of Chester, the king's army made an halt, whilst his majesty, with some prime persons, marched into the city.

Next day a fierce fight happened on the heath, betwixt the King's and Poyntz's forces, the latter going off with the greater loss. Judicious persons conceive that had the royalists pursued this single enemy, as yet unrecruited with additional strength, they had finally worsted him; which fatal omission (opportunities admit of no after-games) proved their overthrow. For next day Colonel Jones drew out his men into the field, so that the royalists, being charged on the heath in front and rear, were put to the worst, the whole body of whose army had wings without legs, horse without foot, whilst the parliament was powerful in both.

Immediately after, a considerable party of horse (the Lord Byron governor of the city being loth to part with any foot, as kept to secure the king's person) came out of Chester, too late to succour their defeated friends, and too soon to engage themselves. Here fell the youngest of the three noble brethren who lost their lives in the king's service, Bernard Stuart earl of Lichfield, never sufficiently to be lamented.

THE WORTHIES

THOMAS OF ECCLESTON (a village in Broxton Hundred) was born in this county, bred a Franciscan in Oxford. Leland saith of him that, under the conduct of prudence and experience, he contended with many paces to pierce into the *penetrales* of learning. He wrote a book of the succession of Franciscans in England, with their works and wonders, from their first coming in to his own time, dedicating the same to (not G. Nottingham, the provincial of his order) but to his friend and fellow-friar; his mortified mind, it seems, not aiming at honour therein. He wrote another book, intituled *De Impugnatione Ordinis sui per Dominicanos* (*Of the Assaults which the Dominicans made on his Order*); these two sorts of friars whipping each other with their cords or knotted girdles, to the mutual wounding of their reputations. [*fl.* 1250]

SIR HUGH CALVELEY, born at Calveley in this county. Tradition makes him a man of teeth and hands, who would feed as much as two, and fight as much as ten men. His quick and strong appetite could digest

(1) In his *Britannia*.

anything but an injury, so that killing a man is reported the cause of his quitting this county, making hence for London, then for France. Here he became a most eminent soldier, answering the character our great antiquary hath given him: *Arte militari ita in Gallia inclaruit, ut vividae ejus virtuti nihil fuit impervium.*[1]

I find five of his principal achievements: 1. When he was one of the thirty English in France, who in a duel encountered as many Bretons. 2. When, in the last of King Edward the Third, being governor of Calais, he looked on (his hands being tied behind him by a truce yet in force for a month) and saw the English slain before his eyes, whose blood he soon after revenged. 3. When, in the first of King Richard the Second, after an unfortunate voyage of our English nobility, beaten home with a tempest, he took the bark Boulogne and five-and-twenty other French ships, besides the castle of Mark, lately lost by negligence, which he recovered. 4. When, in the next year, he spoiled Etaples, at a fair-time, bringing thence so much plunder as enriched the Calicians for many years after. 5. When he married the Queen of Aragon, which is most certain, her arms being quartered on his tomb, though I cannot satisfy the reader in the particulars thereof.[2] [*d.* 1393]

SIR ROBERT KNOLLYS, knight, was born of mean parentage in this county; yet did not the weight of his low extraction depress the wings of his martial mind, who by his valour wrought his own advancement. He was another of the thirty English who, for the honour of the nation, undertook to duel with as many Bretons, and came off with great reputation.

He was afterwards a commander in the French war under King Edward the Third, where, in despite of their power, he drove the people before him like sheep, destroying towns, castles and cities, in such manner and number that, many years after, the sharp points and gable-ends of overthrown houses (cloven asunder with instruments of war) were commonly called Knollys's Mitres.

The last piece of his service was performed in suppressing Wat Tyler and his rebels. Then I behold aged Sir Robert, buckling on his armour, as old Priam at the taking of Troy, but with far better success, as proving victorious; and the citizens of London enfranchised him a member thereof, in expression of their thankfulness.

His charity was as great as his valour; and he rendered himself no less loved by the English, than feared of the French. He gave bountifully to the building of Rochester bridge, founding a chapel and chantry at the east end thereof, with a college at Pontefract in Yorkshire, where Constance his lady was born, endowing it with one hundred and eighty pounds per annum.

He died at his manor of Scunthorpe in Norfolk, in peace and honour, whereas martialists generally set in a cloud, being at least ninety years of age (for he must be allowed no less than thirty years old when, anno

(1) Camden, *Britannia* ["He served with distinction in France, his courage overcoming every difficulty"]. (2) There are no such arms quartered on his tomb. There was no queen of Aragon that he could have married, and probably never married at all.

1352, he was a general under King Edward the Third, and he survived until the 15th of August 1407) being buried in Whitefriars in London, to which he had been a great benefactor.

WILLIAM BOOTH [or BOTHE, *b.* 1390?] was first bred in Gray's Inn in London, in the study of our municipal laws, till he quitted that profession on the proffer of a chancellor's place in Saint Paul's, and took orders upon him. It was not long before he was consecrated bishop of Lichfield, and six years after translated to York. He expended much money in repairing and enlarging his palace at York; and, after twelve years, died, and was buried in Saint Mary's Chapel in Southwell, 1464.

LAWRENCE BOOTH [or BOTHE], brother, but by another mother, to William aforesaid, was bred and became master of Pembroke Hall in Cambridge, and was chancellor of that university. He made the composition betwixt the university and King's College to their mutual advantage; and was an eminent benefactor to his own college, bestowing thereon all the tenements (since alienated) betwixt it and Saint Botolph's Church, amongst which was Saint Thomas Hostel. He exonerated the college of a pension of five pounds which he redeemed, and conferred thereon the manor and patronage of Orton Waterville in Huntingdonshire.

As it is God's, so it is all good men's method, in advancing their servants, "Be faithful in a little, and thou shalt rule over much." Doctor Booth, well performing his chancellor's place in Cambridge, was thence preferred chancellor to Margaret, queen to Henry the Sixth. Well discharging that office, he was, in the 13th of King Edward the Fourth, made lord high chancellor (it seems his public spirit was neither for York nor Lancaster, but England) having first been bishop of Durham, afterwards archbishop of York, and deserving well of both sees, for he built in the first the gate of Auckland College, and bought for the latter the manor of Battersea nigh London.

It must not be forgotten that this archbishop kept the mastership of Pembroke Hall till the day of his death, and so did his successors in the same college, Bishop Foxe and Bishop Ridley; not that they were covetous (what is a molehill to those that have mountains?) of the place, but the place ambitious of them, to be guarded and graced with them, as it is this day by the right reverend father in God, Benjamin Laney, lord bishop of Peterborough. This archbishop died Anno Domini 1480.

JOHN BOOTH [or BOTHE], brother to Lawrence aforesaid, bachelor of laws, was consecrated bishop of Exeter in the sixth of King Edward the Fourth, 1465. He built the bishop's chair, or seat, in his cathedral, which, in the judicious eye of Bishop Godwin, hath not his equal in England. Let me add, that though this be the fairest chair, the soft cushion thereof was taken away when Bishop Vescy alienated the lands thereof. The worst was, when Bishop Booth had finished this chair, he could not quietly sit down therein, so troublesome the times of the civil wars betwixt York and Lancaster; so that, preferring his privacy, he retired to a little place of his own purchasing at Horsley in Hampshire, where he died April the fifth, 1478; and was buried in Saint Clement Danes, London.

SIR HUMPHREY STARKEY was born, with most probability, in this county, where his name is in good, hath been in a better, esteem and estate. He in the study of our laws so profited, that (after some intermediate dignities) he was preferred chief baron of the exchequer.

We need inquire no farther into his ability, finding him, by so wise and frugal a king, employed in a place belonging to his coffers;[1] who, though he was sometimes pleased to be remiss in matters which concerned his subjects, was ever careful in things wherein his own emolument was interested. Wonder not that we have so little left of this judge's actions, because Empson and Dudley (loaders grinding more than the chief miller) were such instruments whose over-activity made all others seem slugs in that court.[2] It doth sound not a little to the praise of our Starkey that, whereas that age was justly complaining of the extortions of the king's officers, nothing of that nature (*no hearing, best hearing* in this kind) is laid to his charge. He was buried in Saint Leonard's, Shoreditch.

[*d.* 1486]

THOMAS SAVAGE was born at Macclesfield in this county. His father, being a knight, bred him a doctor of law in the university of Cambridge. Hence was he preferred bishop of Rochester, and at last archbishop of York. He was a greater courtier than clerk, and most dexterous in managing secular matters, a mighty Nimrod, and more given to hunting than did consist with the gravity of his profession.

No doubt there wanted not those which taxed him with that passage in Saint Jerome, *Penitus non invenimus in scripturis sanctis sanctum aliquem Venatorem, Piscatores invenimus sanctos.* But all would not wean him from that sport to which he was so much addicted.

His provident precedent spared his successors in that see many pounds of needless expenses, by declining a costly installation, being the first who privately was installed by his vicar. Yet was he not covetous in the least degree, maintaining a most numerous family, and building much, both at Scorby and Cawood. Having sate seven years in his see, he died 1507, his body being buried at York, his heart at Macclesfield, where he was born, in a chapel of his own erection, intending to have added a college thereunto, had not death prevented him.

SIR RICHARD SUTTON was born at Prestbury in this county.[3] He is generally believed a knight, though some have suspected the same, but suppose him but esquire. He was one of a plentiful estate and bountiful hand.

It happened that William Smith, bishop of Lincoln, began Brasenose College, but died before he had finished one nostril thereof, leaving this Sutton his executor, who over-performed the bishop's will, and completed

(1) Fuller refers to Henry VII, though Starkey was first appointed chief-baron in 1483. (2) For Edmund Dudley and this incident see Staffordshire, p. 514. Sir Richard Empson's life is in Northamptonshire, p. 432. (3) So my good friend Dr. Yates, principal of Brasenose, hath informed me.

the foundation with his own liberal additions thereunto.[1] When the following verses were composed, in the person of Brasenose College, the muses seemed neither to smile nor frown, but kept their wonted countenance. But take them as they are:

> Begun by one, but finish'd by another,
> Sutton he was my nurse, but Smith my mother:
> Or, if the phrase more proper seem, say rather,
> That Sutton was my guardian, Smith my father;
> 'Cause equal kindness they to me exprest,
> Better I neither love, love both the best;
> If both they may be call'd, who had one will,
> What one design'd, the other did fulfil.
> May such testators live who good intend;
> But, if they die, heaven such exec'tors send.

This worthy knight, being born in this county, deservedly reflected upon his own countrymen, making them (and those of Lancashire) most capable of preferment. [*d.* 1524]

SIR HUGH CHOLMLEY, or CHOLMONDELEY [*b.* 1513]. This worthy person bought his knighthood in the field at Leith in Scotland. He was five times high sheriff of this county (and sometimes of Flintshire) and for many years one of the two sole deputies lieutenants thereof. For a good space he was vice-president of the marches of Wales under the right honourable Sir Henry Sidney, knight; conceive it during his absence in Ireland. For fifty years together he was esteemed a father of his country; and dying anno 1596, was buried in the church of Malpas, under a tomb of alabaster, with great lamentation of all sorts of people, had it not mitigated their mournings that he left a son of his own name, heir to his virtues and estate.

RALPH RADCLIFFE was born [1519?] in this county, who, travelling southward, fixed himself at Hitchin in Hertfordshire, where he converted a demolished house of the Carmelites into a public grammar-school. He here erected a fair stage, whereon, partly to entertain his neighbours, and partly to embolden his scholars in pronunciation, many interludes were acted by them. Pits praiseth him, being a schoolmaster, that he confined himself to his own profession, not meddling with divinity; and yet, amongst his books, he reckoned up a treatise of *The Burning of Sodome*, and another of *The Afflictions of Job*. [*d.* 1559]

SIR HENRY BRADSHAW, knight. This surname being diffused in Derbyshire and Lancashire, as well as in this county, his nativity, advantaged by the alphabet (first come first served) is fixed herein. He became so noted for his skill in our common law, that in the sixth of King Edward the Sixth, in Hilary Term, he was made chief baron of the exchequer, demeaning himself therein to his great commendation.

Pity it is that Demetrius, who is "well reported of all men", should suffer for his namesake Demetrius the silversmith, who made the shrines

(1) Sir Richard Sutton was the first lay founder of a college. For William Smith, see Lancashire, p. 292.

for Diana, and raised persecution against Saint Paul. And as unjust it is, that this good judge, of whom nothing ill is reported, should fare the worse for one of the same surname of execrable memory, of whom nothing good is remembered.[1] I have cause to conceive that this judge was ousted of his place, for protestant inclination, 1 Mariae, finding no more mention of him.

WILLIAM CHADERTON [CHADDERTON, or CHATTERTON, b. 1540?], D.D. Here I solemnly tender deserved thanks to my manuscript author, charitably guiding me in the dark, assuring that this doctor was *ex praeclaro Chadertonorum Cestrensis comitatus stemmate prognatus*.[2] And although this doubtful direction doth not cleave the pin, it doth hit the white; so that his nativity may with most probability (not prejudicing the right to Lancashire when produced) here be fixed. He was bred first fellow, then master of Queens', and never of Magdalen College, in Cambridge (as the reverend Bishop Godwin mistaketh) and chosen first the Lady Margaret's, then king's, professor in divinity; and Doctor Whitaker succeeded him immediately in the chair. He was, anno 1579, made bishop of Chester, then of Lincoln 1595; demeaning himself in both to his great commendation. He departed this life in April 1608.

His grandchild [Elizabeth, 1596-1622], a virtuous gentlewoman of rare accomplishments, married to Torel Joceline, esquire, being big with child, wrote a book of advice, since printed, and intituled *The Mother's Legacy to Her Unborn Child,* of whom she died in travail.

SIR THOMAS EGERTON, knight [BARON ELLESMERE and VISCOUNT BRACKLEY, *b.* 1540?], was extracted from the ancient family of the Egertons of Ridley in this county; bred in the study of the municipal laws of our land, wherein he attained so much eminency, that Queen Elizabeth made him her solicitor, then master of the Rolls, and at last keeper of the great seal May 6, in the thirty-eighth year of the reign, 1596.

Olaus Magnus reporteth that the emperor of Muscovia, at the audience of ambassadors, sendeth for the gravest and seemliest men in Musco and the vicinage, whom he apparelleth in rich vests, and placing them in his presence, pretendeth to foreigners that these are of his privy council, who cannot but be much affected with so many reverend aspects. But surely all Christendom afforded not a person which carried more gravity in his countenance and behaviour than Sir Thomas Egerton, insomuch that many have gone to the Chancery on purpose only to see his venerable garb (happy they who had no other business) and were highly pleased at so acceptable a spectacle.

Yet was his outward case nothing in comparison of his inward abilities; quick wit, solid judgment, ready utterance. I confess Master Camden saith he entered his office *magna expectatione et integritatis opinione* (with a great expectation and opinion of integrity). But no doubt, had he revised his work in a second edition, he would have afforded him a full-

(1) A reference to John Bradshaw the regicide (*d.* 1659) who presided at the trial of Charles I and pronounced the sentence. He was attainted in 1660. (2) R. Parker, in *Sceletos Cantabrigiensis.*

faced commendation, when this lord had turned his expectation into performance.

In the first of King James, of lord keeper he was made lord chancellor, which is only another name for the same office; and on Thursday the 7th of November, 1616, of Lord Ellesmere he was created Viscount Brackley.

It is given to courts whose jurisdictions do border to fall out about their bounds; and the contest betwixt them is the hotter the higher the spirits and parts of the respective judges. Great the contention for many years together betwixt this lord of equity and Sir Edward Coke, the oracle of justice, at Westminster Hall. I know not which of them got the better: sure I am such another victory would (if this did not) have undone the conqueror.

He was attended on with servants of most able parts, and was the sole chancellor since the Reformation who had a chaplain,[1] which (though not immediately) succeeded him in his place. He gave over his office, which he held full twenty years, some few days before his death; and, by his own appointment, his body was brought down and buried at Dodleston in this county, leaving a fair estate to his son, who was afterwards created earl of Bridgwater.

When he saw King James so profuse to the Scots, with the grave fidelity of a statesman he sticked not often to tell him, that as he held it necessary for his majesty amply to remunerate those his countrymen, so he desired him carefully to preserve his crown lands for his own support, seeing he or his successors might meet with parliaments which would not supply his occasions but on such conditions as would not be very acceptable unto him.

It was an ordinary speech in his mouth to say "*frost* and *fraud* both end in *foul*."[2] His death happened Anno Domini 1617.

WILLIAM JAMES, D.D., was born [1542] in this county, bred a scholar in Christ Church in Oxford, and afterwards president of the University College. He succeeded Bishop Matthew in the deanery and bishopric of Durham.

He had been chaplain to Robert Dudley, earl of Leicester; and (I hope) I may lawfully transcribe what I read: "This hope of comfort came to his lordship thereby, that if it pleased God to impart any mercy to him (as his mercy endureth for ever) it was by the especial ministry of this man, who was the last of his coat that was with him in his sickness."[3]

He was a principal means of recovering Durham House unto his see. This house was granted by King Edward the Sixth to the Lady, afterwards Queen, Elizabeth (only for term of life) and lay long neglected during her reign, till Bishop James, about the sixth of King James, regained it, and repaired the chapel (which he found not only profaned, but even defaced) to his great cost, and furnished it very decently.

He once made so complete an entertainment for Queen Elizabeth that her majesty commended the order and manner thereof for many years

(1) Bishop Williams [John Williams—see Wales, p. 697]. (2) Alleged by Sir Francis Bacon, in his censure on the earl of Somerset.—F. (3) Sir J. Harrington, *View of the Church of England*.—F.

after. This maketh me the more to admire at what I have heard reported, that when King James in his progress to Scotland, anno 1617, passed through the bishopric of Durham, some neglect was committed by this bishop's officers, for which the king secretly and sharply checked this bishop, who laid it so to heart, that he survived the same reproof not a full twelvemonth. [*d.* 1617]

JOHN DOD was born [1549?] at Shocklach in this county, where his parents had a complete estate; bred in Jesus College in Cambridge; by nature a witty, by industry a learned, by grace a godly divine; successively minister of Hanwell in Oxford, Fenny Compton in Warwick, Canons Ashby and Fawsley in Northamptonshire, though for a time silenced in each of them.

For the rest, I refer the reader to Master Samuel Clarke, by whom his life is written, wherein are many remarkable passages: I say Master Samuel Clarke, with whose pen mine never did nor shall interfere. Indeed, as the flocks of Jacob were distanced three days' journeys from those of Laban, so (to prevent voluntary or casual commixtures) our styles are set more than a month's journey asunder.[1]

The Jewish Rabbins have a fond and a false conceit, that Methuselah, who indeed died in the very year (and his death a sad prognostic) of the deluge, had a cabin built him in the outside of Noah's ark, where he was preserved by himself. But most true it is that good Father Dod, though he lived to see the flood of our late civil wars, made to himself a cabin in his own contented conscience; and though his clothes were wetted with the waves (when plundered) he was dry in the deluge, such his self-solace in his holy mediations. He died, being eighty-six years of age, anno 1645.

When thieves break in a house and steal, the owner thereof knows for the present that he is robbed, but not of what or how much, till some days after he finds out by the want of such things which were taken from him. The vicinage of Fawsley where Mr. Dod died, knew then they were bereft of a worthy treasure, though ignorant in the particulars of their losses, till daily discovery hath by this time made them sensible thereof.

GEORGE PALIN was (as I have cogent presumptions) born at Wrenbury in this county; bred a merchant in London, free of the Company of Girdlers. Indeed, we may call his benefactions *aureum cingulum charitatis* (the golden girdle of charity). With our Saviour he "went about doing good," completing the circuit of his bounty, continuing till he ended where he began:

1. To Wrenbury (where we believe him born) two hundred pounds to purchase lands for the relief of the poor. 2. Nine hundred pounds for the building of almshouses in or about London. 3. To Trinity College in Cambridge, three hundred pounds. 4. To the college of Saint John the Evangelist in Cambridge, three hundred pounds. 5. To the hospital of Saint Thomas in Southwark, fifty pounds. 6. To the preachers at Paul's Cross, towards the bearing of their charges, two hundred pounds. 7.

(1) The sharpness of this reference to Samuel Clarke (1599—1683) curate of St. Bennet Fink, London, is due to the fact that Clarke had, by implication, accused Fuller of plagiarism.

Toward the making of a sweet chime in Bow Church, one hundred pounds. 8. To six prisons in and about London, sixty pounds. 9. To Brasenose College in Oxford, two scholarships, to each yearly four pounds. 10. To the college of Saint John Baptist in Oxford, two scholarships of the same value. 11. To Christchurch hospital, three hundred pounds. 12. To the church and poor (to buy them gowns) of Wrenbury, seventy pounds. With other benefactions.

Verily, I say unto you, I have not met a more universal and unpartial charity to all objects of want and worth. He died about the beginning of the reign of King James.

WILLIAM SMITH was born [1550?] in this county, wherein his surname hath been of signal note for many ages. His genius inclined him to the study of heraldry, wherein he so profited that, anno 1597, he was made Pursuivant of Arms, by the name of Rouge Dragon. He wrote a description, geographical and historical, of this county, left (it seems) in the hands of Ranulphe Crew, knight, sometime lord chief justice of the king's bench, and lately set forth by the favour of Mr. Randolph Crew,[1] grandchild to that worthy knight. [*d.* 1618]

JOHN SPEED was born [1552?] at Farndon in this county, as his own daughter[2] hath informed me. He was first bred to a handicraft, and as I take it to a tailor. I write not this for his but my own disgrace, when I consider how far his industry hath outstript my ingenious education. Sir Fulke Greville, a great favourer of learning, perceiving how his wide soul was stuffed with too narrow an occupation, first wrought his enlargement, as the said author doth ingeniously confess: "Whose merits to me-ward I do acknowledge, in setting this hand free from the daily employments of a manual trade, and giving it his liberty thus to express the inclination of my mind, himself being the procurer of my present estate."

This is he who afterwards designed the maps and composed the history of England, though much helped in both (no shame to crave aid in a work too weighty for any one's back to bear) by Sir Robert Cotton, Master Camden, Master Barkham and others. He also made the useful genealogies preposed formerly to English Bibles in all volumes, having a patent granted him from King James, in reward of his great labours, to receive the benefit thereof to him and his. This was very beneficial unto them, by composition with the Company of Stationers, until this licentious age, neglecting all such ingenious helps to understand Scripture, and almost levelling (if not prevented) the property of all authors of books. He died in London, anno 1629, and was buried in Saint Giles without Cripplegate, in the same parish with Master John Foxe; so that no one church in England containeth the corpses of two such useful and voluminous historians. Master Josias Shute[3] preached his funeral sermon; and thus we take our leaves of Father Speed, truly answering his name in both acceptions thereof for celerity and success.

(1) See below, p. 77. Smith's work, *The Vale Royal of England*, with maps by Daniel King, was first published in 1656. (2) Mrs. Blackmore, a stationer's wife in Paul's Churchyard.—F. (3) See Yorkshire, p. 663.

SIR RANULPHE CREW was born [1558] in this county; bred in the study of our municipal laws, wherein such his proficiency, that after some steps in his way thereunto, in the twenty-second of King James he was made lord chief justice of the upper bench, and therein served two kings (though scarce two years in his office) with great integrity.

King Charles his occasions calling for speedy supplies of money, some great ones adjudged it unsafe to adventure on a parliament (for fear, in those distempered times, the physic would side with the disease) and put the king to furnish his necessities by way of loan. Sir Ranulphe being demanded his judgment of that design, and the consequence thereof (the imprisoning of recusants to pay it) openly manifested his dislike of such preter-legal courses; and thereupon, November 9, 1626, was commanded to forbear his sitting in the court, and the next day was by writ discharged from his office; whereat he discovered no more discontentment than the weary traveller is offended when told that he is arrived at his journey's end.

The country hath constantly a smile for him for whom the court hath a frown. This knight was out of his office, not out of honour, living long after at his house in Westminster, much praised for his hospitality.

Indeed, he may the better put off his gown (though before he goeth to bed) who hath a warm suit under it; and this learned judge, by God's blessing on his endeavours, had purchased a fair estate, and particularly Crewe Hall in Cheshire (for some ages formerly the possession of the Falshursts) but which probably was the inheritance of his ancestors. Nor must it be forgotten that Sir Ranulphe first brought the model of excellent building into these remoter parts; yea, brought London into Cheshire, in the loftiness, sightliness and pleasantness of their structures.

One word of his lady, a virtuous wife being very essential to the integrity of a married judge; lest what Westminster Hall doth conclude, Westminster Bed-chamber doth revoke. He married Julian, daughter and co-heir of John Clippesby, of Clippesby in Norfolk, esq., with whom he had a fair inheritance.

I saw this worthy judge in health in 1642, but he survived not long after. And be it remembered he had a younger brother, Sir Thomas Crew, a most honest and learned serjeant in the same profession; whose son, John Crew, esquire (of his majesty's privy council) having been so instrumental to the happy change in our nation, is in general report (which no doubt will be effected before these my pains be public) designed for some title of honour.[1] [*d.* 1646]

WILLIAM WEBB, a native of this county, was bred a master in arts, and afterwards betook himself to be a clerk of the mayor's court in Chester. It appeareth also he was under-sheriff to Sir Richard Lee, high-sheriff of this county, in the thirteenth year of King James. He compiled a description of Cheshire and Chester, lately printed by procurement of that no less communicative than judicious antiquary Sir Symon Archer [1581-1662] of Tamworth in Warwickshire.

(1) Created Baron Crew of Stone in 1661.

SIR HUMPHREY DAVENPORT. His surname is sufficient to entitle this county unto him, but I will not be peremptory till better information. He was bred in the Temple, had the reputation of a studied lawyer and upright person; qualities which commended him to be chosen chief baron of the exchequer. How he behaved himself in the case of the ship-money is fresh in many men's memories.[1]

The reader cannot be more angry with me, than I am grieved in myself that, for want of intelligence, I cannot do the right which I would and ought to this worthy judge's memory, who died about the beginning of our civil distempers. [1566-1645]

JOHN BARNSTON, D.D., was born of an ancient family in this county; bred fellow of Brasenose College in Oxford; afterwards chaplain to Chancellor Egerton, and residentiary of Salisbury; a bountiful housekeeper, of a cheerful spirit and peaceable disposition, whereof take this eminent instance. He sat judge in the Consistory, when a churchwarden, out of whose house a chalice was stolen, was sued by the parish to make it good to them, because not taken out of the church chest (where it ought to have been reposited) but out of his private house. The churchwarden pleaded that he took it home only to scour it; which proving ineffectual, he retained it till next morning to boil out the inlaid rust thereof.

"Well," said the doctor, "I am sorry that the cup of union and communion should be the cause of difference and discord between you. Go home, and live lovingly together, and I doubt not but that either the thief out of remorse will restore the same, or some other as good will be sent unto you;" which, by the doctor's secret charity, came to pass accordingly. He founded an Hebrew lecture in Brasenose College; and departed in peace in [1645.]

JOHN SMITH, captain, was born [1580] in this county, as Master Arthur Smith, his kinsman and my schoolmaster, did inform me. But whether or no related unto the worshipful family of the Smiths at Hatherton, I know not.

He spent the most of his life in foreign parts. First in Hungary, under the emperor, fighting against the Turks, three of which he himself killed in single duels, and therefore was authorized by Sigismund King of Hungary to bear three Turks' heads as an augmentation to his arms.[2] Here he gave intelligence to a besieged city in the night, by significant fireworks formed in the air in legible characters, with many strange performances, the scene whereof is laid at such a distance, they are cheaper credited than confuted.

From the Turks in Europe he passed to the pagans in America, where, towards the latter end of the reign of Queen Elizabeth, such his perils, preservations, dangers, deliverences, they seem to most men above belief, to some beyond truth. Yet have we two witnesses to attest them, the prose and the pictures, both in his own book; and it soundeth much to

(1) He maintained that ship-money was legal, but, on a technical point gave judgment for Hampden. (2) So it is writ in the table over his tomb.—F.

the diminution of his deeds, that he alone is the herald to publish and proclaim them.

Two captains being at dinner, one of them fell into a large relation of his own achievements, concluding his discourse with this question to his fellow: "And pray, sir," said he, "what service have you done?" To whom he answered, "Other men can tell that." And surely such reports from strangers carry with them the greater reputation. However, moderate men must allow Captain Smith to have been very instrumental in settling the plantation in Virginia, whereof he was governor, as also admiral, of New England.

He led his old age in London, where his having a prince's mind imprisoned in a poor man's purse rendered him to the contempt of such who were not ingenuous. Yet he efforted his spirits with the remembrance and relation of what formerly he had been, and what he had done. He was buried in Sepulchre's Church quire, on the south side thereof, having a ranting epitaph inscribed in a table over him, too long to transcribe. Only we will insert the first and last verses, the rather because the one may fit Alexander's life for his valour, the other his death for his religion:

> Here lies one conquer'd that hath conquer'd kings . . .
> Oh may his soul in sweet Elysium sleep.

The orthography, poetry, history and divinity in this epitaph are much alike. He [died] on the 21st of June 1631.

JOHN RICHARDSON was, as he told me, born [1580] in this county, of a family of good worship and great antiquity therein. After his hopeful education in country schools, he was bred in the University of Dublin, where he was graduated doctor in divinity, and afterwards was made bishop of Ardagh in Ireland. In the late rebellion he came over into England, continuing for many years therein. Episcopal gravity was written in his countenance, and he was a good divine according to the rule *bonus textuarius, bonus theologus,* no man being more exact in knowledge of Scripture, carrying a concordance in his memory. Great was his pains in the larger annotations, especially on Ezekiel. For let not the cloaks carry away the credit from the gowns and rochet[1] in that work, seeing this bishop might say *pars ego magna fui*; and Doctor Featley, with others of the episcopal party, bare a great share therein. Our Saviour, we know, lived on the charity of such good people as ministered unto him; and yet it may be collected that it was his constant custom (especially about the feast of the Passover) to give some alms to the poor. So our bishop, who was relieved by some, had his bounty to bestow on others; and by his will (as I am informed) he bequeathed no inconsiderable legacy to the college in Dublin. He died anno 1654, in the 74th year of his age.

(1) *Cloak,* a clerical gown, here no doubt means in particular the Geneva (i.e. Calvinist) gown; the *gowns* and *rochet* are also clerical vestments, the latter usually worn by abbots and bishops. Hence, figuratively, the *cloaks* are the Calvinists, the *gowns* and *rochet* the Anglicans.

DANIEL KING. Reader, know this, that I must confess myself advantaged in the description of this county by Daniel King, a native of this county, whence it seems he travelled beyond the seas, where he got the mystery of surveying and engraving; so that he hath both drawn and graven the portraiture of many ancient structures now decayed.

I hope in process of time this Daniel King will outstrip King Edgar, erecting more abbeys in brass than he did in stone, though he be said to have built one for every day in the year. But Cheshire is chiefly beholding to his pains, seeing he hath not only set forth two descriptions thereof, named *The Vale Royal of England,* with the praise to the dead persons the authors thereof duly acknowledged, but also hath enlivened the same with several cuts of heraldry and topography, on whom we will bestow this distich:

Kingus Cestrensi, Cestrensis Patria Kingo,
Lucem alternatim debet uterque suam.

Cheshire to King, and King to Cheshire owes
His light; each doth receive what each bestows.

What is amiss in my poetry, shall be amended in my prayers for a blessing on his and all ingenious men's undertakings. [*d.* 1664?]

RANDOPLH CREW [*b.* 1631], esquire, second son to Sir Clippesby, grandchild to Judge Crew. He drew a map of Cheshire so exactly with his pen that a judicious eye would mistake it for printing, and the graver's skill and industry could little improve it. This map I have seen, and reader, when my eye directs my hand, I may write with confidence. This hopeful gentleman went beyond the seas, out of design to render himself by his travels more useful for his country; where he was barbarously assassinated by some Frenchmen, and honourably buried, with general lamentation of the English, at Paris, 1657.

THE FAREWELL

To take my leave of Cheshire, I could wish that some of their hospitality were planted in the south, that it might bring forth fruit therein; and in exchange I could desire that some of our southern delicacies might prosperously grow in their gardens, and quinces particularly, being not more pleasant to the palate than restorative of the health, as accounted a great cordial; the rather, because a native of this county, in his description thereof, could not remember he ever saw a quince growing therein.[1]

(1) William Smith, in his *Vale Royal*—F.

CHESTER

CHESTER is a fair city on the north-east side of the River Dee, so ancient that the first founder thereof is forgotten, much beholding to the earls of Chester and others for increase and ornaments. The walls thereof were lately in good repair, especially betwixt the New Tower and the Watergate: for I find how, anno 1569, there was a personal fight in this city betwixt the two sheriffs thereof, viz., Richard Massey and Peter Lycherband (who shall keep peace, if aged officers break it?) who deservedly were fined, for the forfeiting of their gravity, to repair that part of the wall. It seems it is more honour to be keeper of a gate in Chester than a whole city elsewhere, seeing East Gate therein was committed to the custody formerly of the earl of Oxford, Bridge Gate to the earl of Shrewsbury, Watergate to the earl of Derby, and North Gate to the mayor of the city.

It is built in the form of a quadrant, and is almost a just square, the four cardinal streets thereof (as I may call them) meeting in the middle of the city, at a place called the Pentise, which affordeth a pleasant prospect at once into all four. Here is a property of building peculiar to the city, called the Rows, being galleries wherein passengers go dry without coming into the streets, having shops on both sides and underneath; the fashion whereof is somewhat hard to conceive. It is therefore worth their pains, who have money and leisure, to make their own eyes the expounders of the manner thereof; the like being said not to be seen in all England; no, nor in all Europe again.

THE BUILDINGS

Saint Werburga's church is a fair structure, and had been more beautiful if the tower thereof (intended some say for a steeple, the first stone whereof was laid 1508) had been finished. It was built long before the Conquest; and being much ruined, was afterwards repaired by Hugh Lupus, first earl of Chester. It was afterwards made by King Henry the Eighth one of his five royal bishoprics: Oxford, Gloucester, Bristol and Peterborough being the other four. I say royal bishoprics, as whose ecclesiastical jurisdictions were never confirmed by the pope, nor baronies by the parliament.

The first is plain, King Henry the Eighth erecting them after he had disclaimed the pope's supremacy; and in the days of Queen Mary, when England was in some sort reconciled to Rome, the pope thought not fit to contest with the queen about that criticism, because these five bishoprics were erected without his consent, but sufficed them to be even as he found them. Their baronies also were not, though their bishoprics were, ever confirmed by act of parliament; so that they owed their beings solely to the king's prerogative, who might as well create spiritual as temporal peers by his own authority; and therefore, when some anti-prelatists, in the late Long Parliament, 1640, endeavoured to overthrow their baronies (as an essay and preludium to the rest of the bishoprics) for want of parliamentary confirmation they desisted from that design, as fond and unfeasable, on better consideration.

PROVERBS

When the daughter is stolen, shut Pepper Gate. Pepper Gate was a postern of this city, on the east side (as I take it) thereof, but in times past closed up and shut upon this occasion. The mayor of the city had his daughter, as she was playing at ball with other maidens in Pepper Street, stolen away by a young man, through the same gate; whereupon, in revenge, he caused it to be shut up, though I see not why the city should suffer in her conveniences for the mayor's want of care, or his daughter's lack of obedience. But what shall we say? Love will make the whole wall a gate to procure its own escape. Parallel to this proverb is the Latin, *Sero sapiunt Phryges* [the Trojans become wise too late] when men, instead of preventing, *postvide* against dangers.

THE WORTHIES

ROGER OF CHESTER was born and bred therein, a Benedictine monk in Saint Werburga's. In obedience to the bishop of Chester, he wrote a *British Chronicle* from the beginning of the world. This was the fashion of all historians of that age, running to take a long rise from the creation itself, that so (it seems) they might leap the further with the greater force. Our Roger's *Chronicle* was like a ship with double decks, first only continuing it to the year 1314, and then, resuming his subject, he superadded five and twenty years more thereunto, entitling it *Polycratica Temporum.*

Both Bale and Pits praise him for pure Latin (a rarity in that age) and assign 1339 the time of his death, Chester the place of his burial.[1]

RANULF HIGDEN (commonly called Ranulf of Chester) was bred a Benedictine in Saint Werburga's. He not only vamped the history of Roger aforesaid, but made a large one of his own, from the beginning of the world, commendable for his method and modesty therein.

Method; assigning in the margent the date of each action. We read, Genesis i, that light was made on the first and the sun on the fourth day of the creation, when the light (formerly diffused and dispersed in the heavens) was contracted, united and fixed in one full body thereof. Thus the notation of times confusedly scattered in many ancient authors (as to our English actions) are by our Ranulphus reduced into an entire bulk of chronology.

Modesty; who, to his great commendation, *unicuique suorum authorum honorem integrum servans,* confesseth himself (to use his own expression), with Ruth the Moabite, "to have gleaned after other reapers." He calleth his book *Polychronicon.*

He continued sixty-four years a monk, and dying very aged, 1364, was buried in Chester.

(1) Roger of Chester is almost certainly the same person as Ranulf Higden, whose life follows immediately below.

WILLIAM ALDERSEY, a pious and godly man, was mayor of the city, 1560, demeaning himself in his place with much gravity and discretion. He caused, with much cost and industry, the catalogue of the mayors of Chester to be completed, and that on this occasion. He found by authentic evidences that one Alan de Whetley had been four times mayor of Chester, and yet his name was never mentioned in the ordinary Book of Mayors. This put this good magistrate on the employment (detection of faults informs little without correction of them) to amend and complete that lame list out of their records. Thus imperfections may occasion perfection; which makes me to hope that hereafter the defects of this my book (without prejudice to my profit or credit) will be judiciously discovered, and industriously amended by others. This William died the twelfth of October, anno 1577, and lieth buried in the chancel of Saint Oswald's under a fair stone of alabaster.

SIR THOMAS OFFLEY, son to William Offley, was born [1505?] in the city of Chester, and bred a Merchant Taylor in London, whereof he became lord mayor anno 1556. The useful custom of the night bellman (preventing many fires and more felonies) began in his mayoralty. He was the Zacchaeus of London, not for his low stature, but his high charity, bequeathing the half of his estate (computed by a reverend divine to amount to five thousand pounds)[1] unto the poor, although he had children of his own. Yea, he appointed that two hundred pounds should be taken out of the other half (left to his son Henry) and employed to charitable uses. He died 1582, and was buried in the church of Saint Andrew Undershaft. I am heartily sorry to meet with this passage in my author:[2] "Sir Thomas Offley bequeathed one half of all his goods to charitable actions. But the parish (meaning St. Andrew Undershaft) receiveth little benefit thereby."

If the testator's will were not justly performed, it soundeth to the shame and blame of his executors. But if the charity of Sir Thomas acted *eminus* not *comminus,* I mean at some distance, and not at his own habitation, it was no injury for any to dispose of his own at his own pleasure.

I believe it was [Sir Thomas Offley] on whom the rhyme was made,

> Offley three dishes had of daily roast;
> An egg, an apple, and (the third) a toast.

This I behold neither sin nor shame in him, feeding himself on plain and wholesome repast, that he might feast others by his bounty, and thereby deserving rather praise than a jeer from posterity.

DAVID MIDDLETON was born in this city, as his kinsman and my friend hath informed me.[3] He was one of those who effectually contributed his assistance to the making of *through lights* in the world; I mean, new discoveries in the East and West Indies, as we may read at large in his own printed relation.[4]

(1) Dr. Willett, in his *Catalogue of Good Works since the Reformation.* (2) Stow's *Survey of London.* (3) Master John Spencer, library keeper of Sion College. (4) Purchas's *Pilgrims.*

The tender-hearted reader, whose affections go along with his eye, will sadly sympathize with his sufferings, so many and great his dangers with cannibals and Portuguese, crocodiles and Hollanders, till at last he accomplished his intentions, and settled the English trade at Bantam.
[*d.* 1615]

SIR HENRY MIDDLETON, knight, was younger brother (as I take it) to the former, deservedly knighted for his great pains and perils in advancing the English trade. Amongst many, most remarkable is his voyage into the Red Sea, which had like to have proved the Dead Sea unto him; I mean cost him his life. Here he was told to land at Mocha, by the treacherous Aga, and then had eight of his men barbarously slain, himself and seven more chained up by the necks. The pretence was, because that port was the door of the holy city, which (though it be Jerusalem in the language of the Scripture) is Mecca in the phrase of the Alcoran, and it is capital for any Christian to come so near thereunto. Then was he sent eight-score miles and upwards to the bashaw at Zenan in Arabia, in the month of January 1611. This city of Zenan lieth but sixteen degrees and fifteen minutes of northern latitude from the equator, and yet was so cold that there was ice of a finger's thickness in one night, as the said Sir Henry did relate. This confuteth the character of these countries, misapprehended by antiquity not to be habitable for the excess of heat therein.

At last the Turkish bashaw gave him leave to depart, and sailing eastwards, he repaired himself, by a gainful composition with the Indians, for the losses he had sustained by the Turks. His ship, called the *Trade's Increase,* well answered the name thereof, until it pleased God to visit his men therein with a strange disease, whereof one hundred English deceased; the grief whereat was conceived the cause of this worthy knight's death, May 24, 1613, whose name will ever survive whilst Middleton's Bay (from him so called) appeareth in the Dutch cards [1]

EDWARD BREREWOOD [or BRYERWOOD] was, as I am informed, born [1565?] in this city, bred in Brasenose College in Oxford. Being candidate for a fellowship, he lost it without loss of credit; for where preferment goes more by favour than merit, the rejected have more honour than the elected.

This ill success did him no more hurt than a rub doth to an overthrown bowl, bringing it the nearer to the mark He was not the more sullen, but the more serious in his studies, retiring himself to Saint Mary Hall, till he became a most accomplished scholar in logic, witness his worthy work thereof; mathematics, being afterwards a lecturer thereof in Gresham College;[1] all learned and many modern languages—hereof he wrote a learned book, called his *Enquiries*: no sacrilegious *enquiries* whereof our age doth surfeit ("it is a snare after vows to make enquiries") but judicious disquisitions of the original and extent of languages.

A little before his death, pens were brandished betwixt Master Byfield[2]

(1) *Cards*=charts. (2) He was the first professor of astronomy at Gresham College, 1596. (2) Nicholas Byfield—see Warwickshire, p. 591.

and him, about the keeping of the sabbath; Master Brerewood learnedly maintaining that the other exacted more strictness therein than God enjoined. I have heard a great scholar in England say that he was the fittest man whom he knew in England to sit at the elbow of a professor to prompt him. But in my opinion, he was a very proper person to discharge the place himself. [*d.* 1613]

GEORGE DOWNHAM [or DOWNAME], D.D., son to William Downham bishop of Chester, was born in this city, as by proportion of time may most probably be collected. He was bred in Christ's College in Cambridge, elected fellow thereof 1585, and chosen logic professor in the university. No man was then and there better skilled in Aristotle, or a greater follower of Ramus,[1] so that he may be termed the top twig of that branch.

It is seldom seen that the clunch-fist of logic (good to knock down a man at a blow) can so open itself as to smooth and stroke one with the palm thereof. Our Downham could do both; witness the oration made by him at Cambridge (preposed to his book of logic) full of flowers of the choicest eloquence. He preached the sermon, April 17, 1608, at the consecration of James Montagu, bishop of Bath and Wells, irrefragably proving therein episcopacy *jure divino*.

"He that receiveth a bishop in the name of a bishop, shall receive a bishop's reward." It was not long before Doctor Downham was made bishop of Derry, in Ireland, then newly augmented with the addition of Londonderry; because so planted with English, it was easy to find London in Derry, but not Derry in Derry, so much disguised from itself with new buildings. But this learned bishop was the greatest beauty thereof, endeavouring by gentleness to cicurate[2] and civilize the wild Irish, and proved very successful therein. [*d.* 1634]

JOHN DOWNHAM [or DOWNAME], younger son to William Downham bishop of Chester, was, as far as my best inquiry can recover, born in this city; bred in Cambridge B.D., and afterwards became a painful and profitable preacher in London. He was the first who commendably discharged that eminent lecture, plentifully endowed by Master Jones of Monmouth;[3] and is memorable to posterity for his worthy work of *The Christian Warfare*. Well had it been for England, had no other war been used therein for this last twenty years, all pious persons being comfortably concerned in the prosecution thereof; seriously considering that their armour is of proof, their quarrel is lawful, their fight is long, their foes are fierce, their company are saints, their captain is Christ, their conquest is certain, their crown is Heaven. This grave divine died, very aged [1652].

THE FAREWELL

And now being to take our leave of this ancient and honourable city, the worst that I wish it is that the distance betwixt Dee and the New Tower

(1) Petrus Ramus (Pierre la Ramée, 1515—1572) famous as an opponent of Aristotelian doctrine. (2) *Cicurate* = to tame. (3) In the church behind the Exchange.—F.

may be made up, all obstructions being removed which cause or occasion the same. That the rings on the New Tower (now only for sight) may be restored to the service for which they were first intended, to fasten vessels thereunto. That the vessels on that river (lately degenerated from ships into barks) may grow up again to their former strength and stature.

CORNWALL

IT hath its name partly from the *form,* partly from the *inhabitants* thereof. From the former it is so called, because narrow in fashion of a horn, which, by the way, is a word of all others passing through both learned and modern languages with the least variation: 1. *Keren,* Hebrew; 2. *Keras,* Greek; 3. *Cornu,* Latin; 4. *Corn,* French; 5. *Cuerno,* Spanish; 6. *Corno,* Italian; 7. *Horn,* English; 8. *Horne,* Dutch; 9. *Kerne,* Welsh.

The latter, *Wale,* signifies *strangers,* for such were the inhabitants of this county reputed by their neighbours.

It hath Devonshire on the west, divided from it generally with the River Tamar, encompassed with the sea on all other sides, affording plenty of harbours; so that foreigners, in their passage to or from Spain, Ireland, the Levant, East or West Indies, sometimes touch herewith; sometimes are driven hither against their will, but never without the profit of the inhabitants, according to the common proverb, "Where the horse lieth down, there some hairs will be found."

The language of the natives is a different *tongue* from the English and *dialect* from the Welsh, as more easy to be pronounced, and is sufficiently copious to express the conceits of a good wit, both in prose and verse. Some have avouched it derived from the Greek, producing for the proof thereof many words of one sense in both, as *kentron,* a spur, *schaphe,* a boat, *ronchi,* snoring, &c. But the judicious behold these as no regular congruities, but the casual coincidences, the like to which may be found in languages of the greatest distance, which never met together since they parted at the confusion of Babel. Thus one would enforce a conformity between the Hebrew and the English, because one of the three giant's sons of *Anak* was called *Ahiman.*

The Cornish tongue affordeth but two natural oaths, or three at most; but whether each of them be according to the kinds of oaths divided by the schoolmen, one *assertory,* the other *promissory,* to which some add a third, *comminatory,* is to me unknown. The worst is, the common Cornish supply this (I will not say defect) not only with swearing the same often over, but also by borrowing other oaths of the English.

NATURAL COMMODITIES

Diamonds

These of themselves sound high, till the addition of Cornish subtracteth from their valuation. In blackness and hardness they are far short of the Indian; yet, set with a good foil (advantaged hypocrisy passeth often for sincerity) may at the first sight deceive no unskilful lapidary. As their lustre is less than orient diamonds, so herein they exceed them, that nature hath made both their face and their dressing, by whom they are pointed and polished. But enough hereof, the rather because some, from the Latin names of jewels, *jocalia,* "things to be jested and played with," and *baubellae,* "things which are trifles and baubles," spitefully collect that stones, accounted precious, are more beholding to the consent of fancy than their own intrinsic worth, for their high valuation.

AMBERGRIS

I confess this precious commodity is fixed to no place in the world, as too great a treasure for any one country to engross; and therefore it is only fluctuating, and casually found by small parcels, sometimes in one place, and sometimes in another; yet because the last, greatest and best quantity thereof that ever this age did behold was found on the coasts of this county, we will here insert a little of the name, nature and use thereof.

It is called *ambra-gresia,* that is, grey amber, from the colour thereof; which modern name, utterly unknown to the ancients, doth speak it to be of later invention; whereof a learned doctor of physic hath assigned this probable reason, because it was never found in the Midland Sea (which was in effect all the seas to the ancients) but only in the main ocean, which was not navigated on till within this last two hundred years, since seamen have gotten the use of the card[1] and compass.

It is almost as hard to know what it is, as where to find it. Some will have it the sperm of a fish, or some other unctuous matter arising from them; others, that it is the foam of the sea, or some excrescency thence, boiled to such a height by the heat of the sun; others, that it is a gum that grows on the shore. In a word, no certainity can be collected herein, some physicians holding one way, and some another. But this is most sure, that apothecaries hold it at five pounds an ounce, which some say is dearer than ever it was in the memory of man.

It is a rare cordial for the refreshing of the spirits, and sovereign for the strengthening the head, besides the most fragrant scent, far stronger in consort when compounded with other things than when singly itself.

A mass of this ambergris was, about the third year of King Charles, found in this county, at low water, close to the shore of the manor of Anthony, then belonging to Richard Carew, esquire.

GARLIC

Here is a great and sudden fall indeed, from the sweetest of gums to the most stinking of roots. Yet is not the distance so great, if the worth of the garlic be such as some have avouched it. Not to speak of the murmuring Israelites, who prized it before manna itself, some avow it sovereign for men and beasts in most maladies. Indeed the scent thereof is somewhat valiant and offensive; but wise men will be contented to hold their noses, on condition they may thereby hold or recover their health. Indeed a large book is written *de usu allii;* which if it hold proportion with truth, one would wonder any man should be sick and die who hath garlic growing in his garden. Sure I am our palate-people are much pleased therewith, as giving a delicious *haut-gout* to most meats they eat, as tasted and smelt in their sauce, though not seen therein. The best garlic is about Stratton in this county.

(1) *Card* = chart.

PILCHARDS

Plenty hereof are taken in these parts, persecuted to the shore by their enemies the tunny and hake, till, in pursuance of their private revenge, they all become a prey to the fishermen. The pilchard may seem contemptible in itself, being so small, though the wit of the vulgar here will tell you they have seen many pilchards an ell long, understand it laid at length, head and tail together. Their numbers are incredible, employing a power of poor people in polling (that is, beheading) gutting, splitting, powdering and drying them; and then, by the name of *fumadoes,* with oil and a lemon they are meat for the mightiest don in Spain. I wish not only their nets, but fish, may hold, suspecting their daily decay, their shoals usually shifting coasts, and verging more westward to Ireland. Other fish here be, which turn to good account; all welcome to fishermen's hooks, save the star-fish, esteemed contagious.

BLUE SLATE

These are commonly found under the walling-slate, when the depth hath brought the workmen to the water. They are thin in substance, clear in colour, light in weight, and lasting in continuance. Generally they carry so good a regard that (besides the supply of home provisions) great store of them are imported into other parts of the land, and transported into France and the Low Countries.

TIN

The most and best in Christendom this county doth produce. Yea, it was the only tin in Europe, until a fugitive miner, running hence, discovered tin in Voigtland, in the confines of Bohemia. God may be said in this county "to rain meat" (such the plenty thereof) "and give dishes too," made of pewter, which hath tin for the father, and lead for the mother thereof, and in our age doth *matrizare* too much. Vast their expense in making their *adits* (understand them addresses and accesses to the mine) with dressing, breaking, stamping, drying, grazing, washing and melting, all plentifully repaid in the selling of it.

The discovery of many of these mines has been very remarkable; for some have gained more sleeping than others waking, having dreamt that in such (improbable) places tin was to be found, and, pursuing such directions, have found it accordingly.

I cannot take my leave of these tinners, until I have observed a strange practice of them, that once in seven or eight years they burn down (and that to their great profit) their own melting houses. I remember a merry epigram in Martial on one Tongilian, who had his house in Rome casually (reputed) burnt, and gained ten times as much by his friends' contribution to his loss:

> *Collatum est decies; rogo non potes ipse videri*
> *Incendisse tuam, Tongiliane, domum.*
>
> Gaining tenfold, tell truly, I desire,
> Tongilian, didst not set thy house on fire?

But here the tinners avow themselves incendiaries of their own houses, on a profitable account; for, during the tin's melting in the blowing-house, diverse light sparkles thereof are, by the forcible wind which the bellows sendeth forth, driven up to the thatched roof on the burning whereof they find so much of this light tin in the ashes, as payeth for the new building, with a gainful overplus.

THE BUILDINGS

Master Attorney Noye[1] was wont pleasantly to say that his house had no fault in it, save only that "it was too near unto London," though indeed distanced thence full three hundred miles in the remoter part of this county. But seriously one may say, and defend it, that the distance of Cornwall from that metropolis is a convenient inconveniency. As for the structure of their houses, they are generally but mean, though the nobility and gentry have handsome habitations, and amongst them none excelleth

MOUNT EDGECUMBE

It was built by Sir Richard Edgecumbe, knight. Take his character from one who very well knew him: "Mildness and stoutness, diffidence and wisdom, deliberateness of undertakings, and sufficiency of effecting, made in him a more commendable than blazing mixture of virtue."[2] In the reign of Queen Mary (about the year 1555) he gave entertainment at one time, for some good space, to the admirals of the English, Spanish and Netherlands, and many noblemen besides. A passage the more remarkable, because I am confident that the admirals of those nations never met since (if ever before) amicably at the same table. Mount Edgecumbe was the scene of this hospitality, a house new built and named by the aforesaid knight, a square structure with a round turret at each end, garreted on the top. The hall (rising above the rest) yieldeth a stately sound as one entereth it; the parlour and dining-room afford a large and diversified prospect both of sea and land. The high situation (cool in summer, yet not cold in winter) giveth health; the neighbour river wealth; two block-houses great safety; and the town of Plymouth good company unto it. Nor must I forget the fruitful ground about it (pleasure without profit is but a flower without a root) stored with wood, timber, fruit, deer, and conies, a sufficiency of pasture, arable and meadow, with stone, lime, marl and what not.

I write not this to tempt the reader to the breach of the tenth commandment, "to covet his neighbour's house," and one line in the prevention thereof. I have been credibly informed that the duke of Medina Sidonia, admiral of the Spanish fleet in the year 88, was so affected at the sight of this house (though but beholding it at a distance from the sea) that he resolved it for his own possession in the partage of this kingdom (blame him not if choosing best for himself) which they pre-conquered in their hopes and expectation. But he had catched a great cold, had he had no other clothes to wear than those which were to be made of a skin of a bear not yet killed.

(1) See below, p. 96. (2) Carew, in his *Survey of Cornwall*.

THE WONDERS

MAIN AMBER

Main is in Cornish the stone, and *Amber,* as some conceive, of Ambrosius that valiant Briton, erected probably by him on some victory achieved against the Romans, or some other enemies. This a masterpiece of mathematics and critical proportions, being a great stone of so exact position on the top of a rock, that any weakness by touching it may move it, and yet no force can remove it, so justly it is poised. I have heard in common discourse, when this Main Amber hath been made the emblem of such men's dispositions, who would listen to all counsel, and seem inclined thereunto, but are so fixed, that no reason can alter them from their first resolution.

But know, reader, that this wonder is now *unwondered;* for I am credibly informed, that some soldiers of late have utterly destroyed it.

PROVERBS

By Tre, Pol, and Pen,
You shall know the Cornish men.

These three words are the dictionary of such surnames which are originally Cornish; and though *nouns* in sense, I may fitly term them *prepositions.*

1. *Tre* signifieth a *town;* hence Tre-fry, Tre-lawny, Tre-vanion, &c. 2. *Pol* signifieth an *head;* hence Pol-whele. 3. *Pen* signifieth a *top;* hence Pen-tire, Pen-rose, Pen-kevil, &c.

Some add to these a fourth inchoation, viz., *Car* (which I guess to signify *rock*); ad Car-mino, Car-zew, &c. But I dare not make additions, but present it as I find it in my author.

To give one a Cornish hug. The Cornish are masters of the art of wrestling; so that if the Olympian games were now in fashion, they would come away with the victory. Their hug is a cunning close with their fellow-combatant; the fruit whereof is his fair fall, or foil at the least. It is figuratively applicable to the deceitful dealing of such who secretly design their overthrow whom they openly embrace.

He is to be summoned before the Mayor of Halgaver. This is a jocular and imaginary court, wherewith men make merriment to themselves, presenting such persons as go slovenly in their attire, untrussed, wanting a spur, &c.; where judgment in formal terms is given against them, and executed more to the scorn than hurt of the persons. But enough hereof, lest I be summoned thither myself.

LAWYERS IN CORNWALL

There passeth a pleasant tradition in this county, how there standeth a man of great strength and stature with a black bill in his hand, at Polston Bridge, the first entrance into Cornwall, as you pass towards Launceston, where the assizes are holden, ready to knock down all the lawyers that should offer to plant themselves in that county. But, in earnest, few of that profession have here grown up to any supereminent height of learning, livelihood or authority; whether because of the far distance of this county from the supremer courts, or because of the multiplicity of petty ones nearer hand, pertaining to the duchy, stanneries[1] and other franchises, enabling attorneys and the like of small reading to serve the people's turn, and so cutting the profit from better-studied councillors.

THE BATTLES

I shall enlarge myself the rather on this subject, because building my discourse therein, not on the floating sands of uncertain relations, but the rock of real intelligence; having gotten a manuscript of Sir Ralph Hopton's, courteously communicated unto me by his secretary Master Tredui, interpolated with his own hand, being a memorial of the remarkables in the west, at which that worthy knight was present in person.

I begin with that which is called the Battle of Liskeard, taking the name from the next town of note thereinto; otherwise Braddock Down was the particular place thereof. Before the fight began, the king's side took it into their seasonable consideration that, seeing by the commission the Lord Mohun brought from Oxford, four persons, viz., the said Lord Mohun, Sir Ralph Hopton, Sir John Berkeley, and Colonel Ashburnham, were equally empowered in the managing of all military matters, and seeing such equality might prove inconvenient (which hitherto had been prevented with the extraordinary moderation of all parties) in ordering a battle, it was fittest to fix the power in one chief; and general consent settled it in Sir Ralph Hopton.

He first gave order that public prayers should be had in the head of every squadron, and it was done accordingly (and the enemy, observing it, did style it saying of mass, as some of their prisoners afterwards did confess). Then he caused the foot to be drawn up in the best order they could; placed a forlorn of musketeers in the little inclosures, winging them with the few horse and dragoons he had.

This done, two small minion drakes,[2] speedily and secretly fetched from the Lord Mohun's house, were planted on a little barrow within random-shot of the enemy; yet so that they were covered from their sight, with small parties of horse about them. These concealed minions were twice discharged with such success that the enemy quickly quitted their ground; and all their army being put to rout, the king's forces had the execution of them, which they performed very sparingly. They took twelve hundred and fifty prisoners, most of their colours, all their cannon, being four brass guns upon carriages, whereof two were twelve-pounders, and one iron saker,[3] all their ammunition, most of their arms; and, marching that night to Liskeard, the king's forces first gave God public thanks, and then took their own private repose.

(1) These cannot now be pretended an hindrance, being put down by the long-lasting parliament. (2) *Minion drakes*=small kind of cannon. (3) *Saker*=cannon of small bore (less than that of demi-culverin, which was about 4½ inches).

STRATTON fight suceeds, on Tuesday, May 16, 1643. But first let us take a true account of the two armies respectively, with the visible inequality betwixt them.

The king's forces were in want of ammunition, and were to hew out their own way up a steep hill with their valour, exposed to all disadvantages and dangers. Their horse and dragoons exceeded not five hundred; their foot about two thousand four hundred in number.

The parliament army had plenty of all provisions, and had advantageously barricaded themselves on the top of a hill. Their horse indeed were not many (having lately sent away twelve hundred to surprise the sheriff and commissioners at Bodmin) but foot were five thousand four hundred by poll, as their major-general did acknowledge.

As for the king's forces, order was given that by four several avenues they should force their passage to the top of the hill, which was very steep; the enemy as obstinately endeavouring to keep them down, as the other did valiantly strive to ascend.

The fight continued doubtful, with many countenances of various events, from five of the clock in the morning till three in the afternoon; amongst which most remarkable the smart charge made by Major-General Chudleigh, with a stand of pikes, on Sir Bevil Grenville, so that the knight was in person overthrown, and his party put into disorder; which would have proved destructive unto it, had not Sir John Berkeley (who led up the musketeers on each side of Sir Bevil Grenville) seasonably relieved it, so reinforcing the charge that Major-General Chudleigh was taken prisoner.

Betwixt three and four of the clock the commanders of the king's forces who embraced those four several ways of ascent, met, to their mutual joy, almost at the top of the hill, which the routed enemy confusedly forsook. In this service, though they were assailants, they lost very few men, and no considerable officer; killing of the enemy about three hundred, and taking seventeen hundred prisoners, all their cannon (being thirteen pieces of brass ordnance) and ammunition (seventy barrels of powder) with a magazine of biscuit, and other provisions proportionable. For this victory public prayer and thanksgiving was made on the hill, and then the army was disposed of, to improve their success to the best advantage. For this good service Sir Ralph Hopton was afterwards, at Oxford, created Baron of Stratton . . . .

As for the general disarming and disbanding of the parliament army in this county, anno 1644, it was a conquest without a battle, on this occasion. I have seen the head bow down to take a thorn out of the foot. Such the proportion of Cornwall to England, and such was the condescension of the king to come into this county. Essex followed him with all his forces, till he penned himself in a narrow place, or rather large pound, so that he was surrounded on all sides with the sea and the king's soldiers.

Hereupon Essex, with some prime commanders, shipped himself for Plymouth, thence for London; whither also their horse forced their passage (without considerable loss) under the conduct of Sir William Balfour, whom the king's horse did *sequi, non assequi* (follow, but not overtake). The foot, left behind, submitted to the king, on such conditions as are generally known.

His majesty, earnestly endeavouring, by the enemy's own confession, the exact observing of articles, which if some unruly royalist did violate (soldiers will hardly wear bad clothes whilst their foes, being in their power, have better on their backs) it was not so much an offering as returning of an injury; some of them having formerly felt the same usage on the like occasion. The parliament foot did not depose their disaffections with their arms, soon resuming (or rather retaining) their former principles, which made them add new arms to their old inclinations in the second battle at Newbury.

THE WORTHIES

URSULA, daughter to Deonotus duke of Cornwall, was born in this county. This is she whose life is loaden with such anticronisms and improbabilities, that it is questionable whether this fable was ever founded in a truth, or hath anything in history for its original.

This Ursula is said to have carried over out of Britain eleven thousand maids of prime quality, besides threescore thousand of meaner rank (seventy-one thousand in all, a prodigious number) to be married to so many in little Britain in France. Preposterous, in my mind, to proffer themselves, and it had argued more modesty if their husbands had fetched them hence.

But blame them not, who paid so dear for their adventures. All shipped from London, some of them were drowned in their passage, the rest slain by the Huns of Cologne, say some; at Rome, say others, by King Attila under Gratian the emperor: *mendacium aequabile,* observing equal temper of untruth, in time, place, and person. However, there is a church at Cologne dedicated to their memories, where the Virgin Earth (let the reporter[1] have the whetstone) will digest no other body, no not the corpse of an infant newly baptised (as good a maid, I believe, as the best of them) but will vomit it up in the night time again as if they had never been buried. [*d.* 238, or 283, or 451]

KING ARTHUR, son of Uther Pendragon, was born in Tintagel Castle in this county; and proved afterwards monarch of Great Britain. He may fitly be termed the British Hercules in three respects: 1. For his illegitimate birth, both being bastards, begotten on other men's wives, and yet their mothers honest women; deluded, the one by miracle, the other by art magic of Merlin, in others personating their husbands. 2. Painful life; one famous for his twelve labours, the other for his twelve victories against the Saxons; and both of them had been greater, had they been made less, and the reports of them reduced within compass of probability. 3. Violent and woeful death; our Arthur's being as lamentable, and more honourable; not caused by feminine jealousy, but masculine treachery, being murdered by Mordred, near the place where he was born:

(1) Richard White of Basingstoke, in *History of British Martyrs.*

As though no other place on Britain's spacious earth
Were worthy of his end, but where he had his birth.[1]

As for his Round Table, with his knights about it, the tale whereof hath trundled along many ages, it never met with much belief amongst the judicious. [*fl.* 5th cent.]

JOHN OF CORNWALL (so called from the county of his nativity) leaving his native soil, studied in foreign universities, chiefly in Rome, where his abilities commended him to the cognizance of Pope Alexander the Third. It argueth his learning that he durst cope with that giant Peter Lombard himself, commonly called the Master of the Sentences; and who on that account expected that all should rather obey than any oppose his judgment. Yea, it appeareth that the judgment of this Peter bishop of Paris was not so sound in all points, by a passage I meet with in Matthew Paris, of Pope Alexander the Third writing a letter to an archbishop of France, "to abrogate the ill doctrine of Peter, sometime bishop of Paris, about Christ's Incarnation." But our John wrote against him, in his lifetime, a book *De Homine Assumpto,* and put Peter's pen to some pains to write his own vindication. He also wrote a book of philosophy and heresies. Wonder not at their conjunction, philosophy being in divinity as fire and water in a family—a good servant, but bad master; so sad it is, when the articles of our creed must be tried by the touchstone of Aristotle. This John flourisheth under King Henry the second, anno 1170.

SIMON OF TOURNAY was born in this county, bred in our English universities until he went over into Paris, where he became so eminent a logician, that all his auditors were his admirers. Most firm his memory, and fluent his expression, and was knowing in all things, save in himself, for profanely he advanced Aristotle above Moses, and himself above both. His pride had a great and sudden fall, losing at the same time both language and memory, becoming completely ἄλογος, without reason or speech. Yet was his dumbness, to all intelligent people, a loud sermon on St. Paul's precept, "Not to think of themselves more highly than they ought to think, but to think soberly." Polydore Vergil saith of him, *Juvene nil acutius, sene nihil obtusius,* whilst others add, he made an inarticulate sound like to lowing. [*fl.* 1180-1200]

BLAUNPAYN MICHAEL, born in Cornwall (some so commonly call him Michael the Master, that he had almost lost his native name) was bred in Oxford and Paris, and became as good a rhyming poet as any in that age. It happened one Henry of Normandy, chief poet to our Henry the Third, had traduced Cornwall as an inconsiderable county, cast out by nature in contempt into a corner of the land. Our Michael could not endure this affront; but, full of poetical fury, falls upon the libeller. Take a taste (little thereof will go far) of his strains:[2]

We need not number up her wealthy store,
Wherewith this helpful land relieves her poor,
No sea so full of fish, of tin no shore.

(1) Drayton's *Polyolbion.* (2) Latin original omitted.

Then, as a valiant champion, he concludeth all with this exhortation to his countrymen:

> What should us fright, if firmly we do stand?
> Bar fraud, and then no force can us command.

His pen, so luscious in praising when so pleased, was as bitter in railing when disposed: witness this his satirical character of his foresaid antagonist:

> Gamb'd like a goat, sparrow-thigh'd, sides as boar,
> Hare-mouth'd, dog-nosed, like mule thy teeth and chin,
> Brow'd as old wife, bull-headed, black as moor.
> If such without, then what are you within?
> By these my signs, the wise will easily conster,
> How little thou didst differ from a monster.

He flourished anno 1250, though the certain time and place of his death is unknown.

JOHN DE TREVISA was born [1326] at Crocadon [St. Mellion] in this county; bred in Oxford; afterwards vicar of Berkeley in Gloucestershire, and chaplain to Thomas Lord Berkeley, at whose instance, besides other histories writ by him, he translated the Bible into English;[1] a daring work for a private person in that age, without particular command from pope or public council.

Some much admire he would enter on this work, so lately performed (about fifty years before) by John Wycliffe. What was this but *actum agere,* to do what was done before? Besides, Wycliffe and Trevisa agreeing so well in their judgments, it was much he would make a re-translation. Such consider not that in that age it was almost the same pains for a scholar to translate as transcribe the Bible.

Secondly, the time betwixt Wycliffe and Trevisa was the crisis of the English tongue, which began to be improved in fifty more than in three hundred years formerly. Many coarse words (to say no worse) used before are refined by Trevisa, whose translation is as much better than Wycliffe's, as worse than Tyndal's. Thus, though the fountain of the original hath always clearness alike therein, channels of translations will partake of more or less purity, according to the translator's age, industry and ability. [*d.* 1412]

MICHAEL TREGURY [or TREVOR] was born in this county, and bred in the university of Oxford, where he attained to such eminence that he was commended to King Henry the Fifth fit to be a foreign professor. This King Henry, desiring to conquer France as well by arts as arms, knowing that learning made civil persons and loyal subjects, reflected on the city of Caen (honoured with the ashes of his ancestors) in Normandy, and resolved to advance it an university, which he did anno 1418, placing this Michael the first professor in the college of his royal erection. Hence King Henry the Sixth preferred him archbishop of Dublin in Ireland, wherein he continued 22 years, deceasing December 1471; and is buried in the church of Saint Patrick in Dublin.

(1) Trevisa is credited by Caxton with a translation of the Bible, but it is not extant. He is chiefly remembered for his translation into English of Higden's *Polychronicon*.

SIR JAMES TYRRELL. This is he so infamous in our English histories for his activity in murdering the innocent sons of King Edward the Fourth; keeping the keys of the Tower, and standing himself at the foot of the stairs, whilst Mr. Forest and J. Dighton stifled them in their beds. I behold this Sir James as an Essex man, though now the prime officer of this county; for King Richard accounted Cornwall the back door of rebellion, and therefore made this knight the porter thereof. Indeed it is remote from London, and the long sides of this county afford many landing places, objected to Britain in France, whence the usurper always feared (and at last felt) an invasion; and therefore he appointed him sheriff, to secure the county, as obliged unto him, by gratitude for favours received, and guilt for faults committed. This Tyrrell was afterwards executed for treason, in the Tower Yard, in [1502].

BARTHOLOMEW TRAHERON. The first syllable of his name, and what is added thereunto by my author, *parentum stemmate clarus,*[1] and the sameness of his name with an ancient family in this county, are a threefold cable to draw my belief that he was this countryman. He was bred in the university of Oxford, and having attained to good learning therein, twice travelled beyond the seas.

Once, for pleasure and curiosity, into France and Italy, whereby he much improved himself. Returning home, he became library-keeper to King Edward the Sixth, and dean of Chichester. The second time, for safety and necessity, in the first of Queen Mary, getting, I believe, his best subsistence (being an exile in Germany) with making and translating books, where he was living 1556, and may be rationally presumed to die before Queen Elizabeth came to the crown, because, being a man of merit, and eccliastically dignified, we hear no more of his preferment. [1510?-1558?]

SIR JOHN TREGONWELL was born in this county; bred in Oxford, where he proceeded doctor of the laws, both canon and civil; and, attaining to great perfection in the theoretic and practical parts of those professions, he was employed to be proctor for King Henry the Eighth in the long and costly cause of his divorce from Queen Catherine dowager. Now, as it was said of the Roman dictator Sylla, *suos divitiis explevit* [he enriches his own] so King Henry full fraught all those with wealth and rewards whom he retained in that employment. This doctor he knighted, and because so dexterous and diligent in his service, gave him a pension of forty pounds per annum; and upon the resignation thereof (with the paying down of a thousand pounds) he conferred on him and his heirs the rich demesne and site of Middleton,[2] a mitred abbey in Dorsetshire, possessed at this day by his posterity. This Sir John died [1565] . . . and is buried under a fair monument in the church of Middleton aforesaid.

RAWE HAYES, a blacksmith by his occupation, and furnished with more learning than is suitable to such a calling; who yet ministered physic for

(1) Bale. (2) Milton Abbas. Tregonwell was an especially active agent in the dissolution of monasteries, in spite of which he found favour with Mary.

many years, with so often success and general applause, that not only the home-bred multitude believed so mainly in him, but even persons of the better calling resorted to him from the remote parts of the realm, to make trial of his cunning by the hazard of their lives; and sundry, either upon just cause, or to cloak their folly, reported that they have reaped their errands' ends at his hands. He flourished Anno Domini 1602.

HUGH ATWELL, born in this county, and parson of St. Tudy therein, was well seen in the theories of physic, and happy in the practice thereof, beyond the belief of most, and the reason that any can assign for the same; for although now and then he used blood-letting, he mostly for all diseases prescribed milk, and often milk and apples, which (although contrary to the judgments of the best esteemed practitioners) either by virtue of the medicine, or fortune of the physician, or fancy of the patient, recovered many out of desperate extremities. This his reputation for many years maintained itself unimpaired, the rather because he bestowed his pains and charge gratis on the poor; and, taking moderately of the rich, left one half of what he received in the households he visited. As for the profits of his benefice, he poured it out with both hands in pious uses. But for the truth of the whole, *sit fides penes authorem.*[1] This Atwell was living in 1602.

VEAL, an old man of Bodmin in this county, was so beholden to Mercury's predominant strength in his nativity, that without a teacher he became very skilful in well-near all manner of handicrafts: a carpenter, a joiner, a millwright, a freemason, a clockmaker, a carver, a metal-founder, architect *et quid non?* Yea, a chirurgeon, physician, alchemist &c. So as that which Georgias of Leontium vaunted of the liberal sciences, he may profess of the mechanical, viz., to be ignorant in none. He was in his eminency anno 1602.

EDWARD BONE, of Ladcock in this county, was servant to Mr. Courtney therein. He was deaf from his cradle, and consequently dumb (Nature cannot give out where it hath not received) yet could learn, and express to his master, any news that was stirring in the country. Especially, if there went speech of a sermon within some miles' distance, he would repair to the place with the soonest, and setting himself directly against the preacher, look him stedfastly in the face while his sermon lasted; to which religious zeal his honest life was also answerable. Assisted with a firm memory, he would not only know any party whom he had once seen for ever after, but also make him known to any other, by some special observation and difference. There was one Kempe, not living far off, defected accordingly, on whose meetings there were such embracements, such strange, often and earnest tokenings, and such hearty laughters and other passionate gestures, that their want of a tongue seemed rather an hindrance to others conceiving them, than to their conceiving one another.

(1) Carew, in his *Survey of Cornwall* ["Have faith in the author."]

RICHARD CAREW, esquire, son to Thomas Carew and Elizabeth Edgecumbe, was born [1555] at Antony in this county, of right worshipful parentage, who honoured his extraction with his learning. He was bred a gentleman commoner in Oxford, where, being but fourteen years old, and yet three years' standing, he was called out to dispute extempore, before the earls of Leicester and Warwick, with the matchless Sir Philip Sidney.

si quaeritis hujus
Fortunam pugnae, non est superatus ab illo.

Ask you the end of this contest?
They *neither* had the better, *both* the best.

He afterwards wrote the pleasant and faithful description of Cornwall . . . This his book he dedicated to Sir Walter Raleigh, with this modest compliment: "That he appealed to his direction, whether it should pass; to his correction, if it might pass; and to his protection, if it did pass"; adding moreover "that duty, not presumption, drawing him to that offering, it must be favour, not desert, must move the other to the acceptance thereof." This survey was set forth 1602, and I collect the author thereof died about the middle of the reign of King James. I know not whether he or his son first brought up the use of gambadoes,[1] much worn in the west, whereby, whilst one rides on horseback, his legs are in a coach, clean and warm, in those dirty countries. [*d.* 1620]

WILLIAM NOYE, born [1577] in this county, was bred in Lincoln's Inn; a most sedulous student, constantly conversant with ancient records, verifying his anagram, WILLIAM NOY, "I MOYL IN LAW."

He was for many years the stoutest champion for the subject's liberty, until King Charles entertained him to be his attorney; after which time, I read this character of him in an history written by an ingenious gentleman:[2] "He became so servilely addicted to the prerogative, as by ferreting old penal statues, and devising new exactions, he became, for the small time he enjoyed that power, the most pestilent vexation to the subjects that this latter age produced."

However, others behold his actions with a more favourable eye, as done in the pursuance of the place he had undertaken, who by his oath and office was to improve his utmost power to advance the profit of his master. Thus I see that after their deaths, the memories of the best lawyers may turn clients, yea and sue too *in forma pauperis,* needing the good word of the charitable survivors to plead in their behalf. He died Anno Domini 1634. Let me add this passage from his mouth that was present thereat. The goldsmiths of London had (and in due time may have) a custom once a year to weigh gold in the Star-chamber, in the presence of the privy council and the king's attorney. This solemn weighing, by a word of art, they call the *pyx;* and make use of so exact scales therein that the master of the company affirmed that they would turn with the two hundredth part of a grain. "I should be loth," said the Attorney Noye standing by, "that all my actions should be weighed

(1) *Gambadoes* = a kind of large boot or gaiter, attached to the saddle. (2) Hamon L'Estrange, esq., in his *Reign of King Charles.*

in those scales." With whom I concur in relation of the same to myself. And therefore, seeing the balance of the sanctuary held in God's hand are far more exact, what need have we of his mercy, and Christ's merits, to make us passable in God's presence?

CHARLES HERLE was born [1598] in this county, of an ancient and worshipful family, bred (though never fellow) in Exeter College, and at last richly beneficed in Lancashire.

We read how Pharaoh removed all the Egyptians, the priests alone excepted, from one end of the borders of the land to the other end thereof; but we, the ministers in England, are of all men most and farthest removeable—three hundred miles and more being interposed betwixt the place of Mr. Herle's birth and benefice.

He was a good scholar, and esteemed by his party a deep divine, and, after the death of Doctor Twisse, president of the assembly. As I dare not defend all the doctrine delivered in his printed books, so I will not inveigh against him, lest in me it be interpreted a revenge on his memory for licensing a book written against me,[1] wherein I was taxed for popish compliance, though since, in myself still the same man, I groan under a contrary representation. The best is, innocence doth turn such groans into songs of gladness. Mr. Herle departed this life [1659].

THE FAREWELL

Being now to part with this county, I wish it all happiness, and particularly that flaws, or flaughs,[2] may either never come thither, or quickly depart thence; which, being a kind of English *hericano,* hath little civility therein, as throwing down some houses, more trees, and making more waste with the blast thereof. And may the same Divine Providence which is their Aeolus, be also Neptune unto it, to secure this county from the fury of water, as well as from the fierceness of the wind, that their *Lioness* may never get a *Lion* unto it, so to propagate inundations betwixt them.[3]

And now, to wish an honour to this duchy, and therewith a happiness both to it and all England, the strength of my weak prayers (twisted with many millions more proceeding from loyal hearts in this land) shall never be wanting, that God would be pleased to bestow a duke of Cornwall of the loins of our gracious sovereign, to be possessed of the virtues, and to be heir apparent to the lands, of his father; a duke, presumed in law to be of full age to all purposes and intents, the first minute of his birth; which happy minute God in due time send, for the comfort of our nation.

(1) By Mr. John Saltmarsh [something of a busybody, of mystical temperament, and well known in his day for his controversies with learned men. He attacked Fuller's *Sermon of Reformation,* and the latter, in his tract *Truth Maintained,* replied with characteristic restraint and charity. See his life in Yorkshire, p. 665]. (2) *Flaughs* = gusts of wind, and metaphorically, quarrels. (3) A playful reference to the lost land of Lyonesse.

CUMBERLAND

CUMBERLAND hath Scotland on the north, Northumberland and Westmorland on the east, Lancashire on the south, and the Irish sea on the west. It is not unlike a half moon in the form thereof; which, from its tips north and south, may be allowed to be somewhat more than forty miles, though east and west it spreadeth not above twenty-six miles. The soil, though generally hard, and exacting much toil to improve it, is pleasant with the varieties, and profitable with these

NATURAL COMMODITIES

Pearls

These are found commonly by the River Irt, where mussels (as also oysters and other shell-fish) gaping for the dew, are in a manner impregnated therewith; so that some conceive that as dew is liquid pearl, so a pearl is dew consolidated in these fishes. Here poor people, getting them at low water, sell to jewellers for pence what they sell again for pounds. Indeed there is a Spanish proverb, that a lapidary who would grow rich must buy of those who go to be executed (as not caring how cheap they sell) and sell to those that go to be married, as not caring how dear they buy. But, waiving these advantages, such of that mystery which trade with country-people herein, gain much by buying their pearls, though far short of the Indian in orientness. But whether not as useful in physic, is not yet decided.

Black-Lead

Plenty hereof is digged up about Keswick, the only place (as I am informed) where it is found in Europe; and various is the use thereof: 1. For painters (besides some mixture thereof in making lead colours) to draw the pictures of their pictures; viz., those shadowy lines made only to be unmade again. 2. For pens, so useful for scholars to note the remarkables they read, with an impression easily delible without prejudice to the book. 3. For feltmakers, for colouring of hats. 4. To scour leaden cisterns, and to brighten things made of iron. 5. In Flanders and Germany they use it for glazing of stuffs.

Besides these visible, surely there are other concealed uses thereof, which causeth it daily to grow the dearer, being so much transported beyond the seas.

Copper

These mines lay long neglected (choked in their own rubbish) till renewed about the beginning of Queen Elizabeth, when plenty of copper was here afforded, both for home use and foreign transportation. But copper itself was too soft for several military services, and could not alone (no single person can prove a parent) produce brass, most useful for that purpose. Here taste and see Divine Providence, which never doth its work by halves, and generally doubleth gifts by seasonable giving them: *Lapis calaminaris* (whereof hereafter in due place[1]) was then first found in England, the mother of brass, as copper the father thereof. Hence came it to pass that Queen Elizabeth left more brass than she found iron-ordnance in the kingdom; and our wooden walls (so our ships are commonly called) were rough-casted over with a coat of a firmer constitution.

We must not forget the names of the two Dutchmen (good frogs by sea, but better moles by land) who re-found out these copper-mines, wherein also some silver (no new milk without some cream therein); viz., Thomas Shurland and Daniel Hechsteller of Augsburg in Germany; whose nephews, turning purchasers of lands hereabouts, prefer easily to take what the earth tenders in her hands above ground, than painfully to pierce into her heart for greater treasure.

I am sorry to hear, and loath to believe, what some credible persons have told me, that within these twenty years the copper within this county hath been wholly discontinued, and that not for want of metal, but mining for it. Sad that the industry of our age could not keep what the ingenuity of the former found out. And I would willingly put it on another account, that the burying of so much steel in the bowels of men, during our civil wars, hath hindered their digging of copper out of the entrails of the earth; hoping that these peaceable times will encourage to the resuming thereof.

THE BUILDINGS

This county pretendeth not to the mode of reformed architecture, the vicinity of the Scots causing them to build rather for strength than state. The cathedral of Carlisle may pass for the emblem of the militant church, black but comely, still bearing in the complexion thereof the remaining signs of its former burning. Rose Castle, the bishop's best seat, hath lately the rose therein withered, and the prickles, in the ruins thereof, only remain.

The houses of the nobility and gentry are generally built castle-wise, and in the time of the Romans this county (because a limitary) did abound with fortifications; Mr. Camden taking notice of more antiquities in Cumberland and Northumberland than in all England besides.

THE WONDERS

Although, if the word Wonders be strained up high and hard, this county affordeth none, yet, if the sense thereof be somewhat let down, the compass thereof fetcheth in

MOSS-TROOPERS

So strange the condition of their living, if considered in their original, increase, height, decay and ruin.

1. *Original.* I conceive them the same, called Borderers, in Mr. Camden, and charactered by him to be a wild and warlike people. They

(1) See Natural Commodities under Somersetshire, p. 486.

are called moss troopers, because dwelling in the mosses, and riding in troops together. They dwell in the bounds or meeting of two kingdoms, but obey the laws of neither. They come to church as seldom as the twenty-ninth of February comes into the calendar.

2. *Increase.* When England and Scotland were united in Great Britain, they that formerly lived by hostile incursions betook themselves to the robbing of their neighbours. Their sons are free of the trade by their fathers' copy; they are like unto Job, not in piety and patience, but in sudden plenty and poverty, sometimes having flocks and herds in the morning, none at night, and perchance many again next day. They may give for their motto, *Vivitur ex rapto,* stealing from their honest neighbours what sometimes they regain. They are a nest of hornets; strike one, and stir all of them about your ears. Indeed, if they promise safely to conduct a traveller, they will perform it with the fidelity of a Turkish janizary; otherwise woe be to him that falleth into their quarters.

3. *Height.* Amounting forty years since to some thousands. These compelled the vicinage to purchase their security by paying a constant rent unto them. When in their greatest height, they had two enemies, the laws of the land, and the Lord William Howard of Naworth. He sent many of them to Carlisle, to that place where "the officer always doth his work by daylight." Yet these moss-troopers, if possibly they could procure the pardon for a condemned person of their company, would advance great sums out of their common stock, who in such a case "cast in their lots amongst themselves, and all have one purse."

4. *Decay;* caused by the wisdom, valour and diligence of the right honourable Charles Lord Howard, now earl of Carlisle, who routed these English tories with his regiment. His severity unto them will not only be excused but commended by the judicious, who consider how our great lawyer[1] doth describe such persons who are solemnly outlawed: "Thenceforward (after they are outlawed) they wear a wolf's head;[2] so that they lawfully may be destroyed, without any judicial inquisition, as who carry their own condemnation about them, and deservedly die without law, because they refused to live according to law."

5. *Ruin.* Such the success of this worthy lord's severity, that he made a thorough reformation amongst them, and, the ringleaders being destroyed, the rest are reduced to legal obedience, and so I trust will continue.

THE WORTHIES

[ANDREW HARCLAY, HARCLA, OR HARTCLA, EARL OF CARLISLE.] Had his latter end answered his beginning, he might deservedly have been ranked amongst the worthies of Westmorland, where he was born, at Hartley; whereas now it shall suffice to make this oblique mention of him in this place.[3]

(1) Bracton [Latin original omitted. *Tories.* At this period the term meant, strictly, the dispossessed Irish, who became outlaws, and lived in much the same way as the moss-troopers. More loosely, it meant bog-trotters, bandits, robbers.] (2) In the laws of King Edward, an out-lawed person is called "Woolfe-hefod." Lambarde. (3) Placed among the sheriffs in the original edition.

He behaved himself right handsomely in the service of King Edward the Second many years before, especially at the battle of Boroughbridge, where he killed Humphrey Bohun earl of Hereford, and took Thomas Plantagenet earl of Lancaster, with many others of the nobility prisoners, and delivered them to the king; in reward whereof he was created, in the 19th year of that king, earl of Carlisle, and had the Isle of Man bestowed upon him. Next year, I know not upon what discontentment, he fell into private confederacy with the king's foes the Scots, for which he was taken and condemned. Now, lest the nobility of others should by secret sympathy suffer in his disgraceful death, the *earl* was first parted from the *man*, and his honour severed from his person, by a solemn degradation, having his knightly spurs hewed off from his heels; which done, he was hanged, drawn and quartered. [*d.* 1323]

JOHN CANON [or CANONICUS]. Some will have him so called because canon of some cathedral church; and if so, there were hundreds of John Canons besides himself; others, because he was doctor of canon law, which leaves as great a latitude as the former for hundreds, with equal right, to jostle with him for the same surname. I have cause to conceive, until I shall be clearly convinced to the contrary, that he was born at Canonsby in this county, *by* being set by for brevity's sake.

Bilious Bale bespattereth him more than any of his order. Hear how he ranteth: "He turned a Minotaur (I should say Minorite) and, with his thrasonical boasting," &c. But I am not bound to believe him, the rather because Trithemius, a foreign, judicious and moderate writer, giveth him great commendation; whence I collect that his worth was not, like a candle in the house, only burning at home in England; but a torch, blazing abroad beyond the seas, the university of Paris and other places taking signal notice of his learning. [*fl.* 1329]

ROBERT OF EGLESFIELD, born in this county, was a pious and learned man, according to the rate of that age; chaplain and confessor to Philippa, queen to Edward the Third. He founded a fair college in Oxford, by the name of Queen's College, for a provost and twelve fellows, whom he ordered to sit in the hall *in purpura*, and that they should be attended on *more curiali*. He appointed that those of Cumberland and Westmorland should be proper for preferment in his foundation, rendering this reason why he reflected most of those northern counties: *propter insolitam vastitatem, et melioris literaturae infrequentiam.*

But, prevented by death, he finished not his intentions; leaving only to the college the manor of Renwick in this county, with the impropriation of Burgh under Stainmore, and which I assure you was considerable, most excellent statutes.

To shew himself both courtier and scholar, he ordered that in the hall they should speak either Latin or French. He bequeathed his college to the honorary patronage of the queens of England; and his surname is still extant in this country in persons of quality, but how to him related to me unknown. [*d.* 1349]

ROGER WHELPDALE was born in the borders of this county (so that Westmorland pretends to a share in him); bred in Balliol College in Oxford, and afterwards became provost of Queen's College in that university. 1. A good logician; 2. A good mathematician; 3. A good divine. Witness his books of 1. *Summulae Logicales;* 2. *De Quanto et Continuo;* 3. *De Deo Invocando.*

Bale ingenuously confesseth that he cannot find where this learned man, after his long labours in Oxford, led the rest of his life; and Pits (who, seeing with Bale's eyes, both are blind or sighted together) is at the same loss. But herein we are able to guide our guides, and light a candle to direct them; for he was by King Henry the Fifth preferred bishop of Carlisle, 1420. He sat three years in that see; and, dying at London, Feb. 4, 1423, was buried in Saint Paul's.

ELIZABETH FOSTER was born at Greystoke in this county, though her maiden surname be unknown. Travelling to London, she was there married to one John Foster, cutler, of the parish of Saint Bride's in Fleet Street; and, being summoned before Bonner for not coming to church, was imprisoned, and strictly examined. Being moved by the bishop to desert her answers, "I will not," said she, "go from them, by God's grace." Hereupon she was condemned; and, being fifty-five years of age, accordingly suffered, with six other martyrs, all in one fire, in Smithfield, Jan. 27, 1557.

EDMUND GRINDAL was born [1519?] at Saint Bees in this county; bred scholar, fellow and master of Pembroke Hall in Cambridge, and proctor of the university. In the reign of Queen Mary he fled beyond the seas, and was no *violento* in the troubles of Frankfurt; but, with all meekness, to his might endeavoured a pacification. Returning home, he was made successively bishop of London, archbishop of York and Canterbury, by Queen Elizabeth, highly favouring him for his learning, piety, modesty and single life; till at last he lost her love by the mischievous practices of his enemies. His fault was, for keeping others from breaking two of God's commandments: "Thou shalt not steal," when he would not let the lord of Leicester have Lambeth House; and "Thou shalt not commit adultery," when he would not permit Julio, the earl's Italian physician, to marry another man's wife.

But it was objected against him to the queen, that he was a fierce defender of factious prophesying, which in process of time would undermine the hierarchy; though moderate men were of the opinion they might prove profitable, as by archbishop Grindal limited and regulated.

Being really blind, more with grief than age (dying at sixty-four) he was willing to put off his clothes before he went to bed, and in his lifetime to resign his place to Doctor Whitgift, who refused such acceptance thereof. And the queen, commiserating his condition, was graciously pleased to say that, "as she had made him, so he should die an archbishop;" as he did, July 6, 1583.

Worldly wealth he cared not for, desiring only to make both ends meet; and as for that little that lapped over, he gave it to pious uses in both universities, and the founding of a fair free-school at Saint Bees, the place of his nativity.

HENRY ROBINSON, D.D., was born [1553?] in Carlisle;[1] bred fellow, and as last provost of Queen's College in Oxford; and afterwards, 1598, was consecrated bishop of the place of his nativity.

When Queen Elizabeth received his homage, she gave him many gracious words of the good opinion which she conceived of his learning, integrity, and sufficiency for that place; moreover adding, that "she must ever have a care to furnish that see with a worthy man, for his sake who first set the crown on her head[2];" and many words to the like purpose.

He was a prelate of great gravity and temperance, very mild in speech, but not of so strong a constitution of body as his countenance did promise, and yet he lived to be a very old man. He died Anno Domini 1616.

RICHARD SENHOUSE, D.D., was born of worshipful parentage at Netherhall in this county; a valiant man in his younger days; and I have heard that in his old age he felt the admonitions of his youthful over-violent exercise. He was bred fellow of Saint John's College in Cambridge, and became an excellent preacher, his sermons losing no lustre by his good utterance and graceful delivering of them. He was chaplain to King Charles whilst prince, and preached his sermon at his coronation. He was preferred bishop of Carlisle, enjoying the place but a short time. He died Anno Domini 1626.

GEORGE PORTER was born at Weary Hall, in the parish of Bolton in this county, of gentle extraction. He was afterward fellow of Queens' College in Cambridge, doctor and professor of civil law therein for above thirty years.

He was of a pitiful nature, and we commonly called him (for I had oft the honour to be in his mess) "the patron of infirmities," whose discourse was always defensive and charitable, either to excuse men's failings, or mitigate their punishments. He was valiant as well as learned; and, with his stern looks and long sword, frighted three thieves from setting upon him. He died Anno Domini 163—; and Doctor Collins (who with Saint Chryostom was *in laudatoriis hyperbolicus*) preaching his funeral sermon, endeavoured to heighten his memory to his soul, mounting it above the skies for his modesty and learning.

SIR RICHARD HUTTON was born [1561?] at Penrith, of a worshipful family (his elder brother was a knight) and bred in Jesus College in Cambridge.[3] He intended his studies for divinity, till, dissuaded by the importunity of his friends (amongst whom George earl of Cumberland most eminent) he became barrister in Gray's Inn. But, in expression of his former affection to divinity, he seldom (if ever) took fee of a clergyman. After-

(1) So Mr. Robinson, stationer, and his countryman, informed me. (2) Owen Oglethorpe (see Oxfordshire, p. 466) the only bishop who agreed to perform the ceremonies of the coronation, though some other bishops did assist him. (3) It is pity his manuscripts on the law should be smothered in private hands, which I hope will hereafter become *publici juris*. [Some of his reports were printed in 1656, and his *Young Clerk's Guide* (conveyancing precedents) in 1658].

wards, being recorder of York, he was knighted, and made judge of the common pleas. In the case of ship money, though he was against the king, or rather for the Commons, yet his majesty manifested not the least distaste, continuing to call him "the honest judge."[1]

This person, so pious to God, and charitable to his poor members, was dissolved about the beginning of our national misery. Thus God, before he new plougheth up a land with the furrows of a civil war, first cutteth down his old crop, and gathereth them like ripe sheaves into his barn. He died at Serjeants' Inn; and was buried, at his earnest desire, without any funeral sermon, save what his own virtues preached to posterity, at St. Dunstan's in the West, on the 27th day of February, Anno Domini 1639.

RICHARD CRAKANTHORPE, D.D., was descended of an ancient family in this county, as appeareth by their frequent being sheriffs thereon. He was bred fellow of Queen's College in Oxford; and afterwards, in the first of King James, went over chaplain to the Lord Evers, sent ambassador to the King of Denmark, and other prime princes of Germany. Here by use he got an easiness in the Latin tongue, and correspondency with several persons of eminent learning.

He was an excellent logician (witness his work in that kind) and became chaplain in ordinary to King James, rector of Black Notley in Essex, greater preferments expecting him, had not his death prevented it.

Pliny observeth that posthume children, born after the death of their father, and *Cæsars* (understand such who are cut out of the womb of their mother) prove very happy in success. What reason soever naturalists assign hereof, divines justly impute it to God's goodness, graciously remembering those orphans which cannot remember their own parents.

The observation may be applied to the books of this worthy doctor, set forth after his death, one called *Vigilius Dormitans,* in defence of the emperor Justinian, and a general council held by him anno 553, set forth by his brother George Crakanthorpe; the other being an answer to the manifesto of the archbishop of Spalato, set forth by that learned antiquary Dr. John Barkham; and both of these books finding an universal and grateful reception among the learned and religious. [1567-1624]

JOHN SALKELD was a branch of a right worshipful family in this county; bred a divine beyond the seas; but whether Jesuit or secular priest I know not. Coming over into England to angle for proselytes, it seems his line broke, and he was cast into prison. Hence he was brought out and presented to King James, by whose arguments (and a benefice bestowed on him in Somersetshire) he became a protestant.

This he used in all companies to boast of, that he was a "royal convert."

—*Nobisque dedit solatia victor.*

And was it not a noble thing,
Thus to be conquer'd by a king?

(1) He gave judgment for Hampden in 1638.

Indeed his majesty in some of his works, styleth him "the learned Salkeld," which the other much vaunted of, often telling it to such who well knew it before, for fear they might forget it. His preaching was none of the best; and he retained some popish (though not *opinions*) *fancies* to the day of his death. I have heard much of his discourse, more *of* his own praise than *to* his own praise, in my judgment. But his true character may be taken out of the book he wrote *Of Angels.* [1576-1660]

SIR JOHN BANKES was born [1589] at Keswick, of honest parents, who, perceiving him judicious and industrious, bestowed good breeding on him in Gray's Inn, in hope he should attain to preferment, wherein they were not deceived. After he was called to the bar, for some years he solicited suits for others, thereby attaining great practical experience. He afterwards might laugh at them, who then did smile at him, leaving many behind him in learning whom he found before him in time, until at last he was knighted by King Charles, made first his attorney, then chief justice of the common pleas, dying in the midst and heat of our civil dissensions.[1]

He ordered by his will (the copy whereof I have received from my good friend[2]) that his body should be buried under some plain monument, at the discretion of his executors; and after an epitaph mentioning the several places he had held, this motto to be added: *Non nobis, Domine, non nobis, sed Nomini tuo da gloriam.*

It must not be forgotten that by his said will he gave to the value of thirty pounds per annum, with other emoluments, to be bestowed in pious uses, and chiefly to set up a manufacture of coarse cottons in the town of Keswick, which, I understand, hath good, and is in hope of better, success. [*d.* 1644]

GERARD LANGBAINE, D.D., was born [1609] at Kirkbampton in this county; bred first fellow in, then provost of, Queen's College in Oxford; a skilful antiquary, ingenious, industrious and judicious in his writings, as by his works will appear.

Whoso shall read over the *History of the Council of Trent,* translated out of Italian by Sir Nathaniel Brent, will conceive it so complete a narration of all the concernments in that council, that nothing of consequence can be added thereunto. Yet this his mistake will be confuted by perusing the works set forth by Doctor Langbaine, of the dissent of the Gallican churches from several conclusions in that council.

As his brain was the mother of some, so was it the midwife to other good books, which he procured to be published; especially a book made by Sir John Cheke, concerning *Rebellion and Loyalty,* seasonably reprinted in the beginning of our civil wars. But alas, such then was the

(1) Bankes represented the crown against Hampden in the case of ship money, his argument lasting for three days. His wife, Lady Mary Bankes (*d.* 1661) the heroine of Corfe Castle, with a small garrison defended the family residence against the parliamentarians in two prolonged sieges in 1643 and 1645-6, when the castle was betrayed through the treachery of an officer of the garrison. (2) Mr. John Myriel, minister at Lamplugh.

noise of men's animosities, that the still voice of truth could not be heard amongst them. More excellent tracts were expected from him (particularly an edition of Brian Twyne, with additions concerning the antiquity of Oxford) when God was pleased, almost in the midst of his days, to put an end to his life, anno 1658.

THE FAREWELL

I understand two small manufactures are lately set up therein; the one of coarse broad-cloth at Cockermouth (vended at home); the other of fustians some two years since at Carlisle; and I wish that the undertakers may not be disheartened with their small encouragement. Such who are ashamed of contemptible beginnings will never arrive at considerable endings. Yea, the greatest giant was (though never a dwarf) once an infant; and the longest line commenced from a little point at the first.

DERBYSHIRE

DERBYSHIRE hath Yorkshire on the north, Nottinghamshire on the east, Leicestershire on the south, Stafford and Cheshire on the west. The river South Derwent, falling into Trent, runneth through the middle thereof. I say *South Derwent,* for I find three more *north* thereof: *Derwent,* which divideth the West from the East Riding in Yorkshire; *Derwent,* which separateth the bishopric of Durham from Northumberland; *Derwent* in Cumberland, which falleth into the Irish ocean.

These I have seen by critical authors written all alike; enough to persuade me that *dower,* the British word for *water,* hath some share in their denomination.

The two extremes of this shire, from north to south, extend to thirty-eight miles, though not fully twenty-nine in the broadest part thereof. The south and east thereof are very fruitful, whilst the north part (called the Peak) is poor above, and rich beneath the ground. Yet are there some exceptions therein. Witness the fair pasture nigh Haddon (belonging to the earl of Rutland) so incredibly battling[1] of cattle, that one proffered to surround it with shillings to purchase it; which, because to be set sideways (not edgeways) were refused.

NATURAL COMMODITIES

Lead

The best in England (not to say Europe) is found in this county. It is not churlish but good-natured metal, not curdling into knots and knobs, but all equally fusile, and therefore most useful for pipes and sheets; yea, the softness thereof will receive any artificial impressions. The miners thereof may be called a commonwealth within our commonwealth, governed by laws peculiar to themselves, often confirmed by act of parliament.

And take a few of them.

1. If any of this nation find a *rake,* or *sione,* or *leading* to the same, he may set in any ground to get lead ore.

2. But churches, houses, and gardens, are free from this custom of the minery.

3. All miners ought to commence their suit for ore-debt in the barmote court; otherwise they must lose their debt, and pay cost too.

4. The barge-master keeps his two great courts twice a year in barmote hall; the steward under him once in three weeks to decide controversies, and punish offences betwixt miners.

(1) *Battling* = nourishing.

5. Plaintiffs or defendants, having three verdicts passed against them, are bound over for ever.

6. He that stealeth ore twice, is fined; and the third time struck through his hand with a knife unto the haft into the stow,[1] and is there to stand until death, or loose himself by cutting off his hand.

7. The lord, for *lot,* hath the thirteenth dish of ore within their mine, and sixpence a load for cope.

Let me add, that whereas miners complain that lead in Somersetshire (as the tin in Cornwall) doth daily decay, here it doth improve and increase; for, as if Phoebus himself had been their Vulcan, massy pieces of lead are frequently found (whereof lately I had one in my hand) so well ripened in the bowels of the earth, that they seemed refined, such the original purity thereof.

THE MANUFACTURES

MALT

Though commonness causeth contempt, excellent the art of the first inventing thereof. I confess it facile to make barley-water, an invention which found out itself, with little more than the bare joining the ingredients together. But to make malt for drink, was a master-piece indeed. How much of philosophy concurred to the first kill of malt! And before it was turned on the floor, how often was it tossed in the brain of the first inventor thereof!

First, to give it a new growth more than the earth had bestowed thereon, swelling it in the water, to make it last the longer by breaking it, and taste the sweeter by corrupting it. Secondly, by making it to pass the fire, the grain (by art fermented) acquiring a lusciousness (which by nature it had not) whereby it doth both strengthen and sweeten the water wherein it is boiled.

ALE

Ceres being our English Bacchus, this was our ancestors' common drink, many imputing the strength of their infantry (in drawing so stiff a bow) to their constant, but moderate, drinking thereof. Yea, now the English begin to turn to ale (may they in due time regain their former vigorousness!); and whereas, in our remembrance, ale went out when swallows came in, seldom appearing after Easter, it now hopeth (having climbed up May hill) to continue its course all the year. Yet have we lost the preservative, whatever it was, which (before hops was found out) made it last so long in our land some two hundred years since, for half a year at the least after the brewing thereof; otherwise of necessity they must brew every day, yea pour it out of the kive[2] into the cup, if the prodigious English hospitality in former ages be considered, with the multitude of menial servants and strangers entertained. Now never was the wine of Sarepta better known to the Syrians, that of Chios to the Grecians, of Falernum to the Latins, than the Canary of Derby is to the English thereabout.

(1) *Stow* = a heated room or chamber. (2) *Kive* = vat.

THE BUILDINGS

Chatsworth, erected by the magnificent Lady Elizabeth Talbot, countess of Shrewsbury, is a stately structure, thus described by the poet:[1]

Stat Chatsworth, praeclara domus, tum mole superba,
Tum Domino magno, celerem Deröentis ad undam.
Miranti similis portam praeterfluit Amnis
Hic tacitus, saxis infra supraque sonorus.

Chatsworth, which in its bulk itself doth pride
And lord (both great) stands Derwent bank beside;
Which slides still by the gate, as full of wonder,
Though loud with stones above the house and under.

The garden on the back side, with an artificial rock and wilderness, accomplisheth the place with all pleasure.

WONDERS

God, who is truly θαυματοῦργος the only worker of wonders, hath more manifested his might in this than in any other county in England; such the heaps of wonders therein, amongst which we take special notice of

Maim Tor, or Mam Tor

Tor is a hill ascending steep, as Glassenbury Tor. *Maim,* saith one,[2] because maimed or broken in the top thereof. Others, following the vulgar pronounciation, will have it *Mam Tor;* that is, the Mother Hill, because it is always delivered, and presently with child again; for incredible heaps of sandy earth constantly fall thence, yet is it not visibly diminished, having, it seems (as a constant stream) such a spring of matter whence it is recruited. It may pass for the emblem of the liberal man, never impoverished by his well-bounded and grounded charity, his expenses being re-supplied by a secret Providence.

MEDICINAL WATERS

Buxton Well, dedicated to St. Anne, sending forth both cold and warm water, is little less than miraculous in the effects, thus described by our author:[3]

Haec resoluta senum confirmat membra trementum,
Et refovet nervos lotrix haec lympha gelatos.
Huc infirma regunt baculis vestigia claudi,
Ingrati referunt baculis vestigia spretis.
Huc, mater fieri cupiens, accedit inanis,
Plenaque discedit, puto, nec veniente marito.

Old men's numb'd joints new vigour here acquire,
In frozen nerves this water kindleth fire.
Hither the cripples halt, some help to find,
Run hence, their crutches unthanked left behind.
The barren wife here meets her husband's love,[4]
With such success she straight doth mother prove.

This well is also famous for the abode of Mary Queen of Scots thereby, who found much refreshing by the waters thereof.

(1) Mr. Hobbes, *De Mirabilibus Pecci.*—F. (2) Mr. Hobbes, ibid.—F. (3) Mr. Hobbes.—F. (4) The translator durst not be so bold as the author.—F.

[THE FREE SCHOOL IN DERBY]

There is a free school in the town of Derby, built, as I understand, by that corporation, and endowed with threescore pounds a year; and I conjecture Mr. R. Fletcher, thrice bailiff of the town (I say, by his laudatory epitaph, I conjecture him) very instrumental to this work. I understand also that the said town hath large privileges, insomuch that Londoners in some cases pay toll at Derby, but Derby men in no case toll at London. I grudge them not their privileges, so long as they employ their public stock to pious uses.

To conclude this topic, I meet with this memorable passage in one who continueth the work of an industrious author,[1] which I will not, yea must not omit:

> Divers well-disposed citizens of London, desirous (as yet) not to be named, being born in or near to Ashbourne in the Peak, in the county of Derby, combining their loving benevolence together, have built there a fair school-house, with convenient lodgings for a master, and liberal maintenance allowed thereto.

I hope that their forwardness hath since provoked many; and that their charity (to allude to their staple commodity of this county) but in the *ore* in the times of our fathers, hath since been refined to perfection.

THE WORTHIES

ROBERT CURSON was born, saith my author, *ex nobili quodam Anglorum genere* (of worshipful English extraction[2]). Now I find none of his surname out of this county (except some branches lately thence derived); but in the same two right ancient families, one formerly at Croxton, whose heir general in our age was married to the earl of Dorset, the other still flourisheth at Kedleston in this county; which moves me to make this Roger a native thereof. Bred he was first a scholar in Oxford, then a doctor in Paris, and lastly a cardinal in Rome, by the title of Saint Stephen in Mount Celius. When the city of Damietta in Egypt was taken under John Brenn king of Jerusalem, our Cardinal Curson was there, accompanying Pelagius the pope's cardinal. He wrote many books, and came over into England as the pope's legate in the reign of King Henry the Third. [*d.* 1218]

THOMAS OF ASHBORNE was born at that well-known market-town in this county (and not in Staffordshire, as both Bale and Pits mistake) and became an Augustinian therein. Going afterwards to Oxford, he was doctorated in divinity. He was a great adversary to Wycliffe, and in that synod wherein his doctrines were condemned for heresy, by ten bishops, twenty lawyers, and four-and-forty divines, our Ashborne made up one of the last number.

Yet once he did some good, or rather diverted much evil. It happened that one Peter Pateshull,[3] an Augustinian, preaching in London, had some passages in favour of Wycliffe, which so displeased those of his order, that they plucked him out of the pulpit, dragged him into the

(1) Stow's *Survey of London*. (2) Bale. (3) See Northamptonshire, p. 429.

convent of Augustines (near Broad Street) intending more violence to his person.

This alarumed the Londoners (amongst whom a considerable party of Wycliffites) to rescue poor Pateshull, who in their rage had burnt the convent about the friar's ears, had not our Ashborne, with his prayers and tears, seasonably interceded. He flourished under King Richard the Second, 1382.

PHILIP [REPINGTON OR REPYNGDON] took, no doubt, his name and birth from Repingdon, commonly contracted and called Repton, in this county; and I question whether any other in England of the same name. He was bred and commenced first bachelor, then doctor of divinity, in Oxford, where he became a great champion and assertor of the doctrine of John Wycliffe, which caused him much trouble and many strict examinations. But alas, he became like the seed on stony ground, "which, not having root in itself, endured but for a while," and withered away in persecution, for he solemnly recanted his opinions, November 18, anno 1382. And, to give the better assurance that he was a true anti-Wycliffite, from a professor he became a persecutor, and afterwards was termed Rampington by those poor people whom he so much molested.

Then preferment flowed in thick and threefold upon him. From a canon he became abbot of Leicester; and, anno 1397, he was made chancellor of Oxford; 1405, bishop of Lincoln; 1408, by Pope Gregory the Twelfth he was created cardinal of Saint Nereus and Achilleis; though that pope had solemnly sworn he would make no more cardinals till the schism in Rome was ended. The best is, the pope, being master of the oath-office, may give himself a pardon for his own perjury. What moved this Repington willingly to resign his bishopric, 1419, is to me unknown. [*d.* 1424]

WILLIAM GREY was son to the Lord Grey of Codnor in this county. He suffered not his parts to be depressed by his nobility, but, to make his mind the more proportionable, he endeavoured to render himself as able as he was honourable. He studied first in Balliol College in Oxford, then at Ferrara in Italy, where he for a long time heard the lectures of Guarino of Verona, that accomplished scholar. No man was better acquainted with the method of the court of Rome, which made our king appoint him his procurator therein. It is hard to say whether Pope Nicholas the Fifth, or our King Henry the Sixth, contributed most to his free election to the Bishopric of Ely; whilst it is out of doubt his own deserts concurred most effectually thereunto. He sat in that see twenty-four years, and wrote many books, which the envy of time hath denied to posterity. Bishop Godwin, by mistake, maketh him chancellor of England, whereas indeed he was lord treasurer in the ninth of King Edward the Fourth, anno 1469. Let me add, he was the last clergyman that ever discharged that office, until Bishop Juxon[1] in our days was preferred thereunto. He died August 4, 1478, and lies buried between two marble pillars in his church, having bestowed much cost in the reparation of the famous belfry thereof.

(1) See Sussex, p. 573.

THOMAS LINACRE, doctor of physic, was born [1460?] in the town of Derby, bred in Oxford, whence he afterwards travelled beyond the seas, residing chiefly at Rome and Florence. Returning into England, he brought languages along with him, and was the first restorer of learning in our nation. It is questionable whether he was a better Latinist or Grecian, a better grammarian or physician, a better scholar or man for his moral deportment. By his endeavours, Galen speaks better Latin in the translation, than he did Greek in the original . . .

No Englishman in that age had so learned masters, viz., Demetrius Chalcondylas, Politian and Hermolaus Barbarus; so noble patrons, viz., Lorenzo de Medici, duke of Florence, whilst he was beyond the seas, King Henry the Seventh and Eighth (to whom he was chief physician) after his return into England; so high-born scholars, Prince Arthur, with many lords' sons his contemporaries; so learned friends, Erasmus, Melancthon, Vives, &c.

This Linacre founded two public lectures in Oxford, and one in Cambridge (dutifully his respect to his mother, double above his aunt) for the study of physic; and that students of that faculty of both universities may meet the more conveniently together, he founded the College of Physicians in London.

I much wonder at what I find in good authors, that Linacre, a little before his death, turned priest, and began to study the Scripture, with which he formerly was unacquainted, insomuch that, reading the fifth, sixth and seventh chapters of Saint Matthew, he vowed "that either this was not the gospel, or we were not Christians," which speech (though much condemned by the relater[1] thereof) is capable of a charitable sense, as taxing men's practice so much different from God's precepts.

He died Anno Domini 1524, on the twentieth of October, and lieth buried in Saint Paul's, under a stately monument built to his memory by Doctor John Caius,[2] and a phoenix is erected on the top thereof. Yea, I may call these two doctors the two phoenixes of their profession in our nation, and justify the expression, seeing the latter in some sort sprang of the ashes of the former, and Caius came not into the general credit till after the decease of Linacre.

SIR ANTHONY FITZHERBERT, son of Ralph Fitzherbert, esquire, was born [1470] at Norbury in this county. He was first the king's serjeant-at-law; and was afterwards, in the fourteenth of King Henry the Eighth, made one of the justices of the common pleas, so continuing until the thirtieth year of the said king, when he died. He wrote the excellent book *De Natura Brevium*, with a great and laborious *Abridgement of the Laws*[3] and a calendar and index thereunto; monuments which will longer continue his memory than the flat blue marble stone in Norbury church under which he lieth interred. [*d.* 1538]

(1) Sir John Cheke, *De Pronunciatione Graeca*.—F. (2) See Norwich, p. 421. (3) The first important attempt to systematize the entire law. Fitzherbert signed the articles of impeachment against Wolsey and was one of the judges who tried Fisher and More.

SIR HUGH WILLOUGHBY was extracted from a right worthy and ancient stock at Risley in this county. He was in the last year of the reign of King Edward the Sixth employed for the north-east passage; and, by the king and merchants of London, made captain-general of a fleet for discovery of regions and places unknown.

Their fleet consisted of three ships, the Bona Esperanza (admiral) of one hundred and twenty tons; the Edward Bonaventure (whereof Richard Chancellor pilot-major) of one hundred and sixty tons; and the Good Confidence, of ninety tons.

A large commission was granted unto them, which commission did not bear date from the year of our Lord, but from the year of the world 5515 because in their long voyage they might have occasion to present it to pagan princes.

They departed at Deptford, May 10, 1553, and, after much foul weather, steered up north-north-east. But, on the second day of August, a tempest arose, and their ships with the violence of the wind were much scattered, and the Bonaventure scattered from the other two ships, which never saw it again.

Sir Hugh, holding on his course, descried a land, which for ice he could not approach, lying from Synam (an island belonging to the King of Denmark) one hundred and sixty leagues, being in latitude seventy-two degrees. This was then called Willoughy Land, as well it might, seeing it had neither then or since any owner or inhabitant pretending to the propriety thereof.

It appeareth by a will found in the ship which was the admiral, in the pocket of a person of quality, how, in January 1554, Sir Hugh and most of his company were then in health, though all soon after frozen to death in a river, or haven, called Arzina in Lapland. We are bound in charity to believe them well prepared for death, the rather because they had with them a minister, Mr. Richard Stafford by name (one of the twelve councillors to manage the design) who read constantly every morning and evening the English service to those who were in the admiral, with the Bible and paraphrases thereon; so that this may be termed the first Reformed Fleet, which had the English prayers and preaching therein.

However, seeing *nocumenta, documenta,* and that the shipwrecks of some are sea-marks to others, even this knight's miscarriage proved a direction to others. As for the Bonaventure, which answering its name, was only found by losing itself, it returned safe, and performed afterwards most excellent service in opening the traffic to Muscovy.

Thus, as the last dog most commonly catcheth the hare which other dogs have turned and tried before, so much who succeed in dangerous and difficult enterprises generally reap the benefit of the adventures of those who went before them. As for Sir Hugh and his company, their discoveries did thaw, though their bodies were frozen to death; the English, the summer following, finding a particular account of all passages of their voyages remaining entire in the ship wherein they perished.

[*d.* 1554]

JOAN WAST was a blind woman in the town of Derby, and on that account the object of any man's alms, rather than the subject of his cruelty. Besides, she was seemingly a silly soul, and indeed an innocent, though no fool. And what saith our Saviour, "For judgment am I come into this world, that they which see not might see, and that they which see might be made blind." This poor woman had a clear apprehension of God's truth, for the testimony whereof she was condemned and burnt at the stake, by the command of Bishop Baynes, who, as he began with the extremes, Mistress Joyce Lewis, one of the best, and this Joan Wast, one of the basest birth in his diocese; so no doubt (had not Queen Mary died) he would have made his cruelty meet in persons of a middle condition. [*fl.* 1553-8]

ELIZABETH HARDWICK [ELIZABETH TALBOT, COUNTESS OF SHREWSBURY] was daughter to John Hardwick, of Hardwick in this county, esquire; a lady of an undaunted spirit, and happy in her several marriages to great persons. First, to Sir William Cavendish, then to Sir William St. Loe, and at last to George earl of Shrewsbury.[1] She left two sacred (besides civil) monuments of her memory in this county; one that I hope will not (her tomb in All Hallows) the other that I am sure cannot, be taken away, as registered in the court of heaven: her stately almshouse for twelve poor people in Derby.

It will not be amiss here to relate a passage which is reported of this countess. Mary Queen of Scots being committed to the keeping of her husband George earl of Shrewsbury, the custody of so great a princess on the earl's cost was found not only chargeable but dangerous, the popish party daily practising her enlargement. Now it happened that this countess coming to court, Queen Elizabeth demanded of her how the Queen of Scots did. "Madam," said she, "she cannot do ill while she is with my husband; and I begin to grow jealous, they are so great together." The queen, who disliked any familiarity of that royal prisoner with so great a peer, presently ordered her removal thence into the custody of others. [1518-1608]

SIR JOHN COKE, younger brother to Sir Francis Coke, was born [1563] at Trusley (in the hundred of Appletree) in this county, of ancient and worshipful parentage, allied to the best family in this county. He was bred fellow of Trinity College in Cambridge, and, being chosen rhetoric lecturer in the university, grew eminent for his ingenious and critical readings in that school on that subject. He then travelled beyond the seas for some years, returning thence rich in foreign language, observations and experience.

Being first related to Sir Fulke Greville Lord Brooke,[2] he was thence preferred to be secretary of the navy, then master of the requests, and at last secretary of state for twenty years together. He was a very zealous

(1) This notorious shrew, perhaps better known as 'Bess of Hardwick', actually married four times, her first husband being Robert Barlow, and, inheriting the whole of the estates from four husbands, had an income estimated at £60,000 a year. She married her daughter to Charles Stuart, younger brother of Darnley, and as a result was imprisoned in the Tower for a short time. (2) See Warwickshire, p. 589.

protestant, and did all good offices for the advancement of true religion, and died the eighth of September 1644.

GEORGE [COKE or] COOKE, D.D., brother to Sir John Coke, secretary of state, was born at Trusley in this county; bred in Pembroke Hall in Cambridge. Afterwards he was beneficed at Bygrave in Hertfordshire, where a lean village (consisting of but three houses) maketh a fat living. Hence he was successively made bishop of Bristol and Hereford. A meek, grave and quiet man, much beloved of such who were subjected to his jurisdiction. He was in the same condemnation with the rest of his brethren, for subscribing the protest in parliament in preservation of their privileges. The times trod so heavily upon him that (though he ever was a thrifty person) they not only bruised the foot, but brake the body of his estate; so that he had felt want, if not relieved by his rich relations, dying [1646].

THE FAREWELL

I understand that it is fashionable in this county for adventurers to begin a mine with this solemn expression:

> For the grace of God, and what I there can find.[1]

By the 'grace of God' understanding good success; otherwise saving grace is not to be sought for by mining of earth, but mounting up to heaven by faith and repentance. This their expression I approve: "The earth being the Lord's, and the fullness thereof (both beneath and above ground) belongeth unto him.

I have read that the vicars in that country do receive every tenth dish of ore for their due, being obliged thereby to pray heartily for the miners. Now though no such place or profit belongeth unto me, yet, treating of this subject, I conceive myself bound, if not in conscience, in courtesy, to wish these workmen a good-speed in their lawful endeavours, whilst they only undermine the earth, and not their neighbours' right, by fraudulent practices. May their lot prove a prize unto them, that they may gain, at the least, no blank to lose thereby. Particularly, may Divine Providence secure the persons of their labours from damps and other casualties, which have happened to many, when the earth (though cruel to kill) was courteous to bury them by the same mischance.

(1) Edward Manlove, esq., in his *Customs of the Barmote Court*.

DEVONSHIRE

DEVONSHIRE hath the narrow sea on the south, the Severn on the north, Cornwall on the west, Dorset- and Somerset-shires on the east. A goodly province, the second in England for greatness, clear in view without measuring, as bearing a square of fifty miles. Some part thereof, as the South Hams, is so fruitful it needs no art; some so barren, as Dartmoor, it will hardly be bettered by art; but generally (though not running of itself) it answers to the spur of industry. No shire shows more industrious, or so many husbandmen, who by marl (blue and white), chalk, lime, sea-sand, compost, soap-ashes, rags, and what not make the ground both to take and keep a moderate fruitfulness; so that Virgil, if now alive, might make additions to his *Georgics* from the plough-practice in this county. As for the natives thereof generally, they are dexterous in any employment; and Queen Elizabeth was wont to say of their gentry: "They were all born courtiers with a becoming confidence."

NATURAL COMMODITIES

Silver

This formerly was found in great plenty in the parish of Combe Martin (miners being fetched out of Derbyshire for the digging thereof) in the reign of King Edward the First, which, as appeareth by record on the account of those trusted therein,[1] turned to a considerable profit. In the two and twentieth year of the reign of King Edward the First, William Wymondham accounted for two hundred and seventy pounds weight of silver. It was forged for the Lady Eleanor, countess of Barre, and daughter to the said king, married the year before. In the twenty-third year of the said king, were fined five hundred and twenty-one pounds ten shillings weight. In the four and twentieth year of his reign, there were brought to London, in fined silver in wedges, seven hundred and four pounds, three shillings and one penny-weight. In the twenty-fifth year of his reign, though three hundred and sixty miners were impressed out of the Peak and Wales, great was that year's profit in silver and lead.

In the reign of Edward the Third, it appeareth by the record of particular accountants, that the profits of the silver were very considerable towards the maintainance of the king's great expenses in the French war.

These mines, long neglected (as I conjecture, by reason of the civil wars betwixt York and Lancaster) were re-entered on by an artist in the reign of Queen Elizabeth, who presented a silver cup made thereof to the earl of Bath, with this inscription:

> In Martin's-Combe long lay I hid, obscure, deprest with grossest soil;
> Debased much with mixed lead, till Bulmer came, whose skill and toil
> Reformed me so pure and clean, as richer nowhere else is seen.

(1) Extant in the Tower, in the years here noted.—F.

These mines have not as yet recovered their former credit, though I understand that some are still pursuing this design, and I do wish well to their endeavours, not that private men should lose by their lead, but the public gain by their silver.

TIN

God said to Israel, by the mouth of his prophet, "And I will take away all thy tin." Sad the case of this county, if so served. But what went before? "Thy silver is become dross." It seemeth the kings of Israel, being reduced to poverty, debased their coin (the last refuge of princes) adulterating it with tin; and herein God promised that their coin should be refined to the true standard. This, the literal meaning of the promise, mystically importeth that God would restore the primitive purity of his service, purged from errors and vices.

In this mystical sense, it will not be amiss to wish that God would take away the tin from Devonshire, seeing such taking it away may consist with the continuance and advance of the metal therein.

As for their literal tin, so plentiful herein, I wish some artifice might be found out (hitherto unknown) to sever the gold and silver from the tin without wasting. Till this be done, I desire some invention might prepare sea coals for the melting thereof; hereby much wood would be saved, and the product of the tin not diminished, and not so much wasted in the blast, which now they are fain to run over three or four times. I am encouraged in the feasibility thereof, because a learned chemist[1] (no empiric, but well experimented) affirmed that it may be done, on his own knowledge, by many trials which he hath made upon it.

HERRINGS

These still are taken in great, and were formerly in greater plenty in this county, for I read of great quantities of them for six or seven years together taken at Lynmouth, until the proctor (as is said) not contented with reasonable and indifferent tithes, vexed the poor fishermen with unusual and extraordinary payment. Whether since the God of Nature, to condemn such covetousness, hath withdrawn such store of fish, or whether the fishermen, disheartened with such exactions, withdrew their own industry, I know not. This I know, that light gains, as in all other commodities, so especially in tithes of this nature, make the heaviest purses. But we shall speak more conveniently of herrings in Norfolk.

STRAWBERRIES

In Latin *fraga,* most toothsome to the palate (I mean if with claret wine or sweet cream) and so plentiful in this county, that a traveller may gather them, sitting on horseback, in their hollow highways. They delight to grow on the north side of a bank, and are great coolers. These, small and sour, as growing wild (having no other gardener than nature) quickly acquire greatness and sweetness if transplanted into gardens, and become as good as those at Portbury in Somersetshire,

(1) Doctor Jorden, in his *Discourse of Natural Baths and Mineral Waters.*

where twenty pounds per annum (thank the vicinity of Bristol) have been paid for the tithe thereof. I would not wish this county the increase of these berries, according to the proverb, "Cut down an oak, and set up a strawberry."

HURTLEBERRIES

In Latin *vaccinia,* most wholesome to the stomach, but of a very astringent nature; so plentiful in this shire, that it is a kind of harvest to poor people, whose children, nigh Axminster, will earn eightpence a day for a month together in gathering them. First they are green, then red, and at last a dark blue. The whitest hands amongst the Romans did not disdain their blackness; witness the poet,

Vaccinia nigra leguntur.[1]

Nothing more have I to observe of these berries, save that the ancient and martial family of the Baskervilles in Herefordshire give a chevron betwixt three *hurts* proper for their arms.

MANUFACTURES

BONE-LACE

Much of this is made in and about Honiton, and weekly returned to London. Some will have it called lace, *à lacinia,* used as a fringe on the borders of cloths. Bone-lace it is named, because first made with bone (since wooden) bobbins. Thus it is usual for such utensils, both in the Latin and English names, gratefully to retain the memory of the first matter they were made of; as *cochleare,* a spoon (whether made of wood or metal) because cockle-shells were first used to that purpose.

Modern the use thereof in England, not exceeding the middle of the reign of Queen Elizabeth; let it not be condemned for a superfluous wearing, because it doth neither hide nor heat, seeing it doth adorn. Besides, though private persons pay for it, it stands the state in nothing; not expensive of bullion, like other lace, costing nothing save a little thread descanted on by art and industry. Hereby many children, who otherwise would be burthensome to the parish, prove beneficial to their parents. Yea, many lame in their limbs and impotent in their arms, if able in their fingers, gain a livelihood thereby; not to say that it saveth some thousands of pounds yearly formerly sent overseas to fetch lace from Flanders.

THE BUILDINGS

BIDEFORD BRIDGE is a stately structure, and remarkable in many respects. 1. It standeth out of, and far from any public road, in a corner of the county, so that Bideford bridge is truely Bideford bridge, intended solely for the convenience of that town 2. It is very long, consisting of twenty-four piers; and yet one William Alford (another Milo) of Bideford, carried on his back, for a wager, four bushels,[2] salt-water measure, all the length thereof. 3. It is very high, so that a barge of sixty tons may pass and repass (if taking down her masts) betwixt the

(1) Virgil, *Eclog.* ii. ["The black whortleberries are picked."] (2) A bushel is two strikes in this county.—F.

piers thereof. 4. The foundation is very firmly fixed, and yet it doth (or seem to) shake at the slightest step of a horse. 5. The builder of so worthy a work is not (the more the pity) punctually known.

Yet tradition (the best author where no better is to be had) maketh that finished by the assistance of Sir Theobold Grenville, the Goldneys and Oketenets (persons of great power in those parts); Peter Quivil, bishop of Exeter, granting indulgences to all such as contributed to the forwarding thereof.

As for the houses of the gentry in this county, some may attract, none ravish the beholder; except it be Wembury, the house of the Heles, near Plymouth, almost corrival with Greenwich itself for the pleasant prospect thereof.

THE WONDERS

Not to speak of a river about Lydford, whose stream sinketh so deep that it is altogether invisible, but supplying to the ear that it denies to the eye, so great the noise thereof.

There is in the parish of North Taunton (near an house called Bath) a pit, but in the winter a pool, not maintained by any spring, but the fall of rain water (in summer commonly dry). Of this pool it hath been observed that before the death or change of any prince, or some other strange accident of great importance, or any invasion or insurrection (though in an hot and dry season) it will, without any rain, overflow its banks, and so continue till it be past that it prognosticated. Be the truth hereof reported to the vicinage (the most competent judges thereof) seeing my author (who finished his book 1648) reporteth that it overfloweth four times within these last thirty years.[1]

Some will be offended at me, if I should omit the Hanging Stone, being one of the bound-stones which parteth Combe Martin from the next parish. It got the name from a thief who, having stolen a sheep and tied it about his own neck to carry it on his back, rested himself for a while upon this stone, which is about a foot high, until the sheep struggling, slid over the stone on the other side, and so strangled the man. Let the lawyers dispute whether the sheep in this case was forfeited to the king's almoner as a deodand. It appeareth rather a providence than a casualty, in the just execution of a malefactor. To these wonders I will add, and hazard the reader's displeasure for the same—

THE GUBBINS

So now I dare call them (secured by distance) which one of more valour durst not do to their face, for fear their fury fall upon him. Yet hitherto have I met with none who could render a reason of their name. We call the shavings of fish (which are little worth) *gubbins;* and sure it is they are sensible that the word importeth shame and disgrace.

I have read of an England beyond Wales, but the Gubbins Land is a Scythia within England, and they pure heathens therein. It lieth nigh Brentor, in the edge of Dartmoor. It is reported that some two hundred years since, two strumpets being with child, fled hither to hide

(1) Manuscript of Baronet Northcott.

themselves, to whom certain lewd fellows resorted, and this was their first original. They are a peculiar of their own making, exempt from bishop, archdeacon and all authority either ecclesiastical or civil. They live in cotes (rather holes than houses) like swine, having all in common, multiplied without marriage into many hundreds. Their language is the dross of the dregs of the vulgar Devonian, and the more learned a man is, the worse he can understand them. During our civil wars, no soldiers were quartered amongst them, for fear of being *quartered* amongst them. Their wealth consisteth in other men's goods, and they live by stealing the sheep on the moor; and vain it is for any to search their houses, being a work beneath the pains of a sheriff, and above the power of any constable. Such their fleetness, they will out-run many horses; vivaciousness, they outlive most men; living in the ignorance of luxury, the extinguisher of life. They hold together like burrs; offend one, and all will revenge his quarrel.

But now I am informed, that they begin to be civilized, and tender their children to baptism, and return to be men, yea Christians again. I hope no *civil* people amongst us will turn barbarians, now these barbarians begin to be *civilized*.[1]

PROVERBS

To Devonshire ground. It is sad when one is made a proverb by way of derision, but honourable to become proverbial by way of imitation, as here Devonshire hath set a copy of industry and ingenuity to all England. To *Devonshire* land is to pare off the surface or top turf thereof, then lay it together in heaps and burn it, which ashes are a marvellous improvement to battle[2] barren ground. Thus they may be said "to stew the land in its own liquor," to make the same ground to find compost to fatten itself; an husbandry which, wherever used, retains the name of the place where it was first invented, it being usual to *Devonshire* land in Dorsetshire and in other counties.

A Plymouth Cloak. That is, a cane, or a staff, whereof this the occasion. Many a man of good extraction, coming home from far voyages, may chance to land here, and being out of sorts, is unable, for the present time and place, to recruit himself with clothes. Here (if not friendly provided) they make the next wood their draper's shop, where a staff cut out serves them for a covering.

First hang and draw,
Then hear the cause by Lydford law.

Lydford is a little and poor, but ancient corporation in this county, with very large privileges, where a court of the Stanneries was formerly kept. This libellous proverb would suggest unto us as if the townsmen thereof, generally mean persons, were unable to manage their own liberties with necessary discretion, administering preposterous and prepoperous justice.

I charitably believe that some tinners, justly obnoxious to censure, and deservedly punished, by fine or otherwise, for their misdemeanours, have

(1) See Kingsley's *Westward Ho!* for further information on this peculiar people.
(2) *To battle* = to make productive.

causelessly traduced the proceedings of that court, when they could not maintain their own innocence.

THE WORTHIES

WYNFRITH [SAINT] BONIFACE was born [675?], at Crediton (corruptly Kirton) once an episcopal see in this county; bred a monk under Abbot Woolfhard in Exeter. Hence he went to Rome, where Pope Gregory the Second (perceiving the ability of his parts) sent him to Germany, for the converting of that stiff-necked nation. This service he commendably performed, baptising not fewer than a hundred thousand, in Barvaria, Thuringia, Hessia, Frisia, Saxony, &c.

But here I must depart from Bale, because he departeth (I am sure) from charity, and I suspect from verity itself. Charity, who (according to his bold and bald apocalyptical conjectures) maketh him "the other beast ascending out of the earth with two horns." And why so? Because, forsooth, he was made by the pope metropolitan of Mainz, and kept the church of Cologne *in commendam* therewith.

Secondly, verity, when saying that he converted men *terrore magis quam doctrina* [more by terror than by teaching] it being utterly incredible that a single man should terrify so many out of their opinions. And if his words relate to his ecclesiastical censures (with which weapons Boniface was well provided) such were in themselves, without God's wonderful improving them on men's consciences, rather ridiculous than formidable to force pagans from their former persuasions. But if Bale (which is very suspicious) had been better pleased with the Germans continuing in their pagan principles than their conversion to corrupted Christianity, he will find few wise and godly men to join with his judgment therein. Yet do I not advocate for all the doctrines delivered and ceremonies imposed by Boniface, beholding him as laying the true foundation, Jesus Christ, which would last and remain, but building much hay and stubble of superstition thereon. But he himself afterwards passed a purging fire in this life, killed at Dockum in Frisia, with fifty-four of his companions, Anno Domini 754, in the sixtieth year of his age, after he had spent thirty six years, six months, and six days, in his German employment.

[SAINT] WILLIBALD, descended of high parentage, was born [700?] in this county, nephew to Saint Boniface aforesaid, whom he followed in all respects; later in time, lower in parts, less in pains, but profitable in the German conversion, wherein he may be termed his uncle's armour-bearer, attending him many a mile, though absent from him at his death. Herein he was more happy than his uncle that, being made bishop of Eichstädt in Germany, as he lived in honour, so he died in peace, Anno Domini 786.

——— CHILDE (whose Christian name is unknown) was a gentleman, the last of his family, being of ancient extraction at Plymstock in this county, and great possessions. It happened that he, hunting in Dartmoor, lost both his company and way in a bitter snow. Having killed his horse he crept into his hot bowels for warmth, and wrote this with his blood:

> He that finds and brings me to my tomb,
> The land of Plymstock shall be his doom.

That night he was frozen to death, and being first found by the monks of Tavistock, they with all possible speed hasted to inter him in their own abbey. His own parishioners of Plymstock, hearing thereof, stood at the ford of the river to take his body from them. But they must rise early, yea not sleep at all, who over-reach monks in matter of profit. For they cast a slight bridge over the river, whereby they carried over the corpse, and interred it. In avowance whereof, the bridge (a more premeditate structure, I believe, in the place of the former extempore passage) is called Guils Bridge to this day. And know, reader, all in the vicinage will be highly offended with such who either deny or doubt the credit of this common tradition. And sure it is, that the abbot of Tavistock got that rich manor into his possession. The exact date of this Childe's death I cannot attain. [11th cent.]

GILBERT FOLIOT was born at Tamerton Foliot in this county; abbot of Gloucester (Bale saith Exeter) then successively bishop of Hereford and London.

He was observed, when a common brother of his convent, to inveigh against the prior; when prior, against the abbot; when abbot, against the pride and laziness of bishops; but when he himself was bishop, all was well, and Foliot's mouth, when full, was silent; whether because all things do rest quiet in their centre, or because age had abated his juvenile animosity, or because he found it more facile to find faults in others than mend them in himself. Indeed oft-times mere moroseness of nature usurps the reputation of zeal, and what is but a bare disgust of men's persons passeth for dislike of their vices. However, our Foliot, the less he had in satires, the more he had of elegies afterwards, secretly bemoaning the badness of the age he lived in. Here a pass betwixt him and a strange voice:

SATAN'S CHALLENGE	FOLIOT'S ANSWER
O Gilberte Foliot, *Dum revolvis tot et tot* *Deus tuus est Ashtarot.*[1] [O Gilbert Foliot while you spin round and round, your God is Ashtaroth.]	*Mentiris, daemon; qui est Deus* *Sabaoth, est ille meus.* [You lie, demon, He who is the God of Sabaoth is my God.]

He finds little favour from our historians of his age, because they do generally *Becketize;* whilst Foliot was all for the king, being a professed enemy to the (not *person*) but *pride* of that prelate.[2] This wise and learned bishop died Feb. 18, 1187.

(1) The goddess of the Sidonians, 1 Kings xi, 5.—F. (2) Foliot had opposed Becket's election to the primacy in 1162, and refused him obedience as metropolitan. Becket twice excommunicated him, though he obtained absolution.

ROBERT FOLIOT, archdeacon of Oxford, was near cousin (and therefore is placed countryman) to Gilbert aforesaid. He was bred first in England, then in France, where he got the surname of Robertus Melundinensis, probably from the place of his longest abode. He was, first, tutor to Becket, and Becket afterwards was patron to him, by whose procurement he succeeded his kinsman in the see of Hereford. He wrote several books, whereof one of the *Sacraments of the Old Law* is most remarkable.

Hitherto we have followed Bale with blind obedience, until Bishop Godwin, whom we rather believe, hath opened our eyes in two particulars: 1. That Robert de Melun (bishop also of Hereford) was a distinct person from our Robert. 2. That our Foliot was advanced bishop after the death of Becket, probably for the affection he bore unto him, not the assistance he received from him. His death happened anno 1186.

HENRY DE LA POMEROY lived at, and was lord of Berry Pomeroy, in this county. This Henry, taking heart at the imprisonment of Richard the First by Leopoldus duke of Austria, surprised and expulsed the monks out of Michael's Mount in Cornwall, that there he might be a petty prince by himself. But, being ascertained of his sovereign's enlargement, and fearing deserved death, to prevent it, he laid violent hands on himself, as Roger Hoveden doth report.

But the descendants from this Pomeroy make a different relation of this accident, affirming that a serjeant-at-arms of the king's came to his castle at Berry Pomeroy, and there received kind entertainment for certain days together, and, at his departure, was gratified with a liberal reward. In counterchange whereof he then, and no sooner, revealing his long-concealed errand, flatly arrested his host, to make immediate appearance before the king to answer a capital crime. Which unexpected and ill-carried message the gentleman took in such despite, that with his dagger he stabbed the messenger to the heart.

Then, despairing of pardon in so superlative an offence, he abandoned his home, and got himself to his sister, abiding in the island of Mount Michael in Cornwall. Here he bequeathed a large portion of his land to the religious people dwelling there, to pray for the redeeming of his soul; and lastly (that the remainder of his estate might descend to this heir) he caused himself to be let blood unto death. [*fl.* 12th cent.]

RICHARD FISHACRE, OR FIZACRE (Matthew Paris termeth him FISHACLE) was, saith Bale, born *in Exoniensi patria,* which I English *in Devonshire.* He was bred first in Oxford, then in Paris, and became a Dominican friar; for his learning and preaching as highly esteemed as any of that age. He was, saith learned Leland, as fast linked in friendship to Robert Bacon (of whom hereafter[1]) as ever Brithus to Bacchius, or Theseus to Perithous; so that one may say of them: *there* were two friends. This Richard, disdaining to survive Robert aforesaid, hearing of his death, expired in the same year, 1248, and was buried at Oxford.

(1) See Oxfordshire, p. 463.

WILLIAM DE RALEIGH was born at that well known town in this county; preferred, first canon of St. Paul's, then successively bishop of Norwich and Winchester; the last of which cost him much trouble, his election being stiffly opposed by King Henry the Third, intending a Valentinian (uncle to the queen) for that bishopric, whom the monks of Winchester refused, terming him *vir sanguinum*, a man of blood. Whether in that sense wherein David is so termed (and on that account prohibited the building of the temple) because a martial man; or whether only because descended of high blood, whose descent was all his desert; so that they rigidly adhered to the election of Raleigh.

King Henry, who seldom used to be angry, and more seldom to swear, sware in his anger "that he would have his will at last, or they should never have bishop;" and how his conscience came off without perjury herein, his own confessor was best able to satisfy him.

Raleigh had (besides his own merits) two good friends, his purse and the pope, the former procuring the latter. He presented his holiness with six thousand marks, which effected his work. Here two persons were at once deceived; the pope not expecting so great a sum should be tendered him, and Raleigh not suspecting he would take all, but leave at least a morsel for manners. But his hands will take whatever is tendered him, if not too hot or too heavy.

Raleigh, thus run in debt, could never creep out thereof, though living very privately, and dying very penitently; for, when the priest brought the eucharist unto him, lying on his death-bed, Raleigh, expressing himself in language like to that of John Baptist, "I have need to come to thee, and comest thou to me?" would rise out of his bed to meet him. His death happened Anno Domini 1250.

JAMES DE AUDLEY is challenged by several counties (Staffordshire, Herefordshire, Dorsetshire, &c.) and that with almost equal probability, to be their native: but my author, well versed in the antiquities of this shire, clearly adjudgeth his birth thereunto, avouching the castle of Barnstaple the place of his principal mansion and inhabitance.

This is that Lord Audley, so famous for his valiant service in France at the battle of Poitiers, where the Black Prince rewarded him with a yearly pension of 500 marks, which presently the Lord Audley gave as freely to his four esquires, having (as he said) received this honour by their means. The news of this largesse being quickly brought to the prince's ears, he questioned the lord, whether he conceived his gift not worthy his esteem, as beneath his acceptance? To whom the lord replied, "These squires have done me long and faithful service, and now especially in this battle, without whose assistance I, being a single man, could have done little. Besides, the fair estate left me by my ancestors enableth me freely to serve your highness, whereas these my men stand in need of some support. Only, I crave your pardon for giving it away without your licence." The prince, highly pleased thereat, praised his bounty as much as his valour, and doubled his former pension into a thousand marks.[1] [1316?—1386]

(1) James de Audley was a 'first founder' of the order of the Garter, instituted in 1348.

JOHN CARY was born at Cockington in this county; and, applying himself to the study of the laws, was made chief baron of the Exchequer in the tenth year of King Richard the Second. The greatest fault I find charged on him was loyalty to his lord and master; which if any dare call a disease, I assure you it is a catching one among conscientious people On this honourable account, this judge lost his office, goods and lands in the first of King Henry the Fourth; whose losses, not long after, providence plentifully repaid to his posterity, on this occasion. A knight-errant of Aragon, coming into England, and challenging any to tilt with him, was undertaken by Sir Robert Cary, son to John Cary aforesaid, who vanquished the vainglorious Don; so that King Henry the Fifth, out of a sympathy of valour, restored all his estate unto him. This judge died about the year of our Lord 1395.

WILLIAM COURTENAY was born [1342?], probably at Okehampton, in this county, son to Hugh Courtenay, earl of Devonshire; successively bishop of Hereford, Winchester and Canterbury. The credit of T. Walsingham, an exact historian (and born before Courtenay was buried) maketh me confident that the pope made him a cardinal; and Ciaconius and Onuphrius, two Italians, confirm the same that a bishop of London (though mistaking his name, Adam for William) was at this time rewarded with a red hat.

How stoutly he then opposed John of Gaunt (Wycliffe's patron) in his church of St. Paul is largely related in my *Church History,* and I can add nothing thereunto.[1] For if the men of Laconia (whose work was to study conciseness) punished him severely for speaking in three what might have been said in two words, critics will severely censure me for such tedious repetition.

Only we may observe that when archbishop of Canterbury, his metropolitical visitation charged through and through every diocese in his own province, no resistance being of proof against him, all opposers giving some trouble to him but disgrace to themselves; soon suppressed by his high blood, strong brains, full purse, skill in law, and plenty of powerful friends in the English and Romish court. The difficulty which he underwent herein made the work easy to his successors ever after. He deceased July 31, Anno Domini 1396.

RICHARD COURTENAY was one of great lineage (allied to the earl of Devonshire) and no less learning (excellently skilled in the knowledge of both laws): so that, at the instant suit of King Henry the Fifth, he was preferred bishop of Norwich, anno 1413. His person (the inn of his soul had a fair sign) was highly favoured by his prince, and beloved by the people; yet all this could not prolong his life, so that he died [1415] of a flux, at the siege of Harfleur in Normandy, in the second year of his consecration; and his corpse, brought over, was honourably entombed in Westminster.

(1) He was a strong opponent of the lollards, proceeded against Wycliffe for heresy in 1372 and repressed his followers a few years later. He had the courage to reprove Richard II for his bad government.

SIR WILLIAM HANKEFORD was born at Annery in this county (a manor which, from owners of the same name, by their daughter and heir, descended to the Hankefords); bred in the study of the laws, till he became chief-justice of the king's bench in the first of King Henry the Fifth; which place he adorned with great learning and integrity, though doleful the manner of his death, on this occasion. Coming home discontented from London, he expressed extreme anger (somewhat trespassing on his judicial gravity) against his keeper; for that (as he said) his deer were stolen, and charged him to shoot any man in the park whom he should find there, and stood not, being spoken unto, and he would discharge him. The next night, being dark, he presents himself, and refusing to stand, the keeper, according to his injunction, shot and killed him. The stump of the oak, nigh which this sad accident happened, hath been shewn to some eminent lawyers, riding that circuit, which are yet alive.

No charitable reader, for one unadvised act will condemn his memory who, when living, was habited with all requisites for a person of his place. [*d.* 1422]

NICHOLAS UPTON was born [1400?] in this county, of an ancient family, still flourishing therein at [Portlinch]. He was bred doctor in the canon law, and became canon of Salisbury, Wells and St. Paul's. Humphrey duke of Gloucester, the Maecenas-general of goodness and learning, had him in high esteem, and gave him great rewards Hereupon Upton, in expression of his gratitude, presented his patron with a book (the first in that kind) of heraldry, and the rules thereof; a book since set forth in a fair impression by Edward Bysshe, esquire, a person composed of all worthy accomplishments. [*d.* 1457]

JOHN STANBURY was (saith Bale out of Leland) *in occidentali regni parte natus*. But the western parts being a wide parish, thanks to our author, who hath particularized the place of his nativity, viz., the farm of Churchill, within the parish of Bratton or Broad Town in this county, where some of his name and kindred remain at this day. He was bred a Carmelite in Oxford, and became generally as learned as any of his order, deserving all the dignity which the university did or could confer upon him. King Henry the Sixth highly favoured and made him the first provost of Eton, being much ruled by his advice in ordering that, his new foundation. He was by the king designed bishop of Norwich; but William de la Pole, duke of Suffolk (see the presumption of a proud favourite, or minion rather) got it from him for his own chaplain, and Stanbury was forced to stay his stomach on the poor bishopric of Bangor, till, anno 1453, he was advanced bishop of Hereford.

Leland doth condemn him for his over-compliance with the pope in all his intolerable taxes; and others commend him as much for his fidelity to his master King Henry, whom he deserted not in all his adversity, so that this bishop was taken prisoner in the battle of Northampton. Say not to this prelate as Eliab to David, "Why camest thou down hither? With whom hast thou left those few sheep in the wilderness? I know the pride and the malice of thy heart, for thou art come down to see the battle." For, Stanbury being confessor to King Henry, he was tied by his oath to such personal attendance. After long durance in Warwick Castle he was set at liberty; and dying anno 1474, was buried in the convent of Carmelites at Ludlow, where his barbarous and tedious epitaph (ill suiting with the author of such learned and pithy books) is not worth the inserting.

SIR JOHN FORTESCUE was born of a right ancient and worthy family in this county, first fixed at Wimpstone in this shire, but since prosperously planted in every part thereof. They give for their motto *Forte scutum salus ducum* [a strong shield is the safety of leaders]; and it is observable that they attained eminency in what profession soever they applied themselves

IN THE FIELD

SIR JOHN FORTESCUE. A valiant and fortunate commander under King Henry the Fifth in the French wars, by whom he was made governor of Meaux.[1] [*fl.* 1394-1421]

SIR ADRIAN FORTESCUE. Porter of the town of Calais; came over with King Henry the Seventh, and effectually assisting him to regain the crown, was by him deservedly created knight banneret.[2] [1476?-1539]

IN WESTMINSTER HALL

SIR HENRY FORTESCUE was lord chief justice of Ireland, and justly of great esteem for his many virtues, especially for his sincerity in so tempting a place[3] [*fl.* 1421-1428]

SIR JOHN FORTESCUE, our present subject, lord chief justice and chancellor of England in the reign of King Henry the Sixth, whose learned commentaries on the law make him famous to all posterity.[4] [1394?-1476?]

IN THE COURT

SIR JOHN FORTESCUE, that wise privy councillor, overseer of Queen Elizabeth's liberal studies; and chancellor of the exchequer and duchy of Lancaster.[5] [1531?-1607]

SIR RICHARD EDGCUMBE. He was a knight, and memorable in his generation, for, being zealous in the cause of Henry earl of Richmond (afterwards King Henry the Seventh) he was in the time of King Richard

(1) Father of Sir Henry and Sir John, chief justices. (2) Fuller's statements have no foundation. This Sir Adrian was grandnephew of Sir John the chief justice; fought against the French 1513 and 1522; attainted 1539 and executed on a charge of treason, the real reason being possibly his near relationship to Anne Boleyn. (3) M.P. for Devonshire, 1421; twice deputed by Irish parliament to lay Irish grievances before Henry VI. (4) Attainted by Edward IV as a Lancastrian and later pardoned; wrote the important works *De Laudibus Legum Angliae* and *On the Governance of the Kingdom of England.* (5) Eldest son of Sir Adrian; intimate friend of Burghley, Bacon, Ralegh and Essex; presented books to his friend Sir Thomas Bodley's library.

the Third so hotly pursued, and narrowly searched for, that he was forced to hide himself in his thick woods, at his house at Cotehele in Cornwall. Here extremity taught him a sudden policy, to put a stone in his cap, and tumble the same into the water, whilst these rangers were fast at his heels who, looking down after the noise, and seeing his cap swimming thereon, supposed that he had desperately drowned himself; and, deluded by this honest fraud, gave over their farther pursuit, leaving him at liberty to shift over into Brittany. Nor was his gratitude less than his ingenuity, who in remembrance of his delivery, after his return, built a chapel (lately extant) in the place where he lurked, and lived in great repute with prince and people. King Henry the Seventh rewarded his loyalty, by bestowing the castle of Totnes in this county upon him.

[*d.* 1489]

SIR LEWIS POLLARD [*b.* 1465?] of King's Nympton in this county, serjeant of the law, and one of the justices of the king's bench in the time of King Henry the Eighth, was a man of singular knowledge and worth, who, by his lady Elizabeth, had eleven sons, whereof four attained the honour of knighthood: Sir Hugh; Sir John, of Ford; Sir Richard; Sir George, who got his honour in the defence of Boulogne; eleven daughters, married to the most potent families in this county, and most of them knights; so that (what is said of Cork in Ireland, that all the inhabitants therein are kin) by this match almost all the ancient gentry in this county are allied.

All the rest, especially John, archdeacon of Sarum and canon of Exeter, were very well advanced.

The portraiture of Sir Lewis and his lady, with their two and twenty children, are set up in a glass window at Bishop's Nympton. There is a tradition continued in this family that the lady, glassing the window in her husband's absence at the term in London, caused one child more than she then had to be set up, presuming (having had one and twenty already, and usually conceiving at her husband's coming home) she should have another child; which, inserted in expectance, came to pass accordingly. This memorable knight died anno 1540.

AGNES PIREST, or PREST, was the sole martyr under the reign of Queen Mary; wherefore, as those parents which have but one child may afford it the better attendance, as more at leisure; so, seeing by God's goodness we have but this single native of this county, yea of this diocese, we will enlarge ourselves on the time, place and cause of her suffering.

1. Her Christian name, which Mr. Foxe could not learn, we have recovered from another excellent author.[1] 2. I am informed by the inhabitants thereabouts, that she lived at Northcott in the parish of Boyton, in the county of Cornwall; but where born is unknown. 3. She was a simple woman to behold, thick, but little and short in stature; about fifty-four years of age. 4. She was indicted on Monday, the fourth week in Lent, an. Philip and Mary 2 and 3, before W. Stanford,[2] justice of the assize (the same, as I conceive, who wrote on the pleas of the crown):

(1) Mr. Vovell, in Holinshed. (2) Sir William Stanford—see Middlesex, p. 392.

so that we may observe more legal formality was used about the condemnation of this poor woman, than any martyr of far greater degree. 5. Her own husband and children were her greatest persecutors, from whom she fled, because they would force her to be present at mass. 6. She was presented to James Tuberville,[1] bishop of Exeter, and by him condemned for denying the sacrament of the altar. 7. After her condemnation she refused to receive any money from well-affected people, saying "she was to go to that city where money had no mastery." 8. She was burnt without the walls of Exeter, in a place called Sothenhay, in the month of November 1558.

She was the only person in whose persecution Bishop Tuberville did appear; and it is justly conceived that Blackstone, his chancellor, was more active than the bishop in procuring her death.

PETER BLUNDELL, of Tiverton in this county, was a clothier by his profession, and through God's blessing on his endeavours therein, raised himself a fair estate. Nor was he more painful and industrious in gaining, than pious and prudent in disposing thereof, erecting a fair free-school in the town of his nativity. By his will he bequeathed thereto a competent maintenance (together with conveniency of lodging) for a master and usher. And, lest such whose genius did incline, and parts furnish them for a further progress in learning, should through want of a comfortable subsistency be stopped or disheartened, he bestowed two scholarships and as many fellowships on Sidney College in Cambridge; carefully providing that the scholars bred in his school at Tiverton should be elected into the same. [1520-1601]

JOHN JEWEL, bearing the Christian name of his father, grandfather, and great-grandfather, was born at Buden (a farm possessed more than two hundred years by his ancestors) in the parish of Berrynarbor, nigh Ilfracombe in this county, on the 24th of May 1522. His mother's surname was Bellamy, who with her husband John Jewel lived happily fifty years together in holy wedlock, and at their death left ten children behind them.

It may be said of his surname, *nomen, omen;* Jewel his name and precious his virtues; so that, if the like ambition led us Englishmen, which doth foreigners, speciously to render our surnames in Greek or Latin, he may be termed *Johannes Gemma,* on better account than Gemma Frisius entituleth himself thereunto.

He was chiefly bred in the school at Barnstaple, where Thomas Harding, afterwards his antagonist, was his schoolfellow, and at fifteen years of age was admitted in Merton College, under the tuition of John Parkhurst, afterwards bishop of Norwich.[2] Such his sedulity, rising always at four of the clock, and not going to bed till ten, that he was never punished for any exercise, and but once for absence from chapel. Hence he was removed to Corpus Christi College, where he proved an excellent poet (having all Horace by heart) linguist and orator.

Thus having touched at all humane arts, he landed at divinity, being

(1) See Dorsetshire, p. 150. (2) See Surrey, p. 549.

much assisted by Peter Martyr, the king's professor therein.[1] Saint Jerome telleth us that so great was the intimacy betwixt Pamphilius that worthy martyr, a priest, and Eusebius the bishop of Caesarea, *ut ab uno alter nomen acceperet* (that they mutually were surnamed the one from the other) Pamphilius Eusebii and Eusebius Pamphilii. No less the unity of affections betwixt these two, who accordingly might be called Martyr's Jewel, and Jewel's Martyr, as seldom in body and never in mind asunder.

What eminent changes afterwards befel him in the course of his life, how he fled into Germany, lived at Zurich, returned into England, was preferred bishop of Salisbury, wrote learnedly, preached painfully, lived piously, died peaceably Anno Domini 1571, are largely related in my *Church History*; and I will trouble the reader with no repetitions.[2]

THOMAS STUKELY [*b.* 1525?]. He was a younger brother, of an ancient, wealthy and worshipful family, nigh Ilfracombe in this county; being one of good parts, but valued the less by others because over-prized by himself. Having prodigally misspent his patrimony, he entered on several projects (the issue-general of all decayed estates) and first pitched on the peopling of Florida, then newly found out in the West Indies. So confident his ambition, that he blushed not to tell Queen Elizabeth that "he preferred rather to be sovereign of a molehill than the highest subject to the greatest king in Christendom;" adding moreover that "he was assured he should be a prince before his death." "I hope," said Queen Elizabeth, "I shall hear from you, when you are stated in your principality." "I will write unto you," quoth Stukely. "In what language?" said the queen. He returned, "In the style of princes: To our dear Sister."

His fair project of Florida being blasted for lack of money to pursue it, he went over into Ireland, where he was frustrate of the preferment he expected, and met such physic that turned his fever into frenzy; for hereafter resolving treacherously to attempt what he could not loyally achieve, he went over into Italy.

It is incredible how quickly he wrought himself through the notice into the favour, through the court into the chamber, yea closet, yea bosom of Pope Pius Quintus; so that some wise men thought his holiness did forfeit a parcel of his infallibility in giving credit to such a *glorioso,* vaunting that with three thousand soldiers he would beat all the English out of Ireland.

The pope, finding it cheaper to fill Stukely's swelling sails with airy titles than real gifts, created him baron of Ross, Viscount Murrough, earl of Wexford, marquess of Leinster; and then furnished this title-top-heavy general with eight hundred soldiers, paid by the King of Spain, for the Irish expedition.

(1) Pietro Martine Vermigli (1500—1562) Augustinian monk, who accepted the reformed faith, and fled from Italy to Strasburg. Brought to London by Cranmer; appointed professor of divinity at Oxford; helped Cranmer with the Second Prayer Book; escaped to Strasburg on Mary's accession. (2) Jewel fled in 1555 to avoid persecution under Mary. He spent much of his life in controversy, ultimately becoming strongly Anglican and an opponent of puritanism. His writings are voluminous.

In passage thereunto Stukely lands at Portugal, just when Sebastian the king thereof, with two Moorish kings, were undertaking of a voyage into Africa. Stukely, scorning to attend, is persuaded to accompany them. Some thought he wholly quitted his Irish design, party because loath to be pent up in an island (the continent of Africa affording more elbow-room for his achievements); partly because so mutable his mind, he ever loved the last project (as mothers the youngest child) best. Others conceive he took this African in order to his Irish design; such his confidence of conquest, that his breakfast on the Turks would the better enable him to dine on the English in Ireland.

Landing in Africa, Stukely gave council, which was safe, seasonable and necessary; namely, that for two or three days they should refresh their land soldiers; whereof some were sick, and some were weak, by reason of their tempestuous passage. This would not be heard; so furious was Don Sebastian to engage, as if he would pluck up the bays of victory out of the ground, before they were grown up; and so, in the battle of Alcazar, their army was wholly defeated, where Stukely lost his life.

> A fatal fight, where in one day was slain,
> Three kings that were, and one that would be fain.

This battle was fought anno 1578, where Stukely, with his eight hundred men, behaved himself most valiantly, till overpowered with multitude.[1]

SIR HUMPHREY GILBERT was born [1539?] at Greenaway in this county, the pleasant seat of his family for a long continuance. He was famous for his knowledge both by sea and land. In the year 1569 he valiantly and fortunately served in Ireland. Afterwards he led nine companies to the assistance of the Hollanders. In the year 1583 he set forth with five ships to make discoveries in the north of America, where he took seisin and possession of Newfoundland (according to the ancient solemn ceremony of cutting a turf) for the crown of England.

He resolved to adventure himself in his return in a vessel of forty tons, and with two ships (the only remains of five) did make for England. In the instant of their winding about (I may confidently report what is generally in this county averred and believed) a very great lion, not swimming after the manner of a beast with the motion of his feet, nor yet diving sometimes under water and rising again (as porpoises and dolphins do) but rather gliding on the water with his whole body except legs in sight, shunned not the ship, nor the mariners, who presented themselves in view; but, turning his head to and fro, yawning and gaping wide, made a horrible roaring. It is conceived no spectrum or apparition, but a real fish; seeing we read that such like a lion in all lineaments was taken at sea, anno 1282, and presented to Pope Martin the Fourth.

Instantly a terrible tempest did arise, and Sir Humphrey said cheerfully to his companions, "We are as near heaven here at sea as at land." Nor

(1) This swashbuckling adventurer had seen service with Protector Somerset, on whose arrest he fled to France. He engaged in privateering in 1563, Elizabeth providing one of the ships, and preyed on the shipping of all nations for a couple of years. The objections of foreign nations obliged Elizabeth to arrest him. He was constantly plotting against England, and accepted a pension from Philip of Spain.

was it long before his ship sank into the sea with all therein, though the other recovered home, like Job's messengers, to bring the tidings of the destruction of their companions. This sad accident happened 1583.[1]

[WILLIAM] COCK. I am sorry I cannot add his Christian name, and more sorry that I cannot certainly avouch his nativity in this county (though inclined with many motives to believe it) being a cock of the game indeed, for in the eighty-eight, *Solus cockus Anglus in sua inter medios hostes navicula, cum laude periit.*[2] And whereas there was not a noble family in Spain but lost either son, brother, or nephew in that fight, this Cock was the only man of note of the English who, fighting a volunteer in his own ship, lost his life, to save his queen and country:

Unus homo nobis pereundo restituit rem.
[One man by his death restored our fortunes.]

Pity it is his memory should ever be forgotten, and my pen is sensible of no higher preferment than when it may be permitted to draw the curtains about those who have died in the bed of honour.

SIR FRANCIS DRAKE.[3] He lived by the sea, died on it, and was buried in it. Thus an extempore performance, scarce heard to be begun before we hear it is ended, comes off with better applause, or miscarries with less disgrace, than a long-studied and openly premeditated action. Besides, we see how great spirits, having mounted to the highest pitch of performance, afterwards strain and break their credits in striving to go beyond it. Lastly, God oftentimes leaves the brightest men in an eclipse, to shew that they do but borrow their lustre from his reflection. We will not justify all the actions of any man, though of a tamer profession than a sea captain, in whom civility is often counted preciseness. For the main, we say that this our captain was a religious man towards God and his houses, generally sparing churches where he came, chaste in his life, just in his dealings, true of his word, and merciful to those that were under him, hating nothing so much as idleness. And therefore lest his soul should rust in peace at spare hours, he brought fresh water to Plymouth. Careful he was for posterity, though men of his profession have as well an ebb of riot as a float of fortune, and providently raised a worshipful family of his kindred. In a word, should those that speak against him fast till they fetch their bread where he did his, they would have a good stomach to eat it. [1540?-1596]

SIR WALTER RALEGH. "The sons of Heth said unto Abraham, Thou art a great prince amongst us; in the choice of our sepulchres bury thy dead; none shall withhold them from thee." So may we say to the memory of this worthy knight, "Repose yourself in this our catalogue under what

(1) Sir Humphrey Gilbert (half-brother to Ralegh) entered parliament in 1571. His first voyage was a failure, but in 1583 he was successful as the first founder of a British colony in North America. (2) Camden's *Elizabeth* ["A solitary English Cock perished honourably in his skiff surrounded by his enemies."] (3) In the original edition Fuller states: "Having formerly, in my *Holy State*, written his life at large, I will forbear any addition." It is too long to quote in full, but the concluding sketch of his character is given above.

topic you please, of statesman, seaman, soldier, learned writer," and what not? His worth unlocks our closest cabinets, and provides both room and welcome to entertain him.

He was born [1552?] at Budleigh in this county[1], of an ancient family, but decayed in estate, and he the youngest brother thereof. He was bred in Oriel College in Oxford; and thence coming to court, found some hopes of the queen's favours reflecting upon him. This made him write in a glass window, obvious to the queen's eye,

Fain would I climb, yet fear I to fall.

Her majesty, either espying or being shown it, did underwrite,

If thy heart fails thee, climb not at all.

However he at last climbed up by the stairs of his own desert. But his introduction into the court bare an elder date, from this occasion. This captain Ralegh, coming out of Ireland to the English court in good habit (his clothes being then a considerable part of his estate) found the queen walking, till meeting with a plashy place, she seemed to scruple going thereon. Presently Ralegh cast and spread his new plush cloak on the ground, whereon the queen trod gently, rewarding him afterwards with many suits, for his so free and seasonable tender of so fair a footcloth.[2] Thus an advantageous admission into the first notice of a prince is more than half a degree to preferment.

It is reported of the women in the Balearic Islands, that to make their sons expert archers, they will not, when children, give them their breakfast before they had hit the mark. Such the dealing of the queen with this knight, making him to earn his honour, and by pain and peril, to purchase what places of credit or profit were bestowed upon him. Indeed it was true of him, what was said of Cato Uticensis, "that he seemed to be born to that only which he went about," so dextrous was he in all his undertakings in court, in camp, by sea, by land, with sword, with pen; witness in the last his *History of the World*, wherein the only default (or defect rather) that it wanteth one half thereof. Yet had he many enemies (which worth never wanteth) at court, his cowardly detractors, of whom Sir Walter was wont to say, "If any man accuseth me to my face, I will answer him with my mouth, but my tail is good enough to return an answer to such who traduceth me behind my back." [*d.* 1618]

RICHARD HOOKER was born [1554?] at Heavitree nigh Exeter; bred in Corpus Christi College in Oxford, and afterwards was preferred by Archbishop Whitgift master of the Temple, whilst at the same time Mr. Walter Travers was the lecturer thereof. Here the pulpit spake pure Canterbury in the morning, and Geneva in the afternoon, until Travers was silenced.[3]

(1) The house its name was called Hayes.—F. (2) The story is generally discredited, but Fuller's uncle Robert Townson (see Cambridgeshire, p. 57) then dean of Westminster and later bishop of Salisbury, attended Ralegh in his last hours, and may very well have heard the story from Ralegh and passed it on to the young Fuller. (3) Walter Travers (1548?—1635), puritan divine, has been passed over for the mastership of the Temple in favour of Hooker. The controversy with Hooker was marked by dignity and mutual respect. Travers subsequently became provost of Trinity College, Dublin.

Hooker's style was prolix, but not tedious, and such who would patiently attend and give him credit, all the reading or hearing of his sentences, had their expectations over-paid at the close thereof. He may be said to have made good music with his fiddle and stick alone, without any resin, having neither pronunciation nor gesture to grace his matter.

His book of *Ecclesiastical Polity* is prized by all generally, save such who out of ignorance cannot, or envy will not understand it. But there is a kind of people who have a pique at him, and therefore read his book with a prejudice;[1] that, as Jephtha vowed to sacrifice the first living thing which met him, these are resolved to quarrel with the first word which occureth therein.

Hereupon it is, that they take exception at the very title thereof, *Ecclesiastical Polity,* as if unequally yoked: church with some mixture of city-ness, that the discipline, *jure divino,* may bow to human inventions. But be it reported to the judicious whether, when all is done, a reserve must not be left for prudential supplies in church government.

True it is, his book in our late times was beheld as an old almanac grown out of date; but, blessed be God, there is now a revolution, which may bring his works again into reputation.

Mr. Hooker leaving London (no inclination of his own, but obedience to others, put him on so public a place) retired to a small benefice in Kent, where he put off his mortality, anno 1600, leaving the memory of an humble, holy and learned divine. Here I must retract (after a father,[2] no shame for a child) two passages in my *Church History.* For, whereas I reported him to die a bachelor, he had wife and children, though indeed such as were neither to his comfort when living, nor credit when dead.[3] But parents cannot stamp their children from their heads or hearts.

JOHN COWELL was born [1554] at Ernsborough in this county; bred first at Eton, then in King's College in Cambridge. He was proctor thereof 1586, doctor of the law, master of Trinity Hall, vice-chancellor in the years 1603 and 1614, doctor of the Arches, and vicar-general to Archbishop Bancroft. Though civil was his profession, such his skill in common law, he was as well able to practise in Westminster Hall as Doctors' Commons.

In his time the contest was heightened betwixt the civilians and common lawyers, Cowell being champion of the former, whom King James countenanced as far as he could with conveniency. Indeed, great were his abilities, though a grand oracle of the common law was pleased to call him Doctor *Cow-heel;* and a *cow-heel* (I assure you) well dressed is good meat, that a cook (when hungry) may lick his fingers after it.[4]

Two chief monuments he hath left to posterity: his book intituled *Institutiones Juris Anglicani,* and his *Interpreter* of the hard words in the common law. Indeed he had both the essentials of an interpreter, who

(1) This may be aimed at the puritans, who attached Hooker's book, the classic defence of Anglicanism. (2) St. Augustine. (3) From the mouth of his sister, lately living at Hoddesdon, nigh London.—F. [The 'judicious' Hooker's 'injudicious' marriage was given currency by Walton's *Life* of him and by this passage of Fuller's. It has lately been questioned.] (4) The 'grand oracle of the common law' was Sir Edward Coke (see Norfolk, p. 414) which makes clear the point of Fuller's joke about the cook licking his fingers.

was both *gnarus* and *fidus*. Many slighted his book who used it, it being questionable whether it gave more information or offence. Common lawyers beheld it as a double trespass against them; first, *pedibus ambulando*, that a civilian should walk in a profession several to themselves; secondly, that he should pluck up the pales of the hard terms wherewith it was enclosed, and lay it open and obvious to common capacities.

But an higher offence was charged upon him, that he made the king to have a double prerogative, the one limited by law, the other unlimited; which being complained of in parliament, his book was called in and condemned. Some other advantages they got against him, the grief whereof (hearts sunk down are not to be buoyed up) hastened his death, Anno Domini 1611; and he lieth buried in Trinity Hall chapel.

SIR JOHN [DODDRIDGE or] DODERIDGE, knight, was born [1555] at [Barnstaple?] in this county; bred in Exeter College in Oxford, where he became so general a scholar that it is hard to say whether he was better artist, divine, civil or common lawyer, though he fixed on the last for his public profession, and became second justice of the king's bench. His soul consisted of two essentials, ability and integrity, holding the scale of justice with so steady an hand, that neither love nor lucre, fear or flattery, could bow him on either side.

It was vehemently suspected, that in his time some gave large sums of money to purchase places of judicature, and Sir John is famous for the expression, that as old and infirm as he was, he would go to Tyburn on foot to see such a man hanged that should proffer money for a place of that nature; for certainly those who buy such offices by wholesale, must sell justice by retail, to make themselves savers. He was commonly called the sleeping judge, because he would sit on the bench with his eyes shut, which was only a posture of attention, to sequester his sight from distracting objects, the better to listen to what was alleged and proved. Though he had three wives successively out of the respectful families of Germain, Bampfylde and Culme, yet he left no issue behind him. He kept a hospitable house at Mount Radford near Exeter; and dying Anno Domini 1628, the thirteenth day of September (after he had been seventeen years a judge) in the seventy-third year of his age, was interred under a stately tomb in our Lady's chapel in Exeter.

WILLIAM BURGOIN, esquire, must not be forgotten; finding this his epitaph on his marble stone in the church of Arlington:

> Here lies Will. Burgoin, a squire by descent,
> Whose death in this world many people lament.
> The rich for his love; the poor for his alms;
> The wise for his knowledge; the sick for his balms.
> Grace he did love, and vice control:
> Earth has his body, and heaven his soul.

He died on the twelfth day of August, in the morning, 1623, as the inscription on his said tomb doth inform us.

ARTHUR CHICHESTER [BARON CHICHESTER of Belfast, *b.* 1563] was descended of a right ancient family, dwelling at Raleigh in this county. He spent his youth first in the university, then in the French and Irish wars, where, by his valour, he was effectually assistant, first to plough and break up that barbarous nation by conquest, and then to sow it with seeds of civility, when by King James made lord deputy of Ireland.

Indeed good laws and provisions had been made by his predecessors to that purpose; but alas they were like good lessons set for a lute out of tune, useless until the instrument was fitted for them. Wherefore, in order to the civilizing of the Irishry, in the first year of his government he established two new circuits for justices of assize, the one in Connaught, the other in Munster. And whereas the circuits in former times only encompassed the English Pale (as the Cynosura doth the Pole) henceforward, like good planets in their several spheres, they carried the influence of justice round about the kingdom. Yea, in short time, Ireland was so cleared of thieves and capital offenders, that so many malefactors have not been found in the two and thirty shires of Ireland, as in six English shires in the western circuit.

He reduced the mountains and glens on the south of Dublin (formerly thorns in the sides of the English Pale) into the county of Wicklow; and in conformity to the English custom, many Irish began to cut their mantles into cloaks. So observant his eye over the actions of suspected persons that Tyrone was heard to complain "that he could not drink a full carouse of sack, but the state was within a few hours advertised thereof."[1]

After he had been continued many years in his deputyship, and deservedly made a lord, King James recalled him home, and (loath to leave his abilities unemployed) sent him ambassador to the emperor, and other German princes. Being besieged in the city of Munich (a place much indebted to his prudence, for seasonably victualling it) by Count Tilly, he sent him word that it was against the law of nations to besiege an ambassador. Tilly returned "that he took no notice that he was an ambassador." The Lord Chichester replied to the messenger: "Had my master sent me with as many hundred men as he hath sent me on fruitless messages, your general should have known that I had been a soldier, as well as an ambassador."

King James at his return entertained him with great commendation, for so well discharging his trust; and he died, in as great honour as any Englishman of our age, Anno Domini 1625.[2]

JOHN MOLLE was born in or nigh South Molton[3] in this county; bred in France, where he attained to such perfection in that tongue, that he made a dictionary thereof for his own use. After his youth spent in some military employments of good trust, he was, in his reduced age,

(1) Sir John Davis, in his *Discovery of Ireland.* (2) Chichester once assaulted a royal purveyor, and prudently withdrawing to Ireland, waited for pardon. He saw service against the Armada, in Drake's 1595 expedition, at Cadiz and in the Low Countries. (3) The ensuing relation I had from his son Mr. Henry Molle, late orator of Cambridge.—F.

made by Thomas Lord Burghley and president of the north, one of the examiners in that court.

Going afterwards governer to the Lord Ross, he passed the Alps (contrary to his own resolution) prizing his fidelity to his charge above his own security. No sooner were they arrived at Rome, but the young lord was courted and feasted, Mr. Molle arrested and imprisoned in the Inquisition. Thus at once did he lose the comfort of his wife, children, friends, own land and liberty, being kept in most strict restraint. Add to all these vexations, visits of importunate priests and Jesuits, daily hacking at the root of his constancy with their objections; till, finding their tools to turn edge, at last they left him to his own conscience.

What saith the Holy Spirit? Revel. xviii. 4: "Come out of Babylon, my people." But here, alas, was he who would but could not come thence, detained there in durance for thirty years together. How great his sufferings were is only known to God who permitted, his foes who inflicted, and himself who endured them, seeing no friend was allowed to speak with him alone. He died in the eighty-first year of his age, about the year of our Lord 1638.

JOHN PRIDEAUX was born [1578] at Harford in the west part of this county; bred scholar, fellow and rector of Exeter College in Oxford, canon of Christ Church, and above thirty years king's professor in that university. An excellent linguist, but so that he would make words wait on his matter, chiefly aiming at expressiveness therein; he had a becoming festivity, which was Aristotle's, not Saint Paul's Εὐτραπελία.

Admirable his memory, retaining whatever he had read. The Welsh have a proverb (in my mind somewhat uncharitable) "He that hath a good memory giveth few alms," because he keepeth in mind what and to whom he had given before. But this doctor crossed this proverb with his constant charity to all in want.

His learning was admired by foreigners, Sixtinus Amama, Rivet &c. He was not vindictive in the least degree, one intimate with him[1] having assured me that he would forgive the greatest injury upon the least show of the party's sorrow, and restore him to the degree of his former favour; and though politicians will thence collect him no prudent man, divines will conclude him a good Christian.

Episcopacy in England being grievously wounded by malevolent persons, King Charles the First conceived that the best wine and oil that could be poured into these wounds was to select persons of known learning and unblameable lives to supply the vacant bishoprics, amongst whom Dr. Prideaux was made bishop of Worcester. But alas, all in vain, such the present fury of the times.

He died of a fever, 1650 . . . He was buried at Bredon in Worcestershire, August the 15th. Such as deny bishops to be peers, would have conceived this bishop a prince, if present at his interment, such the number and quality of persons attending his funeral.

(1) Mr. Joseph Maynard, fellow of Exeter College.

SIR ARTHUR DUCK was born [1580] of wealthy parentage at Heavitree in this county. He was bred in Oxford, fellow of All Souls College, and wrote the life of Archbishop Chichele the founder thereof, in most elegant Latin. Proceeding doctor of law, he became chancellor of Wells and London, and master of the requests; designed also master of the rolls, had not an intervening accident diverted it. One of most smooth language, but rough speech, so that what the comedian saith of a fair maid in mean apparel was true of him:

ni vis boni
In ipsa inesset forma, vestes formam extinguerent.[1]

Had there not been a masculine strength in his matter, it had been marred with the disadvantage of his utterance. He died on the Lord's day, and, in effect, in the church . . . 1648, leaving a great estate to two daughters, since married to two of his name and kindred.

NATHANIEL CARPENTER, son to a minister, was born [1589] in this county; bred fellow of Exeter College in Oxford. He was right-handed in the cyclopaedia of all arts; logic, witness his *Decades;* mathematics, expressed in the book of his *Geography;* and divinity, appearing in his excellent sermons called *Achitophel.* As for his *Optics,* it had been a master-piece in that kind, if truly and perfectly printed.

I have been informed that, to his great grief, he found the written preface thereof casing Christmas pies in his printer's house (pearls are no pearls when cocks or coxcombs find them); and could never after, from his scattered notes, recover an original thereof.

He went over into Ireland, where he became chaplain to James Ussher archbishop of Armagh, and schoolmaster of the king's wards in Dublin; a place of good profit, greater credit, greatest trust; being to bring up many popish minors in the protestant religion, who under his education grew daily out of the nonage of their years and vassalage of their errors.

He died in Dublin. Robert Ussher (soon after bishop of Kildare) preached his funeral sermon, on that text, "Behold a true Israelite, wherein there is no guile;" showing how he was truly a Nathanael, God's gift; and a carpenter, a wise builder of God's house, until the dissolution of his own tabernacle, about the year 1628.

GEORGE MONCK [or MONK, FIRST DUKE OF ALBEMARLE]. Some will say he being (and long may he be) alive, belongs not to your pen, according to your premised rules. But know he is too high to come under the roof of my regulations, whose merit may make laws for me to observe. Besides, it is better that I should be censured, than he not commended. Pass we by his high birth (whereof hereafter) and hard breeding in the Low Countries, not commencing a captain *per saltum* (as many in our civil wars) but proceeding by degrees, from a private soldier, in that martial university. Pass we also by his employment in Ireland, and imprisonment in England for the king, his sea service against the Dutch,

(1) Terentius, in Phormione ["Had there not been great beauty in her very form, these trappings would have extinguished it."]

posting to speak of his last performance, which, should I be silent, would speak of itself.

Being made governor of Scotland, no power or policy of Oliver Cromwell could fright or flatter him thence. Scotland was his castle, from the top whereof he took the true prospect of our English affairs. He secured Scotland in faithful hands, to have all his foes before his face, and leave none behind his back. He entereth England with excellent foot, but his horse so lean, that they seemed tired at their first setting forth.

Now the scales began to fall down from the eyes of the English nation (as from Saul, when his sight was received) sensible that they were deluded, with the pretences of religion and liberty, into atheism and vassalage. They had learnt also from the soldiers (whom they had so long quartered) to cry out "one and all;" each shire setting forth a remonstrance of their grievances, and refusing further payment of taxes.

Lambert cometh forth out of London, abounding with more outward advantages than General Monck wanted; dragonlike he breathed out nought but fire and fury, chiefly against the church and clergy. But he met with a Saint George, who struck him neither with sword nor spear, but gave his army a mortal wound without wounding it. His soldiers dwindled away; and indeed a private person (Lambert at last was little more) must have a strong and long hand on his own account to hold a whole army together.[1]

The hinder part of the parliament sitting still at Westminster, plied him with many messengers and addresses. He returned an answer, neither granting nor denying their desires; giving them hope, too little to trust, yet too much to distrust him. He was an absolute riddle, and no ploughing with his heifer to expound him. Indeed, had he appeared what he was, he had never been what he is, a deliverer of his country. But such must be as dark as midnight who mean to achieve actions as bright as noonday.

Then he was put on the unwelcome office to pluck down the gates of London, though it pleased God that the odium did not light on him that acted, but those who employed him. Henceforward he sided effectually with the City; I say the City, which, if well or ill affected, was then able to make us a happy or unhappy nation.

Since, the honours which he first deserved have been conferred upon him, completed with the title of the duke of Albemarle and master of his majesty's horse, &c. Nor must it be forgotten that he carried the sceptre with the dove thereupon (the emblem of peace) at the king's coronation. But abler pens will improve these short memoirs into a large history. [1608-1670]

THE FAREWELL

I am most credibly informed that a rock, lately (so lately that as yet it is not named) hath been discovered by an Hamburger, being master of a

(1) "Honest John Lambert" (1619—1683) one of Cromwell's ablest major-generals, was brave, rash and, at any rate politically, short-sighted. He fought at Dunbar and Worcester; was a member of the Protector's council of state, but later quarrelled with Cromwell. When Monck declared for the parliament, he was appointed by the army to oppose Monck's advance. After the Restoration he was tried for high treason, sentenced to death but respited, and imprisoned in Guernsey for the rest of his life.

ship, who made the first report thereof, on his own oath, and the oaths of all in his company, to the corporation of seamen at the Trinity House nigh London. It lieth one league off from the Start in Devonshire. It is more than suspicious that many hundreds have here had their silent deaths, never landing to relate the cause of their destruction; for it is very dangerous for a ship that draweth above eleven or twelve foot water, if it should chance to strike upon it at a low water, with an indifferent sea. It is the more dangerous because picked[1] the form thereof, so that if you chance to heave one cast upon it, the next cast shall be no less than fourteen or fifteen fathom water.

I am sorry if the discoverer hereof met not with a proportionable reward, understanding that he had made a better bargain if he had addressed himself first to the Dutch (most bountiful in such cases) though our nation be most concerned therein. Let all ships passing thereby be fore-armed because forewarned thereof, seeing this rock can no otherwise be resisted than by avoiding.

(1) *Picked* = ? peaked.

EXETER

IT is of a circular (and therefore most capable) form, sited on the top of an hill, having an easy ascent on every side thereunto. This conduceth much to the cleanness of this city, Nature being the chief scavenger thereof, so that the rain that falleth there falleth thence by the declivity of the place. The houses stand sideways backward into their yards, and only endways with their gables towards the street. The city therefore is greater in content than appearance, being bigger than it presenteth itself to passengers through the same.

MANUFACTURES

Clothing is plied in this city with great industry and judgment. It is hardly to be believed, what credible persons attest for truth, that the return for serges alone in this city amounteth weekly (even now, when trading, though not dead, is sick) to three thousand pounds, not to ascend to a higher proportion.

But the highest commendation of this city is for the loyalty thereof; presenting us with a pair-royal of services herein, when besieged by—1. Perkin Warbeck, in the reign of King Henry the Seventh; 2. The western rebels, in the reign of King Edward the Sixth; 3. The parliament forces, in the reign of King Charles the First.

Their valour was invincible in the two first, and their loyalty unstained in the last, rewarded by their enemies with the best made and best kept articles.

THE BUILDINGS

The cathedral, dedicated to Saint Peter, is most beautiful, having the west end thereof adorned with so lively statues of stone, that they plainly speak the art of those who erected them.

There is in this city a castle, whitherto King Richard the usurper repaired, and for some days reposed himself therein. He demanded of the inhabitants how they called their castle: who returned the name thereof was Rougemont, though I confess it a rarity that the castle in a city should be called by any other name than a castle. Hereat the usurper was much abashed, having been informed by wizards that he should never prosper after he had met a thing called Rougemont. It seems Satan either spoke this oracle low or lisping, desirous to palliate his fallacy and ignorance, or that King Richard (a guilty conscience will be frighted with little) mistook the word, seeing not Rougemont, but Richmond (the title of King Henry the Seventh) proved so formidable to this usurper.

As for parish churches in this city, at my return thither this year[1] I found them fewer than I left them at my departure thence fifteen years

(1) 1661. Fuller stayed at Exeter 1644-6, when he was chaplain to the infant Princess Henrietta, daughter of Charles I, and where he was "preaching constantly to those loyal citizens," as his anonymous biographer says.

ago. But the demolishers of them can give the clearest account, how the plucking down of churches conduceth to the setting up of religion. Besides, I understand that thirteen churches were exposed to sale by the public crier, and bought by well-affected persons, who preserved them from destruction.

THE WONDERS

When the city of Exeter was besieged by the parliament's forces, so that only the south side thereof towards the sea was open unto it, incredible number of larks were found in that open quarter, for multitude like quails in the wilderness, though (blessed be God) unlike them both in cause and effect, as not desired with man's destruction, nor sent with God's anger, as appeared by their safe digestion into wholesome nourishment: hereof I was an eye and mouth witness. I will save my credit in not conjecturing any number, knowing that herein, though I should stoop beneath the truth, I should mount above belief. They were as fat as plentiful, so that being sold for twopence a dozen, and under, the poor (who could have no cheaper, as the rich no better meat) used to make pottage of them, boiling them down therein. Several natural causes were assigned hereof: 1. That these fowl, frighted with much shooting on the land, retreated to the sea-side for their refuge. 2. That it is familiar with them in cold winters (as that was) to shelter themselves in the most southern parts. 3. That some sorts of seed were lately sown in those parts, which invited them thither for their own repast. However, the Cause of causes was Divine Providence, thereby providing a feast for many poor people, who otherwise had been pinched for provision.

THE WORTHIES

BALDVINUS DEVONIUS [BALDWIN] was born in this city, of poor parentage, save that in some sort a worthy man may be said to be father to himself. His preferment increased with his learning and deserts, being first a schoolmaster, then an archdeacon, then abbot of Ford; afterwards bishop of Worcester, and lastly archbishop of Canterbury. An eloquent man and a pious preacher, according to the devotion of those days, so that the errors which he maintained may justly be accounted the faults of the times, and in him but infirmities. When King Richard the First went to Palestine, he conceived himself bound, both in conscience and credit, to partake of the pains and perils of his sovereign; whom he attended thither, but not thence, dying there, and being buried at Tyre, Anno Domini 1190.

JOSEPHUS ISCANUS [JOSEPH OF EXETER] was born in this city, anciently called Isca, from the river Isc (now named Exe) running thereby. A golden poet in a leaden age, so terse and elegant were his conceits and expressions. This our English Maro had for his Maecenas Baldwin archbishop of Canterbury.[1] But I revoke my words, and desire to turn Maro into Cornelius Nepos, under whose name the Dutchmen have lately printed a poem, made by this Josephus, *De Bello Trojano*. It soundeth much to a man's honour even to be mistaken for another man of

(1) He accompanied Baldwin to Palestine.

eminency; for though there may be much of error in the mistake, there must be something of truth in the error, especially with the judicious; yea, in such case, a general conformity betwixt the persons is not enough to build the mistake on, without some particular assimilation; as here the affinity of phrase and fancy betwixt these two poets. [*fl.* 1190]

WALTER BRONSCOMBE was son to a very mean man in this city, and therefore the more remarkable that, taking no rise from his extraction, he raised himself by his own industry to be bishop of Exeter. Here he built and endowed an hospital for poor people, and also founded a fair college at Perran in Cornwall. The angel Gabriel was very much beholden to him for instituting an annual festival unto him (observed, as I humbly conceive, only in his own cathedral, or own diocese at the most); and lest people should complain of the dearness of their devotion, he left good land to defray the cost of that solemnity. He is much blamed for compassing the manor of Bishop's Clift to his church by indirect means; to which I can say nothing, but only observe that this small city, within eighty years, did afford three eminent prelates (whereof two *Episcopi in Patria*) the natives thereof, which will scarcely be paralleled in any place of the same proportion. He died anno 1280.

WILLIAM OF EXETER was born in this city; bred a doctor of divinity in Oxford, and afterwards became canon of the cathedral in the place of his nativity. Now in his age some Franciscan friars so praised the perfection of poverty, that they touched the pope's copyhold of inheritance; for, if poverty was so essential to piety, papal pomp and plenty must needs argue profaneness. In confutation hereof this William of Exeter undertook William of Ockham, though indeed *impar congressus* betwixt them; for Exeter, a fair city, did not more exceed Ockham, a small village in Surrey, in beauty and building, than that Ockham William excelled this Exeter William in parts and learning. However, what he wanted in brains, he had in a good back to assist him; and William of Exeter, with John the three-and-twentieth pope of Rome, was able to undertake any author of that age. He flourished in the year of our Lord 1330, under the reign of King Edward the Third.

JOAN TUCKVILLE, a merchant's widow in this city, first procured the possession, then the consecration, of a parcel of ground, which she had fairly compassed about, for the interment of such as were executed at Heavitree hard by, allowing land to buy a shrine for every one of them; that such as died malefactors might be buried as men, yea, as Christians; who, having passed under the hand of justice, received a boon from her hand, who was merciful to the dead. This I may call exemplary charity indeed, as which set a copy for others, but such as hitherto hath not (to my knowledge) by any been transcribed. She died about the beginning of the reign of Queen Elizabeth.

WILLIAM [TOOKER or] TUCKER was born [1558?] in this city; bred fellow of New College in Oxford, and after became doctor in divinity, canon of Exeter, archdeacon of Barnstaple, and dean of Lichfield. The purity of his Latin pen procured his preferment, writing and dedicating a book to Queen Elizabeth, *De Charismate* (Of our kings of England their gracious healing the evil) being the best that I have seen on that subject, vindicating such cures from all imposture, unlawful magic, and from some French writers, bold usurpations, who lay claim to it as originally belonging to their kings alone: whereas, under correction, I conceive that the word sovereign, which properly importeth the supreme majesty, doth also in our English tongue, in a secondary sense, signify what is cordial to cure and heal diseases or sores, ever since such sanative power hath been annexed to the crown of England. This doctor may be said to have worn half a mitre, seeing his *congé d'élire* was signed (if not sent) to elect him bishop of Gloucester; but afterwards, by order from King James, it was revoked, on what occasion I list not to enquire.

[*d.* 1621]

WILLIAM MARTYN . . . was born [1562] in this city, and bred a student in the laws of the land. He wrote a short and clear *History of the Kings of England since the Conquest*. I have been credibly informed that King James took some exceptions at a passage therein, sounding either to the derogation of his own family or of the Scotch nation, which he took so tenderly that Mr. Martyn was brought into trouble for the same; and though he weathered out the king's displeasure, and was reconciled to his majesty, yet he never recovered his former cheerfulness. It seems that a prince's anger is a disease which though cured, is not cured, grief for the same being conceived to hasten his death, which happened [1617].

RICHARD MARTIN was born [1570] in this city, and bred partly in the court, partly in the inns of court; and at last betook himself to the study of the law.[1] He was accounted one of the highest wits of our age and his nation, King James being much delighted with his facetiousness: a quality which (with other of his abilities) commended him to be chosen recorder of London. He is eminent, as for many speeches, so especially for that he made in parliament in the tenth year of King James, when account was taken of forty gentlemen in the house which were not twenty, and some of them not sixteen years of age. "Formerly," said this Recorder Martin, "it was the custom of old men to make laws for young ones; but now nature is invaded and inverted, seeing young men enact laws to govern their fathers." He had an excellent pen, and wrote very much, and the more the pity that they are suppressed from public use. His death happened [1618].

JOHN BARKHAM [or BARCHAM], born [1572?] in this city, was bred in Corpus Christi College in Oxford, whereof he was fellow; chaplain afterwards to Archbishop Bancroft, and parson of Bocking in Essex. Much his modesty, and no less his learning, who (though never the public parent of any) was the careful nurse of many books, which otherwise had expired in their infancy, had not his care preserved them. He set forth Richard Crakanthorpe's posthume book against Spalato, and was helpful

(1) He was temporarily expelled from the Middle Temple for riotous behaviour.

to John Speed in the composing of his *English History;* yea, he wrote the whole life of the reign of King John (which is the king of all the reigns in that book, for profound penning) discoverable from the rest [on account] of the different style, and much Scripture cited therein. Mr. Guillim, in his *Heraldry,* was much beholden to this doctor's emendations.

He was a greater lover of coins than of money; rather curious in the stamps than covetous for the metal thereof. That excellent collection in Oxford library was his gift to the archbishop,[1] before the archbishop gave it to the university. He died March 25, 1642.

HENRIETTA [DUCHESS OF ORLEANS], youngest child of King Charles and Queen Mary, was born at Bedford House in this city, anno 1644, on the sixteenth day of June. After her long and sad night of affliction, the day dawned with her, in her brother's happy return. Since, she is married to the duke of Orleans. I hope that I, once related unto her as a chaplain, may ever pray for her, that her soul may be sanctified with true grace, and she enjoy both the blessings of this and a better life.[2]

[*d.* 1670]

THE FAREWELL

Malice knoweth no other heaven than to do mischief to others, though thereby no good to itself. Such the spite of the Cornish rebels besieging Exeter, who, to damnify the city, dammed and stopped up the channel of the river Exe (near to a village thence called Weare at this day) to such a degree that thereby the access of lesser vessels is much hindered, and of the greater ships wholly debarred.

Some, knowing Sir Simon Baskerville[3] (a physician and native of this place) to have a plentiful purse and public spirit, wished he would have taken the work in hand, to cure this obstruction; but it was no physician's work to meddle therewith; nor is it either powder of steel, or gilded pills, which can do the deed; but only pills of massy gold and silver; so expensive is the performance.

Indeed several acts of parliament have ordered the removal of these stoppages; but nothing is effected in this kind, these real *remoraes* remaining as before.

It is urged as an argument of Aristotle, against the conceit of Plato's having all women in common, and their children to be brought up on the public charge, that then the education of such children will be neglected; because what is every man's work is no man's work. The truth hereof appeareth in the slow avoiding of these steam-suffocations.

I could heartily wish that one act of parliament more (an eunuch, yet not barren) may be made; eunuch, that it may beget no more acts to cause the retarding and elongation of this work; yet not barren, that it may effectually remedy this grievance, and that a general good be no longer postponed to men's private profit.

(1) William Laud, archbishop of Canterbury—see Berkshire, p. 32. (2) She married the brother of Louis XIV. A patroness of Molière, Corneille and Racine, she died suddenly, possibly from poisoning, after negotiating the secret treaty of Dover. (3) 1574—1641. Physician to James I and Charles I.

DORSETSHIRE

IT hath Devonshire on the west, Somerset and Wiltshire on the north, Hampshire on the east, and the narrow sea on the south, extending from east to west about forty miles, though not past six-and-twenty the broadest part thereof.

It hath a self-sufficiency of all commodities necessary for man's temporal well-being, and needs not be beholding to any neighbouring county, for it can—1. Feed itself with fine wheat, fat flesh, dainty fowl, wild and tame, fresh fish from sea and rivers. To this meat it yieldeth that sauce without which all the rest is little worth: I mean salt, made here in some measure, but which hath been, and may be, in more abundance. 2. Clothe itself with its own wool, and broadcloth made thereof; and it is believed that no place in England affordeth more sheep in so small a compass as this county about Dorchester. And as they are provided for warmth in their woollen, so for cleanliness with their linen cloth, great store of good flax and hemp growing therein. 3. Build its own houses with good timber out of Blackmore Forest, and with (if not better, I am sure more) freestone out of Portland, most approaching that of Normandy (as in position) so in the purity thereof. Nor wanteth it veins of marble in the Isles of Purbeck. And to all this an excellent air, and the conveniency of a sea, to export for their profit, and import for their pleasure, as whose necessities were provided for before.

NATURAL COMMODITIES

Tenches

Plenty hereof are bred in the river Stour; which is so much the more observable, because generally this fish loveth ponds better than rivers, and pits better than either. It is very pleasant in taste, and is called by some the *physician* of fishes, though in my opinion may better be styled the *surgeon,* for it is not so much a disease as a wound that he cureth; nor is it any potion but a plaster which he affordeth, viz., his natural unctuous glutinousness, which quickly consolidateth any green gash in any fish.

But the pike is principally beholding unto him for cures in that kind; and some have observed that that tyrant, though never so hungry, forbeareth to eat this fish, which is his physician; not that pikes are capable (which many men are not) of gratitude, but that they are endued with a natural policy, not to destroy that which they know not how soon they may stand in need of.

Tobacco-Pipe-Clay

This is a fine clay, which will burn white (while others turn red) found in several parts of England; but so far from the sea, it will not quit cost of portage to London, save from two places: 1. *Poole,* in this county.

This wrought alone makes an hard pipe, but so shrunk and shrivelled it is unhandsome to the eye. 2. *Isle of Wight.* This wrought alone makes a fair and full pipe, but so brittle that it is unserviceable for use.

Both compounded together make these utensils both hard and handsome. This clay brought to London by ship for ballast is there worth about thirty shillings the ton.

HEMP

England hath no better than what groweth here betwixt Beaminster and Bridport, the use whereof is of absolute necessity for cordage, clothing, &c.; so that a man may admire that the seed, being so profitable, and our land affording so much strong and deep ground proper for the same, so little is sown thereof.

The rather because hemp in effect secureth itself, first against cattle, against which it is its own fence, seeing none (deer only excepted) will offer to eat thereof. Secondly, from thieves, not because it is ominous for them to steal that which is the instrument of their execution, but because much pains (which idle persons hate at their hearts) is required to reduce hemp to profit, whilst wheat and barley, left in the field, are more subject to felony, as which, when threshed, will render a present profit.

To these we may add *rubia silvestris,* wild madder, which groweth at Hod Hill in this county, on the next side of the river at Stourpaine (two miles from Blandford); at Wareham likewise, and at other places, and at a place called Somervill, near to Chappel, which, by the landing place, as ye come from Altferry to Chesil, is in great abundance. It is an assumed remedy for the yellow jaundice, openeth the obstructions of the spleen, &c.

THE BUILDINGS

The houses of the gentry herein are built rather to be lived in than to be looked on; very low in their situation (for warmth and other conveniences). Indeed the rhyme holds generally true of the English structures,

> The north for greatness, the east for health;
> The south for neatness, the west for wealth.

However, amongst the houses in this county, Lulworth Castle and Sherborne Lodge are most eminent, escaping pretty well in the late war, so that they have cause neither to brag nor complain.

PROVERBS

As much akin as Lewesdon Hill to Pilsdon Pen. That is, no kin at all. It is spoken of such who have vicinity of habitation or neighbourhood, without the least degree of consanguinity or affinity betwixt them, for these are two high hills, the first wholly, the other partly, in the parish of Broadwindsor, whereof once I was minister.[1]

Yet reader, I assure thee that seamen make the nearest relation betwixt them, calling the one the Cow, the other the Calf; in which forms, it

(1) From 1634 until 1641, when he relinquished the living.

seems, they appear first to their fancies, being eminent sea-marks to such as sail along these coasts. And although there be many hills interposing betwixt these and the sea, which seem higher to a land traveller, yet these surmount them all: so incompetent a judge, and so untrue a surveyor, is an ordinary eye of the altitude of such places.

THE WORTHIES

EDWARD [THE MARTYR], son to Eadgar king of England, was in his childhood bred under the cruel correction of Ælfthryth his mother-in-law,[1] who used for small faults to whip him with wax candles; insomuch that it is reported, it made such an impression in this young prince's memory that, when a man, he could not endure the sight of wax candles.

But Edward afterwards outgrew his mother's tuition, and succeeded his father in his throne. However, such her ambition, that, advantaged with the other's easiness of nature, she managed most matters of state, leaving her son-in-law little more than the bare title of sovereign. Not contented herewith, and to derive the sceptre to her own son Ethelred, caused him to be stabbed at Corfe Castle, in this county, coming in a civil visit unto her. His hidden body, being miraculously discovered, was first buried at Wareham, and thence removed to Shaftesbury, which town for a time was termed Saint Edward's, from his interment.

[963?-978]

THOMAS DE LA LYNDE, a gentleman of a fair estate in this county, killed a white hart in Blackmore Forest, which King Henry the Third by express will had reserved for his own chase. Hereupon a mulct was imposed upon him and the whole county (as accessory for not opposing him) which is paid, called White Hart Silver, to this day into the exchequer. Myself hath paid a share for the sauce, who never tasted any of the meat; so that it seems king's venison is sooner eaten than digested.

JOHN STAFFORD, son to Humphrey Stafford, sixth earl of Stafford, was born at Hooke in this county (then a most stately house belonging to this family) and bred a doctor of the laws in Oxford. He was afterwards dean of the Arches, and dean of Saint Martin's. This was a fair college near Aldersgate in London, founded anno 1056 by Ingelricus and Edvardus his brother; privileged by our kings of England with great immunities, the cause of many and high contests betwixt this college and the city of London. Afterwards he was made bishop of Wells, and for eighteen years (a continuance hardly to be paralleled) was chancellor of England.[2] At last he was advanced archbishop of Canterbury; and no prelate (his peer in birth and preferment) had either less good or less evil recorded of him. He died at Maidstone, 1452, and lies buried in Canterbury.

(1) Mother-in-law = step-mother. (2) The first person in English history to receive the title of 'lord chancellor'.

JOHN MORTON was born [1420?] at Saint Andrew's, Milborne, in this county, of a right worshipful family still extant therein. He was bred in Oxford, and after many mediate preferments, made bishop of Ely, anno 1479. Not long after, when many groaned under the tyranny of King Richard the Third, this prelate first found out the design of marrying Elizabeth, eldest daughter to Edward the Fourth, of the house of York, to Henry earl of Richmond, the last who was left of the line of Lancaster. Indeed the earl's title to the crown was not enough to make a countenance therewith, much less a claim thereto; but as the lady had a title, and wanted a man to manage it, the earl was man enough to manage any design, but wanted a title; and pursuing this advice, by God's blessing he gained the crown, by the name of Henry the Seventh. In expression of his gratitude, he made this bishop chancellor of England, and afterwards archbishop of Canterbury. He was a great instrument in advancing a voluntary contribution to the king through the land; persuading prodigals to part with their money, because they did spend it most, and the covetous, because they might spare it best; so making both extremes to meet in one medium, to supply the king's necessities, who, though prodigiously rich, may be said always to need, because never satisfied. This bishop, with vast cost, cut a new channel in the fens for the public good, but it neither answered his expectation nor expense. He was magnificent in his buildings, and bountiful to poor scholars, enjoining his executors to maintain twenty poor scholars in Oxford, and ten in Cambridge, twenty years after his death, which happened in September 1500.[1]

THOMAS MORE. He dwelt at Melplash in the parish of Netherbury, and by tradition is represented a very humorous person. Aged folks have informed me (whilst I lived in those parts) by report from their fathers, that this Sir Thomas whilst sheriff did, in a wild frolic, set open the prison and let loose many malefactors. Afterwards, considering his own obnoxiousness for so rash an act, he seasonably procured his pardon at court by the mediation of William Paulet, lord treasurer, and afterward marquess of Winchester; and a match was made up betwixt Mary, this sheriff's daughter and co-heir, and Sir Thomas Paulet, second son to the said lord, by whom he had a numerous issue. [*fl.* 1537?]

JOHN RUSSELL [FIRST EARL OF BEDFORD], son of James Russell, esq., was born [1486?] at Kingston Russell in this county;[2] and being bred beyond the seas, arrived at great accomplishments, and returned home about the time when Philip King of Castile (father to Charles the Fifth, emperor) was forced by foul weather into the haven of Weymouth. But "it is an ill wind that blows nobody profit"; this accident proving the foundation of Mr. Russell's preferment.

For when Sir Thomas Trenchard bountifully received this royal guest, Mr. Russell was sent for to complete the entertainment, King Philip

(1) Fuller does not mention that Morton was a Lancastrian and attainted, though the attainder was reversed after his submission following the battle of Tewkesbury. He was an assiduous builder and repairer: the "new channel in the fens" is Morton's Dyke. (2) The inheritance whereof is still possessed by his family.

taking such delight in his company, that at his departure he recommended him to King Henry the Seventh, as a person of abilities, "fit to stand before princes, and not before mean men." Indeed he was a man of spirit, carrying a badge of valour (no blemish, but a beauty) in his face, the loss of an eye at the siege of Montreuil.

King Henry the Eighth much favoured him, making him controller of the household and privy councillor; and anno 1539 created him Lord Russell, and made him keeper of the privy seal. A good share of the golden shower of abbey lands fell into his lap: two mitred ones, viz., Tavistock in Devonshire and Thorney in Cambridgeshire being conferred upon him, and at this day possessed by his posterity. King Edward the Sixth (who made him earl of Bedford) sent him down to suppress the western commotion, and relieve the besieged city of Exeter, which difficult service he performed with no less wisdom than valour, success than either. This worthy lord died in the month of March 1555, and lieth interred at Chenies in Buckinghamshire.

JAMES TURBERVILLE, or *De turbida villa,* was born of a worshipful family, who long have lived in great account in this county. First a monk, but afterwards brought up in New College in Oxford. He was consecrated bishop of Exeter, 1555, and deserved right well of that see. When he entered thereon, it was most true what his successor therein since said, "that the bishop of Exeter was a baron, but a bare one:"[1] so miserably that cathedral had been pilled and polled. But Bishop Turberville recovered some lost lands which Bishop Veysey had *vezed;*[2] and particularly, obtained of Queen Mary the restitution of the fair manor of Crediton. But who can stay what will away? It was afterwards alienated again in the reign of Queen Elizabeth.

This Bishop Turberville carries something of trouble in his name, though nothing but mildness and meekness in his nature. Hence it was that he staved off persecution from those in his jurisdiction, so that not so *many* as properly may be called *some,* suffered in his diocese. He, being deprived in the beginning of Queen Elizabeth, lived peaceably for many years in great liberty; the privacy of whose life caused the obscurity of his death, and the uncertainty of the date thereof. [*d.* 1570?]

SIR RICHARD BINGHAM was born [1528] at Melcombe Bingham in this county, of as ancient a family as any therein, having myself seen an inquisition of lands, taken out of the Tower Rolls, which William de Bingham his ancestor held in Dorsetshire in the reign of King Henry the Third. In his youth he traced most parts of the world to search for service and find fit objects for his valour. He was at the siege of Saint Quentin in France, the sacking of Leith in Scotland, served in Candia under the Venetian against the Turk; then returned into the Netherlands, being observed to be *fortis et felix* in all his undertakings. His judgment was much relied on in eighty-eight about ordering the land army in Tilbury camp.

(1) Bishop Hall, in his asserting Episcopacy. (2) "Driven away," in the dialect of the West.—F.

After long travelling, his feet were fixed in Ireland, where he was not bebogged (as some, otherwise his equals) with ill success; but, being president of Connaught, conquered and drove away O'Rourke, that most dangerous rebel.

Sir William Fitzwilliam,[1] lord deputy of Ireland, was offended at that service, though he could find no fault therewith, save that it was not done by himself. Indeed Bingham met with that which all men of merit must expect (except they will be surprised unawares): envy from others, suspecting that their own bays did wither, because his did seem so verdant. Hereupon they accused him of cruelty, to the queen and her council, who, being employed in Connaught (the very Ireland of Ireland in that age) was necessitated into severity for his own security. For this cause he was brought over into England, ousted his offices, and kept for some time in restraint; all which he, being inured to hardship, as who had not eat his bread, nor fasted neither, all in a place, bare with invincible courage.

But neglected worth will come into fashion once in seven years. Tyrone begins to trouble Munster, and none found fit for to order him but Sir Richard Bingham, who is sent over with more honour and power, marshal of Ireland, and general of Leinster, to undertake that service, whereof no doubt he had given a good account, had not death overtaken him at Dublin. Wherever buried, he hath a monument of mention in the south side of Westminster Abbey. [*d.* 1599]

ROBERT ROGERS, born at Poole in this county, was afterwards a leather-seller in London, and dying a rich bachelor, bequeathed a great part of his estate to pious uses, viz.: For the building of almshouses in Poole, £333. For the relief of poor prisoners (neither atheists nor papists) each man, at the sum of twenty nobles, £150. For poor preachers (allowing to each man ten pound) £100. To decayed artificers, charged with wife and children, £100. To the Merchant Adventurers, for the relief of old, and support of young freemen, £400. To Christ's Hospital, £500. To erect almshouses in and about London, £600. For a weekly dole of bread to the poor, £200. For the maintaining of two scholars in each university, entrusting the Leather-sellers with the managing thereof, £400.

I have only gathered the greatest clusters of his charity which the top boughs thereof did produce, purposely concealing the smaller bunches of his bounty, growing on the under branches. He died Anno Domini 1601, and lieth buried in Christ Church in London.

ARTHUR GREGORY, of Lyme in this county, had the admirable art of forcing the seal of a letter, yet so invisibly that it still appeared a virgin to the exactest beholder. Secretary Walsingham made great use of him about the packets which passed from foreign parts to Mary Queen of Scotland.[2] He had a pension paid unto him for his good service out of the Exchequer, and died at Lyme, about the beginning of the reign of King James.

(1) See Northamptonshire, p. 434. (2) An interesting sidelight on Walsingham's highly efficient secret service system.

GEORGE [SOMERS or] SUMMERS, knight, was born [1554] in or near Lyme, though on my best inquiry (living some years within seven miles of the place) I could not attain the exactness thereof. He afterwards was a successful voyager into far distant countries, and first discovered the Bermudas,[1] from and by him named the Summer Islands; a plantation, though slighted of late (whether for want of industry in the planters, or staple commodities, I know not) yet were it in the hand of the Spaniard (as by God's blessing never shall) it would be over-considerable unto us. Yea, that which now is quarrelled at for not feeding us with any provision, might then stop the mouths, yea knock out the teeth of such who now so undervalue it.

This Sir George Somers was a lamb on the land, so patient that few could anger him; and (as if entering a ship he had assumed a new nature) a lion at sea, so passionate, that few could please him. [*d.* 1610]

WILLIAM ENGLEBERT, born at Sherborne,[2] was an incomparable engineer, and much used in the eighty-eight. Queen Elizabeth (an excellent housewife of her treasure) allowed him a pension of one hundred marks per annum, which was paid him until the day of his death. He requested of King James's privy council leave to serve foreign princes and states (long peace rendering him useless in England) proffering to waive his pension on that condition; but they utterly denied him licence to depart, who lived and died in Westminster, about the year 1634.

THOMAS WINNIFFE was born [1576] at Sherborne in this county, and was bred contemporary with Doctor Hakewill in Exeter College in Oxford; and we may observe a threefold parallel betwixt these two eminent persons. First, they were fellows of the same foundation; secondly, chaplains to the same illustrious master, Prince Charles; thirdly, both out of indiscretion, at the worst (no ill intent) ran on the same rock, though not to the same degree of damage. Dr. Hakewill, for opposing the Spanish match, was unchaplained and banished the court; Dr. Winniffe, for a passage in his sermon, not against, but about Gondomar, was committed close prisoner to the Tower, and there for some days remained.[3]

During which time a great lord (who shall pass nameless) with great importunity endeavoured to beg away all his church-preferment, to dispose of at his pleasure. "No," said King James, "I mean not thus to part with the man." The lord, perceiving his suit hopeless, vowed most solemnly that he did it only to try his royal resolution, protesting that his majesty had not one of more merit amongst all his chaplains. Indeed he was observed to run (with emulation, without envy) in the race of

(1) The Bermudas were first discovered by a Spaniard, Juan de Bermudes, in 1515. They were rediscovered by Somers, who took possession of them for James I, when he was shipwrecked there in 1609. Somers was a founder of the South Virginia Company. (2) So was I informed by Mr. William Swettenham (being himself born in Sherborne) eminently known [as] an under-teller in the exchequer, who for many years paid this pension.—F. (3) George Hakewill, divine (1578—1649); built the chapel for Exeter College. Dr. Johnson's style was influenced by his writings. Gondomar was the Spanish ambassador, active to promote the marriage of Charles I (then Prince Charles) with the Spanish infanta.

virtue even with any of his order, striving to exceed them by fair industry, without offering proudly to jostle their credit, much less falsely to supplant their reputation.

He was, first, dean of Gloucester, afterwards of Saint Paul's, and lastly was chosen bishop of Lincoln, 1642, being one of those six choice persons elected *ut nutantis Episcopatus molem pietatis ac probitatis suae fulcimine sustentarent* [to support the weight of a tottering episcopate with the buttress of their piety and integrity]. All in vain, being borne down under the ruins thereof. Since, that government hath been happily resumed, and long may it flourish in its full lustre. He died Anno Domini 1654, and was buried at Lambourne in Essex, having formerly been the painful minister thereof.

SIR THOMAS RYVES, doctor of the laws, was born [1583?] at Little Langton in this county; bred in New College in Oxford; a general scholar in all polite learning, a most pure Latinist (no hair hanging at the nib of his pen); witness his most critical book of sea battles, a subject peculiar, I think, to his endeavours therein. He was at last made the king's advocate, and indeed he formerly had been advocate to the King of Heaven, in his poor ministers, in his book entituled *The Poor Vicar's Plea,* wherein much law, learning, and reason, and equity is shewn in their behalf; a grievance oftener complained of than heard, oftener heard than pitied, and oftener pitied than redressed, so unequal is the contest betwixt a poor vicar's plea and a wealthy impropriator's purse. He was a man of valour as well as of much learning, and gave good evidence thereof (though well stricken in years) in our late wars.[1] He died in his native county . . . 1652.

THE FAREWELL

And now being to take our leave of this county I should, according to our usual manner, wish it somewhat for the completing of its happiness. But it affording in itself all necessaries for man's subsistence, and being, through the conveniency of the sea, supplied with foreign commodities, I am at a loss what to beg any way additional thereunto. Yet seeing great possessions may be diminished by robbery, may the hemp (the instrument of common execution) growing herein be a constant monitor unto such who are thievishly given, whither their destructive ways tend; and mind them of that end which is due unto them, that they, leaving so bad, may embrace a better (some industrious) course of living.

(1) He fought for Charles I.

DURHAM

THIS bishopric hath Northumberland on the north (divided by the rivers Derwent and Tyne) Yorkshire on the south, the German sea on the east; and on the west (saith Mr. Speed) it is touched by Cumberland (*touched* he may well say, for it is but one mile) and Westmorland. The form thereof is triangular, the sides not much differing, though that along the sea coasts is the shortest, as not exceeding twenty-three miles. However, this may be ranked amongst the middling shires of England. And yet I can remember the time when the people therein were for some years altogether unrepresented in the parliament; namely, in the interval after their bishop was deprived of his vote in the House of Lords, and before any in the House of Commons were appointed to appear for them.[1]

THE WORTHIES

BEDE, and (because some nations measure the worth of the person by the length of the name) take his addition, Venerable. He was born [673] at Gyrwe (now called Jarrow) in this bishropric; bred under Saint John of Beverley,[2] and afterwards a monk in the town of his nativity. He was the most general scholar of that age. Let a sophister[3] begin with his axioms, a bachelor of art proceed to his metaphysics, a master to his mathematics, and a divine conclude with his controversies and comments on Scripture; and they shall find him better in all than any Christian writer in that age in any of those arts and sciences. He expounded almost all the Bible; translated the Psalms and New Testament into English; and lived a comment on those words of the apostle, "shining as a light in the world, in the midst of a crooked and perverse generation." He was no gadder-abroad, credible authors avouching that he never went out of his cell, though both Cambridge and Rome pretend to his habitation. Yet his corpse, after his death, which happened anno 735, took a journey, or rather was removed to Durham, and there enshrined.

RALPH NEVILLE was born at Raby in this bishopric; was lord chancellor under King Henry the Third (none discharging that office with greater integrity and more general commendation) and bishop of Chichester, 1222. He built a fair house from the ground in Chancery Lane, for himself and successors, for an inn, where they may repose themselves when their occasions brought them up to London.

How this house was afterwards aliened, and came into the possession of Henry de Lacy, earl of Lincoln (from whom it is called Lincoln's Inn at this day) I know not. Sure I am, that Mr. Montague (late bishop of Chichester) intended to lay claim thereunto in right of his see. But

(1) Fuller supplied no account of Natural Commodities, etc. for Durham, one of the counties left incomplete at his death. (2) See Yorkshire, p. 642. (3) At Cambridge, a student in his second or third year.

alas, he was likely to follow a cold scent (after so many years' distance) and a colder suit, being to encounter a corporation of learned lawyers so long in the peaceable possession thereof.

Bishop Neville was afterwards canonically chosen by the monks (and confirmed by King Henry the Third) archbishop of Canterbury; being so far from rejoicing thereat, that he never gave any Εὐαγγέλιον (or reward for their good news) to the two monks which brought him tidings, nor would allow anything toward the discharging their costly journey to Rome; forseeing, perchance, that the pope would stop his consecration. For some informed his holiness that this Ralph was a prelate of high birth, haughty stomach, great courtship, gracious with the king, and a person probable to dissuade him from paying the pension (promised by his father King John) to the court of Rome; and then no wonder if his consecration was stopped thereon. But was it not both an honour and happiness to our Neville thus to be crost with the hands of his holiness himself? Yea it seems that no crosier (save only that of Chichester) would fit his hand, being afterwards elected bishop of Winchester, and then obstructed by the king, who formerly so highly favoured him. He built a chapel without the east gate of Chichester, dedicated to St. Michael, and having merited much of his own cathedral, died at London, 1244.

JOHN OF DARLINGTON was born in this bishopric, at a town so called, needing no other indication than the road passing through it into Scotland. He was bred a Dominican, and a great clerk. Matthew Paris giveth him this testimony, that he was one *qui literatura pollebat excellenter et consilio* [whose erudition and counsel were quite outstanding.] King Henry the Third made him his confessor (which argueth his piety, that so devout a prince used him in so conscientious an office) and afterwards he became archbishop of Dublin in Ireland.

A person in whom king and pope met in some equal proportion, seeing he was (as we have said) confessor to the one, and to the other his collector of Peter-pence (as also to his two successors, Nicholas the Third and Martin the Fourth) through all Ireland. Many books he wrote to posterity; and returning into England, sickened, died, and was buried in Preaching Friars in London, 1284.

JOHN WYCLIFFE. It is a great honour to this small county that it produced the last maintainer of religion, before the general decay thereof; understand me, learned Bede; and the firm restorer thereof, I mean this Wycliffe, the subject of our present discourse.

True it is, his nativity cannot be demonstrated in this bishopric, but if such a *scientia media* might be allowed to man, which is beneath certainty, and above conjecture, such should I call our persuasion that Wycliffe was born therein.[1]

Now he was bred in Oxford, some say in Balliol, other more truly in Merton College; and afterwards published opinions distasteful to the

(1) Leland's statement that he was born at Hipswell, near Richmond in Yorkshire, is generally accepted.

church of Rome, writing no fewer than two hundred volumes (of all which largely in our *Church History*) besides his translating of the whole Bible into English.

He suffered much persecution from the popish clergy. Yet after long exile he, by the favour of God and good friends, returned in safety, and died in quietness at his living at Lutterworth in Leicestershire, anno 1384, the last of December; whose bones were taken up and burnt forty-two years after his death.

ALEXANDER NEVILLE, third son of Ralph Neville, was born at Raby; became first, canon, then archbishop, of York, where he beautified and fortified the castle of Cawood with many turrets. He was highly in honour with King Richard the Second, as much in hatred with the party opposing him.

These designed to imprison him (putting prelates to death not yet in fashion) in the castle of Rochester, had not our Alexander prevented them by his flight to Pope Urban to Rome, who, partly out of pity (that he might have something for his support) and more out of policy (that York might be in his own disposal upon the removal of this archbishop) translated him to Saint Andrew's in Scotland, and so dismissed him with his benediction.

Wonder not that this Neville was loath to go out of the pope's blessing into a cold sun, who could not accept this his new archbishopric, in point of credit, profit, or safety. 1. *Credit*. For this his translation was a post-ferment, seeing the archbishopric of Saint Andrew's was subjected in that age unto York. 2. *Profit*. The revenues being far worse than those of York. 3. *Safety*. Scotland then bearing an antipathy to all English (and especially to the Nevilles, redoubted for their victorious valour in those northern parts) and being in open hostility against them.

Indeed half a loaf is better than no bread; but this his new translation was rather a stone than half a loaf, not filling his belly, yet breaking his teeth, if feeding thereon. This made him prefer the pastoral charge of a parish church in Louvain before his arch-no-bishopric, where he died [1392] in the fifth year of his exile, and was buried there in the convent of the Carmelites.

ROBERT NEVILLE [*b.* 1404], fifth son of Ralph first earl of Westmorland by Joan his second wife, daughter of John of Gaunt, bred in the university of Oxford, and provost of Beverley, was preferred bishop of Salisbury in the sixth of King Henry the Sixth, 1427.

During his continuance therein, he was principal founder of a convent at Sonning in Berkshire (anciently the bishops' see of that diocese) valued at the Dissolution (saith Bishop Godwin) at £682 14s. 7d. ob., which I rather observe, because the estimation thereof is omitted in my (and I suspect all other) Speed's Catalogue of Religious Houses.

From Salisbury he was translated to Durham, where he built a place called the Exchequer, at the Castle gate, and gave (in allusion to his two bishoprics, which he successively enjoyed) two annulets innected in his paternal coat. He died Anno Domini 1457.

GEORGE NEVILLE, fourth son of Richard Neville earl of Salisbury, was born [1433?] at Middleham in this bishopric; bred in Balliol College in Oxford; consecrated bishop of Exeter when he was not as yet twenty years of age; so that in the race, not of age, but youth, he clearly beat Thomas Arundel,[1] who at twenty-two was made bishop of Ely. Some say this was contrary not only to the canon law, but canonical scripture; Saint Paul forbidding such a neophyte or novice admission into that office; as if because Richard, the make-king earl of Warwick, was in a manner above law, this his brother also must be above canons. His friends do plead that nobility and ability supplied age in him, seeing five years after, at twenty-five, he was made lord chancellor of England, and discharged it to his great commendation.

He was afterwards made archbishop of York, famous for the prodigious feast at his installing, wherein, besides flesh, fish and fowl, so many strange dishes of jellies.

But the inverted proverb found truth in him, "One glutton meal makes many hungry ones," for some years after, falling into the displeasure of King Edward the Fourth, he was slenderly dieted, not to say famished, in the castle of Calais; and being at last restored by the intercession of his friends, died heartbroken at Blyth, and was buried in the cathedral of York, 1476.

CICELY NEVILLE DUCHESS OF YORK. Though her nativity cannot be fixed with any assurance (whose father's vast estate afforded him a mansion-house for every week in the year); yet is she here placed with most probability, Raby being the prime place of the Nevilles' residence. She may pass for the clearest instance of human frail felicity.

Her happiness. Shs was youngest daughter and child to Ralph earl of Westmorland (who had one and twenty); and exceeded her sisters in honour, being married to Richard duke of York.[2]

She was blessed with three sons (who lived to have issue) each born in a several kingdom: Edward, at Bordeaux, in France; George, at Dublin in Ireland; Richard, at Fotheringhay in England. She beheld her eldest son Edward king of England, and enriched with a numerous posterity.[3]

Her miseries. She saw her husband killed in battle; George duke of Clarence, her third son, cruelly murdered; Edward, her eldest son, cut off by his own intemperance in the prime of his years; his two sons butchered by their uncle Richard, who himself, not long after, was slain at the battle of Bosworth.

She saw her own reputation murdered publicly at Paul's Cross, by the

(1) See Sussex, p. 566. (2) Fuller gives no account of this strange and forceful figure (1411-60) who so much disturbed Henry VI's reign. After serving Henry in France he was virtually banished to Ireland, forced his way back, and was in 1454 elected protector in one of Henry's fits of insanity. Next year, the protectorate being revoked, he was driven from power. He defeated the royal forces in battle, was again proclaimed protector and again discharged, being attainted a few years later. He openly claimed the crown, obtained a promise of it, and was yet again made protector. Soon after he fell in battle. (3) There were four sons, two of whom became kings of England: the eldest became Edward IV; the second, Edmund, earl of Rutland, was killed with his father at Wakefield; the third was George, duke of Clarence; and the youngest became Richard III.

procurement of her youngest son Richard taxing his eldest brother for illegitimate.[1]

Yet our chronicles do not charge her with elation in her good, or dejection in her ill success; an argument of an even and steady soul in all alterations. Indeed she survived to see Elizabeth her grandchild married to King Henry the Seventh; but little comfort accrued to her by that conjunction, the party of Yorkists were so depressed by him.

She lived five and thirty years a widow, and died in the tenth year of King Henry the Seventh, 1495, and was buried by her husband in the quire of the collegiate church of Fotheringhay in Northamptonshire; which quire being demolished in days of King Henry the Eighth, their bodies lay in the churchyard without any monument, until Queen Elizabeth, coming thither in progress, gave order that they should be interred in the church, and two tombs to be erected over them. Hereupon their bodies, lapped in lead, were removed from their plain graves, and their coffins opened. The Duchess Cicely had about her neck, hanging in a silver ribband, a pardon from Rome, which, penned in a very fine Roman hand, was as fair and fresh to be read as if it had been written but yesterday. But alas, most mean are their monuments, made of plaister, wrought with a trowel; and no doubt there was much daubing therein, the queen paying for a tomb proportionable to their personages. The best is, the memory of this Cicely hath a better and more lasting monument, who was a bountiful benefactress to Queens' College in Cambridge.

WILLIAM [SENHOUSE OR] SEVER was born at Shincliffe in this bishopric, where his father was a siveyer or sieve-maker; and I commend his humility in retaining his father's trade for his surname, to mind him of his mean extraction. He was bred in Merton College, whereof he became warden, and provost of Eton, and afterwards bishop of Carlisle, 1495, whence five years after he was translated to Durham. His surname, so contemptible in English, sounds imperially and episcopally when Latinized; in which language he is rendered Gulielmus Severus, severity well agreeing with the gravity of his function. He died Anno Domini 1505.

All I will add is this, that England neither before nor since saw two sieve-makers' sons at the same juncture of time advanced to so high a dignity, this William in the church, Sir Richard Empson[2] in the commonwealth.

ROBERT HORNE was born [1519?] in this bishopric, bred in Saint John's College in Cambridge. Going thence, under the reign of King Edward the Sixth, he was advanced dean of Durham. In the Marian days he fled into Germany; and fixing at Frankfort, became the head of the episcopal party, as in my *Church History* at large doth appear.

Returning into England, he was made bishop of Winchester, Feb. 16, 1560. A worthy man, but constantly ground betwixt two opposite parties, papists and sectaries. Both of these in their pamphlets sported with his

(1) See note 2, p. 292. (2) See Northamptonshire, p. 432.

name, as hard in nature, and crooked in conditions; not being pleased to take notice, how *horn* in Scripture importeth power, preferment and safety, both twitted his person as dwarfish and deformed; to which I can say nothing (none alive remembering him) save that such taunts, though commonly called *ad hominem,* are indeed *ad Deum;* and though shot at man, does glance at "Him who made us, and not we ourselves." Besides, it shews their malice runs low for might (though high for spite) who carp at the *case* when they cannot find fault with the *jewel.* For my part, I mind not the mould wherein, but the metal whereof he was made, and listen to Mr. Camden's character of him, *Valido et foecundo ingenio* (of a sprightful and fruitful wit). He died in Southwark, June 1, 1580; and lieth buried in his own cathedral, near to the pulpit.

RICHARD COSIN, doctor of law, was born [1549?] at Hartlepool (a well known harbour for the safety); and some observe a providence, that he who afterwards was to prove the grand champion of episcopacy, should (amongst all the counties of England) be born in this bishopric. His father was a person of quality, a captain of a company at Musselburgh field, whence his valour returned with victory and wealth, when, crossing the River Tweed (oh, the uncertainty of all earthly happiness!) was drowned therein, to the great loss of his son Richard; and greater, because he was not sensible thereof, as left an infant in the cradle.

His mother afterwards married one Mr. Medhope, a Yorkshire gentleman, who bred this his son-in-law[1] at a school at Skipton in the Craven, wherein such his proficiency that before he was twelve years old (little less than a wonder to me in that age, from so far a country) he was admitted in Trinity College in Cambridge. Some of his friends in Queens' College in that university had a design to fetch him thence, had not Doctor Beaumont prevented the plot, in making him scholar and fellow as soon as by his age, degree, and the statutes, he was capable thereof.

He was a general scholar, geometrician, musician, physician, divine, but chiefly civil and canon lawyer. By Archbishop Whitgift he was preferred to be first, chancellor of Worcester, in that age a place *non tam gratiosus quam negotiosus* [for business rather than pleasure]; and afterwards dean of the Arches, wherein he carried himself without giving (though many took) offence at him.

Of these one wrote a book against him called the *Abstract* (abstracted, saith my author, from all wit, learning and charity); to whom he returned such an answer, in the defence of the high commission, and oath *ex officio,* that he put his adversary to silence.

He gave forty pound to the building of a chamber in Trinity College, and fifteen pound per annum for the maintenance of two scholarships therein: a good gift out of his estate, who left not above fifty pound a year clear to his heir; a great argument of his integrity, that he got no more in so gainful a place. Dying at Doctors Commons, he was buried, by his own appointment, in Lambeth church, and Doctor Andrews preached his funeral sermon. [*d.* 1597]

(1) *Son-in-law* = step-son.

ANTHONY LORD GREY, and eighth earl of Kent of that surname, son of George Grey, esq., and Margery Salvaine his wife, son to Anthony Grey, esq., and Bridget Holland his wife, son to George Grey second earl of Kent of that family (who died in the twentieth year of King Henry the Seventh) was born [1557] at Brancepeth in this bishopric.[1] If any ask what occasion drew his ancestors into the north, know that his grandfather was invited thither to enjoy the company of his friend and kinsman, the earl of Westmorland.

This gentleman being bred in the university of —— applied himself to the study of divinity, and became rector of Aston Flamville in Leicestershire, where he preached constantly, and kept an hospitable house for the poor according to his estate. It happened that, by the death of Henry Grey, his kinsman and the seventh earl of Kent, that earldom descended upon him, Anno Domini 1639.

After the accession of his title [he] did not in the least degree disdain the society of his fellow ministers to converse with the nobility; yea, he abated nothing in the constancy of his preaching, so long as he was able to be led up into the pulpit. He was summoned as a peer to parliament, but excused himself by reason of indisposition and age. Such his humility, that honours did not change manners in him. Thus a mortified mind is no more affected with additions of titles, than a corpse with a gay coffin. By Magdalen his wife he had (besides other children) Henry, ninth earl of Kent. He died Anno Domini 1643.

SAMUEL WARD was born at Bishop Middleham in this county, his father being a gentleman of more ancientry than estate. He was, first, scholar of Christ's, then fellow of Emmanuel, and afterwards master of Sidney College in Cambridge, and Margaret professor therein for above twenty years.

He turned with the times, as a rock riseth with the tide, and, for his uncomplying therewith, was imprisoned in Saint John's College in Cambridge. In a word, he was counted a puritan before these times, and popish in these times; and yet, being always the same, was a true protestant at all times. He died anno 1643, and was the first man buried in Sidney College chapel.[2]

THOMAS JACKSON, born [1579] of a good family in this county, was designed to be a merchant in Newcastle, till his parents were diverted by Ralph Lord Eure and persuaded to make him a scholar. He was admitted first in Queen's College in Oxford, and then became candidate of a fellowship in Corpus Christi; knowing of the election but the day before, he answered to admiration, and was chosen by general consent.

Soon after, in all likelihood, he lost his life, being drowned in the river, and taken out rather for desire of decent burial, than with hope of any recovery. He was wrapped in the gowns of his fellow-students (the best shroud which present love and need could provide him); and,

(1) Out of his private pedigree communicated unto me. (2) He was one of the translators of the Apocrypha in the Authorized Version; and master of Sidney Sussex when Fuller was there

being brought home to the college, was revived, by God's blessing on the care of Doctor Chenil, equally to all people's joy and admiration. His gratitude to the fishermen, who took him up, extended to a revenue unto them during his life. Thus thankful to the instrument, he was more to the principal, striving to repay his life to that God who gave it him.

He was afterwards vicar of Newcastle, a factor for heaven in the place where he was designed a merchant, a town full of men and opinions, wherein he endeavoured to rectify their errors and unite their affections. At this distance was he chosen president of Corpus Christi College, never knowing of the vacancy of the place, till by those letters which informed him it was refilled with his election.

Here he lived piously, ruled peaceably, wrote profoundly, preached painfully. His charity had no fault, if not of the largest size, oftentimes making the receiver richer than it left him that was the donor thereof. [*d.* 1640]

JOHN COSIN, D.D., was born [1594] in the city of Norwich;[1] bred in Caius College in Cambridge, whereof he was fellow. Hence he was removed to the mastership of Peterhouse in the same university. One whose abilities, quick apprehension, solid judgment, variety of reading, &c., are sufficiently made known to the world in his learned books, whereby he hath perpetuated his name to posterity.

I must not pass over his constancy in his religion, which rendereth him amiable in the eyes not of good men only, but of that God with whom there is no variableness, nor shadow of changing. It must be confessed that a sort of fond people surmised as if he had once been declining to the popish persuasion. Thus the dim-sighted complain of the darkness of the room, when alas, the fault is in their own eyes; and the lame of the unevenness of the floor, when indeed it lieth in their unsound legs. Such were the silly folk (their understandings, the eyes of their minds, being darkened, and their affections, the feet of their soul, made lame by prejudice) who have thus falsely conceited of this worthy doctor.

However if any thing that I delivered in my *Church History* (relating therein a charge drawn up against him for urging of some ceremonies, without inserting his purgation, which he effectually made, clearing himself from the least imputation of any fault) hath any way augmented this opinion, I humbly crave pardon of him for the same.

Sure I am, were his enemies now his judges (had they the least spark of ingenuity) they must acquit him, if proceeding according to the evidence of his writing, living, disputing. Yea, whilst he remained in France, he was the Atlas of the protestant religion, supporting the same with his piety and learning, confirming the wavering therein, yea, daily adding proselytes (not of the meanest rank) thereunto.

Since the return of our gracious sovereign, and the reviving of swooning episcopacy, he was deservedly preferred bishop of Durham. And here

(1) It was no doubt inadvertently that Fuller placed a native of Norwich in this county.

the reader must pardon me, if willing to make known my acquaintance with so eminent a prelate. When one in his presence was pleased with some propositions, wherein the pope condescended somewhat to the protestants, he most discreetly returned, in my hearing, "We thank him not at all for that which God hath always allowed us in his Word;" adding withal, "He would allow it us so long as it stood with his policy, and take it away so soon as it stood with his power." And thus we take our leave of this worthy prelate, praying for his long life, that he may be effectual in advancing the settlement of our yet distracted church. [*d.* 1672]

THE FAREWELL

I understand that there is an intention of erecting an university in Durham,[1] and that some hopeful progress is made in order thereunto, which I cannot but congratulate; for I listen not to their objection, alleging it monstrous for one face to have three eyes (one land three universities); seeing I could wish that, Argus-like, it had an hundred in it. Would all men were Moses-minded, "that all the people of God might prophesy;" the rather because I am sure that ignorance is no more the mother of devotion, than the lying harlot, which pleaded before Solomon, was mother to the living child.

I confess I was always much affected with their fears, who suspect that this convenience for the north would be a mischief for the south, and this new one in process of time prove detrimental to the old universities. Nor were these jealousies, when moved, removed in my serious consideration, not being well satisfied of the intentions and design of some prime persons undertaking the same.

But, since this freshman college lived not to be matriculated, much less (not lasting seven years) graduated, God in his wisdom seeing the contrary fitter; the worst I should have wished this new spring (if continuing) was pure water, pious and orthodox professors, to have principled and elemented the members therein with learning and religion.

(1) The letters patent were taken out under Cromwell, but the university was not founded until 1832.

ESSEX

ESSEX hath Kent on the south, divided by the river Thames; Suffolk on the north, served by the river Stour; Cambridge, Hertfordshire and Middlesex on the west, the two latter generally parted by the river Lea; and the German Ocean on the east.

A fair county, bearing the full proportion and five and thirty miles square, plentifully affording all things necessary to man's subsistence, save that the eastern part is not very healthful in the air thereof.

Those parts adjoining to the sea are commonly called the Hundreds of Essex, and are very fruitful in cattle. However, the vulgar wits of this county much astonish strangers with the stock of poor people in these parts: five 'hundred' cows, nine 'hundred' sheep, which indeed are but five cows, and nine sheep, in this part of the county called the Hundreds.

NATURAL COMMODITIES

Saffron

Plenty hereof in this county, growing about Walden, a fair market town, which saffron may seem to have coloured with the name thereof. It is called (as Serapione affirmeth) *sahafaran* by the Arabians, whence certainly our English word is derived. In itself it is a most admirable cordial; and, under God, I owe my life, when sick of the smallpox,[1] to the efficacy thereof.

No precious drug is more adulterated with *cartamus,* the inward pilling of willow, and generally all yellow flowers, when it is brought in great parcels, which ought to quicken the care of chapmen herein. In a word, the sovereign power of genuine saffron is plainly proved by the antipathy of the crocodiles thereunto: for the crocodile's tears are never true, save when he is forced where saffron groweth (whence he hath his name of **Χροκο-δειλος,** or the saffron-fearer) knowing himself to be all poison, and it all antidote.

Oysters

The best in England, fat, salt, green-finned, are bred near Colchester, where they have an excellent art to feed them in pits made for the purpose. King James was wont to say, he was a very valiant man who first adventured on eating of oysters. Most probably mere hunger put men first on that trial. Thus necessity hath often been the purveyor to provide diet for delicacy itself; famine making men to find out those things which afterwards proved not only wholesome, but delicious. Oysters are the only meat which men eat alive, and yet account it no cruelty. Sometimes pearls, considerable both in bulk and brightness, have been found within them.

(1) When Fuller was curate of Waltham Abbey.

HOPS

In Latin *lupulus,* or the little wolf, which made a merry man complain that this wolf did too often devour the innocent malt in beer. Gerard observes they grow best in those countries where vines will not grow, intimating that Nature pointeth at their use therein.

They are not so bitter in themselves as others have been against them, accusing hops for noxious; preserving beer, but destroying those who drink it. These plead the petition presented in parliament in the reign of King Henry the Sixth, against the "wicked weed" called hops. Their back-friends also affirm, the stone never so epidemical in England, as since the general reception and use of hops in the beginning of King Henry the Eighth.

But hops have since outgrown and overtopped all these accusations, being adjudged wholesome, if statutable and "unmixed with any powder, dust, dross, sand, or other soil whatsoever,"[1] which made up two parts of three in foreign hops formerly imported hither.

They delight most in moist grounds. No commodity starteth so soon and sinketh so suddenly in the price; whence some will have them so named from hopping in a little time betwixt a great distance in valuation. In a word, as elephants, if orderly, were themselves enough alone to gain, if disorderly, to lose a victory; so great parcels of this commodity, well or ill bought, in the crisis of their price, are enough to raise or ruin an estate.

PEWITS

There is an island of some two hundred acres, near Harwich, in the parish of Little Oakley, in the manor of Matthew Gilly, esquire, called the Pewit Island, from pewits, in effect the sole inhabitants thereof. Some affirm them called in Latin *upupae,* whilst others maintain that the Roman language doth not reach the name, nor land afford the bird. On Saint George's day precisely they pitch on the island, seldom laying fewer than four, or more than six eggs.[2]

Great their love to their young ones, for, though against foul weather they make to the mainland (a certain prognostic of tempests) yet they always weather it out in the island when hatching their young ones, seldom sleeping whilst they sit on their eggs (afraid, it seems, of spring-tides) which signifieth nothing as to securing their eggs from the inundation, but is an argument of their great affection.

Being young, they consist only of bones, feathers and lean-flesh, which hath a raw gust of the sea. But poulterers take them then, and feed them with gravel and curds (that is, physic and food); the one to scour, the other to fat them in a fortnight, and their flesh thus recruited is most delicious.

Here I say nothing of eryngo roots[3] growing in this county, the candying of them being become a staple commodity at Colchester. These are sovereign to strengthen the nerves, and pity it is that any vigour acquired by them should be otherwise employed than to the glory of God.

(1) See the statute, 1 Jacobi, cap. 18. (2) So am I informed by Captain Farmer, of Newgate Market, copyholder of the island. (3) *Eryngo root*=candied root of the sea holly.

THE MANUFACTURES

This county is charactered like the good wife described by Bathsheba, "She layeth her hand to the spindle, and her hands hold the distaff." *Baize,* and *says,*[1] and *serges,* and several sorts of stuffs, which I neither can nor do desire to name, are made in and about Colchester, Coggleshall, Dedham, &c. I say, desire not to name, because hoping that new kinds will daily be invented (as good reason) and by their inventors intituled. I know not whether it be better to wish them good wares to vent, or good vent for their wares, but I am sure that both together are the best. It will not be amiss to pray that the plough may go along, and wheel around; that so, being fed by the one and clothed by the other, there may be, by God's blessing, no danger of starving in our nation.

GUNPOWDER

Why hereof in this, rather than in other counties? Because more made by mills of late erected on the River Lea, betwixt Waltham and London, than in all England besides. Though some suppose it as ancient as Archimedes in Europe (and ancienter in India) yet generally men behold the friar of Metz the first founder thereof, some three hundred years since.[2] It consisteth of three essential ingredients: 1. *Brimstone,* whose office is to catch fire and flame of a sudden, and convey it to the other two; 2. *Charcoal* pulverized, which continueth the fire and quencheth the flame, which otherwise would consume the strength thereof; 3. *Saltpetre,* which causeth a windy exhalation, and driveth forth the bullet.

This gunpowder is the emblem of politic revenge, for it biteth first, and barketh afterwards, the bullet being at the mark before the report is heard; so that it maketh a noise, not by way of warning, but triumph. As for white powder, which is reported to make no report at all, I never could meet with artist who would seriously avouch it; for, though perchance the noise may be less and lower, yet no sound at all is inconsistent with the nature of saltpetre, and the ventosity[3] thereof, causing the violent explosion of the bullet. It is questionable, whether the making of gunpowder be more profitable or more dangerous, the mills in my parish having been five times blown up within seven years, but blessed be God, without the loss of any one man's life.

THE BUILDINGS

This county hath no cathedral, and the churches therein cannot challenge to themselves any eminent commendation. But as for private houses, Essex will own no shire her superior; whereof three most remarkable: 1. Audley End, built by Thomas Howard, earl of Suffolk and treasurer of England, as without compare the best subject's house in this island. Yet is the structure better than the standing thereof, as low on one side, so that it may pass for the emblem of modest merit, or concealed worth; meaner houses boasting more, and making greater show

(1) *Say*=cloth of fine texture resembling serge. (2) Berthold Schwartz, sometimes, but wrongly, considered to be the inventor of gunpowder, *c.* 1354. (3) *Ventosity*= generation of gases.

afar off in the eyes of passengers. 2. New Hall, built by the Radcliffes, earls of Sussex, but bought from them by George Villiers duke of Buckingham; surpassing for the pleasant shady approach thereunto and for the appurtenances of parks round about it. 3. Copt Hall (in records Coppice Hall, from the woods thereabouts) highly seated on a hill in the midst of a park, built by the abbot of Waltham, enlarged by Sir Thomas Heneage and others; and it is much that multiform fancies should all meet in so uniform a fabric. Herein a gallery, as well furnished as most, more proportionable than any in England.

PROVERBS

Essex calves. A learned author[1] telleth us that Italy was so called, *quasi vitulae,* because the best calves were bred therein. Sure this will be condemned as a far-fetched and forced deduction, but if true, Essex may better pretend to the name of Italy, producing calves of the fattest, fairest and finest flesh in England, and consequently in all Europe; and let the butchers in Eastcheap be appealed unto as the most competent judges therein. Sure it is a Cumberland cow may be bought for the price of an Essex calf, in the beginning of the year. Let me add that it argueth the goodness of flesh in this county, and that great gain was got formerly by the sale thereof, because that so many stately monuments were erected anciently therein for butchers (inscribed *carnifices* in their epitaphs) in Coggeshall, Chelmsford church and elsewhere, made of marble, inlaid with brass (befitting, saith my author,[2] a more eminent man) whereby it appears that these of that trade have in this county been richer (or at least prouder) than in other places.

The weavers' beef of Colchester. These are sprats caught hereabouts, and brought hither in incredible abundance, whereon the poor weavers (numerous in this city) make much of their repast, cutting rands,[3] rumps, sirloins, chines and all joints of beef out of them, as lasting in season well nigh a quarter of a year. They are the minims of the sea, and their cheapness is the worst thing (well considered the best) which can be said of them. Were they as dear, they would be as toothsome (being altogether as wholesome) as anchovies, for then their price would give a high gust unto them in the judgment of palate-men. True it is that within these last sixteen years, better men than weavers have been glad of worse meat than sprats (and thankful to God if they could get it) in the city of Colchester.

He may fetch a flitch of bacon from Dunmow. This proverb dependeth on a custom practised in the priory of Dunmow, which was founded, saith Speed, by Juga, a noble lady, anno 1104, for Black Nuns. But it seems afterwards the property thereof was altered into a male monastery; the mortified men wherein were mirthful sometimes, as hereby may appear.

Any person, from any part of England, coming hither, and humbly kneeling on two stones at the church door (which are yet to be seen) before

(1) Festus, lib. ix. See Mercator's Atlas.—F. (2) Weever's *Funeral Monuments.*
(3) *Rands* = strips or long slices.

the prior or convent, might demand, at his own pleasure, a gammon or flitch of bacon, upon the solemn taking of the ensuing oath:

> You shall swear by the custom of our confession,
> That you never made any nuptial transgression,
> Since you were married man and wife,
> By household brawls, or contentious strife;
> Or otherwise, in bed or at board,
> Offended each other in deed or word:
> Or since the parish clerk said Amen,
> Wished yourselves unmarried again;
> Or, in a twelve-month and a day,
> Repented not in thought any way;
> But continued true and in desire,
> As when you join'd hands in holy quire.
> If to these conditions, without all fear,
> Of your own accord you will freely swear;
> A gammon of bacon you shall receive,
> And bear it hence with love and good leave.
> For this is our custom at Dunmow well known,
> Though the sport be ours, the bacon's your own.

It appeareth in an old book on record[1] that Richard Wright of Badesnorth in Norfolk, in the twenty-third of Henry the Sixth, when John Canon was prior; that Stephen Samuel, of Little Easton in Essex, the seventh of Edward the Fourth, when Roger Rullcot was prior; and that John Ley, of Coggeshall in Essex, the second of Henry the Eighth, when John Taylor was prior, demanded their bacon on the premises, and received it accordingly.

THE BATTLES

Though none in this county (the heart of the eastern association) yet the siege, anno 1648, of Colchester must not be forgotten. Know then that the remnant of the royalists routed in Kent with much difficulty recovered this county, the parliament's forces pursuing them. March much farther they could not, such their weariness and want of accommodation; bid battle to their numerous foes they durst not, which was to run in the jaws of ruin; wherefore they resolved to shelter themselves for a time in Colchester.

Reader, pardon a digression. Winchester castle was by the Long Parliament ordered to be made *untenable;* but the over-officious malice of such who executed the order (wilfully mistaking the word) made it *untenantable.* To apply the distinction to Colchester, all men beheld it as tenantable, full of fair houses, none as tenable in an hostile way for any long time against a great army.

But see what diligence can do. In few days they fortified it even above imagination. Indeed the lining of the wall was better than the facing thereof, whose stone outside was ruinous, but the inside was well filled up with earth, which they valiantly maintained. Nor was it General Fairfax they feared so much as general famine, that grand conqueror of cities; having too much of the best sauce, and too little of the worst meat; insomuch that they were fain to make mutton of those creatures which kill

(1) Now in the possession of the earl of Warwick.—F.

sheep, and beef of cattle which never wore horns, till they were forced to submit to the worst (but best they could get) of conditions.

Here those two worthy knights, Sir Charles Lucas and Sir George Lisle (the one eminently a whole troop of horse, the other a company of foot) were cruelly sentenced, and shot to death; whose bodies have since had a civil resurrection, restored to all possible outward honour by public funeral solemnities.

THE WORTHIES

SAINT OSYTH. She was the daughter to the king of the East Angles, and wife to Sighere last king of East Saxons; by whose consent forsaking the world, she was veiled, and at last became abbess of a monastery of her own founding at Chich [Saint Osyth] in this county; until the Danes, infesting these sea coasts, cut off her head in hatred of religion.

Yet this her head, after it was cut off, was carried by Saint Osyth (oh wonder! oh lie!) three furlongs; and then she fell down and died.

[*fl.* 7th cent.?]

SAINT NEOT (why surnamed Adulphus I know not) was born, saith Bale, either in Essex or Kent; but Pits, who wrote sixty years after him, saith positively he was born in Essex. It seemeth he met with some evidence to sway down the even beam to preponderate on the side of this county. Waiving the pleasures of the world, he lived long an eremite in Cornwall, and then, leaving his solitary life, he became a painful and profitable preacher of the gospel. He was a Zaccheus for his stature, and with him, tall in piety and charity. He moved King Alfred to found, or restore, the university of Oxford, on which account his memory is sacred to all posterity. He died Anno Domini 877, whose body was buried by one Barry, his scholar, in Eynesbury, since St. Neot's, in Huntingdonshire, and some say, was afterwards removed to the abbey of Crowland.

GERVASE OF TILBURY, born at that village in this county (since famous for a camp against the Spaniards in '88) is reported nephew to King Henry the Second. But, though Nepos be taken in the latitude thereof (to signify son to brother, sister or child) I cannot make it out by the door, and am loth to suspect his coming in by the window. This Gervase may be said, by his nativity, to stand but on one foot (and that on tip-toes) in England, being born on the seaside, at the mouth of Thames; and therefore no wonder if he quickly conveyed himself over into foreign parts. He became courtier and favourite to his kinsman Otho the fourth emperor, who conferred on him the marshalship of the archbishopric of Arles (which proveth the imperial power in this age over some parts of Provence); an office which he excellently discharged. Though his person was wholly conversant in foreign air, his pen was chiefly resident on English earth, writing a chronicle of our land, and also adding illustrations to Geoffrey of Monmouth. He flourished, anno 1211, under King John.

ROBERT FITZWALTER. It is observable what I read in my author,[1] that in the reign of King John there was three most eminent knights in the

(1) Stow's *Annals*.

land famous for their prowess, viz., Robert Fitzroger, Richard de Montfichet, and this Robert Fitzwalter; two of which three (a fair proportion) fall to be natives of this county.

This Robert was born at Woodham Walter; and behaved himself right valiantly on all occasions, highly beloved by King Richard the First and King John, until the latter banished him the land, because he would not prostitute his daughter to his pleasure.[1] But worth will not long want a master. The French king joyfully entertained him, till King John recalled him back again, on this occasion: five years' truce being concluded betwixt the two crowns of England and France, an Englishman challenged any of the French to joust a course or two on horseback with him, whom Fitzwalter (then on the French party) undertook and at the first course with his great spear felled horse and man to the ground. Thus then and ever since Englishmen generally can be worsted by none but Englishmen. Hereupon the king next day sent for him, restored his lands, with licence for him to repair his castles (and particularly Baynard's Castle in London) which he did accordingly. He was styled of the common people, "The marshal of God's army and holy church." He died Anno Domini 1235, and lieth buried in the priory of Little Dunmow.

MATILDA FITZWALTER, by some surnamed The Fair, by others The Chaste (qualities admirable when united) was daughter to that strenuous knight, Sir Robert Fitzwalter, of Woodham Walter in this county, of whom before.

Some would persuade us that as the Trojan war was occasioned by Helena in revenge of her wantonness, so the barons' war in the reign of King John by this Matilda, in reward of her chastity, which the king in vain did assault; though surely the same was too private and personal to cause a national engagement; especially the fact being only attempted, not effected.

The king banishing her father beyond the seas (in hope by his absence the easier to compass his desires) renewed his suit with more earnestness, and the same success. For Matilda still answered her anagram, "Tal Maid," both in stature and stoutness of her virtuous resolution; till at last the king, *quia noluit consentire, toxicavit eam* [because she would not consent, poisoned her] procuring one to poison her in a poached egg; meat which in the shell may safely be eaten after a sluttish, out of it, not after a malicious hand.

I much admire she was not made a saint (a dignity in those days conferred on some of less desert) and conceive she had surely been sainted if veiled, and found the less favour for being no votary, but a virgin at large. She was murdered 1213, and lieth buried betwixt two pillars in

(1) And she was supposed also to be murdered by John, but this is legendary (see the amusing account of Matilda Fitzwalter and this episode which follows below). Fitzwalter's daughter was one Christina, who married William Mandeville, earl of Essex. Fitzwalter was exiled for conspiring against John. He was one of the 25 parties who executed Magna Carta, after which he offered the crown to the dauphin. He was defeated and captured at Lincoln in 1217. He joined the fifth crusade, and after his return submitted to the government of Henry III.

the quire of Little Dunmow church. I have nothing to add to this story, save to observe that he who procured her poisoning in her meat was poisoned in his own drink afterwards.

RICHARD DE BARKING took his name (according to the clergymen's heraldry in that age) from that well-noted town in this county. In process of time he became abbot of Westminster for twenty-four years. He was so high in favour with King Henry the Third that he made him one of his special councillors, chief baron of the exchequer, and for a short time lord treasurer of England. He died anno 1246, buried in Westminster church, whose marble tomb, before the middle of the altar, was afterwards pulled down (probably because taking up too much room) by Friar Combe, sacrist of the house, who laid a plain marble stone over him, with an epitaph too tedious and barbarous to be transcribed.

RICHARD BADEW, born of a knightly family at Great Badew (commonly called Great Baddow, nigh Chelmsford) was bred in the university of Cambridge. He so profited in literature that by general consent, anno 1326, the scholars therein chose him their chancellor, in which year this Richard purchased two tenements in Milne Street, and in their place erected a small college, by the name of University Hall, wherein scholars living under a principal had their chambers gratis (a great favour in that age) though otherwise maintaining themselves on their own expenses.

Sixteen years after, by a sad accident, this college was casually burnt down to the ground, whereupon Doctor Badew, with the consent of the university, resigned all his interest therein into the hands of Elizabeth countess of Clare, who fairly refounded this college, as in due place hereafter, God willing, shall be related.[1] [*fl.* 1320-1330]

SIR JOHN DE HAWKWOOD, knight, son to Gilbert de Hawkwood, tanner, was born in Sible Hedingham. This John was first bound an apprentice to a tailor in the city of London; but soon turned his needle into a sword, and thimble into a shield, being pressed in the service of King Edward the Third for his French wars, who rewarded his valour with knighthood. Now that mean men, bred in manual and mechanic trades, may arrive at great skill in martial performances, this Hawkwood, though an eminent, is not the only instance of our English nation.

The heat of the French wars being much remitted he went into Italy, and served the city of Florence, which as yet was a free state. Such republics preferred foreigners rather than natives for their generals, because when the service was ended, it was but disbursing their pay, and then disbanding their power, by cashiering their commission; such foreigners having no advantage to continue their command, and render themselves absolute, because wanting an interest in alliances and relations. Thus a single stake, if occasion serves, is sooner

(1) See Suffolk, p. 525.

plucked up than a tree fastened to the earth, with the many *fibrae* appendant to the root thereof.

Great the gratitude of the state of Florence to this their general Hawkwood, who in testimony of his surpassing valour and singular faithful service to their state, adorned him with the statue of a man of arms, and sumptuous monument, wherein his ashes remain honoured at this present day. Well it is that monument doth remain, seeing his cenotaph, or honorary tomb, which sometimes stood in the parish church of Sible Hedingham (arched over and, in allusion to his name, *berebussed* with *hawks* flying into a *wood*)[1] is not quite flown away and abolished.

This Sir John de Hawkwood married Donnina, daughter of Bernabo the warlike brother of Galeazzo lord of Milan (father to John the first duke of Milan) by whom he had a son named John, born in Italy, made knight and naturalized in the seventh year of King Henry the Fourth.

This valiant knight died very aged, anno 1394, in the eighteenth of King Richard the Second; his friends founding two chantries, to pray for his and the souls of John Oliver and Thomas Newenton, esquires, his military companions, and, which probably may be presumed, born in the same county.

JOHN DE WALTHAM was so named from the place of his nativity; and attained to be a prudent man, and most expert in government of the state, so that he became master of the Rolls, keeper of the privy seal, and anno 1388, was consecrated bishop of Salisbury.

But he missed his mark, and met with one who both matched and mastered him, when refusing to be visited by Courtney, archbishop of Canterbury, on the criticism that Pope Urban the Sixth, who granted Courtney his commission, was lately dead, till the archbishop excommunicated him into more knowledge and humility, teaching him that his visitations had a self-support without assistance of papal power, cast in only by the way of religious compliment. This John of Waltham was afterwards made lord treasurer; and Richard the Second had such an affection for him, that dying in his office, he caused him to be buried (though many muttered thereat) amongst the kings, and next to King Edward the First in Westminster. His death happened 1395.

ROGER WALDEN, taking his name from his birth, in that eminent market-town in this county, was as considerable as any man in his age, for the alternation of his fortune. First, he was the son of a poor man; yet by his industry and ability attained to be dean of York, treasurer of Calais, secretary to the king, and treasurer of England.

Afterwards, when Thomas Arundel, archbishop of Canterbury, fell into the disfavour of King Richard the Second, and was banished the land, this Roger was, by the king, made archbishop of Canterbury, and

(1) Weever's *Funeral Monuments*. At the request of Richard II leave was given to his widow to transfer his body to England, and it was buried probably at Sible Hedingham. Hawkwood was, in Hallam's words, 'the first real general of modern times,' and possessed a genius for organization.

acted to all purpose and intents, calling of synods, and discharging of all other offices. However, he is beheld as a cipher in that see, because holding it by sequestration, whilst Arundel, the true incumbent was alive, who, returning in the first of King Henry the Fourth, resumed his archbishopric.[1]

And now Roger Walden was reduced to Roger Walden, and as poor as at his first beginning, for, though all maintained that the character of a bishop was *indelible,* this Roger found that a bishopric was *dealable,* having nothing whereon to subsist, until archbishop Arundel, nobly reflecting upon his worth, or want, or both, procured him to be made bishop of London. But he enjoyed that place only so long as to be a testimony to all posterity of Arundel's civility unto him, dying before the year was expired, 1406.

He may be compared to one so jaw-fallen with over-long fasting, that he cannot eat meat when brought unto him; and his spirits were so depressed with his former ill fortunes, that he could not enjoy himself in his new unexpected happiness. Why he was buried rather in Saint Bartholomew's in Smithfield than his own cathedral church, is too hard for me to resolve.

THOMAS [NETTER OR] WALDEN was son to John and Matilda Netter, who, declining the surname of his parents, took it from Walden, the noted place in this county of his nativity; so much are they mistaken that maintain that this Walden's name was Vuedale, and that he was born in Hampshire.

In some sort he may be termed Anti-Waldensis, being the most professed enemy to the Wycliffites, who for the main revived and maintained the doctrine of the Waldenses. Being bred a Carmelite in London, and doctor of divinity in Oxford, he became a great champion of, yet vassal to, the pope.

He was in high esteem with three succeeding kings of England; and might have changed his cowl into what English mitre he pleased, but refused it. Under King Henry the Fourth he was sent a solemn ambassador, 1409, about taking away the schism, and advancing an union in the church; and pleaded most eloquently before the pope and Sigismund the emperor. He was confessor and privy councillor to King Henry the Fifth, who died in his bosom, and whom he taxed for too much lenity to the Wycliffites; so that we behold the breath of Walden as the bellows which blew up the coals for the burning of those poor Christians in England, under King Henry the Sixth. He was employed to provide at Paris all necessaries for his solemn coronation; and dying in his journey thither, anno 1430, was buried at Rouen. He was sixteen years provincial of his order throughout all England, and wrote many books against the Wycliffites.

ROBERT D'ARCY. An ancient name in this county, having Danbury (whilst living) for their residence; and the church in Maldon (when dead)

(1) For Thomas Arundel's life see Sussex, p. 566.

for their sepulture, where there be many of their shamefully defaced monuments.

This Robert D'Arcy, afterwards knighted, by his will made the fifth of October 1469, bequeathed his body to be buried in All Hallows church in Maldon, before the altar, where his father lay in a tomb of marble. He willed that forty marks should be disposed for two thousand masses (fourpence a mass) to be said for his soul, and the souls of his relations, within six weeks after his decease; willing also that every priest in Pembroke Hall in Cambridge should have a share of that money, &c. He made Elizabeth his wife and others his executors; the earl of Essex, the Lord Dinham, Thomas Mountgomery, Thomas Terryll, supervisors of his will; beseeching them to help his son Thomas and all his children. He willed the earl of Essex and Lord Dinham should have a butt of malmsey, Sir Thomas Mountgomery and Sir Thomas Terryll, a pipe of red wine, for their pains. Thomas D'Arcy his son, esquire of the body to King Henry the Sixth and Edward the Fourth, married Margaret, one of the daughters and heirs of John Harleton of Suffolk, esquire. He died 25th of September 1485, as appears by his epitaph on his tomb in the church aforesaid.

THOMAS BOURCHIER was son to Sir William Bourchier, who (though but an English knight) was a French earl of Ewe in Normandy, created by King Henry the Fifth, and had a great estate in this county, with many mansion-houses; Halstead being the place of their principal residence, where I presume this prelate was born [1404?]

He was bred in the university of Oxford, whereof he was chancellor 1434; dean of Saint Martin's, then successively bishop of Worcester, Ely, archbishop of Canterbury, and cardinal by the title Saint Cyriacus in the Baths. A prelate, besides his high birth aforesaid, and brotherhood to Henry Bourchier, first earl of Essex of that surname, remarkable on many accounts.

First, for his vivacity, being an old man, and proportionably, an older bishop. 1. Being consecrated bishop of Worcester 1434, the fourteenth of Henry the Sixth. 2. Dying archbishop of Canterbury 1486, the second of King Henry the Seventh. Whereby it appeareth that he wore a mitre full fifty-one years, a term not to be paralleled in any other person. Secondly, he saw strange revolutions in state, the civil wars between Lancaster and York begun, continued and concluded; for though Bishop Morton had the happiness to make the match, Archbishop Bourchier had the honour to marry King Henry the Seventh to the daughter of King Edward the Fourth; so that his hand first solemnly held that sweet posy wherein the white and red roses were tied together. Thirdly, for his wary compliance, that he lost not himself in the labyrinth of such intricate times, applying himself politicly to the present predominant power.

He left no monument to posterity proportionable (what was an hundred pounds and a chest given to Cambridge?) to his great blood, rich place, and long continuance therein. But this my author imputeth unto the troublesomeness of the times, seeing peace was no sooner settled, and the land began to live, but he died, March 30, 1486.

SIR THOMAS AUDLEY, knight [BARON AUDLEY OF WALDEN]; where born [1488] my best industry and inquiry cannot attain. He was bred in the study of the laws till he became attorney of the Duchy of Lancaster, and serjeant-at-law (as most affirm); then speaker of the parliament; knighted and made keeper of the great seal, June 5, 1532, being the twenty-fourth of King Henry the Eighth; and not long after was made lord chancellor of England, and Baron Audley.

In the feast of abbey lands King Henry the Eighth carved unto him the first cut (and that, I assure you, was a dainty morsel); viz., the priory of the Trinity in Aldgate Ward London, dissolved 1531, which as a van-courier fore-ran other abbeys by two years, and foretold their dissolution. This I may call (afterwards called Duke's Place) the Covent Garden within London, as the greatest empty space within the walls, though since filled, not to say pestered with houses. He had afterwards a large partage in the abbey lands in several counties.

He continued in his office of chancellor thirteen years; and had one only daughter, Margaret, who no doubt answered the pearl in her name, as well in her precious qualities, as rich inheritance which she brought to her husband Thomas, last duke of Norfolk. This Lord Audley died April 30, 1544, and is buried in the fair church of Saffron Walden, with this lamentable epitaph:

> The stroke of death's inevitable dart
> Hath now, alas! of life bereft the heart
> Of Sir Thomas Audley, of the Garter knight,
> Late chancellor of England under our prince of might
> Henry the Eighth, worthy of high renown,
> And made him Lord Audley of this town.

This worthy lord took care that better poets should be after than were in his age; and founded Magdalene College in Cambridge, giving good lands thereunto, if they might have enjoyed them according to his donation.[1]

SIR RICHARD MORISON, knight, was born in this county . . . bred probably first in Eton or Winchester, then in Cambridge or Oxford, and at last in the inns of court. In those he attained to great skill in Latin and Greek, in the common and civil law, insomuch that he was often employed ambassador, by King Henry the Eighth and Edward the Sixth, unto Charles the Fifth emperor and other princes of Germany, acquitting himself both honest and able in those negotiations.

He began a beautiful house at Cashiobury in Hertfordshire, and had prepared materials for the finishing thereof; but alas, this house proved like the life of his master who began it, I mean King Edward the Sixth,

(1) This Lord Audley is one of the more significant figures of Henry VIII's reign. As chancellor he sanctioned Henry's divorce from Catherine of Aragon. He presided at the trials of Fisher and More, carried through parliament the act for dissolving Henry's marriage with Anne of Cleves, and passed judgment of death on Catherine Howard.

broken off, not ended, and that before it came to the middle thereof. Yea, he was forced to fly beyond the seas, and returning out of Italy, died at Strasburg, on the 17th of March, Anno Domini 1556, to the grief of all good men.

SIR ANTHONY COOKE, knight, great-grandchild to Sir Thomas Cooke, lord mayor of London, was born [1504] at Gidea Hall in this county, where he finished a fair house, begun by his great-grandfather. . . . He was one of the governors to King Edward the Sixth when prince; and is charactered by Master Camden *vir antiqua severitate* [an old-fashioned disciplinarian.] He observeth him also to be happy in his daughters, learned above their sex in Greek and Latin; namely, 1. Mildred, married unto William Cecil, lord treasurer of England; 2. Anne, married unto Nicholas Bacon, lord chancellor of England; 3, Katharine, married unto Henry Killigrew, knight; 4, Elizabeth, married unto Thomas Hoby, knight; 5. Margaret, married unto Ralph Rowlett, knight. Indeed they were all most eminent scholars (the honour of their own and the shame of our sex) both in prose and poetry.

This Sir Anthony Cooke died in the year of our Lord 1576, leaving a fair estate unto his son, in whose name it continued until our time.

SIR THOMAS SMITH, knight, was born [1513] at Saffron Walden in this county; and bred in Queens' College in Cambridge, where such his proficiency in learning, that he was chosen out by Henry the Eighth to be sent over and brought up beyond the seas. It was fashionable in that age that pregnant students were maintained on the cost of the state, to be merchants for experience in foreign parts; whence returning home with their gainful adventures, they were preferred (according to the improvement of their time) to offices in their own country. Well it were if this good old custom were resumed; for if where God hath given talents, men would give but pounds, I mean encourage hopeful abilities with helpful maintenance, able persons would never be wanting, and poor men with great parts would not be excluded the line of preferment.

This Sir Thomas was afterwards secretary of state to Queen Elizabeth, and a grand benefactor to both universities, as I have formerly declared at large.[1] He died Anno Domini 1577.

HENRY FITZROY [DUKE OF RICHMOND] natural son to King Henry the Eighth. Here we confess our trespass against our own rules, who confined ourselves to the legitimate issue of kings, presuming that the worth of this Henry will make amends for our breach or order herein. He was begotten on the body of the Lady Talboys, and born at Blackmore Manor in this county, anno 1519, being afterwards created earl of Nottingham and Duke of Richmond. He confuted their etymology

(1) In my *History of Cambridge* [Sir Thomas Smith, an upright statesman and fine classical scholar, became regius professor of civil law and vice-chancellor of Cambridge. He lived in retirement in Mary's reign. His important work on the Tudor constitution, *De Republica Anglorum,* was published posthumously.]

who deduced bastard from the Dutch words *boes* and *art*, that is, an abject nature; and verified their deduction deriving it from *besteaerd*, that is, the best disposition: such was his forwardness in all martial activities, with his knowledge in all arts and sciences, learned Leland dedicating a book unto him. He married Mary, daughter to Thomas duke of Norfolk, and dying anno 1536 (in the seventeenth year of his age) was buried at Framlingham in Suffolk with great lamentation.[1]

RICHARD GEORGE, labourer, of West Barfold, is most eminent amongst the many confessors in this shire, for he had successively three wives, whereof two were burnt, and the third imprisoned for religion: viz., 1. Agnes George, burnt at Stratford le Bow, June 27, 1556. 2. Christian George, burnt at Colchester, May 26, 1558. 3. —— George, imprisoned in Colchester, and escaped by Queen Mary's death, November 17, 1558.

Some, who consult the dates of his wives' deaths, will condemn him for over-speedy marriage, and the appetite to a new wife is not comely before the grief for the former be well digested. Such consider not that their glorious death in so good a cause was the subject rather of his joy than grief, and that, being necessitated (for his children's sake) to marry, he was careful, as it appears, to marry in the Lord. Nor did he thrust his wives into the fire, and shrink back from the flames himself, who, being imprisoned in Colchester, had followed his two first, and gone along with his last, to the stake, had not Divine Providence, by Queen Mary's death, prevented it.

SIR WALTER MILDMAY, knight, was born [1520?] at Chelmsford in this county, where he was a younger son to Thomas Mildmay, esquire. He was bred in Christ's College in Cambridge, where he did not (as many young gentlemen) study only in compliment, but seriously applied himself to his book.

Under King Henry the Eighth and King Edward the Sixth, he had a gainful office in the court of augmentations.[2] During the reign of Queen Mary, he practised the politic precept, *Bene vixit qui bene latuit.*[3] No sooner came Queen Elizabeth to the crown, but he was called to state employment, and it was not long before he was made chancellor of the exchequer.

It is observed that "the exchequer never fareth ill, but under a good prince"; such who out of conscience will not oppress their people, whilst tyrants pass not[4] for what they squeeze out of their subjects. Indeed Queen Elizabeth was very careful not to have her coffer swelled with the consumption of her kingdom, and had conscientious officers under her, amongst whom Sir Walter was a principal.

This knight, sensible of God's blessing on his estate, and knowing that *omne beneficium requirit officium* [every benefit has its obligations] cast about to make his return to God. He began with his benefaction to Christ's College in Cambridge, ouly to put his hand into practice;

(1) He may have been poisoned by Anne Boleyn and her brother, and died after witnessing the execution of the former. (2) See note 3, p. 54. (3) Ovid ["He who lives obscurely lives securely."] (4) *Pass not*=care not, reck not.

then his bounty embraced the generous resolution (which the painful piety of Saint Paul propounds to himself) viz., "not to build on another man's foundation"; but, on his own cost, he erected a new college in Cambridge, by the name of Emmanuel.[1]

A right godly gentleman he was, though some of his back-friends suggested to the queen that he was a better patriot than subject; and that he was over-popular in parliaments, insomuch that his life did set *sub nubecula,* under a cloud of the royal displeasure. Yet was not the cloud so great, but that the beams of his innocence, meeting those of the queen's candour, had easily dispelled it, had he survived longer, as appeared by the great grief the queen professed for the loss of so grave a councillor; who, leaving two sons and three daughters, died Anno Domini 1589.

THOMAS TUSSER was born [1524?] at Rivenhall in this county, of an ancient family, since extinct, if his own pen may be believed. Whilst as yet a boy he lived in many schools, Wallingford, Saint Paul's, Eton, whence he went to Trinity Hall in Cambridge; when a man in Staffordshire, Suffolk, Norfolk, Cambridgeshire, London, and where not? so that this stone of Sisyphus could gather no moss. He was successively a musician, schoolmaster, serving man, husbandman, grazier, poet; more skilful in all than thriving in any vocation. He traded at large in oxen, sheep, dairies, grain of all kinds, to no profit. Whether he bought or sold, he lost; and when a renter impoverished himself, and never enriched his landlord. Yet hath he laid down excellent rules in his *Book of Husbandry and Housewifery* (so that the observer thereof must be rich) in his own defence. He spread his bread with all sorts of butter, yet none would stick thereon. Yet I hear no man to charge him with any vicious extravagancy, or visible carelessness, imputing his ill success to some occult cause in God's counsel. Thus our English Columella[2] might say with the poet,

Monitis sum minor ipse meis,

none being better at the theory, or worse at the practice, of husbandry. I match him with Thomas Churchyard; they being marked alike in their poetical parts, living in the same time, and statured alike in their estates; both low enough, I assure you.[3] [*d.* 1580]

THOMAS RADCLIFFE [*b.* 1526?], Lord Fitzwalter, third earl of Sussex of that surname, twice lord-deputy of Ireland, was a most valiant gentleman. By his prudence he caused that actual rebellion brake not out

(1) In his *History of the University of Cambridge,* Fuller tells the following story: "Coming to court after he had founded his college, the queen told him, 'Sir Walter, I hear you have erected a *puritan foundation.*' 'No, madam,' saith he, 'far be it from me to countenance anything contrary to your established laws; but I have set an acorn, which when it becomes an oak, God alone knows what will be the fruit thereof.'" Nevertheless, from its foundation it was puritan in tone. (2) Junius Moderatus Columella, a contemporary of Seneca, famous for his work *De Re Rustica,* dealing with agriculture. *Monitis sum,* etc., "I fall short of my own precepts." (3) Tusser died whilst a prisoner for debt. He is remarkable for introducing the culture of barley. His books, in crude didactic verse, are the source of many proverbial sayings. For Thomas Churchyard, see Shropshire, p. 482.

in Ireland; and no wonder if in his time it rained not war there, seeing his diligence dispersed the clouds before they could gather together. Thus he who cures a disease may be the skilfullest, but he that prevents it is the safest physician.

Queen Elizabeth called him home to be her lord chamberlain, and a constant court faction was maintained betwixt him and Robert earl of Leicester; so that the Sussexians and the Leicesterians divided the court, whilst the Cecilians, as neuters, did look upon them. Sussex had a great estate left him by his ancestors, Leicester as great given or restored him by the queen; Sussex was the honester man and greater soldier, Leicester the more faceit courtier and deep politician, not for the general good, but his particular profit. Great the animosity betwixt them, and what in vain the queen endeavoured death performed, taking this earl away, and so the competition was ended. New Hall in this county was the place, if not (as I believe) of his birth, of his principal habitation. He died Anno Domini 1583.

DOROTHY PETRE, daughter to Sir William Petre, secretary of state, and sister to John Lord Petre, was certainly born [1534] in this county; but uncertain whether at Thorndon, Writtle or Ingatestone, three fair houses in Essex of that wealthy family. Thus variety of habitations render the nativities of great persons doubtful, whilst we are led with more assurance to the cradles of meaner people.

She was married to Nicholas Wadham[1], of Merefield, in Somersetshire, esquire. We read of Ahab, that "he sold himself to work wickedness, whom Jezebel his wife stirred up"; but this worthy man gave himself over to all actions of bounty and charity, whom his wife, answering her name ("a gift of God" indeed) encouraged therein. He founded, she finished, both richly endowed, Wadham College in Oxford; by whose joint bounty it is become as rich as most, more uniform than any college in England.

[*d.* 1618]

RICHARD HOWLAND was born [1540] at Newport Pond in this county; first fellow of Peterhouse, then chosen, 1576, master of Magdalene, and next year master of Saint John's College, in Cambridge. He was twice vice-chancellor of the university; in the year 1584 he was consecrated bishop of Peterborough, in which place he continued sixteen years, and died in June 1600.

WILLIAM GILBERT was born [1540] in Trinity Parish in Colchester[2]; his father being a counsellor of great esteem in his profession, who first removed his family thither from Clare in Suffolk, where they had resided in a genteel equipage some centuries of years.

He had (saith my informer) the clearness of Venice glass, without the brittleness thereof; soon ripe, and long lasting, in his perfections. He commenced doctor in physic, and was physician to Queen Elizabeth, who

(1) See Somerset, p. 497. (2) I received the ensuing intelligence from his near kinsman Mr. William Gilbert, of Brent Eleigh in Suffolk.

stamped on him many marks of her favour, besides an annual pension to encourage his studies. He addicted himself to chemistry, attaining to great exactness therein. One saith of him that he was stoical, but not cynical; which I understand reserved, but not morose; never married, purposely to be more beneficial to his brethren. Such his loyalty to the queen, that as if unwilling to survive, he died in the same year with her, 1603. His stature was tall, complexion cheerful, an happiness not ordinary in so hard a student and retired a person. He lieth buried in Trinity Church in Colchester, under a plain monument.

Mahomet's tomb at Mecca is said strangely to hang up, attracted by some invisible loadstone; but the memory of this doctor will never fall to the ground, which his incomparable book *De Magnete* will support to eternity.[1]

JOHN JEGON was born [1550] in this county at Coggeshall; fellow first of Queens', then master of Benet College in Cambridge, and three times vice-chancellor of the university. A most serious man and grave governor; yet withal of a most facetious disposition, so that it was hard to say wheher his counsel was more grateful for the soundness, or his company more acceptable for the pleasantness thereof. Take one eminent instance of his ingenuity.

Whilst master of the college he chanced to punish all the undergraduates therein for some general offence, and the penalty was put upon their heads in the buttery. And because that he disdained to convert the money to any private use, it was expended in new whiting the hall of the college. Whereupon a scholar hung up these verses on the screen:

> Doctor Jegon, Benet College master,
> Brake the scholar's head, and gave the walls a plaister.

But the doctor had not the readiness of his parts any whit impaired by his age; for, perusing the paper, *extempore* he subscribed,

> Knew I but the wag that writ these verses in a bravery,
> I would commend him for his wit, but whip him for his knavery.

Queen Elizabeth designed him, but King James confirmed him, bishop of Norwich; where, if some in his diocese have since bestowed harsh language on his memory, the wonder is not great, seeing he was a somewhat severe presser of conformity; and died Anno Domini 1618.

SIR FRANCIS and SIR HORACE VERE [BARON VERE OF TILBURY] sons of Geoffrey Vere, esquire, who was son of John de Vere, the fifteenth earl of Oxford, were both born in this county, though several places (Hedingham Castle, Colchester (Tilbury-juxta-Clare) be by sundry men assigned for their nativity. We will first consider them severally, and then compare them together.

(1) *De Magnete*, in which Gilbert declared the earth to be a magnet, was the first great physical work published in England. He was president of the College of Physicians.

SIR FRANCIS was of a fiery spirit and rigid nature, undaunted in all dangers, not over-valuing the price of men's lives to purchase a victory therewith. He served on the scene of all Christendom where war was acted. One master-piece of his valour was at the battle of Nieuport, when his Ragged Regiment (so were the English then called from their ragged clothes) helped to make all whole, or else all had been lost. Another was when for three years he defended Ostend against a strong and numerous army, surrendering it at last a bare skeleton to the king of Spain, who paid more years' purchase for it than probably the world will endure. [1560-1609]

SIR HORACE [*b.* 1565] had more meekness and as much valour as his brother; so pious, that he first made his peace with God before he went out to war with man. One of an excellent temper, it being true of him what is said of the Caspian Sea, that it doth never ebb nor flow; observing a constant tenor, neither elated nor depressed with success. Had one seen him returning from a victory, he would, by his silence, have suspected that he had lost the day; and had he beheld him in a retreat he would have collected him a conqueror, by the cheerfulness of his spirit. He was the first baron of King Charles's creation. Some years after, coming to court, he fell suddenly sick and speechless, so that he died before night, Anno Domini 1635. No doubt he was well prepared for death, seeing such his vigilancy that never any enemy surprised him in his quarters.

Now to compare them together (such their eminency, that they would hardly be paralleled by any but themselves). Sir Francis was the elder brother, Sir Horace lived to be the older man. Sir Francis was more feared, Sir Horace more loved, by the soldiery. The former in martial discipline was oft-times *rigidus ad ruinam,* the latter seldom exceeded *ad terrorem.* Sir Francis left none, Sir Horace no male issue, whose four co-heirs are since matched into honourable families. Both lived in war, much honoured; died in peace, much lamented.

THOMAS HOWARD [FIRST EARL OF SUFFOLK and first BARON HOWARD DE WALDEN], wherever born [1561], is justly reputed of this county, wherein he had his first honour, and last habitation. He was second son to Thomas last duke of Norfolk, but eldest, by his wife Margaret, sole heir to Thomas Lord Audley.

Queen Elizabeth made him baron of Walden and knight of the Garter; and King James (who beheld his father a state-martyr for the Queen of Scots) in the first of his reign, advanced him lord chamberlain and earl of Suffolk; and in the twelfth of his reign, July 11, lord treasurer of England.

He was also chancellor of Cambridge, loving and beloved of the university. When at his first coming to Cambridge Master Francis Nethersole,[1] orator of the university, made a Latin speech unto him, this lord returned, "Though I understand not Latin, I know the sense of your oration is to tell me that I am welcome to you; which I believe

(1) See Kent, p. 282.

verily, thank you for it heartily, and will serve you faithfully in anything within my power."

Doctor Harsnett, the vice-chancellor, laying hold on the handle of so fair a proffer, requested him to be pleased to entertain the king at Cambridge; a favour which the university could never compass from their former great and wealthy chancellors. "I will do it," saith the lord, "in the best manner I may, with the speediest conveniency." Nor was he worse than his word, giving his majesty not long after so magnificent a treatment in the university, as cost him five thousand pounds and upwards.

Hence it was that after his death, Thomas, his second son, earl of Berkshire, not suing for it (not knowing of it) was chosen to succeed him, losing the place (as some suspected) not for lack of voices, but fair counting them. He died at Audley End, Anno Domini 1626, being grandfather to the right honourable James earl of Suffolk.[1]

SAMUEL HARSNETT was born [1561] at Colchester, in the parish of Saint Botolph; bred first, scholar, then fellow, then master, of Pembroke Hall in Cambridge. A man of great learning, strong parts and stout spirit. He was bishop, first of Chichester, then of Norwich, and at last archbishop of York, and one of the privy council of King Charles; the two last dignities being procured by Thomas earl of Arundel, who much favoured him, and committed his younger son to his education.

At Chigwell in this county (the place of his first church preferment) he built and endowed a fair grammar school. He conditionally bequeathed his library to Colchester, where he was born, as by this passage in his will may appear:

Item, I give to the bailiffs and corporation of the town of Colchester all my library of books, provided that they provide a decent room to set them up in, that the clergy of the town of Colchester, and other divines, may have free access for the reading and studying of them.

I presume, the town corresponding with his desire, the legacy took due effect. He died Anno Domini 1631, and lieth buried at Chigwell aforesaid.

AUGUSTINE LINDSELL, D.D., was born at Steeple Bumpstead in this county; bred scholar and fellow in Clare Hall in Cambridge. He applied himself chiefly to the studies of Greek, Hebrew and all antiquity, attaining to great exactness therein. He was very knowing in the ancient practices of the Jews; and from him I learned that they had a custom, at the circumcising of their children, that certain undertakers should make a solemn stipulation for their pious education, conformable to our godfathers in baptism.

He was afterwards made bishop of Peterborough, where (on the joint cost of his clergy) he procured Theophylact on the Epistles, never printed before, to be fairly set forth in Greek and Latin. Hence he was removed to Hereford, where he died 1634.

(1) This Howard distinguished himself against the Armada, and commanded the attack on the Azores fleet in 1591. He was fined and imprisoned in 1619 for accepting bribes when lord treasurer.

RICHARD WESTON [First EARL OF PORTLAND, *b* 1577.] I behold him son to Sir Jerome Weston, sheriff of this county in the one and fourtieth of Queen Elizabeth: and cannot meet with any of his relations to rectify me if erroneous. In his youth he impaired his estate, to improve himself with public accomplishment; but came off both a saver and a gainer at the last, when made chancellor of the exchequer, and afterwards (upon the remove of the earl of Marlborough) July 23, in the fourth of King Charles, lord treasurer of England.

But I hear the cock's crow proclaiming the dawning day, being now come within the ken of many alive; and when men's memories do arise, it is time for history to haste to bed. Let me only be a datary, to tell the reader that this lord was created earl of Portland, February 17, in the eighth of King Charles; and died March 13, Anno Domini 1635, being father to the right honourable Jerome, now earl of Portland.

SIR JOHN BRAMSTON, knight, was born [1577] at Maldon in this county; bred up in the Middle Temple in the study of the common law, wherein he attained to such eminency that he was by King Charles made lord chief justice of the king's bench. One of deep learning, solid judgment, integrity of life, gravity of behaviour; in a word, accomplished with all qualities requisite for a person of his place and profession.

One instance of his integrity I must not forget, effectually relating to the foundation wherein I was bred. Serjeant Brereton bequeathed by will to Sidney College well nigh three thousand pounds; but (for haste or some other accident) so imperfectly done that, as Doctor Samuel Ward informed me, the gift was invalid in the rigour of the law. Now Judge Bramston, who married the serjeant's widow, gave himself much trouble (gave himself indeed, doing all things *gratis*) for the speedy payment of the money to a farthing, and the legal settling thereof on the college, according to the true intention of the dead. He deserved to live in better times; the delivering of his judgment on the king's side in the case of ship-money cost him much trouble.[1] The posting press would not be persuaded to stay till I had received farther instructions from the most hopeful sons of this worthy judge, who died [1654].

JOSEPH [MEAD or] MEDE was born [1586] in this county, a little east of Bishop's Stortford. He was bred in Christ's College in Cambridge, where he attained to great learning by his own industry. 'R' was shiboleth unto him, which he could not easily pronounce; so that a set speech cost him the double pains to another man, being to fit words as well to his mouth as his matter. Yet, by his industry and observation, he so conquered his imperfection, that, though in private discourse he often smiled out his stammering into silence, yet, choosing his words, he made many an excellent sermon without any considerable hesitation.

The first-fruits of his eminent studies was a written treatise, *De Sanctitate Relativa,* which he presented to Bishop Andrewes, who

(1) He was impeached in 1640 by the Commons for the ship-money judgment, removed from office in the king's bench 1642, but shortly after was made serjeant-at-law and restored.

besteaded him with the king's favour, when his election into his fellowship met with some opposition. He afterwards became an excellent linguist, curious mathematician, exact textman, happy in making Scripture to expound itself by parallel places. He was charitable to poor people with his alms, and to all people with his candid censure.

Of one who constantly kept his cell (so he called his chamber) none travelled oftener and farther over all Christendom. For things past he was a perfect historian; for things present, a judicious novilant;[1] and for things to come, a prudential (not to say prophetical) conjecturer.

To his private friends he would often insist on the place of Scripture, Judges iii, 30, "And the land had a rest fourscore years"; which was the longest term of peace which he ever observed the church of God to enjoy; after which many troubles did ensue. And seeing the same lease of halcyon days was expired in England since the first of Queen Elizabeth, he grievously suspected some strange concussion in church and state, which came to pass accordingly. I confess his memory hath suffered much in many men's judgments for being so great a *fautor* of the fanciful opinion of the Millenaries.[2] Yet none can deny but that much is found in the ancient Fathers tending that way. Besides, I dare boldly say that the furious factors for the Fifth Monarchy hath driven that nail which Master Mead did first enter, farther than he ever intended it, and doing it with such violence that they split the truths round about it. Thus when ignorance begins to build on that foundation which learning hath laid, no wonder if there be no uniformity in such a mongrel fabric. He died in the fifty-third year of his age, Anno Domini 1638, leaving the main of his estate to the college, about the value of £300, a large sum to issue out of the purse of a scholar.

FRANCIS QUARLES, esquire, son to James Quarles, esquire, was born [1592] at Stewards, in the parish of Romford in this county, where his son, as I am informed, hath an estate in expectancy. He was bred in Cambridge; and going over into Ireland, became secretary to the Reverend James Ussher, archbishop of Armagh. He was a most excellent poet, and had a mind biased to devotion. Had he been contemporary with Plato (that great back-friend to poets) he would not only have allowed him to live, but advanced him to an office in his commonwealth.

Some poets, if debarred profaneness, wantonness and satiricalness (that they may neither abuse God, themselves. nor their neighbours) have their tongues cut out in effect. Others only trade in wit at the second hand, being all for translations, nothing for invention. Our Quarles was free from the faults of the first, as if he had drank of Jordan instead of Helicon, and slept on Mount Olivet for his Parnassus, and was happy in his own invention. His visible poetry (I mean his *Emblems*) is excellent, catching therein the eye and fancy at one draught, so that he hath *out-Alciated*[3] therein, in some men's judgment. His verses on

(1) *Novilant,* a word used several times in different senses by Fuller, and here probably meaning commentator on current affairs. (2) *Fautor*=partisan, abettor. The Millenary Petition of 1603, presented to James I by about a thousand puritan clergymen, asking for reforms in the church. (3) Andrea Alciati (1492—1550) Italian poet and jurist, perhaps the most famous writer of 'emblems'.

Job are done to the life, so that the reader may see his sores, and through them the anguish of his soul.

The troubles of Ireland, where his losses were great, forced his return hither, bearing his crosses with great patience; so that (according to the advice of Saint Jerome) *verba vertebat in opera*, and practised the Job he had described, dying [1644].

HENRY DE VERE [18th EARL OF OXFORD, *b.* 1593] was son of Edward de Vere, the seventeenth earl of Oxford and Elizabeth Trentham his second lady, whose principal habitation (the rest of his patrimony being then wasted) was at Hedingham Castle in this county. A vigorous gentleman, full of courage and resolution, and the last lord chamberlain of England of this family. His sturdy nature would not bow to court-compliants, who would maintain what he spake, spake what he thought, think what he apprehended true and just, though sometimes dangerous and distasteful.

Once he came into court with a great milk-white feather about his hat, which then was somewhat unusual, save that a person of his merit might make a fashion. The reader may guess the lord who said unto him in some jeer, "My lord, you wear a very fair feather." "It is true," said the earl, "and, if you mark it, there's ne'er a taint in it." Indeed his family was ever loyal to the crown, deserving their motto VERO NIL VERIUS [nothing truer than truth].[1]

Going over one of the four English colonels into the Low Countries, and endeavouring to raise the siege of Breda, he so overheated himself with marching, fighting and vexing (the design not succeeding) that he died a few days after, Anno Domini 1625. He married Diana, one of the co-heirs of William earl of Exeter (afterwards married to Edward earl of Elgin) by whom he left no issue.

THOMAS EDEN, D.L., was born in the south part of Sudbury, within this county,[2] where his name and family are continued in a worshipful degree in Ballingdon Hall. He was bred fellow, and then master of Trinity Hall in Cambridge; a singular good advocate, chancellor of Ely, commisary of Sudbury and Westminster, professor of law in Gresham College, &c.

But, leaving his ability in his own profession to be praised by others, his charity here comes under our cognizance; who bestowed one thousand pounds on Trinity Hall, therewith purchasing lands to maintain wax candles in the chapel, an annual commemoration with a Latin speech, and other excellent benefactions. He died Anno Domini 1645, leaving a considerable estate, and making Mr. James Bunce, alderman of London, his executor (though an utter stranger unto him) on this occasion. The alderman repaired to him for advice on a will, wherein he was an executor, desiring from him the true meaning of a clause therein. The doctor returned that the passage in question was equally capable of two several senses.

(1) The lord was Buckingham, with whom he quarrelled and offended on two occasions, resulting in imprisonment in the tower. (2) Sudbury is now in Suffolk.

"But tell me," said Mr Bunce, "what do you believe in your conscience was the very mind of the testator, being my resolution to perform it whatever it cost me." A speech which stayed with the doctor after the speaker thereof was departed, making such impression in his spirit, that hence he concluded the alderman a conscientious person, and deputed him the executor to his own will. I am informed that since the doctor's death a match hath been made between their nearest relations.

THE FAREWELL

I wish the sad casualties may never return which lately have happened in this county; the one, 1581, in the hundred of Dengie, the other, 1648, in the hundred of Rochford and Isle of Foulness (rented in part by two of my credible parishioners, who attested it, having paid dear for the truth thereof); when an army of mice, nesting in anthills, as conies in burrows, shaved off the grass at the bare roots, which withering to dung was infectious to cattle. The March following, numberless flocks of owls from all parts flew thither, and destroyed them, which otherwise had ruined the country, if continuing another year. Thus, though great the distance betwixt a man and a mouse, the meanest may become formidable to the mightiest creature by their multitudes; and this may render the punishment of the Philistines more clearly to our apprehension, at the same time pestered with mice in their barns, and pained with emerods in their bodies.[1]

(1) 1 Sam. vi. 11 [*Emerods* = haemorrhoids.]

GLOUCESTERSHIRE

GLOUCESTERSHIRE hath Worcester- and Warwick-shires on the north, Oxford- and Wilt-shires on the east, Somersetshire on the south, Herefordshire, with the river Wye, on the west; extending from her South to North Avon 48 miles, but lessened in her broadest part, from east to west, to twenty-eight. The Severn runneth through it, entering this county as a river, increasing in it to an estuary, and becometh little less than a sea before it departs out of it.

Some affirm that this county was anciently like the land of Gerar, wherein Isaac sowed and reaped an hundredfold (the greatest proportion of increase which the good ground in the parable brought forth). But the same men seem to insinuate that this shire, tired out with its over-fruitfulness, hath become barren in these later times. True it is, as lions are said to be tamed by watching, not suffering them to take any sleep, so the most generous and vigorous land will in time be embarrened, when always pinched with the plough and not permitted to slumber at all, and lie fallow some competent time; otherwise, with moderate respite and manuring, some tillage in this county is as fruitful as in any other place. As for pasturage, I have heard it reported from credible persons, that such the fruitfulness of the land nigh Slimbridge, that in spring time, let it be bit bare to the roots, a wand[1] laid along therein overnight will be covered with new-grown grass by the next morning.

NATURAL COMMODITIES

Tobacco

This lately grew in this county, but now may not. It was first planted about Winchcomb, and many got great estates thereby, notwithstanding the great care and cost in planting, replanting, transplanting, watering, snailing,[2] suckering, topping, cropping, sweating, drying, making and rolling it. But it hath been prohibited of late by act of parliament, as hindering our English plantation in the West Indies, abating the revenues of the state in customs and impost, and spoiling much of our good ground, which might be employed for corn or cattle. As for the praise of tobacco, with the virtues thereof, they may better be performed by the pens of such writers whose palates have tasted of the same.

Oak

England hath the best in the world, not for fineness, but firmness. Indeed outlandish oaks have a smaller grain, and therefore fitter for wainscot, and whilst they make the best linings, our English oak is the substantial outside.

The best in England is in Dean Forest in this county, and most serviceable for shipping, so tough, that when it is dry, it is said to be as hard as iron. I have read that in the reign of Queen Elizabeth the Spaniard sent

(1) *Wand*=a young shoot, a sapling. (2) *Snailing*=killing or removing snails.

an ambassador over purposely to get this wood destroyed (by private practices and cunning contrivances) who, had he effected his embassy, deserved a good reward at his return. It is suspicious, if not timely prevented, carelessness and waste will gratify the Spaniard with what then he could not accomplish.

STEEL

It is eldest brother of iron, extracted from the same ore, differing from it not in kind, but degree of purity, as being the first running thereof. It is more hard and brittle (whilst iron is softer and tougher) useful for the making of English knives, scythes, scissors, shears, &c.; but fine edges cannot be made thereof, as lancets for letting of blood, incision knives, dissecting knives, razors, &c. I have been informed that Sir Basil Brook (the great steel-maker in this county) his patent to prohibit the importing of foreign steel was revoked on this account, because that no artist could make the aforesaid instruments of English steel, but must have it from Damascus, Spain, Flanders, &c. As for iron, though plentiful in this, it may be treated of in another county with more conveniency.[1]

THE MANUFACTURES

CLOTHING

As good as any in England, for fineness and colour, is wrought in this county, where the clothiers have a double advantage. First, plenty of the best wool growing therein on Cotswold hills, so that whereas clothiers in some counties fetch their wool far off with great cost, it is here but the removing it from the backs of the sheep into their works-houses. Secondly, they have the benefit of an excellent water for colouring their cloth, being the sweet rivulet of Stroud, which, arising about Brimpsfield, runneth across this shire into the Severn.

Now no rational man will deny occult qualities of perfection in some above other waters (whereby Spanish steel, *non natura sed tinctura,* becomes more tough than ours in England) as the best reds (a colour which always carried somewhat of magistracy therein) are dyed in Stroud water. Hence it is that this shire hath afforded many wealthy clothiers, whereof some may seem in their looms to have interwoven their own names into the clothes, called Webb's cloth and Clutterbuck's, after the names of the first makers of them, for many years after.

MUSTARD

The best in England (to take no larger compass) is made at Tewkesbury in this county. It is very wholesome for the clearing of the head, moderately taken; and I believe very few have ever surfeited thereof, because not granted time, but demanded present payment for the penalty of excess, turning Democritus himself presently to Heraclitus, as the husbandman poet doth observe,

Seque lacessenti fletum factura sinapis.

(1) Under the Natural Commodities in Shropshire and Sussex. (2) Columella, in Hortulo.

It is generally used in England, and the jest is well known of two serving men contesting about superiority: "My master," saith the one, "spends more in mustard than thine does in beef." Whereunto the other returned, "The more *saucy* men his followers."

But seriously, this should raise our gratitude to God for the plentiful provisions of flesh and fish spent in this land, when mustard, a mere complement to both, amounteth to more thousands of pounds by the year than will be believed.

WINE

This formerly grew in this county, but now doth not; witness the many places therein still called Vineyards, whereof one most eminent nigh Gloucester, the palace of the bishop. And it appears by ancient records that some towns in this shire paid rent-wines in great proportions so that England, though it doth not *ferre vinum,* is *ferax vini,* capable (especially in a hot summer) to produce it to good perfection. But in later ages this commodity hath been disused, partly because better and cheaper may be procured from beyond the seas, and partly because experience proveth other native liquors more healthful for our English bodies.

CIDER

We must not forget cider, anciently a native of this, since a free denizen of all other counties, made of apples, here grown in hedgerows (which both fence and feed) in great abundance. Some maintain that the coldness and windiness, easily correctable with spice, is recompensed by the temperate looseness caused by the moderate drinking thereof. But the staple use of cider is at sea, where it quencheth thirst better than other liquor, and if subject to corrupt in hot countries, quickly purgeth itself to a pure constitution.

THE BUILDINGS

The abbey (since cathedral) church of Gloucester is a beautiful building, advanced by several successive abbots. It consisteth of a continued window work, but hath the loudest praises from the whispering-place therein.

The church, in all the siege of the city, and our civil wars, was decently preserved, which I observe to his commendation who was the governor thereof. Since, I have read that, by act of parliament, it was settled on the city to maintain and repair, and hope their practice hath proved precedential to other places in the same nature.

As for civil structures in this county, our late wars laid a finger on Berkeley, their arm on Sudeley Castle (seated where the vales and wolds meet) and the fair clasp to join them together being in part plucked down. But their loins have been laid on Campden House, one of the newest and neatest in England, built by Baptist Hicks, Viscount Campden,[1] pressed down to the very foundation.

(1) Lived 1551—1629; mercer and money-lender, and later contractor for crown lands; M.P. for Tavistock, 1620, and for Shrewsbury 1624-6.

THE WONDERS

THE EAGRE

Men as little know the cause of the name, as the thing thereby signified. It is the confluence or encounter, as supposed, of the salt and fresh water in Severn, equally terrible with its flashings and noise to the seers and hearers, and oh, how much more then to the feelers thereof. If any demand why the Thames hath not an Eagre as well as the Severn, where we find the same cause, and therefore why meet we not with the same effects? I re-demand of them, why is there not an Euripus[1] with the same reciprocation of tides, as well about the other Cyclades, as Euboea alone? Thus in cases of this kind it is easier to ask ten than answer one question with satisfaction.

We will conclude all with that which at first was a wonder's-fellow, until the strangeness thereof abated by degrees. There is a kind of bird, as yet not known by any proper name, which cometh in great companies, but seldom in this county, yet oftener than welcome; in bulk not much bigger than a sparrow, which may seem to carry a saw, or rather a scythe, on his mouth, for with his bill, which is thwarted crosswise at the end, he will shave or cut an apple in two at one snap, eating only the kernels thereof, spoiling more than he doth devour. They come about harvest-time, when apples begin to be ripe, so that these birds may be said to drink up many hogsheads of cider, as destroying them in their causes, and preventing the making thereof. The like have been seen in Cornwall, where at first they were taken (saith my author)[2] for a forboden token, understand him for a presage of ill success.

PROVERBS

The Tracys have always the wind in their faces. This is founded on fond and false tradition, which reporteth that ever since William de Tracy was most active amongst the four knights which killed Thomas à Becket, it is imposed on Tracys for miraculous penance, that whether they go by land or by water, the wind is ever in their faces. If this were so, it was a favour in a hot summer to the females of that family, and would spare them the use of a fan. But it is disproved by daily experience, there being extant at this day in this county two houses, the one honourable, the other worshipful, growing from the same root; so that we see it is not *now*, and therefore believe that it was *never* true. If any say that after so many generations this curse at last is antiquated, know that, according to popish principles, it deserved rather to be doubted of late, seeing no gentle family in England, since the Reformation, have more manifested their cordial disaffection to popery by their sufferings and writings, as hereafter will appear.

THE WORTHIES

CLAUDIANUS OSBERN, or Osbern of Gloucester, was bred a Benedictine monk in the famous convent in that city. He was learned, saith Leland,

(1) *Euripus.* The name of the narrow strait that separates Euboea and Boeotia, and of any part of the sea where the ebb and flow of the tide were remarkably violent. (2) Carew's *Survey of Cornwall.*

praeter illius aetatis sortem (above the standard of that age.) He was a good linguist, philosopher, divine; he used to give clearness to what was obscure, facility to what was difficult, politeness to what was barbarous. Nor wanted he a becoming facetiousness in his dialogues. He wrote many books, dedicating them to Gilbert Foliot bishop of Hereford.

[*fl.* 1148]

WILLIAM DE TRACY, of Toddington in this county, was a gentleman of high birth, state, and stomach, much in favour with King Henry the Second, on whom he was a daily attendant. One fact hath made his memory, call it famous or infamous, because he was the first and forwardest of the four knights who, at the encouragement, if not command, at leastwise at the connivance, if not encouragement, of the aforesaid king, imbrued their hands in the blood of Thomas à Becket.[1] [*d.* 1173]

ALAN OF TEWKESBURY, probably born in this county, though bred at Canterbury, where he became first a monk of Saint Saviour's, and afterwards prior thereof. Very intimate he was with Thomas à Becket, having some reputation for his learning. In his old age, it seems, he was sent back with honour into his native county, and for certain was made abbot of Tewkesbury, when Stephen Langton so much endeavoured, and at last accomplished, the canonizing of Thomas à Becket. Four authors were employed (Becket's Evangelists) to write the history of his mock-passion and miracles, and our Alan made up the *quaternion.* [*fl. 12th cent.*]

ALEXANDER OF HALES was bred up in the famous monastery of Hales, founded by Richard king of the Romans. After his living some time at Oxford, he went over to Paris, it being fashionable for the clergy in that, as for the gentry in our age, to travel into France; that clerk being accounted but half-learned who had not studied some time in a foreign university. But let Paris know that generally our Englishmen brought with them more learning thither, and lent it there, than they borrowed thence.

As for this our Alexander, as he had the name of that great conqueror of the world, so was he a grand captain and commander in his kind, for, as he did follow Peter Lombard, so he did lead Thomas Aquinas, and all the rest of the schoolmen. He was the first that wrote a comment on the Sentences, in a great volume called *The Sum of Divinity*, at the instance of Pope Innocent the Fourth, to whom he dedicated the same. For this, and other of his good services to the church of Rome, he received the splendid title of Doctor Irrefragabilis. He died Anno Domini 1245, and was buried in the Franciscan church in Paris.

ROBERT OF GLOUCESTER, so called because a monk thereof. He is omitted (whereat I wonder) both by Bale and Pits, except disguised under another name, and what I cannot conjecture. They speak truly who term him a rhymer, whilst such speak courteously who call him a

(1) After the murder Tracy surrendered himself to the pope, and set out for the holy land, but died of disease on the way.

poet. Indeed, such his language, that he is dumb in effect to the readers of our age without an interpreter, and such a one will hardly be procured. Antiquaries (amongst whom Mr. Selden) more value him for his history than poetry, his lines being neither strong nor smooth, but sometimes sharp, as may appear by this tetrastic, closing with a pinch at the paunch of the monks, which coming from the pen of a monk is the more remarkable:

> In the citie of Bangor a great hous tho was,
> And ther yndyr vij cellens[1] and ther of ther nas[2]
> That C.C.C. moncks hadde othur mo
> And alle by hure travayle lyvede; loke now if they do so.

[*fl.* 1260-1300]

SIR THOMAS DE LA MORE was, saith my author,[3] born of a knightly family, *patria Gloucestrenci* (a Gloucestershireman by his country); for which his observation I heartily thank him, who otherwise had been at an utter loss for his nativity. He thus further commendeth him:

> *Pacis et armorum vir artibus undique clarus.*
>
> A man whose fame extended far
> For arts in peace, and feats in war.

Indeed he was no carpet knight; as who brought his honour with him out of Scotland on his sword's point, being knighted by King Edward the First for his no less fortunate than valiant service therein. Nor less was his fidelity to his son Edward the Second, though unable to help him against his numerous enemies. But, though he could not keep him from being deposed, he did him the service faithfully to write the manner of his deposition, being a most rare manuscript extant in Oxford library. This worthy knight flourished 1327-1351.

KATHARINE CLIVEDON, better known by the name of Dame KATHARINE BERKELEY, was daughter unto Sir John Clivedon, richly landed in this county. She was first married to Sir Peers le Veel, and after to Thomas, third of that Christian name, baron of Berkeley, whom she survived, living a constant widow for four and twenty years; great her inheritance, augmented with a large jointure, and yet she expended the profits thereof in hospitality and pious uses, amongst which the founding of the fair school of Wotton-under-Edge was most remarkable.

I have sometimes wondered with myself to see the vast donations which the family of the Berkeleys bestowed on monasteries, so that there was no religious house within twenty miles of their castle (besides others at greater distance) which did not plentifully partake of their liberality. All these now are lost and extinct, whilst the endowment of Wotton school doth still continue, whereof I render this private reason to my own thoughts, because monks were not of God's planting, whilst teaching of youth is *jure divino* by a positive precept, "Teach a child in the trade of his youth, and he will remember it when he is old." I behold Wotton school as of great seniority, after Winchester, but before Eton in standing. John Smith, late of Nibley, esquire, was effectually instrumental in

(1) Cells, or portions.—F. (2) Ruler, or governor; *sed quaere*?—F. (3) Pits.

recovering the lands to this school, which since hath been happy in good schoolmasters, as they in pregnant scholars. This lady died March 13, 1385, and is buried by her husband in Berkeley church, in a monument grated about with iron bars.

SIR RALPH BOTELER, knight of the Garter, and Lord Sudeley in this county, was lord treasurer of England about three years, viz., from the seventh of July in the 22nd year of King Henry the Sixth, being the year of our Lord 1444, until the 25th year of that king's reign. This lord built Sudeley castle in this county, which of subjects' castles was the most handsome habitation, and of subjects' habitations the strongest castle. King Edward the Fourth sent for him with such summons that this lord conjectured, and that truly enough, that it was but a preface to his imprisonment; whereupon, going to London, and resting himself on a hill, whence he did behold his own castle: "It is thou, Sudeley, it is thou," said he, "and not I, that am a traitor," and so resigned the same at last into the hand of the king, to procure his own liberty.

SIR WILLIAM HAMPTON, son to John Hampton, was born at Minchinhampton in this county; bred a fishmonger in London, where he thrived so well, that he became lord mayor thereof anno 1472. He was the first that set up stocks in every ward for the punishment of vagabonds and strumpets; on which account I enter him a public benefactor, for an house of correction is a kind of almshouse, it being as charitable a work to reclaim the wicked as to relieve the wanting; and, were it not for prisons, all the land would be but a prison.

JOHN CARPENTER was (as my author[1] rationally collecteth) born at Westbury-on-Trym in this county; bred in Oriel College in Oxford, whereof he became provost, and chancellor of the university; thence preferred prefect of Saint Anthony's in London, and at last bishop of Worcester. He was so indulgent to Westbury, the place of his nativity, that of a mean he made a magnificent convent, more like a castle than a college, walling it about with turrets, and making a stately gate-house thereunto. He had an humorous intent to style himself and successors (in imitation of Bath and Wells) bishops of Worcester and Westbury, which title (though running cleverly on the tongue's end) never came in request, because therein *impar conjunctio*, the matching of a collegiate and cathedral church together. He died Anno Domini 1476, and was buried in his native town of Westbury.

THOMAS RUTHALL [or ROWTHALL], born at Cirencester in this county, bred in Cambridge, where he commenced doctor of the laws, was by King Henry the Seventh, for his great abilities, preferred to be bishop of Durham. King Henry the Eighth made him of his privy council, notwithstanding the hatred which Cardinal Wolsey bare unto him.

It happened King Henry employed him, as a politic person, to draw up a breviate of the state of the land, which he did, and got it fairly trans-

(1) Godwin.

cribed. But it fell out that instead thereof he, deceived with the likeness of the cover and binding, presented the king with a book containing an inventory of his own estate, amounting to an invidious and almost incredible sum of one hundred thousand pounds. Wolsey, glad of this mistake, told the king he knew now where a mass of money was, in case he needed it. This broke Ruthall's heart, who had paid the third part of the cost of making the bridge of Newcastle-over-Tyne, and intended many more benefactions, had not death (1523) on this unexpected occasion surprised him.

THOMAS BELL, born in this county, was twice mayor of the city of Gloucester, and raised his estate by God's blessing on his industry and ingenuity, being one of the first that brought the trade of capping[1] into the city. Hereby he got great wealth, sufficient to maintain the degree of knighthood, which King Henry the Eighth (as I take it) bestowed on him. He bought, from the crown, Blackfriars, by the south gate in this city, and reformed the ruins thereof into a beautiful house for himself, and hard by it erected an almshouse, and endowed it with competent revenues. His daughter and sole heir brought a fair estate into the families of Dennis.

JAMES BAINHAM, esquire, son to Sir Alexander Bainham, knight, was born at ———— in this county, bred in learning and knowledge of the Latin and Greek tongues. He afterwards became a student of the law in the Middle Temple, and when a pleader was charitable to the poor in giving, to the rich in moderating, his fees; and, what was the crown of all the rest, a true lover of the Gospel, in the dawning of Reformation.

Saint Paul saith, "It is appointed for all men once to die," and yet the same apostle saith of himself, "in deaths often," so many and great his pains and perils. And truly our Bainham encountered often with death, so that a little Book of Martyrs might be made of his sufferings.

First, Sir Thomas More sent for him to Chelsea, and tying him to a tree in his garden (called by him the Tree of Truth) caused him to be most cruelly scourged, to make him renounce his opinion. This not succeeding, Sir Thomas himself saw him cruelly racked in the Tower, till at last he was persuaded to abjure, and solemnly carried a torch and a faggot in the church of St. Paul's.

Hereby he rather exchanged than escaped the fire; finding such a fire in his own conscience, he could not be at quiet, till in the church of St. Augustine's, the next parochial church to St. Paul's (that the antidote might be brought as near as he could conveniently to the place of the poison) he publicly recanted his recantation, for which he was afterwards kept a fortnight in stocks in the bishop of London's coal-house, with irons upon him, chained again by Sir Thomas More to a post two nights, cruelly handled for a seven-night at Fulham, scourged for a fortnight in the Tower, and at last sent to a second tree of truth, I mean to the stake, whereat he was burned in Smithfield, April 30, 1532.

(1) *Capping* = cap-making.

EDWARD FOX was born [1496?] in Dursley in this county; bred first in Eton, then in King's College in Cambridge, whereof he was chosen provost, which place he kept until his death. He was afterwards almoner to King Henry the Eighth. He first brought Doctor Cranmer to the knowledge of the king, which doctor first brought the king to the knowledge of himself, how he stood in matter of marriage with the widow of his brother.

This Doctor Fox was after bishop of Hereford, and was (saith my author) *Reformationis ecclesiasticae illius tempore coeptae clanculum fautor.*[1] Let me add, he was the principal pillar of the Reformation as to the managery of the politic and prudential part thereof, being of more activity, and no less ability, than Cranmer himself. Martin Bucer dedicated unto him his *Comment on the Gospels;* yea, this bishop wrote many books, whereof that *De Vera Differentia Regiae Potestatis et Ecclesiae* was his master-piece. He was employed by the king on several embassies into France and Germany; and died, to the great loss of God's church, May 8, 1538.

SIR ANTHONY KINGSTON. This was that terrible provost-marshal of the king's army in the execution of the western rebels, whose memory I find accused by Sir John Heywood for his cruelty, and defended by Mr. Carew. This Sir Anthony, so frightful to all guilty persons, fell himself into the same fear in the reign of Queen Mary, on this occasion. Some were said to have a design to raise war against the queen, and resolved to provide the sinews before the bones of war, money before men. In order whereunto, their design was to rob the exchequer, then furnished with £50,000. This being discovered, many were accused as plotters, more as privy; amongst whom Sir Anthony Kingston, being sent for to come up, he died, for fear of death, some suppose, in his way to London.[2]

[1519-1556]

RICHARD TRACY, esquire, born at Toddington in this county, was son to William Tracy, confessor, of whom before.[3] He succeeded to his father's zeal, in the defence whereof he wrote several treatises in the English tongue, and that most remarkable which is intituled *The Preparation to the Cross.* This he wrote experimentally, having suffered much himself in his estate for his father's reputed heretical will; as also he wrote prophetically, anno 1550, few years before the beginning of Queen Mary; many being fore-warned, and so fore-armed, by his useful endeavours.

It must not be forgotten how, during my abode in Cambridge, on Midsummer Eve, 1626, a book was found in the belly of a cod (brought into the market to be sold) containing therein three treatises, where the

(1) Godwin ["Secretly a promoter of the ecclesiastical reformation which began in his time."] (2) He was charged in 1555 with conspiring to put Elizabeth on the throne, but was soon discharged. The following year he plotted to rob the exchequer for the same purpose, with results made clear by Fuller. (3) Fuller omitted to give an account of the elder Tracy, a justice of the peace under Henry VII and Henry VIII. He was a follower of Luther, and his famous heretical will (in which he declared his disbelief in anything that man could do or say to save his soul, desired no masses said, and left all his goods to his wife and son) became a sort of sacred text to the reformers. His body was exhumed and burned by order of Convocation.

first and largest was intituled *The Preparation to the Cross.* It was wrapped about with canvas, and probably that voracious fish plundered both out of the pocket of some shipwrecked seaman. The wits of the university made themselves merry thereat, one making a long copy of verses thereon, whereof this distich I remember:

> If fishes thus do bring us books, then we
> May hope to equal Bodley's library.[1]

But whilst the youngsters disported themselves herewith, the graver sort beheld it as a sad presage, and some, who then little looked for the cross, have since found it in that place. This book was thereupon reprinted, and the prefacer thereunto entituleth John Frith the author thereof. But no such book appears in Bale (though very accurate to give us a catalogue of his writings). Whereby we conclude, it was the same made by this Richard Tracy, to which another treatise was annexed, *To Teach One to Die,* made likewise by our Tracy, who himself died [1569].

EDWARD PALMER, esquire (uncle to Sir Thomas Overbury[2]) was born at Lemington in this county, where his ancestry had continued ever since the Conquest. Of his breeding I can give no exact account, for, as the growing of vegetables towards perfection is insensible, so (for want of particular information) I cannot trace his gradual motions, but find him at last answering the character given by Mr. Camden, "a curious and a diligent antiquary."

Great his store of coins, Greek and Roman, in gold, silver and brass, and greater his skill in them.

His plentiful estate afforded him opportunity to put forward the ingenuity impressed in him by nature for the public good, resolving to erect an academy in Virginia; in order whereunto he purchased an island, called Palmer's Island unto this day, but in pursuance thereof was at many thousand pounds' expense (some instruments employed therein not discharging their trust reposed in them with corresponding fidelity). He was transplanted to another world, leaving to posterity the memorial of his worthy but unfinished intentions. [*fl.* 1572]

SIR WILLIAM WINTER, knight, and vice-admiral of England, famous in his generation for several performances. 1. Anno 1559, being then but *Machinarum classicarum praefectus* (English it as you please [master of naval ordnance]) he frighted the French in Edinburgh Forth, assaulting their fort in the Island of Inchkeith. 2. Anno 1567, he was sent with Sir Thomas Smith, with the sound of the trumpet, and shooting of some cannon, to demand the restitution of Calais of the French king. 3. Anno 1568, he conducted a great treasure of the Genoan merchants safely into the Netherlands, in despite of the French opposing him. 4. Anno 1576 he, with Robert Beale, clerk of the council, was employed into Zeeland, to demand the restitution of our ships, which they had either taken, or did detain. 5. Anno 1588, he did signal service in the station appointed him, coming in, though not in the heat, in the cool of the day, when the

(1) Thomas Randolph. (2) See p. 196, below.

Spanish fleet was fallen towards the shore of Zeeland, and were sadly sensible of his valour. [*d.* 1589]

THOMAS NEAL was born [1519] at Yate in this county; bred first in Winchester, then New College in Oxford, where he became a great Grecian, Hebritian, and public professor of the latter in the university. He translated some Rabbins into Latin, and dedicated them to Cardinal Pole. He is charactered a man *naturae mirum in modum timidae* (of a very fearful nature) yet always continuing constant to the Roman persuasion. He was chaplain (but not domestic, as not mentioned by Mr. Foxe) to Bishop Bonner, and resided in Oxford. In the first of Queen Elizabeth, fearing his professor's place would quit him, for prevention he quitted it, and built himself an house over against Hart Hall, retaining the name of Neal's House many years after. Papists admire him for his rare judgment, and protestants for his strange invention, in first feigning the improbable lie of Matthew Parker's consecration at the Nag's Head in Cheapside, since so substantially confuted.[1] [*d.* 1590?]

JOHN SPRINT was bred a student in Christ Church in Oxford, and was afterward beneficed at Thornbury in this county; a grave and godly divine, but for a long time much disaffected to the ceremonies of the Church. It happened that Mr. Burton, archdeacon of Gloucestershire, his collegiate and contemporary, took him to task, persuading him seriously to study the point, which he promised, and performed accordingly. He put in the one scale the woe pronounced to such who preach not the gospel, and desert their flocks on pretended scrupulosity; in the other the nature of ceremonies, when things indifferent are enjoined by lawful authority.

Weighing both exactly in the balance of his judgment, he found the former to preponderate, concluding it unlawful for any on such account to leave or lose the exercise of his ministerial function. Hereupon he not only conformed for the future, but also wrote a book (dedicated to Archdeacon Burton) called *Cassander Anglicanus,* to persuade others to conformity. [*d.* 1623]

SIR THOMAS OVERBURY, knight, son to Sir Nicholas Overbury, one of the judges of the Marches, was born [1581] at Bourton-on-the-Hill in this county; bred in Oxford, and attained to be a most accomplished gentleman, which the happiness of his pen, both in poetry and prose, doth declare. In the latter he was the first writer of 'characters' of our nation, so far as I have observed.

But if the great parts of this gentleman were guilty of insolency and petulancy, which some since have charged on his memory, we may charitably presume that his reduced age would have corrected such juvenile extravagancies.

It is questionable whether Robert Carr, earl of Somerset, were more in the favour of King James, or this Sir Thomas Overbury in the favour of

(1) The consecration of Archbishop Parker in 1559, though perfectly well attested, was attacked by Roman controversialists, who invented the fable of a consecration in a tavern. Neal is generally regarded as the ultimate authority for this story.

the earl of Somerset, until he lost it by dissuading that lord from keeping company with a lady (the wife of another person of honour[1]) as neither for his credit here, or comfort hereafter.

Soon after Sir Thomas was by King James designed ambassador for Russia. His false friends persuaded him to decline the employment, as no better than an honourable grave. Better lie some days in the Tower, than more months in a worse prison: a ship by sea, and a barbarous cold country by land. Besides they possessed him that, within a small time, the king should be wrought to a good opinion of him. But he who willingly goes into a prison out of hope to come easily out of it, may stay therein so long till he be too late convinced of another judgment.

Whilst Sir Thomas was in the Tower, his refusal was represented to the king as an act of high contempt, as if he valued himself more than the king's service. His strict restraint gave the greater liberty to his enemies to practise his death, which was by poison performed.

Yet was his blood legally revenged, which cost some a violent, and others a civil death, as deprived of their offices. The earl was soon abated in King James's affection (oh, the short distance betwixt the cooling and quenching of a favourite!) being condemned and banished the court. The death of this worthy knight did happen Anno Domini 1613.

HUGH PIRRY was born in Wotton-under-Edge, a known market-town in this county; bred a merchant in London, whereof he was sheriff Anno Domini 1632. He brought the best servant that ever hath or will come to the town of Wotton; I mean the water, which in his lifetime, on his own cost, he derived thither, to the great benefit of the inhabitants.

He had read how "Job had warmed the poor with the fleece of his sheep," and observed what sheep Job had left, he lost, and what he had laid out, was left him; that wool only remaining his, which he had expended on the poor. Master Pirry, therefore, resolved on pious uses, but prevented by death, bequeathed a thousand pounds and upwards for the building and endowing of a fair almshouse in Wotton aforesaid, which is performed accordingly.

EDWARD TROTMAN, son of Edward Trotman, esquire, was born at Cam nigh Dursley in this county; bred a student of the law till he became a bencher in the Inner Temple. He wrote an abridgment of Sir Edward Coke's eleven volumes of *Reports*, for the benefit of those who had not money to purchase, or leisure to peruse them at large. Yea, such as have both may be profited thereby, for in my own profession, and in the Book of books, even those who are best acquainted with the chapters make also use of the contents. This gentleman, in his title-page, ingeniously wisheth that his *compendium* might not prove *dispendium* to the reader thereof. And I verily believe he hath had his desire, being informed that his endeavours are well esteemed by the learned in that

(1) The countess of Essex, who divorced her husband after Overbury's death and soon after married Robert Carr. He was later accused of poisoning Overbury, his wife pleading guilty, but both were pardoned. Carr's complicity is not certain, but the poisoning was almost certainly arranged by his wife. His life is given by Fuller under York, p. 671.

profession. He was buried in the Temple church, May 29, Anno Domini 1643.

RICHARD CAPEL was born [1586], as I am informed, in the city of Gloucester, whereof his father was alderman, and left him a good temporal estate. He was bred fellow of Magdalen College in Oxford, where he had many pupils of good quality; and among the rest Mr. William Pember, whose books he set forth, and as I remember finished his imperfect comment on *Zachary*.

Leaving the college, he was presented by Mr. Stephens to a good benefice in this county, where he made his excellent book of temptations, full fraught with practical piety, so that what judicious person soever readeth it, will experimentally say unto him, as once the lawyer to our Saviour, "Master, thou hast well spoken:" it carrieth in it such a truth by the confession of his conscience.

When the reading of the Book of Sports on the Lord's day was pressed upon him, he refused the same, as not comporting with his conscience, and willingly resigned his benefice, living afterwards on his temporal means, and preaching *gratis* in neighbouring congregations.[1] He died Anno Domini 1656.

THE FAREWELL

I congratulate the felicity of this county in the return of the episcopal see to the chief city thereof; the rather, seeing some questioned its charter, and would have had it uncitied, because unbishoped in our civil wars; though, with their leave, by the courtesy of England, once a city and ever a city. May the same hereafter ever remain there, to take away all suspicion in that kind for the future.

(1) The 'Book of Sports' was a declaration by James I that those who had attended divine service on Sunday might engage afterwards in certain lawful recreations. Ministers were directed to read it from the pulpit, and it was, of course, a counterblast to the puritans.

HAMPSHIRE

HAMPSHIRE hath Berkshire on the north, Surrey and Sussex on the east, the sea on the south, Dorset and Wiltshire on the west. From north unto south it extendeth unto fifty-four miles, not stretching above thirty miles from the east to the west thereof.

A happy country in the four elements, if culinary fire in courtesy may pass for one, with plenty of the best wood for the fuel thereof. Most pure and piercing the air of this shire; and none in England hath more plenty of clear and fresh rivulets of troutful water, not to speak of the friendly sea conveniently distanced from London. As for the earth, it is both fair and fruitful, and may pass for an expedient betwixt pleasure and profit, where, by mutual consent, they are moderately accommodated.

Yet much of the arable therein is stony ground though not like that in the Gospel, where the grain grew up, and withered so soon, "having no deepness of earth;" this bringing plenty of corn to perfection. Indeed, that in the parable may be presumed inwardly a rock, only faced over with superficial earth; whereas this hath solid earth enough, but abounding with little loose stones lying above it, which are conceived to keep the corn warmer; and therefore some, skilful in husbandry, have maintained that the taking of them away doth more hurt than good to the ground.

The south-west part of this county is called the New Forest, not in the same sense as New College in Oxford, then at the founding the newest, which since hath gained many *puisnes* thereunto; but because the junior of all forests in England, many having been *dis-* none *in*-forested since the Conquest. True it is, King Henry the Eighth made a forest about his palace of Hampton in Middlesex, by the name of Hampton Forest, but it never obtained peaceable possession in *publique pronunciation* (blame not the people thereabout if in point of profit their tongues would not cross their hearts) as this New Forest did. Whereof hereafter.

NATURAL COMMODITIES

Red Deer

Great store of these were lately in New Forest, so called because newly made by King William the Conqueror; otherwise, ten years hence, it will be six hundred years old. Indeed, as Augustus Caesar is said to have said of Herod king of Judea, that it was better to be his hog than his child; so was it most true of that King William, that it was better to have been his stag than his subject; the one being by him spared and preserved, the other ruined and destroyed: such was the devastation he made of towns in this county, to make room for his game.

And now was the south-west of this county made a forest indeed, if, as an antiquary[1] hath observed, a forest be so called, *quia foris est*, because it is set open and abroad. The stags therein were stately

(1) Sir Robert Cotton (under the name of Mr. Speed) in Huntingdonshire.

creatures, jealous, revengeful; insomuch that I have been credibly informed that a stag, unable for the present to master another who had taken his hind from him, waited his opportunity, till his enemy had weakened himself with his wantonness, and then killed him. Their flesh may well be good, whose horns are accounted cordial. Besides, there is a concave in the neck of a green-headed stag, when above his first crossing, wherein are many worms, some two inches in length, very useful in physic, and therefore carefully put up by Sir Theodore Mayerne[1] and other skilful physicians. But, I believe, there be few stags now in New Forest, fewer harts, and not any harts-royal (as escaping the chase of a king) though in time there may be some again.

HONEY

Although this county affordeth not such lakes of honey as some authors relate found in hollow trees in Muscovy, nor yieldeth combs equal to that which Pliny reporteth seen in Germany, eight foot long, yet produceth it plenty of this necessary and profitable commodity.

Indeed Hampshire hath the worst and best honey in England; worst, on the heath, hardly worth five pounds the barrel; best in the champaign, where the same quantity will well nigh be sold for twice as much. And it is generally observed, the finer the wheat and wool, both which very good in this county, the purer the honey of that place.

Honey is useful for many purposes, especially that honey which is the lowest in any vessel. For it is an old and true rule: the best oil is in the top, the best wine in the middle, and the best honey in the bottom. It openeth obstructions, cleareth the breast and lights[2] from those humours which fall from the head, looseneth the belly, with many other sovereign qualities too many to be reckoned up in a winter's day.

However, we may observe three degrees, or kinds rather, of honey: 1. *Virgin honey,* which is the purest, of a late swarm which never bred bees. 2. *Chaste honey,* for so I may term all the rest which is not sophisticated with any addition. 3. *Harlot honey*, as which is adulterated with meal and other trash mingled therewith.

Of the first and second sort I understand the counsel of Solomon: "My son, eat honey, for it is good;" good absolutely in the substance, though there may be excess in the quantity thereof.

WAX

This is the cask, where honey is the liquor; and being yellow by nature, is by art made white, red and green, which I take to be the dearest colours, especially when appendant on parchment. Wax is good by day and by night, when it affordeth light; for sight the clearest, for smell the sweetest, for touch the cleanliest. Useful in law to seal instruments; and in physic, to mollify sinews, ripen and dissolve ulcers, &c. Yea, the ground and foundation of all cerecloth (so called from *cera*) is made of wax.

(1) Lived 1573—1655; qualified in France, and later resident in England. He was physician to James I's queen, an authority on plague, and conducted chemical and physical experiments. Many volumes of his works are preserved in the British Museum. (2) *Lights* = lungs.

HOGS

Hampshire hogs are allowed by all for the best bacon, being our English Westphalian, and which, well ordered, hath deceived the most judicious palates. Here the swine feed in the forest on plenty of acorns (men's meat in the golden, hog's food in this iron age) which, going out lean, return home fat, without either care or cost of their owners. Nothing but fulness stinteth their feeding on the mast falling from the trees, where also they lodge at liberty, not pent up, as in other places, to stacks of pease; which some assign the reason of the fineness of their flesh; which, though not all glore[1] (where no banks of lean can be seen for the deluge of fat) is no less delicious to the taste, and more wholesome for the stomach.

Swine's-flesh, by the way, is observed most nutritive of men's bodies, because of its assimilation thereunto. Yet was the eating thereof forbidden to the Jews, whereof this reason may be rendered (besides the absolute will of the Law-giver) because in hot countries men's bodies are subject to the measles and leprosies, who have their greatest repast on swine's-flesh. For the climate of Canaan was all the year long as hot as England betwixt May and Michaelmas; and it is penal for any butchers with us in that term to kill any pork in the public shambles.

As for the manufacture of CLOTHING in this county (diffused throughout the same) such as deny the goodness of Hampshire cloth, and have occasion to wear it, will be convinced of its true worth by the price which they must pay for it.

THE BUILDINGS

The cathedral in Winchester yieldeth to none in England for venerable magnificence. It could not be *opus unius saeculi,* perfected by the contributive endeavours of several successive bishops, whereof some lie most sumptuously interred in their chapel-like monuments.

On the walls of the quire on each side, the dust of the Saxon kings and ancient bishops of this church were decently entombed (many hundred years after) by Richard Foxe[2] bishop of this see, till, in the beginning of our civil wars, they were barbarously thrown down by the soldiers.

As for the civil structures, Basing, built by the first marquess of Winchester, was the greatest of any subject's house in England, yea larger than most (eagles have not the biggest nests of all birds) of the king's palaces. The motto, "Love Loyalty", was often written in every window thereof, and was well practised in it, when, for resistance on that account, it was lately levelled to the ground.

Next Basing, Bramshill, built by the last Lord Zouche in a bleak and barren place, was a stately structure, especially before part thereof was defaced with a casual fire.

THE WONDERS

There is an oak in this county, which by credible people is generally reported to put forth green leaves yearly on or about Christmas day. It

(1) *Glore* is a verb, from the same root as *glare,* but here meaning *sheen.* (2) See Lincolnshire, p. 332.

groweth nigh Lyndhurst in the New Forest; and perchance I could point more exactly at the position thereof, but am loath to direct some ignorant zealot, lest he cut it down under the notion of superstition, and make timber of this oak, as some lately have made fuel of the hawthorn at Glastonbury.

PROVERBS

Manners make a man, quoth William of Wykeham. This generally was his motto, inscribed frequently on the places of his founding, so that it hath since acquired a proverbial reputation. We commonly say: 1. In the *Church,* "God makes a man," as who truly created him. 2. In the *Court,* "Clothes make a man," as which habit and adorn him. 3. In the *Change,* "Money makes a man," which puts him in a solvable condition. 4. In the *Schools,* "Manners make a man," as which complete and accomplish him.

Grant the two middle expressions, the extravagancy of our pride and covetousness, the first and last must be allowed proportionable to piety and truth. Without manners, one is but a man-beast, or centaur.

Now seeing no man without manners, no manners without some learning, no learning without teaching, no teaching of youth to that in a grammar free-school, of men to that in a college in an university—how much thanks doth posterity owe to this Wykeham's memory.

Canterbury is the higher rack, but Winchester is the better manger. W. Edington,[1] bishop of Winchester, was the author of this expression, rendering this the reason of his refusal to be removed to Canterbury, though chosen thereunto. Indeed, though Canterbury be graced with a higher honour, the revenues of Winchester, lying entirely, are more advantageous to gather riches thereon. The proverb is appliable to such who prefer a wealthy privacy before a less profitable dignity.

Yet know that that manger did once partly maintain that rack, viz., when John White, bishop of Winchester, was enjoined by Queen Mary to pay a thousand pounds a year to Cardinal Pole,[2] archbishop of Canterbury, for the better support of his estate.

[A PLOUGH DRAWN BY DOGS]

We must not forget one (better known to me by his invention than his name) who, dwelling at Stockbridge in this county, made so artificial a plough that, by the help of engines and some contrivances, it might be drawn by dogs, and managed by one man, who would plough in one day well nigh an acre of the light ground in this county. This plough I saw (some thirty years since) at Stockbridge aforesaid.

But the project was not taking, beheld rather as pretty than profitable; though in the judgment of wise men this groundwork might have been built upon, and invention much improved by the skilful in mathematics; for I have heard that some politicians are back-friends (how justly I know not) to such projects which, if accomplished, invite the land to a loss, the fewer poor being thereby set a-work; that being the best way of tillage

(1) See Wiltshire, p. 611. (2) For John White see p. 210, below and for Reginald Pole see Staffordshire, p. 515.

which employeth most about it, to keep them from stealing and starving. So that it would not be beneficial to the state, might a plough be drawn by butterflies, as which would draw the greater burden on the commonwealth, to devise other ways for the maintenance of the poor.

THE WORTHIES

JOHN BASING OR BASINGSTOKE, so called from a fair market town in this county, where he was born. We have a double demonstration of his signal worth; first, because Robert Grosseteste,[1] that pious and learned bishop (who would not advance anything which was under eminency) preferred him archdeacon of Leicester; secondly the pens of Bale and Pits, diametrically opposite one to the other, meet both in his commendation. Being bred first in Oxford, then in Paris, thence he travelled into Athens (Athens as yet was Athens, not routed by Turkish tyranny) where he heard the learned lectures of one Constantina, a noblewoman (not fully twenty years old) of the abstruse mysteries of nature. Coming home, he brought back many precious books, and had good skill in the Greek tongue (whereof he wrote a grammar) and is justly reputed the first restorer thereof in England. He was the author of many works, and died anno 1252.

HENRY III, eldest son of King John and his wife Isabella, born at Winchester, anno 1207, was one, besides the account of longevity, eminent in his generation. He was a most pious king, son to a profane father, King John; a very poor king, brother to a most wealthy, Richard king of the Romans; a very weak king, father to a most wise son, Edward the First. The tragi-comedy of his life was eminent in many particulars. 1. He had scarce half a kingdom in the beginning of his reign: Louis of France being brought in to be king by the English in their hot, and cast out in their cold blood. 2. He had no part of a kingdom in the middle of his reign: embroiled with war with his barons, beaten in battle, imprisoned, and no king in effect. 3. He had all the kingdom in the end of his reign; for as soon as Prince Edward began to man it, this his son may be accounted his father, by whom he attained a comfortable old age.

He was not so weak but that he knew who were wiser than himself, and would be governed by them, one main cause which procured his death in peace, and burial in pomp in the abbey of Westminster of his own foundation, Anno Domini 1272.

WILLIAM OF WYKEHAM was born [1324] at Wickham in this county, being the son of John Long and Sibill his wife (over whose graves he hath erected a chapel at Titchfield in this county) and bred in the university of Oxford. He was otherwise called *Long*, from the height of his stature, as my author conceives,[2] though since it may be applied to the perpetuity of his memory, which will last as long as the world endureth, for his two fair foundations at [1] Oxford, begun 1379. The charter of the foundation of St. Mary's College in Oxford, was dated the 26th of November

(1) See Suffolk, p. 524. (2) Godwin [Fuller gave his father's name as Perot in the original edition, and it has been corrected above.]

1379, in his manor in Southwark, since called Winchester House; finished 1386, the scholars entered thereunto about nine o'clock on the 14th day of April, in the same year; [2] Winchester, begun 1387. The first stone was laid March 26, at nine o'clock in the morning, in the 69th year of the age of the founder; finished 1394.

He died [1404] in the 37th year of his consecration and 80th of his age, in the fifth year of the reign of King Henry the Fourth; and his benefaction to learning is not to be paralleled by any English subject in all particulars.[1]

HENRY BEAUFORT.[2] It will be worth our enquiry who this chief commissioner Henry bishop of Winchester was, with his insolent title of "Cardinal of England." I find many eminent epithets (but none of the quorum of Saint Paul's bishops) meeting in his person; viz., *noble, rich, valiant, politic* and *long-lived*. *Noble,* being son of John of Gaunt,[3] by Catherine Swynford, born at Beaufort in France, whence he had his name; brother to King Henry the Fourth, uncle to King Henry the Fifth, great-uncle to King Henry the Sixth. *Rich,* commonly called the 'Rich Cardinal.' In his time the king and courtiers cast a covetous eye on church-endowments, but were diverted from longer looking on them by the council of Archbishop Chichele and coin of this Bishop Beaufort; the former putting the king upon the war with France, the latter lending him, on good security, twenty thousand pounds, a sum sounding high in those days. He was also called . . . the Cardinal of England, though we had another (and his senior) at the same time of the same order; viz., Thomas Langley, bishop of Durham. *Valiant,* being the pope's legate (in plain English, the pope's general) leading his army into Bohemia, in which service he behaved himself *fortius quam espiscopum decebat* [more stoutly than became a bishop]. *Worldly-politic,* venting words on his death-bed to this purpose: "That if all England" (some reporters take a longer circuit) "would preserve his life, he was able by his purse to purchase or by policy to procure it." *Long life,* having been bishop of Lincoln and Winchester fifty years; yet was he so far from being weaned from the world, he sucked the hardest (as if he would have bit off the nipples thereof) the nearer he was to his grave, dying anno 1447.

He was in his generation (by a charitable *antiperistasis*) fixed betwixt Bishops Wykeham and Wainfleet; but did not equal them in his benefactions to the public, though he founded a fair hospital in Winchester, a work (no doubt) more acceptable to God than when he, anno 1417, undertook and performed a dangerous voyage to Jerusalem.

It is, in my apprehension, very remarkable, that the three aforesaid bishops of Winchester, Wykeham, Beaufort and Wainfleet, sat successively in that see six score years lacking two, not to be paralleled in any other bishopric.

(1) William of Wykeham, one of the greatest pluralists of his age, is more remarkable as statesman than ecclesiastic. Among other important appointments under Edward III he held the chancellorship, was charged with misgovernment, and pardoned under Richard II. He was again chancellor 1389-91. 'St. Mary's College' is of course New College. (2) Placed in the list of Gentry in the original edition. (3) He was the second, and illegitimate son, but declared legitimate by Richard II in 1397.

JOHN RUSSELL was born in this county, in the parish of Saint Peter's in the suburbs of Winchester. He was bred fellow of New College, and when doctor of canon law was chosen chancellor of Oxford. Yea, that office, annual before, was first fixed on him, as in Cambridge on Bishop Fisher, for term of life.

By King Edward the Fourth he was advanced bishop of Lincoln, and by Richard the Third lord chancellor of England, having ability enough to serve any, and honesty too much to please so bad a king. And because he could not bring him to his bent, when the Lord Hastings was killed, this bishop, saith my author,[1] was for a time imprisoned. He died December the 30th, anno 1494.

WILLIAM WARHAM was born [1450?] at Church Oakley, of worshipful parentage, in this county; bred fellow and doctor of the laws in New College; employed by King Henry the Seventh (who never sent sluggard or fool on his errand) to Margaret duchess of Burgundy, and by him advanced bishop of London, then archbishop of Canterbury, living therein in great lustre, till eclipsed in power and profit by Thomas Wolsey, archbishop of York.

It may be said that England then had ten archbishops, if a figure and cipher amount to so many; or else, if it had but two, they were Archbishop Thomas and Archbishop Wolsey, drawing all causes to his court-legatine, whilst all other ecclesiastical jurisdictions in England kept a constant vacation. This Warham bare with much moderation, contenting himself that, as he had less honour, so he had less envy, and kept himself cool, whilst Wolsey, his screen, was often scorched with just and general hatred.

In the case of King Henry his divorce, he was the prime advocate for Queen Catherine; and carried it so cautiously that he neither betrayed the cause of his client, nor incurred the king's displeasure.[2] Nor will any wonder that an archbishop of Canterbury did then plead before an archbishop of York, seeing the king at the same time was summoned before his subject.

He survived Wolsey's ruin, but never recovered his former greatness, blasted with a *praemunire* with the rest of the clergy, and the heavier because the higher in dignity. He is said to have expended thirty thousand pounds in the repair of his palaces, the probable reason why he left no other public monuments, though archbishop twenty-eight years, dying Anno Domini 1532.

ROBERT SHERBORNE [or SHIRBURN] was born [1450?] in this county, and bred first in Winchester, and then in New College; was a great scholar and prudent man, employed in several embassies by King Henry the Seventh, and by him preferred bishop, first of St. David's, then of

(1) Harpsfield, *Historia Ecclesiae Anglicanae* [For William, Lord Hastings, see Leicestershire, p. 315.] (2) A charitable construction not borne out by the facts. Warham, who had originally objected to Henry's marriage with Catherine, was one of the counsel assigned ostensibly for her defence, but was somewhat afraid to act in that capacity, and in fact tried to trap her into making admissions damaging to herself. Henry forced him to advise the pope to annul the marriage.

Chichester;[1] which church he decorated with many ornaments and edifices, especially the south side thereof; where, on the one side, the history of the foundation of the church, with the images of the kings of England; on the other, the statutes of all the bishops of this see, both those of Selsey and of Chichester.

He often inscribed for his motto, *Dilexi decorem domus tuae, Domini* (I have loved the beauty of thy house, O Lord); and sometimes, *Credite operibus* (trust their works). Now although some may like his alms better than his trumpet, charity will make the most favourable construction thereof. Being ninety-six years of age, he resigned his bishopric, and died in the same year, Anno Domini 1536.

WILLIAM LILY was born [1468?] at Odiham, a market-town in this county, and travelled in his youth as far as Jerusalem. In his return he stayed at Rhodes and studied Greek; which will seem strange to some, Rhodes not being Rhodes in that age (except casually some great critic was there); seeing otherwise to find elegance in modern Greek (soured with long continuance) is as impossible as to draw good wine out of a vessel of vinegar.

Hence he went to Rome, where he heard John Sulpitius and Pomponius Laetus, great masters of Latin in those days. After his return, Dean Colet made him the first master of St. Paul's school, which place he commendably discharged for fifteen years. Here he made his Latin grammar, which this great schoolmaster modestly submitted to the correction of Erasmus; and therefore such who will not take it on the single bond of Lily may trust on the security of Erasmus.

Some charge it for surfeiting with variety of examples, who would have had him only set down the bare rules as best for children's remembrance. But they may know that such who learnt grammar in Lily's time were not schoolboys, but schoolmen; I mean arrived at men's estate. Many since have altered and bettered his grammar; and amongst them my worthy friend Dr. Charles Scarburgh,[2] calculating his short, clear and true rules for the meridian of his own son, which in due time may serve for general use. Our Lily died of the plague, and was buried in the porch of Saint Paul's, Anno Domini 1522.

ARTHUR, eldest son to King Henry the Seventh and Queen Elizabeth, was born (being *partus octomestris,* yet vital and vigorous, contrary to the rules of physicians) at Winchester, the 19th day of September 1486. Some will wonder at his name, whereof no alliance, nor English prince, since the unhappy Arthur duke of Brittany, supposed to be made away by King John, his cruel uncle. But because this prince, by his father's side was, with King Arthur, of British extraction, and because born at Winchester where King Arthur kept his court, and his (pretended) Round Table still to be seen, that name was bestowed upon him. He died at Ludlow, in the sixteenth year of his age, anno 1502, and is buried in the cathedral of Worcester; more known to posterity by the widow he left,

(1) He forged the papal bull appointing himself to the former. (2) Lived 1616—1694. An original fellow of the Royal Society, he was physician to Charles II and James II, and knighted by the former. He was with Fuller at the Hague in 1660 to welcome Charles II.

the Lady Catherine Dowager[1] (and the effects ensuing thereon) than by any of his own personal performances.

THOMAS STERNHOLD was born in this county, and was afterwards a servant to King Henry the Eighth. I find him a legatee in his will, thus mentioned: "Item, To Thomas Sternhold, groom of our robes, a hundred mark."

He was afterwards (saith my author[2]) *ab intimo cubiculo* to King Edward the Sixth; though I am not satisfied whether thereby he meant gentleman of his privy chamber, or groom of his bedchamber.

He was a principal instrument of translating the Psalms into English metre; the first twenty-six (and seven-and-thirty in all) being by him performed. Yet had he other assistance in that work.[3] Many a bitter scoff hath since been passed on their endeavours by some wits, which might have been better employed. Some have miscalled these their translations *Geneva gigs;* and, which is the worst, *father,* or *mother* rather, the expression on our Virgin Queen, as falsely as other things have been charged upon her. Some have not sticked to say that "David hath been as much persecuted by bungling translators as by Saul himself." Some have made libellous verses in abuse of them; and no wonder if songs were made on the translators of the psalms, seeing drunkards made them on David the author thereof.

But let these translations be beheld by unpartial eyes, and they will be allowed to go in equipage with the best poems in that age. However, it were to be wished that some bald rhymes therein were bettered; till which time such as sing them must endeavour to amend them by singing them with understanding heads and gracious hearts, whereby that which is bad metre on earth will be made good music in heaven.

As for our Thomas Sternhold, it was happy for him that he died before his good master, anno 1549, in the month of August, so probably preventing much persecution, which had happened unto him if surviving in the reign of Queen Mary.

WILLIAM PAULET, wherever born [1485?] had his largest estate and highest honour (baron of Basing, and marquess of Winchester) in this county. He was descended from a younger house of the Paulets of Hinton St. George in Somersetshire, as by the crescent in his arms is acknowledged. One telleth us[4] that he being a younger brother, and having wasted all that was left him, came to court on trust, where, upon the bare stock of his wit, he trafficked so wisely and prospered so well that he got, spent and left more than any subject since the Conquest.

Indeed he lived at the time of the dissolution of abbeys, which was the harvest of estates; and it argued idleness if any courtier had his barns empty. He was servant to King Henry the Seventh, and for thirty years together treasurer to King Henry the Eighth, Edward the Sixth, Queen Mary and Queen Elizabeth. The latter, in some sort, owed their crowns

(1) Catherine of Aragon. (2) Bale. (3) By John Hopkins (*d.* 1570) a Suffolk schoolmaster, to whom the "Old Hundredth" is often attributed. (4) Sir Robert Naunton, in his *Fragmenta Regalia*.

to his counsel, his policy being the principal defeater of Duke Dudley's design to disinherit them.[1]

I behold this Lord Paulet like to aged Adoram, so often mentioned in Scripture, being over the tribute in the days of King David, all the reign of King Solomon, until the first year of Rehoboam. And though our Lord Paulet enjoyed his place not so many years, yet did he serve more sovereigns, in more mutable times, being, as he said of himself, "no oak, but an osier."

Herein the parallel holds not. The hoary hairs of Adoram were sent to the grave by a violent death, slain by the people in a tumult. This lord had the rare happiness of . . . setting in his full splendour, having lived eighty-seven years, and seen 103 out of his body. He died Anno Domini 1572.

SIR JOHN WALLOP, born in this county of a most ancient and respected family, was directed by his genius to sea-service, at what time our coasts were much infested with French piracies; for there was a knight of Malta, passing in our chronicles by the name of Prior John (more proper, by his profession, to be employed against the Turks, lately so victorious in Hungary) who lived by pickeering,[2] and undoing many English merchants.

But our Sir John made the French pay more than treble damages, who, with eight hundred men, landed in Normandy, burnt one-and-twenty towns, with divers ships in the havens of Traport, Etaples, &c.; and safely returned with wealth and victory.

Methinks the ancient arms of the Wallops appear prophetical herein, viz., Argent, a bend undé Sable; interpreted by my author,[3] a wave, or surge of the sea, raised by some turbulent flaw of wind and tempest, prognosticating the activity of that family in marine performances.

[*d.* 1551]

ROBERT TOMSON, merchant, was born at Andover in this county; bred much at Bristol in sea employment. Hence, anno 1553, he sailed into Spain, and thence two years after shipped himself for Nova Hispania, to make a discovery thereof; on the same token that in his passage thither, in a Spanish ship, a light like a candle (being nothing else but a meteor frequent by sea and land) fell on their mainmast, which the Spaniards on their knees worshipped for St. Elmo, the advocate of sailors. He afterwards wrote the description of New Spain, with the city of Mexico, giving a good and the first account thereof of any Englishman.

During his abode many months in Mexico, at dinner he let fall some discourse against saint-worship, for which he was imprisoned in the holy-house, and enjoined solemn penance by the archbishop of Mexico, this Tomson being the first (reputed) heretic which was ever seen in America on a penitential scaffold. Hence he was sent into Spain, and after three

(1) He held high office under Protector Somerset, but joined John Dudley, duke of Northumberland (see Staffordshire, p. 516) to overthrow him. He was, however, strongly opposed to Northumberland's plot to set his daughter-in-law Lady Jane Grey on the throne. Mary at first was apparently doubtful of his loyalty, although he had proclaimed her, and he was confined, but later admitted to her privy council.
(2) *Pickeering*=pillaging. (3) Gwillim, *Display of Heraldry*.

years' durance in the Inquisition, discharged. Here a Spanish merchant's daughter, Mary de la Barrera by name, fell in love with him, and became his wife, worth to him in bars of gold and silver two thousand five hundred pounds, besides jewels of great price. Returning into England, he lived with great comfort and credit therein, so that it may truly be said of him, "He had been undone, if (by the cruelty of his enemies) he had not been undone."

DAVID WHITEHEAD (where born [1492?] to me unknown) is here placed because I find a worshipful and ancient family of his name in this county. He was bred a bachelor of divinity in Oxford; and, flying into Germany in the reign of Queen Mary, was in high esteem at Frankfort with the English congregation. After his return, Queen Elizabeth proffered him great preferment. And it seems, in the first of her reign, the archbishop of Canterbury went a-wooing to accept thereof, viz., to 1. John de Feckenham, refusing it upon a popish account, because he would not subscribe to the queen's supremacy; 2. Nicholas Wotton, doctor of law, and dean of Canterbury, refusing it on a politic account, suspecting the queen's short life, and fearing alterations in the state; 3. This Whitehead, who declined it out of his desire of privacy, though some causelessly suspected him for disaffection to church discipline. For he was, by Queen Elizabeth, offered the mastership of the hospital of the Savoy, which he might have accepted without any subscription, but would not, affirming he could live plentifully on the preaching of the gospel: a rare example of moderation. He was a deep divine, and was chosen one of the disputants, *primo Elizabethae,* against the popish bishops. His many books, still extant, testify his learning and religion.

Queen Elizabeth highly valued his company, the rather because of his conscientious bluntness, wherein one repartee may be remembered. The queen, who ever was *iniquior in sacerdotes maritatos* [harsher to married priests] said unto him, "Whitehead, I love thee the better, because thou art unmarried." "In truth, Madam," said he, "I love you the worse because you are unmarried." He died Anno Domini 1571.

RICHARD RICH, knight [FIRST BARON RICH] was, in the words of my author, "a gentleman well descended and allied in this county;"[1] bred in the Temple, in the study of our common law, and afterwards became solicitor to King Henry the Eighth. His deposition on oath, upon words spoken to him in the Tower, was the sharpest evidence to cut off the head of Sir Thomas More. He was under Cromwell a lesser hammer to knock down abbeys, most of the grants of which lands going through his hands, no wonder if some stuck upon his fingers.

Under King Edward the Sixth he was made lord chancellor of England, discharging his place with prudence and equity for the term of five years. Forseeing he should be ousted of his office (being of the anti-faction to Duke Dudley) to prevent stripping, he politicly put off his robes of state (resigning his office). Which done, no danger of catching cold, his own undersuit was so well lined, having gotten a fair estate about Leighs

(1) J. Philpot, in his *Catalogue of Chancellors.*

Abbey in Essex, whereof he was created baron. He died in the beginning of the reign of Queen Elizabeth, being direct ancestor unto the right honourable Charles Rich, now earl of Warwick.[1] [1496?-1567]

JOHN WHITE was born [1510?] in this county, of a worshipful house; began on the floor, and mounted up to the roof of spiritual dignity in this diocese. First, scholar in Winchester, then fellow of New College in Oxford, then master of Winchester School, then warden of that college, and at last (taking Lincoln bishopric in his passage) bishop of Winchester, all composed in this distich:

Me puero custos, ludi paulo ante magister,
Vitus, et hac demum praesul in urbe fuit.[2]

I may call the latter a golden verse, for it cost this White many an angel to make it true, entering into his bishopric on this condition: to pay Cardinal Pole a yearly pension of a thousand pounds. Now though this was no better than simony, yet the prelate's pride was so far above his covetousness, and his covetousness so far above his conscience, that he swallowed it without any regret.

He was a tolerable poet, and wrote an elegy on the Eucharist to prove the corporeal presence and confute Peter Martyr,[3] the first and last, I believe, who brought controversial divinity into verses. He preached the funeral sermon of Queen Mary (or, if you will, of public popery in England) praising her so beyond all measure, and slighting Queen Elizabeth without any cause, that he justly incurred her displeasure. This cost him deprivation and imprisonment, straiter than others of his order (though freer than any protestant had under popish persecutors) until his death, which happened at London . . . 1560.

JOHN PHILPOT, son of Sir Peter Philpot, knight, born [1516] in this county; whose family had an ancient habitation at Compton therein. He proceeded master of arts in New College in Oxford; and afterwards, being archdeacon of Winchester, was a zealous promoter of the protestant religion. In the first of Queen Mary, being a member of the convocation, "his heart was hot within; and while he was musing, the fire kindled, and he spake with his tongue," which afterwards occasioned his martyrdom.

If papists account him a distracted man, none will wonder, who consider how the profane captains of Israel called the son of the prophet a mad fellow. And if some vehement expressions fell from him during his imprisonment, his enemies' cruelty was the cause thereof; seeing ill usage, which once made a dumb beast to speak, may make a sober man overspeak in his passion. But all his sufferings are reported by Mr. Foxe so perfectly (*perfectum est cui nihil addi potest*) that it is presumption for

(1) A strangely favourable account of one of the most despicable figures of the period. By base means he procured evidence against John Fisher, bishop of Rochester, perjured himself against Sir Thomas More in court, and deserted Cromwell when he fell. He was severe towards the reformers and protestants, racking one of them with his own hands. He founded Felstead Grammar School. (2) Made by Christopher Johnson, afterwards schoolmaster of Winchester ["White was warden when I was a boy, and a little earlier schoolmaster, and finally bishop in this city."] (3) See note 1, p. 130.

any to hope to make an essential addition thereunto. He was martyred Anno Domini 1555, Dec. 18.

RICHARD WHITE was born [1539] at Basingstoke in this county; bred first in Winchester School, then in New College in Oxford. In the beginning of Queen Elizabeth, leaving the land, he lived first at Louvain, then in Padua in Italy, where he proceeded doctor of the laws. Afterwards he became regius professor at Douay for the space of thirty years and more. He wrote many books, and amongst the rest, a British and English history, which hitherto I have not been so happy as to see, save at the second hand, as often cited by Mr. Selden, which makes me believe much merit therein.

Surely he was better employed in the writing thereof, than in the large comment he hath made on the enigmatical epitaph set up at Bononia: *Aelia Laelia Crispis*, &c., which many think merely made by a conceited brain on design to puzzle intellects, to create sense by their ingenuity and industry, which was never intended therein. For I am clearly of his opinion who said, *Qui ea scribit legi, quar non vult intelligi, debet negligi* [any one who writes what he does not intend to be understood should be ignored].

I have nothing else to observe of this Richard White, save that, after he had successively married two wives, he was made a priest by this special dispensation of Pope Clement the Eighth; and that he was alive at Douay, 1611. [*d.* 1611]

HENRY COTTON was born at Warblington in this county, being a younger son unto Sir Richard Cotton, knight and privy councillor to King Edward the Sixth. Queen (whilst yet but Lady) Elizabeth, being then but twelve years of age, was his godmother. He was bred in Magdalen College in Oxford, and was by the queen preferred bishop of Salisbury; when she pleasantly said "that formerly she had blessed many of her godsons, but now her godson should bless her;" reflecting on the solemnity of episcopal benediction. He was consecrated November the 12th, 1598; at which time William Cotton, of another family, was made bishop of Exeter; the queen merrily saying (alluding to the plenty of clothing in those parts) "that she hoped that now she had well cottoned the west." By his wife, whose name was Patience, he had nineteen children, and died May the 7th, 1615.

THOMAS BILSON was born [1547] in the city of Winchester; bred first, scholar in Winchester School, then (taking New College in his passage) schoolmaster thereof, afterwards warden of the college, and at last (taking Worcester in his way) bishop of Winchester. As reverend and learned a prelate as England ever afforded; witness his worthy works, *Of the Perpetual Government of Christ's Church*, and of *Christ's Descent into Hell;* not (1) *ad patiendum*, to *suffer*, which was concluded on the cross with "It is finished;" nor (2) *ad praedicandum*, to *preach*, useless where his auditory was all the forlorn hope; neither (3) *ad liberandum*, to *free* any, pardon never coming after execution; but (4) *ad possidendum*, to *take possession* of hell, which he had conquered; and (5) *ad triumphandum*, to *triumph*, which is honourable *in hostico*, in the enemies' own country.

The new translation of the Bible was by King James his command ultimately committed to his and Dr. Smith's[1] (bishop of Gloucester) perusal, who put the completing hand thereunto. His pious departure out of this life happened 1616.

NICHOLAS FULLER was, as I have cause to conceive, born [1575?] in this county; and, when a youth, was amanuensis or scribe to Dr. Horne,[2] bishop of Winchester; afterwards he attended, as tutor servant, on Sir Henry Wallop to Oxford; and returning thence, was made minister of Allington nigh Salisbury in Wiltshire, where he had a benefice rather than a living, so small the revenues thereof. But a contented mind extendeth the smallest parish into a diocese, and improveth the least benefice into a bishopric.

Here a great candle was put under a bushel, or peck rather, so private his place and employment. Here he applied his studies in the tongues, and was happy in pitching on, not difficult trifles, but useful difficulties tending to the understanding of Scripture. He became an excellent linguist, and his books found good regard beyond the seas, where they were reprinted.

Drusius, the Belgian critic, grown old, angry and jealous that he should be outshined in his own sphere, foully cast some drops of ink upon him, which the other as fairly wiped off again. He charged Master Fuller for being his plagiary, taking his best notes from him without an acknowledgement thereof. Master Fuller confessed himself always desirous of Drusius his works, but never able, such his poverty, to purchase them, and therefore he could not steal out of those books which his eye never beheld; and (not to be partial to my namesake) let the world judge whether Fuller's *miscellanea* be not so good as Drusius's *wheat*.

Bishop Andrewes[3] came to him, as the queen of Sheba to Solomon, to pose him with hard questions, bringing with him a heap of knots for the other to untie, and departed from him with a good satisfaction. He afterwards bestowed on him a great living in this county, which Master Fuller did not long enjoy. He was most eminent for that grace which is most worth, yet costeth the least to keep it: I mean humility, who in his writings doth as fairly dissent from, as freely concur with, any man's opinions. [*d.* 1626]

JOHN PITS [or PITSEUS] was born [1560] in this county, nigh the market town of Alton; witness his words, *"in vicino cujus oppidi natus sum ego."* Son he was to Henry Pits and Elizabeth his wife, sister to Nicholas Sanders.[4] It is hard to say whether his hands took more pains in writing, or feet in travelling, if the list of his laborious life be perused, whereby he will appear a very aged person. At eleven years of age he went to the school of Winchester, 11; seven years he stayed there, until chosen unto New College, 18; two years he lived in Oxford, and then went beyond the seas, 20; one year he stayed and studied in the college of Rheims, 21; thence going to Rome, he lived seven years there in the English College,

(1) Miles Smith—see Herefordshire, p. 225. Bilson himself had no hand in the Authorized Version. (2) Robert Horne—see Durham, p. 158. (3) Lancelot Andrewes —see London, p. 367. (4) See Surrey, p. 550.

and was ordained priest, 28; returning to Rheims, two years he there taught rhetoric and Greek, 30; then living in Lorraine and in Trèves two years, 32; three years at Ingolstadt in Bavaria, where he was made D.D., 35; made canon of Verdun in Lorraine, and lived there two years, 37; then for twelve years he was confessor to the duchess of Cleves, 49.

Here he wrote many volumes of several subjects, one of the apostolical men, another of the kings and bishops in England; but, because he survived not to see them set forth, he was as good as his word, *mecum morientur et sepelientur* (with him they died, and were buried); only that his book is brought to light, which is intituled *De Illustribus Angliae Scriptoribus,* a subject formerly handled by many, so that some stick not to say J. Leland is the industrious *bee,* working all; J. Bale is the angry *wasp,* stinging all; J. Pits is the idle *drone,* stealing all.

For my part, I have made use of his endeavours to help me with many writers, especially with such English papists as have been since the Reformation. Nor will I pay him with railing from whose pen I have borrowed much information. Some wonder at his invectiveness: I wonder more that he inveigheth so little; and seeing he was sister's son to black-mouthed Sanders, it is much that he doth not more *avunculize* in his bitterness against protestants.

After the death of Antonia duchess of Cleves, he returned the third time into Lorraine, where the bishop of Toul (who formerly had been his scholar) gave him the deanery of Liverdun, a place of good credit and revenue, where quietly he reposed himself for the remainder of his life for many years; and, dying anno 1616, was there buried.

SIR THOMAS LAKE was born [1567?] in the parish of St. Michael in the town of Southampton, and there bred in grammar-learning under Doctor Saravia.[1] By several under-offices he was at last deservedly preferred secretary of state to King James. Incredible his dexterity in dispatch, who at the same time would indite, write, discourse more exactly than most men could severally perform them. Men resembled him to one of the ships-royal of Queen Elizabeth, called the *Swiftsure,* such his celerity and solidity in all affairs. No less his secrecy in concealing, and what was credited to his counsel was always found in the same posture it was left in. Add to all these, he was a good man, and a good man's brother, Dr. Arthur Lake, bishop of Bath and Wells.[2] King James, who always loved what was facile and fluent, was highly pleased with his Latin pen, who by practice had made Tully's phrase his own. He was one of the three noble hands, who at the court first led Mr. George Villiers[3] into the favour of King James.

At last he fell, for the faults of others, into the king's displeasure, being punished for the offences of one of his nearest relations; and of all them fined in the Star-chamber he was the only person generally pitied for his suffering; yet even then King James gave him this public eulogy in open

(1) Hadrian à Saravia (1531—1613) reformist divine; born is Artois, professor of divinity at Leyden, moved to England and held English livings; a friend of Richard Hooker. (2) His life follows immediately below. (3) George Villiers, duke of Buckingham—see Leicestershire, p. 321.

court, "That he was a minister of state fit to serve the greatest prince in Europe." He was ousted his secretary's place, which needed him more than he it, having achieved a fair fortune, which he transmitted to posterity. How long he lived afterwards in a private life, is to me unknown.[1]

[*d.* 1630]

ARTHUR LAKE was born [1569] in the parish of Saint Michael in the town of Southampton; bred first in Winchester School, then fellow of New College. In his own nature he preferred the fruitfulness of the vine, and fatness of the olive (painfulness in a private parish) before the government of the trees, had not immediate Providence, without his suit and seeking, preferred him successively warden of New College, prefect of Saint Cross's nigh Winchester, dean of Worcester, bishop of Bath and Wells.

He continued the same in his rochet what he was in his scholar's gown; and lived a real comment upon Saint Paul's character of a bishop: 1. *Blameless.* Such as hated his order could not cast any aspersion upon him. 2. *The husband of one wife.* He took not that lawful liberty; but led a single life, honouring matrimony in his brethren who embraced it. 3. *Vigilant.* Examining canonically in his own person all those whom he ordained. 4. *Sober, of good behaviour.* Such his austerity in diet, from university-commons to his dying day, that he generally fed but on one, and that no dainty dish, and fasted four times a week from supper. 5. *Given to hospitality.* When master of Saint Cross's, he increased the allowance of the poor brethren in diet and otherwise. When bishop, he kept fifty servants in his family, not so much for state or attendance on his person, but pure charity in regard of their private need. 6. *Apt to teach.* The living, with his pious sermons in his cathedral and neighbouring parishes; and posterity with those writings he hath left behind him. 7. *Not given to wine.* His abstemiousness herein was remarkable. 8. *No striker, not given to filthy lucre.* He never fouled his fingers with the least touch of Gehazi's reward, freely preferring desert. 9. *One that ruleth well his own house.* The rankness of housekeeping brake not out into riot, and a chapter was constantly read every meal, by one kept for that purpose. Every night, besides cathedral and chapel prayers, he prayed in his own person with his family in his dining-room.

In a word, his intellectuals had such predominacy of his sensuals, or rather grace so ruled in both, that the man in him being subordinate to the Christian, he lived a pattern of piety.

I have read of one Arthur Faunt, a Jesuit who, entering into orders, renounced his Christian name, because (forsooth) never legendary saint thereof, and assumed that of Laurence. This gracious Arthur was not so superstitiously scrupulous, and (if none before) may pass for the first saint of his name, dying [1626].

(1) Sir Thomas Lake's fall was due to a family feud. His daughter had married Lord Roos, grandson of the first earl of Exeter. The marriage proved unhappy, and the subsequent quarrels led to an action by the countess of Exeter for defamation of character. Lake, his wife, son and daughter were all imprisoned and heavily fined. Later, on admitting the justice of the sentence, Lake was released.

THOMAS JAMES was born [1573?] in the Isle of Wight; bred first in Winchester, then at New College in Oxford, and afterwards proceeded doctor in divinity. He was chosen by Sir Thomas Bodley the keeper of his inestimable library in Oxford. And, on serious consideration, one will conclude the library made for him, and him for it; like tallies, they so fitted one another. Some men live like moths in libraries, not being better for the books, but the books the worse for them, which they only soil with their fingers. Not so Dr. James, who made use of books for his own and the public good. He knew the age of a manuscript by looking upon the face thereof, and by the form of the character could conclude the time wherein it was written.

He was a member of the Convocation held with the Parliament of Oxford, *primo Caroli,* where he made a motion, that some might be commissioned to peruse the manuscript of Fathers in all public and private English libraries, that thereby the forgery of foreign popish editions might be detected.

I believe his design had formerly been by him pursued for many years, as appears by this passage in Mr. Camden:[1] "Thomas James of Oxford, who may deservedly be styled φιλόβιβλος, as one who is wholly intent upon books and learning; and who is at present (God prosper his endeavours) out of a desire of promoting the public good, employed in searching the libraries of England, on a design that is like to be of singular use to the commonwealth of learning."

He never attained higher preferment than the sub-deanery of Wells; and, dying 1629, was buried in the chapel of New College in Oxford.

CHARLES BUTLER was bred master of arts in Magdalen College in Oxford, and afterwards beneficed in this county. An excellent musician, who wrote a book of the principles of music, in singing and setting, with the twofold use thereof, ecclesiastical and civil; and a critical Englishman, having composed a grammar of our language. He also wrote a book of bees; wherein, as if he had been their secretary, he appears most knowing in the state-mysteries of their commonwealth; whence one, not unhandsomely, on his book:

Aut a consiliis Apibus, Butlere, fuisti;
Aut a consiliis est Apis ipsa tuis.

Butler, he'll say (who these thy writings sees)
Bees counsel thee, or else thou counsellest bees.

I behold these his books as the receptacle of the leakage and superfluities of his study; and it is no trespass on grace for one to walk and take a turn in the field of Nature. He was also a pious man, a painful preacher, and a solid divine: witness his excellent book of the *Marriage of Cousin-Germans,* approved and commended by Doctor Prideaux[2] as the best ever written on that subject. [*d.* 1647]

(1) *Britannia,* in Monmouthshire. [The original Latin is omitted, and the translation is from Bishop Gibson's edition, 1722.] (2) John Prideaux, bishop of Worcester —see Devonshire, p. 137.

THE FAREWELL

When some five years since I visited Winchester, it grieved me at the heart to behold that stately structure so far run to ruin; yea, my thoughts then interpreted those sad schisms and gaping chinks, the heralds of its downfall, deeming with myself that I discovered (as physicians in our bodies do *cadaverosam*) *faciem ruinosam* therein. But it rejoiced me, when coming there this last year, to find it so well amended by the sovereign medicine of gold or silver charitably applied by its good bishop. I wish all cathedrals in England, sick of the same distemper, as quick and happy a recovery.

HEREFORDSHIRE

HEREFORDSHIRE hath Worcestershire and Shropshire on the north, Gloucestershire on the east, Monmouthshire on the south, Brecknock- and Radnor-shires on the west. In form it is almost circular, being from north to south (measured to the best improvement) thirty-five miles, though from east to west not altogether so much.

There cannot be given a more effectual evidence of the healthful air in this shire, than the vigorous vivacity of the inhabitants therein; many aged folk, which in other countries are properties of the chimneys, or confined to their beds, are here found in the field as able (if willing) to work. The ingenious Serjeant Hoskins gave an entertainment to King James, and provided ten aged people to dance the Moorish before him, all of them making up more than a thousand years, so that what was wanting in one was supplied in another: a nest of Nestors not to be found in another place.

This county doth share as deep as any in the alphabet of our English commodities, though exceeding in W for Wood, Wheat, Wool and Water. Besides, this shire better answereth (as to the sound thereof) the name of Pomerania than the dukedom of Germany so called, being a continued orchard of apple-trees, whereof much cider is made, of the use whereof we have treated before.[1]

There is a tract in this county called Golden Vale; and if any demand how much gold is to be found therein, know that even as much as in Chrusaroas, or Golden Stream, the river of Damascus, so called from the yellowness of their water, as this vale is so named either because gilded with flowers in the spring, or because being the best of moulds, as gold is of metals.

Here I cannot but commend Master Camden's cautious commendation of this county: *Secunda fertilitatis laude inter Angliae provincias acquiescere. haud facile est contenta* (it is not willingly content to be accounted the second shire for matter of fruitfulness). But the aforesaid author in his whole book never expresseth which is the first, too politic to adjudge so invidious a pre-eminence. And thus keeping the uppermost seat empty, such competitor counties are allowed leave to put in their several claims which pretend to the prime place of fertility.

Reader, I am sorry that having not hitherto seen the cathedral of Hereford, I must be silent about the buildings in this county.

NATURAL COMMODITIES

Wool

Such as are ignorant of the qualities thereof may inform themselves therein from the common proverbs: 1. "White as wool;" a Scripture phrase, though there be thereof black by nature. 2. "Soft as wool;" and therefore our judges anciently in the parliament-house sat on wool-packs,

(1) In the Manufactures of Gloucestershire.—F.

as well for the easier repose of their age, as to mind them to maintain this staple commodity in its legal privileges. 3. "As warm as wool." And one said merrily, "Wooll must needs be warm, as consisting all of double letters."

Our English garments from head to foot were formerly made thereof, till the beginning of the reign of King Henry the Eighth, when velvet caps becoming fashionable for persons of prime quality, discomposed the proverb, "If his cap be made of wool," as formerly comprising all conditions of people how high and haughty soever.

Great the plenty of wool in this county, and greater God's goodness, that generally our northern lands are well stored therewith. As for the wool in this county, it is best known, to the honour thereof, by the name of Lempster Ore, being absolutely the finest in this county, and indeed in all England, equalling, if not exceeding, the Apulian or Tarentine in the south of Italy, though it cost not so much charge and curiosity in the careful keeping thereof: for good authors inform us, that there the shepherds put in effect a fleece over their fleece, using to clothe their sheep with skins, to preserve their wool from the injury of earth, bushes and weather. How well this requiteth their cost, I know not, but am sure no such trouble is used on our sheep here.

SALMON

A dainty and wholesome fish, and a double riddle in Nature; first, for its invisible feeding, no man alive having ever found any meat in the maw thereof; secondly, for its strange leaping (or flying rather) so that some will have them termed salmons, *a saliendo*. Being both bow and arrow, it will shoot itself out of the water an incredible height and length. I might add the admirable growth thereof, if true what is confidently affirmed that it increaseth from a spawn to a full-grown fish within the compass of a year. Plenty of these in this county, though not in such abundance as in Scotland, where servants (they say) indent with their masters, not to be fed therewith above thrice a week.

Some will say, why salmons in Herefordshire, which are common in other counties? It is answered, in other counties, suitably with the buck, they are seasonable only in summer; whereas here, with buck and doe, they are in season all the year long. This county may say:

Salmo non aestate novus, nec frigore desit.
Salmon in summer is not rare;
In winter, I of them do share.

For the river of Wye affords brumal[1] salmons, fat and sound, when they are sick and spent in other places.

THE WONDERS

There is a little fountain called Bonewell nigh Richard's Castle in this county, the water whereof is always full of bones of little fishes, or as others conceive, of little frogs; seeing, it seems, such their smallness they are hardly to be distinguished. It addeth to the wonder, because this

(1) *Brumal* = belonging to winter.

spring can never be emptied of them, but as fast as some are drawn out, others instantly succeed them.

To this permanent, let us add two transient wonders, on the credit of excellent authors. When a battle was fought in this county, Anno Domini 1461, betwixt Jasper earl of Pembroke and James Butler earl of Ormonde on the one side, and King Edward the Fourth of the other, three suns appeared together in the firmament.

Inquiring into the natural cause hereof, we find it to be nothing else but the image of the sun represented in an equal, smooth, thick and watery cloud, not opposite thereunto (for then it would make the rainbow); nor under the sun (for then it would make those circles called crowns or garlands); but on one or either side thereof, in a competent or moderate distance: for, if it be too far off, then the beams will be too feeble to be reflected; if too near, the sun will disperse it; but in such a middle distance, wherein many suns may appear, as a man's face is expressed in all pieces of a broken glass.

To this wonder add a second, of Marcle Hill, which, Anno Domini 1575, roused itself, as it were, out of its sleep. Yea, in some sort it might seem to be in labour for three days together, shaking and roaring all that while,[1] to the great terror of all that heard or beheld it. It threw down all things that opposed it, and removed itself into an higher place. The best use we can make of such accidents is to fear and not fear thereat, with a reverential awe to God, no servile dread of the thing itself: "Therefore we will not fear, though the earth be removed, and though the mountains be carried into the midst of the sea."

PROVERBS

Lemster bread, and Weobley ale. It seems both these are best in their kinds, though good in other places of the land. Thus, though Palestine was universally termed "a land of wheat," yet the Spirit of God takes signal notice of "the wheat of Minnith and Pannag," as finer than the rest. Yet is there wheat in England which jostleth for pureness with that of Weobley, viz., what groweth about Heston in Middlesex, yielding so fine flour, that for a long time the manchet[2] for the kings of England was made thereof; except any will say it is prized the more for the vicinity to London.

THE WORTHIES

ÆTHELBERHT was king of the East Angles, and went to Offa king of Mercia to treat of the marriage with his daughter; but Queen Cynethryth, wife to Offa, more ambitious of her own unlawful than her daughter's lawful advancement, practised his death at a village now called Sutton Walls, four miles from Hereford. His corpse was afterwards removed by Milfred (a petit prince of that country) to Hereford, where he obtained the reputation of a saint and martyr. His suffering happened Anno Domini 794.

ROSAMOND [CLIFFORD, 'FAIR ROSAMOND'], that is, saith my author,[3] Rosemouth (but by allusion termed Rose of the World) was remarkable on

(1) This kind of earthquake is called Brasmatias.—F. (2) *Manchet*=small loaf of white bread. (3) Verstegan, *Decayed Intelligence*.

many accounts. First, for her father, Walter de Clifford, who had large lands about Clifford's Castle in this county. Secondly, for herself, being the mistress-piece of beauty in that age. Thirdly, for her paramour, King Henry the Second, to whom she was concubine. Lastly, for her son, William Longespée, the worthy earl of Salisbury.

King Henry is said to have built a labyrinth at Woodstock (which labyrinth through length of time hath lost itself) to hide this his mistress from his jealous Juno, Queen Eleanor. But *Zelotypiae nihil impervium.* By some device she got access unto her, and caused her death.

Rosamond was buried in a little nunnery at Godstow nigh Oxford, with this epitaph:

Hic jacet in tumulo Rosa mundi non Rosa munda;
Non redolet sed olet quae redolere solet.

This tomb doth inclose the world's fair rose, so sweet and full of favour;
And smell she doth now, but you may guess how, none of the sweetest savour.

Her corpse may be said to have done penances after her death; for Hugh bishop of Lincoln, coming as a visitor to this nunnery, and seeing Rosamond's body lying in the quire under a silken hearse, with tapers continually burning about it, thought the hearse of an harlot no proper object for eyes of virgins to contemplate on; therefore caused her bones to be scattered abroad. However, after his departure, those sisters gathered her bones together again, put them into a perfumed bag, and enclosed them in lead, where they continued until ousted again in the reign of King Henry the Eighth. [*d.* 1176?]

ROGER OF HEREFORD, born in that city, was bred in the university of Cambridge, being one of the prime promoters of learning therein after the re-foundation of the university by the abbot of Crowland. He was an excellent astronomer, and stars being made for signs, was a good interpreter what by these signs were intended. He wrote a book of *Judicial Astrology;* whether to commend or condemn it, such only can satisfy themselves that have seen his book. He was also skilful in all metals and minerals; and his pretty curiosities made him acceptable to the nobility of England; flourishing under King Henry the Second, Anno Domini 1178.

JOHN LE BRETON, alias BRITTON, doctor of the laws. He meriteth a high place in this catalogue; and yet I am at a perfect loss where to fix his nativity . . . He was a famous lawyer, living in the reign of King Edward the First, at whose commandment, and by whose authority he wrote a learned book of the laws of England, the tenor whereof runneth in the king's name, as if it had been penned by himself.[1]

It is no small argument of the excellency of this book, that notwithstanding the great variation of our laws since his time, that his work still is in great and general repute. Thus a good face conquereth the disadvantage of old and unfashionable clothes. He was preferred bishop of Hereford in the reign of King Henry the Third. And although there be some difference betwixt authors about the time wherein he lived and

(1) Modern scholarship considers this a later work compiled about 1290.

died (some assign a later date) I confide in Bishop Godwin, his successor in the same see, computing his death to happen May 12, in the third of King Edward the First, anno 1275.

THOMAS DE CANTELUPE [*b.* 1218?] was of honourable extraction, whose father William Lord Cantelupe had two fair habitations, Abergavenny Castle in Monmouth, and Harringworth in Northamptonshire, which, by an heir-general of that family, afterwards descended to the Lord Zouche. He was bred in Oxford (whereof at last he became chancellor) and was preferred bishop of Hereford. A charitable man may believe him a person of holy life and great learning; but no wise man will credit what Walsingham writes of him, "That he was never guilty of any mortal sin." Going to (others say returning from) Rome, to assert his church from the encroachment of Peckham, archbishop of Canterbury, he died at a city in Tuscany, where his flesh was taken off his corpse and buried, whilst his bones were sent for relics into England, and enshrined at Hereford. Now, though different dates be assigned of his death, I adhere to Bishop Godwin, noting his dissolution 1282.

He was afterwards canonized by Pope John the Twenty-second, and no fewer than four hundred twenty-five miracles are registered in that church, reported to be wrought at his tomb. I say, just four hundred and twenty-five, which falls out fewer by five-and-twenty than the "prophets of Baal," and more by five-and-twenty than the "prophets of the groves," in a middle number betwixt both, and all of them, I believe, honest and true alike. Yea, it is recorded in his legend that "by his prayers were raised from death to life threescore several persons, one-and-twenty lepers healed, and three-and-twenty blind and dumb men to have received their sight and speech."

No wonder then what Mr. Camden observeth, that in process of time *parum abfuit quin pietatis opinione regio martyri Ethelberto praeluxerit* (he lacked but little to eclipse the lustre of Æthelberht, the royal saint and martyr); formerly buried, as is aforesaid, in the same cathedral. Indeed it is given to superstition always to be fondest of the youngest saint. But long since King Henry the Eighth hath put a period to all emulations betwixt their memories.[1]

ADAM OF ORLTON was born in the city of Hereford. Proceeding doctor of law, he became afterwards bishop in the place of his nativity. This is he so infamous in history for cutting off the life of King Edward the Second with his riddling unpointed answer: *Edwardum regem occidere nolite timere bonum est* (to kill King Edward you need not to fear it is good).

It is hard to say which of these two were the original and which the translation; it being equally probable that the English was Latined as

(1) Cantelupe's career was more colourful than Fuller suggests. A great pluralist and a bitter enemy of the Jews, he led the opposition to Peckham in the synod at Reading summoned to deal with plurality and other abuses, and with intrusions on the privileges of the church. He was excommunicated by Peckham through a dispute over jurisdiction. Popularly regarded as a saint, he was canonized, 1320, as St. Thomas of Hereford

that the Latin was Englished by such authors as relate this transaction.

But to return to Orlton; he made much bustling in the land, passing through the bishoprics of Worcester and Winchester, and died at last, not much lamented, July 18, 1345.[1]

JOHN GRANDISSON was born [1292?] at Ashperton in this county; a person remarkable on several accounts. 1. For his *high birth,* his father William being a baron, and his mother Sybil co-heir to the Lord Tregoz. 2. *Great learning,* being a good writer of that age, though Bale saith of him that he was *orator animosior quam facundior.* 3. *High preferment,* attaining to be bishop of Exeter. 4. *Vivacity,* sitting bishop in his see two and forty years. 5. *Stout stomach,* resisting Meopham archbishop of Canterbury, *vi et armis,* when he came to visit his diocese.[2] 6. *Costly buildings,* arching the beautiful roof of his cathedral, building and endowing a rich college of Saint Mary Ottery.

He was the better enabled to do these and other great benefactions by persuading all the secular clergy in his diocese to make him sole heir to their estates. He died July 15, Anno Domini 1369.

ADAM EASTON. We were at a great loss, had we but his bare surname to direct us to the place of his nativity, seeing scarcely one county in England which hath not one or more Eastons or Eatons (the same in effect) therein. But thanks be to our author, who hath fixed his birth (though but with an *ut videtur*) in this shire.[3]

Pretenders to skill in palmistry would persuade us that such, the table in whose hands is narrow beneath and broad above, are marked out for poverty in their youth, and plenty in their old age. I will not say, such the signature in the hands of our Adam, but sure I am such his success. Mean his birth, homely his breeding, hard his fare, till by his industry he was advanced doctor of divinity in Oxford, wherein he became a great scholar, skilled in Greek and Hebrew (rare accomplishments in that age) and was very dexterous in all civil negotiations. He was afterwards made cardinal, with the title of St. Cecilia, by Pope Urban, against whom Clement the Seventh was elected and erected by others.

Fierce the fight between bears and boars, but far fiercer betwixt two anti-popes, giving no quarter to the opposite party, if brought into their power. Urban, suspecting treachery in some of his cardinals, imprisoned seven of them at once, and putting five of them into sacks, sank them into the sea. Oh, most barbarous *Urbanity!* Our Adam, being the sixth, hardly escaped with his life, and may be said in some sort put into a sack, though of a larger size; I mean a strait dungeon, where he remained half-starved for five years together, till the death of Pope Urban. But Pope Boniface, his successor, restored him to all his honours

(1) He took part in risings against Edward II and was charged with treason and deprived; and was largely reponsible for the king's resignation in 1327. He gained favour under Edward III. (2) This was at a time when laymen were defying ecclesiastical authority, and the clerical order set a bad example in their own discipline. Grandisson closed the doors of his own cathedral against Meopham, his metropolitan, and the king had to interpose in the interests of peace. For Meopham see Kent, p. 262. (3) Bishop Godwin [*Ut videtur* implies hearsay].

and dignities, and sent him over into England to King Richard the Second with most ample commendation.

Returning to Rome, he lived there in all plenty and pomp, and died September the 15th, 1397. He was interred, when dead, in the church of St. Cecilia, which intituled him when alive, though no happiness; an honour which no other Englishman (to my observation) of his order ever enjoyed.

SIR JOHN (son to Sir Thomas) OLDCASTLE was a native of this county, whereof he was sheriff in the seventh of Henry the Fourth; Lord Cobham in the right of his wife; a right valiant man, but great follower of Wycliffe, so that he lost his life on that account.

As his body was hanged and burnt in an unusual posture at Tyburn, so his memory hath ever since been in a strange suspense betwixt malefactor and martyr; papists charging him with treason against King Henry the Fifth, and heading an army of more than ten thousand men, though it wanted nine thousand nine hundred ninety and nine thereof, so far as it appears solidly proved.

But it hath ever been the practice of the devil and his instruments, angry with God's servants for their religion, to accuse them for sedition; perceiving princes generally more jealous of their own honour than God's glory, and most careful to cut off such as oppose their power or persons. Thus Christ was accused for disloyalty to Caesar, and St. Paul for raising of tumults, though they (as it is plain in the text) either raised themselves, or were raised by the Pharisees and Sadducees, Paul's professed enemies. But I have so worn out the nib of my pen in my *Church History* about clearing the innocency of this worthy knight, that I have nothing to add new thereunto.[1] [*d.* 1417]

SIR JAMES CROFT. This worthy knight was accused for complying with Wyatt, and notwithstanding his most solemn oath in his own defence, he was imprisoned by Queen Mary, convicted of high treason; restored by Queen Elizabeth, and made governor of the town and castle of Berwick.

At the siege of Leith he behaved him most valiantly in repelling the foe; and yet, when in a second assault, the English were worsted, the blame fell on him (as if he favoured the French, and maligned the Lord Grey then general) so that he was ousted from his government in Berwick. Yet he fell not so into the queen's final disfavour, but that she continued him privy councillor, and made him comptroller of her household. He was an able man to manage war, and yet an earnest desirer and advancer of peace, being one of the commissioners in '88 to treat with the Spaniards in Flanders. [*d.* 1590]

HUMPHREY ELY, born in this county, was bred in St. John's College in Oxford; whence flying beyond the seas, he lived successively at Douay,

(1) Oldcastle gave good service to Henry IV and Henry V. The latter made vain attempts to convert him to orthodoxy, after which he was tried for heresy. He escaped after condemnation, but was finally captured. Contemporary execrations of him became popular on the Elizabethan stage; cf. Shakespeare's *Henry IV*.

Rome and Rheims, till at last he settled himself at Pont-à-Mousson in Lorraine, where for twenty years together he was professor of canon and civil law; and dying 1604, was buried therein with a double epitaph.

That in verse my judgment commands me not to believe, which here I will take the boldness to translate:

Albion haereseos velatur nocte, viator,
Desine mirari; Sol suus hic latitat.

Wonder not, reader, that with heresies
England is clouded; here her Sun he lies.

The prose part my charity induces me to credit: *Inopia ferme laborabat, alios inopia sublevans* (he eased others of poverty, being himself almost pinched therewith.)[1]

RICHARD HAKLUYT was born [1552?] of an ancient extract in this county, whose family hath flourished at [Eyton] in good esteem. He was bred a student in Christ Church in Oxford, and after was prebendary of Westminster. His genius inclined him to the study of history, and especially to the marine part thereof, which made him keep constant intelligence with the most noted seamen of Wapping until the day of his death.

He set forth a large collection of the English sea voyages, ancient, middle, modern; taken partly out of private letters which never were, or without his care had not been printed; partly out of small treatises, printed and since irrecoverably lost, had not his providence preserved them. For some pamphlets are produced, which for their cheapness and smallness men for the present neglect to buy, presuming they may procure them at their pleasure; which small books, their first and last edition being past (like some spirits that appear but once) cannot afterwards with any price or pains be recovered. In a word, many of such useful tracts of sea adventures, which before were scattered as several ships, Mr. Hakluyt hath embodied into a fleet, divided into three squadrons, so many several volumes; a work of great honour to England, it being possible that many ports and islands in America, which being base and barren, bear only a bare name for the present, may prove rich places for the future. And then these voyages will be produced, and pleaded, as good evidence of their belonging to England, as first discovered and denominated by Englishmen. Mr. Hakluyt died in the beginning of King James's reign, leaving a fair estate to an unthrift son, who embezzled it on this token, that he vaunted that he cheated the covetous usurer, who had given him spick and span new money for the old land of his great-great-grandfather. [*d.* 1616]

JOHN DAVIES of Hereford (for so he constantly styled himself) was the greatest master of the pen that England in his age beheld for 1. *Fast writing,* so incredible his expedition. 2. *Fair writing,* some

(1) In 1580 Ely, disguised as a merchant, together with three priests visited England. On landing at Dover searchers arrested two of the priests; the mayor of Dover, supposing Ely to be a military man, appointed him gaoler of one of them, named Cottam. Out of Dover Ely allowed his prisoner to go at large, but Cottam, fearing for Ely's safety, gave himself up, and was later executed.

minutes' consultation being required to decide whether his lines were written or printed. 3. *Close writing*, a mystery indeed, and too dark for my dim eyes to discover. 4. *Various writing*, Secretary, Roman, Court and Text.

The poetical fiction of Briareus the giant, who had an hundred hands, found a moral in him, who could so cunningly and copiously disguise his aforesaid elemental hands, that by mixing he could make them appear an hundred, and if not so many sorts, so many degrees of writing. Yet had he lived longer he would modestly have acknowledged Mr. Githings (who was his scholar, and also born in this county) to excel him in that faculty, whilst the other would own no such odious eminency, but rather gratefully return the credit to his master again.[1] Sure I am, when two such transcendant penmasters shall again come to be born in the same shire, they may even serve fairly to engross the will and testament of the expiring universe. Our Davies had also some pretty excursions into poetry, and could flourish matter as well as letters, with his fancy as well as with his pen. He died at London, in the midst of the reign of King James, and lieth buried in St. Dunstan's. [1565?-1618]

MILES SMITH, D.D., was born in the city of Hereford,[2] which I observe the rather because omitted in his funeral sermon. His father was a fletcher,[3] and a man of no mean estate, that vocation being more in use formerly than in our age. He was bred first in Brasenose College, then chaplain of Christ Church in Oxford. A deep divine, great linguist, who had more than a single share in the last translation of the Bible, as hereby will appear. 1. More than forty grave divines were employed in several places on that work. 2. When it had passed their hands, it was revised by a dozen select ones. 3. This done, it was referred to the final examination of Bishop Bilson[4] and Dr. Smith. 4. Doctor Smith at last was enjoined to make the preface to the translation, as a comely gate to a glorious city, which remains under his own hand in the university library in Oxford. Yet was he never heard to speak of the work with any attribution to himself more than the rest.

He never sought any preferment he had, and was wont merrily to say of himself that he was *nullius rei praetarquam librorum avarus* (covetous of nothing but books). King James preferred him bishop of Gloucester 1612, wherein he behaved himself with such meekness that, in all matters of doubt, the bias of his inclination did still hang πρὸς τὸ φιλάνθρωπον. He wrote all his books with his own hand (in that faculty not being short of the professors thereof); and, being seventy years of age, died and was buried in his own cathedral, 1624.

JOHN GUILLIM was of Welch extraction, but born [1565] in this county;[6] and became a pursuivant of arms, by the name first of Portsmouth, then Rouge Croix, but most eminent for his methodical *Display of Heraldry* (confusion being formerly the greatest difficulty therein); shewing him-

(1) So informed by Master Cox, draper in London, his executor. (2) So Master Stephens, his secretary, informed me. (3) *Fletcher* = a maker or seller of arrows. (4) See Hampshire, p. 211. (5) See J. Davies of Hereford challenging him for his countryman, in his verses on his *Display of Heraldry*.

self a good logician in his exact divisions, and no bad philosopher, noting the natures of all creatures given in arms, joining fancy and reason therein. Besides his travelling all over the earth in beasts, his industry diggeth into the ground in pursuit of the properties of precious stones, diveth into the water in inquest of the qualities of fishes, flieth into the air after the nature of birds, yea mounteth to the very skies about stars (but here we must call them *estoiles*) and planets, their use and influence. In a word, he hath unmysteried the mystery of heraldry, insomuch that one of his own faculty[1] thus descanteth (in the twilight of jest and earnest) on his performance:

> But let me tell you, this will be the harm
> In arming others you yourself disarm;
> Our art is now anatomizéd so,
> As who knows not what we ourselves do know?
> Our corn in others' mill is ill apaid:
> *Sic vos non vobis* may to us be said.

I suspect that his endeavours met not with proportionable reward.

[*d.* 1621]

ROBERT DEVEREUX [Second EARL OF ESSEX], son to Walter Devereux earl of Essex, was born at Netherwood in this county, November the 10th, 1566, whilst his father as yet was only Viscount Hereford.

He was such a master-piece of court and camp, and so bright a light therein, that we will observe his morning, forenoon, high noon, afternoon and night.

His *morning* began at his first coming to court, the gates whereof he entered with four great advantages, of pity, kindred, favour and merit: pity, on the account of his father lately dead (to say no more) and generally lamented; kindred, on his mother's side, Lettice Knollys, near allied to the queen; favour, being son-in-law to Leicester, and so was a favourite's favourite at the first day, though he quickly stood on his own legs without holding; merit, being of a beautiful personage, courteous nature, noble descent, fair (though much impaired) fortune.

Forenoon, when the queen favourably reflected on him, as a grandmother on a grandchild, making him the wanton to her fond and indulgent affection . . . The earl, in pursuance of his own martial inclination, secretly left the court to see some service in France. The queen, passionately loving his person, grievously complained of his absence, and often said, "We shall have this young fellow knocked on the head, as foolish Sidney was, by his own forwardness," and was restless till his return.

I behold him in his *high noon,* when he brought victory with him home from Cadiz, and was vertical in the esteem of the soldiery, and may be said to awaken the queen's jealousy by his popularity.

His *afternoon* followed when he undertook the Irish action, too knotty service for his smooth disposition, being fitter for personal performance than conduct and managing of martial affairs. And now his enemies' work was half done, having gotten such a gulf betwixt him and the

(1) Sir William Segar, in his verse before his book

queen; for, as Antaeus is said to have recruited strength when he touched his mother earth, so this earl, wrestling with his enemies, suppressed them and supported himself by his daily access to the queen, which distance now denied him.

His *night* approached when, coming over without leave, he was confined by the queen to his house, to reclaim, not ruin him. Hither a miscellaneous crew of swordsmen did crowd, tendering him their service, some of one persuasion, some of another, some of all, some of no religion. Their specious pretence was to take evil counsellors from the queen, though it had been happy if they had been first taken away from the earl. What his company said they would do, the earl knew; but what would have been done by them, God knows. The earl rising, and missing of expected support from the city of London, quickly sunk in the queen's final displeasure, Anno Domini 1601.

He was valiant, liberal to scholars and soldiers, nothing distrustful, if not too confident of fidelity in others. Revengefulness was not bred, but put into his disposition. 'Tis hard to say whether such as were his enemies, or such as should be his friends, did him more mischief. When one flattered him to his face for his valour, "No," said he, "my sins ever made me a coward." In a word, his failings were neither so foul nor so many, but that the character of a right worthy man most justly belongs to his memory. [*d.* 1601]

JOHN WALTER was born in the city of Hereford. Know, reader, I could learn little from the minister[1] which preached his funeral, less from his acquaintance, least from his children. Such his hatred of vainglory, that (as if charity were guiltiness) he cleared himself from all suspicion thereof. Yet is our intelligence of him, though brief, true as followeth.

He was bred in London, and became clerk of Draper's Hall. Finding the world to flow fast in upon him, he made a solemn vow to God, that he would give the surplusage of his estate (whatever it was) to pious uses.[2] Nor was he like to those who at first maintained ten thousand pounds too much for any man; which when they have attained, they then conceive ten times so much too little for themselves; but, after his cup was filled brim-full to the aforesaid proportion, he conscientiously gave every drop of that which overflowed to quench the thirst of people parched with poverty.

I compare him to Elizabeth in the Gospel, who as if "ashamed of her shame" (so then reputed) taken from her, "hid herself five months" (so great her modesty). Such his concealing of his charity, though pregnant with good works; and had not the lanthorn of his body been lately broken, it is believed the light of his bounty had not yet been discovered. He built and endowed a fair almshouse in Southwark, another at Newington (both in Surrey) on which, and other pious uses, he expended well nigh ten thousand pounds, whereof twenty pounds per annum he gave to Hereford, the place of his nativity.

His wife and surviving daughters, so far from grudging at his gifts,

(1) Mr. Richard Henchman, of St. Mary Bothaw. (2) Above ten thousand pounds.—F.

and accounting that lost to them which was lent to God, that they much rejoiced thereat, and deserve to be esteemed joint-givers thereof, because consenting so freely to his charity. He died in the seventy-fourth year of his age, 29th December, Anno Domini 1656, and was solemnly buried in London.

THE FAREWELL

I am credibly informed that the office of the under-sheriff of this county is more beneficial than in any other county of the same proportion; his fees, it seems, increasing from the decrease of the states of the gentry therein. May the obventions[1] of his office hereafter be reduced to a lesser sum. And seeing God hath blessed (as we have formerly observed) this county with so many W's, we wish the inhabitants the continuance and increase of one more, Wisdom, expressing itself both in the improving of their spiritual concernment, and warily managing their secular estates.

(1) *Obventions* = occasional incoming fees or revenues.

HERTFORDSHIRE

HERTFORDSHIRE is so called from Hertford, the chief town therein; as Hartford, so termed from the *Ford* of *Harts,* a hart couchant in the waters being the arms thereof; which convinceth me that HART-, not HERTfordshire, is the orthography of this county. It hath Essex on the east, Middlesex on the south, Buckinghamshire on the west, Bedford and Cambridge-shires on the north thereof. It might be allowed a square of twenty miles, save that the angular insinuations of other counties prejudice the entireness thereof. I have been informed, from an ancient justice therein, that one cannot be so advantageously placed in any part of this shire, but that he may recover another county within the riding of five miles. It is the garden of England for delight, and men commonly say that such who buy a house in Hertfordshire pay two years' purchase for the air thereof.

It falls short in fruitfulness of Essex adjoining thereunto, to which it was also annexed under one sheriff (and one escheator, till after the reign of King Edward the Third) and painful Norden writes a bold truth:[1] "For deep feedings, or sheep pastures, I take notice of few, and those especially about Knebworth. To speak of the soil, as indeed it is most generally, for my part I take it but a barren country in respect of some other shires."

Indeed this forestry ground would willingly bear nothing so well as a crop of wood. But, seeing custom is another Nature, it hath for many years been contented to bring forth good grain, persuaded thereunto by the industrious husbandman. Surely no county can show so fair a bunch of berries; for so they term the fair habitations of gentlemen of remark, which are called places, courts, halls and manors in other shires.

This county affording no peculiar commodity nor manufacture, we may safely proceed to other observations, when first we have given due commendation to the horses of this shire.

Their teams of horses, oft-times deservedly advanced from the cart to the coach, are kept in excellent equipage, much alike in colour and stature, fat and fair; such is their care in dressing and well-feeding them. I could name the place and person (reader, be not offended with an innocent digression) who brought his servant with a warrant before a justice of peace for stealing his grain. The man brought his five horses tailed together along with him, alleging for himself that, if he were the thief, these were the receivers; and so escaped.

THE BUILDINGS

THEOBALDS did carry away the credit, built by Sir William, beautified by Sir Robert Cecil his son, both lord treasurers of England. The last exchanged it, too wise to do it to his loss, with King James for Hatfield House; which king deceased therein, March 27, 1625. Yea, this house

(1) In his Description of Hertfordshire.

may be said to decease about its grand climacterial, some sixty-three years from the finishing thereof, taken down to the ground (for the better partage among the soldiery) anno 1651; and, from the seat of a monarch, is now become a little commonwealth; so many entire tenements, like splinters, have flown out of the materials thereof. Thus our fathers saw it built, we behold it unbuilt; and whether our children shall see it rebuilt, He only knows who hath written, "There is a time to cast away stones, and a time to gather stones together."

HATFIELD HOUSE was first the bishops of Ely, then the kings; afterwards, by exchange, the earls of Salisbury; for situation, building, contrivance, prospect, air and all accommodations, inferior to none in England. Within a little mile thereof lieth a place called the Vineyard, where Nature, by the midwifery of art, is delivered of much pleasure; so that the reader must be a seer before he can understand the perfection thereof. Had this place been in Graecia, or nigh Rome, where the luxuriant fancies of the poets, being subject-bound, improve a tree into a grove, a grove into a forest, a brook into a river, and a pond into a lake; I say, had this vineyard been there, it had disinherited Tempe of its honour; and hence the poets would have dated all their delights as from a little paradise, and staple-place of earthly pleasure.

MEDICINAL WATERS

One hath lately been discovered near Barnet, in a common; as generally sanative springs are found in such places, as if Nature therein intimated her intention, designing them for public profit, not private employment. It is conceived to run through veins of alum, by the taste thereof. It coagulateth milk, and the curd thereof is an excellent plaister for any green wounds, besides several other operations.

But, as Alexander was wont to applaud Achilles, not as the most valiant but the most fortunate of men, having Homer to trumpet forth his actions, so are these waters much advantaged with the vicinity of London, whose citizens proclaim the praise thereof. And indeed London in this kind is stately attended, having three medicinal waters within one day's journey thereof.[1] The catalogue of the cures done by this spring amounteth to a great number; insomuch that there is hope, in process of time, the water rising here will repair the blood shed hard by, and save as many lives as were lost in the fatal battle at Barnet betwixt the two houses of York and Lancaster.

PROVERBS

Hertfordshire clubs and clouted shoon. Some will wonder how this shire, lying so near London, the staple of English civility, should be guilty of so much rusticalness. But the finest cloth must have a list, and the pure peasants are of as coarse a thread in this county as in any other place. Yet, though some may smile at their clownishness, let none laugh at their industry; the rather because the high shoon of the tenants pays for the Spanish leather boots of the landlord.

(1) Tunbridge, Epsom, Barnet.—F.

Ware and Wade's Mill are worth all London. This, I assure you, is a master-piece of the vulgar wits in this county, wherewith they endeavour to amuse travellers, as if Ware, a thoroughfare market, and Wade's Mill (part of a village lying two miles north thereof) were so prodigiously rich as to countervail the wealth of London. The fallacy lieth in the homonymy of Ware, here not taken for that town so named, but appellatively for all vendible commodities. We will not discompose the writ of this proverb, by cavilling that Weare is the proper name of that town (so called anciently from the stoppages which there obstruct the river) but leave it as we found it, and proceed.

THE WORTHIES

SAINT ALBAN, though (as Saint Paul) a Roman by privilege, but Briton by parentage, was born in this county (though many hundreds of years before Hertfordshire had its modern name and dimensions) in the city of Verulam, and was martyred for Christianity under Diocletian, anno 304. The cause and manner whereof (with the martyrdom of Saint Amphibalus hard by Redbourn) I have so largely related in my *Church History* that, as I will repeat nothing, I can add nothing of consequence thereto; except any will conceive this to be remarkable, that good liquorice groweth naturally out of the ruinous walls of Verulam, an old city (the mother of the new town of Saint Alban's) as a skilful eye-witness, antiquary and zealous protestant[1] hath observed. Had some papist taken first notice hereof, he might probably have made it a miracle, and assign the sanctity of this place for the root of this liquorice.

NICHOLAS, son to Robert Breakspear (a lay brother in the abbey of St. Alban's) fetched his name from Breakspears, a place in Middlesex, but was born at Abbots Langley, a town in this county. When a youth, he was put to such servile work in St. Alban's Abbey that his ingenious soul could not comport therewith. Suing to be admitted into that house, he received the repulse, which in fine proved no *mishap,* but a *happy miss* unto him, for, going over into France, he studied so hard and so happily at Paris, that for his worth he was preferred abbot of Saint Rufus near Valence, and afterward, by Pope Eugenius the Third, was made bishop of Albano nigh Rome. *Ad natalis soli memoriam,* saith my author, that he who was refused to be *Monachus Albanensis* in England, should be *Episcopus Albanensis* in Italy. He was employed by the pope for the conversion of the Norwegians; and though Bale saith (he were not Bale if he were not bitter) *anti-christiano charactere Norwegios signavit,* yet his reducing them from paganism to Christianity in the fundamentals was a worthy work, and deserved true commendation. He was afterwards chosen pope of Rome, by the name of Adrian the Fourth. There is a mystery more than I can fathom in the changing of his name, seeing his own font-name was a papal one; yet he preferred rather to be Adrian the Fourth than Nicholas the Third. He held his place four years, eight months, and eight and twenty days, and, anno 1159, as he was drinking,

(1) Norden, in his Description of this country. [St. Alban is the proto-martyr of Britain. He was killed when sheltering a Christian cleric who had converted him.]

was choked with a fly, which in the large territory of St. Peter's patrimony had no place but his throat to get into. But since a fly stopped his breath, fear shall stop my mouth, not to make uncharitable conclusions from such casualties.

ALEXANDER NECKAM, or BAD in English, was born [1157] in St. Albans .. He is known to posterity by the title of *Ingenii Miraculum,* being an excellent philosopher, rhetorician and poet; so true it is what Tully observeth, *Omnes artes quae ad humanitatem pertinent habent quoddam commune vinculum et quasi cognatione quadam inter se continentur* [all the arts that pertain to humanity have a common bond and, as it were, a certain affinity]. Besides, he was a deep divine, as his books do evidence. He was canon of Exeter, and (upon what occasion I know not) came to be buried at Worcester, with this epitaph:

> Wisdom's eclips'd, sky of the sun bereft,
> Yet less the loss if like alive were left.
> A man discreet, in manners debonair,
> Bad name, black face, but carriage good and fair.[1]

Others say he was buried at St. Albans, where he found repulse when living, but repose when dead. [*d.* 1217]

JOHN GILES, or of St. Giles, was born [1180?] at St. Albans in the parish of St. Giles, long since, as some more in that town, demolished. He was bred beyond the seas, where he became so great a scholar, that he was not only physician in ordinary to Philip king of France, but also professor of that faculty in Paris and Montpellier. Then, waiving the care of bodies, he took on him the cure of souls, and was made doctor of divinity. He afterwards became a Dominican, and was the first Englishman that ever entered into that order. In his old age he was famous for his divinity lectures read in Oxford.

But which most persuades me to a venerable reception of his memory is what I read of him in Matthew Paris, how "Robert Grosseteste,[2] the pious and learned bishop of Lincoln, being sick on his death-bed, sent for this Mr. John Giles, learned in physic and divinity, that from him he might receive comfort both for body and soul." [*d.* 1258?]

RICHARD DE WARE, for this is his true name, as appears in his epitaph,[3] though some (pretending his honour, but prejudicing the truth thereby) surname him Warren. He was made abbot of Westminster 1260, and twenty years after treasurer of England under King Edward the First. This Richard, going to Rome, brought thence certain workmen and rich porphyry. And for the rest, hear my author[4]: "By whom and whereof he made the rare pavement to be seen at Westminster, before the communion table, containing the discourse of the whole world, which is at

(1) Latin original omitted. Neckam was born on the same night as Richard I, and his mother was chosen as foster-mother for Richard. Many volumes of Neckam's works exist in MSS. (2) See Suffolk, p. 524. (3) On his tomb, yet well to be seen in Westminster Abbey, on the north side of the tomb of Aymer de Valence, earl of Pembroke.—F. (4) J. Philpot, in his *Treasurers of England.*

this day most beautiful; a thing of that singularity, curiousness and rareness, that England hath not the like again."

See readers, what an enemy ignorance is to art. How often have I trampled on that pavement, so far from admiring, as not observing it; and since, upon serious survey, it will not, in my eyes, answer this character of curiosity. However, I will not add malice to my ignorance (qualities which too often are companions) to disparage what I do not understand; but I take it on the trust of others more skilful for a masterpiece of art. This Richard died on the second of December 1283, the twelfth of King Edward the First; and lieth buried under the foresaid pavement.

RALPH DE BALDOCK, so called from the place of his nativity (a mongrel-market) in this county, was bred in Merton College in Oxford; one not unlearned, and who wrote an *History of England,* which Leland at London did once behold. King Edward the First much prized and preferred him bishop of London. He gave two hundred pounds whilst living, and left more when dead, to repair the east part of St. Paul's, on the same token that, upon occasion of clearing the foundation, an incredible number of heads of oxen were found buried in the ground, alleged as an argument by some to prove that anciently a temple of Diana.[1] Such who object that heads of stags had been more proper for her, the goddess of the game, may first satisfy us whether any creatures *ferae naturae* (as which they could not certainly compass at all seasons) were usually offered for sacrifices. This Ralph died July 24th, 1313, being buried under a marble stone in St. Mary's Chapel in his cathedral.

JOHN DE GATESDEN [JOHN OF GADDESDEN] was undoubtedly born [1280?] in this county, wherein two villages the greater and less of that name. Such who except that they are written Gaddesden will soon be satisfied in their sameness from those who know the sympathy betwixt T and D. He was bred in Merton College in Oxford, where he so profited in the study of physic, that a foreigner, compiling a catalogue of men eminent in that faculty, acknowledgeth him a writer of high esteem therein. By one who hath made a list of learned men, he is styled *Johannes Anglicus.* I am informed that lately his books have been printed in Italy in a folio; no small honour, I assure you, seeing in physic the Italians account all Tramontane doctors but apothecaries in comparison of themselves. The first treatise in his book is termed *Rosa Anglica* (*The English Rose*) and I doubt not but, as it is sweet in the title, so it is sovereign in the matter therein contained.[2] [*d.* 1361]

JOHN BARNET had his name and nativity from a market-town in this county, sufficiently known by the road passing through it. He was first by the pope preferred, 1362, to be bishop of Worcester, and afterwards was

(1) Camden's *Britannia,* in Middlesex. [If these heads of oxen were really found, it was probably a relic of Mithraism. The Roman legions contained many devotees of Mithras, and temples certainly existed on Hadrian's Wall.] (2) Gaddesden practised in London, and treated a son of Edward I for smallpox, and is the 'Gatesden' referred to in the prologue to Chaucer's *Canterbury Tales.*

translated to Bath and Wells. Say not this was a retrograde motion, and Barnet degraded in point of profit by such a removal; for though Worcester is the better bishopric in our age, in those days Bath and Wells (before the revenues thereof were reformed under King Edward the Sixth) was the richer preferment. Hence he was translated to Ely, and for six years was lord treasurer of England. He died at Bishop's Hatfield, June 7, 1373, and was buried there [Ely] on the south side of the high altar, under a monument now miserably defaced by some sacrilegious executioner, who hath beheaded the statue lying thereon.

THOMAS RUDBORNE [or RODEBURNE] no doubt, according to the fashion of those days, took his name from Redbourn, a village within four miles of St. Albans.[1] He was bred in Oxford, and proctor thereof anno 1402, and chancellor 1420. An excellent scholar and skilful mathematician; of a meek and mild temper (though at one time a little tart against the Wycliffites) which procured him much love with great persons. He was warden of Merton College in Oxford, and built the tower over the college gate. He wrote a Chronicle of England; and was preferred bishop of St. David's. [*d.* 1442]

NICHOLAS DIXON, parson for thirty years together of Cheshunt in this county. He was also clerk of the pipe office belonging to the exchequer. See we here why the officers of that place (as also those of the Chancery) were called clerks, because priests in orders with cure of souls did formerly discharge those offices. He was also under-treasurer, and at last baron of the exchequer, when, partly by his own bounty, and partly by collection of others, he built the parish church of Cheshunt (and that, I assure you, is a very fair one) with a chancel to the Virgin Mary. [*d.* 1448]

JOHN WHETHAMSTEDE [or BOSTOCK] was born at Wheathampstead in this county, not so famous for the production of the best wheat, whence the place hath its name, as for this John Whethamstede, who hath his name from that place. He was bred at the priory at Tynemouth in Northumberland (a long stride, I assure you, from the place of his birth) to which he bequeathed a chalice of gold. He was afterwards abbot of St. Albans, and the sixth of that Christian name.

Vast were his expenses in adorning of that church, exceeding six thousand pounds. Two criticisms in his buildings I cannot omit; one, that on the north side of his church (which he enlightened with new windows) he set up the statues of those heathen philosophers which had testified of the incarnation of Christ; two, that in a little chapel he set up the similitudes of all the saints whose Christian names were John, with his own picture, and this prayer in a distich, that though unworthy, he might have a place with his namesakes in heaven.

Besides, he procured from Humphrey the good duke of Gloucester,[2] his great Maecenas, who was buried at St. Albans, a suit of vestments worth three thousand marks, and the manor of Pembroke in South

(1) He was probably a native of Rodbourne, Wiltshire. (2) Youngest son of Henry IV; statesman, soldier and scholar; earned the title of 'the Good Duke' by his munificent patronage of letters.

Wales. Many are the books which he left to posterity, being counted no fewer than fourscore and odd several treatises; and died [1465].

SIR RALPH JOCELYN, son to Geoffrey Jocelyn, was born at Sawbridgeworth in this county; bred a draper in London, whereof he was twice mayor. Once, anno 1463; and ere the end of that year, was made knight of the Bath by King Edward the Fourth, in the field, saith my author.[1] But seeing there is more of the carpet than of the camp in that order, it is more probable what another writes,[2] that he was invested knight of the Bath at the coronation of Elizabeth, queen to the king aforesaid. He was mayor again, anno 1476, when he corrected the bakers and victuallers of the city, and by his diligence were the walls thereof repaired; walls now a mere complement, serving more for the dividing than the defending of the city; so that as some foreign cities cannot be seen for the walls, here the walls cannot be seen for the city. Sad were the case of London, if not better secured with bones within, than stones about it. This Sir Ralph died October the 25th, anno 1478, and was buried in the church of Sawbridgeworth.

JOHN BOURCHIER, Baron Berners [*b.* 1467] was son of John Bourchier Baron Berners in the right of Margery his wife, daughter of Sir Richard Berners of West Horsley in Surrey. Yet had that honourable family of the Berners an ancient habitation at Therfield in this county, which with some probability insinuateth the birth of this noble gentleman therein.

He was a martial man well seen in all military discipline; and when Michael Joseph, the blacksmith, led the Cornish rebels[3] against King Henry the Seventh, anno 1497, no man did better service than this lord in their suppression, for which he was made chief governor of Calais.

Having there gotten a repose, who formerly had been a far traveller and great linguist, he translated many books out of French, Spanish and Italian, besides some of his own making. I behold him as the second, accounting the Lord Tiptoft the first noble hand which, since the decay of learning, took a pen therein to be author of a book. He died on the 16th of March 1533, and is buried in the great church in Calais. And I have read that the estate of the Berners is by an heir-general descended to the Knyvets of Ashwellthorpe in Norfolk.[4]

JOHN INCENT, son of Robert Incent and Catherine his wife, was born at Berkhampstead in this county. He was afterwards a doctor of law, and advanced, anno 1543 (when Richard Sampson was preferred bishop of Coventry and Lichfield) dean of St. Paul's. This John, probably invited by the example of another John (his mediate predecessor) Colet, dean of

(1) Stow's *Survey of London*. (2) Weever's *Funeral Monuments*. (3) The Cornish rising against the taxes imposed for defence against the forays of the Scots who, under their king James IV, were supporting the impostor Perkin Warbeck. The rebels were defeated at Blackheath, but treated leniently by Henry VII. (4) Berners is chiefly remembered for his great translation of Froissart. Fuller is at fault on his genealogy. He was the son of Humphrey Bourchier, first baron (who fell, fighting for the Yorkists, at Barnet in 1471) by Elizabeth, daughter of Sir Frederick Tilney and widow of Sir Thomas Howard. For John, Lord Tiptoft, see Cambridgeshire, p. 53.

Paul's, founded a fair free-school in the town of his nativity, procuring it confirmed by act of parliament, allowing the master twenty, the usher ten pounds per annum. He died, as I collect, in the beginning of the reign of King Edward the Sixth.

SIR THOMAS WHITE, son to William White, was born [1492] at Rickmansworth in this county, and afterwards bred a Merchant Taylor in London, of which city he was lord mayor Anno Domini 1553. He first built Gloucester Hall, and afterwards built and endowed St. John's College in Oxford, the seminary of many flourishing wits. He bestowed also a vast sum of money on several corporations, to be employed circularly for the benefit of the poor freemen therein. I once intended to have presented the reader with an exact particular of his benefactions, till seasonably I reversed my resolution on this consideration. Amongst the Jews it was an injury for one removed further off in blood to do the office of a kinsman to the childless widow, until the next of kin had first disclaimed his interest therein, as in the case of Ruth most plainly appeared. A son, I am sure, is nearer than a nephew, therefore it is a more proper performance for one bred in Oxford to collect the particulars of his bounty (whom whithersoever he went, left the finger-marks of his charity behind him) than for me, distanced a *degree* farther off by my education in another university.[1] [*d.* 1567]

SIR HENRY CAREY, son to William Carey and Mary Boleyn[2] his wife, was, wherever born [1524?] made by Queen Elizabeth lord chamberlain, baron of Hunsdon in this county. A valiant man, and lover of men of their hands; very choleric, but not malicious. Once one Mr. Colt chanced to meet him coming from Hunsdon to London, in the equipage of a lord of those days. The lord, on some former grudge, gave him a box of the ear. Colt presently returned the principal with interest, and thereupon his servants, drawing their swords, swarmed about him. "You rogues," said the lord, "may not I and my neighbour change a blow but you must interpose?" Thus the quarrel was begun and ended in the same minute.

It was merrily said that "his Latin and his dissimulation were both alike, and that his custom of swearing, and obscenity in speaking, made him seem a worse Christian than he was, and a better knight of the carpet than he could be."[3] He might have been with the queen whatsoever he *would* himself, but would be no more than what he was, preferring enough above a feast in that nature.

He hung at court on no man's sleeve, but stood on his own bottom till the time of his death, having a competent estate of his own given him by the queen, who bestowed on him, in the first of her reign, Hunsdon House in this county, with four thousand pounds a year (according to the valuation in that age) in fair desmesnes, parks and lands lying about it. Yet this was rather restitution that liberality in her majesty; seeing he

(1) Sir Thomas White was also one of the founders of Merchant Taylors' School. (2) Sister of Anne Boleyn, and Sir Henry Carey was therefore first cousin to Queen Elizabeth. (3) Sir Robert Naunton, in his *Fragmenta Regalia*.

had spent as great as estate (left him by his father) in her service, or rather relief, during her persecution under Queen Mary.

This lord suppressed the first northern commotion[1] . . . Three times was this lord in election to be earl of Wiltshire, a title which in some sort belonged to him in the right of Mary his mother, but still some intervening accident retarded it. When he lay on his death-bed, the queen gave him a gracious visit, causing his patent for the said earldom to be drawn, his robes to be made, and both to be laid down upon his bed; but this lord, who could dissemble neither *well* nor *sick*: "Madam," said he, "seeing you counted me not worthy of this honour whilst living, I count myself unworthy of it now I am dying." He departed this life Anno Domini 1596; and lieth buried in a most magnificent monument in Westminster Abbey, being the direct ancestor to the earls of Monmouth.

SIR EDWARD WATERHOUSE, knight, was born [1535] at Helmstedbury in this county, of an ancient and worshipful family deriving their descent lineally from Sir Gilbert Waterhouse, of Kirton in Low Lindsey, in the county of Lincoln, in the time of King Henry the Third. As for our Sir Edward, his parents were: John Waterhouse, esquire, a man of much fidelity and sageness; auditor many years to King Henry the Eighth, of whom he obtained (after a great entertainment for him in his house) the grant of a weekly market for the town of Hemel Hempstead; Margaret Turner, of the ancient house of Blunt's Hall in Suffolk, and Cannons in Hertfordshire.

The king, at his departure, honoured the children of the said John Waterhouse, being brought before him, with his praise and encouragement; gave a Benjamin's portion of dignation to this Edward, foretelling, by his royal augury, "that he would be the crown of them all, and a man of great honour and wisdom, fit for the services of princes."

It pleased God afterwards to second the word of the king, so that the sprouts of his hopeful youth only pointed at the growth and greatness of his honourable age; for, being but twelve years old, he went to Oxford, where for some years he glistered in the oratoric and poetic sphere, until he addicted himself to conversation, and observance of state affairs, wherein his great proficiency commended him to the favour of three principal patrons.

One was Walter Devereux, earl of Essex,[2] who made him his bosom friend; and the said earl, lying on his death-bed, took his leave of him with many kisses. "O my Ned," said he, "farewell, thou art the faithfullest and friendliest gentleman that ever I knew."

His other patron was Sir Henry Sidney (so often lord deputy of Ireland) whereby he became incorporated into the familiarity of his son Sir Philip Sidney; between whom and Sir Edward there was so great friendliness, that they were never better pleased than when in one another's companies, or when they corresponded each with other.[3]

(1) The rebellion of the northern earls, 1569, against Elizabeth's religious innovations. It was somewhat severely repressed. (2) See Wales, p. 691. (3) For the Sidneys, see Kent, p. 276.

His third patron was Sir John Perrot, deputy also of Ireland, who so valued his counsel that in state affairs he would do nothing without him. So great his employment betwixt state and state, that he crossed the seas thirty-seven times, until deservedly at last he came into a port of honour, wherein he sundry years anchored, and found safe harbour; for he received the honour of knighthood, was sworn of her majesty's privy council for Ireland, and chancellor of the exchequer therein.

Now his grateful soul, coursing about how to answer the queen's favour, laid itself wholly out in her service, wherein two of his actions most remarkable. First, he was highly instrumental in modelling the kingdom of Ireland into shires as they now are, shewing himself so great a lover of the polity under which he was born, that he advanced the compliance therewith, as commendable and necessary in the dominions annexed thereunto.

His second service was, when many in that kingdom shrouded themselves from the laws, under the target of power, making force their tutelary saint, he set himself vigorously to suppress them. And when many of the privy council, terrified with the greatness of the earl of Desmond, durst not subscribe the instrument wherein he was proclaimed traitor, Sir Edward, among some others, boldly signed the same (disavowing his and all treasons against prince and country) and the council did the like, commanding the publication thereof.

As to his private sphere, God blessed him, being but a third brother, above his other brethren. Now though he had three wives, the first a Villiers, the second a Spilman, the third the widow of Harlackenden, of Woodchurch in Kent, esquire; and though he had so strong a brain and body, yet he lived and died childless, inter-commoning therein with many Worthies, who are, according to Aelius Spartianus, either improlific, or having children in *genitorum vituperium et famarum laesuram*. God thus denying him the pleasure of posterity, he craved leave of the queen to retire himself, and fixed the residue of his life at Woodchurch in Kent, living there in great honour and repute as one who had no design to be popular, and not prudent; rich, and not honest; great, and not good.

He died in the fifty-sixth year of his age, the 13th October 1591, and is buried at Woodchurch under a table marble monument, erected to his memory by his sorrowful lady surviving him.

Reader, I doubt not but thou art sensible of the alteration and improvement of my language in this character, owing both my intelligence and expressions unto Edward Waterhouse,[1] now of Sion College, esquire, who, to revive the memory of his namesake and great-uncle, furnished me with these instructions.

THOMAS CARTWRIGHT was born [1535] in this county, and was admitted in Saint John's College in Cambridge, anno 1550. In the reign of Queen Mary he left the university, being probably one of those scholars which, as Mr. Foxe observeth, went (*alias*, were *driven*) away from this college all at one time, and betook himself to the service of a counsellor. Here

(1) Heraldic and miscellaneous writer, lived 1619—1670.

he got some skill in the common law, which enabled him afterwards to fence the better for himself by the advantage thereof.

In the reign of Queen Elizabeth he returned to Cambridge, was chosen fellow, first of St. John's, then of Trinity. How afterwards he was made Margaret professor, ousted thereof for his nonconformity, travelled beyond seas, returned home, became the champion of the presbyterian party, is largely related in our *Church History*.

Only I will add that the nonconformists, not agreeing which of them (where there is much choice, there is no choice) should answer Dr. Whitgift's Reply, I read that Mr. Cartwright at last was chosen by lot to undertake it.[1]

One saith "for riches he sought them not," and another saith, "that he died rich"; and I believe both say true, God sometimes making wealth to find them who seek not for it, seeing many and great were his benefactors. He died and was buried in Warwick, where he was master of the hospital, anno 1603.

DANIEL DYKE was born at Hempstead [Essex] where his father was a minister silenced for his nonconformity. He was bred in St. John's College in Cambridge, and became afterwards a profitable leader in God's vineyard. Witness, besides his sermons, his worthy books, whereof that is the master-piece which treateth of *The Mystery of Self-Deceiving*, wherein he lays down directions for the discovery thereof; as also how, in other cases, one may be acquainted with his own condition, seeing many men lose themselves in the labyrinths of their own hearts, so much is the *terra incognita* therein. This book he designed for his pious patron John Lord Harington. "But, alas, when the child was come to birth, there was no strength to bring forth!" Before the book was fully finished, the author thereof followed his honourable patron into a better world; so that his surviving brother (of whom immediately) set it forth. And to the Lady Lucy, countess of Bedford, the lord's sister, the same was dedicated. A book which will be owned for a truth whilst men have any badness, and will be honoured for a treasure whilst men have any goodness in them. This worthy man died . . . 1614.

JEREMIAH DYKE, his younger brother, was bred in Sidney College in Cambridge; beneficed at Epping in Essex; one of a cheerful spirit. And know, reader, that an ounce of mirth, with the same degree of grace, will serve God farther than a pound of sadness. He had also a gracious heart, and was very profitable in his ministry. He was a father to some good books of his own; and a guardian to those of his brother, whose posthume works he set forth. He was one "peaceable in Israel," and though no zealot in the practice of ceremonies, quietly submitted to use them. He lived and died piously, being buried in his own parish church, Anno Domini 1620.

(1) In 1572 appeared an anonymous puritan manifesto entitled *An Admonition to the Parliament*, both constructive and abusive, against the established church. It was immediately popular and created a tremendous effect. John Whitgift (then master of Trinity College, and later archbishop of Canterbury) was chosen to reply to it. Cartwright, a man of considerable learning, is the outstanding figure in the early history of puritanism. He was imprisoned 1590-2, and released through the instrumentality of Whitgift.

SIR HENRY CARY, viscount of Falkland in Scotland, and son to Sir Edward Cary, was born at Aldenham in this county. He was a most accomplished gentleman and complete courtier. By King James he was appointed lord deputy of Ireland, and well discharged his trust therein. But an unruly colt will fume and chafe, though neither switched nor spurred, merely because backed. The rebellious Irish will complain, only because kept in subjection, thought with never so much lenity; the occasion why some hard speeches were passed on his government. Some beginning to counterfeit his hand, he used to incorporate the year of his age in a knot flourished beneath his name, concealing the day of his birth to himself. Thus by comparing the date of the month with his own birthday (unknown to such forgers) he not only discovered many false writings which were past, but also deterred dishonest cheaters from attempting the like for the future. Being recalled into England, he lived honourably in this county, until he by a sad casualty brake his leg on a stand in Theobald's Park, and soon after died thereof. He married the sole daughter and heir of Sir Lawrence Tanfield, chief-baron of the exchequer, by whom he had a fair estate in Oxfordshire. His death happened Anno Domini 1633; being father to the most accomplished statesman, Lucius,[1] grandfather to the present Henry Lord Falkland, whose pregnant parts (now clarified from juvenile extravagancies) perform much, and promise more useful service to this nation.

EDWARD SYMONDS, born at Cottered in this county, was bred in Peterhouse in Cambridge, where he commenced master of arts, afterwards minister of Little Rayne in Essex; a man strict in his life and profitable in his preaching, wherein he had a plain and piercing faculty. Being sequestered from his living for siding with the king, with David (1 Sam. xxiii. 13) he went "wheresoever he could go," to Worcester, Exeter, Barnstaple, France, and lastly returned to London. He wrote a book in *Vindication of King Charles,* and was instrumental in setting forth his majesty's book called *Eikon Basilike.* Pens were brandished betwixt him and Mr. Stephen Marshall,[2] though all was fair betwixt them before his death; for Mr. Symonds visited him, lying in his bed at Westminster; told him, "Had I taken you for a wild beast, I would not have roused you in your den." He was very conscientious in discharging his calling. Being once requested by me to preach for me, he excused himself for want of competent warning; and when I pleaded that mine, being a country parish, would be well pleased with his performance, "I can," saith he, "content them, but not mine own conscience, to preach with so little preparation." He died Anno Domini 1649; and was buried in St. Peter's, Paul's Wharf, in London.

ARTHUR CAPEL, esquire [FIRST BARON CAPEL OF HADHAM, *b.* 1610?] of Hadham in this county, was by King Charles the First created a baron, 1641. He served the king with more valour and fidelity than success,

(1) Lucius Cary was the famous Viscount Falkland who deliberately sought death at the battle of Newbury. (2) The great preacher who exercised such a profound influence on the parliamentary side (see Huntingdonshire, p. 248).

during the civil wars, in the Marches of Wales. After the surrender of Oxford he retired to his own house in this shire, and was in some sort well cured of the (so then reputed) disease of loyalty, when he fell into a relapse by going to Colchester, which cost him his life; beheaded in the Palace Yard in Westminster, 1649.

In his lifetime he wrote a book of meditation (published since his death) wherein much judicious piety may be discovered. His mortified mind was familiar with afflictions, which made him to appear with such Christian resolution on the scaffold, where he seemed rather to fright death than to be frighted with it. Hence one not unhappily alluding to his arms (a lion rampant in a field gules betwixt three crosses) thus expresseth himself:

> Thus lion-like Capel undaunted stood,
> Beset with crosses in a field of blood.

A learned doctor in physic (present at the opening and embalming of him and duke of Hamilton) delivered it at a public lecture, that the Lord Capel's was the least heart, whilst the duke's was the greatest, he ever beheld. Which also is very proportionable to the observation in philosophy, that the spirits contracted in a lesser model are the cause of the greater courage.

God hath since been the husband to his widow (who, for her goodness, may be a pattern to her sex) and father to his children, whom not so much their birth, beauty and portions, as *virtues* married to the best bloods and estates in the land, even when the royalists were at the lowest condition.

THE FAREWELL

I am sorry to hear that the fair font of solid brass, brought out of Scotland, and bestowed by Sir Richard Lea on the abbey church in St. Albans, is lately taken away. I could almost wish that the plunderers' fingers had found it as hot as it was when first forged, that so these thieves, with their fault, might have received the deserved punishment thereof.

Had it been returned to the place whence it was taken, to serve for the same use, the matter had not been so much; but, by an usual alchemy, this brass is since turned into silver. But let us not so much condole the late losing of the font, as congratulate our still keeping of baptism; which, if some men might have their minds, should utterly be denied to all infants. I wish all infants to be christened in this county and elsewhere, though not so fair a font, fair water and, which is the best of all, the full concurrence of God's Spirit effectually to complete the sacrament unto them.

HUNTINGDONSHIRE

HUNTINGDONSHIRE is surrounded with Northampton, Bedford and Cambridge-shires; and, being small in extent, hardly stretcheth twenty miles outright, though measured to the most advantage. The general goodness of the ground may certainly be collected from the plenty of convents erected therein, at St. Neot's, Hinchingbrooke, Huntingdon, Sawtry, St. Ives, Ramsey, &c; so that the fourth foot at least in this shire was abbey-land, belonging to monks and friars; and such weeds, we know, would not grow but in rich ground. If any say that monks might not choose their own habitations, being confined therein to the pleasures of their founders, know there were few founders that did not first consult some religious person in the erection of convents; and such would be sure to choose the best for men of their own profession. Sure I am it would set all England hard to show in so short a distance so pleasant a park as Waybridge, so fair a meadow as Portsholme, and so fruitful a town for tillage as Godmanchester; all three within so many miles in this county.

No peculiar commodity or manufacture (save with others equally intercommoning) appearing in this county, let us proceed.

THE BUILDINGS

KIMBOLTON CASTLE. This, being part of the jointure of Queen Catherine dowager, was chosen by her to retire thereunto; as neither too near to London, to see what she would not, nor so far off, but that she might hear what she desired. Here she wept out the remnant of her widowhood (while her husband was yet alive) in her devotions. This castle came afterwards by gift to the Wingfields; from them by sale to the Montagues; Henry late earl of Manchester sparing no cost which might add to the beauty thereof.

HINCHINGBROOKE, once a nunnery, and which I am confident will ever be a religious house whilst it relateth to the truly noble Edward Montagu, earl of Sandwich, the owner thereof. It sheweth one of the most magnificent rooms which is to be beheld in our nation.

We must not forget the house and chapel in Little Gidding (the inheritance of Master Ferrar) which lately made a great noise all over England.[1] Here three numerous female families (all from one grandmother) lived together in a strict discipline of devotion. They rose at midnight to prayers; and other people most complained thereof, whose heads, I dare say, never ached for want of sleep. Sure I am, strangers by them were entertained, poor people were relieved, their children instructed to read, while their own needles were employed in learned and pious work, to bind Bibles; whereof one most exactly done was presented to King Charles. But their society was beheld by some as an embryo nunnery, suspecting that there was a Pope Joan therein;

(1) In the beginning of the Long Parliament.—F

which causeless cavil afterwards confuted itself, when all the younger of those virgins practised the precept of St. Paul, to marry, bear children, and guide their houses.

MEDICINAL WATERS

There is an obscure village in this county, near St. Neot's, called Hail Weston, whose very name soundeth something of sanativeness therein; so much may the adding of what is no letter, alter the meaning of a word; for, 1. *Aile* signifieth a sore or hurt, with complaining the effect thereof. 2. *Haile* (having an affinity with *Heile,* the Saxon idol for Esculapius) importeth a cure, or medicine to a malady.[1]

Now in the aforesaid village there be two fountain-lets, which are not far asunder. 1. One sweet, conceived good to help the dimness of the eyes. 2. The other in a manner salt, esteemed sovereign against the scabs and leprosy.

What saith St. James: "Doth a fountain send forth at the same place sweet water and bitter?" meaning in an ordinary way, without miracle. Now although these different waters flow from several fountains, yet seeing they are so near together, it may justly be advanced to the reputation of a wonder.

PROVERBS

This is the way to Beggar's Bush. It is spoken of such who use dissolute and improvident courses, which tend to poverty; Beggar's Bush being a tree notoriously known, on the left hand of London road from Huntingdon to Caxton. I have heard how King James, being in progress in these parts with Sir Francis Bacon the lord chancellor, and having heard that morning how Sir Francis had prodigiously rewarded a mean man for a small present, "Sir Francis," said he, "you will quickly come to Beggar's Bush, and I may even go along with you, if both be so bountiful."

Ramsey the Rich. This was the *Croesus,* or *Crassus,* of all our English abbeys; for, having but sixty monks to maintain therein, the revenues thereof, according to the standard of those times, amounted unto seven thousand pounds a year, which, in proportion, was a hundred pounds for every monk, and a thousand for their abbot. Yet, at the dissolution of monasteries, the income of this abbey was reckoned but at one thousand nine hundred eighty-three pounds by the year, whereby it plainly appears how much the revenues were under-rated in those valuations.

But how soon is *Crassus* made *Codrus,* and Ramsey the Rich become Ramsey the Poor. The wealth of the town, relative with the abbey, was dissolved therewith, and more the mendicants since in Ramsey than the monks were before. However, now there is great hope that Ramsey, after the two extremes of wealth and want, will at last be fixed in a comfortable mediocrity, the wish of Agur being granted unto him, "Give me neither poverty nor riches," especially since it is lately erected (or rather restored) to the dignity of a market-town. And surely the convenient situation thereof, since the draining of the fens, doth advantage it to be a staple place for the sale of fat and lean cattle.

(1) One of Fuller's most dubious etymologies: Hail Weston means 'dirty stream'.

THE WORTHIES

HENRY OF HUNTINGDON, son to one Nicholas, where born [1084?] unknown, was first a canon of the church of Lincoln, where he became acquainted with one Albinus of Angers, born in France, but fellow-canon with him of the same church. This Albinus he afterwards in his writings modestly owned for his master, having gained much learning from him.

He was afterwards chaplain to Alexander, that great bishop of Lincoln (magnificent unto madness) who made him archdeacon of Huntingdon, whence he took his denomination. A town which hath received more honour from him than ever it can return to him, seeing Huntingdon had never been mentioned in the mouths, nor passed under the pens, of so many foreigners, but for the worthy history of the Saxon kings, written by this Henry. Let me add, that considering the sottishness of superstition in the age he lived in, he is less smutted therewith than any of his contemporaries, and being a secular priest, doth now and then abate the pride of monastical pretended perfection. [*d.* 1155]

WILLIAM OF RAMSEY was born in this county, famous for the richest Benedictines' abbey in England; yet here he would not stay, but went to Crowland, where he prospered so well that he became abbot thereof. He was a natural poet, and therefore no wonder if faults be found in the feet of his verses, for it is given to thorough-paced nags, that amble naturally, to trip much, whilst artificial pacers go surest on foot. He wrote the life of St. Guthlac, St. Neot's, St. Edmund the king, &c., all in verse.

But that which may seem a wonder indeed is this, that being a poet, he paid the vast debts of others, even forty thousand marks, for the engagement of his convent, and all within the compass of eighteen months, wherein he was abbot of Crowland. But it rendereth it the more credible, because it was done by the assistance of King Henry the Second, who, to expiate the blood of Becket, was contented to be melted into coin, and was prodigiously bountiful to some churches. [*fl.* 1219]

GREGORY OF HUNTINGDON, so called from the place of his nativity, was bred a Benedictine monk in Ramsey, where he became prior, or vice-abbot, a place which he deserved, being one of the most learned men of that age for his great skill in languages. For he was thorough-paced in three tongues, Latin, Greek (as appears by his many comments on those grammarians) and Hebrew, which last he learned by his constant conversing with the Jews in England.

But now the fatal time did approach, wherein the Jews (full loath I assure you) must leave the land, and many precious books behind them. Our Gregory, partly by love, partly by the king's power (both together will go far in driving a bargain) purchased many of those rarities, to dispose them in his convent of Ramsey; which, as it exceeded other English monasteries for a library, so for Hebrew books that monastery exceeded itself. [*fl.* 1290]

WILLIAM WHITTLESEY [or WITTLESEY.] No printed author mentioning the place of his birth and breeding, he was placed by us in this county, finding Whittlesey a town therein (so memorable for the Mere) and presuming that this William did follow suit with the best of his coat in that age, surnamed from the places of their nativity. Mr. Parker (I tell you my story and my story's man) an industrious antiquary, collecteth out of the records of the church of Ely, that (after the resignation of Ralph de Holbeach) William Whittlesey, archdeacon of Huntingdon, 1337, was admitted third master of Peterhouse in Cambridge. Yet hath he left more signal testimony of his affection to Oxford, which he freed from the jurisdiction of the bishop of Lincoln, allowing the scholars leave to choose their own chancellor.

He was kinsman to Simon Islip, archbishop of Canterbury, who made him vicar-general, dean of the Arches; and successively he was preferred bishop of Rochester, Worcester, London, archbishop of Canterbury. An excellent scholar, an eloquent preacher; and his last sermon most remarkable, to the convocation, on this text, *Veritas liberabit vos* (the truth shall make you free). It seems by the story, that in his sermon he had a particular reflection of the privileges of the clergy, as exempted by preaching the truth from payment of taxes, save with their own free consent. But all would not serve their turn; for in the contemporary parliament the clergy, unwillingly-willing, granted a yearly tenth to supply the pressing occasions of King Edward the Third. This William died Anno Domini 1374.

FRANCIS WHITE was born [1564?] at St. Neot's in this county, and not in Lancashire, as I and others have been misinformed;[1] witness the admission book of Caius College, and the testimony of his brother's son, still alive. The father to this Francis was a minister, and had five sons, who were divines, and two of them most eminent in their generation. Of these, this Francis was bred in Caius College, on the same token that when he was bishop of Ely (and came to consecrate the chapel of Peterhouse) he received an entertainment at that college, where with a short speech he encouraged the young students to ply their books by his own example, who, from a poor scholar in that house, by God's blessing on his industry, was brought to that preferment.

By the Lord Grey of Groby he was presented to Broughton Astley in Leicestershire, and thence (why should a candle be put under a bushel?) he was brought to be lecturer of St. Paul's in London, and parson of St. Peter's in Cornhill, whence he was successively preferred, first dean, then bishop of Carlisle; after bishop of Norwich and at last Ely.

He had several solemn disputations with popish priests and Jesuits (Father Fisher and others) and came off with such good success, that he reduced many seduced Romanists to our church. He often chose Daniel Featley, D.D.,[2] his assistant in such disputes; so that I may call this prelate and his doctor, Jonathan and his armour-bearer (being con-

(1) By Master Holmes, his secretary, being himself deceived without intent to deceive. [He and his brother John (see below, p. 246) were both born in Eaton Socon, Bedfordshire, and educated at the grammar school in St. Neot's.] (2) See Oxfordshire, p. 469.

fident that the doctor, if alive, would not be displeased with the comparison as any disparagement unto him) jointly victorious over the Romish Philistines. He died anno 1638, leaving some of his learned works to posterity.

RICHARD FISHBOURN was born in the town of Huntingdon; cut out of no mean quarry, being a gentleman by his extraction. Leaving a court-life (as more pleasant than profitable) he became servant to Sir Baptist Hicks, afterwards Viscount Campden,[1] and, by God's blessing on his industry, attained a great estate; whereof he gave two thousand pounds for the buying out of impropriations in the northern parts, and settling a preaching ministry where most want thereof; he bequeathed as much to the company of Mercers, whereof he was free; and the same sum to Huntingdon, the place of his nativity; with one thousand marks to Christ Church Hospital. The whole sum of his benefactions amounted to ten thousand seven hundred pounds and upwards, briefly summed up in his funeral sermon, commonly called *Corona Charitatis,* preached by Master Nathaniel Shute, wherein, to use his expression, "he supped up many things with a very short breath," contracting his deeds of charity to avoid tediousness.

Nor must it be forgotten how this gentleman, lying on his death-bed (when men are presumed to speak with unmasked consciences) did profess that, to his knowledge, he had got no part of his goods unjustly. No man of his quality won more love in health, prayers in sickness, and lamentation at his funeral; dying a single man, and buried in Mercers' Chapel, May the 10th, 1625.

JOHN WHITE, brother to Francis White bishop of Ely, was born [1570] at St. Neot's in this county; bred in Caius College in Cambridge, wherein he commenced master of arts. He did not continue long in the university, but the university continued long in him; so that he may be said to have carried Cambridge with him into Lancashire (so hard and constant in his study) when he was presented vicar of Eccles therein. Afterwards Sir John Crofts, a Suffolk knight, being informed of his abilities, and pitying his remote living on no plentiful benefice, called him into the south, and was the occasion that King James took cognizance of his worth, making him his chaplain in ordinary. It was now but the third month of his attendance at court, when he sickened at London in Lombard Street, died, and was buried in the church of Saint Mary Woolnoth,[2] 1615, without any other monument, save what his learned works have left to posterity, which all who have either learning, piety, or ingenuity do, yea must, most highly commend.

SIR ROBERT BRUCE COTTON, knight and baronet, son to Thomas Cotton, esquire, was born [1571] at Conington in this county; descended by the Bruces from the blood royal of Scotland. He was bred in Jesus College in Cambridge, where, when a youth, he discovered his inclination to the

(1) See p. 188, note 1. (2) So I am informed by his son, Mr. White, a druggist, living in Lombard Street.

study of antiquity (they must spring early who would sprout high in that knowledge) and afterwards attained to such eminency, that sure I am he had no superior, if any his equal, in the skill thereof.

But that which rendered him deservedly to the praise of present and future times, yea the wonder of our own and foreign nations, was his collection of his library in Westminster; equally famous for 1. *Rarity;* having so many manuscript originals, or else copies so exactly transcribed, that, reader, I must confess he must have more skill than I have to distinguish them. 2. *Variety;* he that beholdeth their number would admire they should be rare; and he that considereth their rarity, will more admire at their number. 3. *Method;* some libraries are labyrinths, not for the multitude, but confusion of volumes, where a stranger seeking for a book may quickly lose himself; whereas these are so exactly methodised (under the heads of the twelve Roman emperors) that it is harder for one to miss than to hit any author he desireth.

But what addeth a lustre to all the rest is the favourable access thereunto, for such as bring any competency of skill with them, and leave thankfulness behind them. Some antiquaries are so jealous of their books, as if every hand which toucheth would ravish them; whereas here no such suspicion of ingenious persons. And here give me leave to register myself amongst the meanest of those who through the favour of Sir Thomas Cotton (inheriting as well the courtesy as estate of his father Sir Robert) have had admittance into that worthy treasure.

Yea, most true it is what one saith, that the grandest antiquaries have here fetched their materials:[1]

> *Omnis ab illo*
> *Et Camdene tua, et Seldini gloria crevit.*[2]
> Camden to him, to him doth Selden owe
> Their glory: what they got from him did grow.

I have heard that there was a design driven on in the pope's conclave, after the death of Sir Robert, to compass this library to be added to that in Rome; which, if so, what a Vatican had there been within the Vatican, by the accession thereof. But, blessed be God, the project did miscarry, to the honour of our nation, and advantage of the protestant religion. For therein are contained many privities of princes and transactions of state; insomuch that I have been informed that the fountains have been fain to fetch water from the stream; and the secretaries of state, and clerks of the council, glad from hence to borrow back again many originals, which, being lost by casualty or negligence of officers, have here been recovered and preserved. He was a man of a public spirit, it being his principal endeavour in all parliaments (wherein he served so often) that the prerogative and privilege might run in their due channel; and in truth he did cleave the pin betwixt the sovereign and the subject. He was wont to say, "That he himself had the least share in himself;" whilst his country and friends had the greatest interest in him. He died at his

(1) Cotton gave the free use of his library to Camden (who taught him at Westminster School and laid the foundation of his antiquarian interests) Bacon, Selden, Speed and other scholars. The library was transferred to the nation in 1702, and removed to the British Museum in 1753. (2) Weever's *Funeral Monuments*, in the preface.

house in Westminster, May the 6th, Anno Domini 1631, in the 61st year of his age; though one may say truly, his age was adequate to the continuance of the creation, such was his exact skill in all antiquity. The *opera posthuma* of this worthy knight are lately set forth in one volume, to the great profit of posterity.

RICHARD BROUGHTON was born at Great Stukeley in this county; bred at Rheims in France, where he received the order of priesthood; and was sent over into England for the propagation of his party. Here he gave so signal testimony and fidelity to the cause, that he was, before many others, preferred assistant to the English arch-priest.

He wrote many books, and is most esteemed by those of his own religion for his *Ecclesiastical History of Great Britain,* from the first planting of the Gospel, to the coming in of the Saxons. But in plain truth, there is little milk, no cream, and almost all whey therein, being farced with legendary stuff, taken from authors, some of condemned, most of suspected credit. If by the Levitical law "a bastard should not enter into the congregation of the Lord (understand it, to bear office therein) to the tenth generation," it is pity that adulterated authors, being an illegitimate off-spring, should be admitted to bear rule in church history. [*d.* 1634]

SIR OLIVER CROMWELL, knight, son to Sir Henry Cromwell, knight, of Hinchingbrooke in this county, is remarkable to posterity on a fourfold account. First, for his hospitality and prodigious entertainment of King James and his court. Secondly, for his upright dealing in bargain and sale with all chapmen; so that no man whosoever purchased land of him was put to charge of three-pence to make good his title. Yet he sold excellent pennyworths; insomuch that Sir John Leamon (once lord mayor of London) who bought the fair manor of Warboys in this county of him, affirmed "that it was the cheapest land that ever he bought, and yet the dearest that ever Sir Oliver Cromwell sold." Thirdly, for his loyalty; always beholding the usurpation and tyranny of his nephew, godson and namesake, with hatred and contempt.[1] Lastly, for his vivacity, who survived to be the oldest gentleman in England who was a knight, though not the oldest knight who was a gentleman, seeing Sir George Dalston, younger in years (yet still alive) was knighted some days before him. Sir Oliver died Anno Domini 1654.

STEPHEN MARSHALL was born [1594?] at Godmanchester in this county, and bred a bachelor of arts in Emmanuel College in Cambridge. Thence he went very early a reaper in God's harvest, yet not before he had well sharpened his sickle for that service. He became minister at Finchingfield in Essex; and after many years' discontinuance, came up to Cambridge to take the degree of bachelor of divinity, where he performed his exercise with general applause.

In the late long-lasting parliament, no man was more gracious with the principal members thereof. He was their trumpet, by whom they

(1) Sir Oliver Cromwell's sons in the Civil War fought for the king.

sounded their solemn fasts, preaching more public sermons on that occasion, than any four of his function. In their sickness he was their confessor; in their assembly their counsellor; in their treaties their chaplain; in their disputations their champion.

He was of so supple a soul that he brake not a joint, yea, sprained not a sinew, in all the alteration of times; and his friends put all on the account, not of his inconstancy but prudence, who in his own practice, as they conceive, reconciled the various lections of St. Paul's precept, "serving the lord, and the times."

And although some severely censure him for deserting his principles, yet he is said on his death-bed to have given full satisfaction to such who formerly suspected his sincerity to the presbyterian discipline, dying Anno Domini 1655. He was solemnly buried in the abbey at Westminster.

THE FAREWELL

Much of this county's profit depends on the northern road crossing the body thereof from Godmanchester to Wansford Bridge; a road which in the winter is the ready way, leading not only to trouble but danger, insomuch that here it comes to pass (what war caused in the days of Shamgar) "the highways are unemployed, and travellers walk through byways," to the present prejudice and future undoing of all ancient stages. And indeed though *Stif-clay* (commonly called Stukeley) be the name but of one or two villages in the midst, yet their nature is extensive all over the county, consisting of a deep clay, giving much annoyance to passengers. May a mean man's motion be heard? Let the repairing of bad places in that highway (which is now the parish) be made the county charge, whereby the burden will become the less (borne by more backs) and the benefit the more, when the ways thereby shall effectually be mended and maintained.

KENT

KENT, in the Saxon Heptarchy, was an entire kingdom by itself, an honour which no other sole county attained unto. It hath the Thames on the north, the sea on the east and south, Sussex and Surrey on the west. From east to west it expatiateth itself into fifty-three miles; but from north to south expandeth not above twenty-six miles. It differeth not more from other shires than from itself, such the variety thereof. In some parts of it, health and wealth are at many miles' distance, which in other parts are reconciled to live under the same roof; I mean abide in one place together. Nor is the wonder great, if places differ so much which lie in this shire far asunder, when I have read that there is a farm within a mile of Gravesend, where the cattle, always drinking at one common pond in the yard, if they graze on one side of the house the butter is yellow, sweet and good; but if on the other, white, sourish and naught. Yet needeth there no Oedipus to unriddle the same, seeing one side lieth on the chalk, and hath much trefoil; the other on the gravel, abounding only with couch-grass.

A considerable part of this county is called the Weald; that is, a woodland ground, the inhabitants whereof are called the Wealdish men. And here, reader, I humbly submit a small criticism of mine to thy censure. I read in Master Speed,[1] in Wyatt's rebellion, how Sir Henry Isley and the two Knyvets conducted five hundred Welchmen into Rochester. I much admire how so many Cambro-Britons should straggle into Kent; the rather because that rising was peculiar to that county alone; since I conceive these Welchmen should be Wealdishmen, viz., such who had their habitation in the woody side of this shire.

However, the goodness of the soil generally may be guessed from the greatness of the Kentish breed, where both the cattle and the poultry are allowed the largest of the land. A giant ox, fed in Romney Marsh, was some six years since to be seen in London, so high, that one of the ordinary stature could hardly reach to the top of his back.

Here let me observe a slip of the pen in industrious Master Speed. "The air," saith he, "of Kent, is both wholesome and temperate" (which is confessed most true, but mark what followeth) "as seated nearest to the equinoctial, and farthest from the northern pole." But let his own general map be appealed to as judge, being therein both true and unpartial, and it will appear that some part of Devonshire lieth south of Kent well nigh a whole degree, or threescore miles. Thus we see other men's, other men see our mistakes; so necessary is mutual candour and charity, because he who forgiveth to-day may have need to be forgiven to-morrow. And yet I deny not but that Kent of all English counties is nearest to France; not because southernmost, but because the sea interposed is there the narrowest.

(1) In his *Chronicle*.

NATURAL COMMODITIES

CHERRIES

These were fetched out of Flanders, and first planted in this county by King Henry the Eighth, in whose time they spread into thirty-two parishes, and were sold at great rates. I have read that one of the orchards of this primitive plantation, consisting of thirty acres, produced fruit of one year sold for one thousand pounds; plenty, it seems, of cherries in that garden, meeting with a scarcity of them in all other places.

No English fruit is dearer than those at first, cheaper at last, pleasanter at all times; nor is it less wholesome than delicious. And it is much that of so many feeding so freely on them, so few are found to surfeit. Their several sorts do ripen so successively, that they continue in season well nigh a quarter of a year. It is incredible how many cherries one tree in this county did bear in a plentiful year; I mean not how many pound (being the fruit of other trees) have been weighed thereon (the common fallacy of the word *bear* amongst the country-folk) but simply how many did naturally grow thereupon.

We leave the wholesomeness of this fruit, both for food and physic, to be praised by others, having hitherto not met with any discommending it. As for the outlandish proverb, "He that eateth cherries with noblemen, shall have his eyes spurted out with the stones," it fixeth no fault in the fruit, the expression being merely metaphorical, wherein the folly of such is taxed, who associate themselves equal in expense with others in higher dignity and estate, till they be losers at last, and well laughed at for their pains.

SAINFOIN

SAINFOIN, or HOLY-HAY. Superstition may seem in the name, but I assure you there is nothing but good husbandry in the sowing thereof, as being found to be a great fertilizer of barren ground. It is otherwise called *polygala,* which I may English *much milk,* as causing the cattle to give abundance thereof. Some call it the small clover grass, and it prospereth best in the worst ground.

It was first fetched out of France from about Paris, and since is sown in divers places in England, but especially in Cobham Park in this county, where it thriveth extraordinary well on dry chalky banks, where nothing else will grow. If it prospereth not equally in other dry places, it justly to be imputed to some error in the managing thereof; as, that the ground was not well prepared, or made fine enough; that the seed was too sparing, or else old and decayed; that cattle cropped it in the first year, &c. It will last but seven years, by which time the native grass of England will prevail over this foreigner, if it be not sown again.

TROUTS

We have treated of this fish before,[1] and confess this repetition had been a breach of the fundamental laws, premised to this book, were it not

(1) In Berkshire.

also an addition; Kent affording trouts, at a town called Fordwich, nigh Canterbury, differing from all others in many considerables:

1. *Greatness;* many of them being in bigness near to a salmon. 2. *Colour;* cutting white (as others do red) when best in season. 3 *Cunning;* only one of them ever being caught with an angle;[1] whereas other trouts are easily tickled into taking, and flattered into their destruction. 4. *Abode;* remaining nine months in the sea, and three in the fresh water. They observe their coming up thereinto almost to a day; and the men of Fordwich observe them as exactly, whom they catch with nets, and other devices.

WELD[2] OR WOLD

Know, reader, that I borrow my orthography hereof (if it be so) from the dyers themselves. This is a little seed, sown in this county some forty years since (when first it was brought into England) with barley, the growth whereof it doeth not hinder in any degree; for when the barley is mowed down in harvest, then this weld, or wold, first peeps out of the earth, where it groweth till the May following, when it is gathered; and thus husbandmen with one sowing reap two crops, yet so as it taketh up their ground for two years.

The use hereof is for the dyeing of the best yellow. It hath sometimes been so low as at four pounds a load (which containeth fifteen hundredweight) and sometimes so dear that it was worth fifteen pounds, betwixt which prices it hath its constant motion; and now is in the equator betwixt both, worth seven pounds ten shillings. It was first sown in this county, and since in Norfolk and in other places.

MADDER

This is very useful for dyers, for making of reds and violets. It is a weed whose root only is useful for dyeing (whilst the leaves only of woad are serviceable for that purpose) and there are three kinds thereof: 1. *Crop-Madder,* worth betwixt £4 and £5 the hundred; 2. *Umber-Owe,* worth betwixt £3 and £4; 3. *Pipe,* or *Fat Madder,* worth about £1 10s.

Some two years since, this was sown by Sir Nicholas Crisp[3] at Deptford, and I hope will have good success; first, because it groweth in Zeeland in the same (if not a more northern) latitude; secondly, because wild madder grows here in abundance; and why may not tame madder, if cicurated[4] by art? Lastly, because as good as any grew some thirty years since at Barn-Elms in Surrey, though it quit not cost, through some error in the first planter thereof, which now, we hope, will be rectified.

FLAX

I am informed, by such who should know, that no county in England sends better or more to London; yet doth not our whole land afford the

(1) By Sir George Hastings. Mr. Walton, in his *Compleat Angler.*—F. (2) The plant *Reseda Luteola,* which yields a yellow dye, and the name is used for the dye itself. (3) Lived 1599?—1666; royalist, granted by Charles I exclusive right, with five others, of trading to Guinea. M.P. for Winchelsea, but expelled from parliament as a monopolist. He raised troops for Charles I, and supported Monck at the Restoration. (4) *Cicurate*=to tame.

tenth part of what is spent therein; so that we are fain to fetch it from Flanders, France, yea, as far as Egypt itself. It may seem strange that our soil, kindly for that seed, the use whereof and profit hereby so great, yet so little care is taken for the planting thereof, which, well husbanded, would find linen for the rich and living for the poor. Many would never be indicted spinsters, were they spinsters indeed; nor some to so public and shameful punishments, if painfully employed in that vocation.

When a spider is found upon our clothes, we use to say, "Some money is coming towards us." The moral is this, such who imitate the industry of that contemptible creature, "which taketh hold with her hands, and is in king's palaces," may, by God's blessing, *weave* themselves into *wealth,* and procure a plentiful estate.

MANUFACTURES

Though clothing (whereof we have spoken before) be diffused through many shires of England, yet is it as vigorously applied here as in any other place, and Kentish cloth at the present keepeth up the credit thereof as high as ever before.

Thread

I place this the last, because the least of manufactures, thread being counted a thing so inconsiderable. Abraham said to the king of Sodom, "that he would take nothing, from a thread to a shoe-latchet;" that is, nothing at all. It seems this Hebrew proverb surrounded the universe, beginning at a thread, a contemptible thing, and after the encircling of all things more precious, ended where it begun, at a shoe-latchet, as mean as thread in valuation.

But, though one thread be little worth, many together prove useful and profitable, and some thousands of pounds are sent yearly over out of England to buy that commodity. My author telleth me, that thread is only made (I understand him out of London) at Maidstone in this county, where well nigh a hundred hands are employed about it.[1] I believe a thousand might be occupied in the same work, and many idle women, who now only spin street thread (going tattling about with tales) might procure, if set at work, a comfortable livelihood thereby.

THE BUILDINGS

The cathedral of Rochester is low, and little proportional to the revenues thereof. Yet hath it (though no magnificence) a venerable aspect of antiquity therein.

The king hath (besides other) three fair palaces in this shire: Greenwich, with a pleasant medley prospect of city, country, water and land; Eltham, not altogether so wholesome; and Otford, which Archbishop Warham did so enlarge and adorn with building, that Cranmer, his successor, was in some sort forced to exchange it with King Henry the Eighth on no gainful conditions, to lesson the clergy to content themselves with decency without sumptuousness, lest it awaken envy, and in fine they prove losers thereby.

(1) Hartlib, in his *Legacy*.

THE WONDERS

THE NAVY ROYAL

It may be justly accounted a Wonder of Art. And know, the ships are properly here handled, because the most, best and biggest of them have their birth (built at Woolwich) and winter abode nigh Chatham in the river of Medway in this county. Indeed, before the reign of Queen Elizabeth, the ships royal were so few, they deserved not the name of a fleet; when our kings hired vessels from Hamburg, Lubeck, yea Genoa itself. But such who, instead of their own servants, use char-folk in their houses, shall find their work worse done, and yet pay dearer for it.

Queen Elizabeth, sensible of this mischief, erected a Navy Royal (continued and increased by her successors) of the best ships Europe ever beheld. Indeed much is in the matter, the excellency of our English oak; more in the making, the cunning of our shipwrights; most in the manning, the courage of our seamen; and yet all to God's blessing, who so often hath crowned them with success.

If that man who hath *versatile ingenium* be thereby much advantaged for the working of his own fortune, our ships, so active to turn and wind at pleasure, must needs be more useful than the Spanish galleons, whose unwieldiness fixeth them almost in one posture, and maketh them the steadier marks for their enemies. As for Flemish bottoms, though they are finer built, yet as the slender barbe is not so fit to charge with, they are found not so useful in fight. The great *Sovereign,* built at Woolwich, a lieger-ship for state, is the greatest ship our island ever saw. But great medals are made for some grand solemnity, whilst lesser coin are more current and passable in payment.

I am credibly informed, that that mystery of shipwrights, for some descents hath been preserved successively in families, of whom the Petts[1] about Chatham are of singular regard. "Good success have they with their skill," and carefully keep so precious a pearl, lest otherwise amongst many friends some foes attain unto it. It is no monopoly which concealeth that from common enemies, the concealing whereof is for the common good. May this mystery of ship-making in England never be lost, till this floating world be arrived at its own haven, the end and dissolution thereof.

I know what will be objected by foreigners, to take off the lustre of our Navy Royal; viz., that, though the model of our great ships primitively were our own, yet we fetched the first mould and pattern of our frigates from the Dunkirks, when in the days of the duke of Buckingham (then admiral) we took some frigates from them, two of which still survive in his majesty's navy, by the name of the *Providence* and *Expedition.*

All this is confessed, and honest men may lawfully learn something from thieves for their own better defence. But it is added, we have

(1) Fuller gives no account of any of them. Peter Pett was master-shipwright at Deptford from some time in the reign of Edward VI until his death in 1589. His elder son Phineas (1570-1647) was master-shipwright at Deptford 1605, removed to Woolwich 1607, and commissioner of the navy 1630. Peter Pett (1610-1670?) son of the latter, was commissioner at Chatham 1648-67. The efficiency of the ships during the Dutch wars was largely due to him.

improved our patterns, and the transcript doth at this day exceed the original. Witness some of the swiftest Dunkirks and Ostenders, whose wings in a fair flight have failed them, overtaken by our frigates, and they still remain the monuments thereof in our navy.

Not to disgrace our neighbouring nations, but vindicate ourselves, in these nine following particulars the Navy Royal exceeds all kingdoms and states in Europe;

1. Swift Sailing; which will appear by a comparative induction of all other nations

First, for the Portugal, his *carvels* and *carracks,* whereof few now remain (the charges of maintaining them far exceeding the profit they bring in); they were the veriest drones on the sea, the rather because formerly their ceiling[1] was dammed up with a certain kind of mortar to dead the shot, a fashion now by them disused.

The French (how dextrous soever in land battles) are left-handed in sea fights, whose best ships are of Dutch building.

The Dutch build their ships so floaty and buoyant, they have little hold in the water in comparison of ours, which keep the better wind, and so outsail them.

The Spanish pride hath infected their ships with loftiness, which makes them but the fairer marks to our shot. Besides, the wind hath so much power of them in bad weather, so that it drives them two leagues for one of ours to the leeward, which is very dangerous upon a lee shore.

Indeed the Turkish frigates, especially some thirty-six of Algiers, formed and built much near the English mode, and manned by renegadoes, many of them English, being already too nimble-heeled for the Dutch, may hereafter prove mischievous to us, if not seasonably prevented.

2. Strength

I confine this only to the timber whereof they are made, our English oak being the best in the world. True it is (to our shame and sorrow be it written and read) the Dutch of late have built them some ships of English oak, which (through the negligence or covetousness of some great ones) was bought here and transported hence. But the best is, that, as Bishop Latimer once said to one who had preached his sermon, that he had gotten his fiddlestick but not his rosin, so the Hollanders with our timber did not buy also our art of ship-building.

Now the ships of other countries are generally made of fir and other such slight wood; whereby it cometh to pass that, as in the battle in the forest of Ephraim (wherein Absolom was slain) "the wood devoured more people that day than the sword," the splinters of so brittle timber kill more than the shot in a sea-fight.

3. Comeliness

Our frigates are built so neat and snug, made long and low; so that (as the make of some women's bodies handsomely concealeth their pregnancy or great belly) their contrivance hideth their bigness without

(1) *Ceiling*=foot-waling, i.e., the inside planking or lining of a ship over the floor-timbers.

suspicion, the enemy not expecting thirty, when (to his cost) he hath found sixty pieces of ordnance in them. Our masts stand generally very upright, whereas those of the Spaniards hang over their poop, as if they were ready to drop by the board; their decks are unequal, having many risings and fallings, whereas ours are even. Their ports some higher in a tier than others, ours drawn upon an equal line. Their cables bad (besides subject to rot in these countries) because bought at the second hand, whereas we make our best markets, fetching our cordage from the fountain thereof.

4. Force

Besides the strength inherent in the structure (whereof before) this is accessary, consisting in the weight and number of their guns; those of the

Sixth	Rates, carrying	10, 12, 14, 16, 18, 20,	Ordnance mounted
Fifth		22, 26, 28, 30,	
Fourth		38, 40, 44, 48, 50,	
Third		50, 54, 56, 60,	
Second		60, 64, 70.	

The *Royal Sovereign*, being one of the first rates, when she is fitted for the seas, carrieth one hundred and four pieces of ordnance mounted.

5. Seamen

Courageous and skilful. For the first, we remember the proverb of Solomon: "Let another praise thee, not thy own mouth; a stranger, not thy own lips." The Spaniards with sad shrug, and Dutch with a sorrowful shaking of their heads, give a tacit assent hereunto.

Skilful. Indeed navigation is much improved, especially since Saint Paul's time; insomuch that, when a man goes bunglingly about any work in a ship, I have heard our Englishmen say, "Such a man is one of St. Paul's mariners." For though no doubt they were as ingenious as any in that age to decline a tempest, yet modern experience affords fairer fences against foul weather.

6. Advantageous Weapons

Besides guns of all sorts and sizes, from the pistol to whole cannon, they have round-double-head-bur-spike-crow-bar-case-chain-shot. I join them together, because (though different instruments of death) they all concur in doing execution. If they be windward of a ship, they have arrows made to shoot out of a bow with fireworks at the end, which, if striking unto the enemy's sails, will stick there, and fire them and the ship. If they lie board and board, they throw hand-grenades with stink-pots into the ship, which make so noisome a smell, that the enemy is forced to thrust their heads out of the ports for air.

7. Provision

1. Wholesome our English beef and pork, keeping sweet and sound longer than any flesh of other countries; even twenty-six months to the East and West Indies.

2. More plentiful than any prince or state in all Europe alloweth; the seamen having two beef, two pork, and three fish-days. Besides, every

seaman is always well stored with hooks to catch fish, with which our seas do abound; insomuch that many times six will diet on four men's allowance and so save the rest therewith to buy fresh meat, when landing where it may be procured. I speak not this that hereafter their allowance from the king should be less, but that their loyalty to him, and thankfulness to God, may be the more.

8. Accommodation

Every one of his majesty's ships and frigate officers have a distinct cabin for themselves; for which the Dutch, French and Portuguese do envy them, who for the most part lie *sub dio* under ship-decks.

9. Government

Few offences comparatively to other fleets are therein committed, and fewer escape punishment. The offender, if the fault be small, is tried by a court-martial, consisting of the officers of the ship; if great, by a council of war, wherein only commanders and the judge-advocate. If any sleep in their watches, it is pain of death. After eight o'clock none save the captain, lieutenant and master may presume to burn a candle. No smoking of tobacco (save for the privilege aforesaid) at any time, but in one particular place of the ship, and that over a tub of water. Preaching they have lately had twice a week; praying twice a day; but my intelligencer could never hear that the Lord's Supper for some years was administered aboard of any ship; an omission which I hope hereafter will be amended.

But never did this navy appear more triumphant, than when in May last it brought over our gracious sovereign,[1] being almost becalmed (such the fear of the winds to offend with over roughness); the prognostic of his majesty's peaceable reign.

The Farewell

Being to take our leave of these our wooden walls, first I wish that they may conquer with their mast and sails, without their guns, that their appearance may fright their foes into submission.

But if, in point of honour or safety, they be necessitated to engage, may they always keep the wind of the enemy, that their shot may fly with the greater force, and that the smoke of their powder, pursuing the foe, may drive him to fire at hazard. May their gunner be in all places of the ship, to see where he can make a shot with the best advantage; their carpenter and his crew be always in the hold, presently to drive in a wooden plug (whereas a shot comes betwixt wind and water) and to clap a board with tar and camel's hair upon it till the dispute be over; their chirurgeon and his assistants be in the same place (out of danger of shot) to dress the wounded; their captain to be in the uppermost, the lieutenant in every part of the ship, to encourage the seamen; the chaplain at his devotions, to importune heaven for success, and encouraging all by his good counsel, if time will permit.

(1) Fuller was among those present at the Hague to welcome Charles II, the only occasion he was out of the country. Pepys, in the *Diary*, has a reference to meeting with him there.

MEDICINAL WATERS

TUNBRIDGE WATER

It is usual for Providence, when intending a benefit to mankind, to send some signal chance on the errand, to bring the first tidings thereof; most visible in the news of medicinal waters.

The first discovery of this water (though variously reported) is believed from a footman to a Dutch lord, who passed this way, and drinking thereof found it in taste very like to that at the Spa in Germany.

Indeed, there is a great symbolizing betwixt them in many concurrences; and I believe it is as sovereign as the other, save that it is true of things as of persons, *Major e longinquo reverentia* [respect is greater at a distance]. Surely it runneth through some iron-mine, because so good for splenetic distempers. But I leave the full relation to such who, having experimentally found the virtue of it, can set their seal of *probatum est* unto the commendation thereof.

PROVERBS

A Kentish Yeoman. It passeth for a plain man of a plentiful estate, yeomen in this county bearing away the bell for wealth from all of their rank in England.

Yet such yeomen refuse to have the title of Master put upon them, contenting themselves without any addition of gentility; and this mindeth me of a passage in my memory. One immoderately boasted that "there was not one of his name in all England, but that he was a gentleman." To whom one in the company returned, "I am sorry, sir, you have never a good-man of your name."

Sure am I in Kent there is many an hospitable yeoman of great ability, who though no gentleman by descent and title, is one by his means and state; let me also add by his courteous carriage, though constantly called but Goodman, to which name he desireth to answer in all respects.

A Man of Kent. This may relate either to the liberty or to the courage of this county men; liberty, the tenure of villainage (so frequent elsewhere) being here utterly unknown, and the bodies of all Kentish persons being of free condition. Insomuch that it is holden sufficient for one to avoid the objection of bondage, to say that his father was born in Kent. Now seeing *servi non sunt viri, quia non sui juris* (a bondman is no man, because not his own man) the Kentish for their freedom have achieved to themselves the name of Men.

Kentish long-tails. Let me premise, that those are much mistaken who first found this proverb on a miracle of Austin the monk, which is thus reported. It happened in an English village, where Saint Austin was preaching, that the pagans therein did beat and abuse both him and his associates, opprobriously tying fish-tails to their backsides; in revenge whereof an impudent author relateth (reader, you and I must blush for him who hath not the modesty to blush for himself) how such appendants grew to the hind parts of all that generation.[1] I say they are much mis-

(1) Jerome Porter, in the Flowers of the Lives of the Saints.

taken, for the scene of this lying wonder was not laid in any part of Kent, but pretended many miles off, nigh Cerne in Dorsetshire.

Some will have the English so called from wearing a pouch or poke (a bag to carry their baggage in) behind their backs, whilst probably the proud Monsieurs had their lacqueys for that purpose; in proof whereof, they produce ancient pictures of the English drapery and armory, wherein such conveyances do appear. If so, it was neither sin nor shame for the common sort of people to carry their own necessaries; and it matters not much whether the pocket be made on either side, or wholly behind.

If any demand how this nickname (cut off from the rest of England) continues still entailed on Kent, the best conjecture is, because that county lieth nearest to France, and the French are beheld as the first founders of this aspersion. But if any will have the Kentish so called from drawing and dragging boughs of trees behind them, which afterwards they advanced above their heads, and so partly cozened, partly threatened King William the Conqueror to continue their ancient customs; I say, if any will impute it to this original, I will not oppose.

A jack of Dover. I find the first mention of this proverb in our English Ennius, Chaucer, in his proem to the cook:

> And many a jack of Dover he had sold,
> Which had been two times hot, and two times cold.

This is no fallacy, but good policy, in an household, to lengthen out the provision thereof; and, though less toothsome, may be wholesome enough. But what is no false logic in a family, is false ethics in an inn, or cook's-shop, to make the abused guest to pay after the rate of new and fresh for meat at the second and third hand.

THE WORTHIES

SAINT ALPHEGE [ÆLFHEAH], born [954] of good parentage, had his education during his youth in Gloucestershire; then he became a monk at Glastonbury. But that place not sufficiently suiting the severity of his solitary soul, removing thence he built himself a hut at Bath, which small cell in process of time (the longest line proceedeth from a little point at first) proved the beautiful priory in that place. Hence by Dunstan he was preferred bishop of Winchester, continuing therein twenty-two years; and at last became archbishop of Canterbury.

It happeneth that the cruel Danes seizing on that city put it under decimation. Start not, loyal reader, at the word, if in the late tyranny of the times thou thyself hast been against all right and reason decimated in thy purse, as now the poor citizens of Canterbury were in their persons. For the Danes (under pretence of tribute detained) saved the tenth part of the citizens alive, amounting unto eight hundred and four; destroyed the other nine parts, no fewer than seven thousand two hundred and thirty-six.

As for Archbishop Ælfheah, they demanded of him a greater sum than he could pay or procure, whose wealth consisted chiefly in his piety, no current coin with the pagan Danes; so that, after seven months' imprisonment, they barbarously murdered him, near Greenwich, about the year 1012. His corpse was first buried in St. Paul's, and then removed, by the command of King Canutus, to Canterbury. Impudent monks have almost as much wronged his memory, as the Danes did his person, farcing his life with such abominable lies, that thereby the very truth therein is rendered suspected.

ÆTHELNOTH, son to Count Æthelmær, was a calendared saint in this county, being elected archbishop of Canterbury, from being dean over the canons in that convent.

This is the first time I find the dignity of *Decanus*, or Dean, in England; so called from **Δέκα,** ten, having (it seemeth) at the first inspection just over that number, though since an heteroclite[1] in England; as, either over fewer, but six in Norwich, Bristol, &c., or many more in other cathedrals.

He was so pious in his life, that he was commonly called the Good. And here one may justly wonder; God having two grand epithets, *Optimus* and *Maximus*, most give the former the go-by, and strive only for the latter, to be the greatest; though greatness without goodness is both destructive to him that hath it, and dangerous to all others about him.

Going to Rome to get his pall from the pope, by him he was courteously entertained, and deserved his welcome, who gave him (saith my author[2]) for the arm of Saint Augustine bishop of Hippo, one hundred talents of silver, and one talent of gold, citing Bishop Godwin for his author; but indeed that bishop, though reporting the hundred talents of silver, mentioneth not at all that of gold.

He expended much in repairing (or rather renewing) of his cathedral of Canterbury, lately destroyed by the Danes; assisted therein by the bounty of King Canutus, who, at the instance and by the advice of this prelate, did many worthy works. Our Æthelnoth, after he had sat seventeen years in his see, died October 29, in the year 1038.

HAYMO OF FAVERSHAM both had his first breath at, and fetched his name from Faversham in this county. When a man, he left the land, and repairing to Paris, applied his studies so effectually, that Leland saith he was *inter Aristotelicos Aristotelissimus*.

He became a Franciscan in the church of St. Denys itself, and returning into England, was elected provincial of his order. Afterwards he was called to reside in Rome for his advice, where, quitting his provincialship to his successor, he was chosen general of the Franciscans. Surely he had much real or reputed merit, being so highly prized by the Italians, who generally do as much undervalue us English as they over-admire themselves. *Speculum honestatis* (the glass of honesty) saith one,[3] was the title given unto him; though dark and false this glass, if Bale may be believed, who taxeth him for being an inquisitor after and persecutor of good people, especially when employed by the pope into Grecia. Lying on his death-bed at Anagnia in Italy, the pope in person came to visit him,

(1) *Heteroclite*=irregularly declined, but Fuller uses it in the figurative sense of *irregular*. (2) Weever, *Funeral Monuments*. (3) Pits.

which was no small honour unto him, but all would not prolong his life, which he ended anno 1244; having first, at the command of Pope [Gregory IX] corrected and amended the Roman Breviary.

RALPH OF MAYDENSTAN. I presume this the ancient orthography of Maidstone (a noted town in this county); the rather because I met with no other place in England offering in sound or syllables thereunto.

An author giveth him this short but thick commendation, *Vir magnae literaturae et in theologia nominatissimus.*[1] Insomuch that in the reign of King Henry the Third, 1234, he was preferred bishop of Hereford.

This prelate bought of one Mount-hault, a nobleman, a fair house in, and the patronage of, St. Mary Mount-hault (commonly, but corruptly, called Mount-haw) in London, leaving both to his successors in the see of Hereford. Know, reader, that all English bishops in that age had palaces in London for their conveniency, wherein they resided, and kept great hospitality, during their attendance in parliament.

Now, although the schoolmen generally hold that episcopacy is *Apex consummate religionis,* than which *nihil amplius,* nothing higher or holier in this life; and though many friars have been preferred bishops as a progressive motion both in dignity and sanctity, yet our Ralph was of a different judgment herein. This made him, in the year 1239, turn his mitre into a cowl, and become a Franciscan, first at Oxford, then at Gloucester, where he died [1246].

HENRY DE WINGHAM (a well-known town in this county) was, by King Henry the Third, preferred chancellor both of England and Gascony, dean of Totten-hall (query, where this place is?) and St. Martin's, and twice ambassador into France.

It happened that one Ethelmar, womb-brother to King Henry the Third, was then bishop of Winchester; a person who properly comes not under my pen; first, for his foreign nativity; secondly (so much as he was English) he was an UNWORTHY, wanting age, ability and orders to qualify him in that place.

Hereupon the monks of Winchester, endeavouring to eject him, chose Wingham, a man of merit (and might in the court) to be their bishop, which honour he wisely refused, fearing to incur the king's displeasure. It was not long before his modesty and discretion was rewarded with a peaceable (instead of that litigous) bishopric, when chosen to London 1259.[2] But he enjoyed his see not full two years, dying July 13, 1262, and was buried in his own cathedral.

[SAINT] SIMEON STOCK was born [1165?] in this county, and when but twelve years of age, went into the woods (whereof this shire then afforded plenty) and became a hermit. This Christian Diogenes had for his tub the stock of a hollow tree, whence he fetched his name, and (abating his sex) was like the nymphs called hamadryads, which were the properties of oak trees. Here he had, saith Leland, water for his

(1) Thomas de Wykes, in his *Chronicle of Osney*. (2) He did actually become bishop of Winchester in 1259, and was later translated to London.

nectar, and wild fruits for his ambrosia. One may admire how this man here met with learning, except by inspiration, and except books (as at the original) were written on barks of trees, wherewith he conversed; yet the university of Oxford would force a bachelor of divinity-ship upon him; and many are the superstitious writings he left to posterity.

Reader, behold here how the roaring lion hath translated himself into a mimical ape, endeavouring a mock parallel betwixt this Simeon and Simeon in the Gospel.

Old Simeon had a revelation that he should not die till he had seen our Saviour come in the flesh. This Simeon, aged eighty years, had a revelation that before his death he should behold a holy order of Carmelites come out of Syria, which fell out accordingly.

At their arrival in England, our Simeon quitted his oak, and advanced forward to meet them, as of whom, though he had no sight, he had a vision before, which is probably as true as that he was fed seven years with manna in Mount Carmel. He was chosen the general governor of their order all over Europe; and died in the hundredth year of his age, Anno Domini 1265, and was buried at Bordeaux in France.

SIMON MEOPHAM was born at Meopham in this county. He was bred in Merton College in Oxford. He was a good scholar, as those days went; chosen by the monks of Canterbury, approved by King Edward the Third, and consecrated, by the command of the pope, archbishop of Canterbury. He is only famous for two things: his expensive suit with the monks of Canterbury, wherein at last he got the better, though it cost seven hundred pounds in the court of Rome.[1] Secondly, his magnificent visitation in person of the dioceses south of Thames, till he was restricted by Grandisson bishop of Exeter. This affront did half break Meopham's heart, and the pope siding with the bishop against him, brake the other half thereof, hastening his death, which happened Anno Domini 1333.

SIR JOHN PHILIPOT was born in this county, where his family hath long resided at Upton Court, in the parish of Sibertswold. He was bred a citizen and grocer in London, whereof he became mayor, 1378.

In the second of King Richard the Second our English seas wanted scouring, over-run with the rust of piracies, but chiefly with a canker fretting into them, one John Mercer, a Scot, with his fifteen Spanish ships; to repress whose insolence our Philipot on his own cost set forth a fleet, a project more proportionable to the treasury of a prince than the purse of a private subject. His success was as happy as his undertaking honourable; and Mercer brought his wares to a bad market, being taken with all his ships and rich plunder therein.

Two years after he conveyed an English army into Brittany, in ships of his own hiring, and with his own money released more than 1000 arms there, which the soldiers formerly engaged for their

(1) He did not get the better of it, and was excommunicated for non-payment. He was a good churchman, unworldly, and sought to reform abuses.

victuals. But this industry of Philipot interpretatively taxed the laziness of others, the nobility accusing him (drones account all bees pragmatical) to the king, for acting without a commission. Yea, in that ungrateful age, under a child-king, *pro tantorum sumptuum praemio, veniam vix obtinuit* [instead of a reward for such expenditure he scarcely won a pardon]. However, he who whilst living was the scourge of the Scots, the fright of the French, the delight of the commons, the darling of the merchants, and the hatred of some envious lords, was at his death lamented, and afterwards beloved of all, when his memory was restored to its due esteem.[1] [*d.* 1384]

WILLIAM REDE [or READE]. I place him in this county with confidence, having clearly conquered all suspicions to the contrary: first, because of his name then flourishing at Read in Marden in this county. Secondly, because the provost-place of Wingham College therein was his first public preferment. To which I may add that he was bred fellow of Merton College (abounding with Cantians, since a bishop in Kent was founder thereof); and he merited much of that foundation, not only building a fair library therein, but furnishing it with books, and astronomical tables of his own making, which (they say) are still to be seen therein, with his lively picture inserted.

In his reduced age he applied himself to divinity, and by King Edward the Third was preferred bishop of Chichester. Retaining his mathematical impressions, he commendably expressed them in architecture, erecting a castle *egregii operis,* saith my author,[2] at Amberley in Sussex. His death happened Anno Domini 1385.

RICHARD CLIFFORD. His nativity may bear some debate, Herefordshire pretending unto him; but because Robert Clifford was his brother (in the first of King Henry the Fourth high sheriff of this county, and richly landed therein) I adjudge him a Cantian, and assign Bobbing as the most probable place of his birth. His worth preferred him bishop of London, 1407; and he was sent by King Henry the Fourth as his ambassador to the council of Constance. I could [not] hold my hand from ranking him under the topic of cardinals, confident that no ingenious person would take exception thereat. For, first he was one in merit and desert. Secondly, in general desire and designation. Thirdly (though no actual cardinal) he acted as a cardinal when joined to their conclave to see fair play amongst them at the choosing of a new pope. Yea, some mentioned him for the place, who (counting it more credit to make than be a pope) first nominated Cardinal Colonna, and he clearly carried it by the name of Martin. During his abode at Constance, he preached a Latin sermon before the emperor and pope. He answered his name *de clivo forti,* or of the strong rock indeed, viz., David's, being a most pious[3]

(1) Philipot was twice M.P. for London, and is further memorable for leading the opposition to John of Gaunt and for aiding Richard II during the peasants' revolt of 1381. (2) Bale. (3) Fuller would have written less warmly had he known that Clifford presided at the trial for heresy of Sir John Oldcastle the lollard leader. For an account of Oldcastle see Herefordshire, p. 223.

person. Returning home he lived in good esteem with prince and people, until his death, which happened 1421, being buried nigh the present monument of Sir Christopher Hatton.

WILLIAM WHITE was born in this county; and entering into orders, became a great maintainer of the opinions of Wycliffe. He was the first married priest in England since the pope's solemn prohibition thereof. I find Johan his wife commended for her modesty and patience, and that she was *conjux tali digna marito* [a spouse worthy of such a husband]. Indeed she shared very deep in her husband's sufferings, hardly coming off with her life at the last; for he, though leaving his living (as unsafe to hold) still kept his calling, and preached about all the eastern parts of the land.

The same mouth which commanded the disciples in time of peace, "Go not from house to house," so to avoid the censure of levity, advised them also, "When ye are persecuted in one city, fly to another," so to provide for their own security. Such the constant practice of this William White, who was as a partridge daily on the wing, removing from place to place. At last he was seized on at Norwich by William Alnwick, the cruel bishop thereof, and charged with thirty articles, for which he was condemned, and burnt at Norwich in September 1428. He was the proto-martyr of all born in this county; and had not five before him in all England who suffered merely for religion, without any mixture of matter of state charged upon them.

SIR WILLIAM SEVENOKE was born [1378?] at Sevenoaks in this county; in allusion whereunto he gave seven acorns for his arms, which if they grow as fast in the field of heraldry as in the common field, may be presumed to be oaks at this day. For it is more than 200 years since this William (bred a grocer at London) became, anno 1418, lord mayor thereof. He founded at Sevenoaks a fair free-school for poor people's children, and an almshouse for twenty men and women, which at this day is well maintained. [*d.* 1433?]

JOHN KEMP, son to Thomas, grandchild to Sir John Kemp, nephew to Sir Roger Kemp, both knights, was born [1380?] at Wye in this county (where he built a fair college for seculars); bred also in Merton College in Oxford; successively bishop of Rochester, Chichester and London; afterwards archbishop of York and Canterbury; cardinal, first by the title of Santa Balbina, then of Saint Rufine in Rome. All his preferments are comprehended in the old following verse:[1]

Bis primas, ter praesul erat, bis cardine functus.

He had another honour, to make up the distich, being twice lord chancellor of England, so that I may add:

Et dixit legem bis cancellarius Anglis.

(1) Made by Thomas Kemp, his kinsman, bishop of London. [He is a more important figure than Fuller allows. He played an important part in diplomacy and statecraft under Henry V and VI, and it was he who broke Cade's Rebellion in 1450 by timely pardons. He resisted the Yorkists until his death. His foundation at Wye was also endowed with a grammar school and church.]

Such are mistaken who report him the first raiser of his family to a knightly degree, which he found in that equipage, as is aforesaid, though he left it much improved in estate by his bounty; and some of his name and blood flourish in Kent at this day. He died a very old man, March the 22nd, anno 1454.

RICHARD WALLER. This is that renowned soldier, who in the time of Henry the Fifth, took Charles duke of Orleans, general of the French army, prisoner at the battle of Agincourt, brought him over into England, and held him in honourable restraint or custody at Groombridge, which a manuscript in the Heralds' office notes to be twenty-four years. In the time of which his recess, he newly erected the house at Groombridge upon the old foundation, and was a benefactor to the repair of Speldhurst church, where his arms remain in stonework over the church porch; but, lest such a signal piece of service might be entombed in the sepulchre of unthankful forgetfulness, the prince assigned to this Richard Waller and his heirs for ever an additional crest, viz., the arms or escutcheon of France, hanging by a label on an oak, with this motto affixed, *Haec Fructus Virtutis.*

[1395?-1462?]

THOMAS KEMP, brother's son to John Kemp archbishop of Canterbury, was born of a knightly family in this county; bred in Oxford, whereof he became proctor anno 1437. By papal provision he was made bishop of London, consecrated by his uncle at York House (now Whitehall) and sate in his see forty years, from the twenty-eighth of Henry the Sixth till the fifth of Henry the Seventh; so that he saw the wars between Lancaster and York begun, continued, concluded, and the two Roses tied together in one royal posy. I know not whether his benefactions were adequate to his long possessing of so wealthy a place, finding him to have curiously arched and leaded the Divinity School in Oxford, and built the cross nigh the church of St. Paul's, as it stood in our memories; but lately demolished, though guilty of no other superstition, save accommodating the preacher and some about him with convenient places. Methinks, though idle crosses, standing only for shew, were published for offenders, this useful one, which did such service, might have been spared; but all is fish which comes to the net of sacrilege. This bishop died Anno Domini 1489.

JAMES GOLDWELL was born at Great Chart in this county; bred in All Souls' College in Oxford; promoted first to be dean of Salisbury, and secretary to King Edward the Fourth, and at last made bishop of Norwich. He not only repaired the church at Great Chart, where he was born, but also founded a chapel on the south side thereof, where his picture is in the east window, with his rebus (viz. a *golden well*) in every quarry of the same.[1] He died Anno Domini 1499.

(1) The facts are rather mixed here. The rebus (and Goldwell's tomb) are in Norwich Cathedral. Goldwell completed the tower of the cathedral, and fitted up the quire and chapels.

SIR JOHN [FYNEUX or] FINEUX was by all probability born [1441?] at Swingfield in this county (as I am informed from my good friend Mr. Thomas Fyneux, a descendent from him); a place, saith Mr. Camden, bestowed on his ancestor by T. Criol, a great lord in Kent, about the reign of King Edward the Second. I learned from the same gentleman, that he was eight and twenty years of age before he betook him to the study of the law; that he followed that profession twenty-eight years before he was made a judge; and that he continued a judge for twenty-eight years, whereby it appears that he lived fourscore and four years. This last exactly agrees with Sir Henry Spelman, making him continue lord chief justice of the king's bench from the eleventh of King Henry the Seventh until the seventeenth of King Henry the Eighth.

He was a great benefactor unto Saint Augustine's in Canterbury; whose prior, William Mallaham, thus highly commendeth him in a manuscript instrument: *Vir prudentissimus, genere insignis, justitia praeclarus, pietate refertus, humanitatis splendidus, et charitate foecundus*, &c.

Now though some will say, his convent may well afford him good words who gave them good deeds, yet I believe this character of him can in no part be disproved. He died about the year 1527, and lies buried in Christ Church in Canterbury; who had a fair habitation in this city, and another at Herne in this county, where his motto still remains in each window, *Misericordias Domini cantabo in aeternum.*

SIR EDWARD POYNINGS, knight [*b.* 1459] was in martial performances inferior to none of his age, and a native of this county, as from the catalogue of the sheriffs therein may be collected. We will insist only on his Irish action, being employed by King Henry the Seventh to conjure down the last walking spirits of the house of York which haunted that king; I mean Perkin Warbeck.

Having ferreted him out of Ireland, he seriously set himself to reclaim that barbarous nation to civility; and, in order thereunto, passed an act in parliament, whereby "all the statutes made in England before that time were enacted, established, and made of force in Ireland." He caused also another law to be made, that no act should be propounded in any parliament in Ireland, till first it had been transmitted into England, approved there by the king, and returned thence under his broad seal.[1]

Now though this act seemeth *prima facie* prejudicial to the liberty of the Irish subjects, yet was it made at the request of the commons upon just and important cause, being so sensible of the oppression and laws imposed by private lords, for their particular ends, that they rather referred themselves to the king's justice than to the merciless mercy of so many masters.

Also, to conform Ireland to England, he procured the passing of an act, that the barons should appear in parliament in their robes, which put a face of grandeur and state on their convention. And indeed

(1) Poynings' Law, 1494, repealed 1782.

formalities are more than formalities in matters of this nature, essential to beget a veneration in barbarous people, who carry much of their brain in their eyes.

He thriftily improved the king's revenues, and obtained a subsidy, of twenty-six shillings eight pence, payable yearly for five years, out of every six score acres manured. The worst was, the burden fell on their backs whose islands were most industrious, whereby the sovereign became not more wealthy, but the subjects more lazy, the mischief being as apparent as the remedy impossible. Many more large laws of his making found but narrow performance, viz., only within the Pale. Nor was Henry the Seventh (though in *title*) in *truth* lord of all Ireland, but by the favour of a figure and large synecdoche, of a part for the whole. These things thus ordered, Sir Edward was recalled into England, created a baron, and dying in the beginning of King Henry the Eighth, left a numerous natural but no legitimate issue.[1] [*d.* 1521]

SIMON FISH, esquire, was born in this county, bred a lawyer in Gray's Inn, London. Here he acted that part in a tragedy, wherein the pride of Cardinal Wolsey was personated, and wherewith that prelate was so offended, that Fish was fain to fly, and live two years beyond the seas. There he made, and thence sent over into England, a small but sharp treatise, called *Supplication of the Beggars,* termed by Master Foxe a libel, understand him a little book; otherwise prizing and praising it for a master-piece of wit, learning and religion, discovering the superstition of that age. This by Queen Anne Boleyn was presented to King Henry the Eighth, who therewith was so highly affected, that he sent for the author home, and favoured him in great proportion.

However, many nets were laid by the popish party against him, especially by Sir Thomas More, his implacable enemy; yet Fish had the happiness to escape the hands of men, and to fall into the hand of God more immediately; dying of the plague, 1531, and lieth buried at St. Dunstan in London.

HENRY THE EIGHTH, second son of King Henry the Seventh, was born [1491] at Greenwich. A prince whom some praise to the skies, others depress to the pit, whilst the third (and truer) sort embrace a middle way betwixt both.

Extreme. Some carry him up as the paragon of princes, the great advancer of God's glory and true religion, and the most magnificent that ever sat on the throne. Master Foxe, in his *Acts and Monuments,* is sometimes very superlative in his commendation; and so are most protestant authors who wrote under his reign.

Mean. Polydore Vergil hath an expression of him to this effect: *Princeps in quo aequali quasi temperamento magnae inerant virtutes, ac non minora vitia* (a prince in whom great virtues, and no less vices, were in a manner equally contemperated.)

(1) Henry VIII entertained the idea, never carried out, of creating Poynings a baron. Poynings had one legitimate son, who predeceased him. Of the illegitimate issue, three sons and four daughters, one, Thomas Baron Poynings (*d.* 1545) distinguished himself at the capture of Boulogne, 1544.

Extreme. Sir Walter Ralegh, in his preface to his great *History,* whose words may better be read there than transcribed thence, makes him the truest map of tyranny. Insomuch that King James (who could not abide that any under a king should speak against a king) was much offended thereat. And those words worst became the writer so much advanced by the daughter of the said King Henry.

For mine own part, I humbly conceive, God effected more by his work as the instrument, than he was directed by God's Word as the principal. Indeed he was a man of uncontrollable spirit, carrying a *mandamus* in his mouth, sufficiently sealed when he put his hand to his hilt. He awed all into obedience, which some impute to his skilfulness to rule, others ascribe to his subjects' ignorance to resist.

Let one pleasant passage (for recreation) have its pass amongst much serious matter. A company of little boys were by their schoolmaster not many years since appointed to act the play of *King Henry the Eighth,* and one who had no presence (but an absence rather) as of a whining voice, puling spirit, consumptionish body, was appointed to personate King Henry himself, only because he had the richest clothes, and his parents the best people of the parish; but when he had spoken his speech rather like a mouse than a man, one of his fellow actors told him, "If you speak not *Hoh* with a better spirit, your parliament will not grant you a penny of money."

But it is vain to glean in the stubble, seeing the Lord Herbert hath so largely wrote the life of this king, that nothing of moment can be added thereunto. He died January 28, 1547.

WILLIAM LAMBE, esquire, sometime a gentleman of the chapel to King Henry the Eighth, and in great favour with him, was born [1495] at Sutton Valence in this county, where he erected an almshouse, and a well-endowed school. He was a person wholly composed of goodness and bounty, and was as general and discreet a benefactor as any that age produced. Anno 1557, he began, and within five months finished, the fair conduit at Holborn Bridge, and carried the water in pipes of lead more than two thousand yards at his own cost, amounting to fifteen hundred pounds. The total sum of his several gifts, moderately estimated, exceeded six thousand pounds. He lies buried with his good works in Saint Faith's church under Saint Paul's; where this inscription (set up, it seems, by himself in his lifetime) is fixed on a brass plate to a pillar:

> O Lamb of God, which sin didst take away,
> And (as a Lamb) wast offered up for sin;
> Where I (poor Lamb) went from thy flock astray,
> Yet thou, good Lord, vouchsafe thy Lamb to win
> Home to thy fold, and hold thy Lamb therein,
> That at the day when Goats and Lambs shall sever,
> Of thy choice lambs, Lamb may be one for ever.

[*d.* 1580]

SIR ANTHONY ST. LEGER [*b.* 1496?] is rationally reputed a Kentish man (though he had also a Devonshire relation) as will appear to such who peruse the sheriffs of this county. He was properly the first viceroy of

Ireland, seeing shadows cannot be before their substance; and in his deputyship Henry the Eighth (in the thirty-third year of his reign) assumed the title of King and Supreme Head of the Church of Ireland.

To him all the Irish nobility made their solemn submission, falling down at his feet upon their knees, laying aside their girdles, skeines and caps. This was the fourth solemn submission of the Irish to the kings of England; and most true it is, such seeming submissions have been the bane of their serious subjection; for, out of the Pale, our kings had not power either to punish or protect, where those Irish lords (notwithstanding their complimental loyalty) made their list the law to such whom they could overpower. He caused also certain ordinances of state to be made not altogether agreeable with the rules of the law of England, a satisfactory reason hereof being given in the preamble to them:[1] "Because the Irish as yet do not so savour the laws of England as immediately to live after and be ruled by them."

Thus the greatest statesman must sometimes say "by your leave" to such as are under them, not acting always according to their own ability, but others' capacity.

He seized all the abbey lands in Ireland for the king's use; a flower of the crown which alone had made a posy, if continued thereunto. But alas, the revenues of abbey lands are as ruinous as their buildings, nothing more than the rubbish thereof remaining in the king's exchequer. He made a law that no children should be admitted to church livings, which importeth the frequency of that abuse in former times. He persuaded O'Neill, O'Brien, &c. to go over to England, to surrender their lands into the king's hands; promising they should receive them again from him by letters patent, with the addition of earls, which was done accordingly. At his desire the king conferred on them houses nigh Dublin, that residing there, they might suck in civility with the court air. These things thus settled, he returned into England,[2] and died [1559].

NICHOLAS WOTTON, son to Sir Robert, was born [1497?] at Broughton Malherbe in this county, a place so named, as it seems, from some noxious and malignant herbs growing therein.[3] What the natural plants there may be, I know not. Sure the moral ones are excellent, which hath produced so many of the honourable family of the Wottons; of whom this Nicholas, doctor of civil laws, bred in Oxford, may be termed a centre of remarkables, so many met in his person. 1. He was dean of the two metropolitan churches of Canterbury and York. 2. He was the first dean of those cathedrals. 3. He was privy councillor to four successive sovereigns, King Henry the Eighth, King Edward the Sixth, Queen Mary, Queen Elizabeth. 4. He was employed thirteen several times in embassies to foreign princes.

(1) In the Council Book of Ireland, in the 33rd of King Henry VIII [Latin omitted.] (2) He was recalled in 1551 for alleged papistical practices, acquitted, and reappointed 1553; recalled in 1556 on being charged with falsifying accounts, and died during the proceedings. (3) This is ingenious, for Malherbe was originally an uncomplimentary name; nevertheless the village is called after the Malherbe family.

Now because there are some of so diffident natures, that they will believe no total sum, except they peruse the particulars, let them satisfy themselves with what followeth: Five times to Charles the Fifth, emperor; once to Philip his son, King of Spain; once to Francis the First, King of France; once to Mary Queen of Hungary, governess of the Netherlands; twice to William duke of Cleves; once to renew the peace between England, France and Scotland, Anno Domini 1540; again to the same purpose, at Cambray, 1546; once sent commissioner with others to Edinburgh in Scotland, 1560.

We must not forget how, in the first of Queen Elizabeth, the archbishopric of Canterbury was proffered unto, and refused by him. He died January the twenty-sixth, Anno Domini 1567, being about seventy years of age, and was buried in Canterbury.

SIR THOMAS WYATT, knight, commonly called the elder, to distinguish him from Sir Thomas Wyatt, raiser of the rebellion (so all call it, for it did not succeed) in the reign of Queen Mary, was born [1503?] at Allington Castle in this county, which afterwards he repaired with most beautiful buildings. He was servant to King Henry the Eighth, and fell, as I have heard, into his disfavour about the business of Queen Anne Boleyn, till by his innocence, industry and discretion, he extricated himself.[1]

He was one of admirable ingenuity, and truly answered his anagram, WIAT, "a wit." Camden saith he was *Eques auratus, splendide doctus.*

It is evidence enough of his protestant inclination, because he translated David's Psalms into English metre; and though he be lost both to Bale and Pits in the catalogue of writers, yet he is plentifully found by Leland, giving him this large commendation:

Bella suum merito jacet Florentia Dantem;
Regia Petrarchae carmina Roma probat:
His non inferior patrio sermone Viattus,
Eloquii secum qui decus omne tulit.

Let Florence fair her Dante's justly boast,
And royal Rome her Petrarch's numbered feet;
In English Wyatt both of them doth coast,
In whom all graceful eloquence doth meet.

This knight being sent ambassador by King Henry the Eighth to Charles the Fifth emperor, then residing in Spain, before he took shipping died of the pestilence in the west country, anno 1542.

JOHN [PONET or] POYNET was born [1514?] in this county; bred (say some) in King's College in Cambridge. Sure I am, he was none of the foundation therein, because not appearing in Master Hatcher's exact manuscript catalogue. Bale is rather to be believed herein, making him to be brought up in Queens' College in the same university.

But wherever he had his education, he arrived at admirable learning, being an exact Grecian and most expert mathematician. He presented

(1) A lover of Anne Boleyn before her marriage, he was for a time imprisoned when she came up for trial. Wyatt introduced the sonnet into England. He was the father of the "raiser of the rebellion."

King Henry the Eighth with a *horologium* (which I might English *dial, clock,* or *watch,* save that it is epitheted *scioterícum*) observing the shadow of the sun, and therein shewing not only the hours, but days of the month, change of the moon, ebbing and flowing of the sea, &c. I confess the modern mystery of watchmaking is much completed (men never being more curious to *divide,* more careless to *employ,* their time); but surely this was accounted a master-piece in that age.

His sermons so endeared him to King Edward the Sixth that he preferred him (whilst as yet scarce thirty-six years of age) to the bishopric of Rochester, then of Winchester. But alas! these honours soon got were as soon lost, being forced to fly into High Germany in the first of Queen Mary, where, before he was fully forty, and before he had finished his book begun against Thomas Martin in defence of ministers' marriage, he died at Strasburg, the 2nd of August 1556, and was buried there with great lamentation.

SIR JAMES HALES was born, did live, and was richly landed, in this county, one of the justices of the Common Pleas, a man of most signal integrity. When the rest of the judges (frighted at the frowns of the duke of Northumberland) subscribed the disinheriting of the Lady Mary and Lady Elizabeth, he only refused, as against both law and conscience.

Yet afterwards, in the first of Queen Mary, he fell into the displeasure of Bishop Gardiner (which, like juniper coals, once kindled, hardly quenched) for urging the observations of some laws of King Edward the Sixth. For this he was imprisoned, hardly used, and so threatened by his keeper, that he endeavoured to have killed himself; which, being after let at liberty, he afterwards effected, drowning himself in a small water near his house; fear and melancholy so much prevailing upon him. Mr. Foxe concludeth the sad poem of his final estate with this distich:

Cum nihil ipse vides, propria quin labe laboret,
Tu tua fac cures, caetera mitte Deo.

Seeing nought thou seest, but failing in the best,
Mind thy own matters, and leave God the rest.

We must look on his foul deed with anger, and yet with pity on the doer thereof; frown on the one, and weep for the other; for, seeing he had led a right Godly life, and had suffered so much on the account of his conscience, I hope that his station in this place will not be cavilled at by any charitable persons. He died Anno Domini 1554.

SIR ANDREW JUDD, son of John Judd, was born at Tonbridge in this county, bred a skinner in London, whereof he became lord mayor anno 1553. He built alms-houses nigh Saint Ellen's in London, and a stately free-school at Tonbridge in Kent, submitting it to the care of the company of Skinners. This fair school hath been twice founded in effect, seeing the defence and maintenance whereof hath cost the company of Skinners, in suits of law and otherwise, four hundred pounds. So careful have they been (though to their own great charge) to see the will of the dead performed.

MARY, eldest daughter to King Henry the Eighth and Queen Catherine of Spain, was born at Greenwich, the 18th of February 1516. She did partake of both her parents in her person and properties; having from her father a broad face, big voice, and undaunted spirit; from her mother a swarthy complexion, and a mind wholly devoted to the Romish religion. She attained the crown by complying with the gentry of Norfolk and Suffolk, promising them to continue religion as established by King Edward the Sixth; after the breach of which promise she never prospered. For, first she lost the hearts of her subjects, then her hopes of a child, then the company, not to say affection, of her husband, then the city of Calais, then her mirth, then her health, then her life, which ended on the 17th of November, 1558.

LEONARD DIGGES, esquire, was born in this county; one of excellent learning and deep judgment. His mind most inclined him to mathematics, and he was the best architect in that age for all manner of buildings, for conveniency, pleasure, state, strength, being excellent at fortifications. Lest his learning should die with him, for the public profit he printed his *Tectonicon, Prognostic, General, Stratiotic,* about the ordering of an army, and other works.[1] [*d.* 1571?]

SIR ROGER MANWOOD, born [1525] at Sandwich in this county, applied himself from his youth to the study of the common law; wherein he attained to such eminency, that by Queen Elizabeth he was preferred second justice of the common pleas, in which place he gave such proof of his ability and integrity, that not long after, in Hilary Term in the twenty-first of Queen Elizabeth, he was made chief baron of the Exchequer, discharging that office to his great commendation, full fourteen years, till the day of his death. He was much employed in matters of state, and was one of the commissioners who sat on the trial of the Queen of Scots. In vacation time his most constant habitation was at Saint Stephen's in Canterbury, where, saith my author,[2] the poor inhabitants were much beholding to his bounteous liberality. He erected and endowed a fair free-school at Sandwich, the place of his nativity; and died in the thirty-fifth of Queen Elizabeth, Anno Domini 1592.

THOMAS CHARNOCK was born [1526] in the Isle of Thanet in this county, as by his own words doth appear. He discovereth in himself a modest pride; modest, styling himself (and truly enough) the Unlettered Scholar; pride, thus immoderately boasting of his book discovering the mysteries of the philosopher's stone:

> For satisfying the minds of the students in this art,
> Then thou art worthy as many books as will lie in a cart.

However, herein he is to be commended, that he ingeniously confesseth the persons (viz., William Byrd, prior of Bath, and Sir James, a priest of Salisbury) who imparted their skill unto him.

(1) Digges is said to have anticipated the invention of the telescope. His son Thomas (*d.* 1595) was also a mathematician. Thomas' son, Sir Dudley Digges (1583-1639) was a diplomatist, judge and member of parliament. He was influential in preparing the Petition of Right 1628, and strongly defended the right of the House of Commons to criticise ministers of state. (2) Camden's *Britannia*.

This Charnock, in the pursuance of the said stone (which so many do touch, few catch, and none keep) met with two very sad disasters. One on New Year's day (the omen worse than the accident) anno 1555, when his work unhappily fell on fire. The other three years after, when a gentleman, long owing him a grudge, paid him to purpose, and pressed him a soldier for the relieving of Calais. Whence we observe two things: first, that this Charnock was no man of estate, seeing seldom, if ever, a subsidy-man is pressed for a soldier; secondly, that though he practised surgery, yet he was not free of that society, who by the statute 32 Hen. VIII are exempted from bearing armour.

But the spite of the spite was, that this was done within a month (according to his own computation, which none can confute) of the time wherein certainly he had been made master of so great a treasure. Such miscarriages, frequent in this kind, the friends of this art impute to the envy of evil spirits maligning mankind so much happiness; the foes thereof conceive that chemists pretend (yea, sometimes cause) such casualties to save their credits thereby. [*d.* 1581]

THOMAS GOLDWELL was born at Goldwell in the parish of Great Chart in this county, where his family had long flourished, till lately alienated. He was by Queen Mary preferred bishop of St. David's; and, as a volunteer, quitted the land in the first of Queen Elizabeth. Going to Rome, he made a deal of *do* to *do* just nothing; prevailing by much importunity with the pope to procure large indulgences for such who superstitiously were in pilgrimage to, and offered at, the Well of Saint Winifred in his diocese.[1] [*d.* 1585]

MARY WATERS [HONYWOOD] was born [1527] at Lenham in this county, and how abundantly intituled to memorability, the ensuing epitaph in Markshall church in Essex will sufficiently discover:

Here lieth the body of Mary Waters, the daughter and co-heir of Robert Waters of Lenham in Kent, esquire, wife of Robert Honywood of Charing in Kent, esquire, her only husband, who had at her decease, lawfully descended from her, three hundred sixty-seven children; sixteen of her own body, one hundred and fourteen grandchildren, two hundred twenty-eight in the third generation, and nine in the fourth. She lived a most pious life; and in a Christian manner died here at Markshall, in the ninety-third year of her age, and in the forty-fourth year of her widowhood, the eleventh of May, 1620.

Thus she had a child for every day in the (though leap) year, and one over. Here we may observe, that (generally) the highest in honour do not spread the broadest in posterity. For time was, when all the earls in England (and those then seventeen in number) had not, put together, so many sons and daughters as one of them had, viz., Edward Somerset, earl of Worcester. And yet of both sexes he never had but thirteen. But to return to Mistress Waters; she since hath been much outstript in point of fruitfulness by one still surviving;[2] and therefore this worthy matron (in my mind) is more memorable on another account,

(1) Goldwell was the last of the English Romanist bishops, and the only English bishop present at the council of Trent, 1562, and urged Elizabeth's excommunication. He was attainted in 1539 and 1562. (2) Dame Hester Temple. See Buckinghamshire, p. 42.

viz., for patient weathering out the tempest of a troubled conscience, whereon a remarkable story dependeth. Being much afflicted in mind many ministers repaired to her, and amongst the rest the Reverend Mr. John Foxe, than whom no more happy an instrument to set the joints of a broken spirit. All his counsels proved ineffectual, insomuch that in the agony of her soul, having a Venice glass in her hand, she brake forth into this expression, "I am as surely damned as this glass is broken"; which she immediately threw with violence to the ground.

Here happened a wonder: the glass rebounded again, and was taken up whole and entire. I confess it is possible (though difficult) so casually to throw as brittle a substance, that lighting on the edges, it may be preserved; but happening immediately in that juncture of time, it seemed little less than miraculous.

However, the gentlewoman took no comfort thereat (as some have reported and more believed) but continued a great time after (short is long to people in pain) in her former disconsolate condition without any amendment; until at last God, the great clock-keeper of time, who findeth out the fittest minutes for his own mercies, suddenly shot comfort like lightning into her soul; which once entered, ever remained therein (God doth no palliate cures, what he heals it holds); so that she led the remainder of her life in spiritual gladness. This she herself told to the reverend father, Thomas Morton, bishop of Durham,[1] from whose mouth I have received this relation.

In the days of Queen Mary she used to visit the prisons, and to comfort and relieve the confessors therein. She was present at the burning of Mr. Bradford in Smithfield; and resolved to see the end of his suffering, though so great the press of people, that her shoes were trodden off, and she forced thereby to go barefoot from Smithfield to Saint Martin's, before she could furnish herself with a new pair for her money. Her dissolution happened, as is aforesaid, anno 1620.

RICHARD FLETCHER was born in this county, brother to Doctor Giles Fletcher the civilian and ambassador in Russia,[2] and bred in Benet College in Cambridge.[3] He was afterwards dean of Peterborough at what time Mary Queen of Scots was beheaded at Fotheringhay, to whom he made, saith my author,[4] *verbosam orationem* (a wordy speech) of her past, present and future condition, wherein he took more pains than he received thanks from her who therein was most concerned.

Hence he was preferred bishop of Bristol, and at last of London; my author saith he was *praesul splendidus,* and indeed he was of a comely presence, and Queen Elizabeth knew full well,

Gratior est pulchro veniens e corpore virtus:

The jewel virtue is more grac'd
When in a proper person cas'd.

Which made her always, on an equality of desert, to reflect favourably on such who were of graceful countenance and stature.

(1) See York, p. 669. (2) See below, p. 279. (3) So his near relation informed me. (4) Camden's *Elizabeth.*

In one respect this bishop may well be resembled to John Peckham archbishop of Canterbury, of whom I find this character: "Although he seemed a boaster, and puffed up both in gesture and gait, and sometimes in his speech also; yet was he of a loving disposition and exceeding courteous."[1]

Such a one was Bishop Fletcher, whose pride was rather on him than in him, as only gait and gesture-deep, not sinking to his heart, though causelessly condemned for a proud man, as who was a good hypocrite, and far more humble than he appeared.

He married a lady of this county, who one commendeth for very virtuous; which if so, the more happy she in herself, though unhappy that the world did not believe it. Sure I am, that Queen Elizabeth (who hardly held the second matches of bishops excusable) accounted his marriage a trespass on his gravity, whereupon he fell into her deep displeasure. Hereof this bishop was sadly sensible, and seeking to lose his sorrow in a mist of smoke, died of the moderate taking thereof, June the 15th, 1596.

QUEEN ELIZABETH, second daughter to King Henry the Eighth, was born at Greenwich, September 7, 1533. She was heir only to the eminencies of her father, his learning, bounty, courage and success; besides grace and true goodness, wherein she was daughter to her mother.

Her learning appears in her two Latin speeches to the university, and a third, little better than extempore, to the Poland ambassador. Her bounty was better than her father's, less flowing from humour, and more founded on merit, and ordered with moderation; seeing that is the best liberality that so enricheth the receiver that it doth not impoverish the giver.

Her courage was undaunted, never making herself so cheap to her favourites but that she still valued her own authority, whereof this an eminent instance. A prime officer with a white staff, whose name I purposely forbear, coming into her presence, the queen willed him to confer such a place now void on one of her servants whom she commended unto him. "Pleaseth your highness, madam," said the lord, "the disposal thereof pertaineth to me by virtue of this white staff conferred upon me." "True," said the queen, "yet I never gave you your office so absolutely, but I still reserved myself of the *quorum*." "But of the *quarum*, madam," returned the lord, presuming on the favour of her highness. Hereat the queen, in some passion snatching the staff out of his hand, "You shall acknowledge me," said she, "of the *quorum, quarum, quorum,* before you have it again." The lord waited staff-less almost a day (which seemed so long unto him as if the sun stood still) before the same was re-conferred upon him.

Her success was admirable, keeping the King of Spain at arm's-end all her reign. She was well skilled in the queencraft; and by her policy and prosperity, she was much beloved by her people; insomuch that since it hath been said, "that Queen Elizabeth might lawfully do that which King James might not." For, although the laws were equally the rule to

(1) Bishop Godwin [Latin original omitted.]

them both, yet her popularity sugared many bitter things; her subjects thanking her for taking those taxes which they refused to pay to her successor. She died at Richmond, March 24, Anno Domini 1603.

SIR HENRY SIDNEY [*b.* 1529] was son to Sir William Sidney of Penshurst in this county, who, by his own worth was advanced into the favour of Queen Elizabeth (never a whit less for marrying Mary Dudley, sister to Robert earl of Leicester). He was by her made knight of the Garter, lord president of Wales, and for eleven years (off and on) deputy of Ireland.

Now, though generally the Irish are querulous of their deputies (what patient for the present will praise his chirurgeon, who soundly scratcheth his sore?) yet Sir Henry left a good memory and the monuments of a good governor behind him. 1. He made Annaly, a territory in Leinster by the Sept of O'Farrells, one entire shire by itself, called the county of Longford; he likewise divided the province of Connaught into six counties. 2. In a parliament held the eleventh of Elizabeth, he abolished the pretended and usurped captain-ships, and all extortions incident thereunto. 3. He caused an act to pass, whereby the lord deputy was authorized to accept the surrenders of the Irish seignories, and to regrant estates unto them, to hold of the crown by English tenures and services. 4. Because the inferior sort of the Irish were poor, and not amenable by law, he provided that five of the best persons of every sept should bring in all the persons of their surname, to be justified by the law. 5. A law was made, that for the civil education of the youth, there should be one free school at least in every diocese. 6. To acquaint the people of Munster and Connaught with the English government again (disused amongst them for two hundred years) he instituted two presidency courts in those two provinces. 7. To augment the revenues of the crown, he resumed and vested therein (by the power of the same parliament) more than half the province of Ulster, upon the attainder of Shane O'Neill. 8. He raised customs upon the principal commodities of the kingdom, and reformed the abuses of the exchequer by many good instructions from England. 9. He established the composition of the Pale, in lieu of purveyance and cess of soldiers.

It must not be forgotten that he caused the statutes of Ireland, unto his own time, to be printed; and so, saith my author,[1] *ex umbra in solem eduxit* (he brought them out of the shadow into the sunshine) whereas formerly they were only in manuscript; a sad case, that men should be obliged to the observation of those laws scarce ever seen by one in a hundred subjected thereunto.

Being to leave Ireland, anno 1578, and now ready to go up into his ship, he took his leave thereof with the words of the psalmist, "When Israel came out of Egypt, and Jacob from a strange people"; rejoicing in heart, that he came with a clear conscience from that dangerous employment.[2] He died at Worcester, May 5, 1586, and his corpse being brought to Penshurst, was there solemnly interred amongst his ancestors. I will close his life with this encomium, which I find in a worthy author:[3] "His

(1) Sir James Ware, *De Scriptoribus Hiberniae.* (2) He was recalled because of discontent with his expenditure. Sir Philip Sidney had attempted a masterly defence of his policy before the queen. (3) Doctor Powel, in his *History of Wales.*

disposition was rather to seek after the antiquities and the weal-public of those countries which he governed, than to obtain lands and revenues within the same; for I know not one foot of land that he had, either in Wales or Ireland."

SIR PHILIP SIDNEY. Reader, I am resolved not to part him from his father, such the sympathy betwixt them, living and dying both within the compass of the same year. Otherwise this knight, in relation to my book, may be termed ubiquitary, and appear amongst statesmen, soldiers, lawyers, writers, yea princes themselves, being (though not elected) in election to be king of Poland, which place he declined, preferring rather to be a subject to Queen Elizabeth, than a soverign beyond the seas.

He was born [1554] at Penshurst in this county, son to Sir Henry Sidney (of whom before) and sister's son to Robert earl of Leicester; bred in Christ Church in Oxford. Such his appetite to learning, that he could never be fed fast enough therewith, and so quick and strong his digestion, that he soon turned it into wholesome nourishment, and thrived healthfully thereon.

His home-bred abilities travel perfected with foreign accomplishments, and a sweet nature set a gloss upon both. He was so essential to the English court, that it seemed maimed without his company, being a complete master of matter and language, as his *Arcadia* doth evidence.

I confess I have heard some of modern pretended wits cavil thereat, merely because they made it not themselves: such who say, that his book is the occasion that many precious hours are otherwise spent no better, must acknowledge it also the cause that many idle hours are otherwise spent no worse, than in reading thereof.

At last, leaving the court, he followed the camp, being made governor of Flushing, under his uncle earl of Leicester. But the walls of that city (though high and strong) could not confine the activity of his mind, which must into the field, and before Zutphen was unfortunately slain with a shot, in a small skirmish, which we may sadly term a great battle, considering our heavy loss therein. His corpse, being brought over into England, was buried in the quire of St. Paul's, with general lamentation.

[*d.* 1586]

FRANCES SIDNEY, daughter of Sir William, sister to Sir Henry (lord deputy of Ireland, and president of Wales) aunt to the renowned Sir Philip Sidney, was born (and probably at Penshurst, the ancient seat of the Sidneys) in this county; a lady endowed with many virtues, signally charitable, expending much in large benefactions to the public. She bestowed on the abbey church of Westminster a salary of twenty pounds per annum for a divinity lecture; and founded Sidney Sussex College in Cambridge, of which largely in my *Church History*. She was relict of Thomas Radcliffe, the third earl of Sussex.[1] This worthy lady died childless (unless such learned persons who received their breeding in her foundation may be termed her issue) on the ninth day of May, anno 1589, as appeareth by her epitaph.[2]

(1) See Essex, p. 177. (2) On her monument in Westminster Abbey.—F.

SIR FRANCIS WALSINGHAM, knight, was born [1530?] in this county, wherein his family long flourished at Chislehurst; though I read that originally they fetched their name from Walsingham in Norfolk. He was bred in King's College in Cambridge, and gave the King of Spain's Bible to the library thereof. As a traveller many years beyond the seas, he learnt experience; as an agent, he practised it there; and after his return, as secretary of state, he taught it to many emissaries employed under him.

None alive did better ken the secretary craft, to get counsels out of others, and keep them in himself. Marvellous his sagacity in examining suspected persons, either to make them confess the truth, or confound themselves by denying it to their detection. Cunning his hands, who could unpick the cabinets in the pope's conclave; quick his ears, who could hear at London what was whispered in Rome; and numerous the spies and eyes of this Argus dispersed in all places.

The Jesuits, being outshot in their own bow, complained that he out-equivocated their equivocation, having a mental reservation deeper and farther then theirs. They tax him for making heaven bow too much to earth, oft-times borrowing a point of conscience, with full intent never to pay it again, whom others excused by reasons of state and dangers of the times. Indeed his *simulation* (which all allow lawful) was as like to *dissimulation* (condemned by all good men) as two things could be which were not the same.

He thought that gold might, but intelligence could not, be bought too dear; the cause that so great a statesman left so small an estate, and so public a person was so privately buried in Saint Paul's, Anno Domini 1590. His only daughter Frances was successively matched to three matchless men, Sir Philip Sidney, Robert earl of Essex, and Richard earl of Clanricarde.

ROBERT GLOVER, son to Thomas Glover and Mildred his wife, was born [1544] at Ashford in this county. He addicted himself to the study of heraldry, and in the reward of his pains was first made a pursuivant Portcullis, and then Somerset Herald. When the earl of Derby was sent into France, to carry the Garter to King Henry the Third, Mr. Glover attended the embassage and was, as he deserved, well rewarded for his pains. He by himself in Latin began a book, called *The Catalogue of Honour, or Treasury of True Nobility,* with their arms and matches. Being the first work in that kind, he therein traced untrodden paths, and therefore no wonder if such who since succeeded him in that subject have found a nearer way, and exceed him in accurateness therein. Being old rather in experience than years, he died not forty-six years old, anno 1588, and lieth buried under a comely monument in Saint Giles without Cripplegate, London, on the south wall of the quire.

FRANCIS THYNNE was born [1545?] in this county, and from his infancy had an ingenuous inclination to the study of antiquity, and especially of pedigrees. Herein he made such proficiency, that he was preferred, towards the end of the reign of Queen Elizabeth, to be an herald, by the title of Lancaster. A gentleman painful, and well deserving, not only of his own office, but all the English nation. Whosoever shall peruse the voluminous works of Raphael Holinshed, will find how much he was assisted therein by the help of Mr. Thynne, seeing the shoulders of Atlas himself may be weary, if sometime not beholden to Hercules to relieve them. He died [1608].

GILES FLETCHER (brother of Richard Fletcher, bishop of London) was born [1549?] in this county, as I am credibly informed.[1] He was bred first in Eton, then in King's College in Cambridge, where he became doctor of law. A most excellent poet (a quality hereditary to his two sons, Giles and Phineas); commissioner into Scotland, Germany and the Low Countries, for Queen Elizabeth, and her ambassador into Russia, secretary to the city of London, and master of the court of Requests.

His Russian embassy to settle the English merchandise was his masterpiece, to Theodore Juanowich, duke of Muscovy. He came thither in a dangerous juncture of time, viz., in the end of the year 1588. First, some foreigners (I will not say they were the Hollanders) envying the free trade of the English, had done them bad offices. Secondly, a false report was generally believed, that the Spanish Armada had worsted the English fleet; and the duke of Muscovy (who measured his favour to the English by the possibility he apprehended of their returning it) grew very sparing of his smiles, not to say free of his frowns, on our merchants residing there.

However, our doctor demeaned himself in his embassy with such cautiousness, that he not only escaped the duke's fury, but also procured many privileges for our English merchants, exemplified in Mr. Hakluyt. Returning home, and being safely arrived at London, he sent for his intimate friend Mr. Wayland, prebendary of Saint Paul's, and senior fellow of Trinity College in Cambridge (tutor to my father, from whose mouth I received this report) with whom he heartily expressed his thankfulness to God for his safe return from so great a danger; for the poets cannot fancy Ulysses more glad to be come out of the den of Polyphemus, than he was to be rid out of the power of such a barbarous prince; who, counting himself by a proud and voluntary mistake, emperor of all nations, cared not for the law of all nations; and who was so habited in blood, that, had he cut off this ambassador's head, he and his friends might have sought their own amends; but the question is, where he would have found it?

He afterwards set forth a book called *Of the Russe Commonwealth*, expressing the government, or tyranny rather, thereof; wherein, saith my author,[2] are many things most observable. But Queen Elizabeth, indulging the reputation of the duke of Muscovy as a confederate prince, permitted not the public printing of that which such who have private copies know to set the valuation thereon.[3] [*d.* 1611]

(1) From the mouth of Mr. Ramsey, minister of Rougham in Norfolk, who married the widow of Mr. Giles Fletcher, son to this doctor. [Giles Fletcher was born in Watford, Herts.] (2) Camden, in his *Elizabeth*, anno 1583, when he was agent in Muscovy, as afterward ambassador. (3) Partially available in Hakluyt and Purchas, and published in full in 1856.

SIR HENRY FINCH, knight, was born [1558] in this county, of right worshipful extraction (their ancient surname being Herbert) a family which had, and hath, an hereditary happiness of eminency in the study of the laws. He was serjeant-at-law to King James, and wrote a book of the law, in great esteem with men of his own profession;[1] yet were not his studies confined thereunto: witness his book of the *Calling of the Jews*. And all ingenious persons which dissent from his judgment will allow him learnedly to have maintained an error, though he was brought into some trouble by King James, conceiving that on his principles he advanced and extended the Jewish commonwealth, to the depressing and contracting of Christian princes' free monarchies. He was father unto Sir John Finch,[2] lord chief justice, and for a time lord keeper, and baron of Fordwich, who is still alive. [*d.* 1625]

THOMAS PLAYFERE was born [1561?] in this county, as some of his nearest relations have informed me. He was bred fellow of Saint John's College in Cambridge, and chosen 1596 to succeed Peter Barrow in the place of Margaret professor. His fluency in the Latin tongue seemed a wonder to many, though since such who have seen the sun admire no more at the moon; Doctor Collins not succeeding him so much in age, as exceeding him in eloquence.

The counsel of the apostle is good, Φρονεῖν εἰς τὸ σωφρονεῖν. His foe-friends commending of him, and his own conceiting of himself, made too deep an impression on his intellectuals. It added to his distemper, that when his re-election to his place (after his last two years' end) was put into the Regent House, a great doctor said, *detur digniori*. However, he held his professorship until the day of his death, 1609; and lieth buried, with an hyperbolical epitaph, in St. Botolph's in Cambridge.

WILLIAM ADAMS was (as his own pen reporteth) born at Gillingham in this county; and take the brief account of his life, being the first Englishman who effectually discovered Japan. Twelve years he lived at home with his parents. Twelve years he was apprentice and servant to Nicholas Diggins, a brave seaman. For some time he was master of one of the queen's ships. Ten years he served the English Company of Barbary Merchants. Fourteen years (as I collect it) he was employed by the Dutch in India. For he began his voyage 1598, pilot to their fleet of five sail, to conduct them to Japan; and in order to the settlement of trade, endured many miseries. He who reads them will concur with Cato, and repent that ever he went thither by sea whither one might go by land. But Japan being an island, and inaccessible save by the sea, our Adams' discretion was not to be blamed, but industry to be commended in his adventures. He died at Firando in Japan [1620].

THOMAS MILLES, sister's son to Robert Glover aforesaid,[3] was born [1550?] at Ashford in this county, and following his uncle's direction, applied

(1) A valuable treatise on common law, written in legal French, and an edition appeared as late as 1789. (2) Sir John Finch, Baron Finch of Fordwich (1584-1660) speaker of the House of Commons. He was chiefly responsible for the ship-money judgment in 1637. Impeached in 1640, he fled to Holland, returning at the Restoration. (3) See p. 278, above.

himself to be eminent in the genealogies of our English nobility. If the expression were as properly predicated of a nephew as of the next brother, one might say he raised up seed unto his uncle Glover, in setting forth his *Catalogue of Honour* in English, as more useful therein, because chiefly of our national concernment. He was employed on a message of importance from Queen Elizabeth unto Henry the Fourth, King of France, being then in Normandy; which trust he discharged with great fidelity, and incredible celerity, being returned home with a satisfactory answer to her highness before she could believe him arrived there. In memory of which service he had given him, for the crest of his arms, a chapeau with wings, to denote the *Mercuriousness* of this messenger. He died anno [1627?].[1]

ROBERT FLUDD, who by himself is Latined *Robertus de Fluctibus,* was born [1574] in this county, and that of a knightly family, as I am informed; bred (as I take it) in Oxford, and beyond the seas; a deep philosopher, and great physician, who at last fixed his habitation in Fenchurch Street, London. He was of the order of the Rosicrucians, and I must confess myself ignorant of the first founder and sanctions thereof. Perchance none know it but those that are of it. Sure I am, that a rose is the sweetest of flowers, and a cross accounted the sacredest of forms or figures, so that much of eminency must be imported in their composition.

His books written in Latin are great, many and mystical. The last some impute to his charity, clouding his high matter with dark language, lest otherwise the lustre thereof should dazzle the understanding of the reader. The same phrases he used to his patients; and seeing conceit is very contributive to the well working of physic, their fancy or faith natural was much advanced by his elevated expressions.

His works are for the English to slight or admire, for French and foreigners to understand and use; not that I account them more judicious than our own countrymen, but more inquiring into such difficulties. The truth is, here at home his books are beheld not so good as crystal, which (some say) are prized as precious pearls beyond the seas. He died on the eighth of September, Anno Domini 1637.

WILLIAM HARVEY, son of Thomas Harvey, was born [1578] at Folkestone in this county. His father had a week of sons, whereof this William, bred to learning, was the eldest; his other brethren being bound apprentices in London, and all at last ended in effect in merchants. They got great estates, and made their father treasurer thereof; who being as skilful to purchase land as they to gain money, kept, employed and improved their gainings, to their great advantage; so that he survived to see the meanest of them of far greater estate than himself.

Our William was bred in Caius College in Cambridge, where he proceeded doctor of physic. Five years also he studied at Padua, making a good composition of foreign and domestic learning; so that afterwards he was (for many years) physician to King Charles the First; and not only *doctor medicinae*, but *doctor medicorum.*

(1) Milles held several public appointments, and wrote books on economics.

For this was he that first found out the circulation of the blood, an opinion which entered into the world with great disadvantages. For, first, none will be acquainted with strangers at the first sight, as persons generally suspected; as if to be unknown were part of being guilty. Secondly, the grandees of this profession were of the opposite judgment, heavy enough without any argument to overlay (and so to stifle) any infant opinion by their authority.

But truth, though it may be questioned for a vagrant, carrieth a passport along with it for its own vindication. Such have since shaken friendly hands with Doctor Harvey, which at first tilted pens against him. And amongst the rest Riolanus, that learned physician, if not *ambabus ulnis,* with one arm at the least doth embrace his opinion, and partly consent thereunto.

This doctor, though living a bachelor, may be said to have left three hopeful sons to posterity: his books, 1. *De Circulatione Sanguinis,* which I may call his son and heir, the doctor living to see it at full age, and generally received. 2. *De Generatione;* as yet in its minority, but, I assure you, growing up apace into public credit. 3. *De Ovo;* as yet in the nonage thereof, but infants may be men in due time.

It must not be forgotten, that this doctor had made a good progress, to lay down a practice of physic conformable to his thesis of the circulation of blood, but was plundered of his papers in our civil war. Unhappy dissensions, which not only murdered many then alive, but may be said by this (call it mischief or mischance) to have destroyed more not yet born, whose diseases might have been either prevented or removed, if his worthy pains had come forth into the public; and I charitably presume that grateful posterity will acknowledge the improvements of this opinion, as superstructures on his foundation; and thankfully pay the fruit to his memory, who watered, planted (not to say made) the root of this discovery.

He hath since been a second Linacre and great benefactor to the College of Physicians in London. . . . He died in the eightieth year of his age, June 3, Anno Domini 1657.

SIR FRANCIS NETHERSOLE, knight, born [1587] at [Winghamswood?] in this county, was bred fellow of Trinity College in Cambridge, and afterwards became orator of the university. Hence he was preferred to be ambassador to the princess of the Union, and secretary to the Lady Elizabeth, Queen of Bohemia; it is hard to say whether he was more remarkable for his doings or sufferings in her behalf.[1] He married Lucy, eldest daughter of Sir Henry Goodere of Polesworth in Warwickshire, by whose encouragement (being free of himself to any good design) he hath founded and endowed a very fair school at Polesworth aforesaid, and is still living. [*d.* 1659]

JOHN PHILIPOT was born [1589?] at Folkestone in this county, and from his childhood had a genius inclining him to the love of antiquity. He first was made a pursuivant extraordinary, by the title of Blanch Lion,

(1) He was imprisoned for a short time in 1634 for his over-zealous support of the Electress Palatine, daughter of James I.

then in ordinary, by the name of Rouge Dragon, and afterwards Somerset Herald. He made very pertinent additions to the second edition of Mr. Camden's *Remains;* and deserved highly well of the city of London, proving, in a learned and ingenious book, that gentry doth not abate with apprenticeship, but only sleepeth during the time of their indentures, and awaketh again when they are expired. Nor did he contribute a little to the setting forth of his uncle's *Catalogue of Honour.* He died anno 1645, and was buried in Saint Benet, Paul's Wharf.

THE FAREWELL

Having already insisted on the courage of the Kentish men, and shown how in former ages the leading of the vanguard was entrusted unto their magnanimity, we shall conclude our description of this shire, praying that they may have an accession of loyalty unto their courage, not that the natives of Kent have acquitted themselves less loyal than those of other shires; but, seeing the one will not suffer them to be idle, the other may guide them to expend their ability for God's glory, the defence of his majesty, and maintenance of true religion.

CANTERBURY

CANTERBURY is a right ancient city; and whilst the Saxon Heptarchy flourished, was the chief seat of the kings of Kent. Here Thomas à Becket had his death; Edward, surnamed the Black Prince, and King Henry the Fourth their interment. The metropolitan dignity, first conferred by Gregory the Great on London, was, for the honour of Augustine, afterwards bestowed on this city. It is much commended by William of Malmesbury for its pleasant situation, being surrounded with a fertile soil, well wooded, and commodiously watered by the river Stour, from whence it is said to have had its name *Durwhern;* in British, a swift river. It is happy in the vicinity of the sea, which affordeth plenty of good fish.

THE BUILDINGS

Christ Church, first dedicated, and (after 300 years' intermission to Saint Thomas à Becket) restored to the honour of our Saviour, is a stately structure, being the performance of several successive archbishops. It is much adorned with glass windows. Here they will tell you of a foreign ambassador, who proffered a vast price to transport the east window of the quire beyond the seas. Yet artists, who commend the colours, condemn the figures therein, as wherein proportion is not exactly observed.

According to the maxim, "pictures are the books," painted windows were in the time of popery the library of laymen, and after the Conquest grew in general use in England. It is much suspected annealing of glass (which answereth to dyeing in grain in drapery) especially of yellow, is lost in our age, as to the perfection thereof. Anciently colours were so incorporated in windows, that both of them lasted and faded together; whereas our modern painting (being rather *on* than *in* the glass) is fixed so faintly, that it often changeth, and sometimes falleth away. Now, though some, being only for the innocent white, are equal enemies to the painting of windows as faces, conceiving the one as great a pander to superstition as the other to wantonness; yet others, of as much zeal and more knowledge, allow the historical uses of them in churches.

PROVERBS

Canterbury Tales. So Chaucer calleth his book, being a collection of several tales, pretended to be told by pilgrims in their passage to the shrine of Saint Thomas in Canterbury. But since that time, Canterbury Tales are parallel to *Fabulae Milesiae,* which are charactered *nec verae, nec verisimiles,* merely made to mar precious time, and please fanciful people. Such are the many miracles of Thomas à Becket; some *helpful* (though but narrow, as only for private conveniency) as when perceiving his old palace at Otford to want water, he struck his staff into the dry ground (still called Saint Thomas's Well) whence water runneth plentifully to serve that house (lately rebuilt) unto this day; others spiteful, as when (because a smith dwelling in that town had clogged his horse) he ordered that no smith afterwards should thrive within that parish. But he who shall go about seriously to confute these tales, is as very a fool as he was somewhat else who first impudently invented them.

THE WORTHIES

OSBERN OF CANTERBURY, so called because there he had his first birth, or best being, as chanter of the cathedral church therein. An admirable musician, which quality endeared him (though an Englishman) to Lanfranc, the lordly Lombard and archbishop of Canterbury. He was the English Jubal, as to the curiosity thereof in our churches: an art which never any spake against who undertook it, otherwise Apollo is in a sad case, if Midas's ears must be his judges. However, in divine service, all music ought to be tuned to edification, that all who hear may understand it; otherwise it may tend to delight not devotion, and true zeal cannot be raised where knowledge is depressed. This Osbern wrote the life of Saint Dunstan in pure Latin, according to that age; flourishing . . . anno 1090.

STEPHEN LANGTON. Here we are at a perfect loss for the place of his birth, his surname affording us so much direction; in effect it is none at all. Stephen, born in England, was bred in Paris, where he became one of the greatest scholars of the Christian world in his age. He was afterwards consecrated cardinal of Saint Chrysogonus; and then, by papal power, intruded archbishop of Canterbury, in defiance of all opposition which King John could make against him.

Many are his learned works, writing comments on all the Old, and on some of the New Testament. He was the first that divided the whole Bible into chapters, as Robert Stephens, a Frenchman, that curious critic and painful printer, some six score years since first subdivided into verses. A worthy work, making Scripture more manageable in men's memories, and the passages therein the sooner to be turned to; as any person is sooner found out in the most populous city if methodized into streets and houses with signs, to which the figures affixed do fitly allude.

Say not this was a presumption, incurring the curse denounced to such who add to Scripture, it being no addition, but an illustration thereof. Besides, God set the first pattern to men's industry herein, seeing the distinction of some verses may be said to be *Jure Divino,* as those in the Lamentations and elsewhere, which are alphabetically modelled.

As causeless their complaint who cavil at the inequality of chapters, the eighth of the first of Kings being sixty-six, the last of Malachi but six verses, seeing the entireness of the sense is the standard of their length or shortness. It is confessed some few chapters end, and others begin abruptly; and yet it is questionable whether the alteration thereof would prove advantageous, seeing the reforming of a small fault, with a great change, doth often hurt more than amend; and such alterations would discompose millions of quotations, in excellent authors, conformed to the aforesaid received divisions.

Here it must not be concealed that notwithstanding this general tradition of Langton's chaptering the Bible, some learned men make that design of far ancienter date, and particularly that able antiquary Sir Henry Spelman. This I am confident of, that Stephen Langton did something much material in order thereunto, and the improver is usually called the inventor, by a complimental mistake.

However, though I believe Langton well employed in dividing the Bible, he was ill busied in rending asunder the church and kingdom of England, reducing King John to sad extremities.[1] He died, and was buried at Canterbury, Anno Domini 1228.

SIMON LANGTON was, by his brother Stephen Langton the archbishop, preferred archdeacon of Canterbury; who, *carne et sanguine revelante* (saith the record[2]) made the place much better, both to him and his successors, in revenue and jurisdiction. A troublesome man he was, and on his brother's score, a great adversary to King John, even after that king had altered his copy, and became, of a fierce foe, a son-servant to the pope, by resigning his crown unto him. But our Simon could not knock off when he should, having contracted such an habit of hatred to King John that he could not depose it, though commanded under the pain of excommunication. This caused him to trudge to the court of Rome, where he found little favour. For such who will be the pope's white boys must watchfully observe his signals, and not only charge when he chargeth, but retreat when he retreateth. This Simon (besides others) wrote a book of the penitence of Magdalene, in relation (it seems) to himself, though she found more favour in the court of heaven than he at Rome.[3] He died Anno Domini 1248.

THOMAS NEVILLE, born in this city of most honourable extraction, as his name is enough to notify and avouch. He was bred in Cambridge, and master first of Magdelene, then of Trinity College, and dean of Canterbury. He was the first clergyman (sent by Archbishop Whitgift) who carried to King James tidings of the English crown; and it is questionable whether he brought thither or thence more welcome news (especially to the clergy) acquainting them with the king's full intentions to maintain church discipline, as he found it established.

But the main matter commending his memory is his magnificency to Trinity College, whose court he reduced to a spacious and beautiful quadrangle. Indeed he plucked down as good building as any erected, but such as was irregular, intercepting the sight, disturbing the intended uniformity of the court, whereby the beauty at this day is much advanced; for, as the intuitive knowledge is more perfect than that which insinuates itself into the soul gradually by discourse, so more beautiful the prospect of that building which is all visible at one view, than what discovers itself to the sight by parcels and degrees. Nor was this doctor like those poets good only at translation and bad at invention; all for

(1) He acted as peacemaker in John's quarrel with Pope Innocent III, and mediated during the business of Magna Carta, which he supported. (2) Somner, in his Catalogue of the Archdeacons of Canterbury. (3) Later, under Henry III, he rose to favour with both king and pope.

altering, nothing for adding of his own; who contributed to this college (I will not say a widow's mite) but a bachelor's bounty, a stately new court of his own expence, which cost him three thousand pounds and upwards. Much enfeebled with the palsy he died, an aged man, Anno Domini 1615.

THE FAREWELL

I am heartily sorry that the many laudable endeavours for the scouring and enlargement of the river Stour (advantageous for this city) have been so often defeated, and the contributions given by well-disposed benefactors (amongst whom Mr. Rose, once an alderman of Canterbury, gave three hundred pounds) have missed their ends; praying that their future enterprises in this kind may be crowned with success.

For the rest, I refer the reader to the pains of my worthy friend Mr. William Somner,[1] who hath written *justem volumen* of the antiquities of this city. I am sorry to see him subject-bound (betrayed thereto by his own modesty); seeing otherwise not the city but diocese of Canterbury had been more adequate to his abilities. I hope others, by his example, will undertake their respective counties; it being now, with our age, the third and last time of asking the banns, whether or no we may be wedded to skill in this kind, seeing now "use, or for ever hold your pens"; all church monuments, leading to knowledge in that nature, being daily irrecoverably embezzled.[2]

(1) Lived 1598—1669; Anglo-Saxon scholar and a great antiquary. (2) A reference tc puritan iconoclasm.

LANCASHIRE

LANCASHIRE hath the Irish Sea on the west, Yorkshire on the east, Cheshire (parted with the river Mersey) on the south, Cumberland and Westmorland on the north. It rangeth in length, from Mersey to Windermere, fully fifty-five miles, though the broadest part thereof exceedeth not one and thirty. The air thereof is subtile and piercing, being free from fogs saving in the Mosses; the effects whereof are found in the fair complexions and firm constitutions of the natives therein, whose bodies are as able as their minds willing for any laborious employment. Their soil is tolerably fruitful of all things necessary for human sustenance; and as that youth cannot be counted a dunce, though he be ignorant, if he be docible, because his lack of learning is to be scored on the want of a teacher; so sterility cannot properly be imputed to some places in this county, where little grain doth grow, because capable thereof, as daily experience doth avouch, if it were husbanded accordingly.

This shire, though sufficiently thick of people, is exceedingly thin of parishes, as by perusing this parallel will plainly appear: Rutland hath in it forty-eight parishes; Lancashire hath in it thirty-six parishes. See here how Rutland, being scarce a fifth part of Lancashire in greatness, hath a fourth part of parishes more therein.

But, as it was a fine sight to behold Sir Thomas More, when lord chancellor of England, every morning in term time humbly ask blessing in Westminster Hall of Sir John More his father, then a puisne judge; so may one see in this shire some chapels, exceeding their mother-churches in fairness of structure and numerousness of people, yet owning their filial relation, and still continuing their dutiful dependance on their parents. But for numerosity of chapels, surely the church of Manchester exceedeth all the rest, which, though anciently called but Villa de Manchester, is for wealth and greatness corrival with some cities in England, having no less than nine chapels, which before our civil wars were reputed to have five hundred communicants a-piece. Insomuch that some clergymen, who have consulted God's honour with their own credit and profit, could not better desire for themselves than to have a Lincolnshire church, as best built; a Lancashire parish, as largest bounded; and a London audience, as consisting of most intelligent people.

The people, generally devout, are (as I am informed) northward and by the west, popishly affected; which in the other parts (intended by *antiperistasis*) are zealous protestants. Hence is it that many subtile papists and Jesuits have been born and bred in this county which have met their matches, to say no more, in the natives of the same county; so that thereby it hath come to pass that the house of Saul hath waxed weaker and weaker, and the house of David stronger and stronger.

NATURAL COMMODITIES

OATS

If any ask why this grain, growing commonly all over England, is here entered as an eminent commodity of Lancashire, let him know that here is the most and best of that kind; yea wheat and barley may seem but the adopted, whilst oats are the natural issue of this county, so inclined is its genius to the production thereof. Say not oats are horse-grain, and fitter for a stable than a table; for, besides that the meal thereof is the distinguishing form of gruel or broth from water, most hearty and wholesome bread is made thereof. Yea, anciently, north of Humber, no other was eaten by people of the primest quality; for we read how William the Conqueror bestowed the manor of Castle Bytham in Lincolnshire upon Stephen earl of Albemarle and Holderness, chiefly for this consideration, that thence he might have wheaten bread to feed his infant son, oaten bread being then the diet of Holderness and the counties lying beyond it.

ALUM

I am informed that alum is found at Hoghton in this county, within the inheritance of Sir Richard Hoghton, and that enough for the use of this and the neighbouring shires, though not for transportation. But, because far greater plenty is afforded in Yorkshire, the larger mention of this mineral is referred to that place.

OXEN

The fairest in England are bred (or if you will, made) in this county, with goodly heads, the tips of whose horns are sometimes distanced five foot asunder. Horns are a commodity not to be slighted, seeing I cannot call to mind any other substance so hard that it will not break; so solid, that it will hold liquor within it; and yet so clear, that light will pass through it. No mechanic trade but hath some utensils made thereof, and even now I recruit my pen with ink from a vessel of the same. Yea, it is useful cap-à-pie, from combs to shoeing horns. What shall I speak of the many gardens made of horns, to garnish houses? I mean artificial flowers of all colours. And besides what is spent in England, many thousands' weight are shaven down into leaves for lanthorns and sent daily into France. In a word, the very shavings of horn are profitable, sold by the sack, and sent many miles from London for the manuring of ground. No wonder then that the Horners are an ancient corporation, though why they and the Bottlemakers were formerly united into one company passeth my skill to conjecture. The best horns in all England, and freest to work without flaws, are what are brought out of this county to London, the shop-general of English industry.

THE MANUFACTURES

FUSTIANS

These anciently were creditable wearing in England for persons of the primest quality, finding the knight in Chaucer thus habited:

Of fustian he weared a gippon
All besmottered with his haubergeon.[1]

But it seems they were all foreign commodities, as may appear by their modern names: 1. *Jen Fustians,* which I conceive so called from Jena, a city in Saxony; 2. *Augsburg Fustians,* made in that famous city in Suabia; 3. *Milan Fustians,* brought over hither out of Lombardy.

These retain their old names at this day, though these several sorts are made in this county, whose inhabitants, buying the cotton, wool or yarn coming from beyond the sea, make it here into fustians, to the good employment of the poor and great improvement of the rich therein, serving mean people for their outsides, and their betters for the linings of their garments. Bolton is the staple place for this commodity, being brought thither from all parts of the county.

As for Manchester, the cottons thereof carry away the credit in our nation, and so they did a hundred and fifty years ago. For when learned Leland, on the cost of King Henry the Eighth, with his guide travelled Lancashire, he called Manchester the fairest and quickest town in this county; and sure I am it hath lost neither spruceness nor spirits since that time.

Other commodities made in Manchester are so small in themselves, and various in their kinds, they will fill the shop of an haberdasher of small wares. Being therefore too many for me to reckon up or remember, it will be the safest way to wrap them altogether in some Manchester ticking, and to fasten them with the pins (to prevent their falling out and scattering) or tie them with the tape, and also, because sure bind sure find, to bind them about with points and laces, all made in the same place.

THE BUILDINGS

Manchester, a collegiate as well as a parochial church, is a great ornament to this county. The quire thereof, though but small is exceeding beautiful, and for woodwork, an excellent piece of artifice.

THE WONDERS

About Wigan and elsewhere in this county men go a-fishing with spades and mattocks; more likely, one would think, to catch moles than fishes with such instruments. First, they pierce the turfy ground, and under it meet with a black and deadish water, and in it small fishes do swim. Surely these *pisces fossiles,* or subterranean fishes, must needs be unwholesome, the rather because an unctuous matter is found about them. Let them be thankful to God, in the first place, who need not such meat to feed upon. And next them, let those be thankful which have such meat to feed upon when they need it.

PROVERBS

Lancashire fair women. I believe that the God of Nature having given fair complexions to the women in this county, art may save her pains (not to say her sins) in endeavouring to better them. But let the females of this county know, that though in the Old Testament express notice be

(1) Chaucer, in his Prologue.

taken of the beauty of many women, Sarah, Rebekah, Rachel, Abigail, Thamar, Abishag, Esther; yet in the New Testament no mention is made at all of the fairness of any woman; not because they wanted, but because grace is chief gospel-beauty. Elizabeth's unblameableness; the Virgin Mary's pondering God's word; the Canaanitish woman's faith; Mary Magdalen's charity; Lydia's attention to Paul's preaching; these soul-piercing perfections are far better than skin-deep fairness.

THE BATTLES

At Preston in Amounderness, August 17th, 1648, Duke Hamilton, resolving to play an after-game of loyalty, entered England with an army more numerous than well disciplined. Most beheld him as one rather cunning than wise, yet rather wise than valiant. However, he had officers who did ken the warcraft as well as any of our age. He would accept of no English assistance, so to engross all the work and wages to himself. Some suspect his officers' trust was undermined (or over-moneyed rather); whilst others are confident they were betrayed by none save their own security. Indeed the common soldiers were persuaded that the conquest would be easy; rather to be possessed than purchased. Their van and rear were many miles asunder, and they met the resistance of Major-general Lambert before they expected it. He at Preston gave the Scotch army such a blow as settled or stunned it, though it reeled on some miles more southward into Staffordshire, where at Uttoxeter, the duke was taken prisoner and utterly defeated.

As for the defeat of James earl of Derby in this county, at the end of August, anno 1651, it amounted not to a battle, which properly is the engagement of two formed armies, whereas the forces of the earl were scattered before fully gathered to a firm consistency. Yet this had been a battle, if not prevented by the vigilancy of Colonel Lilburne and others, whose seasonable service to the parliament was not so great in itself, as in the most considerable consequences thereof.

THE WORTHIES

RICHARD ULLERSTON was born in this county, at Ulverston, a well known market-town in Lonsdale hundred. A great antiquary[1] (ambitious of all learned men's acquaintance) complained that he knew him not so well as he desired. He was bred in Oxford, and wrote a book intituled the *Articles of Faith, or the Creed of the Church.* This lay latent a good while till John Stanbury bishop of Hereford rescued it from the moths some thirty years after the author's death, and bestowed a double light upon it; one in producing it into the public, the other illustrating it with a commentary he wrote thereon. Say not this was false heraldry, but true humility, to see a bishop commenting (which is not usual) on the book of a priest. Bale concludeth all thus:

longum
Non doctrina potest obscuro carcere claudi.
nor will worth
Long be confin'd, but make its own way forth.

[*d.* 1423]

(1) Leland.

SIR EDMUND DE TRAFFORD, and SIR THOMAS DE ASHTON [*fl.* 1446], knights, were persons of high esteem, as anciently descended, and richly revenued in this county. How great their skill was in chemistry will appear by the following patent (faithfully transcribed with mine own hand out of the original in the Tower) granted unto them by King Henry the Sixth in the four and twentieth year of his reign:[1]

The king to all unto whom, &c. greeting. Know ye, that whereas our beloved and loyal Edmund de Trafford, knight, and Thomas Ashton, knight, have by a certain petition shown unto us, that although they were willing, by the art or science of philosophy, to work upon certain metals to translate imperfect metals from their own kind, and then to transubstantiate them by the said art or science, as they say, into perfect gold or silver, unto all manner of proofs and trials, to be expected and endured, as any gold or silver growing in any mine; notwithstanding, certain persons, ill-willing and maligning them, conceive them to work by unlawful art, and so may hinder and disturb them in the trial of the said art and science: We, considering the premises, and willing to know the conclusion of the said working or science, of our special grace have granted and given leave to the same Edmund and Thomas, and to their servants, that they may work and try the aforesaid art and science, lawfully and freely, without any hindrance of ours, or of our officers whatsoever; any statute, act, ordinance, or provision, made, ordained, or provided to the contrary notwithstanding. In witness whereof, the king at Westminster, the 7th day of April.

THOMAS PENKETH, so was his true name (though wrested by some Latinists into Penchettus, and miswritten Penthy and Penker by some English) taken from a village in this county. He was bred an Augustinian in Warrington, and a doctor of divinity in Oxford; a deep Scotist, and of so great a memory, that foreigners (amongst whom he lived) report of him that had all the books of Scotus been lost, he could easily have restored every word of them. He was called to be professor at Padua, and returning into England, became provincial of his order.

But his last act stained his former life, who promoted the bastardizing of the issue of King Edward the Fourth; and as Dr. Shaw ushered, his flattery held up the train of the usurper's praises, in a sermon at Saint Paul's; in preaching whereof, he who had formerly forfeited his honesty, lost his voice, a proper punishment for a parasite.[2] His disgrace had some influence on his order, which, then vertical and numerous, daily decayed in England to their dissolution. This Thomas died, and was buried in London, 1487.

WILLIAM SMITH was born [1460?] at Farnworth in this county; bred fellow in Pembroke Hall in Cambridge; and at last, by King Henry the Seventh, preferred bishop of Lichfield and Coventry. That politic prince, to ease and honour his native country of Wales, erected a court of presidency, conformable to the parliaments of France, in the marches

(1) Latin original omitted. (2) On Edward IV's death, his brother Richard duke of Gloucester, was proclaimed protector for the minority of Edward V. The young king, and later his brother, were placed in the Tower. This Dr. Shaw, a brother of the mayor of London, was put up to declare Edward V and his brother illegitimate. Shortly afterwards Gloucester, as Richard III, usurped the crown, following this with the murder of the young princes. The Scotus mentioned above is Duns Scotus (see Northumberland, p. 445).

thereof, and made this bishop first president, those parts lying partly in his diocese. He discharged the place with singular integrity and general contentment (retaining that office till the day of his death) when he was removed to be bishop of Lincoln.

"A good name is an ointment poured out," saith Solomon, and this man, wheresoever he went, may be followed by the perfume of charity he left behind him.

1. At Lichfield he founded an hospital for a master, two priests, and ten poor people. 2. In the same place he founded a school, procuring from King Henry the Seventh that the hospital of Downhall in Cheshire, with the lands thereunto belonging, should be bestowed upon it. Say not this was robbing the spittle, or at the best robbing Peter to pay Paul; seeing we may presume so charitable a prelate would do nothing unjust, though at this distance of time we cannot clear the particulars of his proceedings.

At Farnworth, where he was born, he founded a school, allowing ten pounds annually (in that age no mean salary) for the master thereof.

The university of Oxford discreetly chose him (Oxford being in his diocese of Lincoln) their chancellor, and lost nothing thereby; for he proved a more loving nephew than son, so bountiful to his aunt Oxford, that therein he founded Brasenose College, but died 1514, before his foundation was finished.

JAMES STANLEY, D.D., brother of Thomas earl of Derby, was born [1465?] in this county; and was by King Henry the Seventh (his kinsman by marriage) preferred bishop of Ely, 1506; a man more memorable than commendable, who never resided at his own cathedral. I can partly excuse his living all the summer with the earl his brother in this county, but must condemn his living all the winter at his manor at Somersham in Huntingdonshire with one who was not his sister, and wanted nothing to make her his wife save marriage. However, if Jehu allowed a burial to his most professed enemy, on this account, that she was a king's daughter, none I hope will grudge his memory a room in this book, were it only because he was an earl's brother. He died anno 1515.

HUGH OLDHAM, born in this county at Oldham, a village some six miles from Manchester, bred in Queens' College in Cambridge, was no ill scholar, and a good man, most pious according to and above the devotion of the age he lived in. He was afterwards bishop of Exeter, a foe to monkish superstition, and a friend to university learning. Brasenose College in Oxford, and Corpus Christi College therein, will for ever bear witness of his bounty, to advance religion and learning. Besides, the town of Manchester have good cause to remember him who founded and endowed a school therein, with large revenue, appointing the warden of the college therein *Caput Scholae*.

This bishop having a tough contest with the abbot of Tavistock, was excommunicated for refusing to stand to the decision of the court of Rome. He had formerly built a chapel in the south side of his cathedral; and dying excommunicate (on the aforesaid account) was buried, not in the very church, but brink thereof, and body of the wall. He died Anno Domini 1519.

HENRY STANDISH was, I have just cause to conclude, extracted from the Standishes of Standish in this county; bred a Franciscan and doctor of divinity in Cambridge, and afterwards made bishop of Saint Asaph. I neither believe him so good as Pits doth character him, *pietate et doctrina clarum;* nor so bad as Bale doth decry him, making him a doting fool. Sure I am there was *impar congressus* betwixt him and Erasmus, as unequal a contest as betwixt child and man, not to say dwarf and giant. This Standish is said to have fallen down on his knees before King Henry the Eighth, petitioning him to continue the religion established by his ancestors, and entering into matters of divinity, he cited the Colossians for the Corinthians; which being but a memory-mistake in an aged person, need not to have exposed him so much as it did to the laughter of the standers-by. After he had sat sixteen years bishop of Saint Asaph, he died very aged, 1535.

JOHN ROGERS was born [1500?] in this county, and bred in the university of Cambridge; a very able linguist and general scholar. He was first a zealous papist, till his eyes being opened, he detested all superstition, and went beyond the seas to Wittenburg, where (some years after Tyndale) he translated the Bible, from Genesis till the Revelation, comparing it with the original. Coming to England, he presented it in a fair volume to King Henry the Eighth, prefixing a dedicatory epistle, and subscribing himself (those dangerous days required a disguise) under the name of Thomas Matthew.[1]

Yet this present could not procure Mr. Rogers his security, who, it seems, for fears of the Six Articles,[2] was fain to fly again beyond the seas, and returning in the reign of King Edward the Sixth, became a preacher of London. He and Mr. Hooper were the two greatest sticklers against ceremonies, though otherwise allowing of episcopal government. He was the first martyr who suffered in Smithfield in Queen Mary's days, and led all the rest, of whom we may truly say, that if they had not been flesh and blood, they could not have been burnt; and if they had been no more than flesh and blood, they would not have been burnt.

The nonconformists account it no small credit unto them that one of their opinion (as who could not flinch from the faith) was chosen by Divine Providence the first to encounter the fire. Such may remember that no army is all front, and that as constant did come behind as went before. Had those of an opposite judgment been called first, they had come first to the stake, and in due time the defenders of ceremonies were as substantial in their sufferings. This John Rogers was martyred Feb. 4, 1555.

(1) Rogers did not translate the Bible, but prepared Tyndale's translation (borrowing from Coverdale's translation for the uncompleted portions) for publication at Antwerp in 1537. But to him we owe the valuable prefatory matter and the marginal notes, the latter constituting the first English commentary on the Bible. (2) See p. 30, note 1.

ALEXANDER NOWELL was born [1507?] of a knightly family at Read in this county, and at thirteen years of age being admitted into Brasenose College in Oxford, studied thirteen years therein. Then he became schoolmaster of Westminster.

It happened in the first of Queen Mary he was fishing upon the Thames, an exercise wherein he so much delighted, insomuch that his picture kept in Brasenose College is drawn with his lines, hooks and other tackling lying in a round on one hand, and his angles of several sorts on the other. But, whilst Nowell was catching of fishes, Bonner was catching of Nowell; and understanding who he was, designed him to the shambles, whither he had certainly been sent, had not Mr. Francis Bowyer, then merchant, afterwards sheriff of London, safely conveyed him beyond the seas.

Without offence it may be remembered that, leaving a bottle of ale (when fishing) in the grass, he found it some days after no bottle, but a gun, such the sound at the opening thereof; and this is believed (casualty is mother of more inventions than industry) the original of bottled ale in England.

Returning the first of Queen Elizabeth he was made dean of Saint Paul's; and for his meek spirit, deep learning, prudence and piety, the then parliament and convocation both chose, enjoined and trusted him to be the man to make a catechism for public use, such a one as should stand as a rule for faith and manners to their posterity.

He was confessor to Queen Elizabeth, constantly preaching the first and last Lent sermons before her.[1] He gave two hundred pounds per annum to maintain thirteen scholars in Brasenose College. He died, being ninety years of age, not decayed in sight, February 13, 1602.

JOHN BRADFORD was born [1510?] at Manchester in this county, and bred first a lawyer in the inns of court, and for a time did solicit suits for Sir John Harington; afterwards, saith my author, *ex rixoso causidico mitissimus Christi apostolus.*[2] Going to Cambridge a man in maturity and ability, the university by special grace bestowed on him the degree of master of arts, and so may he be said to commence, not only *per saltum,* but *per volatum.* The Jesuit doth causelessly urge this his short standing for an argument of his little understanding; whereas he had always been a hard student from his youth, and his writings and his disputings give a sufficient testimony of his learning.

It is a demonstration to me that he was of a sweet temper, because Parsons,[3] who will hardly afford a good word to a protestant, saith "that he seemed to be of a more soft and mild nature than many of his fellows." Indeed he was a most holy and mortified man, who secretly in his closet would so weep for his sins, one would have thought he would never have smiled again; and then, appearing in public, he would be so

(1) He fell into disgrace in 1564 after his Lenten sermon at St. Paul's, Elizabeth and the Spanish ambassador being present. Nowell spoke slightingly of the crucifix. Elizabeth called aloud to him, "To your text, Mr. Dean; leave that, we have heard enough of that." Nowell was unable to continue, and Elizabeth left in a rage. (2) Bale ["From being a fractious lawyer he became the gentlest of Christ's apostles."] (3) Robert Parsons, the Jesuit missionary—see Somersetshire, p. 295.

harmlessly pleasant one would think he had never wept before. But Mr. Foxe's pains have given the pens of all posterity a writ of ease, to meddle no more with this martyr, who suffered Anno Domini 1555.

GEORGE MARSH was born [1515] at Dean in this county; bred a good scholar in a grammar school, and then lived in the honest condition of a farmer. After the death of his wife he went to Cambridge, where he followed his studies very close, and afterwards solemnly entering into orders, became a profitable preacher and curate to Mr. Laurence Saunders, the worthy martyr. Causelessly therefore doth Parsons asperse him, that he of a farmer turned a preacher, as if he had done it immediately (with many of our age leaping from the plough to the pulpit) concealing his academical breeding; such is the charity of his Jesuitical reservation.

As little is his charity for condemning him for answering dubiously and fearfully at first to such who examined him about the sacrament of the altar, seeing the said Marsh condemned himself for doing it, as therein too much consulting carnal respects to save his life, as appears in Master Foxe, whence the Jesuit fetcheth all his information. But Marsh made amends for all these failings with his final constancy, being both burnt and scalded to death (having a barrel of pitch placed over his head, an accent of cruelty peculiar to him alone) when he was martyred at Westchester, April 24, 1555.

JOHN CHRISTOPHERSON was born in this county; bred first in Pembroke Hall, then fellow of Saint John's, and afterwards master of Trinity College in Cambridge; an excellent scholar, and linguist especially. I have seen a Greek tragedy, made and written by his own hand (so curiously that it seemed printed) and presented to King Henry the Eighth. He no less elegantly (if faithfully) translated Philo and Eusebius into Latin. Besides his own benefaction to the master's lodgings and library, he was highly instrumental in moving Queen Mary to her magnificent bounty to Trinity College. In the visitation of Cambridge he was very active in burning the bones of Bucer,[1] being then elect bishop of Chichester, scarcely continuing a year in that place.

All expected that, at his first coming in his diocese, he should demean himself very favourably. For why should not the poet's observation of princes be true also of prelates?

Mitissima sors est
Regnorum sub rege novo
Subjects commonly do find
New-made sovereigns most kind.

But he had not so much mercy as Nero, to begin courteously, having no sooner put on his episcopal ring, but presently he washed his hands in the blood of poor martyrs; whereof in due place.[2] In the first of Queen Elizabeth he was deprived and kept in some restraint, wherein he died [1558].

(1) Martin Bucer (1491—1551) converted to protestantism under the influence of Luther; one of the chief protagonists of the English Reformation. Buried in the university church, his body was exhumed by Queen Mary's commissioners in 1557.
(2) See Martyrs in Sussex [p. 562].

EDWIN SANDYS was born [1516?] at Coniston in this county; whose good actions, great sufferings, pious life, and peaceable death, 1588, are plentifully related in our *Church History*.[1]

JAMES PILKINGTON, D.D. [*b.* 1520?] was the third son of James Pilkington of Rivington in this county, esquire, a right ancient family; being informed by my good friend Master William Ryley, Norroy, and this countryman, that the Pilkingtons were gentlemen of repute in this shire before the conquest,[2] when the chief of them, then sought for, was fain to disguise himself a thresher in a barn. Hereupon, partly alluding to the head of the flail (falling sometime on the one, sometime on the other side) partly to himself embracing the safest condition for the present, he gave for the motto of his arms, "Now thus, now thus."

This James, bred fellow of St. John's in Cambridge, was in the first of Queen Mary forced to fly into Germany, where he wrote a comment on Ecclesiastes and both the Epistles of St. Peter. After his return, in the first of Queen Elizabeth, he was chosen master of Saint John's, and March the 2nd, 1561, was consecrated bishop of Durham.

Nine years after, the northern rebels came to Durham, and first tore the Bible, then the English Liturgy, in pieces.[3] Unhappy (though most innocent) book, equally odious to opposite parties; such who account the papists heretics esteeming it popish, whilst the papists themselves account it heretical. The bishop had fared no better than the book, could he have been come by. But when the rebellion was suppressed, the bishop commenced a suit against Queen Elizabeth for the lands and goods of the rebels attainted in the bishopric, as forfeited to him by his charter; and had prevailed, if the parliament had not interposed, and on special consideration, *pro hoc tempore,* adjudged them to the queen. He died Anno Domini 1576.[4]

THOMAS [LEVER or] LEAVER was born [1521] in this county, where his family and name still remain at two villages called Lever at this day. He was bred a fellow and bachelor of divinity of Saint John's College in Cambridge, whereof he was chosen master 1551. He was also preferred master of Sherburn House, or Hospital, in the bishopric; a place, it seems, of good profit and credit, as founded by Hugh de Pudsey, bishop of Durham and earl of Northumberland.

In the beginning of Queen Mary he was forced to fly beyond the seas, and became the principal pastor (for they had three other) of the English exiles at Aarau in Switzerland; which congregation I behold as the least, so the freest, from factions of any in that age of our nation. He was, saith my author,[5] *Virtutum in omni mansuetudine seminator;* and

(1) Sandys was archbishop of York 1576—1588. He had supported the cause of Lady Jane Grey, was imprisoned, and on release escaped to the continent, returning in 1559. (2) Others make this of far later date. [The Pilkingtons were lords of the manor 1202-1605. "My good friend Master William Ryley" was a herald and archivist who supported the parliamentarians, probably treacherously. He proclaimed Charles II at the Restoration, and was buried in Westminster Abbey, 1667.] (3) This was the rebellion of the northern earls, 1569, against Elizabeth's religious innovations. (4) Pilkington was the first protestant bishop of Durham. (5) Bale.

besides some sermons and *A Meditation upon the Lord's Prayer* he wrote a book intituled *The Right Pathway to Christ.* [*d.* 1577]

JOHN DEE, where born [1527] I cannot recover, was a man of much motion and is mentioned in this place, where he had his (though last) best fixation. He was bred, as I believe, in Oxford, and there doctorated, but in what faculty I cannot determine.

He was a most excellent mathematician and astrologer, well skilled in magic, as the ancients did, the Lord Bacon doth, and all may accept the sense thereof, viz., in the lawful knowledge of natural philosophy.

This exposed him, anno 1583, amongst his ignorant neighbours, where he then lived, at Mortlake in Surrey, to the suspicion of a conjurer; the cause, I conceive, that his library was then seized on, wherein were four thousand books, and seven hundred of them manuscripts. This indignity, joined with the former scandal, moved him to leave the land, and go over with Sir Edward Kelley into Bohemia, as hereafter shall be more fully related.[1]

Returning to Mortlake, 1592, the same scandal of being a conjurer haunted him again. Two years after, viz., 1594, he was under a kind of restraint, which caused him to write to the Lady Scydemore to move Queen Elizabeth either that he might declare his case to the council, or have liberty under the broad seal to depart the land. Next year he wrote an apologetical letter to Archbishop Whitgift, which it seems found good reception; yea, at last he gave such satisfaction of the lawfulness and usefulness of his studies, that the queen (besides many considerable new year's gifts sent unto him) presented him warden of Manchester in this county, 1595, where he had many contests and suits with the fellows of that college.

The last mention I find of him is in Mr. Camden, to whom he presented an ancient Roman inscription found about Manchester; and Mr. Camden, in his requital, presented him with this commendation: *Hanc mihi descripsit, qui vidit, Cl. Mathematicus, J. Dee, Collegii Manchestrensis custos.*

And indeed all the books he hath left behind him speak him a *learned,* as those *De usu Globi Terrestris, De Nubium, Solis, Lunae, ac Planetarum distantiis,* &c., an *aged* man, being dedicated to King Edward the Sixth, and he dying about the beginning of King James.[2] [*d.* 1608]

MATTHEW HUTTON. I have given a large account of him formerly in my *Church History*. However, having since received an exact annary, as I may so say, from his nearest relation, of his life, I will here insert an abridgment thereof.

1. Being son to Matthew Hutton of Priest Hutton in this county, he was born Anno Domini 1529. 2. He came to Cambridge in the 17th year

(1) See Sir Edward Kelley's life in Worcestershire [p. 629.] (2) Dee, though shunned by all classes of society because of his evil reputation as a sorcerer (acquired largely through his clever stage effects in a performance of Aristophanes at Cambridge) was a man of remarkable learning, and highly esteemed by Elizabeth. His adaptation of Pope Gregory XIII's calendar, sponsored by the government, was finally rejected by the bishops, and thus delayed reform by 170 years.

of his age, anno 1546, the 38th of King Henry the Eighth. 3. Commenced bachelor of arts 1551; master of arts 1555. 4. Chosen Margaret professor of divinity, December 15, anno 1561, in the 4th of Queen Elizabeth. 5. In the same year commenced bachelor of divinity. 6. Elected master of Pembroke Hall, May the 12th; and the same year, September the fifth, admitted regius professor, anno 1562. 7. Answered a public act before Queen Elizabeth and her court at Cambridge, anno 1564. 8. Married in the same year Catherine Fulmetby (niece to Thomas Goodrich, late bishop of Ely) who died soon after. 9. Made dean of York anno 1567. 10. Married for his second wife Beatrice Fincham, daughter to Sir Thomas Fincham of the Ise of Ely. 11. Resigned his mastership of Pembroke Hall, and his professor's place to Dr. Whitgift, April 12, anno 1567. 12. Married Frances, widow of Martin Bowes, son of Sir Martin Bowes, alderman of London, Nov. 20, 1583. 13. Chosen bishop of Durham, June 9, Anno Domini 1589. 14. Confirmed by the dean and chapter, July 26. 15. Consecrated by John [Whitgift] archbishop of York, July 27. 16. Translated to York, and consecrated at Lambeth, anno 1596, the thirty-seventh of Queen Elizabeth, by John [Whitgift] archbishop of Canterbury and others, March 24. 17. He died in January 1606, in the 76th year of his age.

He gave an hundred marks to Trinity College in Cambridge, and founded an hospital at Warton in this county. In a word, he was a learned prelate, lived a pious man, and left a precious memory.

RICHARD BARNES was born [1532] at Bold near Warrington in this county;[1] bred at Brasenose College in Oxford, and afterwards advanced suffragan bishop of Nottingham; thence he was preferred to Carlisle, 1570, and seven years after to Durham. He was himself one of a good nature (as by the sequel will appear) but abused by his credulity and affection to his brother John Barnes, chancellor of his diocese.

> A man, of whom it is hard to say, whether he was more lustful, or more covetous; who, whereas he should have been the man who ought to have reformed many enormities in the diocese, was indeed the author of them, permitting base and dishonest persons to escape scot-free for a piece of money, so that the bishop had a very ill report everywhere.[2]

By the suggestion of this ill instrument, the patriarchal man Mr. Gilpin[3] fell into this bishop's displeasure, and by him was suspended from his benefice. But the good bishop afterwards restored him, and visiting him at his house, took him aside into the parlour, and thus accosted him: "Father Gilpin, I acknowledge you are fitter to be bishop of Durham than myself to be parson of this church of yours; I ask forgiveness for errors passed; forgive me, father; I know you have hatched up some chickens that now seek to pick out your eyes, but so long as I shall live bishop of Durham, be secure, no man shall injure you."[4]

This bishop sat about eleven years in his see, and died a very aged man, a little before the Spanish invasion, Anno Domini 1587.

(1) Out of a manuscript of the great antiquary, Mr. Dodsworth. (2) Bishop Carleton, in the *Life* of Mr. Gilpin. (3) See Westmorland, p. 599. (4) Bishop Carleton, in the *Life* of Mr. Gilpin.

WILLIAM ALLEN was born [1532] in this county (saith my author[1]) *nobilibus parentibus,* of gentle parentage. He was bred in Oriel College in the university of Oxford, and became head of St. Mary's Hall therein. Then going beyong the seas, he became king's professor at Douay, canon of Cambray and Rheims, and at last, by Pope Sixtus Quintus, made cardinal priest of St. Martin's in Rome, 1587, and deserved his red hat by his good service the year after against his native country.[2] But hear what different characters two authors of several persuasions bestow upon him. "He was somewhat above an ordinary man in stature, comely of countenance, composed in his gait, affable in all meetings; and for the gifts of his mind, pious, learned, prudent, grave, and though of great authority, humble, modest, meek, patient, peaceable; in a word, beautified and adorned with all kinds of virtues."[3] "He was the last of our English cardinals in time, and first in wickedness; deserving not to be counted among Englishmen, who, as another Herostratus, to achieve himself a name amongst the grandees of earth, endeavoured to fire the church of England, the noblest (without envy be it spoken) in the Christian world, so that his memory deserveth to be buried in oblivion."[4]

He collected the English exiles into a body, and united them in a college, first at Douay, then at Rheims; so great an advancer, that we may behold him as founder of that seminary. He died at Rome, anno 1594; and preferred rather to be buried in the English school, than in the church of St. Martin's, which gave him the title of cardinal.

JOHN WOOLTON [or WOLTON] was born [1535?] at Wigan in this county, of honest parents, and worshipful by his mother's side. He was bred a short time in Oxford, and in the reign of Queen Mary, attended his uncle Alexander Nowell in his flight beyond the seas. Returning into England, he was made first canon residentiary, and after, anno 1578, bishop of Exeter, being an earnest assertor of conformity against opposers thereof. He met whilst living with many hard speeches, but after his death (when men's memories are beheld generally in their true colours) he was restored to his deserved esteem, even by those who formerly had been his adversaries. He indited letters, full of wisdom and piety, becoming the strength of one in health, not two hours before his death, which happened March the 13th, 1594. It is a part, though not of his praise, of his happiness, that his daughter was married to Francis Godwin bishop of Hereford,[5] whose learned pen hath deserved so well of the Church of England.

LAURENCE CHADERTON was born [1537?] at Chadderton in this county, of ancient and wealthy parentage, but much nuzzled up in popish superstition. He was intended for a lawyer, and in order thereunto, brought up some time in the Inns of Court, till he changed his profession, and admitted himself in Christ's College in Cambridge. His father, hearing that he had altered his place, studies and religion, sent him a poke with a

(1) Pits. (2) He supported Philip of Spain's claim to the English throne, and was made cardinal so that, should Philip prove successful in conquering England, he could reconcile the country to the Roman church. (3) Pits. (4) Godwin, in his Catalogue of Cardinals. (5) See Northamptonshire, p. 437.

groat therein, for him to go a-begging therewith; disinheriting him of that fair estate which otherwise had descended upon him. But God, who taketh men up when their fathers and mothers forsake them, provided him a comfortable subsistence, when chosen fellow of the college. He was for many years lecturer at Saint Clement's in Cambridge, with great profit to his auditors; afterwards made, by the founder, first master of Emmanuel. He was chosen by the noncomformists to be one of their four representatives in Hampton Court conference, and was afterwards employed one of the translators of the Bible.

He had a plain but effectual way of preaching. It happened that he visiting his friends, preached in this his native county, where the word of God (as in the days of Samuel) was very precious, and concluded his sermon, which was of two hours' continuance at least, with words to this effect, "that he would no longer trespass upon their patience." Whereupon all the auditory cried out (wonder not if hungry people craved more meat) "For God's sake, sir, go on, go on." Hereat Mr. Chaderton was surprised into a longer discourse, beyond his expectation, in satisfaction of their importunity, and (though on a sudden) performed it to their contentment and his commendation. Thus constant preachers, like good housekeepers, can never be taken so unprovided, but that (though they make not a plentiful feast) they can give wholesome food at a short warning.

He commenced doctor in divinity, when Frederick Prince Palatine (who married the Lady Elizabeth) came to Cambridge. What is said of Mount Caucasus, that it was never seen without snow on the top, was true of this reverend father, whom none of our father's generation knew in the university before he was grey-headed, yet he never used spectacles till the day of his death, being ninety-four years of age. [*d.* 1640]

RICHARD BANCROFT was born [1544] at Farnworth in this county,[1] bred in Jesus College in Cambridge, and was afterwards, by Queen Elizabeth, made bishop of London, by King James, archbishop of Canterbury. Indeed he was in effect archbishop whilst bishop, to whom Doctor Whitgift, in his decrepit age, remitted the managing of matters, so that he was the soul of the high commission.

A great statesman he was, and grand champion of church discipline, having well hardened the hands of his soul, which was no more than needed for him who was to meddle with nettles and briars, and met with much opposition. No wonder if those who were silenced by him in the church were loud against him in other places.

He cancelled his first will, wherein he had bequeathed much to the church, which gave the occasion for scurrilous pens to pass on him:

> He who never repented of doing ill,
> Repented that once he made a good will.

Whereas indeed, suspecting an impression of popular violence on cathedrals, and fearing an alienation of what was bequeathed unto them,

(1) So I find in the manuscript of Mr. Dodsworth; and so Mr. Richard Line (this archbishop's servant lately deceased) did inform me.

he thought fit to cancel his own, to prevent others cancelling his testament. This partly appears by his second will, wherein he gave the library at Lambeth, the result of his own and three predecessors' collections, to the university of Cambridge, which now they possess, in case the archiepiscopal see should be extinct.

How came such a jealousy into his mind? What fear of a storm, when the sun shined, the sky clear, no appearance of clouds? Surely his skill was more than ordinary in the complexion of the commonwealth, who did foresee what afterward, for a time, came to pass. This clause, providentially inserted, secured this library in Cambridge during the vacancy of the archiepiscopal see; and so prevented the embezzling, at the least the dismembering thereof, in our late civil distempers. He died Anno Domini 1610, and lieth buried at the church in Lambeth.

WILLIAM WHITAKER,[1] born [1548] at Holme in the county of Lancaster, of good parentage, especially by his mother's side, was allied to two worshipful families. His reverend uncle, Alexander Nowell, dean of St. Paul's (the first fruits of the English confessors in the days of Queen Mary, who after her death first returned into England from beyond the seas) took him young from his parents, sent him first to Paul's school, thence to Trinity College in Cambridge, where he so profited in his studies that he gave great promises of his future perfection.

His prime appearing to the world, was when he stood for the professor's place against two competitors, in age far his superiors. But the seven electors in the university who were to choose the emperor of the schools, preferring a golden head before silver hairs, conferred the place on Whitaker; and the strict form of their election hath no room for corruption. He so well acquitted himself in the place, that he answered expectation, the strongest opponent in all disputes and lectures, and by degrees taught envy to admire him.

He filled the chair with a graceful presence, so that one needed not to do with him as Luther did with Melancthon when he first heard him read, abstract the opinion and sight of his stature and person, lest the meanness thereof should cause an undervaluing of him: for our Whitaker's person carried with it an excellent port. His style was manly for the strength, maidenly for the modesty, and elegant for the phrase thereof, shewing his skill in spinning a fine thread out of coarse wool, for such is controversial matter. He had by his second wife, a modest woman, eight children.

My father hath told me that he often wished that he might lose so much learning as he had gotten in after-supper studies, on condition he might gain so much strength as he had lost thereby. Indeed his body was strongly built for the natural temper, and well repaired by his temperate diet and recreations; but first he foundered the foundation of this house by immoderate study, and at last the roof was set on fire by a hot disease. Thus he lost the health of his body in maintaining that the

(1) Fuller gives no account of him, excusing himself because he had twice previously written of him. The account above is extracted from the life in the *Holy State*. Whitaker was an important exponent of Calvinism in his time. He was regius professor of divinity at Cambridge, 1580-1595.

health of the soul could not be lost. He died in the 47th year of his age, Anno Dom. 1595, and in St. John's College, whereof he was master, was solemnly interred, with the grief of the university and whole church of God.

THOMAS WORTHINGTON was born [1549] in this county, of a gentle family; was bred in the English college at Douay, where he proceeded bachelor in divinity, and a little before the eighty-eight was sent over into England as an harbinger for the Spanish invasion, to prepare his party thereunto. Here he was caught and cast into the Tower of London, yet found such favour that he escaped with his life, being banished beyond the seas.

At Trier he commenced doctor in divinity, and in process of time was made president of the English College at Rheims. When, after long expectation, the Old Testament came out in English at Rheims (permitted with some cautions for our lay-catholics to read) this Worthington wrote his notes thereupon, which few protestants have seen, and fewer have regarded. [*d.* 1622?]

If not the same (which, for his vivaciousness, is improbable) there was a Father Worthington, certainly his kinsman and countryman, very busy to promote the catholic cause in England, about the beginning of King Charles. He dining, some thirty years since, with a person of honour in this land (at whose table I have often eaten) was very obstreperous in arguing the case for transubstantiation and the ubuiquitariness of Christ's body. "Suppose," said he, "Christ were here." To whom the noble master of the house (who till then was silent) returned, "If you were away, I believe he would be here." Worthington perceiving his room more welcome than his company, embraced the next opportunity of departure.

EDWARD RISHTON was born [1550] in this county, and bred some short time in Oxford, till he fled over to Douay, where he was made master of arts. Hence he removed to Rome, and having studied divinity four years in the English college there, was ordained priest 1580. Then was he sent over into England to gain proselytes, in prosecution whereof he was taken and kept prisoner three years. Yet was the severity of the state so merciful unto him, as to spare his life, and only condemn him to banishment.

He was carried over into France, whence he went to the university of Pont-à-Mousson in Lorraine to ply his studies. During his abode there the place was infected with the plague. Here Rishton forgat the physicians' rule, *Cito, procul, longe, tarde* (fly away soon, live far away, stay away long, come again slowly); for he remained so long in the town, till he carried away the infection with him, and, going thence, died at Ste.-Ménehould 1586. I presume no ingenious papist will be censorious on our painful Munster, learned Junius, godly Greenham, all dying of the pestilence, seeing the most conscientious of their own persuasion subject to the same; and indeed neither love nor hatred can be collected from such casualties. [*d.* 1586]

THOMAS JONES was born [1550?] in this county; bred master of arts in Cambridge, but commenced doctor of divinity in the university in Dublin. He was first chancellor, then dean of St. Patrick's in that city, and thence was made bishop of Meath, anno 1584, and the next month appointed by Queen Elizabeth one of her privy council in Ireland. Hence he was translated to be archbishop of Dublin, anno 1605, and at the same time was by King James made chancellor of Ireland, which office he discharged thirteen years, dying April 10, 1619.

As he was a good officer for the king, he was no bad one for himself, laying the foundation of so fair an estate that Sir Roger Jones, his son, was by King Charles created Viscount Ranelagh. Thus, whilst the sons of the clergymen in England never mounted above the degree of knighthood, two of the clergymen in Ireland attained to the dignity of peerage.[1] I say no more, but good success have they with their honour, in their persons and posterity.

MARTIN HETON was born [1552] in this county (as by his epitaph on his monument, lately set up by his daughters in the church of Ely, may appear) and bred first a student, then a canon of Christ Church, on whom Queen Elizabeth bestowed the bishopric of Ely, after twenty years' vacancy thereof. Now although his memory groweth under the suspicion of simoniacal compliance, yet this due the inhabitants of Ely do unto him, that they acknowledge him the best housekeeper in that see within man's remembrance. He died July 14, 1609, leaving two daughters, married in those knightly families of Fish and Filmer.

ROGER FENTON, D.D., fellow of Pembroke Hall in Cambridge, was born [1565] in this county, as appeareth by his epitaph in St. Stephen's, Walbrook, London, being the painful, pious, learned and beloved minister thereof. Little is left of him in print, save a solid treatise against usury.[2] Great was his intimacy with Dr. Nicholas Felton, being contemporaries, collegiates, and city ministers together, with some similitude in their surnames, but more sympathy in their natures.

Once my own father gave Dr. Fenton a visit, who excused himself from entertaining him any longer. "Mr. Fuller," said he, "hear how the passing bell tolls at this very instant for my dear friend Dr. Felton, now a-dying; I must to my study, it being mutually agreed upon betwixt us in our healths, that the survivor of us should preach the other's funeral sermon." But see a strange change. God, "to whom belongs the issues from death," was pleased (with the patriarch Jacob blessing his grandchildren) "wittingly to guide his hands across, reaching out death to the living and life to the dying." So that Dr. Felton recovered, and not only performed that last office to his friend Dr. Fenton, but also survived him more than ten years, and died bishop of Ely. Roger Fenton died in the fiftieth year of his age, Anno Domini 1616, buried in his own church, under a monument at the expense of the parish.

(1) The other, Viscount Loftus of Ely, son [actually nephew] to Archbishop Loftus.—F. (2) He was one of the translators of the Authorized Version.

JOHN SMITH was born at ——— in this county; bred in Magdalene College, in Cambridge, whereof he became fellow, and proctor of the university, when past sixty years of age; when the prevaricators gave him this homonymous salute, "Ave, Pater."

This man could not fiddle, could not tune himself to be pleasant and plausible to all companies, but he could, and did make that little college great wherein he had his education.

Indeed Edward Stafford duke of Buckingham, the first founder thereof, gave it little more than a name. The Lord Audley bestowed on it a new name, with little buildings and less endowment. Magnificent Dr. Neville for a time was master thereof, but (according to the fashion of the world, the rich shall still have more) his affections were all for Trinity College, to which he was afterwards removed.

Only Mr. Smith, by his long life and thrifty living, by what he gave to and what he saved for the college, so improved the condition thereof, that though he left it *lateritium* as he found it, yet what he found poor and empty, he left ruch and full of scholars.

Nor must we forget his painfulness, when with Dr. Gouge he solicited the suit called Magdalene College Case; nor yet his patience when he lay so long in the Fleet for refusing to submit to an order of Chancery (fearing their cause would be prejudiced thereby); so that he may be called the confessor of the college. From inconsiderable income, he raised by his carefulness considerable profit to the fellows of that house; and by observing the statutes, brought the college into such reputation for learning, that yearly it afforded one or more eminent scholars. In a word, he was a true servant to the college all his life, and at his death, to which he bequeathed all he had, six hundred pounds at least, and died Anno Domini 163—.

ROBERT BOLTON was born at Blackburn in this county on Whitsunday 1572, a year as infamous for the massacre of many protestants in France, so for the birth of some eminent in England. His parents having a narrow estate, struggled with their necessities to give him liberal education; and he was bred first in Lincoln, then in Brasenose College in Oxford. His want of means proved an advancement unto him, for, not having whence to buy books, he borrowed the best authors of his tutor, read over, abridged into note-books, and returned them. He was as able to express himself in Latin, or Greek, as English, and that *stylo imperatorio*. He was chosen one of the disputants before King James at his first coming to the university, and performed it with great applause.

Thus far I have followed my author mentioned in the margin,[1] but now must depart from him a little in one particular. Though Mr. Bolton's parents were not overflowing with wealth, they had a competent estate (as I am informed by credible intelligence) wherein their family had comfortably continued long time in good repute.

Sir Augustine Nicolls[2] presented him to the rectory of Broughton in Northamptonshire; sending him his presentation unexpectedly, from

(1) See the particulars justified in his Life at large, written by my worthy friend Edward Bagshawe. (2) See Northamptonshire, p. 436.

his chamber in Sergeant's Inn, where Dr. King, bishop of London, being accidentally present, thanked the judge for his good choice, but told him withal that he had deprived the university of a singular ornament. Besides his constant preaching, he hath left behind him many useful books, the witnesses of his piety and learning, and died in the 59th year of his age, December 17, 1631.

JOHN WEEVER was born [1576] at ——— in this county; bred in Queens' College in Cambridge under Dr. John Person, his worthy tutor. He was very industrious in the study of antiquity, and composed a useful book of *Funeral Monuments* in the diocese of Canterbury, Rochester, London and Norwich. He died in London in the fifty-sixth year of his age, and was buried in St. James's, Clerkenwell, where he appointed this epitaph for himself:

Lancashire gave me breath,
And Cambridge education.
Middlesex gave me death,
And this church my humation.
And Christ to me hath given
A place with him in heaven.

[*d.* 1632]

[LAURENCE] ANDERTON [alias SCROOP], whose Christian name I cannot recover, was born [1577] in this county, and brought up at Blackburn school therein; and (as I have been informed) he was bred in Christ's College in Cambridge, where for his eloquence he was commonly called Golden-mouth Anderton. Afterwards he went beyond the seas, and became a popish priest, and one of the learnedest amongst them.

This is he who, improving himself on the poverty of Mr. Robert Bolton,[1] sometime his schoolfellow (but then not fixed in his religion, and fellow of Brasenose College) persuaded him to be reconciled to the church of Rome, and go over with him to the English seminary, promising him gold enough, a good argument to allure an unstable mind to popery; and they both appointed a meeting. But it pleased the God of heaven, who holdeth both an hour-glass and reed in his hand to measure both time and place, so to order the matter that though Mr. Bolton came, Mr. Anderton came not accordingly; so that Rome lost, and England gained an able instrument. But now I have lost J. Pits to guide me, and therefore it is time to knock off, having no direction for the date of his death. [*d.* 1643]

GEORGE CLARKE, haberdasher, a plain honest man, just, temperate and frugal; and according to his understanding (which in the world's esteem was not great) devout, a daily frequenter of the prayers in the college church, and the hearer of sermons there. Not long before the breaking forth of our civil dissensions, dying without issue, he made the poor his heir, and did give them one hundred pounds per annum in good lands, lying in a place called Crumpsall, within a mile of Manchester. I have not yet attained the certain date of his death.

(1) See p. 305, above.

HUMPHREY CHETHAM, third son of Henry Chetham of Crumpsall, gentleman, is thought (on just ground) to descend from Sir Jeffrey Chetham of Cheetham, a man of much remark in former days; and some old writings, in the hands of worshipful persons not far remote from the place, do evidence as much; but the said Sir Jeffrey falling in troublesome times into the king's displeasure, his family (in effect) was long since ruinated.

But it seems his posterity was unwilling to fly far from their old (though destroyed) nest, and got themselves a handsome habitation at Crumpsall hard by, where James, elder brother to this Humphrey Chetham, did reside. The younger brethren, George, Humphrey and Ralph, betook to the trading of this county, dealing in Manchester commodities sent up to London; and Humphrey signally improved himself in piety and outward prosperity. He was a diligent reader of the scriptures and of the works of sound divines; a respecter of such ministers which he accounted truly Godly, upright, sober, discreet and sincere. He was high sheriff of this county 1635, discharging the place with great honour, insomuch that very good gentlemen of birth and estate did wear his cloth at the assize, to testify their unfeigned affection to him; and two of them, of the same profession with himself, have since been sheriffs of the county.[1]

Grudge not, reader, to go through so long a porch, for I assure thee it leads unto a fair palace, to as great a master-piece of bounty as our age hath afforded. This Mr. Chetham, by his will bearing date the 16th January 1651, gave £7000 to buy a fee-simple estate of £420 for ever, for the education of forty poor children in Manchester at school, from about six till fourteen years of age, when they are to be bound out apprentices. They must be the children of poor but honest parents; no bastards, nor diseased at the time wherein they are chosen; not lame or blind; in regard the town of Manchester hath ample means already (if so employed) for the maintenance of such impotents. Indeed, he intended it for a seminary of religion and ingenuity, where the aforesaid boys were to have diet, lodging, apparel and instruction. He gave £1000 for books to a library, and £100 to prepare a place for them. He bequeathed £200 to buy books (such as he himself delighted in) for the churches of Manchester, Bolton and other chapels thereabouts. He gave the remainder of his estate (debts and legacies first paid) to the increase of the books in the library.

Now as the loaves in the Gospel multiplied in the breaking, so Mr. Chetham's estate did not shrink, but swell, in the calling of it in, insomuch that the aforesaid surplusage is known to be the better part of two thousand pounds. Dying a bachelor, he appointed George Chetham, esquire, citizen and grocer of London (wherefore he was chosen alderman, 1656, and fined[2] for the same) and Edward Chetham, gentleman, executors of his will and testament. God send us more such men, that we may dazzle the eyes of the papists with the light of protestant good works. And know, reader, I am beholding for my exact information

(1) John Huntley and H. Wrigley, esquires. (2) *Fined*=escaped (by payment) the duties of alderman.

herein to my worthy friend Mr. Johnson, late preacher of the Temple, and one of the feoffees appointed by Mr. Chetham for the uses aforesaid. [1580-1653]

GEORGE WALKER was born [1581?] at Hawkshead in Furness of religious parents. Being visited when a child with the smallpox, and the standers-by expecting his dissolution, he started up out of a trance with this ejaculation, "Lord, take me not away till I have shewed forth thy praises," which made his parents devote him to the ministry after his recovery.

He was bred B.D. in St. John's College in Cambridge, where he attained to be well skilled in the oriental tongues, an excellent logician and divine. Mr. Foster (formerly his tutor) resigned unto him his living of St. John the Evangelist, London, wherein Mr. Walker continued the painful preacher well nigh forty years, refusing higher preferment often proffered him. Dr. Felton (the same morning he was elected bishop of Ely) made him his chaplain, and Dr. Featley chose him his second in one of his disputations against Father Fisher; yea, Mr. Walker alone had many encounters with the subtilest of the Jesuitical party.

He was a man of a holy life, humble heart, and bountiful hand, who deserved well of Sion College library; and by his example and persuasion, advanced about a thousand pounds towards the maintenance of preaching ministers in this his native county. He ever wrote all his sermons, though making no other use of his notes in the pulpit than keeping them in his pocket, being wont to say that he thought he should be out if he had them not about him. His sermons, since printed, against the profanation of the sabbath, and other practices and opinions, procured him much trouble, and two years' imprisonment, till he was released by the parliament. He died in the seventieth year of his age, Anno Domini 1651.

THE FAREWELL

I am informed that Pilling Moss is the fountain of fuel (turf) in this county, and is conceived inexhaustible by the vicinage. May it prove so. But if it should chance to fail, may God's grace (which the vulgar, in their profane proverb, equally yoke therewith) I say, may God's grace never be drained to those that stand in need thereof.

And because this county may be called the cockpit of conscience, wherein constant combats betwixt religion and superstition, may the contest betwixt them prove like the morning twilight, wherein, after some equal conflict betwixt them, the light gaineth the final conquest of the darkness.

One word more to this shire, and I have done. Let me be the remembrancer, that Hugh of Manchester in this county wrote a book in the reign of King Edward the First intituled *De Fanaticorum Deliriis* (*Of the Dotages of Fanatics.*) At which time an impostor had almost made Eleanor the queen-mother mad by reporting the posthume miracles done by her husband, King Henry the Third, till this our Hugh settles her judgment aright. I could wish some worthy divine (with such Lancashire doth abound) would resume this subject, and shew how ancient and modern fanatics, though differing much in their wild fancies and opinions, meet together in a mutual madness and distraction.

LEICESTERSHIRE

THIS county is (though not exquisitely) circular in the form, whilst Leicester, the shire town, is almost the exact centre thereof, and the River Soar, diameter-like, divides it into two equal halves, having Lincoln and Rutland on the east, Derby and Nottinghamshire on the north, Warwickshire on the west, and Northamptonshire on the south. It extendeth from north to south thirty and three miles (measured from the utmost angle) but exceedeth not twenty-seven in the breadth thereof.

Here, to avoid all offence, we will collect the quality of this soil from a native thereof,[1] who may be presumed exact in this quadri-partition.

SOUTH-WEST. Rich ground, plentiful in corn and pasture, but wanting wood, forcing the inhabitants to make use of straw, cowshern, &c.

NORTH-WEST. For the most part hard and barren, yielding fruit not without labour and expense, but well stored with wood and pit-coal.

NORTH-EAST. Good soil, apt to bear corn and grass, and sufficiently provided with fuel.

SOUTH-EAST. Much like the last for fruitfulness, and of the two, better furnished with fuel.

However, these four quarters, being put together into the body of one shire, competently supply their mutual defects.

NATURAL COMMODITIES

BEANS

Plenty of these in this county, especially about Barton-on-the-Beans, in the hundred of Sparkenhoe, where they appear like a forest toward the time of harvest. Wherefore the scouts of Charles duke of Burgundy, who mistook a field full of high thistles, near unto Paris, for the army of the king of France with their lances held upright, might here commit the like mistake with more probability. Though beans be generally beheld but as horse and hog-grain, yet were they man's meat even in the plentiful country of Canaan, called *pholl* in the Hebrew, whence some deduce the word *pulse,* though none dare affirm that Daniel's pulse was made thereof. But more of this grain hereafter.[2]

COAL

These are digged up plentifully at Coleorton, in the hundred of West Goscote. I say Coleorton, for there is another village called Cold Overton in this shire, an addition which no less truly than sadly would be prefixed to most towns in this county, if not warmed in winter with this underground fuel, that above ground is so much decayed.

I confess **Θησαυρος ἀνθρακῶν** (a treasure of coals) passeth both in the Greek and Latin proverb for a frustrated expectation; and his hopes

(1) Burton, in his *Description of Leicestershire*. (2) In the proverb of "Bean-belly Leicestershire" p. 312.

fall very low, who, looking for gold, either in specie or in ore, lighteth only on a heap of coals, which anciently used to be buried in the earth, for boundaries or limits of lands. However, such mines of coals are these, without any help of alchemy, are quickly turned into gold and silver, sold at good rates to the counties round about.

THE MANUFACTURES

In this county are not to be expected, for where the husbandman's acre-staff and the shepherd's hook are, as in this county, in *state,* there they engross all to themselves, and command manufactures to observe their distance from them.

THE BUILDINGS

This county affordeth no cathedrals, and as for the parish churches therein, they may take the eye, not ravish the admiration of the beholder. Bottesford is one of the primest, very fair and large, with a high spire steeple. At the suppression of abbeys, many ancient monuments of the Albanies and Rosses were removed hither out of the priory of Belvoir, by the command of Thomas earl of Rutland, and pity it was that his commendable care was not imitated in other places.

As for civil structures, there is a seeming parity betwixt many fair houses in this shire, only something monarchial (above the ordinary aristocracy of fabrics) appears in the height, strength and workmanship of the Stone Tower built by William Lord Hastings at Ashby de la Zouch. Also the fair, large and beautiful palace built at Bradgate by Thomas Grey marquess of Dorset challengeth the pre-eminence above the rest.

THE WONDERS

There is a village in this county named Carlton, surnamed Curlieu, and all that are born therein have a harsh and rattling kind of speech, uttering their words with much difficulty and wharling in the throat, and cannot well pronounce the letter R. Surely this proceedeth not from any natural imperfection in the parents (whence probably the tribual lisping of the Ephraimites did arise); because their children born in other places are not haunted with that infirmity. Rather it is to be imputed to some occult quality in the elements of that place. Thus a learned author informeth us, that some families at Lablonne in Guienne in France do naturally stut and stammer, which he taketh to proceed from the nature of the waters.[1]

As for the inability distinctly to pronounce R, it is a catching disease in other counties. I knew an Essex man,[2] as great a scholar as any in our age, who could not for his life utter *Carolus Rex Britanniae* without stammering. The best was, the king had from him in his hearty prayers what he wanted in his plain pronounciation.

My father hath told me, that in his time a fellow of Trinity College, probably a native of Carlton in this county, sensible of his own imperfection herein, made a speech of competent length, with selected

(1) Jo. Bodin, Method. Hist. (2) Mr. Joseph Mede [see Essex, p. 182.]

words both to his mouth and for his matter, without any R therein, to shew that men may speak without being beholden to the dog's letter.

PROVERBS

Bean-belly Leicestershire. So called from the great plenty of that grain growing therein. Yea, those in the neighbouring counties use to say merrily, "Shake a Leicestershire yeoman by the collar, and you shall hear the beans rattle in his belly"; but those yeomen smile at what is said to rattle in their bellies, whilst they know good silver ringeth in their pockets.

Indeed I read a Latin proverb, *A fabis abstineto* (forbear beans) whereof some make a civil interpretation, "Meddle not with matters of state," because anciently men cast in a bean when they gave their suffrages in public elections. Others expound it physically, because beans are windy, and discompose the tranquillity of men's minds by the flatuous evaporation; the reason assigned for the general report that Pythagoras prohibited the eating of them by his scholars. Yet an excellent author informs me, that Pythagoras had his repast on beans more than on any other kind of pulse.[1]

However, nothing will put Leicestershire men out of conceit of their beloved beans, the rather because their plenty argueth the goodness of their ground, for whereas lean land will serve for puling peas and faint fetches, it must be a strong and fruitful soil indeed where the masculine beans are produced.

THE WORTHIES

WALTER LANGTON was born at West Langton in this county. He was highly in favour with King Edward the First, under whom he was bishop of Coventry and Lichfield, and treasurer of England. He granted him also liberty of free-warren in West and Thorpe Langton in this county, the patrimonial inheritance of this prelate. With his own innocence and friends' assistance, at long sailing he weathered out the tempest of the pope's displeasure. Longer did he groan under the undeserved anger of King Edward the Second, chiefly because this bishop sharply reproved him, when as yet but prince, for his debauchery.

See here the great difference betwixt youth, some hopefully, some desperately riotous. Of the former was Henry the Fifth, who when king is said to have rewarded and advanced such who had reproved and punished him when prince. Of the latter was King Edward, not only wild, but mad in his viciousness. But our Langton at length was bought, saith my author,[2] *in regis semi-gratiam* (into the king's half favour); let me add, *et in populi sesque-gratiam* (and into the people's favour and half) who highly loved and honoured him.

(1) Aristoxenus apud Aulum Gellium. (2) T. Walsingham [Langton was Edward I's favourite but not too scrupulous councillor. In 1301 he was charged with adultery, pluralism, simony and intercourse with the devil, but absolved in 1303. Edward II arrested him, seized his great wealth, and imprisoned him (without regard for a churchman's immunities from secular jurisdiction) for misdemeanours as treasurer, to be released four years later and partly restored to favour because Edward required his able services as treasurer.]

His tragi-comical life had a peaceable end in plenty and prosperity. He found his cathedral of Lichfield mean, and left it magnificent; and it will appear by the instance of our Langton, Jocelin of Wells and others, that bishops continuing unremoved in their see have achieved greater matters than those who have been often translated, though to richer bishoprics. Indeed prodigious was his bounty in building and endowing his cathedral, wherein he continued almost twenty-five years; and dying 1321, was buried in the chapel of Saint Mary, of his own erection.

ROGER DE MARTIVALL, son and heir to Sir Anketin de Martivall, knight (who gave for his arms *Argent a cinquefoil Sable*) was born at Noseley in this county. He was first archdeacon of Leicester, then dean of Lincoln, and at last consecrated bishop of Salisbury in the reign of King Edward the Second, 1315. Now seeing Bishop Godwin hath nothing more of him save his name and date, it is charity further to inform posterity that he was the last heir male of his house, and founded a college at Noseley, temp. Edw. I, for a warden and certain brethren, which in the 24th of Henry VI was valued to dispend yearly (besides all charges) £6 13s. 4d.[1] His estate descended to Joyce de Martivall his sister, married unto Sir Ralph Hastings, lineal ancestor to the now earl of Huntingdon. As for the manor of Noseley, as it came by the mother, so it went away with her daughter, into the family of the Herons; and by her daughter into the family of the Hesilriges, who at this day are possessors thereof. This bishop died in the midst of Lent, 1329.

SIR JOHN DE [PULTENEY or] POULTNEY, knight, was born in this county, at Poultney in the parish of Misterton; bred in the city of London, and became four times lord mayor thereof. He built a college, to the honour of Jesus and Corpus Christi, for a master and seven chaplains in Saint Laurence church in Candleweek Street in London, in the 20th of Edward the Third, which church was after denominated of him Saint Laurence Pountney.

He built the parish church of Allhallows the Less in Thames Street, and the monastery of White Friars in Coventry, and a fair chapel on the north side of Saint Paul's in London, where he lieth buried, who died 1349, the 24th year of Edward the Third. He was a great benefactor to the hospital of Saint Giles by Holborn, and gave many great legacies to the relief of prisoners and the poor.[2]

HENRY KNIGHTON [or CNITTHON] was born at Knighton in this county; sometime abbot of Leicester, who wrote his *History* from William the Conqueror to the time of King Richard the Second, in whose reign he died.[3]

It seemeth *Lelandus non vidit omnia,* nor his shadow Bale, nor his shadow Pits; all three confessing that the history of this Knighton never came to their hands; whereas of late it hath been fairly printed with

(1) This was actually founded by his father. (2) This very wealthy mayor frequently advanced money to Edward III. (3) The 5th book of this history, carrying the story down to 1395, is by another hand. Knighton flourished in Edward III's, not Richard II's reign.

other historians, on the commendable cost of Cornelius Bee. Thus it is some comfort and contentment to such, whom nature hath denied to be mothers, that they may be dry nurses, and dandle babes in their laps, whom they cannot bear in their wombs. And thus this industrious stationer (though no father) hath been foster-father to many worthy books, to the great profit of posterity. [*fl.* 1363]

ROBERT DE WYVILE was born of worthy and wealthy parentage at Staunton Wyville in this county. At the instance of Philippa, queen to King Edward the Third, the pope, anno 1329, preferred him bishop of Salisbury. It is hard to say whether he were more dunce or dwarf, more unlearned or unhandsome, insomuch that T. Walsingham tells us that had the pope ever seen him (as no doubt he felt him in his large fees) he would never have conferred the place upon him.

He sate bishop more than forty-five years, and impleaded William de Montacute earl of Salisbury in a writ of right for the castle of Salisbury. The earl chose the trial by battle, which the bishop accepted of, and both produced their champions into the place. The combatant for the bishop coming forth all clad in white, with the bishop's own arms, viz., *Gules fretty Vaire, a chief Or,* impaled no doubt with them of his see, on his surcoat.

Some highly commended the zeal of the bishop asserting the rights of his church, whilst others condemn this in him as an unprelatical act, God allowing duels no competent deciders of such differences. And moderate men, to find out an expedient, said he did this not as a bishop, but baron. The best was, the matter was taken up by the king's interposing; and the bishop, with 2,500 marks, bought of the earl the quiet possession of the castle; and died Anno Domini 1375, being buried under a marble stone about the middle of the quire.

WILLIAM OF WOODFORD. I cannot fix his nativity with any certainty, because so many Woods and Fords (and would the former did continue as well as the latter) and consequently so many towns called Woodfords in England. He is placed here, because his surname in this age flourished in great eminency in this county. He was bred a Franciscan; and though bilious Bale giveth him the character of *Indocte Doctus,* we learn from Leland that he was one of profound learning, and Thomas Waldensis owneth and calleth him *magistrum suum,* his master.

Indeed Woodford sent him the first copy of railing against Wycliffe, being deputed by Thomas Arundel archbishop of Canterbury to confute, publicly in writing, his opinions. [*fl.* 1381-1390]

SIR ROBERT DE BEALKNAP. Being bred in the study of the laws, he became chief justice of the common pleas, October the 8th, in the 48th of King Edward the Third; and so continued till the general rout of the judges, in the wonder-working parliament, the eleventh of Richard the Second, when he was displaced on this occasion.

The king had a mind to make away certain lords, viz., his uncle the duke of Gloucester, the earls of Arundel, Warwick, Derby, Nottingham,

&c., who in the former parliament had been appointed governors of the kingdom. For this purpose, he called all the judges before him to Nottingham, where the king's many questions in fine were resolved into this, "Whether he might by his regal power revoke what was acted in parliament." To this all the judges, Sir William Skipwith alone excepted, answered affirmatively, and subscribed it.

This Bealknap underwrote unwillingly, as foreseeing the danger, and putting to his seal said these words: "There wants nothing but an hurdle, an horse and an halter to carry me where I may suffer the death I deserve; for if I had not done this, I should have died for it, and because I have done it, I deserve death for betraying the lords."[1]

Yet it had been more for his credit and conscience to have adventured a martyrdom in the defence of the laws, than to hazard the death of a malefactor in the breach thereof. But judges are but men, and most desire to decline that danger which they apprehend nearest unto them.

In the next parliament, all the judges were arrested in Westminster Hall of high treason, when there was a vacation in term time, till their places were re-supplied. Sir R. Tresilian, chief justice of the king's bench, was executed; the rest, thus named and reckoned up in the printed statutes—Robert de Bealknap, John Holt, John Cary, William Burgh, Roger Fulthorp, all judges and knights, with J. Locktan, serjeant-at-law—had their lands (save what were entailed) with their goods and chattels, forfeited to the king; their persons being banished, and they, by the importunate intercession of the queen, hardly escaping with their lives.

[*d.* 1400?]

WILLIAM [BARON] HASTINGS. The reader needeth not my dim candle to direct him to this illustrious person. He was son to Sir Leonard Hastings (sheriff two years before); and was he whom King Edward the Fourth, or rather Edward Plantaganet (because more in his human than royal capacity) so delighted in, that he made him his lord chamberlain, Baron Hastings of Ashby de la Zouche, &c. As he loved the king very well, so after this king's death he is charged to have loved Jane Shore too well; and Richard duke of Gloucester, perceiving him to obstruct the way to his ambitious designs, ordered his removal, causing him to be beheaded, 1 Edward V.[2] As when living he was dear, so being dead his corpse are near to Edward IV, buried under a very fair monument in Windsor Chapel.

[1430?-1483]

JOHN POULTNEY, born in Little Sheppey, was herein remarkable, that in his sleep he did usually rise out of his bed, dress himself, open the doors, walk round about the fields, and return to his bed not wakened. Sometimes he would rise in his sleep, take a staff, fork or any other kind of weapon that was next his hand, and therewith lay about him, now

(1) Bealknap had protested strongly against the whole proceeding, but yielded after being threatened with death. Sir William Skipwith (see Lincolnshire, p. 330) mentioned above was not present. (2) Jane Shore, who had been Edward IV's mistress, was taken into protection by Lord Hastings after the king's death. When Gloucester made himself protector for the minority of Edward V, Hastings was hurriedly executed without a trial. He was a staunch Yorkist and had served Edward IV well.

striking, now defending himself, as if he were then encountered or charged with an adversary, not knowing (being awaked) what had passed. He afterwards went to sea with that famous but unfortunate Sir Hugh Willoughby, knight, and was (together with all the fleet) frozen to death in the north-east passage, about Nova Zembla. [*d.* 1554]

HUGH LATIMER was born [1485?] at Thurcaston in this county. What his father was, and how qualified for his state, take from his own mouth, in his first sermon before King Edward, being confident the reader will not repent his pains in perusing it.

My father was a yeoman, and had no lands of his own; only he had a farm of three or four pounds a year at the uttermost; and hereupon he tilled so much as kept half a dozen men. He had walk for an hundred sheep, and my mother milked thirty kine. He was able, and did find the king an harness, with himself and his horse, whilst he came unto the place that he should receive the king's wages. I can remember I buckled his harness when he went to Blackheath field. He kept me to school, or else I had not been able to have preached before the king's majesty now. He married my sisters with five pounds, or twenty nobles, a-piece, so that he brought them up in godliness and fear of God. He kept hospitality for his poor neighbours, and some alms he gave to the poor. And all this did he of the same farm, where he that now hath it payeth sixteen pounds by the year and more, and is not able to do anything for his prince, for himself, nor for his children, or give a cup of drink to the poor.

He was bred in Christ's College in Cambridge, and converted, under God, by Mr. Bilney, from a violent papist to a zealous protestant. He was afterwards made bishop of Worcester, and four years after ousted for refusing to subscribe the Six Articles.[1] How he was martyred at Oxford, 1555, is notoriously known.

Let me add this appendix to his memory. When the contest was in the House of Lords, in the reign of King Henry the Eighth, about the giving all abbey lands to the king, there was a division betwixt the bishops of the Old and New learning, for by those names they were distinguished. Those of the Old learning, unwillingly willing, were contented that the king should make a resumption of all those abbeys which his ancestors had founded, leaving the rest to continue according to the intention of their founders. The bishops of the New learning were more pliable to the king's desires. Only Latimer was dissenting; earnestly urging, that two abbeys at the least in every diocese, of considerable revenues, might be preserved for the maintenance of learned men therein. Thus swimming a good while against the stream, he was at last carried away with the current.

LADY JANE GREY, eldest daughter of Henry Grey, duke of Suffolk, by Frances Brandon, eldest daughter to Mary, second sister to King Henry the Eighth, was born [1537] at Bradgate, near unto Leicester. No lady, which led so many pious, lived so few pleasant days; whose soul was never out of the nonage of afflictions, till death made her of full years to inherit happiness, so severe her education.

(1) Act of Six Articles—see note, p. 30.

Whilst a child, her father's was to her a house of correction; nor did she write *woman* sooner than she did subscribe *wife;* and in obedience to her parents, was unfortunately matched to the Lord Guildford Dudley; yet he was a goodly, and (for aught I find to the contrary) a godly gentleman, whose worst fault was that he was son to an ambitious father.

She was proclaimed, but never crowned queen, living in the Tower, which place, though it hath a double capacity of a palace and a prison, yet appeared to her chiefly in the latter relation. For she was longer a captive than a queen therein, taking no contentment all the time, save what she found in God and a clear conscience.

Her family, by snatching at a crown which was not, lost a coronet which was their own; much degraded in degree, and more in estate. I would give in an inventory of the vast wealth they then possessed, but am loath to grieve her surviving relations with a list of the lands lost by her father's attainture. She suffered on Tower Hill, 1554, on the twelfth of February.

CATHARINE GREY [COUNTESS OF HERTFORD, *b.* 1538?] was second daughter to Henry duke of Suffolk. 'Tis pity to part the sisters, that their memories may mutually condole and comfort one another. She was born in the same place, and (when her father was in height) married to Henry Lord Herbert, son and heir to the earl of Pembroke; but the politic old earl, perceiving the case altered, and what was the highway to honour, turned into the ready road to ruin, got pardon from Queen Mary, and brake the marriage quite off.

This Heraclita, or Lady of Lamentation, thus repudiated, was seldom seen with dry eyes for some years together, sighing out her sorrowful condition, so that though the roses in her cheeks looked very wan and pale, it was not for want of watering. Afterward Edward Seymour earl of Hertford married her privately without the queen's licence, and concealed, till her pregnancy discovered it.

Indeed our English proverb, "It is good to be near akin to land," holdeth in private patrimonies, not titles to crowns, where such alliances have created to many such molestation. Queen Elizabeth beheld her with a jealous eye, unwilling she should match either foreign prince or English peer, but follow the pattern she set her of constant virginity.

For their presumption, this earl was fined fifteen thousand pounds, imprisoned with his lady in the Tower, and severely forbidden her company. But love and money will find or force a passage. By bribing the keeper, he bought (what was his own) his wife's embraces, and had by her a surviving son, Edward, ancestor to the right honourable the duke of Somerset. She died January 27th, a prisoner in the Tower, 1568, after nine years' durance therein.[1]

MARY GREY [LADY MARY KEYS, *b.* 1540?] the youngest daughter, frighted with the infelicity of her two elder sisters, Jane and this Catherine, forgot her honour to remember her safety, and married one whom she could

(1) Catharine Grey and her husband (who was the son of Protector Somerset) were imprisoned under the act of 1536 which made it treason for a person of royal blood to marry without the sovereign's consent. The marriage was declared invalid. She actually died, still a prisoner, at Cockfield Hall in Suffolk.

love and none need fear, Thomas Keys, of Kent, esq., who was a judge at court (but only of doubtful casts at dice, being serjeant-porter) and died without issue, the 20th of April, 1578.[1]

SIR ROBERT CATLIN, descended from the ancient family of the Catlins of Raunds in Northamptonshire (as doth appear by the heralds' visitation) was born at Beeby in this county.[2] He was bred in the study of the municipal laws, profiting so well therein, that in the first of Queen Elizabeth, he was made lord chief justice of the king's bench. His name hath some allusion to the Roman senator who was the incendiary of that state, though in nature far different, as who by his wisdom and gravity was a great support to his nation.

One point of law I have learned from him, at the trial of Thomas duke of Norfolk, who pleaded out of Bracton that the testimonies of foreigners (the most pungent that were brought against him) were of no validity. Here Sir Robert delivered it for law, "that in case of treason, they might be given in for evidence; and that it rested in the breast of the peers, whether or no to afford credit unto them."

He had one (as what man hath not many) fancy, that he had a prejudice against all those who write their names with an *alias;* and took exceptions at one in this respect, saying "that no honest man had a double name, or came in with an *alias.*" The party asked him what exceptions his lordship could take at Jesus Christ, *alias* Jesus of Nazareth.

He died in the sixteenth year of Queen Elizabeth [1574]; and his coat of arms (viz., Partie per chevron Azure and Or, three lions passant gardant counterchanged, a chief pearl) is quartered by the right honourable the Lord Spencer earl of Sunderland; this judge's daughter and sole heir being married to his ancestor.

Some forty years since, a gentleman of his name and kindred had a cause in the upper bench, to whom the chief justice therein said, "Your kinsman was my predecessor in the court, and a great lawyer." "My lord (replied the gentleman) he was a very honest man, for he left a small estate." But indeed, though his estate was not considerable, compared to his successors then present, it was in itself of a good valuation.

HENRY NOEL, esquire. I will incur the reader's deserved displeasure if he appear not, most memorable in his generation. He was younger son to Sir Andrew Noel of Dalby in this county, who for person, parentage, grace, gesture, valour, and many excellent parts (amongst which, skill in music) was of the first rank in the court. And though his lands and livelihood were small, having nothing known certain but his annuity and pension as gentleman to Queen Elizabeth, yet in state, pomp, magnificence and expenses, did ever equalize the barons of great worth. If any demand whence this preceeded, the Spanish proverb answers him, "That which cometh from above, let no man question."

(1) Keys, a widower with several children, was a huge person, and Mary almost a dwarf. She and her sister Catharine were maids of honour to Queen Elizabeth, who had kept close watch over their matrimonial plans, and was very incensed by the marriage. Keys was sent to the Fleet, and Mary was successively under the charge of various persons. Keys was liberated in 1568 and died in 1571; Mary was allowed out of custody in 1573. (2) So I have learned by his relations.

Being challenged by an Italian gentleman to play balloon,[1] he so heated his blood, that falling into a fever, he died thereof, and, by her majesty's appointment, was buried in the abbey of Westminster, and chapel of Saint Andrew, anno 1597.

JOHN DUPORT, D.D., son to Thomas Duport, esquire, was born at Sheepshed in this county; bred fellow, then master of Jesus College in Cambridge; once proctor, and thrice vice-chancellor of that university. He was one of the translators of the Bible, and a reverend man in his generation, who bestowed the perpetual advowson of the rectory of Harleton on the college. Men generally in Scripture are notified by their fathers, seldom by their sons, as Simon of Cyrene, father of Alexander and Rufus, persons (no doubt) of signal worth in that age. Thus this doctor is remarkable for his son (by Rachel daughter to Richard Cox bishop of Ely) James Duport, D.D., fellow of Trinity College, and lately Greek professor; happy in the education of many hopeful pupils of worship and honour, as they more happy in so able a tutor.[2] His father, Dr. John Duport, deceased 1617.

ROBERT SMITH, citizen and merchant tailor of London, was born at Market Harborough in this county, and became comptroller of the chamber of London, and one of the four attorneys in the mayor's court. A painful person in his place; witness the many remaining monuments of his history, whilst he acted in his office, betwixt the years 1609 and 1617. Nor was his piety any whit beneath his painfulness, who delivered to the chamberlain of London, seven hundred and fifty pounds to purchase lands for the maintenance of a lecturer in the town of his nativity, as also for several other pious uses, as in the settlement of those lands are particularly expressed. He died, as I collect, about 1618.

JOSEPH HALL was born [1574] at Ashby-de-la-Zouch in this county, where his father, under the earl of Huntingdon, was governor or bailiff of the town. So soon almost as Emmanuel College was admitted into Cambridge, he was admitted into that college, within few years after the first foundation thereof. He passed all his degrees with great applause. First noted in the university for his ingenious maintaining (be it truth or paradox) that *mundus senescit* (the world groweth old); yet in some sort his position confuteth his position, the wit and quickness whereof did argue an increase rather than a decay of parts in this latter age.

He was first beneficed by Sir Robert Drury at Hawstead in Suffolk; and thence removed by Edward Lord Denny (afterward earl of Norwich) to Waltham Abbey in Essex. Here I must pay the tribute of my gratitude to his memory, as building upon his foundation, beholding myself as his great-grandchild in that place, three degrees from him in succession, but oh, how many from him in ability! His little catechism hath done great good in that populous parish, and I could wish that ordinance more generally used all over England.

(1) *Balloon* = a game in which a large leather ball was struck to and fro by the arm, which was protected by a stout guard. (2) Lived 1606-1679; ejected from his professorship by the parliamentarians and reinstated at the Restoration.

Being doctor of divinity, he was sent over by King James to the synod of Dort, whence only indisposition of body forced him to return before the rest of his colleagues. He was preferred first, dean of Worcester, then bishop of Exeter, then bishop of Norwich, then bishop of no place, surviving to see his sacred function buried before his eyes.[1] He may be said to have died with his pen in his hand, whose writing and living expired together. He was commonly called our English Seneca[2] for the pureness, plainness and fulness of his style; not unhappy at controversies, more happy at comments, very good in his characters, better in his sermons, best of all in his meditations. Nor will it be amiss to transcribe the following passage out of his will:

> In the name of God, Amen. I Joseph Hall, D.D., not worthy to be called bishop of Norwich, &c. First, I bequeath my soul, &c. My body I leave to be interred, without any funeral pomp, at the discretion of my executors; with this only monition, that I do not hold God's house a meet repository for the dead bodies of the greatest saints.

He died September the 8th, Anno Domini 1656, and was buried at Heigham near Norwich.

WILLIAM BURTON, esquire, son of Ralph Burton of Lindley in this county (who had a more ancient inheritance belonging to his name at Falde in Staffordshire) a place remarkable, because no adder, snake or lizard (common in the confines) were ever seen therein; as if it were a land-island, and an Ireland in England. This William was born at Lindley, August 24, 1575; bred in Brasenose College, and wrote an alphabetical description of the towns and villages in this county, with the arms and pedigrees of the most ancient gentry therein. The sparks of his ingenuity herein have since set fire on Mr. Dugdale, my worthy friend, to do the like to Warwickshire (lately under one sheriff with Leicestershire) and I hope in process of time they may inflame many others into imitation, that so (give me leave to match an English and Greek word together) the *county-graphy* of our land may be completed.[3]

[*d.* 1645]

ROBERT BURTON, his younger brother, born Feb. 8, 1577, afterwards student of Christ Church, Oxon, and bachelor of divinity. He wrote an excellent book, commonly called *Democritus Junior,* of the *Anatomy of Melancholy* (none to the native to describe a country) wherein he hath piled up variety of much excellent learning. On whose tomb is this epitaph:

Paucis notus, paucioribus ignotus;
Hic jacet Democritus junior,
Cui vitam pariter et mortem
Dedit Melancholia.

(1) By 1640 the puritan struggle with episcopacy had provoked a crisis. In 1642 the Long Parliament excluded bishops from the House of Lords and abolished episcopacy. Hall, then Bishop of Norwich, was impeached and imprisoned, his revenues sequestrated and his cathedral desecrated. In 1647 he was expelled from his palace. He has a claim to be considered as the first of English satirists. (2) Sir H. Wotton, in his Letter to Dr. Collins. (3) Burton, author of the *Description of Leicestershire,* presented Leland's invaluable manuscripts to the Bodleian in 1631. Fuller gives no account of Leland, the earliest of modern English antiquaries, to whom he owed a great deal, as his references testify.

Scarce any book of philology in our land hath in so short a time passed so many impressions. He died [1640] rector of Seagrave (presented by his patron George Lord Berkeley) in this county.

GEORGE VILLIERS [DUKE OF BUCKINGHAM] was born [1592] at Brooksby in this county, fourth son to his father Sir George Villiers, and second son to his mother Mary Beaumont. Being debarred (by his late nativity) from his father's lands, he was happy in his mother's love, maintaining him in France, till he returned one of the completest courtiers in Christendom, his body and behaviour mutually gracing one another.

Sir Thomas Lake may be said to have ushered him into the English court, whilst the Lady Lucy, countess of Bedford, led him by the one hand, and William earl of Pembroke by the other, supplying him with a support far above his patrimonial income. The truth is, Somerset's growing daily more wearisome, made Villiers hourly more welcome to King James.

Soon after, he was knighted, created successively baron, Viscount Villiers, earl, marquess, duke of Buckingham; and to bind all his honours the better together, the noble Garter was bestowed upon him. And now offices at court (not being already void) were voided for him. The earl of Worcester was persuaded to part with his place of master of the horse, as the earl of Nottingham with his office of admiral, and both conferred on the duke.

He had a numerous and beautiful female kindred, so that there was hardly a noble stock in England into which one of these his scions was not grafted. Most of his nieces were matched with little more portion than their uncle's smiles, the forerunner of some good office or honour to follow on their husbands. Thus with the same act did he both gratify his kindred, and fortify himself with noble alliance.

It is seldom seen that two kings (father and son) tread successively in the same tract as to a favourite; but here King Charles had as high a kindness for the duke as King James. Thenceforward he became the plenipotentiary in the English court, some of the Scottish nobility making room for him by their seasonable departure out of this life. The earl of Bristol was jostled out, the bishop of Lincoln cast flat on the floor, the earls of Pembroke and Carlisle content to shine beneath him, Holland behind him, none even with, much less before him.

But it is generally given to him who is the little god at the court to be the great devil in the country. The commonalty hated him with a perfect hatred, and all miscarriages in church and state, at home, abroad, at sea and land, were charged on his want of wisdom, valour or loyalty.

John Felton, a melancholy malcontented gentleman, and a sullen soldier, apprehending himself injured, could find no other way to revenge his conceived wrongs, than by writing them with a point of a knife in the heart of the duke, whom he stabbed at Portsmouth, Anno Domini 1628. It is hard to say how many of this nation were guilty of this murder, either by public praising, or private approving thereof.

His person from head to foot could not be charged with any blemish, save that some hypercritics conceived his brows somewhat over-pendulous, a cloud which in the judgment of others was by the beams of his eyes sufficiently dispelled. The reader is remitted for the rest of his character to the exquisite epitaph on his magnificent monument in the chapel of Henry the Seventh.

RICHARD VINES was born [1600?] at Blaston in this county, and bred in Magdalene College in Cambridge, where he commenced master of arts. Now although many healthful souls in their age break out in their youth, he was never given to any extravagance. Hence he was chosen schoolmaster of Hinckley in this county, a profession wherein many a good minister hath been (and it is pity that any but a good man should be) employed. Entering the ministry after other intermediate places (such as are his censurers would be his compurgators, if privy to the weighty causes of his just removal) he was fixed at last at Saint Lawrence Jewry in London.

An excellent preacher, skilful to cut out doctrines in their true shape, naturally raised, to sew them up with strong stitches, substantially proved, and set them on with advantage on such backs who should wear them, effectually applied.

He was one (yea, I may say one of seven score) in the assembly, the champion of their party, therefore called their Luther, much employed in their treaties at Uxbridge and Isle of Wight. His majesty, though of a different judgment, valued him for his ingenuity, seldom speaking unto him without touching (if not moving) his hat; which by Master Vines was returned (though otherwise blunt and unobservant) with most respectful language and gestures; which I will not say was done by all his fellow divines there present.

He was most charitably moderate to such as dissented from him, though most constant to his own principles; witness his forsaking of his mastership of Pembroke Hall for refusing of the 'engagement.'[1] Such who charged him with covetousness are confuted with the small estate he left to his wife and children.

It seemeth that the sand in his hour-glass (though sticking high on each side) was but hollow in the middle, for it sunk down on sudden. Visible decays appeared in him a year before his death, though rather in his limbs than parts, spirits than spirit. But alas, the best mind can not make good music where the instrument of the body is out of tune; his speech grew very low. Not a week before his death, preaching in Saint Gregory's, a rude fellow cried out unto him, "Lift up your voice, for I cannot hear you," to whom Mr. Vines returned, "Lift you up your ears, for I can speak no louder."

Indeed his strength was much spent by his former pains, so that some suppose, had he wrought less, he had lived longer. He was buried Feb. the 7th, 1656, in his own parish church, where Mr. Jacombe modestly and learnedly performed his funeral sermon. Much lamented, as by many others, so by his own parish, where he piously endeavoured to make them all of one piece who were of different colours, and to unite their judgments who dissented in affections.

(1) The "engagement" of 1649 whereby all beneficed clergymen were required to be faithful to the Commonwealth.

JOHN CLEVELAND was born [1613] in this county at Hinckley (where his father was vicar) and bred therein under Mr. Richard Vines his schoolmaster. He was afterwards scholar of Christ's, then fellow of Saint John's, in Cambridge; and during the late civil wars was much conversant in the garrison of Newark, where, as I am informed, he had the place of advocate general.

A general artist, pure Latinist, exquisite orator, and (which was his master-piece) eminent poet. His epithets were pregnant with metaphors, carrying in them a difficult plainness, difficult at the hearing, plain at the considering thereof. His lofty fancy may seem to stride from the top of one mountain to the top of another, so making to itself a constant level and champaign of continued elevations.

Such who have *Clevelandized,* endeavouring to imitate his masculine style, could never go beyond the hermaphrodite, still betraying the weaker sex in their deficient conceits. Some distinguish between the *vein* and *strain* of poetry, making the former to flow with facility, the latter pressed with pains, and forced with industry. Master Cleveland's poems do partake of both, and are not to be the less valued by the reader, because most studied by the writer thereof. As for his anagram, John Cleveland (*Heliconean Dew*) the difficult trifle, I confess, is rather well endeavoured than exactly performed. He died on Thursday morning the 29th of April 1658, at his chamber in Gray's Inn, from whence his body was brought to Hunsdon House, and on Saturday, being May day, was buried at College Hill Church, Mr. John Pearson, his good friend, preaching his funeral sermon. He rendered this reason why he cautiously declined all commending of the party deceased, because such praising of him would not be adequate to any expectation in that auditory, seeing such who knew him not, would suspect it far above, whilst such who were acquainted with him did know it much beneath, his due desert. The selfsame consideration shall put a period to my pen in his present character; only this I will add, that never so eminent a poet was interred with fewer (if any remarkable) elegies upon him.[1]

THE FAREWELL

Being now to take my leave of this county, it is needless to wish it a Friday market (the Leap day therein, and it is strange there should be none in so spacious a shire) presuming that defect supplied in the vicinage. Rather I wish that the leprosy may never return into this county, but if it should return (we carry the seeds of all sins in our souls, sickness in our bodies) I desire that the lands may also (without prejudice to any) return to the hospital of Burton Lazars[2] in this shire, if not entire, yet in such a proportion as may comfortably maintain the lepers therein.

(1) Cleveland was a strong royalist. He had opposed Cromwell's election to the borough of Cambridge in 1640. He was imprisoned in 1655 but released by Cromwell's order. (2) Burton Lazars once possessed a Lazar House or Leper's Hospital (the principal one in England in mediæval times) and a mineral spring supposed to cure leprosy and other skin diseases.

LINCOLNSHIRE

THIS county, in fashion, is like a bended bow, the sea making the back, the rivers Welland and Humber the two horns thereof, whilst Trent hangeth down from the latter like a broken string, as being somewhat of the shortest. Such persecute the metaphor too much who compare the river Witham (whose current is crooked) unto the arrow crossing the middle thereof.

It extendeth 60 miles from south to north, not above 40 in the middle and broadest part thereof. Being too voluminous to be managed entire, it is divided into three parts, each of them corrival in quantity with some smaller shires: Holland on the south-east, Kesteven on the south-west, and Lindsey on the north to them both.

Holland, that is *Hoyland,* or *Hayland,* from the plenty of hay growing therein, may seem the reflection of the opposite Holland in the Netherlands, with which it sympathized in the fruitfulness, low and wet situation. Here the brackishness of the water, and the grossness of the air, is recompensed by the goodness of the earth, abounding with dairies and pasture. And as "God hath," to use the Apostle's phrase, "tempered the body together," not making it all eye or all ear (nonsense that the whole should be but one sense) but assigning each member the proper office thereof; so the same Providence hath so wisely blended the benefits of this county, that take collective Lincolnshire, and it is defective in nothing.

NATURAL COMMODITIES

Pikes

They are found plentifully in this shire, being the freshwater wolves; and therefore an old pond-pike is a dish of more state than profit to the owners, seeing a pike's belly is a little fishpond, where lesser of all sorts have been contained. Sir Francis Bacon alloweth it (though tyrants generally be short-lived) the survivor of all freshwater fish, attaining to forty years, and some beyond the seas have trebled that term. The flesh thereof must needs be fine and wholesome, if it be true what is affirmed, that in some sort it cheweth the cud, and yet the less and middle size pikes are preferred for sweetness before those that are greater. It breedeth but once (whilst other fishes do often) in a year; such the providence of nature, preventing their more multiplying, lest the waters should not afford subjects enough for their tyranny. For want of other fish, they will feed one on another; yea, what is four-footed shall be fish with them, if it once come to their jaws, biting sometimes for cruelty and revenge, as well as for hunger.

I have done with these pikes when I have observed (if I mistake not) a great mistake in Mr. Stow, affirming that pickerels were brought over (as no natives of our land) into England at the same time with carps, and both about the beginning of the reign of King Henry the Eighth. Now if pickerels be the diminutives of pikes (as jacks of pickerels) which none I conceive will deny, they were here many hundred years since, and probably of the same seniority with the rivers of England; for I find, in the bill of fare made at the prodigious feast at the installing of George Neville archbishop of York, anno 1465, that there was spent three hundred *lupi fluviatiles*, that is, river pikes, at that entertainment. Now seeing all are children before they are men, and pikes pickerels at the first, pickerels were more anciently in England than that author affirmeth them.

WILDFOWL

Lincolnshire may be termed the aviary of England for the wildfowl therein, remarkable for their, 1. *Plenty*; so that sometimes in the month of August three thousand mallards, with birds of that kind, have been caught at one draught, so large and strong their nets, and the like must be the reader's belief. 2. *Variety*; no man (no, not Gesmar himself) being able to give them their proper names, except one had gotten Adam's nomenclature of creatures. 3, *Deliciousness;* wildfowl being more dainty and digestible than tame of the same kind, as spending their gross humours with their activity and constant motion in flying.

Now as the eagle is called *Jovis ales,* so here they have a bird which is called the king's bird, namely, *Knut's,* sent for hither out of Denmark, at the charge and for the use of Knut, or Canutus, king of England. If the plenty of birds have since been drained with the fens in this county, what Lincolnshire lacks in her former fowl, is supplied in flesh (more mutton and beef) and a large *first* makes amends for a less *second* course. But amongst all birds we must not forget

DOTTERELS

This is *avis* γελοτοποιος, a mirth-making bird, so ridiculously mimical, that he is easily caught (or rather catcheth himself) by his over-active imitation. There is a sort of apes in India, caught by the natives thereof after this manner: they dress a little boy in his sight, undress him again, leave all the child's apparel behind them in the place, and then depart a competent distance. The ape presently attireth himself in the same garments, till the child's clothes become his chains, putting off his feet by putting on his shoes, not able to run to any purpose, and so is soon taken.

The same humour, otherwise pursued, betrayeth the dotterels. As the fowler stretcheth forth his arms and legs going towards the bird, the bird extendeth his legs and wings approaching the fowler, till surprised in the net. But it is observed, that the foolisher the fowl or fish (woodcocks, dotterels, codsheads, &c.) the finer the flesh thereof.

FEATHERS

It is a pity to part Lancashire ticking (lately spoken of) and Lincolnshire feathers, making so good beds together. I cannot find the first beginning of feather-beds. The Latin word *pulvinar* for a cushion, pillow or bolster, sheweth that the entrails of such utensils amongst the

Romans were made but of dust; and our English plain proverb *de puerperis* (they are in the straw) shows feather-beds to be of no ancient use amongst the common sort of our nation, and beds of down (the cream of feathers) are more modern than they. The feathers of this county are very good (though not so soft as such as are imported from Bordeaux in France); and although a feather passeth for the emblem of lightness itself, they are heavy enough in their prices to such as buy any quantity, and daily grow dearer.

PIPPINS

With these we will close the stomach of the reader, being concluded most cordial by physicians. Some conceive them to be of not above a hundred years seniority in England; however, they thrive best, and prove biggest (not Kentish excepted) in this county, particularly in Holland, and about Kirton therein, whence they have acquired addition of Kirton pippins, a wholesome and delicious apple; and I am informed that pippins grafted on a pippin stock are called *renates,* bettered in their generous nature by such double extraction.

MASTIFFS

This county breedeth choice mastiffs for the bull and bear, and the sport is much affected therein, especially about Stamford, whereof hereafter. What remaineth concerning mastiffs is referred to the same topic in Somersetshire.

Thus the three kinds of hunting,[1] which distinctly require fleetness, scent and strength, are completely performed in this county, by a breed therein which are answerably qualified. This I have inserted, because as to my native county in general, so to this in particular, I would not willingly do less right than what a stranger hath done thereunto.

THE BUILDINGS

Here the complaint of the prophet taketh no place, taxing men to live "in ceiled palaces, whilst the temple of God lay waste," no county affording worse houses, or better churches. It addeth to the wonder, that seeing in this soft county a diamond is as soon found as a flint, their churches are built of polished stones, no natives, but naturalized by importation from foreign parts.

I hope the inhabitants of this shire will endeavour to disprove the old proverb, "the nearer to the church the further from God," because they have substituted a better in the room thereof, viz., "the further from stone, the better the churches."

As for the cathedral of Lincoln, whose floor is higher than the roof of many churches, it is a magnificent structure, proportionable to the amplitude of the diocese. This I dare boldly say, that no diocese in Christendom affordeth two such rivers, Thames and Trent, for the southern and northern bounds; and two such universities, Cambridge

(1) In the original edition Fuller has some remarks on "fleethounds" and greyhounds, here omitted.

and Oxford, both in the content thereof before three small bishoprics[1] were carved out of it.

Amongst the houses of the nobility, I take signal notice of two. One I may call a premeditate building, viz., Tattershall (belonging to the right honourable the earl of Lincoln) advanced by degrees at several times to the modern magnificence thereof. But Grimsthorpe I may term an extempore structure, set up on a sudden by Charles Brandon duke of Suffolk, to entertain King Henry the Eighth in his progress into these parts. The hall therein was fitted to a fair suit of hangings, which the duke had by his wife Mary the French queen, and is now in the possession of the right honourable Montague earl of Lindsey.

THE WONDERS

At Fishtoft in this county, no mice or rats are found, insomuch that barns, built *party per pale*[2] in this and the next parish, on one side are annoyed, on the other side (being Fishtoft moiety) are secured from this vermin. Surely no piper (what is notoriously known of Hamelin in Westphalia) did ever give them this mice-delivery by his music.

It is easier to conjure up many than allay one difficulty; other places in England affording the like. At one of the Rodings in Essex no hogs will root, in another common no mole will cast; in Lindley in Leicestershire no snakes are found. I believe they overshoot the mark who make it a miracle; they undershoot it who make it magic; they come the nearest to truth who impute it to occult qualities.

Let it also pass (for this once) for a wonder, that some seven-score years since, nigh Harlaxton in this shire, there was found (turned up by one ploughing the ground) a golden helmet of antique fashion; I say *cassis non aurata, sed aurea* (a helmet not gilt, but of massive gold) studded with precious stones, probably of some prime Roman commander. Whence I observe, first, that though no edge tool to offend may be made of gold and silver, yet defensive weapons may thereof be compounded. Secondly, that the poetical fiction of Glaucus's golden arms is founded on history; for (not to speak of Solomon's golden shields) great commanders made use of arms of that metal, if not for strength, for state and ornament. Lastly, it was presented to Queen Catherine, first wife to King Henry the Eighth, who, though not knowing to use it as a helmet, knew how to employ it as made of gold and rich jewels.

PROVERBS

Lincolnshire bagpipes. I behold these as most ancient, because a very simple sort of music, being little more than the oaten pipe improved with a bag, wherein the imprisoned wind pleadeth melodiously for the enlargement thereof. It is incredible with what agility it inspireth the heavy heels of the country clowns, overgrown with hair and rudeness, probably the groundwork of the poetical fiction of dancing satyrs. This bagpipe, in the judgment of the rural Midases, carrieth away the credit

(1) Ely, Peterborough and Oxford.—F. (2) *Party per pale*=divided by a vertical line through the middle (heraldic term.)

from the harp of Apollo himself; and most persons approve the blunt bagpipe above the edge-tool instruments of drums and trumpets in our civil dissensions.

As loud as Tom of Lincoln. This shire carries away the *bell* for *round-ringing* from all in England, though other places may surpass it for *changes,* more pleasant for the variety thereof; seeing it may be demonstrated that twelve bells will afford more changes than there have been hours since the creation. Tom of Lincoln may be called the Stentor (fifty lesser bells may be made out of him) of all in this county.

As mad as the baiting bull of Stamford. Take the original hereof. William Earl Warenne, lord of this town in the time of King John, standing upon the castle walls of Stamford, saw two bulls fighting for a cow in the meadow, till all the butchers' dogs, great and small, pursued one of the bulls (being madded with noise and multitude) clean through the town. This sight so pleased the said earl, that he gave all those meadows (called the Castle Meadows) where first the bull duel began for a common to the butchers of the town (after the first grass was eaten) on condition that they find a mad bull, the day six weeks before Christmas day, for the continuance of that sport every year. Some think that the men must be mad as well as the bull, who can take delight in so dangerous a waste-time; whereby that no more mischief is done, not man's care but God's providence is to be praised.

THE WORTHIES

GILBERT OF SEMPRINGHAM . . . born [1083?] in this county, was of noble extraction, Jocelin his father being a knight, to whom he was eldest son, and heir to a great estate. In body he was very deformed, but of subtile wit and great courage. Travelling over into France, there he got good learning, and obtained leave from the pope to be founder of those Epicaene and Hermaphrodite convents, wherein monks and nuns lived together, as under one roof, but with partitions betwixt them.

Sure it was to him a comfort and credit (which is confidently related by credible authors) to see 13 convents, 700 monks, 1100 nuns (women out-superstition men) of his order, being aged one hundred and six years. He appointed the fair convent at Sempringham (his own rich inheritance) to be mother and prime residence of his new-erected order. He died anno 1189.[1]

SIR FREDERIC TILNEY, knight, had his chief residence at Boston in this county. He was a man of mighty stature and strength above the proportion of ordinary persons. He attended King Richard the First, Anno Domini 1191, to the siege of Acre in the Holy Land, where his achievements were such that he struck terror into the infidels. Returning home in safety, he lived and died at Terrington nigh Tilney in Norfolk, where the measure of his incredible stature was for many years preserved. Sixteen knights flourished from him successively in the male

(1) Gilbert of Sempringham's order was that of the Gilbertines, the only monastic order whose origin was purely English. He was a supporter of Becket against Henry II, but was held in great regard by the king and his queen. He was canonised 1202.

line, till at last their heir general being married to the duke of Norfolk, put a period to the lustre of that ancient family.

HUGH [SAINT HUGH OF LINCOLN, *b*. 1246?] was a child, born and living in Lincoln, who by the impious Jews was stolen from his parents, and in derision of Christ and Christianity, to keep their cruel hands in use, by them crucified, being about nine years old. Thus he lost his life, but got a saintship thereby; and some afterwards persuaded themselves that they got their cures at his shrine in Lincoln.

However, this made up the measure of the sins of the Jews in England, for which not long after they were ejected the land, or, which is the truer, unwillingly they departed themselves. And whilst they retain their old manners, may they never return, especially in this giddy and unsettled age, for fear more Christians fall sick of Judaism, than Jews recover in Christianity. This Hugh was martyred Anno Dom. 1255, on the 27th of July.[1]

WILLIAM OF LITTLINGTON was born, say some, at that village in Cambridgeshire; at a village so named in this county say others, with whom I concur, because he had his education at Stamford. He was by profession a Carmelite, and became the fifth provincial of his order in England. Monasteries being multiplied in that age, Gerardus a Frenchman, master-general of the Carmelites, in a synod at Narbonne deputed two English provincials of that order, to the great grievance of our Littlington, refusing to subscribe to the decisions of that synod. His stubbornness cost him an ex-communication from Pope Clement the Fifth, and four years' penance of banishment from his native country. Meantime our Littlington, living at Paris, acquired great credit unto himself by his lectures and disputations. At last he was preferred provincial of the Carmelites in Palestine (whence from Mount Carmel he fetched their original); and he himself best knew whether the depth of his profit answered the height of his honour therein, which I suspect, the rather because returning into England he died and was buried at Stamford, Anno Domini 1312.

JOHN BLOXHAM was born at that town in this county, and bred a Carmelite in Chester. I confess it is a common expression of the country-folk in this county, when they intend to character a dull, heavy, blundering person, to say of him, "he was born at Bloxholm;" but indeed our John, though there first encradled, had acuteness enough, and some will say activity too much for a friar. He advantageously fixed himself at Chester, a city in England, near Ireland, and not far from Scotland, much conducing to his ease, who was supreme prefect of his order through those three nations, for two years and a half; for afterwards he quitted that place, so great was his employment under King Edward the Second and Third, in several embassies into Scotland and Ireland; flourishing anno 1334

(1) The story of the crucifixion by Jews is probably a fabrication. Eighteen Jews were executed for the alleged crime, and about 100 others suffered imprisonment or fine.

WILLIAM AYSCOUGH was descended of a worshipful and very ancient family now living at Kelsey in this county, the variation of a letter importing nothing to the contrary. I have seen at Salisbury his arms, with allusion to the arms of that house, and some episcopal addition. Such likeness is with me a better evidence than the sameness, knowing that the clergy in that age delighted to disguise their coats from their paternal bearing. He was bred doctor of the laws, a very able man in his profession; became bishop of Sarum, confessor to King Henry the Sixth, and was the first (as T. Gascoigne relateth) of bishops who discharged that office, as then conceived, beneath the place. Some will say, if King Henry answered the character commonly received of his sanctity, his confessor had a very easy performance. Not so, for always the most conscientious are the most scrupulous in the confession of their sins, and the particular enumeration of the circumstances thereof.

It happened that Jack Cade with his cursed crew (many of them being the tenants of this bishop) fell foul on this prelate at Edington in this shire. Bishop Godwin saith, *Illi quam ob causam infensi non habeo compertum;* he could not tell "why they should be so incensed against him." But I conceive it was because he was learned, pious and rich, three capital crimes in a clergyman.[1] They plundered his carriages, taking ten thousand marks (a mine of money in that age) from him; and then, to secure their riot and felony, by murder and high treason, dragged him as he was officiating from the high altar. And although they regarded difference of place no more than a wolf is concerned whether he killeth a lamb in the fold or field, yet they brought him out of the church to a hill hard by, and there barbarously murdered him, and tore his bloody shirt in pieces, and left his stripped body stark naked in the place:

Sic concussa cadit populari mitra tumultu,
Protegat optamus nunc diadema Deus.

By people's fury mitre thus cast down,
We pray henceforward God preserve the crown.

This his massacre happened June 29, 1450, when he had sate almost twelve years in the see of Salisbury.

SIR WILLIAM DE SKIPWITH was bred in the study of the laws, profitting so well therein that he was made, in Trinity term, lord chief-baron of the exchequer, in the thirty-fifth, continuing therein until the fortieth, of the reign of King Edward the Third. I meet not with anything memorable of him in our English histories; except this may pass for a thing remarkable, that at the importunity of John of Gaunt duke of Lancaster, this Sir William condemned William of Wykeham, bishop of Winchester, of crimes rather powerfully objected than plainly proved against him; whereupon the bishop's temporals were taken from him, and he denied access within twenty miles of the king's court. [*fl.* 1354-1380]

(1) There was much discontent with bishops at this time of Cade's rebellion. The rioters at Salisbury cried, "He has always stayed at court and never lived among us or kept open house; let him die." In the same year Bishop Moleyns of Chichester was killed by a turbulent mob at Portsmouth.

[JOHN] BOSTON OF BURY, for so he is generally called. I shall endeavour to restore him first to his true name, then to his native county. Some presume Boston to be his Christian, 'of Bury' his surname. But seeing Boston is no font-name, and godfathers were conscientious in those days (I appeal to all English antiquaries) in imposing, if not Scripture or saints' names, yet such as were commonly known (the Christianizing of surnames to baptized infants being of more modern device) we cannot concur with their judgment herein. And now thanks be to Doctor John Caius, who, in the catalogue of his author cited in the defence of the antiquity of Cambridge, calleth him John Boston of Bury, being born at and taking his surname from Boston in this county (which was customary for the clergymen in those days) though he lived a monk in Bury. Thus in point of nativities Suffolk hath not lost, but Lincolnshire hath recovered, a writer belonging unto it.

He travelled all over England, and exactly perused the library in all monasteries, whereby he was enabled to write a catalogue of ecclesiastical writers, as well foreign as English, extant in his age. Such his accurateness, as not only to tell the initial words in every of their books, but also to point at the place in each library where they are to be had. John Leland oweth as much to this John Boston, as John Bale doth to him and John Pits to them both. His manuscript was never printed, nor was it my happiness to see it; but I have often heard the late reverend archbishop of Armagh[1] rejoice in this, that he had, if not the first, the best copy thereof in Europe.

Sure it is that his writings are esteemed the rarity of rarities by the lovers of antiquities; which I speak in humble advice to the reader, if possessed thereof to keep and value them; if not, not to despise his books, if on any reasonable price they may be procured. This John Boston flourished Anno Domini 1410.

HENRY IV, eldest surviving son of John of Gaunt duke of Lancaster, was born [1367] at the castle of Bolingbroke in this county, and bred (according to the discipline of those days) in camp and court, in both which he proved a good proficient. By nature he was made more to command than obey, being ambitious, choleric, and withal courageous, cunning to catch, careful to keep, and industrious to improve all advantages.

Being nettled with some injuries received from King Richard the Second, he complotted with a good party of the nobility to depose him. Miscarriages in his government (many by mismanaging, more by the mis-succeeding of matters) exposed him to just exception, besides his own debauchery; and how easily is a dissolute government dissolved.

Having by the murder of King Richard achieved the government to himself, he reigned with much difficulty and opposition. Though his father was a great patron, *he* was a great persecutor of the Wycliffites, though not so much out of hatred to them as love to himself, thereby to be ingratiated with the clergy, then potent in the land.

(1) James Ussher (1581-1656). Fragments of the catalogue are in the British Museum, and extracts in the Lambeth Library. It was printed in 1748.

When duke he wore on his head an antique hood, which he cast not off when king, so that his picture is generally known by the crown super-added thereon. Lying on his death-bed, he was rather querulous than penitent, much complaining of his sufferings in keeping, nothing bewailing his sin in getting, the crown. Fire and faggot was first kindled in his reign in England to burn (pardon the prolepsis) poor protestants; and happy had it been had they been quenched at his death, which happened Anno Dom. 1413.

WILLIAM LYNDWOOD was born [1375?] at Linwood in this county, and proceeded doctor of the laws (probably rather by incorporation than constant education) in Oxford, long living a commoner in Gonville Hall in Cambridge. He was chancellor to the archbishop of Canterbury, keeper of the privy seal to King Henry the Sixth, and was employed in several embassies into Spain and Portugal. He wrote a learned comment on the English provincial constitutions, from Stephen Langton to Archbishop Chichele: and his pains at last was rewarded with the bishopric of St. David's, where he died 1446.

SIR WILLIAM HUSSEY [or HUSE], knight, was born, as I have cause to believe, in this county, where his name and family flourish in a right worshipful equipage. He was bred in the study of our municipal law, and attained to such eminency therein, that by King Edward the Fourth, in the one and twentieth of his reign, he was made lord chief justice of the king's bench.

King Henry the Seventh (who in point of policy was only directed by himself) in point of law was chiefly ruled by this judge, especially in this question of importance. It happened that in his first parliament many members thereof were returned who, being formerly of this king's party, were attainted, and thereby not legal to sit in parliament, being disabled in the highest degree, it being incongruous that they should make laws for others, who themselves were not inlawed. The king, not a little troubled therewith, remitted it as a case in law to the judges. The judges, assembled in the exchequer chamber, agreed all with Sir William Hussey (their speaker to the king) upon this grave and safe opinion, mixed with law and convenience, "that the knights and burgesses attainted by the course of law should forbear to come into the House, till a law were passed for the reversal of their attainders;" which was done accordingly. When at the same time it was incidentally moved, in their consultation, what should be done for the king himself, who likewise was attainted, the rest unanimously agreed with Sir William Hussey, "that the crown takes away all defects and stops in blood; and that, by the assumption thereof, the fountain was cleared from all attainders and corruptions." He died in Trinity term, in the tenth year of King Henry the Seventh. [*d.* 1495]

RICHARD FOXE was born [1448?] at Grantham in this county, as the fellows of his foundation in Oxford have informed me. Such who make it their only argument to prove his birth at Grantham, because he therein erected a fair free-school, may on the same reason conclude him born at Taunton in Somersetshire, where he also founded a goodly grammar school. But what shall I say? *Ubique nascitur qui orbi nascitur;* he may be said to be born everywhere, who with Foxe was born for the public and general good.

He was very instrumental in bringing King Henry the Seventh to the crown, who afterwards well rewarded him for the same. That politic prince (though he could go alone as well as any king in Europe) yet for the more state in matters of moment he leaned principally on the shoulders of two prime prelates, having Archbishop Morton for his right, and this Foxe for his left supporter, whom at last he made bishop of Winchester. He was bred first in Cambridge, where he was president of Pembroke Hall (and gave hangings thereunto with a fox woven therein) and afterwards in Oxford, where he founded the fair college of Corpus Christi (allowing per annum to it £401 8s. 11d.); which since hath been the nursery of so many eminent scholars. He expended much money in beautifying his cathedral in Winchester, and methodically disposed the bodies of the Saxon kings and bishops (dispersedly buried in this church) in decent tombs erected by him on the walls on each side the quire, which some soldiers, to show their spleen at once against crowns and mitres, valiantly fighting against the dust of the dead, have since barbarously demolished. Twenty-seven years he sat bishop of this see, till he was stark blind with age. All thought him to die too soon, one only excepted, who conceived him to live too long, viz., Thomas Wolsey, who gaped for his bishopric, and endeavoured to render him to the displeasure of King Henry the Eighth, whose malice this bishop, though blind, discovered, and in some measure defeated. He died Anno Domini 1528, and lies buried in his own cathedral.

SIR ROBERT DYMOKE. This Sir Robert Dymoke, at the coronation of King Henry the Seventh, came on horseback into Westminster Hall, where the king dined, and, casting his gauntlet on the ground, challenged any who durst question the king's right to the crown.

King Henry, being pleased to dissemble himself a stranger to that ceremony, demanded of a stander-by what that knight said? To whom the party returned, "He challengeth any man to fight with him, who dares deny your highness to be the lawful king of England." "If he will not fight such a one," said the king, "I will." And so sate down to dinner.[1]

[*d.* 1546]

EDMUND SHEFFIELD [FIRST BARON SHEFFIELD] descended from Robert Sheffield, recorder of London, knighted by King Henry the Seventh, 1487 . . . was born [1521] at Butterwick in the Isle of Axholme in this county, and was by King Edward the Sixth created baron thereof. Great his skill in music, who wrote a book of sonnets according to the Italian fashion. He may seem, swan-like, to have sung his own funeral, being soon after slain (or murdered rather) in a skirmish against the rebels in Norwich;[2]

(1) This Sir Robert Dymoke was also champion at the coronations of Richard III and Henry VIII. He distinguished himself at Tournay, 1513, in the war with France.
(2) Kett's rebellion against inclosures. The sonnets referred to are lost.

first unhorsed and cast unto a ditch, and then slaughtered by a butcher, who denied him quarter, 1549.

THOMAS GOODRICH was son of Edward Goodrich and Jane his wife, of Kirkby in this county, as appeareth by the Yorkshire visitation of heralds; in which county the allies[1] of this bishop seated themselves, and flourish at this day. He was bred in the university of Cambridge, D.D. say some; of law, say others, in my opinion more probable, because frequently employed in so many embassies to foreign princes, and at last made by King Henry the Eighth bishop of Ely (wherein he continued above twenty years) and by King Edward the Sixth lord chancellor of England. Nor will it be amiss to insert and translate this distich made upon him.

Et bonus et dives, bene junctus et optimus ordo;
Praecedit bonitas, pone sequuntur opes.

Both good and rich, well joined, best rank'd indeed:
For grace goes first, and next doth wealth succeed.

I find one pen spirting ink upon him[2] (which is usual in his writings) speaking to this effect, "that if he had ability enough he had not too much to discharge his office." I behold him as one well inclined to the protestant religion; and after his resignation of the chancellor's place to Stephen Gardiner, his death was very seasonable for his own safety, May 10, 1554, in the first of Queen Mary, whilst as yet no great violence was used to protestants.[3]

EDWARD FIENNES DE CLINTON, Lord Clinton, knight of the Garter [FIRST EARL OF LINCOLN, *b.* 1512], was lord admiral of England for more than thirty years; a wise, valiant and fortunate gentleman. The master-piece of his service was in Musselborough field, in the reign of King Edward the Sixth, and the battle against the Scots. Some will wonder, what a fish should do on dry land, what use of an admiral in a land fight. But know, the English kept themselves close to the shore, under the shelter of their ships; and whilst their arrows could do little, their spears less, their swords nothing, against the Scots (who appeared like a hedge of steel, so well armed and closed together) the great ordnance from their ships at first did all, making such destruction in the Scottish army, that though some may call it a land fight, it was first a victory from the sea, and then but an execution on the land.

By Queen Elizabeth (who honoured her honours by bestowing them sparingly) he was created earl of Lincoln, May 4th, 1572; and indeed he had breadth to his height, a proportionable estate, chiefly in this county, to support his dignity, being one of those who, besides his paternal inheritance, had much increased his estate. He died January the sixteenth, 1585, and lieth buried at Windsor in a private chapel, under a

(1) *Allies*=relations. (2) Sir John Hayward, in the *Life of King Edward the Sixth*. (3) Goodrich was a member of the commission that tried Gardiner (see Suffolk, p. 529) who was imprisoned during most of Edward VI's reign for his opposition to doctrinal changes. He was one of the compilers of the Book of Common Prayer.

stately monument, which Elizabeth his third wife, daughter to the earl of Kildare, erected in his remembrance.[1]

THOMAS WILSON, doctor of laws, was born [1525?] in this county; bred fellow of King's College in Cambridge; and afterwards was tutor in the same university to Henry and Charles Brandon, successively dukes of Suffolk. Hard shift he made to conceal himself in the reign of Queen Mary. Under Queen Elizabeth he was made master of the hospital of Saint Catherine's nigh the Tower of London, upon the same token that he took down the quire, which, my author saith (allow him a little hyperbole) was as great as the quire at Saint Paul's.[2] I am loth to believe it done out of covetousness, to gain by the materials thereof, but would rather conceive it so run to ruin that it was past repairing. He at last became secretary of state to Queen Elizabeth for four years together. It argues his ability for the place because he was put into it, seeing in those active times, under so judicious a queen, weakness might despair to be employed in such an office. He died Anno Domini 1581.[3]

ANTHONY GILBY was born in this county, and bred in Christ's College in Cambridge, where he attained to great skill in the three learned languages. But what gave him the greatest reputation with protestants was that in the reign of Queen Mary he had been an exile at Geneva for his conscience. Returning into England, he became a fierce, fiery and furious opposer of the church discipline established in England.[4] [*d.* 1585]

JOHN FOXE was born [1516] at Boston in this county, and bred fellow in Magdalen College in Oxford. He fled beyond the seas in the reign of Queen Mary, where he set forth the first and least edition of the *Book of Martyrs,* in Latin, and afterwards returning into England, enlarged and twice revised the same in our own language.

The story is sufficiently known of the two servants, whereof the one told his master, "he would do everything"; the other (which was even Æsop himself) said "he could do nothing"; rendering this reason, "because his former fellow servant would leave him nothing to do." But in good earnest, as to the particular subject of our English martyrs, Mr. Foxe hath done everything, leaving posterity nothing to work upon; and to those who say he hath overdone something, we have returned our answer before.[5]

He was one of prodigious charity to the poor, seeing nothing could bound his bounty but want of money to give away; but I have largely written of his life and death in my *Church History.* [*d.* 1587]

(1) Clinton's first wife was Elizabeth Blount, mistress of Henry VIII. Neither his conscience nor his abilities were of the highest order, and he managed to secure high office under the various changes of sovereign. He abandoned Lady Jane Grey, made his peace with Mary, and was active in suppressing Wyatt's rebellion. (2) Stow's *Survey of London.* (3) Thomas Wilson was the author, among other works, of the *Art of Rhetoric,* the first systematic work of literary criticism in the English language. (4) Gilby was one of the translators of the Geneva Bible. A "fierce and fiery" puritan, he distinguished himself, in his book *View of Antichrist,* in drawing fourteen parallels between the pope of Rome and the "pope of Lambeth." (5) See the life of John Marbeck, p. 30, in Berkshire.

JANE CECIL, wife of Richard Cecil, esquire, and co-heir to the worshipful families of Heckington and Wallcot, was born [1501?] in this county, and lived the main of her life therein. Job, speaking of parents deceased, "His sons," saith he, "come to honour, and he knoweth it not"; but God gave this good woman so long a life (abating but little of an hundred years) that she knew the preferment of her son, William Cecil, for many years in her life lord treasurer of England. I say she knew it and saw it, and joyed at it, and was thankful to God for it; for well may we conclude her gratitude to God from her charity to man. At her own charges, anno 1561, she leaded and paved the Friday Market Cross in Stamford; besides fifty pounds given to the poor, and many other benefactions. Her last will was made Anno Domini 1588. But she survived some time after, and lies buried in the same vault with her son, in St. Martin's in Stamford. [*d.* 1588]

WILLIAM CECIL [LORD BURGHLEY, *b.* 1520]. Know, reader, before I go farther, something must be premised concerning his position in this topic. Virgil was profane in his flattery to Augustus Caesar, proffering him his free choice after his death to be ranked amongst what heathen gods he pleased, so that he might take his place either amongst those of the land, which had the oversight of men and cities, or the sea-gods, commanding in the ocean, or the sky-gods, and become a new constellation therein. But without the least adulation we are bound to proffer this worthy peer his own election: whether he will be pleased to repose himself under Benefactors to the Public, all England in that age being beholden to his bounty (as well as the poor in Stamford, for whom he erected a fair bead-house) acknowledging, under God and the queen, their prosperity the fruit of his prudence; or else he may rest himself under the title of Lawyers, being long bred in the Inns of Court, and more learned in our municipal law than many who made it their sole profession. However, for the present we lodge this English Nestor (for wisdom and vivacity) under the notion of Statesmen, being secretary and lord treasurer for above thirty years together. Having formerly written his life at large,[1] it will be enough here to observe that he was born at Bourne in this county, being son to Richard Cecil, esquire (of the robes of King Henry the Eighth, and a legatee in his will) and Jane his wife, of whom hereafter.[2] He was in his age *moderator aulae,* steering the court at his pleasure; and whilst the earl of Leicester would endure no equal, and Sussex no superior therein, he, by siding with neither, served himself with both.

Incredible was the kindness which Queen Elizabeth had for him, or rather for herself in him, being sensible that he was so able a minister of state. Coming once to visit him, being sick of the gout at Burghley House in the Strand, and being much heightened with her head attire (then in fashion) the lord's servant who conducted her through the door, "May your highness," said he, "be pleased to stoop." The queen returned, "For your master's sake I will stoop, but not for the king of Spain's." This worthy patriot departed this life in the seventy-seventh year of his age, August the 4th, 1598.

(1) In my *Holy State.* (2) Jane Cecil's life immediately precedes Cecil's.

JOB HARTOP was (as himself affirmeth[1]) born at Bourne in this county, and went anno 1567 (early days, I assure you, for the English in those parts) with Sir John Hawkins, his general, to make discoveries in New Spain. This Job was chief gunner in her majesty's ship called the Jesus of Lubeck, being the queen's by no other title but as hired for her money, who in the beginning of her reign, before her navy royal was erected, had her ships from the Hanse towns.

Long and dangerous was his journey; eight of his men at Cape Verde being killed, and the general himself wounded with poisoned arrows, but was cured by a negro drawing out the poison with a clove of garlic, enough to make nice noses dispense with the valiant smell for the sanative virtue thereof.

He wrote a treatise of his voyage, and is the first I met with who mentioned that strange tree, which may be termed the *tree of food,* affording a liquor which is both meat and drink; the *tree of raiment,* yielding needles wherewith, and thread whereof mantles are made; the *tree of harbour,* tiles to cover houses being made out of the solid parts thereof; so that it beareth a self-sufficiency for man's maintenance.

Job was his name, and patience was with him, so that he may pass amongst the Confessors of this county; for being with some other by this general, for want of provisions, left on land, after many miseries they came to Mexico, and he continued a prisoner twenty-three years, viz., two years in Mexico, one year in the Contraction house in Seville, another in the Inquisition house in Triana, twelve years in the galleys, four years (with the cross of Saint Andrew on his back) in the Everlasting prison, and three years a drudge to Hernando de Soria; to so high a sum did the inventory of his sufferings amount.

So much of his patience. Now see the end which the Lord made with him. Whilst enslaved to the aforesaid Hernando, he was sent to sea in a Flemish, which was afterward taken by an English ship, called the Galleon Dudley; and so was he safely landed at Portsmouth, December the second, 1590; and I believe lived not long after.

JOHN WHITGIFT. Born [1530?] he was of ancient parentage at Great Grimsby in Lincolnshire, bred in Cambridge, admitted in Queens' College, removed scholar to Pembroke Hall (where Mr. Bradford was his tutor) translated fellow to Peterhouse, returned master to Pembroke, thence advanced master of Trinity College; successively parson of Teversham, prebend of Ely, dean of Lincoln, bishop of Worcester, where the queen forgave him his first-fruits, a rare gift for her, who was so good an house-wife of her revenues. Yea, she constantly called him her "little black husband," which favour nothing elated his gravity, carrying himself as one unconcerned in all worldly honour. He survived the queen not a full year, getting his bane by going in a cold morning by barge to Fulham, there to consult with the bishops about managing their matters in the ensuing parliament. And no wonder if those few sparks of natural heat were quickly quenched with a small cold in him, who was then above

(1) In his Travels, inserted in Hakluyt's *Voyages.*

seventy-two years of age. He died of the palsy, one of the worthiest men that ever the English hierarchy did enjoy.

Witness many worthy prelates bred under him in Trinity College, and more elsewhere relieved by him. Yea, his bounty was too large to be confined within the narrow seas; Beza, Drusius and other foreign protestant divines tasting freely thereof. Nor was his liberality only a cistern for the present age, but a running river from a fresh fountain to water posterity in that school of Croydon, which he hath beautifully built and bountifully endowed.[1] [*d.* 1604]

SIR EDMUND ANDERSON, knight, was born [1530] a younger brother of a gentle extract at Flixborough in this county, and bred in the Inner Temple. I have been informed that his father left him £1000 for his portion, which this our Sir Edmund multiplied into many by his great proficiency in the common law, being made in the twenty-fourth of Queen Elizabeth chief justice of the common pleas.

When Secretary Davidson was sentenced in the Star Chamber for the business of the Queen of Scots, Judge Anderson said of him that therein he had done *justum non juste;* and so, acquitting him of all malice, censured him, with the rest, for his indiscretion.[2]

When Henry Cuff was arraigned about the rising of the earl of Essex, and when Sir Edward Coke the queen's solicitor opposed him, and the other answered syllogistically, our Anderson (sitting there as judge of law, not logic) checked both pleader and prisoner, *ob stolidos syllogismos* (for their foolish syllogisms) appointing the former to press the statute of King Edward the Third. His stern countenance well became his place, being a great promoter of the established church discipline, and very severe against all Brownists when he met them in his circuit. He died in the third [1605] of King James, leaving great estates to several sons; of whom I behold Sir Francis Anderson of Eyworth in Bedfordshire the eldest, whose son Sir John, by a second wife Audrey Butler (niece to the duke of Buckingham, and afterwards married to the Lord Dunmore in Warwickshire) was, according to some conditions in his patent, to succeed his father-in-law in that honour, if surviving him. This I thought fit to insert to vindicate his memory from oblivion, who, being a hopeful gentleman (my fellow colleague in Sidney College) was taken away in the prime of his youth.

THOMAS SUTTON, esquire, was born [1532] at Knaith in this county, bred a soldier in his youth, and was somewhat of paymaster by his place; much money therefore passing through, some did lawfully stick on his fingers, which became the bottom of his future estate. He was afterward a merchant in London, and gained great wealth therein. Such who charge him with purblindness in his soul, looking too close on the earth, do themselves acquit him from oppression; that though *tenax,* he was not *rapax;* not guilty of covetousness, but parsimony.

(1) Fuller gives only a bare mention of Whitgift and this account is taken from his *Church History.* For the last twenty years of his life Whitgift was archbishop of Canterbury. He was particularly successful in enforcing Elizabeth's policy of religious uniformity, and though strict, was not harsh, and was a character of conspicuous loftiness and honesty. (2) See note, p. 41.

Indeed there was a merchant, his comrade, whose name I will conceal (except the great estate he left doth discover it) with whom he had company in common; but their charges were several to themselves. When his friend in travel called for two faggots, Mr. Sutton called for one; when his friend for half a pint of wine, Mr. Sutton for a gill, underspending him a moiety. At last, Mr. Sutton, hearing of his friend's death, and that he left but fifty thousand pounds estate, "I thought," said he, "he would die no rich man, who made such needless expenses."

Indeed Mr. Sutton's estate doubled his, and he bestowed it all on Charterhouse, or Sutton's Hospital. This is the master-piece of protestant English charity: designed in his life, completed after his death, begun, continued and finished, with buildings and endowments, *sine causa socia,* solely at his charges; wherein Mr. Sutton appears peerless in all Christendom, on an equal standard and valuation of revenues. As for the canker of popish malice endeavouring to fret this fair flower, we have returned plentiful answers to their cavils in our *Church History*. Mr. Sutton died Anno Domini 1611.[1]

ROBERT JOHNSON was born [1540] at Stamford, whereof Maurice his father had been chief magistrate. He was bred in Cambridge, and entering into the ministry, he was beneficed at Luffenham in Rutland, at what time that little county was at a great loss for the education of the children therein; and Mr. Johnson endeavoured a remedy thereof.

He had a rare faculty in requesting of others into his own desire, and with his arguments could surprise a miser into charity. He effectually moved those of the vicinage to contribute to the building and endowing of schools, money or money worth: stones, timber, carriage, &c., not slighting the smallest gift, especially if proportionable to the giver's estate. Hereby finding none, he left as many free schools in Rutland, as there were market towns therein; one at Oakham, another at Uppingham, well faced with buildings and lined with endowments.

Hitherto he was only a nurse to the charity of others, erecting the schools aforesaid, as my author observeth,[2] who afterwards proved a fruitful parent in his own person, becoming a considerable benefactor to Emmanuel and Sidney Colleges in Cambridge; and though never dignified higher than archdeacon of Leicester, he left an estate of one thousand pounds per annum, which descended to his posterity. [*d.* 1625]

JOHN STILL, D.D. was born [1543?] at Grantham in this county, and bred, first, fellow of Christ's, then master of Saint John's, and afterwards of Trinity College in Cambridge, where I have read in the register this commendation of him, that he was ἀγαθος κουρότροφός, *nec collegio gravis aut onerosus.* He was one of a venerable presence, no less famous for a preacher than a disputant. Finding his own strength, he did not stick to warn such as he disputed with in their own arguments, to take heed to their answers, like a perfect fencer, that will tell aforehand in what button he will give his venue. When, towards the end of the reign

(1) He was probably the richest commoner of his time in England, his estates (leases of land rich in coal in Durham) being worth about £5,000 a year. (2) Camden's *Britannia,* in Rutland, *e stirpe collaticia.*

of Queen Elizabeth, there was an (unsucceeding) motion of a diet, or meeting, which should have been in Germany, for composing matters of religion, Doctor Still was chosen for Cambridge, and Doctor Humphrey for Oxford, to oppose all comers for the defence of the English church.

Anno 1593, being then the second time vice-chancellor of Cambridge, he was consecrated bishop of Bath and Wells, and defeated all causeless suspicion of simoniacal compliance; coming clearly thereunto, without the least scandal to his person or loss to the place. In his days God opened the bosom of the earth, Mendip Hills affording great store of lead, wherewith and with his own providence (which is a constant mine of wealth) he raised a great estate, and laid the foundation of three families, leaving to each of them a considerable revenue in a worshipful condition. He give five hundred pounds for the building of an almshouse in the city of Wells; and dying February 26, 1608, lies buried in his own cathedral, under a neat tomb of alabaster.

THOMAS SPARKE, D.D., was born [1548] at South Somercotes in this county, bred in Oxford, and afterwards became minister of Bletchley in Buckinghamshire: an impropriation which the Lord Grey of Wilton (whose dwelling was at Whaddon hard by) restored to the church.[1] He was a solid divine and learned man, as by his works still extant doth appear. At first he was a non-conformist, and therefore was chosen by that party as one of their champions in the conference of Hampton Court. Yet was he wholly silent in that disputation, not for any want of ability, but because (as afterwards it did appear) he was convinced in his conscience at that conference of the lawfulness of ceremonies, so that some accounted him King James's convert herein. He afterwards set forth a book of *Unity and Uniformity,* and died . . . [1616].

MARTIN FOTHERBY, D.D., was born [1549?] at Great Grimsby in this county, of a good family, as appeareth by his epitaph on his monument in the church of All Hallows, Lombard Street, London. He was bred fellow of Trinity College in Cambridge, and became afterwards one and twenty years prebendary of Canterbury; then he was preferred by King James bishop of Salisbury. He died in his calling, having begun to put in print an excellent book against atheists, most useful for our age, wherein their sin so aboundeth. His death happened March 29, 1619, not two full years after his consecration.

PEREGRINE BERTIE, LORD WILLOUGHBY [DE ERESBY, *b.* 1555], son of Richard Bertie, and Catherine duchess of Suffolk. Reader, I crave a dispensation that I may, with thy good leave, trespass on the premised laws of this book; his name speaking his foreign nativity, born nigh Heidelberg in the Palatinate. Indeed I am loath to omit so worthy a person. Our histories fully report his valiant achievements in France and the Netherlands, and how at last he was made governor of Berwick. He could not brook the obsequiousness and assiduity of the court; and was wont to say "that he was none of the *reptilia* which could creep on the ground."

(1) So am I informed by his grandchild and heir.

The camp was his proper element, being a great soldier, and having a suitable magnanimity.

When one sent him an insulting challenge, whilst he lay sick of the gout, he returned this answer, that "although he was lame of his hands and feet, yet he would meet him with a piece of a rapier in his teeth."

Once he took a jennet,[1] managed for the war, which was intended for a present to the king of Spain; and was desired by a trumpeter from the general to restore it, offering this lord £1000 down for him, or £100 per annum during his life, at his own choice. This lord returned that "if it had been any commander, he freely would have sent him back; but being an horse, he loved him as well as the king of Spain himself, and would keep him." Here I will insert a letter of Queen Elizabeth, written to him with her own hand; and reader, deal in matters of this nature, as when venison is set before thee, eat the one, and read the other, never asking whence either came, though I profess I came honestly by a copy thereof from the original:

Good Peregrine, we are not a little glad that by your journey you have received such good fruit of amendment . . . We must next as seriously recommend to you this consideration: that in these times, when there is such appearance that we shall have the trial of our best and noble subjects, you seem not to affect the satisfaction of your own private contentation, beyond the attending on that which nature and duty challengeth from all persons of your quality and profession . . .

Not doubting but when you have with moderation made trial of the success of these your sundry peregrinations, you will find as great comfort to spend your days at home as heretofore you have done; of which we do wish you full measure, howsoever you shall have cause of abode or return. Given under our signet, at our manor of Nonesuch, the seventh of October 1594, in the 37th year of our reign.

Your most loving Sovereign, E.R.

It appears by the premises that it was written to this lord when he was at the Spa in Lukeland, for the recovery of his health, when a second English invasion of the Spaniard was, I will not say feared, but expected. Now though this lord was born beyond the seas accidentally (his parents flying persecution in the reign of Queen Mary) yet must he justly be reputed this countryman, where his ancestors had flourished so many years, and where he was Baron Willoughby in right of his mother. He died Anno Domini 1601, and lies buried under a stately monument at Eresby in this county.

FYNES MORYSON, brother to Sir Richard Moryson, lord president of Munster, was born [1566] in this county of worshipful extraction, and bred a fellow of Peterhouse in Cambridge. He began his travels May the first, 1591, over a great part of Christendom, and no small share of Turkey, even to Jerusalem, and afterwards printed his observations in a large book,[2] which for the truth thereof is in good reputation; for of so great a traveller, he had nothing of a traveller in him, as to stretch in his reports. At last he was secretary to Charles Blount, deputy of

(1) *Jennet*=a small Spanish horse. (2) The well known *Itinerary*, a valuable source-book for the later Elizabethan and earlier Jacobean period.

Ireland, saw and wrote the conflicts with and conquest of Tyrone, a discourse which deserveth credit, because the writer's eye guided his pen, and the privacy of his place acquainted him with many secret passages of importance. [*d.* 1630]

SIR WILLIAM MONSON, knight [*b.* 1569], was extracted of an ancient family in this shire; and was from his youth bred in sea-service, wherein he attained to great perfection. Queen Elizabeth, having cleared Ireland of the Spanish forces, and desiring carefully to prevent a relapse, altered the scene of war from Ireland to Spain, from defending to invading. Sir Richard Leveson was admiral, our Sir William vice-admiral, anno 1602. These, without drawing a sword, killed trading quite on the coasts of Portugal, no vessels daring to go in or out of their harbours.

They had intelligence of a carrack ready to land in Cezimbra, which was of 1600 tons, richly laden out of the East Indies, and resolved to assault it, though it seemed placed in an invincible posture. Of itself it was a giant in comparison to our pigmy ships, and had in her three hundred Spanish gentlemen; the marquess de Santa Cruz lay hard by with thirteen ships, and all were secured under the command of a strong and well fortified castle. But nothing is impossible to Mars' valour and God's blessing thereon. After a fair dispute (which lasted for some hours) with syllogisms of fire and sword, the carrack was conquered, the wealth taken therein amounting to the value of ten hundred thousand crowns of Portugal account. But, though the goods gotten therein might be valued, the good gained thereby was inestimable; for henceforward they beheld the English with admiring eyes, and quitted their thoughts of invasion. This worthy knight died [1643].

SIR EDWARD HARWOOD was born [1586?] nigh Bourne in this county, a valiant soldier and a gracious man. Such who object that he was extremely wild in his youth, put me in mind of the return which one made to an ill-natured man in a company, who with much bitterness had aggravated the debauched youth of an aged and right godly divine: "You have proved," said he, "with much pains what all knew before, that Paul was a great persecutor before he was converted."

I have read of a bird which hath a face like, and yet will prey upon a man; who coming to the water to drink, and finding there by reflection that he had killed one like himself, pineth away by degrees, and never afterwards enjoyeth himself. Such in some sort the condition of Sir Edward. This accident, that he had killed one in a private quarrel, put a period to his carnal mirth, and was a covering to his eyes all the days of his life. No possible provocations could afterwards tempt him to a duel; and no wonder if one's conscience loathed that whereof he had surfeited. He refused all challenges with more honour than others accepted them; it being well known that he would set his foot as far in the face of an enemy as any man alive. He was one of the four standing colonels in the Low Countries, and was shot at the siege of Maestricht, Anno Domini 1632. Death was so civil to him as to allow him leave to rise up on his knees and to cry "Lord have mercy upon me."

JAMES YORKE, a blacksmith of Lincoln, and an excellent workman in his profession, insomuch that if Pegasus himself would wear shoes, this man alone is fit to make them, contriving them so thin and light, as that they would be no burden to him. But he is a servant as well of Apollo as Vulcan, turning his *stithy* into a *study,* having lately set forth a book of heraldry called *The Union of Honour,* containing the arms of the English nobility and the gentry of Lincolnshire. And although there be some mistake (no hand so steady as always to hit the nail on the head) yet is it of singular use and industriously performed; being set forth anno 1640. [*fl.* 1640]

JERVASIUS SCROOP. He engaged with his majesty in Edgehill fight, where he received twenty-six wounds, and was left on the ground amongst the dead. Next day his son Adrian obtained leave from the king to find and fetch off his father's corpse, and his hopes pretended no higher than to a decent interment thereof.

Hearty seeking makes happy finding. Indeed, some more commended the affection than the judgment of the young gentleman, conceiving such a search in vain amongst many naked bodies, with wounds disguised from themselves, and where pale Death had confounded all complexions together.

However, he having some general hint of the place where his father fell, did light upon his body, which had some heat left therein. This heat was, with rubbing, within few minutes improved into motion; that motion, within some hours, into sense; that sense, within a day, into speech; that speech, within certain weeks, into a perfect recovery; living more than ten years after, a monument of God's mercy and his son's affection.

He always after carried his arm in a scarf; and loss of blood made him look very pale, as a messenger come from the grave, to advise the living to prepare for death. The effect of his story I received from his own mouth, in Lincoln College. [*fl.* 1642-1652]

THE FAREWELL

It is vain to wish the same success to every husbandman in this shire as he had, who some seven score years since, at Harlaxton in this county, found an helmet of gold as he was ploughing in the field.

Besides, in treasure trove, the least share falleth to him who first finds it. But this I not only heartily wish, but certainly promise to all such who industriously attend tillage in this county, or elsewhere, that thereby they shall find (though not gold in specie) yet what is gold worth, and may quickly be commuted into it, great plenty of good grain; the same which Solomon foretold, "He that tilleth his land shall have plenty of bread."

LONDON

IT is the second city in Christendom for greatness, and the first for good government. There is no civilized part of the world but it hath heard thereof, though many with this mistake, that they conceive London to be the country, and England but the city therein.

Some have suspected the declining of the lustre thereof, because of late it vergeth so much westward, increasing in buildings in Covent Garden, &c. But by their favour (to disprove their fear) it will be found to burnish[1] round about, to every point of the compass, with new structures daily added thereunto.

It oweth its greatness, under God's divine providence, to the well-conditioned river of Thames, which doth not (as some tyrant rivers in Europe) abuse its strength in a destructive way, but employeth its greatness in goodness, to be beneficial for commerce, by the reciprocation of the tide therein. Hence it was that when King James, offended with the city, threatened to remove his court to another place, the lord mayor (boldly enough) returned "that he might remove his court at his pleasure, but could not remove the river of Thames."

Erasmus will have London so called from Lindus, a city of Rhodes, averring a great resemblance betwixt the language and customs of the Britons and Grecians. But Mr. Camden (who no doubt knew of it) honoureth not this his etymology with the least mention thereof. As improbable, in my apprehension, is the deduction from Lud's-town, *town* being a Saxon, no British termination. And that it was so termed from Lan Dian, a temple of Diana (standing where now Saint Paul's doth) is most likely, in my opinion.

THE MANUFACTURES

Natural commodities are not to be expected to grow in this place, which is only the field of art, and shop-general of England: Cheapside being called the best garden only by metaphor, seeing otherwise nothing but stones are found therein. As for London manufactures, they are so many, I shall certainly lose myself in this labyrinth, if offering to enter. In leaving therefore all intermediate inventions to others, I will only insist on the Needle and the Engine, as the least and greatest instruments employed therein.

NEEDLES

The use hereof is right ancient, though sewing was before needles; for we read that our first parents made themselves aprons by sewing fig-leaves together, either fastening them with some glutinous matter, or with some sharp thing joining them together.

A pin is a blind needle, a needle a pin with an eye. What nails do in solid, needles do in supple bodies, putting them together; only they remain not there formally, but virtually, in the thread which they leave

(1) *Burnish* = to increase in breadth.

behind them. It is the woman's pencil, and embroidery (*vestis acu picta*) is the master-piece thereof. I say embroidery, much used in former, neglected in our age, wherein modern gallants (affecting variety of suits) desire that their clothes should be known by them, and not, as our ancestors, they by their clothes, one suit of state serving them for several solemnities.

This industrious instrument, *needle,* quasi *ne idle* (as some will have it) maintaineth many millions. Yea, he who desireth a blessing on the plough and the needle (including that in the card and compass) comprehendeth most employments at home and abroad, by land and by sea.

All I will add is this: that the first fine Spanish needles in England were made in the reign of Queen Mary, in Cheapside, by a negro; but such his envy, that he would teach his art to none, so that it died with him. More charitable was Elias Kraus, a German who, coming over into England about the eighth of Queen Elizabeth, first taught us the making of Spanish needles, and since we have taught ourselves the using of them.

THE ENGINE

This general word, communicable to all machines or instruments, *use* in this city hath confined to signify that which is used to quench scare-fires therein. One Mr. Jones, a merchant (living in Austin Friars) fetched the first form thereof from Nuremberg, and obtained a patent of King James, that none should be made without his approbation.

Two were begun but not finished in his lifetime, who died in the great plague, *primo Caroli Primi;* since which time, William Burroughs, city founder, now living in Lathbury, hath so completed this instrument, that his additions amount to a new invention, having made it more secure from breaking, and easy to be cleansed; so that, with the striking out of a wedge, it will cleanse itself, and be fit to work again in four minutes.

Since, the aforesaid party hath made about threescore of these engines for city and country. The cooper, carpenter, smith, founder, brazier and turner contribute their skills to the perfecting of it. Yet may the price thereof be compassed for thirty-five pounds.

It hath gained, because it hath saved, many pounds, and (which is invaluable) many lives of men, in this city. The best, though not the biggest, was lately in the church of Saint James, Clerkenwell, as hath many times been experimented. "A good musician makes a good instrument"; and it was a poor blue-cap,[1] better known by his work than name, who played so well thereon, that (though not, with the left-handed Gibeonites, to hit the mark within a hair's breadth) he could hit within the scantling of a shilling. Since, a newer at Saint Bridget's church is a better; and no wonder if the younger out-active those who are more ancient. All wished this engine may be brought forth once a quarter, to be scoured, oiled and trimmed, but not to be used. But if there be an occasion thereof, may it effectually perform that for which it was intended.

(1) *Blue-cap* = a servant.

THE BUILDINGS

SAINT PAUL'S

This is the only cathedral in Christendom dedicated solely to that saint; great the pillars (little legs will bow under so big a body) and small the windows thereof; darkness in those days being conceived to raise devotion; besides, it made artificial lights to appear with the more solemnity. It may be called the Mother Church indeed, having one babe in her body, Saint Faith's, and another in her arms, Saint Gregory's. Surely such who repair to divine service in Saint Faith's may there be well minded of their mortality, being living people, surrounded with the antiperistasis of the dead both above and beneath them. For the present, I behold Saint Paul's church as one struck with the dead palsy on one side, the east part and quire thereof being quick and alive, well maintained and repaired, whilst the west part is ruinous and ready to fall down. Little hopes it will be repaired in its old decay, which is decayed in its new reparations, and being formerly an ornament, is now an eyesore to the city; not to say unto the citizens in general, some being offended that it is in so bad, and others that it is in no worse condition.

The repairing of this church was a worthy monument of the piety and charity of Archbishop Laud, not only procuring the bounty of others, but expending his own estate thereon. We despair not but that his majesty's zeal, in commending this work to their care, will in due time meet with the forward bounty of the citizens. It is no sin to wish that those who have plundered the cloak and cover of Saint Paul's, not left behind *by*, but violently taken *from* him, might be compelled to make him a new one of their own cost; at leastwise to contribute more than ordinary proportions thereunto.

As for the parochial churches in London, they have all either cast their skins with the snake, or renewed their bills with the eagle, having at the least their fronts beautified, if not their bodies rebuilt; amongst which Saint Clement's, Eastcheap, is not to be forgotten, the monument of the bounty of Baldwin Hamey, doctor of physic.[1]

THE BRIDGE

The middle thereof is properly in none, the two ends in two counties, Middlesex and Surrey. Such who only see it beneath, where it is a bridge, cannot suspect it should be a street; and such who behold it above, where it is a street, cannot believe it is a bridge. It was made with great cost, and is maintained with daily charge against the battery and assault of the tide. The sad riddle is generally known to all, which happened here some twenty years since, when a lamentable fire could not be quenched, because there was such store of water hindering all access thereunto.

(1) Lived 1600-1676; a noted physician of his time; benefactor of the Royal College of Physicians.

THE EXCHANGE

This was built by Sir Thomas Gresham, knight, Anno Domini 1571, in imitation of that at Antwerp, but so that the copy exceedeth the original. Queen Elizabeth named it the Royal Bourse, but it is commonly called the Exchange, or Change, because by bargains driven there, wares are changed for wares, and wares for money, and money for money.[1] Yet, because much of mutability is imported in the word Change, it may be a fit remembrancer to merchants meeting here not to build their hopes of perpetuity on what is so subject to vicissitude and alteration. Well may this place be termed the Change, where poor men so soon become rich by good success, and rich men poor by losses and casualties unexpected.

THE TOWER

This, to waive the fable of Julius Caesar, was first founded by King William the Conqueror, finished by William Rufus, encompassed with a ditch by William Longchamp bishop of Ely, enlarged by King Henry the Third, fortified by King Edward the Fourth, beautified by King Richard the Third, repaired by King Henry the Eighth; since whose time no considerable addition thereunto. The mortar thereof (to make it, belike, the more tenacious) was, saith my author,[2] tempered with the blood of beasts; and this Tower was built to secure London in both senses, to awe or defend it, as occasion should require. It is a palace, prison, a liberty, a town, a castle, and what not, most remarkable for the Armoury, Mint, Wardrobe, and formerly, the unicorn's horn therein.

ARMOURY

I place this before the Mint, because of Solon's speech to Croesus that "he that hath the best steel will command all his gold and silver." Here many justly admire at the prodigious greatness of some ancient corslets. If Tully, seeing a little man wearing a long sword, said pleasantly that he was *alligatus gladio* (tied to his sword) surely at the sight hereof he would conclude wearers imprisoned in their arms. This hath put men on many conjectures; some collecting hence the strength and stature of the former ages far above ours; others parallel them with the shields left by Alexander to lie in India, purposely to possess posterity with an untruth, about the proportion of the persons of his soldiers. If I may interpose my conjecture (and if he may speak of John of Gaunt who never fought in his armour) I conceive those arms, so signally great not made to march in (as too ponderous for any under a giant) but to stand therein in a breach, where they might be serviceable.

MINT

Many of these anciently in most cities and some towns. These afterwards (as so many spangles in one piece of gold) were united in the Tower. Of late it was much employed to coin the plate of our nation, to make state money, whence one said,

Caesaris effigies nulla est, sed imaginis expers,
Crux duplex super est dira, gemensque Lyra.

(1) It was named the Royal Exchange, and not the Royal Bourse, as Fuller states, at a great ceremony in 1571. It was built in the years 1566-68, and destroyed in the fire of 1666. For an account of Sir Thomas Gresham see under Norfolk, p. 411.
(2) Fitzstephen, in his Description of London.

And another,

> May their success like to their coin appear,
> Send double crosses for their single cheer.

Sure I am their coin goeth under a general supicion of being as bad as their cause. But I hope hereafter, when the question is asked of our coiners, "Whose image and superscription is this?" it will be returned, "The *Caesar's* of England."[1]

WARDROBE

This was not that for the king's wearing apparel, or liveries of servants, kept elsewhere in an house so called, in the parish of Saint Andrew's Wardrobe; but for vests or robes of state, with rich carpets, canopies and hangings to be used on great solemnities. Here lately was a rich piece of arras, presenting the sea-fight in eighty-eight, and having the living portraitures of the chiefest commanders wrought in the borders thereof. On the same token, that a captain who highly prized his own service, missing his picture therein, complained of the injury to his friend, professing of himself that he merited a place there as well as some therein remembered, seeing he was engaged in the middle of the fight: "Be content," quoth his friend, "thou hast been an old pirate, and art reserved for another *hanging*."

There were also kept in this place the ancient clothes of our English kings which they wore on great festivals; so that this wardrobe was, in effect, a library for antiquaries, therein to read the mode and fashion of garments in all ages. These King James, in the beginning of his reign, gave to the earl of Dunbar, by whom they were sold, resold and re-resold at as many hands almost as Briareus had, some gaining vast estates thereby.

THE UNICORN'S HORN

Amongst the many precious rarities in the Tower, this (as another in Windsor Castle) was, in my memory, shewn to people.[2] I have done, reader, with this subject, when I have told thee that two of my worthy friends (yea, the friends to mankind by their general generosity) Dr. Baldwin Hamey and Sir Francis Prujean,[3] the one had the horn itself (which to my dim eyes at some distance seemed like a taper of wreathed wax) the other hath the socket, as I may term it, of the fish, into which this horn was fixed. I have heard that, upon experiment, a great cure against poison hath been done with some grains thereof; and it is improbable that the vigour of the vigour of nature should extrude that so specious to sight, which is not also sovereign to service. Since, I am informed that the same Dr. Hamey hath parted with the propriety thereof to the College of Physicians; and they have solemnly presented this unicorn's horn to his majesty, to supply the place of that in the Tower, which our civil wars have embezzled.

(1) A sly hit at Lord Protector Cromwell. (2) The greater portion of Fuller's disquisition on the origin and nature of the unicorn is omitted. (3) Sir Francis Prujean (1593-1666) president of the Royal College of Physicians.

PROVERBS

London Cockneys. Let us observe first the antiquity of this proverb, then the meaning; lastly, the application thereof to Londoners. It is more than four hundred years old; for, when Hugh Bigod added artificial fortifications to the natural strength of his castle at Bungay in Suffolk, he gave out this rhyme, therein vaunting it for impregnable:

Were I in my castle of Bungay,
Upon the river of Waveney,
I would not care for the king of Cockeney.

Meaning thereby King Henry the Second, then peaceably possessed of London, whilst some other places did resist him; though afterwards he so humbled this Hugh, that he was fain, with large sums of money and pledges for his loyalty, to redeem this his castle from being razed to the ground.

I meet with a double sense of this word *Cockney*: some taking it for, 1. One coaxed or cockered (made a wanton or nestle-cock of, delicately bred and brought up) so that when grown men or women they can endure no hardship, nor comport with painstaking. 2. One utterly ignorant of husbandry or housewifery, such as is practised in the country, so that they may be persuaded anything about rural commodities; and the original thereof, and the tale of the citizen's son who knew not the language of a cock, but called it neighing, is commonly known.

Here I take no notice of his fancy who will have it called Cockney by transposition, *quasi incoct* (raw and rude[1]) as forced and far-fetched.

The name is generally fixed on such who are born within the sound of Bow Bell, and are tender enough, and sufficiently ignorant in country businesses. One merrily persuaded a she-citizen, that seeing malt did not grow, the good housewives in the country spin it: "I knew as much," said the cockney, "for one may see the threads hang out at the ends thereof." However, be it known unto all people that as there are delicate and silly folk in the country, so are there as hardy men and skilful housewives in the city, no disparagement to any of what place soever.

Billingsgate language. Billings was formerly a gate, though now rather *portus* than *porta,* being the prime landing-place and market for some sea commodities. Now, although as fashionable people live there as elsewhere in the city, yet much rude folk repair thither, so that one may term this the Esculine Gate of London, from the dross and dregs of the baser people flocking thither. Here one may hear *linguas jurgatrices;* yea, shrewd words are sometimes improved into smart blows betwixt them. I doubt not but that Rome, Venice, Paris and all populous cities have their Billingsgate language in those places where rude people make their rendezvous.

He was born within the sound of Bow Bell. This is the periphrasis of a Londoner at large, born within the suburbs thereof, the sound of this bell exceeding the extent of the lord mayor's mace. It is called Bow Bell because hanging in the steeple of Bow Church, and Bow Church because built upon *bows* or arches. John Dun, mercer,

(1) Minsheu's *Dictionary,* in the word *Cockney.*

gave, 1472, two tenements to maintain the ringing of this bell nightly at nine o'clock, which sounded to servants a retreat from their work, and a march to their supper and bed; and therefore conceived by some masters to ring too soon, by most apprentices too late. William Copland, the king's merchant, about the year 1520 gave a bigger bell for the same purpose, and had the handsel thereof himself, being first rung as a knell at his burial.

To dine with Duke Humphrey. This proverb hath altered the original meaning thereof; for first it signified *aliena vivere quadra,* to eat by the bounty or feed by the favour of another man; for Humphrey duke of Gloucester (commonly called the Good Duke) was so hospitable, that every man of fashion otherwise unprovided was welcome to dine with him, it not being so proper for strangers to sup in those days with the greatest housekeepers. The said duke was so bountiful, that his alms-dish of silver was very massy when empty (what then when full?); which alms-dish came afterwards into the possession of the duke of Somerset, who sent it to Lord Rivers, to sell the same to furnish himself for a sea voyage.

But after the death of good Duke Humphrey (when many of his former alms-men were at a loss for a meal's meat) this proverb did alter its copy: to dine with Duke Humphrey importing to be dinnerless.

THE WORTHIES

NOTHELM. Having casually let slip his *forelock,* I mean his episcopal capacity (being successively bishop of London and archbishop of Canterbury) under which he ought to be entered, we are fain to lay hold on his *hind part* (that his memory may not escape us) taking notice of him as a writer. In his age shined a constellation of three learned men, Bede, Alcuinus and our Nothelm, whom the two former, by their letters, invited to write (a performance proper for his pen) the guests of Gregory the Great, and the disciples sent by him, with Austin the monk, for the conversion of Britain. Nothelm, the more effectually to enable himself for this work, went to Rome, obtained leave from Pope Gregory the Second to peruse his records, then sent his completed collections to Bede, to be inserted in his *Church History*. Bede, in gratitude (according to the courteous custom of the learned exchange) dedicated to him his thirty questions on the Books of Kings. His death happened Anno Domini 739.

THOMAS A BECKET, son of Gilbert Becket, merchant, and Matilda his wife, was born [1118?] in this city, in the place where now Mercers Chapel is erected. I have, reader, been so prodigal in the large description of his life in my *Church History,* that I have no new observable left to present you with. Only when I consider of the multitude of vows, made by superstitious pilgrims to his shrine (where the stones were hallowed with their bended knees) I much admire at their will-worship, no vows appearing in Scripture but what were made to God alone. And therefore most impudent is the attempt of those papists, tampering to corrupt Holy Writ in favour of such vows, reading in the vulgar Latin, Prov. xx. 25: *Ruina est homini devotare sanctos, et post vota retractare* (it is a snare to a man who often maketh vows to saints, and after vows retracteth them); instead of *Ruina est homini devorare sancta, et post vota retractare* (it is a snare to a man who devoureth that which is holy, and after vows to make enquiry.)

This Becket was slain, as is notoriously known, on Innocents' day, in his own church of Canterbury, 1170.

WILLIAM FITZSTEPHEN was descended, saith Leland, of Norman nobility, but born in this city and bred a monk in Canterbury. He wrote many learned works, and one in Latin, of the description of London, since commendably (because rare to come by) translated and added to the *Survey of London.*[1]

Say not that London then was but the suburbs to the London now, for the bigness and populousness thereof; seeing, in Fitzstephen's time, it accounted thirteen conventual and an hundred and six-and-thirty parochial churches, not producing so many at this day; so that it seems, though there be more bodies of men, there be fewer houses of God therein.

As for the populousness thereof in his time, it was able to set forth sixty thousand foot, which I believe it may treble in our time. It could also then raise twenty thousand horsemen, which would pose it at this day to perform. But, as railing Rabshekah made Jerusalem weaker (not able to set two thousand riders on horses) so possibly Fitzstephen might make London stronger than it was. I hope one may safely wish this city may be better in holiness, as bigger in houses, than it was when Fitzstephen flourished, 1190.

RICHARD ANGLICUS was certainly a man of merit, being eminently so denominated by foreigners (amongst whom he conversed) from his country; and he who had our nation for his name, cannot have less than London for his lodging in this our Catalogue of Worthies. He is said to have studied first in Oxford, then in Paris, where he so profited in the faculty of physic, that he is counted, by Simphorianus Champerius (a stranger to our nation, and therefore free from flattery) one of the most eminent writers in that profession. Now, because he was the first Englishman whom I find famous in that calling, may the reader be pleased with a receipt of the several names of the books left by him to posterity: 1. *A Tractate of Urines* 2. *Of the Rules of Urines* 3. *Of the Signs of Diseases* 4. *Of Prognostick Signs* 5. *Of Letting Blood* 6. *Of Anatomy according to Galen* 7. *Of Fevers* 8. *A Correction of Alchemy* 9. *A Mirror of Alchemy* 10. *Of Physic* 11. *Repressive* 12. *Of the Signs of Fevers.*

Leland reporteth that besides these, he wrote other works, which the envy of time hath denied unto us.[2] [*d.* 1252]

(1) This valuable description of London, which Stow printed in his *Survey*, was contained in Fitzstephen's *Life of Becket*. The full work was not published until 1723. (2) This Richard Anglicus is probably identical with Richard of Wendover who was physician to Gregory IX and later canon of St. Paul's. A number of his works, in MS, are preserved chiefly in the libraries of Oxford and Cambridge.

SIMON DE GHENT was born in this city (his mother being an Englishwoman, his father a Fleming); and being bred in good literature, became so famous, that by King Edward the First he was preferred bishop of Salisbury, 1297. He gave the first leave to the citizens thereof to fortify that place with a deep ditch, partly remaining, and a strong wall wholly demolished at this day. Now seeing good laws are the best walls of any foundation, no less was his care for the church than city of Salisbury, making good statutes, whereby it was ordered even unto our age. [*d.* 1315]

NICHOLAS LYRANUS was (as Barnabus a Jew Cypriot, and Saul a Jew Cilician) a Jew Englishman, the first by nation, the second by nativity. He had the Rabbins at his fingers' ends; but conversed so long with, that at last he was converted by, some Franciscans to be a Christian; and I behold Nicholas (conqueror of his people) as his font name then given him, as predictory of those victories he afterwards got, by his disputings and writings, over his own countrymen. Nor doth the church of God more complain of Nicholas, that proselyte of Antioch, the last of the seven deacons, and first founder of the Nicholaitans whom God hated, than it doth commend our Nicholas, who vigorously confuted the Jews, who expect the rising of the sun in the afternoon, waiting for Messias still to come.

I read how, some fifty years before, Henry the Third founded a house called *Domus Conversorum* (where now the office of the rolls is kept in Chancery Lane) where converted Jews were accommodated with lodging and a small salary. But I believe Lyranus made no use thereof, contenting himself to live first in Oxford, then in Paris, a Franciscan friar; and wrote comments on all the Old and New Testament; whereof so different the editions, that I am certainly informed, one is so bad, one can hardly give too little, and one is so good, one can hardly give too much for it. Though sometimes he may be wide of the mark, and this harp be out of tune, yet uncharitable their censure of *Lyra delirat*, whilst Luther highly praiseth him, because his wanton wit did not gad after empty allegories, but with the good housekeeper stays at home, keeping himself close to the text in his literal interpretations. Now though there were many Jewish synagogues in England, at York, Cambridge, Northampton, &c., yet the Old Jewry in London equalling all the rest in numerousness, Lyranus' birth is here assigned with the best assurance, though dying in Paris about the year 1340.

WILLIAM SAWTREY, alias Chatris, parish priest of the church of Saint Osyth's, London, was the first Englishman that was put to death by fire, for maintaining the opinions of Wycliffe.

In the primitive times (pardon, reader, no impertinent digression) such the lenity and tenderness of the fathers of the church towards heretics, that, contenting themselves with condemning their blasphemous opinions, they proceeded to no penalty on their persons. Yea, in after ages, when the Christian emperor would have punished the furious Donatists with a pecuniary mulct, the holy men of those times so earnestly interceded, as to procure the remission. And St. Augustine himself, who was most zealous in his writing against these Donatists, professeth he had rather be himself slain by them, than by detecting them be any cause they should undergo the punishment of death; whereas henceforward in England many were brought to the fire by the bishops and others of the clergy, whose opinions were neither so blasphemous, nor deportment so inhuman, as ancient heretics.

I confess, not only simple heresy was charged on this Sawtrey, but also a relapse thereinto after abjuration; in which case such is the charity of the canon law, that such a person is *seculari judicio sine ulla penitus audientia relinquendus*[1] (not affording any audience to one relapsed, though he should revoke his opinions.) Quite contrary to the charitable judgment of Saint Chrysostum, who sticked not to say . . . "if thou fall a thousand times, and repent thee of thy folly, come boldly into the church."

There is some difference amongst authors, about the legal proceedings against this Sawtrey, by what power he was condemned to die. Walsingham will have him die during the sitting of the parliament, secundo Henrici Quarti, by virtue of the law then made against heretics. Others will have him put to death, not by any statute-law then made, but as convicted in a provincial council of the archbishop of Canterbury.

The latter seemeth most true, because the writ *De Haeretico Comburendo* (sent down by the advice of the lords temporal to the mayor of London, to cause his execution) bare date the 26th of February; whereas it was ordered in that parliament that the penal statutes made therein should not take effect till after Whitsuntide.

But, by what power soever it was done, poor Sawtrey was burnt in Smithfield, about the 28th February, 1401. One criticism of cruelty and hypocrisy is most remarkable. The close of the archbishop's sentence of degradation, when Sawtrey was committed over to the secular court, endeth with this expression: "Beseeching the court aforesaid, that they will receive favourably the said William, unto them thus re-committed."

We have been the larger upon this Sawtrey's death, because he was the English protestant (pardon the *prolepsis*) proto-martyr.

JOHN BADBY was an artificer in Blackfriars in London, condemned and burned in Smithfield [1410]. Henry Prince of Wales (afterwards King Henry the Fifth) happened to be present at his execution, who not only promised him pardon on his recantation, but also a stipend out of the king's treasury sufficient for his support; all which Badby refused. He was put into an empty tun (a ceremony peculiar to him alone) and the fire put therein.

At the first feeling thereof he cried "Mercy, mercy," begging it of God of heaven, which noble Prince Henry mistook for a kind of revocation of his opinions, and presently caused the fire round about him to be quenched, renewing his promises unto him with advantage; which Badby refused the second time, and was martyred.

(1) *De Haeretico Comburendo* [Sawtrey was the first victim of this statute, which enacted that an offender, if still impenitent after conviction by a spiritual court, was to be handed to the secular power and burned in public.]

JULIANA BERNERS was born [1388?] *ex antiqua et illustri domo.* Understand it not in the sense wherein the same was said of a certain pope, born in a ruinous cottage, where the sun did shine through rotten walls and roof thereof. But indeed she was descended of a respectable family . . .

She was the Diana of her age for hunting and hawking; skilful also in fishing, and wrote three of these exercises, commending the practice thereof to the gentry of England.

Our Juliana also wrote a book of heraldry. Say not the needle is the most proper pen for the woman, and that she ought to meddle with making no coats, save such as Dorcas made for the widows, seeing their sex may be not only pardoned, but praised for such lawful diversions.

JOHN PHREAS [or FREE] was born in this city, bred fellow of Balliol College in Oxford, where he contracted familiarity with his colleague and Maecenas, J. Tiptoft earl of Worcester.[1] He afterwards travelled into Italy, and at Ferrara was a constant auditor of Gwarinus, an old man and famous philosopher.

Hitherto our Phreas made use only of his ears, hereafter of his tongue, when of hearer he turned a teacher; and see the stairs whereby he ascended. 1. He read physic at Ferrara, concerning medicinal herbs; 2. Then at Florence, well esteemed by the duke thereof; 3. Then at Padua, beneath Florence in beauty, above it in learning, an university where he proceeded doctor of physic; 4. Then at Rome, where he was gracious with Pope Paul the Second, dedicating unto him many books translated out of Greek.

The pope rewarded him with the bishopric of Bath and Wells; dying before his consecration, poisoned (as is vehemently suspected) by some who maligned his merit; *Heu mihi quod nullis livor medicabilis herbis*!

Solomon himself, who wrote of all simples, from the cedar in Lebanus to the hyssop on the wall, could find no defensative against it, which made him cry out, "But who can stand before envy?" No wonder, therefore, if our Phreas (though a skilful botanist) found man's malice mortal unto him. He died at Rome, Anno Domini 1465.

ROBERT FABYAN was born and bred in this city, whereof he became sheriff 1493. Treating his guests with good cheer and welcome, he doubled his dishes with pleasant discourse, being an excellent historian, witness two chronicles of his own writing: 1. From Brutus to the death of King Henry the Second; 2. From the first of King Richard to the death of King Henry the Seventh. He was also an excellent poet, both in Latin, French and English.

A modern master wit,[2] in the contest betwixt the poets of our age for the laurel, maketh Apollo to adjudge it to an alderman of London, because to have most wealth was a sign of most wit. But had the scene of this competition been laid seven-score years since, and the same remitted to the umpirage of Apollo, in sober sadness he would have given the laurel to this our alderman.

(1) See Cambridgeshire, p. 53. (2) Sir John Suckling ["A Session of the Poets."]

As for his histories, if the whole strain of them doth λονδινίζειν, it must be indulged to him that followed the genius of his own education. He died at London, 1513; and was buried in the church of All Hallows, where he hath a tedious and barbarous epitaph, as commonly (reader, I should be glad to have my observation confuted) who hath worse poetry than poets on their monuments? After his death, Cardinal Wolsey caused so many copies of this book as he could come by to be burnt, because therein he had opened the coffers of the church too wide, and made too clear discovery of the revenues of the clergy.

CHRISTOPHER SAINT-GERMAN. Reader, wipe thine eyes, and let mine smart, if thou readest not what richly deserves thine observation, seeing he was a person remarkable for his gentility, piety, chastity, charity, ability, industry and vivacity.

1. *Gentility;* descended from a right ancient family, born [1460?] as I have cause to believe, in London, and bred in the Inner Temple in the study of our laws. 2. *Piety;* he carried Saint in his nature as well as in his surname, constantly reading and expounding every night to his family a chapter in the Bible. 3. *Chastity;* living and dying unmarried, without the least spot on his reputation. 4. *Charity;* giving *consilia* and *auxilia* to all his people gratis. Indeed I have read of a company of physicians in Athens, called ἀνάργυροι, because they would take no money of their patients; and our Saint-German was of their judgment as to his clients. 5. *Ability;* being excellently skilled in civil, canon and common law; so that it was hard to say wherein he excelled. Add to these his skill in Scripture, witness his book called the *Doctor and Student,* where the former vies divinity with the law of the latter. 6. *Industry;* he wrote several works, wherein he plainly appeareth not only a favourer of but champion for the Reformation. 7. *Vivacity;* living to be above eighty years old, and dying Anno Domini 1540, was buried at St. Alphage, London, near Cripplegate.

JOHN RASTELL was a citizen and printer of London; by marriage a kin to Sir Thomas More; and when the said Sir Thomas and Bishop Fisher wrote in defence of purgatory, to prove it by Scripture, Rastell undertook to maintain it by reason. Surely he that buys the two former books deserveth to have this last given him, to make him a saver. Some will say the former two endeavoured to prove the fire, and Rastell the smoke, of purgatory. But to pass by his works in divinity, he was a good mathematician; and made a comedy of Europe, Asia and Africa, which, my author saith,[1] was very witty, and very large, and I can believe the latter, seeing he had three parts of the world for his subject; and how long would it have been had America been added? He wrote a book against John Frith, but afterwards (convinced with his adversary's arguments) recanted it of his own accord; the cause why we have placed him since the Reformation. He wrote a book of the terms of law, and made an index to Justice Fitzherbert; yea, I behold this John as father to Rastell the famous lawyer, of whom before.[2] He died and was buried at London 1536.

(1) Bale. (2) Placed below, p. 362, in this edition.

JOHN KITE was born in London, bred in Oxford, sent ambassador into Spain, made a Grecian titulary archbishop (receiving thence as much profit as men shear wool from hogs) and at last the real bishop of Carlisle; yet is his epitaph, in the church of Stepney, neither good English, Latin, Spanish or Greek, but a barbarous confusion, as followeth:

Under this stone closyd et marmorate
Lyeth John Kite, Londoner natiffe.
Encreasing in virtues, rose to hygh estate
In the fourth Edward's chappel by his young life,
Sith which the Seuinth Henries service primatife
Proceeding still in virtuous efficase
To be in favour with this our king's grase.
With witt endewyed chosen to be legate
Sent into Spain, where he right joyfully
Combined both princes in pease most amate.
In Grece archbishop elected worthely
And last of Carlyel ruling postorally:
Keeping nobyl houshold with great hospitality.
One thousand fyve hundred thirty and seuyn
Inuyterate with carys consumed with age,
The nineteeth of Jun, reckonyd full euyn
Passed to Heauyn from worldly pylgramage,
Of whose soul good peopul of Cherite
Prey, as ye wold be preyd for, for thus must you lye;
Jesu mercy, Lady help.

These if made 300 years ago had been excusable; but such midnight verses are abominable, made, as it appears, in the dawning of good learning and pure language. Yet, because some love poetry, either very good or very bad, that if they cannot learn from it, they may laugh at it, they are here inserted. [*d.* 1537]

WILLIAM KNIGHT was born [1476] in this city, bred fellow of New College in Oxford, on the same token that there have been ten of his surname, fellows of that foundation. He proceeded doctor of law, and a noble pen[1] makes him secretary to King Henry the Eighth. Sure it is he was the first person employed to the pope to motion to him the matter of his divorce; advertising the king, by his weekly dispatches, how slowly his cause (though spurred with English gold) crept on in the court of Rome. After his return, the king rewarded his industry, fidelity and ability with bestowing the bishopric of Bath and Wells upon him.

In Wells (with the assistance of Dean Wolman) he built a stately covered cross in the market-place, for the glory of God and conveniency of poor people, to secure them from the weather; adding this inscription, *Laus Deo, pax vivis, requies defunctis.* He died September 29, anno 1547.

SIR THOMAS MORE[2] was, Anno Domini 1478, born in Milk Street, London, the brightest star that ever shined in that *via lactea,* sole son to Sir John More, knight, one of the justices of the king's bench.

Some have reported him of mean parentage, merely from a mistake of

(1) Lord Herbert, in the *Life of Henry VIII.* (2) The sum hereof is taken out of his printed Life (rare to be had) written by a nephew of his, more fairly and unpartially than any would expect from so near a relation. [Fuller refers to the life by William Roper, More's son-in-law.]

a modest word, in an epitaph of his own making, on his monument in Chelsea Church; where *nobilis* is taken not in the civil but common-law sense, which alloweth none noble under the degree of barons. Thus men cannot be too wary what they inscribe on tombs, which may prove a record, though not in law, in history, to posterity.

He was bred first in the family of Archbishop Morton, then in Canterbury College (now taken into Christ Church) in Oxford, where he profited more in two than many in ten years' continuance. Thence he removed to an inn of Chancery called New Inn, and from thence to Lincoln's Inn, where he became a double reader. Then did his worth prefer him to be judge in the sheriff of London's court, whilst a pleader in others. And although he only chose such causes which appeared just to his conscience, and never took fee of widow, orphan or poor person, he gained in those days four hundred pounds per annum.

Being made a member of the House of Commons, he opposed King Henry the Seventh, about money for the marriage of his daughter Margaret, whereat the king was much discontented, when a courtier told him that a beardless boy (beard was never the true standard of brains) had obstructed his desires; which king, being as certain, but more secret than his son in his revenge, made More the mark of his displeasure, who, to decline his anger, had travelled beyond the seas, had not the king's going into another world stopped his journey.

King Henry the Eighth coming to the crown, and desirous to ingratiate himself by preferring popular and deserving persons, knighted Sir Thomas, and made him chancellor of the duchy of Lancaster, the king's personal patrimony. Finding him faithful in lesser matters (according to the method of the Gospel) he made him in effect ruler of all when lord chancellor of England; a place wherein he demeaned himself with great integrity, and with no less expedition. In testimony of the latter, it is recorded that, calling for the next cause, it was returned unto him, "There are no more to be heard, all suits in that court depending, and ready for hearing, being finally determined." Whereon a rhythmer:

> When *More* some years had chancellor been,
> No more suits did remain;
> The same shall nevermore be seen
> Till *More* be there again.

Falling into the king's displeasure for not complying with him about the queen's divorce, he seasonably resigned his chancellor's place, and retired to his house in Chelsea, chiefly employing himself in writing against those who were reputed heretics. And yet it is observed to his credit (by his great friend Erasmus) that, whilst he was lord chancellor, no protestant was put to death; and it appears by some passages in his *Utopia* that it was against his mind that any should lose their lives for their consciences.

He rather soiled his fingers than dirtied his hands in the matter of the Holy Maid of Kent, and well wiped it off again.[1] But his refusing,

(1) This holy maid, Elizabeth Barton, was subject to trances, during which her sayings had such a profound effect on her audience that she was led to believe, or feigned, that she had direct revelations. An unwise pronouncement on Henry VIII's proposed divorce from Catherine of Arragon led to her trial and execution. More had seen her, but was cautious.

or rather not accepting the oath of supremacy, stuck by him, for which he was sixteen months imprisoned in the Tower, bearing his afflictions with remarkable patience. He was wont to say that his natural temper was so tender, that he could not endure a fillip; but a supernatural principle, we see, can countermand, yea help natural imperfections.

In his time (as till our memory) Tower prisoners were not dieted on their own, but on the king's charges; the lieutenant of the Tower providing their fare for them. And when the lieutenant said that he was sorry that commons were no better, "I like," said Sir Thomas, "your diet very well, and if I dislike it, I pray turn me out of doors."

Not long after, he was beheaded on Tower Hill, 1535. He left not above one hundred pounds a year estate, perfectly hating covetousness, as may appear by his refusing four or five thousand pounds offered him by the clergy. Among his Latin books his *Utopia* beareth the bell, containing the idea of a complete commonwealth in an imaginary island, but pretended to be lately discovered in America, and that so lively counterfeited, that many at the reading thereof mistook it for a real truth; insomuch that many great learned men, as Budaeus, and Johannes Paludanus, upon a fervent zeal, wished that some excellent divines might be sent thither to preach Christ's Gospel; yea, there were here amongst us at home sundry good men and learned divines, very desirous to undertake the voyage, to bring the people to the faith of Christ, whose manners they did so well like.

By his only son, Mr. John More, he had five grandchildren, Thomas and Augustin, born in his lifetime, who proved zealous Romanists; Edward, Thomas and Bartholomew (born after his death) were firm protestants; and Thomas, a married minister of the Church of England.

MARGARET ROPER. Excuse me, reader, for placing a lady among men and learned statesmen. The reason is because of her unfeigned affection for her father from whom she would not willingly be parted (and for me shall not be) either living or dead.

She was born [1505] in Bucklersbury in London, at her father's[1] house therein, and attained to that skill in all learning and languages that she became the miracle of her age. Foreigners took such notice hereof that Erasmus hath dedicated some epistles unto her. No woman that could speak so well did speak so little, whose secrecy was such, that her father entrusted her with his most important affairs.

Such was her skill in the Fathers that she corrected a depraved place in St. Cyprian, for whereas it was corruptly written *Nisi vos sinceritatis*, she amended it *Nervos sinceritatis*. Yea, she translated Eusebius out of Greek; but it was never printed, because I. Christopherson had done it so exactly before.

She was married to William Roper, of Eltham in Kent, esquire, one of a bountiful heart and plentiful estate. When her father's head was set up on London Bridge, it being suspected it would be cast into the Thames, to make room for divers others (then suffering for denying

(1) Sir Thomas More—see above, p. 356. The beautiful story of Margaret Roper's affection for her father is told with striking pathos in Roper's life of More.

the king's supremacy) she bought the head, and kept it for a relic, which some called affection, others religion, others superstition in her; for which she was questioned before the council, and for some short time imprisoned, until she had buried it; and how long she herself survived afterwards, is to me unknown. [*d.* 1544]

ANDREW BOORDE, doctor of physic, was (I conceive) bred in Oxford, because I find his book called *The Breviary of Health* examined by that university. He was physician to King Henry the Eighth, and was esteemed a great scholar in that age. I am confident his book was the first written of that faculty in English, and dedicated to the College of Physicians in London.

Take a taste out of the beginning of his dedicatory epistle: "Egregious doctors and masters of the eximious and arcane science of physic, of your urbanity exasperate not yourselves against me for making this little volume of physic, &c."

Indeed his book contains plain matter under hard words; and was accounted such a jewel in that age (things whilst the first are esteemed the best in all kinds) that it was printed, *cum privilegio ad imprimendum solum,* for William Middleton, anno 1548.[1] [1490?-1549]

JOHN HEYWOOD was born [1497?] in London, and was most familiar with Sir Thomas More, whom he much resembled in quickness of parts, both undervaluing their friend to their jest, and having *ingenium non edentulum, sed mordax.* I may safely write of him, what he pleasantly writes of himself, that "he applied mirth more than thrift; many mad plays, and did few good works." He hath printed many English proverbial epigrams; and his *monumenta literaria* are said to be *non tam labore condita, quam lepore condita.* He was highly in favour with Queen Mary, and after her death fled for religion beyond the seas.

It is much that one so fanciful should be so conscientious. He lived and (for ought I find) died at Malines, about the year 1580. Jasper Heywood, his son, was a great Jesuit, and executed here in Queen Elizabeth's reign.[2]

THOMAS LUPSET was born [1498?] in this city, and was related to most English and some foreign learned eminencies of his age: 1. Bred a child in the house of Dean Colet. 2. Under William Lily in St. Paul's School. 3. Sent to Oxford, where he became Greek professor. 4. Resigns his place to his friend Ludovicus Vives. 5. Travelled into Italy, and at Padua was familiar with Cardinal Pole. 6. Was known unto Erasmus, who giveth him this character: *Hujus ingenio nihil gratius, nihil amantius.* 7. Intended divinity, diverted by Cardinal Wolsey. 8. At Paris was tutor to Thomas Winter, a ward to the cardinal. 9. Returning into England,

(1) Boorde was suffragan bishop of Chichester about 1521. He was sent abroad by Cromwell to find out the state of feeling about Henry VIII. At the end of his life he was imprisoned in the Fleet, possibly for behaviour over loose women. (2) Jasper Heywood (1535-1598) translator of Seneca, was leader of the Jesuit mission to England in 1581; arraigned in 1584 with five other priests who were executed, but he was withdrawn from the trial, for some unknown reason, and deported the next year. He died at Naples.

was known to King Henry the Eighth. 10. Began to grow into his favour, when cut off with a consumption, 1530, in the prime of his life.

He died in London, and lieth buried in the church of Saint Alphage nigh Cripplegate, without a monument.

EDWARD HALL [*b.* 1498/9]. We may trace him from his cradle to his coffin, as followeth: 1. He was a citizen of London by his birth. 2. He was bred a scholar at Eton. 3. Thence he removed, and was one of the foundation of King's College. 4. Thence he went to Gray's Inn, and studied the municipal law. 5. He became common serjeant of London; for the well discharging whereof he, 6. Was advanced to be one of the judges of the sheriff's court. 7. Wrote an elegant history of the wars of York and Lancaster, from King Henry the Fourth, till the end of King Henry the Eighth.[1] 8. Died a very aged man, 1547.

He was, as by some passages in his book may appear, in that age well affected to the Reformation. He lieth buried in the church of Saint Sithes (contracted, I think, for Saint Osyth's) where I cannot recover any epitaph upon him.

NICHOLAS HEATH was born [1501?] and had his childhood in the city of London, being noted for one of St. Anthony's Pigs therein (so were the scholars of that school commonly called, as those of St. Paul's, Paul's Pigeons); and bred first in Christ's College, then fellow of Clare Hall in Cambridge. By King Henry the Eighth (to whom he was almoner) he was preferred bishop, first of Rochester, then of Worcester; deprived by King Edward the Sixth, restored by Queen Mary, who advanced him archbishop of York, and lord chancellor of England. A moderate man, who would not let the least spark of persecution be kindled in his diocese, if any in his province.

In the conference at Westminster betwixt papists and protestants, *primo Elizabethae,* he was a kind of moderator, but interposed little. Infected by his fellow-prisoner-popish-prelates, he could not be persuaded to take the oath of supremacy, for which he was deprived. He led a pious and private life, on his own lands, at Chobham in Surrey, whither Queen Elizabeth came often to visit him; and died [1578].

ANNE BOLEYN, daughter of the Lord Thomas Boleyn, earl of Wiltshire, was (as some of her honourable relations still surviving do conjecture) born [1507] in London, and became second wife to King Henry the Eighth. Indeed he passionately affected her when but a lord's daughter, but did not marry her till she was a princess; created by him marchioness of Pembroke, partly to make her the more proportionable match, and partly to try how she would become a coronet before she wore a crown.

The papists much disparage her memory (malice will lie, or must be dumb) making all her wit to consist in boldness, her beauty in a French garb, and her modesty in a cunning coyness; whereas indeed she was a lady accomplished in body (was it likely King Henry would love what

(1) Hall's valuable chronicle of the period, *The Union of the Noble and Illustrious Families of Lancaster and York,* first published in 1542, was prohibited by Queen Mary because of its protestant tone, and not reprinted till 1809.

was not lovely?) and virtuous in mind, and whilst a favourite of the king's a favourer of all good men, and great promoter of the Gospel. The inconstancy of her husband's affection is conceived by most moderate men (what else soever was pretended) her chiefest crime, and cause of her death, which happened anno 1536.

CATHERINE HOWARD, daughter to the Lord Edmund Howard, son to Thomas duke of Norfolk, was (though her father had large lands and houses in many places) probably born in London, and at last became fifth wife to King Henry the Eighth. Such as desire to know the names, number and success of all six, may conceive King Henry thus speaking on his death-bed:

> Three Kates, two Nans, and one dear Jane I wedded;
> One Spanish, one Dutch, and four English wives:
> From two I was divorced, two I beheaded,
> One died in childbed, and one me survives.

Of this Catherine Howard little is reported, and yet too much, if all be true, of her incontinency, which cost her her life. The greatest good the land got by this match was a general leave to marry cousins-german, formerly prohibited by the canon, and hereafter permitted by the common law; a door of lawful liberty left open by God in Scripture, shut by the pope for his private profit, opened again by the king, first for his own admittance (this Catherine being cousin-german to Anne Boleyn, his former wife) and then for the service of such subjects as would follow him upon the like occasion. This lady was beheaded Anno Domini 1542.

THOMAS WRIOTHESLEY [FIRST EARL OF SOUTHAMPTON], knight of the Garter, was born [1505] in Barbican, son to William Wriothesley, York herald, and grandchild to John Wriothesley (descended from an heir general of the ancient family of the Dunstervilles) king of arms. He was bred in the university of Cambridge . . . He afterwards effectually applied his studies in our municipal law, wherein he attained to great eminency. He was by King Henry the Eighth created baron of Titchfield at Hampton Court, January the first, 1544, and in the next year, about the beginning of May, by the said king made chancellor of England. But in the first of King Edward the Sixth he was removed from that place, being a conscientiously rigorous Romanist, though in some reparation he was advanced to be earl of Southampton. He died at his house, called Lincoln's Place, in Holborn, 1550, the 30th of July, and lies buried at Saint Andrew's in Holborn.

WILLIAM PAGET, knight [FIRST BARON PAGET], was born [1505] in this city, of honest parents, who gave him pious and learned education, whereby he was enabled to work out his own advancement; privy councillor to four successive princes, which, though of different persuasions, agreed all in this, to make much of an able and trusty minister of state. 1. King Henry the Eighth made him his secretary, and employed him ambassador to Charles the emperor, and Francis king of France. 2. King Edward the Sixth made him chancellor of the duchy, comptroller of his household, and created him baron of Beaudesert. 3. Queen Mary made him keeper of her privy seal. 4. Queen Elizabeth dispensed with his attendance at court, in favour to his great age, and highly respected him.

Indeed, Duke Dudley, in the days of King Edward, ignominiously took from him the Garter of the order, quarrelling that by his extraction he was not qualified for the same. But if all be true which is reported of this duke's parentage,[1] he of all men was most unfit to be active in such an employment. But no wonder if his pride wrongfully snatched a Garter from a subject, whose ambition endeavoured to deprive two princes of a crown. This was restored unto him by Queen Mary, and that with ceremony and all solemn accents of honour, as to a person who by his prudence had merited much of the nation. He died very old, anno 1563; and his corpse (as I remember) is buried in Lichfield, and not in the vault under the church of Drayton in Middlesex, where the rest of that family, I cannot say lies (as whose coffins are erected) but are very completely reposed in a peculiar posture, which I meet not with elsewhere; the horror of a vault being much abated with the lightness and sweetness thereof.

THOMAS POPE, knight, was born [1507?] in this city, as my worthy friend Doctor Seth Ward,[2] the head, and others of the Society of Trinity College in Oxford, have informed me. I behold him as *Fortunae suae fabrum,* the smith who, by God's blessing, hammered out his own fortune without any patrimonial advantage. Indeed he lived in an age which one may call the harvest of wealth, wherein any that would work might get good wages, at the dissolution of abbeys.

Herein he was much employed, being, under the Lord Cromwell, an instrument of the second magnitude, and lost nothing by his activity therein. However, by all the printed books of that age, he appeareth one of a candid carriage; and in this respect stands sole and single by himself, that of the abbey-lands which he received, he refunded a considerable proportion for the building and endowing of Trinity College in Oxford. [*d.* 1559]

WILLIAM RASTELL was born [1508?] in this city (sister's son to Sir Thomas More) and was bred in the study of our common law; and whoever readeth this passage in Pits, will thence conclude him one of the two chief justices of England: *Factus est civilium et criminalium causarum alter ex duobus per Angliam supremis judicibus;* whereas indeed he was but one of the justices of the king's bench, yet his ability and integrity did incapacitate him for higher preferment, being also a person of industry.

He wrote the life, and set forth the works, of his uncle More; and made a collection of, and comment on, the statutes of England.

Great was his zeal to the Romish religion, flying into Flanders; with the changing of his country under King Edward the Sixth, he changed

(1) See Edmund Dudley, in our Description of Staffordshire, p. 516. (2) Lived 1617-1689; bishop of Salisbury; famous in his day as mathematician and astronomer.

the nature of his studies; but then wrote worse books on a better subject, I mean divinity. He undertook Bishop Jewel, as much his over-match in divinity, as Rastell was his in common law. The papists are much pleased with him for helping their cause, as they conceive; and we are not angry with him, who hath not hurt ours in any degree.

He died at Louvain, 1565, and lieth buried with his wife in the same tomb, and this epitaph may be bestowed on him:

Rastallus tumulo cum conjuge dormit in uno,
Unius carnis pulvis et unus erit.

Know that Winifred Clement, his wife, was one of the greatest female scholars, an excellent Grecian, and, the crown of all, most pious according to her persuasion.

JOHN STOW, son to Thomas Stow, who died anno 1559, grandchild to Thomas Stow, who died 1526 (both citizens of London, and buried in Saint Michael's in Cornhill) was born [1525?] in this city, bred at learning no higher than a good grammar scholar; yet he became a painful, faithful and (the result of both) useful historian.

I confess I have heard him often accused that (as learned Guicciardini is charged for telling *magnarum rerum minutias*) he reporteth *res in se minutas* (toys and trifles) being such a smell-feast that he cannot pass by Guildhall but his pen must taste of the good cheer therein. However, this must be indulged to his education, so hard it is for a citizen to write an history but that the fur of his gown will be felt therein. Sure I am, our most elegant historians who have wrote since his time (Sir Francis Bacon, Master Camden, &c.) though throwing away the basket, have taken the fruit; though not mentioning his name, making use of his endeavours. Let me add of John Stow that however he kept tune, he kept time very well, no author being more accurate in the notation thereof.

Besides his chronicle of England, he hath a large *Survey of London,* and I believe no city in Christendom, Rome alone excepted, hath so great a volume extant thereof. Plato was used to say that many good laws were made, but still one was wanting, viz., a law to put all those good laws in execution. Thus the citizens of London have erected many fair monuments to perpetuate their memories; but still there wanted a monument to continue the memory of their monuments (subject by time and otherwise to be defaced) which at last by John Stow was industriously performed.

He died in the eightieth year of his age, April 6, 1605, and is buried at the upper end of the north aisle of the quire of Saint Andrew's Undershaft; his *Chronicle* since continued by another, whose additions are the lively emblem of the times he writeth of, as far short of Master Stow in goodness, as our age is of the integrity and charity of those which went before it.

MAURICE CHAUNCY, most probably born in this city, was bred a friar in Charterhouse, now called Sutton's Hospital. He was imprisoned for refusing the oath of supremacy, with eighteen of his order, all which lost their lives for their obstinacy, whilst our Maurice (like Job's messenger) "only escaped alone" to tell of his fellows' misfortune, and write the history of the execution. Some of Chauncy's party report to his praise that martyrdom was only wanting to him, and not he to martyrdom. Others more truly tax him, for warping to the will of King Henry the Eighth, not so much to decline his own death, as to preserve his convent from destruction, who sped in the first, and failed in the latter. However, fearing some after-claps, he fled beyond the seas, passing the rest of his life in the Low Countries, dying Anno Domini 1581.

JOHN YOUNG, D.D., was born [1534?] in Cheapside,[1] and bred in Pembroke Hall in Cambridge, whereof he became master; hence he was preferred rector of Saint Giles, Cripplegate, and at last bishop of Rochester; a constant preacher, and to whose judgment Queen Elizabeth ascribed much in church matters.

Better bishoprics were often offered to, and often refused by him; particularly when Norwich was proffered to him, by one who affirmed it to be a higher seat, Bishop Young pleasantly returned, "Yea, but it is a harder, and not so easy for an old man, since the cushion was taken away from it"; meaning, since Dr. Scambler had *scambled* away the revenues thereof.[2] He died Anno Domini 1605; and lieth buried at Bromley Church in Kent, where his son most solemnly and sumptuously interred him, though he enjoined all possible privacy, and on his death-bed forbad all funeral expenses. But in such cases it may become the charity and affection of the survivors to do what beseems not so well the modesty and discretion of the dying to desire.

WILLIAM FULKE, D.D., was born [1538] in this city; bred first fellow of Saint John's, then master of Pembroke Hall in Cambridge. His studies were suitable to his years: when young, a good philosopher, witness his book of *Meteors;* afterwards his endeavours ascended from the middle region of the air to the highest heavens, when he became a pious and solid divine.

Now the Romanists, seeing they could no longer blindfold their laity from the Scriptures, resolved to fit them with false spectacles, and set forth the Rhemish translation, which by Doctor Fulke was learnedly confuted, though he never attained any great preferment in the church.

Here it is worth our pains to peruse the immediate succession of masters in Pembroke Hall, because unparalleled in any English foundation: Edmund Grindall, archbishop of Canterbury; Matthew Hutton, archbishop of York; John Whitgift, archbishop of Canterbury; John Young, bishop of Rochester; William Fulke, D.D.; Lancelot Andrewes, bishop of Winchester; Samuel Harsnett, archbishop of York; Nicholas Felton, bishop of Ely.

Here, though all the rest were episcopated, Doctor Fulke was but Doctor Fulke still, though a man of great merit. This proceeded not from any disaffection in him to the hierarchy, as some would fain suggest,

(1) So I am informed by Sir John Young, his grandchild. (2) Edmund Scambler (1510?-1594) bishop of Peterborough, then of Norwich; one of the translators of the "Bishops' Bible."

but principally from his love of privacy, and place of Margaret professor, wherein he died Anno Domini 1589.[1]

EDMUND CAMPION was born [1540] in this city, and bred fellow in Saint John's College in Oxford, where he became proctor anno 1568, when Queen Elizabeth visited that university. Being made deacon by the protestant church, he afterwards renounced that order, and fled beyond the sea. A man of excellent parts; though he who rode post to tell him so, might come too late to bring him tidings thereof, being such a valuer of himself that he swelled every drop of his ability into a bubble by his vain ostentation. And indeed few who were reputed scholars had more of Latin, or less of Greek, than he had.

He was sent over with Father Parsons into England to reduce it to the church of Rome; to this purpose he set forth his *Ten Reasons,* so purely for Latin, so plainly and pithily penned, that they were very taking, and fetched over many (neuters before) to his persuasion.

It was not long before he was caught by the setters of the Secretary Walsingham, and brought to the Tower, where one of his own religion said that he was *exquisitissimis cruciatibus tortus* (racked with most exquisite torments).

Yet the lieutenant of the Tower truly told him that he had rather seen than felt the rack, being so favourably used therein, that being taken off, he did presently go to his lodging without help, and used his hands in writing. Besides, as Campion confessed, he was not examined upon any point of religion, but only upon matters of state.

Some days after he was engaged in four solemn disputations, to make good that bold challenge he had made against all protestants: place, the chapel in the Tower; auditors, the lieutenant of the Tower, Mr. Beale, clerk of the council, with many protestants and papists.

An authentic author[2] giveth this unpartial account of Campion in his disputation: *ad disputandum productus, expectationem concitatam aegre sustinuit;* and, in plain truth, no man did ever boast less when he put it off. Within a few days the queen was necessitated, for her own security, to make him the subject of severity, by whose laws he was executed in the following December [1581].

EDMUND SPENSER, born [1552?] in this city, was brought up in Pembroke Hall in Cambridge, where he became an excellent scholar; but especially most happy in English poetry, as his works do declare, in which the many *Chaucerisms* used (for I will not say affected by him) are thought by the ignorant to be blemishes, known by the learned to be beauties to his book; which notwithstanding had been more saleable if more conformed to our modern language.

There passeth a story commonly told and believed that Spenser, presenting his poems to Queen Elizabeth, she, highly affected therewith, commanded the Lord Cecil, her treasurer, to give him an hundred

(1) Fulke was never considered for election to the bench of bishops, the real reason being probably his strong puritan opinions, expressed frequently in strident championship. Contrary to Fuller's statement, he failed to secure election as regius professor of divinity. (2) Camden, in his *Elizabeth*.

pounds; and when the treasurer (a good steward of the queen's money) alleged that sum was too much, "Then give him," quoth the queen, "what is reason," to which the lord consented, but was so busied, belike, about matters of higher concernment, that Spenser received no reward; whereupon he presented this petition in a small piece of paper to the queen in her progress:

> I was promis'd on a time,
> To have reason for my rhyme;
> From that time unto this season,
> I receiv'd nor rhyme nor reason

Hereupon the queen gave strict order (not without some check to her treasurer) for the present payment of the hundred pounds she first intended unto him.

He afterwards went over into Ireland, secretary to the Lord Grey, lord deputy thereof; and though that his office under his lord was lucrative, yet got he no estate; but, saith my author, *peculiari poetis fato, semper cum paupertate conflictatus est.*[1] So that it fared little better with him than with William Xilander the German (a most excellent linguist, antiquary, philosopher and mathematician) who was so poor that, as Thuanus saith, he was thought, *fami non famae scribere.*

Returning into England, he was robbed by the rebels of that little he had; and dying for grief in great want, anno 1599, was honourably buried nigh Chaucer in Westminster, where this distich concludeth his epitaph on his monument:

> *Anglica te vivo vixit plausitque poesis,*
> *Nunc moritura timet te moriente mori.*
> Whilst thou didst live, liv'd English poetry,
> Which fears, now thou art dead, that she shall die.

Nor must we forget, that the expense of his funeral and monument was defrayed at the sole charge of Robert, first of that name earl of Essex.

WILLIAM COTTON, D.D., was born in this city (though his infancy was much conversant about Finchley in Middlesex) as his nearest relation hath informed me.[2] He was bred in Queens' College in Cambridge; preferred by Queen Elizabeth archdeacon of Lewes and canon residentiary of Saint Paul's. Hence he was advanced and consecrated bishop of Exeter, November the 12th, 1598.

During his sitting there, Mr. Snape,[3] a second Cartwright (not for abilities but activity) came out of Jersey, and plentifully sowed the seeds of non-comformity in his diocese, which the vigilancy of this stout and prudent prelate plucked up by the roots, before they could come to perfection.

In his old age he was apoplectical, which malady deprived him of his speech some days before his death; so that he could only say "Amen, amen," often reiterated. Hereupon some scandalous tongues broached

(1) Camden's *Elizabeth.* ["He suffered the usual fate of poets, having a continual struggle against poverty."] (2) Edward Cotton, D.D., his son. (3) Edmund Snape (fl. 1576-1608) puritan, imprisoned for a short time for attempting to introduce presbyterian usages into England. For Thomas Cartwright see Hertfordshire, p. 238.

this jeer, "that he lived like a bishop, and died like a clerk"; and yet let such men know, that no dying person can use any one word more expressive, whether it be an invocation of his help in whom all the promises are Amen, or whether it be a submission to the Divine Providence in all, by way of approbation of former, or option of future things.

I will only add and translate his epitaph, transcribed from his monument.

A Paulo ad Petrum pia te Regina vocavit:
Cum Petro et Paulo coeli Rex arce locavit.

Whom th' queen from Paul to Peter did remove:
Him God with Paul and Peter plac'd above.

He lieth buried in the north side of the quire of Exeter, but his monument is distanced from the place of his interment, in a north-east chapel. His death happened Anno Domini 1621.

LANCELOT ANDREWES, D.D., was born [1555] in this city, in Tower Street, his father being a seaman of good repute belonging to Trinity House. He was bred scholar, fellow and master of Pembroke Hall in Cambridge.

He was an unimitable preacher in his way, and such plagiaries who have stolen his sermons could never steal his preaching, and could make nothing of that whereof he made all things as he desired. Pious and pleasant Bishop Felton (his contemporary and colleague) endeavoured in vain in his sermon to assimilate his style; and therefore said merrily of himself, "I had almost marred my own natural trot, by endeavouring to imitate his artificial amble." But I have spoken largely of this peerless prelate in my *Church History*. He died Anno Domini 1626.[1]

THOMAS DOVE, D.D., was born [1555] in this city, as a credible person of his nearest relation hath informed me, bred a *tanquam* (which is a fellow's fellow) in Pembroke Hall in Cambridge. He afterwards became an eminent preacher, and his sermons, substantial in themselves, were advantaged by his comely person and graceful elocution. Queen Elizabeth was highly affected, and anno 1589 preferred him dean of Norwich, advancing him eleven years after to the bishopric of Peterborough. He departed this life 1630, in the thirtieth year of his bishopric, on the thirtieth of August, who kept a good house whilst he lived, and yet raised a family to knightly degree.

JOHN HOWSON, D.D., was born [1557?] in Saint Bride's parish in this city;[2] bred a scholar in Saint Paul's School, whence going to Oxford, he became a student and canon of Christ Church, and afterwards was consecrated bishop of Oxford, May 9, 1619, being his birthday in his climacterical, then entering upon the 63rd year of his age.

(1) Andrewes was bishop of Chichester, of Ely, and finally of Winchester. He was renowned for his patristic learning, and was first on the list of divines appointed to make the Authorized Version of the Bible. (2) So am I informed by his own daughter, the widow of famous Master Farnaby, since remarried to Mr. Cole in Suffolk. [Thomas Farnby (1575?-1647) who sailed in Drake and Hawkins' last voyage, was the chief classical scholar and schoolmaster of his time, and secured an European reputation.]

His learned book, *In What Case a Divorce is Lawful,* with his sermons against sacrilege, and stating of the pope's supremacy, in four sermons, enjoined on him by King James (to clear his causeless aspersion of favouring popery) and never since replied by the Romish party, have made him famous to all posterity. He was afterwards removed to the bishopric of Durham, but continued not long therein, for he died, in the 75th year of his age, 6th of February Anno Domini 1632, and was buried in Saint Paul's in London.

SIR HENRY MARTEN, knight, was born [1562?] in this city, where his father left him forty pounds a year; and he used merrily to say that if his father had left him fourscore he would never have been a scholar, but lived on his lands; whereas this being (though a large encouragement) but a scant maintenance, he plied his book for a better livelihood. He was bred fellow in New College in Oxford; and by the advice of Bishop Andrewes, addressed himself to the study of the civil law.

By the advice of the said bishop, Master Marten had weekly transmitted unto him, from some proctors at Lambeth, the brief heads of the most important causes which were to be tried in the high commission. Then, with some of his familiar friends in that faculty, they privately pleaded those causes amongst themselves, acting in their chamber what was done in the court. But Mr. Marten, making it his work, exceeded the rest in amplifying and aggravating any fault, moving of anger and indignation against the guilt thereof; or else in extenuating and excusing it: procure pity, obtain pardon, or at least prevail for a lighter punishment. Some years he spent in this personated pleading, to enable himself against [the time when] he was really called to that profession.

Hence it was that afterwards he became so eminent an advocate in the high commission that no cause could come amiss to him; for he was not to make new armour, but only to put it on and buckle it; not to invent, but apply arguments to his client. He was at last knighted, and made judge of the prerogative for probate of wills, and also of the admiralty in causes concerning foreign traffic; so that, as King James said pleasantly, "he was a mighty monarch in his jurisdiction over land and sea, the living and dead." He died, very aged and wealthy, Anno Domini 1641.[1]

EDWARD ALLEYN was born [1566] in the aforesaid parish [Saint Botolph] near Devonshire House, where now is the sign of The Pie. He was bred a stage-player; a calling which many have condemned, more have questioned, some few have excused, and far fewer conscientious people have commended. He was the Roscius of our age, so acting to the life that he made any part (especially a majestic one) to become him. He got a very great estate, and in his old age, following Christ's counsel, on what forcible motive belongs not to me to inquire, "he made friends of his unrighteous mammon," building therewith a fair college at Dulwich in Kent, for the relief of poor people.

Some, I confess, count it built on a foundered foundation, seeing in a spiritual sense none is good and lawful money save what is honestly and

(1) He was the father of Henry Marten the famous regicide.

industriously gotten. But perchance such who condemn Master Alleyn herein, have as bad shillings in the bottom of their own bags, if search were made therein. Sure I am, no hospital is tied with better or stricter laws, that it may not *sag* from the intention of the founder. The poor of his native parish Saint Botolph Bishopsgate, have a privilege to be provided for therein before others. Thus he, who out-acted others in his life, out-did himself before his death, which happened Anno Domini 1626.

THOMAS CURSON, born in All Hallows, Lombard Street, armourer, dwelt without Bishopsgate. It happened that a stage-player borrowed a rusty musket, which had lain long ledger[1] in his shop. Now, though his part was comical, he therewith acted an unexpected tragedy, killing one of the standers-by, the gun casually going off on the stage, which he suspected not to be charged.

Oh the difference of divers men in the tenderness of their consciences! Some are scarce touched with a wound, whilst others are wounded with a touch therein. This poor armourer was highly afflicted therewith, though done against his will, yea without his knowledge, in his absence, by another, out of mere chance. Hereupon he resolved to give all his estate to pious uses. No sooner had he gotten a round sum, but presently he posted with it in his apron to the court of aldermen, and was in pain till by their direction he had settled it for the relief of poor in his own and other parishes; and disposed of some hundreds of pounds accordingly, as I am credibly informed by the then churchwardens of the said parish. Thus, as he conceived himself casually (though at great distance) to have occasioned the death of one, he was the immediate and direct cause of giving a comfortable living to many. He died Anno Domini 16—.

JOHN DONNE was born [1571/2] in this city, of wealthy parentage extracted out of Wales; one of an excellent wit, large travel and choice experience. After many vicissitudes in his youth, his reduced age was honoured with the doctorship of divinity and deanery of Saint Paul's.

Should I endeavour to deliver his exact character (who willingly would not do any wrong) should do a fourfold injury: 1. To his worthy memory, whose merit my pen is unable to express. 2. To myself, in undertaking what I am not sufficient to perform. 3. To the reader, first in raising, then in frustrating his expectation. 4. To my deservedly honoured Master Izaak Walton, by whom his life is so learnedly written.

It is enough for me to observe he died March 31, Anno Domini 1631, and lieth buried in Saint Paul's, under an ingenious and choice monument, neither so costly as to occasion envy nor so common as to cause contempt.

LIONEL CRANFIELD [EARL OF MIDDLESEX], son to Randal Cranfield, citizen, and Martha his wife, daughter to the Lady Dennis of Gloucestershire (who by her will, which I have perused, bequeathed a fair estate unto her) was born [1575] in Basinghall Street, and bred a merchant, much conversant in the custom-house.

(1) *Lain long ledger*=long remained stationary.

He may be said to have been his own tutor, and his own university. King James being highly affected with the clear, brief, strong, yea and profitable sense he spake, preferred him lord treasurer 1621, baron of Cranfield and earl of Middlesex. Under him it began to be *young flood* in the exchequer, wherein there was a very *low ebb* when he entered on that office; and he possessed his treasurer's place some four years, till he fell into the duke of Buckingham's (the best of friends' and the worst of foes') displeasure. Some say this lord, who rose chiefly by the duke, whose near kinswoman he married, endeavoured to stand without, yea, in some cases (for the king's profit) against him; which independency and opposition that duke would not endure. Flaws may soon be found, and easily be made breaches, in great officers, who being active in many, cannot be exact in all matters.[1]

However, this lord, by losing his office, saved himself, departing from his treasurer's place, which in that age was hard to keep; insomuch that one asking "what was good to preserve life?" was answered, "Get to be lord treasurer of England, for they never die in their place;" which indeed was true for four successions.

Retiring to his magnificent house at Copt Hall, he there enjoyed himself contentedly, entertained his friends bountifully, neighbours hospitably, poor charitably. He was a proper person, of comely presence, cheerful yet grave countenance, and surely a solid and wise man. And though their soul be the fattest who only suck the sweet milk, they are the healthfullest who (to use the Latin phrase) have tasted of both the breasts of fortune. He died, as I collect, anno 1645, and lieth interred in a stately monument in the abbey at Westminster.

JOHN DAVENANT, D.D., born [1576] in Watling Street, was son to John Davenant, a wealthy citizen, whose father was of Davenant's lands in Essex. When an infant newly able to go, he fell down a pair of stairs, and rising up at the bottom smiled, without having any harm; God and his good angels keeping him for further service in the church.

When a child he would rather own his own forwardness than another's flattery; and when soothed up by the servants, "that not John but some other of his brothers did cry," he would rather appear in his own face than wear their disguise, returning, "that it was none of his brothers, but John only cried."

He was bred first, fellow-commoner, then fellow, then Margaret professor, then master of Queens' College in Cambridge. At a public election, he gave his negative voice against a near kinsman, and a most excellent scholar:[2] "Cousin," said he, "I will satisfy your father, that you have worth, but not want enough to be one of our society."

Returning from the synod of Dort, he was elected bishop of Sarum, 1621. After his consecration, being to perform some personal service to King James at Newmarket, he refused to ride on the Lord's day, and came, though a day later to the court, no less welcome to the king, not

(1) In 1624 he was charged with corrupt practices and condemned, but pardoned the following year. (2) Mr. John Gore (afterwards knighted) of Gilston in Hertfordshire.

only accepting his excuse, but also commending his seasonable forbearance.

Taking his leave of the college, and of one John Rolfe, an ancient servant thereof, he desired him to pray for him, and when the other modestly returned, that he rather needed his lordship's prayers: "Yea, John," said he, "and I need thine too, being now to enter into a calling wherein I shall meet with many and great temptations." *Praefuit qui profuit* was the motto written in most of his books, the sense whereof he practised in his conversation.

He was humble in himself, and, the consequence thereof, charitable to others. Indeed, once invited by Bishop Field, and not well pleased with some roisting company there, he embraced the next opportunity of departure after dinner. And when Bishop Field proffered to light him with a candle down stairs, "My lord, my lord," said he, "let us lighten others by our unblameable conversation;" for which speech some since have severely censured him, how justly I interpose not. But let others unrelated unto him write his character, whose pen cannot be suspected of flattery, which he when living did hate, and dead did not need.[1]

We read of the patriarch Israel, that the time drew nigh that he must die; *must,* a necessity of it. Such a decree attended this bishop, happy to die, before his order (for a time) died, April 1641, and with a solemn funeral he was buried in his own cathedral; Dr. Nicholas (now dean of Saint Paul's) preaching an excellent sermon at his interment.

MATTHEW WREN, D.D., was born [1585] in this city, not far from Cheapside; but descended (as appears by his arms) from the worshipful family of the Wrens in Northumberland. He was bred fellow of Pembroke Hall in Cambridge, where he kept the extraordinary philosophy act[2] before King James. I say kept it, with no less praise to himself than pleasure to the king; where if men should forget, even dogs would remember his seasonable distinction, what the king's hounds could perform above others by virtue of their prerogative.

He afterwards became an excellent preacher, and two of his sermons in the university were most remarkable. One preached before the judges on this text, "And let judgment run down like waters, and righteousness as a mighty stream," at what time the draining of the fens was designed, suspected detrimental to the university. The other, when newly returned from attending Prince Charles into Spain, on the words of the psalmist, *Abyssus abyssum invocat* (one depth calleth another.)

He was afterwards preferred master of Peterhouse, dean of Windsor, bishop of Norwich, and Ely. Some in the Long Parliament fell so heavily on him that he was imprisoned in the Tower almost fifteen years, and his cause never heard. Surely, had the imposers been the sufferers hereof, they would have cried it up for a high piece of injustice; but, as St. Paul had the credit to be brought with entreaties out of prison by those who sent him thither, so this prelate hath had the honour, that the

(1) Davenant was Fuller's uncle on his mother's side. The Bishop Field referred to above was Theophilus Field (1574-1636) impeached by the Commons for bribery before his promotion to the see of Llandaff. (2) *Act*=a thesis publicly maintained by a candidate for a degree.

same parliamentary power (though not constituted of the same persons) which committed him, caused his enlargement.[1] [*d.* 1667]

GILES FLETCHER was born [1588?] in this city,[2] son to Giles Fletcher, doctor in law, and ambassador into Russia, of whom formerly in Kent. From Westminster School he was chosen first, scholar, then fellow of Trinity College in Cambridge; one equally beloved of the Muses and the Graces, having a sanctified wit, witness his worthy poem intituled *Christ's Victory,* made by him being but bachelor of arts, discovering the piety of a saint and divinity of a doctor. He afterwards applied himself to school-divinity (cross to the grain of his genius, as some conceive) and attained to good skill therein. When he preached at St. Mary's, his prayer before his sermon usually consisted of one entire allegory, not driven, but led on, most proper in all particulars. He was at last, by exchange of his living, settled in Suffolk, which hath the best and worst air in England; best about Bury, and worst on the sea-side where Master Fletcher was beneficed. His clownish and low-parted parishioners (having nothing but their shoes high about them) valued not their pastor according to his worth, which disposed him to melancholy, and hastened his dissolution. I behold the life of this learned poet, like those half-verses in Virgil's *Aeneid,* broken off in the middle, seeing he might have doubled his days according to the ordinary course of nature; whose death happened [1623]. He had another brother, Phineas Fletcher, fellow of King's College in Cambridge, and beneficed also in Norfolk; a most excellent poet, witness his *Purple Island* and several other pieces of great ingenuity.

THOMAS WENTWORTH [FIRST EARL OF STRAFFORD] was born [1593], his mother coming casually to London, in Chancery Lane, in the parish of St. Dunstan's in the West. Yet no reason Yorkshire should be deprived of the honour of him, whose ancestors long flourished in great esteem at Wentworth-Woodhouse in that county.

He was bred in St. John's College in Cambridge, and afterwards became a champion patriot on all occasions. He might seem to have a casting voice in the House of Commons, for where he was pleased to dispose his yea or nay, there went the affirmative or negative. It was not long before the court gained from the country, and then honours and offices were heaped on him, created Baron and Viscount Wentworth, earl of Strafford, and lord deputy of Ireland.

When he went over into Ireland, all will confess he laid down to himself this noble foundation: vigorously to endeavour the reduction of the Irish to perfect obedience to the king, and profit to the exchequer. But many do deny the superstructure (which he built thereon) was done by legal line and plummet.

(1) Following on Hampden's report to the House of Lords, after Laud's impeachment, that the Commons had received information against Wren, the commons declared him unfit to hold any office, and he was imprisoned in the Tower. Cromwell more than once offered him his liberty (on one occasion through his nephew Sir Christopher Wren) but he declined to acknowledge Cromwell's authority. He was released in 1660. (2) So was I informed by Mr. John Rainsey, who married his relict.

A parliament was called in England, and many crimes were by prime persons of England, Scotland and Ireland charged upon him. He fenced skilfully for his life, and his grand guard was this, that, though confessing some misdemeanors, all proved against him amounted not to treason. And indeed *number* cannot create a *new kind;* so that many trespasses cannot make a riot, many riots one treason, no more than many frogs can make one toad. But here the distinction of accumulative and constructive treason was coined, and caused his destruction. Yet his adversaries politicly brake off the edge of the axe which cut off his head, by providing his condemnation should not pass into precedent to posterity; so that his death was remarkable, but not exemplary. Happy had it been, if (as it made no precedent on earth) so no remembrance thereof had been kept in Heaven.

Some hours before his suffering, he fell fast asleep, alleged by his friends as an evidence of the clearness of his conscience, and hardly to be paralleled, save in St. Peter, in a dead sleep the night before he was to die, condemned by Herod. His death happened in 1641.

He hath an eternal monument in the matchless meditations of King Charles the First, and an everlasting epitaph in that weighty character there given him, "I looked upon my lord of Strafford as a gentleman, whose abilities might make a prince rather afraid than ashamed, in the greatest affairs of state, &c."[1]

God alone can revive the dead. All that princes can perform is to honour their memory and posterity, as our gracious sovereign King Charles hath made his worthy son knight of the Garter.

ALEXANDER STRANGE, son to a doctor in law, was born in London,[2] bred in Peterhouse in Cambridge, where he commenced bachelor of divinity, and afterwards for forty-six years was vicar of Layston,[3] and prebendary of Saint Paul's, where his *prebenda-submersa,* the corpse whereof was drowned in the sea, afforded him but a noble a year.

Now, because Layston Church stood alone in the fields, and inconveniently for such who were to repair thereunto, he built at Buntingford (a through-road market, mostly in his parish) a neat and strong chapel, *e stipe collatitia,* from the bounty others gave and he gathered. Wherefore, having laid the foundation, before well furnished for the finishing thereof, he gave for his motto, "Beg hard, or beggard."

None could tax him (with the Scribes and Pharisees) for "binding heavy burthens and grievous to be borne, and laying them on other men's shoulders, whilst he himself would not move them with one of his fingers." First, because the burthens were not heavy, being light in the particulars, though weighty in the total sum. Secondly, he bound them on none, but professed himself bound unto them, if pleased to take them up for a public good. Thirdly, he put his, and that a bountiful hand unto them, purchasing land out of his own purse to pay for the daily reparation thereof. He also promoted the building of a free school in the said place, to which some sisters, worshipfully born in the same town,

(1) *Eikon Basilike.* (2) So was I informed by his careful executors. (3) So read I in his epitaph in the chapel.

wealthily and honourably married, were the foundresses; yet so as it will still be thankful to contributors thereunto for better accommodation.

This Master Strange, being no less prosperous than painful in compounding all differences among his neighbours, being a man of peace, went to eternal peace December 8, in the eightieth year of his age, 1650.

THE FAREWELL

And now, being to take my farewell of this great city, I cannot forget the verse, which I find, amongst others, in Master Camden's commendation thereof:

Urbs pietate potens, numeroso cive superba
Potent in piety, in her people proud.

But see the Romish charity, who confine all piety to popery. The *Index Expurgatorius,* printed at Madrid by Lewes Sanchez 1612, commandeth the fore part of the verse, concerning their piety, to be expunged; letting the latter moiety, of their pride, to remain.

May I in this particular be the humble remembrancer of the city (without the least entrenching on his place who worthily dischargeth that office) to cross and confute that peevish and partial *Index.* Let it be their endeavours to delete out of their hearts all high conceits of their populousness, and effectually to express grace and goodness in their conversations.

Nor let the city of London ever forget *quantillum interfuit inter maximam civitatem et nullam* (how little distance there lately was betwixt the greatest city and none at all) if gates and bars, as it is generally received, be the essential difference of a city. But God, who can produce light out of darkness, can make the plucking down of the gates to be the setting up of the city. Wherefore though the eleventh day of March be generally beheld as the first day of Spring, London may date her Spring from the eleventh day of February, 1660, when she effectually felt the vernal heat after a long winter of woe and misery.[1]

I heartily wish this honourable city whatever may conduce to the continuance and increase of the happiness thereof. Especially that the river of Thames, the life of London (as which easeth, adorneth, enricheth, feedeth and fortifieth it) may have its channel constantly continued. The miller's riddle, "If I have water I will drink wine; but if I have no water, I must drink water," is applicable to this city: so long as Thames water continues, Londoners may *wine* it; but should it fail, they must drink water indeed, and some perchance brackish too, as made of their tears.

I will not pry too nearly and narrowly into the fancy of our poet, speaking of the ruins of old Rome:

Ne ought, save Tiber hasting to his fall,
O world's inconstancy! Remains of all;
That which is firm doth flit and fall away.
And that is flitting doth abide and stay.[2]

(1) The Restoration of Charles II. (2) Du Bellay, in his *Ruins of Rome,* translated by Spenser.

And yet, by his leave, greater rivers than Tiber have in process of time had their streams, by casualties or neglect, partly drained, wholly dried or otherwise diverted. My humble request therefore to the officers of the city is, effectually to own their concernment in the river of Thames, in clearing and cleansing it from shoals, sands and other obstructing enroachments, that they may leave it as well to posterity, as they found it from their fathers.

WESTMINSTER

WESTMINSTER is the greatest city in England next London, not only in position, but by the dimensions thereof. For let it be taken, as truly it ought, extensively with the liberty of Lancaster from Temple Bar, and it filleth as much ground (not to say containeth more reasonable souls) than any city in the land. But as a proper man seemeth a dwarf when placed next to a giant, such the infelicity of Westminster, whose due greatness, devoured by the vicinity of London, is insensible in the eyes of beholders.

It was anciently called Thorney, and afterwards Westminster, for distinction from St. Paul's, called in ancient times Eastminster.

THE BUILDINGS

The abbey church is beheld as a rare structure, with so small and slender pillars (greater legs argue not the strongest man) to support so weighty a fabric; built by King Henry the Third, and afterwards much enlarged and beautified by the abbots thereof.

Adjoining to it is the chapel of King Henry the Seventh, which Leland calls "the miracle of the world." Indeed, let the Italians deride our English, and condemn them for Gothish buildings; this they must admire, and may here take notes of architecture (if their pride would permit them) to perfect theirs accordingly.

In this chapel the founder thereof, with his queen, lieth interred under a monument of solid brass,[1] most richly guilded and artificially carved. Some slight it for the cheapness, because it cost but a thousand pounds in the making thereof. Such do not consider it as the work of so thrifty a prince, who would make a little money go far, besides that it was just at the turning of the tide (as one may term it) of money, which flowed after the finding out of the West Indies, though ebbing before.

Amongst the civil structures, Westminster Hall is eminent, erected by King William Rufus for the hall to his own court, built with cobwebless beams, conceived of Irish wood. Sure I am, we then had no command in that island, as first subdued by King Henry the Second. It is one of the greatest rooms in Christendom; and indeed it needeth to be of good capacity, to receive so many plaintiffs and defendents being at such mututal distance of affection.

Next is Whitehall, the palace of our English kings, which one termed a good hypocrite, promising less than it performeth, and more convenient within than comely without; to which the nursery of St. James's was an appendant.

As for the houses of noblemen all along the Strand, I desire to be excused from commending some, lest it should by cavilling spirits be

(1) Or copper rather.—F.

implicitly interpreted a dispraise of the rest. Besides, I am ignorant under what name to commend them to posterity, so many houses daily, new-dipt, assume to themselves new names according to the alteration of their owners. I conclude them therefore *all best,* and *best of all* whilst they continue in the hands of their present possessors.

PROVERBS

There is no redemption from Hell. There is a place partly under, partly by the exchequer court, commonly called Hell; I could wish it had another name, seeing it is ill jesting with edge-tools, especially with such as are sharpened by Scripture. I am informed that formerly this place was appointed a prison for the king's debtors, who never were freed thence until they had paid their uttermost due demanded of them. If so, it was no Hell, but might be termed purgatory, according to the popish erroneous persuasion. But, since, this proverb is applied to moneys paid into the exchequer, which thence are irrecoverable upon what plea or pretence whatsoever.

THE WORTHIES

EDWARD THE FIRST was born [1329] in Westminster, being a prince placed by the posture of his nativity, betwixt a weak father and a wilful son.[1] Yet he needed no such advantage for foils to set forth his real worth. He was surnamed Longshanks, his step being another man's stride, and was very high in stature. And though ofttimes such who are built four storeys high are observed to have little in their cock-loft, yet was he a most judicious man in all his undertakings; equally wise to plot, as valiant to perform; and (which under Divine Providence was the result of both) happy in success at sea, at land, at home, abroad, in war, in peace. He was so fortunate with his sword at the beginning of his reign that he awed all his enemies with his scabbard before the end thereof. In a word, he was a prince of so much merit, that nothing under a chronicle can make his complete character. [*d.* 1307]

MATTHEW WESTMINSTER was bred a monk therein, and as accomplished a scholar as any of his age. Observable is the grand difference betwixt our English history as he found it, and as he left it. He found it like Polyphemus when his eye was bored out, a big and bulky body, but blind. Memorable actions were either presented without any date, which little informed, or too many dates, which more distracted the reader. Our Matthew reduced such confused sounds to an articulate and intelligible voice, regulating them by a double directory of time, viz., the beginnings and deaths of all the kings of England and archbishops of Canterbury. He wrote one history from the beginning of the world to Christ; a second, from Christ's Nativity to the Norman Conquest; a third, from thence to the beginning of King Edward the Second, augmenting it afterwards with the addition of his life, and King Edward the Third's. He named his book *Flores Historiarum;* and if sometimes

(1) The "weak father" being Henry III, and the "wilful son" Edward II.

(for it is but seldom) he presenteth a flower less fragrant, or blasted bud, the judicious reader is not tied to take what he tenders, but may select for his own ease a nosegay of the choicest flowers thereof.[1]

EDWARD [PRINCE OF WALES], sole son to King Henry the Sixth and Margaret his queen, was born at Westminster, on the 13th day of October 1453. Now, when his father's party was totally and finally routed in the battle at Tewkesbury, this prince, being taken prisoner, presented to King Edward the Fourth, and demanded by him, on what design he came over into England, returned this answer, "That he came to recover the Crown, which his ancestors for three descents had no less rightfuly than peaceably possessed."

An answer, for the truth, befitting the son of so holy a father as King Henry the Sixth; for the boldness thereof, becoming the son of so haughty a mother as Queen Margaret. But presently King Edward dashed him on the mouth with his gauntlet, and his brother Richard Crookback stabbed him to the heart with his dagger.[2] A barbarous murder, without countenance of justice in a legal, or valour in a military way. And his blood then shed was punished not long after.

Here I am not ashamed to make this observation, that England had successively three Edwards, all Princes of Wales, sole or eldest sons to actual kings; two dying violent, all untimely deaths, in their minority, before they were possessed of the crown: viz., 1. Edward, son to Henry VI, stabbed in the seventeenth year of his age; 2. Edward, son to Edward IV, stifled in the tenth year of his age; 3, Edward, son to Richard III, pined away in the eleventh year of his age.

The murder of the second may justly be conceived the punishment of the murder of the first, and the untimely death of the last (of whom more in Yorkshire) a judgment for the murder of the two former. [*d*. 1471]

EDWARD V, eldest son to Edward the Fourth and Elizabeth his queen, was born in the sanctuary of Westminster, November 2/3, 1470. His tender years are too soft for a solid character to be fixed on him. No hurt we find done by him, but too much on him, being murdered in the Tower by the procurement of his uncle protector. Thus was he born in a spiritual, and killed in a temporal prison. He is commonly called King Edward the Fifth, though his head was asked, but never married to the English crown; and therefore, in all the pictures made of him, a distance interposed forbiddeth the banns betwixt them. [*d*. 1483]

ELIZABETH [OF YORK], eldest daughter of King Edward the Fourth and Elizabeth his queen, was born in Westminster on the eleventh of February 1465. She was afterwards married to King Henry the Seventh; and so the two houses of York and Lancaster united first hopefully in their bed, and afterwards more happily in their issue. Besides her duti-

(1) Matthew Westminster is now considered an imaginary writer. The *Flores Historiarum* mentioned by Fuller was compiled by several writers at the abbeys of St. Albans and Westminster. (2) This version gained currency in Tudor times, but he was probably killed in the rout following the victory of the Yorkists at Tewkesbury.

fulness to her husband, and fruitfulness in her children, little can be extracted of her personal character. She died (though not in child-bearing) in childbed, being safely delivered on Candlemas day, anno 1503, of the Lady Catherine; and afterwards falling sick, languished until the eleventh of February, and then died, in the thirty-seventh year of her age, on the day of her nativity. She lieth buried with her husband in the chapel of his erection, and hath an equal share with him in the use and honour of that his most magnificent monument.

CECILY, [third] daughter to King Edward the Fourth by Elizabeth his queen, bearing the name of Cecily duchess of York, her grandmother and godmother, was born [1469] at Westminster. In her childhood mention was made of a marriage betwixt her and James (son to James the Third) prince of Scotland. But that motion died with her father; heaven (wherein marriages are made) reserving that place for Margaret her eldest sister's eldest daughter.

She long led a single life, but little respected of King Henry the Seventh her brother-in-law. That politic king, knowing that if he had none or no surviving issue by his queen, then the right of the crown rested in this Cecily, sought to suppress her from popularity or any public appearance. He neither preferred her to any foreign prince, nor disposed of her to any prime peer of England, till at last this lady wedded herself to a Lincolnshire lord, John Baron Wells, whom King Henry advanced viscount, and no higher. After his death, my author[1] saith, she was remarried, not mentioning her husband's name;[2] whence I conclude him an obscure person, and this lady rather married than matched, such the distance betwixt their degrees. Probably this Cecily, consulting her comfort more than her credit, did it of design, so to be beneath the jealousy of King Henry the Seventh. [*d.* 1507]

CHRISTOPHER TYE, doctor of music, flourished in the reign of King Henry the Eighth and King Edward the Sixth, to whom he was one of the gentlemen of their chapel, and probably the organist. Music, which received a grievous wound in England at the dissolution of the abbeys, was much beholding to him for her recovery; such his excellent skill and piety, that he kept it up in credit at court and in all cathedrals during his life. He translated the Acts of the Apostles into verse; and let us take a taste of his poetry:[3]

> In the former treatise to thee
> Dear friend Theophilus;
> I have written the veritie
> Of the Lord Christ Jesus.

Pass we now from this poetry (being music in words) to his music (being poetry in sounds) who set an excellent composition of music of four parts to the several chapters of his aforementioned poetry, dedicating the same to King Edward the Sixth, a little before the death of

(1) Speed's *Chronicle*. (2) Some say his name was Kymbe [or Kyne, of the Isle of Wight.] (3) Fuller quotes five other stanzas which are here omitted. Some of Tye's compositions have become well-known hymn-tunes, among them "Winchester", sung to "While shepherds watched."

that good prince, and printed it Anno Domini 1553. He also did compose many excellent services and anthems of four and five parts, which were used in cathedrals many years after his death, the certain date whereof I cannot attain. [1497?-1572]

EDMOND DOUBLEDAY, esquire, was of a tall and proper person, and lived in this city. Nor had this large case a little jewel, this long body a lazy soul, whose activity and valour was adequate to his strength and greatness, whereof he gave this eminent testimony.

When Sir Thomas Knyvet was sent, November 4, 1605, by King James, to search the cellar beneath the Parliament House, with very few, for the more privacy, to attend him, he took Master Doubleday with him. Here they found Guy Fawkes, with his dark lanthorn, in the dead of the night, providing for the death of many the next morning. He was newly come out of the Devil's Closet (so I may fitly term the inward room where the powder lay and the train was to be laid) into the outward part of the cellar. Fawkes beginning to bustle, Master Doubleday instantly ordered him, at his pleasure, up with his heels, and there with the traitor lay the treason flat along the floor, by God's goodness detected, defeated. Fawkes vowed (and though he was a false traitor, herein I do believe him) that, had he been in the inner room, he would have blown up himself and all the company therein. Thus it is pleasant music to hear disarmed malice threaten, when it cannot strike. Master Doubleday lived many years after, deservedly loved and respected, and died about the year of our Lord 1618.

SIR FRANCIS BACON, knight, youngest son to Sir Nicholas Bacon, lord keeper, was born in York House, anno 1561; for, being demanded his age by Queen Elizabeth, he returned that he was two years younger than her majesty's reign. He was bred in Trinity College in Cambridge, and there first fell into a dislike of Aristotle's philosophy, as barren and jejune, enabling some to dispute, more to wrangle, few to find out truth, and none, if confining themselves to his principles.

Hence it was that afterwards he traded so largely in experiments; so that, as Socrates is said to be the first who stooped towering speculations into practical morality, Sir Francis was one of the first who reduced notional to real and scientifical philosophy.

He was afterwards bred in Gray's Inn in the study of our municipal law, attaining to great eminency, but no preferment therein, during the reign of Queen Elizabeth; imputable to the envy of a great person, who hindered his rising, for fear to be hindered by him if risen, and eclipsed in his own profession.[1] Thus the strongest wing of merit cannot mount if a stronger weight of malice doth depress it. Yet was he even then favourite to a favourite, I mean the earl of Essex, and more true to him than the earl was to himself, for, finding him to prefer destructive before displeasing counsel, Sir Francis fairly forsook not his person (whom his

(1) Although William Cecil, Lord Burghley, was his uncle, Bacon's advancement was slow. When the attorney-generalship was vacant in 1593, Bacon's claim was strongly pressed by Essex, but Elizabeth, whom Bacon had offended, preferred Sir Edward Coke for the position.

pity attended to the grave) but practices; and herein was not the worse friend for being the better subject.

By King James he was made his solicitor, and afterwards his attorney (then privileged, contrary to custom, to sit a member *in Dom. Com.*) and at last lord chancellor of England. His abilities were a clear confutation of two vulgar errors, libels on learned men: first, that judgment, wit, fancy and memory cannot eminently be in conjunction in the same person; whereas our knight was a rich cabinet, filled with all four, besides a golden key to open it, elocution. Secondly, that he who is something in all, is nothing in any one art; whereas he was singular *in singulis,* and, being in-at-all, came off with credit.

Such who condemn him for pride, if in his place, with the fifth part of his parts, had been ten times prouder themselves. He had been a better master if he had been a worse, being too bountiful to his servants, and either too confident of their honesty, or too conniving at their falsehood. The story is told to his advantage, that he had two servants, one in all causes patron to the plaintiff, whom his charity presumed always injured, the other to the defendant, pitying him as compelled to law; but taking bribes of both, with this condition, to restore the money received if the cause went against them. Their lord, ignorant hereof, always did unpartial justice; whilst his men (making people pay for what was given them) by compact shared the money betwixt them, which cost their master the loss of his office.

Leading a private life, he much delighted to study in the shade of solitariness; and many useful discoveries in nature were made by him, so that he may be said to have left nothing to his executors, and all to his heirs, under which notion the learned of all ages may be beheld. His vast bounty to such who brought him presents from great persons occasioned his want afterwards, who, in rewarding them, so remembered that he had been lord chancellor, that he forgot that he was but the Lord Verulam.

He died, Anno Domini 1626, in the house of the earl of Arundel at Highgate, and was buried in Saint Michael's Church in Saint Alban's, Master Mutis his grateful servant erecting a monument for him. Since, I have read that his grave being occasionally opened, his skull (the relic of civil veneration) was by one King, a doctor of physic, made the object of scorn and contempt; but he who then derided the dead is since become the laughing-stock of the living.

RICHARD NEILE was born [1562] in King Street in this city, and was bred in St. John's College in Cambridge; he was afterwards vicar of Cheshunt in the county of Hertford, presented thereunto by the honourable family of the Cecils. He was the first and last native of this city who became the dean, and so the supreme magistrate thereof. Through many bishoprics, of Coventry and Lichfield, Durham and Winchester, he was at last preferred archbishop of York, being also privy councillor to King James and King Charles. He died Anno Domini 1640.

JOHN DOWLAND was, as I have most cause to believe, born [1563?] in this city; sure I am he had his longest life and best livelihood therein, being servant in the chapel to Queen Elizabeth and King James. He was the rarest musician that his age did behold; having travelled beyond the seas, and compounded English with foreign skill in that faculty, it is questionable whether he excelled in vocal or instrumental music. A cheerful person he was, passing his days in lawful merriment, truly answering the anagram made of him,[1] JOHANNES DOULANDUS (*annos ludendo hausi.*)

Christian the Fourth, king of Denmark, coming over into England, requested him of King James, who unwillingly willing parted with him. Many years he lived (as I am credibly informed) in the Danish court, in great favour and plenty, generally employed to entertain such English persons of quality as came thither.[2] [*d.* 1626?]

BENJAMIN JONSON was born [1573?] in this city. Though I cannot, with all my industrious inquiry, find him in his cradle, I can fetch him from his long-coats. When a little child, he lived in Hartshorn Lane near Charing Cross, where his mother married a bricklayer for her second husband.

He was first bred in a private school in Saint Martin's church, then in Westminster school, witness his own epigram:

> Camden, most reverend head, to whom I owe
> All that I am in arts, all that I know;
> How nothing's that to whom my country owes
> The great renown and name wherewith she goes, &c.[3]

He was statutably admitted into Saint John's College in Cambridge (as many years after incorporated an honorary member of Christ Church in Oxford) where he continued but few weeks for want of further maintenance, being fain to return to the trade of his father-in-law. And let not them blush that have, but those that have not, a lawful calling. He helped in the new structure of Lincoln's Inn, when, having a trowel in his hand, he had a book in his pocket.

Some gentlemen, pitying that his parts should be buried under the rubbish of so mean a calling, did by their bounty manumit him freely to follow his own ingenious inclinations. Indeed his parts were not so ready to run of themselves, as able to answer the spur; so that it may be truly said of him, that he had an elaborate wit wrought out by his own industry. He would sit silent in learned company, and suck in (besides wine) their several humours into his observation. What was *ore* in others, he was able to refine to himself.

He was paramount in the dramatic part of poetry, and taught the stage an exact conformity to the laws of comedians. His comedies were above the *volge* (which are only tickled with downright obscenity) and took not so well at the first stroke as at the rebound, when beheld the second time; yea, they will endure reading, and that with due commendation, so long as either ingenuity or learning are fashionable in our nation. If his later be not so spriteful and vigorous as his first pieces,

(1) By Ralph Sadler, esq., of Standon in Hertfordshire, who was with him at Copenhagen. (2) Subsequently he became lutenist to Charles I. (3) William Camden was at that time usher, and later headmaster, of Westminster School. To Camden Jonson owed his later eminence in learning.

all that are old will, and all that desire to be old should, excuse him therein.

He was not very happy in his children, and most happy in those which died first, though none lived to survive him. This he bestowed as part of an epitaph on his eldest son, dying in infancy:

> Rest in soft peace; and, ask'd, say here doth lye,
> Ben Jonson his best piece of poetry.

He died Anno Domini 1637; and was buried about the belfry in the abbey church at Westminster.

JOHN WARNER, D.D., was born [1581] in the parish of Saint Clement Danes,[1] within the precincts of this city; bred in Magdalen College in Oxford; at last preferred bishop of Rochester.

This worthy bishop, perceiving the want of a fixed font in the cathedral church of Canterbury, bestowed one upon it; whether more curious or costly my author[2] could not decide, it being both ways so excellent and exquisite; a gift the more remarkable, because the first which hath been offered by any private hand to that church of later times. But I suspect now this font itself is washed away, in the deluge of our late wars, under the notion of superstition.

God hath given him a great estate, and a liberal heart to make use of it; keeping good hospitality in the Christmas at Bromley. As he fed many poor, so he freed himself from much trouble; being absent when the rest of the bishops subscribed their protest in parliament, whereby he enjoyed liberty in the restraint of others of his order. He was an able and active advocate for episcopacy in the House of Lords, speaking for them as long as he had any voice left him, and then willing to have made signs in their just defence, if it might have been permitted him.[3]

[*d.* 1666]

JAMES PALMER, B.D., was born [1585] in this city, and bred in Magdalene College in Cambridge. The company of Carpenters in London gave him an exhibition towards his maintenance there, or lent it him rather; for, since his bounty hath repaid them the principal with plentiful consideration. He was afterwards for many years the constant preacher of Saint Bridget's in Fleet Street, the only church preferment he enjoyed. I perceive thus craft and cruelty may raise a quick and great, but plain frugality (especially if vivacious) will advance a better and surer estate. Though sequestered in these times, what he had formerly gained in his place he hath since bestowed in building and endowing, over against the new chapel in Westminster, a fair almshouse for twelve poor people. Besides this, many and great have his gifts been to ministers' poor widows. And wonder not, reader, if they be unknown to me, which were unknown to his own left hand. All this he did in his lifetime. Oh, it giveth the best light, when one carrieth his lanthorn before him! The surest way that one's will shall be performed is to see it performed. Yea, I may say

(1) So informed from his own mouth. (2) W. Somner, in *The Antiquities of Canterbury*. (3) He was an ardent royalist, impeached and imprisoned in 1641, and later ejected from his see, to which he was restored in 1660.

that his poor people in his almshouse are in some sort provided for, not only from head to foot, but also from body to soul, he constantly preaching to them twice a week. He died anno 1660.

CHARLES THE SECOND (son to King Charles the First, of blessed memory, and Mary youngest daughter to Henry the Fourth, king of France) was born at Saint James's, May 29, 1630. Great was the general rejoicing thereat. The university of Oxford congratulated his birth with printed poems; and it was taken ill, though causelessly, by some that Cambridge did not do the like; for then the wits of the university were sadly distracted into several counties, by reason of the plague therein.

He was, on the first of January 1651, at Scone, crowned king of Scotland; being before invaded by an army under the conduct of Oliver Cromwell. Soon after quitting that kingdom, he marched for England; and on the third of September 1651, nigh Worcester,[1] was fought, and lost the day, though he, to use my author's expression, "acted beyond the expectation of his friends, and to the great applause of his very enemies."[2] Narrow search was made after his person, yea a thousand pounds (a bait his politic enemies made sure would have been bit at) promised to such who should betray him. Yet God (whose angels were his life-guard) miraculously preserving him out of the hands of his enemies, he safely passed over into France to the queen his mother.

During his continuance beyond the seas, great were the proffers tendered unto him if forsaking the protestant religion; but, alas! as soon might the impotent waves remove the most sturdy rocks, as they once unfix him; such his constancy, whom neither the frowns of his afflictions, nor smiles of secular advantages, could make to warp from his first principles.

At length his piety and patience were rewarded by God, with a happy restitution to his undoubted dominions; and he, after a long and tedious exile, landed at Dover, May 26, 1660, to the great joy of this three kingdoms. [*d.* 1685]

MARY [PRINCESS OF ORANGE], eldest daughter of King Charles the First and Queen Mary, was born at Saint James's, November 4, 1631. When her royal father, out of his paternal love, began to cast about for a fitting consort, this peerless princess (though tender in years, rich in piety and wisdom) made it her humble request she might be matched as well in her religion as affection; which happened answerable to her desires, for not long after, a marriage treated betwixt her and Count William of Nassau, eldest son to Henry Prince of Orange, was concluded; and this royal pair wedded accordingly, May 2, 1641. The February following, having at Dover taken her leave of the king her father (the last time she ever saw him on earth) she embarked for, and within few days landed in Holland.

His majesty's affairs in England daily growing worse and worse, at length the sad news of his horrid murder arrived at her ears; this was

(1) See Battles in Worcestershire, p. 621. (2) Doctor Heylyn, in his *Life of King Charles*.

seconded with the loss of her husband the Prince of Orange, who deceased October 8, 1650. Yet such her signal patience that she underwent the weight of so many heavy afflictions, sufficient to break the back of a mean Christian, with a courage far surpassing the weakness of her sex. But, amidst these her calamities, God was pleased to remember mercy, blessing her the November ensuing with a hopeful son.[1]

The complexion of the times being altered in England, she came over to congratulate the happiness of her brother's miraculous restitution; when, behold, sickness arrests this royal princess, no bail being found by physic to defer the execution of her death, which happened 1660. On the 29th December following she was honourably (though privately) interred at Westminster, in the chapel of King Henry the Seventh; and no eye so dry but willingly afforded a tear to bemoan the loss of so worthy a princess.

THE FAREWELL

Seeing the well-being, yea, being, of this city consisteth in the king's court and in the courts of justice, I congratulate the happy return of the one, praying for the long continuance of the other; yea, may the lawyers in Westminster Hall never again plead in their armour (as they did in the time of Wyatt's rebellion) but in their peaceable gowns and legal formalities. Nor doth this wish only extend to the weal of Westminster, but all England; for no such dearth in a land, as what is caused from a drought of justice therein; for if "judgment do not run down as waters, and righteousness as a mighty stream," injustice, like an ocean, will drown all with its inundation.

(1) Who became William III of England.

MIDDLESEX

IT is in effect but the suburbs at large of London, replenished with the retiring houses of the gentry and citizens thereof, besides many palaces of noblemen, and three (lately) royal mansions. Wherefore much measure cannot be expected of so fine ware; the cause why this county is so small, scarce extending, east and west, to 18 miles in length, and not exceeding north and south 12 in the breadth thereof.

It hath Hertfordshire on the north, Buckinghamshire on the west, Essex parted with Lea on the east, Kent and Surrey (severed by the Thames) on the south. The air generally is most healthful, especially about Highgate, where the expert inhabitants report "that divers that have been long visited with sickness, not curable by physic, have in short time recovered by that sweet salutary air."[1]

NATURAL COMMODITIES

Wheat

The best in England groweth in the Vale lying south of Harrow on the Hill nigh Heston (where Providence for the present hath fixed my habitation[2]); so that the king's bread was formerly made of the fine flower thereof. Hence it was that Queen Elizabeth received no composition-money from the villages thereabouts, but took her wheat in kind for her own pastry and bakehouse.

There is an obscure village hereabouts, called Perivale, which my author[3] will have more truly termed Purevale (an honour I assure you unknown to the inhabitants thereof) because of the clearness of the corn growing therein, though the purity thereof is much subject to be humbled with the mildew, whereof hereafter.[4]

Tamarisk

It hath not more affinity in sound with *tamarind* than sympathy in extraction (both originally Arabic) general similitude in leaves and operation; only tamarind in England is an annual (dying at the approach of winter) whilst tamarisk lasteth many years. It was first brought over by Bishop Grindal out of Switzerland (where he was exile under Queen Mary) and planted in his garden at Fulham in this county; where the soil, being moist and fenny, well complied with the nature of this plant, which since is removed, and thriveth well in many other places. Yet it groweth not up to be timber, as in Arabia, though often to that substance that cups of great size are made thereof. Dioscorides saith it is good for the toothache (as what is not, and yet indeed what is good for it?) but it is especially used for mollifying the hardness and opening the stopping of the belly.

(1) John Norden, Speculum Britanniae. (2) Fuller was rector of Cranford, near Heston, from 1658 until his death. (3) Norden. (4) In the Farewell to this county [p. 394.]

THE MANUFACTURES

LEATHER

This, though common to all counties, is entered under the manufactures of Middlesex, because London therein is the staple-place of slaughter; and the hides of beasts there bought are generally tanned about Enfield in this county.

A word of the antiquity and usefulness of this commodity. Adam's first suit was of leaves, his second of leather. Hereof girdles, shoes and many utensils (not to speak of whole houses of leather, I mean coaches) are made. Yea, I have read how Frederick the Second, emperor of Germany, distressed to pay his army, made *monetam coriaceam* (coin of leather) making it current by his proclamation; and afterwards, when his soldiers repaid it into his exchequer, they received so much silver in lieu thereof.

Many good laws are made (and still one wanting to enforce the keeping of them) for the making of this merchantable commodity; and yet still much unsaleable leather is sold in our markets.

The lord treasurer Burghley (who always consulted artificers in their own art) was indoctrinated by a cobbler in the true tanning of leather. This cobbler, taking a slice of bread, toasted it by degrees at some distance from the fire, turning many times till it became brown and hard on both sides. "This, my lord," saith he, "we good fellows call a tanned toast, done so well that it will last many mornings' draughts"; and leather, thus leisurely tanned and turned many times in the fat, will prove serviceable, which otherwise will quickly fleet and rag out. And although that great statesman caused statutes to be made according to his instructions, complaints in this kind daily continue and increase. Surely, were all of that occupation as honest as Simon the tanner (the entertainer of Simon Peter in Joppa) they would be more conscientious in their calling. Let me add, what experience avoweth true, though it be hard to assign the true cause thereof, that when wheat is dear, leather always is cheap; and when leather is dear, then wheat is cheap.

THE BUILDINGS

HAMPTON COURT was built by that pompous prelate Cardinal Wolsey; one so magnificent in his expenses, that whosoever considereth either of these three, would admire that he had anything for the other two left unto him: viz., his house-building, housekeeping, house-furnishing.

He bestowed it on King Henry the Eighth, who, for the greater grace thereof, erected it (princes can confer dignities on houses as well as persons) to be an honour, increasing it with buildings till it became more like a small city than a house. Now whereas other royal palaces (Holdenby, Oatlands, Richmond, Theobald's) have lately found their fatal period, Hampton Court hath happiness to continue in its former estate.

Non equidem invideo: miror magis, undique totis
Usque adeo spoliatur agris.

I envy not its happy lot, but rather thereat wonder;
There's such a rout, our land throughout, of palaces by plunder.

Let me add that Henry the Eighth enforested the grounds hereabouts (the last of that kind in England) though they never attained the full reputation of a forest in common discourse.

OSTERLEY HOUSE (now Sir William Waller's) must not be forgotten, built in a park by Sir Thomas Gresham, who here magnificently entertained and lodged Queen Elizabeth. Her majesty found fault with the court of this house as too great, affirming that it would appear more handsome if divided with a wall in the middle.

What doth Sir Thomas, but in the night-time sends for workmen to London (money commands all things) who so speedily and silently apply their business, that the next morning discovered that court double, which the night had left single before. It is questionable whether the queen next day was more contented with the conformity to her fancy, or more pleased with the surprise and sudden performance thereof; whilst her courtiers disported themselves with their several expressions, some avowing it was no wonder he could so soon *change* a building, who could build a *Change;* others (reflecting on some known differences in this knight's family) affirmed that any house is easier divided than united.[1]

PROVERBS

When Tottenham Wood is all on fire,
Then Tottenham Street is nought but mire.

I find this proverb in the *Survey of Tottenham,* written by Mr. William Bedwell, one of the most learned translators of the Bible.[2] And seeing so grave a divine stooped to so low a subject, I hope I may be admitted to follow him therein. He thus expoundeth the proverb: "When Tottenham Wood, of many hundred acres, on the top of an high hill in the west end of the parish, hath a foggy mist hanging and hovering over it, in manner of a smoke, then generally foul weather followeth; so that it serveth the inhabitants instead of a prognostication." I am confident there is as much mire now as formerly in Tottenham Street, but question whether so much wood now as anciently on Tottenham Hill.

Tottenham is turned French. I find this in the same place of the same author, but quoting it out of Mr. Heywood. It seems, about the beginning of the reign of King Henry the Eighth, French mechanics swarmed in England, to the great prejudice of English artizans, which caused the insurrection in London, on ill May day, Anno Domini 1517. Nor was the city only, but country villages for four miles about, filled with French fashions and infections. The proverb is applied to such who, contemning the custom of their own country, make themselves more ridiculous by affecting foreign humours and habits.

THE BATTLES

BRENTFORD FIGHT, November the 12th, 1642. It began on the south-west side of the town, near Syon House, some execution being done by great

(1) Sir Thomas Gresham (for an account of him see under Norfolk, p. 411) founded the Royal Exchange, hence the play on "change." (2) Bedwell (1561/2-1632) was the father of Arabic studies in England, and a mathematician.

guns, and a boat on the Thames with many therein sunk, and Captain Quarles (an active citizen on the parliament side) drowned before he could recover the shore.

Soon was the scene of this tragedy removed to the north of the town, near Acton; and the king's forces fell fiercely on the regiment of Colonel Denzil Holles, then present in parliament, and put them to the worst.

Here the Welch, under Colonel William Salisbury their leader, made true the Greek proverb . . . "he that flieth will fight again."

These who shewed swift heels at Edgehill battle, use as stout arms as any in this fight; for formerly they were little better than naked, whereas since they had recovered armour to fence their bodies, and resolutions to arm their minds.

Next day, being Sunday, marched out the militia of London; but both armies may be said to have kept the Sabbath, facing each other without any considerable action. It is incredible how many cart-loads of victuals were carried out from London, enough to have feasted their soldiers for some days, and fed them for some weeks. In the evening the king's forces drew off towards Kingston.

The number of the slain on both sides amounted not to a thousand; and the reputation of the victory on the king's side was more than the effect thereof; for then the royalists did *nose* and *beard* the populous city of London, and did *triumphare* (though not *in*) *sub hostico*. Indeed the accession of citizens to the king answered not rational expectation; wealth, though loyal, being always fearful, and loth to hazard a certain estate.

This is most sure, that many scores of prisoners taken by the king were by him freely dismissed, without other ransom than a strict oath to serve no more against him. Now, what oath-office is kept in London I know not, nor what pope therein had power to dispense with so sacred an obligation. But these met with such confessors, who seemingly satisfied them in the violation of this oath, so that some weeks after they appeared on the same side as fierce as before.

THE WORTHIES

FALKES DE BREAUTE. This Falkes was a minion to King John, whose dangers endeared martial men unto him; who, the more to oblige his fidelity, gave him in marriage Margaret the daughter of Warin Fitzgerald his chamberlain, late wife to Baldwin of Redvers, many muttering thereat, and the lady herself (it seems) not well satisfied therewith, as beneath her deserts.

Hereupon our author:[1]

> Now both of them being brought into a bed,
> By law, and love, and concord joined are:
> What law? what love? what concord did them wed?
> Law lawless, loathed love, concord which did jarr.

This Falkes was highly in favour with King Henry the Third, who, by the valour of this his general, obtained the great victory at Lincoln.

But afterwards, when the land was settled in peace, Falkes found him-

(1) Matthew Westminster. [Latin original omitted.]

self less respected, *set by*, and not *sett by*,[1] hung up like the axe, when it hath hewn all the hard timber, on the wall unregarded. He endeavoured therefore to embroil the nation in a new war, and, like a dishonest chirurgeon, wilfully to blister the sound flesh into a sore, to gain by the curing thereof. This not succeeding (all being weary of civil war) he, presuming on the king's lenity and his own merit (accounting himself too high to come under the roof of any law) committed many outrages of felonies and murders. He was esteemed too bad to live, such his present desperateness; yet too good to be put to death, such his former deserts; and therefore (as an expedient between both) he was condemned to perpetual banishment. He went to Rome (none had more need to confess his faults) where he lived obscurely, died miserably, and was buried ignobly, anno 1226.

ROGER TWYFORD. I find eleven towns so named in England (probably from the confluence of two fords thereabouts) and two in this county. He was bred an Augustinian friar, studied in both universities, and became a doctor of divinity. In his declining age he applied himself to the reading of the Scripture and the Fathers, and became a painful and profitable preacher. I find him not fixed in any one place, who is charactered, *Concionum propalator per dioecesin Norvicensem* (an itinerant, no errant preacher through the diocese of Norwich.) He was commonly called Goodluck ("and good luck have he with his honour") because he brought good success to others (and consequently his own welcome) with him whithersoever he went, which made all places and persons ambitious and covetous of his presence. He flourished about the year of our Lord 1390.

RICHARD NORTHALIS was, saith my author, born in this county, adding moreover *Praetoris Londinensis, ejusdem cognominis ut fertur, filius*.[2] But take *praetor* either for mayor or sheriff, and no such man appeareth in Stow's exact *Survey of London;* so that one may thence safely conclude the negative, no such person in those places, though probably he might hold some other eminent office in that city.

By the way, the applying the names of Roman magistrates to our English officers, wherein every one followeth their own fancy in assigning the correspondency, hath caused much uncertainty in matters of this nature. But we willingly believe this Robert of wealthy extraction, though he became a Carmelite, and afterwards chaplain to King Richard the Second, who for his good preaching preferred him bishop of Ossory, for a time chancellor of Ireland, and at last archbishop of Dublin. He wrote a set of sermons for the whole year, lived much beloved for his learning and virtues, and died, no less lamented, Anno Domini 1397, on the 20th day of July.

ROBERT HOUNSLOW was born in this county at Hounslow, a village well known for the road through and the heath besides it. He was a friar of the order of the Holy Trinity, which chiefly employed themselves for the

(1) There used to be a difference in meaning: *sett,* thus spelt, implying expectation.
(2) Bale.

redemption of captives. Indeed locusts generally were the devourers of all food; yet one kind of locusts were themselves wholesome though coarse food, whereon John Baptist had his common repast. Thus friars, I confess, generally were the pests of the places they lived in; but to give this order their due, much good did redound from their endeavours; for this Robert being their provincial for England, Scotland and Ireland, rich people by him were affectionately exhorted, their alms industriously collected, such collections carefully preserved, till they could be securely transmitted, and thereby the liberty of many Christian captives effectually procured. He wrote also many synodal sermons, and epistles of consequence to several persons of quality, to stir up their liberality. He flourished, says Pitseus, Anno Domini 1430.

PETER FABELL. I shall probably offend the gravity of some to insert, and certainly curiosity of others, to omit him. Some make him a friar, others a lay gentleman; all a conceited person, who with his merry devices deceived the devil, who by grace may be resisted, not deceived by wit. If a grave bishop, in his sermon, speaking of Brute's coming into this land, said it was but a *bruit,* I hope I may say, without offence, that this *Fabell* was but a *fable,* supposed to live in the reign of King Henry the Sixth.[1] [*fl.* 15th cent.]

SIR THOMAS FROWYK, knight, was born at Ealing in this county, son to Thomas Frowyk, esquire, by his wife, who was daughter and heir to Sir John Sturgeon, knight (giving for his arms, Azure, three sturgeons Or, under a fret Gules); bred in the study of our municipal law, wherein he attained to such eminency that he was made lord chief justice of the common pleas, on the 30th of September in the eighteenth year of the reign of King Henry the Seventh.

Four years he sat in his place, accounted the oracle of law in his age, though one of the youngest men that ever enjoyed that office. He is reported to have died *florida juventute,* before full forty years old, and lieth buried, with Joan his wife, in the church of Finchley in this county, the circumscription about his monument being defaced; only we understand that his death happened on the seventeenth of October, 1506.

SIR RALPH SADLER, son of Henry Sadleir, esquire, was born [1507] at Hackney in this county, where he was heir to a fair inheritance. He first was servant to Lord Cromwell, and by him advanced into the service of King Henry the Eighth; a prince judicious in men and meat (and seldom deceived in either) who made him chief secretary of state. He was much knowing (and therefore most employed) in the Scotch affairs, much complicated with state intricacies, which he knew well to unfold. It is seldom seen that the pen and sword, gown and corslet, meet eminently, as here, in the same person; for, in the battle of Musselborough, he ordered and brought up our scattered troops (next degree

(1) This Peter Fabell, a native of Edmonton, was a magician and dabbler in alchemy. He figures as the hero in the play *The Merry Devil of Edmonton,* formerly attributed to Shakespeare. Brute is the legendary founder of the British race.

to a rout) inviting them to fight by his own example; and so for his valour was made a knight banneret. Of these two kinds, one by way of encouragement made before, the other by way of reward after a field victory, more safe and no less honourable in my opinion. Sir Ralph was of the second sort, and the last which survived in England of that order. Yet he was little in stature, tall not in person but performance. Queen Elizabeth made him chancellor of the duchy.

During his last embassy in Scotland, his house at Standon in Hertfordshire was built by his steward, in his absence, far greater than himself desired; so that he never joined therein, and died soon after, anno 1587, in the 80th year of his age. However, it hath been often filled with good company; and they feasted with great cheer by the hereditary hospitality therein.

SIR WILLIAM STANFORD, knight, was of Staffordian extraction, Robert his grandfather living at Rowley in that county. But William his father was a merchant in London, and purchased lands at Hadley in Middlesex, where Sir William was born August 22, 1509.

He was bred in the study of our municipal laws, attaining so much eminence therein that he was preferred one of the judges of the common pleas. His most learned book of the *Pleas of the Crown* hath made him for ever famous amongst men of his own profession. There is a spirit of retraction of one to his native country, which made him purchase lands, and his son settle himself again in Staffordshire. This worthy judge died August 28th, and was buried at Hadley in this shire, in the last year of the reign of Queen Mary, 1558.

EDWARD VI, sole surviving son of King Henry the Eighth and Jane his wife, was born at Hampton Court in this county, Anno Domini 1537. He succeeded his father in the kingdom, and was most eminent in his generation; seeing the kings of England fall under a fivefold division: 1. Visibly vicious, given over to dissoluteness and debauchery, as King Edward the Second. 2. *Potius extra vitia quam cum virtutibus* (rather free from vice than fraught with virtue) as King Henry the Third. 3. *In quibus aequali temperamento magnae virtutes inerant, nec minora vitia* (in whom vices and virtues were so equally matched, it was hard to decide which got the mastery) as in King Henry the Eighth. 4. Whose good qualities beat their bad ones quite out of distance of competition, as in King Edward the First. 5. Whose virtues were so resplendent, no faults (human frailties excepted) appeared in them, as in this King Edward.

He died July 6, 1553, and pity it is that he who deserved the best should have no monument erected to his memory. Indeed, a brass altar of excellent workmanship, under which he was buried (I will not say sacrificed with an untimely death by the treachery of others) did formerly supply the place of his tomb; which since is abolished under the notion of superstition.

WILLIAM WICKHAM, born [1539] at Enfield in this county, bred in King's College, was bishop first of Lincoln, then of Winchester, where he may be termed William Wickham junior, in distinction of his namesake and predecessor; one equal to any of his order in piety and painfulness (though little of him extant in print); superior to all in patience, dying anno 1595 of the strangury, when he had not made water for fourteen days together. This mindeth me of an usual prayer amongst the modern Jews (had they no worse customs their company would be welcome unto us) praising God as well for their vents of ejection, as mouths for the admission of nourishment.

ALICE [OWEN], daughter of Thomas Wilkes, was a poor maid born in Islington, where her cap was casually shot through with an arrow without any hurt to her head. She afterwards was thrice married to wealthy husbands (whereof Justice Owen[1] the last); and built at Islington, near to the place of her deliverance, a proper almshouse, by her well endowed. This lady expended to charitable uses, here and elsewhere, what amounted to the full sum of two thousand three hundred pounds and upwards; and lieth buried, as I take it, in Islington. [*d.* 1613]

———— TRESTRAM was a gardener by his occupation, living at Brentford in this county. This man, Anno Domini 1609, fell into a most violent inflammation of the lungs, accompanied with a terrible fever, shortness of breath, stitch of both sides, dry cough, and an unquenchable thirst. Doctor Theodore Diodati,[2] being his neighbour (then physician to Prince Henry and the Lady Elizabeth) beholding him of a ruddy and sanguine complexion, adventured to let him blood, though he was of threescore and sixteen years of age.

Once he let him blood about twenty ounces, by which evacuation (his blood being extremely putrefied) he felt ease for three hours; but afterwards all his accidents returned as violent as before. Next morning he repeated the bleeding in the same quantity, whereby the patient only found a momentary ease, his pain returning as violent as before. The third day, remembering the rule of Hippocrates, that blood must be let to the changing of the colour, he adventured again on as copious a phlebotomy as before; whereby the sick man found an extraordinary ease, who in three days had lost more than sixty ounces of blood.

This Trestram survived eight years after, and died anno 1619, a most eminent instance against those who endeavour to prove the decay of the world, because men cannot spare so much by blood-letting as in former ages.

SIR JULIUS CAESAR, knight, was born [1558] in this county, his father having a house nigh unto Tottenham. His father was a doctor of physic to Queen Elizabeth, and descended of the ancient family of the Dalmarii in Italy. This his son was bred in Oxford; and after other intermediate preferments, was advanced chancellor of the duchy of Lancaster, and sworn a privy councillor on Sunday the 6th of July 1607, and afterwards was preferred master of the rolls.

(1) Thomas Owen (*d.* 1598) M.P. for Shrewsbury and later judge of common pleas; buried in Westminster Abbey. (2) From his own letter, printed in Dr. Hakewill's *Apology*. [This Dr. Diodati was the father of Charles Diodati (1608?-1638) the friend of Milton, who lamented his death in the Latin poem *Epitaphium Damonis*.

A person of prodigious bounty to all of worth or want, so that he might seem to be almoner-general of the nation. The story is well known of a gentleman, who once borrowing his coach (which was as well known to poor people as any hospital in England) was so rendezvoused about with beggars in London, that it cost him all the money in his purse to satisfy their importunity, so that he might have hired twenty coaches on the same terms. Sir Francis Bacon, Lord Verulam, was judicious in his election, when perceiving his dissolution to approach, he made his last bed in effect in the house of Sir Julius.

He continued more than twenty years master of the rolls; and though heaved at by some expectants, sate still in his place, well poised therein with his gravity and integrity: *Vir tantarum elemosynarum non movebitur* (a man of so great alms and prayers, made by him and for him, shall not be removed.) Nor was it without a prosperous omen, that his chief house in Hertfordshire was called Bennington; that is, *Villa benigna* (the bountiful village) as one author will have it; or as another *Villa beneficii* (the town of good turns) from the river so named running by it. What shall I speak of his arms, viz., Gules, three roses Argent; on a chief of the first so many roses of the second; embleming the fragrancy of the memory he hath left behind him.

He died the twenty-eighth day of April, Anno Domini 1636, in the seventy-ninth of his age.

WILLIAM GOUGE, born [1578] at Stratford-le-Bow in this county, bred in King's College in Cambridge, where he was not once absent from public service morning and evening the space of nine years together. He read fifteen chapters in the Bible every day; and was afterwards minister of Blackfriars in London. He never took a journey merely for pleasure in all his life; he preached so long, till it was a greater difficulty for him to go up into the pulpit, than either to make or preach a sermon; and died aged seventy-nine years, leaving the examples of his humility, faith patience, &c., to the imitation of posterity; being buried in his own church, December 16, 1653.[1]

THE FAREWELL

This county is much infested with the mildew. That it is, I know to my cost, but could not purchase the knowledge what it is, much less how it might be prevented at the same price, though having diligently inquired into the name and nature thereof.

Some will have it called *mildew,* quasi *maldew,* or *ill-dew;* others *meldew,* or *honey-dew,* as being very sweet (oh, how luscious and noxious is flattery!) with the astringency thereof causing an atrophy, a consumption in the grain. His etymology was peculiar to himself who would have it termed *mildew,* because it grindeth the grain aforehand, making it to dwindle away almost to nothing.

It falleth (be it mist or dew) when corn is almost ripe for the sickle,

(1) These memoirs are extracted out of the sermon preached at his funeral. [This remarkable puritan once served a term of imprisonment. Although he took the covenant, he denounced the trial of Charles I.]

and antedateth the harvest, not before it is welcome, but before it is wished by the husbandman, grain being rather withered than ripened thereby. If, after the fall, a good rain or strong wind cometh, it washeth and wipeth it off, so that no mischief is done; otherwise the hot sun arising sealeth (to use the husbandman's phrase) the mildew upon the straw, and so intercepteth the nourishment betwixt the root and the ear, especially if it falleth not on the hoase (which is but another case, and hath another tunicle under it) but on the stripped straw near to the top of the stalk.

Grain growing under hedges (where the wind hath least power) is most subject thereunto; though wheat of all grain is most, bearded wheat of wheat is least, liable unto it; not that the haulms thereof are spears to fright the mildew from it, but advantageous gutters, to slide it away the sooner, which sticketh on notted or pollard wheat.

Inland counties, Northamptonshire, Bedfordshire, &c., complain the least, maritime the most, of mildew, which insinuateth the vapours of the sea to be causal thereof. Some hold that, seeing it falls from the skies, earth hath no guard for heaven's blow, save prayer, which in this very case is prescribed by Solomon. But others conceive that human may be subordinate to spiritual means; to prevent, not the falling but the hurting of this dew in such a degree, and hopefully expect the remedy from the ingenuity of the next generation.

I am the rather confirmed in my hopes, because a help hath been found out against the smutting of wheat, at leastwise in some good proportion; I say the smutting of wheat, which makes it a negro, as mildew makes it a dwarf; viz., by mingling the seed with lime, as your husbandman will inform you.

And for my *vale* to this county, I heartily desire that either God would of his goodness spare the fruits of the earth from so hurtful a casualty, or put it into the minds of men (if it may stand with His will) to find out some defensative, in some part to abate the malignity thereof.

MONMOUTHSHIRE

I MAY fitly call this an English-Welsh county; for, though it lie west of Severn, yea of Wye itself, and though the Welsh be the common language thereof, yet it doth wear a double badge of English relation. First, whereas formerly all Welsh counties sent but one knight to the parliament, this had the privilege of two, conformable to the shires of England. Secondly, it is not subject to the Welsh jurisdiction, but such itinerant judges as go Oxford Circuit have this county within the compass of their commission.

MANUFACTURES

Caps

These were the most ancient, general, warm and profitable coverings of men's heads in this island. It is worth our pains to observe the tenderness of our kings to preserve the trade of cap-making, and what long and strong struggling our state had to keep up the using thereof, so many thousands of people being maintained thereby in the land,[1] especially before the invention of fulling-mills, all caps before that time being wrought, beaten and thickened by the hands and feet of men, till those mills, as they eased many of their labour, ousted more of their livelihood. Thus ingenious inventions conducing to the compendious making of commodities, though profitable to private persons, may not always be gainful to the public, to which what employs most is most advantageous; as capping anciently set fifteen distinct callings on work, as they are reckoned up in the statute:[2] 1. Carders; 2. Spinners; 3. Knitters; 4. Parters of Wool; 5. Forcers; 6. Thickers; 7. Dressers; 8. Walkers; 9. Dyers; 10. Battelers; 11. Shearers; 12. Pressers; 13. Edgers; 14. Liners; 15. Band-makers; and other exercises.

The best caps were formerly made at Monmouth, where the Cappers' Chapel doth still remain, being better carved and gilded than any other part of the church. But, on the occasion of a great plague happening in this town, the trade was some years since removed hence to Bewdley in Worcestershire, yet so that they are called Monmouth caps unto this day. Thus this town retains, though not the profit, the credit of capping; and seeing the child still keeps the mother's name, there is some hope in due time she may return unto her.

All I will add is this: if at this day the phrase of "wearing a Monmouth cap" be taken in a bad acception, I hope the inhabitants of that town will endeavour to disprove the occasion thereof.

(1) Eight thousand in London, Stat. 13 Elizabeth, cap. 19; and probably twice as many in the land beside. (2) 13 Elizabeth, cap. 19.

THE WORTHIES

GEOFFREY OF MONMOUTH was born [1100?] in, and named from Monmouth. He was also called ap Arthur, from his father, as I suppose; though others say, because he wrote so much of King Arthur, but, by the same proportion Homer may be termed Achillides, and Virgil the son of Aeneas. Yea, this Geoffrey, by an ancienter title, might be surnamed ap Bruit, whose story he asserteth. He translated and compiled the various British authors into one volume.

I am not so much moved at William of Newburgh calling this his book *ridicula figmenta,* as that Giraldus Cambrensis, his countryman, and (as I may say) *con-sub-temporary,* should term it *fabulosam historiam.* Indeed he hath many things from the British bards, which, though improbable, are not *ipso facto* untrue. We know Herodotus, nicknamed by some *Pater Fabularum,* is by others acknowledged to be *Pater Historiarum.*

The truth is that both novelants and antiquaries must be content with many falsehoods; the one taking reports at the first rebound, before come to, the other raking them out of the dust, when past their perfection.

Others object that he is too hyperbolical in praising his own country; a catching disease, seeing Livy mounts Italy to the skies, and all other authors respectively. And why should that be mortal in our Monmouth, what is but venial in others? And if he be guilty in mistiming of actions, he is not the only historian without company in that particular.

However, on the occasion of the premises, his book is prohibited by his holiness, whilst the lying legend is permitted to be read without control. Thus Rome loves *questuosa, non inutilia figmenta,* falsehoods whereby she may gain. Some conceive it to be his greatest fault that he so praiseth the ancient church in Britain, making it independent from the see of Rome, before Augustine the monk came hither. One maketh him a cardinal, which is improbable; whilst it is more certain that he was bishop of St. Asaph, and flourished anno 1152. [*d.* 1154]

RICHARD DE CLARE was born (as from all concentred probalities may be conjectured) at Striguil Castle in this county, and had the title of earl of Pembroke and Strigul. He was otherwise surnamed Strongbow, from drawing so strong a bow, and had *brachia projectissima,* saith my author;[1] though I can hardly believe that Reacher, which another writeth of him, that "with the palms of his hands he could touch his knees, though he stood upright."[2] More applicable to him is the expression of Tully, *Nihil egit levi brachio,* being a person of effectual performance.

It happened that MacMurrough lord of Leinster, in the year of our Lord 1166, being expelled his territory for several tyrannies, by the lords of Meath and Connaught, repaired to our King Henry the Second, and invited him to invade Ireland. But that politic king, fearing, if failing in success, to forfeit the reputation of his discretion, would not engage in the design; but permitted such subjects of his who had a mind *militare propriis stipendiis,* to adventure themselves therein.

(1) Camden's *Britannia.* (2) Milles, in his *Catalogue of Honour.*

Amongst these Richard Strongbow was the principal, going over into Ireland with twelve hundred men (too great for an earl's train, yet too little for a general's army) to make a national invasion; yet so great his success, that in a short time he possessed himself of the ports of Leinster and Munster, with large lands belonging thereunto; insomuch that King Henry grew jealous of his greatness, remanded him home, and commanded him to surrender his acquests into his hands; which done, he received them again by re-grant from the king, save that Henry reserved the city of Dublin for himself.

This Strongbow is he who is commonly called *Domitor Hiberniae,* "the Tamer of Ireland;" though the natives thereof then, and many hundred years after, paid rather verbal submission than real obedience to our English kings. Yea, some of their great lords had both the power and title of kings in their respective territories; witness the preface in the commission whereby King Henry the Second made William FitzAldhelm his lieutenant of Ireland: *Archiepiscopis, Episcopis, Regibus, Comitibus, Baronibus, et omnibus fidelibus suis in Hibernia, salutem;* where kings are post-posed to bishops, which speaketh them *royolets* by their own ambition, and by no solemn inauguration. This Earl Richard died at Dublin 1176; and lieth buried in Trinity Church therein.

WALTER DE CANTELUPE was son to William (the elder) Lord Cantelupe, whose prime residence was at Abergavenny in this county. One of high birth, higher preferment (made, by King Henry the Third, bishop of Worcester) and highest spirit. In his time the pope's legate came into England, and complained of many clergymen keeping their livings against the canons, intending either to force such irregular incumbents into avoidance (so to make room for the pope's favourites) or else to compound for their continuance at his arbitrary price. But our Walter would not yield to such extortion. Indeed he was one of a keen nature; and his two-edged spirit did cut on both sides, against:—

The Pope. Telling Rustand, his legate, coming hither 1255, that he would prefer to be hanged on the gallows, rather than ever consent to such expilation[1] of the church.

The King. Siding with the barons, he encouraged them in their civil wars, promising heaven for their reward, though this doctrine cost him an excommunication from the pope.

Lying on his death-bed, he was touched with true remorse for his disloyalty, and, upon his desire, obtained absolution. He died February the twelfth, 1266, whom I behold as uncle unto Thomas Cantelupe, the sainted bishop of Hereford.[2]

HENRY [OF LANCASTER], first duke of Lancaster, was born [1299?] in Monmouth Castle, the chief seat of his barony. He is commonly surnamed *de torto collo,* or the wry-neck, and by others the good duke of Lancaster, by which name we entitle him, it being fitter to call men from what was to be praised, than what to be pitied in them, not from their natural defects, but moral perfections. His bounty commends him to

(1) *Expilation* = pillage, plunder. (2) See Herefordshire, p. 221.

our mention in this place, being head of the guild of Corpus Christi in Cambridge, and the first founder of a college so called in that university. Indeed the land was but little he conferred thereon, but great the countenance of so eminent a person in procuring and settling their mortmain. He died in the year of our Lord 1361; and was buried in the collegiate church at Leicester, which he founded.[1] Blanche, his only daughter which had issue, was married to John of Gaunt, duke of Lancaster.

HENRY OF MONMOUTH [HENRY V, *b.* 1387] so called from that well-known town wherein he was born . . . He was son to King Henry the Fourth (by Mary, one of the daughters and heirs of Humphrey de Bohun earl of Hereford) and whom he succeeded on the throne, being the fifth of that name; and began his reign March 20, anno 1413.

He cannot be excused from extravagancies in his youth, seeing the king his father expelled him his council (substituting his younger brother the duke of Clarence president in his stead) for the same. Yet as those bodies prove most healthful which break out in their youth, so was his soul the sounder for venting itself in its younger days; for no sooner was his father dead, but he reclaimed himself, and became a glory to his country, and a constant terror to his enemies. Yea, he banished all his idle companions from court, allowing them a competency for their subsistence.

When the lord chief justice (who had secured him when prince for striking him for the commitment of some of his lewd companions) begged his pardon for the same, he not only forgave him, but rewarded his justice, for distributing it without fear or partiality.[2]

In his reign a supplication was preferred, that the temporal lands given to pious uses, but abusively spent, might have been seized by the king. This was wisely awarded by Chichele, archbishop of Canterbury, by putting the king on the design of recovering France. Yea, this king, by his valour reduced Charles the Sixth, king of France to such a condition, that he in a manner resigned his kingdom into his hand.

And here the Frenchmen found him as good, or rather worse, as his promise, which he made to the dauphin (who sent him a barrel of Paris tennis-balls) sending such English balls that they proved to their great loss.

He died at Bois de Vincennes in France, the last day of August, anno 1422; and was brought over with great solemnity, and interred in Westminster Abbey.

SIR WILLIAM HERBERT, earl of Pembroke, with SIR RICHARD HERBERT his brother, were both undoubtedly born in this county; but whether or no at Raglan Castle is uncertain. Both valiant men, and as fast friends to King Edward the Fourth, as professed foes to Richard Neville earl of Warwick. They gave the last and clearest evidence hereof in the battle

(1) Henry of Lancaster served on many a battlefield, and was regarded in his day throughout western Europe as a perfect knight. He was Edward III's most trusted counsellor. Contrary to Fuller's statement, he was not the founder of Corpus Christi. (2) The story is told of Sir William Gascoigne (see Yorkshire, p. 648) but it is without foundation.

of Banbury, where we find it reported, that these two leading the army of the Welsh, with their pole-axes, twice made way through the battle of the northern men (which sided with King Henry the Sixth) without any mortal wound.

There passeth a tradition in the noble family of the Herberts of Cherbury, that this Sir Richard their ancestor slew that day one hundred and forty men with his own hands; which, if done in charging, some censure as an act of impossibility; if after a rout in an execution, as a deed of cruelty. But others defend both truth and courage therein, as done in passing and repassing through the army. Indeed guns were, and were not, in fashion in that age, used sometimes in sieges, but never in field service; and next the gun, the pole-axe was the mortal weapon, especially in such a dead hand as this knight had, with which, *Quot icti, tot occisi.* He is reported also to be of a giant's stature, the peg being extant in Montgomery Castle whereon he used to hang his hat at dinner, which no man of an ordinary height can reach with his hand at this day.

However, both these brave brethren, circumvented with the subtlety of their foes (odds at any time may be bet on the side of treachery against valour) were brought to Banbury, beheaded, and buried, the earl at Tintern, and Sir Richard at Abergavenny, in this county.[1] [*d.* 1469]

SIR ROGER WILLIAMS, born [1540?] of an ancient family at Penrhos in this county, was first a soldier of fortune under Duke d'Alva, and afterwards successfully served Queen Elizabeth; having no fault, save somewhat over-free and forward to fight.

When a Spanish captain challenged Sir John Norris to fight a single combat (which was beneath him to accept, because a general) this Roger undertook the don. And after they had fought some time (both armies beholding them) without any hurt, they pledged each other a deep draught of wine, and so friendly departed.

Another time, at midnight, he assaulted the camp of the prince of Parma, nigh Venloo, slew some of the enemy, and pierced to the tent of the general, as highly blamed by some for rashness, as commended by others for his valour. He bravely defended Sluys, whilst any hope of help. [*d.* 1595]

WILLIAM JONES was a native of the town of Monmouth; a person whose estate was very considerable in several respects; viz., in 1. His *emptiness;* being forced out of Monmouth for not being able to pay ten groats, as the late recorder of that corporation hath informed me. How had he been *undone,* if he had *not* been undone! 2. His *filling;* flying to London, he became first a porter, and then (his brains being better than his back) a factor; and going over to Hamburg, by his industry and ingenuity made such a vent for Welsh cottons, that what he found *drugs* at home, he left *dainties* beyond the sea. 3. His *re-funding,* founding a fair schoolhouse in the place of his nativity, allowing fifty pounds yearly for the

(1) Pembroke, a prominent Yorkist, did good service for Edward IV against Jasper Tudor (father of Henry VII) in the wars of the Roses. The rebellion of the northern men referred to above was fomented largely by Warwick the "King-maker", who was at this time changing from Yorkist to Lancastrian.

master, thirty for the usher, with one hundred marks salary to a lecturer; besides a stately almshouse for twenty poor folk, each of them having two rooms and a garden, with half a crown a week, besides other conveniences.

All which his benefactions, and many more, he by will submitted to the oversight of the honourable company of Haberdashers in London, who at this day right worthily discharge their trust herein. [*fl.* 1614]

WILLIAM EVANS was born in this county, and may justly be accounted the giant of our age for his stature, being full two yards and a half in height. He was porter to King Charles the First, succeeding Walter Persons in his place, and exceeding him two inches in height, but far beneath him in an equal proportion of body; for he was not only what the Latins call *compernis*, knocking his knees together, and going out squalling with his feet, but also halted a little; yet made he a shift to dance in an antimasque[1] at court, where he drew little Jeffery the dwarf[2] out of his pocket, first to the wonder, then to the laughter of the beholders. He died Anno Domini 163—.

THE FAREWELL

I understand that, in January 1607, part of this county which they call the Moor sustained a great loss by the breaking-in of the Severn sea, caused by a violent south-west wind, continuing for three days together. I heartily desire the inhabitants thereof may for the future be secured from all such dangerous inundations (water being a good servant, but bad master) by His providence, who bindeth the sea in a girdle of sands, and saith to the waves thereof, Thus far shall ye go, and no further.

(1) *Antimasque*=a grotesque interlude between the acts of a masque. (2) Jeffery Hudson—see Rutland, p. 474

NORFOLK

NORFOLK hath the German Ocean on the north and east thereof; Suffolk, severed by the river Waveney, on the south side; Cambridgeshire, parted by the river Ouse, and a small part of Lincolnshire, on the west. It extendeth full fifty miles from east to west; but from north to south stretcheth not above thirty miles.

All England may be carved out of Norfolk, represented therein not only to the kind but degree thereof. Here are fens and heaths, and light and deep, and sand and clay ground, and meadows and pasture, and arable and woody, and (generally) woodless land; so grateful is this shire with the variety thereof. Thus, as in many men, though perchance this or that part may justly be cavilled at, yet all put together complete a proper person: so Norfolk, collectively taken, hath a sufficient result of pleasure and profit, that being supplied in one part which is defective in another.

This county hath the most churches of any in England (six hundred and sixty) and, though the poorest livings, yet, by some occult quality of their good husbandry, and God's blessing thereon, the richest clergymen. Nor can there be given a greater demonstration of the wealth and populousness of this county, than that in the late act for an assessment upon England, at the rate of sixty thousand pounds by the month, for three months, Norfolk, with the city of Norwich, is rated at three thousand two hundred sixty-six pounds, thirteen shillings and fourpence, the highest proportion of any shire in England. And, though Norfolk hath little cause to please and less to pride itself in so dear purchased pre-eminence, yet it cannot but account it a credit to see itself not undervalued.

NATURAL COMMODITIES

It shareth plentifully in all English commodities, and aboundeth with the best and most

Rabbits

These are an army of natural pioneers, whence men have learned *cuniculos agere,* the art of undermining. They thrive best on barren ground, and grow fattest in the hardest frosts. Their flesh is fine and wholesome. If Scottish men tax our language as improper, and smile at our wing of a rabbit, let us laugh at their shoulder of a capon.

Their skins were formerly much used when furs were in fashion; till of late our citizens of Romans are turned Grecians, have laid down their grave gowns, and took up their light cloaks; men generally disliking all habits, though emblems of honour, if also badges of age.

Their rich or silver-hair-skins, formerly so dear, are now levelled in prices with other colours; yea, are lower than black in estimation, because their wool is most used in making hats, commonly (for the more credit)

called half-beavers, though many of them hardly amount to the proportion of semi-demi-casters.[1]

HERRINGS

Great store and very good of these are caught nigh Yarmouth, where once every year, on the feast of Saint Michael, is a fair held for the sale of fish; and such the plenty of herrings there constantly vended, that incredible the sum which is raised thereby. Indeed, the fishing for herrings is a most gainful trade; fish, though contemptible in itself, considerable in its company, swimming in shoals, that what the whale hath in bigness the herring hath in number. (It may well mind such who excel in strength and valour, not to boast or be proud thereof, seeing the greatest courage may be soon pressed to death under unequal number.) Yea, red herrings, in England mostly eaten for sauce to quicken the appetite, serve in Holland and elsewhere for food to satisfy hunger.

THE MANUFACTURES

WORSTEDS

These first took their name from Worstead, a village in this county. Originally it is nothing but woollen thread spun very fine, and for the more strength twisted together. But oh! it surpasseth my skill to name the several stuffs (being worsted disguised with weaving and colouring) made thereof.

It argueth the usefulness and public profit of this commodity, which first found a general repute in England toward the end of the reign of King Henry the Sixth, that there are no fewer than fourteen statutes now in force in the well-ordering thereof to merchantable proof; and appointing which of them may, which may not, be transported. Not to speak of four wardens of worsted weavers to be chosen yearly within the city of Norwich, and other four out of the county of *Northfolk*, with their solemn oath, office and authority.

As for worsted stockings, they were first made in England, anno 1564, by William Ryder,[2] an ingenious apprentice living against Saint Magnus Church, at the foot of London Bridge. This William, chancing to see a pair of knit worsted stockings in the lodging of an Italian merchant, who had brought them from Mantua, borrowed them; and, making the like by that pattern, presented them to William earl of Pembroke, who first wore them in England.

SEAMEN OF NORFOLK

No county in England doth carry a *top* and *top-gallant* more high in maritime performances than Norfolk. Witness the proportion of Yarmouth alone in the ensuing catalogue of ships, used by King Edward the Third against Calais:

(1) *Caster*=beaver, which makes the point of Fuller's remarks clearer. (2) Stow's *Chronicle*. [Sir William Ryder, or Rither (1544?-1611) apprenticed as haberdasher; lord mayor of London 1600, and knighted by Elizabeth for his loyalty during Essex's rebellion.]

The South-fleet ships, 493; the mariners thereof, 9630. The North-fleet ships, 217; the mariners thereof, 4521. Ships of London, 25; mariners of London, 662. Ships of Yarmouth, 43; mariners of Yarmouth, 1950 or 1075.

Know, reader, I cannot with all my diligence and interest recover the original of this catalogue, as extant, not in the Tower (where by my friend's favour I could do something) but in the king's great wardrobe in London, out of which it is cited by our author.[1] But our times (I fear) have brushed it away with the rest of the wardrobe. However, give me leave to make some annotations thereon:

1. These ships, as by their great number appeareth, were small vessels; yet as good as any in that age of England, and better (witness their victories) than any in France.

2. The proportion may seem strange, that Yarmouth should afford well nigh twice as many ships and mariners as London itself.

3. Except it was that the king spared London at this time, as the sure reserve for his navy on all occasions.

4. Or except there be a mistake in the numbers (figures in writing, as well as figures in rhetoric, may, with a small dash, have their *meiosis* made an *hyperbole*). And the various lections[2] in the mariners of Yarmouth doth something shake (though not shatter) the credit of the account.

5. The numbers may be very true, Yarmouth in that age being so populous a place that (though but one parish) a lamentable plague in one year did sweep thence 7000 men to the grave.

Thus, though the church (and that very large) could never hold their living, the churchyard could contain the dead; seeing persons alive will not be pressed in their pews so close, as corpses may be crowded together in their graves.

PROVERBS

Norfolk dumplings. This cannot be verified of any dwarfish or diminutive stature of people in this county, being as tall of their bodies, and as tall of their arms too, I assure you, as any in England. But it relates to the fare they commonly feed on, so generally called. I wish much good may it do them, and that their bodies thereby may be enabled of all natural, civil and spiritual performances.

He is arrested by the bailie of Marshland. The air of Marshland in this county is none of the wholesomest, being surrounded with the sea and fens on all sides. Hence it is that strangers coming hither are clapt on the back with an ague, which sometimes lasts them longer than a stuff suit. The best is when such prisoners have paid the bailiff's fees and garnish, and with time and patience have weathered out the brunt of that disease, they become habited to the air of the country, and arrive in health at a very great age.

(1) Hakluyt. (2) *Lection* = interpretation.

THE WORTHIES

RALPH DE HENGHAM, so named from a fair market town in this county, was made lord chief-justice of the king's bench in Michaelmas Term in the second year of King Edward the First, when the king was newly returned from the Holy Land. He sat sixteen years in that place (saving that one Winborne was, for a year or two, interposed) and, at the general purging and garbling[1] of the judges, which happened in the 18th year of the aforesaid king, when all the judges (except two, John de Metingham and Elias de Bekingham) were cast out by the parliament for their corruption, fined, banished and imprisoned; then this Ralph was amerced in seven thousand marks for bribery, and ejected out of his place.

Some will say, let him wither in silence; why do you mention him amongst the Worthies of our nation? I answer, penitence is the second part of innocence; and we find this Ralph, after his fine paid, made chief-justice of the common pleas, *sub resipiscendi fiducia* (under the confidence generally conceived of his amendment). He died [in 1311, and] lies buried in the church of Saint Paul, where he hath, or had, this epitaph:

Per versus patet hos Anglorum quod jacet hic flos
Legum, qui tuta dictavit vera statuta.
Ex Hengham dictus Radulphus vir benedictus.

One must charitably believe that he played a good after-game of integrity; and, if enjoying longer life, he would have given a clearer testimony thereof.

JOHN BACONTHORPE was born in a village so called in this county; bred a Carmelite in the convent of Blakeney, and afterwards studied first in Oxford, then in Paris; one remarkable on many accounts. First, for the dwarfishness of his stature,

Scalpellum calami atramentum charta libellus.

His penknife, pen, ink-horn, one sheet of paper, and any of his books, would amount to his full height. As for all the books of his own making, put together their burden were more than his body could bear.

Secondly, for his *high* spirit in his *low* body. Indeed his soul had but a small diocese to visit, and therefore might the better attend the effectual informing thereof. I have heard it delivered by a learned doctor in physic (at the anatomy lecture in London) who a little before had been present at the embowelling and embalming of Duke Hamilton and the Lord Capel, that the heart of the former was the largest, the latter the least, he had ever beheld; inferring hence that contracted spirits act with the greatest vigorousness.

Thirdly, for his high title, wherewith he was generally termed the Resolute Doctor. Two sorts of people he equally disliked: sceptics who are of none, and unconstant people who are (successively) of all opinions; and whilst others turned about like the wheel, he was as fixed as the axle-tree in his own judgment. Yet this his resoluteness was not attended with censuring of such who were of another opinion, where equal probability on either side allowed a latitude to dissent.

(1) *Garbling* = sifting.

He groped after more light than he saw, saw more than he durst speak of, spake of more than he was thanked for by those of his superstitious order; amongst whom (saith Bale) neither before, nor after, arose the like for learning and religion. Most agree in the time of his death, anno 1346, though dissenting in the place of his burial; assigning Blakeney, Norwich, London, the several places of his interment.[1]

NICHOLAS OF LYNNE, born in that town; bred in Oxford, and is generally accounted a Franciscan friar. But my author, being a Carmelite himself, makes him one of his own order.[2] And all acknowledge him an excellent musician, mathematician and astrologer.

It is reported of him how, in the year 1330, being the thirtieth year of the reign of King Edward the Third, he sailed with others to the most northern islands in the world. Then leaving his company, and taking his astrolabe, he, by the help of art-magic (so mathematicians are nick-named by the ignorant) went as far as the pole itself, where he discovered four indraughts of the ocean, from the four opposite quarters of the world, from which many did conceive, as well the flowing of the sea, as blasts of the winds to have their original. Were these things true, and had they been known to the ancients (as it would have spared philosophers much pains in disputing the moon the cause of the motion of the tide in the sea) so had it spoiled Virgil's fancy in making the country of Aeolia the only magazine of the winds.

Sure I am, Gerardus Mercator hath so graced the fancy of this friar, that he made his description of the countries about the Arctic Pole conformable to this his imaginary discovery, preferring to fill that his map with a fiction, than otherwise to leave it altogether empty. But the other parts of his book have more solid and substantial truths, or else weak the shoulders of his Atlas to support the world therewith.

But to return to Friar Nicholas. One tells us[3] he wrote a book of his discoveries, and intituled it *Inventio Fortunata*. Sure it is, he was highly honoured by our learned Chaucer; witness his testimony of him, styling "Freere N. Linne a reverend clerk." [*fl.* 1386]

JOHN COLTON, born at Terrington in this county, was chaplain to William Bateman, bishop of Norwich, and first master (by the appointment of the founder) of Gonville Hall in Cambridge. Leland allows him a man *plus quam mediocriter doctus et bonus*; for which good qualities King Henry the Fourth advanced him archbishop of Armagh and primate of Ireland.[4] He was employed to the court of Rome in the heavy schism between Pope Urban the Sixth and Clement the Seventh, which occasioned his writing of his learned treatise, *De Causa Schismatis;* and because, knowing the cause conduceth little to the cure without applying the remedy, he wrote another book *De Remediis ejusdem*. It seemeth he resigned his archbishopric somewhat before his death, which happened in the year of our Lord 1404.

(1) Baconthorpe was the grandnephew of the great Roger Bacon. (2) Bale. (3) Dr. John Dee [the mathematician and astrologer—see Lancashire, p. 298.] (4) So saith Pits, but mistaken, for it was King Richard the Second.

ALAN OF LYNN was born in that famous mart-town in this county, and brought up in the university of Cambridge, where he proceeded doctor of divinity and afterwards became a Carmelite in the town of his nativity. Great his diligence in reading many and voluminous authors; and no less his desire that others with him should reap the fruit of his industry, to which end he made indexes of the many writers he perused.

An index is a necessary *implement,* and no *impediment* of a book, except in the same sense wherein the carriages of an army are termed *impedimenta.* Without this, a large author is but a labyrinth without a clue to direct the reader therein. I confess there is a lazy kind of learning, which is only *indical;* when scholars (like adders which only bite the horse's heels) nibble but at the tables, which are *calces librorum,* neglecting the body of the book. But, though the idle deserve no crutches (let not a staff be used *by* them, but *on* them) pity it is the weary should be denied the benefit thereof, and industrious scholars prohibited the accommodation of an index, most used by those who most pretend to condemn it.

To return to our Alan: his Herculean labour in this kind doth plainly appear to me, who find it such a toil and trouble to make but an index of the indexes he had made of the authors following.[1] All these J. Bale professeth himself to have seen in the Carmelites' library at Norwich, acknowledging many more which he saw not.

Now, although it be a just and general complaint, that indexes for the most part are heteroclites, I mean either redundant in what is needless, or defective in what is needful, yet the collections of this Alan were allowed very complete. He flourished anno 1424; and was buried at Lynn, in the convent of Carmelites.

WILLIAM PASTON, esq., son of Clement Paston, esq., and Beatrix his wife (sister and heir to Geoffrey de Somerton, esq.) was born [1378] at Paston in this county. He was learned in the laws of this realm, and first was serjeant to King Henry the Sixth, and was after by him preferred second judge of the common pleas. I confess, having confined our catalogue to capital judges or writers on the law, he falls not under our method in the strictness thereof. But I appeal to the reader himself, whether he would not have been highly offended with me, had I in silence passed over a person so deserving his observation.[2]

He was highly in favour with King Henry the Sixth, who allowed him, besides the ordinary salary assigned to other judges, one hundred and ten marks (reader, behold the standard of money in that age, and admire) with two gowns, to be taken yearly out of the exchequer.

I wonder the less at these noble favours conferred on the said William Paston, judge, for I find him in grace with the two former kings, being made serjeant by King Henry the Fourth, and of his council for the duchy of Lancaster; and in the reign of King Henry the Fifth, he was in such esteem with Sir John Fastolf, knight, that he appointed him one

(1) The names of 33 Fathers and other writers are here omitted. (2) He was known as the "Good Judge."

of his feoffees, whom he enabled, by a writing under his hand, to recover debts from the executors of King Henry the Fifth.

This William Paston married Agnes, daughter and heir of Sir Edmund Berry, by which marriage the Pastons rightly quarter at this day the several coats of Hetherset, Wachesham, Craven, Gerbredge, Hemgrave and Kerdeston; and received both advancement in blood and accession of estate. This said William Paston died at London, August 13, 1444, and lies buried in Norwich, so that his corpse, by a peculiar exception, do straggle from the sepulchre of their ancestors, who from Wolstan de Paston (who three years after the Conquest came into England to William earl of Glandwill[1]) were all interred at Paston. He left rich revenues to John Paston, esquire, his eldest son, who married Margaret daughter and heir of John Mauteby; and no mean estate to William his second surviving son, who married Anne daughter to Edmund duke of Somerset.

JOHN FASTOLF, knight [b. 1378] was a native of this county, as I have just cause to believe, though some have made him a Frenchman, merely because he was baron of Silly-Guillem in France, on which account they may rob England of many other worthies. He was a ward (and that the last) to John duke of Bedford, a sufficient evidence, to such who understand time and place, to prove him of English extraction. To avouch him by many arguments valiant is to maintain that the sun is bright, though since the stage hath been over-bold with his memory, making him a thrasonical puff, and emblem of mock valour.

True it is, Sir John Oldcastle did first bear the brunt of the one, being made the make-sport in all plays for a coward. It is easily known out of what purse this black penny came: the papists railing on him for a heretic, and therefore he must also be a coward, though indeed he was a man of arms, every inch of him, and as valiant as any in his age.

Now as I am glad that Sir John Oldcastle is put out, so I am sorry that Sir John Fastolf is put in, to relieve his memory in this base service, to be the anvil for every dull wit to strike upon. Nor is our comedian excusable, by some alteration of his name, writing him Sir John Falstaff, and making him the property of pleasure of King Henry the Fifth to abuse, seeing the vicinity of sounds entrench on the memory of that worthy knight, and few do heed the inconsiderable difference in spelling of their name.[2] He was made knight of the Garter by King Henry the Sixth; and died [1459].

GEOFFREY BOLEYN, knight, son of Geoffrey Boleyn, was born at Salle in this county. Being but a second brother, he was sent into the city to acquire wealth, *ad aedificandum domum antiquam;* unto whose achievements fell in both the blood and inheritance of his eldest brother, for want of issue male; by which accumulation he attained great wealth, and Anno Domini 1457 was lord mayor of London. By his testament,

(1) Out of the book of William Botoner, fol. 20, sometime herald to Sir John Fastolf, written in the reign of King Henry VI, and containeth all the ancient gentry of this county. (2) The few resemblances between Fastolf and Shakespeare's Falstaff are generally considered coincidental. This Fastolf distinguished himself at Agincourt and on other fields. For Sir John Oldcastle see Herefordshire, p. 223.

made in the next year, he gave liberally to the prisoners, hospitals and lazar-houses. Besides, he gave one thousand pounds (the greatest sum I meet with in that age to pious uses) to poor householders in London, and two hundred pounds to those in Norfolk. But it was the height of his and our happiness that he was great-grandfather, by the mother's side, to Queen Elizabeth.

SIR JAMES HOBART was born in this county, though I dare not say at Hales Hall, which he left to his posterity. He was attorney-general, and of the privy council, to King Henry the Seventh; by him dubbed knight at such time as he created Henry his son Prince of Wales. This worthy patriot (besides his many benefactions to his parish church in London) built a fair bridge over the river Waveney, betwixt this county and Suffolk, and a firm causeway thereby, with many other works of charity, so that the three houses of his issue, planted in this county, with fair possessions, may be presumed to prosper the better for the piety of this their ancestor. [*d.* 1507]

JOHN SKELTON [*b.* 1460?] is placed in this county, on a double probability. First, because an ancient family of his name is eminently known long fixed therein. Secondly, because he was beneficed at Diss, a market-town in Norfolk. He usually styled himself, and that *nemine contradicente* for ought I find, "the king's orator and poet laureate."[1] We need go no further for a testimony of his learning than to Erasmus, styling him, in his letter to King Henry the Eighth, *Britannicarum literarum lumen et decus.*

Indeed he had scholarship enough and wit too much; seeing one saith truly of him, *Ejus sermo salsus in mordacem, risus in opprobrium, jocus in amaritudinem.*[2] Yet was his satirical wit unhappy to light on three *Noli me tangere's;* viz., the rod of a schoolmaster, the cowls of friars, and the cap of a cardinal. The first gave him a lash, the second deprived him of his livelihood, the third almost ousted him of his life.

William Lily[3] was the schoolmaster whom he fell foul with, though gaining nothing thereby, as may appear by his return. And this I will do for W. Lily (though often beaten for his sake) endeavour to translate his answer:

> With face so bold, and teeth so sharp
> Of viper's venom, why dost carp?
> Why are my verses by thee weigh'd
> In a false scale? May truth be said?
> Whilst thou, to get the more esteem,
> A learned poet fain wouldst seem;
> Skelton, thou art, let all men know it,
> Neither learned, nor a poet.

The Dominican friars were the next he contested with, whose viciousness lay pat enough for his hand; but such foul lubbers fell heavy on all which found fault with them. These instigated Nix bishop of Norwich to call him to account for keeping a concubine, which cost him (as it seems) a suspension from his benefice.

(1) Not poet laureate in the character which it assumed from Ben Jonson onwards, though he was created so by both universities, and possibly by the crown. (2) Pits. (3) See Hampshire, p. 206.

But Cardinal Wolsey (*impar congressus* betwixt a poor poet and so potent a prelate) being inveighed against by his pen, and charged with too much truth, so persecuted him that he was forced to take sanctuary at Westminster, where Abbot Islip used him with much respect. In this restraint he died, June 21, 1529; and is buried in Saint Margaret's chapel with this epitaph:

J. Skeltonus Vates Pierius hic situs est.

The word *vates* being poet or prophet, minds me of this dying Skelton's prediction, foretelling the ruin of Cardinal Wolsey. Surely one unskilled in prophecies, if well versed in Solomon's Proverbs, might have prognosticated as much, that "Pride goeth before a fall."

We must not forget how, being charged by some on his death-bed, for begetting many children on the aforesaid concubine, he protested that in his conscience he kept her in the notion of a wife, though such his cowardliness, that he would rather confess adultery (then accounted but a *venial*) than own marriage, esteemed a *capital* crime in that age.

JOHN BARRET was born of an honest family at Lynn in this county; bred a Carmelite of White Friars in Cambridge, when learning ran low, and degrees high, in that university; for many usurped scarlets, qualified only with ignorance and impudence (properties seldom parted) so that a scholar could scarcely be seen for doctors, till the university, sensible of the mischief thereby, appointed Doctor Cranmer (afterwards archbishop of Canterbury) to be the *poser-general* of all candidates in divinity; amongst whom he stopped Barret for insufficiency.

Back goes Barret to Lynn, turns over a new, yea many new leaves, plying his book to purpose, whose former ignorance proceeded from want of pains, not parts; and in short time became a tolerable, a good, an excellent and admirable scholar; and, commencing doctor with due applause, lived many years a painful preacher in Norwich, always making honourable mention of Doctor Cranmer as the means of his happiness. Indeed he had been ever, if not once, a dunce who, if not debarred, had never deserved his degree. Bale saith that in the reign of Queen Mary he returned to his vomit, and became a great papist. But his praises are better to be believed than his invectives; and seeing wood, not growing crooked, but warping with weight, may be straightened again, we charitably believe that, though complying in times of persecution, he returned to the truth in the reign of Queen Elizabeth, in the beginning whereof he died [1563].

PETER READ. What he was his ensuing epitaph on his monument, in the south aisle in Saint Peter's Church in Norwich, will fully acquaint you:

Here under lieth the corpse of Peter Read, esquire, who hath worthily served not only his prince and country, but also the Emperor Charles the Fifth, both at his conquest of Barbary, and his siege at Tunis, as also in other places. Who had given him by the said emperor, for his valiant deeds, the order of Barbary. Who died the 29th day of December, in the year of our Lord God, 1566.

It is observable that this Sir Peter, knighted by the emperor, as appears in his epitaph (let me add anno 1538) is only styled, not less modestly than truly, 'esquire' upon his monument. I confess some maintain that though higher honours (baron, count, &c.) are only local, to be owned by the person receiving them in that place where they are given him; yet that knighthood given by a sovereign prince is universal, and passeth current through all Christendom. But others, their equals, as stiffly deny it; and one who is their superior (I mean Queen Elizabeth) who, in the case of Count Arundel, would not admit of any foreign honour conferred on any of her subjects, avowing that her sheep should only be known by her own mark.

CLEMENT PASTON, fourth son to Sir William Paston, son to Sir John Paston, a famous soldier, and favourite to King Edward the Fourth (sent by him with the Lord Scales to conduct the Lady Margaret, the sister of the king, to her husband Charles duke of Burgundy) son to Sir William Paston the judge, was born [1515?] at Paston in this county. When a youth he was at the burning of Conques in France; and afterwards by King Henry the Eighth was made captain of one of his ships of war; and in a sea-fight took a French galley, and therein the admiral of France prisoner, called Baron St. Blancard, whom he brought into England, and kept at Caister nigh Yarmouth, till he had paid 7000 crowns for his ransom, besides the spoil of the galley, wherein he had a cup and two snakes of gold, which were the admiral's, and which Paston used during his life on festivals, and at his death bequeathed them to his family for a monument. He received divers wounds, and was left for dead at Musselborough field in Scotland. When Sir Thomas Wyatt,[1] in the reign of Queen Mary, was worsted at Ludgate, and desired, for the more civil usage, to render himself to a gentleman, he submitted himself (saith our historian) to Clement Paston. He served at Newhaven, having command of some ships of Queen Elizabeth; and was pensioner to two kings and two queens successively. So rare was his happiness, that he spent his old age honourably, quietly, and in good house-keeping in this county, where, at Oxnead, he built a goodly house for hospitality; and an hospital hard by, for six poor serving-men, retainers to his name and family, allowing them convenient maintenance. He died Anno Domini 1597; and lieth buried in a fair tomb in the church at Oxnead.

SIR THOMAS GRESHAM was born [1519?] in this county; bred a mercer and merchant in the city of London, where God so blessed his endeavours, that he became the wealthiest citizen in England of his age, and the founder of two stately fabrics, the Old Exchange, a kind of college for merchants, and Gresham College, a kind of Exchange for scholars.

I have learned from goldsmiths that vessels made of silver and gilt are constantly burnished; seldom or never those few which are made of massy gold, whose real intrinsic worth disdaineth to borrow any foil

(1) Sir Thomas Wyatt, the younger (1521?-1554) who joined the earl of Devonshire in "Wyatt's Rebellion" to prevent the marriage of Mary with Philip of Spain, and on the failure of the rising was executed for high treason.

from art. Let lesser donations be amplified with rhetorical praises. Nothing need be said of this worthy knight's gifts but his *gifts* . . . This worthy knight completed his second change, I mean of a mortal life for a blessed eternity, on the 21st of November 1579, and lieth buried in the parish church of Saint Helen's[1].

ANDREW PERNE was born [1519?] at Bilney; bred in Peterhouse, whereof he was fellow and master, as also proctor and vice-chancellor of Cambridge and dean of Ely. Very bountiful he was to his college, wherein he founded a fellowship and scholarships; besides many rare manuscripts he acquired to their library.[2] But his memory ought most to be honoured (saving God's living temples is better than building dead colleges) on this account because, in the days of Queen Mary, he was the screen to keep off the fire of persecution from the faces and whole bodies of many a poor protestant; so that by his means no gremial[3] of the university was martyred therein.

I know he is much taxed for altering his religion four times in twelve years, from the last of King Henry the Eighth to the first of Queen Elizabeth: a papist, a protestant, a papist, a protestant, but still Andrew Perne.[4] However, be it known that though he was a *bending* willow, he was no *smarting* willow, guilty of compliance, not cruelty, yea preserving many who otherwise had been persecuted.

He was of a very facetious nature, excellent at *blunt-sharp* jests, and perchance sometimes too tart in true ones. One instance of many: this dean chanced to call a clergyman *fool,* who indeed was little better, who returned that he would complain thereof to the lord bishop of Ely. "Do," said the dean, "when you please, and my lord bishop will *confirm* you."

Yet was Doctor Perne himself at last heart-broken with a jest, as I have been most credibly informed from excellent hands, on this occasion. He was at court with his pupil Archbishop Whitgift in a rainy afternoon, when the queen was, I dare not say wilfully, but really resolved to ride abroad, contrary to the mind of her ladies, who were on horseback (coaches as yet being not common) to attend her. Now one Clod the queen's jester was employed by the courtiers to laugh the queen out of so inconvenient a journey. "Heaven," saith he, "Madam, dissuades you, it is cold and wet; and earth dissuades you, it is moist and dirty. Heaven dissuades you, this heavenly-minded man Archbishop Whitgift; and earth dissuades you, your fool Clod, such a lump of clay as myself. And if neither will prevail with you, here is one that is neither heaven nor earth, but hangs betwixt both, Doctor Perne, and he also dissuades you." Hereat the queen and the courtiers laughed heartily, whilst the Doctor looked sadly and, going over with his grace to Lambeth, soon saw the last of his life. [*d.* 1589]

(1) Sir Thomas Gresham was influential in his day: he was appointed the king's merchant in 1552, and attended Elizabeth's first council. He established at Osterley the first English paper-mills. He was born in London, and not in Norfolk as stated above. For Fuller's account of the Royal Exchange see under London, p. 347. (2) Some have questioned whether the MSS were his gift.—F. (3) *Gremial* = a resident member (of the university). (4) He was known in his day as "Old Andrew Turncoat", "Judas", etc., and it was usual to refer to a cloak that had been turned as having been "Perned."

JOHN AYLMER, brother to Sir Robert Aylmer, knight, was born [1521] at Aylmer Hall, in the parish of Tilney in this county, as his nearest surviving relations have informed me, from whom I have received the following information.

When he was but a child, going toward school, Henry Grey, duke of Suffolk, having some discourse with, took so much liking unto him that, after he had been bred some years in the university of Cambridge, he made him his chaplain, and committed his daughter the Lady Jane Grey to his tuition.

In the reign of Queen Mary he fled over beyond sea, and was little less than miraculously saved from the searchers of the ship by the ingenuity of a merchant, who put him into a great wine-butt, which had a partition in the middle, so that Master Aylmer sate in the hind part, whilst the searchers drank of the wine which they saw drawn out of the head or other end thereof.

Returning into England, he was made archdeacon of Lincoln, and at last bishop of London. He was happy in a meet yoke-fellow, having a gracious matron to his wife, by whom he had many children, and one son to which Archbishop Whitgift was godfather, and named him Tob-el; that is, The Lord is Good, in memorial of a great deliverence bestowed on this child's mother; for, when she was cast out of her coach in London (by a mastiff casually seizing upon the horses) she received no harm at all, though very near to the time of her travail.

Bishop Aylmer was well learned in the languages, a ready disputant and deep divine. He was eighteen years bishop of London; and, dying anno 1594, in the 73rd year of his age, had this for part of his epitaph, which Bishop Vaughan[1] (sometime his chaplain, afterwards his successor) made upon him:

Ter senos annos praesul, semel exul, et idem
Bis pugil in causa religionis erat.

Eighteen years bishop, and once banished hence,
And twice a champion in the truth's defence.

I understand it thus: once a champion in suffering, when an exile for religion, and again in doing, when chosen one of the disputants at Westminster against the popish bishops *primo Elizabethae;* except any expound it thus: once champion of the doctrine against papists, and afterwards against the discipline of the non-conformists, none more stoutly opposing, or more foully belibelled of them.[2]

SIR WILLIAM PASTON, knight, son and heir to Erasmus Paston, of Paston, esquire, is justly recounted a public benefactor. True it is, the family whence he was extracted were always forward in deeds of charity, according to the devotion of the days they lived in. Witness their bountiful donations to the abbeys of Saint Benet, in the Holme and the Bromholm in this county. After the Reformation, they had not (with too many) less heat because more light; but continued the stream, though they

(1) Richard Vaughan—see Wales, p. 693. (2) Bishop Aylmer was unconciliatory towards the puritans, and in the Marprelate tracts scurrilous attacks were made upon him.

changed the channel, of charity. This Sir William erected a very fair school, with thirty pounds per annum for the maintenance thereof, at North Walsham in this county; a deed, no doubt, acceptable to the God of heaven.

Solomon saith, "Teach a child in the trade of his youth." But, alas! it is above the reach of poor parents to teach their children, lacking learning to do it themselves, and livelihood to hire others, save where such good persons as this worthy knight have made provision for them. This Sir William married Frances the daughter of Sir Tho. Clere of Stokesby; and was great-grandfather to Sir William Paston, the bountiful promoter of all my weak endeavours.[1] [1528-1610]

HENRY HOWARD [FIRST EARL OF NORTHAMPTON] youngest son of Henry Howard, earl of Surrey, and brother to Thomas Howard, last duke of Norfolk, was born [1540] at Shotesham in this county. He was bred a serious student for many years in King's College in Cambridge, then in Trinity Hall, going the ordinary path and pace to the degree of mastership, without any honorary advantage. Here he became a great and general scholar; witness his large and learned work intituled *A Dispensative against the Poison of supposed Prophecies,* and dedicated to Sir Francis Walsingham. His fortune, left him by his father, was not great; and he lived privately all the reign of Queen Elizabeth, till King James advanced him in honour and wealth.

Here, for variety sake, and the better to methodize our matter, we will make use of a distinction, common in the custom-house about bills of lading, *Inwards* and *Outwards,* observing what greatness were *imported* on him, what gratitude was *exported* and performed by him.

Inwards. 1. King James created him baron of Marnhull in Dorsetshire. 2. Earl of Northampton. 3. Lord Privy Seal. 4. Lord Warden of the Cinque Ports. 5. Knight of the Garter. 6. Cambridge chose him her chancellor.

Outwards. 1. He founded and endowed an hospital, for twelve poor women and a governor, at Rising in this county. 2. Another for twelve poor men and a governor, at Clun in Shropshire. 3. Another at Greenwich in Kent, for a governor and twenty poor men, of whom eight are to be chosen out of Shotesham the place of his nativity.

He died the 15th of June 1614; and was buried in the ancient chapel of the castle of Dover.[2]

SIR EDWARD COKE, knight, son to Robert Coke, esquire, and of Winefred Knightly his wife, was born [1552] at Mileham in this county; bred, when ten years of age, at Norwich school, and thence removed to Trinity College in Cambridge. After four years' continuance there, he was admitted into Clifford's Inn, London, and the year following entered a student of the municipal law in the Inner Temple. Such his proficiency

(1) An antiquary (*d.* 1662) one of Fuller's literary patrons. (2) Northampton was a Roman catholic and found it difficult to make headway at Elizabeth's court, but his supple temperament and lack of principle served him well. Under James I he did well, as Fuller states. He was a commissioner for the trials of Ralegh and Guy Fawkes. He was reputed the most learned noble of his time.

therein, that at the end of six years (exceeding early in that strict age) he was called to the bar, and soon after for three years chosen reader in Lyon's Inn. Here his learned lectures so spread forth his fame that crowds of clients sued to him for his counsel, and his own suit was the sooner granted, when tendering his affections in order to marriage, unto Bridget daughter and co-heir of John Paston, esquire.

She was afterwards his incomparable wife; whose portion, moderately estimated, *viis et modis,* amounted unto thirty thousand pounds, her virtues not falling under valuation; and she enriched her husband with ten children.

Then began preferment to press upon him; the city of Norwich choosing him recorder, the county of Norfolk their knight to parliament, the queen her speaker therein, as also successively her solicitor and attorney. King James honoured him with knighthood, and made him chief-justice, first of the common pleas, then of the king's bench. Thus, beginning on a good bottom left him by his father, marrying a wife of extraordinary wealth, having at the first great and gainful practice, afterwards many and profitable offices, being provident to choose good pennyworths in purchases, leading a thrifty life, living to a great age, during flourishing and peaceable times (born as much after the persecution under Queen Mary, as dying before our civil wars) no wonder if he advanced a fair estate, so that all his sons might seem elder brethren, by the large possessions left unto them.

Some falsely character him a back-friend to the church and clergy, being a grand benefactor to the church of Norwich . . . As for the many benefices in his own patronage, he freely gave them to worthy men, being wont to say, in his law-language that he would have church-livings pass by livery and seisin, not bargain and sale.

Five sorts of people he used to fore-design to misery and poverty: chemists, monopolizers, councillors, promoters and rhyming poets. For three things he would give God solemn thanks: that he never gave his body to physic, nor his heart to cruelty, nor his hand to corruption. In three things he did much applaud his own success: in his fair fortune with his wife,[1] in his happy study of the laws, and in his free coming by all his offices, *nec prece, nec pretio,* neither begging nor bribing for preferment.

His parts were admirable: he had a deep judgment, faithful memory, active fancy; and the jewel of his mind was put into a fair case, a beautiful body, with a comely countenance; a case which he did wipe and keep clean, delighting in good clothes well worn, and being wont to say "that the outward neatness of our bodies might be a monitor of purity to our souls."

In his pleadings, discourse and judgments, he declined all circumlocutions, usually saying, "The matter lies in a little room." In all places, callings and jurisdictions he commended modesty and sobriety within their boundaries, saying, "If a river swells beyond its banks, it loseth its own channel."

(1) This, his first wife, died in 1598. In the same year he married Lady Elizabeth Hatton, Burghley's granddaughter, from whom he separated in 1617 after a violent quarrel about the marriage of their youngest daughter.

If any adverse party crossed him, he would patiently reply, "If another punisheth me, I will not punish myself." In the highest term of business, he made vacation to himself at his table; and would never be persuaded privately to retract what he had publicly adjudged, professing he was a judge in a court and not in a chamber. He was wont to say, "No wise man would do that in prosperity whereof he should repent in adversity." He gave for his motto, *Prudens qui patiens,* and his practice was accordingly, especially after he fell into the disfavour of King James.

The cause hereof the reader may find in our English chronicles,[1] whilst we behold how he employed himself when retired to a private life, when he did *frui suo infortunio,* and improved his loss to his advantage. He triumphed in his own innocency, that he had done nothing illegally, calling to mind the motto which he gave in his rings when made serjeant, *Lex est tutissima cassis* (the law is the safest helmet.)

And now he had leisure to peruse what formerly he had written, even thirty books, with his own hand; most pleasing himself with a manual which he called his *Vade mecum,* from whence, at one view, he took a prospect of his life passed, having noted therein most remarkables. His most learned and laborious works on the laws will last to be admired by the judicious posterity whilst Fame hath a trumpet left her, and any breath to blow therein. His judgment lately passed for an oracle in law; and if since the credit thereof hath causelessly been questioned, the wonder is not great. If the prophet himself, living in an incredulous age, found cause to complain, "Who hath believed our report?" it need not seem strange, that our licentious times hath afforded some to shake the authenticalness of the "reports" of any earthly judge.

He constantly had prayers said in his own house, and charitably relieved the poor with his constant alms. The foundation of Sutton's Hospital (when indeed but a foundation) had been ruined before it was raised, and crushed by some courtiers in the hatching thereof, had not his great care preserved the same. The free-school at Thetford was supported in its being by his assistance, and he founded a school, on his own cost, at Godwick in this county.

It must not be forgotten that Dr. Whitgift[2] (afterwards archbishop of Canterbury) was his tutor, who sent unto his pupil, when the queen's attorney, a fair New Testament, with this message: "He had now studied common law enough, let him hereafter study the law of God."

Let me add to this, that when he was under a cloud at court, and ousted of his judge's place, the lands belonging to the church of Norwich, which formerly he had so industriously recovered and settled thereon, were again called into question, being begged by a peer, who shall pass nameless. Sir Edward desired him to desist, telling him that otherwise he would put on his gown and cap, and come into Westminster Hall once again, and plead there in any court in justification of what he had done. He died [1634] at Stoke Poges in Buckinghamshire, on Wednesday the

(1) More than once Coke had fallen foul of James I, and in 1613 James removed him from the common pleas to the king's bench and later dismissed him. Whatever the immediate cause, the quarrel was one of principle, Coke asserting the independence of the judicature, and the king attempting to make law subserve his own purposes. (2) See Lincolnshire, p. 337.

3rd of September, being the 83rd year of his age, whose last words were, "Thy kingdom come, Thy will be done."

SIR THOMAS RICHARDSON, knight, was born [1569] at Mulbarton in this county, his father being minister thereof. He was bred in the study of our municipal law, and became the king's serjeant therein. Afterwards, on the 28th of November 1626, he was sworn chief-justice of the common pleas, that place having been void ten months before.

But coming now to our own times, it is safest for me to break off. Virgil, I remember, put a period to his *Eclogue* with

Et Hylax in limine latrat.

We'll verify no more,
For do but hark, Hylax doth bark at th' entrance of the door.

Seeing many will be ready to carp, it is safest for me to be silent[1]. . . This judge married, for his second lady, Elizabeth Beaumont, the sister (as I take it) of Mary countess of Buckingham, and the relict of Sir John Ashburnham, knight. She was by King Charles created baroness of Cramond in Scotland, and (though issueless by the judge) the honour descended to his grandchild. [*d.* 1635]

EDMUND GURNEY, born in this county, was bred in Queens' and Benet College in Cambridge, where he commenced bachelor of divinity, and afterwards was beneficed in this shire. An excellent scholar, who could be humorous, and would be serious, as he was himself disposed; his humours were never profane towards God, or injurious towards his neighbours; which premised, none have cause to be displeased if in his fancies he pleased himself.

Coming to me in Cambridge when I was studying, he demanded of me the subject whereon I studied. I told him I was collecting the witnesses of the truth of the protestant religion through all ages, even in the depth of popery, conceiving it feasible though difficult to evidence them.

"It is a needless pains," said he, "for I know that I am descended from Adam, though I cannot prove my pedigree from him." And yet, reader, be pleased to take notice he was born of as good a family as any in Norfolk. His book against Transubstantiation, and another on the Second Commandment are learnedly and judiciously written. [*d.* 1648]

JOHN TOWERS was born in this county, bred fellow of Queens' College in Cambridge, and became chaplain to William earl of Northampton, who bestowed on him the benefice of Castle Ashby in Northamptonshire. He was preferred dean, and at last bishop, of Peterborough.

He was a good actor when he was young, and a great sufferer when he was old;[2] dying [1649] rich only in children and prudence. Nothing but sin is a shame in itself; and poverty as poverty (especially since our Saviour hath sanctified it by suffering it) is no disgrace.

(1) Fuller's diffidence is curious. This judge refused to allow Felton (the assassin of the duke of Buckingham) to be racked to induce confession, which marked a step in the history of criminal jurisprudence. Later he came into conflict with Laud for suppressing Sunday revels. (2) He was imprisoned by Parliament in 1641.

THE FAREWELL

And now being to take my leave of this county, I wish the inhabitants thereof may make good use of their so many churches, and cross that pestilent proverb, "The nigher to the church, the farther from God;" substituting another (which will be a happy change) in the room thereof, viz., "The more the churches, the more sincere the devotion."

NORWICH

NORWICH is (as you please) either a city in an orchard, or an orchard in a city, so equally are houses and trees blended in it, so that the pleasure of the country and the populousness of the city meet here together. Yet, in this mixture, the inhabitants participate nothing of the rusticalness of the one, but altogether of the urbanity and civility of the other.

NATURAL COMMODITIES

FLOWERS

The Dutch brought hither with them, not only their profitable crafts, but pleasureable curiosities. They were the first who advanced the use and reputation of flowers in this city. A flower is the best-complexioned grass, as a pearl is the best-coloured clay; and daily it weareth God's livery, for "He clotheth the grass in the field." Solomon himself is outbraved therewith, as whose gallantry only was adopted, and *on* him, theirs innate, and *in* them. In the morning, when it groweth up, it is a lecture of Divine Providence. In the evening, when it is cut down withered, it is a lecture of human mortality.

Single flowers are observed much sweeter than the double ones (poor may be more fragrant in God's nostrils than the rich) and let florists assign the cause thereof, whether because the sun doth not so much dry the intricacies of such flowers which are duplicated.

Great the art in meliorating of flowers; and the rose of roses (*rosa mundi*) had its first being in this city. As Jacob used an ingenious invention to make Laban's cattle speckled or ring-streaked, so, much the skill in making tulips feathered and variegated with stripes of divers colours.

In my judgment those flowers carry it clearly which acquire themselves to a double sense, sight and smell; for though in some things it may be true, *optime quae minime olent,* yet in flowers (besides a negation of an ill) the position of a good scent is justly required.

THE MANUFACTURES

STUFFS

"It is an ill wind which bloweth no man good." Even storms brings wrecks to the admiral. The cruelty of Duke d'Alva, as it blew the Dutch out of their own, brought them into this city, and with them their manufactures, which the English quickly learned from them, until Norwich became the staple of such commodities for the whole land. For the nimble woof, its artificial dancing in several postures about the standing warp produceth infinite varieties in this kind.

Expect not I should reckon up their several names, because daily increasing, and many of them are *binominous,* as which, when they began to tire in sale, are quickened with a new name. In my childhood there was one called *stand-far-off* (the emblem of hypocrisy) which seemed pretty at competent distance, but discovered its coarseness when nearer to the eye: also *perpetuano,* so called from the lasting thereof (though but a counterfeit of the cloths of the Israelites, which endured in the wilderness forty years); *satinisco, bombicino, Italiano,* &c. Comineus saith that a favourite must have an handsome name which his prince may easily call on all occasions; so a pretty pleasing name, complying with the buyer's fancy, much befriendeth a stuff in the sale thereof.

By these means Norwich hath beaten Sudbury out of distance in the race of trading. Indeed in the starting (the south having the better of the north, and *bury,* or city, being before *wich,* or *vicus,* a village) Sudbury had the advantage; but now Norwich is come first to their mark.

THE BUILDINGS

The cathedral therein is large and spacious, though the roof in the cloisters be most commended. When, some twenty years since, I was there, the top of the steeple was blown down; and an officer of the church told me "that the wind had done them much wrong, but they meant not to put it up;" whether the wrong or the steeple he did not declare.

Amongst private houses, the duke of Norfolk's palace is the greatest I ever saw in a city out of London. Here a covered bowling-alley (the first, I believe, of that kind in England) on the same token that when Thomas last duke of Norfolk was taxed for aspiring, by marriage of the queen, to the crown of Scotland, he protested to Queen Elizabeth that when he was in his bowling-alley at Norwich he accounted himself as a king in Scotland.

As for the bishop's palace, it was formerly a very fair structure, but lately *unleaded,* and new covered with *tile* by the purchasers thereof; thereon a wag, not unwittily,

> Thus palaces are altered; we saw
> John *Leyden,* now Wat *Tyler,* next Jack *Straw.*

Indeed there be many thatched houses in the city; so that Luther (if summoned by the emperor to appear in this place) would have altered his expression, and said, instead of "*tiles* of the house," that "if every *straw* on the roof of the houses were a devil, notwithstanding he would make his appearance." However, such thatch is so artificially done (even sometimes on their chancels) that it is no eyesore at all to the city.

THE WORTHIES

WILLIAM BATEMAN was born [1298?] in this city, bred in Cambridge, and afterwards became first archdeacon, and then by King Edward the Third made bishop of this his native see. One of an high spirit to maintain the profit and privileges of his place; and I charitably presume him watchful over his sheep (souls subjected to his charge) because he was so careful of his deer; for the stealing whereof he enjoined penance to Robert Lord Morley, and made him perform them in the cathedral of Norwich, notwithstanding the king's threatening letters to the contrary.

This prelate, in his travels beyond the seas, perceiving that our English common law was *outlawed* in those parts, and apprehending the absolute necessity that the English should have skill in the canon law and civil laws (for the managing of foreign negotiations) erected a college in Cambridge, called Trinity Hall, for the study thereof. As he was father to Trinity, he was foster-father to Gonville Hall in the same university, removing it to a more convenient place, building and settling the revenues thereof, according to the will of the founder. King Edward the Third, resolving to follow his title to the crown of France, sent this bishop to the pope to acquaint him with his intentions, in which embassage he died, at Avignon, 1355.

JOHN CAIUS, born [1510] in this city, son to Robert Caius, was bred fellow in Gonville Hall in Cambridge. Hence he travelled into Italy, where he studied much, and wrote several learned treatises; returned home, became physician to Queen Mary, and improved Gonville Hall into a college. He bestowed good land on, erected fair buildings in, bequeathed thrifty statutes to, produced a proper coat of arms for, and imposed a new name on this foundation: Gonville and Caius College. He wrote an excellent book of the antiquity of Cambridge. When King James passed through this college, the master thereof presented him a Caius *De Antiquitate Cantabridgiae* fairly bound; to whom the king said, "What shall I do with this book? Give me rather Caius' *De Canibus*," a work of the same author, very highly praised, but very hardly procured.[1] Few men might have had a longer, none ever had a shorter epitaph, FUI CAIUS. [*d.* 1573]

THOMAS LEGGE was born [1535] in this city; bred first fellow in Trinity, then Jesus College in Cambridge, until he was chosen by Doctor Caius (then surviving) the nineteenth master of Gonville Hall, and the second of Gonville and Caius College. He was doctor of the law and Arches, one of the masters of the Chancery, twice vice-chancellor of the university, and thirty-four years master of his college therein.

This doctor, though himself a serious man, used to recreate himself with delightful studies, observing gravity in his very pleasures. He composed a tragedy of the destruction of Jerusalem, and having at last refined it to the purity of the public standard, some plagiary filched it from him, just as it was to be acted. He formerly had made a tragedy of the life of King Richard the Third, presented with great applause (Queen Elizabeth, I suppose, being a beholder thereof) in Saint John's College Hall. On the same token that John Palmer (afterwards dean of Peterborough) who acted King Richard therein, had his head so possessed with a prince-like humour, that ever after he did what then he acted, in his prodigal expenses; so that (the cost of a sovereign ill befitting the purse of a subject) he died poor in prison, notwithstanding his great preferment.

Great the bounty of Doctor Legge unto his college, bequeathing 600 pounds for the building of the east part thereof, besides several lesser

(1) James's request implied a compliment to a good naturalist and excellent physician and scholar. Caius' medical writings have a high value, and his classic works on the sweating sickness are the most important in England before the time of Harvey.

liberalities. Yea, be it remembered that after Thomas Bacon, fifteenth master of the college, had been a malefactor thereunto, leaving it much indebted, the four succeeding masters (ill examples avoided do good) Doctor Caius, Legge, Branthwaite, Gostlin (all natives of Norwich) were signal benefactors; though masters of, but stewards for, the house; making it, for the main, their heir at their decease. Doctor Legge died July 12, 1607, in the 72nd year of his age.

JOHN GOSTLIN, born [1566?] in this city, was first fellow, and afterwards master of Caius College in Cambridge, proctor of the university, and twice vice-chancellor thereof; a general scholar, eloquent Latinist, a rare physician, in which faculty he was regius professor. A strict man in keeping, and magistrate in pressing, the statutes of college and university, and a severe punisher of the infringers thereof. And here, courteous reader, let me insert this pleasant passage (seeing Cato himself may sometimes smile) without offence.

I remember, when this doctor was last vice-chancellor, it was highly penal for any scholar to appear in boots, as having more of the gallant than civil student therein. Now a scholar undertook for a small wager, much beneath the penalty, to address himself *ocreated*[1] unto the vice-chancellor, which was beheld by others as a desperate adventure. Carrying his state in his urinal,[2] he craved his advice for an hereditary numbness in his legs (and something of truth therein) which made him, in his habit, to trespass on the university's statutes, to keep them warm. The vice-chancellor, pitying instead of punishing him, prescribed him his best receipts; and so, by this *fraus honesta,* he effected his desires.

This doctor was a worthy benefactor to Catherine Hall (to which he had no relation, save what his bounty created) bestowing thereon the fair Bull Inn, of considerable value.[3] If he who giveth a night's lodging to a servant of God shall not lose his reward, certainly he that bestoweth inn and all upon the sons of the prophets shall find full compensation; the rather because that hall, pent formerly for lack of ground, and complaining with the sons of prophets, "The place where we dwell is too strait for us," may now say with Isaac, "The Lord hath made room for us" by this convenient addition. He died in his vice-chancellorship, anno 1626.

THE FAREWELL

I heartily wish that this city may long flourish in its full lustre. In tendency whereunto, may the thatch of all their houses, by Divine Providence, be effectually secured from the merciless element of fire (as which knoweth not to be a king, but must be tyrant) whose furious raging is seldom bounded, unless by the want of fuel to feed on. Yea, may their straw in due time advance into tile, that thereby their houses may for the future be better fenced for another element; I mean the injury of wind and rain.

(1) *Ocreate* = wearing an ocrea, greave, or legging, i.e., being booted. (2) Presumably nervous frequency of micturition. (3) At one time the fellows of Caius used to drink "to the unhappy memory of Dr. Gosling, who was such a goose as to leave the bull to Catherine."

NORTHAMPTONSHIRE

NORTHAMPTONSHIRE, being a long narrow inland county, is stretched from north-east to south-west, and bordereth on more counties than any other in England, being nine in number: viz., on the east, 1. Cambridgeshire; 2. Huntingdonshire; on the west, 3. Warwickshire; on the north, 4. Lincolnshire; 5. Rutland; 6. Leicestershire; on the south, 7. Bedfordshire; 8. Buckinghamshire; 9. Oxfordshire.

It is as fruitful and populous as any in England, insomuch that sixteen several towns with their churches have at one view been discovered therein by my eyes, which I confess none of the best; and God grant that those who are sharper-sighted may hereafter never see fewer.[1]

Sure I am there is as little waste ground in this as in any county in England, no mosses, meres, fells, heaths (Wittering, but a beauty-spot) which elsewhere fill so many shires with much emptiness; Northamptonshire being an apple without core to be cut out, or rind to be pared away.

Northamptonshire challengeth that all the rivers running through or by it are its natives, as bred in it (which argueth the elevation and height of the ground thereof) which I believe no other county in England can say. Besides, it lendeth two considerable rivers, Avon to Warwick, and Cherwell to Oxfordshire.

The language of the common people is generally the best of any shire in England. A proof whereof, when a boy, I received from a hand-labouring man herein, which since hath convinced my judgment: "We speak, I believe," said he, "as good English as any shire in England, because, though in the singing psalms some words are used to make the metre unknown to us, yet the last translation of the Bible, which no doubt was done by those learned men in the best English, agreeth perfectly with the common speech of our country."

Know, reader, that Doctor Bowle, my worthy friend, and most skilful botonographist,[2] hath taken notice of a heath in this county nigh to Stamford, where he giveth this commendation: "As fine a place for variety of rare plants as ever I beheld;"[3] who, I am sure, hath seen, in this kind, as much, both here and beyond the seas, as any of his age and profession.

NATURAL COMMODITIES

Now though this shire shares as largely as any in those profits which are general to England, grass, corn, cattle &c., yet it is most eminent for

SALTPETRE

In Latin *sal petrae*, rather so called because *exudat e petris* (it usually sweats out of rocks) than because it is wrought up at the last to a rocky or a stony consistency. Some conceive it utterly unknown to the ancients,

(1) Other men have discovered two and thirty. (2) The word is Fuller's own invention. He means, of course, *botanist*. (3) *Phytologia Britannica.*

which learned Hoffman will not allow, only it was disguised unto them under the name of *sal nitrum,* though our modern use was unknown to them, that *pulvis nitrosus,* or gunpowder, might be made thereof. It is ἐνφλώγιστος, what will easily take fire, the best test of the goodness thereof.

But why is saltpetre (common to all counties) insisted on in Northamptonshire? Because most thereof is found in dove-houses, and most dove-houses in this great corn county. Yet are not those emblems of innocency guilty in any degree of those destructions, which is made by that which is made thereof. All that I will add of saltpetre is this. I have read in a learned writer that "saltpetre men, when they have extracted saltpetre out of a floor of earth one year, within three or four years after they find more generated there, and do work it over again."[1]

PIGEONS

These of all fowls live most sociably in a commonwealth together, seeing their government is not, as bees, monarchical. They are generally reported without gall; understand it, their gall is not sequestered into a distinct vessel, as in other creatures. Otherwise we find the effects thereof in their animosities among themselves (whose bills can peck as well as kiss) as also, if their crops be not clearly drawn, in the bitterness of their flesh. They are most swift in flight, and the steerage of their tails conduceth much to their steady mounting upright. An envious man, having caught his neighbour's pigeons in a net, feeding on his stack, plucked off their tails, and let them go; which, though they could fly forward home, yet were soon after found dead in the dovecote, famished for want of food, as unable to fly perpendicularly, and so out at the louver.[2]

Pigeons, against their wills, keep one Lent for seven weeks in the year, betwixt the going out of the old and growing up of the new grain. Probably our English would be found as docible and ingenious as the Turkish pigeons, which carry letters from Aleppo to Babylon, if trained up accordingly. But such practices, by these *wing-posts,* would spoil many a *foot-post* living honestly by that painful vocation.

I find a grievous indictment drawn up against the poor pigeons for felony, as the grand plunderers of grain in this land. My author, computing six and twenty thousand dove-houses in England and Wales, and allowing five hundred pair in each house, four bushels yearly for each pair, hath mounted the annual waste they make to an incredible sum.[3] And if the moiety of his proportions hold true, doves may be accounted the causers of dearth, and justly answer their etymology in Hebrew, *Jonah,* which is deduced from a root, signifying to spoil or to destroy. The advocates for pigeons plead that they pick up such loose corn which otherwise would be lost, and uselessly trodden into the earth; that probably Divine Providence, which feedeth the fowls, by some natural instinct directeth them to such grain which would be barren and fruitless; that their dung, incredibly fruitful for the manuring of ground, abundantly recompenseth the spoil done by them.

(1) Dr. Jorden, *Discourse of Natural Baths and Mineral Waters.* (2) *Louver* = dome-like dovecote. (3) Samuel Hartlib, of Husbandry, his *Legacy*

However, if pigeons be guilty of so great stealth, they satisfy the law for the same, being generally killed for man's meat; and a *corrected pigeon* (let blood under both wings) is both pleasant and wholesome nourishment.

THE MANUFACTURES

This county can boast of none worth naming, whereof this the reason: sufficient the fruitfulness thereof in corn, grass (and what not, necessary for nature) for its plentiful subsistence. The elder brother who hath the inheritance of his own to maintain him, need not to be bound an apprentice; let the younger turn tradesman, and enlarge his narrow portion by his industry. It is enough for Northamptonshire to sell their wool, whilst that other countries make cloth thereof. I speak not this (though it be my native county) to praise Northamptonshire men for not *using*, but that Northamptonshire men may praise God for not *needing* manufactures. However, the town of Northampton may be said to stand chiefly on other men's legs; where, if not the best, the most and cheapest boots and stockings are bought in England.

I am credibly informed by a good friend that the manufacture of clothing hath, by prudent and able persons, been endeavoured effectually (understand me, in design, not success) in this county; and yet, though fine their wool, their cloth ran so soarse, it could not be sold without loss. Thus God hath innated every country with a peculiar genius; and when art crosseth nature, neither succeed; but both exceed where both concur.

THE BUILDINGS

As Saint Peter hath the primacy of all the other apostles, so the CATHEDRAL dedicated unto him in this county challengeth the precedency of all in England, for a majestic western front of *columel*[1] work. But, alas! this hath lately felt the misfortune of other fabrics in this kind. Yea, as in gangrene one member is cut off to preserve the rest; so I understand the cloisters of this cathedral were lately plucked down to repair the body thereof; and am heartily glad God in his mercy hath restored the only remedy (I mean its lands) for the cure thereof.

As for civil structures, HOLDENBY HOUSE lately carried away the credit, built by Sir Christopher Hatton, and accounted by him the last monument of his youth. If Florence be said to be a city so fine that it ought not to be shown but on holidays, Holdenby was a house which should not have been shown but on Christmas day. But, alas! Holdenby House is taken away, being the emblem of human happiness, both in the beauty and brittleness, short flourishing, and soon fading thereof. Thus one demolishing hammer can undo more in a day than ten edifying axes can advance in a month.

Next is BURGHLEY HOUSE nigh Stamford, built by William Lord Cecil. Who so seriously compareth the (late) state of Holdenby and Burghley, will dispute with himself whether the offices of the lord chancellor or treasurer of England be of greater revenues; seeing Holdenby may be

(1) *Columel* = a small column.

said to show the seal, and Burghley the purse, in their respective magnificence, proportionable to the power and plenty of the two great officers that built them.

WOTHORPE must not be forgot (the least of noble houses, and best of lodges) seeming but a dim reflection of Burghley, whence it is but a mile distant. It was built by Thomas Cecil earl of Exeter, "to retire to," as he pleasantly said, "out of the dust, whilst his great house of Burghley was a-sweeping."

CASTLE ASHBY, the noble mansion of the earl of Northampton, succeeds, most beautiful before a casual fire deformed part thereof. But seeing fire is so furious a plunderer, that it giveth whatsoever it taketh not away, the condition of this house is not so much to be condoled as congratulated.

Besides these, there be many others, no county in England yielding more noblemen; no noblemen in England having fairer habitations. And although the freestone, whereof they be built, keepeth not so long the white innocence as brick doth the blushing modesty thereof, yet, when the fresh lustre is abated, the full state thereof doth still remain.

THE WONDERS

There is within the demesnes of Boughton (the barony of the right honourable Edward Lord Montagu) a spring which is conceived to turn wood into stone. The truth is this: the coldness of the water incrustateth wood (or what else falleth into it) on every side with a stony matter, yet so that it doth not transubstantiate wood into stone; for the wood remaineth entire within. until at last wholly consumed, which giveth occasion to the former erroneous relation. The like is reported of a well in Candia, with the same mistake, that *quicquid incidit lapidescit*. But I have seen, in Sidney College in Cambridge, a skull brought thence, which was candied over with stone, within and without, yet so as the bone remained entire in the middle, as by a casual breach thereof did appear. This skull was sent for by King Charles; and whilst I lived in the house, by him safely again returned to the college, being a prince desirous in such cases to preserve others' propriety, as to satisfy his own curiosity.

MEDICINAL WATERS

WELLINGBOROUGH WELL

Some may conceive it called Wellingborough, from a sovereign well therein anciently known, afterwards obstructed with obscurity, and rediscovered in our days. But Master Camden doth *marr* their *mart,* avouching the ancient name thereof Wedlingburough. However, thirty years since, a water herein grew very famous, insomuch that Queen Mary lay many weeks thereat. What benefit her majesty received by the spring here, I know not. This I know, that the spring received benefit from her majesty; and the town got credit and profit thereby. But it seems all waters of this kind have, though far from the sea, their ebbing and flowing; I mean in esteem. It was then full tide with Wellingborough Well, which ever since hath abated, and now I believe is at low water in its reputation.

PROVERBS

The mayor of Northampton opens oysters with his dagger.

This town being eighty miles from the sea, sea-fish may be presumed stale therein. Yet have I heard that oysters (put up with care, and carried in the cool) were weekly brought, fresh and good, to Althorp, the house of the Lord Spencer, at equal distance. Sweeter, no doubt, than those oysters commonly carried over the Alps, well nigh 300 miles, from Venice to Vienna, and there reputed (far-fetched and dear-bought) dainties to great persons, though sometimes very valiant their savour. Nor is this a wonder, seeing Pliny tells us that our English oysters did *Romanis culinis servire* (serve the kitchens of Rome); pickled as some suppose, though others believe them preserved by an ingenious contrivance (epicures bear their brains in their bowels); and some conceive them carried in their shells. But, seeing one of their own emperors gave for his motto, *Bonus odor hostis, melior civis occisi* (good is the smell of an enemy, but better the smell of a citizen of Rome killed); I say unto such a Roman nose, stinking may be better than sweet oysters; and to their palates we'll leave them.

MARTYRS

This county affordeth no Marian martyrs, thanks be to a good and gracious God; a meek and moderate man, David Pole,[1] bishop of Peterborough; whom I here mention the more willingly, not knowing where to fix his nativity. However, *unus homo nobis*.

One martyr we had, not chargeable on the bishop, but his bloody archdeacon's account: John Curd of Syresham, a shoemaker, burnt in Northampton.

As for Augustine Dudley, parson of Castor, though some of his family credibly informed me that he was martyred, yet, on inquiry, his sufferings amounted not to loss of life; and therefore the less wonder that they escaped the drag-net of Master Foxe's diligence.

THE WORTHIES

SAINT WERBURGA was daughter to Wulfhere prince of Mercia, who had his chief palace of residence at Weedon-in-the-Street in this county, which place her father bestowed on her for her portion. She was bred a nun, under Saint Sexburga her aunt, and abbess at Ely, until such time that she was able, of herself, to go alone without leading in a monastical life. Returning to Weedon, she turned that place, which had been her father's palace, into a monastery.

Besides Weedon, she had the inspection of two other monasteries, Threckingham in Lincolnshire, and Hamburge, noted by my author[2] near Ely in Cambridgeshire, though no such place appear in any modern maps or catalogue. She parted herself, whilst living, successively betwixt these three places; but on her death-bed, commanded her body to be

(1) Second bishop of Peterborough, deprived on Elizabeth's accession. He died in 1568. (2) The English Martyrology [Hamburge is a mistake for Hanbury, Staffordshire.]

buried at Hamburge, when, contrary to her will, it was carried to the monastery of Threckingham, and the gates thereof fast locked, and carefully watched, to keep so great a treasure.

Wonder not they were so ambitious for her body; for, as Werburga was her name, which by a great antiquary[1] is interpreted the keeper or conserver of a burgh or town, so all presumed she would prove a tutelary patroness to the place which possessed her body, seeing some have reported that she hath miraculously driven away all geese from Weedon, that they shall destroy no grain thereabout. If this be true, then, as a certain Jupiter amongst the heathens was called Jupiter Απόμυιος, Jupiter the fly-trapper, who drave away those offensive insects, let this saint, hereafter be termed Werburga Αποχήνιος, the chaser-away of noisome geese, which spoil grain, grass and water, where they come. She died Anno Domini 700. Her body was afterwards taken up and translated to Chester, where Hugh Lupus, somewhat after the Conquest, built the fair monastery of Saint Werburga's to her memory, converted into a cathedral by King Henry the Eighth.

MARTIN DE PATESHULL. Let him remain here, till any shall show me a town called Pattishall in any other county of England; which village in this shire gave the name, and afforded the habitation to that ancient family. Though a clergyman, he was, in the first of King Henry the Third, made justice of the lower bench, or common pleas, wherein he continued for twelve years and upwards, as appeareth by the date of his death.

He was the fourth dean of Saint Paul's, as reckoned up in Bishop Godwin's catalogue. In that age, we see, clergymen were not only trusted with the spirit (I mean the equity) but also with the letter of the law, being judges in those courts wherein were the most strict proceedings. [*d.* 1229]

ROBERT OF HOLCOT was born in a village of this county so named, bred in the university of Oxford, and afterwards became a Dominican in Northampton. A deep scholar, and yet commended to be prudent *in rebus agendis,* and accounted one of the greatest schoolmen in that age. Nor was he only a candle, or domestic light, confined within the walls of his own country; but his learning was a public luminary to all Christendom.

He died at Northampton of the plague, anno 1349, before he had finished his lectures on the seventh of Ecclesiastes. I say of the plague, which at that time so raged in England, that our chroniclers affirm scarce a tenth person of all sorts was left alive; insomuch that the churches and churchyards in London not sufficing for their interments, a new churchyard was consecrated in west Smithfield, wherein fifty thousand were buried who at that time died of the pestilence.

WILLIAM LA ZOUCHE, son to William Lord Zouch, was born at Harringworth in this county, as a branch of that honourable family,[2] still alive,

(1) R. Verstegan. (2) Dr. Richard Zouche, professor of law in Oxford. [Lived 1590-1661; supported Charles I in the civil war; his treatise on *Jus Feciale* was the first work to exhibit the law of nations as a well-ordered system.]

and critical in their pedigrees, hath credibly informed me. From dean he became archbishop of York, 1342.

King Edward the Third, going over to France, committed the north to the care of this prelate. Soon after, David king of Scots with a great army invaded it. He promised himself Caesar's success, to come and conquer, see and subdue; the rather because he believed that the flower of the English chivalry being gone into France, only priests and peasants were left behind. Our archbishop, with such forces as he could suddenly provide, bid him battle at Durham, on Saint Luke's eve; whereon the Scotch king found such a *fast,* he had little list to *feast* the day following, being routed and taken prisoner.[1] Hence a poet of that age,

Est pater invictus, sicco de stipite dictus:

Zouch in French signifying the dry stump of a stick. However, his honourable family flourished as a green tree for many years, till withered in our memory, when Edward the last Lord Zouche died, without male issue, in the beginning of King Charles.

To return to our prelate; he began a beautiful chapel on the south side of his cathedral, intending to be interred therein, but dying before the finishing thereof, was buried before the altar of Saint Edward, 1352.

PETER PATESHULL was no doubt born in that village not far from Northampton; bred an Augustinian in Oxford. However, falling afterwards into some dislike of his order, he procured from Walter Diss (legate to Pope Urban the Sixth) a dispensation to relinquish it, and was made the pope's honorary chaplain. Afterwards, by often reading the works of Wycliffe (but especially his book of *Real Universals*) he became of his judgment; and after the death of Wycliffe, preached and promoted his doctrine. He wrote an exposition of the prophecy of Hildegarde's (a stinging comment on a nettling text) and so taxed the pride and laziness of all friars, that his book was burnt by command from the pope; and the writer thereof had been burnt also, had he not seasonably secured himself by his flight beyond the seas.

This mindeth me of a passage of a friar who burned a book of Peter Ramus, after the death of the author thereof, and then and there used this distich, in some imitation of Ovid:

Parve, nec invideo (sine me) liber ibis in ignem,
Hei mihi quod domino non licet ire tuo.

Small book, thy fate I envy not,
(Without me) feel the flame;
Oh had it been thy master's lot,
He might have felt the same.

But our Pateshull was out of reach in Bohemia, betwixt which and England a great intercourse in that age, since King Richard had married a sister of Wenceslaus king of Bohemia. We behold him as an advancer of Wycliffism in that country, for which John Hus and Jerome of Prague were afterwards condemned. He flourished in the year of our Lord 1387.

(1) The archbishop commanded one of the three divisions of the army at this battle of Neville's Cross. The king warmly praised him for his action, and by the northern clergy he was regarded as a hero.

HENRY CHICHELE, son of Thomas and Agnes Chichele, was born [1362?] at Higham Ferrers in this county; bred in Oxford, and designed by Wykeham himself (yet surviving) to be one of the fellows of New College. He afterwards became chaplain to R. Mitford bishop of Sarum, who made him archdeacon, which he exchanged for the chancellor's place of that cathedral. This bishop at his death made him his chief executor, and bequeathed him a fair gilt cup for a legacy. By King Henry the Fourth he was sent to the council of Pisa, 1409, and by the pope's own hands was consecrated bishop of Saint David's at Lucca, and thence was advanced archbishop of Canterbury by King Henry the Fifth.

During his reign, in the parliament at Leicester, a shrewd thrust was made at all abbeys, not with a rebated point, but with sharps indeed, which this archbishop, as a skilful fencer, fairly put by, though others will say he guarded that blow with a silver buckler; the clergy paying to the king vast sums of money to maintain his wars in France, and so made a foreign diversion for such active spirits, which otherwise, in all probability, would have antedated the dissolution of monasteries.

Under King Henry the Sixth he sat sure in his see, though often affronted by the rich Cardinal Beaufort of Winchester, whom he discreetly thanked for many injuries. A cardinal's cap was proffered to and declined by him; some putting the refusal on the account of his humility, others of his pride (loth to be junior to the aforesaid cardinal); others of his policy, unwilling to be more engaged to the court of Rome. Indeed he was thorough-paced in all spiritual popery which concerned religion, which made him so cruel against the Wycliffites; but in secular popery (as I may term it, touching the interest of princes) he did not so much as rack, and was a zealous assertor of the English liberties against Romish usurpation.

Great his zeal to promote learning, as appears by three colleges erected and endowed at his expense and procurement: 1. One, with an hospital for the poor, at Higham Ferrers, the place of his nativity. 2. Saint Bernard's in Oxford, afterwards altered and bettered by Sir Thomas White into Saint John's College. 3 All Souls in Oxford, the fruitful nursery of so many learned men.

He continued in his archbishopric longer than any of his predecessors for 500 years—full twenty-nine years; and died April 12, 1443.

ELIZABETH, daughter of Sir Richard Woodville by the Lady Jacquetta his wife (formerly the relict of John duke of Bedford) was born [1437?] at Grafton Regis in this county; in proof whereof many strong presumptions can be produced.[1] Sure I am, if this Grafton saw her not first a child, it beheld her first a queen, when married to King Edward the Fourth.

This Elizabeth was widow to Sir John Grey, who lost his life for the house of Lancaster, and petitioned King Edward to take off the sequestration from her jointure.

Beauty is a good solicitress of an equal suit, especially where youth is

(1) The Woodvilles had formerly, for four generations, lived at Grafton, as appears by the ledger-book [records, accounts, etc.] of Pipewell Abbey.—F.

to be the judge thereof. The king fell much enamoured with her feature; whilst the lady put herself into a chaste posture, and kept a discreet distance, neither forward to accept, nor froward to decline his favour. She confessed herself too worthless to be his wife, yet pleaded too worthy to be his wanton; till at last the king was content to take her upon her own terms, though a widow, and his subject. She got more greatness than joy, height than happiness, by her marriage; her husband keeping company with others for his pleasure, her for posterity. Nor was it long before the tempest of his lust drave him to another Shore,[1] which had a greater share in his affections.

This lady lived to see the death of her husband, murder of her two sons, restraint of herself, and rest of her children. And though her condition was altered and bettered by the marriage of her eldest daughter to King Henry the Seventh, yet that cunning king (who always weighed his love in the balance of policy) was not over-dutiful to her, nor over-loving to her daughter. She died Anno Domini 1492.

But her memory is most remarkable to posterity for finishing Queens' College in Cambridge (wherein I had my first breeding, and for it, and all therein, shall ever have an unfeigned affection); begun by Queen Margaret (wife to King Henry the Sixth) an implacable enemy to her husband, so that the two houses of Lancaster and York had their first amity in that foundation; a comfortable presage that in process of time they should be publicly and effectually united.

LIONEL WOODVILLE was born [1446?] at Grafton (since called Grafton Regis) in this county; bred in the university of Oxford, whereof for a time he was chancellor; then made bishop of Salisbury, 1482. As he was at first preferred, so his memory is still supported from sinking in silence, rather by the buttresses of his great relations, than the foundation of his own deserts; for he was son to Jacquetta duchess of Bedford, and Richard Woodville Earl Rivers; brother to Elizabeth queen of England; brother-in-law to King Edward the Fourth; uncle to King Edward the Fifth; and father (say some) to Stephen Gardiner, bishop of Winchester. Heart-broken with grief, with the tragedies he beheld in his own family, caused by the cruelty of King Richard the Third, he died . . . 1484.[2]

RICHARD III, son to Richard Plantagenet duke of York, was born [1452] at Fotheringhay Castle in this county. He was somewhat rumpled in his mother's womb, which caused his crooked back; otherwise handsome enough for a soldier. Ajax and Ulysses, valour and eloquence, met in his person, having as well a tongue to flatter, as an arm to fight.

He compassed the crown by cruelty, and the killing of his nephews, the two sons of King Edward the Fourth. When king he made good laws, which never procured him the people's love, as who beheld vice for his

(1) Meaning Jane Shore, his mistress. (2) He was one of the leaders in the Duke of Buckingham's rebellion in 1483. Buckingham had helped Richard III in his bloody passage to the throne, then, for some reason not clear now, raised a force against Richard. The floods of the Wye and Severn rendered his army useless, and he was captured and beheaded. Woodville fled to Henry of Richmond (later Henry VII) in Brittany.

native colour, and virtue for his painted complexion, on design to make himself popular.

He lost the crown and his life in the battle of Bosworth; where it may be verified of him, what Livy saith of Hannibal, when beaten by Scipio, that "in that fight he performed all the offices of a wise general and valiant soldier; only fortune did not befriend him."

If any except that King Richard in this battle was too prodigal of his own person, engaging it too far for a general; his condition did excuse him herein, with whom it was all one to die as to survive success. His memory hath since met with a modern pen,[1] who hath not only purged, but praised it to the height; and pity it is, that so able an advocate had not a more meriting person to his client. He was slain Anno Domini 1485.

WILLIAM CATESBY was born in this county, where his family long flourished at Ashby St. Ledgers. He was first advanced by William Lord Hastings, by whose countenance he came to the notice, then favour, of Richard the Third, though ill requiting it, when betraying him who caused his preferment. Take his character (transcribing in this kind is safer than indicting) from an author above exception. "This Catesby was a man well learned in the laws of this land; and surely great pity it was that he had not more truth, or less wit."[2]

If any object that being neither lord chief justice, chief baron, nor any writer on the law, he falleth not under my pen, by the charter of method prefixed to this catalogue, know that, though formerly *none,* he was eminently *all* officers, in every court of judicature, all the judges shaking at his displeasure. Witness the libel which Colyngbourne made, and which cost him his life for the same:

> The Rat,[3] and the Cat,[4] and Lovell the Dog,
> Do govern all England under the Hog.[5]

The time of his death is uncertain;[6] but, because we find him not molested in the reign of King Henry the Seventh (which, had he survived, surely had happened) it is probable he died before his patron and preferrer, King Richard the Third. [*d.* 1485]

SIR RICHARD EMPSON. It is pity to part them, seeing Empson may be called the Catesby to King Henry the Seventh, as Catesby the Empson to King Richard the Third; both countrymen, eminent for having, odious for abusing, their skill in law; active for the prince, injurious to the people. This Sir Richard was chancellor of the duchy of Lancaster; and from a sieve-maker's son (at Towcester in this county, where he was born) came to *sift* the estates of the most wealthy men in England.

For King Henry the Seventh, vexed that he had refused Columbus's proffer (whereby the West Indies, being found out fortunately, fell to

(1) George Buck, esquire [Sir George Buc, *d.* 1623.] (2) Sir Thomas More, printing the continuation of John Hardyng's *Chronicle.* (3) Ratcliffe [Sir Richard Ratcliffe, favourite of, and loaded with honours by, Richard III. Killed at Bosworth 1485.] (4) Catesby. (5) King Richard the Third, who gave a boar for his crest [Lovell is Francis, first Viscount Lovell, supporter of Richard III, attainted by Henry VII after Bosworth. He fought for Lambert Simnel, escaped and probably died of starvation in 1487.] (6) He was taken prisoner at Bosworth and beheaded.

Ferdinand king of Spain) resolved to discover Indies in England; and to this purpose, made Empson promoter general, to press the penal statutes all over the land.

Empowered hereby, this prowling knight did grind the faces of rich and poor, bringing the grist thereof to the king, and keeping the toll thereof to himself, whereby he advanced a vast estate, which now, with his name, is reduced to nothing. He united the two houses of York and Lancaster in the king's coffers, taking no notice of parties or persons for their former good services, but making all equally obnoxious to fines and forfeitures. But in the beginning of the reign of King Henry the Eighth he was arraigned, condemned, and beheaded, August the 17th, 1510.[1] Say not that princes, if sacrificing their ministers to popular fury, will want persons faithfully to serve them, seeing such exemplary justice will rather fright officers from false-deserving them; for, in fine, no real profit can redound to the sovereign which resulteth from the ruin of his subjects.

I must not forget how there was an old man in Warwickshire, accounted very judicious in judicial astrology, of whom Sir Richard Empson (then in his prime) did scoffingly demand, "When the sun would change?" To whom the old man replied, "Even when such a wicked lawyer as you go to heaven." But we leave him to stand and fall to his own Master, and proceed.

SIR WILLIAM LAXTON, son to John Laxton of Oundle in this county, was bred a grocer in London, where he so prospered by his painful endeavours, that he was chosen lord mayor, Anno Domini 1544. He founded a fair school and almshouse at Oundle in this county, with convenient maintenance, well maintained at this day by the worshipful company of Grocers; and hath been, to my knowledge, the nursery of many scholars most eminent in the university.

These Latin verses are inscribed in the front of the building:

Oundellae natus, Londini parta labore,
Laxtonus posuit senibus puerisque levamen.

At Oundle born, what he did get
In London with great pain.
Laxton to young and old hath set
A comfort to remain.

He died Anno Domini 1556, the 29th of July; and lieth buried under a fair tomb in the chancel of Saint Mary's, London.

SIR EDWARD MONTAGU, son of Thomas Montagu, born at Brigstock in this county, was bred in the Inner Temple in the study of the laws, until his ability and integrity advanced him lord chief justice of the king's bench, in the thirtieth of Henry the Eighth. He gave for his motto *Equitas Justitiae Norma*. And although equity seemeth rather to resent of the chancery than the king's bench, yet the best justice will be wormwood without a mixture thereof. In his times, though the golden

(1) Empson and Edmund Dudley (see Staffordshire, p. 514) his associate in the exaction of taxes, were beheaded for constructive treason.

showers of abbey lands rained amongst great men, it was long before he would open his lap (scrupling the acceptation of such gifts) and at last received but little in proportion to others of that age.

In the thirty-seventh of King Henry the Eighth, he was made chief justice of the common pleas, a descent in honour, but ascent in profit; it being given to old age rather to be thrifty than ambitious.

In drawing up the will of King Edward the Sixth, and settling the crown on the Lady Jane, for a time he swam against the tide and torrent of Duke Dudley, till at last he was carried away with the stream, as in our *Church History* is largely related.[1]

Ousted of his judge's office in the first of Queen Mary, he returned into Northamptonshire; and what contentment he could not find in Westminster Hall his hospitable hall at Boughton afforded unto him. He died anno 1557; and lieth buried in the parish church of Weekley.

ROBERT CROWLEY was born [1518] in this county; bred master of arts in Magdalen College in Oxford. It happened that one Miles Huggarde, whom Pits maketh a learned writer, and intituleth him *Virum doctum, pium, et in fide Catholica mire zelosum* (though in Master Foxe it appeareth, by his own confession, that he was but an hosier in London) wrote railing books against the poor protestants. Our Crowley took him to task, and confuted him in several treatises. Under Queen Mary, he fled over to Frankfort; and returning under Queen Elizabeth, was made vicar of Saint Giles without Cripplegate, London, where he lieth buried under a fair plated stone in the chancel. He died on the 18th of June, 1588.

SIR WILLIAM FITZWILLIAM, born [1526] at Milton Malsor in this county, married the sister of Sir Henry Sidney, lord deputy of Ireland. Yea, he himself was five times lord deputy of that kingdom; a sufficient evidence of his honesty and ability, seeing Queen Elizabeth never trusted twice, where she was once deceived in a minister of state. She so preserved him in the power of his place, that, sending over Walter earl of Essex (a person higher in honour) to be governor of Ulster, it was ordered that the earl should take his commission from the lord deputy.

An intelligent pen[2] alloweth him serviceable towards the reduction of that kingdom, in two eminent particulars. First, in raising a composition in Munster, then in settling the possessions of the lords and tenants in Monaghan, one of the last acts of state (tending to the reformation of the civil government) performed in the reign of Queen Elizabeth. His vigilancy was most conspicuous in the eighty-eight, when the routed Armada in its return did *look*, dared not to *land* in Ireland, except against their wills driven by tempest, when they found the shore worse than the sea unto them. I confess, some impute the Irish rebellion which afterwards broke out to this deputy's severity in imprisoning suspected persons

(1) For the indiscretion of drafting these clauses in favour of Lady Jane Grey in Edward VI's will he was fined £1,000 on Mary's accession. For John Dudley Duke of Northumberland see Staffordshire, p. 516. (2) Sir John Davies in his *Discovery of the State of Ireland*.

for concealing Spanish goods, though this only gave the Irish a mantle for their intended wickedness. He died Anno Domini 1599.[1]

SIR CHRISTOPHER HATTON was born [1540] I collect at Holdenby in this county, of a family rather ancient than wealthy, yet of no mean estate. He rather took a bait than made a meal at the inns of court whilst he studied the laws therein. He came afterwards to court in a masque, where the queen first took notice of him, loving him well for his handsome dancing, better for his proper person, and best of all for his great abilities. His parts were far above his learning, which mutually so assisted each other, that no manifest want did appear; and the queen at last preferred him lord chancellor of England.

The gown-men, grudging hereat, conceived his advancement their injury, that one not thoroughly bred in the laws should be preferred to the place. How could he cure diseases unacquainted with their causes, who might easily mistake the justice of the common law for rigour, not knowing the true reason thereof? Hereupon it was that some sullen serjeants at the first refused to plead before him, until, partly by his power, but more by his prudence, he had convinced them of their errors and his abilities. Indeed he had one Sir Richard Swale, doctor of the civil laws (and that law, some say, is very sufficient to dictate equity) his servant-friend, whose advice he followed in all matters of moment.

A scandal is raised that he was popishly affected; and I cannot blame the Romanists, if desirous to countenance their cause with so considerable a person. Yet most true it is that his zeal for the discipline of the church of England gave the first being and life to this report.

One saith that he was "a mere vegetable of the court, that sprung up at night, and sunk again at his noon";[2] though indeed he was of longer continuance. Yet it brake his heart that the queen (which seldom gave boons, and never forgave due debts) rigorously demanded the present payment of some arrears, which Sir Christopher did not hope to have remitted, but did only desire to be forborne; failing herein in his expectation, it went to his heart, and cast him into a mortal disease. The queen afterwards did endeavour what she could to recover him, bringing, as some say, cordial broths unto him with her own hands; but all would not do. Thus no pulleys can draw up a heart once cast down, though a queen herself should set her hand thereunto. He died Anno Domini 1591; and is buried, under a stately monument, in the quire of Saint Paul's.

NICHOLAS LATHAM was born at Brigstock[3] in this county, and afterwards became minister of All Saints' church in Barnwell. This man had no considerable estate left him from his father, nor eminent addition of wealth from his friends, nor enjoyed any dignity in the church of England, nor ever held more than one moderate benefice. And yet, by

(1) Fitzwilliam was one of Elizabeth's ablest viceroys, though much vilified and misrepresented. He was governor of Fotheringhay Castle at the time of the execution of Mary Queen of Scots, and was the only person to shew her any respect. She presented him with a picture of her son, James I. (2) Sir Robert Naunton, *Fragmenta Regalia*. (3) So saith the inscription of his monument.

God's blessing on his vivacious frugality, he got so great an estate that he told a friend he could have left his son, had he had one, land to the value of five hundred pounds by the year. But though he had no issue, yet making the poor his heirs, he left the far greatest part of his estate to pious uses; founded several small schools with salaries in country villages, and founded a most beautiful almshouse at Oundle in this county, and I could wish that all houses of the like nature were but continued and ordered so well as this is, according to the will of the founder. He died Anno Domini 1620; and lieth buried in the chancel of his own parish, having lived seventy-two years.

SIR AUGUSTINE NICOLLS, son to Thomas Nicholls, serjeant-at-law, was born [1559] at Ecton in this county. He was bred in the study of the common law, wherein he attained to such knowledge, that Queen Elizabeth made him *a*, King James *his own*, serjeant; whence he was freely preferred one of the judges of the common pleas; I say freely, King James commonly calling him "the judge that would give no money." Not to speak of his moral qualifications and subordinate abilities, he was renowned for his special judiciary endowments: patience to hear both parties all they could say, a happy memory, a singular sagacity to search into the material circumstances; exemplary integrity, even to the rejection of gratuities after judgment given.

His forbearing to travel on the Lord's day wrought a reformation on some of his own order. He loved plain and profitable preaching, being wont to say, "I know not what you call puritanical sermons, but they come nearest to my conscience."

Of this man it may be said *judex mortuus est jura dans,* dying in his calling, as he went the northern circuit; and hath a fair monument in Kendal church in Westmorland. [*d.* 1616]

MATTHEW KELLISON was born [1560?] in this county, at Harrowden, his father being a servant and tenant of the Lord Vaux, in whose family his infancy did suck in the Romish persuasions. He afterwards went beyond the sea, and was very much in motion. 1. He first fixed himself at the college of Rheims in France; 2. Thence removed to the English college at Rome, where he studied in philosophy and divinity; 3. Returned to Rheims, where he took the degree of doctor; 4. Removed to Douay, where for many years he read school-divinity; 5. Re-returned to Rheims, where he became king's professor, and rector of the university.

So much for the travails of his feet; now for the labours of his hands (the pains of his pen) those of his own opinion can give the best account of them. He wrote a book to King James, which his majesty never saw; and another against Sutcliffe,[1] with many more. [*d.* 1642]

NICHOLAS ESTWICK, B.D., was born at Harrowden (the barony of the Lord Vaux) in this county. A solid protestant, to counterpoise Kellison, a violent papist, and native of the same village. He was bred fellow of Christ's College in Cambridge, being there beheld as a pious and judicious

(1) Matthew Sutcliffe (1550?-1629) dean of Exeter; protestant controversialist.

divine, always cheerful without the least levity, and grave without any moroseness. He was afterwards presented by the Lord Montagu parson of Warton, where he lived a painful preacher 40 years, less than a deacon in his humility, and more than an archbishop in his own contentment. Hence he was (unwillingly-willing) preferred by the earl of Rutland to Bottesford in Leicestershire, where he had hardly inned one harvest, before, like a ripe sheaf, he was brought into the barn of the grave. Thus, though young trees are meliorated with transplanting, yet old ones seldom live, and never flourish after their removal. Let his works witness the rest of his worth, some of whose books are published, others prepared for the press; and I wish them a happy nativity, for the public good. Coming to take his farewell of his friends, he preached on the forenoon of the Lord's day, sickened on the afternoon; and was buried with his wife in the same grave, in Warton chancel, the week following, 1657.

SIR ROBERT DALLINGTON, knight, was born [1561] at Geddington in this county; bred a Bible clerk (as I justly collect) in Benet College, and after became a schoolmaster in Norfolk. Here having gained some money, he travelled over all France and Italy, being exact in his observations; and was, after his return, secretary to Francis earl of Rutland. He had an excellent wit and judgment, witness his most accurate aphorisms on Tacitus. At last he was knighted, and preferred master of the Charterhouse, where the schoolmaster, at his first entering, welcomed him with a speech in Latin verse, spoken by a schoolboy; but sure he was more than a boy who indited it. It is hard to say, whether Sir Robert was more pleased or displeased with the last distich therein:

Partem oneris vestri minimam ne despice, curam
Nec pueros iterum taediat esse tuam.

Do not the least part of your trust disdain,
Nor grudge of boys to take the care again.

He lived to be a very aged man, past seventy-six, and died Anno Domini 1637.[1]

FRANCIS GODWIN, son to Thomas Godwin,[2] bishop of Bath and Wells, was born at Hannington in this county; bred in Christ Church in Oxford; doctor of divinity, and sub-dean of Exeter. He was born in the fourth year of the reign of Queen Elizabeth, anno 1562; and in the fortieth year of his age, 1601, by her majesty made bishop of Llandaff; a bishopric better proportioned to his modesty than merits, as which was much impaired by his predecessor; so that one did truly say, "A bad Kitchin did for ever spoil the good meat of the bishops of Llandaff."[3] He was a good man, grave divine, skilful mathematician, pure Latinist, and incomparable historian. The church of Llandaff was much beholding

(1) He left a sum of money for the distribution of loaves every Sunday in his native village, which practice still continues. (2) See Berkshire, p. 29. Francis Godwin is Fuller's chief authority for the accounts of bishops in this work. (3) Anthony Kitchin, who marred this see with selling and letting long leases. [Kitchin (1477-1563) clung to his bishopric through all the changes from Henry VIII to Elizabeth, reducing it from one of the wealthiest to one of the poorest sees. He was one of the two Roman catholic bishops who took the oath of supremacy at Elizabeth's accession.]

to him; yea, the whole church of England; yea, the whole church militant; yea, many now in the church triumphant had had their memories utterly lost on earth, if not preserved by his painful endeavours in his *Catalogue of English Bishops*. I am sorry to see that some have made so bad use of his good labours, who have lighted their candles from his torch, thereby merely to discover the faults of our bishops, that their personal failings may be an argument against the prelatical function. He was translated by King James to the bishopric at Hereford, and died, very aged, in the reign of King Charles, Anno Domini 1633.

EDWARD MONTAGU [FIRST LORD MONTAGU OF BOUGHTON] second son to Sir Edward Montagu, knight, was born [1562] in this county; a pious, peaceable and hospitable patriot. It was not the least part of his outward happiness that, having no male issue by his first wife, and marrying when past fifty years of age, he lived to see his son enriched with hopeful children. I behold him, as bountiful Barsillai, superannuated for courtly pleasures, and therefore preferring to live honourably in his own county, wherein he was generally beloved, so that popularity may be said to have affected him, who never affected it; for in evidence of the vanity thereof, he used to say, "Do the common sort of people nineteen courtesies together, and yet you may lose their love if you do but go over the stile before them." He was a bountiful benefactor to Sidney College, and builded and endowed an almshouse at Weekley in this county.

"To have no bands in their death" is an outward favour many wicked have, many godly men want; amongst whom this good lord, who died in restraint in the Savoy, on the account of his loyalty to his sovereign. Let none grudge him the enjoyment of his judgment, a purchase he so dearly bought, and truly paid for, whose death happened in the year of our Lord 1644.

SIR HENRY MONTAGU [FIRST EARL OF MANCHESTER] fourth son to Sir Edward Montagu, knight, grandchild to Sir Edward Montagu, knight, lord chief justice of the king's bench, was born [1563?] at Boughton in this county. One skilful in mysterious arts, beholding him when a schoolboy, foretold that by the pregnancy of his parts he would raise himself above the rest of his family; which came to pass accordingly. He was bred first in Christ's College in Cambridge, then in the Middle Temple, where he attained to great learning in the laws, and passed through many preferments, viz., 1. Serjeant-at-law; 2. Knighted by King James, July 23, 1603; 3. Recorder of London; 4. Lord chief justice[1] of the king's bench, November 16, 1616; 5. Lord treasurer of England, December 16, 1620; 6. Baron of Kimbolton; 7. Viscount Mandeville; 8. President of the council, September 29, 1621; 9. Earl of Manchester; 10. Lord privy seal.

He wisely perceiving that courtiers were but as counters in the hands of princes, raised and depressed in valuation at pleasure, was contented rather to be set for a smaller sum, than to be quite put up into the box. Thus, in point of place and preferment, being pleased to be what the

(1) As chief justice he passed sentence of death on Ralegh.

king would have him (according to his motto *Movendo non mutando me*) he became almost what he would be himself, finally advanced to an office of great honour. When lord privy seal, he brought the court of requests into such repute, that what formerly was called the alms-basket of the chancery, had in his time well nigh as much meat in, and guests about it (I mean suits and clients) as the chancery itself. His *Meditations on Life and Death,* written in the time of his health, may be presumed to have left good impressions in his own soul, preparatory for his dissolution, which happened 1642.

JAMES MONTAGU, son to Sir Edward Montagu, knight, was born [1568?] at Boughton in this county; bred in Christ's College in Cambridge. He was afterwards master, or rather nursing-father, to Sidney College; for he found it in bonds to pay twenty marks per annum to Trinity College for the ground whereon it was built, and left it free, assigning it a rent for the discharge thereof. When the King's Ditch[1] in Cambridge, made to *defend* it by its *strength,* did in his time *offend* it with its *stench,* he expended an hundred marks to bring running water into it, to the great conveniency of the university. He was afterwards bishop, first of Bath and Wells, then of Winchester, being highly in favour with King James, who did ken a man of merit as well as any prince in Christendom. He translated the works of King James into Latin, and improved his greatness to good offices therewith. He died Anno Domini 1618; and lieth buried within his fair monument, within his fairer monument, I mean a goodly tomb in the church of Bath, which oweth its well-being and beauty to his munificence.

JOHN FLETCHER, son of Richard Fletcher, D.D.,[2] was, as by proportion of time is collectible, born [1579] in this county, before his father was bishop of Bristol or London, and whilst as yet he was dean of Peterborough. He had an excellent wit, which the back-friends to stage plays will say was neither idle nor well employed; for he and Francis Beaumont, esquire, like Castor and Pollux (most happy when in conjunction) raised the English to equal the Athenian and Roman theatre; Beaumont bringing the ballast of judgment, Fletcher the sail of phantasy; both compounding a poet to admiration.

Meeting once in a tavern, to contrive the rude draft of a tragedy, Fletcher undertook to kill the king therein; whose words being overheard by a listener (though his loyalty not to be blamed herein) he was accused of high treason; till the mistake soon appearing, that the plot was only against a dramatic and scenical king, all wound off in merriment.

Nor could it be laid to Fletcher's charge what Ajax doth to Ulysses,[3]

Nihil hic Diomede remoto

When Diomede was gone,
He could do nought alone,

for, surviving his partner, he wrote good comedies himself, though inferior to the former; and no wonder, if a single thread was not so strong as a

(1) Constructed as a defence of the town by King John in 1215. (2) See Kent, p. 274. (3) Ovid. *Metam.* lib. 13.

twisted one. He died (as I am informed) in London, of the plague, in the first of King Charles, 1625.

SIR ISAAC WAKE was born [1580?] in this county, whose father, Arthur Wake, clerk, was parson of Billing, master of the hospital of Saint John's in Northampton, and canon of Christ Church, and son to John Wake of Salcey Forest, esquire, of a most ancient and honourable family.[1] He was bred fellow of Merton College in Oxford, proctor and orator of that university. He was afterwards secretary to Sir Dudley Carleton, secretary of state; and from his, was advanced into the king's service, and employed ambassador to Venice, where he neglected his own commodity to attend his majesty's employment; the reason that he died rich only to his own conscience. Coming from Venice, he was appointed lieger for France, and designed secretary of state, had not death prevented him at Paris. He was accomplished with all qualifications requisite for public employment: learning, languages, experience, abilities and what not.

King Charles, hearing of his death, commanded his corpse to be decently brought from Paris into England, allowing the expenses for his funeral, and enjoining his nearest relations to attend the performance thereof. These accordingly met his body at Boulogne in France, and saw it solemnly conveyed into England, where it was interred in the chapel of the castle of Dover, Anno Domini 1632.

JOHN OWEN was born [1580] at Burton Latimer in this county; his father being the worthy and grave minister thereof. He was bred a fellow in Jesus College in Cambridge, where he commenced doctor of divinity; and was chaplain to King Charles whilst he was a prince. A modest man, who would not own the worth he had in himself; and therefore others are the more engaged to give him his due esteem.

In the vacancy of the bishopric of Saint Asaph, King Charles, being much troubled with two competitors, advanced Doctor Owen (not thinking thereof) as an expedient to end the contest. Indeed his majesty was mistaken in his *birth*, accounting him a Welshman; but not in his *worth*, seeing he deserved a far better preferment. Besides he was, though not *ortus, oriundus e Wallia*, and by his father (being a Welshman) he was related to all the best families in north Wales. He outlived his vote in parliament, and survived to see all contempt cast on his order, which he bare with much moderation, and died Anno Domini 1651.

JOHN PRESTON, D.D., was born [1587] at Heyford in this county; bred in Queens' College in Cambridge, whose life (interwoven much with church and state matters) is so well written by his pupil, Master Thomas Ball, that all additions thereunto may seem carrying of coals to Newcastle. However, seeing he who carrieth charcoal (a different kind from the native coal of that place) may meet with a chapman there, on the same confidence a word or two of this doctor.

Before he commenced master of arts, he was so far from eminency, as

(1) So am I informed from Mr. George Wake, late fellow of Magdalen College in Oxford, and his near kinsman.

but a little above contempt. Thus the most generous wines are the most muddy before they are fine. Soon after, his skill in philosophy rendered him to the general respect of the university.

He was the greatest pupil-monger in England in man's memory, having sixteen fellow commoners (most heirs to fair estates) admitted in one year in Queens' College, and provided convenient accommodations for them. As William, the popular earl of Nassau, was said to have won a subject from the king of Spain to his own party every time he put off his hat, so was it commonly said in the college that every time when Master Preston plucked off his hat to Doctor Davenant the college-master, he gained a chamber or study for one of his pupils; amongst whom one Chambers, a Londoner (who died very young) was very eminent for his learning.

Being chosen master of Emmanuel College, he removed thither with most of his pupils; and I remember when it was much admired where all these should find lodgings in that college, which was so full already, "Oh!" said one, "Master Preston will carry *Chambers* along with him."

The party called puritan then being most active in parliament, and Doctor Preston most powerful with them, the duke[1] rather used than loved him, to work that party to his compliance. Some thought the doctor was unwilling to do it; and no wonder he *effected* not what he *affected* not. Others thought he was unable, that party being so diffusive, and then, in their designs, as since in their practices, divided. However, whilst any hope, none but Doctor Preston with the duke, set by and extolled, and afterwards, set by and neglected, when found useless to the intended purpose. In a word, my worthy friend fitly calls him the court-comet, blazing for a time, and fading soon afterwards.

He was a perfect politician, and used, lapwing-like, to flutter most on that place which was furthest from his eggs; exact at the concealing of his intentions, with that simulation which some make to lie in the marches of things lawful and unlawful. He had perfect command of his passion; with the Caspian Sea never ebbing nor flowing, and would not alter his composed pace for all the whipping which satirical wits bestowed upon him. He never had wife, or cure of souls; and leaving a plentiful, no invidious estate, died Anno Domini 1628, July 20.

THOMAS RANDOLPH, born [1605] at Houghton in this county, was first bred in Westminster School, then fellow in Trinity College in Cambridge. The Muses may seem not only to have smiled, but to have been tickled at his nativity, such the festivity of his poems of all sorts. But my declining age, being superannuated to meddle with such ludicrous matters, consigneth the censure and commendation of his poems (as also of his countryman Peter Hausted, born at Oundle in this county) to younger pens, for whom it is most proper. Master Randolph died Anno Domini 1635.[2]

(1) i.e., the duke of Buckingham, who appointed him about 1620 chaplain in ordinary to Prince Charles as a conciliatory gesture to the puritans. (2) Randolph, a friend of Ben Jonson, is now best remembered by his plays *Amyntas* and *The Muses' Looking Glass*. The Peter Hausted mentioned was a minor dramatist and divine who died in the castle at Banbury during the siege of 1645.

THE FAREWELL

The worst I wish to this my native county is, that Nene (a river which some will have so termed from *nine* tributary rivulets) were Ten; I mean, made navigable from Peterborough to Northampton; a design which hath always met with many back-friends, as private profit is (though a secret) a sworn enemy to the general good.

Sure I am the Hollanders (the best copy of thrift in Christendom) teach their little ditches to bear boats. Not that their waters are more docible in this kind than ours; but they are the more ingenious and industrious schoolmaster of the lesson of public advantage, making every place in their province to have access unto every place therein by such cheap transportation.

NORTHUMBERLAND

NORTHUMBERLAND hath the bishopric of Durham (separated by the River Derwent running into Tyne) on the south; Cumberland on the south-west; the German Ocean on the east; and Scotland on the north and west, parted with the River Tweed, Cheviot Hills, and elsewhere (whilst our hostility with the Scots) *mutuo metu,* with mutual fear, now turned into mutual faith, both nations knowing their own, and neither willing to invade the bounds of others.

It is somewhat of a pyramidal form, whose basis, objected to the south, extendeth above forty, whilst the shaft thereof, narrowing northward, ascendeth to full fifty miles. Nature hath not been over-indulgent to this county in the fruitfulness thereof; yet it is daily improved, since (to use the prophet's expression) they have beat their swords into ploughshares, and spears into pruning-hooks; and surely such ploughshares make the best furrows, and such comfortable pruning-hooks cut with the best edge.

It must not be forgotten, how before the uniting of England with Scotland, there lay much waste ground in the northern part of this county, formerly disavowed (at leastwise not owned by any) only to avoid the charges of the common defence. But afterwards so great, sudden and good the alteration, that the borders becoming safe and peaceable, many gentlemen inhabiting thereabouts, finding the ancient waste ground to become very fruitful, in the fourth of King James put in their claims, and began to contend in law about their bounds, challenging their hereditary right therein.

THE BUILDINGS

One cannot rationally expect fair fabricks here, where the vicinity of the Scots made them to build not for state but strength. Here it was the rule with ancient architects, "what was firm, that was fair;" so that it may be said of the houses of the gentry herein, *Quot mansiones, tot munitiones,* as either being all castles or castle-like, able to resist, though no solemn siege, a tumultuary incursion.

Before we come to the Worthies of this county, be it premised that Northumberland is generally taken in a double acception: first, as a county, whose bounds we have fore-assigned; and secondly, as a kingdom, extending from Humber to Edinburgh Forth, and so taking in the southern part of Scotland. Here then we have an opportunity to cry quits with Dempster the Scottish historian, and to repair ourselves of him for challenging so many Englishmen to be Scots, should we bring all them in for Northumberlanders which were born betwixt Berwick and Edinburgh, whose nativities we may, in the rigour of right, justify to be English, if born therein whilst the tract of ground was subjected to the Saxon heptarchy. But, because we will have an unquestionable title to what we claim to be ours, we are content to confine ourselves to Northumberland in the county capacity thereof.

PROVERBS

To carry coals to Newcastle. This is to do what was done before, or to busy one's self in a needless employment. Parallel to the Latin, *Aquam mari infundere, Sidera coelo addere, Noctuas Athenas* (to carry owls to Athens) which place was plentifully furnished before with fowl of that feather.

To take Hector's cloak. That is, to deceive a friend who confideth on his faithfulness; and hereon a story doth depend. When Thomas Percy, earl of Northumberland, anno 1569, was routed in the rebellion which he had raised against Queen Elizabeth, he hid himself in the house of one Hector Graham, of Harlow in this county, having confidence he would be true to him, who, notwithstanding, for money betrayed him to the regent of Scotland. It was observed that Hector, being before a rich man, fell poor of a sudden, and so hated generally, that he never durst go abroad, insomuch that the proverb "To take Hector's cloak," is continued to this day among them, when they would express a man that betrayed his friend who trusted him.

THE WORTHIES

SAINT EBBA was born in Northumberland, being daughter to Æthelfrith the king thereof. When her father was taken prisoner, she got hold of a boat in Humber, and passing along the raging ocean, she safely landed at a place in Merch in Scotland, which is called the promontory of Saint Abb unto this day.

Becoming prioress of Coldringham in that country, to preserve her own and fellow-nuns' chastity from the pagan Danes, she cut off her own nose, and persuaded the rest to do the like, that their beauty might be no bait, whilst their deformity did secure their virginity. Sure I am, that since, more have lost their noses in prosecution of their wantonness, than in preservation of their chastity. As for the Danes, being offended that these nuns would not be the objects of their lusts, they made them the subjects of their fury, burning them and their monastery together.

But such the reputed holiness of Saint Ebba, that many churches, commonly called Saint Tabbs, are in North England dedicated unto her, and her memory is continued in the name of Ebchester, a little village in the bishopric of Durham. [*d.* 679?]

RALPH FRESBORN was born in this county, bred a soldier, scholar, traveller (being a man of great estate) and at last turned a friar. He attended Richard, earl of Cornwall and king of the Romans, into the Holy Land. Here he came acquainted with the friars living on Mount Carmel, which were then much molested with the inroads of pagans. Our Ralph, pitying their condition, and much taken with their sanctity and (as some say) miracles, brought them over with him into England, and built them an house at Hulne, nigh Alnwick in Northumberland, *in loco Carmelo Syriae non dissimili,* saith my author, in a place not unlike Carmel in Syria.[1] Thus pence are like shillings; and as Carmel

(1) Bale.

had an hill, with the river Kishon running under it, a forest beside it, and the midland sea some three miles from it; so this had the river Aln, a park adjoining, and the German Sea at the same distance.[1]

But Northumberland was but a cold Carmel for these friars; who soon got themselves warmer nests, in Kent, Essex, London, and where not, multiplying more in England than in any other country, as Mantuan observeth, and hath not ill expressed[2]:

> Hear, why that they so much in England thriv'd:
> When th' English erst in Palestine arriv'd,
> The city Acon on the shore of Tyre,
> As next at hand, with arms did soon acquire.

And after some verses interposed:

> The captains, seeing so great wonders wrought,
> These friars with them into England brought;
> What was denied at home, they here anew
> Churches and houses built. In years but few,
> Increasing twig-like set by happy band,
> Or tree transplanted to a fruitful land.

This Ralph wrote books of pious exhortations and epistles; and, after he had been fourteen years provincial of his own order, died and was buried at Hulne aforesaid, Anno Domini 1274.

JOANNES SCOTUS [DUNS SCOTUS]. He was born [1265?] at Dunstar, a village in the parish of Embleton in this county, as appeareth by a writing in a book of his in Merton College, wherein he was bred. He was a Franciscan by order; and of such nimble and solid parts, that he got the title of Doctor Subtilis.

Hitherto all schoolmen were, like the world before the building of Babel, "of one language, and of one speech," agreeing together in their opinions; which hereafter were divided into two regiments, or armies rather, of Thomists and Scotists, under their several generals opposing one another. Scotus was a great stickler against the Thomists for that sinful opinion, that the Virgin Mary was conceived without sin; which if so, how came she to "rejoice in God her Saviour?" He read the sentences thrice over in his solemn lectures, once at Oxford, again at Paris, and last at Cologne, where he died, or was killed rather, because falling into a strong fit of an apoplexy, he was interred whilst yet alive, as afterwards did appear. Small amends were made for his hasty burial, with an handsome monument erected over him, at the cost of his order (otherwise whether as Scot, scholar or Franciscan, he had little wealth of his own) in the quire before the high altar. On his monument are inscribed the names of fifteen Franciscans, viz., three popes and two cardinals on the top, and ten doctors (whereof six English) on the sides thereof; all his contemporaries, as I conceive. He died Anno Domini 1308.

ROBERT WODELARKE was born, saith my author,[3] at Wakerley in this county. True it is in my late *Church History* I have challenged him for Northamptonshire, because there is no Wakerley in Northumberland,

(1) The Lord Vesey was so great a benefactor to this convent that by some he is reputed the founder thereof. (2) *Fastorum*, lib. viii. [Latin original omitted.] (3) John Scot, in his Tables of Cambridge.

because there is a Wakerley in Northamptonshire. But on second thoughts, I resign him clear to his county, loth to higgle for a letter or two (misprinted perchance) in the name of a town. This Wodelarke was the last of the first original fellows, and third provost, of King's College in Cambridge. He bought three tenements in Milne Street, and by a mortmain procured from King Edward the Fourth, erected of them a small college, by the name of Saint Catherine's Hall.

"As is the man, so is his strength." Great matters cannot be expected from so private a person, who never attained to any prelatical preferment, who was bountiful to his foundation to the utmost of his ability. Herein he stands alone, without any to accompany him, being the first and last who was master of one college, and at the same time founder of another.[1] This his *Zoar* hath since met with many worthy benefactors, who have advanced it to be considerable both in buildings and revenues. [*d.* 1479]

WILLIAM TURNER was born at Morpeth in this county; bred in the university of Cambridge, where he became an excellent Latinist, Grecian, orator and poet. He was very zealous in the protestant religion, writing many books in the defence thereof, and much molested for the same by Bishop Gardiner and others. He was kept long in durance; and escaping at last by God's providence, fled over beyond sea. At Ferrara in Italy he commenced doctor of physic, there gaining his degree with general applause. He wrote a great *Herbal,* and a book of physic for the English gentry, as also several treatises of plants, fishes, stones, metals, &c. He went afterwards into Germany, where he lived in great credit and practice; and, as I conjecture, died there in the reign of Queen Mary. Reader, I conceive him worthy of thy special notice, because he was both a confessor and physician, qualifications which meet not every day in the same person.[2] [*d.* 1568]

THOMAS GIBSON. It is a pity to part him from the former, because symbolising in many particulars of concernment, both 1. Born in this county, and in the same town of Morpeth; 2. Flourishing at the selfsame time; 3. Physicians by profession; and it is said of this Thomas that he did *aegritudinum sanationes incredibiles* (incredible cures of diseases); 4. Writing of the same subject, of the nature of herbs; 5. Professed enemies to popery.

This Thomas wrote many other books, and one intituled *The Treasons of the Prelates since the Conquest,* which work, had it come to the hand of a modern author,[3] happily it might have much helped him in that subject. He was alive in the last of Queen Mary; and Bale sendeth forth a hearty prayer for the continuance of his health and happiness.[4] [*d.* 1562]

(1) He was also twice chancellor of the university. (2) Actually he returned after Elizabeth's accession and was reinstated in the deanery of Wells, of which he had been deprived by Mary. In 1564 he was suspended for nonconformity. His *Herbal* marks the beginning of scientific botany in England. (3) Master William Spring. (4) Gibson was also a printer, printing his own work, and commended to Cromwell by Latimer as "an honest poor man, who will set it forth in a good letter, and sell it good cheap." His *Concordance of the New Testament* is the earliest printed concordance in the English language.

VALENTINE CARY was born at Berwick, which, though north of Tweed, is reduced to this county; extracted from the Careys, barons of Hunsdon. He was first, scholar of Saint John's College in Cambridge, then fellow of Christ's College, afterwards of St. John's again, and at last master of Christ's College; so that I meet not with any his peer herein, thus bounded and rebounded betwixt two foundations. But the best is, they both had one and the same foundress, Margaret countess of Richmond. He was vice-chancellor of Cambridge, anno 1612, dean of Saint Paul's, and at last bishop of Exeter; a complete gentleman and excellent scholar. He once unexpectedly owned my nearest relation in the high commission court, when in some distress; for which courtesy I, as heir to him who received the favour, here publicly pay this my due thanks unto his memory.[1]

Though some contest happened betwixt him and the city of Exeter; yet, I am credibly informed, when that city was visited with the sickness, he was bountiful above expectation, in relieving the poor thereof. He died Anno Domini 1626; and lies buried under a plain stone in the church of Saint Paul's, London, though he hath another monument of memorial in the church of Exeter.

GEORGE CARLETON was born [1559] in this county, nigh the borders of Scotland, at Norham, his father being the keeper of the important castle therein; bred in Merton College in Oxford. Hear what our English antiquary[2] saith of him, "Whom I have loved in regard of his singular knowledge in divinity, which he professeth; and in other more delightful literature, and am loved again of him," &c. He was one of the four divines sent by King James to the synod of Dort, each of them there observed in their respective eminencies: *In Carletono praelucebat episcopalis gravitas, in Davenantio subactum judicium; in Wardo multa lectio; in Hallo expedita concionatio.* Doctor Carleton was then bishop of Llandaff, and afterwards of Chichester. His good affections appear in his treatise intituled *A Thankful Remembrance of God's Mercy;* solid judgment in his *Confutation of Judicial Astrology;* and clear invention in other juvenile exercises. Indeed, when young, he was grave in his manners; so when old he was youthful in his parts, even unto his death, which happened [1628].

RICHARD HOLDSWORTH, D.D., was born [1590] at Newcastle in this county; preferred fellow of Saint John's College in Cambridge, rector of St. Peter-le-Poer of London, archdeacon of Huntingdon, and at last master of Emmanuel College.

During his continuance in London, he did *dominari in concionibus;* and although it be truly observed, that the people in London honour their pastors (as John Baptist) πρὸς ὥραν for an hour (or short time) yet this Doctor had his hour measured him by a large glass, continuing in public esteem till the beginning of these civil wars, when the times turned and he, standing still, was left to the censure of factious innovators.

(1) The elder Fuller, like his son, was a man of moderation (in his time implying someone not pressing puritans towards conformity with the Anglican church) and came under the cognizance of the court of high commission, and was probably passed to the court of Star Chamber for punishment. (2) Camden's *Britannia.*

Most candid his disposition; and if he had the infirmity of ingenuous persons to be choleric, he prevented others checking it in him, by checking it first in himself.

He suffered long imprisonment in Ely House and the Tower for a sermon he made when vice-chancellor of Cambridge; and at last, restored to his liberty, waited on his majesty in the Isle of Wight. He is here entered amongst the bishops, because proffered Bristol, but refused it; and such who know least of his mind, are most bold to conjecture the cause of it. He slighted not the smallness thereof; because such his manners, loyalty and conscience, that he would have thanked his sovereign for an injury, much more for a smaller courtesy. Wherefore such only shoot by the aim of their own fancies, who report him to have said, he would not "wear a Bristol stone."

Sure I am that England had, if any more able, none more zealous to assert episcopacy; and let that suffice us, that he esteemed the acceptance thereof, in that juncture of time, unsafe and unseasonable for himself. He afterwards took the deanery of Worcester; though he received no profit, the place received honour from him, being the last who was intituled (and indeed it was no more) with that dignity.

Pity it is so learned a person left no monuments, save a sermon, to posterity; for I behold that posthume work as a scripture none of his, named by the transcriber *The Valley of Vision,* a scripture expression, but here misplaced. *Valley* it is indeed, not for the fruitfulness but lowness thereof (especially if compared to the high parts of the pretended author) but little vision therein. This I conceived myself in credit and conscience concerned to observe, because I was surprised to *preface* to the book; and will take the blame, rather than clear myself, when my innocency is complicated with the accusing of others.[1]

Dying [1649] he was buried in his own parish church, in Saint Peter's, Broad Street; his ancient friend Doctor Jefferies of Pembroke Hall taking for his text, "My days are like a shadow that decline;" Thomas Rich and Richard Abdi, esquires, his executors and worthy friends, ordering his funeral with great solemnities and lamentation.

Machell Vivan is a Scottish man by his birth; but, because beneficed in this county so many years, shall (by the reader's leave) pass for an Englishman, so far as to be here inserted; the rather, because he will minister to the present and future ages just matter of admiration, as, by the perusing of the ensuing letter from my credible friend, well known in London (where his surviving father was not long since the prime magistrate thereof) will appear:

There is an acquaintance of mine, and a friend of yours, who certified me of your desire of being satisfied of the truth of that relation I made, concerning the old minister in the north. It fortuned in my journey to Scotland, I lay at Alnwick in Northumberland, one Sunday by the way; and understanding from the host of the house where I lodged, that this minister lived within three miles of that place, I took my horse after dinner, and rid thither to hear him preach, for my own satisfaction. I found him in the desk,

(1) In 1651 Fuller was trapped into writing a preface to the collection of sermons purporting to be by Holdsworth, and discovered, too late, that only one was genuine. Holdsworth was one of the most eloquent and popular preachers of his day.

where he read unto us some part of the Common Prayer, some of holy David's Psalms, and two chapters, one out of the Old, the other out of the New Testament, without the use of spectacles. The Bible, out of which he read the chapters, was a very small printed Bible. He went afterwards into his pulpit, where he prayed and preached to us about an hour and half. His text was, "Seek you the kingdom of God, and all things shall be added unto you." In my poor judgment, he made an excellent good sermon, and went cleverly through without the help of any notes.

After sermon I went with him to his house, where I proposed these several following questions to him. Whether it was true, the book reported of him concerning his hair? Whether or no he had a new set of teeth come? Whether or no his eyesight ever failed him? And whether in any measure he found his strength renewed unto him? He answered me distinctly to all these; and told me, he understood the news-book reported his hair to become a dark brown again, but that is false: he took his cap off, and shewed me it. It is come again like a child's, but rather flaxen than either brown or grey. For his teeth, he hath three come within these two years, not yet to their perfection; while he bred them he was very ill. Forty years since he could not read the biggest print without spectacles, and now (he blesseth God) there is no print so small, no written hand so small, but he can read it without them. For his strength, he thinks himself as strong now as he hath been these twenty years. Not long since he walked to Alnwick to dinner and back again, six north-country miles. He is now an hundred and ten years of age, and ever since last May, a hearty body, very cheerful, but stoops very much. He had five children after he was eighty years of age, four of them lusty lasses now living with him, the other died lately; his wife yet hardly fifty years of age. He writes himself *Machell Vivan.* He is a Scottish man, born near Aberdeen. I forget the town's name where he is now pastor; he hath been there fifty years.

Your assured loving friend, THOMAS ATKIN. Windsor, 28 September, 1657.

THE FAREWELL

Being now to take our leave of Northumberland, I remember what I have read of Sir Robert de Umfraville, a native of this county, how he was commonly called Robin Mendmarket, so much he improved trading hereabouts, in the reign of King Henry the Fourth. It will not be amiss to wish this county more Mendmarkets, that the general complaint of the decay of traffic may be removed. I confess the knight bettered the markets by selling therein the plentiful plunder which he had taken from the Scots; but I desire it done by some ingenuous and not injurious design, that none may have just cause to complain.

NOTTINGHAMSHIRE

NOTTINGHAMSHIRE hath Yorkshire on the north, Lincolnshire on the east, Leicestershire on the south, and Derbyshire on the west. Nor can I call to mind any county besides this, bounded with four, and but four shires, and those towards the four cardinal points, without any parcels of other shires interposed. The pleasantness thereof may be collected from the plenty of noblemen, many having their baronies, and more their residence therein. It is divided into two parts, the sand and the clay, which so supply the defects one of another, that what either half doth afford, the whole county doth enjoy.

NATURAL COMMODITIES

Glycyrize, or Liquorice

England affordeth hereof the best in the world for some uses; this county the first and best in England. Great the use thereof in physic, it being found very pectoral[1] and sovereign for several diseases. A stick hereof is commonly the spoon prescribed to patients, to use in any lingences or loaches.[2] If (as Aeneas's men were forced to eat their own trenchers) these chance to eat their spoons, their danger is none at all. But liquorice, formerly dear and scarce, is now cheap and common, because growing in all counties. Thus plenty will make the most precious thing a drug; as silver was nothing respected in Jerusalem in the days of Solomon.

THE WONDERS

We must not forget how two aeries of lanners were lately found in Sherwood Forest. These hawks are the natives of Saxony; and it seems, being old and past flying at the game, were let or did set themselves loose; where meeting with *lannerets,* enlarged on the same terms, they did breed together, and proved as excellent in their kind, when managed, as any which were brought out of Germany.

PROVERBS

Many talk of Robin Hood, who never shot in his bow. That is, many discourse, or prate rather, of matters wherein they have no skill or experience. This proverb is now extended all over England, though originally of Nottinghamshire extraction, where Robin Hood did principally reside in Sherwood Forest. He was an *arch*-robber, and withal an excellent *archer;* though surely the poet gives a twang to the loose of his arrow, making him shoot one a cloth-yard long, at full forty score mark, for compass never higher than the breast, and within less than a foot of the mark. But herein our author hath verified one proverb, talking at large of Robin Hood, in whose bow he never shot.

(1) *Pectoral* = good for affections of the chest. (2) *Lingence* = a linctus. Loach appears to be a synonym.

One may justly wonder that this archer did not at last hit the mark; I mean, come to the gallows for his many robberies. But see more hereof in the memorable persons of this county.

The little smith of Nottingham,
Who doth the work that no man can.

England hath afforded many rare workmen in this kind; whereof he may seem an apprentice to Vulcan, and inferior only to his master (in making the invisible net) who made a lock and key, with a chain of ten links, which a flea could draw. But what this little smith and great workman was, and when he lived, I know not; and have cause to suspect that this of Nottingham is a periphrasis of *nemo,* or a person who never was. And the proverb, by way of sarcasm, is applied to such who, being conceited of their own skill, pretend to the achieving of impossibilities.

THE WORTHIES

ROBIN HOOD was, if not by birth, by his chiefest abode this countryman. Camden calls him *praedonem mitissimum,* the gentlest thief that ever was; and know, reader, he is entered into our catalogue not for his thievery, but for his gentleness. Take the character of his (though not good) less bad behaviour from the pen of our poet.[1]

From wealthy abbots' chests, and churls' abundant store,
What oftentimes he took, he shar'd amongst the poor;
No lordly bishop came in lusty Robin's way,
To him before he went, but for his pass must pay,
The widow in distress he graciously reliev'd,
And remedied the wrongs of many a virgin griev'd.

But who made him a judge? Or gave him a commission to take where it might best be spared, and give where it was most wanted? His principal residence was in Sherwood Forest in this county, though he had another haunt (he is no fox that hath but one hole) near the sea in the North Riding in Yorkshire, where Robin Hood's Bay still retaineth his name. Not that he was any pirate, but a land thief, who retreated to those unsuspected parts for his security.

One may wonder how he escaped the hand of justice, dying in his bed for ought is found to the contrary; but it was because he was rather a merry than a mischievous thief, complimenting passengers out of their purses; never murdering any but deer, and this popular robber feasted the vicinage with his venison. He played his pranks in the reign of King Richard the First.

SIR JOHN MARKHAM, descended of an ancient family, was born at Markham in this county, and brought up in the municipal law, till, being knighted by Edward the Fourth, he was made lord chief justice of the king's bench, in the place of Sir John Fortescue. These I may call the two chief justices of the chief justices, for their signal integrity; for, though the one of them favoured the house of Lancaster, the other of

(1) Drayton's *Polyolbion.*

York, in the titles to the crown, both of them favoured the House of Justice in matters betwixt party and party.

It happened that Sir Thomas Cooke, late lord mayor of London, one of vast wealth, was cast beforehand at the court (where the Lord Rivers and the rest of the queen's kindred had pre-devoured his estate) and was only, for formality's sake, to be condemned in Guildhall, by extraordinary commissioners in Oyer and Terminer,[1] whereof Sir John Markham was not the meanest. The fact for which he was arraigned, was for lending money to Margaret the wife of Henry the Sixth. This he denied; and the single testimony of one Haukins, tortured on the rack, was produced against him.

Judge Markham directed the jury (as it was his place, and no partiality in point of law to do) to find it only misprision of treason; whereby Sir Thomas saved his lands, though heavily fined, and life, though long imprisoned. The king was highly displeased at him, and vowed he should never sit on the bench any more. And here I hope it will not trespass on the grave character of this judge, to insert a modern and pleasant passage, being privy myself to the truth thereof.

A lady would traverse a suit of law, against the will of her husband, who was contented to buy his quiet by giving her her will therein, though otherwise persuaded in his judgment the cause would go against her.

This lady, dwelling in the shire-town, invited the judge to dinner, and, though thrifty enough of herself, treated him with sumptuous entertainment. Dinner being done, and the cause being called, the judge clearly gave it against her. And when in passion she vowed never to invite any judge again, "Nay, wife," said he, "vow never to invite a *just* judge any more."

Well, King Edward was so vexed, that Sir John Markham was ousted of his chief-justiceship, and lived privately, but plentifully, the remainder of his life, having fair lands by Margaret his wife (daughter and coheir of Sir Simon Leke, of Cottam in this county) besides the estate acquired by his practice and paternal inheritance.[2] [*d.* 1479]

THOMAS MAGNUS. He was an exposed child left by his mother in the parish of Newark. What the poet[3] saith of the father of Cadmus (commanding his son to find his lost sister Europa, or else never to return) that he was

Facto pius et sceleratus eodem,

Expressing in one act a mind,
Which was both cruel and was kind,

may be applied to the mother of this and all such foundlings. Now it happened that some Yorkshire clothiers coming in the dark (very early or late) did light on this child, and resolved to pay both for his nursing

(1) A commission of Oyer and Terminer was, formerly, a commission directed to the king's judges, serjeants, etc., empowering them to hear and determine indictments on treasons, felonies, etc. (2) Sir John Markham is said to have earned the name of the "upright judge." Arising out of the case of Sir Thomas Cooke, Markham laid down the maxim of our jurisprudence that "a subject may arrest for treason, the king cannot, for if the arrest be illegal the party has no remedy against the king." (3) Ovid, *Metamorphoses.*

and education, the charge whereof would not be great, equally divided betwixt them, according to the proverb.

Multorum manibus grande levatur onus.

An heavy work is light to do,
When many hands are put thereto.

First then they took order he should be baptized in Newark by the name of Thomas (probably the best person in their company); and because all of them had interest alike in him, for his surname they assigned him *Amang-us,* which is *amongst us* in the northern pronunciation.

They were very careful in his breeding. I confess Aristotle urgeth it as an argument against the breeding of children in common, that the care of all will effectually be the care of none, and so the children be neglected. Not so here, where this Thomas, though he had a commonwealth of foster-fathers, was very well brought up in learning, and became an excellent scholar and statesman, being employed in many foreign embassies. Then took he on him the name of Dr. Magnus, and was famous thereby both at home and beyond the seas; on which account he might claim kindred with Pompeius Magnus, Carolus Magnus, and Albert Magnus, and whom not, who was great for arts, arms, or otherwise? It soundeth much in his commendation that he forgot not his gratitude to the town of his nativity, where he erected a fair school, with other benefactions.[1]

[*d.* 1550]

THOMAS CRANMER was born [1489] at Aslockton in this county; and being bred in Jesus College in Cambridge, became archbishop of Canterbury; and at last (after some intermediate failings) valiantly suffered for the truth at Oxford, Anno Domini 1556, March 21.

"Two hungry meals," saith our English proverb, "make the third a glutton." This may also be inverted, "Two glutton meals require the third an hungry one;" fasting being then necessary, lest Nature be surcharged. If the reader hath formerly perused Mr. Foxe's *Acts and Monuments* and my *Church History,* Cranmer's story is so largely related in those two books, there is danger of his surfeit if I should not now be short and sparing therein; only one memorable passage omitted by Mr. Foxe (and that's a wonder) I must here insert out of an excellent author:[2] "After his whole body was reduced into ashes, his heart was found entire and untouched." Which is justly alleged as an argument of his cordial integrity to the truth, though fear too much and too often prevailed on his outward actions; so that what the Holy Spirit recordeth of King Asa was true of him: "Nevertheless the heart of Asa was perfect all his days;" though, good man, he was guilty of many and great imperfections.

(1) Among other distinctions, Thomas Magnus was present at the Field of the Cloth of Gold, canon of Windsor for many years, custodian of St. Leonard's Hospital, York, and a privy councillor. The story of his being a foundling may be true, but it is known that his parents were John and Alice Magnus of Newark.
(2) Godwin.

JOHN PLOUGH was born in this county, a pious and learned minister of the word, who for his conscience fled over into Basle in the reign of Queen Mary.

It happened that a book came over into the hands of the English exiles, written against the marriage of ministers, by one Miles Huggarde,[1] a silly hosier in London, but highly opinioned of his learning. It was debated amongst the English whether this book should be passed over with neglect, or answered. And here the reader is requested to pardon this digression, as proper enough for my profession. Solomon hath two proverbs, the one immediately succeeding, yet seemingly crossing the other: "Answer not a fool according to his folly, lest thou also be like unto him;" "Answer a fool according to his folly, lest he be wise in his own conceit."

Some will have the first precept given to magistrates, who are not to make their authority cheap by engaging against fools, and the latter to belong to all Christians. Others distinguish that an answer according to his folly may be twofold: by way of complying with it, which may not, and confuting of it, which ought to be done. Most make a difference between the railing fool and the reasoning fool; the former to be ordered, as Hezekiah did Rabshakeh, "Answer him not a word." But, if he be a reasoning fool, who will offer to argue, conceited of himself, take him off his speed with a short and seasonable return.

Such a fool this Huggarde was adjudged, whom John Plough undertook to answer, and cut his comb so close, that the other appeared no more. [*d.* 1562]

THOMAS BRIGHTMAN was born [1562] in Nottingham, where some of his brethren were lately alive; bred fellow of Queens' College in Cambridge, and afterwards beneficed at Hawnes in Bedfordshire. No lover of conformity, yet no hater of conformists, being charitable to such who in judgment dissented from him. His memory is most remarkable for his comment on the Revelation, by some protestants approved, praised, admired; by others slighted, contemned,[2] condemned.

Pro.—1. His very name, *Brightman*, imports something of illumination and clearness therein. 2. He makes many hard places to be plain, and mysteries to be his histories, by his comment. 3. He foretold many things forty years ago, which we see performed in our days.

Con.—1. Names are casual; and even *Lucian* himself, as bad as he was, had as much of light and lustre in his name. 2. He makes many plain places hard, and histories to be mysteries by his misinterpretation; expounding the seven Asian churches, then literally extant, to be Germany, France, England, &c. 3. Shooting so many arrows, no wonder if some few, rather by hap than aim, hit the mark.

Sure I am that time and Mr. Brightman will expound the hardest places in the Revelation; but what credit is to be given to the latter alone I will not engage.

Such who dislike Mr. Brightman's writing, could not but commend his angelical living, who had so much of heaven in his heart. Walking

(1) A writer against the Reformation, flourished 1557. (2) *Contemned* here means "treated as of small value."

through the vineyard of this world, he plucked and eat a few grapes, but put up none in his vessel, using wealth as if he used it not. His clay-cottage did crack and fall down in the same minute, so sudden was his death; but he who died daily could on no day be said to die suddenly, being always prepared for his dissolution, which happened Anno Domini 1607.

WILLIAM CHAPPELL was born [1582] at Laxton in this county, and bred a fellow in Christ's College in Cambridge, where he was remarkable for the strictness of his conversation. No one tutor in our memory bred more and better pupils, so exact his care in their education.[1] He was a most subtle disputant, equally excellent with the sword and the shield, to reply or answer. He was chosen provost of Trinity College in Dublin, and afterwards bishop of Cork and Ross. Frighted with the rebellion in Ireland, he came over into England, where he rather exchanged than eased his condition, such the woefulness of our civil wars. He died anno 1649, and parted his estate almost equally betwixt his own kindred and distressed ministers; his charity not impairing his duty, and his duty not prejudicing his charity.

THE FAREWELL

There is in this county a small market town called Blyth, which my author[2] will have so named *a jucunditate,* from the mirth and good fellowship of the inhabitants therein. If so, I desire that both the name and the thing may be extended all over the shire, as being confident that an ounce of mirth, with the same degree of grace, will serve God more and more acceptably than a pound of sorrow.

(1) He was Milton's tutor, and is supposed to have whipped him. (2) John Norden, in his Description of Hertfordshire, *voce* Benington.

OXFORDSHIRE

OXFORDSHIRE hath Berkshire (divided first by the Isis, then by the Thames) on the south, Gloucestershire on the west, Buckinghamshire on the east, Warwick and Northampton-shires on the north. It aboundeth with all things necessary for man's life, and I understand that hunters and falconers are nowhere better pleased. Nor needeth there more pregnant proof of plenty in this place, than that lately Oxford was for some years together a court, a garrison and an university; during which time it was well furnished with provisions on reasonable rates.

NATURAL COMMODITIES

Fallow Deer

And why of these in Oxfordshire? Why not rather in Northamptonshire, where there be the most, or in Yorkshire, where there be the greatest parks in England? It is because John Rous of Warwick[1] telleth me that at Woodstock in this county was the most ancient park in the whole land, encompassed with a stone wall by King Henry the First.

Let us premise a line or two concerning parks, the *case,* before we come to what is contained therein. 1. The word *parcus* appears in Varro (derived, no doubt, *a parcendo,* to spare or save) for a place wherein such cattle are preserved. 2. There is mention once or twice in Domesday Book of *parcus silvestris bestiarum,* which proveth parks in England before the Conquest. 3. Probably such ancient parks (to keep J. Rous in credit and countenance) were only paled, and Woodstock the first that was walled about. 4. Parks are since so multiplied that there be more in England than in all Europe besides.

The deer therein, when living, raise the stomachs of gentlemen with their sport; and when dead, allay them again with their flesh. The fat of venison is conceived to be (but I would not have deer-stealers hear it) of all flesh the most vigorous nourishment, especially if attended with that essential addition which Virgil coupleth therewith:

Implentur veteris Bacchi pinguisque ferinae.

Old wine did their thirst allay, fat venison hunger.

But deer are daily diminished in England since the gentry are necessitated into thrift, and forced to turn their pleasure into profit: *Jam seges est ubi parcus erat;* and, since the sale of bucks hath become ordinary, I believe, in process of time, the best stored park will be found in a cook's shop in London.

Wood

Plenty hereof doth, more hath grown in this county, being daily diminished. And indeed the woods therein are put to too hard a task in their daily duty (viz., to find fuel and timber for all the houses in, and

(1) See Warwickshire, p. 582.

many out of the shire); and they cannot hold out, if not seasonably relieved by pit-coal found here, or sea-coal brought hither. This minds me of a passage wherein Oxford was much concerned. When Shotover Woods (being bestowed by King Charles the First on a person of honour) were likely to be cut down, the university by letters laboured their preservation; wherein this among many other pathetical expressions: "That Oxford was one of the eyes of the land, and Shotover Woods the hair of the eyelids; the loss whereof must needs prejudice the sight, with too much moisture flowing therein." This retrenched that designed for the present; but in what case those woods stand at this day, is to me unknown.

THE BUILDINGS

The colleges in Oxford, advantaged by the vicinity of fair freestone, do for the generality of their structure carry away the credit from all in Christendom, and equal any for the largeness of their endowments.

It is not the least part of Oxford's happiness that a moiety of her founders were prelates (whereas Cambridge hath but three episcopal foundations, Peterhouse, Trinity Hall and Jesus) who had an experimental knowledge what belonged to the necessities and conveniences of scholars, and therefore have accommodated them accordingly; principally in providing them the patronages of many good benefices, whereby the fellows of those colleges are plentifully maintained, after their leaving of the university.

Of the colleges, University is the oldest, Pembroke the youngest, Christ Church the greatest, Lincoln (by many reputed) the least, Magdalen the neatest, Wadham the most uniform, New College the strongest, and Jesus College (no fault, but its unhappiness) the poorest; and if I knew which was the richest, I would not tell, seeing concealment in this kind is the safest. New College is most proper for southern, Exeter for western, Queen's for northern, Brasenose for north-western men; Saint John's for Londoners, Jesus for Welshmen; and at other colleges almost indifferently for men of all counties. Merton hath been most famous for schoolmen, Corpus Christi (formerly called Trilingue Collegium) for linguists, Christ Church for poets, All Souls for orators, New College for civilians, Brasenose for disputants, Queen's College for metaphysicians, Exeter for a late series of regius professors; Magdalen for ancient, Saint John's for modern prelates; and all eminent in some one kind or other. And if any of these colleges were transported into foreign parts, it would alter its kind (or degree at least) and presently of a college proceed an university, as equal to most, and superior to many academies beyond the seas.

Before I conclude with these colleges, I must confess how much I was posed with a passage which I met with in the epistles of Erasmus, writing to his familiar friend Ludovicus Vives, then residing in Oxford, *in Collegio Apum*, in the College of Bees, according to his direction of his letter. I knew all colleges may metaphorically be termed the College of Bees, wherein the industrious scholars live under the rule of one master, in which respect Saint Jerome advised Rusticus the monk to busy himself in making beehives, that from thence he might learn *monasteriorum ordinem et regiam disciplinam* (the order of monasteries and discipline of kingly government). But why any one college should be so signally called, and which it was, I was at a loss; till at last seasonably satisfied that it was Corpus Christi; whereon no unpleasant story doth depend.

In the year 1630, the leads over Vives' study being decayed, were taken up, and new cast; by which occasion the stall was taken, and with it an incredible mass of honey. But the bees, as presaging their intended and imminent destruction (whereas they were never known to have swarmed before) did that spring, to preserve their famous kind, send down a fair swarm into the president's garden; the which, in the year 1633, yielded two swarms, one whereof pitched in the garden for the president; the other they sent up as a new colony into their old habitation, there to continue the memory of this mellifluous doctor, as the university styled him in a letter to the cardinal.

It seems these bees were *aborigines* from the first building of the college, being called *Collegium Apum* in the founder's statutes; and so is John Claymond,[1] the first president thereof, saluted by Erasmus.

THE LIBRARY

If the schools may be resembled to the ring, the library may the better be compared to the diamond therein; not so much for the bunching forth beyond the rest, as the preciousness thereof, in some respects equalling any in Europe, and in most kinds exceeding all in England: yet our land hath been ever φιλοβιβλος, much given to the love of books; and let us *fleet the cream* of a few of the primest libraries in all ages.

In the infancy of Christianity, that at York bare away the bell, founded by Archbishop Egbert (and so highly praised by Alevinus in his epistle to Charles the Great) but long since abolished.

Before the dissolution of abbeys, when all cathedrals and convents had their libraries, that at Ramsey was the greatest Rabbin, spake the most and best Hebrew, abounding in Jewish and not defective in other books.

In that age of lay-libraries (as I may term them, as belonging to the city) I behold that pertaining to Guildhall as a principal, founded by Richard Whittington, whence three cart-loads of choice manuscripts were carried in the reign of King Edward the Sixth, on the promise of (never performed) restitution.

Since the Reformation, that of Benet in Cambridge hath for manuscripts exceeded any (thank the cost and care of Matthew Parker) collegiate library in England.

Of late, Cambridge library, augmented with the arch-episcopal library of Lambeth, is grown the second in the land.

As for private libraries of subjects, that of treasurer Burghley was the best, for the use of a statesman, the Lord Lumley's for an historian, the late earl of Arundel's for an herald, Sir Robert Cotton's for an antiquary, and Archbishop Ussher's for a divine.

Many other excellent libraries there were of particular persons: Lord

(1) John Claymond (1457?-1537) was formerly president of Magdalen; a benefactor of Brasenose, Magdalen and Corpus Christi.

Brudenell's, Lord Hatton's &c., routed by our civil wars; and many books which scaped the execution are fled (transported) into France, Flanders and other foreign parts.

To return to Oxford library, which stands like Diana amongst her nymphs, and surpasseth all the rest for rarity and multitude of books; so that, if any be wanting on any subject, it is because the world doth not afford them. This library was founded by Humphrey the good duke of Gloucester; *con*-founded in the reign of King Edward the Sixth, by those who I list not to name; *re*-founded by worthy Sir Thomas Bodley, and the bounty of daily benefactors.

As for the king's houses in this county, Woodstock is justly to be preferred, where the wood- and water-nymphs might equally be pleased in its situation. Queen Elizabeth had a great affection for this place, as one of her best remembrancers of her condition when a prisoner here (in none of the best lodgings) in the reign of her sister. Here she escaped a dangerous fire, but whether casual or intentional God knoweth. Here, hearing a milkmaid merrily singing in the park, she desired exchange of estates, preferring the poorest liberty before the richest restraint. At this day it is a fair, was formerly a fairer fabric, if the labyrinth built here by King Henry the Second answered the character of curiosity given it by authors. But long since the labyrinth (Time, without the help of Ariadne her clue of silk, can unravel and display the most intricate building) is vanished away.

Nor must Enstone hard by be forgotten; which, though some sullen soul may recount amongst the costly trifles, the more ingenious do behold as Art's pretty comment, as Nature's pleasant text; both so intermingled, that art in some sort may seem natural, and nature artificial therein. It was made by Thomas Bushell, esq., sometime servant to Francis Bacon Lord Verulam. Now, because men's expectations are generally tired with the tedious growing of wood, here he set hedges of full growth, which thrived full well, so that where the former left no plants, the following year found trees grown to their full perfection. In a word, a melancholy mind may here feast itself to a surfeit with variety of entertainments. But rarities of this nature are never sufficiently described till beheld.

PROVERBS

Banbury zeal, cheese and cakes. I admire to find these joined in so learned an author as Mr. Camden, affirming that town famed for these three things (*quam male conveniunt*) and though zeal be deservedly put first, how inconsistent is it with his gravity and goodness, to couple a spiritual grace with matters of corporeal repast, so that, if spoken in earnest, it hath more of a profane than pious pen; if in jest, more of a libeller than historian.

But, to qualify the man, no such words are extant in the Latin Camden, where only we read, *Nunc autem conficiendo caseo oppidum notissimum, castrum ostendit,* &c.

Secondly, it being in the English translated by Philemon Holland, was at the first (as I have been credibly informed) a literal mistake of the printers (though not confessed in the errata) set forth in Anno Domini 1608; *zeal* being put for *veal* in that place.

But what *casual* in that may be suspected *wilful* in the next and last edition, anno 1637, where the error is continued out of design to nick the town of Banbury, as reputed then a place of precise people, and not over-conformable in their carriage. Sure I am that Banbury had a gracious, learned and painful minister;[1] and this town need not be ashamed of, nor grieved at, what scoffers say or write thereof; only let them add knowledge to their zeal, and then the more of zeal the better their condition.

THE WORTHIES

SAINT FRIDESWIDE was born in the city of Oxford, being daughter to Didanus the duke thereof. It happened that one Algar, a noble young man, solicited her to yield to his lust, from whom she miraculously escaped, he being of a sudden struck blind. If so, she had better success than as good a virgin, the daughter to a greater and better father; I mean Thamar daughter of King David, not so strangely secured from the lust of her brother.

She was afterwards made abbess of a monastery, erected by her father in the same city, which since is become part of Christchurch, where her body lieth buried.

It happened in the first of Queen Elizabeth, that the scholars of Oxford took up the body of the wife of Peter Martyr,[2] who formerly had been disgracefully buried in a dunghill, and interred it in the tomb with the dust of Saint Frideswide. Sanders added that they wrote this inscription (which he calleth *impium epitaphium*): *Hic requiescit Religio cum Superstitione;*[3] though, the words being capable of a favourable sense on his side, he need not have been so angry. However, we will rub up our old poetry, and bestow another upon them.

> Entomb'd with Frideswide, deem'd a sainted maid,
> The wife of Peter Martyr here is laid.
> And reason good, for women chaste in mind
> The best of virgins come no whit behind.
> Should popery return (which God forefend!)
> Their blended dust each other would defend.

Yet was there more than eight hundred years betwixt their several deaths, Saint Frideswide dying anno 735, and is remembered in the Romish calendar on the nineteenth day of October.

SAINT EDWARD THE CONFESSOR was born at Islip in this county, and became afterwards king of England, sitting on the throne for many years, with much peace and prosperity; famous for the first founding of Westminster Abbey, and many other worthy achievements.

By Bale he is called *Edvardus simplex,* which may signify either *shallow* or *single;* but (in what sense soever he gave it) we take it in the latter. Sole and single he lived and died, never carnally conversing with Saint Edith his queen: which is beheld by different persons according

(1) Mr. William Whately, of whom hereafter in this county. (2) See editorial note, p. 130. (3) Sanders, *De Schismate Anglicana.*

to their different judgments (coloured eyes make coloured objects); some pitying him for defect or natural impotence; others condemning him as affecting singleness for want of conjugal affection; others applauding it as an high piece of holiness and perfection. Sure I am, it opened a door for foreign competitors, and occasioned the conquest of this nation. He died Anno Domini 1066, and lieth buried in Westminster Abbey.

HERBERT DE LOSINGA was born [1054?] in Oxford, his father being an abbot, seeing wives in that age were not forbidden the clergy; though possibly his father turned abbot of Winchester in his old age, his son purchasing that preferment for him. But this Herbert bought a better for himself, giving nineteen hundred pounds to King William Rufus for the bishopric of Thetford. Hence the verse was made,

Filius est praesul, pater abbas, Simon uterque,

meaning that both of them were guilty of simony, a fashionable sin in the reign of that king, preferring more for their gifts than their endowments.

Reader, pardon a digression. I am confident there is one, and but one sin frequent in the former age, both with clergy and laity, which in our days our land is not guilty of, and may find many compurgators of her innocence therein: I mean the sin of simony; seeing none in our age will give anything for church-livings, partly because the persons presented thereunto have no assurance to keep them, partly because of the uncertainty of tithes for their maintenance. But whether this our age hath not added in sacrilege what it wanteth in simony, is above my place to discuss, and more above my power to decide.

To return to our Herbert, whose character hitherto cannot entitle him to any room in our Catalogue of Worthies; but know that afterwards he went to Rome (no such clean washing as in the water of Tiber) and thence returned as free from fault as when first born. Thus cleansed from the leprosy of simony, he came back into England, removed his bishopric from Thetford to Norwich, laid the first stone, and in effect finished the fair cathedral therein, and built five beautiful parish churches. He died Anno Domini 1119.

ROBERT PULLEN, or Pullain, or Pulley, or Puley, or Bullen, or Pully; for thus variously is he found written. Thus the same name, passing many mouths, seems in some sort to be declined into several cases, whereas indeed it still remaineth one and the same word, though differently spelled and pronounced.

In his youth he studied at Paris; whence he came over into England in the reign of King Henry the First, when learning ran very low in Oxford, the university there being first much afflicted by Harold the Dane, afterwards almost extinguished by the cruelty of the Conqueror. Our Pullen improved[1] his utmost power with the king and prelates for the restoring thereof; and, by his praying, preaching and public reading, gave a great advancement thereunto. Remarkable is his character in

(1) *Improved* = exerted.

the Chronicle of Osney: *Robertus Pulenius Scripturas Divinas quae in Anglia obsolverant apud Oxoniam legere cepit* (Robert Pullen began to read at Oxford the Holy Scriptures, which were grown out of fashion in England).

The fame of his learning commended him beyond the seas; and it is remarkable that whereas it is usual with popes (in policy) to unravel what such weaved who were before them, three successive popes continued their love to, and increased honour upon him: 1. Innocent courteously sent for him to Rome. 2. Celestine created him cardinal of Saint Eusebius, anno 1144. 3. Lucius the Second made him chancellor of the Church of Rome.

He lived at Rome in great respect, and although the certain date of his death cannot be collected, it happened about the year of our Lord 1147.

RICHARD I, son to King Henry the Second and Queen Eleanor, was (the sixth king since the Conquest, but second native of England) born in the city of Oxford, anno 1157. Whilst a prince he was undutiful to his father, or, to qualify the matter, over-dutiful to his mother, whose domestic quarrels he always espoused. To expiate his offence, when king he, with Philip King of France, undertook a voyage to the Holy Land where, through the treachery of *Templary* cowardice of the Greeks, diversity of the climate, distance of the place, and differences betwixt Christian princes, much time was spent, a mass of money expended, many lives lost, some honour achieved, but little profit produced. Going to Palestine, he suffered shipwreck and many mischiefs on the coast of Cyprus; coming for England through Germany, he was tossed with a worse land tempest, being (in pursuance of an old grudge betwixt them) taken prisoner by Leopoldus duke of Austria. Yet this *Coeur de Lion,* or *lion-hearted king,* for so was he commonly called, was no less *lion* (though now in a grate) than when at liberty, abating nothing of his high spirit in his behaviour. The duke did not undervalue this his royal prisoner, prizing his person at ten years' purchase, according to the (then) yearly revenue of the English crown. This ransom of an hundred thousand pounds being paid, he came home; first reformed himself, and then mended many abuses in the land; and had done more, had not an unfortunate arrow, shot out of a besieged castle in France, put a period to his life, Anno Domini 1199.

JOHN OF OXFORD was, no doubt, so named from his birth in that city; otherwise, had he only had his education or eminent learning therein, there were hundreds [of] Johns of Oxford as well as himself. Hector Boethius surnamed him a *Vado Boum,* and owneth him the next historian to Geoffrey of Monmouth in age and industry. He was a great anti-Becketist, as many more in that age of greater learning (except stubbornness be made the standard thereof) than Becket himself. Being dean of Old Sarum and chaplain to King Henry the Second, he was by him employed, with others, to give an account to the pope (but I question whether he would take it) of the king's carriage in the business of Becket. He was preferred, anno 1175, bishop of Norwich, where he repaired his cathedral, lately defaced with fire; built a fair almshouse, and Trinity Church in Ipswich. His death happened Anno Domini 1200.

ROBERT BACON, first scholar of, afterward a familiar friend to, Saint Edmund archbishop of Canterbury, was bred a doctor of divinity in Oxford; and when aged became a Dominican or preaching friar; and for his sermons he was highly esteemed by King Henry the Third. He was *lepidus et cynicus,* and a most professed enemy to Peter de Roches bishop of Winchester.

Matthew Paris gives him and another (viz., Richard de Fishacre) this praise: *Quibus non erant majores, imo nec pares* (*ut creditur*) *viventes in theologia, et aliis scientiis;* and I listen the rather to his commendation because, being himself a Benedictine monk, he had an antipathy against all friars. I behold this Robert Bacon as the senior of all the Bacons, which, like tributary streams, disembogued themselves, with all the credit of their actions, into Roger Bacon who, in process of time, hath monopolized the honour of all his surname-sakes in Oxford. Our Robert died Anno Domini 1248.[1]

THOMAS JOYCE, or JORZ, a Dominican, proceeded doctor of divinity in Oxford; and, living there, he became provincial of his order, both of England and Wales. From this place, without ever having any other preferment, Pope Clement the Fifth created him cardinal of Saint Sabina; though some conceive he wanted breadth proportionable to such an height of dignity, having no other revenue to maintain it, cardinals being accounted kings' fellows in that age. Others admire at the contradiction betwixt friars' profession and practice, that persons so low should be so high, so poor so rich; which makes the same men to suspect, that so chaste might be so wanton.

He is remarkable on this account, that he had six brethren all Dominicans. I will not listen to their comparison, who resemble them to the seven sons of Sceva,[2] which were exorcists; but may term them a week of brethren, whereof this rubricated cardinal was the Dominical letter. There want not those who conceive great virtue in the youngest son of these seven, and that his touch was able to cure the pope's evil. This Thomas, as he had for the most time lived in Oxford, so his corpse by his own desire was buried in his convent therein. [*d.* 1310]

EDMUND [OF WOODSTOCK], youngest son to King Edward the First by Queen Margaret, was born at Woodstock, Aug. 5, 1301. He was afterwards created earl of Kent, and was tutor to his nephew King Edward the Third; in whose reign, falling into the tempest of false, injurious and wicked envy, he was beheaded, for that he never dissembled his natural brotherly affection toward his brother deposed, and went about when he was (God wot) murdered before (not knowing so much) to enlarge him out of prison, persuaded thereunto by such as covertly practised his

(1) Robert Bacon, the first Dominican writer in England, was either the brother or uncle of the great Roger Bacon. He publicly rebuked Henry for his partiality to foreign favourites, chiefly Peter de Roches mentioned above. (2) Acts xix, 14.

destruction. He suffered at Winchester, the nineteenth of March, in the fourth of Edward the Third.[1] [*d.* 1330]

EDWARD, eldest son of King Edward the Third, was born [1330] at Woodstock in this county, and bred under his father (never abler teacher met with an apter scholar) in martial discipline.

He was afterwards termed the Black Prince; not so called from his complexion, which was fair enough (save when sunburnt in his Spanish expedition); not from his conditions, which were courteous (the constant attender of valour); but from his achievements, dismal and black, as they appeared to the eyes of his enemies, whom he constantly overcame.[2]

But grant him black in himself, he had the fairest lady to his wife this land and that age did afford; viz., Joan countess of Salisbury and Kent, which, though formerly twice a widow, was the third time married unto him. This is she whose Garter (which now flourisheth again) hath lasted longer than all the wardrobes of the kings and queens in England since the Conquest, continued in the knighthood of that order.

This prince died, before his father, at Canterbury, in the 46th year of his age, Anno Domini 1376; whose maiden success attended him to the grave, as never foiled in any undertakings. Had he survived to old age, in all probabilities the wars between York and Lancaster had been ended before begun; I mean prevented in him, being a person of merit and spirit, and in seniority before any suspicion of such divisions. He left two sons: Edward, who died at seven years of age, and Richard, afterwards king, second of that name; both born in France, and therefore not coming within the compass of our catalogue.

GEOFFREY CHAUCER was, by most probability, born [1340?] at Woodstock in this county, though other places lay stiff claim to his nativity.

Berkshire's title. Leland confesseth it likely that he was born in *Barochensi provincia;* and Mr. Camden avoweth that Donnington Castle, nigh Newbury, was anciently his inheritance. There was lately an old oak standing in the park, called Chaucer's Oak.

London's title. The author of his life, set forth 1602, proveth him born in London, out of these his own words in the *Testament of Love*[3]: "Also in the Citie of London, that is to mee soe deare and sweete, in which I was foorth grown; and more kindely love have I to that place than to any other in yerth (as every kindely creature hath full appetite to that place of his kindly ingendure)."

Besides, Mr. Camden praiseth Mr. Edmund Spenser, the Londoner, for the best poet: *Ne Chaucero quidem concive excepto* (Chaucer himself, his fellow-citizen, not being excepted).

Oxfordshire's title. Leland addeth a probability of his birth in Oxfordshire; and Camden saith of Woodstock, *Cum nihil habeat quod ostentet,*

(1) In 1326 this Edmund conspired against his brother Edward II, who was deposed the year following. Trying to resist the ascendency of Edward III's mother, Isabella, and Mortimer over young Edward III, he got into treasonable courses and suffered death. (2) Quite possibly he appeared in black armour after Creçy, being named the Black Prince after that battle. (3) This work is now considered to be by Thomas Usk (*d.* 1388). It is, however, considered fairly certain that Chaucer was born in London.

Homerum nostrum Anglicum, Galfredum Chaucerum, alumnum suum fuisse gloriatur. Besides, J. Pits is positive that his father was a knight, and that he was born at Woodstock. And Queen Elizabeth passed a fair stone house next to her palace in that town unto the tenant by the name of Chaucer's House, whereby it is also known at this day.

Now, what is to be done to decide the difference herein? Indeed Apion the grammarian would have Homer (concerning whose birthplace there was so much controversy) raised *ab Inferis* that he might give a true account of the place of his nativity. However, our Chaucer is placed here (having just grounds for the same) until stronger reasons are brought to remove him.

He was a terse and elegant poet (the Homer of his age) and so refined our English tongue, *ut inter expolitas gentium linguas potuit recte quidem connumerari.*[1] His skill in mathematics was great (being instructed therein by Joannes Sombus and Nicholas of Lynn) which he evidenceth in his book *De Sphaera.* [*d.* 1400]

THOMAS OF WOODSTOCK, youngest son of King Edward the Third and Queen Philippa, was surnamed of Woodstock from the place of his nativity. He was afterward earl of Buckingham and duke of Gloucester; created by his nephew King Richard the Second, who summoned him to the parliament by the title of the King's Loving Uncle. He married Isabel, one of the co-heirs of Humphrey de Bohun earl of Essex, in whose right he became constable of England: a dangerous place, when it met with an unruly manager thereof.

But this Thomas was only guilty of ill-tempered loyalty, loving the king well, but his own humours better; rather wilful than hurtful; and presuming on the old maxim, *Patruus est loco parentis* (an uncle is in the place of a father). He observed the king too nearly, and checked him too sharply; whereupon he was conveyed to Calais, and there strangled; by whose death King Richard, being freed from the causeless fear of an uncle, became exposed to the cunning plots of his cousin-german Henry duke of Lancaster, who at last deposed him. This Thomas founded a fair college at Pleshey in Essex, where his body was first buried with all solemnity, and afterward translated to Westminster. [1355-1397]

ANNE DE BEAUCHAMP [ANNE NEVILLE, COUNTESS OF WARWICK] was born at Caversham in this county. Let her pass for a princess (though not formally) reductively, seeing so much of history dependeth on her; as,

Elevated.—1. Being daughter (and in fine sole heir) to Richard de Beauchamp, that most martial earl of Warwick. 2. Married to Richard Neville earl of Salisbury and Warwick, commonly called the Make-king; and may not she then, by a courteous proportion, be termed the Make-queen. 3. In her own and husband's right she was possessed of one hundred and fourteen manors in several shires. 4. Isabel, her eldest daughter, was married to George duke of Clarence; and Anne, her younger, to Edward Prince of Wales, son of Henry the Sixth, and afterwards to King Richard the Third.

(1) Bale.

Depressed.—1. Her husband being killed at Barnet fight, all her land by act of parliament was settled on her two daughters, as if she had been dead in nature. 2. Being attainted (on her husband's score) she was forced to fly to the sanctuary at Beaulieu in Hampshire. 3. Hence she got herself privately into the north, and lived there a long time in a mean condition. 4. Her want was increased after the death of her two daughters, who may be presumed formerly to have secretly supplied her.

I am not certainly informed when a full period was put by death to these her sad calamities. [*d.* 1490?]

OWEN OGLETHORPE was (saith my author[1]) born of good parentage, and, I conjecture, a native of this county, finding Owen Oglethorpe his kinsman twice high-sheriff thereof in the reign of Queen Elizabeth. He was president of Magdalen College in Oxford, dean of Windsor, and at last made bishop of Carlisle by Queen Mary. A good-natured man, and when single by himself very pliable to please Queen Elizabeth, whom he crowned queen, which the rest of his order refused to do; but, when in conjunction with other popish bishops, such principles of stubbornness were distilled unto him, that it cost him his deprivation. However, an author[2] tells me that the queen had still a favour for him, intending his restitution either to his own or a better bishopric, upon the promise of his general conformity, had he not died suddenly, of an apoplexy, 1559.

SIR JOHN NORRIS [*b.* 1547?]. He was a most accomplished general, both for a charge, which is the sword, and a retreat, which is the shield of war. By the latter he purchased to himself immortal praise, when in France he brought off a small handful of English from a great armful of enemies, fighting as he retreated, and retreating as he fought, so that always his rear affronted the enemy: a retreat worth ten victories got by surprise, which speak rather the fortune than either the valour or discretion of a general.

He was afterwards sent over with a great command into Ireland, where his success neither answered to his own care, nor others' expectation. Indeed hitherto Sir John had fought with right-handed enemies in France and the Netherlands, who was now to fight with left-handed foes, for so may the wild Irish well be termed (so that this great master of defence was now to seek a new guard) who could lie on the coldest earth, swim through the deepest water, run over what was neither earth nor water, I mean bogs and marshes. He found it far harder to find out than fight his enemies, they so secured themselves in fastnesses. Supplies, sown thick in promises, came up thin in performances; so slowly were succours sent unto him.

At last a great lord was made lieutenant of Ireland, of an opposite party to Sir John; there being animosities in the court of Queen Elizabeth (as well as of later princes) though her general good success rendered them the less to the public notice of posterity. It grieved Sir John to the heart, to see one of an opposite faction should be brought over his head, insomuch that some conceive his working soul broke the cask of his body, as wanting a vent for his grief and anger; for, going up into

(1) Godwin. (2) Sir John Harrington, in his Addition to Bishop Godwin.

his chamber, at the first hearing of the news, he suddenly died, Anno Domini 1597.

SIR RICHARD BAKER, knight [*b.* 1568] was a native of this county, and high sheriff thereof in the 18th of King James, Anno Domini 1620. His youth he spent in learning, the benefit whereof he reaped in his old age, when his estate through surety-ship (as I have heard him complain) was very much impaired. But God may smile on them on whom the world doth frown; whereof his pious old age was a memorable instance, when the storm on his estate forced him to fly for shelter to his studies and devotions. He wrote an *Exposition on the Lord's Prayer,* which is corrival with the best comments which professed divines have written on that subject. He wrote a chronicle of our English kings, embracing a method peculiar to himself, digesting observables under several heads, very useful for the reader. This reverend knight left this troublesome world about the beginning of our civil wars.[1] [*d.* 1645]

THOMAS LYDIAT [*b.* 1572]. Now I find the old sentence to be true, *Difficile fugitivas mortuorum memorias retrahere,* seeing all my industry and inquiry can retrieve very little of this worthy person; and the reader, I hope, will not be angry with me, who am so much grieved with myself for the same. Indeed contradicting qualities met in him, *eminency* and *obscurity;* the former for his learning, the latter for his living. All that we can recover of him is as followeth. He was born at Alkerton in this county; bred first in Winchester school, then in New College in Oxford, being admitted therein June 22, 1593. An admirable mathematician, witness these his learned works, left to posterity: 1. *De variis Annorum Formis;* 2. *De natura Coeli, et conditione Elementorum;* 3. *Praelectio Astronomica;* 4. *De origine Fontium;* 5. *Disquisitio Physiologica;* 6. *Explicatio et additamentum Arg. Temp. Nativitatis et Ministerii Christi.*

In handling these subjects, it seems, he crossed Scaliger, who was highly offended thereat, conceiving himself such a prince of learning, it was high treason for any to doubt of, much more deny his opinion. Yea, he conceited his own judgment so canonical, that it was heresy for any inferior person to differ from the same. Shall Scaliger write a book of *The Emendation of Times,* and should any presume to write one of *The Emendation of Scaliger*? Especially one no public professor, and so private a person as Lydiat? However, this great bugbear critic, finding it more easy to contemn the person than confute the arguments of his adversary, slighted Lydiat as inconsiderable, jeering him for a prophet, who indeed somewhat traded in the apocalyptical divinity.

Learned men of unbiassed judgments will maintain, that Lydiat had the best in that contest; but here it came to pass what Solomon had long before observed, "Nevertheless the poor man's wisdom is despised, and his words are not heard."

He never attained higher church-preferment than the rectory of Alkerton, the town of his nativity; and deserted that (as I have cause to suspect) before his death.

(1) He died in the Fleet prison, where he was confined for debt for the last ten years of his life.

Impute his low condition to these causes: 1. The nature of his studies, which, being mathematical and speculative, brought not πρὸς ἄλφιτα (grist to the mill). 2. The nature of his *nature,* being ambitious of privity and concealment. 3. The death of Prince Henry (whose library keeper he was) and in whose grave Lydiat's hopes were interred. 4. His disaffection to church discipline, and ceremonies used therein; though such wrong his memory who represent him an Anabaptist.

His modesty was as great as his want, which he would not make known to any. Sir William Boswell, well understanding his worth, was a great friend unto him; and so was Bishop Williams. He died about Westminster, as I take it, in the year of our Lord 1646. Happy had it been for posterity, if on his death-bed he could have bequeathed his learning to any surviving relation.

SIR DUDLEY CARLETON, knight [VISCOUNT DORCHESTER], was born [1573] in this county; bred a student in Christ Church in Oxford. He afterwards was related as a secretary to Sir Ralph Winwood, ambassador in the Low Countries, when King James resigned the 'cautionary' towns to the states.[1] Here he added so great experience to his former learning, that afterwards our king employed him for twenty years together ambassador in Venice, Savoy and the United Provinces; Anne Gerrard his lady (co-heir to George Gerrard esq.) accompanying him in all his travels, as is expressed in her epitaph in Westminster Abbey.

He was by King Charles the First created baron of Imbercourt in Surrey, and afterwards Viscount Dorchester; marrying for his second wife the daughter of Sir Henry Glemham, the relict of Paul Viscount Bayning, who survived him. He succeeded the Lord Conway (when preferred president of the council) in the secretaryship of state, being sworn at Whitehall, December 14, 1628. He died without issue, Anno Domini 1632, assigning his burial (as appears on her tomb) with his first wife, which no doubt was performed accordingly.

JOHN BANCROFT was born [1574] at Asthall in this county; and was advanced, by Archbishop Bancroft[2] his uncle, from a student in Christ Church, to be master of University College in Oxford. Here it cost him much pains and expense in a long suit to recover and settle the ancient lands of that foundation. Afterwards he was made bishop of Oxford; and, during his sitting in that see, he renewed no leases, but let them run out for the advantage of his successor. He obtained the royalty of Shotover for, and annexed the vicarage of Cuddesdon to his bishopric; where he built a fair palace and a chapel, expending on both about three thousand five hundred pounds; *cujus munificentiae* (said the Oxford Orator of him to the king at Woodstock) *debemus, quod incerti laris mitra surrexerit e pulvere in Palatium.* But now, by a retrograde motion, that fair building *e Palatio recidit in pulverem,* being burned down to the ground in the late wars; but for what advantage, as I do not know, so I list not to inquire.[3] This bishop died Anno Domini 1640.

(1) The three "cautionary" towns of Flushing, Brill and Enckhuizen were pledged as security by the Dutch in their alliance with England embodied in the treaty of 1598. (2) See Lancashire, p. 301. (3) The bishop's palace was intentionally burned in 1644 to prevent its use as a garrison by the parliamentarians.

JOHN WHITE (descended from the Whites in Hampshire) was born [1575] at Stanton Saint John[1] in this county; bred first in Winchester, then New College in Oxford, whereof he was fellow; and fixed at last a minister at Dorchester in Dorsetshire well nigh forty years. A grave man, yet without moroseness, as who would willingly contribute his shot of facetiousness on any just occasion. A constant preacher, so that in the course of his ministry he expounded the Scripture all over, and half over again; having an excellent faculty in the clear and solid interpreting thereof. A good governor, by whose wisdom the town of Dorchester (notwithstanding a casual merciless fire) was much enriched; knowledge causing piety, piety breeding industry, and industry procuring plenty unto it. A beggar was not then to be seen in the town, all able poor being set on work, and impotent maintained, by the profit of a public brew-house, and other collections.

He absolutely commanded his own passions, and the purses of his parishioners, whom he could wind up to what height he pleased on important occasions. He was free from covetousness, if not trespassing on the contrary, and had a patriarchal influence both in Old and New England;[2] yet, towards the end of his days, factions and fond opinions crept in his flock; a new generation arose, which either did not know, or would not acknowledge this good man: disloyal persons, which would not pay the due respect to the crown of his old age, whereof he was sadly and silently sensible.

He was chosen one of the assembly of divines, and his judgment was much relied on therein. He married the sister of Dr. Burges, the great non-conformist (who afterwards, being reclaimed, wrote in the defence of ceremonies) by whom he left four sons; and died quietly at Dorchester, Anno Domini 1648.

I hope that Solomon's observation of the poor wise man, who saved the little city, "yet no man remembered him," will not be verified of this town, in relation to this their deceased pastor, whom I hope they will not, I am sure they should not forget, as a person so much meriting of them in all considerations. His comment on some part of Genesis is lately set forth, and more daily expected.

DANIEL FEATLEY [or FAIRCLOUGH], D.D., was born [1582] in, or very near to, the city of Oxford, his father being a servant of Corpus Christi College, and this his son fellow thereof. Here he had the honour to make the speech in the college, at the funeral of Dr. Reynolds.

Some men may be said to have mutinous parts, which will not obey the commands of him who is the owner of them. Not so this doctor, who was perfect master of his own learning. He did not, as Quintilian saith of some, *occultis thesauris incumbere;* but his learning was *in numerato,* for his present using thereof. He was as good in the schools as in the pulpit, and very happy in his disputes with papists; for in the conference with F. Fisher (when Fisher was caught in his own net) though Dr.

(1) Where his father held a lease from New College. (2) John White used to be known as the Patriarch of Dorchester. He sent out a colony of Dorset men to Massachusetts and, bringing about the formation of the Massachusetts Company, was the virtual founder of that colony.

White did wisely cast that net, Dr. Featley did help strongly to draw it to the shore.

It seems, though he was *in*, yet he was not *of*, the late assembly of divines; as whose body was with them, whilst his heart was at Oxford. Yea, he discovered so much in a letter to the archbishop of Armagh; which, being intercepted, he was proceeded against as a spy, and closely imprisoned, though finding some favour at last. He died in the prison college at Chelsea, Anno Domini 1645. His wife's son hath since communicated to me his pocket manual of his memorable observations, all with his own hand, but alas, to be read by none but the writer thereof.

WILLIAM WHATELEY was born [1583] in Banbury (whereof his father was twice mayor) and bred in Christ's College in Cambridge. He became afterwards minister in the town of his nativity; and though generally people do not respect a prophet or preacher when a *man*, whom they knew whilst a *child*, yet he met there with deserved reverence to his person and profession. Indeed he was a good linguist, philosopher, mathematician, divine, and (though a poetical satirical pen is pleased to pass a jeer upon him) free from faction. He first became known to the world by his book called *The Bride-Bush*, which some say hath been more condemned than confuted, as maintaining a position rather odious than untrue; but others hold that blows given from so near a relation to so near a relation, cannot be given so lightly, but they will be taken most heavily.[1] Other good works of his have been set forth since his death, which happened in the 56th year of his age, Anno Domini 1639.

JOHN BALL was born [1585] at Cassington (four miles north-west of Oxford) in this county; an obscure village, only illustrated by his nativity. He proceeded bachelor of arts in Brasenose College in Oxford (his parents' purse being not able to maintain him longer) and went into Cheshire, until at last he was beneficed at Whitmore in the county of Stafford. He was an excellent schoolman and schoolmaster, qualities seldom meeting in the same man, a painful preacher and a profitable writer; and his *Treatise of Faith* cannot sufficiently be commended. Indeed he lived by faith, having but small means to maintain him (but 20 pounds yearly salary, besides what he got by teaching and boarding his scholars) and yet was wont to say he had "enough, enough, enough." Thus contentment consisteth not in heaping on more fuel, but in taking away some fire. He had an holy facetiousness in his discourse. When his friend, having had a fall from his horse, and said that he never had the like deliverance, "Yea," said Mr. Ball, "and an hundred times when you never fell;" accounting God's preserving us from, equal to his rescuing us out of, dangers. He had an humble heart, free from passion; and, though somewhat disaffected to ceremonies and church-discipline, confuted such as conceived the corruptions therein ground enough for a separation. He hated all new lights and pretended inspirations besides Scripture; and when one asked him whether he at any time had experience thereof in his own heart, "No," said he, "I bless God; and if I should

(1) Whateley maintained adultery or desertion to be a valid reason for divorce.

ever have such phantasies, I hope God would give me grace to resist them." Notwithstanding his small means, he lived himself comfortably, relieved others charitably, left his children competently, and died piously, October the 20th, Anno Domini 1640.

WILLIAM CHILLINGWORTH was born [1602] in the city of Oxford; so that, by the benefit of his birth, he fell from the lap of his mother into the arms of the Muses. He was bred in Trinity College in this university; an acute and subtle disputant, but unsettled in judgment, which made him go beyond the seas, and in some sort was conciled to the church of Rome; but whether because he found not the respect he expected (which some shrewdly suggest) or because his conscience could not close with all the Romish corruptions (which more charitably believe) he returned into England; and in testimony of his true conversion, wrote a book entituled *The Religion of Protestants a Safe way to Salvation,* against Mr. Knott the Jesuit. I will not say *Malo nodo malus quaerendus est cuneus* [for a hard knot a hard tool must be sought] but affirm no person better qualified than this author with all necessary accomplishments to encounter a Jesuit. It is commonly reported that Dr. Prideaux compared his book to a lamprey, fit for food, if the venomous string were taken out of the back thereof: a passage, in my opinion, inconsistent with the doctor's approbation prefixed in the beginning of his book. This William Chillingworth was taken prisoner by the parliament forces at Arundel Castle, and not surprised and slain in his studies, as Archimedes at the sacking of Syracuse (as some have given it out) but was safely conducted to Chichester where, notwithstanding, hard usage hastened his dissolution. [*d.* 1644]

ANNE GREENE, a person unmarried, was indicted, arraigned, cast, condemned and executed for killing her child, at the assizes at Oxford, December 14, 1650. After some hours, her body being taken down, and prepared for dissection in the anatomy schools, some heat was found therein, which, by the care of the doctors, was improved into her perfect recovery. Charitable people interpret her so miraculous a preservation a compurgator of her innocence. Thus she, intended for a *dead,* continues a *living* anatomy of Divine Providence, and a monument of the wonderful contrivances thereof. If Hippolytus, revived only by poetical fancies, was surnamed *Virbius,* because twice a man; why may not *Mulierbia,* by as good proportion, be applied to her, who is since married, and liveth in this county in good reputation.[1]

THE FAREWELL

As for the poorer sort of husbandmen in this county, I wish there may be more Sir Henry Kebles for their sakes. This knight (though a native of London, and lord mayor thereof) had such an affection for this and Warwickshire, that he singled out an hundred and fifty of the poorest husbandmen therein, and gave each of them a new ploughshare and a new coulter of iron; and, in my mind, that is the most charitable charity which enableth decayed industry to follow its vocation.

(1) The story of Anne Greene is authentic.

RUTLAND

RUTLAND is, by a double diminutive, called by Mr. Camden *Angliae provinciola minima.* Indeed it is but the pestle of a lark, which is better than a quarter of some bigger bird, having the most cleanly profit in it; no place, so fair for the *rider,* being more fruitful for the *abider* therein.

Banishing the fable of King Rott, and their fond conceit who will have Rutland so called from *rouet,* the French word for a wheel, from the rotundity thereof (being in form almost exactly orbicular); it is so termed *quasi Red-land*, for as if Nature kept a *dye-vat* herein, a reddish tincture discoloureth the earth, stones, yea the very fleeces of the sheep feeding therein. If the Rabbins' observation be true, who distinguish betwixt *Arets,* the general element of the earth, and *Adamah,* red ground, from which Adam was taken and named (making the latter the former refined) Rutland's soil, on the same reason, may lay claim to more than ordinary purity and perfection.

THE BUILDINGS

Burley-on-the-Hill belonged formerly to the Lords Harington, but since so beautified with buildings by the duke of Buckingham, that it was inferior to few for the *house,* superior to all for the *stable;* where horses (if their *pabulum* so plenty as their *stabulum* stately) were the best accommodated in England. But alas, what saith Menedemus to Chremas in the comedy? *Filium unicum adolescentulum habeo. Ah, quid dixi habere me? immo habui.* So may Rutland say, "I have, yea I had, one most magnificent house:" this Burley being since demolished in our civil war; so just was the poet's ancient invective,

> Mars, Mars, bane of men, slaughter-stain'd spoiler of houses.

But when we have first sufficiently bemoaned the loss of so many worthy men in our late war, if then we have still any sorrow left, and tears to spare, we will spend them in lamenting the raising and ruining of so many stately structures.

THE WONDERS

How it will appear to the reader I know not; but it is wonderful in my apprehension, that this county, so pleasant, so fruitful, almost in the middle of England, had not one absolute or entire abbey therein; producing only two small appurtenances (of inconsiderable value) to convents in other counties, viz.: *Oakham,* under the custody of the priory of Saint Anne by Coventry, founded by William Dalby, for two chaplains and twelve poor; receiving in all one and twenty pounds per annum; *Brooke,* a cell to Killingworth, founded by Walkelin de Ferrers, baron of Oakham, for black canons, valued at the dissolution at forty-three pounds thirteen shillings and four-pence.

The like cannot be paralleled in England, choose so great a parcel of good ground where you please. Shew me so fair a bunch of sweet grapes which had no more flies to suck them. Nor can I conjecture any competent cause thereof, except because Edward the Confessor, by his will, gave all Rutland to Westminster church; which, though rescinded by King William the Conqueror, yet other convents perchance might be scrupulous to accept what once belonged to another foundation.

PROVERBS

Rutland Raddleman. I meet in an author[1] with this blazon, as he terms it, of Rutland, though I can scarcely recover the meaning thereof.

Rad here is the same with *red* (only more broadly pronounced); as *Radcliffe, de rubro clivo, Redcliffe. Raddleman* then is a *Reddleman,* a trade (and that a poor one) only in this county, whence men bring on their backs a pack of red stones, or ochre, which they sell to their neighbouring counties for the marking of sheep, well nigh as discernible (and far less hurtful to the wool) as pitch-brands made on their fleeces.

THE WORTHIES

WILLIAM BROWNE, esq., twice alderman of Stamford, merchant of the Staple, was (as I am credibly informed) extracted from the ancient family of Brownes of Tolethorpe in this county. He built, on his own proper cost, the beautiful steeple, with a great part of the church, of All Saints in Stamford; and lieth therein, with his wife, buried in a chapel proper to his family. He also erected, anno 1485, the old bede-house in that town, for a warden, confrator, twelve poor old men, with a nurse-woman to attend them; to this he gave the manor of Swayfeld (seven miles from Stamford) worth four hundred pounds per annum, besides divers lands and tenements elsewhere. I am loath to insert, and loath to omit, what followeth in my author, viz., "That the pious and liberal gift is much abused by the avarice and mis-employment of the governors thereof,"[2] and charitably do presume that such faults (if any) are since, or will be suddenly, amended [*d.* 1489?]

JOHN HARINGTON the elder [First BARON HARINGTON] son to Sir James Harington, was born at Exton in this county, where their ancient family had long flourished. A bountiful housekeeper, dividing his hospitality between Rutland and Warwickshire, where he had a fair habitation. He was one of the executors to the Lady Frances Sidney, and a grand benefactor to the college of her founding in Cambridge. King James created him baron of Exton; and his lady, a prudent woman, had the Princess Elizabeth committed to her government. When the said princess was married to Frederick Prince Palatine, this lord (with Henry Martin, doctor of the laws) were sent over to the Palatinate, to see her highness settled at Heidelburg, and some formalities about her dowry and jointure performed.[3] This done (as if God had designed this for his last work) he sickened on the first day of his return, and died at Worms in Germany,

(1) Drayton's *Polyolbion.* (2) Mr. Richard Butcher, in his *Survey of Stamford.* (3) The Gunpowder plotters planned to abduct the princess and proclaim her queen, but Harington prevented them by escaping with his charge to Coventry. Through her extravagance he was considerably in debt, and he begged a royal patent to coin brass farthings, known as "Haringtons."

on Saint Bartholomew's day, Anno Domini 1613. The Lord John his son (of whom in Warwickshire) did not survive him a year; both of them signally eminent, the one a pattern for all good fathers, the other for all gracious sons; and pity it is the last had not issue to be a precedent to all grandchildren; but God thought it fit that here the male issue of that honourable family should expire.

JEFFERY HUDSON was born [1619] in the parish of Oakham in this county, where his father was a very popular man, broad-shouldered and chested, though his son never arrived at a full ell in stature. It seems that families sometimes are chequered, as in brains so in bulk, that no certainty can be concluded from such alterations.

His father, who kept and ordered the baiting bulls for George duke of Buckingham (a place, you will say, requiring a robustious body to manage it) presented him, at Burley-on-the-Hill, to the duchess of Buckingham, being then nine years of age, and scarce a foot and half in height, as I am informed by credible persons then and there present, and still alive. Instantly Jeffery was heightened (not in stature) but in condition, from one degree above rags into silk and satin, and two tall men to attend him.

He was, without any deformity, wholly proportionable, whereas often dwarfs, pigmies in one part, are giants in another. It was not long before he was presented in a cold baked pie to King Charles and Queen Mary at an entertainment; and ever after lived (whilst the court lived) in great plenty therein, wanting nothing but humility (high mind in a low body) which made him that he did not know himself, and would not know his father, and which by the king's command caused justly his sound correction. He was, though a dwarf, no dastard, a captain of horse in the king's army in these late civil wars, and afterwards went over to wait on the queen in France.

Here being provoked by Mr. Crofts, who accounted him the object not of his anger but contempt, he shewed to all that *habet musca suum splenum* [even a fly has its temper] and they must be little indeed that cannot do mischief, especially seeing a pistol is a pure leveller, and puts both dwarf and giant into equal capacity to kill and be killed. For the shooting of the same Mr. Crofts he was imprisoned. And so I take my leave of Jeffery, the least man of the least county in England.[1]

THE FAREWELL

Let not the inhabitants of Rutland complain that they are pinned up within the confines of a narrow county, seeing the goodness thereof equals any shire in England for fertility of ground; but rather let them thank God, who hath cast their lot into so pleasant a place, giving them a goodly heritage.

(1) Fuller's facts are well authenticated. For killing Crofts (who had foolishly armed himself with only a squirt) the dwarf was not imprisoned, as Fuller states, but was saved probably by Henrietta Maria. His subsequent career was somewhat chequered. He was captured by pirates off the coast of France and sold as a slave, managed to escape and returned to England. He was imprisoned because of supposed complicity in the Popish Plot of 1678, but released shortly after. His height was eighteen inches until he was thirty, subsequently growing to about three feet six inches.

SHROPSHIRE

SHROPSHIRE hath Cheshire on the north, Staffordshire on the east, Worcester, Hereford and Radnor-shires on the south, Montgomery and Denbigh-shires on the west. The length thereof from north to south is 34 miles, and the general breadth thereof about 26 miles. I behold it really, though not so reputed, the biggest land-lock-shire in England; for although (according to Mr. Speed's measuring) it gathereth but one hundred thirty-four miles (short of Wiltshire by five) in circumference; yet, though less in compass, it may be more in content, as less angular in my eye, and more approaching to a circle, the form of greatest capacity. A large and lovely county, generally fair and fruitful, affording grass, grain and all things necessary for man's sustenance, but chiefly abounding with

NATURAL COMMODITIES

Iron

It is the most impure of metals, hardly meltable but with additaments; yea malleable and ductible with difficulty. Not like that at Damascus, which they refine in such sort, that it will melt at a lamp, and yet so tough that it will hardly break. Some impute the grossness of our English iron to our water, not so proper for that purpose as in Spain and other parts; and the poet telleth us of Turnus's sword:

> *Ensem quem Dauno igni potens Deus ipse parenti*
> *Fecerat, et Stygia candentem extinxerat unda.*[1]
> Sword which god Vulcan did for Daunus fix,
> And quenched it when fiery hot in Styx.

However, many utensils are made of the iron of this county, to the great profit of the owners, and no loss (I hope) of the commonwealth.

Coal

One may observe a threefold difference in our English coal. 1, *Sea-coal,* brought from Newcastle; 2. *Land-coal,* at Mendip, Bedworth, &c., and carted into other counties; 3. What one may call *river or fresh-water coal,* digged out in this county, at such a distance from Severn that they are easily ported by boat into other shires.

Oh if this coal could be so charked as to make iron melt out of the stone, as it maketh it in smiths' forges to be wrought in the bars. But Rome was not built all in one day, and a new world of experiments is left to the discovery of posterity.

THE MANUFACTURES

This county can boast of no one her original, but may be glad of one to her derivative, viz., the Welsh friezes brought to Oswestry, the staple of that commodity, as hereafter shall be observed.

(1) Virgil *Aeneid*, xii.

THE BUILDINGS

No county in England hath such a heap of castles together, insomuch that Shropshire may seem on the west divided from Wales with a wall of continued castles. It is much that Mr. Speed, which alloweth but one hundred and eighty-six in all England, accounteth two and thirty in this county. But as great guns, so useful in the side of a ship, are useless in the middle thereof, so these castles, formerly serviceable whilst Shropshire was the verge of English dominions, are now neglected, this shire being almost in the middest of England since Wales was peacably annexed thereunto. As for the houses of the gentry of this county, as many of them are fair and handsome, so none amount to an extraordinary eminence.

MEDICINAL WATERS

There is a spring at Pitchford, in this shire, which hath an oily unctuous matter swimming upon the water thereof. Indeed it is not in such plenty as in a river near to Solos in Cilicia, so full of that liquid substance, that such as wash therein seem anointed with oil; nor so abundant as in the springs near the Cape of St. Helen, wherewith (as Josephus Acosta reports) men use to pitch their ropes and tackling. I know not whether the sanative virtue thereof hath been experimented; but am sure that if it be bitumen, it is good to comfort the nerves, supple the joints, dry up rheums, cure palsies and contractions. I have nothing more to say of bitumen, but that great the affinity thereof is with sulphur, save that sulphur hath ingression into metal, and bitumen none at all. Here I purposely pass by Oakengates in this county, where are alum springs, whereof the dyers of Shrewsbury make use instead of alum.

PROVERBS

The case is altered, quoth Plowden. This proverb referreth its original to Edmund Plowden, an eminent native and great lawyer of this county, though very various the relations of the occasion thereof.[1] Some relate it to Plowden's faint pleading at the first for his client, till spurred on with a better fee; which, some will say, beareth no proportion with the ensuing character of his integrity. Others refer it to his altering of his judgment upon the emergency of new matter formerly undiscovered; it being not constancy, but obstinacy, to persist in an old error, when convinced to the contrary by clear and new information. Some tell it thus, that Plowden being of the Romish persuasion, some setters[2] trepanned him (pardon the prolepsis) to hear mass. But afterwards Plowden understanding that the pretender to officiate was no priest, but a mere layman —on design to make a discovering—"Oh! the case is altered," quoth Plowden, "no priest, no mass." As for other meaner origination of this proverb, I have neither list nor leisure to attend unto them.

THE WORTHIES

OSWALD [*b.* 605?] was king of Northumberland, who, after many fortunate battles fought, was vanquished and slain at last by Penda, the pagan king

(1) See p. 481 below for an account of Plowden. (2) *Setters*=informers.

of the Mercians, at a place in this county called after his name, Oswestry, now a famous market town in the Marches; thereby procuring to his memory the reputation of saint and martyr.

Be pleased, reader, to take notice that all battles of this nature, though there were quarrels or armed suits, commenced on a civil or temporal account, for the extending or defending their dominions; yet were they conceived (in that age especially) to have a mixture of much piety and church concernment therein, because fought against infidels, and so conducing consequently to the propagation of the faith; the reason that all kings killed in such service, achieved to themselves the veneration of saints and martyrs. Say not that King Saul might be sainted on the same account, mortally wounded in a pitched field fought against the uncircumcised Philistines; both because in fine he slew himself, and his former life was known to be notoriously wicked; whereas our Oswald was always pious, and exceedingly charitable to the poor. [*d.* 641]

MILBURG, daughter to Merewalh prince of Mercia, had the fair manor of Wenlock in this county given to her by her father for her portion. She, quitting all worldly wealth, bestowed her inheritance on the poor, and answered her name of Milburg, which (as an antiquary interpreteth) is good or gracious to town and city. Living a virgin, she built a monastery in the same place, and departed this life about the year 722.

Four hundred years after, in the reign of William the Conqueror, her corpse, discovered by miracles wrought thereby, was taken up sound and uncorrupted, to the admiration of the beholders (saith my author[1]); and surely, had I seen the same, I would have contributed my share of wondering thereunto. This I am sure of, that as good a saint, Lazarus by name, by the confession of his own sister, did stink when but four days buried. Her relics, enshrined at Wenlock, remained there in great state, till routed in the reign of King Henry the Eighth.

ROBERT BURNELL was son to Robert, and brother to Hugh Lord Burnell, whose prime seat was at Acton Burnell Castle in this county. He was, by King Edward the First, preferred bishop of Bath and Wells; and first treasurer, then chancellor, of England. He was well versed in the Welsh affairs, and much used in managing them; and that he might the more effectually attend such employment, caused the court of chancery to be kept at Bristol. He got great wealth, wherewith he enriched his kindred, and is supposed to have rebuilt the decayed castle of Acton Burnell on his own expense. And, to decline envy for his secular structures left to his heirs, he built for his successors the beautiful hall at Wells, the biggest room of any bishop's palace in England, plucked down by Sir John Gates (afterwards executed for treason) in the reign of King Edward the Sixth.[2]

English and Welsh affairs being settled to the king's contentment, he employed Bishop Burnell in some business about Scotland, in the Marches

(1) The English Martyrology. (2) Sir John Gates (1504?-1553) one of the worst iconoclasts under Edward VI. He was executed by Mary for complicity in Northumberland's rebellion.

whereof he died Anno Domini 1292; and his body, solemnly brought many miles, was buried in his own cathedral.[1]

RALPH OF SHREWSBURY, born therein, was, in the third of King Edward the Third, preferred bishop of Bath and Wells. Being consecrated without the pope's privity (a daring adventure in those days) he paid a large sum to expiate his presumption therein. He was a good benefactor to his cathedral, and bestowed on them a chest, portcullis-like, barred with iron, able to hold out a siege in view of such as beheld it. But what is proof against sacrilege? Some thieves (with what engine unknown) in the reign of Queen Elizabeth forced it open.

But this bishop is most memorable for erecting and endowing a specious structure for the vicars-choral of his cathedral to inhabit together, which in an old picture is thus presented:

THE VICARS' HUMBLE PETITION ON THEIR KNEES.

Per vicos positi villae, pater alme, rogamus
Ut simul uniti, te dante domos, maneamus.

To us dispers'd i'th streets, good father, give
A place where we together all may live.

THE GRACIOUS ANSWER OF THE BISHOP, SITTING.

Vestra petunt merita quod sint concessa petita,
Ut maneatis ita, loca fecimus haec stabilita.

Your merits crave that what you crave be yielded,
That so you may remain, this place we've builded.

Having now made such a palace, as I may term it, for his vicars, he was (in observation of a proportionable distance) necessitated in some sort to enlarge the bishop's seat, which he beautified and fortified castle-wise with great expense. He much ingratiated himself with the country people by disforesting Mendip, beef better pleasing the husbandman's palate than venison, He sat bishop thirty-four years; and dying August 14, 1363, lieth buried in his cathedral, where his statue is done to the life.

WILLIAM LANGLAND. He was born [1330?] at Cleobury Mortimer in this county, eight miles from Malvern Hills; was bred a priest, and one of the first followers of John Wycliffe, wanting neither wit nor learning, as appears by his book called *The Vision of Piers Plowman;* and hear what character a most learned antiquary giveth thereof:[2] "It is written in a kind of English metre, which for discovery of the infecting corruptions of those times I prefer before many of the more seemingly serious invectives, as well for invention as judgment."

It is observable that Pits (generally a perfect plagiary out of Bale) passeth this Langland over in silence. And why? Because he wrote *in*

(1) This Burnell was a great minister of state, but somewhat lacking as a churchman, being covetous and ambitious (he owned 28 manors in 19 counties). Edward I tried unsuccessfully to secure the primacy for him, going so far as to burst into the chapter-house at Canterbury during the election of 1270 and to dare the monks to brave his and his father's displeasure, which they proceeded to do. (2) Mr. Selden, in his notes on *Polyolbion*.

oppositum to the papal interest. Thus the most light-fingered thieves will let that alone which is too hot for them. [*d.* 1400?]

SIR JOHN TALBOT [FIRST EARL OF SHREWSBURY] was born [1388?] as all concurring indications do avouch, at Blackmere in this county, the then flourishing (now ruined) house, devolved to his family by marrying the heir of Lord Strange of Blackmere,

Many honourable titles deservedly met in him, who was 1. Lord Talbot and Strange, by his paternal extraction. 2. Lord Furnivall and Verdun, by marriage with Maud, the daughter of Thomas Neville. 3. Earl of Shrewsbury in England, and Waterford in Ireland, by creation of King Henry the Sixth.

This is that terrible Talbot, so famous for his sword, or rather whose sword was so famous for his arm that used it; a sword with bad Latin[1] upon it, but good steel within it, which constantly conquered where it came, insomuch that the bare fame of his approach frighted the French from the siege of Bordeaux. Being victorious for twenty-four years together, success failed him at last, charging the enemy near Castillon on unequal terms, where he, with his son the Lord Lisle, were slain with a shot, July 17, 1453. Henceforward we may say, "Good night to the English in France," whose victories were buried with the body of this earl, and his body was interred at Whitchurch in this county.

RICHARD TALBOT was born of honourable parentage in this county, as brother unto John Talbot, the first earl of Shrewsbury. Being bred in learning, he was consecrated archbishop of Dublin in Ireland in 1417. He sat two and thirty years in that see (being all that time a privy councillor to King Henry the Fifth and Sixth) twice chief justice, and once chancellor of Ireland.

He deserved well of his church, founding six petty canons, and as many choristers therein; yea, generally of all Ireland, writing a book against James earl of Ormonde, wherein he detected his abuses during his lieutenancy in Ireland. He died August the 15th, 1449; and lieth buried in Saint Patrick's in Dublin under a marble stone, whereon an epitaph is written not worthy the inserting.

The said Richard was unanimously chosen archbishop of Armagh, a higher place, but refused to remove, wisely preferring safety above either honour or profit.

RICHARD PLANTAGENET, second son to Edward the Fourth and Elizabeth his queen, was born at Shrewsbury 1472. He was created by his father duke of York, and affianced to Anne, daughter and heir to John Mowbray duke of Norfolk. But before the nuptials were solemnized, his cruel uncle, the duke of Gloucester, married him to a grave in the Tower of London. The obscurity of his burial gave the advantage to the report, that he lived in Perkin Warbeck, one of the idols which put polite King

(1) *Sum Talboti pro vincere inimicos meos.* [His dash and daring made a great impression upon the French, and the legends of Guienne still commemorate "le roi Talabot."]

Henry the Seventh to some danger, and more trouble, before he could finally suppress him. [*d.* 1483]

SIR GILBERT TALBOT. He was son to John Talbot, second earl of Shrewsbury of that name. In the time of his shrievalty, Henry earl of Richmond (afterwards King Henry the Seventh) marching with his men to give battle to King Richard the Third, was met at Shrewsbury by the same Sir Gilbert, with two thousand men well appointed; most of them tenants and retainers to his nephew George fourth earl of Shrewsbury, then in minority; whenceforward, and not before, his forces deserved the name of an army. For this and his other good service in Bosworth Field, King Henry rewarded him with fair lands at Grafton in Worcestershire; made him governor of Calais in France, and knight of the Garter; and from him the present earl of Shrewsbury is descended.

I conceive it was rather his son than himself, to whom King Henry the Eighth (fearing a sudden surprise from the French) wrote briefly and peremptorily, "That he should instantly fortify the castle of Calais." To whom the Governor Talbot, unprovided of necessaries, as briefly as bluntly replied, "That he could neither *fortify* nor *fiftyfy* without money." [*d.* 1517]

THOMAS PARR ['OLD PARR'], son of John Parr, born at Alberbury in the parish of Winnington in this county, lived to be above one hundred and fifty years of age, verifying his anagram, THOMAS PARRE (*most rare hap*). He was born in the reign of King Edward the Fourth, one thousand four hundred eighty-three; and, two months before his death, was brought up by Thomas earl of Arundel (a great lover of antiquities in all kinds) to Westminster. He slept away most of his time, and is thus charactered by an eye-witness of him:

> From head to heel his body had all over
> A quick-set, thick-set, nat'ral hairy cover.

Change of air and diet (better in itself but worse for him) with the trouble of many visitants, or spectators rather, are conceived to have accelerated his death; which happened at Westminster, November the 14th, 1635, and he was buried in the abbey church; all present at his burial doing homage to this our aged Thomas de Temporibus.[1]

SIR ROWLAND HILL, son of Richard Hill, was born [1492?] at Hodnet in this county; bred a mercer in London, whereof he was lord mayor 1549. Being sensible that God had given him a great estate, he expressed his gratitude unto him, in giving maintenance to a fair school at Drayton in this county, which he built and endowed; besides six hundred pounds to Christchurch Hospital, and other benefactions; in forgiving at his death all his tenants in his manors of Aldersey and Sponely a year's rent; also enjoining his heirs to make them new leases of one and twenty years, for two years' rent.

(1) The great age of Parr is attested only by the gossip of his village, though no doubt he was very old. He is supposed to have done penance at the age of 105 for begetting a bastard. The great William Harvey performed an autopsy on his body, and pronounced his chief organs to be in a singularly healthy condition.

As for the causeways he caused to be made, and bridges built (two of stone containing eighteen arches in them both) seeing hitherto it hath not been my hap to go over them, I leave his piety to be praised by such passengers who have received safety, ease and cleanness by such conveniences. He died Anno Domini 1561.[1]

GEORGE DAY was born [1501?] in this county, and successively scholar, fellow and provost of King's College in Cambridge, which he retained with the bishopric of Chichester, to which he was consecrated 1543. A most pertinacious papist, who, though he had made some kind of recantation in a sermon (as I find it entered in King Edward the Sixth's own diary) yet either the same was not satisfactory, or else he relapsed into his errors again, for which he was deprived under the said king, and restored again by Queen Mary. He died Anno Domini 1556.

WILLIAM DAY [*b.* 1529] was brother to the aforesaid George Day . . . Not so great was the difference betwixt their vivacity as distance betwixt their opinions; the former being a rigid papist, the latter a zealous protestant, who, requesting of his brother some money to buy books therewith and other necessaries, was returned with this denial, "That he thought it not fit to spend the goods of the church on him who was an enemy of the church."

However, this William found the words of Solomon true, "And there is a friend who is nearer than a brother," not wanting those who supplied his necessities. He was proctor of Cambridge 1558, and afterwards was made by Queen Elizabeth (who highly esteemed him for his learning and religion) provost of Eton and dean of Windsor, fair preferments, parted with Thames, but united in his person. The bishopric of Winchester he enjoyed scarcely a whole year; and died . . . 1596.[2]

EDMUND PLOWDEN was born [1518] at Plowden in this county; one who excellently deserved of our municipal law, in his learned writings thereon . . . We must add a few words out of the character Mr. Camden gives of him: *Vitae integritate inter homines suae professionis nulli secundus.* And how excellently a medley is made, when honesty and ability meet in a man of his profession! Nor must we forget how he was treasurer for the Honourable Society of the Middle Temple, anno 1561, when their magnificent hall was builded, he being a great advancer thereof.[3] [*d.* 1585]

THOMAS GATACRE, younger son of William Gatacre, was a branch of an ancient family, so firmly planted by Divine Providence at Gatacre Hall in this county, that they have flourished the owners thereof, by a non-

(1) Sir Rowland Hill was probably the first protestant to become lord mayor of London. (2) William Day is noteworthy in the history of Eton for destroying all traces of catholicism in Eton College chapel. (3) Plowden sat in parliament in Mary's reign, but being a Roman catholic public life was closed to him on Elizabeth's accession. It is said that Elizabeth offered him the lord chancellorship if he would renounce his religion, but he refused. He had such fame as a jurist that his name was embodied in the proverb, "The case is altered, quoth Plowden," which is commented on by Fuller on p. 476 above.

interrupted succession, from the time of King Edward the Confessor. This Thomas, being designed a student for the law, was brought up in the Temple, where in the reign of Queen Mary he was often present at the examination of persecuted people. Their hard usage made him pity their persons, and admirable patience to approve their opinions. This was no sooner perceived by his parents (being of the old persuasion) but instantly they sent him over to Louvain in the Low Countries, to win him to a compliance to the popish religion; and for his better encouragement, settled on him an estate of one hundred pound per annum, old rent. All would not do. Whereupon his father recalled him home, and revoked his own grant; to which his son did submit, as unwilling to oppose the pleasure of his parents, though no such revocation could take effect without his free consent. He afterwards diverted his mind from the most profitable to the most necessary study, from law to divinity; and finding friends to breed him in Oxford, he became the profitable pastor of St. Edmund's in Lombard Street, London, where he died anno 1593, leaving Thomas Gatacre, his learned son . . . heir to his pains and piety.

THOMAS CHURCHYARD was born [1520?] in the town of Shrewsbury, as himself doth affirm in his book made in verse of *The Worthines of Wales,* taking Shropshire within the compass; making (to use his own expression) Wales the park, and the Marches to be the pale thereof. Though some conceive him to be as much beneath a poet as above a rhymer, in my opinion his verses may go abreast with any of that age, writing in the beginning of Queen Elizabeth. It seems by this his epitaph, in Mr. Camden's *Remains,* that he died not guilty of much wealth:

Come, Alecto, lend me thy torch,
To find a *church-yard* in a *church-porch,*
Poverty and poetry his tomb doth enclose;
Wherefore, good neighbours, be merry in prose.

[*d.* 1604]

SIR THOMAS BROMLEY was born [1530] at Bromleghe in this county, of a right ancient family, I assure you; bred in the Inner Temple, and general solicitor to Queen Elizabeth. He afterwards succeeded Sir Nicholas Bacon in the dignity of lord chancellor, April 26, 1579.

Now although it was difficult to come after Sir Nicholas Bacon, and *not* to come after him, yet such was Sir Thomas's learning and integrity, being charactered by my author *vir jurisprudentia insignis,*[1] that [the] court was not sensible of any considerable alteration. He possessed his place about nine years, dying anno 1587, not being sixty years old. Hereby the pregnancy of his parts doth appear, seeing by proportion of time he was made the queen's solicitor before he was forty, and lord chancellor before he was fifty years old. Learning in law may seem to run in the veins of that name, which since had a baron of the exchequer of his alliance.

(1) Camden, in his *Elizabeth.*

THOMAS HOLLAND, D.D., was born in this county, *in finibus et limitibus Cambriae* (in the confines and Marches of Wales); bred in Exeter College in Oxford, and at last became rector thereof. He did not, with some, only sip of learning, or at the best but drink thereof, but was *mersus in libris* (drowned in his books) so that the scholar in him almost devoured all other relations. He was, saith the author of his funeral sermon, so familiar with the Fathers, as if he himself had been a Father. This quality commended him to succeed Dr. Laurence Humphrey in the place of regius professor, which place he discharged with good credit for twenty years together. When he went forth of his college on any journey for any long continuance, he always took this solemn valediction of the fellows: "I commend you to the love of God, and to the hatred of popery and superstition."

His extemporaries were often better than his premeditations; so that he might have been said "to have been out, if he had not been out." He died in March, Anno Domini 1612, and was buried in Oxford with great solemnity and lamentation.[1]

SIR CLEMENT EDMONDES was born [1564?] at Shrawardine in this county;[2] and bred fellow in All Souls' College in Oxford, being generally skilled in all arts and sciences; witness his faithful translations of, and learned illustrations on, Caesar's *Commentaries.* Say not that comment on commentary was false heraldry, seeing it is so worthy a work, that the author thereof may pass for an eminent instance to what perfection of theory they may attain in matter of war, who were not acquainted with the practical part thereof; being only once employed by Queen Elizabeth, with a dispatch to Sir Francis Vere, which occasioned his presence at the battle of Nieuport; for he doth so smartly discuss *pro* and *con,* and seriously decide many martial controversies, that his judgment therein is praised by the best military masters.

King James, taking notice of his abilities, made him clerk of the council, and knighted him; and he was at last preferred secretary of state in the vacancy of that place, but prevented by death, acted not therein. He died anno 1622; and lies buried at Preston in Northamptonshire, where he purchased a fair estate, which his grandchild doth possess at this day.

SIR JOHN WALTER, son to Edmund Walter, chief justice of south Wales, was born [1566] at Ludlow in this county, and bred a student of our common laws, wherein he attained to great learning, so that he became, when a pleader, eminent; when a judge, more eminent; when *no* judge, most eminent.

1. *Pleader.* The character that learned James Thuanus gives of Christopher Thuanus his father, being an advocate of the civil law, and afterwards a senator of Paris, is exactly agreeable to this worthy knight: *Ut bonos a calumniatoribus, tenuiores a potentioribus, doctos ab ignorantibus, opprimi non pateretur* (that he suffered not good men to

(1) Thomas Holland was one of the translators of the Authorized Version. (2) So his near kinsman informed me.

be borne down by slanderers, poor men by more potent, learned men by the ignorant.)

2. *Judge.* Who (as when ascending the bench, entering into a new temper) was most passionate as Sir John, most patient as Judge Walter, and great his gravity in that place. When Judge Denham, his most upright and worthy associate in the western circuit, once said unto him, "My lord, you are not merry." "Merry enough," returned the other, "for a judge."

3. *No judge.* Being ousted of his place, when chief baron of the exchequer, about the illegality of the loan, as I take it.

He was a grand benefactor (though I know not the just proportion) to Jesus College in Oxford; and died anno 1630, in the parish of Savoy, bequeathing £20 to the poor thereof.[1]

SIR THOMAS ADAMS, knight,[2] was born [1586] at Wem in this county; bred a draper in London, where God so blessed his honest industry, that he became lord mayor thereof 1645. A man who hath drunk of the bitter waters of Meribah without making a bad face thereat, cheerfully submitting himself to God's pleasure in all conditions.

He gave the house of his nativity to be a free school (that others might have their breeding where he had his birth) and hath liberally endowed it. He liveth in due honour and esteem, and, I hope, will live to see many years, seeing there is no better collirium, or eye-salve to quicken and continue one's sight, than in his lifetime to behold a building erected for the public profit. [*d.* 1668]

SIR EDWARD LITTLETON [FIRST BARON LITTLETON], born [1589] at Munslow in this county,[3] was the eldest son to Sir Edward Littleton, one of the justices of the Marches, and chief justice of north Wales. He was bred in Christ Church in Oxford, where he proceeded bachelor of arts, and afterwards one of the justices of north Wales, recorder of London, and solicitor to King Charles. From these places he was preferred to be chief justice of the common pleas, when he was made privy councillor; thence advanced to be lord keeper and baron of Munslow, the place of his nativity. He died in Oxford, and was buried in Christ Church, anno 1645.

ABRAHAM WHEELOCKE was born [1593] in Whitchurch parish in this county; bred fellow of Clare Hall, library-keeper, Arabic professor, and minister of Saint Sepulchre's in Cambridge. Admirable his industry, and no less his knowledge in the oriental tongues; so that he might serve for the interpreter to the Queen of Sheba coming to Solomon, and the wise men of the east who came to Herod, such his skill in the Arabian

(1) Sir John Walter had concurred with Charles I on questions of taxation but opposed him on the law of treason, and was ordered in 1630 to cease his judicial functions. (2) Dubbed by King Charles II at the Hague, when sent thither a commissioner for the City of London. [During the Commonwealth he had been imprisoned in the Tower for his loyalty to Charles II. He founded an Arabic lecture at Cambridge, and Abraham Wheelocke, whose life follows below, was the first reader.] (3) So am I informed by his two surviving brothers, the one a serjeant-at-law, the other a doctor in divinity.

and Persian languages. Amongst the western tongues he was well versed in the Saxon, witness his fair and true edition of Bede.

He translated the New Testament into Persian, and printed it, hoping in time it might tend to the conversion of that country to Christianity. Such as laugh at his design as ridiculous, might well forbear their mirth; and seeing they expended neither penny of cost nor hour of pains therein, might let another enjoy his own inclination. True it is, he that sets an acorn, sees it not a timber-oak, which others may behold; and if such Testaments be conveyed into Persia, another age may admire what this doth deride. He died, as I take it, Anno Domini 1653.

WILLIAM ADAMS, esq., was born at Newport in this county; bred by trade a haberdasher in London, where God so blessed his endeavours, that he fined for alderman[1] in that city. God had given him an heart and hand proportionable to his estate, having founded in the town of his nativity a school-house in the form following.

1. The building is of brick, with windows of freestone, wherein the school is threescore and ten in length, and two and twenty foot in breadth and height. 2. Over it a fair library, furnished with plenty and choice books. At the south end, the lodgings of the schoolmaster, whose salary is sixty; on the north the usher's, whose stipend is thirty pounds per annum. 3. Before the front of the school a stately *crypto-porticus,* or fair walk all the length of the school, with pillars erected, and on the top thereof a leaden terrace, with rails and balusters. 4. Two almshouses for poor people, at convenient distance from the school, with competent maintenance. 5. Two gardens apiece, for schoolmaster and usher, with well nigh two acres of ground for a place for the scholars to play in. 6. The rent for the maintenance thereof deposed in the hands of trustees a year before, that, in case of casualty, there may be no complaint. 7. More intended for the settlement of exhibitions to scholars chosen hence to the university, as God hereafter shall direct the founder. But who for the present can hold from praising so pious a performance?

[*fl.* 1656]

THE FAREWELL

May this shire, by Divine Providence, be secured from the sweating-sickness, which first began and twice raged in the town of Shrewsbury. The cure was discovered too late to save many, yet soon enough to preserve more thousands of men, viz., by keeping the patient in the same posture wherein he was seized, without food or physic; and such who weathered out the disease for twenty-four hours did certainly escape.

(1) *Fined for alderman,* i.e., escaped (by payment) the duties of alderman.

SOMERSETSHIRE

SOMERSETSHIRE hath the Severn sea on the north, Gloucestershire on the north-east, Wiltshire on the east, Dorsetshire on the south, and Devonshire on the west. Some will have it so called from the *summerliness,* or temperate pleasantness thereof; with whom we concur, whilst they confine their etymologies to the air; dissent, if they extent it to the earth, which in winter is as winterly, deep and dirty as any in England. The truth is, it is so named from Somerton, the most ancient town in the county. It stretcheth from east to west fifty-five miles, and from north to south forty-two miles.

No shire can shew finer ware which hath so large measure; being generally fruitful, though little moisture be used thereon.

The inhabitants will tell you that there be several single acres in this shire (believe them of the larger size, and *sesquijugera,* if measured) which may serve a good round family with bread for a year, as affording a bushel of wheat for every week therein, a proportion not easily to be paralleled in other places.

NATURAL COMMODITIES

Lead

Plenty of the best (for the kind thereof) is digged out of Mendip Hills. Indeed it is not so soft, pliant and equally fusile as that in Derbyshire; not so proper for sheeting, because when melted it runs into knots, and therefore little known to, and less used by, our London plumbers; for, being of a harder nature, it is generally transported beyond the seas, and employed to make bullets and shot, for which purpose it is excellent. May foreigners enjoy *wild* lead to kill men, whilst we make use of *tame* lead to cover houses, and keep people warm and dry therein.

It is almost credible what great sums were advanced to the bishops of Bath and Wells by the benefit of lead, since the latter end of Queen Elizabeth. Bishop Still is said to have had the harvest, Bishop Montagu the cleanings, Bishop Lake the stubble thereof; and yet considerable was the profit of lead to him and his successors.[1]

Lapis Calaminaris[2]

Plenty hereof is also found in Mendip Hills; and it is much used in physic (being very good, as artificially ordered, for the clearing of the sight) and more by metallists; for brass, no original, but a compound metal, is made of this stone and copper; and becometh more hard than copper alone, and therefore the more serviceable for many other purposes.

And now the riddle in nature, which so long hath posed me, is at last explained: viz., how it can come to pass that brass, being made of the

(1) For accounts of these bishops see John Still under Lincolnshire, James Montagu under Northamptonshire, and Arthur Lake under Hampshire. (2) *Calaminaris* = an ore of zinc (an earlier form of the word calamine).

best copper with much art and industry, is notwithstanding afforded some pence in the pound cheaper than copper itself. This cometh to pass, because calaminary-stone, being of itself not worth above sixpence in the pound, doth in the composition *metalescere,* turn metal, in the mixture thereof, whereby the mass and bulk of brass is much advanced.

I have no more to observe of this stone, save that it was first discovered in this county in that juncture of time when the copper mines were newly re-discovered in Cumberland, God doubling his gift by the seasonable gift thereof.

CHEESE

The best and biggest in England are made at Cheddar in this county. They may be called Corporation Cheeses, made by the joint dairies of the whole parish putting their milk together; and each one, poor and rich, receive their share according to their proportion; so that some may think that the unity and amity of those female neighbours, living so lovingly together, giveth the better runnet[1] and relish to their handiwork.

If any ask why as good cheese may not be made in the vicinage, where the soil is as rich, and the same housewifery, it will be demanded of them, why (nails must be driven out with nails) the like cheese, in colour, taste and tenderness, may not be made at Cremona as at Parma, both lying in Lombardy near together, and sharing equally in all visible advantages of fatness and fruitfulness. The worst fault of Cheddar cheese is they are so few and dear, hardly to be met with, save at some great man's table.

WOAD

In Latin *glastum* or *glaustum,* was much used by the ancient Britons for the painting of their faces; for I believe it will hardly be proved that they dyed their whole bodies. Say not painted terribleness is no terribleness, rather ridiculous than formidable, seeing vizards are more frightful than men's own faces. This woad gave the Britons a deep black tincture, as if they would blow up their enemies with their sulphureous countenances.

Our dyers make much use thereof, being *color ad colorem,* the stock (as I may say) whereon other colours are grafted. Yea, it giveth them truth and fruitfulness, who without it prove fading and hypocritical.

This herb doth greatly impair the ground it groweth on; profitable to such to set who have land to let without impeachment of waste,[2] it being long before it will recover good grass therein. I have placed woad, which groweth in all rich places, in this county because, as I am informed, it groweth naturally therein, hardly to be destroyed, especially about Glastonbury; insomuch that a learned critic, and my worthy good friend,[3] had almost persuaded me that from this *glastum* that town taketh its denomination.

(1) *Runnet.* A form of the word *rennet,* which means curdled milk found in the stomach of an unweaned calf or other animal, used for curdling milk in cheese-making. (2) i.e., without being answerable for spoil to the detriment of persons subsequently entitled to the inheritance. (3) Mr. John Langley, late schoolmaster of Paul's.

MASTIFFS

Smile not, reader, to see me return to coarse creatures amongst the commodities of this county. Know they are not, like apes, the fools and jesters, but the useful servants in a family, viz., the porters thereof. Pliny observes that Britain breeds cowardly lions and courageous mastiffs, which to me seems no wonder, the former being whelped in prison, the latter at liberty. An English mastiff, anno 1602, did in effect worst a lion, on the same token that Prince Henry allowed a kind of pension for his maintenance, and gave strict order, "that he that had fought with the king of beasts should never after encounter any inferior creatures."

THE MANUFACTURES

Taunton serges are eminent in their kind, being a fashionable wearing, as lighter than cloth, yet thicker than many other stuffs. When Dionysius sacrilegiously plundered Jove's statue of his golden coat (pretending it too cold for winter, and too hot for summer) he bestowed such a vestment upon him as to fit both seasons. They were much sent into Spain before our late war therewith, wherein trading (long since complained of to be dead) is now lamented generally buried, though hereafter it may have a resurrection.

THE BUILDINGS

Of these the churches of Bath and Wells are most eminent. Twins are said to make but one man, as these two churches constitute one bishop's see. Yet, as a twin oft-times proves as proper a person as those of single births, so these severally equal most, and exceed many, cathedrals in England.

We begin with Bath, considerable in its several conditions, viz., the beginning, obstructing, decaying, repairing and finishing thereof.

1. It was begun by Oliver King, bishop of this diocese, in the reign of King Henry the Seventh, and the west end most curiously cut and carved with angels climbing up a ladder to heaven. But this bishop died before the finishing thereof.

2. His death obstructed this structure, so that it stood a long time neglected, which gave occasion for one to write on the church wall with a charcoal.

> O church, I wail thy woeful plight,
> Whom king, nor cardinal, clerk, or knight,
> Have yet restored to ancient right.

Alluding herein to Bishop King, who began it; and his four successors, in thirty-five years, viz., Cardinal Adrian, Cardinal Wolsey, Bishop Clerk, and Bishop Knight, contributing nothing to the effectual finishing thereof.

3. The decay and almost ruin thereof followed, when it felt in part the hammers which knocked down all abbeys. True it is the commissioners proffered to sell the church to the townsmen under 500 marks. But the townsmen, fearing if they bought it so cheap to be thought to cozen the king, so that the purchase might come under the compass of concealed lands, refused the proffer. Hereupon the glass, iron, bells and

lead (which last alone amounted to 480 tons) provided for the finishing thereof, were sold and sent beyond the seas, if a shipwreck (as some report) met them not by the way.

4. For the repairing thereof, collections were made all over the land in the reign of Queen Elizabeth, though inconsiderable, either in themselves, or through the corruptions of others. Only honest Mr. Billet (whom I take to be the same with him who was designed executor to the will of William Cecil Lord Burghley) disbursed good sums to the repairing thereof; and a stranger, under a feigned name, took the confidence thus to play the poet and prophet on this structure:

> Be blithe, fair Kirck, when *Hempe* is past,
> Thine *Olive*, that ill winds did blast,
> Shall flourish green for age to last.
> (*Subscribed* Cassadore.)

By *Hempe* understand Henry the Eighth, Edward the Sixth, Queen Mary, King Philip, and Queen Elizabeth. The author, I suspect, had a *tang of the cask;* and being parcel-popish, expected the finishing of this church at the return of their religion; but his prediction was verified in a better sense, when this church

5. Was finished by James Montagu, bishop of this see, disbursing vast sums in the same, though the better enabled thereunto by his mines at Mendip; so that he did but remove the lead from the bowels of the earth to the roof of the church, wherein he lies interred under a fair monument.

This church is both *spacious* and *specious,* the most lightsome as ever I beheld, proceeding from the greatness of the windows and whiteness of the glass therein.

As for the cathedral of Wells, it is a greater, so darker than that of Bath; so that Bath may seem to *draw* devotion with the pleasantness, Wells to *drive* it with the solemnity thereof; and ill-tempered their minds who will be moved with neither. The west front of Wells is a masterpiece of art indeed, made of imagery in just proportion, so that we may call them *vera et spirantia signa.* England affordeth not the like, for the west end of Exeter beginneth accordingly, it doth not like Wells persevere to the end thereof.

As for the civil habitations in this county (not to speak of Dunster Castle, having a high ascent, and the effect thereof, a large prospect by sea and land) Montacute, built by Sir Edward Phelips, master of the rolls, is a most magnificent fabric.[1] Nor must Hinton St. George, the house of the Lord Poulett, be forgotten, having every stone in the front shaped doul-ways, or in the form of a cart-nail. This I may call a charitable curiosity, if true what is traditioned, that, about the reign of King Henry the Seventh, the owner thereof built it in a dear year, on purpose to employ the more poor people thereupon.

THE WONDERS

Wookey Hole, in Mendip Hills, some two miles from Wells. This is an underground concavity, admirable for its spacious vaults, stony walls,

(1) Sir Edward Phelips (1560?-1614) was also speaker of the House of Commons. Montacute House was acquired by the National Trust in 1946.

creeping labyrinths; the cause being unimaginable, how and why the earth was put in such a posture, save that the God of nature is pleased to descant on a plain hollowness with such wonderful contrivances.

MEDICINAL WATERS

Bath is well known all England and Europe over; far more useful and wholesome, though not so stately, as Diocletian's bath in Rome (the fairest amongst 856 in that city, made only for pleasure and delicacy) beautified with an infinity of marble pillars (not for support but ostentation) so that Salmuth saith fourteen thousand men were employed for some years in building thereof. Our Bath waters consist of 1. *Bitumen,* which hath the predominancy; sovereign to discuss, glutinate, dissolve, open obstructions, &c. 2. *Nitre;* which dilateth the bitumen, making the solution the better, and water the clearer. It cleanseth and purgeth both by stool and urine, cutteth and disolveth gross humours. 3. *Sulphur;* in regard whereof they dry, resolve, mollify, attract, and are good for uterine effects, proceeding from cold and windy humours.

But how these waters came by their great heat is rather controverted than concluded amongst the learned. Some impute it to wind, or airy exhalations, included in the bowels of the earth, which by their agitation and attrition (upon the rocks and narrow passages) gather heat, and impart it to the waters.

They are used also inwardly, in broths, beer, juleps, &c., with good effect. And although some mislike it, because they will not mix medicaments with aliments, yet such practice beginneth to prevail.

PROVERBS

Where should I be born else than in Taunton Dean. This is a parcel of ground round about Taunton, very pleasant and populous, as containing many parishes; and so fruitful, to use their phrase, with the *zun* and *zoil* alone, that it needs no manuring at all. The peasantry therein are as rude as rich, and so highly conceited of their good country (God make them worthy thereof) that they conceive it a disparagement to be born in any other place, as if it were eminently all England.

The beggars of Bath. Many in that place, some natives there, others repairing thither from all parts of the land; the poor for alms, the pained for ease. Whither should fowl flock in an hard frost but to the barn door? Here, all the two seasons, being the general confluence of gentry. Indeed laws are daily made to restrain beggars, and daily broke by the connivance of those who make them; it being impossible, when the hungry belly barks, and bowels sound, to keep the tongue silent. And although oil of whip be the proper plaister for the cramp of laziness, yet some pity is due to impotent persons. In a word, seeing there is the Lazars-bath in this city, I doubt not but many a good Lazarus, the true object of charity, may beg therein.

THE BATTLES

None have been fought in this county which come properly under this notion. Indeed the skirmish at Martial's Elm (something military and ominous in the name thereof) fought 1642, made much noise in men's ears (a musket gave then a greater report than a cannon since); and is remembered the more, because conceived first to break the peace of this nation, long restive and rusty in ease and quiet.

As for the encounter at Langport, where the king's forces under the Lord Goring were defeated by the parliament's, July 12, 1645, it was rather a flight than a fight, like the battle of Spurs, fought many years since; the horse, by their speed, well saving themselves, whilst the poor foot (pawned in the place) paid dearly for it. And henceforward the sun of the king's cause declined, verging more and more westward, till at last it set in Cornwall, and since (after a long and dark night) rose again by God's goodness in the east, when our gracious sovereign arrived at Dover.

THE WORTHIES

GILDAS, surnamed the Wise, was born [516?] in the city of Bath; and therefore it is that he is called *Badonicus*. He was eight years junior to another Gildas, called *Albanius*, whose nativity I cannot clear to belong to our Britain. He was also otherwise sur-styled *Querulus*, because the little we have of his writing is only a *Complaint*. Yet was he none of those whom the apostle condemneth. These are "murmurers, complainers" &c., taxing only such who either were impious against God, or uncharitable against men; complaining of them either without cause or without measure; whilst our Gildas only inveigheth against the sins, and bemoaneth the sufferings, of that wicked and woeful age wherein he lived; calling the clergy *Montes Malitiae*, the Britons generally *Atramentum Seculi*.

He wrote many books, though we have none of them extant at this day (some few fragments excepted, inserted amongst the manuscript canons) but his aforesaid history. This makes me more to wonder that so learned a critic as Dr. Gerrard Vossius should attribute the comedy of *Aulularia* in Plautus to this our Gildas, merely because that comedy is otherwise commonly called *Querulus;* whereas indeed their language is different: that in *Aulularia* tolerably pure, though perchance coarser than the rest in Plautus; whilst the style of Gildas is hardly with sense to be climbed over, it is so harsh and barbarous. Besides, I do not believe that Gildas had a drop of comical blood in his veins, or any inclination to mirth and festivity; and if he had prepared anything scenical to be acted on the theatre, certainly it would have been a tragedy relating to the ruin and destruction of his nation. Some variety there is about the date of his death, which most probably is assigned anno 570.

SAINT DUNSTAN was born [910?] in the town of Glastonbury in this county. He afterwards was abbot thereof, bishop of London and Worcester, archbishop of Canterbury, and at last, for his promoting of monkery, reputed a saint. I can add nothing to, but must subtract something from, what I have written of him in my *Church History*. True it is, he was first abbot of England, not in time but in honour, Glastonbury being the *proto-abbaty* then and many years after, till Pope Adrian advanced Saint Albans above it. But, whereas it followeth in my book "that the title of abbot till his time was unknown in England," I admire by what casualty it crept in, confess it a foul mistake, and desire the reader with his pen to delete it. More I have not to say of Dunstan, save that he died Anno Domini 988; and his skill in smithery was so great, that the goldsmiths in London are incorporated by the name of the Company of Saint Dunstan.

JOHN DE COURCI, baron of Stoke Courcy in this county, was the first Englishman who invaded and subdued Ulster in Ireland; therefore deservedly created earl thereof. He was afterward surprised by Hugh de Lacy (corrival for his title) sent over into England, and imprisoned by King John in the Tower of London.

A French castle, being in controversy, was to have the title thereof tried by combat, the kings of England and France beholding it. Courci, being a lean lank body, with staring eyes (prisoners, with the wildness of their looks, revenge the closeness of their bodies) is sent for out of the Tower to undertake the Frenchman; and because enfeebled with long durance, a large bill of fare was allowed him to recruit his strength. The monsieur, hearing how much he had eat and drunk, and guessing his courage by his stomach, or rather stomach by his appetite, took him for a cannibal who would devour him at the last course; and so he declined the combat.

Afterwards the two kings, desirous to see some proof of Courci's strength, caused a steel helmet to be laid on a block before him. Courci, looking about him with a grim countenance (as if he intended to cut with his eyes as well as with his arms) sundered the helmet at one blow into two pieces, striking the sword so deep into the wood that none but himself could pull it out again.

Being demanded the cause why he looked so sternly, "Had I," said he, "failed of my design, I would have killed the kings and all in the place;" words well spoken because well taken, all persons present being then highly in good humour. Hence it is, that the Lord Courci, baron of Kingrone, second baron in Ireland, claimed a privilege (whether by patent or prescription, charter or custom, I know not) after their first obeisance, to be covered in the king's presence, if process of time had not antiquated the practice.

His devotion was equal to his valour, being a great founder and endower of religious houses. In one thing he foully failed, turning the church of the Holy Trinity in Down into the church of Saint Patrick, for which (as the story saith) he was condemned never to return into Ireland, though attempting it fifteen several times but repelled with foul weather. He afterwards went over and died in France, about the year 1219.

ALEXANDER OF ASHBY is (saith my author[1]) by some accounted a Somerset, by others a Staffordshire man; and therefore by our fundamental laws (laid down in our preface,[2] to decide differences about nativities) falls to the share of this county. He was the prince of English

(1) Bale. (2) This portion of the preface is omitted in this edition.

poets in his age; and in imitation of Ovid *De Fastis,* put our Christian festivals into verse, setting a copy therein to Baptista Mantuanus.

Then leaving Ovid, he aspired to Virgil, and wrote the history of the Bible (with the lives of some saints) in an heroical poem; and, though falling far short of Virgil, went beyond himself therein. He afterward became prior of Ashby Abbey, belonging to the Augustines; and flourished under King Henry the Third, Anno Domini 1220.

JOCELIN OF WELLS. Bishop Godwin was convinced, by such evidences as he had seen, that he was both born and bred in Wells, becoming afterwards the bishop thereof.

Now whereas his predecessors styled themselves bishops of Glaston (especially for some few years after their first consecration) he first fixed on the title of Bath and Wells, and transmitted it to all his successors. In his time the monks of Glastonbury, being very desirous to be only subjected to their own abbot, purchased their exemption by parting with four fair manors to the see of Wells.

This Jocelin, after his return from his five years' exile in France (banished with Archbishop Langton on the same account of obstinacy against King John) laid out himself wholly on the beautifying and enriching of his cathedral. He erected some new prebends; and to the use of the chapter, appropriated many churches, increasing the revenues of the dignities (so fitter called than profits, so mean then their maintenance); and to the episcopal see he gave three manors of great value. He, with Hugh bishop of Lincoln, was the joint founder of the hospital of Saint John in Wells; and on his own sole cost, built two very fair chapels, one at Wookey, the other at Wells. But the church of Wells was the master-piece of his works, not so much repaired as rebuilt by him, and well might he therein have been afforded a quiet repose. And yet some have plundered his tomb of his effigies in brass, being so rudely rent off, it hath not only defaced his monument, but even hazarded the ruin thereof. He sat bishop, which was very remarkable, more than thirty-seven years (God, to square his great undertakings, giving him a long life to his large heart) and died 1242.

ADAM DE MARISCO, or ADAM OF MARSH, was born in this county, where there be plenty of marshes in the fenny part thereof. But I take Brentmarsh as the principal, the most probable place for his nativity. It seemeth that a foggy air is no hindrance to a refined wit, whose infancy and youth in this place was so full of pregnancy. He afterwards went to Oxford, and there became D.D. It is argument enough to persuade any indifferent man into a belief of his abilities, because that Robert Grosseteste, that learned and pious bishop of Lincoln, made use of his pains, that they might jointly peruse and compare the Scripture. He became afterwards a Franciscan friar in Worcester, and furnished the library thereof with most excellent manuscripts; for then began the emulation in England betwixt monasteries, which should outvie other for most and best books. He flourished Anno Domini 1257. I cannot grieve heartily for this Adam's loss of the bishopric of Ely, because Hugh de Balsham his corrival got it from him, the founder of Peterhouse in Cambridge.[1]

SIR MATTHEW GOURNEY was born [1310?] at Stoke-under-Hamdon in this county, where his family had long flourished since the Conquest, and there built both a castle and a college. But our Matthew was the honour of the house, renowned under the reign of King Edward the Third, having fought in seven several signal set battles, viz., 1. At the siege of Algeciras, against the Saracens; 2. At the battle of Benemazin, against the same. 3. Sluys, a sea-fight against the French; 4. Crecy, a land-fight against the same; 5. Ingen; 6. Poitiers, pitched fights against the French; 7. Najára, under the Black Prince, in Spain. His armour was beheld by martial men with much civil veneration, with whom his faithful buckler was a relic of esteem.

But it added to the wonder that our Matthew, who did lie and watch so long on the bed of honour, should die [1406] in the bed of peace, aged ninety and six years, about the beginning of King Richard the Second. He lieth buried under a fair monument in the church of Stoke aforesaid, whose epitaph, legible in the last age, is since (I suspect) defaced.

THOMAS BECKINGTON was born [1390?] at Beckington in this county; bred in New College, doctor in the laws, and dean of the Arches, till by King Henry the Sixth he was advanced bishop of Bath and Wells.

1. A good *statesman;* having written a judicious book to prove the right of the kings of England to the crown of France, notwithstanding the pretenced Salic law. 2. A good *churchman,* in the then notion of the word; professing in his will that he had spent six thousand marks in the repairing and adorning of his palaces. 3. A good *townsman;* besides a legacy given to the town where he was born, he built at Wells, where he lived, a fair conduit in the market-place. 4. A good *subject;* always loyal to King Henry the Sixth even in the lowest condition. 5. A good *kinsman;* plentifully providing for his alliance with leases, without the least prejudice to the church. 6. A good *master;* bequeathing five pounds apiece to his chief, five marks apiece to his meaner servants, and forty shillings apiece to his boys. 7. A good *man;* he gave for his rebus (in allusion to his name) a *burning beacon,* to which he answered in his nature, being a burning and shining light: witness his many benefactions to Wells Church, and the vicars therein; Winchester, New, Merton, but chiefly Lincoln College, in Oxford, being little less than a second founder thereof.

A *beacon* (we know) is so called from *beckoning;* that is, making signs, or giving notice to the next beacon. This bright Beacon doth nod, and give hints of bounty to future ages; but it is to be feared, it will be long before his signs will be observed, understood, imitated. Nor was it the least part of his prudence, that (being obnoxious to King Edward the Fourth) in his lifetime he procured the confirmation of his will under the broad seal of England, and died January the 14th, 1465.

(1) Adam died during the long-disputed election, in which the monastic orders mocked at the ambition of a friar in aspiring to a bishopric. For Hugh de Balsam see Cambridgeshire, p. 52.

RICHARD FITZJAMES, doctor at law, was born at Redlynch in this county, of right ancient and worshipful extraction; bred at Merton College in Oxford, whereof he became warden; much meriting of that place, wherein he built most beautiful lodgings, expending also much on the repair of Saint Mary's in Oxford. He was preferred bishop, first of Rochester, next of Chichester, last of London.

He was esteemed an excellent scholar, and wrote some books, which if they ever appeared in public, never descended to posterity. He cannot be excused for being over-busy with fire and faggot in persecuting the poor servants of God in his diocese. He deceased anno 1522; lieth buried in his cathedral (having contributed much to the adorning thereof) in a chapel-like tomb, built, it seems, of timber, which was burnt down when the steeple of Saint Paul's was set on fire, anno 1561. This bishop was brother to Judge Fitzjames, lord chief justice, who with their mutual support much strengthened one another in church and state.[1]

SIR JOHN FITZJAMES, knight, was born [1470?] at Redlynch in this county, of right ancient and worthy parentage; bred in the study of our municipal laws, wherein he proved so great a proficient, that by King Henry the Eighth he was advanced chief justice of the king's bench. There needs no more be said of his merit, save that King Henry the Eighth preferred him, who never used either dunce or drone in church or state, but men of ability and activity. He sat above thirteen years in his place demeaning himself so, that he lived and died in the king's favour.

He sat one of the assistants when Sir Thomas More was arraigned for refusing the oath of supremacy, and was shrewdly put to it to save his own conscience, and not incur the king's displeasure; for Chancellor Audley, supreme judge in that place (being loath that the whole burthen of More's condemnation should lie on his shoulders alone) openly in court asked the advice of the lord chief justice, Fitzjames, "Whether the indictment were sufficient or no?" To whom our judge warily returned: "My lords all, by Saint Gillian," which was ever his oath, "I must needs confess that if the act of parliament be not unlawful, then the indictment is not in my conscience insufficient."

He died [1542?] in the thirtieth year of King Henry the Eighth; and although now there be none left at Redlynch of his name and family, they flourish still at Leweston in Dorsetshire, descended from Alured Fitzjames (brother to this judge and to Richard bishop of London) whose heir in a direct line, Sir John Fitzjames, knight, I must acknowledge a strong encourager of my weak endeavours.

JOHN HOOPER was born in this county; bred first in Oxford, then beyond the seas. A great scholar and linguist; but suffering under the notion of a proud man only in their judgments who were unacquainted with him. Returning in the reign of King Edward the Sixth, he was elected bishop of Gloucester; but for a time scrupled the acceptance thereof, on a double account.

(1) Actually uncle of the worthy that follows. He built Fulham Palace.

First because he refused to take an oath tendered unto him. This oath I conceived to have been the oath of canonical obedience; but since (owing my information to my worthy friend the learned Doctor John Hacket) I confess it the oath of supremacy, which Hooper refused, not out of lack of loyalty but store of conscience: for the oath of supremacy, as then modelled, was more than the oath of supremacy enjoining the receivers thereof conformity to the king's commands in what alterations soever he should afterwards make in religion; which implicit and unlimited obedience learned casuists allow only due to God himself. Besides, the oath concluded with "So help me God, and all his angels and saints"; so that Hooper had just cause to scruple the oath, and was the occasion of the future reforming, whilst the king dispensed with his present taking thereof.

The second thing he boggled at was the wearing of some episcopal habiliments; but at last, it seemeth, consented thereunto, and was consecrated bishop of Gloucester.

His adversaries will say that the refusing of one is the way to get two bishoprics, seeing afterward he held Worcester *in commendam* therewith. But be it known, that as our Hooper had double dignity, he had treble diligence, painfully preaching God's word, piously living as he preached, and patiently dying as he lived, being martyred at Gloucester, anno 1555.

SIR JOHN CHAMPNEYS, son of Robert Champneys, was born at Chew in this county; but bred a skinner in London, and lord mayor thereof, 1534. Memorable he is on this account, that whereas before his time there were no turrets in London (save what in churches and public structures) he was the first private man who, in his house, next Clothworkers' Hall, built one to oversee his neighbours in the city, which delight of his eye was punished with blindness some years before his death. But seeing "prying into God's secrets is a worse sin than overlooking men's houses," I dare not concur with so censorious an author,[1] because every consequent of a fact is not the punishment of a fault therein. [*d.* 1556]

SIR JAMES DYER, knight, younger son to Richard Dyer, esquire, was born [1512] at Roundhill in this county, as may appear to any by the heralds' visitation thereof, and doth also to me by particular information from his relations.

He was bred in the study of our municipal law; and was made lord chief justice of the common pleas, *primo* Eliz., continuing therein twenty-four years, longer (if my eye or arithmetic fail me not) than any in that place before or after him. When Thomas duke of Norfolk was, anno 1572, arraigned for treason, this judge was present thereat on the same token, that when the duke desired counsel to be assigned him, pleading that it was granted to Humphrey Stafford in the reign of King Henry the Seventh, our judge returned unto him "that Stafford had it allowed him only as to point of law, then in dispute, viz., whether he was legally taken out of the sanctuary; but as for matter of fact, neither

(1) Stow's *Survey of London*.

he nor any ever had, or could have, any counsel allowed him": a course observed in such cases unto this day.

But "let his own works praise him in the gates" is known for the place of public justice amongst the Jews; let his learned writings, called his *Commentaries* or *Reports,* evidence his abilities in his profession.

[*d.* 1582]

SIR JOHN POPHAM, of most ancient descent, was born [1531?] at Huntworth in this county. In his youthful days he was as stout and skilful a man at sword and buckler as any in that age, and wild enough in his recreations. But oh! if quicksilver could be really fixed, to what a treasure would it amount? Such is wild youth seriously reduced to gravity, as by this young man did appear. He applied himself to a more profitable fencing, the study of the laws, therein attaining to such eminency that he became the queen's attorney, and afterwards lord chief justice of England.

Being sent, anno 1600, by the queen, with some others, to the earl of Essex, to know the cause of the confluence of so many military men unto his house, the soldiers therein detained him for a time, which some did make to tantamount to an imprisonment. This his violent detention Sir John deposed upon his oath at the earl's trial, which I note the rather for the rarity thereof, that a lord chief justice should be produced as witness in open court.

In the beginning of the reign of King James, his justice was exemplary on thieves and robbers. The land then swarmed with people which had been soldiers, who had never *gotten* (or else quite *forgotten*) any other vocation. Hard it was for peace to feed all the idle mouths which a former war did breed; being too proud to beg, too lazy to labour. Those infected the highways with their felonies; some presuming on their multitudes, as the robbers on the northern road, whose knot (otherwise not to be untied) Sir John cut asunder with the sword of justice.

He possessed King James how the frequent granting of pardons was prejudicial to justice, rendering the judges to the contempt of insolent malefactors, which made his majesty more sparing afterward in that kind. In a word, the deserved death of some scores preserved the lives and livelihoods of more thousands; travellers owing their safety to this judge's severity, many years after his death, which happened Anno Domini 1607.

NICHOLAS WADHAM [*b.* 1532] of Merefield in this county, esquire, had great length in his extraction, breadth in his estate, and depth in his liberality. His hospitable house was an inn at all times, a court at Christmas. He married Dorothy, daughter to the secretary, sister to the first Lord Petre.

Absalom, having no children, reared up for himself a pillar to perpetuate his name. This worthy pair, being issueless, erected that which hath, doth, and will afford many pillars to church and state, the uniform and regular (nothing defective or superfluous therein) college of Wadham in Oxford. Had this worthy esquire, being a great patron of church-livings, annexed some benefices thereunto (which may be presumed rather forgotten than neglected by him) it had, for completeness of fabric and endowment, equalled any English foundation.

If he was (which some suggest) a Romanist in his judgment, his charity is the more commendable, to build a place for persons of a different persuasion. Whilst we leave the invisible root to the Searcher of hearts, let us thankfully gather the good fruit which grew from it. He died [1609] before his college was finished, his estate by co-heirs descending to Strangeways, Windham, White, &c.; and he lieth buried with his wife under a stately monument in the fair church of Ilminster.[1]

SIR AMIAS [PAULET or] POULET, son to Sir Hugh, grandchild to Sir Amias Paulet (who put Cardinal Wolsey, then but a schoolmaster, in the stocks) was born [1536?] at Hinton Saint George in this county. He was chancellor of the Garter, governor of the Isles of Jersey and Guernsey, and privy councillor to Queen Elizabeth, who chiefly committed the keeping of Mary Queen of Scots to his fidelity, who faithfully discharged his trust therein.[2]

I know the Romanists rail on him as over-strict in his charge; but indeed without cause, for he is no unjust steward who to those under him alloweth all his master's allowance, though the same be but of the scantiest proportion. Besides, it is no news for prisoners (especially if accounting their restraint unjust) to find fault with their keepers merely for keeping them. And such who complain of him, if in his place, ought to have done the same themselves.

When Secretary Walsingham moved this knight to suffer one of his servants to be bribed by the agents of the Queen of Scots, so to compass the better intelligence, he would in no terms yield thereunto. Such conniving at, was consenting to; and such consenting to, in effect, was commanding of such falsehood. Whereupon the secretary was fain to go further about, and make use of an instrument at a greater distance, who was no menial servant to Sir Amias.

He died Anno Domini 1588; and was buried in London, in Saint Martin's-in-the-Fields, where his epitaph is all an allusion to the three swords in his arms, and three words in his motto, *Gardez la Foy* (Keep the Faith). Which harping on that one string of his fidelity, though perchance harsh music to the ears of others, was harmonious to Queen Elizabeth.

JOHN FENN was born at Montacute in this county; bred in New College in Oxford, where he proceeded bachelor in laws, continuing there till, Anno Domini 1562, for his popish activity he was ejected by the queen's commissioners. Then for a time he lived schoolmaster at St. Edmundsbury, till ousted there on the same account. Hence he fled over into Flanders; thence into Italy; whence returning, at last he was fixed at Louvain. He wrote many, and translated more books; living to finish his jubilee, or fiftieth year of exile, beyond the seas, where he died . . . [1615].

(1) For Dorothy his wife see Essex, p. 178. (2) Paulet was keeper of Mary Queen of Scots for the last three years of her life, and was ordered to keep a much stricter watch on her than her previous gaolers.

JOHN GIBBONS was undoubtedly born [1544] in this county, though herein Pits presents us with an untoward and left-handed direction: *Patrica Somersetensis, Diocesis Wintoniensis.* Now either Winchester is imprinted for Wells, or he was born in this county in some peculiar belonging to Winchester, which see hath large revenues about Taunton. Leaving the land for his religion, Pope Gregory XIII collated on him a canon's place in the church of Bonn. This he soon quitted, and became rector of the Jesuit's College in Trèves. He wrote a book against G. Sohn, professor at Heidelberg, in vindication that the pope was not Antichrist. Being indisposed in health, his hearing of the defeat of the Spanish Armada was no cordial unto him, and died anno 1589.

ROBERT PARSONS was born [1546] in this county; bred in Balliol College in Oxford, till for his viciousness he was expelled thence with disgrace.[1] Running to Rome, and there finishing the course of his studies, he with Campion[2] were the first brace of English Jesuits, who returned hither 1580 to preserve this nation. Two years after he escaped hence, and got beyond the seas.

One of a troublesome spirit, wherewith some moderate Romanists were so offended, that, during his abode here, they once resolved to resign him up to the queen's officers. He had an ill-natured wit, biassed to satiricalness. A great statesman, and it was not the least part of his policy to provide for his own safety; who would look on, direct, give ground, abet on other men's hands, but never played so as to adventure himself into England.

He wrote a shrewd book of the *Succession to the English Crown,* setting it forth under the false name of Doleman (a dull secular priest, guilty of little learning and less policy); dedicating the same to the earl of Essex. He had an authoritative influence on all English catholics; nothing of importance being agitated by them but Parsons had a finger, hand, arm therein. He was for twenty-three years rector of the college at Rome, where he died Anno Domini 1610.

SIR JOHN HARINGTON, knight; where born [1561] I know not; sure I am he had a fair estate at Kelston near Bath in this county; and is eminent for his Confessor extraction.

His father, only for carrying a letter to the Lady (afterwards Queen) Elizabeth, [was] by Bishop Gardiner kept twelve months in the Tower, and made to spend 1000 pounds ere he could get free of that trouble.

His mother, servant to the Lady Elizabeth, was, by Gardiner's command, sequestered from her as an heretic, and her husband enjoined not to keep company with her.

Queen Elizabeth was godmother to this Sir John; and he was bred in Cambridge, where Doctor Still was his tutor; but whether whilst he was fellow of Christ's or master of Saint John's, is to me unknown. He afterward proved one of the most ingenious poets of our English nation;

(1) This is unjust. He distinguished himself as a tutor, was popular with his pupils, and was for a time dean and bursar. He was at enmity with the master and fellows, and as a result left or was dismissed. (2) Edmund Campion—see London, p. 365.

witness his translation of *Orlando Furioso* out of the Italian, dedicated to the Lady Elizabeth, since queen of Bohemia, and the several pieces of his own invention.

It happened that while the said Sir John repaired often to an ordinary in Bath, a female attendress at the table, neglecting other gentlemen which sat higher, and were of greater estates, applied herself wholly to him, accommodating him with all necessaries, and preventing his asking anything with her officiousness. She, being demanded by him the reason of her so careful waiting on him, "I understand," said she, "you are a very witty man, and if I should displease you in anything, I fear you would make an epigram of me."

A posthume book of his is come forth as an addition to Bishop Godwin's *Catalogue of Bishops;* wherein (besides mistakes) some tart reflections *in uxoratos episcopos* might well have been spared. In a word, he was a poet in all things save in his wealth, leaving a fair estate to a learned and religious son, and died about the middle of the reign of King James.[1] [*d.* 1612]

SAMUEL DANIEL was born [1562] not far from Taunton in this county;[2] whose faculty was a master of music, and his harmonious mind made an impression on his son's genius, who proved an exquisite poet. He carried in his Christian and surname two holy prophets, his monitors, so to qualify his raptures, that he abhorred all profaneness.

He was also a judicious historian; witness his lives of our English kings, since the Conquest until King Edward the Third; wherein he hath the happiness to reconcile brevity with clearness, qualities of great distance in other authors; a work since commendably continued (but not with equal quickness and judgment) by Mr. Trussell.

He was a servant in ordinary to Queen Anne, who allowed him a fair salary. As the tortoise buried himself all the winter in the ground, so Mr. Daniel would lie hid at his garden-house in Old Street, nigh London, for some months together (the more retiredly to enjoy the company of the Muses) and then would appear in public, to converse with his friends, whereof Doctor Cowel and Mr. Camden were principal.

Some tax him to smack of the old cask, as resenting of the Romish religion; but they have a quicker palate than I who can make any such discovery. In his old age he turned husbandman, and rented a farm in Wiltshire nigh the Devizes. I can give no account how he thrived thereupon; for though he was well versed in Virgil, his fellow husbandman poet, yet there is more required to make a rich farmer than only to say his *Georgics* by heart; and I question whether his Italian will fit our English husbandry. Besides, I suspect that Mr. Daniel's fancy was too fine and sublimated to be wrought down to his private profit.

(1) Harington is now best remembered for his *Metamorphosis of Ajax,* in which he projects the modern privy, and for which Elizabeth banished him from court, not on account of his book's frankness, but because of a supposed innuendo about Leicester. He was deputed by Essex, whom he had accompanied in the ill-starred Irish expedition, to appease Elizabeth's anger, but was ordered, and was very glad, to leave her presence. He charmed by his ready wit, frankness and literary brilliance. Elizabeth referred to him as "that saucy poet, my godson." (2) So am I certified by some of his (late surviving) acquaintance.

However, he had neither a *bank* of *wealth* or *lank*[1] of *want*, living in a competent condition. By Justina his wife he had no child; and I am unsatisfied both in the place and time of death, but collect the latter to be about the end of the reign of King James. [*d.* 1619]

HENRY CUFF was born [1563] at Hinton St. George in this county, as the late Lord Paulet, baron thereof, did inform me, though none of that name left there at this day. He was afterwards fellow of Merton College in Oxford, and secretary to Robert earl of Essex, with whom he engaged in his rising, anno 1600, being arraigned at Westminster for his life. Sir Edward Coke (then but the queen's attorney) disputed syllogistically against him; whom Cuff, an admirable logician, could, *caeteris paribus,* well have encountered. But power will easily make a solecism to be a syllogism. The most pregnant proof brought against him was a verse out of Lucan alleged by him; for when the earl, sitting in consultation with his complices, demanded their advice, whether he should proceed in their design, or desist, Mr. Cuff returned,

> *Viribus utendum est quas fecimus; arma ferenti*
> *Omnia dat qui justa negat.*[2]

This, I may say, proved his neck-verse, being attested against him; for which he suffered. He wrote an excellent book of *The Differences of the Ages of Man's Life;* a rare piece indeed, though not altogether so hard to be procured, as worthy to be perused. [*d.* 1601]

SIR AMYAS DE PRESTON, knight, was descended of an ancient family, who have an habitation at Cricket, nigh Crewkerne in this county. He was a valiant soldier and active seaman; witness in 88, when he seized on the admiral of the galliasses,[3] wherein Hugh de Moncada the governor, making resistance, with most of his men, were burnt or killed, and Mr. Preston (as yet not knighted) shared in a vast treasure of gold taken therein.

Afterwards, anno 1595, he performed a victorious voyage to the West Indies, wherein he took by assault the isle of Porto Santo, invaded the isle of Cocke, surprised the fort and town of Coro, sacked the stately city of Santiago, put the town of Cumana to ransom, entered Jamaica with little loss, some profit and more honour; safely returned, within the space of six months, to Milford Haven in Wales.

I have been informed, from excellent hands, that on some distaste, he sent a challenge to Sir Walter Ralegh; which Sir Walter declined, without any abatement to his valour (wherein he had abundantly satisfied all possibility of suspicion) and great advancement of his judgment; for, having a fair and fixed estate, with wife and children, being a privy councillor, and lord warden of the Stannaries, he thought it an uneven lay to stake himself against Sir Amyas, a private and (as I take it) a single person; though of good birth and courage, yet of no considerable estate. This also is consonant to what he hath written so judiciously

(1) *Lank*=scarcity, leanness. (2) The words of the poet are somewhat different.—F.
(3) *Galliass*=a heavy, low-built vessel, impelled by sail and oars.

about duels, condemning those for ill honours "where the hangman gives the garland."[1] However, these two knights were afterwards reconciled, and Sir Amyas (as I collect) died about the beginning of the reign of King James. [*d.* 1617?]

THOMAS CORYATE. Though some will censure him as a person rather ridiculous than remarkable, he must not be omitted; for first, few would be found to call him fool, might none do it save such who had as much learning as himself. Secondly, if others have more wisdom than he, thankfulness and humility is the way to preserve and increase it.

He was born [1577?] at Odcombe nigh Yeovil in this county; bred at Oxford, where he attained to admirable fluency in the Greek tongue. He carried folly (which the charitable called merriment) in his very face. The shape of his head had no promising form, being like a sugar-loaf inverted, with the little end before, as composed of fancy and memory, without any common sense.

Such as conceived him fool *ad duo,* and something else *ad decem,* were utterly mistaken; for he drave on no design, carrying for coin and counters alike; so contented with what was present, that he accounted those men guilty of superfluity who had more suits and shirts than bodies, seldom putting off either till they were ready to go away from him.

Prince Henry allowed him a pension, and kept him for his servant. *Sweetmeats* and *Coryate* made up the last course at all court entertainments. Indeed he was the courtiers' anvil to try their wits upon; and sometimes this anvil returned the hammers as hard knocks as it received, his bluntness repaying their abusiveness.

His book, known by the name of *Coryate's Crudities,* nauseous to nice readers for the rawness thereof, is not altogether useless, though the porch be more worth than the palace, I mean the preface of other men's mock-commending verses thereon.

At last he undertook to travel into the East Indies by land, mounted on an horse with ten toes, being excellently qualified for such a journey; for rare his dexterity (so properly as consisting most in manual signs) in interpreting and answering the dumb tokens of nations whose language he did not understand. Besides, such his patience in all distresses, that in some sort he might seem cooled with heat, fed with fasting, and refreshed with weariness. All expecting his return with more knowledge, though not more wisdom, he ended his earthly pilgrimage in the midst of his Indian travel [1617].

THE FAREWELL

May He who bindeth the sea in a girdle of sand, confine it within the proper limits thereof, that Somersetshire may never see that sad accident return, which happened here 1607, when by the irruption of the Severn sea, much mischief was, more had been done, if the west wind had

(1) *History of the World.*

continued longer with the like violence. The country was overflowed, almost twenty miles in length, and four in breadth, and yet but eighty persons drowned therein. It was then observable that creatures of contrary natures, dogs, hares, foxes, conies, cats, mice, getting up to the tops of some hills, dispensed at that time with their antipathies, remaining peaceably together, without sign of fear or violence one towards another: to lesson men in public dangers, to depose private differences, and prefer their safety before their revenge.

BRISTOL

BRISTOL, more truly *Brightstow,* that is, *illustrious* or *bright dwelling,* answers its name in many respects: *bright* in the situation thereof, conspicuous on the rising of a hill; *bright* in the buildings, fair and firm; *bright* in the streets, so cleanly kept, as if scoured (where no carts, but sledges, are used); but chiefly *bright* for the inhabitants thereof, having bred so many eminent persons.

It standeth both in Somerset and Gloucester-shires, and yet in neither, it being a liberty of itself; divided into two parts by the river Avon, conjoined with a bridge which, being built on both sides, counterfeiteth a continued street, for which strangers at the first sight do mistake it. The houses of the merchants herein are generally very fair; and their entries, though little and narrow, lead into high and spacious halls; which form may mind the inhabitants thereof of their passage to a better place.

NATURAL COMMODITIES

Diamonds

These are the stars of the earth, though such but dim ones, which Saint Vincent's Rock, near to this city, doth produce.[1] Their price is abated by their paleness and softness, to which we may add their number and nearness; for were they but few and far fetched, their value would be advanced. They are not those unions, pearls so called, because thrifty Nature only affordeth them by one and one; seeing that not only twins, but bunches and clusters of these are found together.

Were this rock of raw diamonds removed into the East Indies, and placed where the beams of the sun might sufficiently concoct them; probably in some hundreds of years they would be ripened into an orient perfection. All I will add is this: a lady in the reign of Queen Elizabeth would have as patiently digested the lie, as the wearing of false stones or pendants of counterfeit pearl, so common in our age; and I could wish it were the worst piece of hypocrisy in fashion.

THE MANUFACTURES

Grey Soap

I behold Bristol as the staple place thereof, where alone it was anciently made; for though there be a place in London, nigh Cheapside, called Soper Lane, it was never so named from that commodity made therein (as some have supposed) but from Alen le Sopar, the long since owner thereof. Yea, it is not above an hundred and fifty years, by the confession of the chronicler of that city, since the first soap was boiled in London; before which time the land was generally supplied with *Castile* from Spain, and grey soap from Bristol. Yea, after that London

(1) These "diamonds" were probably zircon, topaz or fluor-spar.

meddled with the making thereof, Bristol soap (notwithstanding the portage) was found much the cheaper. Great is the necessity thereof, seeing without soap our bodies would be no better than dirt, before they are turned into dust; men, whilst living, become noisome to themselves and others. Nor less its antiquity; for although our modern soap, made of pot-ashes and other ingredients, was unknown to the ancients, yet had they τὸ ἀνάλογον something which effectually supplied the place thereof, making their woollen clear, their linen cloth cleanly. Christ is compared by the prophet to Fuller's soap, in Hebrew *borith,* which word Arias Montanus, in his Interlineary Bible, retaineth untranslated; but in his comment (following the example of St. Jerome) on the place rendereth it *herba fullonum,* expounding it to be *saponaria,* in English *soapwort.* Indeed, both Dodoneus and Gerardus write thereof: "This plant hath no use in physic." Yet, seeing Nature made nothing in vain, soapwort cannot justly be charged as useless, because purging, though not the body, the clothes of a man, and conducing much to the neatness thereof.

THE BUILDINGS

Redcliffe Church in this city clearly carrieth away the credit from all parish churches in England. It was founded by Canynges (first a merchant, who afterwards became a priest) and most stately the ascent thereunto by many stairs, which at last plentifully recompenseth their pains who climb them up, with the magnificent structure both without and within.

If any demand the cause why this church was not rather made the see of a bishop than Saint Augustine's in this city, much inferior thereunto, such may receive this reason thereof: that this, though an entire stately structure, was not conveniently accommodated like Saint Augustine's (formerly a monastery) with public buildings about it, for the palace of a bishop and the reception of the dean and chapter. However, as the town of Hague in Holland would never be walled about, as accounting it more credit to be the biggest of villages in Europe, than but a lesser city; so Redcliffe Church esteemeth it a greater grace to lead the van of all parochial, than to follow in the rear after many cathedral churches in England.[1]

MEDICINAL WATERS

Saint Vincent's Well, lying west of the city, under Saint Vincent's Rock, and hard by the river, is sovereign for sores and sicknesses; to be washed in, or drunk of, to be either outwardly or inwardly applied. Undoubtedly the water thereof runneth through some mineral of iron, as appeareth by the rusty ferruginous taste thereof, which it retaineth though boiled never so much. Experience proveth that beer brewed thereof is wholesome against the spleen; and Dr. Samuel Ward,[2] afflicted with that malady, and living in Sidney College, was prescribed the constant drinking thereof, though it was costly to bring it through the

(1) Yet some have informed me that it only is a chapel-of-ease to the mother-church of Bedminster. (2) See Durham, p. 160.

Severn and narrow seas to Lynn, and thence by the river to Cambridge. But men in pain must not grudge to send far to purchase their ease, and thank God if they can so procure it.

PROVERBS

Bristol milk. Though as many elephants are fed as cows grassed within the walls of this city, yet great plenty of this metaphorical milk, whereby *Xeres* or *sherry sack* is intended. Some will have it called milk, because (whereas nurses give new-born babes in some places pap, in others water and sugar) such wine is the first moisture given to infants in this city. It is also the entertainment of course which the courteous Bristolians present to all strangers when first visiting their city.

SEAMEN

No city in England (London alone excepted) hath, in so short a time, bred more brave and bold seamen, advantaged for western voyages by its situation. They have not only been merchants, but adventurers, possessed with a public spirit for the general good; aiming not so much to return wealthier as wiser; not always to enrich themselves as inform posterity by their discoveries. Of these, some have been but merely casual; when going to fish for cod they have found a country, or some eminent bay, river or haven of importance, unknown before. Others were intentional, wherein they have sown experiments, with great pains, cost and danger, that ensuing ages may freely reap benefit thereof.

THE WORTHIES

THOMAS NORTON was born in this city; and, if any doubt thereof, let him but consult the initial syllables in the six first, and the first line in the seventh chapter of his *Ordinal,* which put together compose,

Thomas Norton of Briseto
A parfet master you may him trow.

Thus his modesty embraced a middle way betwixt concealing and revealing his name; proper for so great a professor in chemistry as he was, that his very name must from his book be mysteriously extracted.

He was scarcely twenty-eight years of age, when in forty days (believe him, for he saith so of himself) he learned the perfection of chemistry, taught, as it seems, by Mr. George Ripley.[1] But what saith the poet?

Non minor est virtus, quam quaerere, parta tueri

[To preserve knowledge is no less a virtue than to seek fresh discoveries]

The spite is, he complaineth that a merchant's wife of Bristol stole from him the elixir of life. Some suspect her to have been the wife of William Canynges (of whom before) contemporary with Norton, who started up to so great and sudden wealth, the clearest evidence of their conjecture.

(1) For George Ripley the alchemist see Yorkshire, p. 650. This Thomas Norton was M.P. for Bristol in 1436, and was employed by Edward IV on embassies.

The admirers of this art are justly impatient to hear this their great patron traduced by the pen of J. Pits and others, by whom he is termed *Nugarum opifex in frivola scientia* [a maker of trifles in a frivolous science]; and that he undid himself, and all his friends who trusted him with their money, living and dying very poor about the year 1477.

JOHN MILVERTON. Having lost the *fore* I must play an *after* game, rather than wholly omit such a man of remark. The matter is not much if he, who was lost in Somersetshire, where indeed he was born, at Milverton, be found in Bristol, where he first fixed himself a friar Carmelite. Hence he went to Oxford, Paris, and at last had his abode in London.

He was provincial-general of his order through England, Scotland and Ireland; so that his jurisdiction was larger than King Edward the Fourth's under whom he flourished. He was a great anti-Wycliffite, and champion of his order both by his writing and preaching. He laboured to make all believe that Christ himself was a Carmelite (professor of wilful poverty) and his high commending of the poverty of friars tacitly condemned the pomp of the prelates. Hereupon the bishop of London (being his diocesan) cast him into the gaol, from whom he appealed to Paul the Second; and coming to Rome, he was for three years kept close in the prison of Saint Angelo. It made his durance the more easy, having the company of Platina the famous papal biographist, the nib of whose pen had been too long in writing dangerous truth. At last he procured his cause to be referred to seven cardinals, who ordered his enlargement.

Returning home into England, he lived in London in good repute. I find him nominated bishop of Saint David's; but how he came to miss it, is to me unknown. Perchance he would not bite at the bait; but whether because too fat to cloy the stomach of his mortified soul, or too lean to please the appetite of his concealed covetousness, no man can decide. He died and was buried in London, 1487.

WILLIAM GROCYN was born [1446?] in this city, and bred in Winchester School, where he, when a youth, became a most excellent poet. Take one instance of many. A pleasant maid (probably his mistress, however she must be so understood) in a love frolic pelted him with a snowball, whereon he extempore made this Latin tetrastic:—

Me nive candenti petiit mea Julia: rebar
Igne carere nivem, nix tamen ignis erat.
Sola potes nostras extinguere Julia flammas,
Non nive, non glacie, sed potes igne pari.

A snowball white at me did Julia throw;
Who would suppose it? Fire was in that snow.
Julia alone can quench my hot desire,
But not with snow, or ice, but equal fire.

He afterwards went over into Italy, where he had Demetrius Chalcondyles and Politian for his masters; and returning into England, was public professor of the Greek tongue in Oxford. There needs no more to be added to his honour, save that Erasmus in his *Epistles* often owns him *pro patrono suo et praeceptore.* He died anno 1519.

ROBERT THORNE was born in this city . . . I see it matters not what the name be, so the nature be good. I confess, thorns came in by "man's curse;" and our Saviour saith, "Do men gather grapes of thorns?" But this our Thorne (God send us many coppices of them) was a blessing to our nation, and wine and oil may be said freely to flow from him. Being bred a merchant tailor in London, he gave more than four thousand four hundred forty-five pounds to pious uses; a sum sufficient therewith to build and endow a college, the time being well considered, being towards the beginning of the reign of King Henry the Eighth.

I have observed some at the church door cast in sixpence with such ostentation, that it rebounded from the bottom, and rung against both sides of the bason, so that the same piece of silver was the alms and the giver's trumpet; whilst others have dropped down silent five shillings without any noise. Our Thorne was of the second sort, doing his charity effectually, but with a possible privacy. Nor was this good Christian abroad worse, in the apostle-phrase, than an infidel at home in not providing for his family, who gave to his poor kindred (besides debt forgiven unto them) the sum of five thousand one hundred forty-two pounds.

He died a bachelor, in the fortieth year of his age, Anno Domini 1532, and lies buried in Saint Christopher's, London.

HUGH ELLIOTT, a merchant of this city who was, in his age, the prime pilot of our nation. He first (with the assistance of Mr. Thorne his fellow-citizen) found out Newfoundland, anno 1527. This may be called Old-found-land, as senior, in the cognizance of the English, to Virginia and all our other plantations.

Had this discovery been as fortunate in public encouragement as private industry, probably before this time we had enjoyed the kernel of those countries, whose shell only we now possess. It is to me unknown when Elliott deceased.

JOHN FOWLER was born [1537] in Bristol; bred a printer by his occupation, but so learned a man, that (if the character given him by one of his own persuasion be true) he may pass for our English Robert or Henry Stephens, being skilful in Latin and Greek, and a good poet, orator and divine. He wrote an abridgment of Thomas [Aquinas'] *Summes,* the translation of Orosius into English, &c. Being a zealous papist, he could not comport with the Reformation; but conveyed himself and his press over to Antwerp, where he was signally serviceable to the catholic cause in printing their pamphlets, which were sent over and sold in England. He died at Namur 1579, and lies there buried in the church of Saint John the Evangelist.

MARY DALE, better known by the name of Mary Ramsey, daughter of William Dale, merchant, was born in this city. She became afterwards second wife to Sir Thomas Ramsey, grocer and lord mayor of London, anno 1577; and surviving him, was thereby possessed of a great estate, and made good use thereof. She founded two fellowships and scholarships in Peterhouse in Cambridge, and proffered much more, if on her terms it might have been accepted. For most certain it is that she would have settled on that house lands to the value of five hundred pounds per annum and upwards, on condition that it should be called the college of Peter and Mary. This Doctor Soams, then master of the house, refused, affirming that "Peter, who so long lived single, was now too old to have a feminine partner," a dear jest to lose so good a benefactress.[1]

This not succeeding, the stream of her charity was not peevishly dried up, with those who in matters of this nature will do nothing, when they cannot do what they would do; but found other channels therein to derive itself. She died Anno Domini 1596, and lieth buried in Christ's Church in London.

TOBIE MATTHEW, D.D. He was born [1546] in the Somersetshire side of Bristol, and in his childhood had a marvellous preservation, when with a fall he brake his foot, ankle and small of his leg, which were so soon recovered to eye, use, sight, service, that not the least mark remained thereof. Coming to Oxford, he fixed at last in Christ Church, and became dean thereof. He was one of a proper person (such people, *caeteris paribus,* and sometimes *caeteris imparibus* were preferred by the queen) and an excellent preacher, Campion himself confessing that he did *dominari in concionibus* [always to the forefront in gatherings of men]. He was of a cheerful spirit, yet without any trepass on episcopal gravity, there lying a real distinction between facetiousness and nugacity.[2] None could condemn him for his pleasant wit, though often he would condemn himself as so habited therein, he could as well not *be,* as not be *merry,* and not take up an innocent jest as it lay in the way of his discourse.

One passage must not be forgotten. After he had arrived at his greatness, he made one journey into the west to visit his two *mothers*: her that bare him at Bristol, and her that bred him in learning, the university of Oxford. Coming near to the latter, attended with a train suitable to his present condition, he was met almost with an equal number who came out of Oxford to give him entertainment. Thus augmented with another troop, and remembering he had passed over a small water a poor scholar when first coming to the university, he kneeled down and took up the expression of Jacob: "With my staff came I over this Jordan, and now I am become two bands."

He died yearly in report, and I doubt not but that in the apostle's sense he died daily in his mortifying meditations. He went over the graves of many who looked for his archbishopric; I will not say they catched a cold in waiting barefoot for a living man's shoes. His wife, the daughter of Bishop Barlow (a confessor in Queen Mary's days) was a prudent and provident matron. Of this extraction came Sir Tobie Matthew, having all his father's name, many of his natural parts, few

(1) So was I informed by Dr. Seaman, late master of that college. [Lazarus Seaman (*d.* 1675) master of Peterhouse 1644-1660.] (2) *Nugacity*=trifling or frivolous idea.

of his moral virtues, fewer of his spiritual graces, as being an inveterate enemy to the protestant religion.[1] [d. 1628]

THOMAS WHITE, D.D., was born [1550?] in this city, and bred in Oxford. He was afterwards related to Sir Henry Sidney, lord deputy of Ireland, whose funeral sermon he made, being accounted a good preacher in the reign of Queen Elizabeth.

Indeed he was accused for being a great pluralist, though I cannot learn that at once he had more than one cure of souls, the rest being dignities. As false is the aspersion of his being a great usurer, but one bond being found by his executors amongst his writings, of one thousand pounds, which he lent *gratis* for many years to the company of Merchant Taylors, whereof he was free, the rest of his estate being in land and ready money. Besides other benefactions to Christ Church, and a lecture in Saint Paul's, London, he left three thousand pounds for the building of Sion College to be a Ramah for the sons of the prophets in London. He built there also a fair almshouse for twenty poor folk, allowing them yearly six pounds apiece; and another at Bristol, which, as I am informed, is better endowed.[2]

Dr. Thomas White died Anno Domini 1624.

THE FAREWELL

I am credibly informed that one Mr. Richard Grigson, citizen, hath expended a great sum of money in new casting of the bells of Christ Church, adding tunable chimes unto them. Surely he is the same person whom I find in the printed list of compounders to have paid one hundred and five pounds for his reputed delinquency in our civil wars; and am glad to see one of his persuasion (so lately purified in Goldsmith's Hall) able to go to the cost of so chargeable a work.

I wish Bristol may have many more to follow his example; though perchance, in this our suspicious age, it will be conceived a more discreet and seasonable desire, not to wish the increase, but the continuance, of our bells; and that (though not taught the descant of chimes) they may retain their plainsong for that public use to which they were piously intended.

(1) This account of Tobie Matthew is extracted from the *Church History*. Early in life he attracted Queen Elizabeth's notice, was preferred bishop of Durham 1596 and archbishop of York 1606. He was entrusted with the detention of Lady Anabella Stuart (next heir to the English throne after James I) who however escaped. The son referred to above is better known than his father. He was a courtier, diplomatist and writer, converted to Roman catholicism and suspected by the puritans as a papal spy. He lived 1577-1655. (2) Thomas White was also founder of the chair of moral philosophy at Oxford.

STAFFORDSHIRE

STAFFORDSHIRE hath Cheshire on the north-west, Derbyshire on the east and north-east, Warwick and Worcester-shires on the south, and Shropshire in the west. It lieth from north to south in form of a lozenge, bearing forty in the length from the points thereof, whilst the breadth in the middle exceeds not twenty-six miles.

A most pleasant county, for though there be a place therein still called Sinai Park (about a mile from Burton) at first so named by the abbot of Burton, because a vast, rough, hilly ground, like the wilderness of Sinai in Arabia; yet this, as a small mole, serves for a foil to set off the fair face of the county the better.

Yea, this county hath much beauty in the very solitude thereof; witness Beaudesert, or the Fair Wilderness, being the beautiful barony of the Lord Paget.

> And if their deserts have so rare devices:
> Pray then, how pleasant are their paradises.

Indeed most fruitful are the parts of this shire above the banks of Dove; butchers being necessitated presently to kill the cattle fatted thereupon, as certainly knowing that they will fall in their flesh if removed to any other pasture, because they cannot but change to their loss.

NATURAL COMMODITIES

The best alabaster in England (know reader, I have consulted with curious artists in this kind) is found about Heighley Castle in this county. It is but one degree beneath white marble, only more soft and brittle. However, if it lie dry fenced from weather, and may be let alone, long the during thereof. Witness the late statue of John of Gaunt in Paul's, and many monuments made thereof in Westminster, remaining without breck[1] or blemish to this day. I confess Italy affords finer alabaster (whereof those *imagilets* wrought at Leghorn are made) which indeed apes ivory in the whiteness and smoothness thereof. But such alabaster is found in small bunches and little proportions; it riseth not (to use the language of workmen) in great blocks, as our English doth. What use there is of alabaster calcined in physic, belongs not to me to dispute. Only I will observe, that it is very cool, the main reason why "Mary put her ointment so precious into an alabaster box," because it preserved the same from being dried up, to which such liquors in hot countries were very subject.

MANUFACTURES

NAILS

These are the accommodators general to unite solid bodies, and to make them to be continuous; yea, coin of gold and silver may be better

(1) *Breck*=breach, blemish.

spared in a commonwealth than nails; for commerce may be managed without money by exchange of commodities, whereas hard bodies cannot be joined together so fast, and fast so soon and soundly, without the mediation of nails.

Such their service for firmness and expedition, that iron nails will fasten more in an hour than wooden pins in a day, because the latter must have their way made, whilst the former make way for themselves.

THE BUILDINGS

I have presented the portraiture of the church of Lichfield in my *Church History,* with the due praise of the neatness thereof. But now, alas! the body thereof is become a very carcase, ruined in our late civil wars. The like fate is likely to fall on the rest of our cathedrals, if care be not taken for their reparations.

TUTBURY CASTLE is a stately place; and I dare take it on the credit of an excellent witness,[1] that it hath a brave and large prospect, *to* it, *in* it, and *from* it: northward it looks on pleasant pastures; eastward on sweet rivers and rich meadows; southward on a goodly forest, and many parks, lately no fewer than twelve, belonging thereto or holden thereof. It was formerly the seat of the Lord Ferrers earl of Derby; and how it was forfeited to the crown is worth our observing.

Robert Ferrers earl of Derby, siding with Simon Montfort against King Henry the Third, was fined at fifty thousand pounds, to be paid *pridie Johannis Baptistae* next following. I know not whether more to admire at the suddenness of payment, or vastness of the sum, seeing an hundred thousand pounds was the ransom set by the emperor on our King Richard the First; and it shaked all the coffers of England in that age (without help of church plate to make it up).

But Earl Robert, unable to advance the money at the time appointed, and unwilling to leave the lords, his bail, under the king's lash, surrendered his lands, and Tutbury Castle amongst the rest, to the clear yearly value of three thousand pounds into the king's hands; redeemable, when he or his heirs should pay down on one day fifty thousand pounds, which was never performed.

The English clergy much pitied John the son of this Earl Robert, who presented a petition to the pope, informing his holiness that the English clergy were willing to give him money by way of contribution to redeem his estate, but durst not, because commanded to the contrary under the pain of the pope's curse; and therefore he craved his apostolical indulgence therein.

Something I find was restored unto him, but Tutbury was too sweet a morsel to return, being annexed to the Duchy of Lancaster. John of Gaunt built a fair castle there, walled on three sides by art, and the fourth by its natural steepness.

DUDLEY CASTLE must not be forgotten, highly and pleasantly seated; and in the reign of King Edward the Sixth well built and adorned by

(1) Sampson Erdeswicke, in his manuscript survey of this shire.

John Dudley duke of Northumberland, whereon a story worth the reporting doth depend.

The aforesaid duke, deriving himself (how truly not yet decided) from a younger branch of the Lord Dudley, thirsted after this castle in regard of the name and the honourableness of the house, some having avouched that the barony is annexed to the lawful possession thereof, whether by purchase or descent. Now finding John de Sutton the Lord Dudley (grandfather to the last baron) a weak man, exposed to some wants, and entangled with many debts, he, by the help of those money-merchants, wrought him out of his castle. So that the poor lord, turned out of doors and left to the charity of his friends for subsistence, was commonly called the Lord Quondam. But, after the execution of that duke, Queen Mary, sympathizing with Edward the son of this poor lord (which Edward had married Katherine Brydges her maid of honour and sister to the Lord Chandos) restored him to the lands and honour which justly belonged to his father.

PROVERBS

Wooton under Weever,
Where God came never.

It is time that this old profane proverb should die in men's mouths for ever. I confess, in common discourse, God is said to *come* to what he doth approve; to *send* to what he only permits; and neither to *go* nor *send* to what he doth dislike and forbid. But this distinction, if granted, will help nothing to the defending of this profane proverb, which it seems took its wicked original from the situation of Wootton, so covered with hills from the light of the sun, a dismal place, as report representeth it. But were there a place indeed where God came never, how many years' purchase would guilty consciences give for a small abode therein, thereby to escape divine justice for their offences.

THE WORTHIES

Edmund de Stafford [*b.* 1344] was brother to Ralph first earl of Stafford, and consequently must be son to Edmund Baron Stafford. His nativity is rationally with most probability placed in this county, wherein his father (though landed everywhere) had his prime seat and largest revenues.

He was by King Richard the Second preferred bishop of Exeter, and under King Henry the Fourth, for a time, was chancellor of England. I meet with an author who doth make him bishop first of Rochester, then of Exeter, and lastly of York.[1] But of the first and last *altum silentium* in Bishop Godwin, whom I rather believe. He was a benefactor to Stapeldon Hall in Oxford, on a three-fold account, viz., 1. *Of Credit;* first calling it Exeter College, whereby he put an obligation on the bishops of that see favourably to reflect thereon. 2. *Of Profit;* adding two fellow-

(1) Mr. Philpot, in his Catalogue of Lord Chancellors. [Edmund de Stafford was the grand-nephew, and not, as stated in the first paragraph, the brother of the first earl of Stafford.]

ships unto it, and settling lands to maintain them. 3. *Of Safety;* which consisteth in good statutes, which here he wisely altered and amended. He sat in his see twenty-four years; and, dying 1419, was buried under an alabaster tomb in his own cathedral.

WILLIAM LICHFIELD, so termed from the place of his nativity, applied himself to a study of divinity, whereof he became doctor, and afterwards rector of All Hallows the Great, in Thames Street, London. He was generally beloved for his great learning and Godly life. He wrote many books, both moral and divine, in prose and verse, one intituled *The Complaint of God unto Sinful Men.* There were found in his study after his death three thousand four score and three sermons of his own writing. He died Anno Domini 1447, being buried under a defaced monument in the quire of his own church.

EDMUND DUDLEY, esq., [*b.* 1462?] was son to John Dudley, esq., second son to John Sutton, first baron of Dudley, as a learned antiquary[1] hath beheld his pedigree derived. But his descent is controverted by many, condemned by some, who have raised a report that John, father to this Edmund, was but a carpenter, born in Dudley town (and therefore called John Dudley) who, travelling southward to find work for his trade, lived at Lewes in Sussex, where they will have this Edmund born, and for the pregnancy of his parts brought up by the abbot of Lewes in learning. But probably some who afterwards were pinched in their purses by this Edmund, did in revenge give him this bite in his reputation, inventing this tale to his disparagement. I must believe him of noble extraction, because qualified to marry the daughter and heir of the Viscount Lisle, and that before this Edmund grew so great with King Henry the Seventh, as by the age of John his son (afterwards duke of Northumberland) may probably be collected.

He was bred in the study of the laws, wherein he profited so well, that he was made one of the *puisne* judges, and wrote an excellent book, compounded of law and policy, which hitherto I have not seen, intituled *The Tree of the Commonwealth.*[2]

But what saith Columella? *Agricolam arbor ad fructum perducta delectat* (a husbandman is delighted with the tree of his own planting when brought to bear fruit.) Judge Dudley knew well how to turn a land into the greatest profit of his prince, which made him employed by King Henry the Seventh to put his penal statutes in execution; which he did, with severity, cruelty and extortion; so that, with Sir Richard Empson, *viis et modis* (*vitiis et modis* rather) they advanced a mighty mass of money to the king, and no mean one to themselves.

King Henry the Eighth coming to his crown, could not pass in his progress for complaints of people in all places, against these two wicked instruments who, with the two "daughters of the horse leech," were always crying, Give, Give; and therefore he resolved to discharge their

(1) Sampson Erdeswicke, MS. (2) This work, in which Dudley argued for absolute monarchy, was not printed until 1859.

protection, and to resign them to justice; so that they were made a peace-offering to popular anger 1510, and were executed at Tower Hill.[1]

ROBERT WHITTINGTON, born at Lichfield, was no mean grammarian. Indeed, he might have been greater, if he would have been less; pride prompting him to cope with his conquerors, whom he mistook for his match. The first of these was William Lily, though there was as great difference betwixt these two grammarians as betwixt a verb defective and one perfect in all the requisites thereof. The two other were William Horman, and Aldrich, both eminent in the Latin tongue; but some will carp at the best, who cannot mend the worst line in a picture, the humour of our Whittington, who flourished 1519.

EDMUND AUDLEY, son to the Lord Audley of Hely in this county, whose surname was Touchet. I am informed by my worthy friend, that skilful antiquary Mr. Thomas Barlow of Oxford, that this Edmund in one and the same instrument writeth himself both Audley and Touchet. He was bred in the university of Oxford; and, in process of time, he built the quire of Saint Mary's therein anew on his own charge, adorning it *organis hydraulicis*, which, I think, imports no more than a musical organ.

He was preferred bishop, first of Rochester, then of Hereford, and at last of Salisbury. He died at Ramsbury, August 23, 1524; and is buried in his own cathedral, on the south side of the altar, in a chapel of excellent artifice of his own erection.

REGINALD POLE was born at Stourton Castle in this county, anno 1500. He was second son into Sir Richard Pole, knight of the Garter, and *frater consobrinus* (a relation which I cannot make out in reference to him) to Henry the Seventh. His mother, Margaret countess of Salisbury, was niece to King Edward the Fourth, and daughter to George duke of Clarence.

This Reginald was bred in Corpus Christi College in Oxford; preferred afterward dean of Exeter. King Henry the Eighth highly favoured and sent him beyond the seas, allowing him a large pension, to live in an equipage suitable to his birth and alliance. He studied at Padua, conversing there so much with the patricians of Venice, that at last he degenerated into a perfect Italian; so that neither love to his country, nor gratitude to the king, nor sharp letters of his friends, nor fear to lose his present, nor hopes to get future preferments, could persuade him to return into England, but that his pensions were withdrawn from him.

This made him apply his studies the more privately in a Venetian monastery, where he attained great credit for his eloquence, learning and good life. Such esteem foreign grandees had of his great judgment, that Cardinal Sadolet, having written a large book in the praise of philosophy, submitted it wholly to his censure. Pole as highly com-

(1) Dudley and Empson were executed on a trumped-up charge of constructive treason, having advised their friends, it was alleged, to arm themselves in the event of Henry VII's death. For an account of Sir Richard Empson see Northamptonshire, p. 432.

mended the work, as he much admired that a cardinal of the church of Rome would conclude his old age with writing on such a subject, applying unto him the verses of Virgil,

Est in conspectu Tenedos notissima fama
Insula, dives opum, Priami dum regna manebant,
Nunc tantum sinus, et statio malefida carinis.

From Troy may th' isle of Tenedos be spied,
Much fam'd when Priam's kingdom was in pride,
Now but a bay where ships in danger ride.

These far-fetched lines he thus brought home to the cardinal, that though philosophy had been in high esteem whilst paganism was in the prime thereof, yet was it but a bad harbour for an aged Christian to cast his anchor therein.

It was not long before he was made deacon-cardinal, by the title of St. Mary in Cosmedin, by Pope Paul the Third, who sent him on many fruitless and dangerous embassies to the emperor and the French King, to incite them to war against King Henry the Eighth. Afterwards he retired himself to Viterbo in Italy, where his house was observed the sanctuary of Lutherans, and he himself became a racking, but no thorough-paced protestant;[1] insomuch that being appointed one of three presidents of the council of Trent, he endeavoured (but in vain) to have justification determined by faith alone.

During his living at Viterbo, he carried not himself so cautiously, but that he was taxed for begetting a base child, which Pasquil[2] published in Latin and Italian verses, affixed in the season of liberty on his lawless pillar.

This defamation made not such an impression on Pole's credit, but that after the death of Paul the Third, he was at midnight, in the conclave, chosen to succeed him. Pole refused it, because he would not have his choice a deed of darkness, appearing therein not perfectly Italianated in not taking preferment when tendered; and the cardinals beheld his refusal as a deed of dulness. Next day, expecting a re-election, he found new morning new minds; and, Pole being reprobated, Julius the Third, his professed enemy, was chosen in his place.

Yet afterwards he became *alterius orbis Papa,* when made archbishop of Canterbury by Queen Mary. He was a person free from passion, whom none could anger out of his ordinary temper. His youthful books were full of the flowers of rhetoric, whilst the withered stalks are only found in the writings of his old age, so dry their style and dull their conceit. He died few hours after Queen Mary, November the 17th, anno 1558.[3]

JOHN DUDLEY, duke of Northumberland, where born [1502?] uncertain, was son to Edmund Dudley, esq. . . . and would willingly be reputed of this county, a descendant from the Lord Dudley therein, whose memory we will gratify so far as to believe it.

(1) By a "racking protestant" is probably meant a protestant only by a strained meaning or stretched interpretation. (2) *Pasquil,* or *Pasquin,* was the name under which anonymous authors of lampoons, etc., shielded themselves. (3) Fuller overlooks the single purpose to which Pole devoted his life, the reconciliation of England with Rome.

He lived long under King Henry the Eighth, who much favoured him; and the servant much resembled his master in the equal contemperament of virtues and vices, so evenly matched that it is hard to say which got the mastery in either of them. This John was proper in person, comely in carriage, wise in advising, valiant in adventuring, and generally, till his last project, prosperous in success. But he was also notoriously wanton, intolerably ambitious, a constant dissembler, prodigiously profuse; so that he had sunk his estate, had it not met with a seasonable support of abbey land, he being one of those who well warmed himself with the chips which fell from the felling of monasteries.

King Henry the Eighth first knighted, then created him Viscount Lisle, earl of Warwick, and duke of Northumberland.[1] And under Queen Mary he made himself almost king of England, though not in title, in power, by contriving the settling of the crown on Queen Jane, his daughter-in-law, till success failed him therein. And no wonder if that design missed the mark, which, besides many rubs it met with at hand, was thrown against the general bias of English affection. For this his treasonable practices he was executed [1553] in the first of Queen Mary, much bemoaned by some martial men, whom he had formerly endeared in his good service in the French and Scottish wars.

RICHARD TARLTON. My intelligence of the certainty of his birthplace coming too late . . . I fix him here, who indeed was born at Condover in the neighbouring county of Shropshire, where still some of his name and relations remain. Here he was in the field, keeping his father's swine, when a servant of Robert earl of Leicester (passing this way to his lord's lands in his barony of Denbigh) was so highly pleased with his *happy unhappy* answers, that he brought him to court, where he became the most famous jester to Queen Elizabeth.

Many condemn his (vocation I cannot term it, for it is a *coming* without a *calling*) employment as unwarrantable. Such maintain that it is better to be a fool of God's making, born so into the world, or a fool of man's making, jeered into it by general derision, than a fool of one's own making, by his voluntary affecting thereof. Such say also he had better continued in his trade of swine-keeping, which, though more painful, and less profitable, his conscience changed to loss for a jester's place in the court, who, of all men, have the hardest account to make for every idle word that they abundantly utter.

Others allege, in excuse of their practices, that princes in all ages were allowed their ἀρητόλογιο whose virtue consisted in speaking anything without control; that jesters often heal what flatterers hurt, so that princes by them arrive at the notice of their errors, seeing jesters carry about with them an act of indemnity for whatsoever they say or do; that princes, overburdened with state business, must have their diversions; and that those words are not censurable for absolutely idle which lead to lawful delight.

Our Tarlton was master of his faculty. When Queen Elizabeth was

(1) These latter creations were under Edward VI.

serious (I dare not say sullen) and out of good humour, he could *undumpish* her at his pleasure. Her highest favourites would, in some cases, go to Tarlton before they would go to the queen, and he was their usher to prepare their advantageous access unto her. In a word, he told the queen more of her faults than most of her chaplains, and cured her melancholy better than all of her physicians.

Much of his merriment lay in his very looks and actions, according to the epitaph written upon him:

Hic situs est cujus poterat vox, actio, vultus,
Ex Heraclito reddere Democritum.

Indeed the selfsame words, spoken by another, would hardly move a merry man to smile; which, uttered by him, would force a sad soul to laughter.

This is to be reported to his praise, that his jests never were profane, scurrilous nor satirical; neither trepassing on piety, modesty or charity, as in which *plurimum inerat salis, multum aceti, aliquid sinapis, nihil veneni.* [*d.* 1588]

SAMPSON ERDESWICKE, esq., was born at Sandon near Stafford in this county, of a right worshipful and ancient extraction. He was a gentleman accomplished with all noble qualities, affability, devotion and learning. 'Tis hard to say whether his judgment or industry was more in matters of antiquity.

Bearing a tender respect to his native county, and desiring the honour thereof, he began a description intituled *A View of Staffordshire,* Anno Domini 1593, continuing the same till the day of his death. A short, clear, true, impartial work, taken out of ancient evidences and records, the copies whereof in manuscripts are deservedly valued for great rarities.[1] This is he who, when I often groped in the dark, yea, feared to fall in matters concerning this county, took me by the hand (oh! for the like conductors in other counties) and hath led me safe by his direction. He was much delighted with decency of God's house, which made him on his own cost to repair and new glaze the church of Sandon, wherein (to prevent neglect of executors) he erected for himself a goodly monument of freestone, with his proportion cut out to the life, and now lieth therein interred. He died April 11, 1603; and let his elogy of Mr. Camden serve for his epitaph, *Venerandae Antiquitatis fuit cultor maximus.*

THOMAS ALLEN was born [1542] in this county, deriving his original from Henry Allan, lord of Bucknall in the reign of King Edward the Second. He was bred in [Trinity College] in Oxford; a most excellent mathematician, where he succeeded to the skill and scandal of Friar Bacon (taken at both, but given I believe by neither) accounted a conjuror. Indeed vulgar eyes, ignorant in optics, conceit that raised which is but reflected, fancy every shadow a spirit, every spirit a devil. And when once the repute of a conjuror is raised in vulgar esteem, it is not in the power of the greatest innocence and learning to allay it. He was

(1) The earliest book devoted solely to the county, and not published until 1717.

much in favour with Robert earl of Leicester;[1] and his admirable writings of mathematics are latent with some private possessors, which envy the public profit thereof. [*d.* 1632]

WILLIAM GIFFORD. Though this ancient and worshipful name be diffused in several counties, I have satisfied myself in fixing him here, as an extract of the family of Chillington. He was a man of much motion, and my pen is resolved to follow him, as able to travel with more speed, less pain and cost.

1. From his father's house he went to, and lived four years in Oxford. 2. Thence (with his schoolmaster) he went over to Louvain, where he got *lauream doctoralem in artibus,* was made master of arts. 3. Then, studying divinity there under Bellarmine, was made bachelor in that profession. 4. Frighted hence with war, went to Paris. 5. Removed to Rheims, where he eleven years professed divinity. 6. Doctorated at Pont-à-Mousson in Lorraine. 7. Highly prized by Henry duke of Guise, and Cardinal Louis his brother, who gave him a pension of two hundred crowns a year. 8. After their death, he went to Rome, where he became dean of St. Peter's [at Lille] for ten years. 9. Returning to Rheims, he was made rector of the university therein. 10. At fifty years of age, bidding farewell to the world, he became a Benedictine at Dieulewart in Lorraine.

Thus far Pitseus (acquainting us that he was alive 1611) on whose stock give me leave to graft what followeth. This Dr. Gifford was afterwards advanced archbishop of Rheims by the favour of the duke of Guise, who is shrewdly suspected to have quartered too heavily on the profit of that place.

However, our Gifford gained so much, as therewith to found not only a convent for English monks at Saint Malo in France, but also at Paris for those of the same profession. Remarkable charity that an exile, who properly had no home of his own, should erect houses for others.

[1554-1629]

WALTER PARSONS, born in this county, was first apprenticed to a smith, when he grew so tall in stature, that a hole was made for him in the ground, to stand therein up to the knees, so to make him adequate with his fellow-workmen. He afterwards was porter to King James; seeing as gates generally are higher than the rest of the building, so it was sightly that the porter should be taller than other persons. He was proportionable in all parts, and had strength equal to height, valour to his strength, temper to his valour, so that he disdained to do an injury to any single person. He would make nothing to take two of the tallest yeoman of the guard (like the gizzard and liver) under his arms at once, and order them as he pleased.

Yet were his parents, for ought I do understand to the contrary, but of an ordinary stature; whereat none will wonder who have read what Saint Augustine reports of a woman which came to Rome (a little before the sacking thereof by the Goths) of so giant-like a height, that she was

(1) Leicester offered him a bishopric, which he refused.

far above all who saw her, though infinite troops came to behold the spectacle. And yet he addeth, *Et hoc erat maximae admirationis, quod ambo parentes ejus* &c. (this made men most admire that both her parents were but of ordinary stature.)

This Parsons is produced for proof that all ages afford some of extraordinary height, and that there is no general decay of mankind in their dimensions; which if there were, we had ere this time shrunk to be lower than pygmies, not to instance in a less proportion. This Parsons died Anno Domini 162-.

WILLIAM MYNERS. Reader, I remember how, in the case of the ship-money, the judges delivered it for law that England being an island, the very middle-land shires therein are all to be accounted as maritime. Sure I am, the genius even of land-lock counties acteth the natives with a maritime dexterity. The English generally may be resembled to ducklings which, though hatched under a hen, yet naturally delight to dabble in the water. I mean, though born and bred in inland places (where neither infancy nor childhood ever beheld ship or boat) yet have they a great inclination and aptness to sea-service. And the present subject of our pen is a pregnant proof thereof.

This William, son to Richard Myners, gent., of Hallenbury Hall, was born at Uttoxeter in this county; who afterwards coming to London, became so prosperous a mariner, that he hath safely returned eleven times from the East Indies, whereas, in the days of our grandfathers, such as came thence twice were beheld as rarities; thrice, as wonders; four times, as miracles.

Much herein, under Divine Providence, is to be attributed to the make of our English ships, now built more advantageous for sailing than in former ages. Besides, the oftener they go, the nearer they shape their course, use being the mother of perfectness.

Yet, whilst others wonder at his happiness in returning so often, I as much commend his moderation in going no oftener to the East Indies. More men know how to get enough, than when they have gotten enough, which causeth their covetousness to increase with their wealth. Mr. Myners, having advanced a competent estate, quitted the water to live on the land; and now peaceably enjoyeth what he painfully hath gotten, and is living in or near Hertford at this present year 1660.

THE FAREWELL

To take our *vale* of Staffordshire. I wish that the pit-coal (wherewith it aboundeth) may seasonably and safely be burnt in their chimneys, and not have their burning ante-dated, before they be digged out of the bowels of the earth. The rather because I have read how, in the year 1622, there was found a coal-mine actually on fire between Willenhall and Wednesbury in this county. I find not by what casualty this English Etna was kindled, nor how long it did continue. And although such combustions be not so terrible here as in the south of Italy, where the sulphureous matter more enrageth the fury of the fire, yet it could not but cause much fright and fear to the people thereabouts.

SUFFOLK

SUFFOLK hath Norfolk on the north, divided with the rivers of Little Ouse and Waveney, Cambridgeshire on the west, the German ocean on the east, and Essex, parted with the river Stour, on the south thereof. From east to west it stretcheth forty-five miles, though the general breadth be but twenty, saving by the sea-side where it runneth out more by the advantage of a corner. The air thereof generally is sweet, and by the best physicians esteemed the best in England, often prescribing the receipt thereof to the consumptionish patients. I say generally sweet, there being a small parcel nigh the sea-side not so excellent, which may seem left there by Nature, on purpose to advance the purity of the rest.

NATURAL COMMODITIES

Cheese

Most excellent are made herein, whereof the finest are very thin, as intended not for food but digestion. I remember, when living in Cambridge, the cheese of this county was preferred as the best. If any say that scholars' palates are incompetent judges, whose hungry appetites make coarse diet seem delicates unto them, let them know that Pantaleon, the learned Dutch physician, counted them equal at least with them of Parma in Italy.

Butter

For quantity and quality this county doth excel, and venteth it at London and elsewhere. The child not yet come to, and the old man who is past the use of teeth, eateth no softer, the poor man no cheaper (in this shire) the rich no wholesomer food, I mean in the morning. It was half of our Saviour's bill of fare in his infancy: "Butter and honey shall He eat."

It is of a cordial or, if I may say, antidotal nature. The story is well known of a wife which, desiring to be a widow, incorporated poison in the butter, whereon her husband had his principal repast. The poor man, finding himself strangely affected, repaired to a physician, who by some symptoms suspecting poison, demanded of his patient which was his chiefest diet. The sick man told him that he fed most constantly on butter. "Eat butter still," returned the physician, "which hitherto hath saved your life;" for it corrected the poison, that neither the malignity thereof, nor the malice of the wife, could have their full operation.

THE MANUFACTURES

Clothing

Here it will not be amiss to insert a passage which I meet with in an industrious antiquary, as relating to the present subject.

The manufacture of clothing in this county hath been much greater, and those of that trade far richer, I persuade myself, heretofore than in these times;

or else the heirs and executors of the deceased were more careful that the testator's dead corpse should be interred in more decent manner than they are nowadays; otherwise I should not find so many marbles richly inlaid with brass, to the memory of clothiers in foregoing ages, and not one in these later seasons. All the monuments in the church of Nayland, which bare any face of comeliness and antiquity, are erected to the memory of clothiers, and such as belong to that mystery.[1]

Some perchance would assign another reason, viz., because monuments formerly were conceived to conduce much to the happiness of the deceased, as bespeaking in their epitaphs the suffrages of the living in their behalf; which error is vanished away since the Reformation; all which being fully believed, weakeneth not the observation, but that Suffolk clothiers were wealthier in former than in our age.

THE BUILDINGS

This county hath no cathedral therein, and the parochial churches, generally fair, no one of transcendant eminency. But formerly it had so manificent an abbey church in Bury, the sun shined not on a fairer, with three lesser churches waiting thereon in the same churchyard.

Of these but two are extant at this day, and those right stately structures:

> And if the servants we so much commend,
> What was the mistress whom they did attend?

Here I meet with a passage that affected me with wonder, though I know not how the reader will resent it. It is avouched by all authors, that Mary, youngest sister to King Henry the Eighth, relict to Louis the Twelfth, king of France, afterwards married to Charles Brandon duke of Suffolk, died on Midsummer Eve, 1533, and was buried in the abbey church in Bury. But, it seems, her corpse could not protect that church from demolishing, which in few years after was levelled to the ground. I read not that the body of this princess was removed to any other place; nor doth any monument here remain to her memory, though her king-brother and second husband survived the destruction of that church.[2] A strange thing! save that nothing was strange in those days of confusion.

As for the town of Bury, it is sweetly seated and fairly built, especially since the year 1608; about which time it was lamentably defaced with a casual fire, though since God hath given them "beauty for ashes." And may the following distich (set up therein) prove prophetical unto the place:

> *Burgus ut antiquus violento corruit igne,*
> *Hic stet dum flammis terra polusque flagrent.*
>
> Though furious fire the old town did consume,
> Stand this, till all the world shall flaming fume.

Nor is the school a small ornament to this town, founded by King Edward the Sixth, being itself a corporation, now (as well as ever) flourishing under Mr. Stephens, the able master thereof.

(1) Weever's *Funeral Monuments*. (2) At the Dissolution her remains were removed to St. Mary's Church, where they now lie.

Amongst the many fair houses of the gentry in this county, Long Melford must not be forgotten, late the house of the Countess Rivers, and the FIRST FRUITS of PLUNDERING[1] in England; and Somerleyton Hall (nigh Yarmouth) belonging to the Lady Wentworth, well answering the name thereof: for here *summer* is to be seen in the depth of *winter* in the pleasant walks, beset on both sides with fir-trees green all the year long, besides other curiosities. As for merchants' houses, Ipswich town (corrival with some cities for neatness and greatness) affordeth many of equal handsomeness.

PROVERBS

Suffolk fair maids. It seems the God of Nature hath been bountiful in giving them beautiful complexions, which I am willing to believe so far forth as it fixeth not a comparative disparagement on the same sex in other counties. I hope they will labour to join gracious hearts to fair faces; otherwise, I am sure, there is a divine proverb of infallible truth, "As a jewel of gold in a swine's snout, so is a fair woman which is without discretion."

THE WORTHIES

SAINT EDMUND, king of the East Angles [*b.* 841]. Hear what falsehoods are huddled together in our English martyrology, written, as he terms himself, "by a catholic priest, permissu superiorum, 1608," page 319, on the 20th November: "At Hexham in Northumberland, the passion of Saint Edmund, king and martyr, who being a Saxon by blood, born in the city of Nuremburg in that province, and nephew to Offa king of the East Angles."

First, Hexham in Northumberland should be Hoxne in this county, where Saint Edmund was martyred. Secondly, there is no city Nuremburg in Britain, nor Europe, save that in Germany.

This is enough to make us distrust what he writeth afterwards, viz., that when the said Saint Edmund was cruelly murdered by the Danes, and when the Christians, seeking his corpse, were lost in a wood, did call one to another, "Where art? Where art? Where art?" the martyred head answered, "Here, here, here." However, God forbid that this author's falsities should make us undervalue this worthy king and martyr, cruelly tortured to death by the pagan Danes, and by an old author thus not unhandsomely expressed:[2]

> As Denis by his death adorneth France:
> Demetrius Greece: each credit to his place:
> So Edmund's lustre doth our land advance,
> Who with his virtues doth his country grace.
> Sceptre, crown, robe, his hand, head, corpse renowns,
> More famous for his bonds, his blood, his wounds.

(1) Fuller probably had in mind the plundering of the house of Lady Rivers, a Roman catholic, at Colchester in 1642. Property valued at £40,000 was destroyed or removed. The House of Commons sent two of its members to restore order in Colchester. (2) *Ex Libro Abbathiae de Rufford*, in Bibl. Cott. [Latin original omitted.]

His death happened Anno Domini 870, whose body was placed in a goodly shrine, richly adorned with jewels and precious stones, at Bury in this county. These all are vanished, whilst the name of Saint Edmund will ever remain in that town's denomination.

ROBERT GROSSETESTE. Possibly the reader, seeing such swarms of popish saints in England, will demand, "Is there not yet a saint of the Lord besides?" And I conceive myself concerned to return a true answer, that there is Robert Grosseteste by name, whom now we come to describe.

He was born [1175?] in this county, bred in Oxford, where he became most eminent for religion, and learning in all kind of languages, arts and sciences; and at last was preferred bishop of Lincoln, 1235. He wrote no fewer than three hundred treatises, whereof most are extant in manuscript in Westminster library, which Dr. Williams (his successor in the see of Lincoln) intended to have published in three fair folio volumes,[1] had not the late troublesome times disheartened him. Thus our civil wars have not only filled us with legions of lying pamphlets, but also deprived us of such a treasure of truth, as this worthy man's works would have proved to all posterity.

He was a stout opposer of popish oppression in the land, and a sharp reprover of the corruptions of the court of Rome, as we have largely declared in our *Church History*. Such the piety of his life and death that, though loaded with curses from the pope, he generally obtained the reputation of a saint.

Bellarmine starts a question, whether one may pray lawfully to him, and paint his picture in the church, who is not canonized by the pope? And very gravely he determineth (a short line will serve to fathom a shallow water) that privately he may do it; and that a picture of such a man may be painted in the church, provided his head be not encompassed with a radiated circle as particular to canonized saints. Thus our learned and pious Robert must want that addition of a glory about his picture; and the matter is not much, seeing, no doubt, having "turned many to righteousness, he doth shine in Heaven as the brightest of the firmament;" whose death happened Anno Domini 1253.

HUMPHREY NECTON [or NECHODUN] was born (though Necton be in Norfolk) in this county; and, quitting a fair fortune from his father, professed poverty, and became a Carmelite in Norwich.

Two *firstships* met in this man, for he hanselled[2] the house-convent, which Philip Warin of Cowgate, a prime citizen (and almost I could believe him mayor of the city) did, after the death of his wife, in a fit of sorrow give with his whole estate to the Carmelites.

Secondly, he was the first Carmelite who in Cambridge took the degree of doctor in divinity; for some boggled much thereat, as false heraldry in devotion, to superinduce a doctoral hood over a friar's cowl, till our Necton adventured on it. For, though poverty might not affect pride, yet

(1) So Mr. Goland, the learned library keeper (lately deceased) informed me.
(2) *Hanselled* = performed the inaugural ceremony.

humility may admit of honour. He flourished, under King Henry the Third and Edward the First, at Norwich; and was buried with great solemnity by those of his order, Anno Domini 1303.

RICHARD DE BURY, son to Sir Richard Aungerville, knight, was born [1281] at Bury in this county, and bred in Oxford, where he attained to great eminency in learning. He was governor to King Edward the Third whilst prince, and afterwards advanced by him to be successively his cofferer, treasurer of his wardrobe, dean of Wells, bishop of Durham, chancellor, and lastly treasurer of England. He bestowed on the poor every week eight quarters of wheat baked in bread. When he removed from Durham to Newcastle (twelve short miles) he used to give eight pounds sterling in alms to the poor, and so proportionably in other places betwixt his palaces. He was a great lover of books, confessing himself *extatico quodam librorum amore potenter abreptum*,[1] insomuch that he alone had more books than all the bishops of England in that age put together, which stately library by his will he solemnly bequeathed to the university of Oxford. The most eminent foreigners were his friends, and the most learned Englishmen were his chaplains until his death, which happened anno 1345.

ELIZABETH DE CLARE, third daughter of Gilbert earl of Clare, and wife to John de Burgh earl of Ulster in Ireland, I dare not say born at, but surely had her greatest honour, from Clare in this county. Blame me not, reader, if I be covetous on any account to recover the mention of her memory, who, anno 1338, founded Clare Hall in Cambridge, since augmented by many benefactors. [1291?-1360]

RICHARD LAVENHAM was born at a market town well known for clothing in this county, and bred, when young, a Carmelite in Ipswich. He made it his only request to the prefect of his convent, to have leave to study in Oxford; which was granted him, and deservedly, employing his time so well there, that he proceeded doctor with public applause. Leland's pencil paints him pious and learned; but Bale cometh with his sponge, and in effect deletes both, because of his great antipathy to the Wycliffites. However his learning is beyond contradiction, attested by the books he left to posterity. Much difference about the manner and place of his death; some making him to decease in his bed at Bristol, others to be beheaded in London (with Sudbury archbishop of Canterbury, and Hales master of St. John's of Jerusalem) by the rebellious crew of Wat Tyler, who being a *misogrammatist* (if a good Greek work may be given to so barbarous a rebel) hated every man that could write or read, and was the more incensed against Lavenham for his eminent literature. [*fl.* 1380]

SIMON OF SUDBURY, alias Tybald, was born at Sudbury, as great as most and ancient as any town in this county. After many mediate preferments (let him thank the pope's provisions) at last he became archbishop of Canterbury. He began two synods with Latin sermons in his own person, as rare in that age as blazing-stars, and as ominous; for they portended

(1) In his book called *Philobiblon*.

ill success to Wycliffe and his followers. However, this Simon of Sudbury, overawed by the God of heaven and John duke of Lancaster, did not (because he could not) any harm unto him. He was killed in the rebellion of Jack Straw and Wat Tyler, Anno Domini 1381.

And although his shadowy tomb (being no more than an honorary cenotaph) be shown at Christ Church in Canterbury, yet his substantial monument, wherein his bones are deposited, is to be seen in Saint Gregory's in Sudbury, under a marble stone sometime inlaid all over with brass, some four yards long and two broad, saith mine eye-witness author,[1] though I confess I never met with any of like dimension; so that in some sense I may also call this a cenotaph, as not proportioned to the bulk of his body, but height of his honour and estate.

SIR JOHN CAVENDISH, knight, was born at Cavendish in this county, where his name continued until the reign of King Henry the Eighth; bred a student of the municipal law, attaining to such learning therein, that he was made lord chief justice of the king's (or upper) bench, July 15, in the 46th of King Edward the Third; discharging his place with due commendation, until his violent death, on the fifth of King Richard the Second, on this occasion.

John Wrawe, a priest, contemporary with Jack Straw and Wat Tyler, advanced Robert Westbroome, a clown, to be king of the commons in this county, having no fewer than fifty thousand followers. These, for eight days together, in savage sport, caused the heads of great persons to be cut off, and set on poles to kiss and whisper in one another's ears.

Chief Justice Cavendish chanced then to be in the county, to whom they bare a double pique; one, because he was honest, the other, learned. Besides, they received fresh news from London, that one John Cavendish, his kinsman, had lately killed their idol, Wat Tyler, in Smithfield.[2] Whereupon they dragged the reverend judge, with Sir John of Cambridge, prior of Bury, into the market-place there, and beheaded them; whose innocent blood remained not long unrevenged by Despencer the warlike bishop of Norwich, by whom this rascal rabble of rebels was routed and ruined, 1381. [*d.* 1381]

THOMAS EDWARDSTON, so named from his birth-place, Edwardstone in this county, a village formerly famous for the chief mansion of the ancient family of Montchensy; bred first in Oxford, then an Augustinian eremite in Clare. He was a great scholar, as his works evidence, and confessor to Lionel duke of Clarence, whom he attended into Italy, when he married Violante, daughter to John Galeazzo, duke of Milan.

J. Pits conceiveth him to have been an archbishop in Ireland, which is utterly disowned by judicious Sir James Ware.[3] And indeed if Bale's words (whence Pits deriveth his intelligence) be considered, it will appear he never had title of an archbishop, *Sed cujusdam Archi-episcopatus curam accepit* (he undertook care of some archbishopric) probably com-

(1) Weever's *Funeral Monuments.* (2) The name of the man who gave the final blow that killed Wat Tyler was actually John Standwich. (3) *De Scriptoribus Hiberniae.*

mended in the vacancy thereof to his inspection. And why might not this be some Italian archbishopric, during his attendance on his patron there, though afterwards (preferring privacy before a pompous charge) he returned into his native country, and died at Clare, anno 1396.

THOMAS PEVERELL was born of good parentage in this county; bred a Carmelite, and D.D. in Oxford. He was afterwards, by King Richard the Second, made bishop of Ossory in Ireland. I say by King Richard the Second, which minds me of a memorable passage which I have read in an excellent author.

It may justly seem strange, which is most true, that there are three bishoprics in Ireland, in the province of Ulster, by name Derry, Raphoe and Clogher, which neither Queen Elizabeth, nor any of her progenitors, did ever bestow, though they were the undoubted patrons thereof; so that King James was the first king of England that did ever supply those sees with bishops; so that it seems, formerly, the great Irish lords in those parts preferred their own chaplains thereunto.

However, the bishoprics in the south of the land were ever in the disposal of our kings, amongst which Ossory was one, bestowed on our Peverell. From Ireland he was removed to Landaff in Wales, then to Worcester in England, being one much esteemed for learning, as his books do declare. He died, according to Bishop Godwin's account, March 1, 1419, and lieth buried in his own cathedral.

JOHN LYDGATE was born [1370?] in this county at a village so called, bred a Benedictine monk in Saint Edmundsbury. After some time spent in our English universities, he travelled over France and Italy, improving his time to his great accomplishment. Returning, he became tutor to many noblemen's sons; and, both in prose and poetry, was the best author of his age. If Chaucer's coin were of a greater weight for deeper learning, Lydgate's was of a more refined standard for purer language, so that one might mistake him for a modern writer.

He lived to be 60 years of age; and died about the year 1451, and was buried in his own convent with this epitaph:

Mortuus saeclo, superis superstes,
Hic jacet Lydgate *tumulatus urna,*
Qui fuit quondam celebris Britanniae
Fama poesis.

Dead in this world, living above the sky,
Intombed within this urn doth Lydgate lie,
In former time famed for his poetry
All over England.

As for the numerous and various books which he wrote of several subjects, Bale presenteth us with their perfect catalogue.[1]

(1) Lydgate is now best remembered for his minor poem *London Lickpenny*, a vivid description of contemporary manners. He described himself as a disciple of Chaucer, and was a voluminous but not a great poet.

SIR SIMON EYRE, son of John Eyre, was born at Brandon in this county; bred in London, first an upholsterer, then a draper; in which profession he profited, that he was chosen lord mayor of the City, 1445. On his own cost he built Leadenhall (for a common garner of corn to the city) of squared stone in form as it now sheweth, with a fair chapel in the east side of the quadrant; over the porch of which he caused to be written, *Dextra Domini exaltavit me* (the Lord's right hand hath exalted me.) He is elsewhere styled *Honorandus et famosus Mercator*. He left five thousand marks, a prodigious sum in that age, to charitable uses; so that, if my sight mistake not (as I am confident it doth not) his bounty, like Saul, stands higher than any others from the shoulders upwards. He departed this life the 18th of September, Anno Domini 1459; and is buried in the church of St. Mary Woolnoth, in Lombard Street, London.

THOMAS SCROPE was born at Bradley in this county (but extracted from the Lord Scrope in Yorkshire) who rolled through many professions: 1. He was a Benedictine, but found that order too loose for his conscience; 2. A Carmelite at Norwich, as a stricter profession; 3. An anchorite (the dungeon of the prison of Carmelitism) wherein he lived twenty years; 4. Dispensed with by the pope, he became bishop of Dromore in Ireland; 5. Quitting his bishopric, he returned to his solitary life; yet so, that once a week he used to walk on his bare feet, and preach the decalogue in the villages round about.

He lived to be extremely aged; for, about the year 1425, clothed in sackcloth and girt with an iron chain, he used to cry out in the street, "That new Jerusalem, the bride of the Lamb, was shortly to come down from heaven, prepared for her spouse; *Revel.* xxi, and that with great joy he saw the same in the spirit."

Thomas Walden,[1] the great anti-Wycliffite, was much offended thereat; protesting it was a scandal and disgrace to the church. However, our Scrope long outlived him, and died aged well nigh 100 years, *non sine sanctitatis opinione,* say both Bale and Pits; and it is a wonder they meet in the same opinion. He was buried at Lowestoft in this county, Anno Domini 1491.

THOMAS WOLSEY was born [1472?] in the town of Ipswich, where a butcher, a very honest man, was his father, though a poet be thus pleased to descant thereon:

> Brave priest, whoever was thy sire by kind,
> Wolsey of Ipswich ne'er begat thy mind.

One of so vast undertakings, that our whole book will not afford room enough for his character; the writing whereof I commend to some eminent person of his foundation of Christ Church in Oxford.

He was made cardinal of Saint Cecily, and died heart-broken with grief at Leicester 1530, without any monument, which made a great wit[2] of his own college thus lately complain:

(1) See Essex, p. 172. (2) Dr. Corbet, in his *Iter Boreale*.

And though for his own store Wolsey might have
A palace, or a college for his grave,
Yet here he lies interred, as if that all
Of him to be remembered were his fall.
Nothing but earth to earth, nor pompous weight
Upon him but a pebble or a quoit,
If thou art thus neglected, what shall we
Hope after death, that are but shreds of thee?

This may truly be said of him, he was not guilty of mischievous pride, and was generally commended for doing justice when chancellor of England.

STEPHEN GARDINER was born [1483?] in Bury St. Edmund's, one of the best airs in England, the sharpness whereof he retained in his wit and quick apprehension. Some make him base-son to Lionel Woodville,[1] bishop of Salisbury; which I can hardly believe, Salisbury and St. Edmundsbury being six score miles asunder. Besides, *time* herein is harder to be reconciled than *place*. For it being granted an error of youth in that bishop, and that bishop vanishing out of this world 1484, Gardiner in all probability must be allowed of greater age than he was at his death.

It is confessed by all that he was a man of admirable natural parts, and memory especially; so conducible to learning, that one saith, *Tantum scimus quantem meminimus.* He was bred doctor of laws in Trinity Hall in Cambridge; and, after many state embassies and employments, he was by King Henry the Eighth made bishop of Winchester. His malice was like what is commonly said of white powder, which surely discharged the bullet, yet made no report, being secret in all his acts of cruelty. This made him often chide Bonner,[2] calling him ass, though not so much for killing poor people, as not for doing it more cunningly.

He was the chief contriver of what we may call Gardiner's Creed, though consisting but of Six Articles,[3] which caused the death of many, and trouble of more protestants. He had almost cut off one who was, and prevented another for ever being, a queen, I mean Catherine Parr and the Lady Elizabeth, had not Divine Providence preserved them. He complied with King Henry the Eighth, and was what he would have him; opposed King Edward the Sixth, by whom he was imprisoned and deprived; acted all under Queen Mary, by whom he was restored, and made lord chancellor of England.

He is reported to have died more than half a protestant, avouching that he believed himself and all others only to be justified by the merits of Christ; which if so, then did he verify the Greek and Latin proverb:

The *'Gardiner'* oft-times in due season
Speaks what is true, and solid reason.

He died at Whitehall of the gout, November the 12th, 1555; and is buried, by his own appointment, on the north side of the quire, over against Bishop Foxe, in a very fair monument. He had done well, if he

(1) See Northamptonshire, p. 431. (2) See Worcestershire, p. 626. (3) The Act of Six Articles, explained in note, p. 30.

had paralleled Bishop Foxe, founder of Corpus Christi College in Oxford, in erecting some public work; the rather because he died so rich, being reported to have left forty thousand marks in ready money behind him.

However, on one account his memory must be commended, for improving his power with Queen Mary to restore some noble families formerly depressed. My author[1] instanceth in some descendants from the duke of Norfolk, in the Stanhopes, and the Arundels of Wardour Castle. To these give me leave to add, the right ancient family of the Hungerfords, to whom he procured a great part of their patrimony, seized on by the crown, to be restored.

ROWLAND TAYLOR. Where born, unknown, though some, without any assurance, have suggested his nativity in Yorkshire; was bred in Cambridge, and became head of Borden Hostel, nigh, if not partly in, Caius College, where he commenced doctor of the laws. Hence he was, by Archbishop Cranmer, presented to the rectory of Hadleigh in this county. He was a great scholar, painful preacher, charitable to the poor, of a comely countenance, proper person (but inclining to corpulency) and cheerful behaviour. The same devotion had different looks in several martyrs, frowning in stern Hooper, weeping in meek Bradford, and smiling constantly in pleasant Taylor.

Indeed some have censured his merry conceits, as trepassing on the gravity of his calling, especially when just before his death. But surely such Romanists, who admire the temper of Sir Thomas More jesting with the axe of the executioner, will excuse our Taylor for making himself merry with the stake. But though it be ill jesting with edged tools (whereof death is the sharpest) yet since our Saviour hath blunted it, his servants may rather be delighted than dismayed with it. No long after, Doctor Taylor set Archbishop Cranmer, who was his patron, a copy of patience, who indeed wrote after it, but not with so steady a hand, and so even a character of constancy. Taylor was martyred at Hadleigh, February 9, 1555.

ROBERT SAMUEL was minister of Bergholt in this county, who, by the cruelty of Hopton bishop of Norwich, and Downing his chancellor, was tortured in prison, not to *preserve* but to *reserve* him for more pain. He was allowed every day but three mouthfuls of bread, and three spoonfuls of water. Fain would he have drunk his own urine, but his thirst-parched body afforded none.

I read how he saw a vision of one all in white, comforting and telling him that after that day he never should be hungry or thirsty; which came to pass accordingly, being within few hours after martyred at Ipswich, August 31, 1555. Some report that his body, when burnt, did shine as bright as burnished silver. *Sed parcius ista.* Such things must be sparingly written by those who would not only avoid untruths, but the appearance thereof. Thus, loth to lengthen men's tongues reporting what may seem improbable, and more loth to shorten God's hand in what might be miraculous, I leave the relation as I found it.

(1) Sir John Harington, in the Bishops of Winchester.

JOHN BALE was born [1495?] at Cove in this county, five miles from Dunwich; and was brought up in Jesus College in Cambridge, being before, or after, a Carmelite in Norwich. By the means of Thomas Lord Wentworth he was converted to be a protestant. This is that Bale who wrote a book *De Scriptoribus Britannicis,* digested into nine centuries, not more beholding to Leland than I have been to Bale in this work and my *Church History*. Anno 1553, February the 2nd, he was consecrated at Dublin bishop of Ossory in Ireland, whence on the death of King Edward the Sixth, he was forced to fly, some of his servants being slain before his eyes; and, in his passage over the sea, was taken prisoner by pirates, sold, ransomed, and after many dangers safely arrived in Switzerland.

After the death of Queen Mary, he returned into England, but never to his Irish bishopric, preferring rather a private life, being a prebendary of the church of Canterbury. One may wonder that, being so learned a man, who had done and suffered so much for religion, higher promotion was not forced upon him, seeing, about the beginning of Queen Elizabeth, bishoprics went about begging able men to receive them. But probably he was a person more learned than discreet, fitter to write than to govern, as unable to command his own passion; and *Biliosus Balaeus* passeth for his true character. He died in the sixty-eighth year of his age, at Canterbury, Anno Domini 1563, in the month of November; and was buried in the cathedral church therein.

SIR NICHOLAS BACON, knight, was born [1509] in this county, not far from the famous abbey of Saint Edmundsbury; and I have read that his father was an officer belonging thereunto. His name, I assure you, is of an ancient gentry in this shire as any whatsoever. He was bred in Benet College in Cambridge, to which afterwards he proved a bountiful benefactor, building a beautiful chapel therein.

He afterwards applied himself to the study of the common law, and was made attorney to the court of wards, whence he was preferred lord keeper of the great seal in the first of Queen Elizabeth, 1558. He married Anne, second daughter to Sir Anthony Cooke of Gidea Hall in Essex, governor to King Edward the Sixth.

He was *condemned* by some who seemed wise, and *commended* by them that were so, for not causing that statute to be repealed (the queen relying on him as her oracle of law) whereby the queen was made illegitimate in the days of her father. For this wise statesman would not open that wound which time had partly closed, and would not meddle with the variety, yea, contrariety of statutes in this kind, whereby people would rather be perplexed than satisfied; but derived her right from another statute which allowed her succession, the rather because lawyers maintain that a "crown once worn cleareth all defects of the wearer thereof."

He continued in his office about eighteen years, being a man of rare wit and deep experience:

Cui fuit ingenium subtile in corpore crasso.

For he was loaden with a corpulent body, especially in his old age, so that he would be not only out of breath, but also almost out of life, with going from Westminster Hall to the Star Chamber; insomuch, when sitting down in his place, it was some time before he could recover himself; and therefore it was usual in that court that no lawyer should begin to speak, till the lord keeper held up his staff as a signal to him to begin.

He gave for his motto, *Mediocria Firma;* and practiced the former part thereof, *mediocria;* never attaining, because never affecting, any great estate. He was not for invidious structures (as some of his contemporaries) but delighted in *domo domino pari;* such as was his house at Gorhambury in Hertfordshire. And therefore when Queen Elizabeth, coming thither in progress, told him, "My lord, your house is too little for you;" "No, madam," returned he, no less wittily than gratefully, "but it is your highness that hath made me too great for mine house." Now as he was a just practiser of the first part of this motto, *mediocria,* so no doubt he will prove a true prophet in the second part thereof, *firma,* having left an estate, rather good than great, to his posterity, whose eldest son, Sir Nicholas Bacon, in this county, was the first baronet in England. He died on the 20th of February, 1579, and lieth buried in the quire of Saint Paul's. In a word, he was a good man, a grave statesman, a father to his country, and father to Sir Francis Bacon.[1]

SIR WILLIAM CORDELL, knight. Wherever he was born, he had a fair estate at Long Melford in this county, and lieth buried in that fair church under a decent monument. We will translate his epitaph, which will perfectly acquaint us with the great offices he had, and good offices he did to posterity:

Here William Cordell doth in rest remain,
Great by his birth, but greater by his brain.
Plying his studies hard his youth throughout,
Of causes he became a pleader stout.
His learning deep such eloquence did vent,
He was chose speaker of the parliament.
Afterwards knight Queen Mary did him make,
And councillor, state-work to undertake;
And master of the Rolls. Well worn with age,
Dying in Christ, heaven was his utmost stage.
Diet and clothes to poor he gave at large,
And a fair almshouse founded on his charge.[2]

He was made master of the Rolls, November 5th, the fifth of Queen Mary, continuing therein till the day of his death, the 23rd of Queen Elizabeth. [*d.* 1581]

SIR THOMAS WENTWORTH [Second BARON WENTWORTH, *b.* 1525] of Nettlestead in this county, of a younger family (confessed by the crescent in his coat) descended from the Wentworths of Wentworth Woodhouse in Yorkshire, was created Baron Wentworth by King Henry the Eighth[3]. He was a stout and valiant gentleman, a cordial protestant, and his family a sanctuary of such professors; John Bale comparing him to the good centurion in the Gospel, and gratefully acknowledging him the cause of his conversion from a Carmelite.

(1) See Westminster, p. 380. (2) At Melford aforesaid. (3) Actually his father was created Baron Wentworth under Henry VIII, and the facts of this first paragraph apply to the father.

The memory of this good lord is much, but unjustly blemished, because Calais was lost, the last of Queen Mary, under his government. It not only abated the queen's cheer, the remnant of Christmas, but her mirth all the days of her life. Yet might she thank herself for losing this key of France, because hanging it by her side with so slender a string, there being but five hundred soldiers effectually in the garrison, too few to manage such a piece of importance.

The Lord Wentworth, the second of June following, was solemnly condemned for treason, though unheard, as absent in France; which was not only against Christian charity, but Roman justice; Festus confessing it was not fashionable amongst them "to deliver any man to die before he, which is accused, have the accusers face to face, and have licence to answer for himself concerning the crime laid against him."[1]

It was well for this lord that he was detained in France till his ransom was paid, and Queen Mary dead, who otherwise probably had lost his life, if he had had his liberty. But Queen Elizabeth coming to the crown, he found the favour, or rather had the justice, to be tried again; and was acquitted by his peers, finding it no treachery, cowardice or carelessness in him, but in Sir John Harlston and Sir Ralph Chamberlain, the one governor of Ruisbank, the other of Calais Castle, for which they were both condemned to die, though their judgment was remitted.[2] This lord was the only person I have read of, who thus in a manner played *rubbers* when his *head lay at stake;* and having lost the *fore* recovered the *after-game.* [*d.* 1584]

SIR WILLIAM DRURY was born [1527] in this county, where his worshipful family had long flourished at Hawstead. His name in Saxon soundeth a *pearl,* to which he answered in the preciousness of his disposition, clear and hard, innocent and valiant, and therefore valued deservedly by his queen and country.

His youth he spent in the French wars, his middle in Scotland, and his old age in Ireland. He was knight marshal of Berwick, at what time the French had possessed themselves of the castle at Edinburgh, in the minority of King James. Queen Elizabeth employed this Sir William, with 1500 men, to besiege the castle, which service he right worthily performed, reducing it within few days to the true owner thereof.

Anno 1576 he was appointed lord president of Munster, whither he went with competent forces, and executed impartial justice, in despite of the opposers thereof. For as the sign of *Leo* immediately precedeth *Virgo* and *Libra* in the Zodiac, so no hope that innocency will be protected, or justice administered in a barbarous country where power and strength do not first secure a passage unto them. But the earl of Desmond opposed this good president, forbidding him to enter the county of Kerry, as a palatinate peculiarly appropriated unto himself.

Know by the way, as there were but four palatinates in England, Chester, Lancaster, Durham and Ely (whereof the two former, many years since, were in effect invested in the crown) there were no fewer

(1) Acts xxv. 16. (2) Both the government and Wentworth were incompetent in the matter, the former tardy in supplies, and the latter neglecting warnings of imminent French attack.

than eight palatinates in Ireland, possessed by their respective dynasts, claiming regal rights therein, to the great retarding of the absolute conquest of that kingdom. Amongst these (saith my author) Kerry became the sanctuary of sin and refuge of rebels, as outlawed from any English jurisdiction.

Sir William, no whit terrified with the earl's threatening, entered Kerry with a competent train, and there dispensed justice to all persons, as occasion did require. Thus, with his seven score men, he safely forced his return through seven hundred of the earl's who sought to surprise him. In the last year of his life, he was made lord deputy of Ireland; and no doubt had performed much in his place, if not afflicted with constant sickness, the forerunner of his death, at Waterford, 1579.

WILLIAM BUTLER was born [1535] at Ipswich in this county, where he had one only brother who, going beyond sea, turned papist, for which cause this William was so offended with him, that he left him none of his estate.[1] I observe this the rather, because this William Butler was causelessly suspected for popish inclinations. He was bred fellow of Clare Hall in Cambridge, where he became the Aesculapius of our age. He was the first Englishman who quickened Galenical physic with a touch of Paracelsus, trading in chemical receipts with great success. His eye was excellent at the instant discovery of a cadaverous face, on which he would not lavish any art. This made him, at the first sight of sick Prince Henry, to get himself out of sight. Knowing himself to be the prince of physicians, he would be observed accordingly. Compliments would prevail nothing with him, entreaties but little; surly threatenings would do much, and a witty jeer do anything. He was better pleased with presents than money, loved what was pretty rather than what was costly; and preferred rarities before riches. Neatness he neglected into slovenliness; and accounting cuffs to be manacles, he may be said not to have made himself ready for some seven years together. He made his humoursomeness to become him, wherein some of his profession have rather aped than imitated him, who had *morositatem aequabilem,* and kept the tenor of the same surliness to all persons.

He was a good benefactor to Clare Hall; and dying 1618, he was buried in the chancel of Saint Mary's in Cambridge, under a fair monument. Mr. John Crane,[2] that expert apothecary and his executor, is since buried by him; and if some eminent surgeon was interred on his other side, I would say that physic lay here in state, with its two pages attending it.

THOMAS CAVENDISH, of Trimley in this county, esquire, in pursuance of his generous inclination to make foreign discoveries for the use and honour of his nation, on his own cost victualled and furnished three ships (the least of fleets) as followeth: 1. The *Desire,* admiral, of 120 tons; 2. The *Content,* vice-admiral, of 40 tons; 3. The *Hugh Gallant,* rear-admiral, of 40 tons; all three managed by 123 persons, with which he set sail from Plymouth the 21st of July, 1586.

(1) So I am informed by Mrs. Crane in Cambridge, to whose husband he left his estate. (2) See Cambridgeshire, p. 60.

So prosperous their winds, that by the 26th of August they had gone nine hundred and thirty leagues to the south of Africa. Then bending their course south-west, January the 7th they entered the mouth of the Magellan Straits; *straits* indeed, not only for the narrow passage, but many miseries of hunger and cold which mariners must encounter therein. Here Mr. Cavendish named a town Port Famine; and may never distressed seamen be necessitated to land there. It seems the Spaniards had a design so to fortify these straits in places of advantage, as to engross the passage, that none save themselves should enter the southern sea. But God, the promoter of the public good, destroyed their intended monopoly, sending such a mortality amongst their men, that scarce five of five hundred did survive.

On the 24th of February they entered the South Sea, and frequently landed as they saw occasion. Many their conflicts with the natives, more with the Spaniards; coming off gainers in most, and savers in all encounters, that alone at Quintero excepted, April 1, 1587, when they lost twelve men of good account, which was the cause that the June following they purposely sunk the rear-admiral, for want of men to manage her.

Amongst the many prizes he took in his passage, the *Great Saint Anna* was the most considerable, being the Spanish admiral of the southern seas, of seven hundred tons. However, our Cavendish boarded her with his little ship (a chicken of the game will adventure on a greater fowl, and leap where he cannot reach) and mastered her, though an hundred and ninety persons therein. There were in the ship an hundred and two and twenty thousand pezos[1] (each worth eight shillings) of gold; the rest of the lading being silks, satins, musks and other rich commodities. Mr. Cavendish his mercy after, equalled his valour in the fight, landing the Spaniards on the shore, and leaving them plentiful provisions.

Surrounding the East Indies, and returning for England, the ship called the *Content* did not answer her name, whose men took all occasions to be mutinous, and stayed behind in a road with Stephen Hare their master; and Mr. Cavendish saw her not after. But he, who went forth with a fleet, came home with a ship, and safely landed in Plymouth, Sep. 10, 1588. Amongst his men, three most remarkable; Mr. John Way their preacher; Mr. Thomas Fuller, of Ipswich, their pilot; and Mr. Francis Pretty, of Eye in this county, who wrote the whole history of their voyage.

Thus having circumnavigated the whole earth, let his ship no longer be termed the *Desire,* but the *Performance.* He was the third man, and second Englishman, of such universal undertakings.

Not so successful his next and last voyage, begun the 26th of August, 1591, when he set sail with a fleet from Plymouth, and coming in the Magellan Straits, near a place by him formerly named Port Desire, he was, the November following, casually severed from his company, not seen or heard of afterward. Pity so illustrious a life should have so obscure a death. But all things must be as Being itself will have them to be. [1560-1592]

(1) In English money 48,800 pounds.—F.

JOHN OVERALL, D.D., born [1560] at Hadleigh in this county, was bred in the free-school therein, till sent to Saint John's; then to Trinity College in Cambridge, whereof he was fellow, and there chosen regius professor, one of the most profound school divines of the English nation. Afterwards, by the queen's absolute mandate, to end a contention betwixt two corrivals, not much with his will, he was made master of Catherine Hall; for, when Archbishop Whitgift joyed him of the place, he returned that it was *terminus diminuens,* taking no delight in his preferment. But his Grace told him, "that if the injuries, much more the less courtesies of princes, must be thankfully taken," as the ushers to make way for greater, as indeed it came to pass. For, after the death of Dr. Nowell, he was, by the especial recommendation of Sir Fulke Greville, made dean of Saint Paul's. Being appointed to preach before the queen, he professed to my father (most intimate with him) that he had spoken Latin so long, it was troublesome to him to speak English in a continued oration. He frequently had those words of the psalmist in his mouth, "When thou with rebukes dost correct man for iniquity, thou makest his beauty to consume away like a moth; surely every man is vanity."

I cite it the rather out of the new translation (something different from the old) because he was so eminent an instrument employed therein. King James made him bishop of Norwich, where he was a discreet presser of conformity, on which score he got the ill-will of many disaffected thereunto, and died anno 1619.

LEONARD MAWE was born at Rendlesham in this county, a remarkable place I assure you, which, though now a country village, was anciently the residence of the kings of the East Angles; where King Redwald, a mongrel Christian, kept at the same time *altare et arulam,* the communion table, and altars for idols.

He was bred in Cambridge; where he was proctor of the university, fellow and master of Peterhouse, after of Trinity College, whereof he deserved well, shewing what might be done in five years by good husbandry to disengage that foundation from a great debt.

He was chaplain to King Charles whilst he was a prince, and waited on him in Spain, by whom he was preferred bishop of Bath and Wells. He had the reputation of a good scholar, a grave preacher, a mild man, and one of gentle deportment. He died Anno Domini 1629.

JOHN BOIS, born [1561] at Elmsett in this county, being son of the minister thereof. He was bred first in Hadleigh school, then in Saint John's College in Cambridge, and was deservedly chosen fellow thereof. Here he (as a volunteer) read in his bed a Greek lecture to such young scholars who preferred *antelucana studia* before their own ease and rest. He was afterwards of the quorum in the translating of the Bible; and whilst Saint Chrysostom lives, Mr. Bois shall not die; such his learned pains on him in the edition of Sir Henry Savile.[1] Being parson of Boxworth in Cambridgeshire, and prebendary of Ely, he made a quiet end about the beginning of our warlike disturbances. [*d.* 1644]

(1) See Yorkshire, p. 659.

SIR ROBERT NAUNTON was born [1563] in this county, of right ancient extraction; some avouching that his family were here before, others that they came in with the Conqueror, who rewarded the chief of that name for his service with a great inheritrix given him in marriage, insomuch that his lands were then estimated at (a vast sum in my judgment) seven hundred pounds a year. For a long time they were patrons of Alderton in this county, where I conceive Sir Robert was born.

He was first bred fellow commoner in Trinity College, and then fellow of Trinity Hall, in Cambridge. He was proctor of the university, Anno Domini 1600-1, which office, according to the Old Circle, returned not to that college but once in forty-four years. He addicted himself from his youth to such studies as did tend to accomplish him for public employment. I conceive his most excellent piece, called *Fragmenta Regalia,* set forth since his death, was a fruit of his younger years.

He was afterwards sworn secretary of state to King James on Thursday the eighth of January, 1618; which place he discharged with great ability and dexterity. And I hope it will be no offence here to insert a pleasant passage. One Mr. Wiemark, a wealthy man, great novilant,[1] and constant Paul's walker, hearing the news that day of the beheading of Sir Walter Ralegh, "His head," said he, "would do very well on the shoulders of Sir Robert Naunton, secretary of state." These words were complained of, and Wiemark summoned to the privy council, where he pleaded for himself that he intended no disrespect to Mr. Secretary, whose known worth was above all detraction; only he spake in reference to an old proverb, "Two heads are better than one." And so for the present he was dismissed. Not long after, when rich men were called on for a contribution to Saint Paul's, Wiemark at the council-table subscribed a hundred pounds, but Mr. Secretary told him two hundred were better than one; which, betwixt fear and charity, Wiemark was fain to subscribe.

He died Anno Domini 1635, leaving one daughter, Penelope, who was first married to Paul Viscount Bayning, and after to Philip Lord Herbert, eldest son to Philip fourth earl of Pembroke.

WILLIAM ALABASTER was born [1567] at Hadleigh in this county, and by marriage was nephew to Doctor John Still,[2] bishop of Bath and Wells. He was bred fellow in Trinity College in Cambridge. A most rare poet as any our age or nation hath produced; witness his tragedy of *Roxana,* admirably acted in that college, and so pathetically, that a gentlewoman present thereat (reader, I had it from an author whose credit it is sin with me to suspect) at the hearing of the last words thereof, *sequar, sequar,* so hideously pronounced, fell distracted, and never after fully recovered her senses.

He attended chaplain in [the] Calais voyage on Robert earl of Essex, where he was so affected with the beauty of popish churches, and the venerable respect the papists gave to their priests, that he staggered in his own religion. There wanted not those of the Romish party to force his

(1) *Novilant,* here probably meaning a commentator on current affairs or a gossip.
(2) See Lincolnshire, p. 339.

fall whom they found reeling; working on his ambition, who complained of the slowness of preferment in England, which followed not so fast as in due time to overtake his deserts; so that soon after he turned a papist.

Yet it was not long before he was out of love with that persuasion; so that, whether because he could not comport with their discipline, who would have made him (who conceived himself at the top) begin again, according to their course, at the bottom of humane learning; or because (which I rather charitably believe) that upon second thoughts he seriously disgusted the Romish superstition, he returned into his own country.

It was not long before he was made prebendary of Saint Paul's, and rector of the rich parsonage of Therfield in Hertfordshire. He was an excellent Hebrician, and well skilled in cabalistical learning; witness his *clerum*[1] in Cambridge, when he commenced doctor in divinity, taking for his text the first words of the first book of Chronicles, "Adam, Seth, Enos."

Besides the literal sense, as they are proper names of the patriarchs, he mined for a mystical meaning: man is put or placed for pain and trouble.

How well this agreeth with the original belongs not to me to inquire. This I know, it had been hard (if not impossible) for him to hold on the same rate, and reduce the proper names in the genealogies following to such an appellativeness as should compose a continued sense. He died Anno Domini 1640.

SIR ROBERT HITCHAM, knight, and serjeant-at-law, was born [1572?] if not at, near Nacton in this county, and was very skilful in our common law. By his practice he got a great estate, and purchased the fair manor of Framlingham of the earl of Suffolk. Herein he met with many difficulties, knots which would have made another man's axe turn edge to hew them off; so that, had he not been one of a sharp wit, strong brains, powerful friends, plentiful purse and indefatigable diligence, he had never cleared the title thereof to him and his heirs.

I am willing to believe that gratitude to God (who gave him to wade through so many incumbrances, and land safely at last on the peaceable possession of his purchase) was the main motive inclining him to leave a great part of his estate to pious uses, and principally to Pembroke Hall in Cambridge. [*d.* 1636]

RICHARD SIBBES was born [1577] in the edge of this county (yet so that Essex seemeth to have no share in him) nigh Sudbury, and was bred fellow of Saint John's College in Cambridge. He proved afterwards a most profitable preacher to the Honourable Society of Grays Inn, whence he was chosen master of Saint Catherine's Hall in Cambridge. He found the house in a mean condition, the wheel of Saint Catherine having stood still (not to say gone backwards) for some years together; he left it replenished with scholars, beautified with buildings, better endowed with revenues. He was most eminent for that grace which is most worth, yet cost the least to keep it, viz., Christian humility. Of all

(1) *Clerum* = a Latin sermon preached on certain occasions.

points of divinity he most frequently pressed that of Christ's Incarnation; and if the angels desired to pry into that mystery, no wonder if this angelical man had a longing to look therein. A learned divine imputed this good doctor's humility to his much meditating on that point of Christ's humiliation, when he took our flesh upon him. If it be true what some hold in physic, that *omne par nutrit suum par* (that the vitals of our body are most strengthened by feeding on such meat as are likest unto them) I see no absurdity to maintain that men's souls improve most in those graces whereon they have most constant meditation, whereof this worthy doctor was an eminent instance. He died in the 58th year of his age, Anno Domini 1635.

SAMUEL WARD was born [1577] at Haverhill in this county, where his father had long been a painful minister of the place and I remember I have read this epitaph written on his monument in the chancel there, which I will endeavour to translate:

> *Quo si quis scivit scitius,*
> *Aut si quis docuit doctius;*
> *At rarus vixit sanctius,*
> *Et nullus tonuit fortius.*
> Grant some of knowledge greater store,
> More learned some in teaching;
> Yet few in life did lighten more,
> None thundered more in preaching.

He bred his son Samuel in Cambridge, in Sidney College, whereof he became fellow, being an excellent artist, linguist, divine and preacher. He had a sanctified fancy, dexterous in designing expressive pictures, representing much matter in a little model.

From Cambridge he was preferred minister *in* or rather *of* Ipswich, having a care over, and a love from, all the parishes in that populous place. Indeed he had a magnific virtue (as if he had learned it from the loadstone, in whose qualities he was so knowing) to attract people's affections. Yet he found foes as well as friends, who complained of him to the high commission, where he met with some molestation.

He had three brethren ministers, on the same token that some have said, that these four put together would not make up the abilities of their father. Nor were they themselves offended with this hyperbole, to have the branches lessened to greaten their root. One of them, lately dead, was beneficed in Essex; and, following the counsel of the poet,

> *Ridentem dicere verum,*
> *Quis vetat?*
> What doth forbid but one may smile,
> And also tell the truth the while?

hath in a jesting way, in some of his books, delivered much smart truth of the present times. Mr. Samuel died 1640.

RALPH BROWNRIG, D.D., was born [1592] at Ipswich, of parents of merchantly condition. His father died in his infancy, and his mother did not carelessly cast away his youth (as the first broachings of a vessel[1])

(1) i.e., as liquor is spilled when a barrel is tapped.

but improved it in his education at school, till he was sent to Pembroke Hall in Cambridge, and afterwards became scholar and fellow thereof.

King James, coming to Cambridge, was (amongst others) entertained with a philosophy act and Mr. Brownrig was appointed to perform the *joco-serious* part thereof; who did both, to the wonder of the hearers.

Herein he was *like* himself, that he could on a sudden be so *unlike* himself, and instantly vary his words and matter from mirth to solidity. No man had more ability, or less inclination, to be satirical, in which kind *posse et nolle* is a rarity indeed. He had wit at will, but so that he made it his page, not privy councillor, to obey, not direct his judgment. He carried learning enough *in numerato* about him in his pockets for any discourse, and had much more at home in his chests for any serious dispute. It is hard to say whether his loyal memory, quick fancy, solid judgment or fluent utterance were most to be admired, having not only *flumen* but *fulmen eloquentiae,* being one who did teach with authority.

When commencing bachelor in divinity, he chose for his text, *Vobis autem,* &c. (it is given to you, not only to believe but suffer in the behalf of Christ) a text somewhat prophetical to him, who in the *sequele* of his life met with affronts to exercise his prudence and patience, being afterwards *defied* by some, who almost *deified* him before, in whose eyes he seemed the *blacker* for wearing *white* sleeves when, 1641, made bishop of Exeter.

I was present at his consecration sermon, made by his good friend Doctor Young, taking for his text, "The waters are risen, O Lord, the waters are risen," &c.; wherein he very gravely complained of the many invasions which popular violence made on the privileges of church and state. This bishop himself was soon sadly sensible of such inundations; and yet, by the *procerity*[1] of his parts and piety, he not only safely waded through them himself, but also (when vice-chancellor of Cambridge) by his prudence raised such banks, that those overflowings were not so destructive as otherwise they would have been to the university.

He continued constant to the church of England, a champion of the needful use of the liturgy, and for the privileges of ordination to belong to bishops alone. Unmoveable he was in his principles of loyalty; witness this instance. O.P.,[2] with some shew of respect unto him, demanded the bishop's judgment (non-plussed it seems himself) in some business; to whom he returned, "My lord, the best counsel I can give you is, Give unto Caesar the things that are Caesar's, and unto God the things that are God's;" with which free answer O.P. was rather silenced than satisfied.

About a year before his death, he was invited by the Society of both Temples to be their preacher, admirably supplying that place, till strong fits of the stone, with hydropical inclinations, and other distempers incident to plethoric bodies, caused his death.

I know all accidents are minuted and momented by Divine Providence; and yet I hope I may say without sin, his was an untimely death, not to himself (prepared thereunto) but as to his longer life; which the prayers of pious people requested, the need of the church required, the date of

(1) *Procerity* = loftiness. (2) i.e., Oliver the Protector.

nature could have permitted, but the pleasure of God (to which all must submit) denied. Otherwise he would have been most instrumental to the composure of church differences, the deserved opinion of whose goodness had peaceable possession in the hearts of the presbyterian party. I observed at his funeral that the prime persons of all persuasions were present, whose judgments going several ways met all in a general grief for his decease. He was buried on the cost of both Temples, to his great but their greater honour.

The reader is referred for the rest to the memorials of his life, written by the learned Doctor John Gauden, who preached his funeral sermon, and since hath succeeded him both in the Temple, and bishopric of Exeter. His dissolution happened in the 67th year of his age, December 7, 1659; and was buried the week following in the Temple Church.

SIR SIMONDS D'EWES [b. 1602]. This Sir Simonds was grandchild unto Gerard D'Ewes, descended of the ancient stem of Des Ewes, dynasts or lords of the Dition of Kessel in the Duchy of Guelderland; who came first thence when that province was wasted with civil war, in the beginning of King Henry the Eighth.

He was bred in Cambridge, as appeared by his printed speech (made in the Long Parliament) wherein he endeavoured to prove it more ancient than Oxford. His genius addicted him to the study of antiquity; preferring rust before brightness, and more conforming his mind to the garb of the former than mode of the modern times. He was studious in Roman coin, to discriminate true ones from such as were cast and counterfeit. He passed not for price to procure a choice piece; and was no less careful in conserving, than curious in culling, many rare records. He had plenty of precious medals, out of which a methodical architect might contrive a fair fabric for the benefit of posterity. His treasury afforded things as well new as old, on the token that he much admired that the ordinances and orders of the late Long Parliament did in bulk and number exceed all the statutes made since the Conquest. He was loving to learned men, to whom he desired to do all good offices.[1]

[*d.* 1650]

THE FAREWELL

To conclude our description of Suffolk, I wish that therein grain of all kinds may be had at so reasonable rates, that rich and poor may be contented therewith. But if a famine should happen here, let the poor not distrust Divine Providence, whereof their grandfathers had so admirable a testimony, 1586, when, in a general dearth all over England, plenty of pease did grow on the sea-shore near Dunwich (never set or sown by human industry) which, being gathered in full ripeness, much abated the high prices in the markets, and preserved many hundreds of hungry families from famishing.

(1) D'Ewes was high sheriff for Suffolk, 1639; M.P. for Sudbury, and expelled from parliament in Pride's Purge, 1648. He was the author of *Journals of all the Parliaments during the Reign of Queen Elizabeth* and an *Autobiography*, documents of primary importance for their respective periods.

SURREY

SURREY hath Middlesex (divided by the Thames) on the north, Kent on the east, Sussex on the south, Hampshire and Berkshire on the west. It may be allowed to be a square (besides its angular expatiation in the south-west) of two-and-twenty miles; and is not unproperly compared to a cinnamon tree, whose bark is far better than the body thereof; for the skirts and borders bounding this shire are rich and fruitful, whilst the ground in the inward parts thereof is very hungry and barren, though, by reason of the clear air and clean ways, full of many genteel habitations.

NATURAL COMMODITIES

Fuller's Earth

The most and best of this kind in England (not to say Europe) is digged up nigh Reigate in this county. It is worth 4d. a bushel at the pit, 16d. at the wharf in London, 3s. at Newbury, and westward twice as dear. Double the use thereof in making cloth, to scour out stains and to thicken it, or (to use the tradesman's term) to bring it to proof. Though the transporting thereof be by law forbidden, yet private profit so prepondereth the public, that ships ballasted therewith are sent over into Holland, where they have such magazines of this earth, that they are ready (on their own rates) to furnish us therewith, if there should be any occasion.

And now we are mentioning of earth, near Nonsuch is a vein of potter's earth, much commended in its kind, of which crucibles are made for the melting of gold, and many other necessary utensils.

Walnuts

As in this county, and in Carshalton especially, there be excellent trouts, so are there plenty of the best walnuts in the same place, as if nature had observed the rule of physic, *post pisces nuces.* Some difficulty there is in *cracking* the name thereof: why *walnuts,* having no affinity with the *wall,* whose substantial trees need to borrow nothing thence for their support? Nor are they so called because *walled* with shells, which is common to all other nuts. The truth is, *gual* or *wall* in the old Dutch signifieth *strange* or *exotic* (whence *Welsh,* that is, *foreigners*); these nuts being no natives of England or Europe, and probably first fetched from Persia, because called *nux Persique* in the French tongue.

Surely, some precious worth is in the kernels thereof (though charged to be somewhat obstructive, and stopping of the stomach) because provident nature hath wrapped them in so many coverts; a thick green one (falling off when ripe) an hard yellowish and a bitter blackish one. As for the timber of the walnut tree, it may be termed an English Shittim-wood for the fineness, smoothness and durableness thereof; whereof the best tables, with stocks of guns, and other manufactures, are made.

Box

The best which England affords groweth about Dorking in this county, yet short in goodness of what is imported out of Turkey. Though the smell and shade thereof be accounted unwholesome, not only pretty toys for children, but useful tools for men, and especially mathematical instruments, are made thereof. But it is generally used for combs, as also by such as grave pictures and arms in wood, as better because harder than pear-tree for that purpose. For mine own part, let me speak it with thankfulness to two good lords and patrons, it hath not cost me so much in wood and timber of all kinds, for the last ten years, as for box for one twelvemonth.

MANUFACTURES

Gardening

I mean not such which is only for pleasure (whereof Surrey hath more than a share with other shires) to feast the sight and smell with flowers and walks, whilst the rest of the body is famished, but such as is for profit, which some seventy years since was first brought into this county, before which time great deficiency thereof in England.

For we fetched most of our cherries from Flanders, apples from France; and hardly had a mess of rathripe pease but from Holland, which were dainties for ladies: they came so far, and cost so dear. Since gardening hath crept out of Holland to Sandwich in Kent, and thence into this county, where though they have given six pounds an acre and upward, they have made their rent, lived comfortably, and set many people on work.

Oh, the incredible profit by digging of ground! For though it is confessed that the plough beats the spade out of distance for speed (almost as much as the press beats the pen) yet what the spade wants in the quantity of the ground it manureth, it recompenseth with the plenty of the fruit it yieldeth; that which is set multiplying a hundred-fold more than what is sown.

'Tis incredible how many poor people in London live thereon, so that in some seasons gardens feed more poor people than the field. It may be hoped that in process of time aniseeds, cumin seeds, caraway seeds (yea, rice itself) with other garden ware now brought from beyond the seas, may hereafter grow in our land, enough for its use, especially if some ingenious gentlemen would encourage the industrious gardeners by letting ground on reasonable rates unto them.

Tapestry

Pass we from gardening, a kind of *tapestry* in earth, to tapestry, a kind of *gardening* in cloth. The making hereof was either unknown or unused in England, till about the end of the reign of King James, when he gave two thousand pounds to Sir Francis Crane, to build therewith a house at Mortlake for that purpose.[1] Here they only imitated old

(1) Sir Francis Crane (*d.* 1636) was director of the tapestry works set up at Mortlake by James I.

patterns until they had procured one Francis Clein, a German, to be their designer.

This F. Clein was born at Rostock, but bred in the court of the king of Denmark at Copenhagen. To improve his skill he travelled into Italy, and lived at Venice, and became first known unto Sir Henry Wotton, who was the English lieger there. Indeed there is a stiff contest betwixt the Dutch and Italians, which should exceed in this mystery; and therefore Clein endeavoured to unite their perfections. After his return to Denmark, he was invited thence into England by Prince Charles, a virtuoso, judicious in all liberal mechanical arts, which proceeded on due proportion. And though Clein chanced to come over in his absence (being then in Spain) yet King James gave order for his entertainment, allowing him liberal accommodations.

THE BUILDINGS

There are two most beautiful palaces in this county, both built by kings. First, *Richmond,* by King Henry the Seventh, most pleasantly seated on the Thames; a building much beholding to Mr. Speed representing it in his map of this county. Otherwise (being now plucked down) the form and fashion thereof had for the future been forgotten.

Nonsuch, the other, built by King Henry the Eighth, whereof our English antiquary[1] hath given such large commendations. Indeed, what Sebastianus Cerlius, most skilful in building, spake of the Pantheon at Rome, may be applied to this pile, that it is *ultimum exemplar consummatae architecturae.*

But grant it a *none-such* for building, on which account this and Windsor Castle are only taken notice of in the description of Sebastian Braune; yet, in point of clean and neat situation, it hath *some-such,* not to say some *above-such.* Witness Wimbledon in this county, a daring structure, built by Sir Thomas Cecil in eighty-eight, when the Spaniards invaded, and (blessed be God) were conquered by our nation.

MEDICINAL WATERS

Epsom

They were found on this occasion some two-and-forty years since (which falleth out to be 1618). One Henry Wicker, in a dry summer and great want of water for cattle, discovered, in the concave of a horse or neat's footing, some water standing. His suspicion that it was the stale of some beast was quickly confuted by the clearness thereof. With his pad-staff he did dig a square hole about it, and so departed.

Returning the next day, with some difficulty he recovered the same place (as not sufficiently particularized to his memory in so wide a common) and found the hole he had made, filled and running over with most clear water. Yet cattle, though tempted with thirst, would not drink thereof, as having a mineral taste therein.

It is resolved that it runneth through some veins of alum, and at first was only used outwardly for the healing of sores. Indeed simple wounds

(1) Camden's *Britannia.*

have been soundly and suddenly cured therewith, which is imputed to the abstersiveness[1] of this water, keeping a wound clean, till the balsam of Nature doth recover it. Since, it hath been inwardly taken, and (if the inhabitants may be believed) diseases have here met with their cure, though they came from contrary causes. Their convenient distance from London addeth to the reputation of these waters; and no wonder if citizens coming thither, from the worst of smokes into the best of airs, find in themselves a perfective alteration.

THE WONDERS

There is a river in this county which, at a place called the Swallow, sinketh unto the earth, and surgeth again some two miles off, nigh Leatherhead; so that it runneth (not in an entire stream) but as it can find and force its own passage the interjacent distance under the earth. I listen not to the country people telling it was experimented by a goose, which was put in, and came out again with life, though without feathers; but hearken seriously to those who judiciously impute the subsidency of the earth in the interstice aforesaid to some underground hollowness made by that water in the passage thereof. This river is more properly termed *Mole,* than that in Spain is on the like occasion called *Anas,* that is a duck or drake. For *moles* (as our Surrey river) work under ground, whilst *ducks* (which *Anas* doth not) dive under water; so that the river Alpheus may more properly be intituled *Anas,* if it be true, what is reported thereof, that, springing in Peloponnesus, it runneth under the sea, and riseth up again in Sicily.

Nor may we forget a vault (wherein the finest sand I ever saw) nigh Reigate, capable conveniently to receive five hundred men; which subterranean castle in ancient time was the receptacle of some great person, having several rooms therein. If it be merely natural, it doth curiously imitate art; if purely artificial, it doth most lively simulate Nature.

PROVERBS

The vale of Holmsdale
Never won, ne ever shall.

This proverbial rhyme hath one part of history, the other of prophecy therein; and if, on examination, we find the first to be true, we may believe the other the better.

Holmsdale lieth partly in this shire, and partly in Kent; and indeed hath been happy in this respect, that several battles being fought therein and thereabouts, betwixt our Saxon kings, the true owners of the land, and the Danes, the former proved victorious. Thus was not Holmsdale won *pro una et altera et tertia vice.*

But I hope I may humbly mind the men of Holmsdale, that when King William the Conqueror had vanquished King Harold at Battle in Sussex, he marched with his army directly to London, through the very middle and bowels of Holmsdale; and was it not won at that time? However, if this vale hath not been won hitherto, I wish and hope it never may be hereafter, by a foreign nation invading it.

(1) *Abstersiveness* = having the quality of cleansing or purging.

THE WORTHIES

NICHOLAS DE FARNHAM, or de Fileceto, was born at Farnham in this county, and bred a physician in Oxford. Now our nation esteemeth physicians, little physic, little worth, except far fetched from foreign parts. Wherefore this Nicholas, to acquire more skill and repute to himself, travelled beyond the seas. First he fixed at Paris, and there gained great esteem, accounted *Famosus Anglicus*. Here he continued until that university was in effect dissolved, through the discords betwixt the clergy and the citizens. Hence he removed, and for some years lived in Bologna. Returning home, his fame was so great, that he became physician to King Henry the Third. The vivacity and health of this patient (who reigned longer than most men live) was an effect of his care. Great were the gifts the king conferred upon him, and at last made him bishop of Chester. Wonder not that a physician should prove a prelate, seeing this Farnham was a general scholar. Besides, since the Reformation, in the reign of Queen Elizabeth, we had J. Coldwell, doctor of physic, a bishop of Sarum. After the resignation of Chester, he accepted of the bishopric of Durham. This also he surrendered (after he had sitten nine years in that see) reserving only three manors for his maintenance. He wrote many books, much esteemed in that age, of the practice in physic and use of herbs, and died in a private life 1257.

WALTER DE MERTON was born at Merton in this county, and in the reign of King Henry the Third, when chancellors were chequered in and out, three times he discharged that office: 1. Anno 1260, placed in by the king; displaced by the barons, to make room for Nicholas of Ely; 2. Anno 1261, when the king (counting it no equity or conscience that his lords should obtrude a chancellor on him) restored him to his place, continuing therein some three years; 3. Anno 1273, when he was replaced in that office for a short time.

He was also preferred bishop of Rochester, that a rich prelate might maintain a poor bishopric. He founded Merton College in Oxford, which hath produced more famous schoolmen than all England (I had almost said Europe) besides. He died in the year 1277, in the fifth of King Edward the First.

WILLIAM OCKHAM was born in this county, in a village so called of oaks; and indeed our William was all heart of oak, as soon will appear.

He was first bred under John Scotus,[1] and afterwards served him as Aristotle did his master Plato, disproving his principles, and first setting on foot a new sort of sophistry. Then it was hard to hear anything in the schools for the high railing betwixt the *Reals,* headed by John Duns Scotus; *Nominals,* fighting under their general Ockham; neither of them conducing much to the advance of religion.

Our Ockham, flushed with success against John Scotus, undertook another John, of higher power and place, even Pope John the Two-and-twentieth, and gave a mortal wound to his temporal power over princes. He got a good guardian, viz., Lewis of Bavaria the emperor, whose court

(1) See Northumberland, p. 445.

was his sanctuary, so that we may call him a schoolman courtier. But he was excommunicated by the pope, and the masters of Paris condemned him for a heretic, and burnt his books. This, I conceive, was the cause why Luther was so versed in his works, which he had at his fingers' ends, being the sole schoolman in his library whom he esteemed.

However, at last the pope took wit in his anger, finding it no policy to enrage so sharp a pen; and though I find no recantation or public submission of Ockham, yet he was restored to his state, and the repute of an acute schoolman. Now because he is generally complained of, for his soul of opposition (gain-saying whatever Scotus said) it will serve to close his epitaph, what was made on a great paradox-monger, possessed with the like contradicting spirit:

> *Sed jam est mortuum, ut apparet,*
> *Quod si viveret id negaret.*
> But now he's dead, as plainly doth appear;
> Yet would *deny* it, were he *living* here.

He flourished under King Edward the Third; and, dying 1349, was buried at Munich in Bavaria.

THOMAS CRANLEY was in all probability born [1337?] at and named from Cranleigh (in Blackheath Hundred) in this county. It confirmeth the conjecture, because I cannot find any other village so named in all England. Bred he was in Oxford, and became the first warden of New College; thence preferred archbishop of Dublin in Ireland. Thither he went over 1397, accompanying Thomas Holland, duke of Surrey and lieutenant of Ireland; in that kingdom our Cranley was made by King Henry the Fourth chancellor, and by King Henry the Fifth chief justice thereof. It seems, he finding the Irish possessed with a rebellious humour, bemoaned himself to the king in a terse poem of 106 verses, which Leland perused with much pleasure and delight. Were he but half so good as some make him, he was to be admired. Such a case, and such a jewel, such a presence, and a prelate clear in complexion, proper in stature, bountiful in house-keeping and house-repairing; a great clerk, deep divine, and excellent preacher. Thus far we have gone along very willingly with our author,[1] but now leave him to go alone by himself, unwillingly to follow him any farther, for fear of a *tang* of blasphemy, when bespeaking him, "Thou art fairer than the children of men; full of grace are thy lips," &c.

Anno 1417 he returned into England, being fourscore years old; sickened, and died at Faringdon; and lieth buried in New College Chapel, and not in Dublin, as some have related.

NICOLAS WEST was born [1461] at Putney in this county; bred first at Eton, then at King's College in Cambridge, where (when a youth) he was a rake-hell in grain; for, something crossing him in the college, he could find no other way to work his revenge than by secret setting on fire the master's lodgings, part whereof he burnt to the ground. Immediately after, this incendiary (and was it not high time for him?) left the college;

(1) T. Marleburgensis, of the Writers of Ireland.

and this little Herostratus[1] lived for a time in the country, debauched enough for his conversation.

"But they go far who turn not again;" and in him the proverb was verified, "Naughty boys sometimes make good men." He seasonably retrenched his wildness, turned hard student, became an eminent scholar and most able statesman; and, after smaller promotions, was at last made bishop of Ely, and often employed in foreign embassies. And now, had it been possible, he would have quenched the fire he kindled in the college with his own tears; and, in expression of his penitence, became a worthy benefactor to the house, and rebuilt the master's lodgings firm and fair from the ground. No bishop of England was better attended with menial servants, or kept a more bountiful house, which made his death so much lamented, Anno Domini 1533.[2]

SIR NICHOLAS CAREW. He was a jolly gentleman, fit for the favour of King Henry the Eighth, who loved active spirits, as could keep pace with him in all achievements, and made him knight of the Garter, and master of his horse.

This Sir Nicholas built a fair house, or palace rather, at Beddington in this county, which, by the advantage of the water, is a paradise of pleasure.

Tradition in this family reporteth how King Henry, then at bowls, gave this knight opprobrious language, betwixt jest and earnest; to which the other returned an answer rather true than discreet, as more consulting therein his own animosity than allegiance. The king, who in this kind would give and not take, being no good fellow in tart repartees, was so highly offended thereat that Sir Nicholas fell from the top of his favour to the bottom of his displeasure, and was bruised to death thereby. This was the true cause of his execution, though in our chronicles all is scored on his complying in a plot with Henry marquis of Exeter, and Henry Lord Montague.[3] [*d* 1539]

WILLIAM HOWARD [*b.* 1510?] son to Thomas Howard, second of that surname duke of Norfolk, was by Queen Mary created baron of Effingham in this county, and by her made lord admiral of England, which place he discharged with credit. I find he was one of the first favourers and furtherers, with his purse and countenance, of the strange and wonderful discovery of Russia. He died Anno Domini 1573.

CHARLES HOWARD, son to the Lord William aforesaid, succeeded him (though not immediately) in the admiralty. An hearty gentleman, and cordial to his sovereign; of a most proper person, one reason why Queen Elizabeth (who, though she did not value a jewel *by*, valued it the more *for*, a fair case) reflected so much upon him. The first evidence he gave of his prowess was when the emperor's sister, the spouse of Spain, with a fleet of 130 sails, stoutly and proudly passed the narrow seas, his lordship,

(1) An Ephesian who set fire to the temple of Artemis at Ephesus, on the night that Alexander the Great was born, in order to secure immortal fame. (2) He was chaplain to Catherine of Aragon, and opposed to the divorce proceedings. (3) On this plot see note to life of Margaret Pole in Wiltshire, p. 612.

accompanied with ten ships only of her majesty's navy royal, environed their fleet in a most strange and warlike sort, enforced them to *stoop-gallant,* and to vail[1] their bonnets for the queen of England.

His service in the eighty-eight is notoriously known, when, at the first news of the Spaniards' approach, he towed at a cable with his own hands to draw out the harbour-bound ships into the sea. I dare boldly say he drew more, though not by his person, by his presence and example, than any ten in the place. True it is, he was no deep seaman (not to be expected from one of his extraction) but had skill enough to know those who had more skill than himself, and to follow their instructions; and would not starve the queen's service by feeding his own sturdy wilfulness, but was ruled by the experienced in sea-matters; the queen having a navy of oak, and an admiral of osier.

His last eminent service was, when he was commander of the sea, as Essex of the land forces, at the taking of Cadiz, for which he was made earl of Nottingham, the last of the queen's creation.

His place was of great profit (prizes being so frequent in that age) though great his necessary and vast his voluntary expenses, keeping, as I have read, seven standing houses at the same time, at London, Reigate, Effingham, Blechingley, &c.; so that the wonder is not great if he died not very wealthy.

He lived to be very aged, who wrote *man* (if not married) in the first of Queen Elizabeth, being an invited guest at the solemn consecration of Matthew Parker at Lambeth; and many years after, by his testimony, confuted those lewd and loud lies which the papists tell of the Nag's Head in Cheapside.[2] He resigned his admiralty in the reign of King James to the duke of Buckingham. [1536-1624]

JOHN PARKHURST was born [1512?] at Guildford in this county; bred first in Magdalen, then in Merton College, in Oxford. Here it was no small part of praise, that he was tutor, yea Maecenas, to John Jewel.[3] After his discontinuance, returning to Oxford, it was no small comfort unto him to hear his pupil read his learned humanity lectures to the Somato Christians (reader, I coin not the word myself, but have took it in payment from a good hand[4]); that is, to those of Corpus Christi College, to which house then Jewel was removed. Hereupon Mr. Parkhurst made this distich:

Olim discipulus mihi, chare Juelle fuisti;
Nunc ero discipulus, te renuente, tuus.

Dear Jewel, scholar once thou wast to me,
Now 'gainst thy will I scholar turn to thee.

Indeed he was as good a poet as any in that age; and delighted to be an anti-epigrammatist to John White, bishop of Winchester;[5] whom, in my opinion, he far surpassed both in phrase and fancy.

(1) *To stoop-gallant*=something that humbles "gallants." *To vail*=to lower. *Bonnet* is an additional piece of canvas laced to the foot of a sail to catch more wind. *To vail bonnets* is to make a sign of respect. (2) See note to life of Thomas Neal in Gloucestershire, p. 196. (3) Bishop of Salisbury (see Devonshire, p. 129). (4) Dr. Humphrey, in the Latin life of Jewel. (5) See Oxfordshire, p. 469.

Mr. Parkhurst, when leaving Oxford, was presented parson, shall I say, or bishop of Cleeve in Gloucestershire; as which may seem rather a diocese than a parish, for the rich revenue thereof. But let none envy *beneficium opimum beneficiario optimo* (a good living to an incumbent who will do good therewith.) He laid himself out in works of charity and hospitality. He used to examine the pockets of such Oxford scholars as repaired unto him, and always recruited them with necessaries; so that such who came to him with heavy hearts and light purses, departed from him with light hearts and heavy purses.

But see a sudden alteration. King Edward the Sixth dies; and then he, who formerly entertained others, had not a house to hide himself in. Parkhurst is forced to post speedily and secretly beyond the seas, where he remained all the reign of Queen Mary; and, providing for his return in the first of Queen Elizabeth, was robbed of that little he had by some searchers appointed for that purpose. Were not these thieves themselves robbed, I mean of their expectation, who hoped to enrich themselves by pillaging an exile and a poet? It grieved him most of all that he lost the fair copy of his Epigrams, though afterwards with much ado he recovered them from his foul papers. These at last he put in print, *et juvenilem foetum senex edidit,* without any trespass on his gravity; such his poems being so witty that a young man, so harmless that an old man, need not be of them ashamed.

Being returned into England, he was by Queen Elizabeth preferred to the bishopric of Norwich; and was consecrated September 1, 1560. Fourteen years he sat in that see, and died 1575.

NICHOLAS SANDERS was born [1530?] at Charlwood in this county, where his family still continueth worshipful; bred bachelor of the laws in New College. Going over beyond the seas he was made D.D. at Rome, and afterwards king's professor thereof at Louvain.

Pity it was he had not more honesty, or less learning, being master of art in malice; not hoping the whole body of his lies should be believed, but, being confident the least finger thereof finding credit could prove heavy enough to crush any innocence with posterity; presuming the rather to write passages without truth, because on a subject beyond memory.

He thought it would much advantage his cause to call the church of England schismatic first in that his libellous treatise. Indeed the controversy consisting much in matter of fact, let records and histories be perused; and it will appear that our English kings, after many intolerable provocations, and entrenchments on their crown from the church of Rome, at last, without the least invading of others, conserved their own right; partly as supreme princes calling together their clergy, by their advice to reform the errors therein; partly to protect their subjects from being ruined by the canons and constitutions of a foreign power.

But this subject hath lately been so handled by that learned baronet Sir Roger Twysden,[1] that, as he hath exceeded former, he hath saved all

(1) Historian and antiquary; lived 1597-1672. Like Hampden, he refused to pay ship-money. Fuller refers to his *Historical Vindication of the Church of England.*

future pains therein. To return to Sanders, it is observable, that he who surfeited with falsehoods was famished for lack of food in Ireland. We must be *sensible*, but may not be *censorious* on such accidents; those deserving to forfeit the eyes of their souls, who will not mark so remarkable a judgment, which happened Anno Domini 1581.

THOMAS RAVIS was born [1560?] of worthy parentage at Malden in this county;[1] bred in Christ Church in Oxford, whereof he was dean, and of which university he was twice vice-chancellor. Afterwards, when many suitors greedily sought the bishopric of Gloucester then vacant, the lords of the council requested Dr. Ravis to accept thereof.

As he was not very willing to go thither, so (after his three years' abode there) those of Gloucester were unwilling he should go thence, who in so short a time had gained the good liking of all sorts, that some who could scant brook the name of bishop were content to give (or rather to pay) him a good report.

Anno 1607 he was removed to London, and there died on the 14th of December 1609; and lieth buried under a fair tomb in the wall at the upper end of the north part of his cathedral.[2]

ROBERT ABBOT, D.D., was born [1560] at Guildford in this county; bred in Balliol College in Oxford, whereof he became principal, and king's professor of divinity in that university. What is said of the French, so graceful is their garb, that they make any kind of clothes become themselves; so in general was his learning, he made any liberal employment beseem him; reading, writing, preaching, opposing, answering and moderating; who could disentangle truth, though complicated with errors on all sides. He so routed the reasons of Bishop,[3] the Romish champion, that he never could rally them again. Yet preferment (which is ordered in heaven) came down very slowly on this doctor, whereof several reasons are assigned: 1. His humility affected no high promotion. 2. His foes traduced him for a puritan, who indeed was a right godly man, and cordial to the discipline, as doctrine of the church of England. 3. His friends were loth to adorn the church with the spoil of the university, and mar a professor to make a bishop.

However, preferment at last found him out, when he was consecrated bishop of Salisbury, December 3, 1615. Herein he equalled the felicity of Seffrid bishop of Chichester, that, being himself a bishop, he saw his brother George at the same time archbishop of Canterbury.[4] Of these two, George was the more plausible preacher, Robert the greater scholar; George the abler statesman, Robert the deeper divine; gravity did frown in George, and smile in Robert.

But alas! he was hardly warm in his see before cold in his coffin, being one of the five bishops which Salisbury saw in six years. His death happened anno 1617.

(1) So expressed in his epitaph on his monument in St. Paul's. (2) Bishop Ravis was one of the translators of the Authorized Version of the Bible. (3) William Bishop—see Warwickshire, p. 588. (4) His life follows immediately below.

GEORGE ABBOT was born [1562] at Guildford in this county, being one of that happy ternion of brothers; whereof two, eminent prelates, the third, lord mayor of London.[1] He was bred in Oxford, wherein he became head of University College; a pious man, and most excellent preacher, as his lectures on Jonah do declare.

He did first creep, then run, then fly into preferment, or rather preferment did fly upon him without expectation. He was never incumbent on any living with cure of souls, but was mounted from a lecturer to a dignitary; so that he knew well what belonged to the stipend and benevolence of the one and the dividend of the other; but was utterly unacquainted with the taking of tithes, with the many troubles attending it, together with the causeless molestations which persons presented meet with in their respective parishes. And because it is hard for one to have a fellow-suffering of that whereof he never had a suffering, this (say some) was the cause that he was so harsh to ministers when brought before him.

Being chaplain to the earl of Dunbar, then omni-prevalent with King James, he was unexpectedly preferred archbishop of Canterbury, being of a more fatherly presence than those who might almost have been his fathers for age in the church of England.[2] I find two things much charged on his memory: first, that in his house he respected his secretary above his chaplains, and out of it always honoured cloaks above cassocks, lay above clergymen; secondly, that he connived at the spreading of nonconformity, insomuch that I read in a modern author, "Had Bishop Laud succeeded Bancroft, and the project of conformity been followed without interruption, there is little question to be made but that our Jerusalem (by this time) might have been a city at unity in itself."[3]

Yet are there some of Archbishop Abbot's relations, who (as I am informed) will undertake to defend him, that he was in no degree guilty of these crimes laid to his charge.

This archbishop was much humbled with a casual homicide of a keeper of the Lord Zouch's in Bramshill Park, though soon after he was solemnly quitted from any irregularity thereby.

In the reign of King Charles, he was sequestered from his jurisdiction; say some, on the old account of that homicide, though others say for refusing to license a sermon of Dr. Sibthorpe's.[4] Yet there is not an express of either in the instrument of sequestration; the commission only saying, in the general, "That the said archbishop could not at that present, in his own person, attend those services which were otherwise proper for his cognizance and jurisdiction."

For my own part, I have cause to believe that as *vulnus semel sanatum novo vulnere recrudescit,* so his former obnoxiousness for that casualty

(1) Sir Maurice Abbot (1565-1642) an eminent merchant, one of the original directors of the East India Company. (2) His previous preferments had been dean of Winchester, thrice vice-chancellor of Oxford, bishop of Coventry and Lichfield, and bishop of London. He was one of the translators of the Authorized Version of the Bible. It was Abbot that introduced George Villiers, the famous duke of Buckingham, to court, a step he later regretted. (3) The Observator Rescued. (4) A sermon exalting the royal prerogative and its right to arbitrary taxation. The prime mover in Abbot's sequestration was Buckingham, who was jealous of his influence.

was renewed on the occasion of his refusal to license that sermon, with some other of his court-uncompliances. This archbishop died Anno Domini 1633, having erected a large hospital with liberal maintenance at Guildford, the place of his nativity.

SIR ROBERT DUDLEY, knight, son to Robert Dudley earl of Leicester by Douglas Sheffield (whether his mistress or wife God knoweth, many men being inclinable charitably to believe the latter[1]) was born [1574] at Sheen in this county, and bred by his mother, out of his father's reach, at Offington in Sussex. He afterwards became a most complete gentleman in all suitable accomplishments. Endeavouring, in the reign of King James, to prove his legitimacy, and meeting with much opposition from the court, in distaste he left his land, and went over into Italy. But worth is ever at home, and carrieth its own welcome along with it. He became a favourite to the duke of Florence, who highly reflected on his abilities, and used his directions in all his buildings. At this time Leghorn, from a child started a man without ever being a youth, and of a small town grew a great city on a sudden; and is much beholding to this Sir Robert for its fairness and firmness, as chief contriver of both.

But by this time his adversaries in England had procured him to be called home by a special privy seal, which he refused to obey, and thereupon all his lands in England were seized on by the king, by the statute of fugitives. These his losses doubled the love of the duke of Florence unto him. And indeed Sir Robert was a much meriting person on many accounts, being: 1. An excellent mathematician, especially for the practical part thereof in architecture; 2. An excellent physician, his *Catholicon* at this day finding good esteem amongst those of that faculty; 3. An excellent navigator, especially in the western seas.

Indeed long before his leaving of England, whilst as yet he was *rectus in curia,* well esteemed in Queen Elizabeth's court, he sailed with three small ships to the Isle of Trinidad, in which voyage he sunk and took nine Spanish ships, whereof one an armada of 600 tons.

It must not be forgotten how he was so acceptable to Ferdinand the Second, emperor of Germany, that by his letters patent bearing date at Vienna, March the 9th, 1620, he conferred on him and his heirs the title of a duke of the Sacred Empire. Understand it a title at large (as that of Count Arundel's) without the assignation of any proper place unto him.

[*d.* 1649]

ELIZABETH JANE WESTON. We must gain by degrees what knowledge we can get of this eminent woman, who no doubt was: 1. Of *gentle extraction,* because her parents bestowed on her so liberal and costly education; 2. A *virgin,* because she wrote a book of poetry, called *Parthenicon;*[2] 3. A great scholar, because commended by two grand critics.

It seems her fame was more known in foreign parts than at home. And I am ashamed that, for the honour of her sex and our nation, I

(1) She was the widow of John, second Baron Sheffield, and daughter of William, first Lord Howard of Effingham. The earl of Leicester apparently went through a form of marriage with her, but Dudley's legitimacy was never legally established.
(2) The Parthenon being the "Virgin's Chamber."

can give no better account of her. However, that her memory may not be harbourless, I have lodged her in this county (where I find an ancient and worshipful family of the Westons flourishing at Sutton) ready to remove her at the first information of the certain place of her nativity.

Here we may see how capable the weaker sex is of learning, if instructed therein. Indeed, when a learned maid was presented to King James for an English rarity because she could speak and write pure Latin, Greek and Hebrew, the king returned, "But can she spin?" However, in persons of birth and quality, learning hath ever been beheld as a rare and commendable accomplishment.[1] [1582-1612]

HENRY SMITH, who was born at Wandsworth in this county.[2] Now, reader, before I go any further, give me leave to premise and apply a passage in my apprehension not improper in this place.

Luther, commenting on those words, Gen. i, 21, "And God created great whales," rendereth this reason why the creation of whales is specified by name: *ne, territi magnitudine, crederemus ea spectra esse* (lest, affrighted with their greatness, we should believe them to be only visions or fancies). Indeed many simple people who lived, where Luther did, in an inland country, three hundred miles from the sea, might suspect that whales (as reported with such vast dimensions) were rather fables than realities. In like manner, being now to relate the bounty of this worthy person, I am afraid that our infidel age will not give credit thereunto, as conceiving it rather a romanza or fiction than a thing really performed, because of the prodigious greatness thereof. The best is, there are thousands in this county can attest the truth therein. And such good deeds publicly done are a pregnant proof to convince all deniers and doubters thereof.

This Henry Smith, esq., an alderman of London, gave, to buy lands for a perpetuity for the relief and setting the poor to work: in Croydon, one thousand pounds; in Kingston, one thousand pounds; in Guildford, one thousand pounds; in Dorking, one thousand pounds; in Farnham, one thousand pounds; in Reigate, one thousand pounds; in Wandsworth, to the poor, five hundred; besides many other great and liberal legacies bequeathed to pious uses, which I hope by his executors are as conscionably employed as by him they were charitably intended.

He departed this life the 13th of January 1628, in the seventy-ninth year of his age; and lieth buried in the chancel of Wandsworth.

RICHARD CORBET, D.D., was born [1582] at Ewell in this county, and from a student in, became dean of Christ Church, then bishop of Oxford. An high wit and most excellent poet; of a courteous carriage, and no destructive nature to any who offended him, counting himself plentifully repaid with a jest upon him. He afterwards was advanced bishop of Norwich, where he died Anno Domini 1635.

(1) This learned lady was born in London and removed with her parents to Bohemia. She married the jurist Johann Leon. The two "grand critics" who praised her were Scaliger and Dousa. She addressed Latin letters to princes and scholars. (2) So testifieth his monument in the upper end of the chancel of Wandsworth.

HENRY HAMMOND, D.D., was born [1605] at Chertsey in this county, his father being doctor of physic, and physician to King James. He was bred in Eton school, where judicious Mr. Bust (so skilful in *reading* other boys) could not *spell* his nature; but, being posed with the riddle of his portentous wit, at last even left him to himself, which proved the best. Hence he became fellow of Magdalen College in Oxford, till preferred canon of Christ Church and orator of the university.

He may be called an 'angelical doctor', as justly as he who is generally so styled.[1] First, for his countenance and complexion, white and ruddy, resembling the common portraitures of the cherubims. Secondly, his sanctity, spending his life in devotion. His eating and drinking were next to nothing, so exemplary his abstinence, and he always embraced a single life. Thirdly, meekness. "Michael durst not (the valour of an archangel is frighted at a sin) bring a railing accusation against Satan." Herein only our doctor was a coward: he feared to revile any of an opposite judgment. Fourthly, his charity; he was the tutelar angel, to keep many a poor royalist from famishing; it being verily believed that he yearly gave away more than two hundred pounds. Lastly, for his knowledge; such the latitude of his learning and languages. As distillers extract *aqua vitae,* or living water, from the dregs of dead beer, so he, from the rotten writings of the Rabbins, drew many observations to the advance of Christianity.

He could turn his ploughshares and pruning-hooks into swords and spears in his controversial treatises; and could again at pleasure convert his swords and spears into ploughshares and pruning-hooks in his comments and practical catechism.

He was well versed in all modern pamphlets touching church discipline. When some of the royal disputants (in the treaty at Uxbridge) in some sort did overshoot their adversaries, this doctor could lay his arguments level against them, and discourse with the parliament divines in their own dialect.

But, alas! he was an angelical man, no angel; witness his death of the student's disease, the stone. He died at Westwood in Worcestershire, at the house of the Lady Pakington; his Pella,[2] where he peacably reposed himself whilst all our English Jerusalem was in combustion. One thousand pounds well nigh were due unto him at his death; yet there appeared neither speciality, nor any man's hand amongst his writings; so confident he was that his conscientious debtors would faithfully pay what was freely lent them. By his will he empowered Dr. Humphrey Henchman (since bishop of Sarum) his sole executor, to expend according to his discretion, in the relief of poor people, not exceeding two hundred pounds. Let this his short character be pitched up like a tent for a time, to be taken down when a firmer fabric (which, as I am informed, a more able pen is about) shall be erected to his memory.[3] He died Anno Domini 1660.

(1) i.e., Thomas Aquinas. (2) i.e., his retreat. (Pella, a city of Palestine, to which the Christians fled from Jerusalem before its capture by the Romans). Hammond was deprived and imprisoned by the parliamentarians, but later was allowed to live with Sir Philip Warwick and Sir John Pakington. (3) His life was written in 1662 by John Fell, later bishop of Oxford.

HENRY OF OATLANDS (so I have heard him called in his cradle) [third] and youngest son to King Charles the First and Queen Mary, was born at Oatlands in this county, anno 1639. This I thought fit to observe, both because I find Saint James's by some mistaken for the place of his birth, and because that house wherein he was born is buried in effect; I mean, taken down to the ground. He was commonly called duke of Gloucester, by a court prolepsis (from the king manifesting his intentions in due time to make him so) before any solemn creation. Greatness being his only guilt, that he was the son of a good king (which many men would wish, and no child could help.)

The then present power, more of covetousness than kindness (unwilling to maintain him either like or unlike the son of his father) permitted him to depart the land, with scarce tolerable accommodations, and the promise of a (never performed) pension for his future support. A passage I meet with in my worthy friend, concerning this duke, deserveth to be written in letters of gold:[1] "In the year 1654, almost as soon as his two elder brethren had removed themselves into Flanders, he found a strong practice in some of the queen's court to seduce him to the church of Rome, whose temptations he resisted beyond his years, and thereupon was sent for by them into Flanders."

He had a great appetite to learning, and a quick digestion, able to take as much as his tutors could teach him. He fluently could speak many, understood more modern tongues. He was able to express himself in matters of importance presently,[2] properly, solidly, to the admiration of such who trebled his age. Judicious his curiosity to inquire into navigation, and other mathematical mysteries. His courtesy set a lustre on all, and commanded man's affections to love him.

His life may be said to have been all in the night of affliction, *rising* by his birth a little before the *setting* of his father's, and *setting* by his death a little after the *rising* of his brother's peacable reign. It seems Providence, to prevent excess, thought fit to temper the general mirth of England with some mourning. He deceased at Whitehall on Thursday the 13th of September 1660, and was buried (though privately) solemnly, *veris et spirantibus lacrymis,* in the chapel of King Henry the Seventh.

THE FAREWELL

I have been credibly informed, that one Mr. Clarke, some seven-score years since, built at his charges the market-house of Farnham in this county. Once, reproving his workmen for going on so slowly, they excused themselves that they were hindered with much people pressing upon them, some liking, some disliking, the model of the fabric.

Hereupon Mr. Clarke caused this distich (hardly extant at this day) to be written in that house:

> You who do like me give money to end me;
> You who dislike me give money to mend me.

I wish this advice practised all over this county, by those who vent their various verdicts in praising or reproving structures erected *gratis* for the general good.

(1) Dr. Heylin, in his *Life and Reign of King Charles.* (2) *Presently*=immediately.

SUSSEX

SUSSEX hath Surrey on the north, Kent on the east, the sea on the south, and Hampshire on the west. It is extended along the sea-side three-score miles in length, but is contented with a third of those miles in the breadth thereof. A fruitful county, though very dirty for the travellers therein, so that it may be better measured to its advantage by days' journeys than by miles. Hence it is that, in the late order for regulating the wages of coachmen, at such a price a day and distance from London, Sussex alone was excepted, as wherein shorter way or better pay was allowed. Yet the gentry of this county well content themselves in the very badness of passage therein, as which secureth their provisions at reasonable prices; which, if mended, *higglers* would mount, as *bajulating*[1] them to London.

It is peculiar to this county that all the rivers (and those, I assure you, are very many) have their fountains and falls in this shire, though one may seem somewhat suspicious, as being bred, living (though not to their full strength and stature of being navigable) and dying therein, swallowed up by the sea.

It is sufficient evidence of the plenty of this county that the toll of the wheat, corn and malt, growing or made about and sold in the city of Chichester, doth amount yearly, at a halfpenny a quarter, to sixty pounds and upwards,[2] as the gatherers thereof will attest; and the numbers of the bushels we leave to be audited by better arithmeticians.

It hath been said that the first baron, viscount and earl in England,[3] all three have, and have had for some term of time their chief residence in this county; and it is more civility to believe all than to deny any part of the report, though sure I am this observation was discomposed at the death of the earl of Essex, since which time Viscount Hereford is the first person in England of that dignity.

NATURAL COMMODITIES

Iron

Great the necessity hereof, some nations having lived in the ignorance of gold and silver, scarce any without the use of iron. Indeed we read not of it in making the Tabernacle (though from no mention no use thereof therein cannot infallibly be inferred) which being but a slight and portable building, brass might supply the want thereof. But in the Temple, which was a firmer fabric, we find "iron for the things of iron," and a hundred thousand talents of that metal employed therein.

Great the quantity of iron made in this county; whereof much used therein, and more exported thence into other parts of the land and beyond the seas. But whether or no the private profit thereby will at

(1) Hence *Badgers*. [*Bajulate*=to carry, especially as a badger.] (2) So was I informed by Mr. Peckham, the recorder of Chichester. (3) Lord Abergavenny, Viscount Montacute, and the earl of Arundel.

long-running countervail the public loss in the destruction of woods, I am as unwilling to discuss as unable to decide. Only let me add the ensuing complaint, wherein the timber-trees of this county deplore their condition, in my opinion richly worth the reader's perusal:

> Jove's oak, the warlike ash, veined elm, the softer beech,
> Short hazel, maple plain, light asp, the bending wych,
> Tough holly, and smooth birch, must altogether burn:
> What should the builders serve, supplies the forgers' turn;
> When under public good, base private gain takes hold,
> And we poor woeful Woods to ruin lastly sold.

But it is to be hoped that a way may be found out, to *chark*[1] sea-coal in such a manner as to render it useful for the making of iron. All things are not found out in one age, as reserved for future discovery, and that perchance may be easy for the next which seems impossible to this generation.

TALC

Talc (in Latin *talchum*) is a cheap kind of mineral, which this county plentifully affords, though not so fine as what is fetched from Venice. It is white and transparent like crystal, full of streaks or veins, which prettily scatter themselves. Being calcined and variously prepared, it maketh a curious whitewash, which some justify lawful, because clearing, not changing complexion. It is a great astringent, yet used but little in physic. Surely Nature would not have made it such an hypocrite to hang out so fair a sign, except some guest of quality were lodged therein; I mean, it would not appear so beautiful to the eye, except some concealed worth were couched therein, inclining me to believe that the virtue thereof is not yet fully discovered.

WHEATEARS

Wheatears is a bird peculiar to this county, hardly found out of it. It is so called, because fattest when wheat is ripe, whereon it feeds; being no bigger than a lark, which it equalleth in the fineness of the flesh, far exceedeth in the fatness thereof. The worst is that being only seasonable in the heat of summer, and naturally larded with lumps of fat, it is soon subject to corrupt, so that (though abounding within forty miles) London poulterers have no mind to meddle with them, which no care in carriage can keep from putrefaction. That palate-man shall pass in silence, who, being seriously demanded his judgment concerning the abilities of a great lord, concluded him a man of very weak parts, "because once he saw him, at a great feast, feed on chickens when there were wheatears on the table."

I will add no more in praise of this bird, for fear some female reader may fall in longing for it, and unhappily be disappointed of her desire.

CARPS

It is a stately fish, but not long naturalized in England; and of all freshwater fishes (the eel only excepted) lives longest out of his proper

(1) *Chark* = to char; to coke.

element. They breed, which most other fishes do not, several months in one year; though in cold ponds they take no comfort to increase. A learned writer[1] observeth they live but ten years; though others assign them a far longer life.

They are better for their age and bigness, a rule which holds not in other fishes, and their tongues by ancient Roman palate-men were counted most delicious meat; though, to speak properly, they have either no tongues in their mouths, or all their mouths are tongues, as filled with a carneous substance, whilst their teeth are found in their throats. There is a kind of frog which is a professed foe unto them; insomuch, that of an hundred carps put into a pond, not five of them have been found therein a year after. And though some may say, perchance two-legged frogs stole them away, yet the strict care of their owners in watching them disproved all suspicion thereof.

Now as this county is eminent for both sea and river fish, namely an Arundel mullet, a Chichester lobster, a Selsey cockle, and an Amberly trout, so Sussex aboundeth with more carps than any other of this nation. And though not so great as Jovious reporteth to be found in the Laurian lake in Italy, weighing more than fifty pounds, yet those generally of great and goodly proportion. I need not add that physicians account the galls of carps, as also a stone in their heads, to be medicinable; only I will observe, that because Jews will not eat caviare made of sturgeon (because coming from a fish wanting scales, and therefore forbidden in the Levitical law) therefore the Italians make greater profit of the spawn of carps, whereof they make a red caviare, well pleasing the Jews both in palate and conscience.

All I will add of carps is this, that Ramus himself doth not so much redound in dichotomies as they do; seeing no one bone is to be found in their body which is not forked or divided into two parts at the ends thereof.

THE MANUFACTURES

GREAT GUNS

It is almost incredible how many are made of the iron in this county. Count Gondomar[2] well knew their goodness, when of King James he so often begged the boon to transport them.

A monk of Metz (some three hundred years since) is generally reputed the first founder of them. Surely ingenuity may seem transposed, and to have crossed her hands, when about the same time a soldier found out printing; and it is questionable which of the two inventions hath done more good, or more harm. As for guns, it cannot be denied that, though most behold them as instruments of cruelty, partly because subjecting valour to chance, partly because guns give no quarter, which the sword sometimes doth, yet it will appear that, since their invention, victory hath not stood so long a neuter, and hath been determined with the loss of fewer lives. Yet do I not believe what soldiers commonly say, that "he was cursed in his mother's belly, who is killed with a cannon," seeing many prime persons have been slain thereby.

(1) Sir Francis Bacon, in his *History of Life and Death*. (2) The Spanish ambassador.

Such as desire to know the pedigree and progress of great guns in England may be pleased to take notice, 1. Anno 1535, John Oaven was the first Englishman who in England cast brass ordnance, cannons, culverins &c. 2. Peter Baud, a Frenchman, in the first of King Edward the Sixth, was the first who in England cast iron ordnance, falcons, falconers, minions &c. 3. Thomas Johnson, covenant-servant to Peter aforesaid, succeeded and exceeded his master, casting them clearer and better. He died about 1600.

Some observe, that God hath so equally divided the advantage of weapons between us and Spain, that their steel makes the best swords, our iron the most useful ordnance.

GLASS

Plenty hereof is made in this county, though not so fine as what Tyre afforded, fetched from the River Belus and the Cendevian lake; nor so pure as is wrought at Chiosa nigh Venice, whereof the most refined falls but one degree short of crystal; but the coarse glasses here serve well enough for the common sort, for vessels to drink in. The workmen in this mystery are much increased since 1557, as may appear by what I read in an author writing that very year:[1]

> As for glass-makers they be scant in this land,
> Yet one there is as I do understand,
> And in Sussex is now his habitation,
> At Chiddingfold he works of his occupation.

These brittle commodities are subject to breaking upon any casualty; and hereupon I must transmit a passage to posterity, which I received from an author beyond exceptions.

A nobleman, who shall be nameless, living not many miles from Cambridge (and highly in favour with the earl of Leicester) begged of Queen Elizabeth all the plate of that university, as useless for scholars, and more for state than service, for superfluity than necessity. The queen granted his suit, upon condition to find glasses for the scholars. The lord, considering this might amount to more than his barony would maintain (except he could compass the Venetian artist, who, as they say, could make *vitra sine vitio fragilitatis pellucida,* yea, could consolidate glass to make it malleable) let his petition, which was as charitable as discreet, sink in silence.

By the way be it observed, that though coarse glass-making was, in this county, of great antiquity, yet "the first making of Venice glasses in England began at the Crutched Friars in London, about the beginning of the reign of Queen Elizabeth, by one Jacob Venaline, an Italian."[2]

THE BUILDINGS

CHICHESTER Cathedral is a fine fabric, built (after it had been twice consumed with fire) by Bishop Seffrid, the second of the name, about the year 1193. Country folk are confident in their tradition, that the master-workman built Salisbury, and his man the church of Chichester; and if

(1) Thomas Charnock [see Kent, p. 272] in his *Breviary of Philosophy*. (2) Stow's *Chronicle*.

so, *sequitur Dominum non passibus aequis.* But proportion of time confuteth the conceit, seeing Seffrid flourished under King John, and Bishop Poor (the founder of Salisbury) lived much later, under King Henry the Third.

Now though Seffrid bestowed the cloth and making on the church, Bishop Sherborne gave the trimming and best lace thereto in the reign of King Henry the Seventh. I am sorry I can follow the allegory so far, being informed that now it is not only seam-ript, but torn in the whole cloth, having lately a great part thereof fallen down to the ground.

ARUNDEL Castle is of great esteem, the rather because a local earldom is cemented to the walls thereof. Some will have it so named from Arundel, the horse of Bevis the great champion. I confess it is not without precedent in antiquity, for places to take names from horses, meeting with the promontory Bucephalus in Peloponnesus, where some report the horse of Alexander buried; and Bellonius will have it for the same cause called Cavalla at this day. But this castle was so called long before that imaginary horse was foaled, who cannot be fancied elder than his master Bevis, flourishing after the Conquest, long before which Arundel was so called from the river Arun running hard by it.

PETWORTH, the house of the earls of Northumberland, is most famous for a stately stable, the best of any subject's in Christendom. Comparisons must move in their own spheres, and princes only are meet to measure with princes. Tell me not therefore of the duke of Saxony's stable at Dresden, wherein are an hundred twenty and eight horses of service, with a magazine out of which he can arm thirty thousand horse and foot at a day's warning; that elector being the most potent prince in the empire. But is not the proportion fair, that Petworth stable affordeth standing in state for three-score horse, with all necessary accommodations?

WONDERS

Expect not here I should insert what William of Newbury writeth (to be recounted rather amongst the untruths than wonders) viz., "That in this county, not far from Battle Abbey, in the place where so great a slaughter of the Englishmen was made, after any shower, presently sweateth forth very fresh blood out of the earth, as if the evidence thereof did plainly declare the voice of blood there shed, and crieth still from the earth unto the Lord."

This is as true, as that in white chalky countries (about Baldock in Hertfordshire) after rain run rivulets of milk; neither being anything else than the water discoloured, according to the complexion of the earth thereabouts.

PROVERBS

He is none of the Hastings. This proverb, though extended all over England, is properly reduceable to this county, as originated there; for there is a haven town named Hastings therein, which some erroneously conceive so called from *haste* or *speed,* because William the (afterwards)

Conqueror, landing there did, as Matthew Paris sayeth, with *haste,* or speedily, erect some small fortification. But sure it is that there is a noble and ancient family of the Hastings in this land (I will not say first taking their name from this town) who formerly were earls of Pembroke, and still are of Huntingdon.

Now men commonly say, 'They are none of the Hastings,' who being slow and slack go about business with no agility. Such they also call *dull dromedaries* by a foul mistake, merely because of the affinity of that name to our English word *dreaming,* applied to such who go slowly and sleepily about their employment; whereas indeed dromedaries are creatures of a constant and continuing swiftness, so called from the Greek word *dremo,* to run; and are the cursitors for travel for the eastern country.

MARTYRS

Grievous the persecution in this county under John Christopherson[1] the bishop thereof. Such his havoc in burning poor protestants in one year, that had he sat long in that see, and continued after that rate, there needed no iron mills to rarefy the woods of this county, which this Bonner junior would have done of himself.

I confess the papists admire him as a most able and profound divine; which mindeth me of an epigram made by one who, being a suitor to a surly and scornful mistress, after he had largely praised her rare and divine perfections, concluded,

> She hath too much divinity for me:
> Oh! that she had some more humanity!

The same may this diocese say of Christopherson who, though carrying much of Christ in his surname, did bear nothing of him in his nature; no meekness, mildness or mercy, being addicted wholly to cruelty and destruction; burning no fewer than ten in one fire in Lewes, and seventeen others at several times in sundry places.

THE WORTHIES

HERBERT OF BOSHAM was born at Bosham, a goodly manor in this county (which Earl Godwin craftily kissed out of the archbishop of Canterbury); and, being a good scholar, he was a *manubus* (I mean to *write,* not to *fight* for him) unto Thomas à Becket archbishop of Canterbury. He was present at his murder-martyring; and had the discretion to make no resistance, lest he had been sent the same way with his master. However, amongst many other books, he wrote the story of his master's death. Going over into Italy he was, by Pope Alexander the Third, made archbishop of Beneventum; and, in the month of December 1178, created cardinal; but by what title it is unknown, as also is the exact date of his death. [*fl.* 1162-1186]

JOHN PECKHAM, born of obscure parents in this county; bred, when a boy, in Lewes; when a youth, a Franciscan in Oxford; when a young man,

(1) See Lancashire, p. 296.

in Paris; when a man, he lived in Lyons, where he became canon; when a grave man, in Rome, there made auditor of causes in that court; when an old man, in Canterbury, preferred against his will (except out of cunning he would seem courted into what he coveted) by the pope's plenary power to be archbishop thereof.

Peckham believed the pope invited him freely to that place, when soon after he was called upon to pay a sad reckoning, no less than four thousand marks. A worthy man he was in his place, who neither feared the laity nor flattered the clergy, unpartially imposing on both (if appearing peccant) most severe penance. He was a great punisher of pluralists, and enjoiner of residence.

His canon's place at Lyons he not only kept during his life, but left it to his successors, who held it *in commendam* some hundred years afterwards. Loth they were to part with it, as a safe retreating place in case our English kings should banish them the realm; besides it was a convenient inn for them to lodge at, as almost in the midway of their journeys betwixt Canterbury and Rome.

He sat archbishop almost fourteen years; built and endowed a college at Wingham; yet left a great estate to his kindred. I believe his wealth well gotten, because the land purchased therewith hath lasted so long in the lineage of his allies, in this and the next county, even to our age. He died Anno Domini 1292.

ROBERT DE WINCHELSEA. Although Bishop Godwin saith, *Ubi natus traditur, opinor, a nemine,* yet, considering the custom of the clergy in that age, none can doubt his birth in this county, except any should deny Winchelsea to be therein. He was bred in the neighbouring shire of Kent, where he was such a proficient in grammar learning, all did foretell that he, then the *arch-scholar* in the school, in due time would be *archbishop* of the see of Canterbury.

He was afterwards admitted in Merton College in Oxford; went thence to Paris, where he took the degree of master of arts, and became rector (perchance no more than a regent amongst us) of that university. Returning to Oxford, he there proceeded doctor of divinity, and became chancellor thereof; successively canon of Paul's, archdeacon of Essex, and archbishop of Canterbury. He went to Rome, to procure his pall of Pope Celestine.

He easily obtained his pall, and refused a cardinal's cap offered unto him. Returning to Canterbury, he was there solemnly enthroned, and on the same day consecrated one bishop, bestowed twelve rich benefices on twelve doctors, and twelve meaner livings on as many bachelors in divinity.

Confiding in the canon of the council of Lyons, which forbad the clergy to pay any taxes to princes without the consent of the pope, he created much molestation to himself, King Edward the First using him very harshly, till at last he overcame all with his patience. For the main, he was a worthy prelate, excellent preacher; being learned himself, he loved and preferred learned men. Prodigious his hospitality, being reported that Sundays and Fridays he fed no fewer than four thousand men when corn was cheap, and five thousand when it was dear; and because it shall not be said but my belief can be as large as his bounty, I give credit thereunto. Otherwise it seemeth suspicious, as a mock-imitation of those selfsame numbers of persons, which Christ, at two several times, miraculously fed with loaves and fishes. His charity went home to them which could not come to it, sending to such who were absented by their impotencies.

After his death, happening Anno Domini 1313, he was accounted, though not the pope's, the poor man's saint (bountiful men will always be canonized in the calendar of beggars); poor people repairing in flocks to the place of his burial, and superstitiously praying unto him; and they could best tell whether they found as much benefit from his tomb when dead, as at his table when living.

THOMAS BRADWARDINE [*b.* 1290?] was descended of an ancient family at Bredwardine in Herefordshire, who removing thence had settled themselves for three generations in this county, where this Thomas was born, in or near the city of Chichester. He was bred fellow of Merton College in Oxford, where he became a most exquisite mathematician and deep divine, being commonly called Doctor Profundus. He was confessor to King Edward the Third; and some impute our great conquest in France, not so much to the prowess of that king, as to the prayers of this his chaplain. He constantly preached in the camp, industry to officers, obedience to common soldiers, humility to all in good, patience in bad success. He exhorted them to be pious to God, dutiful to their king, pitiful to all captives; to be careful in making, faithful in keeping articles with their enemies. After the death of Stratford,[1] he was made archbishop of Canterbury; and at Avignon (where the pope then resided) received his consecration. Here he was accounted ἀγροικότερος, somewhat clownish, by the Romish court; partly because he could not mode it with the Italians, but chiefly because money being the general turnkey to preferment in that place, he was merely advanced for his merit.

But that which most recommended his memory to posterity, is that worthy book he made *de Causa Dei,* wherein speaking of Pelagius, he complaineth in his second book that *totus paene mundus, ut timeo et doleo, post hunc abiit, et erroribus ejus favet* (I fear and lament that almost the whole world runs after him, and favours his errors.) Bradwardine, therefore, undertook to be champion for grace and God's cause, against such who were not *defensores, sed deceptores, sed inflatores, sed praecipitatores liberi arbitrii,* as Augustine calleth them; and as the same father said of Cicero, *dum liberos homines esse volunt, faciunt sacrilegos.* He died at Lambeth, in October, Anno Domini 1349.

THE ABBOT OF BATTLE. He is a pregnant proof that one may leave no name and yet a good memory behind him. His Christian or surname cannot be recovered out of our chronicles which hitherto I have seen. But take his worth as followeth.

(1) John de Stratford—see Warwickshire, p. 581.

King Richard the Second, in the beginning of his reign, was in *nonage,* and his council, some will say, in *dotage,* leaving the land and sea to defend themselves, whilst they indulged their private factions.

This invited the French to invade this county, where they did much mischief, plundering (the thing was known in England before the name) the people thereof, and carrying away captive the prior of Lewes.[1] And no wonder if our abbot was startled therewith, seeing it may pass for a proverb in these parts:

> Ware the abbot of Battle,
> When the prior of Lewes is taken prisoner.

Wherefore, though no sheriff, he got together, as well as he might, the *posse comitatus;* and, putting it in as good a posture of defence as the time would permit, marched to Winchelsea and fortified it.

Some condemned him herein, it being incongruous for a clergyman to turn soldier. They objected also, that he ought to have expected orders from above; doing *rectum* but not *recte* for want of a commission.

Others commended him; to save and preserve being the most proper performance of a spiritual person, that *in hostes publicos, omnis homo miles;* that, though it be treason for any to fight a foe in a set field without command from the Supreme Power, yet one may (if he can) repel a rout of armed thieves invading a land; the first being the fittest time for such a purpose, the occasion itself giving (though no *express*) an *implicit* commission for the same. This abbot used rather the shield than the sword, being only on the defensive side.

Well, the French followed the abbot, and besieged him in the town of Winchelsea. In bravado they dared him to send out one, two, three, four or more, to try the mastery in fight, to be encountered with an equal number. But the abbot refused to retail his men out in such parcels, alleging that he was a spiritual person, not to challenge but only defend.

Then the French let fly their great guns; and I take it to be the first and last time they were ever planted by a foreign enemy on the English continent, and then roared so loud that they lost their voice, and have been (blessed be God) silent ever since.

The enemy, perceiving that the country came in fast upon them, and suspecting they should be surrounded on all sides, were fain to make for France as fast as they could, leaving the town of Winchelsea behind them, in the same form and fashion wherein they found it.

I behold this abbot as the saver, not only of Sussex, but England. For as dogs, who have once gotten an haunt[2] to worry sheep, do not leave off till they meet with their reward, so, had not these French felt the *smart* as well as the *sweet* of the English plunder, our land (and this county especially) had never been free from their incursions. All this happened in the reign of King Richard the second, Anno Domini 1377.

(1) At this period we were at a low ebb in our war with France, having for some years lost command of the channel. The French sacked Rye, ravaged the Isle of Wight and burned Hastings. The earl of Arundel, who should have commanded the shire levies, had fled to London, leaving the prior to face the enemy.
(2) *Haunt* = habit.

THOMAS ARUNDEL was the fourth archbishop of Canterbury who was born [1353] in this county; son he was to Richard, brother to Richard Fitzalan, both earls of Arundel. Herein he standeth alone by himself, that the name Arundel speaks him both nobleman and clergyman; the title of his father's honour, and place of his own birth, meeting both in the castle of Arundel.

It was either his nobility, or ability, or both, which in him did *supplere aetatem,* qualifying him to be bishop of Ely at twenty-two years of age. He was afterwards archbishop of York, and at last of Canterbury, 1396; and three several times lord chancellor of England, viz., in the tenth of Richard the Second, 1386; in the fifteenth of Richard the Second, 1391; the eleventh of Henry the Fourth, 1410.[1]

By King Richard the Second, when his brother the earl of Arundel was beheaded, this Thomas was banished the land. Let him thank his orders for saving his life, the tonsure of his hair for the keeping of his head, who otherwise had been sent the same path and pace with his brother.

Returning in the first of King Henry the Fourth, he was restored to his archbishopric. Such who commend his courage for being the church's champion, when a powerful party in parliament pushed at the revenues thereof, condemn his cruelty to the Wycliffites, being the first who persecuted them with fire and faggot. As for the manner of his death, we will neither carelessly wink at it, nor curiously stare on it, but may with a serious look solemnly behold it. He who had stopped the mouths of so many servants of God from preaching his word, was himself famished to death by a swelling in his throat. But seeing we bear in our bodies the seeds of all sickness (as of all sins in our souls) it is not good to be overbold and busy in our censures on such casualties. He died February 20, 1414, and lieth buried in his cathedral at Canterbury.

JOHN, HENRY, and THOMAS PALMER, sons unto Edward Palmer, esq., of Angmering in this county; a town so called, as I am informed, from *aqua marina,* or the water of the sea, being within two miles thereof, and probably, in former ages, nearer thereunto.

Their mother was daughter to one Clement of Wales, who, for his effectual assisting of King Henry the Seventh, from his landing at Milford Haven until the battle of Bosworth, was brought by him into England, and rewarded with good lands in this and the next county.

It happened that their mother, being a full fortnight inclusively in labour, was on Whit Sunday delivered of John her eldest son, on the Sunday following of Henry her second son, and the Sunday next after of Thomas her third son. This is that which is commonly called *superfoetation,* usual in other creatures, but rare in women; the cause whereof we leave to the disquisition of physicians.

These three were knighted for their valour by King Henry the Eighth, who never laid his sword on his shoulders who was not a man; so that they appear as remarkable in their success as their nativities. The

(1) Actually chancellor on five occasions: 1386-9, 1391-6, 1399, 1407 and 1412.

truth hereof needed no other attestation than the general and uncontrolled tradition of their no less worshipful than numerous posterity in Sussex and Kent; amongst whom I instance in Sir Roger Palmer, aged eighty years, lately deceased, and cofferer to our late king, averring to me the faith hereof on his reputation.[1]

WILLIAM BARLOW, D.D. My industry hath not been wanting in quest of the place of his nativity; but all in vain. Seeing therefore I cannot fix his character on his cradle, I am resolved (rather than omit him) to fasten it on his coffin, this county wherein he had his last preferment.

A man he was of much *motion* and *promotion*. First, I find him canon regular of St. Osyth's in Essex, and then prior of Bisham in Berkshire; then preferred by King Henry the Eighth, bishop of St. Asaph, and consecrated February 22, 1525; translated thence, the April following, to St. David's, remaining thirteen years in that see. In the third of King Edward the Sixth, he was removed to the bishopric of Bath and Wells. Flying the land in the reign of Queen Mary, he became superintendent of the English congregation at Emden. Coming back into England, by Queen Elizabeth he was advanced bishop of Chichester.

It is a riddle, why he chose rather to enter into new first-fruits, and begin at Chichester, than return to Bath, a better bishopric. Some suggest that he was loth to go back to Bath, having formerly consented to the expilation of that bishopric; whilst others make his consent to signify nothing, seeing empowered sacrilege is not so mannerly as to ask any "by your leave."

He had a numerous and prosperous female issue, as appeareth by the epitaph on his wife's monument, in a church in Hampshire, though one shall get no credit in translating them:

Hic Agathae tumulus Barloi, praesulis inde,
Exulis inde, iterum praesulis, uxor erat.
Prole beata fuit, plena annis; quinque suarum,
Praesulibus vidit, praesulis ipsa, datas.

Barlow's wife Agatha doth here remain;
Bishop, then exile, bishop then again.
So long she lived, so well his children sped,
She saw five bishops her five daughters wed.

Having sat about ten years in his see, he peaceably ended his life, December 10, 1568.

JOHN JEFFREY was born in this county, as I have been informed. It confirmeth me herein, because he left a fair estate in this shire (judges generally building their nest near the place where they were hatched)

(1) Whatever doubts there may be regarding the 'superfoetation', these three brothers are historical figures. Sir Thomas was a soldier of unbounded courage who held important appointments under Henry VIII. He conspired with, but disclosed, Protector Somerset's treasonable plot, was pardoned and in 1553 executed as an adherent of Lady Jane Grey. Sir Henry was a distinguished soldier who served at Boulogne and Calais, and on the fall of the latter was taken prisoner, ransomed, and died in 1559. The eldest, Sir John, was sheriff successively of Surrey and Sussex. He was a noted dicer, habitually won money from Henry VIII at cards, and was hanged, upon what grounds it is now not known. The facts of their parentage need correction. The father was Sir Edward Palmer, who married the sister and coheiress of Sir Richard Clement, who probably built the chapel of the manor-house of Igtham Mote, Kent.

which descended to his daughter. He so profited in the study of our municipal laws, that he was preferred secondary judge of the common pleas; and thence advanced by Queen Elizabeth, in Michaelmas term, the nineteenth of her reign, to be lord chief baron of the Exchequer, which place he discharged for the term of two years, to his great commendation. This worthy judge died in [1578].

GREGORY MARTIN was born at Maxfield in this county; bred (contemporary with Campion[1]) fellow of Saint John's College in Oxford. He was chosen by Thomas duke of Norfolk to be tutor to his son Philip earl of Arundel, and well discharged his trust therein.

Going afterwards beyond the seas, and living some time in Douay and Rome, he fixed at last in the English College at Rheims, where he was professor of divinity. As he was papal both in his Christian and surname, so was he deeply dyed with that religion, writing many books in the defence thereof, and one most remarkable, intituled *A Detection of the Corruptions in the English Bible.* Athaliah did craftily cry out first, "Treason, treason," when she was the greatest traitor herself;[2] and this Martin, conscious of the many and foul corruptions in his own Rhemish translation, politicly complained of the faults in our English Bible.[3] He died the 28th of October 1582; and lieth buried in the parish church of St. Stephen's in Rheims.

SIR WILLIAM PELHAM, knight, was a native of this county, whose ancient and wealthy family hath long flourished at Laughton therein. His prudence in peace, and valour in war, caused Queen Elizabeth to employ him in Ireland, where he was, by the privy council, appointed lord chief justice to govern that land, in the interim betwixt the death of Sir William Drury and the coming of Arthur Grey, lord-lieutenant of Ireland.

Say not that he did but stop a gap for a twelvemonth at the most; seeing it was such a *gap*, destruction had entered in thereat to the final ruin of that kingdom, had not his providence prevented it. For, in this juncture of time, Desmond began his rebellion, 1579, inviting Sir William to side with him, who wisely gave him the hearing, with a smile into the bargain. And although our knight (for want of force) could not cure the wound, yet he may be said to have washed and kept it clean, resigning it in a recovering condition to the Lord Grey, who succeeded him. Afterwards he was sent over into the Low Countries, 1581, being commander of the English horse therein; and my author[4] saith of him, *Brabantiam persultabat* (he leaped through Brabant) importing celerity and success, yea as much conquest as so sudden an expedition was capable of. I suspect he survived not long after, meeting no more mention of his martial activity. [*d.* 1587]

LEONARD MASCALL, of Plumpton in this county, being much delighted in gardening, man's original vocation, was the first who brought over

(1) Edmund Campion the Jesuit martyr—see London, p. 365. (2) Kings xi, 14. (3) He was the chief translator of the Douay Bible. (4) Camden's *Elizabeth.*

into England, from beyond the seas, carps and pippins; the one well cooked delicious, the other cordial and restorative. For the proof hereof, we have his own word and witness;[1] and did it, it seems, about the fifth year of the reign of King Henry the Eighth, Anno Domini 1514. [*d.* 1589]

THOMAS STAPLETON was born [1535] at Henfield in this county, as Pits, his familiar friend, doth inform us. Object not that it is written on his tomb at Saint Peter's at Louvain,

Thomas Stapletonus, qui Cicestriae in Anglia nobili loco natus.

Chichester there not being taken restrictively for the city, but extensively for the diocese. His bare surname is sufficient proof of his gentle birth.

Those of his own persuasion please themselves much to observe, that this Thomas was born in the same year and month wherein Sir Thomas More was beheaded, as if Divine Providence had purposely dropped from heaven an acorn in place of the oak that was felled.

He was bred in New College in Oxford, and then by the bishop (Christopherson, as I take it) made canon of Chichester, which he quickly quitted in the first of Queen Elizabeth. Flying beyond the seas, he first fixed at Douay, and there commendably performed the office of catechist, which he discharged to his commendation.

Reader, pardon an excursion caused by just grief and anger. Many, counting themselves protestants in England, do slight and neglect that ordinance of God, by which their religion was set up, and gave credit to it in the first Reformation: I mean Catechising. Did not our Saviour say even to Saint Peter himself, "Feed my lambs, feed my sheep." And why *lambs* first? 1. Because they were *lambs* before they were *sheep*. 2. Because, if they be not fed whilst *lambs,* they could never be *sheep*. 3. Because *sheep* can in some sort feed themselves, but *lambs* (such their tenderness) must either be *fed* or *famished.* Our Stapleton was excellent at this *lamb-feeding,* from which office he was afterwards preferred king's professor of divinity in Louvain, and was for forty years together *Dominus ad oppositum,* the undertaker-general against all protestants. Dr. Whitaker, professor in Cambridge, experimentally professed that Bellarmine was the *fairer* and Stapleton the *shrewder* adversary.

His preferment (in mine eyes) was not proportionable to his merit, being no more than canon and master of a college in Louvain. Many more admired that Stapleton missed, than that Allen got, a cardinal's cap, equalling him in strictness of life, exceeding him in gentility of birth, and painfulness of writing for the Romish cause. Such consider not that Stapleton's ability was drowned with Allen's activity; and one *grain* of the statesman is too heavy for a pound of the student; practical policy, in all ages, beating pen-pains out of distance in the race of preferment.[2] Stapleton died, and was buried in Saint Peter's in Louvain, anno 1598.

(1) In his book on Fishing, Fowling, and Planting. [Mascall was clerk of the kitchen to Archbishop Parker. It is unlikely that he introduced carps and pippins into England, but he was an ingenious horticulturist.] (2) William Whitaker and William Allen—see both under Lancashire.

THOMAS SACKVILLE [First EARL OF DORSET, *b.* 1536] son and heir to Sir Richard Sackville (chancellor and sub-treasurer of the exchequer, and privy councillor to Queen Elizabeth) by Winifred his wife, daughter to Sir John Bruges, was bred in the university of Oxford, where he became an excellent poet, leaving both Latin and English poems of his composing to posterity. Then studied he law in the Temple, and took the degree of barrister; afterward he travelled into foreign parts, detained for a time prisoner in Rome, whence his liberty was procured for his return into England, to possess the vast inheritance left him by his father, whereof in short time, by his magnificent prodigality, he spent the greatest part, till he seasonably began to spare, growing near to the bottom of his estate.

The story goes, that this young gentleman coming to an alderman of London, who had gained great pennyworths by his former purchases of him, was made (being now in the wane of his wealth) to wait the coming down of the alderman so long, that his generous humour being sensible of the incivility of such attendance, resolved to be no more beholding to wealthy pride, and presently turned a thrifty improver of the remainder of his estate. If this be true, I could wish that all aldermen would *state* it on the like occasion, on condition their noble debtors would but make so good use thereof.

But others make him a convert of Queen Elizabeth (his cousin-german once removed) who by her frequent admonitions diverted the torrent of his profusion. Indeed she would not know him, till he began to know himself, and then heaped places of honour and trust upon him, creating him, 1. Baron of Buckhurst in this county (the reason why we have placed him therein) Anno Domini 1567. 2. Sending him ambassador into France, anno 1571; into the Low Countries, anno 1587. 3. Making him knight of the order of the Garter, anno 1589. 4. Appointing him treasurer of England, 1599.

He was chancellor of the university of Oxford, where he entertained Queen Elizabeth with a most sumptuous feast. His elocution was good, but inditing better; and therefore no wonder if his secretaries could not please him, being a person of so quick dispatch (faculties which yet run in the blood.) He took a roll of the names of all suitors, with the date of their first addresses; and these in order had their hearing, so that a fresh man could not leap over the head of his senior, except in urgent affairs of state.

Thus having made amends to his house for his mis-spent time, both in increase of estate and honour, being created earl of Dorset by King James, he died on the 19th of April, 1608.[1]

ROBERT SACKVILLE [Second EARL OF DORSET, *b.* 1561] eldest son of Thomas earl of Dorset, by Cecily his wife, had his *barony,* if not his birth, at Buckhurst in this county. A gentleman of singular learning in many sciences and languages, so that the Greek and Latin were as familiar unto him as his own native tongue.[2] Succeeding his father in that

(1) Sackville wrote the 'Induction' to the *Mirror for Magistrates* and part of the *Tragedy of Gorboduc.* His father was first cousin of Anne Boleyn. (2) He was educated by Roger Ascham. He was several times M.P. for Sussex.

earldom, he enjoyed his dignity not a full year, as lacking seven weeks thereof. Yet is there no fear that the shortness of his earlship will make his name forgotten, having erected a monument which will perpetuate his memory to all posterity, viz., a college at East Grinstead in this county, for one-and-thirty poor people to serve almighty God therein; endowing the same with three hundred and thirty pounds a year out of all his land in England. By Margaret sole daughter to Thomas duke of Norfolk he left two surviving sons, Richard and Edward, both persons of admirable parts, successively earls after him; and, dying 1609, was buried at Withyham in this county.

SIR ANTHONY SHIRLEY [*b.* 1565] second son to Sir Thomas, set forth from Plymouth, May the 21st, 1596, in a ship called the *Bevis* of Southampton, attended with six lesser vessels. His design for San Thome was violently diverted by the contagion they found on the south coast of Africa, where the rain did stink as it fell down from the heavens, and within six hours did turn into maggots. This made him turn his course to America, where he took and kept the city of Santiago two days and nights, with two hundred and eighty men, whereof eighty were wounded in the service, against three thousand Portugals.

Hence he made for the Isle of Fuego, in the midst whereof a mountain, Etna-like, always burning; and the wind did drive such a shower of ashes upon them, that one might have wrote his name with his finger on the upper deck. However, in this fiery island they furnished themselves with good water, which they much wanted.

Hence he sailed to the island of Margarita, which to him did not answer its name, not finding here the pearl dredgers which he expected. Nor was his gain considerable in taking the town of Saint Martha, the isle and chief town of Jamaica, whence he sailed more than thirty leagues up the River Rio-dolci, where he met with great extremity.

At last, being diseased in person, distressed for victuals, and deserted by all his other ships, he made by Newfoundland to England, where he arrived June 15, 1597. Now although some behold his voyage, begun with more courage than counsel, carried on with more valour than advice, and coming off with more honour than profit to himself or the nation (the Spaniard being rather frighted than harmed, rather braved than frighted therewith) yet unpartial judgments, who measure not worth by success, justly allow it a prime place amongst the probable (though not prosperous) English adventures.[1] [*d.* 1635?]

SIR ROBERT SHIRLEY [*b.* 1581?] youngest son to Sir Thomas, was by his brother Anthony entered in the Persian court. Here he performed great service against the Turks, and shewed the difference between Persian and English valour; the latter having therein as much courage, and more

(1) Fuller knew only what Hakluyt relates of this single episode of this extraordinary adventurer's life. Prior to this voyage he served in the Netherlands and in Normandy. He accompanied Essex on the unsuccessful Azores expedition in 1597. After a mission to Persia, where he was created mirza, or prince, he returned to Europe as the shah's envoy. Later, suspected of treason, he was disavowed by the English government, created a count of the Empire, served the king of Spain, and died in poverty at Madrid.

mercy, giving quarter to captives who craved it, and performing life to those to whom he promised it. These his actions drew the envy of the Persian lords, and love of the ladies, amongst whom one, reputed a kinswoman to the great Sophy, after some opposition was married unto him. She had more of *ebony* than *ivory* in her complexion; yet amiable enough, and very valiant, a quality considerable in that sex in those countries. With her he came over into England, and lived many years therein. He much affected to appear in foreign vests; and, as if his clothes were his limbs, accounted himself never ready till he had something of the Persian habit about him.

At last a contest happening betwixt him and the Persian ambassador (to whom some reported Sir Robert gave a box on the ear) the king sent them both into Persia, there mutually to impeach one another, and joined Doctor Gough (a senior fellow of Trinity College in Cambridge) in commission with Sir Robert. In this voyage (as I am informed) both died on the seas, before the controverted difference was ever heard in the court of Persia, about the beginning of the reign of King Charles.[1]

[*d.* 1628.]

SIR THOMAS SHIRLEY [*b.* 1564]. I name him the last, though the eldest son of his father, beiause last appearing in the world, men's activity not always observing the method of their register. As the trophies of Miltiades would not suffer Themistocles to sleep, so the achievements of his two younger brethren gave an alarum unto his spirit. He was ashamed to see them worn like flowers in the breasts and bosoms of foreign princes, whilst he himself withered upon the stalk he grew on. This made him leave his aged father and fair inheritance in this county, and to undertake sea voyages into foreign parts, to the great honour of his nation, but small enriching of himself; so that he might say to his son, as Aeneas to Ascanius:

> *Disce, puer, virtutem ex me verumque laborem,*
> *Fortunam ex aliis.*
>
> Virtue and labour learn from me thy father;
> As for success, child, learn from others rather.

As to the general performances of these three brethren, I know the affidavit of a poet carrieth but a small credit in the court of history; and the comedy made of them is but a friendly foe to their memory, as suspected more accommodated to please the present spectators, than to inform posterity. However, as the belief of Miltio, when an inventory of his adopted son's misdemeanours was brought unto him, embraced a middle and moderate way, *Nec omnia credere nec nihil* (neither to believe all things nor nothing) of what was told him, so in the list of their achievements we may safely pitch on the same proportion, and when

(1) Sir Robert Shirley, half-brother to Sir Anthony, remained in Persia when the latter left. He was Persian envoy at various European courts, created count palatine, and was received by James I in 1624, but later, quarrelling with another envoy from Persia, both were dismissed. Contrary to Fuller's statement, both envoys reached Persia, where the Persian acknowledged himself in the wrong by committing suicide. Shirley himself was in disgrace and, broken-hearted, died shortly afterwards.

abatement is made for poetical embellishments, the remainder will speak them worthies in their generations.[1] [*d.* 1630?]

WILLIAM PEMBLE was born [1592?] in this county, where his parents had no plentiful estate; but their wants were supplied (as to this their son's education in learning) by the bounty of John Barker, of Mayfield in this shire, esquire, as by the following passage may appear, written by Mr. Capel, his worthy tutor:[2]

> You are the man who supported the vine that bore this and many excellent grapes. His studies had shrunk and withered, even then when they were about to knit, had it not been for you and your exhibitions, who have raised up an able scholar, a learned divine, a well-studied artist, a skilful linguist, and (which is the soul of all) a very godly minister.

So then, if I have missed Master Pemble's native county, yet I shall be excused by the known proverb, *Non ubi nascor, sed ubi pascor;* Sussex affording him his most effectual maintenance. He was *bred in* (or if you will *he bred*) Magdalen Hall in Oxford; that house owing its late lustre to his learned lectures, the gravest in the university not disdaining their presence thereat. He was an excellent orator indeed, as who spake *non ex ore sed ex pectore,* many excellencies being in him; but above all, this was his crown, that he unfeignedly sought God's glory, and the good of men's souls. He died in the flower of his age, as he was making his lectures on the prophecy of Zechariah (finishing but nine chapters of fourteen) Anno Domini [1623] of a burning fever.

WILLIAM JUXON was born [1582] at Chichester in this county, bred fellow in Saint John's College in Oxford, where he proceeded bachelor of law; very young, but very able for that degree, and afterwards became doctor in the same faculty, and president of the college.

One in whom nature had not omitted, but grace hath ordered, the tetrarch humour of choler, being admirably master of his pen and his passion. For his abilities, he was successively preferred, by King Charles the First, bishop of Hereford and London, and for some years lord treasurer of England: a troublesome place in those times, it being expected that he should make much *brick,* though not altogether without, yet with very little *straw* allowed unto him. Large then the expenses, low the revenues of the Exchequer. Yet those coffers which he found empty, he left filling; and had left full, had peace been preserved in the land, and he continued in his place. Such the mildness of

(1) Sir Thomas Shirley served in the Netherlands. He angered and was imprisoned by Elizabeth for a secret marriage. He was M.P. for Hastings 1601. He was captured by the Turks when privateering in the Levant, and after an appeal by James I and bribes to gaolers, he was at length released. Later he was imprisoned in the Tower for illegal interference with the Levant Company. The father of these three brothers was Sir Thomas Shirley (1542-1612) M.P. and sheriff of Sussex and Surrey. When treasurer-at-war to the English army in the Netherlands he involved himself in debts to the Crown. Committed to the Fleet he claimed privilege as M.P., and parliament in a notable case decided that members were secure from arrest except for treason, felony and breach of the peace. The home of the Shirleys was at Wiston near Steyning. (2) In the Epistle Dedicatory, before his Lectures on the Sacrament.

his temper, that petitioners for money (when it was not to be had) departed well pleased with his denials, they were so civilly languaged. It may justly seem a wonder that whereas few spake well of bishops at that time, and lord treasurers at all times are liable to complaints of a discontented people, though both offices met in this man, yet, with Demetrius, "he was well reported of all men, and of the truth itself."[1]

He lived to see much shame and contempt undeservedly poured on his function, and all the while possessed his own soul in patience. He beheld those of his order to lose their votes in parliament; and their insulting enemies hence concluded (loss of speech being a sad symptom of approaching death) that their final extirpation would follow, whose own experience at this day giveth the lie to their malicious collection. Nor was it the least part of this prelate's honour that, amongst the many worthy bishops of our land, King Charles the First selected him for his confessor at his martyrdom. He formerly had had experience (in the case of the earl of Strafford) that this bishop's conscience was bottomed on piety, not policy; the reason that from him he received the sacrament, good comfort and counsel, just before he was murdered. I say just before that royal martyr was *murdered;* a fact so foul, that it alone may confute the error of the Pelagians, maintaining "that all sin cometh by imitation," the universe not formerly affording such a precedent; as if those regicides had purposely designed to disprove the observation of Solomon, that "there is no new thing under the sun." King Charles the Second, Anno Domini 1660, preferred him archbishop of Canterbury; which place he worthily graceth at the writing hereof, February 1, 1661. [*d.* 1663]

JOHN SELDON, son of Thomas Selden, was born [1584] at Salvington, within the parish of West Tarring in this county. He was first bred in Hart Hall in Oxford, then in the Inner Temple in London, where he attained great skill in the law and all antiquity. His learning did not live in a lane, but traced all the latitude of arts and languages, as appeared by the many and various works he hath written, which people *affect* as they stand affected either by their fancy or function. Lay gentlemen prefer his *Titles of Honour;* lawyers his *Mare Clausum;* antiquaries his *Spicilegium ad Edmearum;* clergymen like best his book *De Diis Syris,* and worst his *History of Tithes.*

Indeed, the body of that history did not more offend them in point of profit, than the preface thereof in matter of credit, such his insolent reflections therein. Nor will it be impertinent here to insert a passage of consequence, which I find in a modern author of good intelligence:

> Master Selden was no friend to bishops, as constituted and established in the Church of England. For, being called before the High Commission, and forced to make a public acknowledgment of his error and offence given unto the church in publishing a book entituled *The History of Tithes,* it sunk so deep into his stomach, that he never after affected the men, or cordially approved the calling, though many ways were tried to gain him to the church's interest.[2]

(1) 3 John 12. (2) Extraneus Vapulans, made by an *Alter-idem* to Doctor Heylin.

To this his public acknowledgment I can say nothing. This I know, that a friend of mine, employed on a fair and honest account to peruse the library of Archbishop Laud, found therein a large letter written to him, and subscribed with Master Selden's own hand, wherein he used many expressions of his contrition, much condemning himself for setting forth a book of that nature; which letter my aforesaid friend gave back again to Master Selden, to whom, I assure you, it was no unacceptable present.[1]

But that which afterwards entituled him to a general popularity, was his pleading with Master Noye for a *habeas corpus* of such gentlemen which were imprisoned for the refusal of the loan.[2] Hence was it that most men beheld Master Selden as their common counsel, and themselves as his clients, conceiving that the liberty of all English subjects was concerned in that suit.

He had very many ancient coins of the Roman emperors, and more modern ones of our English kings; dying exceeding wealthy; insomuch that naked charity both wished and hoped for a good new coat at his hands, but missed of its expectation. The archbishop of Armagh (to whom he was always most civil and respectful) preached his funeral sermon. The large library which he left is a jewel indeed; and this jewel long looked to be put into a new cabinet, when one of the inns of court (on which it was bestowed) should be pleased to provide a fair and firm fabric to receive it; but now is reposited (*Bodley* within a *Bodley*) in the matchless library of Oxford. [*d.* 1654]

ACCEPTED FREWEN, D.D., was born [1588] at Northiam in this county, bred fellow of Magdalen College in Oxford, and afterwards became president thereof; and, after some mediate preferments, was by King Charles the First advanced bishop of Coventry and Lichfield; and since, by King Charles the Second, made archbishop of York.

But the matter whereof porcelain or china dishes are made, must be ripened many years in the earth before it comes to full perfection. The living are not the proper objects of the historian's pen, who may be misinterpreted to flatter, even when he falls short of their due commendation, the reason why I add no more in praise of this worthy prelate.

As to the nativities of archbishops, one may say of this county, "Many shires have done worthily, but Sussex surmounteth them all;" having bred *five* archbishops of Canterbury, and at this instant claiming for her natives the two metropolitans of our nation. [*d.* 1664]

THOMAS MAY was born [1595] in this county, of a worshipful but decayed family; bred fellow-commoner in Cambridge, in Sidney College, where he seriously applied himself to his studies. He afterwards lived

(1) Mr. Spencer, keeper of the library at Jesus College. [*The History of Tithes* was later suppressed by public authority. Selden's labitudinarian and somewhat sceptical mind, detached and judical, irritated an age of fierce religious controversy. He stung many with his *dicta*, learned and barbed. His profound knowledge of the common law made him a formidable antagonist of Charles I's prerogative.] (2) The case of the five knights, who were imprisoned for refusing to subscribe to the forced loan of 1627.

in Westminster, and about the court. He was an elegant poet, and translated Lucan into English. Now though Scaliger be pleased to say hypocritically of Lucan, *Non canit, sed latrat,* yet others (under the rose) as judicious, allow him an excellent poet, and losing no lustre by Mr. May's translation.

Some disgust at court was given to, or taken by him (as some will have it) because his bays were not gilded richly enough, and his verses rewarded by King Charles according to his expectation. He afterwards wrote a history of this state,[1] in the beginning of our civil wars; and being myself (for my many writings) one under the authority of the tongues and pens of others, it ill becometh me to pass any censure on his performance therein. Sure I am, if he were a biassed and partial writer, he lieth buried near a good and true historian indeed (I mean Mr. Camden) in the west side of the north aisle of Westminster Abbey, dying suddenly in the night, Anno Domini 1650, in the 55th year of his age.

THE FAREWELL

For my *vale* to this county, I desire to be their remembrancer of the counsel which their countryman William earl of Arundel gave to his son, Henry Fitzalan, last earl of that surname, viz., "Never to trust their neighbours the French." Indeed for the present they are at amity with us; but foreign friendship is ticklish, temporary, and lasteth no longer than it is advantaged with mutual interest. May never French land on this shore, to the loss of the English. But if so sad an accident should happen, send then our Sussexians no worse success than their ancestors of Rye and Winchelsea had, 1378, in the reign of Richard the Second, when they embarked for Normandy; for, in the night, they entered a town called Peter's Port, took all such prisoners who were able to pay ransom, and safely returned home without loss, and with much rich spoil; and amongst the rest they took down out of the steeple the bells, and brought them into England; bells which the French had taken formerly from these towns, and which did afterwards ring the more merrily, restored to their proper place, with addition of much wealth to pay for the cost of their recovery.

(1) His *History of the Long Parliament* is a useful source for the period.

WARWICKSHIRE

WARWICKSHIRE hath Leicester and Northampton-shires on the east, Oxford and Gloucester-shires on the south, Worcester on the west, and Staffordshire on the north thereof. In form, at the first view in a map, it doth pretend to some circularness, but attaineth no exactness therein, as extending thirty-three miles from north to south, though from east to west not distanced above twenty-six.

One said no less truly than merrily, "It is the *heart* but not the *core* of England," having nothing coarse or choky therein. The woodland part thereof may want what the fielden[1] affords, so that Warwickshire is defective in neither. As for the pleasure thereof, an author is bold to say that from Edgehill one may behold it another Eden,[2] as Lot did the plain of Jordan; but he might have put in, "It is not altogether so well watered."

NATURAL COMMODITIES

Sheep

Most large for bone, flesh and wool in this county, especially about Wormleighton. In this shire the complaint of J. Rous[3] continueth and increaseth, that sheep turn cannibals, eating up men, houses and towns: their pastures make such depopulation.

But, on the other side, it is pleaded for these enclosures that they make houses the fewer in this county, and the more in the kingdom. How come buildings in great towns every day to increase (so that commonly tenants are in before tenements are ended) but that the poor are generally maintained by clothing, the staple trade of the nation?

Indeed corn doth visibly employ the poor in the place where it groweth, by ploughing, sowing, mowing, inning,[4] threshing; but wool invisibly maintaineth people at many miles' distance, by carding, spinning, weaving, dressing, dyeing it. However, an expedient might be so used betwixt tillage and pasturage, that Abel should not kill Cain, the shepherd undo the husbandman, but both subsist comfortably together.

Ash

It is the prince (oak being allowed the king) of English timber, growing plentifully in the woodland part of this county. I confess it far short in sovereignness, against serpents, of the Italian ash, if true what Pliny reporteth (making affidavit thereof on his own experience, *experti prodimus*) that a serpent, encircled with fire and boughs of ash will, in this dilemma, put himself rather on the hazard of fire, than adventure on the fence of ashen boughs. It is also far inferior in toughness to the Spanish ash; and yet a stand of pikes made of English ash, and

(1) *Fielden*=open, consisting of fields. (2) J. Speed, in his Description of Warwickshire. (3) See p. 582 below. (4) *Inning*=ingathering, harvesting.

managed with Englishmen's arms, will do very well. But, to waive the warlike, and praise the peaceable use of the ash, it is excellent for plough-timber, besides many utensils within a family. Being cut down green, it burneth (a peculiar privilege of this wood) clear and bright, as if the say thereof had a fire-feeding unctuousness therein. The fruit thereof is good in physic, whose keys are opening of obstructions arising from the spleen.

COAL

Much hereof is digged up at Bedworth, which (in my measuring) of all coal-mines north of Thames is the most southward, adding much to their price and owners' profit. The making such mines destroyeth much, but when made preserveth more timber. I am sorry to hear that those *black Indies,* both in quantity and quality, fall short of their former fruitfulness; and I wish they may recover their lost credit, being confident the earth there will bleed profit as plentifully as any, had the miners but the good hap to hit the right vein thereof.

As for manufactures in this county, some broadcloths are made in Coventry, and ten might be made for one, if the mystery thereof were vigorously pursued.

THE BUILDINGS

Coventry, much beholding to the Lady Godiva (who took order that her charity should not prejudice her modesty, when she purchased the privileges of this place) sheweth two fair churches close together. How clearly would they have shined, if set at competent distance! Whereas now, such their vicinity, that the Archangel eclipseth the Trinity.[1]

SAINT MARY'S in Warwick, a beautiful structure, owes its *life* to the monuments of the *dead* therein, most being earls of Warwick. Of these, that in the body of the church is the oldest, that in the chancel is the largest, that in the chapel (of gilt brass) the richest, that in the chapter-house (of Fulke Lord Brooke) the latest. Greatness may seem in some sort to be buried in the tomb of the earl of Leicester, and goodness in that of the earl of Warwick. Women are most delighted with the statue of the infant baron of Denbigh, and scholars most affected with the learned epitaph of Sir Thomas Puckering. In a word, so numerous is the church with its appendances, as I am informed by my worthy friend the minister,[2] that he can accommodate one clergyman, of all dignities and degrees, to repose them in several chapels or vestries by themselves.

KENELWORTH, alias KENILWORTH. It had the strength of a castle and beauty of a prince's court. Though most fair the porch, no danger of the castle's running out thereat (like that of Mindus at the gate) as most proportionable to the rest of the fabric. I confess *handsome* is an

(1) Fuller means *St. Michael's* (later the cathedral church, destroyed in the air raid of 1940) and the church of the *Holy Trinity.* Lady Godiva and her husband, the earl of Mercia, founded the great Benedictine monastery of Coventry in 1043.
(2) Mr. Venour.

unproper epithet of a giant, yet neatness agreeth with the vastness of this structure.

Some castles have been demolished for security, which I behold destroyed, *se defendendo,* without offence; others demolished in the heat of the wars, which I look upon as castle-slaughter. But I cannot excuse the destruction of this castle from wilful murder, being done in cold blood since the end of the wars.

I am not stocked enough with charity to pity the ruiners thereof, if the materials of this castle answered not their expectation who destroyed it.

Pass we now from the preterperfect to the present tense, I mean from what was once to what now is most magnificent, the castle of Warwick. It overlooketh the town, which is washed and swept by nature; so sweet, on a rising hill, is the situation thereof. The prospect of this castle is pleasant in itself, and far more to the present owner thereof, the right honourable Robert Lord Brooke, seeing the windows look into lands mostly of his possession.

We will conclude the buildings of this county, with the beautiful Cross of Coventry; *a reformed cross* (or *standard* rather) without any cross thereon, being a master-piece, all for ornament, nothing for superstition; so that the most curious hath just cause to commend, the most conscientious to allow, none to condemn it.

It was begun 1541, the 33d, and finished 1544, the 36th of King Henry the Eighth, at the sole cost of Sir William Holles, lord mayor of London, great-grandfather to the right honourable the earl of Clare.

THE WONDERS

At Leamington, within two miles of Warwick, there issue out, within a stride, of the womb of the earth two twin-springs, as different in taste and operation, as Esau and Jacob in disposition, the one salt, the other fresh. Thus the meanest countryman doth plainly see the effects, whilst it would pose a consultation of philosophers to assign the true cause thereof.

To this permanent let me enjoy a transient wonder, which was some fifty years since. The situation of Coventry is well known, on a rising hill, having no river near it, save a small brook, over which generally one may make a bridge with a stride. Now here happened such an inundation, on Friday, April the seventeenth, 1607 (attested under the seal of the city, in the mayoralty of Henry Sewel) as was equally admirable: 1. In coming about eight o'clock in the morning, no considerable rain preceding, which might suggest the least suspicion thereof. 2. In continuance, for the space of three hours, wherein it overflowed more than two hundred and fifty dwelling houses, to the great damage of the inhabitants. 3. In departure, or vanishing rather, sinking as suddenly as it did rise.

MEDICINAL WATERS

At Newnham Regis there is a spring, the water whereof drunk with salt looseneth, with sugar bindeth the body. It is also very sovereign against ulcers, impostumes and the stone. This last I commend to the reader's choice observation; the same author affirming that it turneth sticks into stone, and that he himself was an eyewitness thereof.[1] Now, how it should dissolve the stone in the body of a man, and yet turn wood into stone, I leave to such who are *Naturae a sanctioribus consiliis,* at their next meeting at their council table to discuss and decide.

PROVERBS

He is the Black Bear of Arden. Arden is a forest, anciently occupying all the woodland part of this county. By the Black Bear is meant Guy de Beauchamp earl of Warwick, who (besides the allusion to his crest) was grim of person and surly of resolution; for, when this bear had gotten Piers Gaveston (that monkey and minion of King Edward the Second) into his chambers, he caused his death at a hill within two miles of Warwick, notwithstanding all opposition to the contrary. The proverb is applicable to those who are not *terriculamenta* but *terrores,* no fancy-formed bugbears, but such as carry fear and fright to others about them.

THE WORTHIES

SAINT WULFSTAN [*b.* 1012?]. There is some difference, but what is easily reconcileable, about the place of his nativity: *Sanctus Wolstanus, natione Anglus, Wigorniensis.*[2] "Saint Wulfstan was born in Warwickshire, of worthy and religious parents."[3]

The accommodation is easy, seeing a Warwickshire man by his county may be a Worcester man by his diocese, to which see the western moiety of that county doth belong. Since, I have learned from my worthy friend[4] that Long Itchington in this shire may boast of the birth of Saint Wulfstan. He afterwards began bishop of Worcester, and for his piety and holiness was generally reverenced.

Indeed he was, like Jacob, a plain man, with Nathanael an Israelite, without guile, welt or guard.[5] He could not mode it, or comport, either with French fickleness or Italian pride; which rendered him at once hated by two grandees, King William the Conqueror, and Lanfranc the lordly Lombard, archbishop of Canterbury.

These resolved on his removal,[6] quarrelling with him that he could not speak French (a quality which much commended the clergy in that age to preferment) and command him to give up his episcopal staff and ring into the hands of the king. But old Wulfstan trudged to the tomb of King Edward the Confessor in Westminster, who had been his patron, and there offered up his episcopal habiliments. "These," said he, "from you I received, and to you I resign them."

(1) Speed, in his Description of Warwickshire. (2) J. Pits. (3) Jerome Porter, in the Flowers of the Lives of English Saints. (4) Mr. Dugdale, in his *Illustrations* of this county. (5) *Welt or guard.* Probably used in the sense of *amour-propre.* (6) The story has been disproved. Although the Conqueror was not in the habit of appointing Englishmen to bishoprics, Wulfstan had submitted to him and was unmolested. Wulfstan is remarkable for having preached against the slave trade practised by English merchants against their countrymen and women, and secured its abandonment.

This his plain dealing so wrought on his adversaries (honesty at long running is the best policy) that he was not only continued, but countenanced, in his bishopric; yea, acquired the reputation of a saint. The greatest fault which I find charged on his memory is his activity in making William Rufus king, to the apparent injury of Robert his elder brother. But it is no wonder if clergymen betray their weakness, who, being bred in a convent, quit church business to intermeddle with secular matters. He died January 18, 1095.

JOHN DE STRATFORD, son of Robert and Isabella de Stratford, is notoriously known to be born at Stratford-on-Avon, an eminent market in this county. Being, by papal provisions, preferred bishop of Winchester, without the royal consent, he fell into the disfavour of King Edward the Second, regaining his good will by the intercession of Archbishop Meopham; and being a subject, not to the prosperity but person of his prince, he forsook him not in the greatest extremity. This cost him the displeasure of the queen mother and King Edward the Third, till at last, converted by his constancy, they turned their frowns into smiles upon him.

When archbishop of Canterbury, he persuaded King Edward the Third to invade France, promising to supply him with competent provisions for the purpose; a promise not so proportionable to his archiepiscopal capacity as to him, as he had been twice treasurer of England, and skilful in the collecting and advancing of money, so that he furnished the king with great sums at his first setting forth for France.

These being spent before the year ended, the king sends over for a supply. Stratford, instead of coin, returns counsel, advising him to alter his officers; otherwise, if so much was spent at a breakfast, the whole wealth of the land would not suffice him for dinner.

Over comes the angry king, from whose fury Stratford was forced to conceal himself until, publicly passing his purgation in parliament, he was restored to the reputation of his innocence, and rectified in the king's esteem. He built, and bountifully endowed, a beautiful college in the town of his nativity; and, having sat archbishop fifteen years, died anno 1348, leaving a perfumed memory behind him for his bounty to his servants, charity to the poor, meekness and moderation to all persons.

ROBERT DE STRATFORD (brother to the archbishop aforesaid) was, in the reign of King Edward the Third, made bishop of Chichester. He was at the same time chancellor of Oxford (wherein he was bred) and of all England; honourable offices, which sometimes have met in the same person, though never more deservedly than in the present enjoyer[1] of them both.

In his time there was a tough contest betwixt the south and northern men in that university. They fell from their pens to their hands, using the contracted fist of martial logic, bloody blows passing betwixt them. This bishop did wisely and fortunately bestir himself an arbitrator in

(1) Edward Hyde, earl of Clarendon (1609-1674).

this controversy, being a proper person for such a performance, born in this county (in the very navel of England) so that his nativity was a natural expedient betwixt them, and his judgment was unpartial in compromising the difference.

He was accused to the king for favouring the French, with his brother archbishop; contented patiently to attend till pregnant *Time* was delivered of *Truth* her daughter; and then this brace of prelates appeared brethren in integrity. He died at Aldingbourne, April 9, 1362.

RALPH DE STRATFORD (kinsman to the foresaid archbishop[1]) was born in the town of Stratford-on-Avon, where he built a chapel to the honour of Saint Thomas. He was first canon of Saint Paul's; and afterwards, May 12, 1340, was consecrated at Canterbury bishop of London.

During his sitting in that see, there happened so grievous a pestilence[2] in London, that hardly the tenth person in some places did escape. Then each churchyard was indeed a *polyandrum,* so that the dead might seem to justle one another for room therein. Yea, the dead did kill the living, so shallowly were their heaped corpses interred.

Whereupon this bishop charitably bought a piece of ground nigh Smithfield. It was called No Man's Land, not *a parte ante,* as formerly without an owner (seeing it had a proprietary of whom it was legally purchased) but *de futuro,* none having a particular interest therein, though indeed it was All Men's Land, as designed and consecrated for the general sepulture of the deceased. This bishop, having continued about fourteen years in his see, died at Stepney 1354.

JOHN ROUS, son of Geoffrey Rous, was born [1411?] at Warwick, but descended from the Rouses of Brinklow in this county. He was bred in Oxford, where he attained to great eminency of learning. He afterwards retired himself to Guy's Cliffe, within a mile of Warwick.

A most delicious place, so that a man in many miles' riding cannot meet so much variety as there one furlong doth afford. A steep rock, full of caves in the bowels thereof, washed at the bottom with a crystal river, besides many clear springs on the side thereof, all overshadowed with a stately grove; so that an ordinary fancy may here find to itself Helicon, Parnassus and what not. Many hermits (and Guy earl of Warwick himself) being sequestered from the world, retreated hither. Some will say it is too gaudy a place for that purpose, as having more of a paradise than wilderness therein, so that men's thoughts would rather be *scattered* than *collected* with such various objects. But, seeing hermits deny themselves the company of men, let them be allowed to converse with the rarities of Nature; and such are the fittest texts for a solitary devotion to comment upon.

To this place came our John Rous; and, by leave obtained from King Edward the Fourth, immured himself therein that he might apply his studies without distraction. Here he wrote of *The Antiquities of Warwick,* with a catalogue of the earls thereof, a chronicle of our English

(1) He was probably the nephew of Robert de Stratford. (2) The Black Death.

kings, and a history of our universities. He was as good with the pencil as the pen, and could draw persons as well as describe them, as appears by lively pictures limned with his own hand. He died, a very aged man, Anno Domini 1491.

SIR HUGH CLOPTON was born at Stratford, a fair market town in this county, bred a mercer in London, and at last lord mayor thereof anno 1492. Remembering that his native town stood on Avon, a river in summer and little sea in winter, troublesome for travellers to pass over, he, in lieu of the former inconvenient conveyance, built a stately and long stone bridge, of many arches, over the channel and overflowings thereof.

I behold this bridge more useful, though less costly, than what Caligula made, termed by Suetonius *novum et inauditum spectaculi genus,* reaching from Putzel to Bauly, three miles and a quarter. This was only a pageant bridge for pomp, set up to be soon taken down, whereof Lipsius said well, *laudem immenso operi vanitas detrahit.* But our Clopton's bridge remaineth at this day, even when the college in the same town, built by Archbishop Stratford, is (as to the intended use thereof) quite vanished away. Indeed bridges are the most lasting benefactions, all men being concerned in their continuance, lest by destroying of them they destroy themselves, not knowing how soon, for their own safety, they may have need to make use thereof. Many other charities he bestowed, and deceased anno 1496.[1]

ANNE NEVILLE, daughter and coheir to Richard Neville earl of Warwick, was most probably born [1456] in Warwick Castle. She was afterward married, with a great portion and inheritance, to Edward Prince of Wales, sole son to King Henry the Sixth;[2] a prince, neither dying of disease, nor slain in battle, nor executed by justice, but barbarously butchered by Richard duke of Gloucester.

Was it not then a daring piece of courtship in him, who had murdered her husband, to make love unto her in way of marriage? And was not his success strange in obtaining her, having no beauty to commend his person to her affection? Oh the impotency of the weaker sex to resist the battery of a princely suitor, who afterwards became king by his own ambition! However, her life with him proved neither long nor fortunate.

It happened that there was the muttering of a marriage between Henry earl of Richmond and Elizabeth eldest daughter to Edward the Fourth, so to unite the houses of Lancaster and York. To prevent this, King Richard the Third intended to marry the lady himself; so methodical he was in breaking the commandments of the second table. First, "Honour thy father and mother," when he procured his mother to be proclaimed a harlot, by a preacher at Paul's Cross. Secondly, "Thou shalt not kill," when he murdered his nephews. Thirdly, "Thou shalt not commit adultery," being now in pursuit of an incestuous copulation.

(1) Clopton built New Place, the house Shakespeare bought on retiring to Stratford, and rebuilt the nave and added a tower to Trinity Chapel. (2) Fuller is at fault. She was betrothed in 1470 to the Prince of Wales, to be married should Warwick (the 'King-Maker') prove successful in restoring Henry VI, but the prince and Warwick were slain in the battle of Tewkesbury, 1471. The story that the prince was murdered is probably an invention of Tudor times.

Say not that this match would nothing confirm his title, seeing formerly he had pronounced all the issue of King Edward the Fourth as illegitimate; for first, that design was rather endeavoured than effected; most men remaining (notwithstanding this bastardizing attempt) well satisfied in the rightfulness of their extraction. Secondly, they should or should not be bastards, as it made for his present advantage; tyrants always driving that nail which will go, though it go cross to those which they have driven before. Lastly, if it did not help him, it would hinder the earl of Richmond, which made that usurper half wild till he was wedded.

But one thing withstood his desires. This Anne his queen was still alive, though daily quarrelled at, and complained of (her son being lately dead) for barren; and oh, what a loss would it be to nature itself, should her husband die without an heir unto his virtues! Well, this lady understanding that she was a burthen to her husband, for grief soon became a burthen to herself, and wasted away on a sudden. Some think she went her own pace to the grave, while others suspect a grain was given her, to quicken her in her journey to her long home; which happened Anno Domini 1485.

EDWARD PLANTAGENET [EARL OF WARWICK] son to George duke of Clarence, may pass for a prince, because the last male heir of that royal family. Yea, some of his foes feared, and more of his friends desired, that he might be king of England. His mother was Isabel, eldest daughter to Richard Neville earl of Warwick, and he was born [1475] in Warwick Castle.

As his age increased, so the jealousy of the kings of England on him did increase, being kept close prisoner by King Edward the Fourth, closer by King Richard the Third, and closest by King Henry the Seventh. This last, being of a new lineage and surname, knew full well how this nation hankered after the name of Plantagenet; which, as it did out-syllable Tudor in the mouths, so did it outvie it in the affections of the English. Hence it was that the earl was kept in so strict restraint, which made him very weak in his intellectuals; and no wonder, being so sequestered from human converse.

It happened, a marriage was now in debate betwixt Prince Arthur[1] and Catherine daughter to Ferdinand king of Spain, and the latter would not consent thereunto until, to clear all titles, this Edward Plantagenet were taken out of the way. Thereupon he was charged for intending an escape out of the Tower (was he not a very fool indeed, if not desiring his own liberty?) which far-fetched deduction was heightened into high treason. The simple earl was persuaded, by his friend-pretending foes, to confess the fact, as the only way to find favour; and so, freely acknowledging more against himself than others could prove, yea, or himself did intend, soon after found the proverb true, "Confess, and be beheaded."

However, the blood of this innocent (so may he truly be termed, take

(1) Arthur (see Hampshire, p. 206) eldest son of Henry VII, married Catherine of Aragon in 1501.

the word in what sense you please) did not pass unpunished; and the Lady Catherine dowager was wont to acknowledge the death of her two sons[1] an ill success of her match, as heaven's judgment on her family for the murdering of this earl, which happened Anno Domini 1499.

JOHN VEYSEY, alias HARMAN, doctor of law, was born [1465?] at Sutton Coldfield in this county, bred in Oxford; a most vivacious person, if the date of these remarks be seriously considered. 1. In the twentieth year of King Henry the Sixth, he was appointed to celebrate the divine service in the free chapel of Saint Blaise of Sutton aforesaid.[2] 2. In the twenty-third year of Henry the Seventh, he was made vicar of Saint Michael's Church in Coventry. 3. Under King Henry the Eighth, he was made dean of the chapel-royal, tutor to the Lady Mary, and president of Wales. 4. In the eleventh of King Henry the Eighth, 1519, he was advanced to be bishop of Exeter. Which bishopric he destroyed, not only shaving the hairs (with long leases) but cutting away the limbs with sales outright, insomuch that Bishop Hall, his successor in that see, complaineth in print that the following bishops were *barons,* but *bare-ones* indeed.

Some have confidently affirmed, in my hearing, that the word *to veize* (that is, in the west, to drive away with a witness) had its original from his profligating of the lands of his bishopric; but I yet demur to the truth thereof.

He robbed his own cathedral to pay a parish church, Sutton in this county, where he was born, whereon he bestowed many benefactions, and built fifty-one houses. To enrich this his native town, he brought out of Devonshire many clothiers, with desire and hope to fix the manufacture of clothing there. All in vain; for, as Bishop Godwin observeth, *Non omnis fert omnia tellus.* Which, though true *conjunctively,* that all countries put together bring forth all things to be mutually bartered by a reciprocation of trade, is false *disjunctively,* no one place affording all commodities, so that the cloth-workers here had their pains for their labour, and sold for their loss.

It seems, though he brought out of Devonshire the *fiddle* and *fiddle-stick,* he brought not the *resin* therewith to make good music; and every country is innated with a peculiar genius, and is left-handed to those trades which are against their inclinations.

He quitted his bishopric (not worth keeping) in the reign of King Edward the Sixth; and no wonder he resumed it not[3] in the reign of Queen Mary, the bone not being worth the taking, the marrow being knocked out before. He died (being 103 years old) in the reign of Queen Mary; and was buried in his native town, with his statue mitred and vested.

[*d.* 1554]

(1) She married Henry VIII, and the four children born in the years 1510-14 all died in infancy. (2) Fuller is careless here. He states below that Veysey died aged 103 (more probably 90) in Mary's reign, which would be about 130 years after this supposed appointment. The first ascertainable facts regarding Veysey are that he was fellow of Magdalen College 1486-7, that he adopted the name of Veysey or Voysey about 1488, and that he was chaplain to Henry VII's consort in 1489. (3) He was restored to the bishopric by Mary in 1553.

JOHN BIRD was born in the city of Coventry; bred a Carmelite at Oxford, and became afterwards the thirty-first (the head game) and last provincial of his order. He preached some smart sermons before King Henry the Eighth against the primacy of the pope; for which he was preferred (saith Bishop Godwin) to be successively bishop of Ossory in Ireland, Bangor in Wales, and Chester in England.

To the two last we concur; but dissent to the former, because John Bale, contemporary with this John Bird, and also bishop of Ossory (who therefore must be presumed skilful in his predecessors in that see) nameth him not bishop of Ossory, but *Episcopum Pennecensem in Hibernia.*[1] The same Bale saith of him, *Audivi eum ad Papismi vomitum reversum* (I have heard that in the reign of Queen Mary he returned to the vomit of popery) which my charity will not believe. Indeed in the first of Queen Mary he was ousted of his bishopric for being married; and all that we can recover of his carriage afterwards is this passage at the examination of Master Thomas Haukes, martyr; when John Bird (then very old) brought Bonner a bottle of wine, and a dish of apples, probably a present unto him for a *ne noceat;* and therefore not enough to speak him a papist in his persuasion.

Bishop Bonner desired him to take Haukes into his chamber, and to try if he could convert him; whereupon, after Bonner's departure out of the room, the quondam bishop accosted Haukes as followeth: "I would to God I could do you some good. You are a young man, and I would not wish you to go too far, but learn of the elders to bear somewhat." He enforced him no further; but, being a thorough old man, even fell fast asleep. All this, in my computation, amounts but to a passive compliance, and is not evidence enough to make him a thorough-paced papist; the rather because John Pits omitteth him in the *Catalogue of English Writers,* which no doubt he would not have done, had he any assurance that he had been a radicated Romanist. Nothing else have I to observe of him, but only that he was a little man, and had a pearl in his eyes;[2] and, dying 1558, was buried in Chester.

SIR NICHOLAS THROCKMORTON, knight [*b.* 1515] fourth son of Sir George Throckmorton of Coughton in this county, was bred beyond the seas, where he attained to great experience. Under Queen Mary he was in Guildhall arraigned for treason (compliance with Wyatt) and, by his own wary pleading, and the jury's upright verdict, hardly escaped. Queen Elizabeth employed him for her leiger a long time, first in France, then in Scotland, finding him a most able minister of state; yet got he no great wealth, and no wonder, being ever of the opposite party to Burghley, lord treasurer; chamberlain of the Exchequer, and chief butler of England, were his highest preferments. I say chief butler, which office, like an empty covered cup, pretendeth to some state, but affordeth no considerable profit. He died at supper with eating of salads, not without suspicion of poison, the rather because happening in the house of one no mean artist in that faculty, Robert earl of Leicester. His death, as it was

(1) He was suffragan to the bishop of Llandaff, with the title of bishop of Penrith.
(2) A kind of cataract.

sudden, was seasonable for him and his, whose active (others will call it turbulent) spirit had brought him into such trouble as might have cost him, at least, the loss of his personal estate. He died, in the fifty-seventh year of his age, February the 12th, 1571; and lieth buried in the south side of the chancel of St. Katherine Cree Church, London.

THOMAS UNDERHILL, esq., was born at Nether Eatington in this county. It is pity to part him from Elizabeth his wife, seeing the poetical fiction of Philemon and Baucis found in them an historical performance with improvement:

> But good old Baucis with Philemon, match'd
> In youthful years, now struck with equal age,
> Made poorness pleasant in their cottage thatch'd,
> And weight of want with patience did assuage.

Whereas this our Warwickshire pair, living in a worshipful equipage, and exemplary for their hospitality, did teach others, not how poverty might be borne, but wealth well used (by their example) for the owners' and others' good.

The Ovidian couple appear issueless, whereas twenty children, viz., thirteen sons and seven daughters, were begotten and born by this Thomas and Elizabeth, living sixty-five years together in marriage.

Indeed, the poetical pair somewhat outstripped them in the happiness of their death, their request being granted them:

> Because we liv'd and lov'd so long together,
> Let's not behold the funerals of either;
> May one hour end us both; may I not see
> This my wife buried, nor wife bury me.

However, these Underhills deceased in one year; she in July, he in October following, 1603.

PHILEMON HOLLAND, where born [1552] is to me unknown, was bred in Trinity College in Cambridge a doctor in physic, and fixed himself in Coventry. He was the translator general in his age, so that those books alone of his turning into English will make a country gentleman a competent library for historians; insomuch that one saith,

> Holland with his translations doth so fill us,
> He will not let *Suetonius* be *Tranquillus.*

Indeed some decry all translators as interlopers, spoiling the trade of learning, which should be driven amongst scholars alone. Such also allege that the best translations are works rather of industry than judgment, and (in easy authors) of faithfulness rather than industry; that many be but bunglers, forcing the meaning of the authors they translate, "picking the lock when they cannot open it."

But their opinion resents too much of envy, that such gentlemen who cannot repair to the fountain should be debarred access to the stream. Besides, it is unjust to charge all with the faults of some; and a distinction must be made amongst translators betwixt cobblers and workmen, and our Holland had the true knack of translating.

Many of these his books he wrote with one pen, whereon he himself thus pleasantly versified:

> With one sole pen I writ this book,
> Made of a grey goose quill;
> A pen it was when it I took,
> And a pen I leave it still.

This monumental pen he solemnly kept, and shewed to my reverend tutor Doctor Samuel Ward. It seems he leaned very lightly on the nib thereof, though weightily enough in another sense, performing not slightly but solidly what he undertook.

But what commendeth him most to the praise of posterity is his translating Camden's *Britannia,* a translation more than a translation, with many excellent additions, not found in the Latin, done fifty years since in Master Camden's lifetime, not only with his knowledge and consent, but also, no doubt, by his desire and help. Yet such additions (discoverable in the former part with asterisks in the margin) with some antiquaries obtain not equal authenticalness with the rest. This eminent translator was translated to a better life, Anno Domini 1637.[1]

WILLIAM BISHOP was born [1554] in this county, saith my author,[2] *ex nobili familia.* Inquiring after his surname in this shire, I find one John Bishop, gentleman, patron of Brailes in this county, who died anno 1601, aged 92, being a protestant, as appeareth by his epitaph; who, according to proportion of time, might in all probability be his father, the rather because he is said *parentes et ampli patrimonii spem reliquisse* (to have left his parents and the hope of a fair inheritance.)

Reader, a word by the way of the word *nobilis,* which soundeth high in English ears, where barons' youngest children are the lowest step to nobility; whilst *nobilis* from the pen of a foreigner generally importeth no more than an ordinary gentleman.[3]

It was not long since my weakness was employed to draw up, in Latin, a testimonial for a High German, who indeed was of honourable extraction; and, according to direction, I was advised to style him *Generosissimum ac Nobilissimum.* For *Generosus* (which runneth so low in England) in Saxony doth carry it clear as the more honourable epithet. Thus words, like counters, stand for more or less according to custom. Yea, Latin words are bowed in their modern uses, according to the acception of several places.

This Bishop, leaving the land, went first to Rheims, then to Rome, where he was made priest; and, being sent back into England, met with variety of success: 1. Being seized on, he was brought before the secretary Walsingham, and by him committed to the Marshalsea; 2. After three years, being banished the realm, he became a doctor of Sorbonne; 3. He returned into England, and for nine years laboured in the popish harvest;

(1) Philemon Holland was born in Chelmsford, and spent the greater part of his life in Coventry. After trying medicine, he became for thirty years an usher at the free school, was promoted headmaster in 1628, and in 1632 the city awarded him a pension. He had received the freedom of the city in 1612, and when James I visited Coventry Holland was chosen to present the loyal address. (2) Pits. (3) Our countryman, Pits, did *foreignize* with long living beyond the seas.

4. By their clergy he was employed a messenger to Rome, about some affairs of importance; 5. His business dispatched, he returned the third time into England; and, after eight years' industry therein to advance his own cause, was caught and cast into prison at London, where he remained about the year 1612; 6. Soon after he procured his enlargement; and, anno 1615, lived at Paris, in *Collegio Atrebatensi*.

Men of his persuasion cry him up for a most glorious confessor of their popish faith, who, if any goodness in him, should also be a thankful confessor of the protestant charity, permitting him twice to depart prison (on hope of his amendment) though so active an instrument against our religion. No such courtesy of papists to protestants; *vestigia nulla restrorsum;* no return (especially the second time) out of durance; the first disease being dangerous, but deadly their relapse into a prison. But perchance this William Bishop found the more favour, because our churchmen, accounting it too much severity to take away both his credit and his life, both to conquer and kill him, seeing this priest, whilst in prison, was often worsted (though his party bragged of victory) both by tongues and pens, in disputings and writings, of several protestants, amongst whom Robert Abbot (afterwards bishop of Salisbury) gave him the most fatal defeat. [*d*. 1624]

SIR FULKE GREVILLE, knight [First BARON BROOKE, *b*. 1554] son to Sir Fulke Greville the elder, of Beauchamp Court in this county. He was bred first in the university of Cambridge. He came to the court, backed with a full and fair estate; and Queen Elizabeth loved such substantial courtiers as could plentifully subsist of themselves. He was a good scholar, loving much to employ, and sometimes to advance learned men, to whom worthy Bishop Overall[1] chiefly owed his preferment, and Mr. Camden (by his own confession) tasted largely of his liberality.

His studies were most in poetry and history, as his works do witness. His style, conceived by some to be swelling, is allowed for lofty and full by others. King James created him Baron Brooke of Beauchamp Court, as descended from the sole daughter and heir of Edward Willoughby, the last Lord Brooke, in the reign of King Henry the Seventh.

His sad death, or murder rather, happened on this occasion. His discontented servant, conceiving his deserts not soon or well enough rewarded, wounded him mortally; and then (to save the law the labour) killed himself, verifying the observation that he may when he pleaseth be master of another man's life, who contemneth his own.

He lieth buried in Warwick Church, under a monument of black and white marble, whereon he is styled "servant to Queen Elizabeth, councillor to King James, and friend to Sir Philip Sidney." Dying anno 1628 without issue, and unmarried, his barony, by virtue of entail in the patent, descended on his kinsman Robert Greville Lord Brooke, father to the right honourable Robert Lord Brooke.[2]

(1) John Overall—see Suffolk, p. 536. (2) Fulke Greville is best remembered as the friend of Sidney, whose life he wrote. Nearly all his work—the most remarkable being the sonnet sequence *Caelica*—was published posthumously.

MICHAEL DRAYTON, born [1563] in this county at Atherstone, as appeareth in his poetical address thereunto:

My native county,
If there be virtue yet remaining in thy earth,
Or any good of thine thou breath'st into my birth,
Accept it as thine own, whilst now I sing of thee,
Of all thy later brood th' unworthiest though I be.[1]

He was a pious poet, his conscience having always the command of his fancy; very temperate in his life, slow of speech, and inoffensive in company. He changed his laurel for a crown of glory, anno 1631; and is buried in Westminster Abbey, near the south door, with this epitaph:

Do, pious marble, let thy readers know,
What they and what their children owe
To Drayton's name, whose sacred dust
We recommend unto thy trust.
Protect his memory, and preserve his story,
Remain a lasting monument of his glory.
And when thy ruins shall disclaim
To be the treasurer of his name;
His name that cannot fade, shall be
An everlasting monument to thee.

He was born within a few miles of William Shakespeare, his countryman and fellow poet; and buried within fewer paces of Geoffrey Chaucer and Edmund Spenser.

WILLIAM SHAKESPEARE was born [1564] at Stratford-on-Avon in this county; in whom three eminent poets may seem in some sort to be compounded: 1. *Martial,* in the warlike sound of his surname (whence some may conjecture him of a military extraction) *Hasti-vibrans,* or Shake-speare; 2. *Ovid,* the most natural and witty of all poets; and hence it was that Queen Elizabeth, coming into a grammar school, made this extemporary verse,

Persius a crab-staffe, bawdy *Martial, Ovid* a fine wag;

3. *Plautus,* who was an exact comedian, yet never any scholar, as our Shakespeare (if alive) would confess himself. Add to all these, that though his genius generally was jocular, and inclining him to festivity, yet he could, when so disposed, be solemn and serious, as appears by his tragedies; so that Heraclitus himself (I mean if secret and unseen) might afford to smile at his comedies, they were so merry; and Democritus scarce forbear to sigh at his tragedies, they were so mournful.

He was an eminent instance of the truth of that rule, *Poeta non fit sed nascitur* (one is not made but born a poet.) Indeed his learning was very little; so that, as Cornish diamonds are not polished by any lapidary, but are pointed and smoothed even as they are taken out of the earth, so Nature itself was all the art which was used upon him.

Many were the wit-combats betwixt him and Ben Jonson; which two I behold like a Spanish great galleon and an English man-of-war; Master Jonson (like the former) was built far higher in learning; solid, but slow

(1) *Polyolbion.*

in his performances. Shakespeare, with the English man-of-war, lesser in bulk, but lighter in sailing, could turn with all tides, tack about and take advantage of all winds by the quickness of his wit and invention. He died Anno Domini 1616, and was buried at Stratford-upon-Avon, the town of his nativity.

FRANCIS HOLYOAKE (Latining himself *de sacra quercu*), and minister of Southam, born [1567] at Whitacre in this county. He set forth that staple-book which schoolboys called *Rider's Dictionary*. This Rider did borrow (to say no worse) both his saddle and bridle from Thomas Thomatius, who, being bred fellow of King's College in Cambridge, set forth that dictionary known by his name; than which men have not a better and truer, children no plainer and briefer. But Rider, after Thomas his death, set forth his dictionary, the same in effect, under his own name, the property therof being but little disguised with any additions.

Such plagiaryship ill becometh authors or printers; and the dove being the crest of the Stationers' arms, should mind them, not, like rooks, to filch copies one from another. The executors of Thomas Thomatius entering an action against Rider, occasioned him, in his own defence, to make those numerous additions to his dictionary, that it seems to differ rather in kind than degree from his first edition.

I am forced to place this child rather with his guardian than father; I mean, to mention this dictionary rather under the name of Master Holyoake than Rider, both because the residence of the latter is wholly unknown to me, and because Mr. Holyoake added many (as his learned son hath since more) wonders thereunto. This Master Holyoake died November 13, Anno Domini 1653.

NICHOLAS BYFIELD was born [1579] in this county, as his son[1] hath informed me; bred (as I remember) in Exeter College in Oxford. After he had entered into the ministry, he was invited into Ireland, to a place of good profit and eminency; in passage whereunto, staying wind-bound at Chester, his inn proved his home for a long time unto him, preaching a sermon there with such approbation, that he was chosen minister in the city; not without an especial providence, seeing the place promised in Ireland would have failed him, and his going over had been a labour in vain. The Cestrians can give the best account of his profitable preaching and pious life, most strict in keeping the Lord's day, on which occasion pens were brandished betwixt him and Mr. Brerewood.[2]

In his declining age he was presented to the benefice of Isleworth in Middlesex, where for fifteen years together he preached twice every Lord's day, and expounded Scripture every Wednesday and Friday, till five weeks before his death, notwithstanding there was *mors in olla* (a stone in his bladder) which, being taken out, weighed and measured after his death, was found of these prodigious proportions: 1. In weight, thirty-

(1) Mr. Adoniram Byfield, who promised to leave larger instructions of his father's life, but I received them not. [Adoniram Byfield (*d.* 1660) a puritan, like his father, and better known. He was chaplain to a parliamentary regiment and, later, on the Wiltshire Committee for ejecting clergymen.] (2) Edward Brerewood—see Chester, p. 81.

three ounces and more; 2. In measure about the edge, fifteen inches and a half; 3. In measure about the length, thirteen inches and above; 4. In measure about the breadth, almost thirteen inches. It was of a solid substance to look upon, like a flint. "Lo, here is the patience of the saints." All I will add is this: the Pharisee said proudly, "I thank thee, Lord, I am not as this publican;" let writer and reader say humbly and thankfully to God, "We are not as this truly painful preacher;" and let us labour, that as our bodies are more healthful, our souls may be as holy as his, who died [1622] and was buried at Isleworth.

EDWARD CONWAY, knight [FIRST VISCOUNT CONWAY] son to Sir John Conway, knight, lord and owner of Ragley in this county. This Sir John, being a person of great skill in military affairs, was made by Robert earl of Leicester (general of the English auxiliaries in the United Provinces) governor of Ostend. His son Sir Edward succeeded to his father's martial skill and valour, and twisted therewith peaceable policy in state affairs; so that the gown and the sword met in him in most eminent proportion; and thereupon King James made him one of the principal secretaries of state.

For these his good services he was by him created Lord Conway of Ragley in this county; and afterwards, by King Charles, Viscount Killultagh in the county of Antrim; and lastly, in the third of King Charles, Viscount Conway of Conway in Carnarvonshire; England, Ireland, and Wales mutually embracing themselves in his honours. He died January the third, anno 1631.

JOHN DIGBY, baron of Sherborne, and earl of Bristol was born [1580] in this county, a younger son of an ancient family, long flourishing at Coleshill therein. To pass by his infancy (all children being alike in their long coats) his youth gave pregnant hopes of that eminency which his mature age did produce.

He did ken the ambassador-craft as well as any in his age; employed by King James in several services to foreign princes, recited in his patent (which I have perused) as the main motives of the honours conferred upon him. But his managing the *matchless match* with Spain was his master-piece, wherein a good, I mean a great, number of state-traverses were used on both sides.[1]

His contest with the duke of Buckingham is fresh in many men's memories, charges of high treason mutually flying about. But this lord fearing the duke's power, as the duke this lord's policy, it at last became a drawn battle between them; yet so that this earl lost the love of King Charles, living many years in his disfavour; but such as are in a court-*cloud* have commonly the country's *sunshine;* and this peer, during his eclipse, was very popular with most of the nation.

It is seldom seen that a favourite once broken at court sets up again for himself; the *hap* rather than *happiness* of this lord; the king graciously

(1) After two fruitless embassies for Spanish matches for Prince Henry and Prince Charles, Digby negotiated a match for the latter in 1617, but it was eventually broken off by James I because of the severe conditions demanded by Spain.

reflecting on him, at the beginning of the Long Parliament, as one best able to give him the safest counsel in those dangerous times. But how he incensed the parliament so far as to be excepted pardon, I neither do know nor dare inquire.[1] Sure I am, after the surrender of Exeter, he went over into France, where he met with due respect in foreign, which he missed in his native country. The worst I wish such who causelessly suspect him of popish inclinations is that I may hear from them but half so many strong arguments for the protestant religion as I have heard from him, who was, to his commendation, a cordial champion of the Church of England. He died in France [1653].

JOHN LORD HARINGTON, son to John Lord Harington,[2] was born [1592] at Coombe Abbey in this county (accruing unto him by his mother, heiress of Kelway) as by a property of that family, lately, or still surviving, I have, on very strict inquiry, been certainly informed.

He did not count himself privileged from being good, by being great; and his timely piety rising early, did not soon after go to bed (as some young saints, beheld under another notion) but continued watchful during his life.

He was one of the first who began the pious fashion (since followed by few of his quality) of a diary, wherein he registered, not the injuries of others done unto him (a work of revenge, not devotion) but of his failings and infirmities toward his Master. Thus making even with the God of Heaven, by repentance in Christ at the end of every day, "he had," to use the expression and counsel of the reverend archbishop of Armagh, "but one day to repent of before his death."

He lived out all his days in the appointment of Divine Providence, not half of them according to the course and possibility of Nature, not half a quarter of them according to the hopes and desires of the lovers and honourers of virture in this nation, especially of the society in Sidney College in Cambridge, whereto he was a most bountiful benefactor. [*d.* 1614]

JAMES CRANFORD was born [1592?] at Coventry in this county, where his father was a divine and schoolmaster of great note; bred in Oxford, beneficed in Northamptonshire, and afterwards removed to London, to Saint Christopher's. A painful preacher and exact linguist, subtil disputant, orthodox in his judgment, sound against sectaries, well acquainted with the Fathers, not unknown to the schoolmen, and familiar with the modern divines. Much his humility, being James the Less in his own esteem, and therefore ought to be the greater in ours. He had, as I may say, a broad-chested soul, favourable to such who differed from him. His moderation increased with his age, charity with his moderation; and

(1) Parliament demanded, as one of the conditions for the peace proposed in 1643, that Digby be expelled from court. He had offended parliament, among other matters, by refusing to vote on the attainder against Strafford. Digby invited Fuller to accompany him to France, and promised the latter (as he relates in his *Appeal of Injured Innocence*) that "I should have half a loaf with him, so long as he had a whole one to himself," but the offer was declined. (2) For the first Lord Harington, see Rutland, p. 473.

he had a kindness for all such who had any goodness in themselves. He had many choice books, and (not like to those who may lose themselves in their own libraries, being owners, not masters, of their books therein) had his books at such command as the captain has his soldiers, so that he could make them, at pleasure, go or come, and do what he desired. This lame and loyal Mephibosheth (as I may term him) sadly sympathizing with the suffering of church and state, died rather infirm than old, anno 1657.

THE FAREWELL

I cannot but congratulate the happiness of this county in having Master William Dugdale (now Norroy) my worthy friend, a native thereof; whose *Illustrations* are so great a work, no young man could be so bold to begin, or old man hope to finish it, whilst one of middle age fitted the performance.[1] A well-chosen county for such a subject, because lying in the centre of the land, whose lustre diffuseth the light, and darteth beams to the circumference of the kingdom. It were a wild wish, that all the shires in England were described to an equal degree of perfection, as which will be accomplished when each star is as big and bright as the sun. However, one may desire them done *quoad speciem,* though not *quoad gradum,* in imitation of Warwickshire. Yet is this hopeless to come to pass, till men's pains meet with proportionable encouragement; and then the poet's prediction will be true:

Sint Maecenates, non desint, Flacce, Marones;
Virgiliumque tibi vel tua Rura dabunt.

Let not Maecenases be scant,
And Maroes we shall never want;
For, Flaccus, then thy country-field
Shall unto thee a Virgil yield.

And then would our little (divided) world be better described than the great world by all the geographers who have written thereof.

(1) Sir William Dugdale (1605-1686) one of the greatest of English antiquaries. He wrote or compiled, among other works, *Antiquities of Warwickshire Illustrated, Monasticon* and *Baronage of England*. He was a royalist, and proclaimed Charles II at Coleshill in 1660. Appointed Norroy in 1660, he became Garter King-of-Arms in 1677.

WESTMORLAND

WESTMORLAND hath Cumberland on the west and north, Lancashire on the south, bishopric [of Durham] and Yorkshire on the east thereof. From north to south it extendeth thirty miles in length, but is contented in the breadth with twenty-four.

As for the soil thereof, to prevent exceptions, take its description from the pen of a credible author:[1] "It is not commended either for plenty of corn or cattle, being neither stored with arable ground to bring forth the one, nor pasturage to breed up the other; the principal profit that the people of this province raise unto themselves is by clothing."

Here is cold comfort from nature, but somewhat of warmth from industry. That the land is barren, is God's pleasure; the people painful, their praise. That thereby they grow wealthy, shews God's goodness, and calls for their gratefulness.

However, though this county be sterile by general rule, it is fruitful by some few exceptions, having some pleasant vales, though such ware be too fine to have much measure thereof; insomuch that some back-friends to this country will say, that though Westmorland hath much of *Eden* (running clean through it) yet hath little of *delight* therein.

I behold the barrenness of this county as the cause why so few friaries and convents therein; Master Speed (so curious in his catalogue in this kind) mentioning but one religious house therein. Such lazy folk did hate labour as a house of correction, and knew there was nothing to be had here but what art with industry wrested from nature.

The reader perchance will smile at my curiosity in observing that this small county, having but four market towns, three of them are Kirkby Stephen, Kirkby Lonsdale, Kirkby Kendal; so that so much of kirk or church argueth not a little devotion of the ancestors in these parts, judiciously expressing itself, not in building convents for the ease of monks, but churches for the worship of God.

THE MANUFACTURES

Kendal cottons are famous all over England; and Master Camden termeth that town *Lanificii gloria, et industria praecellens.* I hope the townsmen thereof (a word is enough to the wise) will make their commodities so substantial, that no southern town shall take an advantage, to gain that trading away from them. I speak not this out of the least distrust of their honesty, but the great desire of their happiness, who, being a Cambridge man, out of sympathy wish well to the clothiers of Kendal, as the first founder of our Stourbridge fair.

(1) J. Speed, in the description of this county.

THE WORTHIES

JOHN DE KIRKBY, born at one of the two Kirkbys (Lonsdale or Stephen) in this county, was first canon, and afterwards bishop of Carlisle, anno 1332. This is that stout prelate who, when the Scots invaded England, anno 1345, with an army of thirty thousand, under the conduct of Sir William Douglas, and had taken and burnt Carlisle with the country thereabouts; I say, this John de Kirkby was he who, with the assistance of Thomas Lucy, Robert Oggill, persons of prime power in those parts, fighting in an advantageous place, utterly routed and ruined them. Such as behold this act with envious eyes, cavilling that he was non-resident from his calling when he turned his mitre into a helmet, crosier-staff into a sword, consider not that true maxim, *In publicos hostes omnis homo miles;* and the most conscientious casuists, who forbid clergymen to be military plaintiffs, allow them to be defendants. He died Anno Domini 1352.

WILLIAM STRICKLAND, descended of a right worshipful family in this county, anno 1396, by joint consent of the canons, chosen bishop of Carlisle. However, by the concurrence of the pope and King Richard the Second, one Robert Reade was preferred to the place; which injury and affront Strickland bare with much moderation. Now it happened that Reade was removed to Chichester, and Thomas Merke his successor translated to a Grecian bishopric, that Strickland was elected again (patience gains the goal with long running) and consecrated bishop of Carlisle, anno 1400. For the town of Penrith in Cumberland he cut a passage with great art, industry, and expense, from the town into the River Petteril, for the conveyance of boatage into the Irish Sea. He sate bishop 19 years, and died Anno Domini 1419.

RICHARD KENDALE. I place him here with confidence, because no Kendal in England save what is the chief town of this county. He was an excellent grammarian, and the greatest instructor (shrewd and sharp enough) of youth in his age. He had a vast collection of all Latin grammars, and thence extracted a *quintessence,* whereof he was so highly conceited, that he publicly boasted that Latin only to be elegant which was made according to his rules, and all other to be base and barbarous; which, reader, I conceive, being out of *his,* though under *thy* correction, a proud and pedantic expression. [*d.* 1431]

CHRISTOPHER BAINBRIDGE, born [1464?] near Appleby in this county, was bred doctor of law in Queen's College in Oxford. He was afterwards dean of York, bishop of Durham, and at last archbishop of York. Being employed an ambassador to Rome, he was an active instrument to procure our King Henry the Eighth to take part with the pope against Louis king of France, for which good service he was created cardinal of Saint Praxedis, a title some say he long desired; let me add, and little enjoyed; for, falling out with his steward Rinaldo de Modena, an Italian, and fustigating him for his faults, the angry Italian poisoned him.

But grant him greatly faulty, it were uncharitable in us to beat his memory with more stripes, who did then suffer so much for his own indiscretion. His death happened July 14, 1514; and was buried at Rome, not in the church of Saint Praxedis, which entitled him, but in the hospital of the English.

CATHERINE PARR, daughter of Sir Thomas Parr, was born [1512] at Kendal Castle in this county, then the prime seat of that (though no parliamentary) barony, devolved to her father by inheritance from the Bruces and Rosses of Werk. She was first married unto John Neville Lord Latimer,[1] and afterwards to King Henry the Eighth.

This king first married half a maid (no less can be allowed to the Lady Catherine, the relict of Prince Arthur) and then he married four maids successively. Of the two last he complained, charging the one with impotency, the other with inconstancy; and being a free man again, resolved to wed a widow who had given testimony of her fidelity to a former husband.

This lady was a great favourer of the Gospel, and would earnestly argue for it, sometimes speaking more than her husband would willingly hear of. Once, politic Gardiner (who spared all the weeds, spoiled the good flowers and herbs) had almost got her into his clutches, had not Divine Providence delivered her. Yet a Jesuit tells us that the king intended, if longer surviving, to behead her for an heretic; to whom all that I will return is this, that he was neither confessor nor privy councillor to King Henry the Eighth.

This queen was afterwards married to Thomas Seymour, baron of Sudeley and lord admiral;[2] and died in childbed of a daughter, Anno Domini 1548; her second husband surviving her.

SIR EDWARD BELLINGHAM, knight, was born of an ancient and warlike family in this county;[3] servant of the privy chambers of King Edward the Sixth, who sent him over, anno 1548, to be lord deputy of Ireland; whose learning, wisdom and valour made him fit to discharge that place.

Hitherto the English pale had been hidebound in the growth thereof, having not gained one foot of ground in more than two hundred years, since the time of King Edward the Third. This Sir Edward first extended it, proceeding against the Irishry in a martial course, by beating and breaking the Mores and O'Connors, two rebellious septs.

And, because the poet saith true,

> It proves a man as brave and wise
> To keep, as for to get the prize;

he built the forts of Leix and Offaly, to secure his new acquisition. Surely, had he not been suddenly revoked into England, he would have perfected the project in the same sort as it was performed by his successor the earl of Sussex, by settling English plantations therein.

Such his secrecy (the soul of great designs) that his soldiers never

(1) Lord Latimer was her second husband, the first being Edward Borough, of whom nothing is known. (2) See Wiltshire, p. 613. (3) Though Sussex (where his surname is of good esteem) may pretend unto him, I am confident of his right location.

knew whither they went, till they were come whither they should go. Thus he surprised the earl of Desmond, being rude and unnurtured; brought him up to Dublin, where he *informed* and *reformed* him in manners and civility; sometimes making him to kneel on his knees an hour together, before he knew his duty, till he became a new man in his behaviour. This earl all his life after highly honoured him; and at every dinner and supper, would pray to God for good Sir Edward Bellingham, who had so much improved him.

This deputy had no faults on his deputyship but one, that it was so short; he being called home before two years were expired. Surely this hath much retarded the reducing of the Irishry, the often shifting of their deputies (too often change of the kinds of plaisters, hinders the healing of the sore) so that as soon as they had learned their trade, they must resign their shop to another; which made King James continue the Lord Chichester so long in the place, for the more effectual performance therein.

Coming into England, he was accused of many faults; but cleared himself as fast as his adversaries charged him, recovering the king's favour in so high a degree, that he had been sent over deputy again, save that he excused himself by indisposition of body, and died not long after. [*d.* 1549]

HUGH COREN, or CURWEN, was born in this county, and made by Queen Mary archbishop of Dublin; Browne, his immediate predecessor, being deprived, for that he was married. Here it is worthy of our observation, that though many of the protestant clergy in that land were imprisoned, and otherwise much molested, yet no one person, of what quality soever, in all Ireland, did suffer martyrdom; and hereon a remarkable story doth depend; a story which hath been solemnly avouched by the late reverend archbishop of Armagh[1] in the presence of several persons, and amongst others unto Sir James Ware, knight (that most excellent antiquary) and divers in the university of Oxford, who wrote it from his mouth, as he received the same from ancient persons of unquestionable credit.

About the third of the reign of Queen Mary, a pursuivant was sent with a commission into Ireland, to empower some eminent persons to proceed, with fire and faggot, against poor protestants. It happened, by Divine Providence, this pursuivant at Chester lodged in the house of a protestant innkeeper who, having gotten some inkling of the matter, secretly stole his commission out of his cloak-bag, and put the knave of clubs in the room thereof. Some weeks after, he appeared before the lords of the privy council at Dublin (of whom Bishop Coren a principal) and produced a card for his pretended commission. They caused him to be committed to prison for such an affront, as done on design to deride them. Here he lay for some months, till with much ado at last he got his enlargement. Then over he returned for England; and quickly getting his commission renewed, makes with all speed for Ireland again.

But, before his arrival there, he was prevented with the news of Queen Mary's death; and so the lives of many, and the liberties of more, poor servants of God were preserved.

(1) James Ussher (1581-1656) whose chronology is used in Bibles.

To return to our Coren; though a moderate papist in Queen Mary's days, yet he conformed with the first to the Reformation of Queen Elizabeth, being ever sound in his heart. He was for some short time chief justice and chancellor of Ireland, till he quitted all his dignities in exchange for the bishopric of Oxford. It may seem a wonder that he should leave one of the best archbishoprics in Ireland for one of the worst bishoprics in England. But oh, no preferment to quiet; and this politic prelate, very decrepit, broken with old age and many state affairs, desired a private repose in his native land before his death, which happened Anno Domini 1568.[1]

BERNARD, son of Edwin GILPIN, esquire, was born at Kentmere in this county, anno 1517. At sixteen years old (very young in that age from those parts) his parents sent him to Queen's College in Oxford; whence his merit advanced him one of the first students in the new foundation of Christ Church.

Hitherto the heat of Gilpin was more than his light; and he hated vice more than error; which made him so heartily dispute against Master Hooper (who afterwards was martyred) when indeed he did follow his argument with his affections.

How afterwards he became a zealous protestant, I refer the reader to his life, written at large by Bishop Carleton. He was rector of Houghton in the north, consisting of fourteen villages.

In his own house he boarded and kept full four and twenty scholars. The greater number of his boarders were poor men's sons, upon whom he bestowed meat, drink, and cloth, and education in learning. He was wont to entertain his parishioners and strangers at his table, not only at the Christmas time, as the custom is; but, because he had a large and wide parish, a great multitude of people, he kept a table for them every Sunday from Michaelmas to Easter. He had the gentlemen, the husbandmen, and the poorer sort, set every degree by themselves, and as it were ordered in ranks. He was wont to commend the married state in the clergy; howbeit himself lived and died a single man. He bestowed, in the building, ordering and establishing of his school, and in providing yearly stipends for a schoolmaster and an usher, the full sum of five hundred pounds; out of which school he supplied the Church of England with great store of learned men. He was careful to avoid not only all evil doing, but even the lightest suspicions thereof. And he was accounted a saint in the judgments of his very enemies, if he had any such. Being full of faith unfeigned, and of good works, he was at the last put into his grave, as a heap of wheat in due time swept into the garner. He died the 4th of March 1583, and in the 66th year of his age.[2]

RICHARD MULCASTER was born [1530?] of an ancient extract in the north; but whether in this county or Cumberland, I find not decided. From

(1) Curwen was the only possessor of an Irish see who changed his religion when Elizabeth came to the throne, and was very much 'a complier in all reigns.' He was uncle to Richard Bancroft, archbishop of Canterbury (see Lancashire, p. 301).
(2) Gilpin earned the title 'Apostle of the North.' He was, though a firm protestant and unsparing of abuses, a man of moderation, much the same as Fuller himself. He refused the see of Carlisle in 1559.

Eton school he went to Cambridge, where he was admitted into King's College, 1548; but, before he was graduated, removed to Oxford. Here such his proficiency in learning, that by general consent he was chosen the first master of Merchant Taylors' School in London, which prospered well under his care, as, by the flourishing of Saint John's in Oxford, doth plainly appear.

The Merchant Taylors, finding his scholars so to profit, intended to fix Mr. Mulcaster as his desk to their school, till death should remove him. This he perceived, and therefore gave for his motto, *Fidelis servus, perpetuus asinus.* But after twenty-five years he procured his freedom, rather increasing than mitigating his severity on their offending child.

His method in teaching was this. In a morning he would exactly and plainly construe and parse the lessons to his scholars; which done, he slept his hour (custom made him critical to proportion it) in his desk in the school; but woe be to the scholar that slept the while. Awaking, he heard them accurately; and Atropos might be persuaded to pity, as soon as he to pardon, where he found just fault. The prayers of cockering mothers prevailed with him as much as the requests of indulgent fathers, rather increasing than mitigating his severity on their offending child.

In a word he was *plagosus Orbilius*[1]; though it may be truly said (and safely for one out of his school) that others have taught as much learning with fewer lashes. Yet his sharpness was the better endured, because unpartial; and many excellent scholars were bred under him, whereof Bishop Andrewes[2] was most remarkable.

Then quitting that place, he was presented to the rich parsonage of Stanford Rivers in Essex. I have heard from those who have heard him preach, that his sermons were not excellent, which to me seems no wonder; partly because there is a different discipline in teaching children and men; partly because such who make divinity not the choice of their youth, but the refuge of their age, seldom attain to eminency therein.

[*d.* 1611]

BARNABY POTTER was born in this county, 1577, within the barony of Kendal, in which town he was brought up, until he was sent to Queen's College in Oxford, becoming successively scholar, fellow and provost thereof. He was chosen the last with the unanimous consent of the fellows when, being at great distance, he never dreamed thereof.

Then, resigning his provost's place, he betook himself to his pastoral charge in the country. He was chaplain in ordinary to Prince Charles, being accounted at court the penitential preacher, and by King Charles was preferred bishop of Carlisle, when others sued for the place, and he little thought thereof. He was commonly called the puritanical bishop, and they would say of him, in the time of King James, that organs would blow him out of the church; which I do not believe, the rather because he was loving of and skilful in vocal music, and could bear his own part therein.

(1) Orbilius Pupillus, Roman grammarian and schoolmaster, given the epithet *plagosus* by Horace because of the floggings received by his pupils, the poet being one of them. (2) See London, p. 367. Spenser may have been one of his earliest pupils.

He was a constant preacher, and performer of family duties; of a weak constitution, melancholy, lean, and a hard student. He died in honour, being the last bishop that died a member of parliament, in the year of our Lord 1642.

CHRISTOPHER POTTER, D.D., kinsman to Bishop Potter (of whom before) was born [1591] in this county, bred fellow of Queen's College in Oxford, and at last was chosen provost thereof; chaplain in ordinary to King Charles, and dean of Worcester. One of a sweet nature, comely presence, courteous carriage, devout life and deep learning. He wrote an excellent book, entituled *Want of Charity*, containing impregnable truth, so that malice may snarl at but not bite it, without breaking its own teeth. Yet a railing Jesuit wrote a pretended confutation thereof, to which the doctor made no return; partly because the industrious bee would not meddle with a wasp, or hornet rather; partly because Mr. Chillingworth, a great master of defence in school divinity, took up the cudgels against him. [*d.* 1646]

ANNE CLIFFORD, sole daughter and heir to George earl of Cumberland, wife first to Richard earl of Dorset, then to Philip earl of Pembroke and Montgomery, though born [1590] and nursed in Hertfordshire, yet because having her greatest residence and estate in the north, is properly referable to this county. The proverb is, *Homo non est ubi animat, sed amat* (one is not to be reputed there where he lives, but where he loves) on which account this lady is placed, not where she first took life, but where she hath left a more lasting monument of her love to the public. This is that most beautiful hospital, stately built and richly endowed, at her sole cost, at Appleby in this county.

It was conceived a bold and daring part of Thomas Cecil (son to Treasurer Burghley) to enjoin his masons and carpenters not to omit a day's work at the building of Wimbledon House in Surrey, though the Spanish Armada, anno 1588, all that while shot off their guns, whereof some might be heard to the place. But Christianly valiant is the charity of this lady, who in this age, wherein there is an earthquake of ancient hospitals, and as for new ones they are hardly to be seen for new lights; I say, courageous this worthy lady's charity, who dare *found* in this *confounding* age, wherein so much was demolished and aliened, which was given to God and his church. Long may she live in wealth and honour, exactly to complete whatsoever her bountiful intentions have designed.[1] [*d.* 1676]

THE FAREWELL

Reader, I must confess myself sorry and ashamed that I cannot do more right to the natives of this county, so far distanced north, that I never had yet the opportunity to behold it. Oh that I had but received some

(1) Samuel Daniel, the poet (see Somersetshire, p. 500) was Anne Clifford's tutor. She erected his monument in Beckington Church, Somersetshire. She was unhappy in both her marriages. She wrote her autobiography, which was first published in 1916.

intelligence from my worthy friend Doctor Thomas Barlow[1], provost of Queen's College in Oxford, who, for his religion and learning, is an especial ornament of Westmorland. But time, tide and a printer's press are three unmannerly things that will stay for no man; and therefore I request that my defective endeavours may be well accepted.

I learn out of Master Camden, that in the River Kent, in this county, there be two *catadupae,* or waterfalls; whereof the northern, sounding clear and loud, foretokeneth fair weather; the southern, on the same terms, presageth rain. Now I wish that the former of these may be vocal in hay-time and harvest, the latter after great draught, that so both of them may make welcome music to the inhabitants.

(1) Barlow (1607-1691) a very learned man, but a time-server, became bishop of Lincoln in 1675. He helped Fuller with his *Church History.*

WILTSHIRE

WILTSHIRE hath Gloucestershire on the north, Berkshire and Hampshire on the east, Dorsetshire on the south, and Somersetshire on the west. From north to south it extendeth thirty-nine miles, but abateth ten of that number in the breadth thereof.

A pleasant county, and of great variety. I have heard a wise man say that an ox left to himself would, of all England, choose to live in the north, a sheep in the south part hereof, and a man in the middle betwixt both, as partaking of the pleasure of the plain, and the wealth of the deep country.

Nor is it unworthy the observing, that of all inland shires (no ways bordered on salt water) this gathereth the most in the circumference thereof, as may appear by comparing them, being in compass one hundred and thirty-nine miles. It is plentiful in all English, especially in the ensuing commodities.

NATURAL COMMODITIES

Wool

The often repetition hereof (though I confess against our rules premised) may justly be excused. Well might the French ambassador return, "France, France, France," reiterated to every petty title of the king of Spain. And our English "wool, wool," &c. may counterpoise the numerous but inconsiderable commodities of other countries. I confess a lock thereof is most contemptible; *non flocci te facio,* passing for an expression of the highest neglect; but a quantity thereof quickly amounteth to a good valuation.

THE MANUFACTURES

Clothing

This mystery is vigorously pursued in this county; and I am informed, that as Medleys are most made in other shires, as good Whites as any are woven in this county.

This mentioning of *whites* to be vended beyond the seas minds me of a memorable contest in the reign of King James betwixt the merchants of London and Sir William Cokayne, once lord mayor of that city, and as prudent a person as any in that corporation. He ably moved, and vigorously prosecuted the design, that all the cloth which was made might be dyed in England; alleging, that the wealth of a country consisteth in driving on the natural commodities thereof, through all manufactures, to the utmost, as far as it can go, or will be drawn. And by the dyeing of all English cloth in England, thousands of poor people would be employed, and thereby get a comfortable subsistence.

The merchants returned that such home dyeing of our cloth would prove prejudicial to the sale thereof, foreigners being more expert than we are in the mystery of fixing colours. Besides, they can afford them far cheaper than we can, much of dyeing stuff growing in their countries; and foreigners bear a great affection to white or virgin cloth, unwilling to have their fancies prevented by the dyeing thereof; insomuch that they would like it better (though done worse) if done by themselves; that Sir William Cokayne had got a vast deal of dyeing stuff into his own possession, and did drive on his own interest under the pretence of the public good. These their arguments were seconded with good store of good gold on both sides, till the merchants prevailed at last (a shoal of herrings is able to beat the whale itself) and clothing left in the same condition it was before.

Tobacco-Pipes

The best for shape and colour (as curiously sized) are made at Amesbury in this county. They may be called chimneys portable in pockets, the one end being the hearth, the other the tunnel thereof. Indeed, at the first bringing over of tobacco, pipes were made of silver and other metals; which, though free from breaking, were found inconvenient, as soon fouled, and hardly cleansed.

These clay pipes are burnt in a furnace for some fifteen hours, on the selfsame token that if taken out half an hour before that time, they are found little altered from the condition wherein they were when first put in. It seems all that time the fire is working itself to the height, and doth its work very soon when attained to perfection. Gauntlet-pipes, which have that mark on their heels, are the best; and hereon a story doth depend.

One of that trade observing such pipes most saleable, set the gauntlet on those of his own making, though inferior in goodness to the other. Now the workman who first gave the gauntlet sued the other, upon the statute which makes it penal for any to set another's mark on any merchantable commodities. The defendant being likely to be cast (as whose counsel could plead little in his behalf) craved leave to speak a word for himself, which was granted. He denied that he ever set another man's mark: "For the thumb of his gauntlet stands one way, mine another; and the same hand given dexter or sinister in heraldry is a sufficient difference." Hereby he escaped; though surely such who bought his pipes never took notice of that criticism, or consulted which way the thumb of his gauntlet respected.

THE BUILDINGS

The Cathedral of Salisbury (dedicated to the Blessed Virgin) is paramount in this kind, wherein the doors and chapels equal the months, the windows the days, the pillars and pillarets of fusile marble (an ancient art now shrewdly suspected to be lost) the hours of the year; so that all Europe affords not such an almanac of architecture.

Once walking in this church (whereof then I was prebendary) I met a countryman wondering at the structure thereof. "I once," said he to me, "admired that there could be a church that should have so many pillars as there be hours in the year; and now I admire more that there should be so many hours in the year as I see pillars in this church."

The cross aisle of this church is the most beautiful and lightsome of any I have yet beheld. The spire steeple (not founded on the ground, but for the main supported by four pillars) is of great height and greater workmanship. I have been credibly informed that some foreign artists, beholding this building, brake forth into tears, which some imputed to their admiration (though I see not how wondering can cause weeping); others to their envy, grieving that they had not the like in their own land.

Nor can the most curious (not to say cavilling) eye desire anything which is wanting in this edifice, except possibly an ascent; seeing such who address themselves hither for their devotions can hardly say with David, "I will go up into the house of the Lord."

Amongst the many monuments therein, that of Edward earl of Hertford is most magnificent; that of Helena Suavenberg, a Swede (the relict of William marquess of Northampton, and afterwards married to Sir Thomas Gorges) is most commended for its artificial plainness.

But the curiosity of critics is best entertained with the tomb in the north of the nave of the church, where lieth a monument in stone of a little boy, habited all in episcopal robes, a mitre upon his head, a crozier in his hand, and the rest accordingly. At the discovery thereof (formerly covered over with pews) many justly admired, that either a bishop could be so small in person, or a child so great in clothes; though since all is unriddled; for it was fashionable in that church (a thing rather deserving to be remembered than fit to be done) in the depth of popery, that the choristers chose a boy of their society to be a bishop among them from St. Nicholas' till Innocents' day at night, who did officiate in all things bishop-like, saying of mass alone excepted, and held the state of a bishop, answerably habited, amongst his fellows the counterfeit prebends. One of these, chancing to die in the time of his mock-episcopacy, was buried with crozier and mitre, as is aforesaid. Thus superstition can dispense with that which religion cannot, making piety pageantry, and subjecting what is sacred to lusory[1] representations.

As for civil buildings in this county, none are such giants as to exceed the standard of structures in other counties. Longleat, the house of Sir James Thynne, was the biggest, and Wilton is the stateliest and pleasantest for gardens, fountains, and other accommodations.

Nor must the industry of the citizens of Salisbury be forgotten, who have derived[2] the river in every street therein; so that Salisbury is a heap of islets thrown together. This mindeth me of an epitaph made on Mr. Francis Hyde, a native of this city, who died secretary unto the English lieger in Venice:

> Born in the English Venice, thou didst die,
> Dear friend, in the Italian Salisbury.

The truth is, that the strength of this city consisted in the weakness thereof, incapable of being garrisoned, which made it, in our modern wars, to escape better than many other places of the same proportion.

(1) *Lusory* = used as a pastime; of the nature of play. (2) *Derived* = to conduct from the source to or into another place.

THE WONDERS

KNOT-GRASS

This is called in Latin *gramen caninum supinum longissimum,* and groweth nine miles from Salisbury, at Master Tucker's at Maddington. It is a peculiar kind; and of the ninety species of grasses in England, is the most marvellous. It groweth ordinarily fifteen feet in length; yea, I read of one four-and-twenty foot long, which may be true, because as there are giants amongst men, so there are giants amongst giants, which even exceed them in proportion.

The place whereon it groweth is low, lying some winters under water, having hills round about it, and a spacious sheep-common adjoining; the soil whereof by every hasty shower is brought down into this little meadow, which makes it so incredibly fruitful. This grass being built so many stories high, from knot to knot, lieth matted on the ground, whence it is cut up with sickles, and bound into sheaves. It is both hay and provender, the joint-like knots whereof will fat swine.

Some conceive that the seed thereof, transplanted, would prosper plentifully, though not to the same degree of length, in other places; from whose judgment other husbandmen dissent, conceiving it so peculiar to this place, that ground and grass must be removed both together. Or else it must be set in a paralleled position, for all the particular advantages aforesaid, which England will hardly afford. So that Nature may seem mutually to have made this plant and this place one for another.

THE BATTLES

LANDSDOWNE FIGHT. This was fought in the confines of this county and Somerset, the 5th of July 1643. It was disputed by parcels and piecemeals, as the place and narrow passages would give leave; and it seemed not so much one entire battle, as a heap of skirmishes huddled together. It may be said in some sort of both sides,

Victus uterque fuit, victor uterque fuit.

For the parliament forces five times, by the confession of the royalists, beat them back with much disorder, Sir Bevil Grenville being slain in the head of his pikes; Major Lowre in the head of his party of horse. Yet the king's forces allege demonstration of conquest, that Prince Maurice and Sir Ralph Hopton remained in the heads of their troops all night, and next morning found themselves possessed of the field and of the dead, as also of three hundred arms and nine barrels of powder the enemy had left behind them.

ROUNDWAY FIGHT. Five days after, Prince Maurice with the earl of Carnarvon returning, and the Lord Wilmot coming from Oxford, with a gallant supply of select horse, charged the parliament forces under the conduct of Sir William Waller. With him were the horse of Sir Arthur Hesilrige, so well armed that (if of proof as well within as without) each soldier seemed an impregnable fortification. But these were so smartly charged by the prince that they fairly forsook the field, leaving their foot, which in English battles bear the heat of the day, to shift for themselves.

In the meantime Sir Ralph Hopton, hurt lately (with the blowing up of powder) lay sick and sore in the town of the Devizes. His men wanted match, whom Sir Ralph directed to beat and to boil their bed-cords (necessity is the best mother of ingenuity) which so ordered did them good service; when, marching forth into the field, they effectually contributed to the total routing and ruining of the parliament foot which remained.

THE WORTHIES

ALDHELM [*b.* 640?], son to Centwine, nephew to Ine king of the West Saxons, was bred in foreign parts; and returning home, was abbot of Malmesbury thirty years, a person memorable on several accounts. 1. He was the first Englishman who ever wrote in Latin. 2. He was the first that ever brought poetry into England. 3. The first bishop of the see of Sherborne.

Bede giveth him a large commendation for his learning, the rather because he wrote a book for the reducing the Britons to observe Easter according to the church of Rome.

Impudent monks have much abused his memory with shameless lies, and amongst the rest with a wooden miracle, that a carpenter having cut a beam for his church too short, he by his prayers stretched it out to the full proportion. To this I may add another lie as clear as the sun itself, on whose rays (they report) he hung his vestment, which miraculously supported it, to the admiration of the beholders.

Coming to Rome, to be consecrated bishop of Sherborne, he reproved Pope Sergius his fatherhood, for being a father indeed to a base child, then newly born; and returning home, he lived in great esteem until the day of his death, which happened Anno Domini 709.

His corpse, being brought to Malmesbury, was there enshrined, and had in great veneration; who having his longest abode whilst living, and last when dead, in this county, is probably presumed a native thereof.

SAINT EDITH [or EADGYTH, *b.* 962?], natural daughter of King Eadgar, by the lady Wulfthryth, was abbess of Wilton, wherein she demeaned herself with such devotion, that her memory obtained the reputation of saintship. And yet an author telleth us that being more curious in her attire than beseemed her profession, Bishop Ethelwold sharply reproved her, who answered him roundly, "That God regardeth the heart more than the garment, and that sins might be covered as well under rags as robes."

One reporteth that after the slaughter of her brother Edward, holy Dunstan had a design to make her queen of England (the veil of her head, it seems, would not hinder the crown) so to defeat Ethelred the lawful heir, had she not declined the proffer, partly on pious, partly politic, dissuasions. She died Anno Domini 984; and is buried in the church of Saint Dionysius at Wilton, of her own building.

OLIVER OF MALMESBURY was, saith my author,[1] *in ipsius monasterii territorio natus;* so that there being few paces betwixt his cradle and

(1) Pits.

that convent, he quickly came thither, and became a Benedictine therein. He was much addicted to mathematics and to judicial astrology. A great comet happened in his age, which he entertained with these expressions: *Venisti? venisti? multis matribus lugendum malum! Dudum te vidi; sed multo jam terribilius, Angliae minans prorsus excidium.* (Art thou come? Art thou come? Thou evil to be lamented by many mothers! I saw thee long since; but now thou art much more terrible, threatening the English with utter destruction.)

Nor did he much miss his mark herein; for, soon after, the coming in of the Norman conqueror deprived many English of their lives, more of their laws and liberties, till, after many years, by God's goodness they were restored.

This Oliver, having a mind to try the truth of poetical reports, *an facta vel ficta,* is said to have tied wings to his hands and feet, and taking his rise from a tower in Malmesbury, flew, as they say, a furlong, till something failing him, down he fell, and brake both his thighs. Pity it is but that, Icarus-like, he had not fallen into the water; and then

OLIVER OL'VARIS nomina fecit aquis.

I find the like recorded in the ecclesiastical history of Simon Magus, flying from the Capitol in Rome high in the air, till at last, by the prayers of Saint Peter, he fell down, and bruised himself to death. But that Simon did it by the *black,* our Oliver by the *white* art; he being supported by ill spirits, this by mere ingenuity, which made him the more to be pitied. [*fl.* 1066]

WILLIAM, quitting his own name of SUMMERSET, assumed that of MALMESBURY, because there he had (if not born) his best preferment. Indeed he was a *duallist* in that convent, and if a pluralist no ingenious person would have envied him, being chanter of that church, and library-keeper therein. Let me add, and library-maker too; for so may we call his history of the Saxon kings and bishops before the Conquest, and after it until his own time; an history to be honoured, both for the truth and method thereof. If any fustiness be found in his writings, it comes not from the grape, but from the cask. The smack of superstition in his books is not to be imputed to his person, but to the age wherein he lived and died, viz., Anno Domini 1143, and was buried in Malmesbury.

ROBERT CANUTUS [ROBERT OF CRICKLADE]. His surname might justly persuade us to suspect him a Dane, but that Bale doth assure him born at Cricklade in this county, and further proceedeth thus in the description of the place: "Leland, in the life of great King Alfred, informs us that during the flourishing of the glory of the Britons, before the university of Oxford was founded, two scholars were famous both for eloquence and learning, the one called *Greeklade,* where the Greek, the other *Latinlade,* where the Latin tongue was professed; since corruptly called *Cricklade* and *Lechlade* at this day."

Having so good security, I presumed to print the same in my *Church History,* and am not as yet ashamed thereof. But since, my worthy friend Doctor Heylyn (whose relations, living thereabouts, gave him the opportunity of more exactness) thus reporteth it that Cricklade was the place for the profession of Greek, Lechlade for physic and Latin, a small village (small indeed, for I never saw it any map) hard by the place where Latin was professed.

But to proceed: our Canute went thence to Oxford, and there became chief of the canons of Saint Frideswide. He gathered the best flowers out of Pliny his *Natural History,* and, composing it into a *Garland,* as he calleth it, dedicated the book to King Henry the Second. He wrote also his comments on the greater part of the Old and New Testament; and flourished [1157-1170].

JOHN OF SALISBURY was born at, and so named from, Old Sarum in this county; though I have heard of some of the Salisburies in Derbyshire, who essay to assert him to their family; as who would not recover so eminent a person?

Leland saith that he seeth in him *omnem scientiae orbem* (all the world, or, if you will the whole circle of learning). Bale saith that he was one of the first who, since Theodorus archbishop of Canterbury, living five hundred years before him (oh the μέγα κάσμα of barbarism in England!) endeavoured to restore the learned languages to their original purity, being a good Latinist, Grecian, musician, mathematician, philosopher, divine, and what not?

What learning he could not find at home, he did fetch from abroad, travelling into France and Italy, companion to T. Becket in his exile, but no partner in his protervity[1] against his prince, for which he sharply reproved him. He was highly in favour with Pope Eugenius the Third and Hadrian the Fourth; and yet no author in that age hath so pungent passages against the pride and covetousness of the court of Rome. Take a taste of them:

> Scribes and Pharisees sit in the church of Rome, putting unbearable burthens on men's backs. His legates do so swagger, as if Satan were gone forth from the face of the Lord to scourge the church.
>
> They eat the sins of the people; with them they are clothed, and many ways riot therein, whilst the true worshippers worship the Father in spirit. Whoso dissent from their doctrine are condemned for heretics or schismatics. Christ therefore will manifest himself, and make the way plain, wherein we must walk.[2]

How doth our author *Luther* it (before Luther) against their errors and vices? The more secure for the general opinion men had of his person, all holding our John to be, though no prophet, a pious man King Henry the Second made him bishop of Chartres in France, where he died 1180.

RICHARD OF DEVIZES. A word of the place of his nativity. The Vies, or Devizes, is the best and biggest town for trading (Salisbury being a

(1) He left England probably because of his strong support of Becket. He was present at the latter's murder, wrote his life and urged his canonization. *Protervity*= waywardness, frowardness. (2) John of Salisbury, in *Polycratico.* [Latin original omitted.]

city) in this shire; so called because anciently divided betwixt the king and the bishop of Salisbury, as *Mine-Thine* (corruptly called *Minden*) a city in Westphalia, had its name from such a partition. Now because the Devizes carrieth much of strange conceits in the common sound thereof, and because Stonehenge is generally reputed a wonder, country people who live far off in our land misapprehend them (distanced more than twelve miles) to be near together. Our Richard, born in this town, was bred a Benedictine in Winchester, where his learning and industry rendered him to the respect of all in that age. He wrote a history of the reign of King Richard the First, under whom he flourished, and an epitome of the British affairs, dedicating them both to Robert prior of Winchester. His history I could never see but at the second-hand, as cited by others, the rarity thereof making it no piece for the shop of a stationer, but a property for a public library. [*fl.* 1189-1192]

RICHARD POOR, dean of Salisbury, was first, bishop of Chichester, then of Salisbury, or Old Sarum rather. He found his cathedral most inconveniently seated for want of water and other necessaries; and therefore removed it a mile off, to a place called Merryfield (for the pleasant situation thereof) since Salisbury; where he laid the foundation of that stately structure which he lived not here to finish.

Now as the place whence he came was so dry, that as Malmesbury saith, *miserabili commercio ibi aqua veneat* (by sad chaffer they were fain to give money for water) so he removed to one so low and moist, men sometimes, upon my own knowledge, would give money to be rid of the water. I observe this for no other end but to shew that all human happiness, notwithstanding often exchange of places, will still be an heteroclite,[1] and either have too much or too little for our contentment.

This Poor was afterwards removed to the bishopric of Durham, and lived there in great esteem; Matthew Paris characterising him *eximiae sanctitatis et profundae scientiae virum.* His dissolution, in a most pious and peaceable manner, happened April 5, Anno Domini 1237. His corpse, by his will, was brought and buried at Tarrant in Dorsetshire, in a nunnery of his own founding; and some of his name, and probably alliance, are still extant in this county.

WALTER WINTERBOURNE was born [1225?] at Salisbury in this county, and bred a Dominican friar. He was an excellent scholar in all studies suitable to his age, when a youth; a good poet and orator, when a man; and acute philosopher, *Aristotelicarum doctrinarum heluo,* saith he who otherwise scarce giveth him a good word,[2] when an old man; a deep controversial divine and skilful casuist, a quality which commended him to be confessor to King Edward the First.

Now news being brought to Pope Benedict the Eleventh that William Mykelfeld, provincial of the Dominicans, and designed cardinal of Saint Sabin, was dead and buried at London before his cap could be brought

(1) i.e. (happiness) is uneven, fitful. (2) Pits.

to him, he appointed this Walter to be heir to his honour. The worst is, as medlars are never ripe till they are rotten, so few are thought fit to be cardinals but such as are extremely in years. Mykelfeld had all his body buried, and our Winterbourne had one foot in the grave, being seventy-nine years of age before he was summoned to that dignity.

However, over he went with all haste into Italy; and though coming thither too late to have a sight of Pope Benedict the Eleventh, came soon enough to give a suffrage at the choice of Clement the Fifth. This Walter's cardinal's cap was never a whit the worse for wearing, enjoying it but a year. In his return home he died, and was buried at Genoa; but afterwards his corpse was brought over, and re-interred most solemnly in London, anno 1305.

WILLIAM OF EDINGTON was born at Edington in this county; bred in Oxford, and advanced by King Edward the Third to be bishop of Winchester and lord treasurer of England. During his managing of that office, he caused new coins (unknown before) to be made, groats and half-groats, both readier for change and fitter for charity. But the worst was, *imminuto nonnihil pondere* (the weight was somewhat abated). If any say this was an unepiscopal act, know he did it not as bishop but as lord treasurer; the king, his master, having all the profit thereby. Yea, succeeding princes, following this pattern, have sub-diminished their coin ever since. Hence is it that our nobility cannot maintain the port of their ancestors with the same revenues; because *so many pounds* are not *so many pounds,* though the same in noise and number, not the same in intrinsical valuation.

He was afterwards made lord chancellor, and erected a stately convent for Bonhommes[1] at Edington in this county, the place of his nativity, valued at the Dissolution per annum at five hundred twenty-one pounds, twelve shillings, five-pence halfpenny. Some condemn him for robbing St. Peter (to whom, with St. Swithin, Winchester church was dedicated) to pay all saints collectively, to whom Edington convent was consecrated, suffering his episcopal palaces to decay and drop down, whilst he raised up his new foundation. This he dearly paid for after his death, when his executors were sued for dilapidations by his successor William of Wykeham, an excellent architect, and therefore well knowing how to proportion his charges for reparations, who recovered of them one thousand six hundred sixty-two pounds ten shillings, a vast sum in that age, though paid in the lighter groats and half-groats. Besides this, his executors were forced to make good the standing stock of the bishopric, which in his time was impaired: viz., oxen, 1556; wethers, 4717; ewes, 3521; lambs, 3521; swine, 127.

This Edington sat in his bishopric twenty-one years; and dying 1366, lieth buried on the south side, in the passage to the quire, having a fair monument of alabaster, but an epitaph of coarse stone; I mean, so barbarous that it is not worth the inserting.

(1) Austin friars, known as such, previously settled in England at Ashridge, Hertfordshire, by the Black Prince, and Edington's foundation was at the former's request.

MARGARET PLANTAGENET [MARGARET POLE, COUNTESS OF SALISBURY] daughter to George duke of Clarence and Isabella Neville eldest daughter and coheir of Richard Neville earl of Warwick, was born August 14, 1473, at Farley Castle in this county.[1] Reader, I pray thee, let her pass for a princess, because daughter to a duke, niece to two kings, Edward the Fourth and Richard the Third, mother to Cardinal Reginald Pole; but chiefly because she was the last liver of all that royal race which from their birth wore the name of Plantagenet. By Sir Richard Pole, a knight of Wales, and cousin-german to King Henry the Seventh, she had divers children, whereof Henry Lord Montague was the eldest; he was accused of treason, and this lady his mother charged to be privy thereunto, by King Henry the Eighth, who (as his father was something too slow) was somewhat too quick in discovering treasons, as soon as, if not before, they were. On the scaffold, as she stood, she would not gratify the executioner with a prostrate posture of her body.[2]

Some beheld this her action as an argument of an erected soul, disdaining pulingly to submit to an infamous death, showing her mind free, though her body might be forced, and that also it was a demonstration of her innocence. But others condemned it as a needless and unseasonable animosity in her, who, though supposed innocent before man for this fact, must grant herself guilty before God, whose justice was the supreme judge condemning her. Besides, it was indiscreet to contend where it was impossible to prevail, there being no guard against the edge of such an axe, but patience; and it is ill for a soul to go reeking with anger out of this world.

Here happened an unequal contest betwixt weakness and strength, age and youth, nakedness and weapons, nobility and baseness, a princess and an executioner, who at last dragging her by the hair, grey with age, may truly be said to have took off her head, seeing she would neither give it him, nor forgive him the doing thereof. Thus died this Lady Margaret, heir to the name and stout nature of Margaret duchess of Burgundy, her aunt and godmother, whose spirits were better proportioned to her extraction than estate; for, though by special patent she was created countess of Salisbury, she was restored but to a small part of the inheritance she was born unto. She suffered in the twenty-third year of the reign of King Henry the Eighth. [*d.* 1541]

T. STUMPE, of the town of Malmesbury in this county, was in his age one of the most eminent clothiers in England; of whom there passeth a story, told with some variation of circumstances, but generally to this purpose.

(1) Actually at Farley Castle near Bath. (2) Margaret Pole's position had been compromised by her son Cardinal Pole's book *De Unitate Ecclesiastica*, a strong criticism of Henry VIII's conduct. Because of their opposition to the divorce and to his policy generally, finally sealed by this book, and because they had a claim to the throne, Henry was determined to exterminate the Poles. Henry Pole, Lord Montague was, with others, accused of treason and executed; his brother Sir Geoffrey, whose confessions implicated his brother, tried to commit suicide, was pardoned, and escaped to Rome. The cardinal (see Staffordshire, p. 515) was abroad at the time. Margaret Pole was included in the act of attainder of 1539 and imprisoned for two years before execution.

King Henry the Eighth, hunting near Malmesbury in Braden Forest, came with all his court train, unexpected, to dine with this clothier. But great housekeepers are as seldom surprised with guests as vigilant captains with enemies. Stumpe commands his little army of workmen, which he fed daily in his house, to fast one meal until night, which they might easily do without endangering their health, and with the same provision gave the king and his court train (though not so delicious and various) most wholesome and plentiful entertainment.

But more authentic is what I read in the great antiquary,[1] speaking of the plucking down of Malmesbury monastery: "The very minster itself should have sped no better than the rest, but been demolished, had not T. Stumpe, a wealthy clothier, by much suit, but with a greater sum of money, redeemed and bought it for the townsmen his neighbours, by whom it was converted to a parish church, and for a great part is yet standing at this day."

I find one William Stumpe, gentleman, who, in the one-and-thirtieth year of King Henry the Eighth, bought of him the demesnes of Malmesbury abbey for fifteen hundred pounds two shillings and a halfpenny.[2] Now how he was related to this T. Stumpe, whether son or father, is to me unknown. It will not be a sin for me to wish more branches from such Stumpes, who by their bounty may preserve the monuments of antiquity from destruction.

EDWARD SEYMOUR and THOMAS SEYMOUR, both sons of Sir John Seymour, of Wolfhall, knight, in this county. I join them together, because whilst they were united in affection they were invincible; but when divided, easily overthrown by their enemies.

EDWARD SEYMOUR, duke of Somerset, lord protector and treasurer of England, being the elder brother, succeeded to a fair paternal inheritance. He was a valiant soldier for land-service, fortunate, and generally beloved by martial men. He was of an open nature, free from jealousy and dissembling, affable to all people. He married Anne, daughter of Sir Edward Stanhope, knight, a lady of a high mind and haughty undaunted spirit. [1506?-1552]

THOMAS SEYMOUR, the younger brother, was made baron of Sudeley. By offices and the favours of his nephew, King Edward the Sixth, he obtained a great estate. He was well experienced in sea affairs, and made lord admiral of England. He lay at a close posture, being of a reserved nature, and was more cunning in his carriage. He married Queen Catherine Parr, the widow of King Henry the Eighth [1508?-1549].

Very great the animosities betwixt their wives; the duchess refusing to bear the queen's train, and in effect justled with her for precedence; so that what betwixt the train of the queen, and long gown of the duchess, they raised so much dust at the court, as at last put out the eyes

(1) Camden's *Britannia*. (2) I perused the original in the Remembrancer's (or Sir Thomas Fanshawe's) Office, C. vii. Par. rot. 147. [Something is known of this last Stumpe, a rich clothier who bought the abbey. He set up his looms in the monastic buildings, and did a tremendous amount of damage, including the destruction of MSS, but to him we owe the survival of the building as it now stands.]

of both their husbands, and occasioned their executions, as we have largely declared in our *Church History*.

Thus the two best bulwarks of the safety of King Edward the Sixth being demolished to the ground, Duke Dudley had the advantage the nearer to approach and assault the king's person, and to practise his destruction, as is vehemently suspected.[1]

JANE SEYMOUR, daughter to Sir John Seymour, knight (honourably descended from the lords Beauchamps) was, as by all concerning probabilities is collected, born [1509?] at Wolfhall in this county, and after was married to King Henry the Eighth.

It is currently traditioned that at her first coming to court, Queen Anne Boleyn, espying a jewel pendant about her neck, snatched thereat (desirous to see, the other unwilling to show it) and casually hurt her hand with her own violence; but it grieved her heart more, when she perceived it the king's picture by himself bestowed upon her, who from this day forward dated her own declining, and the other's ascending, in her husband's affection.

It appeareth plainly by a passage in the act of parliament, that the king was not only invited to his marriage by his own affections, but by the humble petition and intercession of most of the nobles of his realm, moved thereunto, as well by the conveniency of her years, as in respect that by her excellent beauty and pureness of flesh and blood (I speak the very words of the act itself) she was apt, God willing, to conceive issue. And so it proved accordingly.

This queen died some days after the birth of Prince Edward her son, on whom this epitaph:

Phoenix Jana jacet, nato Phoenice; dolendum
Saecula Phoenices nulla tulisse duas.

Soon as her Phoenix bud was blown,
Root-Phoenix Jane did wither:
Sad, that no age a brace had shown
Of Phoenixes together.

Of all the wives of King Henry, she only had the happiness to die in his full favour, the 24th of October, 1537; and is buried in the quire of Windsor Chapel, the king continuing in real mourning for her, even all the festival of Christmas.

SIR JAMES LEY, knight and baronet [FIRST EARL OF MARLBOROUGH], son of Henry Ley, esquire (one of great ancestry, who on his own cost, with his men, valiantly served King Henry the Eighth at the siege of Boulogne) was born [1550] at Treffont in this county. Being his father's sixth son, and so in probability barred of his inheritance, he endeavoured to make himself an heir by his education, applying his book in Brasenose College, and afterwards studying the laws of the land in Lincoln's Inn,

(1) John Dudley, duke of Northumberland (see Staffordshire, p. 516) attempted to alter the succession in favour of his own family by marrying his son to Lady Jane Grey. Jane Seymour, whose life follows below, was sister to Edward and Thomas Seymour. After Catherine Parr's death, Thomas Seymour sought the hand of Queen (then Princess) Elizabeth.

wherein such his proficiency, King James made him lord chief justice in Ireland.

Here he practised the charge King James gave him at his going over, yea, what his own tender conscience gave himself, namely, "not to build his estate on the ruins of a miserable nation"; but aiming by the unpartial execution of justice not to enrich himself but civilize the people, he made a good progress therein. But the king would no longer lose him out of his own land, and therefore recalled him home about the time when his father's inheritance, by the death of his five elder brethren, descended upon him.

It was not long before offices and honour flowed in fast upon him, being made, by King James, 1. Attorney of the court of wards; 2. Chief justice of the upper bench, 18th of his reign, Jan. 29; 3. Lord treasurer of England, in the 22nd of his reign, December 22; 4. Baron Ley of Ley in Devonshire, the last of the same month; by King Charles, 1. Earl of Marlborough in this county, immediately after the king's coronation; 2. Lord president of the council; in which place he died, Anno Domini 1629.

He was a person of great gravity, ability and integrity; and as the Caspian Sea is observed neither to ebb nor flow, so his mind did not rise or fall, but continued the same constancy in all conditions.

JOHN THORNBOROUGH, B.D., was born [1551] as I am credibly informed, in the city of Salisbury, bred in Magdalen College in Oxford. He did εὐπροσοπῆσαι ἐν σαρκὶ, and his goodly presence made him more acceptable to Queen Elizabeth, preferring him dean of York, and bishop of Limerick in Ireland, where he received a most remarkable deliverance, in manner as followeth.

Lying in an old castle in Ireland, in a large room, partitioned but with sheets or curtains, his wife, children and servants, in effect a whole family in the dead time of the night, the floor overhead being earth and plaster, as in many places is used, overcharged with weight, fell wholly down together, and crushing all to pieces that was above two feet high, as cupboards, tables, forms, stools, rested at last on certain chests, as God would have it, and hurt no living creature.

In the first of King James, 1603, he was consecrated bishop of Bristol; and held his deanery and Irish bishopric *in commendam* with it, and from thence was translated to Worcester. I have heard his skill in chemistry much commended; and he presented a precious extraction to King James, reputed a great preserver of health, and prolonger of life. He conceived by such helps to have added to his vigorous vivacity, though I think a merry heart, whereof he had a great measure, was his best elixir to that purpose. He died, exceeding aged, Anno Domini 1641

SIR OLIVER ST. JOHN, knight, Lord Grandison, &c., was born [1559] of an ancient and honourable family, whose prime seat was at Lydiard Tregoze in this county. He was bred in the wars from his youth, and at last by King James was appointed lord deputy of Ireland, and vigorously pursued the principles of his predecessors for the civilizing thereof.

Indeed the Lord Mountjoy reduced that country to obedience, the Lord Chichester to some civility, and this Lord Grandison first advanced it to considerable profit to his master. I confess T. Walsingham writeth that Ireland afforded unto Edward the Third thirty thousand pounds a year paid into his exchequer; but it appears by the Irish records (which are rather to be believed) that it was rather a burden, and the constant revenue thereof beneath the third part of that proportion. But now, the kingdom being peaceably settled, the income thereof turned to good account, so that Ireland (called by my author[1] the land of *Ire,* for the constant broils therein for four hundred years) was now become the land of *concord.* Being recalled into England, he lived many years in great repute, and dying without issue left his honour to his sister's son by Sir Edward Villiers; but the main of his estate to his brother's son Sir John St. John, knight and baronet. [*d.* 1630]

JOHN BUCKERIDGE was born [1562?] at Draycot nigh Marlborough in this county;[2] and bred under Master Mulcaster in Merchant Taylors' School; from whence he was sent to Saint John's College in Oxford, where, from a fellow, he became doctor of divinity, and president thereof. He afterwards succeeded Doctor Lancelot Andrewes in the vicarage of Saint Giles, Cripplegate, in which cure they lived one-and-twenty years a-piece; and indeed great was the intimacy betwixt these two learned prelates. On the 9th of June 1611, he was consecrated bishop of Rochester; and afterwards set forth a learned book, in opposition of John Fisher, *De Potestate Papae in Rebus Temporalibus.*

He was afterwards preferred bishop of Ely; and having preached the funeral sermon of Bishop Andrewes (extant in print at the end of his works) survived him not a full year, dying Anno Domini 1631.[3] He was decently interred, by his own appointment, in the parish church of Bromley in Kent; the manor thereof belonged to the bishopric of Rochester.

SIR NICHOLAS HYDE, knight, was born at Wardour in this county, where his father, in right of his wife, had a long lease of that castle from the family of the Arundels. His father, I say (descended from an ancient family in Cheshire) a fortunate gentleman in all his children, and more in his grandchildren; some of his under-boughs outgrowing the top branch, and younger children, amongst whom Sir Nicholas, in wealth and honour exceeding the heir of the family.[4]

He was bred in the Middle Temple, and was made serjeant-at-law the first of February 1627; and on the eighth day following was sworn lord chief justice of the king's bench, succeeding in that office, next save one, unto his countryman Sir James Ley (then alive, and preferred lord treasurer, born within two miles one of another) and next of all unto Sir Ranulphe Crew,[5] lately displaced. Now, though he entered on his place with some disadvantage, Sir Ranulphe being generally popular, and

(1) Sir John Davies, in *Discovery of Ireland.* (2) So am I informed by Mr. Anthony Holmes, his secretary, still alive. (3) Lancelot Andrewes died in 1626. (4) This Sir Nicholas was uncle to Edward Hyde, earl of Clarendon. (5) See Cheshire, p. 74.

though in those days it was hard for the same person to please court and country, yet he discharged his office with laudable integrity, and died 1631.

HENRY DANVERS [EARL OF DANBY]. His ensuing epitaph on his monument in the church of Dauntsey in this shire, will better acquaint the reader with his deserts, than any character which my pen can give of him:

"Here lieth the body of Henry Danvers, second son to Sir John Danvers, knight, and Dame Elizabeth, daughter and coheir to Neville Lord Latimer. He was born at Dauntsey in the county of Wilts., Jan., Anno Domini 1573, being bred up partly in the Low Country wars under Maurice earl of Nassau, afterward Prince of Orange; and in many other military actions of those times, both by sea and by land. He was made a captain in the wars of France, and there knighted for his good service under Henry the Fourth, the then French king. He was employed as lieutenant of the horse, and serjeant-major of the whole army in Ireland, under Robert earl of Essex, and Charles baron of Mountjoy, in the reign of Queen Elizabeth. By King James the First he was made baron of Dauntsey, and peer of this realm, as also lord president of Munster, and governor of Guernsey. By King Charles the First he was created earl of Danby, made of his privy council, and knight of the most noble order of the Garter. In his latter time, by reason of imperfect health, considerably declining more active employments, full of honours, wounds, and days, he died Anno Domini 1644. *Laus Deo.*"

For many years before, St. George had not been more magnificently mounted, I mean the solemnity of his feast more sumptuously observed, than when this earl, with the earl of Morton, were installed knights of the Garter. One might have there beheld the abridgment of English and Scottish in their attendance: the Scottish earl, like Zeuxis his picture, adorned with all art and costliness; whilst our English earl, like the plain sheet of Apelles, by the gravity of his habit got the advantage of the gallantry of his corrival with judicious beholders.[1]

WILLIAM LAWES, son of Thomas Lawes, a vicar-choral of the church of Salisbury, was bred in the Close of that city, being from his childhood inclined to music. Edward earl of Hertford obtained him from his father, and bred him at his own cost in that faculty under his master Giovanni Coperario, an Italian, and most exquisite musician.[2] Yet may it be said that the scholar in time did equal, yea exceed his master.

He afterwards was of the private music to King Charles; and was respected and beloved of all such persons who cast any look towards virtue and honour. Besides his fancies of the three, four, five and six parts to viol and organ, he made above thirty several sorts of music for voices and instruments; neither was there any instrument then in use, but he composed to it so aptly, as if he had only studied that.

(1) Danvers served as page to Sir Philip Sidney in the Low Countries. In 1594, arising out of a family feud, he and his brother Sir Charles Danvers were involved in the death of a Henry Long, and both were outlawed, but later pardoned. Sir Charles was executed in 1601 for complicity in Essex's rebellion. (2) Coperario (d. 1626) said to be an Englishman of the name of Cooper, was composer to Charles I, and taught both William and Henry Lawes.

In these distracted times his loyalty engaged him in the war for his lord and master; and though he was by General Gerard made a commissary, on design to secure him (such officers being commonly shot-free by their place, as not exposed to danger) yet such the activity of his spirit, he disclaimed the covert of his office, and betrayed thereunto by his own adventurousness, was casually shot at the siege of Chester the same time when the Lord Bernard Stuart lost his life.

Nor was the king's soul so engrossed with grief for the death of so near a kinsman and noble a lord, but that hearing of the death of his dear servant William Lawes, he had a particular mourning for him when dead, whom he loved when living, and commonly called the Father of Music. I leave the rest of his worth to be expressed by his own works of composures of Psalms done jointly by him and his brother, Master Henry Lawes,[1] betwixt which two no difference, either in eminency, affection, or otherwise considerable, save that the one is deceased, and the other still surviving. Master William Lawes died in September 1645.

SIR FRANCIS COTTINGTON [BARON COTTINGTON] was born [1578?] nigh Mere in this county, and bred, when a youth, under Sir Edward Stafford. He lived so long in Spain, till he made the garb and gravity of that nation become his, and become him. He raised himself by his natural strength, without any artificial advantage; having his parts above his learning, his experience above his parts, his industry above his experience, and (some will say) his success above all; so that at the last he became chancellor of the exchequer, baron of Hanworth in Middlesex, and upon the resignation of Doctor Juxon, lord treasurer of England, gaining also a very great estate. But what he got in few years he lost in fewer days since our civil wars, when the parliament was pleased (for reasons only known to themselves) to make him one of the examples of their severity, excluding him pardon, but permitting his departure beyond the seas, where he died [1652].[2]

THE FAREWELL

This county, consisting so much of sheep, must honour the memory of King Edgar, who first freed the land from all wolves therein. For the future, I wish their flock secured, 1. From *two-legged* wolves, very destructive unto them; 2. From Spanish ewes, whereof one being brought over into England, anno ...... brought with it the first general contagion of sheep; 3. From hunger-rot, the effect of an over-dry summer.

I desire also, that, seeing these seem to be of the same breed with Laban's and Jethro's sheep, which had their solemn times and places of drinking (which in other shires I have not observed) that they may never have any want of wholesome water.

(1) William Lawes' younger brother, the friend of Milton, who wrote *Comus* at his suggestion, and for which he composed the music. He lived 1596-1662. (2) He joined Charles II abroad; tried, unsuccessfully, to raise money for him in Spain, embraced Roman Catholicism, and settled and died at Valladolid. He never became lord treasurer, as Fuller states, but was for a short time a commissioner of the treasury.

WORCESTERSHIRE

WORCESTERSHIRE hath Staffordshire on the north, Warwickshire on the east, Gloucestershire on the south, Hereford and Shrop-shires on the west. It is of a triangular but not equilateral form; in proportion, stretching from north to south, twenty-two miles; south to north-west, twenty-eight miles; thence to her north-east point, twenty-eight miles. Be this understood of the continued part of this shire, which otherwise hath snips and shreds cut off from the whole cloth, and surrounded with the circumjacent countries, even some in Oxfordshire distanced, by Gloucestershire interposed.

What may be the cause hereof, it were presumption for me to guess, after the conjectures of so many learned men. Some conceive that such who had the command of this county (probably before the Conquest) and had parcels of their own land scattered in the vicinage, desired to unite them to this county, so to make their own authority the more entire. Or else as a worthy writer will have it (rendering a reason why part of Devonshire straggleth into Cornwall) it was done that "there might rest some cause of intercourse betwixt this and the neighbouring counties;" adding moreover that a "late great man ensued and expressed the like consideration, in the division of his lands betwixt two of his sons."[1] All I will say is this, that God, in the partage of Palestine (reader, if you forget, I must remember my own profession) betwixt the twelve tribes, on the same account, as the learned conceive, made some tribes to have in-lots within another: "And Manasseh had in Issachar and in Asher, Bethshean and her towns, and Ibleam and her towns, &c."

This county hath a child's portion (and that, I assure you, a large one) in all English, and especially in these

NATURAL COMMODITIES

Lampreys

In Latin *Lampetrae, a lambendo petras* (from licking the rocks) are plentiful in this and the neighbouring counties in the river of Severn. A deformed fish, which for the many holes therein, one would conceive Nature intended it rather for an instrument of music than for man's food. The best manner of dressing whereof, saith my author, is " to kill it in malmsey, close the mouth thereof with a nutmeg, the holes with so many cloves; and when it is rolled up round, putting in thereto filbert-nut kernels stamped, crumbs of bread, oil, spices, &c."[2] Others but those miso-lampreys) do add that after all this cost, even cast them away, seeing money is better lost than health; and the meat will rather be delicious than wholesome, the eating whereof cost King Henry the First his life. But, by their favour, that king did not die of lampreys, but of excess in eating them; and I am confident the Jews might surfeit of manna itself, if eating thereof above due proportion.

(1) Carew, in his *Survey of Cornwall*. (2) Camden's *Britannia*.

PERRY

This is a drink, or a counterfeit wine, made of pears, whereof plenty in this county, though such which are least delicious for taste, are most proper for this purpose. Such the providence of Nature, to design all things for man's service. Peter Martyr, when professor in Oxford, and sick of a fever, would drink no other liquor, though it be generally believed both cold and windy, except corrected with spice, or some other addition.

SALT

I have twice[1] formerly insisted hereon, and do confess this repetition to be flatly against my own rules, laid down for the regulating of this work, save that the necessity of this commodity will excuse it from any offence. I beheld England as a long well-furnished table, and account three principal salt-cellars set at a distance thereon. Worcestershire I fancy the trencher salt, both because it is not so much in quantity (though very considerable) and because it is whiter, finer and heavier than any other. Cheshire, I conceive, deserveth to be reputed the grand salt-cellar, placed somewhat beneath the middle; whilst the third is the salt of Newcastle, set far north, at the lower end of the table, for the use of those who otherwise cannot conveniently reach to the former. The usefulness of this not-duly-valued blessing may be concluded from the Latin word *salarium,* so usual in ancient and modern authors, which importeth the entertainment or wages of soldiers, anciently paid chiefly (if not only) in victuals, and taketh its name, by a synecdoche, from *sal,* or salt, as of all things most absolutely needful; without which condiment nothing can be wholesome nutriment.

I read in a modern author, describing his own county of Cheshire, and measuring all things to the advantage thereof, that "there is no shire in England, or in any other country beyond the seas, where they have more than one salt-well therein; neither at Droitwich in Worcestershire is there more than one; whereas in Cheshire there be four, all within ten miles together."[2]

Here let me enter this caveat in preservation of the right of Worcestershire, that many salt-fountains are found therein, but stopped up again for the preservation of woods; so that the making of salt at one place alone proceeds not from any *natural* but a *politic* restriction. Nor must I forget how our German ancestors (as Tacitus reports) conceited such places where salt was found to be nearest to the heavens, and to ingratiate men's prayers to the gods; I will not say, founding their superstition on the misapprehension of the Jewish worship, "Every sacrifice shall be salted with salt."

THE BUILDINGS

I am sorry I have never seen the cathedral of Worcester, so that I cannot knowingly give it a due recommendation; and more sorry to hear that our late civil wars have made so sad an impression thereon.

The market-towns are generally handsomely built; and no shire in

(1) Actually once only, in Cheshire (p. 61). (2) William Smith, in the *Vale Royal of England.*

England can shew a brace of them so neat and near together as Bewdley and Kidderminster in this county, being scarcely two miles asunder.

THE BATTLES

WORCESTER FIGHT. Many smart skirmishes have happened in this county, and near this city. We only insist on that fatal fight, September the third, 1651.

Know then (as introductory thereunto) that his majesty, on the first of August foregoing, began his march from Edinburgh into England, not meeting with any considerable opposition (those at Warrington being soon put to flight by his presence) until he came to Worcester. His army consisted of twelve thousand effectual fighting men, whereof two thousand English, the rest of the Scottish nation; but neither excellently armed nor plentifully stored with ammunition, whilst the parliament forces under Cromwell more than doubled that number, wanting nothing (but a good cause) that an army could wish or desire.

The royalists' chiefest strength consisted in two passes they possessed over the river of Severn, which proved not advantageous according to expectation; for the enemy found the river fordable elsewhere; and the bridge and pass at Upton, though valiantly defended by Major-General Massey (who received a shot in his hand) was forced by Lambert pouring in unequal numbers on the king's forces. Besides, Cromwell finished a bridge of boards and planks over the main river, with more celerity, and less resistance than could have been expected in a matter of such importance.

Then began the battle wherein his majesty, to remember his subjects' good, forgot his own safety, and gave an incomparable example of valour to the rest, by charging in his own person. This was followed by few to the same degree of danger; but imitated in the greatest measure by the Highlanders, fighting with the butt-ends of their muskets when their ammunition was spent. But new supplies constantly charging them, and the main body of the Scotch horse not coming up in due time from the city to his majesty's relief, his army was forced to retreat in at Sidbury Gate in much disorder.

If there were (which some more than whisper) false and foul play in some persons of principal trust; as they have had a great space seasonably, God grant them his grace sincerely, to repent for their treacherous retarding the happiness, prolonging and increasing the miseries, of a gracious king and three great nations! Sure it is, here were slain the flower of the Scottish loyal gentry, with the most illustrious William (formerly earl of Lanark) duke of Hamilton. As for common soldiers, some few who escaped had a longer life to have a sadder death, wandering in the country till other men's charity and their own strength failed them.

THE WORTHIES

FLORENCE OF WORCESTER was probably born near, certainly bred *in* that city, one eminent in learning as any of his age, and no less industrious. Many books are extant of his making, and one most useful, beginning at the Creation, and continued till his death. This he calleth *Chronicum Chronicorum,* which some esteem an arrogant title, and an insolent defiance of all authors before and after him, as if (as the rose is *flos florum*) so his were the superlative chronicle of all that are extant. But others meet with much modesty in the title *Chronicum Chronicorum,* as none of his own making, but only gathered both for matter and language out of others, he being rather the collector than the original composer thereof. He died Anno Domini 1118.

JOHN COMYN. It must cost us some pains (but the merit of the man will quit cost) to clear him to be of English extraction. For the proof whereof, we produce the testimony of Giraldus Cambrensis, his contemporary and acquaintance, who saith he was *vir Anglicus natione.* Hereby the impudent falsehood of Thomas Dempster the Scottish historian doth plainly appear, thus expressing himself: "John Comyn, descended from the most noble stock of the earls of Buchan, born at Banff, is most falsely set down amongst the English; seeing I myself lately saw some of his writings at Paris, in the library of Paulus Petavius, senator of Paris, in which he recommended the cause of his countrymen to Pope Lucius."

In plain English, this Scottish Dempster is an arrant rook, depluming England, Ireland and Wales of famous writers, merely to feather his own country therewith; so that should he, according to the Jewish law, be forced to make fourfold restitution for his felony, he would be left poor enough indeed.

Besides, Alexander Comyn was created first earl of Buchan by King Alexander the Second, who began to reign Anno Domini 1214; whereas Comyn (by the testimony of Dempster himself) died 1212; and therefore could not properly descend of their stock who were not then in being.

I cannot certainly avouch him a Worcestershire man; but know that he was bred a monk at Evesham therein, whence he was chosen (the king procuring it) *a clero Dublinensi consone satis et concorditer,* archbishop of Dublin. He endowed Trinity Church in Dublin with two-and-twenty prebends; and was made by Pope Lucius cardinal of St. Vellit in Italy.[1]

SAINT RICHARD DE WYCHE, born [1197?] at Wich (alias Droitwich) from which he took his name, was bred in Oxford, afterwards at Paris, and lastly at Bononia in Italy, where for seven years together he heard and read the canon law. Having thus first plentifully *laid in,* he then began to *lay out,* in his lectures in that university; and returning home, became chancellor of Oxford, then of Canterbury, till at last chosen bishop of Chichester. He was a great Becketist, viz., a stout opposer of regal power over spiritual persons; on which and other accounts, he wrote a book to Pope Innocent the Fourth, against King Henry the Third. These his qualities, with the reputation of his holy life, so commended his memory to the notice of Pope Urban the Fourth, that seven years after his death, viz., anno 1262, he canonized him for a saint. It seems men then arrived sooner at the maturity of (popish) saintship than nowadays, more dis-

(1) John Comyn was opposed to, and excommunicated by, Becket. In Henry II's struggle with the latter he used Comyn as his emissary to the pope.

tance being now required betwixt their death and canonization. As for their report that the *wiches* or salt-pits in this county were miraculously procured by his prayers, their unsavoury lie hath not a grain of probability to season it; it appearing by ancient authors that salt water flowed there time out of mind, before any sweet milk was given by mother or nurse to this Saint Richard. [*d.* 1253]

HUGH OF EVESHAM, so called from the place of his nativity in this county, applied himself to the study of physic with so good success that he is called the Phoenix in that faculty. Great also was his skill in the mathematics, and especially in astrology. Some questions arising at Rome about physic (which consequently were of church government) Pope Martin the Fourth sent for our Hugh, to consult with him; who gave such satisfaction to his demands, that in requital he created him cardinal of St. Laurence, 1281. But so great the envy of his adversaries at his preferment, that seven years after, he was put to death by poison; and let none say he might have foreseen his fate in the stars, seeing hell, and not the heavens, brooded that design. Neither say, "Physician, cure thyself," seeing English antidotes are too weak for Italian poisons. But Ciaconius, to palliate the business, saith he died of the plague; and thus I believe him, of the plague of hatred in the hearts of such who contrived his death; which happened Anno Domini 1287.

WILLIAM PAKINGTON. I confess two villages (the less and greater) of this name in Warwickshire; and yet place this Pakington here, with no discredit to myself, and greater grace to him. For, first, I behold him as no clergyman (commonly called from their native places) but have reasons to believe him rather a layman, and find an ancient family of his name (not to say alliance) still flourishing in this county. He was secretary and treasurer to Edward the Black Prince; and his long living in France had made the language of his nurse more natural to him than the tongue of his mother. Hence it was that he wrote in French the story of five English kings (King John, Henry the Third, Edwards First, Second and Third) and a book of the achievements of the Black Prince. [*d.* 1390]

RICHARD DE BEAUCHAMP, earl of Warwick, was born at the manor house of Salwarpe in this county, January the 28th, 1382. King Richard the Second and Richard Scrope, then bishop of Coventry (afterwards archbishop of York) were his godfathers. A person so redoubted for martial achievements, that the poetical fictions of Hercules' labours found in him a real performance.

1. Being hardly twenty-two years old, in the fifth of King Henry the Fourth, at the queen's coronation, he jousted, and challenged all comers.

2. He bid battle to Owen Glendower the Welsh rebel; put him to flight, and took his banner with his own hands.

3. He fought a pitched field against the two Percys at Shrewsbury, and overcame them.

4. In his passage to the Holy Land (whither he went on pilgrimage) he was challenged at Verona, by an Italian, Sir Pandolph Malatete, to fight

with him at three weapons; viz., with axes, arming swords and sharp daggers; whom he had slain at the second weapon, had not some seasonably interceded.

5. Fighting at jousts in France with Sir Collard Fiennes, at every stroke he bare him backward to his horse; and when the French suspected that he was tied to his saddle, to confute their jealousies, our earl lighted, and presently remounted.

6. He was eminently active in the king's victorious battles in France, and might truly say, *Quorum pars magna fui* [whereof I was no small part].

7. He was one of those whom King Henry the Fifth sent to the council of Constance, whose whole retinue amounted unto eight hundred horse.

8. Here he killed a Dutch duke who challenged him, Sigismund the emperor and his empress beholding it.

9. The empress, affected with his valour, took the badge from one of the earl's men (being a plain bear of silver) and wore it on her shoulder. But the next day our earl presented her with a bear (which was his crest) made of pearls and precious stones.

10. Being sent by King Henry the Fifth, with a thousand men in arms, to fetch Queen Catherine, sole daughter to the king of France, he fought with the earls of Vendôme and Linosin, killed one of them with his own hand, routed the forces of five thousand men, and brought the lady, whom he saw safely married to the king.

11. He was, by the said king's will, appointed governor to his son in his minority, and made lieutenant of all France.

12. During his life our success in France was progressive, and retrograde after his death.

It must not be forgotten how Sigismund the emperor, coming into England, told King Henry the Fifth that no Christian king had such another knight for wisdom, nurture and manhood.

He obtained leave of the king (because in his dominions) that he might by imperial authority fix a title of honour upon him; and caused him to be named the Father of Courtesy, as indeed true courage and courtesy are undivided companions.

The last time he went over into Normandy, he was tossed with a hideous tempest; so that, despairing of life, he caused himself to be bound (for who could bind him against his will?) with his lady and infant son, to the mainmast, on this design, that having his armour and coat of arms upon him, he might thereby he known, that such who should light on his corpse, if either noble or charitable, might afford him a Christian burial.

Yet he, escaping the tempest, and landing safely in France, died in his bed (no usual repose for so restless and active a spirit) at Rouen, of a lingering disease, April 30, 1439; and lieth buried in a smost stately tomb, in a chapel of the collegiate church of Warwick, where his epitaph, graven in brass is pointed with bears, serving for commas, colons, periods and all distinctions thereof. His deeds of charity (according to the devotion of those days) were little inferior to the achievements of his valour.

JOHN LOWE was born in this county; bred an Augustinian friar at Wich therein; afterwards he went to the universities, and then settled himself in London. Hence he was preferred by King Henry the Sixth to Saint Asaph, and thence was removed (desiring his own quietness) from one of the best bishoprics in Wales, to Rochester, the meanest in England. He was a great book-monger; and on that score, Bale, no friend to friars, giveth him a large testimonial, that Bishop Godwin borroweth from him (the first and last in that kind) the whole character of his commendation, and this amongst the rest, *Opuscula quaedam scripsit purgatis auribus digna.*

He deserved well of posterity in preserving many excellent manuscripts, and bestowing them on the magnificent library which he furnished at Saint Augustine's in London. But alas! that library, at the Dissolution, vanished away, with the fine spire-steeple of the same church (oh, the wide swallow of sacrilege!); one person, who shall be nameless, embezzling both books and buildings to his private profit. He died Anno Domini 1467; and lieth buried in his own cathedral (over against Bishop Merton) under a marble monument.

SIR THOMAS LITTLETON, knight. Reader, the nimiety[1] of my cautiousness (loth to prejudice the seeming right of any) made me to bestow part of his character on Staffordshire, who since am convinced that he wholly and solely belongeth to this shire, as born [1422] at Frankley therein; and I request the reader to rectify some mistakes I formerly wrote by that which followeth. He was a man remarkable in many respects.

First, for his extraction. He was son to Thomas Wescote, esquire, and Elizabeth Littleton his wife, who, being a double inheritrix, by her father to the Littletons, mother to the Quatremains, indented with her husband that her heritable issue should assume her surname. Say not her husband might say, *Accepi dotem, cognomen perdidi,* seeing it was done before Scripture itself, Joab being constantly named the son of his mother Zeruiah.

Secondly, for his happiness, that two great kings had a great sympathy to him, who had an antipathy each to other: Henry the Sixth, whose serjeant he was, and rode judge of the northern circuit; and Edward the Fourth, who made him a judge, and in his reign he rode the Northamptonshire circuit.

Thirdly, for his exquisite skill in the laws; witness his book of *Tenures,* which, though writ about two hundred years since, yet at this day retaineth an authentical reputation. Insomuch that when in the reign of King James, it came in question upon a demurrer in law, "Whether the release to one trepasser should be available or no to his companion?" Sir Henry Hubbard, and Judges Warburton, Winch, and Nicolls, his companions, gave judgment according to the opinion of our Littleton, and openly said that "they would not have HIS CASE disputed or questioned."

Lastly, for his happy posterity, having left three families, signally fixed and flourishing, in this and the neighbouring counties of Stafford and

(1) *Nimiety* = excess, redundancy.

Salop. And one[1] saith very truly, that these quarter the arms of many matches after the best manner of quartering them (other are scarce half-half-quartering them); viz., they possess at this day good land on the same account.

Indeed the Lord Coke observeth that our lawyers seldom die either without wills or heirs. For the first, I believe it, for our common lawyers will not have their estates come under the arbitrary disposal of a civilian judge of the prerogative, and therefore wisely prevent it. For the second, the observation as qualified with seldom may pass; otherwise our grandfathers can remember Sir James Dyer, lord chief justice, and Periam, lord chief baron, both dying without issue. His book of *Tenures* hath since been commented on by Sir Edward Coke's most judicious pen.

He died [1481] in the 21st year of King Edward the Fourth; and lieth buried in the cathedral of Worcester, having formerly constituted Doctor Alcock (his faithful friend, and then bishop of Worcester) supervisor of his will, who saw it performed to all critical particulars.

RICHARD SMITH, D.D., was born [1500] in this county, bred in the university of Oxford, where he became king's professor, and was fit for that place in all things, if, as one of his own persuasion avoweth, *non obstitisset laterum debilitas, et vocis exilitas* (the weakness of his sides and lowness of his voice had not hindered him.)

King Edward the Sixth afterwards sent for Peter Martyr over to be his professor in this university, betwixt whom and Dr. Smith so great the contest that, waiving all engagements, it is best to state it to the eye of the reader, as it is represented by authors of both sides.

In public disputations he convicted Peter Martyr the apostate monk, and a follower of the Zwinglian heresy, thrust in by King Edward the Sixth into the divinity chair in Oxford, and being conqueror did require his own chair to be restored to him; which he obtained not, because the king did withstand him.

But this valiant Achilles, when he did not appear on the day appointed for him to dispute, fled to Saint Andrew's in Scotland, conceiving that in a case of this kind he lived best who lay hid the closest.[2]

From St. Andrew's he afterwards conveyed himself into the Low Countries. But this Smith returned afterwards in the reign of Queen Mary, when Peter Martyr was glad to get leave to fly from that university. Thus we see (as to speak unbiassed without reflection on the cause) that, in such controversies, it mattereth little who are the disputants on either side, whilst the prevalent power is the moderator.

Doctor Smith, flying again over into the Low Countries, was made dean of Saint Peter's in Douay, and the first professor in the university founded therein. He died Anno Domini 1563.

EDMUND BONNER, alias SAVAGE. He had to his father, John Savage, a priest, richly beneficed and landed in Cheshire, son to Sir John Savage,

(1) Lord Coke, in his Preface to Littleton's *Tenures*. [The *Tenures*, with Coke's commentary, for long remained the chief authority on English real property law. For Sir Edward Coke see Norfolk, p. .] (2) The first quotation is from Pits, the second from Laurence Humphrey's Latin *Life of Jewel*. The Latin originals are omitted. This Dr. Smith retracted his opinions under Edward VI, but soon returned to the old theology.

knight of the Garter, and privy councillor to King Henry the Seventh. His mother, concubine to this priest (a dainty dame in her youth, and a jolly woman in her age) was sent out of Cheshire, to cover her shame, and lay down her burthen at Elmley in this county, where this bouncing babe Bonner was born.[1] The history of his life may be methodized according to the five princes under whom he lived.

He was born [1500?] under King Henry the Seventh, and bred a bachelor in the laws in Broadgates Hall[2] in Oxford.

Under King Henry the Eighth he was made doctor of laws, archdeacon of Leicester, master of the faculties under Archbishop Cranmer, and employed in several embassies beyond seas. All this time Bonner was not Bonner, being as yet meek, merciful, and a great Cromwellite, as appeared by some tart printed repartees betwixt him and Bishop Gardiner. Indeed he had *sesqui corpus,* a body and half (but I hope that corpulency without cruelty is no sin) and towards his old age he was overgrown with fat, as Master Foxe, who is charged to have persecuted persecutors with ugly pictures, doth represent him. Not long after, he was consecrated bishop of London.

Under King Edward the Sixth, being deputed to preach publicly concerning the Reformation, his faint and frigid expressions thereof manifested his mind rather to betray than defend it, which cost him a deprivation and imprisonment. Then it was when one jeeringly saluted him, "Good morrow, *bishop quondam*!" To whom Bonner as tartly returned, "Good morrow, *knave semper*!"

Being restored under Queen Mary to his bishopric, he caused the death of twice as many martyrs as all the bishops in England besides, justly occasioning the verses made upon him:

> If one by shedding blood for bliss may hope,
> Heaven's widest gate for Bonner doth stand ope.
>
> *Nobody speaking to Bonner.*
> All call thee cruel, and the sponge of blood;
> But, Bonner, I say, thou art mild and good.

Under Queen Elizabeth he was deprived and secured in his castle: I mean the Marshalsea in Southwark; for as that prison kept him from doing hurt to others, it kept others from doing hurt to him; being so universally odious he had been stoned in the streets if at liberty. One great good he did, though not intentionally, accidentally, to the protestant bishops of England; for, lying in the Marshalsea, and refusing to take the oath of supremacy tendered to him by Horne, then bishop of Winchester, he pleaded for himself that Horne was no lawful bishop, which occasioned the ensuing parliament to confirm him and the rest of his order to all purposes and intents.

After ten years' soft durance in all plenty (his face would be deposed for his whole body that he was not famished) enjoying a great temporal estate left him by his father, he died 1569; and was buried, saith Bishop Godwin, in Barking churchyard, amongst the thieves and murderers,

(1) Manuscript Collections of the industrious antiquary Mr. Dodsworth, extant in the library of the Lord Fairfax. [This story of Bonner's birth is somewhat doubtful.] (2) Which became Pembroke College in 1624.

being surely a mistake in the printer; All Hallows Barking being on the other side of the Thames, nothing relating to the Marshalsea. And I have been credibly informed that he was buried in the churchyard of St. George's in Southwark. But, so long as Bonner is dead, let him choose his own grave where he will be buried. But enough, if not too much, of this Herostratus, who burnt so many living temples of the Holy Ghost, and who, had he not been remembered by other writers, had found no place in my history.

JOHN DE FECKENHAM was born [1518?] of poor parents in Feckenham Forest in this shire. He was the last clergyman I find (and therefore memorable) who locally was surnamed; and was bred a Benedictine in Evesham, and at the dissolution thereof received an annual pension of an hundred florins, which (in my accounting) make up some twenty pounds. This maintained him when afterwards he went and studied in Oxford, attaining to eminent learning therein.

In the reign of King Edward the Sixth, he was imprisoned in the Tower, until Sir Philip Hoby, to use Feckenham's own words, *quasi mutuatum accepit* (borrowed him of the Tower.) Being at liberty, he had frequent disputations in the earnest yet modest defence of his religion.

By Queen Mary he was made abbot of Westminster, being the last mitred abbot (and therefore more memorable) who sat in parliament. He was very gracious with the queen, and effectually laid out all his interest with her, sometime even to offend, but never to injure her, to procure pardon of the faults, or mitigation of the punishments, for poor protestants.

By Queen Elizabeth he was highly honoured, and proffered, as is currently traditioned, the see of Canterbury, which he refused, and was kept in easy restraint; for, although he found not the same favour with Joseph, to whom the gaoler committed the care of all his family, making him superintendent of all other prisoners, yet had he always respective usage, and oft-times liberty on his parole. By his bounty to the poor, he gained the good will, saith Master Camden, of all persons; whilst I behold his bounty to others as the queen's bounty to him, *enabling,* because not *disenabling* him for the same, and permitting him peaceably to possess his estate. He died, a very aged man, in Wisbech Castle, as I collect, anno 1585.

JOHN WATSON was born [1520] at Bengeworth in this county,[1] where some of his name and relations remain at this day; bred (I believe) in Oxford, and afterwards became prebendary, then dean of Winchester. Hence he was advanced bishop of that see; and the ensuing passage (which I expect will meet with many infidels, though to me credibly attested) will acquaint us with the occasion thereof, and suspecting the bishopric of Winchester, when vacant, would be offered unto him.

Dean Watson, aged sixty years, and desirous to lead a private life, in the sickness of Bishop Horne, privately promised the earl of Leicester

(1) So was I informed by Mr. Venners, the minister of St. Mary's in Warwick, whose father was nephew and steward to this bishop.

(in that age the *Dominus fac multum,* if not *totum,* in the disposal of church dignities) two hundred pounds that he might not be made bishop of Winchester, but remain in his present condition.

The bishopric falling void, and the queen expressing her intention to confer it on Watson, the foresaid earl requested the contrary; acquainting the queen with the passage betwixt them, how otherwise it would be two hundred pounds out of his way.

"Nay then," said the queen, "Watson shall have it, he being more worthy thereof who will give two hundred to decline, than he who will give two thousand pounds to attain it."

I confess, such who have read so much of the corruption of the earl of Leicester, and heard so little of the integrity of Watson, will hardly credit this story, which I am ready to believe. [*d.* 1584]

JOHN [MARTIALL or] MARSHALL was born [1534] at Daylesford in this county, as New College register doth attest, which is to be credited before J. Pits, making him to be born in Dorsetshire. He was bred at New College in Oxford, where he proceeded bachelor of laws and for his gravity and learning was chosen second master of Winchester school. But in the first of Queen Elizabeth he left the land with Thomas Hyde, chief schoolmaster thereof; so that now their scholars had a *sat otium,* and in both their absence might play with security, till a successor received their sceptre. He became afterwards canon of Lille in Flanders, though a long time disturbed in his quiet possession thereof. He wrote a book, much prized by men of his persuasions, against John Calfhill, an English protestant. At his death he bequeathed a ring with a rich stone to adorn a piece of the cross in his cathedral (which by Doctor Gifford[1] was solemnly applied thereunto) and died Anno Domini 1597.

RICHARD BRISTOW was born [1538] in this county; bred first in Oxford, in Exeter College, whence he conveyed himself over beyond the seas, living first at Louvain, then in the English college at Douay. He was the first of that foundation that was made priest, being the right hand of Cardinal Allen who, departing to Rheims, left Bristow prefect of Douay College. Afterwards he was sent for to Rheims, where he wrote his book, say the papists, *contra futilem Fulkum* (against foolish Fulke)[2]—railing is easier than reasoning with such mouths—who indeed was a grave and godly divine. Being very sickly, he was advised for his health to return into his native country, where having the good hap to miss that which cureth all diseases, he died in his bed near London, 1581.

SIR EDWARD KELLEY (alias TALBOT) was born at Worcester (as I have it from the scheme of his nativity, graved from the original calculation of Doctor Dee) Anno Domini 1555, August the first, at four o'clock in the afternoon, the Pole being there elevated 52° 10′. Thus, reader, I hope that my exactness herein will make some reparation for my uncertainties and looser intelligence in the births of other persons.

(1) William Gifford—see Staffordshire, p. 519. (2) That worthy confuter of the Rhemish Testament [William Fulke—see London, p. 364.]

He was well studied in the mysteries of nature, being intimate with Doctor Dee, who was beneath him in chemistry, but above him in mathematics. These two are said to have found a very large quantity of elixir in the ruins of Glastonbury Abbey. Indeed I have read how William Bird, the prior of the Bath, left and lost the elixir in the walls of his priory; and it may seem strange that what was lost at Bath was found at Glastonbury, in the same county indeed, but sixteen miles asunder. But so long as Kelley had this treasure, none need trouble themselves how or where he came by it.

Afterwards (being here in some trouble) he went over beyond the seas, with Albert a Laski, a Polonian baron, who gave for his arms the hull of a ship, having only a mainmast and a top, without any tackling, and gave for his motto *Deus dabit vela* (God will send sails). But it seems this lord had formerly carried too high a sail, of whom a good author reporteth that *Aere alieno oppressus, clam recessit;*[1] and now, it seems, sought to repair his fortunes by associating himself with these two archchemists of England.

How long they continued together is to me unknown. Sir Edward (though I know not how he came by his knighthood) with the doctor, fixed at Trebona in Bohemia, where he is said to have transmuted a brass warming-pan (without touching or melting, only warming it by the fire, and putting the elixir thereon) into pure silver, a piece whereof was sent to Queen Elizabeth. He had great converse with Rudolph, the second emperor.

I have seen a voluminious manuscript in Sir Thomas Cotton's library of the particulars of their mysterious proceedings; where, amongst many strange passages, I find this ensuing monstrosity. They kept constant intelligence with a messenger, or spirit, giving them advice how to proceed in their mystical discoveries; and enjoining them that by way of preparatory qualification for the same, they should enjoy their wives in common. Though boggling hereat at first, they resolved to submit thereunto, because the law-giver might dispense with his laws in matters of so high a nature. Hereby may the reader guess the rest of their proceedings.

This probably might be the cause why Doctor Dee left Kelley and returned into England. Kelley, continuing still in Germany, ranted it in his expenses (say the brethren of his own art) above the sobriety befitting so mysterious a philosopher. He gave away, in gold-wire rings, at the marriage of one of his maid-servants, to the value of four thousand pounds. As for the high conceit he had of his own skill in chemistry, it appeareth sufficiently in the beginning of his own works, though I confess myself not to understand the gibberish of his language:

> All you that fain philosophers would be,
> And night and day in *Geber's* kitchen broil,
> Wasting the chips of ancient Hermes' tree;
> Weening to turn them to a precious oil;
> The more you work, the more you lose and spoil:
> To you I say, how learn'd so e'er you be,
> Go burn your books, and come and learn of me.

(1) Camden's *Elizabeth.*

Come we now to his sad catastrophe. Indeed the curious had observed that in the scheme of his nativity, not only the dragon's-tail was ready to promote abusive aspersions against him (to which living and dead he hath been subject) but also something malignant appears posited in Aquarius, which hath influence on the legs, which accordingly came to pass. For, being twice imprisoned (for what misdemeanor I know not) by Rudolph the emperor, he endeavoured his escape out of a high window, and tying his sheets together to let him down, fell (being a weighty man) and brake his leg, whereof he died 1595.

I believe him neither so bad as some, nor so good as others do character him. All know how separation is of great use amongst men of his profession; and indeed, if his pride and prodigality were severed from him, he would remain a person, on other accounts, for his industry and experience in practical philosophy, worthy recommendation to posterity.[1]

SIR EDWIN SANDYS, son to Edwin Sandys, D.D., was, in all probability, born [1561] in this county, whilst his father was bishop of Worcester. He was bred in Cambridge, and attained to be a most accomplished person.

I have known some pitiful in affection, but poor in condition, willing but unable to relieve one in greater want than themselves, who have only gotten an empty purse, and given it to others to put their charity therein for the purpose aforesaid. Such my case: I can only present the reader with a place in this my book for the character of this worthy knight, but cannot contribute any coin of memoirs or remarkables to the furnishing thereof. Only let me add, he was περιδέξιος, right-handed to any great employment; and was as constant in all parliaments as the speaker himself, being beheld by all as an excellent patriot, faithful to his country, without being false to his king, in all transactions. He was the treasurer to the undertakers for the western plantations, which he effectually advanced; the Bermudas (the firmest though not the fairest footing the English have in the West Indies) owing their happiness to his care, and Sandys' tribe is no contemptible proportion therein. He had a commanding pen, witness his work of the *Religion of the Western World* (many in one book) so much matter is stowed therein. I have been informed that he bequeathed by his will a considerable sum to the building of a college in Cambridge; but debts not coming in according to expectation, his good intention failed in the performance thereof. He died, much lamented of all good men [in 1629].[2]

SIR THOMAS COVENTRY, knight [FIRST BARON COVENTRY] was born [1578] at Croome in this county, eldest son to Sir Thomas Coventry, knight, one of the justices of the common pleas. He was bred in the Inner Temple

(1) Kelley is said to have studied at Oxford under an *alias*. Early in his career he was pilloried at Lancaster either for fraud or coining. For his colleague John Dee see Lancashire, p. 298. (2) Besides his part in the development of Virginia (he was possibly instrumental in the introduction of popular government in the colony) Sandys has an important place in the constitutional history of England. He became virtually the leader of the opposition in the House of Commons, and in 1613 enunciated the important principle that there were certain reciprocal conditions of the constitution which neither the monarchy nor the people might violate with impunity.

a student in the laws, and in the year 1617 was treasurer of the said Temple; and attorney-general to King James. He was afterwards made lord keeper of the great seal of England, the first day of November, in the first year of King Charles. He was by the same king created, in the fourth of his reign, April 10, Baron Coventry of Aylesborough in this county.

An ingenious gentleman in his history giveth him this character, in relation to his keepership, that "he enjoyed that dignity fifteen years, if it was not more proper to say, that dignity enjoyed him; this latter age affording none better qualified for the place;" adding that "he knew enough, and acted conformable to his knowledge, so that captious malice stands mute to blemish his fame."

He died about the beginning of January 1640, before our civil distempers began, so that it is hard to say whether his honourable life or seasonable death was the greater favour which God bestowed upon him.

I must not forget, that it hath been observed, that never lord keeper made fewer orders which afterwards were reversed than this Lord Coventry, which some ascribe to his discretion, grounding most of his orders on the consent and compromise of the parties themselves interested therein, whose hands, so tied up by their own act, were the more willing to be quiet for the future.

RICHARD DUGARD, B.D., was born at Grafton Flyford in this county; bred, under Master Henry Bright, in the king's school at Worcester. I name him the rather, because never did Master Calvin mention his master Corderius with more honour, than Master Dugard gratefully remembered Master Bright. He was chosen fellow of Sidney College, where in my time (for I had the honour of his intimate acquaintance) he had a moiety of the most considerable pupils, whom he bred in learning and piety, in the golden mean betwixt superstition and faction. He held a gentle-strict hand over them, so that none presumed on his lenity to offend, or were discouraged by his severity to amend. He was an excellent Grecian, and general scholar; old when young, such his gravity in behaviour; and young when old, such the quickness of his endowments. He bestowed on the college an hundred and twenty pounds for some perpetual use for the master and fellows, and ten pounds for books for the library. At last he was surprised with a presentation of the rectory of Fulletby in Lincolnshire, where, by his constant preaching and pious living, he procured his own security; a rare happiness in those troublesome times. He died January 28, Anno Domini 1653; and lies buried under a marble stone in his chancel.[1]

THE FAREWELL

I read in a good author how the state of Luneburg in Germany, whose chief revenues arise from the sale of salt, prohibited poor people the profit thereof. Whereupon Divine Providence, offended that a monopoly was made of his mercy, stopped the flowing of those salt-springs for a

(1) Richard Dugard was an intimate friend of Milton. He gave much help to distressed royalists.

time, till the poor were restored to their partage therein. I am not particularly instructed what share the poor have in the salt of this shire, not knowing how their interest is stated therein; but I presume the concernments of the poor are well cared for, and all things equally ordered betwixt them and rich people, grounding my confidence on the long and large continuance of the salt-pits amongst them. All I will add is this; I shall pray that they may endeavour for spiritual-soul-savouriness, "that their speech may be always with grace seasoned."

As for the loyal city of Worcester (which deserves a particular farewell by itself) I heartily desire that God would be pleased to restore unto it the years which the locust, caterpillar and palmer-worm have devoured. And how quickly can He do it, as by infinite other ways, so by blessing the clothing, the staple commodity in this county? Not formerly omitted by me, but pretermitted till this occasion. Sure it is, that the finest (though this may seem a word of challenge) cloth of England is made at Worcester; and such, I believe, was that which Erasmus that great critic (who knew fine cloth as well as pure Latin) calleth *pannus Britannicus;* Leominster wool, in the neighbouring county of Hereford, being here made into (pardon the prolepsis till it be dyed) the purest scarlet.

YORKSHIRE

YORKSHIRE hath the bishopric of Durham and Westmorland on the north; Lancashire and a snip of Cheshire on the west; Derby, Nottingham and Lincolnshire (divided by the Humber) on the south; and the German Ocean on the east thereof. It extendeth (without any angular advantages) unto a square of fourscore and ten miles, adequate in all dimensions unto the dukedom of Wurtemburg in Germany. Yea, on due consideration I am confident that all the seven United Provinces cannot present such a square of solid continent without any sea interposed.

One may call and justify this to be the best shire of England, and that not by the help of the general catachresis[1] of *good* for *great* (a good blow, good piece, &c.) but in the proper acception thereof. If in Tully's *Orations* (all being excellent) that is adjudged *optima quae longissima* (the best which is the longest) then, by the same proportion, this shire, partaking in goodness alike with others, must be allowed the best, seeing Devonshire itself, the next in largeness, wisely sensible of the visible inequality betwixt them, quits all claims of corrivality (as a case desperate) and acknowledgeth this as paramount in greatness.

Indeed, though other counties have more of the warm sun, this hath as much as any of God's (temporal) blessings. So that let a surveyor set his centre at Pontefract or thereabouts, and take thence the circumference of twenty miles, he there will meet with a tract of ground not exceeded for any, nor equalled for the goodness and plenty of such commodities. I would term it the Garden of England, save because it is so far from the Mansion House, I mean the city of London; insomuch that such sullen dispositions who do not desire to go thither only because of the great distance, the same if settled there would not desire to come thence, such the delight and pleasure therein.

Most true it is that when King Henry the Eighth, anno 1537, made his progress to York, Doctor Tunstall, bishop of Durham, then attending on him, shewed the king a valley (being then some few miles north of Doncaster) which the bishop avowed to be the richest that ever he found in all his travels through Europe; for, within ten miles of Hazelwood, the seat of the Vavasours, there were 165 manor-houses of lords, knights and gentlemen of the best quality; 275 several woods, whereof some of them contain five hundred acres; 32 parks and two chases of deer; 120 rivers and brooks, whereof five be navigable, well stored with salmon and other fish; 76 water-mills, for the grinding of corn on the aforesaid rivers; 25 coal-mines, which yield abundance of fuel for the whole county; 3 forges for the making of iron, and stone enough for the same.

And within the same limits as much sport and pleasure for hunting, hawking, fishing and fowling, as in any place of England besides.

(1) *Catachresis* = improper use of words.

NATURAL COMMODITIES

GEAT[1]

A word of the name, colour, virtues and usefulness thereof. In Latin it is called *gagates* (as different in nature, as alike in name to the precious stone called *gagites,* only found in an eagle's nest) whence our English word *geat* is deduced. But be it remembered, that the *agate,* vastly distinct from *geat,* is also named *gagates.*

It is found in this county, towards the sea-side, in the clefts of the rocks, whose gaping chaps are filled up therewith. It is naturally of a reddish and rusty colour, till it becomes black and bright by polishing. Indeed the lustre consists of the blackness thereof (negroes have their beauties as well as fair folk) and vulgar eyes confound the inlayings made of black marble (polished to the height) with touch,[2] geat and ebony, though the three former be stones, the last a kind of wood.

The virtues of geat are hitherto concealed. It is the lightest of all solid (not porous) stones, and may pass for the emblem of our memories, attracting trifles thereto, and letting slip matters of more moment. Rings are made thereof (fine foils to fair fingers) and bracelets with beads, here used for ornament, beyond the sea for devotion; also small utensils, as salt-cellars, and the like.

ALUM

This was first found out nigh Guisborough in this county, some sixty years since, by that worthy and learned knight Sir Thomas Chaloner (tutor to Prince Henry) on this occasion. He observed the leaves of trees thereabouts more deeply green than elsewhere; the oaks broad-spreading, but not deep-rooted, with much strength, but little sap; the earth clayish, variously coloured, here white, there yellowish, there blue, and the ways therein a clear night glistering like glass; symptoms which first suggested unto him the presumption of minerals, and of alum most properly.

Yet some years interceded betwixt the discovery and perfecting thereof; some of the gentry of the vicinage burying their estates here under earth before the alum could be brought to its true consistency. Yea, all things could not fadge[3] with them, until they had brought (not to say stolen) over three prime workmen in hogsheads from Rochelle in France; whereof one, Lambert Russell by name, and a Walloon by birth, not long since deceased. But when the work was ended, it was adjudged a *mine-royal,* and came at last to be rented by Sir Paul Pindar, who paid yearly to the king £12500; to the earl of Mulgrave £1640; to Sir William Pennyman £600; besides large salaries to numerous clerks and daily wages to rubbish-men, rockmen, pit-men, and house-men or fire-men; so that at one time, when the mines were in their majesty, I am credibly informed he had in pay no fewer than eight hundred by sea and land.

Yet did not the knight complain of his bargain, who having the sole sale of the commodity to himself, kept up the reputation thereof, and the price of alum at six-and-twenty pounds the ton. This he did the easier,

(1) Obsolete form of the word "Jet." (2) *Touch* = touchstone. (3) *Fadge,* in the context, means either 'agree' or 'succeed.'

because no better, and scarce other (save what from Rome and Rochelle) alum in all Europe.

But the late long-lasting parliament voted it a monopoly; and restored the benefit thereof to the former proprietaries. Such now the emulation betwixt these owners to undersell one another, that the commodity is fallen to thirteen pounds the ton.

Great use thereof in physic and surgery, as a grand astringent. Besides, much thereof is daily employed by clothiers, glovers, dyers, &c., so that some will maintain, that another thing in England, as white and far sweeter than alum, may of the two be better spared, with less loss to the commonwealth.

LIME

I am credibly informed that, within few miles of Pontefract, no less than twenty thousand pounds' worth of this coarse commodity is yearly made, and vended in the vicinage. It is a great fertilizer of ground, if judiciously disposed of. Indeed the laying of lime on light and sandy ground (like the giving hot cordials to persons in high fevers, enough to drive them into a frenzy) will soon burn out the heart thereof; which bestowed on cold and chill ground brings it to a fruitful consistency, and prudently ordered, it will for a long time retain the same.

HORSES

These are men's wings, wherewith they make such speed. A generous creature a horse is, sensible in some sort of honour, made most handsome by that which deforms man most, pride. The kings of Israel were not forbidden (as some may mistake) the having, but the multiplying of them; chiefly because they were a foreign, yea, an Egyptian commodity, and God would cut off from his children all occasion of commerce with that country, which was the staple-place of idolatry.

Our English horses have a mediocrity of all necessary good properties in them; as neither so slight as the barb, nor so slovenly as the Flemish, nor so fiery as the Hungarian, nor so airy as the Spanish jennets (especially if, as reported, they be conceived of the wind) nor so earthly as those in the Low Countries, and generally all the German horse. For stature and strength they are of a middle size, and are both seemly and serviceable in a good proportion. And whilst the seller praiseth them too much, the buyer too little, the indifferent stander-by will give them this due commendation.

It is confessed that our English horse never performed any eminent and signal service beyond the seas, in comparison of the achievements of their infantry. Partly because our horses, sent over many together in ships, beat and heat themselves, and are not for sudden use in the field after their transportation, so that some time of rest must be allowed them for their recovery; partly because the genius of the English hath always more inclined them to the foot service, as pure and proper manhood indeed without any mixture; whilst in a victory on horse-back, the credit thereof ought in equity to be divided betwixt the man and his horse.

Yorkshire doth breed the best race of English horses, whose keeping commonly in steep and stony ground bringeth them to firmness of footing and hardness of hoof; whereas a stud of horses bred in foggy fenny ground and soft rotten morasses (delicacy mars both man and beast) have often a fen in their feet, being soft, and soon subject to be foundered. Well may Philip be so common a name amongst the gentry of this county, who are generally so delighted in horsemanship.

THE MANUFACTURES

KNIVES

These are the teeth of old men, and useful to those of all ages; for, though some think themselves scarce gentlemen with knives, as good as they conceive themselves scarce men without them, so necessary they are on all occasions. The most of these for common use of country people are made in this county; whereof the bluntest, with a sharp stomach, will serve to cut meat if before them. Sheffield, a remarkable market, is the staple town for this commodity, and so hath been these three hundred years; witness Chaucer, speaking of the accoutrements of the miller,

A Sheffield whitel bare he in his hose

One may justly wonder how a knife may be sold for one penny, three trades anciently distinct concurring thereunto: bladers, haft-makers, and sheath-makers, all since united into the Corporation of Cutlers. Nor must we forget that, though plain knife-making was very ancient in this county, yet Thomas Matthews on Fleet Bridge, London, was the first Englishman who (*quinto Elizabethae*) made fine knives, and procured a prohibition that no more ship-lading of hafts should be brought from beyond the seas.

PINS

A pin passeth for that which is next to nothing, or (if you will) is the *terminus a quo* from which something doth begin, and proceed from a pin to a pound, &c. However it is considerable both as hurtful and useful; hurtful, if advantageously placed, it may prove as mortal as a poignard, the life of the greatest man lying at the mercy of the meanest thing; useful, not only to fasten our ornaments, but fill up the chinks betwixt our clothes, lest wind and weather should shoot through them.

Many and very good of these are made in this county; a commodity not to be slighted, since the very dust that falls from them is found profitable. We commonly say that it is not beneath a proper person to stoop to take up a pin, until he be worth ten thousand pounds, according to the thrifty rule in Latin, *Qui negligit minima nunquam ditescet.* Such who admire that so many millions of pins, made, sold, used and lost in England, should vanish away invisible, may rather wonder how so many that wear them (being no more than pins in the hands of their Maker) do decay, die and slip down in the dust, in silence and obscurity. I will add, that the world is well altered with England as to this commodity, now exporting so much of them into foreign parts; whereas formerly "strangers have sold pins in this land to the value of threescore thousand pounds a year."[1]

(1) Stow's *Chronicle.*

MEDICINAL WATERS

About a mile and a half from Knaresborough westward, in a moorish boggy ground, ariseth a spring of a vitrioline taste and odour. It was discovered by one Master Slingsby about the year 1620, and is conceived to run parallel with the Spa waters in Germany.

Not far off is a sulphur well, which hath also the qualities of saltness and bitterness; the stench whereof though offensive (patients may hold their nose, and take wholesome physic) is recompensed by the virtues thereof; insomuch, as my author[1] saith, "It heateth and quickeneth the stomach, bowels, liver, spleen, blood, veins, nerves, and indeed the whole body; insomuch that it consumes crudities, rectifieth all cold distempers in all parts of the body, causeth a good digestion, cureth the dropsy, spleen, scurvy, green-sickness, gout." And here it is high time to hold still; for, if this last be true, let that disease, which formerly was called *dedecus medicinae,* be hereafter termed *decus fontis Knaresburgensis.*

In the same parish, over against the castle (the River Nid running betwixt) ariseth a spring which runneth a little way in an entire stream, till, dammed at the brow of the descent with ragged rocks, it is divided into several trickling branches, whereof some drop, some stream down, partly over, partly through a jetting rock. This is called the Petrifying Well (how grammatically I will not engage) because it converteth spongy substances into stone, or crusteth them over round about.

We must not forget Saint Mungus's Well which some have slighted as an ineffectual superstitious relic of popery, whilst others maintain it hath regained its reputation, and is of sovereign virtue. Some will have the name thereof mistaken for Saint Magnus, which in my opinion was rather so called from Saint Mungo (Kentigernus in Latin) a Scottish saint, and much honoured in these northern parts. I believe no place in England can shew four springs, so near in situation, so distant in operation.

Such as desire to know more of the nature and use of these springs; of the time, manner and quantity wherein the waters are to be taken, and how the patient is to be dieted for his greater advantage, may inform themselves by perusing two smaller treatises, one set forth anno 1626, by Edmund Dean, doctor of physic, living in York, called *Spadsacrena Anglica;* the other written some six years since by John French, doctor of physic, and is very satisfactory on that subject.

THE BUILDINGS

The church of Beverley is much commended for a fine fabric; and I shall have a more proper occasion to speak hereafter of the collegiate church in Ripon.

But, amongst ancient civil structures, we must not forget WRESSELL CASTLE. It is seated in the confluence of Derwent and Ouse. In what plight it is now I know not; but hear how Leland commendeth it in his *Itinerary* through this county. It is built of square stone, which some

(1) John French, doctor of physic, in his *Yorkshire Spa.* [This John French (1616?-1657) was physician to the parliamentary army.]

say was brought out of France; it hath four fair towers, one at each corner, and a gatehouse (wherein are chambers five stories high) which maketh the fifth. In Leland's time it looked as new built, though then one hundred years old, as being erected by the Lord Percy earl of Winchester in the reign of King Richard the Second. Without the walls (but within the moat) gardens done *opere topiario*. In a word, he termeth it one of the properest buildings north of Trent.

But that which most affected him was a study, in an eight-square tower, called Paradise, furnished with curious and convenient desks, loaden with variety of choice books.

PROVERBS

From Hell, Hull, and Halifax,——deliver us. This is part of the beggars' and vagrants' litany. Of these three frightful things unto them, it is to be feared that they least fear the first, conceiting it the furthest from them. Hull is terrible unto them, as a town of good government,[1] where vagrants meet with punitive charity, and 'tis to be feared are oftener corrected than amended. Halifax is formidable unto them for the law thereof, whereby thieves taken ἐπαυτοφώρῳ, in the very act of stealing cloth, are instantly beheaded with an engine, without any further legal proceedings.

A Yorkshire way-bit. That is, an overplus not accounted in the reckoning, which sometimes proveth as much as all the rest. Ask a countryman here on the highway, how far it is to such a town, and they commonly return, "So many miles and a way-bit;" which *way-bit* is enough to make the weary traveller surfeit of the length thereof. If such over-measure be allowed to all yards, bushels, &c., in this shire, the poor therein have no cause to complain of their pennyworths in buying any commodities.

But hitherto we have run along with common report and false spelling (the way not to win the race) and now return to the starting-place again. It is not *way-bit,* though generally so pronounced, but *wee-bit,* a pure Yorkshireism, which is a *small bit* in the northern language.

THE BATTLES

Many engagements (as much above skirmishes as beneath battles) happened in this shire. But that at Marston Moor, July 2, 1644, was our English Pharsalian fight, or rather the fatal battle of Cannae to the loyal cavaliers.

Know then that Prince Rupert, having fortunately raised the siege at York, drew out his men into the Moor, with full intention to fight the enemy. Discreet persons, beholding the countenance of the present affairs with an unpartial eye, found out many dissuasives for the prince to hazard a battle. 1. He had done his work by relieving York; let him digest the honour thereof and grasp at no more. 2. His wearied soldiers wanted refreshing. 3. Considerable recruits were daily expected out of the north, under Colonel Clavering.

(1) Others conceive it only to relate to the dangerous haven thereof.

Add to all these, that such were the present animosities in the parliament army, and so great their mutual dissatisfactions when they drew off from York, that (as a prime person since freely confessed) if let alone they would have fallen foul amongst themselves, had not the prince, preparing to fight them, cemented their differences to agree against a general enemy. But a blot is no blot if not hit; and an advantage no advantage if unknown; though this was true, the prince was not informed of the differences aforesaid.

However, he did not so much run out of his own ambition of honour, as answer the spur of the king's command, from whom he had lately received a letter (still safe in his custody) speedily to fight the enemy if he had any advantage, that so he might spare and send back some supplies to his majesty's perplexed occasions at Oxford.

Besides, the prince had received certain intelligence that the enemy had, the day before, sent away seven thousand men, now so far distanced that they were past possibility of returning that day. The former part hereof was true, the latter false, confuted by the great shout given this day in the parliament's army at the return of such forces unto them.

But now it was too late to draw off the parliament forces, necessitating them to fight. A summer's evening is a winter's day, and about four o'clock the battle began.

Some causelessly complain of the marquess of Newcastle, that he drew not his men soon enough, according to his orders, out of York, to the prince's seasonable succour. Such consider not that soldiers newly relieved from a nine weeks' siege will a little indulge themselves. Nor is it in the power of a general to make them at such times to march at a minute's warning, but that such a minute will be more than an hour in the length thereof.

The Lord General Goring so valiantly charged the left wing of the enemy that they fairly forsook the field. General Leslie, with his Scottish ran away more than a Yorkshire mile and a *wee-bit*. Fame with her trumpet sounded their flight as far as Oxford, the royalists rejoicing with bonfires for the victory. But within few days their bays, by a mournful metamorphosis, were turned into willow; and they sunk the lower in true sorrow for being mounted so high in causeless gladness. For Cromwell, with his cuirassiers, did the work of that day. Some suspected Colonel Hurry (lately converted to the king's party) for foul play herein; for he divided the king's Old Horse, so valiant and victorious in former fights, into small bodies, alleging this was the best way to break the Scottish lancers. But those horse, always used to charge together in whole regiments or greater bodies, were much discomposed with this new mode, so that they could not find themselves in themselves. Besides, a right valiant lord, severed (and in some sort secured) with a ditch from the enemy, did not attend till the foe forced their way unto him, but gave his men the trouble to pass over that ditch, the occasion of much disorder.

The van of the king's foot being led up by the truly honourable Colonel John Russell, impressed with unequal numbers, and distanced from seasonable succour, became a prey to their enemy. The marquess of Newcastle's Whitecoats (who were said to bring their winding-sheet about them into the field) after thrice firing, fell to it with the butt ends of their muskets, and were invincible, till mowed down by Cromwell's cuirassiers. With Job's servants, they were all almost slain, few escaping to bring the tidings of their overthrow.

Great was the execution on that day, Cromwell commanding his men to give no quarter. Various the numbering of the slain on both sides; yet I meet with none mounting them above six, or sinking them beneath three thousand.

THE WORTHIES

SAINT HILD [*b.* 614] was daughter unto Prince Hereric, nephew to Edwin king of Northumberland; and may justly be counted our English Huldah, not so much for sameness of sex, and name-sounding similitude, as more concerning conformities. Huldah lived in a college; Hild in a convent at Strensall in this county. Huldah was the oracle of those times, as Hild of her age, being a kind of a moderatress in a Saxon synod (or conference rather) called to compromise the controversy about the celebration of Easter. I behold her as the most learned English female before the Conquest, and may call her the She-Gamaliel, at whose feet many learned men had their education. She ended her holy life with a happy death, about the year of our Lord 680.[1]

BENEDICT BISCOP was born [628?] saith Pits, amongst the East Saxons; saith Jerome Porter in Yorkshire, whom I rather believe; first because, writing his life *ex professo,* he was more concerned to be curious therein; secondly because this Benedict had much familiarity with, and favour from, Oswiu king of Northumberland, in whose dominions he fixed himself, building two monasteries, the one at the influx of the River Wear, the other at the River Tyne into the sea, and stocking them in his lifetime with 600 Benedictine monks.

He made five voyages to Rome, and always returned full fraught with relics, pictures and ceremonies.

He left religion in England braver, but not better, than he found it. Indeed, what Tully said of the Roman lady, that she danced better than became a modest woman, was true of God's service as by him adorned, the gaudiness prejudicing the gravity thereof. He made all things according (not to the pattern in the mount with Moses) but the precedent of Rome; and his convent, being but the Romish transcript, became the English original to which all monasteries in the land were suddenly conformed.

In a word, I reverence his memory, not so much for his first bringing over painted glass into England, as for his bringing up pious Bede in his monastery. Being struck beneath the girdle with the dead palsy, his soul retired into the upper rooms of his clay cottage, much employed in meditation, until the day of his death, which happened anno 690.[2]

(1) St. Hild, the foundress of the monastery at Whitby (later destroyed by the Danes) is the greatest of all English abbesses. Huldah is the prophetess (see 2 Chronicles xxxiv, 22). (2) Benedict Biscop brought together remarkable libraries, unparalleled in England in his time, at Wearmouth and Jarrow. These libraries made possible the great work of Bede.

SAINT JOHN OF BEVERLEY may be challenged by this county on a threefold title, because therein he had his—1. Birth, at Harpham in this county, in the East Riding; 2. Life, being three and thirty years and upwards archbishop of York; 3. Death, at Beverley in this county, in a college of his own foundation.

I remember his picture in a window in the library at Salisbury, with an inscription under it (whose character may challenge to itself three hundred years' antiquity) affirming him the first master of arts in Oxford; and Alfredus Beverlacensis reporteth as much. Arts indeed were, and Oxford was (though hardly an university) in that age; but seeing the solemnity of graduating was then unknown, a judicious Oxonian[1] rejecteth it as a fiction. More true it is that he was bred at Strensall under Hild aforesaid, which soundeth something to her honour and nothing to his disgrace, seeing eloquent Apollos himself learned the primer of his Christianity partly from Priscilla. He was afterwards educated under Theodorus, the Grecian, and archbishop of Canterbury. Yet was he not so famous for his teacher as for his scholar, venerable Bede, who wrote this John's life, which he hath so spiced with miracles that it is of the hottest for a discreet man to digest into his belief.

Being very aged, he resigned his archbishopric, that he might the more effectually apply his private devotions in his college at Beverley, for which he procured the freed-stool from King Athelstan. Yet such sanctuaries (though carrying something of holiness in their name) had a profane abuse for their very use, making malefactors with their promise of impunity, and then protecting them from justice. Saint John died May 7, 721; and was buried in the porch of his collegiate church. A synod held at London 1416, assigned the day of his death an anniversary solemnity to his memory.

HENRY I, youngest son to William duke of Normandy, but eldest to King William the Conqueror (by whom he was begotten after he was crowned king) on which politic criticism he claimed and gained the crown from Duke Robert his eldest brother, was, Anno Domini 1068, born at Selby in this county. If any ask what made his mother travel so far north from London, know, it was to enjoy her husband's company, who, to prevent insurrections, and settle peace, resided many months in these parts, besides his peculiar affection to Selby, where after he founded a mitred abbey.

This Henry was bred (say some) in Paris, say others in Cambridge, and I may safely say in both; wherein he so profited, that he attained the surname of Beauclerk. His learning may be presumed a great advantage to his long and prosperous reign for thirty-five years and upwards, wherein he remitted the Norman rigour, and restored to his subjects a great part of the English laws and liberties.

Indeed his princely virtues, being profitable to all, did with their lustre so dazzle the eyes of his subjects, that they did not see his personal vices, as chiefly prejudicial to himself. For he was very wanton, as appeareth by his numerous natural issue, no fewer than fourteen, all by him

(1) Bishop Godwin.

publicly owned; the males highly advanced, the females richly married, which is justly reported to his praise, it being lust to beget, but love to bestow them. His sobriety otherwise was admirable, whose temperance was of proof against any meat objected to his appetite, lampreys alone excepted, on a surfeit whereof he died, Anno Domini 1135. He had only two children, William dying before, and Maud surviving him, both born in Normandy, and therefore omitted in our catalogue.

ETHELRED, abbot of Rievaulx [*b.* 1109?] was one eminent in his generation for piety and learning. He was most intimate with David king of Scotland, and had the rare felicity to adventure on desperate differences betwixt great persons, and yet, above human hope, to complete their agreement. He had Saint Augustine's *Confessions* both *by* heart and *in* his heart; yet generally he is accounted the English Saint Bernard, and wrote very many books, whereof one, *De Virginitate Mariae,* and another *De Abusionibus Claustri,* shewing twelve abuses generally committed in that kind of life. Yet, as Saint Paul honoured widows that were widows indeed, he had a high esteem for monks who were monks indeed, so addicted to a solitary life that he refused all honours and several bishoprics proffered unto him. He died in the 57th year of his age, 1166; and after his death attained with many the reputation of a saint.

ROBERT THE SCRIBE (but no Pharisee, such his *humility;* not hypocrite, such his *sincerity*) was the fourth prefect of Canon Regulars at Bridlington in this county. He had his surname from his dexterity in writing, not a little beneficial in that age; Erasmus ingenuously confessing that his father Gerard got a handsome livelihood thereby. But our Robert, in fair and fast writing, did reach a note above others, it being true of him what was said,

> *Nondum lingua suum dextra peregit opus.*
>
> The tongue her task hath not yet done,
> When that the hand her race hath run.

And he may be said to have had the *longhand* of *shorthand,* such the swiftness of his pen, though I confess brachygraphy was not then, nor many years after, invented. But he, though a quick scribe, is but a dull one who is good only at facsimile, to transcribe out of an original; whereas our Robert left many books of his own making to posterity. He flourished Anno Domini 1170, and lieth buried before the doors of the cloister of his own convent.

ROGER OF HOVEDEN [or HOWDEN] was born in this county, of the illustrious family of the Hovedens, saith my author;[1] bred first in the study of the civil, then of the canon law; and at last, being servant to King Henry the Second, he became a most accomplished courtier. He is the chiefest, if not sole, lay historian of his age; who, being neither priest nor monk, wrote a *Chronicle of England,* beginning where Bede ended, and continuing the same until the fourth of King John. When King Edward the First laid claim to the crown of Scotland, he caused the

(1) Bale.

Chronicles of this Roger to be diligently searched, and carefully kept many authentical passages therein tending to his present advantage. [*d.* 1201?]

JOHN [HOLYWOOD OR] HALIFAX, commonly called De Sacro Bosco, was born in that town, so famous for clothing; bred first in Oxford, then in Paris, being the prime mathematician of his age. All students of astronomy enter into that art through the door of his book *De Sphaera*. He lived much beloved, died more lamented, and was buried with a solemn funeral, on the public cost of the university of Paris. [*fl.* 1230]

THOMAS PLANTAGENET [*b.* 1277?]. He was earl of Derby, Lancaster, Leicester, and in the right of Alice his wife, of Lincoln. A popular person, and great enemy of the two Despensers, minions to King Edward the Second, who being hated as devils for their pride, no wonder if this Thomas was honoured as a saint and martyr by the common sort. Indeed he must be a good chemist who can extract *martyr* out of *malefactor;* and our chronicles generally behold him put to death for treason against King Edward the Second. But let him pass for a saint in this shire, though never solemnly canonized, it being true of such local saints what Servius Honoratus observeth of topical gods: *Ad alias regiones nunquam transibant* (they travelled not so far as to be honoured in other countries). His beheading, alias his martyrdom, happened at Pontefract, Anno Domini 1322.[1]

ROBERTUS PERSCRUTATOR [ROBERT THE ENGLISHMAN] was born in this county; bred a Dominican; great mathematician and philosopher. He got the surname of Searcher because he was in the constant quest and pursuit of the mysteries of Nature; a thing very commendable, if the matters we seek for, and means we seek with, be warrantable.

Yea Solomon himself, on the same account, might be entituled Searcher, who, by his own confession, "applied his heart to know, and to search, and to seek out wisdom, and the reason of things."

But curiosity is a kernel of the forbidden fruit, which still sticketh in the throat of a natural man, sometimes to the danger of his choking. It is heavily laid to the charge of our Robert that he did light his candle from the devil's torch, to seek after such secrets as he did desire: witness his work of *Ceremonial Magic,* which a conscientious Christian would send the same way with the Ephesian conjuring books, and make them fuel for the fire. However, in that age he obtained the reputation of a great scholar, flourishing under King Edward the Second, 1326.

WILLIAM DE MELTON was born in this county (wherein are four villages so named) and preferred therein provost of Beverley, and canon, then archibshop of York. He went to Avignon, there to procure his consecration. I say to Avignon, whither then the court was removed

(1) Thomas Plantagenet was the son of Edmund, earl of Lancaster ('Crouchback') brother of Edward I. He became bitterly hostile to Piers Gaveston, foster-brother and great favourite of Edward II, was instrumental in bringing about Gaveston's death, pardoned by Edward II, but refused to be reconciled to the Despensers. An unscrupulous career led finally to capture and execution.

from Rome, and continued about threescore and ten years, on the same token that those remaining at Rome (almost starved for want of employment) called this the "seventy years' captivity of Babylon."

Consecrated after two years' tedious attendance, he returned into England, and fell to finish the fair fabric of his cathedral, which John Romanus had begun, expending seven hundred marks therein. His life was free from scandal, signal for his chastity, charity, fasting and praying. He strained up his tenants, so as to make good music therewith, but not break the string; and surely church-lands were intended, though not equally, yet mutually, for the comfortable support both of landlord and tenants.

Being unwilling that the infamy of infidel should be fixed upon him, according to the apostle's doctrine, for not "providing for his family," he bought three manors in this county, from the archbishop of Rouen, with the pope's confirmation, and settled them on his brother's son, whose descendant, William Melton, was high sheriff of this county in the fiftieth of King Edward the Third.

There is a place in York, as well as in London, called the Old Bailey; herein more remarkable than that in London, that Archbishop Melton compassed it about with a great wall. He bestowed also much cost in adorning the *feretrum* (English it the *bier* or the *coffin*) of Saint William, a person purposely omitted by my pen, because no assurance of his English extraction. Archbishop Melton died, after he had sat two-and-twenty years in his see, Anno Domini 1340; entombed in the body of his church, nigh the font (whereby I collect him buried below in the bottom of the church) that instrument of Christian initiation anciently advancing but a little above the entrance into the church.[1]

RICHARD ROLLE, alias HAMPOLE [*b.* 1290?] had his first name from his father, the other from the place, three miles from Doncaster, where living he was honoured, and dead was buried and sainted. He was an eremite, led a strict life, and wrote many books of piety, which I prefer before his prophetical predictions, as but a degree above almanac prognostications. He threatened the sins of the nation with future famine, plague, inundations, war and general calamities, from which no land is long free, but subject to them in some proportion. Besides, his predictions, if hitting, were heeded; if missing, not marked.

However, because it becomes me not ἁγιομαχεῖν, let him pass for a saint. I will add, that our Saviour's dilemma to the Jews may partly be pressed on the papists his contemporaries. If Hampole's doctrine was of men, why was he generally reputed a saint; if from God, why did they not obey him, seeing he spake much against the viciousness and covetousness of the clergy of that age? He died Anno Domini 1349.

SIR WILLIAM DE LA POLE, born at Ravenser Odd in this county, was, for wealth and skill in merchandise, inferior to none in England. He made

(1) Melton was a considerable statesman, being, among other appointments, keeper of the great seal and twice treasurer of England. In 1319, when the Scots ravaged Yorkshire, Melton led hastily assembled forces against them. He was utterly routed, and escaped with great difficulty.

his abode at Kingston upon Hull, and was the first mayor of that town. When King Edward the Third was at Antwerp, and much necessitated for money (no shame for a prince always in war to be sometimes in want) this William lent him many thousand pounds of gold; in recompense whereof the king made him his valet (equivalent to what afterward was called gentleman of the bedchamber) and lord chief baron of his exchequer, with many other honours, amongst which this was one, that he should be reputed a banneret, not that he was really made one, seeing the flourishing of a banner over his head, in the field, before or after a fight, was a ceremony essential thereunto; but he had the same precedency conferred upon him.[1] [*d.* 1366]

SAINT JOHN OF BRIDLINGTON was born hard by that town; bred two years in Oxford, where he profited in piety and learning above his age and equals. Returning home, for a short time he was teacher to a gentleman's sons, until the twentieth year of his age he entered himself a canon regular in the convent of Bridlington, where he grew eminent for his exemplary holiness.

It was his happiness that such offices always fell to his share as did not retard but quicken his devotion, as chanter, almoner, &c. At last he was chosen prior, but refused the place, alleging his own unworthiness, professing he had rather be beaten in pieces with blows than accept thereof; so that another was put into the place. This new elect dying soon after, our John was chosen again in the vacancy, and then took it, fearing there might be as much peevishness in rejecting as pride in affecting it, and hoping that providence, which fairly called him to, would freely fit him for the discharge of that office.

He used to treat strangers at his table with good cheer, and seemingly kept pace with them in eating morsel for morsel, whilst he had a secret contrivance wherein he conveyed his exceedings above his monastical pittance. Being demanded of one why he did not enter into more strict and austere order: "Surely," said he, "a man may lead a sincere and acceptable life in any order; and it were arrogancy in me to pretend to a severer discipline, when I cannot observe as I ought this easier course of life." My author[2] saith that Martha and Mary were both compounded in him, being as pious, so provident to husband the revenues of their house to their best advantage.

He was a holy man, and could one light on his life unleavened, before heaved up with the ferment of monkish fiction, it would afford many remarkables. He died in the sixtieth year of his age, 1379, and was reputed (though I believe not solemnly canonized) a saint amongst his own countrymen.[3]

HENRY WAKEFIELD is here placed with assurance, there being three towns of that name in, and none out of this county. Indeed his is an episcopal name, which might mind him of his office, the diocese of Worcester (to

(1) Sir William de la Pole was the first English merchant to found a noble house. His family became a great force in English life until finally exterminated by Henry VIII (see note—page 612). (2) Harpfield's *Ecclesiastical History,* out of whom his life is extracted. (3) He was canonized in 1401.

which he was preferred anno 1375, by King Edward the Third) being his *field,* and he by his place to *wake* or watch over it; nor hear I of any complaints to the contrary, but that he was very vigilant in his place. He was also for one year lord treasurer of England. Dying March 11, 1395, he lieth covered in his own church, *ingenti marmore;* and let none grudge him the greatness of his gravestone, if two foot larger than ordinary, who made the body of this his church two arches longer westward than he found it, besides a fair porch added thereunto.

RICHARD LE SCROPE [*b.* 1350?] son to the Lord Scrope of Masham in this county, brother to William earl of Wiltshire, was bred a doctor of divinity in Cambridge, attaining to be a man of great learning and unblameable life. Nor was it so much his high extraction as his own abilities causing him to be preferred bishop first of Coventry and Lichfield, then archbishop of York. Being nettled with the news of his earl brother's beheading, he conjoined with the earl of Northumberland, the earl marshal, Lord Bardolf, and others, against King Henry the Fourth, as an usurper and invader of the liberties of church and state. The earl of Westmorland, in outward deportment, complied with him, and seemed to approve a writing wherein his main intentions were comprised so to trepan him into his destruction; toling[1] him on, till it was too late for him either to advance or retreat, the king with his army being at Pontefract.

Bishop Godwin saith it doth not appear that he desired to be tried by his peers; and I believe it will appear that nothing was then calmly or judiciously transacted, but all being done in an hurry of heat, and by martial authority.[2] The executioner had five strokes at his neck before he could sunder it from his body, imputable not to his cruelty but ignorance, it not being to be expected that one nigh York should be so dexterous in that trade as those at London. His beheading happened anno 1405.

JOHN MARRE (by Bale called MARREY, and by Trithemius MARRO) was born at Marr, a village in this county, three miles west from Doncaster, where he was brought up in learning. Hence he went to Oxford, where, saith Leland, the university bestowed much honour upon him for his excellent learning.

He was by order a Carmelite; and in one respect it was well for his memory that he was so, which maketh John Bale (who generally falleth foul on all friars) to have some civility for him, as being once himself of the same order, allowing him subtily learned in all secular philosophy. But what do I instance in home-bred testimonies? Know, reader, that, in the character of our own country writers, I prize an inch of foreign above an ell of English commendation; and outlandish writers, Trithemius, Sixtus Senensis, Petrus Lucius, &c., give great encomiums of his ability; though I confess it is chiefly on this account, because he wrote

(1) *Toling*=enticing, alluring. (2) Scrope's trial was irregular, an act of vengeance which made him a martyr, and in the north he was called Saint Richard Scrope. He is vividly portrayed in Shakespeare's I *Henry IV*.

against the opinions of John Wycliffe. He died on the eighteenth of March, 1407; and was buried in the convent of Carmelites in Doncaster.

JOHN GOWER was born [1325?] saith Leland, at Stittenham (in the North Riding in Bulmer Wapentake) of a knightly family. He was bred in London student of the laws, till, prizing his pleasure above his profit, he quitted pleading to follow poetry. He was the first refiner of our English tongue, effecting much but endeavouring more therein. Thus he who sees the whelp of a bear but half licked, will commend it for a comely creature, in comparison of what it was when first brought forth. Indeed Gower left our English tongue very bad, but found it very very bad.

Bale makes him *equitem auratum et poetam laureatum,* proving both his ornaments on his monumental statue in Saint Mary Overies, Southwark. Yet he appeareth there neither laureated nor hederated[1] poet (except the leaves of the bays and ivy withered to nothing since the erection of the tomb) but only roseated, having a chaplet of four roses about his head. Another author unknighted him,[2] allowing him only a plain esquire; though in my apprehension the collar of SSS. about his neck speaks him to be more. Besides (with submission to better judgments) that collar hath rather a civil than military relation, proper to persons in places of judicature; which makes me guess this Gower some judge in his old age, well consisting with his original education.

He was before Chaucer, as born and flourishing before him, yea by some accounted his master; yet he was after Chaucer, as surviving him two years, living to be stark blind, and so more properly termed our English Homer. Many the books he wrote, whereof three most remarkable, viz., *Speculum Meditantis* in French, *Confessio Amantis* in English, *Vox Clamantis* in Latin. His death happened 1408.

STEPHEN PATRINGTON was born in the village so called, in the East Riding of this county. He was bred a Carmelite and doctor of divinity in Oxford, and the three-and-twentieth provincial of his order throughout England for fifteen years. It is incredible (saith Leland) what multitudes of people crowded to his sermons, till his fame preferred him chaplain and confessor to King Henry the Fifth. He was deputed of the king commissioner at Oxford, to inquire after and make process against the poor Wycliffites; and as he was busied in that employment, he was advanced to the bishopric of Saint David's. Hence he was sent over to the council of Constance, and therein (saith Walsingham) gave great testimony of his ability. Returning into England, he was made bishop of Chichester; but dying before his translation was finished, 1417, was buried in Whitefriars in Fleet Street.

SIR WILLIAM GASCOIGNE was born [1350?] at Gawthorpe in Harewood parish[3] (in the midway betwixt Leeds and Knaresborough) and afterwards was student of the law in the Inner Temple in London; wherein he so profited, that being knighted, the sixth of King Henry the Fourth, he

(1) *Hederated*=adorned or crowned with ivy. (2) Stow, in his *Survey of London.* (3) So am I informed by Mr. Richard Gascoigne, one descended from him, an accomplished antiquary in record heraldry.

was made chief justice of the king's bench, November 15, and therein demeaned himself with much integrity, but most eminent for the following passage.

It happened that a servant of Prince Henry, afterwards the fifth English king of that Christian name, was arraigned before this judge for felony, whom the prince, then present, endeavoured to take away, coming up in such fury that the beholders believed he would have stricken the judge. But he, sitting without moving, according to the majesty he represented, committed the prince prisoner to the king's bench, there to remain until the pleasure of the king his father were farther known; who, when he heard thereof by some pickthank courtier, who probably expected a contrary return, gave God thanks for his infinite goodness, who at the same instant had given him a judge who could minister, and a son who could obey justice.[1]

I meet in J. Stow with this marginal note: "William Gascoigne was chief justice of the king's bench from the sixth of Henry the Fourth till the third of Henry the Fifth." And another historian maketh King Henry the Fifth, in the first of his reign, thus expressing himself in relation to that lord chief justice: "For which act of justice I shall ever hold him worthy of the place, and my favour, and wish all my judges to have the like undaunted courage, to punish offenders of what rank soever."[2] Hence our comedian (fancy will quickly blow up a drop in history into a bubble in poetry) hath founded a long scene on the same subject.[3]

Give me leave, for my love to truth, to rectify these mistakes out of authentic records. First, Gascoigne was made judge not in the sixth but first of King Henry the Fourth, on the first of November. Secondly, he died December 17th, in the fourteenth of King Henry the Fourth; so that, in a manner, his sitting on the bench ran parallel to the king's sitting on the throne.

This date of his death is fairly written in his stately monument in Harewood Church.[4]

[*d.* 1419]

JOHN HARDYNG was born [1378] saith my author,[5] in the northern parts, and I have some cause to believe him this countryman. He was an esquire of ancient parentage, and bred from his youth in military employment; first under Robert de Umfraville, governor of Roxborough Castle, and did good service against the Scots. Then he followed the standard of King Edward the Fourth, adhering faithfully unto him in his deepest distress.

But the master-piece of his service was his adventuring into Scotland, not without the manifest hazard of his life; where he so cunningly demeaned himself, that he found there, and fetched thence out of their records, many original letters, which he presented to King Edward the

(1) Sir Thomas Elyot, in his *Governor*, out of whom our modern historians have transcribed it [This story is without foundation.] (2) J. Trussell, in his continuation of Daniel. (3) W. Shakespeare, in his second part of the Life of *King Henry the Fourth*.—F. (4) Contrary to Fuller's statement, Gascoigne survived well into the reign of Henry V, though he ceased to be chief justice soon after the king's accession. (5) Bale.

Fourth. Out of these he collected an history of the several solemn submissions publicly made, and sacred oaths of fealty, openly taken from the time of King Athelstan, by the kings of Scotland; although the Scotch historians stickle with might and main that such homage was performed only for the county of Cumberland, and some parcels of land their kings had in England south of Tweed.[1] He wrote also a *Chronicle* of our English kings, from Brutus to King Edward the Fourth, and that in English verse; and, in my judgment, he had drank as hearty a draught of Helicon as any in his age. [*d.* 1465?]

THOMAS GASCOIGNE, eldest son to Richard (the younger brother unto Sir William Gascoigne,[2] lord chief justice) was born at Hunslet in this county; bred in Oriel College in Oxford, where he proceeded doctor in divinity, and was commissioner of that university Anno Domini 1434. He was well acquainted with the maids of honour, I mean humane arts and sciences, which conducted him first to the presence, then to the favour of divinity, the queen. He was a great Hieronymist, perfectly acquainted with all the writings of that learned father, and in expression of his gratitude for the good he had gotten by reading his works, he collected out of many authors and wrote the life of Saint Jerome. He made also a book called *Dictionarium Theologicum,* very useful to, and therefore much esteemed by, the divines in that age. [*d.* 1458]

GEORGE RIPLEY (whether knight or priest, not so soon decided) was undoubtedly born at Ripley in this county, though some have wrongfully entituled Surrey to his nativity. Leaving this land, he went over into Italy, and there studied twenty years together in pursuance of the philosopher's stone, and found it in the year 1470, as some collect from those his words then written in his books, *Juveni quem diligit anima mea* (spoken by the spouse, Canticles, iii, 4) so bold is he with Scripture in that kind.

An English gentleman of good credit reported that in his travels abroad he saw a record in the isle of Malta, which declares that Sir George Ripley gave yearly to those knights of Rhodes one hundred thousand pounds towards maintaining the war (then on foot) against the Turks. This vast donation makes some suspect this Sir George for a knight (who by this might have been *eques auratus*) though indeed never more than Sir Priest, and canon of Bridlington.

Returning into his native country, and desiring to repose his old age (no philosopher's stone to quiet retirement) he was dispensed with by the pope to leave his canon's place (as too full of employment) and became a Carmelite-anchorite at Boston in Lincolnshire, where he wrote no fewer than 25 books, though his *Compound of Alchemy* carrieth away the credit of all the rest.

It presenteth the reader with the twelve gates leading to the making of the philosopher's stone, which are thus reckoned up in order: 1.

(1) Hardyng invented and inserted false documents to strengthen the claim of the English crown to the suzerainty over the crown of Scotland. (2) See p. 648 above. Thomas was not a nephew of Sir William, though probably related.

Calcination; 2. Solution; 3. Separation; 4. Conjunction; 5. Putrefaction; 6. Congelation; 7. Cibation; 8. Sublimation; 9. Fermentation; 10. Exaltation; 11. Multiplication; 12. Projection.

Oh for a key, saith the common reader, to open these gates, and expound the meaning of these words, which are familiar to the knowing in this mystery! But such who are disaffected thereunto (what art hath not enemies?) demand whether these gates be to let in, or let out the philosopher's stone; seeing *projection,* the last of all, proves but a project, producing nothing in effect.

We must not forget how the said Sir George beseecheth all men, wheresoever they shall meet with any of his experiments written by him, or that go under his name (from the year 1450 to the year 1470) either to burn them, or afford them no credit, being written according to his esteem, not proof; and which, upon trial, he afterwards found false and vain.

For mine own part, I believe his philosophy truer than his chemical divinity; for so may I call his work, wherein he endeavours to equal in merit for mankind, the compassion of the Virgin Mary with the passion of Christ. He died about the year of our Lord 1490; and some of his works are since exactly set forth by my worthy and accomplished friend Elias Ashmole, esquire, in his *Theatrum Chymicum Britannicum.*[1]

THOMAS SCOTT [THOMAS ROTHERHAM] was born [1423] at Rotherham, no obscure market in this county. Waiving his paternal name, he took that of Rotherham from the place of his nativity. This I observe the rather, because he was (according to my exactest inquiry) the last clergyman of note with such an assumed surname; which custom began now to grow out of fashion, and clergymen, like other men, to be called by the name of their fathers.

He was first, fellow of King's College, afterwards master of Pembroke Hall in Cambridge, and chancellor of that university. Here he built on his proper cost (saving something helped by the scholars) the fair gate of the school, with fair walks on each side, and a library on the east thereof. Many have mistaken this for the performance of King Richard the Third, merely because his crest, the boar, is set up therein. Whereas the truth is that Rotherham, having felt the sharp tusks of that boar (when imprisoned by the aforesaid king for resigning the great seal of England to Queen Elizabeth, the relict of King Edward the Fourth) advanced his arms thereon merely to ingratiate himself. He went through many church preferments, being successively provost of Beverley, bishop of Rochester, Lincoln, and lastly archbishop of York. Nor less was his share in civil honour: first, keeper of the privy seal, and last, lord chancellor of England. Many were his benefactions to the public, of which none more remarkable than his founding five fellowships in Lincoln College in Oxford. He deceased, in the 76th year of his age, at Cawood, of the plague, Anno Domini 1500.

(1) Antiquary and astrologer, who bequeathed his library to Oxford University. He lived 1617-1692.

JOHN ALCOCK was born [1430] at Beverley in this county, where he built a chapel and founded a chantry for his parents. He was bred a doctor of divinity in Cambridge, and at last became bishop of Ely. His prudence appeared in that he was preferred lord chancellor of England by King Henry the Seventh, a prince of an excellent palate to taste men's abilities, and a dunce was no dish for his diet. His piety is praised by the pen of J. Bale, which, though generally bitter, drops nothing but honey on Alcock's memory, commending him for a most mortified man, "given to learning and piety from his childhood, growing from grace to grace, so that in his age none in England was higher for holiness." He turned the old nunnery of St. Rhadegund into a new college called Jesus, in Cambridge. Surely, had Malcolm king of Scots, first founder of that nunnery, survived to see this alteration, it would have rejoiced his heart to behold lewdness and laziness turned out for industry and piety to be put in their place. This Alcock died October 1, 1500. And had saintship gone as much by merit as favour, he deserved one as well as his namesake Saint John, his predecessor in that see.

JOHN FISHER was born [1459] in the town of Beverley in this county. His father, Robert Fisher, was by condition a merchant, and lived in good reputation. He was afterwards bred in Michaelhouse in Cambridge, whereof he was the first chancellor *pro termino vitae,* and bishop of Rochester. How this Fisher was caught afterwards in the net of Elizabeth Barton, commonly called the Holy Maid of Kent,[1] thereby made accessary to her dissembling; how stiff he was against King Henry's divorce, and title of supreme head of the church; how the pope sent him a cardinal's cap, and the king cut off his head, hath been so largely related in my *Church History;* and being, I hope, pardoned by the reader for my former tediousness, I will not now contract a new guilt by offending in prolixity on the same person; the rather because his manuscript life, written eighty years since by Richard Hall in Christ's College in Cambridge, is lately set forth in print under the name of Thomas Baily, D.D.; in which book, as I do not repine at any passages (though hyperbolical) to the praise of this prelate, so I cannot but be both angry and grieved at the many false and scandalous reflections therein on the worthy instruments of our Reformation. This learned bishop was beheaded in the year 1535, the three-score and seventeenth year of his age.

WILLIAM HUGH was born in this county, and bred in Corpus Christi College in Oxford, where he attained to great eminency in learning. In his time the consciences of many tender parents were troubled about the final estate of infants dying unbaptised, as posting from the womb to the winding-sheet in such speed that the sacrament could not be fastened upon them. To pacify persons herein concerned, this William wrote and dedicated a book to Queen Catherine Parr, entituled *The Troubled Man's Medicine.* He died, of the breaking of a vein, Anno Domini 1549.

CUTHBERT TUNSTALL was born [1474] at Hackforth in Richmondshire in this county, of a most worshipful family (whose chief seat at Tunstall

(1) See footnote to Sir Thomas More's life in London, p. 357.

Thurland not far off) and bred in the university of Cambridge, to which he was in books a great benefactor. He was afterwards bishop of London, and at last of Durham. A great Grecian, orator, mathematician, civilian, divine, and (to wrap up all in a word) a fast friend to Erasmus.

In the reign of King Henry the Eighth he publicly confuted the papal supremacy in a learned sermon, with various and solid arguments, preached on Palm Sunday, before his majesty, Anno Domini 1539. And yet (man is but man) he returned to his error in the reign of King Edward the Sixth, continuing therein in the first of Queen Elizabeth, for which he was deprived of his bishopric. He shewed mercy when in power, and found it in his adversity, having nothing but the name of a prisoner, in which condition he died, and was buried at Lambeth 1559.[1]

MILES COVERDALE was born [1488] in this county; bred in the university of Cambridge, and afterwards became an Augustine friar; till, his eyes being opened, he quitted that superstitious profession. Going into Germany, he laboured greatly in translating of the Bible and in writing many books, reckoned up by John Bale. He was made doctor of divinity in the university of Tübingen; and returning into England, being incorporated in Cambridge, was soon after made bishop of Exeter by King Edward the Sixth, 1551.

But alas, he was not comfortably warm in his place, before his place by persecution grew too hot for him; and in the first of Queen Mary, he was cast into prison, a certain forerunner of his martyrdom, had not Frederic king of Denmark seasonably interposed. This good king, with great importunity, hardly obtained this small courtesy, viz., that Coverdale should be enlarged, though on this condition, to be banished out of his country; in obedience whereunto he went over into Germany. In the first of Queen Elizabeth he returned to England, but not to Exeter, never resuming that or accepting any other bishopric. Several men assigned several causes hereof, but Coverdale only knew the true reason himself.

Some will say that for the books he made he had better been placed under the title of Learned Writers; or, for the exile and imprisonment he suffered, ranked under Confessors, than under the title of Prelates, manifesting an averseness of his own judgment thereunto by not returning to his bishopric. But be it known that Coverdale in his judgment approved thereof; being one of those bishops who solemnly consecrated Matthew Parker archbishop of Canterbury at Lambeth. Now *quod efficit tale, magis est tale;* I understand it thus: "He that makes another archbishop is abundantly satisfied in his judgment and conscience of the lawfulness thereof;" otherwise such dissembling had been inconsistent with the sincerity of so grave and godly a person. He died Anno Domini 1568, and lies buried in Saint Bartholomew's behind the Exchange, under a fair stone in the chancel.[2]

(1) Tunstall throughout his life remained a catholic, but always passively obeyed the civil power. He was bishop of London 1522-30, of Durham 1530-1552 and 1553-9. He refrained from persecution in Mary's reign. (2) In the last years of his life Coverdale's sympathies became increasingly puritan, resigning on that account his rectorship (1563-6) of St. Magnus, London Bridge, and preached privately.

RALPH BAYNES was born in this county, bred fellow of Saint John's College in Cambridge. An excellent linguist in Latin, Greek and Hebrew; I say Hebrew, then in its nonage, whereof Baynes was a good guardian, first in learning, then in teaching the rules thereof. Hence he went over into France, and became Hebrew professor at Paris. He wrote a comment on the Proverbs in three volumes, and dedicated it to King Francis the First of France, that grand patron of good men and great scholars.

Pits telleth us *ferunt* (it is reported) "that the ministers of Geneva have much depraved many of his writings in several places," which I do not believe; such passages (doubtlessly according to the author's own writing) being reducible to two heads. First, his fair mentioning of some learned linguists, though protestants, with whom he kept an epistolary correspondency. Secondly, some expressions in preferring the original of Scripture to the diminution of the vulgar translation.

Returning into England, he was, by Queen Mary, 1554, made bishop of Coventry and Lichfield. Hitherto no ill could be spoken of his intellectuals; and hereafter no good of his morals, in point of his cruelty—he caused such persecution in his diocese. His greatest commendation is, that though as bad a bishop as Christopherson, he was better than Bonner.[1] In the first of Queen Elizabeth he was deprived of his bishopric; and dying not long after of the stone, was buried in Saint Dunstan's, 1559.

THOMAS BENTHAM was born [1513] in this county; bred fellow of Magdalen College in Oxford. Under King Henry the Eighth he was a complier with, no promoter of popery. In the first of Queen Mary, repenting of his former, he resolved not to accumulate sin, refusing not only to say mass, but also to correct a scholar in the college (though urged thereto by Sir Robert Reed, the prime visitor) for his absence from popish prayers, conceiving it injurious to punish in another that omission for a fault which was also according to his own conscience. He also then assisted Henry Bull (one of the same foundation) to wrest out, and throw down out of the hands of the choristers, the censer, when about to offer their superstitious incense.

No wonder then if he was fain to fly into foreign parts, and glad to get over into Germany, where he lived at Basle, preacher to the English exiles, to whom he expounded the entire book of the Acts of the Apostles. Now seeing the apostles' suffering was above all their doing, it was a proper portion of Scripture for him hence to press patience to his banished countrymen.

Towards the end of Queen Mary, he was secretly sent for over to be superintendent of the London conventicle (the only true church in time of persecution) where, with all his care and caution, he hardly escaped. In the second of Queen Elizabeth he was consecrated bishop of Coventry and Lichfield, succeeding Ralph Baynes therein (one of the same county with him, but a different judgment) and died on the 21st of February 1578.

(1) For John Christopherson see Lancashire, p. 296, and Edmund Bonner see Worcestershire, p. 626.

THOMAS ROBERTSON [or ROBINSON] was born in this county; and, being doctor of divinity in Oxford, was one of the best grammarians for Greek and Latin in that age. He had an admirable faculty in teaching youth; for every boy can teach a man, whereas he must be a man who can teach a boy. It is easy to inform them who are able to understand, but it must be a master-piece of industry and discretion to descend to the capacity of children. He wrote notes upon the grammar of Lily; and, besides others, one book *De Nominibus Heteroclitis*; and another *De Verbis Defectivis;* so that by his pains the hardest parts of grammar are made the easiest, and the most anomalous reduced to the greatest regularity by his endeavours. [*fl.* 1520-1561]

SIR ROGER CHOLMLEY, knight. He is placed in this county with moderate assurance; for his father (as I am instructed by those of his family) lived in this county, though branched from Cheshire, and much conversant in London, being lieutenant of the Tower under King Henry the Seventh. By his will he bequeathed a legacy to Roger his natural son, then student of the laws, the selfsame with our Roger, as proportion of time doth evince.

He applied his studies so effectually that in the 37th of King Henry the Eighth, in Michaelmas Term, he was made chief baron of the exchequer; and in the sixth of Edward the Sixth, chief justice of the king's bench.

In the first of Queen Mary, July 27, he, with Sir Edward Montagu,[1] lord chief justice of the common pleas, was committed to the Tower, for drawing up the testament of King Edward the Sixth, wherein his sisters were disinherited. Yet Sir Roger's activity amounted no higher than to a compliance and a subscription of the same. He afterwards was enlarged, but lost his judge's place, living some years in a private condition.

When William Flower was burnt in Westminster, Sir Roger being present (though called by Master Foxe but plain Master Cholmley) "willed him to recant his heresy;" which I impute rather to his carnal pity than great affection to popery.

He built a free school of brick at Highgate, about the year 1562; the pension of the master being uncertain, and the school in the disposition of six governors; and I believe he survived not long after, and have some ground for my suspicion that he died without issue. [*d.* 1565]

ARMAGIL WAAD [or WADE] born of an ancient family in Yorkshire, as I am informed from his epitaph on his monument at Hampstead in Middlesex, wherein he is termed *Hen.* 8 *et Edw.* 6 *regum secretiori concilio ab epistolis,* which I took the boldness to interpret, not secretary but clerk of the council.

He was the first Englishman that discovered America, and his several voyages are largely described in Mr. Hakluyt's *Travels.* This English Columbus had by two wives twenty children, whereof Sir William Waad was the eldest, a very able gentleman, and clerk of the council to Queen

(1) Northamptonshire, p. 433.

Elizabeth. This Armagil died June 20, 1568, and was buried as is aforesaid.[1]

JOHN YOUNG was born [1514] in this county. His life appeareth to me patched up of unsuiting pieces, as delivered by several authors. A judicious antiquary,[2] seldom mistaken, will have him a monk of Ramsey, therein confounding him with his namesakes many years more ancient. Another[3] will have him bred doctor of divinity in Trinity College in Cambridge, though that foundation (suppose him admitted the first day thereof) affordeth not seniority enough to write doctor before the reign of Queen Mary, except we understand him bred in some of the hostels afterwards united thereunto. So that I rather concur herein with the forenamed antiquary, that he was fellow of Saint John's College in that university.

It is agreed that, at the first, he was at the least a parcel protestant, translating into English the book of Archbishop Cranmer, of the Sacrament. But afterwards he came off with a witness, being a zealous papist and great antagonist of Martin Bucer, and indeed as able a disputant as any of his party.

He was vice-chancellor of Cambridge anno 1553, master of Pembroke Hall, king's professor of divinity, and rector of Landbeach nigh Cambridge; but lost all his preferment in the first of Queen Elizabeth. Surely more than ordinary obstinacy appeared in him, because not only deprived, but imprisoned; and in my judgment, more probably surprised before he went than after his return from foreign parts. He died under restraint, in England, 1580.

ROGER ASCHAM was born [1515] at Kirkby Wiske in this county; and bred in Saint John's College in Cambridge, under Doctor Metcalfe, that good governor, who, whetstone-like, though dull in himself, by his encouragement set an edge on most excellent wits in that foundation.[4] Indeed Ascham came to Cambridge just at the dawning of learning, and stayed therein till the bright day thereof, his own endeavours contributing much light thereunto. He was orator and Greek professor in the university (places of some sympathy, which have often met in the same person); and in the beginning of the reign of Queen Mary, within three days wrote letters to forty-seven several princes, whereof the meanest was a cardinal. He travelled into Germany, and there contracted familiarity with John Sturm and other learned men; and after his return, was a kind of teacher to the Lady Elizabeth, to whom (after she was queen) he became her secretary for her Latin letters.

In a word, he was an honest man and a good shooter; archery, whereof he wrote a book called *Toxophilus*, being his only exercise in his youth, which in his old age he exchanged for a worse pastime, neither so

(1) Armagil Waad cheaply earned the name of 'the English Columbus', to which he was no more entitled than his companions, through a voyage to N. America in 1536. Cabot and his father and brothers had discovered Nova Scotia in 1497.
(2) Parker, *Skeletos Cantabrigensis*. (3) J. Pits. (4) Nicholas Metcalfe (1475?-1539) was master of St. John's for over twenty years. He opposed Henry VIII's divorce and his claims to supremacy in doctrinal matters. Fuller gives an account of him in his *Holy State*.

healthful for his body nor profitable for his purse: I mean cock-fighting, and thereby, being neither greedy to get nor careful to keep money, he much impaired his estate.

He had a facile and fluent Latin style; not like those who, counting obscurity to be elegancy, weed out all the hard words they meet in authors; witness his *Epistles,* which some say are the only Latin ones extant of any Englishman, and if so, the more the pity. What loads have we of letters from foreign pens, as if no author were complete without those necessary appurtenances; whilst surely our Englishmen write, though not so many, as good as any other nation. In a word, his *Toxophilus* is accounted a good book for *young* men, his *Schoolmaster* for *old* men, his *Epistles* for *all* men, set out after his death, which happened Anno Domini 1568, December 30, in the 53rd year of his age; and he was buried in Saint Sepulchre's in London.

EDMUND GUEST was born [1518] at Northallerton in this county; bred fellow of King's College in Cambridge, where he proceeded doctor of divinity. He was afterwards almoner to Queen Elizabeth, and he must be both a wise and good man whom she would trust with her purse. She preferred him bishop, first of Rochester, then of Salisbury. John Bale (saith my author[1]) reckoneth up many books made by him of considerable value. He died February 28, 1577.

SIR CHRISTOPHER WRAY, knight, was born [1524] in the spacious parish of Bedale; the main motive which made his daughter Frances countess of Warwick scatter her benefactions the thicker in that place. But I have been informed that his ancestor, by some accident, came out of Cornwall, where his name is right ancient. He was bred in the study of our municipal law; and such his proficiency therein, that in the sixteenth of Queen Elizabeth, in Michaelmas Term, he was made lord chief justice of the king's bench.

He was not like that judge who feared neither God nor man, but only one widow (lest her importunity should weary him) but he heartily feared God in his religious conversation. Each man he respected in his due distance off the bench, and no man on it to bias his judgment. He was, *pro tempore,* lord privy seal, and sat chief in the court, when Secretary Davison was sentenced in the Star Chamber. Sir Christopher, collecting the censures of all the commissioners, concurred to fine him, but with this comfortable conclusion, "that as it was in the queen's power to have him punished, so her highness might be prevailed with for mitigating or remitting of the fine." And this our judge may be presumed no ill instrument in the procuring thereof.[2]

He bountifully reflected on Magdalene College in Cambridge, which infant foundation had otherwise been starved at nurse for want of maintenance. We know who saith, "the righteous man leaveth an inheritance to his children's children;" and the well thriving of his third generation

(1) Bishop Godwin. [Edmund Guest, a friend of Bacon, Hatton and Cecil, left his library to Salisbury Cathedral. He translated the Psalms in the Bishops' Bible.] (2) See Note 1, p. 41, on the incident of Davison. Sir Christopher Wray was assessor to the tribunal which tried Mary Queen of Scots.

may be an evidence of his well gotten goods. This worthy judge died May 7, in the thirty-fourth of Queen Elizabeth [1592].

ADAM LOFTUS was born [1533?] in this county, and bred in Trinity College in Cambridge, where he commenced doctor of divinity the same year with John Whitgift, afterwards archbishop of Canterbury. He was chaplain to Robert earl of Sussex, deputy of Ireland; and was first made archbishop of Armagh, anno 1563; and afterwards archbishop of Dublin, anno 1567.

Wonder not that he should desire his own degradation, to be removed from Armagh, then primate of Ireland, to Dublin, a subordinate archbishopric, seeing herein he consulted his safety (and perchance his profit) more than his honour, Armagh being then infested with rebels, whilst Dublin was a secure city.

After the death of Sir William Gerard, he was made chancellor of Ireland, which place he discharged with singular ability and integrity until the day of his death.

And that which in my judgment commendeth him most to the notice of posterity, and most engageth posterity in thankfulness to his memory, is that he was a profitable agent in, yea, a principal procurer of the foundation of the university and college of Dublin (where Dermitius, son of Mercard king of Leinster, had formerly founded a convent for canons regular) and the first honorary master thereof, being then archbishop (if not chancellor of Ireland) to give the more credit and countenance to that foundation. He died April 5, anno 1605; and was buried in the church of Saint Patrick, having been archbishop from his consecration eight months above two-and-forty years.

SIR MARTIN FROBISHER, knight, was born [1535?] nigh Doncaster in this county. I note this the rather, because learned Mr. Carpenter, in his *Geography*, recounts him amongst the famous men of Devonshire (but why should Devonshire, which hath a flock of worthies of her own, take a lamb from another county?) because much conversing therein.

He was from his youth bred up in navigation; and was the first Englishman that discovered the north way to China and Cathay, whence he brought great store of black soft stone, supposing it silver or gold ore; yet will no wise man laugh at his mistake, because in such experiments they shall never hit the mark who are not content to miss it.[1]

He was very valiant, but withal harsh and violent (faults which may be dispensed with in his profession) and our chronicles loudly resound his signal service in eighty-eight, for which he was knighted. His last service was the defending of Brest haven in Brittany, with ten ships against a far greater power of Spaniards. Here he was shot into the side, the wound not being mortal in itself; but swords and guns have not made more mortal wounds than probes in the hands of careless and skill-less chirurgeons, as here it came to pass. The chirurgeon took out only the bullet, and left the bombast[2] about it behind, wherewith the sore festered, and the worthy knight died at Plymouth, anno 1594.

(1) From one voyage he did bring back 200 tons of gold. (2) *Bombast* = wadding.

SIR JOHN PUCKERING, knight, was born [1544] at Flamborough Head in this county, as I have learned out of the notes of that industrious and judicious antiquary Mr. Dodsworth. He was second son to his father, a gentleman who left him neither plentiful nor penurious estate. His breeding was more beneficial to him than his portion; gaining thereby such skill in the common law that he became queen's serjeant, speaker in the House of Commons, and at last lord chancellor of England. How he stood in his judgment in the point of church discipline, plainly appeareth by his following speech, delivered in the House of Lords, 1588, the original whereof was courteously communicated unto me.[1]

He died Anno Domini 1596, charactered by Mr. Camden *Vir Integer*. His estate is since descended, according to the solemn settlement thereof, the male issue failing, on Sir Henry Newton, who, according to the condition, hath assumed the surname of Puckering; and I can never be sufficiently thankful to him and his relations.[2]

SIR HENRY SAVILE, knight, was born [1549] at Bradley in the parish of Halifax, in this county, of ancient and worshipful extraction. He was bred in Oxford, and at last became warden of Merton College, and also provost of Eton. Thus this skilful gardener had at the same time a nursery of young plants and an orchard of grown trees, both flourishing under his careful inspection.

This worthy knight carefully collected the best copies of Saint Chrysostom, and employed learned men to transcribe and make annotations on them; which done, he fairly set it forth, on his own cost, in a most beautiful edition; a burden which he underwent without stooping under it, though the weight thereof would have broken the back of an ordinary person. But the papists at Paris had their emissaries in England, who surreptitiously procured this knight's learned labours, and sent them over weekly by the post into France, *schedatim*, sheet by sheet, as here they passed the press. Then Fronton Du Duc (a French cardinal as I take it) caused them to be printed there with implicit faith and blind obedience, letter for letter as he received them out of England, only joining thereunto a Latin translation and some other inconsiderable additions. Thus two editions of Saint Chrysostom did together run a race in the world, which should get the speed of the other in public sale and acceptance.

Sir Henry's edition started first by the advantage of some months. But the Parisian edition came up close to it, and advantaged with the Latin translation (though dearer of price) outstript it in quickness of sale; but of late the Savilian Chrysostom hath much mended its pace, so that very few are left of the whole impression.

It must not be forgotten that he was a most excellent mathematician, witness his learned lectures on Euclid. Yet once happening casually into the company of Master Briggs of Cambridge, upon a learned encounter betwixt them, Master Briggs demonstrated a truth, besides (if not against) the judgment of Sir Henry, wherewith that worthy knight was so highly

(1) The speech, directed against the puritans, is here omitted. (2) The family were literary patrons of Fuller.

affected that he chose him one of his mathematic professors in Oxford, wherein he founded two, allowing a liberal salary unto them.[1] [*d.* 1622]

JOHN MUSH was born [1552] in this county; bred first in the English College at Douay, and then ran his course of philosophy in their college at Rome. Afterwards, being made priest, he was sent over into England, to gain people to his own persuasion, which he did without and within the prison for twenty years together, but at last he got his liberty.

In his time the Romish ship in England did spring a dangerous leak, almost to the sinking thereof, in the schism betwixt the priests and the Jesuits. Mush appeared very active and happy in the stopping thereof; and was by the English popish clergy sent to Rome to compose the controversy, behaving himself very wisely in that service. Returning into his own country, he was for fourteen years together assistant to the English archpriest, demeaning himself commendably therein. He wrote many books, and one whose title made me more to mind it, *Vitam et Martyrium D. Margaretae Clithoroae.*

Now whether this *D.* be for *Domina* or *Diva,* for *Lady* or *Saint,* or both, I know not. I take her for some gentlewoman in the north, which, for some practices in the maintenance of her own religion, was obnoxious to, and felt the severity of our laws.[2] [*d.* 1617]

GEORGE CLIFFORD, Lord Clifford, Vesci, &c., earl of Cumberland [*b.* 1558] was son to Henry, second earl of that family, by his second lady; a person wholly composed of true honour and valour, whereof he gave the world a clear and large demonstration.

It was resolved by the judicious in that age, the way to humble the Spanish greatness was, not by pinching and pricking him in the Low Countries, which only emptied his veins of such blood as was quickly refilled; but the way to make it a cripple for ever was by cutting off the Spanish sinews of war, his money from the West Indies. In order whereunto, this earl set forth a small fleet at his own cost, and adventured his own person therein, being the best-born Englishman that ever hazarded himself in that kind.

His fleet may be said to be bound for no other harbour but the port of honour, though touching at the port of profit in passage thereunto; I say *touching,* whose design was not to enrich himself but impoverish the enemy. He was as merciful as valiant (the best metal bows best) and left impressions of both in all places where he came.

Queen Elizabeth, anno 1592, honoured him with the dignity of the Garter. When King James came first out of Scotland to York, he attended him with such an equipage of followers, for number and habit, that he seemed rather a king than earl of Cumberland. Here happened a contest between the earl and the lord president of the north, about carrying the sword before the king in York; which office, upon due

(1) Now known as the Savilian professorship of astronomy and the Savilian professorship of geometry. Sir Henry Savile was also tutor in Greek to Queen Elizabeth, and one of the translators of the Authorized Version. (2) Mrs. Margaret Clitherow, the 'martyr of York,' wife of a butcher; embraced Roman catholicism, and barbarously executed for harbouring priests.

search and inquiry, was adjudged to the earl as belonging unto him; and whilst Clifford's Tower is standing in York, that family will never be therein forgotten. He died 1605, leaving one daughter and heir, the Lady Anne, married to the earl of Dorset.[1]

GEORGE [MONTAIGNE or] MOUNTAIN was born [1569] in this county, at Cawood, and bred in Queens' College in Cambridge, where he became fellow and proctor of the university. He was chaplain to the earl of Essex, whom he attended on his voyage to Cadiz, being indeed one of such personal valour, that out of his gown he would turn his back to no man. He was afterwards made dean of Westminster, then successively bishop of Lincoln and London. Whilst residing in the latter, he would often pleasantly say that of him the proverb would be verified, "Lincoln was, and London is, and York shall be;"[2] which came to pass accordingly, when he was removed to the archbishopric of York, wherein he died; through which sees never any prelate so methodically passed but himself alone. He was a good benefactor to the college wherein he was bred, whereon he bestowed a fair piece of plate, called *poculum charitatis,* with this inscription, INCIPIO (I begin to thee) and founded two scholarships therein. [*d.* 1628]

THOMAS TAYLOR was born [1576] at Richmond in this county, where his father (a bountiful entertainer of people in distress) was recorder of the town. He was afterwards bred in Christ's College in Cambridge, and chosen a fellow thereof.

This Timothy, grave when green, entered very young but not raw into the ministry, at twenty-one years of age; and continued in the same at Reading and London for the space of thirty-five years. His sermons were generally well studied; and he was wont to say that oft-times he satisfied himself the least when he best pleased his people, not taking such pains in his preaching. His flock was firmly founded and well bottomed on catechistical divinity; it being observed that his auditors stuck close to their principles in this age, wherein so many have reeled into damnable errors. He was a great giver of alms, but without a trumpet, and most strict in his conversation.

Zeal for the house of God may be said in some sort to have consumed him, dying in the fifty-sixth year of his age, Anno Domini 1633, comfortably avowing at his death, that we serve such a Master "who covereth many imperfections," and giveth "much wages for a little work."

GEORGE SANDYS, youngest son of Edwin Sandys, archbishop of York,[3] was born [1578] at Bishopthorpe in this county. He proved a most accomplished gentleman, and an observant traveller, who went as far

(1) Clifford fitted out ten privateering expeditions, going on four of them himself. A gambler who wasted his estates, he was an accomplished courtier and romantic buccaneer. He was of fine appearance, possessed great courage, and was popular. For his daughter Anne Clifford see Westmorland, p. 601. (2) The proverb runs thus:

Lincoln was, London is, York will be
The greatest city of all the three.

(3) See Lancashire, p. 297.

as the Sepulchre at Jerusalem; and hath spared other men's pains in going thither by bringing the Holy Land home to them, so lively is his description thereof, with his passage thither and return thence.

He most elegantly translated Ovid's *Metamorphoses* into English verse; so that, as the soul of Aristotle was said to have transmigrated into Thomas Aquinas (because rendering his sense so naturally) Ovid's genius may seem to have passed into Master Sandys. He was a servant, but no slave, to his subject; well knowing that a translator is a person in *free custody; custody,* being bound to give the true sense of the author he translated; *free,* left at liberty to clothe it in his own expression.

Nor can that in any degree be applied to Master Sandys, which one rather bitterly than falsely chargeth on an author, whose name I leave to the reader's conjecture:

> We know thou dost well
> As a translator,
> But where things require
> A genius and a fire,
> Not kindled before by others' pains,
> As often thou hast wanted brains.

Indeed some men are better nurses than mothers of a poem, good only to feed and foster the fancies of others; whereas Master Sandys was altogether as dexterous at inventing as translating, and his own poems as spriteful, vigorous and masculine. He lived to be a very aged man, whom I saw in the Savoy, anno 1641, having a youthful soul in a decayed body; and I believe he died soon after. [*d.* 1644]

SIR GEORGE CALVERT, knight [FIRST BARON BALTIMORE] was born [1580?] at Kipling, near Richmond, in this county; had his education first in Trinity College in Oxford, then beyond the seas. His abilities commended him first to be secretary to Robert Cecil, earl of Salisbury, lord treasurer of England. Afterwards he was made clerk of the council, and at last principal secretary of state to King James, succeeding Sir Thomas Lake in that office anno 1619.

Conceiving the duke of Buckingham highly instrumental in his preferment, he presented him with a jewel of great value; which the duke returned him again, not owning any activity in his advancement, whom King James, *ex mero motu,* reflecting on his ability, designed for the place.

This place he discharged above five years, until he willingly resigned the same, 1625, on this occasion. He freely confessed himself to the king that he was then become a Roman catholic, so that he must either be wanting to his trust, or violate his conscience in discharging his office. This his ingenuity so highly affected King James, that he continued him privy councillor all his reign (as appeareth in the council book) and soon after created him Lord Baltimore of Baltimore in Ireland.

During his being secretary he had a patent to him and his heirs to be *absolutus dominus et proprietarius,* with the royalties of a count palatine, of the province of Avalon in Newfoundland; a place so named by him in imitation of old Avalon in Somersetshire, wherein Glastonbury stands:

the first fruits of Christianity in Britain, as the other was in that part of America. Here he built a fair house in Ferry Land, and spent five-and-twenty thousand pounds in advancing the plantation thereof. Indeed his public spirit consulted not his private profit, but the enlargement of Christianity and the king's dominions. After the death of King James he went twice in person to Newfoundland. Here, when Monsieur de l'Arade, with three men-of-war, sent from the king of France, had reduced our English fishermen to great extremity, this lord, with two ships manned at his own charge, chased away the Frenchmen, relieved the English, and took sixty of the French prisoners.

He removed afterwards to Virginia, to view those parts; and afterwards came into England, and obtained from King Charles (who had as great an esteem of and affection for him as King James) a patent to him and his heirs for Maryland on the north of Virginia, with the same title and royalties conferred on him as in Avalon aforesaid, now a hopeful plantation peopled with eight thousand English souls, which in process of time may prove more advantageous to our nation.

Being returned into England, he died in London, April 15, 1632, in the 53rd year of his age, lying buried in the chancel of Saint Dunstan's in the West, leaving his son, the right honourable Cecil Calvert, now Lord Baltimore, heir to his honour, estate and noble disposition.

NATHANIEL SHUTE was born at Giggleswick in this county; Christopher Shute his father being the painful vicar thereof.[1] He was bred in Christ's College in Cambridge; a most excellent scholar and solid preacher, though nothing of his is extant in print, save a sermon called *Corona Charitatis,* preached at the funeral of Master Fishbourn. But the goodness of the land of Canaan may as well be guessed from one great bunch of grapes, as if the spies had brought whole vineyards along with them. Indeed he was a profound and profitable preacher for many years together at Saint Mildred Poultry in London.

One in the university being demanded his judgment of an excellent sermon in Saint Mary's, returned that "it was an uncomfortable sermon, leaving no hope of imitation for such as should succeed him." In this sense alone I must allow Master Nathaniel Shute an uncomfortable preacher (though otherwise a true Barnabas and son of consolation) possessing such as shall follow him in time with a despair to equal him in eminency.

He died Anno Domini 1638, when our English sky was clouded all over, and set to rain, but before any drops of water fell down amongst us, Doctor Holdsworth most excellently preached his funeral sermon, taking for his text, "We have this our treasure in earthly vessels."

JOSIAS SHUTE [*b.* 1588] brother to Nathaniel aforesaid, was bred in Trinity College in Cambridge, and became afterwards minister of Saint Mary Woolnoth in London; and was (reader, I do say, and will maintain

(1) So I am informed by Mr. Christopher Shute, minister of Saint Vedast in London, heir to his father's virtues.

it) the most precious jewel that was ever shewn or seen in Lombard Street. All ministers are God's husbandmen; but some of them can only plough in soft ground, whose shares and coulters will turn edge in a hard point of divinity. No ground came amiss to Master Shute, whether his text did lead him to controversial or positive divinity; having a strain, without straining for it, of native eloquence, he spake that which others studied for. He was for many years, and that most justly, highly esteemed of his parish; till in the beginning of our late civil wars some began to neglect him, distasting wholesome meat well dressed by him merely because their mouths were out of taste, by that general distemper which in his time was but an ague, afterwards turned to a fever, and since is turned into a frenzy in our nation.

Master Shute died Anno Domini 1643, and was buried with great solemnity in his own church, Master Udall preaching his funeral sermon. Since his death his excellent sermons are set forth on some part of Genesis, and pity it is there is no more extant of his worthy endeavours.

It must not be forgotten how, retiring a little before his death into the country, some of his parishioners came to visit him, whom he cheerfully entertained with this expression: "I have taught you, my dear flock, for above thirty years, how to live, and now I will shew you in a very short time how to die." He was as good as his word herein; for within an hour he in the presence of some of them was peaceably dissolved.

Be it also known, that besides these two brothers, Nathaniel and Josias, fixed in the city of London, there were three more, bred and brought up in the ministry: viz., Robert, preacher at Lynn; Thomas, minister for a good time in Chester; and Timothy, lately, if not still alive, a preacher in Exeter.

All great (though not equal) lights are set up in fair candlesticks; I mean, places of eminency, and conveniently distanced one from another, for the better dispersing of their light; and good housewives tell me old candles are the best for spending. Happy their father, who had his quiver full with five such sons. He need not be ashamed "to see his enemies in the gate." It is hard to say whether he was more happy in his sons, or they in so good a father; and a wary man will crave time to decide the doubt, until the like instance doth return in England.

THOMAS JOHNSON was born in this county, not far from Hull;[1] bred an apothecary in London, where he attained to be the best herbalist of his age in England, making additions to the edition of Gerard. A man of such modesty that, knowing so much, he would own the knowledge of nothing. The university of Oxford bestowed on him the honorary degree of doctor in physic; and his loyalty engaged him on the king's side in our late civil war. When in Basing House a dangerous piece of service was to be done, this doctor, who publicly pretended not to valour, undertook and performed it. Yet afterwards he lost his life in the siege of the same house, and was (to my knowledge) generally lamented of those who were of an opposite judgment. But let us bestow this epitaph upon him:

(1) So his near kinsman, an apothecary living on Snow Hill, informed me.

Hic, Johnsone, jaces; sed, si mors cederet herbis,
Arte fugata tua, cederet illa tuis.

Here Johnson lies; could physic fence Death's dart,
Sure Death had been declined by his art.

His death happened Anno Domini 1644.[1]

JOHN SALTMARSH was extracted from a right ancient (but decayed) family in this county; and I am informed that Sir Thomas Metham, his kinsman, bountifully contributed to his education. He was bred in Magdalene College in Cambridge. Returning into this his native county, was very great with Sir John Hotham the elder. He was one of a fine and active fancy, no contemptible poet, and a good preacher, as by some of his profitable printed sermons doth appear. Be it charitably imputed to the information of his judgment and conscience, that of a zealous observer he became a violent oppressor of bishops and ceremonies.

He wrote a book against my sermon of *Reformation,* taxing me for many points of popery therein. I defended myself in a book called *Truth Maintained,* and challenged him to an answer, who appeared in the field no more, rendering this reason thereof, that "he would not shoot his arrows against a dead mark," being informed that I was dead at Exeter.

I have no cause to be angry with fame (but rather to thank her) for so good a lie. May I make this true use of that false report, "to die daily." See how providence hath crossed it. The dead (reported) man is still living,[2] the then *living* man *dead*; and seeing I survive to go over his grave, I will tread the more gently on the mould thereof, using that civility on him which I received from him.

He died in or about Windsor, as he was riding to and fro in the parliament army, of a burning fever, venting on his death-bed strange expressions, apprehended (by some of his party) as ecstatical, yea prophetical raptures; whist others accounted them (no wonder if outrages in the city, when the enemy hath possessed the castle commanding it) to the acuteness of his disease, which had seized his intellectuals. [*d.* 1647]

JEREMIAH WHITAKER was born [1599] at Wakefield in this county; bred master of arts in Sidney College, and after became schoolmaster of Oakham, then minister of Stretton in Rutland. He was chosen to be one of the members of the late assembly, wherein he behaved himself with great moderation; at last he was preacher of Saint Mary Magdalen, Bermondsey, well discharging his duty, being a solid divine, and a man made up of piety to God, pity to poor men, and patience in himself. He had much use of the last, being visited with many and most acute diseases.

Sure I am, this good Jeremiah was tormented with gout, stone, and one ulcer in his bladder, another in his kidneys; all which he endured with admirable and exemplary patience, though God of his goodness grant that (if it may stand with His will) no cause be given that so sad a copy

(1) He published the first local catalogue of plants issued in England; the genus *Johnsonia* is named after him. (2) May 20, 1661, at the writing hereof.

be transcribed. Thus God, for reasons best known unto himself, sent many and the most cruel bailiffs to arrest him to pay his debt to nature, though he always was ready to tender the same at their single summons. His liberality knew no bottom but an empty purse, so bountiful he was to all in want. He was buried on the 6th of June, anno 1654, in his own parish of Southwark, much lamented; Master Simeon Ashe preaching his funeral sermon, to which the reader is referred for his further satisfaction. I understand some sermons are extant of his preaching.

THE FAREWELL

As I am glad to hear the plenty of a coarser kind of cloth is made in this county at Halifax, Leeds and elsewhere, whereby the meaner sort are much employed, and the middle sort enriched; so I am sorry for the general complaints made thereof; insomuch that it is become a general byword "to shrink as northern cloth" (a giant to the eye, and dwarf in the use thereof) to signify such who fail their friends in deepest distress, depending on their assistance. Sad that the sheep, the emblem of innocence, should unwillingly cover so much craft under the wool thereof; and sadder that fullers, commended in Scripture for making cloth *white,* should justly be condemned for making their own consciences *black* by such fraudulent practices. I hope this fault, for the future, will be amended in this county and elsewhere; for sure it is that the transporting of wool and fuller's-earth (both against law) beyond the seas, are not more prejudicial to our English clothing abroad, than the deceit in making cloth at home, debasing the foreign estimation of our cloth, to the unvaluable damage of our nation.

YORK

YORK is an ancient city, built on both sides of the river Ouse, conjoined with a bridge, wherein there is one arch, the highest and largest in England. Here the Roman emperors had their residence (Severus and Valerius Constantius their death) preferring this place before London, as more approaching the centre of this island; and he who will hold the ox-hide from rising up on either side, must fix his foot in the middle thereof.

What it lacketh of London in bigness and beauty of buildings, it hath in cheapness and plenty of provisions. The ordinary in York will make a feast in London; and such persons, who in their eating consult both their purse and palate, would choose this city as the staple place of good cheer.

THE MANUFACTURES

It challengeth none peculiar to itself; and the foreign trade is like their river (compared with the Thames) low and little. Yet send they coarse cloth to Hamburg, and have iron, flax and other Dutch commodities in return.

But the trade which indeed is but driven on at York, runneth of itself at Hull, which, of a fisher's town, is become a city's fellow within three hundred years, being the key of the north. I presume this key (though not new made) is well mended, and the wards of the lock much altered, since it shut out our sovereign from entering therein.[1]

THE BUILDINGS

The cathedral in this city answereth the character which a foreign author[2] giveth it, *Templum opere et magnitudine toto orbe memorandum*: the work of John Romanus, William de Melton, and John Thoresby, successive archbishops thereof; the family of the Percys contributing timber, of the Vavasours stone thereunto.

Appending to this cathedral is the chapter-house; such a master-piece of art, that this golden verse (understand it written in golden letters) is engraved therein:

> *Ut rosa flos florum, sic est domus ista domorum.*
>
> Of flowers that grow the flower's the rose;
> All houses so this house out-goes.

Now as it follows not that the usurping tulip is better than the rose, because preferred by some foreign fancies before it, so is it as inconsequent that modish Italian churches are better than this reverend magnificent structure, because some humorous travellers are so pleased to esteem them.

(1) In 1642, at the beginning of the Civil War, when Charles I was anxious to secure the arms stored there. (2) The writer of the life of Aeneas Sylvius, or Pope Pius Secundus.

One may justly wonder how this church, whose edifice woods (designed by the devotion of former ages for the repair thereof) were lately sold, should consist in so good a condition. But, as we read that "God made all those to pity his children, who carried them captive," so I am informed that some who had this cathedral in their command favourably reflected hereon, and not only permitted but procured the repair thereof; and no doubt he doth sleep the more comfortably, and will die the more quietly for the same.

THE WORTHIES

FLACCUS ALBINUS, more commonly called ALCUIN, was born [735] say some, nigh London, say others, in York; the latter being more probable, because befriended with his northern education under Venerable Bede, and his advancement in York. Here he so plied the well furnished library therein (much praised by him) that he distilled it into himself, so great and general his knowldge. Bale ranketh him the third Englishman for learning, placing Bede and Aldhelm before him; and our Alcuin's humility is contented with the place, though he be called up higher by the judgments of others.

Hence he travelled beyond the seas, and what Aristotle was to Alexander he was to Charles the first emperor. Yea, Charles owed unto him the best part of his title, the Great, being made great in arts and learning by his instructions.

This Alcuin was the founder of the university in Paris;[1] so that, whatsoever the French brag to the contrary, and slight our nation, their learning was *lumen de lumine nostro,* and a taper lighted at our torch.

He was made first, abbot of Saint Augustine's in Canterbury, and afterward of Saint Martin's in the city of Tours in France; and dying anno 804, he was buried in a small convent appendant to his monastery.

SEWALL DE BOVILL had his nativity probably in these parts. But he was bred in Oxford, and was a scholar to Saint Edmund, who was wont to say to him, "Sewall, Sewall, thou wilt have many afflictions, and die a martyr." Nor did he miss much of his mark therein, though he met with peace and plenty at first when archbishop of York. The occasion of his trouble was when the pope, *plenitudine potestatis,* intruded one Jordan an Italian to be dean of York, whose surprised installing Sewall stoutly opposed. Yea at this time there were in England no fewer than three hundred benefices possessed by Italians, where the people might say to them, as the eunuch to Philip, "How can we understand without an interpreter?" Yea, which was far worse, they did not only not teach in the church, but mis-teach by their lascivious and debauched behaviour. As for our Sewall, Matthew Paris saith plainly that he would not "bow his knee to Baal;" so that, for this his contempt, he was excommunicated and cursed by bell, book and candle, though it was not the bell of Aaron's garment, nor book of Scripture, nor the candle of an unpartial judgment. This brake his heart; and his memory lieth in an intricate

(1) Though for centuries a centre of teaching, a university did not come into being at Paris until the latter part of the twelfth century.

posture (peculiar almost to himself) betwixt martyr and no martyr, a saint and no saint. Sure it is, Sewall, though dying excommunicated in the Romish, is reputed saint in vulgar estimation; and some will maintain that the pope's solemn canonization is no more requisite to the making of a saint, than the opening of a man's windows is necessary to the lustre of the sun. Sewall died Anno Domini 1257.

JOHN ROMANUS, so called because his father was born in Rome, though living a long time in this city, being treasurer of the cathedral therein; and I conjecture this John his son born in York, because so indulgent thereunto; for generally *pure pute* Italians, preferred in England, transmitted the gain they got by bills of exchange or otherwise into their own country; and those outlandish mules, though lying down in English pasture, left no hairs behind them; whereas this Romanus had such affection for York, that being advanced archbishop, he began to build the body of the church, and finished the north part of the cross-aisle therein. Polydore Vergil praised him (no wonder that an Italian commended a Roman) for a man of great learning and sincerity.

He fell into the disfavour of King Edward the First, for excommunicating Anthony Bek bishop of Durham, and it cost him four thousand marks to regain his prince's goodwill. He died Anno Domini 1296; and let none grudge his burial in the best place in the church, who was so bountiful a builder thereof.

ROBERT WALDBY, born in this city, was therein bred an Augustinian friar. He afterwards went over into France, where he so applied his studies, that at last he was chosen divinity professor in the city of Toulouse. He was chaplain to the Black Prince, and after his death, to his father King Edward the Third. Now as his master enjoyed three crowns, so under him in his three kingdoms this his chaplain did partake successively of three mitres, being first a bishop in Gascony, then archbishop of Dublin in Ireland, and afterwards bishop of Chichester in England; not grudging to be degraded in dignity to be preferred in profit. At last he was consecrated archbishop of York; and was the first and last native which that city saw the least of infants and, in his time, when man, the greatest therein. Yet he enjoyed his place but a short time, dying January 6, Anno Domini 1398.

THOMAS MORTON was born, anno 1564, in the city of York, whose father Richard Morton, allied to Cardinal Morton archbishop of Canterbury, was a mercer (I have been informed the first of that calling, in that city sure) of such repute that no mercers for many years by-past were of any eminency, but either immediately or mediately were apprentices unto him. He was bred in York School, where he was schoolfellow with Guy Fawkes, which I note, partly to shew that loyalty and treason may be educated under the same roof, partly to give a check to the received opinion that Fawkes was a Fleming, no native Englishman.

He was bred in Saint John's College in Cambridge, and chosen fellow thereof, to a fellowship to which he had no more propriety than his own merit, before eight competitors for the place, equally capable with himself, and better befriended.

He was successively preferred dean of Gloucester, Winchester; bishop of Chester, Coventry and Lichfield, and Durham. The foundation which he laid of foreign correspondency with eminent persons of different persuasions, when he attended as chaplain to the Lord Eure (sent by King James ambassador to the king of Denmark and many princes of Germany) he built upon unto the day of his death.

In the late Long Parliament the displeasure of the House of Commons fell heavy upon him; partly for subscribing the bishops' protestation for their votes in parliament, partly for refusing to resign the seal of his bishopric, and baptizing a daughter of John earl of Rutland with the sign of the cross; two faults which, compounded together, in the judgment of honest and wise men, amounted to a high innocence.

Yet the parliament allowed him eight hundred pounds a year (a portion above any of his brethren) for his maintenance. But alas, the trumpet of their charity gave an uncertain sound, not assigning by whom or whence this sum should be paid. Indeed the severe votes of the parliament ever took full effect, according to his observation who did anagram it, VOTED (OUTED). But their merciful votes found not so free performance. However, this good bishop got a thousand pounds out of Goldsmiths' Hall, which afforded him his support in his old age.

The nib of his pen was unpartially divided into two equal moieties; the one writing against faction, in defence of three innocent ceremonies; the other against superstition, witness *The Grand Imposture,* and other worthy works.

He solemnly proffered unto me (pardon me, reader, if I desire politicly to twist my own with his memory, that they may both survive together) in these sad times to maintain me to live with him; which courteous offer, as I could not conveniently accept, I did thankfully refuse. Many of the nobility deservedly honoured him, though none more than John earl of Rutland, to whose kinsman, Roger earl of Rutland, he formerly had been chaplain. But let not two worthy baronets be forgotten: Sir George Savile, who so civilly paid him his purchased annuity of two hundred pounds, with all proffered advantages; and Sir Henry Yelverton, at whose house he died, aged 95, at Easton Maudit in Northamptonshire, 1659.

RICHARD STOCK was born [1569?] in this city; bred scholar of the house in Saint John's College in Cambridge, and designed fellow of Sidney, though not accepting thereof. He was afterwards minister of All Hallows, Bread Street, in London, by the space of thirty-two years, till the day of his death; where, if in health, he omitted not to preach twice every Lord's day, with the approbation of all that were judicious and religious.

No minister in England had his pulpit supplied by fewer strangers. Doctor Davenant,[1] afterwards bishop of Sarum (whose father was his parishioner) was his constant auditor, while lying in London. His

(1) John Davenant (1576-1641) Fuller's uncle.

preaching was most profitable, converting many and confirming more in religion; so that, appearing with comfort at the day of judgment, he might say, "Behold, I and the children that God hath given me." He was zealous in his life, a great reformer of profanations on the Sabbath, prevailing with some companies to put off their wonted festivals from Mondays to Tuesdays, that the Lord's day might not be abused by the preparation for such entertainments. Though he preached oft in neighbouring churches, he never neglected his own, being wont to protest that it was more comfortable to him to win one of his own parish than twenty others.

Preaching at Saint Paul's Cross when young, it was ill taken at his mouth that he reproved the inequality of rates in the city (burdening the poor to ease the rich); and he was called a *green-head* for his pains. But, being put up in his latter days to preach on the lord mayor's election, and falling on the same subject, he told them, "That a *grey-head* spake now what a *green-head* had said before." He died April 20, Anno Domini 1626, with a great lamentation of all, but especially of his parishioners.

Sir Robert Carr [Earl of Somerset] was born in this city, on this occasion. Thomas Carr, his father, laird of Ferniehurst, a man of great lands and power in the south of Scotland, was very active for Mary Queen of Scots; and on that account forced to fly his land, came to York. Now although he had been a great inroader of England, yet, for some secret reason of state, here he was permitted safe shelter; during which time Robert his son was born. This was the reason why the said Robert refused to be naturalized by act of our parliament, as needless for him born in the English dominions.

I have read how his first making at court was by breaking of his leg at a tilting in London, whereby he came first to the cognizance of King James. Thus a fair starting with advantage in the notice of a prince is more than half way in the race to his favour. King James reflected on him whose father was a kind confessor for the cause of the queen his mother. Besides, the young gentleman had a handsome person, and a conveniency of desert. Honours were crowded upon him; made baron, viscount, earl of Somerset, knight of the Garter, warden of the Cinque Ports, &c.

He was a well-natured man, not mischievous with his might, doing himself more hurt than any man else. For, abate one foul fact,[1] with the appendance and consequences thereof, notoriously known, and he will appear deserving no foul character to posterity; but for the same he was banished the court, lived and died very privately [1645].

THE FAREWELL

To take our leave of this loyal city, I desire that some lucrative trade may be set up therein to repair her former losses with advantage. Meantime I

(1) The imprisonment of his friend Sir Thomas Overbury (see Gloucestershire, p. 196). Carr was James I's great favourite until displaced by Buckingham.

rejoice that the archiepiscopal see is restored thereunto; not despairing but that, in due time (if the supreme authority adjudge it fit) the court of the presidency of the north may be re-erected therein, presuming the country will be eased and city enriched thereby, as the loadstone which will attract much company, and by consequence commodity thereunto.

Let me add, I am informed that Sir Thomas Widdrington, a person accomplished in all arts (as well as in his own profession of the laws), hath made great progress in his exact description of this city.[1] Nor do I more congratulate the happiness of York coming under so able a pen, than condole my own infelicity, whose unsuccessful attendance hitherto could not compass speech with this worthy knight. Sure I am, when this his work is set forth, then indeed York shall be—what? a city most completely illustrated in all the antiquities and remarkables thereof.

(1) Sir Thomas Widdrington (*d.* 1664) speaker of the House of Commons, who held important offices under Charles I and during the Protectorate. His history of York was not published until 1897.

WALES

THIS principality hath the Severn sea on the south; Irish ocean on the west and north; England on the east, anciently divided from it by the river Severn, since by a ditch drawn with much art and industry from the mouth of Dee to the mouth of Wye. From east to west (Wye to Saint David's) is an hundred, from north to south (Carlion to Holyhead) is an hundred and twenty miles.

The ditch, or trench, lately mentioned, is called Clauhd-Offa, because made by King Offa, who cruelly enacted, that what Welshman soever was found on the east side of this ditch should forfeit his right hand. A law long since cancelled, and for many ages past the Welsh have come peaceably over that place; and good reason, bringing with them both their right hands and right hearts, no less loyally than valiantly to defend England against all enemies, being themselves under the same sovereign united thereunto.

It consisteth of three parts, the partition being made by Roderic the Great, about the year 877, dividing it betwixt his three sons: 1. *North Wales,* whose princes chiefly resided at Aberfrow; 2. *Powys,* whose princes resided at Mathravall; 3. *South Wales,* whose princes resided at Dynefar.

This division, in fine, proved the confusion of Wales; whose princes were always at war, not only against the English, their common foe, but mutually with themselves, to enlarge or defend their dominions.

Of these three, North Wales was the chief as doth plainly appear: first, because Roderic left it [to] Merfin his eldest son. Secondly, because the princes thereof were by way of eminency styled the Princes of Wales, and sometimes Kings of Aberfrow. Thirdly, because, as the king of Aberfrow paid to the king of London yearly three-score and three pounds by way of tribute, so the same sum was paid to him by the princes of Powys and South Wales.

However, South Wales was of the three the larger, richer, fruitfuller; therefore called by the Welsh *Deheubarth;* that is, "the right side," because nearer the sun. But that country, being constantly infested with the invasions of the English and Flemings, had North Wales preferred before it, as more entire, and better secured from such annoyances. Hence it was, that whilst the Welsh tongue in the south is so much mingled and corrupted, in North Wales it still retaineth the purity thereof.

The Soil

It is not so champaign and level, and by consequence not so fruitful as England; mostly rising up into hills and mountains of a lean and hungry nature; yet so that the ill quality of the ground is recompensed by the good quantity thereof.

A right worshipful knight in Wales, who had a fair estate therein, his rents resulting from much barren ground, heard an English gentleman (perchance out of intended opposition) to brag that he had in England so much ground worth forty shillings an acre. "You," said he, "have ten yards of velvet, and I have ten score of frieze; I will not exchange with you." This is generally true of all Wales, that much ground doth make up the rent; and yet in proportion they may lose nothing thereby, compared to estates in other countries.

However, there are in Wales most pleasant meadows along the sides of rivers; and as the sweetest flesh is said to be nearest the bones, so most delicious valleys are interposed betwixt these mountains.

NATURAL COMMODITIES

SILVER

Tully (a better orator than historian, yet better historian than metallist) affirmeth that Britain affordeth *ne micam auri vel argenti,* (not a grain of gold or silver); understand him what in his age was discovered. Otherwise Wales, and especially Cardiganshire, yields ROYAL MINES, where the silver holds standard, and pays with profit for the separation from lead, and the refining thereof, as by the ensuing particulars will appear.

1. Six mountains there are in Cardiganshire (pardon, British reader, if I spell them rather after our English pronunciation than the Welsh orthography); viz. Comsomelock, Tallabant, Gadarren, Bromefloid, Geginnon, and Cummerum.

2. The Romans first began to mine here, as appears by their coins found therein, working in trenches, not above twenty or four-and-twenty fathom deep, and found plenty of lead.

3. The Danes and Saxons were wrought by *sheafts;* so they call what is long and narrow; whether mounting into the air (as spires of steeples) or sinking into the earth, as their pits here, an hundred fathoms deep.

4. They found great plenty of lead; but at last deserted their works, either because the vein of metal failed, or they drowned with the irruption of water.

5. Customer Smith, about the latter end of the reign of Queen Elizabeth, discovered silver in Comsomelock; and sent it up to the Tower of London, with great expense, to be coined.

6. After his death, the design was prosecuted, and more perfected by Sir Hugh Myddelton, knight; coining the silver to his great charge, as his predecessor, at the Tower.

7. After the death of Sir Hugh, Sir Francis Godolphin of Cornwall, knight, and Thomas Bushell, esquire, undertook the work.

8. King Charles, for their greater encouragement, and sparing their expense, granted them power of coinage at Aberrusky in this county.

9. Thomas Bushell (Sir Francis dying soon after, and Comsomelock being deserted) adventured on the other five mountains.

10. Not disheartened that the first year and half afforded no effectual discovery, at last these mines yielded one hundred pounds a week (besides lead amounting to half as much) coined at Aberrusky aforesaid.

11. The pence, groats, shillings, half-crowns, &c. of this silver, had the ostrich feathers (the arms of Wales) for distinction stamped on them.

Then came our civil wars, and discomposed all the work; when mattocks must be turned into spears, and shovels into shields; or else probably before this time the project had arrived at a greater perfection.

Here, by the way, it is richly worth the observing, how the modern manner of mining exceedeth what was formerly used; for, thirty years since, they began at the top of a mountain, digging directly downwards with their shafts, which was subject to a double mischief, of damps and drowning. Besides, vast was the expense before they could come to the bowels of the mountain, wherein the ore (if any) was most probably expected.

Since, they have gone a more compendious way by adits, making their entrance some five feet and a half high (and perchance as broad) into the mountain, at the lowest level thereof, so that all the water they meet with conveyeth itself away, as in a channel, by the declivity of the place. And thus they penetrate the most expeditious way athwart the middle thereof, which bringeth them to the speediest discovery of the metal therein.

But the rarest invention is the supplying of the miners with fresh air, which is performed by two men's blowing wind by a pair of bellows on the outside of the adit, into a pipe of lead, daily lengthened as the mine is made longer, whereby the candle in the mine is daily kept burning, and the diggers recruited constantly with a sufficiency of breath. This invention was the master-piece of Sir Francis Bacon, Lord Verulam; and not only acknowledged by Thomas Bushell, his grateful servant, but also effectually prosecuted by him; a person innated with a public spirit, if he might meet with proportionable encouragement.[1]

And here methinks, it were fitting (pardon, reader, a short digression) that rewards should be given to such undertakers who are the discoverers of profitable projects; and not only to such who exactly hit the mark, but even to those who ingeniously miss it, because their aberrations may be directions to others. And though many tympanies and false conceptions would happen, yet, amongst many miscarriages, some pregnant wits would happily be delivered of rare invention; especially if the state would be pleased to be their midwife, favourably to encourage them.

LEAD

This is found in many places in Wales, but in Carnarvonshire the best in many respects. First, because so near the sea, so that they may cast the ore into the ship. Metals elsewhere are digged, as out of the bowels of the earth, so out of the bowels of the land; I mean, so far from any conveyance by water, that the expense of the portage swallows much of the profits thereof; which charge is here avoided. Secondly, for the plenty. Lastly, for the purity thereof, insomuch that there was great probability for a long time that it would have proved a mine royal, which hope was frustrated at last, to the great gain of the owners thereof.

(1) Thomas Bushell (1594-1674) was a mining engineer of great resourcefulness. He became page to Bacon, who taught him what was then known of mineralogy. Several times Bacon paid debts for Bushell's various experiments and speculations. He was patronised by Charles I, and was a devoted royalist in the Civil War; but managed, however, to lease crown mines from Cromwell.

For a leaden mine is a silver mine to such subjects as possess it; whilst a silver mine is but a leaden one unto them from whom the property is taken, as then accruing to the crown or state, by virtue of its prerogative.

GOATS

In Latin *capri, a carpendo,* from cropping (therefore forbidden to be kept in some places, because destructive to young woods) are, when young, most nimble and frisking (whence our English phrase *to caper*); but afterwards put on so great gravity, that an he-goat is recounted by wise Agur amongst "the four creatures which are comely in going." Yea, if that ornamental excrement which groweth beneath the chin be the standard of wisdom, they carry it from Aristotle himself. They are strong above their proportion, and an he-goat will beat a ram of equal bigness, Hence it is that, in Daniel, the Persian monarchy is compared to a ram, and the Macedonian, which subdued the Persian, resembled to a goat. They can clamber the highest hills, without help of a ladder; delighting in steep and craggy places, seeming rather to hang than stand, as they are feeding.

Their flesh, disguised with good cookery, may deceive a judicious palate, as it did Isaac's, for venison. Of their skins excellent gloves are made, which may be called our English cordovan, soft, supple and stretching, whence the expression of cheverel-consciences, which will stretch any way for advantage.[1] Coarse coverings are made of their shag; God himself not despising the present of goat's hair, which made the outward case of the tabernacle. Their milk is accounted cordial against consumptions; yea, their very stench is used for a perfume in Arabia the Happy, where they might surfeit of the sweetness of spices, if not hereby allayed. In a word, goats are best for food, where sheep cannot be had.

Plenty of these are bred in Wales, especially in Montgomeryshire, which mindeth me of a pleasant passage during the restraint of Lady Elizabeth. When she was so strictly watched by Sir Henry Bedingfield that none were admitted access unto her, a goat was espied by a merry fellow (one of the warders) walking along with her. Whereupon, taking the goat on his shoulders, he in all haste hurried him to Sir Henry. "I pray, Sir," said he, "examine this fellow, whom I found walking with her grace; but what talk they had I know not, not understanding his language. He seems to me a stranger, and I believe a Welshman by his frieze coat."

To return to our subject; I am not so knowing in goats, as either to confirm or confute what Pliny reports, that *adhuc lactantes generant* (they beget young ones, whilst they themselves as yet suck their dams.) He addeth that they are great enemies to the olive trees (which they embarren with licking it) and therefore are never sacrificed to Minerva. Sure I am, a true deity accepted them for his service; as many kids well nigh as lambs being offered in the Old Testament.

(1) *Cordovan* is Spanish goat-skin leather, made at Cordova; *cheverel* is literally kid, used in the sense of kid-leather, easily stretched.

THE MANUFACTURES

The British generally bearing themselves high on the account of their gentle extraction, have spirits which can better comport with designs of sudden danger than long difficulty; and are better pleased in the employing of their valour than their labour. Indeed some souls are over-lovers of liberty, so that they mistake all industry to be degrees of slavery. I doubt not but posterity may see the Welsh commodities improved by art far more than the present age doth behold; the English as yet as far excelling the Welsh, as the Dutch exceed the English, in manufactures. But let us instance in such as this country doth afford.

FRIEZE

This is a coarse kind of cloth, than which none warmer to be worn in winter, and the finest sort thereof very fashionable and genteel. Prince Henry had a frieze suit, by which he was known many weeks together; and when a bold courtier checked him for appearing so often in one suit, "Would," said he, "that the cloth of my country (being Prince of Wales) would last always." Indeed it will daily grow more into use, especially since the gentry of the land, being generally much impoverished, abate much of their gallantry, and lately resigned rich clothes to be worn by those, not whose persons may best become them, but whose purses can best pay for the price thereof.

CHEESE

This is milk, by art so consolidated that it will keep uncorrupted for some years. It was anciently, and is still the staple food for armies in their marching; witness when David was sent with ten cheeses to recruit the provisions of his brethren; and when Barzillai with cheeses (amongst other food) victualled the army of king David. Such as are made in this country are very tender and palatable; and once one merrily (without offence, I hope) thus derived the pedigree thereof:

> Adams nawn Cusson was her by her birth,
> Ap curds, ap milk, ap cow, ap grass, ap earth.

Foxes are said to be the best tasters of the fineness of flesh, flies of the sweetest grapes, and mice of the tenderest cheese; and the last (when they could compass choice in that kind) have given their verdict for the goodness of the Welsh. What should be the reason that so many people have an antipathy against cheese (more than any one manner of meat) I leave to the skilful in the mysteries of nature to decide.

METHEGLEN

Some will have this word of Greek extraction from μέθυ αἰγλήεν, contracted αἰγλῆν. But the British will not so let go their non-countryman Matthew Glin, but will have it *purum potum Cambricum,* wholly of Welsh original. Whencesoever the word is made, the liquor is compounded of water, honey and other ingredients, being most wholesome for man's body. Pollio Romulus, who was an hundred years old, being asked of Augustus Caesar by what means especially he had so long preserved his vigour both of mind and body, made answer, *Intus mulso, foris oleo* (by taking metheglen inward, and oil outward.)

It differeth from mead, *ut vinum a lora,* as wine from that weak stuff which is the last running from the grapes pressed before. It is a most generous liquor, as it is made in this country; insomuch that had Mercator, who so highly praised the mead of Egra, for the best in the world; I say, had he tasted of this Welsh hydromel, he would have confined his commendation to Germany alone, and allowed ours the precedency. Queen Elizabeth, who by the Tudors was of Welsh descent, much loved this her native liquor, recruiting an annual stock thereof for her own use; and here take, if you please,

The receipt thereof. First, gather a bushel of sweet-briar leaves, and a bushel of thyme, half a bushel of rosemary, and a peck of bay-leaves. Seethe all these (being well washed) in a furnace of fair water; let them boil the space of half an hour, or better, and then pour out all the water and herbs into a vat, and let it stand till it be but milk-warm; then strain the water from the herbs, and take to every six gallons of water one gallon of the finest honey, and put into the *boorn,*[1] and labour it together half an hour; then let it stand two days, stirring it well twice or thrice each day. Then take the liquor, and boil it anew; and when it doth seethe, skim it as long as there remaineth any dross. When it is clear, put it into the vat as before, and there let it be cooled. You must then have in readiness a kind of new ale or beer, which, as soon as you have emptied, suddenly whelm it upside down, and set it up again, and presently put in the metheglen, and let it stand three days a-working. And then tun it up in barrels, tying at every tap-hole (by a pack-thread) a little bag of beaten cloves and mace,[2] to the value of an ounce. It must stand half a year before it be drunk.

THE BUILDINGS

For their buildings, generally they are like those of the old Britons, neither big nor beautiful, but such as their ancestors in this isle formerly lived in; for when Caratacus, that valiant British general (who for nine years resisted here the Romans' puissance) after his captivity and imprisonment was enlarged, and carried about to see the magnificence of Rome, "Why do you," said he, "so greedily desire our poor cottages, whereas you have such stately and magnificent palaces of your own?"

The simplicity of their common building for private persons may be conjectured by the palaces of their princes; for Hoell Dha prince of Wales, about the year 800, built a house for his own residence of white hurdles, or watling; thereof called Ty-Gwin, that is, the White House, or White Hall if you please.

However there are brave buildings in Wales, though not Welsh buildings, many stately castles which the English erected therein. And though such of them as survive at this day may now be beheld as beauties, they were first intended as bridles to their country. Otherwise their private houses are very mean indeed. Probably they have read what

(1) That is the *wort* or boiled liquor.—F. (2) *Mace* = a spice consisting of the dried outer covering of the nutmeg

Master Camden writes, that the building of great houses was the bane of good housekeeping in England; and therefore they are contented with the worse habitations, as loath to lose their beloved hospitality; the rather because it hath been observed that such Welsh buildings as conform to the English mode have their chimneys, though more convenient, less charitable, seeing as fewer eyes are offended, fewer bellies are fed, with the smoking thereof.

But, though the lone houses in Wales be worse than those in England, their market towns generally are built better than ours; the gentry, it seems, having many of their habitations therein.

PROVERBS

As long as a Welsh pedigree. Men (who are made heralds in other countries) are born heralds in Wales; so naturally are all there inclined to know and keep their descents, which they derive from great antiquity; so that any Welsh gentleman (if this be not a tautology) can presently climb up, by the stairs of his pedigree, into princely extraction. I confess, some Englishmen make a mock of their long pedigree (whose own, perchance, are short enough if well examined.) I cannot but commend their care in preserving the memory of their ancestors, conformable herein to the custom of the Hebrews. The worse I wish their long pedigree, is broad possessions, that so there may be the better symmetry betwixt their extractions and estates.

THE WORTHIES

SAINT PEDROG was a Welsh-Irish-Cornish man. He had his birth in Wales, but breeding in Ireland, according to the mode of that age, wherein all British sailed over into Ireland (as the English in after-ages did into France) there to have their education in all learned sciences. Who would have thought to have found Helicon among the bogs, as indeed it was at that time? Pedrog, after twenty years reading good authors there, came over into Cornwall, and fixed himself nigh the Severn sea, in a small oratory called Petrok-stow (the station or abiding-place of Pedrog), now corruptly Padstow, where many eminent scholars were brought up under him. He wrote a book of *Solitary Life,* whereto he was much addicted.

I confess Pedrog is somewhat degraded, as entered under the topic of writers, who is reputed a saint; and I remember a handsome church in Exeter dedicated to his memory, who flourished anno 550.

[NEST or] NESTA. Hunger maketh men eat what otherwise they would let alone, not to say cast away: the cause I confess (wanting matter to furnish out our description) inviting me to meddle with this *memorable* (not *commendable*) person.

1. She was daughter to Gruffydd, prince of Wales; 2. Wife to Bernard de Newmarch, a noble Norman, and lord by conquest of this county; 3. Mother to Mahel, an hopeful gentleman, and Sibyl his sister; 4. Harlot to a young man, whose name I neither do, nor desire to know.

It happened, Mahel having got this stallion into his power, used him very hardly, yet not worse than he deserved. Nesta, madded hereat, came into open court, and on her oath, before King Henry the Second, publicly protested (no manna like revenge to malicious minds, not caring to wound their foes, though through themselves) that "Mahel was none of Newmarch's son, but begotten on her in adultery."

This, if true, spake her dishonesty; if false, her perjury; true or false, her peerless impudence. Hereby she disinherited her son, and settled a vast territory on Sibyl her sole daughter, married afterwards to Milo earl of Hereford.[1] [*c.* 1095—*c.* 1114]

GIRALDUS CAMBRENSIS, whose surname, say some, was Fitz-Gerald, say others, was De Barri; and I believe the latter, because he saith so himself in his book, *De Vita Sua;* and was born [1146] at Tenby in Pembrokeshire.

His father, William de Barri, an Englishman; his mother, Angareth, the daughter of Nesta, daughter of Rhys, prince of South Wales.

He was nephew to David, the second bishop of Saint David's, by whom he was made archdeacon of Brecknock. He was wont to complain that the English did not love him because his mother was a Welsh woman; and the Welsh did hate him because his father was an Englishman; though, by his excellent writings, he deserved of England well, of Wales better, and of Ireland best of all; making a topographical description of all three; but acting in the last as a secretary under King John, with great industry and expense. Yea, he was a great traveller, as far as Jerusalem itself, and wrote *De Mirabilibus Terrae Sanctae,* so that he might be styled Giraldus Anglicus, Hibernicus, Hierosolymitanus, though it was his mind and modesty only to be Cambrensis.

One may justly wonder that, having all dimensions requisite to preferment, his birth, broad acquaintance, deep learning, long life (living above seventy years) he never attained to any considerable dignity. Indeed for a long time no preferment was proffered him above a beggarly bishopric in Ireland; and at last the see of Saint David's was the highest place he attained. Whilst some impute this to his *planet,* the malignant influence whereof hath blasted men of the most merit; his *pride,* some men counting it their due for preferment to court them, and that it is enough for them to *receive,* too much to *reach* after it; his *profitableness* to be employed in meaner places; some having gotten an useful servant, love to wear them out in working, and (as gardeners keep their hedges close cut, that they may spread the broader) maintain them mean, that they may be the more industrious.

Giraldus himself tells us the true reason that he was ever beheld *oculo novercali,* because being a Welshman by the surer side; and then such the antipathy of the English, they thought no good could come out of Wales. Sad, that so worthy a man should *poenas dare patriae et matris suae.*

Being at last, as we have said, made bishop of Saint David's, he went to Rome, and there stickled for an exemption of that his see from Canterbury, and to make it an absolute metropolitan, whereby he highly offended

(1) Fuller has hopelessly confused the mistress of Henry I with two other women, but the story is retained for its characteristic touches.

Hubert archbishop of Canterbury. But Giraldus, after long debates, being rather over-borne with bribes than overcome in cause, returned *re infecta,* died, and was buried in his own cathedral, about the year 1220.

MADOG, son to Owain Gwynedd ap Gruffyth ap Conan, and brother to David ap Owain Gwynedd, prince of North Wales, was born [1150] probably at Aberfraw in Anglesey (now a mean town) then the principal palace of their royal residence. He made a sea voyage westward; and by all probability, those names of Cape de Breton in Noruinberg, and Penguin in part of the Northern America (for a white rock and a white-headed bird, according to the British) were relics of this discovery. If so, then let the Genoese and Spaniards demean themselves as younger brethren, and get their portions in pensions in those parts paid as well as they may, owning us Britons (so may the Welsh and English as an united nation style themselves) for the heirs, to whom the solid inheritance of America doth belong, for the first discovery thereof. The truth is, a good navy, with a strong land army therein, will make these probabilities of Madog evident demonstrations; and without these, in cases of this kind, the strongest arguments are of no validity. This sea voyage was undertaken by Madog about the year 1170.[1] [*d.* 1180?]

WALTER DE COUTANCES. Who would not conclude him, from his surname, born at Constance on the Boden Zee in Switzerland? But we have a *constat* for his British nativity. He was preferred first, archdeacon of Oxford, then bishop of Lincoln, then archbishop of Rouen, by King Richard the First. A man of much merit, besides his fidelity to his sovereign, whom he attended to Palestine, through many perils by sea and by land; insomuch that there want not those who will have him named De Constantiis, from the expressive plural, relating to his constancy to his master in all conditions.

No doubt he had waited on him in his return through Austria, and shared with him the miseries of his captivity, if not formally remanded into England, to retrench the tyranny of William of Longchamp bishop of Ely, which he effectually performed. He had afterwards a double honour, first to inter King Richard at Fontevrault, then to invest King John with the principality of Normandy, as being the prime prelate therein. [*d.* 1207]

EDWARD II, the fourth (but first surviving) son of King Edward the First and Queen Eleanor, was born at Carnarvon in this county, April 25, 1284. No prince ever ascended the English throne with greater, or used it with less advantage to himself.

First, though his father had in a manner surprised the Welsh to accept him for their prince (pleading his royal extraction, birth in Wales, inability to speak a word of English, and innocence that none could tax him with actual sin); yet I find them not for his father's fallacy to think the worse of his son—*sic juvat esse deceptos*—and generally they accepted

(1) Madog is a very shadowy figure, and his supposed discovery of America now receives less support than formerly. Southey's *Madoc* is based on his adventures.

him, as preferring that a prince should be put with wit rather than with violence upon them.

In England he succeeded to a wise and victorious father, who happily had hit the expedient to be both beloved and feared by his subjects, leaving the land in so good a posture for government, that touch the wheel, and it would turn in the right track itself. But this Edward first estranged himself from his subjects, and in effect, subjected himself to a stranger, Piers Gaveston, his French minion, and after his execution, to the two Despensers, who, though native Englishmen, were equally odious to the English for their insolence.

Hence it was that he first lost the love of his subjects, then of his queen (the vacuity of whose bed was quickly filled up) then his crown, then his life. Never any English king's case was so pitiful, and his person less pitied, all counting it good reason that he should give entertainment to that woe which his wilfulness had invited home to himself. His violent death happened at Berkeley Castle, September 21, 1327.

WILLIAM [BRITON or] BRETON was born (saith Bale and Pits, the latter alleging one Willot for his author) in Wales; bred a Franciscan at Grimsby in Lincolnshire. I will not quarrel his Cambrian extraction; but may safely remind the reader, that there was an ancient family of the Britons at Ketton in Rutland next Lincolnshire, where this William had his education.

But let this Breton be Brito (believing the allusion in sound not the worst evidence for his Welsh original) sure it is, he was a great scholar and deep divine; the writer of many books both in verse and prose; and of all, his master-piece was an exposition of all the hard words of the Bible, which thus begins:

Difficiles studio partes quas Biblia[1] *gestat,*
Pandere; sed nequeo, latebras nisi qui manifestat,
Auxiliante qui cui vult singula praestat,
Dante juvamen eo, nihil insuperabile restat, &c.

Hard places which the Bible doth contain,
I study to expound; but all in vain,
Without God's help, who darkness doth explain,
And with His help nothing doth hard remain, &c.

Such the reputation of his book, that in the controversy betwixt Standish bishop of Saint Asaph and Erasmus (unequal contest) the former appeals to Breton's book about the interpretation of a place in Scripture. This William died at Grimsby, Anno Domini 1356.

OWEN GLENDOWER was born [1359?] in his ancient patrimony of Glendower Wye in Flintshire; then bred in London a student in the common law, till he became a courtier, and servant to King Richard the Second; after whose death, this Owen being then on the wrong side of preferment, retired to this his native county, where there arose a difference betwixt him and his neighbour the Lord Grey of Ruthin about a piece of common, which Owen by force recovered, and killed the Lord Grey.

(1) A nominative case singular, according to the barbarism of that age.

There wanted not many to spur his posting ambition, by telling him that he was the true heir to all North Wales, and now or never the time to regain it; that the injuries he had already offered the English were above pardon, and no way left to secure himself, but by committing greater. There needeth no torch to light tinder, where a spark will do the deed; and hereupon Owen brake out into open rebellion.

The worst was, being angry with the king, his revenge fell upon God, burning down the fair cathedrals of Bangor and Saint Asaph. His destructive nature delighted in doing mischief to others, though no good to himself. King Henry the Fourth found it more facile by far to depose King Richard than subdue this Owen, who had taken Roger Mortimer earl of March (and next heir to the crown) prisoner. [*d.* 1416?]

NICHOLAS OF HEREFORD. I have presumptions to persuade myself (though possibly not to prevail with the reader) to believe him of British extraction. He was bred doctor of divinity in Oxford, and a secular priest, betwixt whose profession and friary there was an ancient antipathy. But our Hereford went higher, to defy most popish principles, and maintain, 1. That in the Eucharist, after the consecration of the elements, bread and wine still remained; 2. That bishops and all clergymen ought to be subject to their respective princes; 3. That monks and friars ought to maintain themselves by their own labour; 4. That all ought to *regle* their lives, not by the pope's decrees, but Word of God.

From these his four cardinal positions many heretical opinions were by his adversaries deduced (or rather detracted); and no wonder they did rack his words, who did desire to torture his person.

From Oxford he was brought to London; and there, with Philip Repington, was made to recant his opinions publicly at Saint Paul's Cross, 1382. See their several success. REPINGTON, like a violent renegado, proved a persecutor of his party, for which he was rewarded, first with the bishopric of Lincoln, then with a cardinal's cap. HEREFORD did too much to displease his conscience, and yet not enough to please his enemies; for the jealousy of Archbishop Arundel persecuted and continued him always a prisoner.

The same with the latter was the success of John Purvey, his partner in opinions, whom T. Walden termeth the Lollards' Library. But they locked up this library, that none might have access unto it, keeping him and Hereford in constant durance. I will say nothing in excuse of their recantation; nor will I revile them for the same, knowing there is more requisite to make one valiant under a temptation, than only to call him coward who is foiled therewith. Yet I must observe, that such as consult carnal councils to avoid afflictions (getting out by the window of their own plotting, not the door of Divine Providence) seldom enjoy their own deliverance. In such cases our Saviour's words are always (without parties' repentance) *spiritually* and often *literally* true: "He that findeth his life shall lose it." And although we read not that this Hereford was put to death, he lost the life of his life, his liberty and lustre, dwindling away in obscurity as to the time and place of his death.

[*fl.* 1390-1417]

DAVID BOYS [or BOSCHUS]. Let not Kent pretend unto him, wherein his surname is so ancient and numerous, our author assuring us of his British extraction.[1] He studied in Oxford (saith Leland) no less to his own honour, than the profit of others reaping much benefit by his books. Having his breeding at Oxford, he had a bounty for Cambridge; and compassing the writings of John Barningham his fellow-Carmelite, he got them fairly transcribed in four volumes, and bestowed them on the library in Cambridge, where Bale beheld them in his time. He was very familiar (understand it in a good way) with Eleanor Cobham, duchess of Gloucester, whence we collect him at least a parcel-Wycliffite. Of the many books he wrote, fain would I see that intituled *Of Double Immortality,* whether intending thereby the immortality of soul and body, or of the memory here and soul hereafter. I would likewise satisfy myself in his book about the madness of the Hagarens, whether the Mahometans be not meant thereby, pretending themselves descended from Sarah, when indeed they are the issue of the bond-woman. He was prefect of the Carmelites in Gloucester, where he died 1451.

REGINALD PECOCK was born [1395?] in Wales; bred in King's (commonly, saith Bale, called Oriel) College in Oxford, where for his learning and eloquence, he proceeded doctor in divinity; bishop first of Saint Asaph, then of Chichester. For twenty years together he favoured the opinions of Wycliffe, and wrote many books in defence thereof, until, in a synod held at Lambeth by Thomas Bourchier archbishop of Canterbury, 1457, he was made to recant at Paul's Cross (his books being burnt before his eyes) confuted with seven solid arguments, thus reckoned up, *authoritate, vi, arte, fraude, metu, terrore, et tyrannide.*[2]

Charitable men behold this his recantation as his suffering, and the act of his enemies; some account it rather a slip than a fall; others a fall, whence afterwards he did arise. It seems his recanting was little satisfactory to his adversaries, being never restored to his bishopric, but confined to a poor pension in a mean monastery, where he died obscurely; though others say he was privily made away in prison. He is omitted by Pitseus in his catalogue of writers, a presumption that he apprehended him finally dissenting from the popish persuasion. [*d.* 1460?]

HENRY STAFFORD, duke of Buckingham [*b.* 1454?]. Though Humphrey his father had a fair castle at, and large lands about Stafford (whereof he was earl) yet his nativity is most probably placed in Brecknockshire, where he had Brecknock castle, and a principality about it. This was he who with both his hands set up Richard the Third on the throne; endeavouring afterwards, with his hands and teeth too, to take him down, but in vain.

He was an excellent spokesman, though I cannot believe that his long oration (to persuade the Londoners to side with the usurper) was ever uttered by him *in terminis* as it lieth in Sir Thomas More's history.

(1) Bale. (2) Pecock never supported the lollards and frequently wrote against them. By his writings, in magnificent 15th century English, he managed to alienate all sections of theological opinion. For the last few years of his life he lived and died probably at Thorney Abbey.

Thus the Roman generals provided themselves of valour; and Livy (as he represented them) stocked them with eloquence. Yet we may be well assured that this our duke either did or would have said the same; and he is the orator who effects that he aimeth at, this duke being unhappily happy therein.

Soon after, not remorse for what he had done, but revenge for what King Richard would not do (denying his desire) put him on the project of unravelling what he had woven before. But his fingers were entangled in the threads of his former web; the king compassing him into his clutches, betrayed by Ralph Bannister his servant. The sheriff seized this duke in Shropshire, where he was digging a ditch in a disguise. How well he managed the mattock and spade, I know not. This I know, that in a higher sense, "He had made a pit (to disinherit his sovereign) and digged it, and is falled into the ditch which he had made;"[1] being beheaded at Salisbury, without any legal trial, anno 1483.

SIR [RHYS OR] RICE AP THOMAS was never more than a knight, yet little less than a prince in Carmarthenshire, if the author of *Proelia Anglorum* may not be believed,

Ricius Thomas flos Cambro-Britannum.

King Henry the Seventh will himself witness his worth. To him, lately landed at Milford Haven with contemptible forces, this Sir Rice repaired with a considerable accession of choice soldiers, marching with them to Bosworth field, where he right valiantly behaved himself. That thrifty king, according to his cheap course of remuneration (rewarded gownmen in orders, by him most employed, with church livings, and swordsmen with honour) afterwards made Sir Rice knight of the order; and well might he give him a Garter, by whose effectual help he had recovered a crown.

Elmelin in this county was one of his principal seats, whose name and nature he altered, building and calling it Newcastle; and I believe it one of the latest castles in Wales, seeing since that time it hath been fashionable to demolish, not to erect, fortified houses.

As he appeared early, so he continued long in military action; for I find him, in the fourth year of King Henry the Eighth, conductor of five hundred light horse, at the pompous and expensive siege of Therouenne, where I meet his last mention in our English chronicles. [1449-1525]

HENRY TUDOR, son to Edmund earl of Richmond and Margaret his lady, was born at Pembroke in this county, Anno Domini 1457. In the reign of King Henry the Sixth, he was bred a child at court; when a young man he lived an exile in France, where he so learned to live of a little, that he contracted a habit of frugality, which he did not depose till the day of his death. Having vanquished King Richard the Third in the battle of Bosworth, and married Elizabeth eldest daughter to King Edward the Fourth, he reigned king of England by the name of Henry the Seventh.

(1) Psalms vii. 15.

He is generally esteemed the wisest of our English kings; and yet many conceive, that the Lord Bacon, writing his life, made him much wiser than he was, picking more prudence out of his actions than the king himself was privy to therein; and not content to allow him politic, endeavoured to make him policy itself.

Yet many think his judgment failed him, when refusing the fair proffer of Columbus for the discovery of America, who might therein have made a secret adventure, without any prejudice to the reputation of his wisdom. But such his wariness, he would not tamper with costly contingencies, though never so probable to be gainful; nor would he hazard a hook of silver to catch a fish of gold. He was the first king who secretly sought to abate the formidable greatness (the parent of many former rebellions) in the English peerage, lessening their dependencies, countenancing the commons, and encouraging the yeomanry with provisions against depopulations. However, hereby he did not free his successors from fear, but only exchanged their care, making the commons (who because more numerous, less managable) more absolute, and able in time to contest with sovereignty.

He survived his queen, by whom he had the true title to the crown, about five years. Some will say, that all the time he was king only by the courtesy of England, which I am sure he was loath to acknowledge. Others say he held the crown by conquest, which his subjects were as unwilling to confess. But let none dispute how he held, seeing he held it; having pope, parliament, power, purse, success, and some shadow of succession, on his side.

His greatest fault was grinding his subjects with grievous exactions. He was most magnificent in those structures he hath left to posterity; amongst which, his devotion to God is most seen in two chapels, the one at Cambridge, the other at Westminster; his charity to the poor in the hospital of the Savoy; his magnificence to himself in his own monument of gilded copper; and his vanity to the world, in building a ship called the Great Harry, of equal cost, saith some, with his chapel, which afterwards sunk into the sea, and vanished away in a moment.

He much employed bishops in his service, finding them honest and able. This politic king, at his palace at Richmond, April 21, 1509, ended his life, and was buried in the magnificent chapel aforesaid; on the same token that he ordered, by his last will and testament, that none save such of the blood royal (who should descend from his loins) should be buried in that place; straightly forbidding any other, of what degree or quality soever, to be interred therein. But only the will of the King of Heaven doth stand inviolable, whilst those of the most potent earthly princes are subject to be infringed.

ARTHUR BULKELEY [or BOKELEY] bishop of Bangor, was born either in Cheshire, or more probably in Anglesey. But it matters not much had he never been born, who, being bred doctor of the laws, had either never read, or wholly forgotten, or wilfully would not remember, the chapter "De Sacrilegio;" for he spoiled the bishopric, and sold the five bells; being so over-officious, that he would go down to the sea to see them shipped, which, in my mind, amounted to a second selling of them.

We have an English proverb of him who maketh a detrimental bargin to himself, "That he may put all the gains gotten thereby into his eye, and see nothing the worse." But Bishop Bulkeley saw much more the worse by what he had gotten, being himself suddenly deprived of his sight, who had deprived the tower of Bangor of the tongue thereof. Thus having ended his credit before his days, and his days before his life, and having sate in that see fourteen years, he died 1553.

WILLIAM GLYN, D.D., was born [1504?] at Heneglwys in Anglesey; bred in Queens' College in Cambridge, whereof he was master, until in the second of Queen Mary, he was preferred bishop of Bangor. An excellent scholar, and I have been assured by judicious persons, who have seriously perused the solemn disputations (printed in Master Foxe) betwixt the papists and protestants, that of the former none pressed his arguments with more strength and less passion than Doctor Glyn. Though constant to his own, he was not cruel to opposite judgments, as appeareth by the appearing of no persecution in his diocese, and his mild nature must be allowed at least *causa socia,* or the fellow cause thereof. He died in the first of Queen Elizabeth; and I have been informed that Jeffry Glyn, his brother, doctor of laws, built and endowed a free school at Bangor.

[*d.* 1558]

ROBERT RECORDE was born [1510?] in this country, *ex claris parentibus;* bred in Oxford where he proceeded doctor of physic. His soul did not live in the lane of a single science, but traversed the latitude of learning; witness his works. In *Arithmetic;* not so absolute in all numbers, before his time, but that by him it was set forth more complete. *Astrology;* the practical part whereof hath so great an influence upon physic. *Geometry;* whereof he wrote a book called *The Pathway to Knowledge,* and that easier and nearer than any before. *Physic; The Urinal of Physic*; and though it be commonly said, *Urina Meretrix,* yet his judicious rules have reduced that harlot to honesty, and in a great measure fixed the uncertainty thereof. *Metals;* his sight may seem to have accompanied the sunbeams into the bowels of the earth, piercing into those penetrales in his discoveries of, and discourses on, gold and silver (wherewith I believe him well stored) brass, tin, lead, and what not.

What shall I speak of his skill in anatomy, cosmography, music, whereof he read public lectures in Oxford?

As for his religion (say not this is of no concernment in a physician) I conjecture him to be a protestant; first, because he wrote of auricular confession, and *De Negotio Eucharistiae,* each whereof is a *noli me tangere* for a Romish layman to meddle with, according to popish principles; secondly, because so largely commended by Bale. But I dare conclude nothing herein, having not hitherto seen his treatises in divinity.[1]

[*d.* 1558?]

(1) Recorde was the first writer in English on arithmetic, geometry and astronomy, and first introduced algebra into England. He died in prison, probably in debt.

THOMAS PHAER [or PHAYER] was born [1510?] in Wales; and bred (I believe) first in Oxford, then in London; a general scholar, and well versed in the common law, wherein he wrote a book, *De Natura Brevium* (*Of the Nature of Writs*). Strange that he would come after Justice Fitzherbert, who formerly had written on the same subject. But probably Phaer's book (having never seen any who have seen it) treateth of writs in the court of Marches (whereto Wales was then subjected) and where the legal proceedings may be somewhat different from ours in England.

But the study of the law did not fadge[1] well with him, which caused him to change his copy, and proceeded doctor in physic. Now (though he made none) he, out of French, did translate many useful books. 1. *Of the Pestilence, and the Cure thereof.* 2. *A Book of Children.* 3. *Of the Nature of Simples.* 4. *The Regiment of Life.* He had also his diversion, some excursion into poetry, and translated Virgil's Æneid, *magna gravitate* (saith my author[2]) which our modern wits *will render with great dulness,* and avouch that he, instead of a Latin Virgil, hath presented us with an English Ennius, such the rudeness of his verse. But who knoweth not that English poetry is improved fifty in the hundred in this last century of years? He died, and was buried in London . . . [1560]

ALBAN HILL [or HYLL] was Britannus by birth. I confess Britannus doth not clearly carry his nativity for Wales, except it were additional Cambro-Britannus. But according to our peaceable promise premised, let him pass for this countryman, the rather because so many hills (and mountains too) therein. He was bred a doctor of physic, professing and practising most beyond the seas, more famous in foreign parts than in his native country. I find two eminent outlandishman, viz., Josias Simler, an Helvetian of Zurich, and Bassianus Landus, an Italian of Piacenza, charactering him to be *medicus nobilissimus ac optimus, et in omni disciplinarum genere optime versatus;* and that he wrote much upon Galen, and the anatomical part of physic; so that we may say with the poet,[3]

Ut littus, Hyla, Hyla, omne sonaret.

The shore resounded still,
Nothing but *Hill* and *Hill.*

I find no time affixed wherein he flourished; but, according to the received rule, *noscitur e socio,* he may, from his contemporaries, be collected in full lustre anno 1550. And it is remarkable that Wales had three eminent physicians, writers all in the same age [*d.* 1550]

SIR EDWARD CARNE is here placed with confidence, because assured to be a Welshman; and I find his family flourishing at Wenny in Glamorganshire. He was bred (I believe in Oxford) doctor of the civil law; and was knighted by Charles the Fifth, emperor.

The first public service he eminently appeared in was when King Henry the Eighth, having intelligence of the pope's intention shortly to cite him to appear at Rome, either in person or proxy, despatched him thither

(1) *Fadge*=agree. (2) Pits. (3) Virgil, *Ecloga* sexta.

for his excusator, to remonstrate that his grace was not bound by law so to appear.

This he effectually performed, pleading, that the emperor was so powerful at Rome, that he could not expect justice; declaring that, unless they desisted, he must appeal thence to the able men in some indifferent universities; and if this were refused, he protested a nullity in all that they did; a behaviour which spake him of no less valour than ability.

Queen Mary highly prized him, and no whit the less for his cordial appearing for King Henry in the matter of her mother's divorce; imputing it to the discharge of his credit and calling, in him who otherwise was a thorough-paced Romanist, and whom she employed her ambassador to the pope.

After her death, he still resided at Rome; and by command from Queen Elizabeth, repaired to Pope Paul the Fourth, to give him an account that his mistress was called to the crown of England; to whom the pope returned that "England was a fee of the church of Rome; and that she could not succeed, as illegitimate." A strange reply to a civil message, and fitting his mouth with whom it was a usual saying, "that he would have no prince in his compagnion, but all subject under his foot."

Besides, he commanded Sir Edward Carne to lay down the office of an ambassador; and under the pain of the greater excommunication, and confiscation of all his goods, not to go out of the city, but to take on him the regiment of the English hospital therein. So that I see not how Queen Elizabeth can be taxed by the papists for a schismatic, and wilful breach from the church of Rome, being thrust away thence by the pope himself, so barbarously treating her ambassador (whilst as yet she had made no alteration in religion) against the law of nations; though I confess, some conceive that the crafty old knight was (such his addiction to popery) well contented with his restraint, wherein he died, 1561.

RICHARD CLOUGH was born at Denbigh in Flintshire, whence he went to be a chorister in the city of Chester. Some were so affected with his singing therein, that they were loath he should lose himself in empty air (church music beginning then to be discountenanced) and persuaded, yea, procured his removal to London, where he became an apprentice to, and afterwards partner with Sir Thomas Gresham. He lived some years at Antwerp; and afterwards travelled as far as Jerusalem, where he was made a knight of the Sepulchre, though not owning it after his return under Queen Elizabeth (who disdained her subjects should accept of such foreign honour). He afterwards, by God's blessing, grew very rich; and there want not those who will avouch that some thousands of pounds were disbursed by him for the building of the Bourse, or Royal Exchange. Such maintain that it was agreed betwixt him and Sir Thomas Gresham, that the survivor should be chief heir to both; on which account they say that the knight carried away the main of the estate. How much the new church in Denbigh was beholden to his bounty, I am not as yet certainly informed. This is true, that he gave the impropriation of Kilken in Flintshire, worth an hundred pounds per annum, to the free school in Denbigh; and if the same at this day be aliened, I question whether repentance without restitution will secure such who are the causers thereof. He died Anno Domini 1570.[1]

SIR JOHN PRICE, *alias* AP RICE, knight, was born in Wales; noble by his lineage, but more by his learning. He was well versed in the British antiquities, and would not leave a hoof of his country's honour behind, which could be brought up to go along with him. Now so it was that Polydore Vergil, that proud Italian, bare a pique to the British, for their ancient independency from the pope. Besides, he could not so easily compass the Welsh records into his clutches, that so he might send them the same way with many English manuscripts, which he had burnt to ashes. This made him slight the credit of Welsh authors, whom our Sir John was a zealot to assert, being also a champion to vindicate the story of King Arthur. Besides, he wrote a treatise of the Eucharist; and by the good words Bale bestoweth upon him, we believe him a favourer of the Reformation.[2] [*d.* 1573?]

WILLIAM SALESBURY was born [1520?] in Denbighshire, where his family flourisheth at this day. This gentleman, out of a love to his native language, *amor patriae ratione valentior omni,* composed a short English and Welsh dictionary, first privately presented to and approved by King Henry the Eighth (being a Tudor by his father's side of Welsh extraction) and then publicly printed Anno Domini 1547.

Some captious spirits will quarrel the usefulness thereof, seeing the Welsh did not want, and the English did not wish, a book of that nature. But let them know that it is useful for both nations; to the English for *attaining,* to the Welsh for *retaining,* that language.

Attaining. For, being an original tongue, an antiquary is lame without it (which I find by my own defect) to understand the (few of many) remaining monuments of that nation.

Retaining. That tongue, as well as others, by disuse being subject not only to corruption but oblivion, by the confession of the natives of that country. Indeed all dictionaries of languages are very useful: words bringing matter to the tongue, and, as Plato well observed, ὄνομα ἐςὶ ὄργανον διδασκαλικὸν a name or word is an instrument of instruction) and ushereth knowledge into our understanding.

However, seeing nothing can be begun and finished at once, Salesbury's book (as the first in this kind) did rather essay than effect the work, and since hath been completed by others. He died about the year 1600.[3]

GABRIEL GOODMAN, son of Edward Goodman, esq., was born [1529?] at Ruthin in Denbighshire; afterwards doctor of divinity in Saint John's College in Cambridge, and dean of Westminster, where he was fixed for

(1) It was Richard Clough that urged Sir Thomas Gresham (see London, p. 347) to fulfil the elder Gresham's idea of a bourse or exchange for merchants, and the Royal Exchange was the result. Clough's great wealth gave rise to the Welsh proverb, 'He is become a Clough.' Arthur Hugh Clough the poet was descended from his illegitimate son. (2) Sir John Price was appointed in 1535, together with Sir Thomas Legh, as a visitor to the monasteries, a step preliminary to their dissolution. (3) Salesbury was a pioneer in philology, skilled in nine languages, and besides much other work translated the New Testament into Welsh.

full forty years; though by his own parts and his friends' power, he might have been what he would have been in the church of England. Abigail said of her husband, "Nabal is his name, and folly is with him." But it may be said of this worthy dean, *Goodman* was his name, and goodness was in his nature, as by the ensuing testimonies will appear.

1. The Bible was translated into Welsh on his cost, as by a note in the preface thereof doth appear.

2. He founded a school-house, with a competent salary, in the town of his nativity; as also erected and endowed an almshouse therein for twelve poor people.

3. He repaired the house for the minister (there called the warden) of Ruthin, furnishing it with plate and other utensils which were to descend to his successors.

4. He purchased a fair house with land thereunto at Chiswick in Middlesex, where with his own hands he set a fair row of elms, now grown up to great beauty and height, for a retiring place for the masters and scholars at Westminster in the heat of summer, or any time of infection. If these lands at this day be not so profitably employed, as they were by the donor piously intended, it is safer to bemoan the sad effect, than accuse the causers thereof.

There needs no other testimony of his honesty and ability, than that our English Nestor, the lord treasurer Cecil, made him one of the executors of his will, to dispose of great sums of charitable uses; which trust he most faithfully discharged. He died in the year 1601; and is buried in the collegiate church of Westminster, whereof he so well deserved, as of all England, Mr. Camden performing his perambulation about it on his expenses.

WALTER DEVEREUX [FIRST EARL OF ESSEX] son of Sir Richard Devereux and Dorothy his wife (sole sister to Thomas Bourchier last earl of Essex) was born [1541?] in the town of Carmarthen, and by Queen Elizabeth in his maternal right created earl of Essex. One martially minded, and naturally hating idleness, the rust of the soul.

Though time hath silenced the factions, and only sounded the facts of Queen Elizabeth's court, no place had more heart-burnings therein; and it was a great part of God's goodness and her prudence that no more hurt was done thereby. Many maligned our earl—*tantaene animis aularibus irae*? [can courtly minds cherish resentment so dire?]—desirous to thrust him on dangerous designs. Nor need we consult the oracle of Apollo to discover his chief adversary, seeing he was a prime favourite,[1] who loved the earl's nearest relation better than he loved the earl himself, whom he put on the project of Ireland.

Yet was not our Walter surprised into that service, seeing *injuria non fit volenti* [no injury is done to a consenting party]; and being sensible that his room was more welcome to some than his company at court, he willingly embraced the employment. Articles (the first and last, I believe, in that kind) are drawn up betwixt the queen and him, who was to maintain such a proportion of soldiers on his own cost, and to have part

(1) Robert Dudley, earl of Leicester.

of the territory of Clandeboy in Ulster for the conquering thereof. So much for the bear's-skin. Now all the craft will be to catch, kill and flay the bear himself.

Well, to maintain an army (though a very little one) is a sovereign's and no subject's work, too heavy for the support of any private man's estate, which cost this earl first the mortgaging, then the selling outright his fair inheritance in Essex. Over he goeth into Ireland with a noble company of kindred and friends, supernumerary volunteers above the proportion of soldiers agreed upon.

Sir William Fitzwilliam, lord deputy of Ireland, hearing of his coming, and suspecting (court jealousy riseth very early, or goeth not to bed at all) to be eclipsed by this great earl, solicits the queen to maintain him in the full power of his place, without any diminution; alleging this much to conduce to the honour of her majesty, whom he represented. Hereupon it was ordered that the earl should take his commission from this lord deputy, which with much importunity and long attendance, he hardly obtained, and that with no higher title than governor of Ulster.

After many impressions (not-over successfully) made in Ulster, he was by the deputy remanded in the south of Ireland, where he spent much time (take much in little in my author's words as to his general performance) *nullis bono, sed magno suo damno.*[1] His friends in the English court grew few and cold, his foes many and active; affronts were plentifully poured upon him, on purpose either to drown him in grief, or burn him in his own anger. From Munster he was sent back into Ulster, where he was forbidden to follow his blow, and use a victory he had gotten; yea, on a sudden stript out of his commission, and reduced to be governor of three hundred men; yet his stout stomach (as true tempered steel) bowed without breaking; in all these afflictions embracing all changes with the same tenor of constancy. Pay-days in Ireland came very thick, moneys out of England very slow; his noble associates began to withdraw, common men to mutiny; so that the earl himself was at last recalled home.

Not long after, he was sent over the second time into Ireland with a loftier title than (the length of the feather makes not the heap the higher) of earl marshal of Ireland, where he fell into a strange looseness (not without suspicion of poison) and he died anno 1576. His soul he piously resigned to God; his lands (much impaired) descended to his son Robert, but ten years of age. His body was brought over, and buried in Carmarthen, the place of his nativity; and his widow lady (to say no more) was soon re-married to Robert earl of Leicester. Let me add, that he died in the 36th year of his age, fatal to his family, his father and grandfather dying in the same; which year Robert earl of Essex his son never attained to; and whether it had not been as honourable for his grandchild Robert earl of Essex to have died in the same year of his age, or to have lived longer, let others decide.[2]

(1) Camden's *Elizabeth.* (2) The leader of the parliamentary forces 1642-5. This brilliant little life of Walter Devereux gives too favourable a view of an Irish adventurer who wasted a large fortune in an ambitious project. He was a man of great courage, but could be treacherous and ruthless. He died of dysentery, and not through poisoning.

HUGH BROUGHTON was born [1549] in Wales, but very nigh unto Shropshire. He used to speak much of his gentility, and of his arms, which were the owls, presaging, as he said, his addiction to the study of Greek, because those were the birds of Minerva, and the emblem of Athens. I dare not deny his gentle extraction, but it was probable that his parents were fallen to great decay, as by the ensuing story will appear.

When Mr. Bernard Gilpin,[1] that apostolic man, was going his annual journey to Oxford, from his living at Houghton in the north, he spied by the way-side a youth, one while walking, another while running; of whom Mr. Gilpin demanded whence he came. He answered, out of Wales, and that he was a-going to Oxford with intent to be a scholar.

Mr. Gilpin, perceiving him pregnant in the Latin, and having some smattering in the Greek tongue, carried him home to Houghton, where being much improved in the languages, he sent him to Christ's College in Cambridge. It was not long before his worth preferred him fellow of the house.

This was that Broughton so famous for his skill in the Hebrew; a great ornament of that university, and who had been a greater, had the heat of his brain and peremptoriness of his judgment been tempered with more moderation; being ready to quarrel with any who did not presently and perfectly embrace his opinions. He wrote many books, whereof one, called *A Concent of Scripture,* carrieth the general commendation.

As his industry was very commendable, so his ingratitude must be condemned, if it be true what I read, that when Master Gilpin, his Maecenas (by whose care, and on whose cost he was bred, till he was able to breed himself) grew old, he procured him to be troubled and molested by Doctor Barnes, bishop of Durham, in expectation of his parsonage, as some shrewdly suspect.

At last he was fixed in the city of London, where he taught many citizens and their apprentices the Hebrew tongue. He was much flocked after for his preaching, though his sermons were generally on subjects rather for curiosity than edification. [*d.* 1612]

RICHARD VAUGHAN, born [1550?] at Nyffryn in Carnarvonshire, was bred fellow in Saint John's College in Cambridge, and was afterwards successively bishop of Bangor, Chester, and lastly of London; a very corpulent man, but spiritually minded; an excellent preacher and pious liver, on whom I find this epigram, which I will endeavour to English:

Praesul es (o Britonum decus immortale tuorum)
Tu Londinensi primus in urbe Brito.
Hi mihi Doctores semper placuere, docenda
Qui faciunt, plus quam qui facienda docent.
Pastor es Anglorum doctissimus, optimus ergo,
Nam facienda doces ipse, docenda facis.

Prelate of London (O immortal grace
Of thine own Britons) first who had that place.
He's good who what men ought to do doth teach;
He's better who doth do what men should preach.
You best of all, preaching what men should do.
And what men ought to preach that doing too.

(1) See Westmorland, p. 599.

Here to justify the observation, *praesul* must be taken for a plain bishop, and *primus* accounted but from the conversion of the Saxons to Christianity; for otherwise we find no fewer than sixteen archbishops of London before that time, and all of the British nation. He was a most pleasant man in discourse, especially at his table, maintaining that truth, "At meals be glad, for sin be sad," as indeed he was a mortified man. Let me add, nothing could tempt him to betray the rights of the church to sacrilegious hands, not sparing sharply to reprove some of his own order on that account. He died March 30, 1607, being very much lamented.

HENRY ROWLANDS, born [1551] in Carnarvonshire, bred in the university of Oxford, was consecrated bishop of Bangor, November 12, 1598. We have formerly told how Bishop Bulkeley plundered the tower of Saint Asaph of five fair bells; now the bounty of this bishop brought four new ones for the same (the second edition, in case of this kind, is seldom as large as the first) whereof the biggest cost an hundred pounds. He also gave to Jesus College in Oxford means for the maintenance of two fellows. He died Anno Domini 1616.

JOHN PHILLIPS [*b.* 1555?] was a native of Wales; had his education in Oxford, and was afterwards preferred to be *Episcopus Sodorensis,* or bishop of Man. Out of his zeal for propagating the Gospel he attained the Manx tongue, and usually preached therein.

Know by the way, reader, that the king of Spain himself (notwithstanding the vastness of his dominions) had not in Europe more distinct languages spoken under his command, than had lately the king of Great Britain, *seven* tongues being used in his territories; viz., 1. *English,* in England; 2. *French,* in Jersey and Guernsey; 3. *Cornish,* in Cornwall; 4. *Welsh,* in Wales; 5. *Scotch,* in Scotland; 6. *Irish,* in Ireland; 7. *Manx,* in the Isle of Man.

This Doctor Phillips undertook the translating of the Bible into the Manx tongue, taking some of the islanders to his assistance, and namely Sir Hugh Cannell, minister of the Gospel, and lately (if not still) vicar of Kirk Michael. He perfected the same work in the space of twenty-nine years; but, prevented by his death, it was never put to press. I know not whether the doing hereof soundeth more to the honour of the dead, or the not printing thereof since his death to the shame of the living, seeing surely money might be procured for so general and beneficial a design; which makes some the less to pity the great pains of the ministers of the Isle of Man, who, by double labour, read the Scriptures to the people out of the English in the Manx tongue. This singularly learned, hospitable, painful and pious prelate died Anno Domini 1633.

SIR HUGH [MYDDELTON or] MIDDLETON, son of Richard Middleton, was born [1560?] at Denbigh, and bred in London. This is that worthy knight, who hath deserved well of London, and in it, of all England. If those be recounted amongst David's worthies, who, breaking through the army of the Philistines, fetched water from the well of Bethlehem, to satisfy the longing of David (founded more on fancy than necessity) how meritorious a work did this worthy man perform, who, to quench the thirst of thousands in the populous city of London fetched water on his own cost, more than twenty-four miles, encountering all the way with an army of oppositions, grappling with hills, struggling with rocks, fighting with forests, till, in defiance of difficulties, he had brought his project to perfection.[1] [*d.* 1631]

HUGH HOLLAND was born in Wales, and bred first a scholar in Westminster, then fellow in Trinity College in Cambridge. No bad English but a most excellent Latin poet. Indeed he was addicted to the *new-old* religion: *new,* in comparison of truth itself; yet *old,* because confessed of long continuance. He travelled beyond the seas, and in Italy (conceiving himself without ear-reach of the English) let fly freely against the credit of Queen Elizabeth. Hence he went to Jerusalem, though there he was not *made,* or he would not *own* himself, knight of the Sepulchre. In his return he touched at Constantinople, where Sir Thomas Glover, ambassador for King James, called him to an account for his *scandalum reginae* at Rome, and the former over-freedom of his tongue cost him the confinement for a time in prison. Enlarged at last, returning into England with his good parts bettered by learning, and great learning increased with experience in travel, he expected presently to be chosen clerk of the council at least; but preferment not answering his expectation, he grumbled out the rest of his life in visible discontentment. He made verses in description of the chief cities in Europe, wrote the chronicle of Queen Elizabeth's reign (believe him older and wiser, not railing as formerly) and a book of the Life of Master Camden, all lying hid in private hands, none publicly printed. This I observe the rather, to prevent plagiaries, that others may not *imp* their credit with stolen feathers, and wrongfully with ease pretend to his painful endeavours. He had a competent estate in good candle-rents in London; and died about the beginning of the reign of King Charles.[2] [*d.* 1633]

LAUNCELOT BULKELEY was born [1568?] in Anglesea, of a then right worshipful (since honourable) family, who have a fair habitation (besides others) near Beaumaris. He was bred in Brasenose College in Oxford; and afterwards became first, archdeacon, then archbishop in Dublin. He was consecrated, the third of October, 1619, by Christopher archbishop of Armagh. Soon after he was made by King James one of his privy council in Ireland, where he lived in good reputation till the day of his death, which happened some ten years since. [*d.* 1650]

(1) Sir Hugh Myddelton's great achievement was the New River, running from near Ware, Herts, to London. Begun in 1609, and completed in 1613, landlords strongly opposed the scheme, and Myddelton applied to James for money. The latter supplied half the capital and received half the profits. Myddelton also began the reclamation of Brading Harbour, Isle of Wight. He was several times M.P. for Denbigh. (2) Holland is now chiefly remembered as the writer of a sonnet prefixed to the first folio of Shakespeare, 1623. He was a member of the Mermaid Club, and possibly knew Shakespeare. *Candle-rent* is rent from house property (which constantly deteriorates).

JULINES HERRING was born at Flambere-Mayre in Montgomeryshire, 1582. His father returned hence to Coventry, to which he was highly related; Coventry, whose ancestors (for the space of almost two hundred years) had been in their course chief officers of that city. Perceiving a pregnancy in their son, his parents bred him in Sidney College in Cambridge. He became afterwards a profitable and painful preacher at Calke in Derbyshire, in the town of Shrewsbury, and at Wrenbury in Cheshire, being one of a pious life, but in his judgment disaffected to the English church discipline.

[His] Christian name is very usual in the country amongst people of quality, in memory of Julins Palmer (in the Marian days martyred) and a native of that city [Coventry]. He, being prohibited his preaching here for his non-conformity, was called over to Amsterdam, where he continued preacher to the English congregation some years, well respected in his place; and died in the year of our Lord 1644.

GEORGE HERBERT was born [1593] at Montgomery Castle, younger brother to Edward Lord Herbert (of whom immediately); bred fellow of Trinity College in Cambridge, and orator of the university, where he made a speech no less learned than the occasion was welcome, of the return of Prince Charles out of Spain.

He was none of the nobles of Tekoa, who, at the building of Jerusalem, "put not their necks to the work of the Lord;" but waiving worldly preferment, chose serving at God's altar before state employment. So pious his life that, as he was a copy of primitive, he might be a pattern of sanctity to posterity. To testify his independency on all others, he never mentioned the name of Jesus Christ, but with this addition, "My Master." Next God the Word, he loved the Word of God; being heard often to protest, that he "would not part with one leaf thereof for the whole world."

Remarkable his conformity to church discipline, whereby he drew the greater part of his parishioners to accompany him daily in the public celebration of Divine service. Yet had he (because not desiring) no higher preferment than the benefice of Bemerton nigh Salisbury (where he built a fair house for his successor) and the prebend of Leighton (founded in the cathedral of Lincoln) where he built a fair church, with the assistance of some few friends' free offerings. When a friend on his death-bed went about to comfort him with the remembrance thereof, as an especial good work, he returned, "It is a good work if sprinkled with the blood of Christ." But his *Church* (that inimitable piece of poetry) may outlast this in structure. His death happened Anno Domini 1633.

EDWARD HERBERT [FIRST BARON HERBERT OF CHERBURY], son of Richard Herbert, esquire, and Magdalen Newport his wife, was born [1583] at Montgomery Castle; knighted by King James, who sent him over ambassador into France.[1] Afterwards King Charles the First created him baron of Castleisland in Ireland, and some years after baron of

(1) So was I informed by Sir Henry Herbert, his younger brother, late master of the revels.

Cherbury in this county. He was a most excellent artist and rare linguist, studied both in books and men, and himself the author of two works most remarkable, viz., *A Treatise of Truth,* written in French, so highly prized beyond the seas, that (as I am told) it is extant at this day with great honour in the pope's Vatican.

He married the daughter and sole heir of Sir William Herbert of St. Julians in Monmouthshire, with whom he had a large inheritance both in England and Ireland. He died in August, Anno Domini 1648; and was buried in St. Giles's in the Fields, London, having designed a fair monument, of his own invention, to be set up for him in the church of Montgomery, according to the model following:

> Upon the ground a halpace[1] of fourteen foot square, on the midst of which is placed a Doric column, with its rights of pedestal basis and capital, fifteen foot in height; on the capital of the column is mounted an urn with an heart flamboul supported by two angels. The foot of this column is attended with four angels placed on pedestals at each corner of the said halpace, two having torches reversed, extinguishing the motto of mortality; the other two holding up palms, the emblems of victory.[2]

This monument hath not hitherto been (by what obstruction I list not to inquire) and I fear will not be finished; which hath invited me the rather to this description, that it might be erected in paper when it was intended in marble.[3]

JOHN WILLIAMS was born [1582] at Conway in Carnarvonshire; bred fellow of St. John's College in Cambridge, proctor of the university, dean of Westminster, bishop of Lincoln, lord keeper of the great seal of England, and lastly archbishop of York. In my *Church History* I have offended his friends, because I wrote so little in his praise; and distasted his foes, because I said so much in his defence. But I had rather live under the indignation of others, for relating what may offend, than die under the accusation of my own conscience for reporting what is untrue. He died on the 25th day of March, 1650.[4]

GODFREY GOODMAN was born [1583] of wealthy parentage in Denbighshire; bred under his uncle (of whom hereafter)[5] in Westminster school; then in Trinity College in Cambridge, where he commenced doctor of divinity; successively preferred prebendary of Windsor, dean of Rochester, and bishop of Gloucester. He might have been joined to the

(1) This word appears in the original edition as *hath pace,* but Fuller probably had in mind the word as amended (somteimes spelt *haltpace*) from the French *hault (haut) pas,* a 'high step.' (2) Courteously communicated unto me by Mr. Stone, the stone-cutter, at his house in Long Acre. (3) Lord Herbert wrote an entertaining *Autobiography,* first printed by Horace Walpole in 1764, characterized by his child-like vanity and passion for duelling. His chief philosophical work, *De Veritate,* is the first purely metaphysical work by an Englishman. (4) Williams was well involved in the complex politics of his day. He tried to moderate Charles I's attitude towards parliament, but Charles did not care for his counsels, and removed him from the lord keepership. Later he was charged with betraying secrets of the privy council, and imprisoned in the Tower. On the outbreak of the Civil War he retired to Conway. In 1645, after Naseby, the Welsh put him forward as their leader, and he made terms with the parliamentary leader. Among other charities, Williams gave a large sum for the building of St. John's, Cambridge. (5) Gabriel Goodman [placed above, on p. 690, in this edition.]

prelates before (though he lived long since) the Reformation, because he agreed with them in judgment, dying a professed Romanist, as appeareth by his will. Yet the adversaries of our hierarchy have no cause to triumph thereat, who slanderously charge popish compliance on all his order, being able to produce, of two hundred bishops since Queen Elizabeth, but this only instance, and him a person of no great eminency; not only disavowed by his fellow prelates, but imprisoned in the late convocation for his erroneous opinions.

Indeed, in his discourse he would be constantly complaining of our first reformers; and I heard him once say, in some passion, that Bishop Ridley was a very odd man; to whom one presently returned, "He was an odd man indeed, my lord; for all the popish party in England could not match him with his equal in learning and religion." To give Goodman his due, he was a harmless man, hurtful to none but himself, pitiful to the poor, hospitable to his neighbours, against the ruining of any of an opposite judgment, and gave the most he left to pious uses. He was no contemptible historian; but I confess an undermatch to Doctor Hakewill. But I remember the ring bequeathed to me in his will, with the posy thereof, *Requiem defunctis;* and therefore I will no longer be troublesome to his memory, who was made bishop 1642, and some seven years since deceased in Westminster, almost 80 years of age. [*d.* 1656]

THOMAS HOWELL was born [1588] at Llangammarch in Brecknockshire,[1] within few miles of Brecknock; bred fellow of Jesus College in Oxford, and became afterwards a meek man, and most excellent preacher. His sermons, like the waters of Siloah, did run softly, gliding on with a smooth stream; so that his matter, by a lawful and laudable felony, did steal secretly into the hearts of his hearers. King Charles made him the last bishop of Bristol, being consecrated at Oxford. He died Anno Domini 1646, leaving many orphan children behind him.

I have been told that the honourable city of Bristol hath taken care for their comfortable education; and am loath to pry too much into the truth thereof, lest so good a report should be confuted.[2]

(1) So was I told by his brother, Mr. James Howell [author of *Epistolae Hoeliane: Familiar Letters.*] (2) Thomas Howell was the last bishop consecrated in England for sixteen years. In 1645, a year after his election, Bristol was surrendered by Rupert to the parliamentarians; all the royalist clergy were violently ejected, and Howell was so roughly handled that he died the following year.

GLOSSARY

THE WORDS given here are those used more than once in this work, and of which definitions are given, if at all, only where they first occur.

ALLIES. Relations

ARTIFICIAL. Made by or resulting from the handiwork of man (as opposed to 'natural')

BY. Beside

CASUAL. Accidental

CASUALTY. Accident; chance

CORDIAL. Stimulating; restorative; 'comforting' or invigorating the heart

CREDIBLE. Trustworthy

ENLARGED. Set free

ENLARGEMENT. Freedom (from restraint)

FACEIT. Fuller's own spelling for FACETE: elegant, graceful, polished

FACETIOUS. According to the context, polished, urbane, or given to pleasantry, jocularity, waggishness

FLAUGH, FLAW. Gust of wind

HARDLY. With difficulty

HETEROCLITE. A thing or person that deviates from the ordinary rule

IMPROVE. (1) To disprove, refute, confute a statement or person; (2) to disapprove as bad, to reprove, to disallow, to blame. (But Fuller has his own variants according to the context.)

IN COMMENDAM. As commended or entrusted. A *commendam* is a licence to hold a living jointly with some benefice of higher rank

INGENIOUS, INGENUITY. Having good intellectual capacity, talented, or possessing genius; but sometime (e.g., p. 662) mistakenly used for ingenuous—open, frank

IN-LAW. Implying step relationship, e.g., *father-in-law* for *step-father*

LEGATE A LATERE. Papal legate

MARK. A money of account, originally representing the value of a mark weight of pure silver, and in England worth 13s. 4d. (O.E.D.)

MORTIFIED. Dead to the world; having the passions and appetites in control; ascetic

NOVELANT, NOVILANT. A relater of current events; a newsmonger. But see definitions in notes for varying shades of meaning

PAINFUL. Painstaking

PALATE-MEN. Epicures

PRESENTLY. Immediately

PROPRIETY. Property

REDUCED AGE. The age of gravity and composure; in other words, old age. (This particular meaning is found only in Fuller.)

VIVACITY. Longevity; vitality

BIBLIOGRAPHY

FOR A FULL bibliography of Fuller's work the reader is referred to Strickland Gibson's *Bibliography of the Work of Thomas Fuller* (1936) with biographical introduction by Geoffrey Keynes. It supersedes all other bibliographies. The short list below aims to point out the more useful biographical and critical work.

I

ADDISON, WILLIAM. *Worthy Dr. Fuller.* London, 1951. A sound, clear, illustrated account of Fuller's life and work.

ANONYMOUS. *The Life of that Reverend Divine and Learned Historian, Dr. Thomas Fuller.* London, 1661; Oxford, 1662. All later work is based on this *Life,* the author of which apparently knew Fuller well in his later years. Reprinted in vol. I of J. S. Brewer's edition of the *Church History,* Oxford, 1845.

BAILEY, J. E. *The Life of Thomas Fuller.* London, 1874. A prolix work, but the standard authority, and with a good bibliography.

LYMAN, D. B. *The Great Tom Fuller.* Berkeley, California, 1935. A short and quite sound biographical study, somewhat lyrical in tone, and with no critical estimate.

II

BUSH, DOUGLAS. *English Literature in the Earlier Seventeenth Century,* 1600-1660 (Oxford History of English Literature). Oxford, 1945. Excellent short critical summaries in chapters 6 and 7.

COLERIDGE, S. T. *Notes on English Divines.* The relevant comments are available in *Select Prose and Poetry of Coleridge,* edited by Stephen Potter, London, 1933.

CROSSLEY, JAMES. *Fuller's Holy and Profane States.* Article in The Retrospective Review, vol. III, 1821. Short extracts in Bailey's *Life* and in *Selections* from Fuller edited by E. K. Broadus, Oxford, 1928.

HOUGHTON, W. E. *The Formation of Thomas Fuller's "Holy and Profane States".* Harvard, 1938. A good critical study of Fuller's sources, and of the place of the work in 17th century literature.

JESSOPP, AUGUSTUS. Biographical and critical introduction to *Wise Words and Quaint Counsels of Thomas Fuller.* Oxford, 1892.

KELLETT, E. E. *Reconsiderations* ("A Church Historian"). London, 1928.

LAMB, CHARLES. *Specimens from the Writings of Fuller, the Church Historian,* with Lamb's penetrating notes. Available in complete editions of Lamb edited by Ainger, Lucas, &c.

ROGERS, HENRY. *An Essay on the Life and Genius of Thomas Fuller.* Edinburgh Review, 1842, and afterwards reprinted in the Traveller's Library, with selections, London, 1856.

SAINTSBURY, GEORGE. *A History of Elizabethan Literature,* ch. 12. London, 1887.
——————— In *The Cambridge History of English Literature,* vol. VII, ch. 10. Cambridge, 1911.

STEPHEN, SIR LESLIE. Article in the Cornhill Magazine, January, 1872. Extract in *Selections,* ed. Broadus.

——————— Article in the *Dictionary of National Biography.* Excellent short life.

THOMPSON, E. N. S. *Literary Bypaths of the Renaissance* ("A Representative Man of Letters"). New Haven, Conn., 1924.

WALTEN, M. G. *Thomas Fuller's "The Holy and Profane State,"* 2 vols., Columbia, 1938. Facsimile of the first edition, with full critical apparatus.

A note on the reprints of the *Worthies* is not out of place here. J. Nichols' edition in two volumes, retaining Fuller's orthography, was followed by P. Austin Nuttall's in modern orthography, three volumes, in 1840. The latter has generally been preferred, but a careful examination by the present editor shews that Nuttall reproduces Nichols' edition to the extent of repeating Nichols' errors and using his notes almost verbatim.

INDEX TO WORTHIES

N.B. Worthies only mentioned by Fuller, but about whom a few particulars are given by the editor, are denoted by the contraction *n.* following the page reference.

INDEX OF TOPICS AND PLACES

GEORGE ALLEN & UNWIN LTD
London: 40 Museum Street, W.C.1
Cape Town: 58–60 Long Street
Sydney, N.S.W.: 55 York Street
Toronto: 91 Wellington Street West
Calcutta: 17 Central Ave., P.O. Dharamtala
Bombay: 15 Graham Road, Ballard Estate
Wellington, N.Z.: 8 Kings Crescent, Lower Hutt